KU-165-718

Burke's
Guide to the
Royal Family

BURKE'S GENEALOGICAL SERIES

Founded 1826 by John Burke and Sir Bernard Burke CB LLD
(Ulster King of Arms 1853-92)

Editorial Director: Hugh Montgomery-Massingberd

Anthony Buckley

HER MAJESTY QUEEN ELIZABETH II

This special commemorative volume in Burke's Genealogical Series is being published 6 February 1973 to mark the twenty-first anniversary of Her Majesty's accession to the Throne.

Burke's
Guide to the
Royal Family

FIRST EDITION

MCMLXXIII

LONDON

Burke's Peerage Limited

First published Tuesday 6 February 1973.

Publishers's Note
Every care has been taken to check the information supplied for this book but the Publishers cannot accept responsibility for mis-statements, omissions or other inaccuracies which may appear in this work.

ISBN 0 220 66222 3

This book has been set in 9 pt Times Roman on 12 pt body, printed and bound in England by Walter Smith at Herald Printers (Westminster Press Ltd), York, for the publishers, Burke's Peerage Limited in conjunction with Shaw Publishing Company Limited, London, England (registered office: 180 Fleet Street, London EC4).
Publishing and Editorial Offices:
Mercury House, Waterloo Road, London SE1 8UL.

Production Manager: Paul Smith.

Book Designer: Geoffrey Wadsley.

MADE AND PRINTED IN GREAT BRITAIN

Foreword

BY ADMIRAL OF THE FLEET
THE EARL MOUNTBATTEN OF BURMA
KG PC GCB OM GCSI GCIE GCVO DSO FRS

I have lived in six reigns. It is true I don't actually remember Queen Victoria though I am told I knocked her spectacles off her nose when she held me at my christening but I have clear recollections of the Kings who followed.

I have no doubt that in spite of the disappearance of so many monarchies during this century the British Monarchy has gone from strength to strength under the wise rule of our successive sovereigns. Perhaps the most remarkable aspect of our Queen's reign is how she and her husband and children have succeeded in moving with the times without detracting from the dignity of their duties or sacrificing the royal ceremonial which other countries envy.

I have read Dermot Morrah's article "Twenty-one years a Queen" with great interest. He refers to the fact that at the height of the First World War King George V and his closest relations agreed to abandon all their styles and titles originating from German sources, the King himself taking the new English name of Windsor for his dynasty. At this time Queen Mary's family the Tecks took the name Cambridge and my father (who was Prince Philip's grandfather) took the name Mountbatten in place of Battenberg for our family. The two senior members of each of these two families received British Peerages in place of their Princely titles.

In the Summer of 1917 my father was staying at my elder brother's house, and while there heard that the change of titles had been approved by the King. With his irrepressible sense of humour he wrote in the visitors' book "June 9th arrived Prince Hyde, June 19th departed Lord Jekyll."

As President of the Society of Genealogists I welcome Burke's new *Guide to the Royal Family* as I regard this publication as a further manifestation of public feeling towards The Queen herself and to the Monarchy as a whole.

Mountbatten of Burma

Preface

"As well for his faithfulness and good affection to us and his country, as for his descent, patrimony, ample estate and ingenious education, every way answerable, who out of a liberal mind . . . ." (and worse), Henry Massingberd was created a baronet by Oliver Cromwell. Fervent monarchists reading this book edited by his descendant need not be alarmed, for the undersigned does not share these republican sympathies—nor for that matter the attributes alleged to have been enjoyed by Sir Henry in the Patent of 1658—and in fact the Interregnum of 1649-1660 is not dealt with in these pages.

If the Monarchy in this country were ever to be overthrown again—which God forbid—it would probably be on a permanent rather than on a temporary basis like last time. That is why we must always be on our guard against the conditions under which its demise could occur. The greatest danger to the Monarchy lies not from attacks by anarchists and others hostile to its survival; nor from the obsessive outpourings of republicans and periodic displays of bad manners by a few pampered adolescents at provincial universities; nor indeed from rational criticism. The over-reaction to such criticism in the past has possibly done the Monarchy more harm than the original remarks in question—which the hysterical vilifiers of their authors had often never even read. For criticism of the Monarchy is to be welcomed provided that it is constructive and directed at the institution of Monarchy, not at individuals who can fairly be said to be beyond criticism because they cannot answer back. The time to worry is when intellectuals do not consider the Monarchy worth criticising any longer; when young people simply do not care about it. Those who claim that the Monarchy means nothing to them invariably have no coherent idea as to what they might wish to see replace it. Others take the Monarchy entirely for granted, without any active appreciation. Thus, in short, the greatest danger to the Monarchy is apathy. If ever apathy were to set in, the way would be open to republicanism and the rude awakening might come too late.

Happily public feeling towards the Monarchy, as shown during the recent Silver Wedding Celebrations, seems to be tending not to apathy but to ever-increasing warmth. Lord Mountbatten concludes his Foreword by saying that he regards this book as a further manifestation of such feeling and that is certainly what we would like it to be. This book is offered as proof of the endless fascination of the Monarchy and its history. Interest in them must be kept alive and the manifold advantages of the present system must be promoted. Discussion and argument are very healthy things in this context. It is hoped that reference to the wealth of authoritative material in this book will become an essential aid to any such discussion in the future.

Hitherto the Royal Family has been included in a small section of its own in *Burke's Peerage, Baronetage and Knightage.* As has been announced in the press this enormous book will not be published again in its old format. Sad though this may be, it will nevertheless mean that we are now free to produce a series covering the same and also more general fields, in greater depth, but in compacter individual volumes. These will be complete in themselves and it is hoped that they will be found even more reliable and readable than in the past. We trust that this variegated and greatly expanded new list of books will continue to be indispensable for reference and, moreover, reach a wider public that is interested in history—for that is what our books are about.

Burke's Guide to the Royal Family is the first volume in the new Genealogical Series. Those under the impression that it may merely be a re-hash of what used to appear in *Burke's Peerage* should glance at the five pages devoted to the Contents and List of Illustrations and they will be swiftly disillusioned. We say "First Edition" on the title page and we mean it: this is a freshly researched and newly written work comprehensively covering the Royal Family and aspects of the Monarchy in Britain throughout its history down to the present day. The day of publication is in fact the twenty-first anniversary of Her Majesty Queen Elizabeth II's accession to the Throne and this is a special commemorative edition.

As one looks forward to future anniversaries, it is interesting to ponder the significance of Britain's entry into the European Economic Community with regard to the Monarchy. The British Monarchy is, of course, very closely linked to its European counterparts—as "The Royal Lineage" makes abundantly clear—and taken with the other European countries which have monarchies, the long term effects for Monarchy in general should be most beneficial. If and when the dream of a Federal Europe comes true presumably a Head will be needed and the possibility of the British Sovereign occupying the post should not be precluded.

Basically *Burke's Guide to the Royal Family* can be split into four sections: first, twelve essays on "The Monarchy in Britain", past and present, by a collection of justly celebrated writers and historians; second, the section on "The Royal Family" featuring very full biographies of its members, the factual content of which reflects the wonderful service that they give to the country; third, a complete account of "The Royal Lineage" tracing the narrative pedigrees of the Royal Houses from their beginnings down to the present (and including entries for all the descendants, living and dead, of King George II); and fourth, various Appendices of interest. Each section is self-contained with its own Introduction and really requires nothing further to be said here.

Finally, we would like to express a deep debt of gratitude to all the people and institutions that have assisted in the preparation of this book. We are most grateful to Her Majesty The Queen for her gracious permission to reproduce the illustrations shown, and to the other owners of copyright material who have kindly agreed to its reproduction. We thank Lord Mountbatten for generously writing the Foreword, and every one of our contributors for their time and trouble. We have tried to give the credit due to all concerned by making individual acknowledgments throughout the book, but will anyone who has helped in any way, and is not mentioned elsewhere, please accept our warmest thanks.

HUGH MONTGOMERY-MASSINGBERD
Editorial Director
Burke's Genealogical Series

November 1972

Contents

The publishers gratefully acknowledge the advice given on The Royal Residences *by Mr Robert Mackworth-Young, Librarian Windsor Castle and Assistant Keeper of The Queen's Archives and Mr John Charlton, Chief Inspector of Historic Monuments, Department of the Environment; and on* The Counsellors of State *by the Home Office.* The Kings in Shakespeare *authology was compiled by Mr John James.*

List of Illustrations

The picture research for this book was undertaken by Hugo Vickers, Christine Massingberd and Andrew Wells.

Abbreviations

NB *This list is not intended to indicate a complete list of abbreviations, nor of those in general use; but it is a guide to those largely in use in this work (particularly in* THE ROYAL LINEAGE, *p* 185).

The symbol • denotes that a person is living.

AAF Auxiliary Air Force
AAG Assistant Adjutant-General
Acad Academy
ACA Associate of Institute of Chartered Accountants
A/Cdre Air Commodore
A/C/M Air Chief Marshal
ADC Aide-de-Camp
addl Additional
Adjt Adjutant
Adm Admiral
Admin Administration,-or,-ive
Admon Administration (wills)
Adv Advisor,-ory
AEA Air Efficiency Award
AEF Australian Expeditionary Force
AFC Air Force Cross
AFRAeS Associate Fellow of Royal Aeronautical Society
AG Adjutant General
Agric Agriculture,-al
Ald Alderman
A/M Air Marshal
AM Albert Medal
Amb Ambassador
AMICE Associate Member of the Institution of Civil Engineers
AMIMarE Associate Member of Institute of Marine Engineers
AMIMechE Associate Member of Institute of Mechanical Engineers
AOC Air Officer Commanding
AOC-in-C Air Officer Commanding-in-Chief
apptd Appointed
AQMG Assistant Quarter-Master-General
ARA Associate of the Royal Academy
ARCS Associate of the Royal College of Science
ARAeS Associate of the Royal Aeronautical Society
Arb Arbitrator,-te,-ion
arg argent
ARIBA Associate of the Royal Institute of British Architects
ARICS Associate of Royal Institute of Chartered Surveyors
ARP Air Raid Precautions
ARRC Associate of the Royal Red Cross
Art Artillery
ARWS Associate of the Royal Society of Painters in Water Colours
ASC Army Service Corps
Assist Assistant
Assoc Associate,-d
AssocStJ Associate of the Order of St John
Assocn Association
A/V/M Air Vice Marshal
az azure

B Baron
b born
BA Bachelor of Arts
Bach Bachelor
BAOR British Army On the Rhine
bapt baptized
Batt Battery
BCh Bachelor of Surgery
BCL Bachelor of Civil Law
BCS Bengal Civil Service
BD Bachelor of Divinity
Bd Board
Bde Brigade
Bldg Building
BEF British Expeditionary Force
BEM British Empire Medal
BLA British Liberation Army
Bn Battalion
Brev Brevet
BSc Bachelor of Science
BSC Bengal Staff Corps
Bt Baronet
bur buried

C Count
CA County Alderman
ca *circa* (about)
Camb Cambridge
Capt Captain
CAS Chief of the Air Staff
Cav Cavalry
CB Companion of the Order of the Bath
CBE Commander of the Order of the British Empire
CC County Councillor
CD Civil Defence
Cdre Commodore
CEF Canadian Expeditionary Force
Cent Central
CF Chaplain to the Forces
CFA Canadian Field Artillery
CH Member of the Order of Companions of Honour
ChCh Christ Church
ChapStJ Chaplain of the Order of St John of Jerusalem
ChB Bachelor of Surgery
Chm Chairman
CI Channel Islands; Lady of the Imperial Order of the Crown of India
CIE Companion of the Order of the Indian Empire
CIGS Chief of Imperial General Staff
C-in-C Commander-in-Chief
cl Class
Cllr Councillor
CMG Companion of the Order of St Michael and St George
CP Central Provinces (India); Cape Province (S Africa)
CS Civil Service
CSI Companion of the Order of the Star of India
CStJ Companion of the Order of St John of Jerusalem
cmdg commanding
cmd command
cmd'd commanded
Cmdr Commander

Cmdt Commandant
Co Company
co County
Col Colonel
Coll Collector, College
Commn Commission
commn'd commissioned
Commr Commissioner
Compt Comptroller
Corpn Corporation
Corres Correspondent,-ing
cr Created
CS Civil Service
Cttee Committee
CVO Commander of the Royal Victorian Order

D Duke
d died
DAAG Deputy Assistant Adjutant General
DAG Deputy Adjutant General
dau Daughter
DBE Dame Commander of the Order of the British Empire
DCH Diploma in Childrens' Health
DCL Doctor of Civil Law
DCLI Duke of Cornwall's Light Infantry
DCM Distinguished Conduct Medal
DCMG Dame Commander of the Order of St Michael and St George
DCVO Dame Commander of the Royal Victorian Order
DD Doctor of Divinity
Def Defence
Deleg Delegate, delegation
Dep Deputy
Des Designate
DFC Distinguished Flying Cross
DGStJ Dame of Grace of the Order of St John of Jerusalem
Dir Director
diss Dissolved
Dist District
Div Division
div Divorce
DJAG Deputy Judge Advocate General
DJStJ Dame of Justice of the Order of St John of Jerusalem
DL Deputy Lieutenant
DLI Durham Light Infantry
DMus Doctor of Music
DOMS Diploma in Ophthalmic Medicine and Surgery
DPH Diploma of Doctor of Public Health
DSC Distinguished Service Cross
DSc Doctor of Science
DSO Companion of the Distinguished Service Order
dsp *decessit sine prole* (died without issue)
dspl *decessit sine prole legitima* (died without legitimate issue)
dspm *decessit sine prole mascula* (died without male issue)
dspms *decessit sine prole mascula superstita* (died without surviving male issue)
dsps *decessit sine prole superstita* (died without surviving issue)
dunm died unmarried
dvp *decessit vita patris* (died in the lifetime of the father)
dvm *decessit vita matris* (died in the lifetime of the mother)
dvu *decessit vitae uxoris* (died in the lifetime of the husband/wife)

E Earl
ED Efficiency Decoration
Eccles Ecclesiastic,-al
Edcn Education
Edcnalist Educationalist
Edin Edinburgh
Edn Edition
educ Educated at
Elect Electric,-al
EM Efficiency Medal
empd Employed
Engr Engineer
Engrg Engineering
ER East Riding
Exam Examiner,s,-ation
Exec Executive
Exor Executor
Expdn,-y Expedition,-ary
Extraord Extraordinary

FAA Fleet Air Arm
FAMS Fellow of the Ancient Monuments Society
FANY First Aid Nursing Yeomanry
FBA Fellow of the British Academy
Fell Fellow
FCA Fellow of the Institute of Chartered Accountants
FEIS Fellow of the Educational Institute of Scotland
FFR Fellow of the Faculty of Radiologists
FIA Fellow of the Institute of Actuaries
FM Field Marshal
FLAS Fellow of (Chartered) Land Agents' Society
FLS Fellow of the Linnean Society
FRAS Fellow of the Royal Astronomical Society
FRCO Fellow of the Royal College of Organists
FRCP Fellow of the Royal College of Physicians
FRCS Fellow of the Royal College of Surgeons
FRES Fellow of the Royal Empire Society
FREconS Fellow of the Royal Economic Society
FRGS Fellow of the Royal Geographical Society
FRMS Fellow of the Royal Microscopical Society
FRS Fellow of the Royal Society
FRSA Fellow of the Royal Society of Arts
FSA Fellow of the Society of Antiquaries
FSAScot Fellow of the Society of Antiquaries (Scotland)
FZS Fellow of the Zoological Society
Fedn Federation
Fus Fusiliers
F/Lt Flight Lieutenant
F/O Flying Officer
FRHS Fellow of the Royal Horticultural Society
FRSE Fellow of the Royal Society of Edinburgh
FRTPI Fellow of the Royal Institute of Town Planning

GBE Knight (or Dame) Grand Cross of the Order of the British Empire
GC George Cross
G/Capt Group Captain
GCB Knight Grand Cross of the Order of the Bath
GCH Knight Grand Cross of the Hanoverian Guelphic Order
GCIE Knight Grand Commander of the Order of the Indian Empire
GCMG Knight (or Dame) Grand Cross of the Order of St Michael and St George
GCSI Knight Grand Commander of the Order of the Star of India
GCStJ Bailiff (or Dame) Grand Cross of the Order of St John of Jerusalem
GCVO Knight (or Dame) Grand Cross of the Royal Victorian Order
Glas Glasgow
GM George Medal
GOC General Officer Commanding
Gov Governor
Govt Government
Gren Grenadier
Grm Grammar (School)
GSO General Staff Officer

gu gules
HBM His or Her Britannic Majesty
HCM His or Her Catholic Majesty [Spain]
HE His or Her Excellency
HEICS Honourable East India Company Service
HG Home Guard
HH His or Her Highness
HI & RH His or Her Imperial and Royal Highness
HIH His or Her Imperial Highness
H Ill H His or Her Illustrious Highness
Highrs Highlanders
HIM His or Her Imperial Majesty
Hist History,-orical
HLI Highland Light Infantry
HM His or Her Majesty
HMCM His or Her Most Christian Majesty [France]
HMFM His or Her Most Faithful Majesty [Portugal]
HMS His or Her Majesty's Ship
HMSO His or Her Majesty's Stationery Office
HRH His or Her Royal Highness
HSH His or Her Serene Highness
Hon The Honourable
hon honorary
Hosp Hospital
Hus Hussars
Hy Heavy

IA Indian Army
IARO Indian Army Reserve of Officers
ICI Imperial Chemical Industries
ICS Indian Civil Service
idc Passed Imperial Defence College
Ind India,-n
ISC Indian Staff Corps: Imperial Service Coll
ISO Imperial Service Order
i/c In charge of
Imp Imperial
Inf Infantry
inf Infant
Inst Instructor, Institute
Instn Institution
Internat International
IoW Isle of Wight

Jnr Junior
JP Justice of the Peace
Jt Joint
Jtly Jointly

k Killed
KA Knight of the Order of St Andrew [Russia]
KAR King's African Rifles
KB Knight of the Order of the Bath (before the reorganization of the Order into classes)
KBE Knight Commander of the Order of the British Empire
KC King's Council
KCB Knight Commander of the Order of the Bath
KCH Knight Commander of the Hanoverian Order
KCIE Knight Commander of the Order of the Indian Empire
KCMG Knight Commander of the Order of St Michael and St George
KCSG Knight Commander of the Order of St Gregory the Great
KCSI Knight Commander of the Order of the Star of India
KCVO Knight Commander of the Royal Victorian Order
KE Knight of the Order of the Elephant [Denmark]
KG Knight of the Order of the Garter
KGF Knight of the Order of the Golden Fleece [Austria and Spain]
KGStJ Knight of Grace of the Order of St John of Jerusalem
KH Knight of the Hanoverian Guelphic Order
K-i-H Kaisar-i-Hind Medal
KJStJ Knight of Justice of the Order of St John of Jerusalem
KOSB King's Own Scottish Borderers
KOYLI King's Own Yorkshire Light Infantry
KP Knight of the Order of St Patrick
KPM King's Police Medal
KR Knight of the Order of the Redeemer [Greece]
KRRC King's Royal Rifle Corps
KSA Knight of the Order of St Anne [Russia]
KSLI King's Shropshire Light Infantry
KSV Knight of the Order of St Vladimir [Russia]
KT Knight of the Order of the Thistle
Kt Knight
ktd Knighted

Leg Legislation
LG *Landed Gentry* (BURKE'S)
LI Light Infantry
Lieut Lieutenant
LLB Bachelor of Laws
LLD Doctor of Laws
LLM Master of Laws
LO Lyon Office
Lond London (not in addresses)
Lord Lieut Lord Lieutenant
LRCP Licentiate of the Royal College of Physicians
LRAM Licentiate of the Royal Academy of Music
LSA Licentiate of Society of Apothecaries
Lt-Col Lieutenant-Colonel
Lt-Cmdr Lieutenant-Commander
Lt-Gen Lieutenant-General

M Marquess
m married
MA Master of Arts
Mag Magistrate
Man Manager
Man Dir Managing Director
MB Bachelor of Medicine
MBE Member of the Order of the British Empire
MC Military Cross
MCh Master of Surgery
MCSP Member of Chartered Society of Physiotherapists
MD Doctor of Medicine
Med Medicine, Medical
mem Member
Met Metropolitan
Mfrs Manufacturers
MFH Master of Fox Hounds
MGC Machine Gun Corps
Mgr-s Manager,-s; Monsignor,-s
MI Military Intelligence
Mil Military
Min Minister,-ry
MInstCE Member, Institute of Civil Engineers
MInstT Member, Institute of Transport
MLA Member, Legislative Assembly
MLC Member, Legislative Council
MO Medical Officer
MOH Medical Officer of Health
MP Member of Parliament
MRCP Member of the Royal College of Physicians
MRCS Member of Royal College of Surgeons
MRCVS Member of the Royal College of Veterinary Surgeons
Munic Municipal
MVO Member of the Royal Victorian Order

Nat National
NI Native Infantry

nr	Near
NR	North Riding (Yorks)
NSW	New South Wales
NWFP	North West Frontier Province (India)
NZ	New Zealand
OBE	Officer of the Order of the British Empire
Offg	Officiating
Offr	Officer
OM	Order of Merit
Org	Organization
OStJ	Officer of the Order of St John of Jerusalem
Parl	Parliament,-ary
PC	Privy-Councillor
Perm	Permanent
Plen	Plenipotentiary
PMO	Principal Medical Officer
PMRAFNS	Princess Mary's Royal Air Force Nursing Service
P/O	Pilot Officer
pr	proved
ppr	proper
Preb	Prebendary
Pres	President
Prin	Principal
Priv	Private
Prob	Probate,-ion,-ionary
Prod	Production
Prof	Professor,-ional
Prov	Province
psa	Passed Staff College, Andover
psc	Passed Staff College, Camberley
QC	Queen's Counsel
QAIMS	Queen Alexandra's Imperial Military Nursing Service
QAINNS	Queen Alexandra's Imperial Naval Nursing Service
QALAS	Qualified Associate of the Land Agents' Society
QO	Queen's Own
QPM	Queen's Police Medal
RA	Royal Artillery; Royal Academician
RAAF	Royal Auxilliary Air Force; Royal Australian Air Force
RAC	Royal Armoured Corps
RAF	Royal Air Force
RAFVR	Royal Air Force Volunteer Reserve
RAMC	Royal Army Medical Corps
RAOC	Royal Army Ordnance Corps
RASC	Royal Army Service Corps
RAVC	Royal Army Veterinary Corps
RBA	Royal Society of British Artists
RCA	Royal College of Art; Royal Company of Archers
RCAS	Royal Central Asian Society
RCNVR	Royal Canadian Naval Volunteer Reserve
RCT	Royal Corps of Transport
RD	Rural Dean
RDC	Rural District Council
RE	Royal Engineers
regd	Registered
Regnl	Regional
Regt	Regiment
Rep	Representative
Res	Reserve; Resident
ret	Retired
Rev	Reverend
RFA	Royal Field Artillery
RFC	Royal Flying Corps
RGA	Royal Garrison Artillery
RHG	Royal Horse Guards
RHA	Royal Horse Artillery
RI	Rhode Island
RIC	Royal Irish Constabulary
RIE	Royal Indian Engineers
RIN	Royal Indian Navy
RINVR	Royal Indian Naval Volunteer Reserve
RL	Royal Licence
Rly-s	Railway,-s
RM	Royal Marines
RMA	Royal Military Academy
RMC	Royal Military College
RMLI	Royal Marine Light Infantry
RN	Royal Navy
RNR	Royal Naval Reserve
RNVR	Royal Naval Volunteer Reserve
RofO	Reserve of Officers
RP	Royal Society of Portrait Painters
RRC	Royal Red Cross
RSA	Royal Scottish Academy, Academician
Rt	Right
RTC	Royal Tank Corps
RTR	Royal Tank Regt
RWS	Member of Royal Society of Painters in Water Colours
s	Succeeded
sa	Sable
SA	South Africa
SAAF	South African Air Force
SASO	Senior Air Staff Officer
SBStJ	Serving Brother of the Order of St John of Jerusalem
ScD	Doctor of Sciences
Sch	School
Scot	Scotland; Scottish
Sett	Settlement
Snr	Senior
Soc	Society
S/Ldr	Squadron Leader
Sqdn	Squadron
SR	Supplementary (or Special) Reserve
SRN	State Registered Nurse
SSStJ	Serving Sister of the Order of St John of Jerusalem
Surg	Surgeon
surv	Surviving
SWBdrs	South Wales Borderers
T/	Temporary
TA	Territorial Army
T&AVR	Territorial and Army Volunteer Reserve
TARO	Territorial Army Reserve Officers
TD	Territorial Decoration
Tech	Technical
temp	Living in time of (*tempore*)
trans	Transferred
Treas	Treasurer,-y
Trib	Tribune
Trin	Trinity
Trop	Tropical
UDC	Urban District Council
Univ	University
UNO	United Nations Organisation
UP	United Provinces (India)
USA	United States of America
USAF	United States Air Force
USAAF	United States Army Air Force
v	*versus* (against)
V	Viscount
VA	Lady of the Royal Order of Victoria and Albert
VAD	Voluntary Aid Department
VC	Victoria Cross
VD	Volunteer Officers' Decoration
Ven	Venerable
Visn	Visitation
Vol	Volunteer
VRD	Volunteer Reserve Decoration (RN)
WAAF	Womens Auxiliary Air Force
W/Cmdr	Wing Commander
WO	Warrant Officer; War Office
WR	West Riding (Yorks)
WRAC	Women's Royal Army Corps
WRAF	Women's Royal Air Force
WRNS	Women's Royal Naval Service
WS	Writer to the Signet
Yeo	Yeomanry
yr	Younger
yst	Youngest

The Monarchy in Britain

Introduction

This section comprises twelve specially commissioned articles which examine the Monarchy—past and present—and discuss some of its features. As this book is being published to coincide with the twenty-first anniversary of Her Majesty Queen Elizabeth II's accession to the Throne it is fitting to begin with "Twenty-one Years a Queen", a review of her reign by Mr Dermot Morrah, Arundel Herald of Arms Extraordinary and a distinguished writer on Royalty.

Then come a succession of Historical Views in which the development of the Monarchy in this country, from the earliest times to the present, is traced by historians with particular knowledge of the various periods. Professor Henry Loyn, of the University of Wales, looks at the Monarchy from the Age of Settlement down to 1485 in "Medieval Monarchy", and then Dr A. L. Rowse discusses "The Monarchy under the Tudors". Dr Rowse, incidentally, rightly says that "Shakespeare expresses the whole pageant, the role and range of kingship", and to further illustrate his point an anthology, "The Kings in Shakespeare" has been included as an Appendix. "The Monarchy under the Stuarts" is the first article in this section by Mr Mark Bence-Jones, a versatile writer and a regular contributor to *Burke.* Two eminent Royal biographers, Mr Roger Fulford and Sir Philip Magnus-Allcroft, Bt (Philip Magnus), view the periods from the accession of King George I to the death of Prince Albert and from Queen Victoria's widowhood to King George V's death respectively in "The Monarchy 1714-1861" and "The Monarchy 1861-1936".

Another distinguished historian, Sir Charles Petrie, Bt, discusses the modern concept of Monarchy in a general article on "The Monarchy in the Twentieth Century". It is appropriate that the survey of "The Monarchy and the Constitution" should have been undertaken here by Mr Norman St John-Stevas, MP, the leading authority on Walter Bagehot and himself a member of the Select Committee on The Civil List (Session 1971-72) whose *Report* is so invaluable a document. The Countess of Longford, whose recent work (as Elizabeth Longford) has indubitably stamped her as an historian of the first rank, has written on an important and interesting aspect of the Monarchy, "The Role of the Prince Consort".

Next there are three articles with illustrations. Dr Roy Strong, Director of the National Portrait Gallery and a highly talented writer and broadcaster on Royalty, discusses "The Royal Image"; Mr Mark Bence-Jones describes the palaces and houses where reigning Sovereigns have lived in "The Royal Residences", and, finally, Mr John Brooke-Little, Richmond Herald at the College of Arms gives the history and development of royal arms in Great Britain in his article on "Royal Heraldry". This last article leads in to a colour section featuring illustrations of the armorial bearings of the Royal Family.

The authors were invited to contribute articles on chosen subjects but the views they express and the conclusions to which they come are their own. No attempt was made to impose strict limits as to what they could write about within certain broadly specified themes—by no means mutually exclusive—and what they could not. It is felt that although an occasional overlap may occur and sometimes a basically similar point is brought out in different articles—though not necessarily in the same way—this only serves to emphasise the significance of the matter in question. Thus the reader is advised, to an extent, to regard this collection of essays more in the light of a symposium on the Monarchy than as a ruthlessly dovetailed series of set pieces.

The articles which now follow need no further introduction as they speak, in an illuminating and thought-provoking way, for themselves.

Twenty-one Years a Queen

BY DERMOT MORRAH

Arundel Herald of Arms Extraordinary

As Queen Elizabeth II completes twenty-one years on the Throne, memory travels back to the day, 21 April 1947, when The Princess Elizabeth completed twenty-one years of life and, according to the law of that time, came of age. Broadcasting from Cape Town her vow of personal dedication to the service of all her father's subjects in the Empire and Commonwealth, the Heiress Presumptive rejoiced in her inherited privilege, that in each and all of their many countries she was entitled to feel, as she then felt in South Africa, at home.

It was in fact the last occasion on which, with formal constitutional propriety, any member of the royal House could make such an assertion. Before the year was out another historic coming-of-age was recorded. The leaders of the Indian people, who had been preparing themselves for nearly a century, with the active good will of Queen Victoria and all her successors, for responsible self-government, declared that the process was now complete and claimed their right to sovereign independence within the Commonwealth. King George VI, with the concurrence of his Ministers in all his other self-governing dominions, readily acceded to the request. But then the Indian statesmen asked for something further: that, while remaining in the Commonwealth and according to its royal Head a place of unchallengeable honour, they need not accept him—as Canada, Australia and other nations had done—as supreme representative of their own community, but set at its head a President, not subordinate to the King but elected by themselves. After some debate this desire also was conceded, with only the implied instruction to the constitutional lawyers that they must somehow adapt their doctrine to the new political fact of life.

Hitherto the canonical teaching had been that though the Commonwealth had many independent governments there was only one Crown, to which all were formally subject. The King reigned by the same title everywhere, and therein lay the expression and warranty of the organic union of the whole. But now the theory had to be restated, as if a number of separate Crowns were worn on a single brow. So when the death of King George summoned his daughter home from her travels to succeed him, she was proclaimed by different titles in six different places. From the balcony of St James's Palace Garter King of Arms declared the accession of "Elizabeth the Second, by the Grace of God of the United Kingdom of Great Britain and Northern Ireland and of her other Realms and Territories Queen, Head of the Commonwealth, Defender of the Faith". Southern Rhodesia used the same form of words. But Canada, Australia, New Zealand, South Africa, Pakistan and Ceylon all varied it slightly, each naming its own country and each including the expression "Head of the Commonwealth". India, which was to regard her not as head of its own nation but as external chairman of a society to which India subscribes, did not proclaim her at all.

This current of constitutional change, which George VI did not personally set in motion and Elizabeth II, even if she wished, would be powerless to stem, has been gathering force through the first twenty-one years of her reign. One after another the formerly dependent territories of Africa, Asia and the scattered islands of the Victorian Empire have celebrated their promotion to independent status by electing Presidents and ceasing to be governed "in the name of The Queen". The most recent to become a Republic is Ceylon; South Africa and only last year Pakistan have withdrawn from the Commonwealth altogether. These are symbolic acts, but they express realities. The Queen is the symbol of the spirit of the Commonwealth, or at least of the British culture and way of life. She has been offered to every emergent nation as its representative head, in the hope of consolidating such a Commonwealth culture; the majority of them, while remaining in the Commonwealth but politely declining to inscribe the name of its Head in their own constitutions, are in effect declaring that they wish to continue in political association but have and intend to develop an indigenous culture of their own, which no one not of their own blood can even symbolically represent.

Thus Queen Elizabeth in 1973 bears nominal rule over a much smaller area than King George in 1945 or even she herself in 1952. It does not follow that she is a less real and vivid figure in the thoughts of the young nations of the Commonwealth than was her predecessor. His legal authority has been surrendered without ill will; but the inspiration of monarchy is not sustained or communicated by lawyers. As far as the legal theory goes, the relation of the Head of the Commonwealth to its republican members—which are now the majority—is solely with the Governments; the subjects owe no allegiance, and need concern themselves as little with the personality of The Queen as with the constantly shifting names which appear annually as chairmen of the Security Council or the General Assembly of the United Nations. But here we are in the domain, not of constitutional formulae, but of human understanding and intercourse; and considered under that light it may be said that Elizabeth II stands for more in the public and even private life of the Commonwealth at large than did any of the crowned Sovereigns of the Empire since the chiefs of Africa commended themselves to the protection of the almost divine Great White Queen at Windsor and the Maharajahs and Nawabs of India tendered their homage to George V at the Delhi Durbar of 1912.

This is not because of any failure of The Queen's ancestors to make good their claim to personal allegiance, or of their Ministers and Proconsuls to impress the royal image upon their age. It is due to the fortunate accidents of the phase in history into which The Queen has been born—accidents in the sense that they come to her through no design or volition of her own, though it should also be said that she has shown herself ready and eager to turn to good account the opportunities that good fortune has offered. Hers is conspicuously a twentieth-century royalty: the great achievements and potencies of the new age have been powerfully enlisted to enhance the moral stature and authority of the ancient monarchy in the hearts of modern men and women.

The first of these mighty potencies is the new mobility. In less than sixty years from the date in the reign of George V when the pioneer Blériot fluttered precariously across the English Channel, American astronauts (or selenonauts) landed confidently on the Moon.

George V, who may be regarded as the founder of the modern social monarchy, certainly desired to be mobile. Turning deliberately away from the European preoccupations of his father, he charged himself at the beginning of his reign to cultivate personal intercourse with his compatriots, whom he felt his subjects throughout his Empire to be. But he was too speedily hurled into the maelstrom of world war; his health began to fail before the post-war world was clearly shaped; and there was no successor to the Delhi Durbar. His plans for the development of relations between royalty and the peoples oversea were partly delegated to his heir apparent; but the short reign of Edward VIII offered no time for their enlargement. George VI in his turn, nursing the same high hopes of closer intercourse with the peoples of the now rapidly changing Commonwealth, was thwarted, first by long immersion in world war (and "cold war" to follow), and then by grave illness. He had nevertheless made his preparations for a great Royal Tour throughout the whole Commonwealth; and it was in fact from an attempt to carry through that project on her sick father's behalf that his daughter was summoned back to mourn his death and take up his burden. By her the thing at last was done. She has been granted good health and more than twenty years of peace—troubled though that peace may have been; and at the beginning of those years, in 1954, she inscribed her name triumphantly in the history books as the first monarch of any nationality to circumnavigate the globe, scarcely setting foot in the entire voyage on any soil not belonging to the Commonwealth of which she is the Head. Since that memorable achievement she has made use of all the resources, denied to her ancestors, that the age of the jet aircraft can bring to the assistance of human intercourse. So favoured by the climate of her age, she has been enabled to visit and make herself known in:

Canada (five times), Australia (three times), New Zealand (three times), Malta (twice), Jamaica (twice), Tonga (twice), Ghana, Nigeria, Fiji (three times), Aden, Gibraltar, Uganda, India, Pakistan, Ceylon, Trinidad, Bermuda, Bahamas, Barbados, Turks and Caicos Islands, St Kitts and Nevis, St Lucia, St Vincent, Dominica, Montserrat, Grenada, Trinidad and Tobago, The Gambia, Sierra Leone and the Cocos Islands.

(Since this list, drawn up in the Royal Household, was laid before a Select Committee of the House of Commons in 1971, Pakistan has renounced membership of the Commonwealth.) What is remarkable in retrospect to those who followed these tours is the difficulty of collating memory with the records of constitutional status, of remembering any appreciable difference in the reception of The Queen between those countries which had become republics before the time of the visit and those which retained the monarchial forms. Of course the courtesies paid by a President were distinguishable from the obeisance of a Governor General. But to the people everywhere, whether the symbolic Crown had or had not been repudiated as an emblem of alien dominion, the person of The Queen made the same direct and immediate appeal. Even in India, the first and greatest of the republics, those who accompanied her reported that she seemed still to command the same romantic reverence that was due to the Queen Empress she had never been.

Twentieth-century mobility, then, has enhanced the emollient influence of the monarchy upon human relations even in those many regions of the old Empire over which its formal authority has been relinquished. The question how long this influence can survive its original institutional basis does not belong to the theme of an essay concerned with the first phase of the reign.

A word, however, needs to be said about the effect of the new mobility in the three major Commonwealth nations of European settlement—Canada, Australia and New Zealand. For each of these the Head of the Commonwealth has remained the nominal head of society in all its aspects, of which the state (or society organized for politics) is only one. There is no doubt that the sense of loyal devotion to the far-away King contributed largely to the patriotic fervour that brought the forces of these kindred nations to the aid of the Mother Country in two world wars. Nevertheless thoughtful students of Commonwealth affairs, as sovereign self-government came to maturity, continued to feel anxiety throughout the reigns of George V and George VI, about the possibility of maintaining this loyalty over the generations by faith and not by sight. In George VI's time, at least, it began to be suggested that the King could not for ever remain a credible head of society in, say, Australia unless he could occasionally go and live among his subjects there for a substantial continuous period. The idea was canvassed, but received little support, partly because of the feeling that the Commonwealth must have a centre where visitors, public or private, might normally expect to meet or see its Head; and though the problem it was designed to meet remained, this problem has gone far to solve itself through the new mobility of the following reign. Dispensing for the most part with the pomp and circumstance of royal tours, The Queen has been enabled to pay flying visits to provincial cities oversea on local occasions such as centenaries, to mix with her subjects and share their celebrations, and leave behind her the impression that nowadays a citizen of Brisbane need not regard himself as separated from his sovereign more than his cousin at Brighton, and that a subject in Manitoba has nearly as good a chance of contact with her as one in Manchester. The notion of a monarch occasionally resident in Ottawa or Wellington has lost its specious attraction. It could revive, now that The Queen has an adult heir apparent fully competent to discharge, in the capacity of first Counsellor of State, all the royal functions in the United Kingdom; but that is a hypothesis that has not needed consideration in these first twenty-one years of the reign.

The other great factor by which the scientific achievement of the twentieth century has enhanced the influence of the monarchy is the new ease of communication, as distinct from personal mobility. It has given to the people an unprecedented sense of participation in The Queen's life, and that equally in both the correlative aspects that, in a sort of stereoscopic sense, combine to make the image of a social monarchy. These aspects are The Queen's grandeur and her simplicity.

For the first time in history the most august ceremonies of Church and State could be made fully visible and audible to all subjects—and to countless millions who were not of The Queen's obedience. On 11 May 1973, just a thousand years will have elapsed since the first recorded coronation, of King Edgar the Peaceful, was celebrated at Bath. In all that time the essential structure of the rite has remained the same, and even some of the words (only translated from the Latin) such as the famous anthem *Unxerunt Salomonem*—"Zadok the priest and Nathan the prophet anointed Solomon king"—which is sung over the crowned King or Queen. But hitherto this solemn consecration of the new reign has necessarily been within the experience only of a limited congregation of highly privileged persons. But when the sacring of Queen Elizabeth II was communicated by the revolutionary invention of television to a watching world, there were many who believed themselves aware of a quite new sense of corporate exaltation in the body of the people when they saw The Queen anointed as their supreme representative; it even seemed not altogether fanciful that the look of dedicated joy that shone in her eyes as she sat enthroned was in some way reflected in the hearts of the spectators far away.

Thus the traditional splendour by which the visible monarchy has always sustained the pride of a nation and the unity of loyal subjects has gained new power in this reign. Many other displays in the same tradition have helped to express these sentiments—most notably, perhaps, when the Investiture of The Queen's eldest son as Prince of Wales at Caernarvon in 1969 was made visible in colour far and wide. This was not an ancient ceremony: it had been devised half a century before at the instigation of David Lloyd George, with political motives that were suspect to many, and to the scarcely veiled distaste of the central figure in the proceedings. In 1969 a new spirit was breathed into the celebration, largely derived from the genuine enthusiasm with which the Prince himself approached his inheritance. More than six centuries after the first English Prince of Wales was created (at Lincoln in 1301) an heir to the Throne deliberately set out to identify himself with the country from which he took his principal title. He demonstrated his resolution by entering a Welsh university to acquire a working knowledge of the national language, and by travelling through the whole country after the formal ceremonies, to seek direct acquaintance with the people. At a time when the growing warmth of Welsh national sentiment had caused some fears of racial disharmony within the triune Kingdom, this dramatic royal irruption into public ceremony and private intercourse, accepted by the great majority of the Welsh in the spirit in which it was offered, afforded a notable exhibition of the reconciling influence of the Throne.

This reference to the less formal appearances of the newly invested Prince anticipates consideration of the second mode in which modern richness of communication has enlarged the scope of royalty. The continuity and harmony of aim between The Queen, her father and her grandfather, which has been so marked a characteristic of the family through these three generations, is nowhere more conspicuous than in the progressive efforts of all three to bring the Throne closer to the life of the people at large. Whatever hopes egalitarian reformers may hold for the future, to ignore in 1973 the evident continued prevalence of a graded society is a fiction against which the very existence of a series of volumes such as this is a confutation. So long as certain groups and types of people are marked out as more publicly important than others, whether their eminence derives from their heredity, their wealth, their intellectual attainments or their political power, so long the Sovereign, the most important personage of all, inevitably has more frequent contact with those at the top than at the bottom of the scale—however the scale is graduated. For that very reason Queen Elizabeth, carrying on a continuous process from where her father left it, has been at pains to emphasize that she is the representative not of the great and the highly connected, but of the whole nation. To that end she has abandoned or modified old institutions and customs which might seem to mark her as particularly the leader of a governing class. A good example is the cessation of the presentation parties, in which the daughters of great families, on their emergence from the schoolroom into social life, were brought, arrayed in their costliest finery, to make their obeisance before their King and Queen. (The tradition that the original purpose of this ceremony was to offer the cadets of the royal house a parade of the most eligible brides is difficult to reconcile with the fact that it flourished most conspicuously in a time when these exalted young men almost invariably married foreign princesses, and were pursued with every weapon of the royal displeasure, even with Acts of Parliament, if they dared suggest "making an honest woman" of a compatriot.) Instead of these glittering entertainments, The Queen has stabilized (she did not originate) the routine of entertaining in the summer months as many thousands of every rank and grade as can be crowded into the acres of garden at Buckingham Palace and Holyroodhouse.

Signs of closer sympathy between the Sovereign and the masses of the people may also be traced in the changing emphasis of the Birthday and New Year Honours lists, in which popular enthusiasm for the leaders of sport and light entertainment has been accepted with increasing frequency as good grounds for royal favour and titular distinction. That these lists are issued on Ministerial advice does not alter the fact that their style affects the public conception of The Queen who bestows the decorations.

Another large step in participation in the national life was involved in the decision—taken in consultation with high statesmanship but not under political pressure—to pass the heir apparent through very much the course of training of ordinary boys of good social standing, and encourage him to mix on equal terms with his contemporaries all the way from pre-preparatory school to university. His sister was receiving substantially the same sort of education, modified by the change of gender. In extension of this it is to be noted that The Prince of Wales, by his prolonged incursions before graduation into his own Principality and his mother's Commonwealth of Australia, came of age with already a familiarity with peoples outside England unique in the reigning House since Charles II, under duress, went on his "travels" three centuries before.

These two elder children of The Queen may now be considered full members of the family "team" which from the days of George VI has been so conscious of its mission to bring royalty progressively nearer to the life of the people. Chief after the Sovereign herself from her accession, and likely to continue as such at least until The Prince of Wales has completed the apprentice stages of his training as a naval officer, has been The Duke of Edinburgh—whose powerful contribution to the life and service of the monarchy is separately assessed elsewhere in this volume.

The mention of the part to be played by The Queen's kindred in support of her public work makes this perhaps the appropriate place to mention briefly a secondary family matter, which has evidently confronted Her Majesty with something of a problem before a final solution could be reached. A reigning Sovereign has such very rare occasion to use a surname that there was considerable doubt what such name properly belonged to the Saxe-Coburg dynasty, which ascended the Throne in the person of King Edward VII in the first year of the century. That discussion lost relevance, when, at the height of the First World War, George V and his closest relations agreed to abandon all their styles and titles originating from German sources, the King himself taking the new English name of Windsor for the dynasty.

In the course of nature a queen regnant is the last of her dynasty: her successor will inaugurate a new dynasty, taking its surname from her consort. Thus upon the accession of Elizabeth II, all the descendants of The Queen's marriage, born and unborn, male and unmarried female, in the male line, were clearly—at common law—surnamed Mountbatten. The common law has since been modified by two successive prerogative acts. A Declaration in Council in the first year of The Queen's reign stated that it was the intention that The Queen and her descendants should be known as the House and Family of Windsor. On further reflection, however, Her Majesty decided that this ruling, evidently dictated by respect for her father's memory, did less than justice to her husband as the progenitor of the dynasty to come. So in 1960, shortly before the birth of Prince Andrew, she made a second declaration affecting the as yet unborn cadet lines of the royal family descending from her marriage.

By the ruling of George V the first two generations in the male line from The Queen or The Prince of Wales are princes or princesses with the style of his or her royal highness. They use no surname in private or public life: even their most formal correspondence is signed with a Christian name alone. But in the next generation these exalted designations lapse, and they need to use a surname like any other subject, embellished of course in some cases with a substantive or courtesy title derived from the peerage. Under the declaration of 1960 this surname is to be Mountbatten-Windsor.

The declaration of 1960 expressly excepts from its terms the bearers of the princely title, from whom these commoners will descend. No doubt for all ordinary purposes these stand in no need of a surname. But even they must occasionally be described in some document—such as the registration of a marriage or birth—on which a surname is required by law. In the absence of any authoritative declaration to the contrary it would seem natural for Their Royal Highnesses to presume that the name they will be transmitting to their posterity is already theirs to bequeath, and accordingly to sign themselves on those rare occasions as, for example, Charles or Anne Mountbatten-Windsor. This interpretation of the slightly ambiguous declaration of 1960 is made more plausible by a semi-official notice issued the same day from Buckingham Palace, which described as "close to The Queen's heart" her desire "to associate the name of her husband with her own and his *descendants*"—not, be it noted, their descendants three generations hence. It seems safe to adopt it unless and until the pleasure of The Queen or some future Sovereign is declared in different terms.

For The Queen herself the desire to establish and maintain the sense of common humanity uniting her with all her subjects is an inheritance from at least three generations of her ancestors; but its expression differs from theirs not in direction but in degree. The movement was thus summarized by her Private Secretary, Sir Michael Adeane (now Lord Adeane), presenting to the Select Committee on the Civil List in 1971 an account of her daily labours obviously summarizing the collective judgment of her personal staff:

> The Queen has come to stand much nearer to her people in all her realms than her predecessors . . . Much has been written about the increased informality of The Queen and her entourage and some of this may be exaggerated. The importance of any such change lies in the considerable extent to which any gulf, real or imaginary, between Her Majesty and her subjects has decreased. Not only does The Queen meet many more people from all sections of the community than her predecessors, but she does so in many different ways and on many different occasions. To give only two examples: Garden Parties which were once exclusive now include people of many different occupations from all parts of the country, while the frequent Provincial visits which once centred round Mayors, Guards of Honour, formal Addresses and the presentation of Aldermen and Councillors, now usually include public meetings and informal walks where The Queen can talk to anyone among the citizens and their families who happen to catch her eye.

Sir Michael went on to say: "there is also television and this, more than anything else, has made The Queen, as she follows her various daily duties and interests, familiar to her people and has brought her into their homes".

Here indeed is a factor in daily life which has made the reign of Elizabeth II so far unique. George V, in his old age, began to address his subjects collectively through the medium of sound broadcasting. George VI made his annual addresses at Christmas an institution for the Commonwealth, and, as many judged, a true promoter of fellow-feeling between its peoples. By the time Queen Elizabeth had been enabled on these occasions to make herself not only audible but visible to her subjects, first in black and white and presently in colour, the annual message had become so much part of the whole Commonwealth's pattern of life that an attempt to break the stereotype by interrupting the routine had to be promptly countermanded in response to widespread protests. Later on, the enormous success of the officially authorized film, intimately depicting the domestic life of the Royal Family, interspersed with some of the ceremonial observances, which has been exhibited on the television screens of nations far beyond the boundaries or sympathies of the Commonwealth, has made The Queen the best known woman in the world. To quote Sir Michael Adeane once more, now under examination by the Chairman of the Select Committee:

"I do not think that when The Queen came to the Throne anyone thought of television as being part of what you might describe as the apparatus of royalty. Now it is very much part of it, and one can see when one goes to some of these rather remote parts of the Commonwealth with The Queen, what the impact of it is, because all sorts of people who would hardly have known The Queen existed turn out to be as familiar with the everyday life of her family and children and even animals as if they lived in Westminster."

With some justification the most distinguished of the small group of writers who during the reign have argued the case for a republic—the late Kingsley Martin in *The Crown and the Establishment*—heads the central chapter "TV Monarchy".

Comparatively little needs to be said, because so little has changed, about The Queen's work as head of the state in the United Kingdom, that is, of her relation to politics, which has long ceased to be the most important, while remaining the most laborious, of the Sovereign's functions. Guided at first, as the young Victoria was guided by Lord Melbourne, by the affectionate loyalty of the veteran Winston Churchill, Queen Elizabeth slipped into the political routine of her father without jolt or jar. She has been served by six Prime Ministers, five of them Conservatives; but in the division of years in office between the two principal parties there has been no comparable disproportion. Each has been in power for long enough to give The Queen mature understanding of its ideas and purposes—and to have the benefit of The Queen's experience gained while the other side has been in occupation of Whitehall. Foreign inquirers into the British monarchy generally ask if it is possible for a Queen to work harmoniously with Labour Ministers. They are often surprised by the answer that no problem has ever arisen; that Parliament is not a theatre of class war nor the Sovereign the leader or patron of an established caste. Any early embarrassment there may have been was overcome long ago between George V and Ramsay MacDonald; and Queen Elizabeth has taken for granted a uniformly easy relationship with her accredited advisers, whatever party they represent and in whatever social background they were bred. She may or may not have personal preferences in politics: she never expresses them in public. In dealing with her Ministers she recognizes, as all Sovereigns in this century has done, that her function is not to impose her views but to help them realize their own.

Five times in the reign so far she has been called upon to exercise what is commonly described as the last remnant of direct royal authority in politics—the choice of a new Prime Minister when the office falls vacant. On three of these occasions her act was purely formal, there being obviously only one possible appointment. But when Sir Anthony Eden (now the Earl of Avon) resigned there was acute tension within the Conservative party over the rival claims of his Cabinet colleagues Mr Butler (now Lord Butler of Saffron Walden) and Mr Harold Macmillan. Sir Anthony's frail health, however, had caused the emergency to be foreseen some months earlier, during which The Queen's Household staff had taken pains to keep her in touch with all the important people who could inform her of the movement of opinion in the Conservative party. When Sir Anthony actually resigned, therefore, she was quickly able to make her choice, which was for Mr Macmillan, quite independently—not in any arbitrary sense, but in the sense that the friends she had consulted gave their advice informally, and were in no way to be held responsible for her eventual decision.

When Mr Macmillan himself was forced to resign, also on grounds of ill health, the circumstances were quite different. The sudden announcement took the Conservative party by surprise, and threw its counsels into confusion, for there were three or four candidates who might have justifiable ambitions to succeed him, and, moreover, it was by no means certain at first that, if his surgical operation were successful, Mr Macmillan himself might not be persuaded to resume his responsibilities. This time The Queen wisely decided to wait and let the Conservative leaders iron out their differences among themselves. This they did in several days of consultation or, as some described it, of intrigue. Only after their arguments had converged upon the name of a compromise candidate did The Queen act upon the long-established constitutional principle which lays down that she may, though she need not, seek the advice of the outgoing Prime Minister. She visited Mr Macmillan on his sickbed, accepted his resignation, and received from him the agreed name of the Earl of Home, who renounced his ancient dignities in the peerage and re-entered the House of Commons as Sir Alec Douglas-Home, KT.

After this embarrassing exposure of their internal dissensions, the Conservatives, following the example of their rivals on the Labour side, decided henceforth to elect their Leader by ballot of the parliamentary party. At first sight it appeared to many that thereby they in effect diminished the prerogative by extinguishing the last personal act of the Sovereign in government—her independent choice of a new Prime Minister*. Further consideration confirms that this was neither the intention nor the probable effect of the new machinery, whose authors were loyal monarchists. They were chiefly contemplating the choice of a leader when their party is out of office, which has never been of concern to the Sovereign. When a Leader of Opposition comes newly victorious from a general election, his moral claim to receive the royal commission has never been disputed. There remains the situation in which an undefeated Prime Minister is removed by death, disablement, or personal decision to retire. Here the circumstances may vary as widely as they did on the resignations of Sir Anthony Eden and Mr Macmillan, and in other possible directions which cannot be foreseen. (There might, for example, be a coalition in office, with more than one party to consider.) All that can be said is that the Minister has to be found under whom the government can most contentedly and efficiently continue its administration; and there may as often as ever be occasions on which the Sovereign can help it to make up its collective mind. She may wait until its internal discussions or votes have eliminated all candidates but one, but she is under no obligation to do so. She may still with perfect constitutional propriety invite a person of her own choice to take the vacant office. With equal propriety he may make his acceptance conditional on his finding sufficiently weighty support to make an effective Cabinet; this has long been normal practice, and if he adds that he must first make sure of a position as leader of his party, there is precedent also for that. He may therefore decide to submit himself to the new ballot procedure—in which very probably the fact of The Queen's prior approval will give him an advantage—perfectly legitimate—over any rivals. The effect of the new system can only be judged

* This interpretation was given in two contributions to the symposium called *The Monarchy and its Future* (Allen & Unwin, 1969) by Mr Paul Johnson (*p* 122) and the present writer (*p* 169). The different view now embodied in the text is the result of successive discussions with two Privy Councillors, each with special but quite different qualifications to speak with authority on this subject.

when it has been used in this way: it may be found in practice to confine the prerogative, but there is as yet no evidence that it is likely to do so.

Thus the residuary right and duty of The Queen on certain rare occasions to intervene personally in government remains formally, and it would seem substantially, what it was in the reigns of George V and George VI. For the rest, the political outline of the monarchy has continued from the previous reigns without a break. Though unseen by the world, it imposes upon The Queen a heavy burden, from which there is no complete relief even in holiday time, and no prospect of eventual retirement. The main purpose is to maintain regular contact and consultation, not only with Ministers in the United Kingdom, but with the leaders or representatives of all the countries of the Commonwealth. The Queen may spend two or three hours a day merely reading State Papers. A great part of her time is devoted to conferring with the endless series of incoming and outgoing Governors, High Commissioners, Ambassadors and other important functionaries with whom she does not merely exchange formal compliments: she uses these official receptions as a means of informing herself of the realities of life in the countries they serve. The work has increased during the reign, and seems likely to increase further. One reason is that, though the scope of authority has narrowed, the number of separate units in the Commonwealth, requiring the attention of its Head, multiplies. There are now thirty-one. All these manage their own affairs. But they would manage them less well if their rulers did not know that at the centre of the Commonwealth there is one person who has some knowledge of each of them, is the friend of all, and is always ready to extend sympathy, consultation and, if need be, advice in any situation that may threaten or perplex them.

Medieval Monarchy

BY H. R. LOYN

The Monarchy from the Age of Settlement to the Reign of Edgar (959-75)

The nature of kingship changed greatly during these centuries. There is no recognisable link with kingship as exercised in the ancestral Germanic homelands on the Continent. Only the Mercians claimed in their royal genealogies descent from kings who flourished when the English were still in Denmark: and the Mercians consisted of the greatest racial hotchpotch of all English peoples. The English settlement was an agrarian migration. Its history is to be found in place-name patterns that tell of river-valley communities, pioneering farming, building up tribal communities within the eastern lowlands of Britain. The English tribes were made in Britain; and so were the English ruling dynasties.

In these early days kingship was still essentially kingship over peoples, rather than over territories. The king was an active war-leader. He would exact tribute for himself or on behalf of the folk. He would preside over tribunals at which law was declared and judgements made. It is uncertain how strong his religious attributes were. Bede tells us that a ceremonial standard, a *tufa,* was borne before the high-king, Edwin, on his progress through the land. Elaborate jewelled harness and equipment, possibly to be associated with the East-Anglian high-king, Rædwald, has been discovered in the great grave-mound at Sutton Hoo in Suffolk. A special peace and protection was allotted the king in early recorded law. Pagan sanctions to monarchy may not have been given time to develop into truly significant historical attributes as in parts of Continental Germany and in Scandinavia. In the seventh century England was converted to Christianity. Thereafter the religious sanctions of kingship were closely associated with the new religion, with the Church and its bishops. Issuing of lawcodes, promulgation of charters to ensure stability in landholding, education of the young in English and in Latin, became symptoms of active co-operation of King and Church. As the kings extended their range beyond simple tribal units, developing into rulers of elaborate territorial communities, they drew more heavily on church support. A high point was reached at the end of the eighth century when Offa's son, Ecgfrith, was consecrated King. This ceremony, based on immediate precedent in Carolingian Frankia, is the first recorded ceremony of this type in English history. The West Saxon house carried on the principles of active co-operation with the Church to its ultimate point. King Alfred (871-99), the greatest of kings of the period, emerged from his fierce campaigns against the Danes as the true defender of Christian England. A further advance came in the reign of Edgar, the first King of England in recognisable modern form. Contemporaries and later chroniclers (with suitable poetic embroideries) made much of his solemn coronation. Edgar was effective King of an England that embraced all settled Christian English peoples. He was consecrated and crowned King. He was also recognised (if precariously) as a superior ruler by many of the Celtic rulers in Britain.

The Last Phase of the Old English Monarchy

There was a tendency in late Anglo-Saxon England to look back on Edgar's reign as a Golden Age in the past. The unhappy reign of Ethelred (978-1016) casts gloom on the later history of the West Saxon dynasty, but the achievements of Edgar and his predecessors were permanent. England had become a territorial kingdom, fully developed out of the tribal stage. The country was divided into shires, and the shires further divided into hundreds or wapentakes. Courts held regularly in these divisions helped to preserve a measure of peace. A second wave of Scandinavian invasion brought temporary disaster to the dynasty but not to the monarchy. The Danish victor, Cnut (1016-35), proved more English than the English. His law-codes were treated as a model for the following century and more. Special pleas were reserved for royal jurisdiction. Edgar's work was carried that stage further, and the King was universally regarded as special guardian of some aspects of the law. After a brief interlude under Cnut's sons the ancient dynasty itself was restored in the person of Edward the Confessor (1042-66) whose formative years had been spent in exile in Normandy.

During this late Anglo-Saxon period we find much active speculation about the nature of kingship. Earlier thought had drawn heavily from Old Testament precedent, and to some extent from immediate continental parallels. Edgar appears to have sworn a coronation oath which had the heart of the matter in it. He promised to protect the Church, to put down malefactors and evil-doing, and to uphold justice. Archbishop Wulfstan of York (1002-23), a homilist, scholar, and close adviser first to Ethelred and then to Cnut, wrote a tract on the rights and duties of men in the course of which he exhorted kings to be a comfort to their people and a righteous head over the Christian flock. Their prime duty was to protect the Church and all Christian people, to help the just and to put down evil-doers, to eschew heathenism and to support book-learning. His contemporary and friend, Aelfric, the greatest stylist in Anglo-Saxon prose, also concerned himself with the monarchy. In a famous sermon, written for delivery on Palm Sunday, he declared:

> No man can make himself king, but the people has the choice to select as king whom they please; but after he is consecrated king, he then has dominion over the people, and they cannot shake his yoke from off their necks.

To some extent this remained standard ecclesiastical theory until well after the Norman Conquest. The king was to be elected from the royal kin but, once consecrated, he should not be deposed. A wicked ruler was to be suffered as the penalty for sin.

The Norman Kings

Edward the Confessor died in early January 1066, and was succeeded by the strongest man in the kingdom, Harold son of Godwin, elected and crowned as Harold II even though he was not of the blood royal. After a brief troubled reign Harold was defeated and killed by William, Duke of Normandy on 14 October 1066. William's claims to the English throne rested not on blood, but on what he saw as an act of designation on Edward's part, on Harold's apparent solemn promise to agree to his succession, and on legal decision of the papal court in his favour. None of these claims would have been heard of again if it had not been for his military strength. The battle of Hastings, not shadowy promises and dubious law, made William King of England. Representatives of the old dynasty went into exile in Scotland. The marriage of Henry I, the Conqueror's youngest son, with Edith, the daughter of Queen Margaret of Scotland, a descendant of Ethelred through his son, Edmund Ironside, brought the ancient royal blood back into the English ruling stock.

The Norman Kings, William the Conqueror and his sons William Rufus (1087-1100) and Henry I (1100-1135) were careful to stress the legitimacy of their succession and so the continuity with the Anglo-Saxon past. The criterion of good law was the law of Edward the Confessor (in practice the laws of Cnut). By the intrusion of a new feudal aristocracy from Normandy, by castle-building and general concentration on military virtues, they brought however a new discipline into the executive government of an old community. The *Anglo-Saxon Chronicle* summed up William I's character and achievements at his death in 1087, describing him as harsh and so stern and relentless that no one dared act against his will. The Chronicler praised his good order but criticised him for his avarice and greed. Strong government remained the dominant characteristic of the reigns of the Conqueror's two sons. Henry I in his coronation charter, promulgated to gain support after his doubtful accession in 1100, pledged himself to protect the Church, to put down evil customs (mostly abuses of the feudal order), and to uphold good laws, even new law made by his father with the common counsel of the realm, but responsibility for executive government rested completely with the King. Increasing complexity of business, however, led steadily to the evolution of new permanent institutions of royal government. The King's household, though retaining its residual powers, was no longer enough. Financial affairs demanded special attention and the development in the early twelfth century of the Exchequer with its elaborate methods of accounting and its permanent records signifies an important stage in the growth of monarchical institutional life.

Part of the reason for increasing complexity in business must be attributed to involvement in continental affairs. The Norman Kings of England did not cease to be Normans and, apart from a spasmodic interlude between 1087 and 1106 Normandy and England were governed by the same men. The physical absence of the English Kings on visits, often protracted, to their Norman lands had consequences for the monarchy in accustoming England to occasional delegation of authority to justiciars, and favoured great magnates. Such delegation did not in this period weaken monarchy. It took the civil wars of Stephen's reign (1135-54) to bring the phase of powerful feudal government to an end. At the heart of discontent was uncertainty over hereditary succession not only to the monarchy but also to the baronial estates created as a result of the Norman Conquest. Henry I left only one legitimate child, a daughter, Matilda, married to the unpopular Geoffrey Plantagenet, Count of Anjou. In spite of the old King's efforts the community proved unwilling at this date (and throughout the Middle Ages) to accept a woman ruler. There was still no recognised order of precedence among possible male heirs, and it was the vigour and popularity of Henry I's younger nephew, Stephen of Blois, that brought him the crown. In time a party formed around Matilda.

Stephen retained his throne but was forced ultimately to a compromise solution over succession by which, on Stephen's death, the powerful Henry of Anjou, Matilda's son, became King of England in 1154.

The Angevin Monarchy

The family name of Henry of Anjou, Henry II of England, was Plantagenet, and the name Angevin or Plantagenet is used interchangeably by modern historians to describe Henry II and his sons, Richard and John. After the loss of Anjou and Normandy to the French crown in the early thirteenth century Angevin is rarely used in spite of the unbroken line of descent from the House of Anjou. For half a century after 1154, however, England was part of a vast complex of Angevin lands covering more of the map of France than that under the effective authority of the French King himself. Many of the Angevin territories, it is true, were fiefs of the French crown, and Philip II, King of France, 1180-1223, was able to reclaim lordship in Maine, Touraine, the greater part of Aquitaine, Brittany, and even Anjou and Normandy themselves by 1204; but the effort of holding these great territorial possessions on the English monarchy should not be underestimated. The efficiency of royal government in England under Henry II and both his royal sons owed much to the need for peace and resources at home so that the continental position could be stabilised; and the discontent resulting from the military disasters of John's reign was no small factor in determining the events leading to *Magna Carta.*

Royal institutions grew particularly strong in the legal and financial fields. Responsibility for government rested with the king and his court. Consent and advice were taken on matters of importance in the Great Council. Itinerant justices on regular circuits, helped by new more efficient legal procedures, made royal justice more accessible. Continuous series of records of their own indicate, by the beginning of the thirteenth century, the vigour of central institutions of government. John, in many respects a capable ruler, abused royal power to the point where he provoked rebellion. The resulting forced issue of *Magna Carta* marks an important stage in the development of English monarchy. The barons made no significant attempt to reduce the authority of the King. They showed themselves willing to accept the legal innovations of Henry II which had served to strengthen rather than weaken monarchy. Implicit in their demands, and even in the final version of *Magna Carta* in Henry III's reissue of 1225, was nevertheless the belief that the king governed under law, and that unlawful royal action could not be tolerated. No effective machinery was set up for bringing an unlawful monarch to book, but the later history of *Magna Carta* shows its importance as a symbol of restriction on royal power. Constitutional movements of the later Middle Ages tended to put confirmation of *Magna Carta* and allied documents high on their list of aims.

Monarchy in the Thirteenth Century: Henry III and Edward I

A further great crisis in the development of English monarchy occurred late in the reign of John's son and successor, Henry III, 1216-1272. Under the leadership of Simon de Montfort an attempt was made in 1258-65 to initiate what was virtually government by council as a safeguard against arbitrary royal rule. The attempt failed but not before Montfort, in his efforts to win support, had summoned representatives of the middle sort of men, knights from the shires and burgesses from the towns, to a central assembly of the realm. The victor in the Barons' War and ultimate heir in this respect both of his father, Henry III, and of Simon de Montfort was the Prince Edward, later to be Edward I, 1272-1307, one of the strongest of all English Kings. He conquered Wales, was less successful against Scotland, and within England brought up to date the instruments of government, increasing conciliar efficiency, initiating a fine legislative programme that helped among other things to stabilize land law and systematize police activities. Above all he continued the process of summoning representatives of the shires and towns to national assemblies, known as parliaments. Edward I and his successors came to rely more and more on parliament for financial aid in extraordinary circumstances. Edward himself drew counsel from parliament, and found it convenient and important as a place to announce legislation and to do justice. Not until after 1325, however, can it be said that the presence of "Commons" in parliament was customary and normal.

The Later Plantagenets

(a) MONARCHY IN THE FOURTEENTH CENTURY

England remained a monarchy in the full sense of the word, that is to say it depended for its healthy functioning on the will and capacity of the king. Dynastically it was fortunate in producing heirs in the male line: son succeeded father in unbroken succession from 1216 to 1377. Not all heirs were satisfactory and the fourteenth century experienced two major crises not over succession as such but over the capacity of the kings. Early in the reign of Edward II (1307-27) attempts were made to control the King by conciliar government. The attempts failed and he ruled with the help of his favourites, the Despensers, until (surprised by a conspiracy in which the leading figure was his wife) he was overthrown by an invasion from France, forced to abdicate, and murdered in prison in September 1327. During the following long reign of Edward III (1327-77), war with France, the first stages of the so-called Hundred Years' War, was the dominant political theme. Early sensational successes at Crecy and Poitiers were followed by set-backs and severe financial strains. Under pressure of military events the panoply of monarchy grew: the Order of the Garter dates from this reign. The kingship passed to Edward's young grandson, Richard II, but it was something of a perilous inheritance. The involved, complicated, ultimately excessively autocratic king overreached himself and brought retribution in 1399 in the shape of armed rebellion, military defeat, forced abdication and probable murder in 1400.

The fourteenth century had proved a century of chequered fortune for the monarchy. Two kings had been deposed, the one by faction, the other (Richard) by faction combined with constitutional acts which involved the consent of the realm as expressed in Parliament. Kings were still held to rule by grace of God and to exercise extensive powers by royal prerogative. Attempts to substitute council for king had failed. Yet even when a king was undoubtedly master of his council he was forced by the complexity of business to rely heavily on the councillors and others for carrying out royal commands. Parliament was increasingly accepted as a permanent part of government, with the knights and the burgesses (the "Commons") normally deliberating together and increasingly influential in financial affairs.

(b) MONARCHY IN THE FIFTEENTH CENTURY TO 1485

Henry IV (1399-1413) was the son of John of Gaunt, Duke of Lancaster, the fourth of Edward III's sons. He was succeeded by his son Henry V (1413-22), and in turn by his grandson, Henry VI (1422-61) and again for a brief unhappy interlude (1470-71). The title of Henry IV, and so of the Lancastrian house, rested on military success and also on parliamentary support, though the older view that the Lancastrians represented constitutional monarchy while their ultimate rivals and supplanters of York stood for a more arbitrary form of royal government is no longer tenable. The political and dynastic crises which erupted after 1455 into the civil wars commonly known as the "Wars of the Roses" compelled much hard thought about kingship, the royal prerogative, and the limitations in royal power, but they cannot be explained away by a simplified antithesis between York and Lancaster. The King was held to govern under law, whether of Lancaster or of York, and practical limitations in the exercise of his prerogative were imposed by the existence of institutions with a life and continuous history of their own, foremost among them parliament with its established methods of providing the assent of the realm to the *magna negotia* of the kingdom. In practical matters concerning finance and local government the King had also to rely on parliament and the great ones of the realm.

The first two Lancastrian Kings were both powerful rulers, though Henry V's ventures in France placed heavy strains on the machinery of royal government. His early death in 1422 initiated a long period of crisis in the monarchy. The dynasty was so well established that England acquiesced in the succession of an infant heir, Henry VI, acclaimed king of France as well as England. His physical and mental weaknesses led to what was at worst an unhappy travesty of medieval monarchy between 1437 and 1453; and yet constitutional historians have been quick to point out that the reign was not without promise for the monarchy. The long minority gave opportunity for what was virtually a continual royal administrative council to thrive. Henry's early acts after he came of age suggest that he and his close advisers, intent on re-establishing the force of royal prerogative, made important steps towards the creation of instruments of royal government that were later vigorously exploited by Yorkists and Tudors. The professional administrative element in the council was strengthened, and extensive use made of grants and warrants issued under the sign manual or signet seal. But sheer personal incapacity, coupled with lamentable political and military failures in the last flickers of the Hundred Years' War brought disaster to the Lancastrian monarchy. The last of the French territories (except Calais) was lost in 1453, and the king himself suffered his first and most severe attack of paralysis and insantity. The birth of a Lancastrian heir, Prince Edward, on 13 October 1453, complicated the situation further. Somewhat reluctantly—a measure of the respect for legitimate kingship—Henry's strongest kinsman, Richard, Duke of York, made a bid first for the regency and finally for the Throne itself. Richard was killed in 1460 but his son, Edward, helped by the powerful Earl of Warwick, overthrew the Lancastrians and was crowned King as Edward IV, March 1461. There was one brief flurry of Lancastrian revival in 1470-71. The pathetic Henry VI was taken from his prison in the Tower and placed on the throne. The adventure ended in a Lancaster holocaust; Edward, the Lancastrian heir, was put to death, his mother, Margaret of Anjou, was imprisoned, and Henry VI himself, still under fifty years of age, died in the Tower, so it was said, "of pure displeasure and melancholy". Edward IV thereafter ruled virtually without opposition.

Edward IV was descended in the male line from Edward III's fifth son and in the female from Clarence, the third of Edward III's sons. He therefore had a good claim to the Throne by right of blood. Edward IV was no new Italianate despot, rather a successful and vigorous exploiter of well-established principles of conciliar government. He worked his council hard, re-established (although comparatively slowly) royal solvency, exploited crown lands (swollen by attainders of the 1460s) and feudal rights, and controlled overmighty subjects with the possible exception of his own brother Richard of Gloucester. His death in 1483 at the age of forty provoked the final and strangest phase in medieval dynastic history. His twelve-year-old son, Edward V, was proclaimed King but immediately became the victim of a power struggle. Before he could be crowned he was imprisoned (together with his younger brother) in the Tower, declared illegitimate, and either died or was murdered there in the course of the succeeding years. The traditional villain of the piece was his uncle, Richard of Gloucester, who was crowned King at Westminster as Richard III in early July 1483. Richard had won a good reputation in his earlier days as a soldier and administrator in the North, and as a loyal servant of his brother, Edward IV; but opposition quickly mounted against him among disaffected Yorkists and Lancastrians alike. The death of Richard's only son in 1484 further weakened his position. A leader was found in the exiled Lancastrian Welshman, Henry Tudor, who could trace his descent to John of Gaunt and to Henry V's Queen, Catherine of France. In August 1485 Henry landed near Milford Haven, and started the campaign which ended in victory at Bosworth. He owed much to his Yorkist predecessors, and a vigorous new dynasty was now to take the monarchy a stage further along the paths that led to strong central government by means of a compact subservient royal council.

The monarchy thus experienced in the fifteenth century an even more alarming sequence of events than in the fourteenth: a long minority, erratic fitful personal rule followed by insanity on the part of the monarch, no fewer than five depositions (Henry VI twice, Edward IV once, Edward V, Richard III), and constant uncertainty and agitation over long periods concerning the nature of the monarchy and the legitimacy of the King. It is a tribute to the inherent strength of royal institutions and to the need of the English community for a focus for loyalty and authority that the monarchy survived so well. When the constitutionalists of the seventeenth century sought precedents they turned naturally to the period before the Tudor dynasty, to what they saw as the abortive Lancastrian constitutional experiments, to the growth of parliamentary privilege and power, and ultimately, of course, to *Magna Carta* and the rule of law itself.

The Monarchy under the Tudors

BY A. L. ROWSE

In most people's minds the English monarchy reached its apogee under the Tudors. The lasting impression made by the outsize personalities of Henry VIII and Elizabeth I may be taken to confirm it—and both of them took every care to stamp their image unforgettably upon the mind of their people. Of course both of them had the advantage, which not all our royal Houses have had, of being dominantly and exceptionally English. Hence both had an instinctive understanding of their people: whatever Henry VIII did he was always popular and has come down in the nation's memory as such ("bluff King Hal" indeed!—a singular foreshortening of the facts). The historian Creighton made Queen Elizabeth I's almost tactile sense of national feeling—she certainly had it at her finger-tips—the clue to her legendary success as a ruler.

Both father and daughter are living memories still—in itself a significant achievement when so much of the stuff of history is forgotten dust.

There is also the factor of sheer ability. Many historians would agree that the Tudor monarchs provided the ablest of our dynasties. Three out of the five were rulers of the first rank: Henry VII, Henry VIII and Elizabeth I. Edward VI was a youth of sixteen when he died, but he had already shown uncommon intelligence and a masterful will; he would have made his mark had he lived: the Elizabethan Age would have been the Edwardian Age. (Most of the great Elizabethans were Edwardians in origin and stamp.) Mary Tudor certainly made her mark; for all that her reign was tragic for herself and her people, the forceful little woman was no negligible figure.

But there is a more subtle consideration, a more important historical point, about the Tudor period: paradoxical as it may seem, it really saw, in a sense, the transition from medieval to modern monarchy. One might say, from power-monarchy to popular monarchy. This point will require some elucidation in its place.

For all Henry VII's being thought of as a Renaissance ruler, he was essentially a medieval man, still entirely circumscribed by medieval ideas and beliefs, like all the Lancastrian family abnormally religious. His own personality is all the more fascinating because so secret, little appreciated or understood in his own day or ours. He was deep and scheming, as he needed to be; a sage and cautious inward-looking man; far-seeing, with none of the Yorkist extrovert confidence in life, which his son inherited through his mother. The canny wise Welshman had little reason to trust anybody; he one day said to Polydore Vergil, with pardonable exaggeration, that he had spent the first fourteen years of his life in confinement, and the next fourteen in exile. In the end, he over-compensated his sense of insecurity by heaping up millions.

But that was able policy, too; in fact his personal control of the nation's finances—he was his own finance minister—was essential to good government. Observers saw—what Fortescue diagnosed in his famous book—that the weakness of the monarchy that led to the Wars of the Roses was in part financial. The monarchy could not properly function as custodian of the interests of the whole nation, when a number of "overmighty subjects" were powerful enough to take the law into their own hands. Henry VII and the Tudor monarchs put a stop to that. Henry VII was a humane man and accomplished it largely by financial measures; Henry VIII was not a humane man—he inherited the Yorkist capriciousness and cruelty—but whenever he executed one of the overmighty, not a town-cat mewed. Fundamentally he had the nation with him.

I find the personality of Henry VII more fascinating because so much less obvious—yet there it is all written in the wonderful Torrigiani portrait-bust of him: the lean, ascetic features, the deep-sunk eyes, the sad watchfulness. His racial mixture is so interesting: Welsh on one side, French and Italian blood of Valois and Visconti; his only English royal descent through his remarkable mother, the Lady Margaret Beaufort, undoubted heiress-general of John of Gaunt—without her astute Beaufort brain Henry would never have achieved the throne.

I have sometimes wondered if he spoke English with a Welsh accent—more likely with a French one: he did his serious reading (he was well educated) in French. His idea of kingship must have been influenced by the most successful exponent of it in the generation senior to his, Louis XI. Though so careful about money—his meanness deserves to be inscribed in letters of gold in the annals of the country, for he made it prosperous by trade instead of wasting its wealth by wars (like his son)—yet Henry VII had a royal magnificence, not only in his surroundings but in his foundations. What could be more magnificent than Henry VII's Chapel at Westminster?

His rule, as with his son, was personal; the well-being, the interests, of the nation were never in better hands; he saw to everything with his unpopular memorandum-books. For all his services to the country, and his fame abroad as a successful ruler, he never had the popularity he so well deserved. Absolute master in his house, depending on no-one, all his ministers really his agents, he yet ruled constitutionally. As Bacon summed him up—one subtle man summing up another: "He was ever an observer of formality in all his proceedings, which notwithstanding was no impediment to the working of his will."

Henry VII was not only the founder of the Tudor dynasty, but a far-seeing creator to whose plans—it is too often overlooked—the present royal family owe their possession of the throne. He had his eye on the eventual unification of Scotland with England. To that end he negotiated the marriage of his daughter Margaret with James IV of Scotland; it was through that marriage that the Stuarts—much less successful as rulers—succeeded to the throne of the Tudors, and thence to the present line.

Henry VIII makes much more of a figure in people's minds for, after all, he carried through a revolution—a revolution from on top, with his subordination of the Church to the State, nationalizing perhaps one-third of the Church's lands and revenues altogether, and uniting the powers of both in his capacious hands. From our particular point of view, the evolution of the monarchy, the apex of monarchical power since medieval times was reached under him.

To such an extent that people often think of him as a despot, and talk and write of the Tudor Despotism. But this is inaccurate. A despot is an arbitrary ruler unrestrained by law, a despotism means properly rule without law. And this was not true even of Henry VIII, the most "despotic" by nature of the family, let alone of the others. They were all authoritarian and temperamentally autocratic, but it was their business to be so: we see how difficult it is to keep any semblance of order in society today—still more so in the more primitive conditions of the sixteenth century.

In fact Henry VIII was no dictator—unlike Oliver Cromwell, whose rule rested on the Army, totally unrepresentative of the nation. Henry VIII was careful to make his revolutionary changes—the breach with the Papacy, the assumption of headship of the Church, the dissolution of the monasteries—along with and through Parliament. Rather legalistic in mind, he never overstepped the bounds of constitutionality. These decisive changes, however, greatly increased the power of the monarchy in the short run, and the efficiency of the state in the long run.

With part of the proceeds of the dissolution Henry built his Navy—the effective beginning of the Royal Navy. Another part of the Church's ancient non-productive wealth went into the fortifications all round the southern coast. Henry was as keenly interested in naval shipbuilding as he was in military engineering. These are two crucial interests that serve to illustrate his personal activity and intervention in practically all sides of government. He not only gave political leadership, himself set the directives and the pace, but was the executive, the boss—like a Stalin in more ways than one. In the last years of his life, in his last French war, Henry had himself carried in a chair—a great hulk of a man, swollen with his glandular condition, in pain from the ulcer in his leg—down to Portsmouth to direct operations himself.

He certainly identified the state with himself, but then so did everybody around him (except Sir Thomas More, who paid for that with his life): no ruler could ever have claimed more entirely, "L'état, c'est moi". With his ruthless and insatiable egoism, there was very much a personality cult around him. He called in the genius of Holbein to create the image, paint the portraits, stamp upon people's minds the persona still so familiar to us.

He kept his grip on power to the last, playing cat-and-mouse with the factions waiting for the succession. In his last year, an ambassador described "the old fox, surrounded by men of great ability". Henry could dominate and drive them all. He specifically left the masterful Bishop Gardiner out of the Council that was to govern for his young son: "Marry, I could control him; but so shall not any of you". He meant to control what should happen after his death by his Will, which he held up to the last moment, keeping everybody on tenterhooks lest he should recover and pounce again. With his last pounce, the old tiger destroyed the Howards, and left the way open for his new deal and the Protestant dynamic to go forward together.

With the minority of the boy-king Edward VI, we have a striking object-lesson of what the monarchy was for the nation: the true guardian of its interests and protector of the people at large. For, the moment Henry was dead, the rapacious oligarchy around his son joined together to help themselves right and left to the Crown's, *i.e.* the nation's, wealth. There was a grand hand-out all round not only of peerages and titles but, more important, of lands and revenues. Little Edward's Seymour uncle, who had started as just a country gentleman, became Lord Protector and a Duke; his income shot up from £2500 to £7500 (multiply by 100 for contemporary valuation). The rest of the reptiles gorged themselves similarly while the going was good, *i.e.* while the King was a minor, in no position to protect his own or the country's.

If Edward had lived, he would have got some of it back. His attempt to alter the succession, when he was dying, showed a glimpse of Tudor will-power. The design to keep his half-sisters out and put Lady Jane Grey on the throne has always been blamed on Northumberland, but Edward was at least as responsible and bullied the Council into signing the "Devise". He said that his sisters, Mary and Elizabeth, were but of the half-blood and both had at one time been declared illegitimate: there was no doubt about the legitimacy of Lady Jane Grey, Henry's niece.

What the nation, however, showed upon Edward's death was that it wanted Henry's children, not his niece. That in itself was another tribute to the astonishing force of personality of the dead Henry. Queen Jane would have made an able and excellent Queen; both Mary and Elizabeth could hardly have been legitimate—Catholics thought Mary, Protestants thought Elizabeth. No matter; such was the charisma of this man that, as he willed the succession, so it came about—each of his children in turn, Edward, Mary, Elizabeth.

Mary I came to the throne with a certain amount of good will—except for the supporters of the new deal, who had been in power since Henry's later years. But Mary had been out of the centre of politics for twenty years, put aside—it had not been expected that she would succeed to the throne and attempt to reverse the whole course set during that time. It was yet another tribute to the force of monarchical power that the country should have accepted the reversal, simply because the new Queen was an unreconstructed Catholic. She had never accepted the new deal in her heart and, though her father had forced her to subscribe, she would not accept her brother's further changes. She intended to put the clock back to where it had ceased to be; the effort broke her heart and dissipated the good will of the nation. But it did not break the monarchy—for there was an alternative already on the stage, and in people's minds.

Mary Tudor was quite as authoritarian as any of her family, and even more obstinate—no sense of compromise, so necessary in politics, and in which her sister was so adept. Mary detested the new deal and all its works, disapproved of the whole course the nation had taken in the past twenty years, and put down all its ills to this. She intended to have her way, as her father had done—without any of his political flair—and at once met with resistance. In the first year of her reign Wyatt's Rebellion might have overthrown her, but for her royal courage. The tiny figure went down to the Guildhall and, in her singularly deep voice, made a personal appeal to the citizens of London to save her throne—and their own property.

I admire her for her spirit and could almost love her for the magnificent rebuke she administered to the Council when they opposed her wishes: "My father made the more part of you out of almost nothing". Observe the moral scrupulousness of "the more part", not every one of them, and again not out of nothing but out of "almost" nothing. Still more, she gave the grandest royal snub when, as Princess, she was asked by Protector Somerset's brother to advance his candidature for the hand of Henry's widow: "If the remembrance of the King's Majesty my father (whose soul God pardon) will not suffer her to grant your suit, I am nothing able to persuade her to forget the loss of him, who is as yet very ripe in mine own remembrance".

It somehow evokes that terrifying shade of "the King's Majesty my father", very vividly.

But where Henry could terrify, Mary could not, for all her burnings. This is where the Spanish fanaticism in her character came out: she regarded Protestantism as a deviation which she could burn out, as Spain succeeded in doing. But in England it could not be done: Protestantism had the future with it. All that Mary succeeded in doing was in finishing Catholicism effectively, and in alienating the nation from herself and branding her memory. In the end it was impossible to govern the country any longer on that basis, she could not even maintain order in London. She had divided the country by her inflexible fixation; her refusal to contemplate any attempt to find a consensus meant a (temporary) loss of authority and power to the Crown.

It was Elizabeth I's prime business to repair the damage and recover the position—much as it fell to George VI and his Queen to repair the damage wrought by the episode of Edward VIII. There was such a reaction against the bankruptcy and bitterness of Mary's rule, especially in London, that Elizabeth I on her accession was swept further to the left, in a Protestant direction, than she wished. But, like her father and grandfather—she more closely resembled Welsh Henry VII in character—she was an astute politician and knew when she had to compromise.

This common sense at once began to pay dividends. The Spanish ambassador, Feria, soon noticed that she was much more readily obeyed than her sister and was in a position to exert something of her father's authority. A London citizen, as he watched her go by in her coronation procession, was heard to say, "Remember old King Harry?" (Henry was always pronounced Harry then.)

There is this great difference to be observed. Machiavelli, whose tractate *The Prince* was a text-book of Renaissance statecraft, has a chapter on "Whether it is better that a Prince should be loved or feared", and he concluded in favour of the latter. Henry VIII deliberately and consciously opted to be feared—and was so effective a ruler that he lost no popularity in consequence. Elizabeth I from the very beginning set out to be loved; she made an art of cultivating popularity, she always played to the gallery; someone at the time said she was a fisherman who fished for men's hearts with sweet bait. This was true from beginning to end of her reign, and received final expression in her famous last Address to the Commons, the Golden Speech: "Though God hath raised me high, yet this I count the glory of my crown: that I have reigned with your loves".

This policy became second nature to her, perhaps the real and enduring love of her life; it was no less effective than her father's option to rule *in terrorem*. Though we cannot say that she was exactly feared, her authority was thoroughly respected.

She was very watchful to see that it was, and there is historical proof of its effectiveness. She would allow no interference in what she regarded as the proper sphere of her prerogative. First, with regard to the Church, of which she was Supreme Governor—she certainly acted in every way as its Supreme Governess. Having accepted the return to Edwardian Protestantism in 1559, inevitably, she stood pat on that position for the rest of her life, resisting any further changes in a Protestant direction or any attempt of Parliament to interfere. She was the real obstacle to Puritanism, the effective enemy of the Puritan minority. If the laity in Parliament had had their way, the Church of England would have been more Protestant, possibly more Presbyterian. Its catholic and comprehensive character is a standing proof of her effective role in government.

There are many others. There was her steady refusal to marry, despite the pressure put on her by Parliament. Herewith another resounding royal snub, this time to the whole assembly: "I am your anointed Queen. I will never be by violence constrained to do anything. I thank God I am endued with such qualities that if I were turned out of the Realm in my petticoat I were able to live in any place in Christendom". With that she dismissed them.

Her aim from the beginning was to recover, and then maintain, the maximum of national unity; to this end she disapproved public discussion of divisive issues, for example religion. She was more conservative socially, as a woman would be, than her father, who had made his two chief ministers of a disreputable butcher's son (Wolsey) and a brewer's son of Putney (Cromwell). Sir Robert Naunton observed that she never made a favourite of a mere mechanic. She was consciously conservative of the peerage; frequently we find her refusing to allow a young peer who had as yet no heir to serve abroad and risk his life. At the same time she would not cheapen titles and honours by profuse creations and awards—as the Stuarts immediately did, and for money.

In government she had the last word, hers was the final court of appeal—as her great ministers, Lord Burghley and his son, Robert Cecil, always recognised. The essential quality in which they were at one with the Queen was the ability to think always in terms of the central well-being of the state and its long-term interests, without fear or favour, without partisan deviation. The Queen took full part in discussions in Council, and in negotiations with foreign ambassadors—here her linguistic abilities were a great advantage, speaking Latin, French, or Italian. (No foreigner spoke English in those days.) Her temper was as autocratic as her father's, though more humane and reasonable—a fine outburst was a way of keeping people on their toes. Robert Cecil said that in her last years, "no one durst oppose anything the Queen said, unless I bestow half-a-dozen words upon it".

Over the crucial personal issue of Mary Stuart's execution the whole Council virtually took the decision, though not the responsibility, out of Elizabeth's hands. Her last showdown was with Essex, and this was specifically over the *arcana imperii*. He intended to control James's accession to the English throne. Dangerous in itself, this was a challenge to what the Queen most held at heart, the independence of the Crown, the sacred rights of monarchy—fatal to the whole function of monarchy to have it controlled by a subject.

We may say that just as the power of the monarch reached its apex with Henry VIII, so the cult of monarchy achieved its apotheosis with Elizabeth I. Its expressions indeed offer a foremost chapter in English culture. In literature the Queen is immortalised in Spenser's *Faerie Queene*, and many another work; in art by Hilliard and other painters and jewellers; in music by Tallis and Byrd's *Cantiones Sacrae* announcing the maturity of a new school to Europe, and at the end by *The Triumphs of Oriana* in which all the composers united to do her honour; the drama, which owed so much to her encouragement and protection, is starred with tributes to her.

Shakespeare displays the whole pageant, the role and range of kinship. There is the religious aura, the sacramental character of the anointing of a king:

Not all the water in the rough rude sea
Can wash the balm from an anointed King . . .

Even the Protestant Edward VI had been anointed, though Archbishop Cranmer was careful to explain that its purpose was symbolic, not a sacrament in itself. We are reminded that Elizabeth I performed the sacred rite of touching for the King's Evil, just as the Catholic Mary did. All these paraphernalia of monarchy we should recognise today as having an anthropological significance for primitive societies, even if emptied of religious content.

Shakespeare characteristically expresses all aspects of monarchy, from the sacramental to the utilitarian. On the one hand,

There's such divinity doth hedge a king;

on the other, if a king does not properly fulfil his function and do his job, he goes, like Richard II; his place is taken by the next member of the royal family who can, Henry IV. It is all chiefly summed up in the play Shakespeare devoted to kingship, *Henry V;* for, to the Elizabethans, Henry V was the ideal hero-king, taking upon himself the burdens of society, caring for all his people, in himself representing them all. That was what Elizabeth I tried to be and do, with the success that has given her an enduring place in the memory of her people.

And yet—we come to the explanation of the paradox with which we began—for all her fame, she left the monarchy less powerful than it had been under her father and grandfather. It could hardly have been otherwise. For one thing, society had become less primitive, evolved a stage further. For another, during the second half of the Tudor period, with a minor then two women on the throne, they could hardly conduct the actual business of government, give the active day by day supervision that Henry VII and Henry VIII had done. It is in this sense that we may say that the Tudor period saw the transition from medieval monarchy, where government was the king's personal affair, to the more modern idea where the role of the monarch is to be representative, to represent in his or her person the whole society. In that sense Elizabeth I was on the way to that idea so well exemplified in her successor by name.

The Monarchy under the Stuarts

BY MARK BENCE-JONES

When James VI of Scotland ascended the English throne as James I, the prevailing sentiment among his new subjects was one of relief that the country had been spared the evils of a disputed succession. In the words of Bacon, "it rejoiced all men to see so fair a morning of a Kingdom, and to be thoroughly secured of former apprehensions; as a man that awaketh out of a fearful dream". A hundred years later, James's great-grandson, namesake and rightful heir was living in exile, destined never to regain the throne which his father had lost. And between the "fair morning" of James I's accession and the December's day in 1688 when James II sailed away for good aboard a fishing-smack, lay the tragedy of Charles I. One can ascribe the misfortunes of the seventeenth century Stuart kings to the notorious ill-luck of their House; one can take the traditional Whig view of history and blame their downfall on their obstinate determination to resist the growth of English parliamentary democracy. Or one can see the Stuarts as a line of conscientious monarchs, most of them notable characters in their own right, but with the exception of Charles II—and William III, who was only half a Stuart—lacking the statesmanship necessary for guiding the barque of monarchy through the extremely difficult times in which it was their fate to live.

It was unfortunate for the Stuarts that by the time they ascended the English throne, the country was growing less afraid of the might of Spain. The threat from abroad had united Elizabeth's subjects behind her; making for an amenable Parliament, with all other issues subordinate to foreign policy, in which, since it was part of the Royal prerogative, the Queen had a free hand. The Stuarts had no military glory to compare with the Armada; that sad and ailing mother of twelve dead children, Queen Anne, being hardly in a position to derive much personal benefit from Blenheim and Ramilles, which did not happen until the fate of the dynasty was already virtually sealed. The nearest was the great naval victory of 1665 against the Dutch; which, as well as bringing glory to Charles II—in any case the most successful of all the Stuarts—enabled his brother, James, Duke of York, the future James II, to show his courage and leadership as commander of the British fleet.

Without the distraction of foreign affairs, the Stuarts faced a Parliament that had grown greatly in stature during the past century. Not only did the Tudors strengthen the constitutional position of Parliament by making full use of it as a backing to their rule; but their social, economic, religious and foreign policy had enriched the country gentry and merchant classes, giving a new importance to the House of Commons. Almost inevitably, there would have been some conflict between the Stuarts and Parliament; if it had not happened on account of James I's Scottish upbringing, which made him ignorant of English institutions, it would have been caused by a British monarch of the later seventeenth century becoming imbued with the ideas of kingship fashionable on the Continent, of which the chief protagonist was Louis XIV. But the conflict might never have assumed the proportions it did—plunging the country into civil war, sending one king to the scaffold and another into exile—had the Stuarts not been chronically short of money; and if they and the Commons had not been on opposite sides in the religious controversies which loomed so large in seventeenth century Britain.

Even under the frugal Elizabeth I, the permanent revenue of the Crown was not enough to meet the ordinary expenses of government. As the seventeenth century progressed, the cost of government increased; with additional expenditure on account of the Irish troubles. Then there was the extravagance of the Stuarts, who kept up a far larger household than that of Elizabeth I; built palaces and made substantial purchases of jewels and plate. Charles I spent money on pictures; he was the first British monarch to do so, building up a collection which would now be the finest in the world had it not been dispersed under the Commonwealth.

The Stuarts were thus obliged to call Parliament frequently, and ask for subsidies towards ordinary expenditure; whereas Parliament was theoretically supposed to meet on great occasions only, to vote money for wars and other national emergencies. These frequent sittings gave Parliament plenty of opportunities to criticise the King's government, and in particular to demand the redress of grievances in the ecclesiastical field. To avoid calling Parliament and being faced with such grievances, the Crown looked for ways of increasing its ordinary revenue, which inevitably created further grievances for Parliament to redress when it was next called; causing its relations with the Crown to deteriorate still further.

Used as we are to the monstrous taxation of today, we nevertheless tend to think like the seventeenth century merchants and gentry and regard Ship Money, Forced Loans and the other means by which the Stuarts extracted additional funds from their subjects as intolerable and crushing burdens. In fact, considering how the country had grown in wealth under Elizabeth, and continued to grow richer throughout the Stuart period—with the East India and Levant Companies capturing the trade of distant parts of the world—the scale of taxation was absurdly low, even by the standards of the time; as Sir Walter Raleigh had pointed out shortly before the death of the old Queen. When people paid taxes according to a fixed assessment, which remained unchanged even though their incomes might have greatly increased, the Stuart Kings were justified in attempting to make them pay more. Of the Royal revenues, only the customs kept pace with the rising national wealth; until, towards the end of the reign of Charles II, the finances of the Crown were at last on a satisfactory footing. Earlier in his reign, Charles II had been as short of money as either his father or grandfather. He had been obliged to stop paying interest to his bankers and to accept subsidies from Louis XIV, who considered it worth handing out large sums to keep the predominantly anti-French Parliament from sitting. Ironically, James II was alone among the first four Stuart Kings in having no financial troubles, only to founder on the other reef which had all along been a menace to the Stuart monarchy. That was religion.

At the beginning of the seventeenth century, the Church of England was predominantly Calvinistic, or Puritan; with a small Arminian or High Church party led by Lancelot Andrewes. Having had all too much experience of the Presbyterians of Scotland, James I did not take kindly to Puritanism, even in its milder English form. "A Scottish Presbytery agreeth as well with a monarchy as God and the Devil" he exclaimed angrily after hearing the English Puritan point of view at the conference which he called at Hampton Court in 1604; and for the rest of his reign he was on the side of the Arminians. Charles I went further in his espousal of the High Church cause; not merely through a distaste for Puritanism, as had been largely the case with his father, but because he sincerely believed in the teachings of Andrewes and of Andrewes' more celebrated disciple, William Laud, whom he made Archbishop of Canterbury in 1633. In this lay the roots of the conflict between Charles I and Parliament, which was overwhelmingly Puritan. It has been widely held that Charles I died for his religious beliefs; for had he, after being defeated in the Civil War, agreed to Parliament's demand that Presbyterianism should be established, he might have preserved his throne as well as his life. Until last century the Church of England venerated him as Charles, King and Martyr, and kept his feast every year.

The cult of the Royal Martyr—furthered by such books as *Eikon Basilike*—and the inevitable reaction to the unbridled Puritanism of the Commonwealth, made the Church of England far more Arminian after the Restoration than it had been before; so that if Charles II and James II had adhered to the same beliefs as their father and grandfather, they might have had no religious troubles. Instead, they moved away from the Church of England towards Catholicism. James II's conversion to Rome, which took place during the reign of his brother, nearly cost him his succession to the Throne, and lost him the Throne three years after he had succeeded to it. Charles II prudently avoided being received into the Catholic Church until he was on his death-bed; but his obvious Catholic sympathies aroused the suspicions of his more bigotted Protestant subjects. He also laboured under the disadvantage of having a Catholic Queen, Catherine of Bragança; just as his staunchly Anglican father had been suspected of Popery through being married to the French Catholic Queen Henrietta Maria.

The anti-Catholic prejudices of seventeenth century England were exacerbated by the Irish bogey, which, in the form of the rising of 1641, made matters much worse for Charles I on the eve of the Civil War. Charles II was fortunate in having a peaceful Ireland throughout his reign; but James II's policy of redressing the wrongs of the Irish Catholics, while being morally justifiable, was a grave tactical error, for it brought a stream of disgruntled Anglo-Irish Protestants over to England, whose stories awakened the fears of 1641 all over again. English Francophobia did not take kindly to Charles I's French Queen and Charles II's private negotiations with the King of France; but Charles II suffered far less as the supposed lackey of Louis XIV than did James II from being regarded as the ally of the Irish: it is significant that *Lillibulero,* the song alleged to have sung him out of his three kingdoms, is about the machinations of his Irish henchman, Richard Talbot, Earl of Tyrconnell.

In fact James II was not the Catholic bigot he was popularly supposed to be. His aim was not to overthrow the Church of England but to restore to his Catholic subjects the rights which had been taken away from them by the Test Act and other legislation during the previous reign. The Quaker, William Penn, saw in him "a true spirit of toleration and a real desire to grant to all men freedom of worship in their own way"; for his toleration, like that of Charles II, extended to the Non-Conformist Dissenters, who suffered from the same disabilities as the Catholics. It might be said that this was merely in order to gain the support of the Dissenters against the Church of England; yet there is no reason why James should not have resembled his brother, his father and his grandfather who were all genuinely tolerant in matters of religion—a rare virtue among monarchs of the seventeenth century, when it was generally accepted that the subject should hold the same religious beliefs as his Prince. Charles II tried to counter the penal legislation of his reign by his two Declarations of Indulgence, but was obliged to withdraw them owing to the strength of Parliament. Charles I, though personally devoted to High Anglicanism, showed, in the words of a modern Catholic writer, "a cool and dignified forbearance towards the adherents of the old religion"*. James I, though his attitude towards Catholics appeared to harden at the time of the Gunpowder Plot, relaxed the severity of the anti-Catholic laws as soon as the immediate panic was over.

Far more serious than the Gunpowder Plot in the effect it had on James I's thinking was the attempt by Father Robert Parsons and other Catholic controversialists to dispute his title to the English throne, which James answered by claiming that his right to the Throne came from Heaven—a claim also made in support of Henri Quatre. Thus did the Stuart monarchy take unto itself the doctrine of Divine Right, formerly exclusive to Popes and Emperors. Had Divine Right been limited to the matter of succession, and to such outward signs of "the divinity that doth hedge a King" as touching for the King's Evil, it might not have caused any constitutional problems; but the logical inference of the doctrine that the King held his power of God was that to disobey him was to disobey God's Will. Or as James himself put it in his speech to the Judges in 1616, "That which concerns the mystery of the King's power is not lawful to be disputed; for that is to wade into the weakness of Princes, and to take away the mystical reverence that belongs unto them that sit in the throne of God". Hence the "absolute power" of the Stuarts, which in effect was no more extensive and nothing like as tyrannical as the "Royal prerogative" of the Tudors; but whereas the latter was within the framework of the law, the former, since it was supposed to derive from Heaven, knew no bounds, and was regarded as a potential threat to the English Parliamentary system; providing the Parliamentarians with a reason for fighting the Civil War. Needless to say, the doctrine of Divine Right did not lack its champions among the intelligensia, who carried it much further than the Stuarts themselves ever did: writers like Dr John Cowell and Sir Robert Filmer, High Church ecclesiastics such as Archbishop Laud, whose teachings gave rise to the corollary of Non-Resistance, which caused the Anglican clergy so many heart-searchings at the time of the Revolution.

James I was aware that there were those among his subjects who went too far in attributing supernatural powers to the King. "I am neither a god nor an angel, but a man like any other" he told his Council, with some of the smugness inherent in his nature. The traditional picture of the "Wisest Fool in Christendom", that ungainly monarch who made puns, was inclined to dribble at the mouth and whose hands were white and soft like "satin sarsaparilla" is not an attractive one; his weakness for favourites, which saddled the country with Robert Carr and the egregious Buckingham, has given rise to unpleasant insinuations; while it is hard to forget his indifference to the fate of his mother, Mary Queen of Scots. Yet he cannot have been so ponderous

* Archbishop David Mathew, *Catholicism in England*.

when he first ascended the English throne, for he was then only thirty-seven and passionately addicted to hunting; and if he was a pedant, we must remember that pedantry in a monarch was better than either tyranny or nonentity. He may not have quite lived up to his own concept of himself as a philosopher-king, but he was genuinely learned and a ruler of ability; showing himself to be statesmanlike and in advance of his time in wishing for a real instead of just a personal union with Scotland, and in his toleration of Catholics. His sayings, such as his celebrated condemnation of Sir Walter Raleigh's habit of smoking, might to us seem laboured; but to most of his contemporaries they would have passed as wit. In an age much given to polemics, there was something to be said for a King who could meet the lawyers and Puritan divines on their own ground.

Charles I's troubles might have been less had he been able to lecture his adversaries in the way that his father would have done. Instead, he faced them with infinite sadness and dignity. Unlike his father, who had the self-confidence born of being a King from infancy, Charles did not become heir to the Throne until the death of his brilliant and popular elder brother, Prince Henry. As well as lacking experience, he suffered from a stammer, and from the disadvantage of being under-sized, having been sickly as a child—some believe him to have been a victim of polio.

As a King, his worst fault was his weakness. He was unable to stand by his word, as when he sacrificed that most able servant of the Stuart monarchy, the Earl of Strafford, to the wrath of Parliament, having previously assured him of his safety. Like so many weak men, he was obstinate; and when he found himself in a difficult situation, he would resort to duplicity. At the same time, Charles did not lack courage, as can be seen from the manner in which he faced death. Though his enemies called him "Charles Stuart, that man of blood", he was by nature humane; when his nephew, Prince Rupert, attempted to introduce some of the harsher methods of the Thirty Years War into the English civil conflict, he was as angry as James II was fifty years later when one of his foreign generals behaved with an un-British brutality at the siege of Derry. Charles's greatest virtue was his conscientiousness. He was also, as we have seen, deeply religious; he had exquisite taste in art and architecture and was a devoted family man.

Domesticity is not something which we associate with Charles II, though he was fond of children and loved his sister, Minette; he might have been more of a family man had he been blessed with legitimate offspring. It is, moreover, to his credit that he steadfastly refused to listen to those who suggested that he should divorce his Queen on account of her childlessness. He was fond of the rather plain Catherine of Bragança, however unfaithful he may have been to her; and he never failed to treat her with kindness.

Physically, Charles II was in complete contrast to his father: tall and strong, with swarthy and slightly coarse good looks that were very different from his father's over-refined beauty. He had charm, energy and an abundance—perhaps an excess—of animal spirits; he got on with people and was witty; his sayings, unlike those of his grandfather, are still fresh and show a broad understanding of humanity. Behind his gaiety and love of pleasure lay a sense of purpose and a capicity for the business of ruling. He resembled his father in his toleration and in his love of art and architecture, to which he added an interest in science. As a present-day writer has put it, he brought a stylishness to the monarchy. The same writer sees a resemblance between him and his maternal grandfather, Henri Quatre; but while Charles may have inherited something of his grandfather's character, he seems closer to our idea of a modern English king than to a French king of the sixteenth century. We see him visiting the Navy, entertaining ambassadors aboard his yacht (often to their discomfiture), racing at Newmarket, going to the theatre; conversing on easy terms with any of his subjects who happen to be present. During the Fire of London, he personally took charge of the fire-fighting, assisted by his brother, the Duke of York; the people, who earlier had taken no notice of the City Fathers in the prevailing panic, willingly obeyed orders when they came from him.

As a ruler, Charles showed great political ability combined with a certain lack of scruple, which was apparent in his secret negotiations with Louis XIV, as well as in his use of corrupt methods—distributing pensions and places, even direct bribery—to build up a party in Parliament. He also had a talent for choosing the right ministers: Clarendon, the faithful old servant of the House of Stuart in its adversity for the first halcyon years following the Restoration; the clever men of the Cabal for when he was playing high, endeavouring to free himself from Parliamentary control and to pursue a policy of toleration; the reliable if uninspiring Danby for the years when he was on the defensive. Then, in the fevered months following the Popish Plot, when the Shaftesbury faction attempted to exclude the Catholic Duke of York from the succession to the Throne, and grew so powerful that the outbreak of a new civil war seemed imminent, Charles became his own minister and showed a superb sense of timing in the way that he allowed his enemies to overplay their hand, so that he not only restored his kingdom to sanity and saved the succession for his brother, but scored such a victory over Parliament that he was able to do without it for the remaining four years of his reign.

That James II should so quickly have thrown away the advantage bequeathed to him by his brother was due primarily to his tactlessness, and to his possessing even more than his father's share of obstinacy. He resembled his father in having plenty of courage, but was a much more straightforward character; he lacked the charm with which, in different ways, both his father and his brother were amply endowed. In James's defence, it must be said that if only Parliament had agreed to repeal the Test Act, he might never have embarked on his disastrous policy of appointing Catholics to key positions, which he did in order to demonstrate the right of his co-religionists to serve their King and country. It was also unfortunate that his Queen, Mary of Modena, should have borne him a son and heir just as he was at his most unpopular: the prospect of a Catholic dynasty proving at this juncture too much for most of his subjects.

The reigns of William and Mary and Queen Anne seem little more than the epilogue of the Stuart monarchy. The Revolutionary Settlement had extinguished the doctrine of Divine Right, which had been replaced, in Whig philosophy, by the no less unhistorical theory of the "Original Contract" between King and people. The Royal prerogative, which formed the basis of Stuart absolutism, had been greatly curtailed: the Crown could no longer raise and keep a standing army in time of peace without the consent of Parliament; while Parliaments had to be summoned at least every three years, and could not continue for longer than this period. Nevertheless, Mary II and Queen Anne were as much Stuarts as any of their predecessors, being the daughters of James II—they were, incidentally, the grand-daughters of Clarendon, since James had, contrary to what was by his time the accepted custom for Royal princes, married the commoner Anne Hyde as his first wife—while William III was the son of Charles I's daughter Mary, who became Princess of Orange.

After the first flush of the "Glorious Revolution" had died down, the nation's enthusiasm for "Dutch William" quickly waned. He was a foreigner, he did not bother to understand the British people and their customs, his manner was chilling. Like James I, he had his favourites, whom he brought with him from Holland; though neither Bentinck nor Keppel ever threatened to become a new Carr, still less a Buckingham. William was a European statesman of the first magnitude; respected as such by Louis XIV, whom he in turn respected as an adversary worthy of himself. He regarded his accession to the British throne as a move on the European chessboard: in order to be able to face the French King with the might of Britain behind him, he was willing to stand as the defender of the Protestant faith, though he was personally inclined to toleration—it is ironical that the name of his House should, in later centuries, have become a byword for religious bigotry. In Mary II, who reigned jointly with him, William had a devoted wife, a handsome, warm-hearted, intelligent if not very well-educated Princess who until her untimely death from smallpox in 1694 did much to make up for her husband's lack of popularity with his British subjects.

Queen Anne had none of her sister's attractive qualities. She is a classic example of the dull, spoilt rich woman, indolent and discontented, mainly concerned with her creature comforts and with being amused. Between endless card-games, and listening to trivial books being read aloud to her, she gave some thought to her prerogative, which she was eager to enlarge. Her other object was to increase the power of the Church of England; but while being a devoted Anglican, even to the point of bigotry, she wished to be succeeded on the Throne not by the Protestant George of Hanover, but by her Catholic half-brother James, "The Old Pretender"—perhaps this was to atone for having deserted her father in the crisis of his reign. She allowed herself to be dominated by her two successive women favourites, Sarah, Duchess of Marlborough and Mrs Masham; which was perhaps as well, for in each case the favourite was associated with the political faction in power—the Duchess of Marlborough with the Whigs and Mrs Masham with the Tories—and was able to secure the Queen's acquiescence to measures which she might otherwise have opposed. So instead of there being a head-on collision between the Queen and Parliament—which might easily have happened, for she had all the obstinacy of her father and grandfather—the reign of Queen Anne was in some ways a precursor of the modern parliamentary monarchy.

In judging Queen Anne, the last and least notable of the Stuarts, we must remember her personal misfortunes; her ill-health, the loss of all her children, her marriage to the dreary nonentity, George of Denmark. And she deserves some credit from the fact that her reign was a period of national glory: the victories of Marlborough, the wit of Steele, Addison and Defoe. She may have had nothing to do with all this, but at least she did not have a stultifying effect on the nation, which would have been the case with a really bad monarch.

This is something that may be said for the Stuart monarchs in general. With all their faults, they did not prevent Britain from becoming much greater during the century of their rule. There was tremendous economic growth; the foundations of the Empire were laid; the arts, sciences and literature flourished. If we look for a more positive contribution by the Stuarts to Britain's greatness, we find that Charles I and Charles II both encouraged colonization; Charles II built up the Navy which was essential if the newly-acquired overseas possessions were to be held. James I, Charles I and Charles II were all patrons of art and architecture: James I and Charles I employed Inigo Jones, Charles II gave Wren the support he needed when rebuilding London after the Fire. If the Church of England enriched the life of the nation during the golden days of Tillotson, Stillingfleet and the other "Caroline Divines", this was thanks to the first two Stuart Kings' espousal of Arminianism; while James I's conference at Hampton Court bore fruit in the Authorized Version of the Bible. Charles II took an interest in the Royal Society; which, ten years after he had given it its charter, elected Isaac Newton as a Fellow.

It can also be said of the Stuarts that their humbler subjects were reasonably contented under their rule. There was none of the social unrest which occurred during the Tudor period on account of the enclosures, or under the Hanoverians with the onset of the Industrial Revolution. The Londoners rioted in support of Pym and Parliament, or because they were stirred up by Titus Oates, or by Shaftesbury and his minions; not because they were hungry. The Whig view of history makes it seem as if Parliament defended the ordinary people against the oppression of Charles I; but it is just as fair to see Charles I as the champion of the poor against the rich vested interests. During the eleven years of his personal rule, there were instances of action being taken to prevent the exploitation of workmen by their masters.

Charles I's "Rule of Thorough" ended through shortage of money. Charles II, when he ruled without Parliament after 1681, did not have his father's financial problem; and he benefited from the fact that the country, having experienced a republican dictatorship during the Commonwealth, was far more ready to tolerate a growth of the Royal prerogative after the Restoration than it was before the Civil War. Had Charles II lived longer, or had James II avoided his religious troubles, it is possible that Britain might have ended with an absolute monarchy similar to the Continental monarchies of the day. One feels, however, that if the Stuarts had really been able to wield the absolute power to which they aspired, they would not have used it to win military glory at the expense of their subjects in the manner of Louis XIV; rather, they would have resembled the "Benevolent Despots" of the eighteenth century. This is perhaps the role which they would have liked most to have played: concerning themselves with all aspects of their subjects' welfare; while if there had been a Voltaire at the beginning of the seventeenth century, James I would surely have corresponded with him. It can be argued that the Stuarts suffered from being too much in advance of their times.

The Monarchy 1714-1861

BY ROGER FULFORD

Throughout the seventeenth century the Royal Family of England was—for all practical purposes—confined to only two branches. One branch consisted of King Charles I and his descendants while the other branch consisted of his sister, Elizabeth Queen of Bohemia, and her descendants. Supposing that some calamity had overtaken both branches we should have had to find a sovereign among the obscure descendants of King Henry VII in the families of Percy or Stanley. Thus isolated from relations, rivals or family factions the two branches were drawn closely together: unencumbered by collaterals, they represented the Royal Family of England. After the Restoration of King Charles II, Prince Rupert, one of the three surviving sons of the Queen of Bohemia, came to live in London, was an Admiral in the Royal Navy and was created Duke of Cumberland. His youngest sister, Sophia, gifted and intelligent, was warmly attached to the reigning branch of her family, and when she wrote to congratulate King William III on becoming King after the flight of James II she added "Yet—I lament King James—for he honoured me with his friendship". Her husband was Duke of Brunswick and Elector of Hanover, and her eldest son, afterwards King George I, spent many months in London as a young man and was canvassed as a possible husband for Queen Anne. This close link between the reigning family and their cousins was of course well known to public men at the time. It explains why, at the beginning of the Civil War, it was mooted that the English crown should be removed from Charles I and his family and pass to one of the sons of the Queen of Bohemia, and it also explains why Parliament at the end of the century was anxious to name Princess Sophia, who was the only surviving Protestant child of the Queen of Bohemia, as the eventual successor to the throne. Her niece wrote to her: "You are the one person in all the world worthy of being a great Queen"[1]. She loved England.

1 *Letters from Liselotte, Elizabeth Charlotte, Princess Palatine and Duchess of Orleans* by Maria Kroll (Gollancz, 1970).

When Queen Anne died in 1714, her cousin "worthy of being a great Queen" had just died and her son, King George I came to the Throne: he was treated by many English people, then and since, as a foreigner carved as King out of a forgotten pedigree. This was propaganda; it was unjust. This propaganda wrongly included the country, Hanover, of which he was the sovereign. Patriotism or propaganda, as the reader prefers, depicted Hanover as a mendicant, eager for alms and oblations from England; it also depicted its elector as a ruler of laughable unimportance. Such national partiality, though understandable, is not acceptable. In 1814 on the centenary of the accession of the Brunswick family to the English throne London celebrated the occasion in gay and triumphant style. A few weeks later the electorate was elevated into a Kingdom and it was stated then that the House of Brunswick-Luneburg was one of the most illustrious and ancient in Europe. In fact the Stuarts from Scotland and the Tudors from Wales looked a trifle regional beside a family which had been given the Dukedom of Brunswick by a famous Emperor of the Holy Roman Empire in the thirteenth century.

The attacks on the King's origins were superficial. His personality drove them more deeply into the minds of his new subjects. He arrived with a troupe of German advisers and mistresses but again that was not very important though it makes an easy subject for quip and jest. One mistress was tall and was called the Maypole, the other was portly and was called the Elephant. But what the King lacked were the graces of the Stuarts and the intelligence of his mother. He was a fighting prince with the character of a soldier, and the outlook of the parade ground. Moreover he was dull, and at fifty-four, when he ascended the throne he was too old to adapt himself, too old to change. But he displayed some of the habits of a King of England. He went racing at Newmarket, visiting the Master of Trinity College, Cambridge, on the way. He went down to Windsor, was extremely delighted with it and planned to make a garden below the Terrace. He had a sound appreciation of music, and Handel wrote *The Water Music* in his honour when he went on the Thames from Whitehall to Limehouse. But with the majority of his new subjects—or more exactly the interests of the influential majority of his new subjects—he was out of sympathy. Commerce meant little enough to him. Scholarship, literature, and religious discussion, which had all brought the intellectual life of the nation to a high pitch, were matters in which he was not interested. The wrangles of English politicians likewise bored him. He was no linguist, and spoke virtually no English. He was never really at home in England, and, as Lord Rosebery has amusingly said, "only breathed by the dykes of Holland or the waters of the Leine". His best language was French, and it is possible that amusing descriptions of his difficulties of communications with his English subjects are exaggerated. The effect of his absence in Hanover may likewise have been exaggerated. The matter was neatly expressed by the University of Cambridge in an address to the King after the Jacobite rising in 1715. After noticing his absence abroad the University said—"And indeed we can scarce deem it absence while you only cross your own seas to visit your own hereditary countries".

The history of the power of the English sovereign in the century and a half after George I's accession might be likened to the flow of a stream, inevitably and inexorably moving away from the throne towards Parliament but here and there perhaps seeming to glide so sluggishly that the tide and movement are lost. But with the accession of the first George the movement away from the Crown went briskly. This was not wholly caused by the inability of the King to speak English, by his no longer presiding over the Cabinet or by his love for the banks of the Leine. Rather it was that his personality, together with the points just mentioned, combined to bring the monarchy down to earth. The mystic majesty of the earlier kings—vice-regents of the deity—had vanished. The Stuarts, down to Queen Anne's time, as Dr Johnson well remembered, had all "touched" for scrofula or the King's evil. King George I ceased to "touch". Charles II, on the other hand, is said to have "touched" 100,000 times. With the Hanoverian dynasty, we enter a more practical role for the kingship.

George II succeeding his father in 1727 was forty-four—old enough to be wise and too old to be romantic. Yet romance did not wholly elude him. At the age of sixty-one he took part in the Battle of Dettingen against the French. At the beginning of the battle his horse bolted, but on foot and brandishing his sword he called to his men "Now boys for the honour of England". He shared to the full his father's partiality for Hanover. When George I died, his will was handed to George II by the Archbishop of Canterbury at a meeting of the Council. George II thrust it into his pocket and, without reading it, stalked from the room. It is now known that in this suppressed will George I had made arrangements for separating Hanover from England[1]. George I saw how difficult it would always be for the Dynasty if it was forever attached to the *gemütlich* electorate. But George II could not reconcile himself to a separation from what he enjoyed and loved. About King George II there are more ludicrous anecdotes than any other of our kings. They are familiar to all readers of Horace Walpole or Lord Hervey. He was impatient and peppery—two qualities which tend to make all who are in authority comical. He was courageous. Once he was about to sail for Germany when a storm developed. The Admiral wished him to delay his start. To this the King replied "Faugh—did you ever hear of a King being drowned?" The reply was immediate, "Yes, your Majesty, Pharaoh".

He had one characteristic which was possibly unexpected by those who only remember funny stories about him; he was gentlemanly. Lord Chesterfield, then the greatest living authority on manners and behaviour, wrote "Nobody is more exact in all points of good breeding than the King". He was the most fortunate of our Hanoverian sovereigns in that the fates had given him an attractive wife endowed with an intelligence which was commanding. Queen Caroline is our oustanding Queen Consort. She enjoyed and was able to conduct discussions on affairs, philosophy and religion with the leaders of thought in England. The King himself praised her as a good wife and always accompanied the praise by making it clear that he deserved a good one: he likewise praised her intellect but at the same time made it clear that he did not think it had suffered from companionship with his for many years. Such masculine self-confidence is endearing.

In politics King George II was adaptable. The politicians prominent in his long reign, Walpole, Newcastle, the Pelhams, Carteret and the elder Pitt owed their position to other reasons than royal favour. He would have liked Carteret as his Prime Minister but lack of parliamentary support made this impossible; he had, later in his reign, to accept the elder Pitt as Prime Minister (though reluctantly) because of his strength in Parliament. In conversation he may have called his Ministers Liars, Knaves and Poltroons (a favourite word) and described their policy as "stuff and nonsense"—and his language implies that he spoke English better than is sometimes believed—but in the end he bowed before the superior force of Parliament. He saw the necessity of accepting the wishes of "that damn'd House of Commons"[2], as he called it. We should not be exaggerating if we agreed that King George II established the foundations of our constitution. The testimony to him from Pitt is fair and memorable, "the late good

1 *Lord Hervey's Memoirs* Edited by R. R. Sedgwick (1931).
2 *The Whig Supremacy* by Basil Williams (Oxford, 1939).

old King possessed justice, truth and sincerity in an eminent degree". A glance at the map proclaims that the reign of George II was the most successful in modern history. The French had been humbled, and we had supplanted them in Canada, India and the West Indies.

The King died with a groan in his water-closet at Kensington Palace, and was succeeded by his grandson, George III, on 25 October 1760. The new King's father, Frederick Prince of Wales—probably christened Frederick after the King of Bohemia—has been the target for some malevolent ridicule but dying before he was forty-five he had no chance to show his capacity in a position of authority. George III always spoke highly of the character of George I, whom he had been taught to revere by his father[1], but it is fair to say that the sincerity and outspokenness of the earlier Georges was not inherited by him. The history of his relations with the politicians from his accession to his madness in 1788 has been the subject of exhaustive (and exhausting) research by historians and scholars for many years. The relations of George III with the Pitts, George Grenville, Rockingham, Shelburne and Lord North can be unravelled from many a text-book. Earlier historians and those remembering the golden age of the Whig Party believed that the King had attempted to re-establish the personal rule of the sovereign through a too compliant Prime Minister (North). Such doctrines are no longer acceptable. Rather it would be fair to say that the quarter of a century after George III's accession was a period of political confusion, with no man emerging such as Walpole or the younger Pitt to form a government commanding the support of Parliament. This quarter of a century was a time of strain at home—the disturbances which centred round John Wilkes—and of humiliation overseas—the American War of Independence. One of the greatest of King George's subjects (Edmund Burke) said during these years, "A great Empire and little minds go ill together". There were plenty of little minds among the politicians, and we can justly say of the King that he lacked the resilience of a statesman.

In the autumn of 1788 the King went mad; "he is a complete lunatic"[2]. Some attempts have been made to show that the King was not, in the accepted sense, mad but was the victim of a taint in the hereditary system of everyone descended from King James I. That may or may not be correct: the important point, again to quote his son, was that he was afflicted by "a total loss of all rationality". His recovery was gradual, but he was never able to exert himself fully again in public life. After his recovery he wrote to a political friend "I must decline entering into a pressure of business, and indeed for the rest of my life, shall expect others to fulfil the duties of their employments, and only keep that superintending eye which can be effected without labour or fatigue"[3]. After one or two further attacks he lapsed into final imbecility at the end of 1810. Though muted compared with the powers of our earlier kings, those of King George III were considerable until his reason collapsed. No government could expect to survive without the support of the King, and this was still true even after 1788. An example will show this. After seventeen years, he withdrew his support from Pitt, over the question of the emancipation of the Roman Catholics from their political disabilities. That was in 1801. He felt that he would have violated the oath which he made at his Coronation if he had agreed to any easing of these restrictions. Pitt resigned.

Yet whatever the anxieties and tribulations of the King's public life he had large compensations in private. He was the only member of the Hanoverian Dynasty whose

1 Mrs Harcourt's *Diary of the Court of King George III.*

2 The Duke of York writing to one of his younger brothers. Professor Aspinall *The Correspondence of George, Prince of Wales* (Cassell) vol *i* 405.

3 *Diaries and Correspondence of George Rose* vol *i* 97.

domestic life gave no tremor to even the most censorious of mortals. He was deeply religious and, away from politics, he had the pastimes of a squire and the tastes and interests of a country clergyman. A member of the Court who knew him really well said that when the King was a young man Lord Bute had taught him to believe that the motives of all mankind were selfish[1]. He may never have thought otherwise of politicians but meeting ordinary people at Windsor, Weymouth, Kew and in his journeys through the South of England, he realised that Bute was wrong. Above all he had the gratification of knowing that he was popular for himself. His popularity owed little to hopes of favour, nothing to fear but he was the most widely liked and respected sovereign which, up to that time, the country had known.

His successor, who was much criticised and ridiculed, proved that his father's popularity was personal not dynastic; that it was for the man and not the office. The weaknesses of King George IV were conspicuous ones. He was extravagant. Since most of his money was derived from the nation and frugality at that time was a high virtue which could not flourish amidst high taxation, he was pilloried. He had several mistresses with one of whom (Mrs Fitzherbert) he went through a form of marriage. His own marriage with his first cousin Queen Caroline was a public disaster—culminating in a case before Parliament based on her infidelities in Italy. Now all these matters were exacerbated by an extraordinary outpouring of pamphlets, squibs and caricatures against George IV—especially when he became Regent at the breakdown of his father's reason. Moreover they were re-inforced by weightier attacks (though not necessarily better-informed) in the newspapers and by the poets. In 1813 when he was present at the opening of Charles I's coffin, which rested near that of Henry VIII at Windsor, Byron wrote:

"Ah! what can tombs avail! — since those disgorge
The blood and dust of both — to mould a George."

Yet George IV was our most gifted king since Charles II: his extremely important additions to the royal collections enable us to class him in this respect with Charles I. His architectural experiments in Brighton and Windsor Castle, together with the buildings in London associated with his name show that much of his extravagance was devoted to a single end—the creation of a background worthy of the English Monarchy.

He inherited the Monarchy when it had been weakened by the afflictions of his father, and though he made it more splendid he could not make it more politically powerful. He himself had always supported the Whig Party, and when he became Regent it was clear that he could not install his Party friends in power—even if he had wished—because of the uncertainty of their following in Parliament. In moments of irritation—especially over Crown appointments and the handling of the case against his wife—he might threaten to dismiss the Prime Minister (Liverpool). Writing to the Duke of Wellington in 1823 he said, "Depend upon it, that Lord Liverpool, if he lives till Dooms Day, will never be corrected, or made fit for the high office to which I raised him"[2]. But these were threats; they were remote from reality. He made alarming scenes against Catholic Emancipation at the end of his life, but in 1829 the Act was passed with the sanction of the King.

In society George IV could, without exaggeration, be called scintillating. J. P. Curran, the Irish wit and lawyer, who frequently stayed at the Brighton Pavilion said that he had never met anything superior to the colloquial liveliness of the Prince. He was himself a practised talker and humorist but he said that with a little practice the Prince

1 Mrs Harcourt's *Diary*.

2 *Correspondence of George Prince of Wales*, vol *viii*, *p* 447 edited by Professor Aspinall (1971).

"would have fairly kept up at saddle-skirts with him"[1]. But on ceremonial occasions his dignity was incomparable. Before his reign at Levees and Drawing Rooms the King was not stationary but perambulated round the room. George IV seems to have originated the idea of receiving the company seated. At a Drawing Room at the close of his life "he sat on an elevated armchair, and looked like a King in a play, or in a wooden cut in the History of England and what can be more truly royal and dignified"?[2]

The next King, who succeeded George IV on 26 June 1830, was less dignified. King William was three years younger than his brother, had been in the Royal Navy and perhaps rightly felt that he lacked the capacity for wrestling with party politicians. He had married Adelaide of Saxe-Meiningen by whom he had two daughters who did not survive infancy. He had formerly lived with the actress, Dorothy Jordan, by whom he had numerous children. Before 1830 he was regarded in his family and by London society as a fit subject for friendly jests and laughter; he completely lacked the authority of the former Kings of his House. He showed this on his accession when he decided to walk down St James's Street, arm in arm with an old friend. He was speedily encompassed by a motley crowd of sightseers and prostitutes. "Oh, never mind all this," he was heard to say, "when I have walked about a few times they will get used to it." But he never promenaded the streets of London thereafter, and in fact as is true of most of our sovereigns called unexpectedly to the succession, the office changed the man and moulded the King.

He had to guide the monarchy through one of those periods in English history when party feeling was at its zenith. Within a few months of his accession he had to face a Whig Government (the first for half a century) committed to a far-reaching measure of Parliamentary Reform. In 1834, two years after the Reform Bill was carried, he dismissed the Whig Government and he was the last sovereign in English history to use this constitutional weapon. But with this important exception he showed that he had mastered one important doctrine of the constitution—namely that the Sovereign should show to the world outside that the Government was his government and was fully supported by the Sovereign. He showed this when at short notice he drove to Westminster to dissolve Parliament in accordance with the wishes of the Whig Government. When all kinds of difficulties were raised about getting the state coach ready in time, he is believed to have retorted "Then I will go in a hackney-cab". He was even prepared—though with the greatest reluctance—to create sufficient peers or at least to use his influence with existing peers to force the Bill through the House of Lords. As his latest biographer points out he discharged his constitutional duties "with honesty and good will"[3].

He was succeeded by his niece, Queen Victoria, on 20 June 1837. She was just eighteen and therefore eligible to rule without a Regency. On coming to the throne she fell victim to the charms of her Whig Prime Minister, Lord Melbourne. At the end of his reign King William had remained outwardly loyal to the Whig Government but his growls, grumbles and resistance to some of their measures did not pass unnoticed. The Queen partly because of youthful enthusiasm and partly because of affection for Melbourne exaggerated support of the Government into partisanship. She confessed later that owing to her youth "she plunged too ardently into support of the Whigs". On New Year's Day, 1840, she wrote in her journal "I implore Providence to grant that the true and good cause may prosper for this year and many to come under the guidance of my kind Lord Melbourne". This partisanship might not have

1 Croly's *Life of George IV*, *p* 113.
2 Lord Palmerston—quoted in Lord Ashley's *Life of Palmerston*.
3 *King William IV* by Philip Ziegler (Collins, 1971).

been serious if she had managed to hide her feelings for the Tories. When the Whigs were defeated and Peel was trying to form a Government she refused to change her Whig Ladies of the Court for Tory ones. At a Levee it was noticed that when a distinguished Tory lawyer came to make his bow "she drew herself up as though she had seen a snake".

On 10 February 1840, she married her first cousin, Prince Albert of Saxe-Coburg-Gotha. He was a remarkable man—handsome, clever, industrious and devoted to his wife and family. For the twenty-one years of his mature life he had an important influence on the constitutional development of the Monarchy. First he guided the Queen away from her partisanship with the Whigs, and substituted for it the idea that whatever party was in power the Crown should be absolutely impartial. He then encouraged the belief that the Sovereign would expect to be kept fully informed on all questions of policy and to be given the chance—especially in foreign affairs—to express a point of view even if it ran counter to what the Government planned. Through his origins and connections in Europe the Prince had often a deeper knowledge of the current problems in foreign affairs than had the Cabinet. This led to serious clashes between the Court and the Foreign Office and the indignation of the Court at finding the Foreign Secretary (Palmerston) deaf to their warnings was the main cause of his dismissal by the Prime Minister (Russell) in 1851. The work of the Prince Consort, as a kind of fifth wheel to the coach of government, was important, culminating in the last official act of his life—the modification of the Despatch to the American Government after an American warship had taken passengers off the British Steamer Trent. Disraeli, after the Prince's death, told the Saxon Minister in London, "This German Prince has governed England for twenty-one years with a wisdom and energy such as none of our Kings had ever shown"[1]. Disraeli was given to flowery language, but here he was saying what was exact and true. But during the twenty years after the Prince Consort came to England political parties were weak and confused. What would happen when they recovered their strength and the monarchy no longer had the support of a man of exceptional capacity?

1 Monypenny and Buckle's *Life of Benjamin Disraeli, Earl of Beaconsfield* (1929) *ii*, 117.

The Monarchy 1861-1936

BY PHILIP MAGNUS

At the start of the nineteenth century it was an undisputed constitutional axiom that a British sovereign had the personal right and duty to decide policy. He was expected to choose ministers to carry it out and to dismiss and replace them when necessary. But by 1861, when the Prince Consort died, the crown's relationship to the executive had been transformed. A new constitutional axiom, first formulated in 1867 by Walter Bagehot, became accepted as authoritative. It limited a sovereign's constitutional role to the right to be consulted, the right to encourage and the right to warn.

During the previous three quarters of a century the industrial revolution, reinforcing the effects of the American and French revolutions, had disseminated a great body of doctrines and objectives. These competed for the support of an increasingly aroused and informed public opinion which parliament could not reflect adequately without the aid of disciplined political parties. After a series of extensions of the franchise—1832, 1867, 1884—a modern party system became securely based upon a numerous electorate thinking and voting for the first time in British history in nation-wide political terms.

A sovereign attempting to continue to control the executive in those radically changed conditions would have found his position untenable. Party leaders contending about political issues could succeed each other as prime minister. But an embattled monarch would have been compelled, in Sir Lewis Namier's words, either to incur the risk and odium of leading a party himself; or to jettison principle, pass freely from side to side and "in turn captain opposite teams". That insoluble dilemma caused the entire royal family to quit the political arena.

At the start of her reign Queen Victoria was embarrassed when her government changed. She explained that she felt "guilty of dishonesty in giving her confidence suddenly to persons who had been acting in opposition to those to whom she had hitherto given it". Stockmar brashly advised her that since the death of George IV in 1830 "the executive power has been entirely in the hands of the ministry", but Lord Melbourne was more cautious. He told the Queen that "the work of conducting the executive government has rested so much on practice, on usage, on understanding, that there is no publication to which reference can be made for an explanation or description of it. It is to be sought in debates, in protests, in letters, in memoirs, and wherever it can be picked up".

Those and other sources of nineteenth century constitutional history are currently being explored by the authors of *The History of Parliament.* But they may find it difficult to pinpoint precisely the critical moments when the monarchy underwent the most profound process of successful adaptation to altered conditions which it has experienced. Its foundations in public opinion remained undisturbed, and the advantages of an unwritten constitution were never illustrated more clearly.

Victoria and her husband wrongly attributed the drastic diminution of the royal prerogative during the previous half century to the distrust which the sons of George III had inspired. They hoped to restore some portion of it by restoring full confidence in the sovereign's character and capacity. For that reason they subjected their eldest son to an extraordinarily ambitious educational experiment. It was designed to enable the future King Edward VII to display, like his father, qualities of intellect, initiative, thoroughness and drive at least equal to those possessed by an average cabinet minister.

Victoria knew that it was not flattery but the truth when Lord John Russell told her that her husband was "an informal but potent member of all cabinets"; when Lord Clarendon declared that the Prince's knowledge was astonishing, and that "there is not a department of the government regarding all the details of which he is not much better informed than the minister at the head of it"; and when Lord Granville confirmed that in foreign affairs the Prince had "kept the government out of innumerable scrapes", besides writing "some of the ablest papers" which ministers had ever read.

In those circumstances the Prince Consort's efforts to mould the monarchy into an indispensable cautionary department of state achieved considerable success. But that position could not be maintained after his death. Victoria and her heir, whom she sometimes dubbed in moments of depression "a caricature" of herself, lacked the necessary capacity, and the pattern of British constitutional monarchy evolved on different lines.

The Queen's mind was set hard at the time of her husband's death, and she never became a strictly constitutional sovereign. As late as July 1892, for example, she announced in the court circular that she had received "with regret" Lord Salisbury's resignation as prime minister. He had been ousted by Mr Gladstone at a general election, and the Queen informed her daughter, the Empress Frederick, that the "much famed" British constitution was defective. She explained that she had had to part with an "admirable" Conservative government "for no question of any importance, or any particular reason, merely on account of the majority of votes".

Victoria would have liked statesmen to form coalitions and to imitate the elevated detachment enjoined upon her. She failed sometimes to preserve it, and she disliked the party system. In matters of detail there remained throughout the century a shrinking conventional borderland in which it was open to a resolute sovereign to assert personal authority, and Disraeli restored the Queen's self-confidence by encouraging her to assert it, especially when Gladstone was in power. She became in consequence partisan, and was uninhibited in seeking clandestine advice from Conservative friends in opposition. Her weight, such as it was, was hurled impetuously on occasion against aspects of her Liberal governments' policies, but the ineffectiveness of those interventions was their most remarkable feature.

Concentrating conscientiously upon desk work which helped to soothe her nerves, Victoria turned too sternly attentive an eye upon an excessive amount of detail, without contriving to influence significantly the course of events. She refused after her husband's death to perform any public duties, but lived in eccentric seclusion, plunged apparently into eternal mourning, at Osborne or Balmoral, while Buckingham

Palace remained untenanted for years on end. That selfish neglect of the visible aspects of sovereignty, coupled with frequent importunate demands upon parliament for money grants for her children and relatives, provoked widespread criticism.

The Queen became unpopular in consequence, and by 1870 the institution of monarchy was being subjected to a more concentrated and direct attack than at any time since its temporary abolition in the seventeenth century. A blind revolutionary agitation during the late 1820s and early 1830s had menaced the entire structure of society. But it was not aimed specifically at the throne; the Chartists had not demanded its overthrow; and no revolutionary situation existed during the 1870s. There arose instead a call for a republic on cool rational grounds. Joseph Chamberlain told cheering crowds in Birmingham that this was inevitable, and some fifty republican clubs were established in large towns throughout the country. An ugly situation was aggravated when the French monarchy collapsed, and when the Prince of Wales was cited as a co-respondent in a divorce suit. Although proved innocent, his pleasure-seeking way of life affronted serious-minded people.

"We have arrived," Gladstone wrote, "at a great crisis of royalty. The Queen is invisible: the Prince of Wales is not respected." He devised, accordingly, during his first period as prime minister, a plan for solving what he termed privately "the royalty question". He fought with unrelenting persistance to force that solution upon the Queen, who never forgave what she regarded as a dictatorial attempt to govern her domestic life.

Gladstone invited the Queen to inform the nation unequivocally that precarious health precluded her from performing her public duties, and that the Prince and Princess of Wales would in future perform them on her behalf. He asked that the Prince should deputize for the Queen during the summer months at Buckingham Palace, and that he should spend the winter months in Dublin as permanent Viceroy of Ireland, aided by a responsible Secretary of State. After suggesting that the Prince should train annually for one month with the army, the Prime Minister indicated ways in which all remaining fractions of the Prince's time could be utilized in the nation's best interest.

That brash attempt to link the royalty and the Irish problems, and to settle both at one stroke, was killed by the invincible hostility of Queen Victoria and the Prince of Wales. But the monarchy was, and is, marvellously resilient. Its popularity was not merely restored but enhanced year by year in the sunshine of late Victorian prosperity and expansion. As Prince of Wales and as King, Edward VII employed an unchallenged social sovereignty, which he exercised with huge enjoyment for half a century, to democratize royalty by broadening in innumerable personal contacts the basis of its appeal.

He carried that process to the extreme limit possible in that age. But he could not overstep it. Many human aspects of democracy, which Americans absorbed in their struggle to tame a continent, left the Edwardians untouched. They seeped into England belatedly during the reign of George V, after experience of a community of suffering and death in the trenches of World War One.

In the meantime Edward VII delighted the nation by staging a splendid show. He hated to be unoccupied; his vitality appeared inexhaustible; and he performed with gusto a great number of public engagements. Exaggerated rumours about gambling hurt his reputation a little, but rumours about amorous adventures were less damaging. Those private sectors of highly-placed lives were protected from public criticism by a taboo which the press observed loyally; Edward VII had learnt discretion; and Jupiter himself had given vicarious satisfaction to millions of humble worshippers by descending occasionally from Olympus in a shower of gold.

Edward VII never doubted that the mass of all classes among his subjects shared his earthy tastes and interests, except when inhibited by economic difficulties. A popular king, trailing a breath of the raffish air of Merrie England, he fulfilled adequately his role. But he could not match the veneration and affection which his mother commanded before she died. The immense prestige which attached itself to her sixty-three years' tenure of "the noblest office upon earth" led Victoria through years of secluded eccentricity to an apothesis unparalleled since the reign of Elizabeth I.

The hold upon public opinion which Queen Victoria and her successors have enjoyed is independent of the possession of outstanding personal attributes. Those invaluable ancillary aids were powerless to prevent a popularity bordering upon idolatry, which Edward VIII had earned as Prince of Wales, from dissolving almost overnight like a pricked bubble in 1936, when he recklessly flouted the royal mystique which is the monarchy's ultimate bedrock. By the start of the twentieth century the crown had been transformed into a human symbol of authority which its wearer cannot exercise personally, and which, as an article of faith, defies rational analysis. As such it meets a psychological need, and manifests a built-in capacity for continuous successful adaptation to an economic, political and social framework which has assumed with ever-increasing and bewildering rapidity the appearance of a series of dissolving views.

In discharging a sovereign's duties Edward VII departed in significant respects from the methods consecrated by his mother. Detesting desk work, he led an exhausting social life. He spent three months annually abroad, dined out constantly in subjects' houses in London and spent weekends in their houses in the country. He found it convenient, therefore, to bring his cardinal attribute of forcefulness to bear on matters which interested him most—foreign affairs and the armed services—in informal talks and meetings with ministers and others on purely social occasions.

He had had to wait until his sixtieth year to pick up the art of constitutional government. Queen Victoria had not attempted to initiate him into the nature of his future duties, and had refused him access to cabinet papers. But King Edward shared all secrets with his only surviving son whom he dearly loved, and from whom he hated to be parted. In intimate talk King George V used to acknowledge with tears in his eyes the debt which he owed to his father, and that happy relationship, which George V failed to repeat in his relationship with his own children, was unique at that time in the annals of the royal family during the previous two hundred years.

The visible aspects of sovereignty, which Victoria had neglected, were discharged by Edward VII with inimitable panache. In crude films which have survived his every gesture and movement appear to exude an incomparable and irresistible warmth. Ill-provided at his accession with friends among leading politicians, he made his influence felt behind the scenes through an inner circle of trusted advisers.

They included Lord Fisher, First Sea Lord; Lord Hardinge of Penshurst, Permanent Secretary of the Foreign Office and subsequently Viceroy of India; and Lord Esher, chairman of the War Office reconstruction committee, and an *eminence grise* who refused the Indian Viceroyalty and other offers of high official employments. They included also Mrs George Keppel, whose special position was welcomed by ministers because she smoothed their relations with King Edward while displaying exemplary discretion. Her liberal political views were particularly helpful from 1906 onwards, when the King became increasingly anxious, irritable and asthmatic as a result of a head-on collision between his Liberal government and the House of Lords.

The twenty-six years' reign of King George V was much more troubled than the nine years' reign of his father. Its most conspicuous feature was the enhanced emphasis laid upon the imperial aspect of the monarchy, partly in consequence of the great contribution of blood and treasure made by the self-governing dominions, and by India, to Great Britain's war effort during the terrible years of military attrition between 1914 and 1918.

It had long been evident that the mother country was forfeiting the lead which she had acquired over all rivals during the early decades of the industrial revolution. The growing wealth, armaments and populations of other great powers seemed to menace British security. In those circumstances the once despised overseas dependencies offered a means of restoring the balance. The crown came accordingly to be valued increasingly as the supreme constitutional bond uniting in a single empire many important and growing communities of free men, and of others under tutelage, separated geographically from each other by half the circumference of the globe. The British sovereign was formally proclaimed Emperor of India; the Boer republics in South Africa, rich in gold, diamonds and wide open spaces, were subjugated after a costly three years' war; and all the patriotic sentiment which made such a disparate and far-flung empire possible was centred upon its sovereign.

Edward VII had embarked when young upon educational and pleasure expeditions to Canada, the United States and India. But a journey undertaken by the future King George V in 1901 to Australia, where he inaugurated in Melbourne the first parliament of the newly formed Australian Commonwealth, and to New Zealand, South Africa and Canada, provided a much more emphatic and significant expression of the new ideal of empire founded upon a dual loyalty. Loyalty was owed firstly to a local individual nation, and secondly to a powerful union of nations symbolized by a common dynasty and crown.

After visiting India as Prince of Wales in 1905-06, George V returned as King-Emperor in 1911-12. In December, 1911, he and Queen Mary, robed and crowned as Emperor and Empress of India, accepted in person the homage of the princes of India at a ceremony of unparalleled magnificence in Delhi. Before it ended the King-Emperor rose himself to proclaim two major political boons—the transfer of the capital from Calcutta to Delhi, and the revision of the partition of Bengal.

When many ancient dynasties were toppled in the catastrophe of World War One, the British throne remained virtually unshaken under King George V. As a constitutional sovereign he could not be faulted; he became even better loved than his father; and he commanded more respect. He was modestly surprised by the upsurge of affection and esteem which greeted his Silver Jubilee in 1935, less than a year before he died. He owed it, in the lapidary words of Sir Harold Nicolson's model biography[1], to "the candour of his approach, the probity of his nature, and the straightness of all his thoughts and actions".

A bearded father-figure with children and grandchildren, George V followed a slowly turning wheel of fashion as he passed from one royal residence and dignified pursuit to another in unchanging rotation throughout the year. Bred in the navy, where he became a thoroughly competent professional officer, he was by temperament a reactionary martinet. But in public he dutifully "subordinated his own preferences and prejudices, his many unconcealed likes and dislikes, to an excellent conception of his duty". His principles were fixed; his reactions were predictable; his routine never varied. "Under his wise guidance the British monarchy emerged from a period of international convulsion, from a period at home of slow silent revolution, with enhanced influence and repute".

1 *King George V: His Life and Reign*, Harold Nicolson (1952).

The Monarchy in the Twentieth Century

BY SIR CHARLES PETRIE

If a modern Rip van Winkle had gone to sleep in 1901 on the death of Queen Victoria and woken up to-day he would have been in doubt, where the monarchy is concerned, at which to wonder the more—how much was apparently the same and how much was actually different. When the Queen died the great prerogatives of the Crown were those of mercy, the dissolution and convocation of Parliament, the dismissal and selection of ministers, the declaration of war and peace, the making of treaties, the cession of territory, the creation of peers, and the nomination to official appointments. In addition, the monarch could refuse his or her assent to a Bill, even if it had passed both Houses of Parliament, but this right had not been exercised since the reign of Anne, and might therefore be said to be obsolete. Such, in theory, is the position to-day, for in the last seventy years there has been no legislation framed with the express purpose of limiting the power of the Crown, but the Constitution has been worked by all parties in such a way as to achieve that end.

The gains and losses of the monarchy during the reign of King Edward VII are not easy to assess. He certainly raised it in the public esteem by reviving the old pageantry which had been associated with it in the past, but the prerogative of the cession of territory was successfully challenged, and, it is not uninteresting to note, by a Conservative government. On the other hand in foreign affairs the King played a part which had not been played by any British ruler since William III. Lord Esher, from whom little was hidden concerning monarchs and their ways, said of him, "He had an instinct for statecraft which carried him straight to the core of a great problem without deep or profound knowledge of the subject. He had one supreme gift, and this was his unerring judgment of men and women." Perhaps his reign can best be summed up by saying that whatever might have been the ups and downs of the monarchy as such he showed that even in the political field the monarch himself could, under the Constitution, play a very influential part in the national life.

His role in the conclusion of the Anglo-French Entente in 1903-04 is too well known for detailed description here, but when in due course the time came to include Russia the King once more did everything in his power to help the Government of the day. In June 1908, the year after the conclusion of the Anglo-Russian agreement, he and Queen Alexandra met the Tsar and the Russian Imperial Family off Reval, and the proceedings which followed are conclusive evidence of the free hand which he enjoyed in matters of foreign policy for he was not accompanied by any of his Ministers, yet he had political discussions both with the Russian Premier, the ill-fated Stolypin, and the Russian Foreign Minister, the somewhat slippery Isvolsky. It was almost as if Queen Elizabeth II were to go to Madrid to talk politics with General Franco in the absence of Mr Heath or Sir Alec Douglas-Home. It is little wonder that a Belgian diplomatist should have written about this time, "The English are getting more and more into the habit of regarding international problems as being almost exclusively the province of King Edward, for whose profound political instinct and fertile diplomacy they very rightly feel great respect."

King George V as Prince of Wales had always been very much under the shadow of his father, and it was therefore more than a little unfortunate that at the very beginning of his reign he should have been plunged into two domestic crises, namely the Constitutional one in 1910-11 and the Irish in 1914, in both of which the politicians went out of their way to humiliate him, Bonar Law even going so far as to write of one audience, "I think I have given the King the worst five minutes that he has had for a long time." No man would have spoken like that to his father, and the difference in treatment must have rankled: indeed, it was not until 1931 that he again ventured to take the initiative in the political field.

Lord Blake has well written that "royal influence is the most intangible influence in politics", and it is not easy to decide whether the First World War, which in general dealt a very heavy blow to the monarchical principle, strengthened or weakened the British monarchy. It certainly enabled all the members of the Royal Family to come into personal contact with the mass of the people in a way and to an extent that had been unknown since the fall of the Stuarts, while the King and Queen personally set an example of devotion to duty which secured for them widespread respect.

It was not, however, until the politico-economic crises of 1931 that King George V was able to show of what he was capable, for of one thing there can be no doubt, and it is that the formation of the National Government, which saved the country, was his work. He had twenty-one years' experience of kingship behind him, and he did not hesitate: his behaviour recalls that of his great-great-grandfather at the time of the Gordon Riots, for he rose to the occasion.

At this point it may not be out of place to reflect upon what might have happened had Great Britain been a republic at that time. The President might well have been either a colourless nonentity or a violent partisan. If he had been the former he would never have dared to adopt a policy of his own, and at a moment when every hour was of supreme importance if catastrophe was to be avoided, precious days, and probably weeks, would have been wasted in consultations with the various party leaders before a new administration could have been formed. If the President had been a partisan he would not have possessed the confidence of the nation as a whole, and his chief concern would most likely have been, not the future of the country, but that of his own political associates. In either case it is difficult to see how disaster could have been avoided, and from this the country was saved by the monarchy as it would not have been saved by a republic.

With the short and unhappy reign of King Edward VIII we come to the greatest crisis through which the British monarchy has passed in modern times, for because it was not of long duration, and because it was in the main skilfully handled, this does not mean that there are any grounds for the assumption that it was not of the utmost gravity: in slightly different circumstances that abdication might have rendered the position of the throne so insecure that its collapse could not have been averted, and the late Sir Arnold Wilson, MP, gave it as his opinion that if a straight vote of the House of Commons had been taken there would have been forty of fifty votes in favour of a republic. That matters were not pushed to extremes was due in the main to three men, namely the Prime Minister, the Leader of the Opposition, and the King himself. In the case of the first of these his behaviour was the more surprising in view of his mismanagement of the crisis over the Hoare-Laval Pact twelve months earlier, and it was largely due to his initiative that the relevant proceedings were dignified; in fact, during the three Premierships of Mr Baldwin nothing became him better. Mr Attlee, too, deserves high praise for refraining from any attempt to make party capital out of the crisis. Finally, tribute must be paid to King Edward himself, for his decision to remain at Fort Belvedere prevented any extension of those demonstrations which might so easily have developed into something very much worse had he returnd to London.

It would, as we have seen, be idle to deny that monarchical feeling in Britain received a severe shock from the circumstances of the abdication of King Edward VIII and it was indeed fortunate that his successor was a man of the stamp of his brother: if ever there was the right King at the right time it was he. With all his father's virtues without his father's weaknesses he was too well acquainted with the century in which he lived to be at war with it as King George V had been accused of being, and he left the monarchy a great deal stronger than he found it in spite of the fact that he reigned during the extremely difficult years of the Second World War and its immediate aftermath. The great contribution which the throne made to the national life during his reign was to provide a symbol of stability and continuity in a revolutionary age. On all sides, once hostilities were at an end, there was a deplorable lack of unity, and everywhere the so-called leaders of public opinion were stressing what keeps men apart rather than what brings them together, but King George VI did all in his power to draw attention to the fact that the Crown was at once the emblem and the hope of a more sane state of affairs. It was nothing less than a national tragedy that his reign was so short.

Yet with all his solid virtues the King's approach to strangers was somewhat hesitant, and it was here that his wife, now Queen Elizabeth The Queen Mother, proved a pillar of the monarchy, and that it recovered so rapidly from the injury which it had received was largely due to her personality, for she was always singularly successful in eradicating any unfortunate impression to which this weakness of her husband might from time to time give rise. After the sixteen strenuous years through which she had lived as Queen Consort she would have been fully justified in going into a well earned retirement, but she did no such thing: rather she has placed all her great qualities at the disposal of her daughter as she had formerly placed them at that of her husband. No one is likely to question the loyal way in which she has served Queen Elizabeth II, or the affection which is well expressed in the name by which she is so widely known—"the Queen Mum". Above all, she so clearly enjoys life, and not even the dullest of public duties appears to bore her. This makes a special to the British public who have always liked to see their rulers enjoying themselves, whether it was King Charles II feeding the ducks in St James's Park or King Edward VII leading in a winner at Epsom.

The premature demise of King George VI was as much a misfortune for his elder daughter as for his subjects: he had looked forward to spending a number of years in bringing her up to cope with her responsibilities when she should succeed him, but this time was denied him, and as a result she was condemned to learn by experience. Napoleon once said that to be royal was like playing a part at a theatre, with the exception that kings and queens are always on the stage, and the present Queen has had plenty of light on that lesson during a very difficult period in the life of the monarchy.

In days gone by Queen Victoria was able to reign by remote control: once she had created the image of "The Widow of Windsor" all she had to do was to live up to it, and this she did so successfully that by the time of her death she was a legend to the overwhelming majority of her subjects: they had never seen her, save perhaps in the odd photograph, nor were they ever likely to do so. During the reign of her great-great-granddaughter hardly a day goes by that she is not seen on television or on a newsreel, while she is continually appearing in person all over the kingdom—one had almost written all over the world: with considerable justification she might echo the words of her predecessor Queen Elizabeth I, "To be a king and wear a crown is a thing more glorious to them that see it than it is pleasant to them that wear it." The problem that she has had to face has been primarily that of combining dignity with friendliness—no easy task in this permissive age when dignity is at a discount, and when the leaders of the world only too often think it necessary to play the buffoon. How successful she has been was summed up a few years ago by an American professor who commented, "On our side of the Atlantic we have a great respect for your Queen. She seems to be the only person in this goddam country who is trying to keep up any standards."

When one passes to a consideration of The Queen's position as a constitutional monarch it is to be confronted with the fact that many years must inevitably elapse before the evidence upon which to base a judgment can become available, though in the latest volume of his autobiography, *Pointing the Way*[1], Mr Harold Macmillan has lifted the curtain to a slight extent upon the role of the monarchy in modern Britain, when he says of an audience which he once had on his return from the United States in 1960, "I was astonished at Her Majesty's grasp of all the details set out in various messages and telegrams," and on the following year when on grounds of security many voices were raised against her visit to Ghana he comments that she "means to be a Queen and not a puppet." The lack of a written Constitution has made her position the more difficult, for she cannot refer to a book to see what she is to do in an emergency. As King Charles I once rightly observed, "The English are a sober people", but there are occasions when they lose their heads, and it is at such moments that their monarchs have to be most careful. Nobody can say that The Queen has failed in that respect.

There is no organized republican party in Britain to-day even if there was a temporary upsurge of republican feeling at the time of the abdication of King Edward VIII, but there is undoubtedly a widespread conviction that monarchy is a lost cause, and in some ways that is more dangerous. This attitude is almost wholly due to the fixed belief of the modern world that progress must necessarily be uninterrupted and that all changes are for the good. After all, our grandfathers travelled in coaches, while we ride in motor-cars, and they had neither television nor aeroplanes, so it is but natural—thus the argument runs—that we should be superior to them in other ways. We have progressed from the ape in the forest to the moron in the suburb, and to suggest that there can be any looking back now is an insult to the dignity of man. From this it follows that when any survival from the past is discarded, it is a sign of progress. If our forbears, after the nightmare of the Dark Ages, settled down under hereditary monarchy it was because they knew no better, just as they admired Titian and Velasquez because

1 *Pointing the Way*, Harold Macmillan (Macmillan, 1972).

they were unacquainted with the superior excellence of the Impressionists. Since the end of the First World War this contempt for the legacy of the past has become increasingly more pronounced, and the desire to hail "new dawns", to begin "new eras", and to turn over "new pages" has become almost feverish; because we can move over the ground more quickly than our forefathers, therefore we are wiser than they, and when we overthrow the forms of government they set up it is a sign of progress.

In reality nothing could be further from the truth, for the eclipse of hereditary monarchy inevitably coincides with an era of retrogression and chaos. Since 1918 there has been a wholesale exchange of monarchies for republics, and with definitely disastrous consequences, for the last fifty years have been the most unsettled that Europe has known since the French Revolution, when the principle of hereditary monarchy was also called in question. The reason is not far to seek, for in a republic the centrifugal forces have free play, and in their embittered strife they waste the national resources at home and perpetuate the feeling of insecurity abroad. Moreover, under a republican regime there is a complete lack of continuity, and continuity is the crying need for our time.

For example, Queen Victoria, owing to the accumulated experience of so many years, was able to exercise very considerable influence over her ministers, and in the later part of her life she could quote from personal experience precedents relating to events that had occurred before some of them were even born, and this was an enormous advantage both to them and to her subjects. As an illustration of this, when Campbell-Bannerman, the future Prime Minister, was Secretary of State for War in the nineties of last century he took some Army schemes to the Queen for approval, and explained that they were entirely new ones. "No, Mr Bannerman," was the reply, "Lord Palmerston proposed exactly the same thing to me in '52, and Lord Palmerston was wrong." Such being the case it is difficult to believe that the ordinary statesman is not considerably the better, when in office, for the advice of a monarch whose training and experience give him a great advantage when any fresh problem comes up for examination. If this was so in the past when ministers were drawn from a class of the community which had always been accustomed to public life it is more so today, when the majority of those who hold high office have not been trained to politics since early years. A Sovereign can cite precedents, and can adduce arguments, which would otherwise not be recalled until it was too late, and in any event he is likely to take a much wider view than his ministers.

Sometimes one wonders if the members of the British Royal Family realize how popular most of them are with the country as a whole. The mass of the people appreciate that the Crown stands above all party bickerings, and when, say The Prince of Wales or The Duke of Edinburgh, give their views on a subject it knows that he is speaking with sincerity, and that, as the saying goes, he has no axe to grind. In the past—at any rate—the usual criticisms of a royal speech was that it was too vague, for what the ordinary citizen wants to know are the real views of the person who is making it, for on account of the wide knowledge of men and matters which the members of the Royal Family must necessarily accumulate their opinions should be of great value: they are daily meeting people from all over the world, and are thus cosmopolitan in the best sense of that much-abused term. The Secretary of State for Foreign and Commonwealth Affairs may, while he is in office, be in closer touch officially with what is going on abroad, but as he was probably at Environment in the last administration, and may be at Education in the next, his personal interest in overseas affairs can never be so great as that of the Sovereign. One would like to think that the members of the Royal Family are encouraged by the constitutional advisers of the Crown to use their knowledge in the national interest.

An argument which is often advanced against hereditary monarchy, though it is many years since even the most fanatical republican could use it in Britain, is that there is no guarantee of the ability of a king or queen to fulfil adequately the functions of their office. This is true, but the advocates of republicanism can hardly maintain that it brings better men—in Europe and America it rarely brings women at all—to the top than does monarchy. There would, let it be frankly admitted, be a strong case for republicanism could it be proved that it placed the helm of State in the most capable hands, but even its apologists do not claim that it does any such thing. It is also objected that a hereditary monarch may be mad or vicious, or he may become such. This is true, but kingship provides against manifestations of this sort, which are anyhow extremely rare. The eldest son of King Charles III of Spain was so unbalanced a nympholept that he was quite unable to refrain from an attempt upon the virtue of any attractive female that he saw, and he was accordingly excluded from the succession both to Spain and the Two Sicilies. Moreover, republicanism is no guarantee against the insanity of the Head of the State, as the case of Paul Deschanel in France clearly proved.

Finally, however much the cynic may scoff, there is the sentimental appeal of monarchy, for self-interest is never in the long run enough, and human nature craves for some pageantry in its public life. The modern world has been so mechanised that its inhabitants are clutching at every chance which presents itself to escape from its monotony, and he is a wise ruler who surrounds his power with a certain amount of pomp and circumstance. This is the strength of the Church of Rome. It was the same in the Middle Ages, when the sordidness of everyday existence was relieved by religious festivals and knightly tournaments. In monarchy this very natural craving can be satisfied, and King Edward VII showed great wisdom in reviving so much of the external glory attaching to the British Crown. It may be regrettable, but it is certainly indisputable, that a regime which appeals to the head alone is nothing like so strong as one which appeals both to head and heart.

The monarchy provides that element of colour and romance for which mankind craves, but which is rapidly vanishing from the drab world of modern times, and if proof of this be required it can be found in the enormous crowds which every year flock to the Birthday Parade. The ordinary citizen looks upon it as a link with the past, and whatever his political opinions he rarely wants to break such links; nor is the plight of those nations which have done so any great encouragement to him to follow their example. "The councils to which Time is not called," wrote Sir Walter Raleigh, "Time will not ratify." In this mechanical and materialistic age such manifestations of Royalty as the Birthday Parade are a reminder of what Time represents in the life of a nation, and they impress upon the least imaginative the fact that the history of Great Britain did not begin yesterday.

The Monarchy and the Constitution

BY NORMAN ST JOHN-STEVAS, MP

The British monarchy today is both one of the most venerable and the most practical institutions of the modern world. Based upon sentiment and utility it is an asset of incalculable value to Britain, making a major contribution to the national life and raising the prestige and influence of Britain throughout the world.

The Monarchy as Symbol

The principal functions of the monarchy today are symbolic and religious although the monarch has certain constitutional functions as well. In a sense the monarchy should not have to explain itself but in a utilitarian age this cannot be avoided altogether. The relevance of the monarchy to the country today is that the monarch symbolizes the nation. The Queen has to represent both the contemporary life of the nation and its historic past, a dual function which can cause conflict. The monarchy must change with the times and symbolize the present national aspirations: to become a museum piece would be fatal: yet at the same time an essential function of the monarch is to remind the country that there is more to the nation than the present generation and to link it both with the past and with the future. By assuming this role of national symbol the monarchy strengthens the nation. In Britain, however fierce the party strife—no-one ever has to be against the country. The contrast in this respect between ourselves and the United States, for example, is marked. There, because the president is both a symbolic embodiment of the country and a partisan figure, one half of the nation finds itself in the embarrassing position of appearing to be opposed to the aspirations of the country when in fact they are merely rejecting the nominee of a particular party. The loyalty which constellates round the monarch in Britain finds a centre in the United States in the flag, but an abstract piece of bunting is no substitute for a symbol of flesh and blood. Countries which separate the head of the executive from the head of the state by artificial means do not fare much better, since the president is either an extremely dim and shadowy figure or, if not, tends to become a focus of political divisiveness instead of national unity[1]. This is not to say that I believe that monarchy is suitable for every country or that monarchy on the British model can be exported. One should simply recognize that for historical and other reasons the British nation has an almost unique natural advantage in its monarchical constitution.

1 The whole world knows who is Queen of England, but how many people could name the President of Germany?

The British monarchy is in one sense a conservative force but by this very fact it paradoxically facilitates change. A nation has two basic needs, that for stability and that for change, and the monarchy by preserving the idea of continuity in the life of the country enables it to absorb more radical changes in its political and social structure than would otherwise be possible without real risk of disorder. It moderates the bitterness of party strife by providing a focus of loyalty which is common to all parties in the state and by judicious intervention it can at a time of extreme party conflict be an effective moderating influence, as was shown on a number of occasions during the reign of King George V. Similar circumstances might well arise in the future.

The monarchy symbolizes not only the political life of the nation but its moral and religious life as well. This, of course, has not always been so. The Stuart Kings by their Laudian Anglicanism and Roman Catholicism repelled many and, until the accession of Queen Victoria, the Hanoverian dynasty did not exactly provide a model of domestic rectitude; but Queen Victoria and in particular her successors George V and George VI imparted a moral force to the monarchy which has been maintained by the present Queen. Indeed this aspect of the monarchy is more important than ever today when both the established Church and nonconformity are in decline. The association of monarchy with religion strengthens both[1]. Again in a society which has grown steadily more permissive (a process which is both good and bad) the example of a united family life set by The Queen, her husband, children, and her close relations is a real contribution to the nation's morality. The influence of the crown, declared Disraeli in 1872, "is not confined merely to political affairs. England is a domestic country. Here the home is revered and the hearth sacred. The nation is represented by a family—the Royal Family; and if that family is educated with a sense of responsibility and a sentiment of public duty, it is difficult to exaggerate the salutary influence they may exercise over a nation." "A *family* on the throne," noted Bagehot, "is an interesting idea also." "The women—one half of the human race at least—care fifty times more for a marriage than a ministry . . . a princely marriage is the brilliant edition of a universal fact, and, as such, it rivets mankind"[2].

The English monarch is of course a constitutional sovereign but that is a very different thing from being a cypher. The best description of the general constitutional rights of the sovereign is still that given by Bagehot in his *English Constitution.*

1 Under the Constitution it is a condition of title to the Crown that the sovereign should "join in communion with the Church of England as by law established". Under the Bill of Rights and Act of Settlement, succession to the throne is restricted to Protestants and Catholics are specifically excluded. The Sovereign may not be married to a Catholic. These provisions are open to objection on two grounds: (*a*) they discriminate against Catholics. (*b*) They derogate from the basic human rights of the sovereign and infringe his religious liberty.
These objections are theoretically valid, but the relation of Crown and Church is the creation of history, not logic. As long as the royal supremacy over the Church is retained and the sovereign remains "supreme governor" of the Church, obligatory membership of the Church of England is not unreasonable. On the other hand, the provisions *explicitly* excluding Catholics from the succession to the throne might with advantage be done away with. If the Church were to be separated from the state and the royal supremacy abolished then the case for doing away with the restrictions on the sovereign's religion would be greatly strengthened. At the same time it should be recognized that it is probably an advantage to have a Protestant sovereign (Anglican in England, Presbyterian in Scotland) as the United Kingdom is largely Protestant and a Catholic monarch would be separated by religion from the majority of his subjects.

2 *The English Constitution.*

Constitutional Rights

Perhaps Bagehot's most signal contribution to the lore of the Constitution was his formulation of the rights of a constitutional sovereign which has ever since been accepted by constitutional authorities and acted on by successive sovereigns. The monarch, he maintained, under the English system, has three rights: "the right to be consulted, the right to encourage, the right to warn". And, he added, "a king of great sense and sagacity would want no others. He would find that his having no others would enable him to use these with singular effect. A wise king would gradually acquire a fund of knowledge and experience which few ministers could rival." The king, Bagehot points out, would have the advantage which a permanent under-secretary has over his superior, the parliamentary secretary, "that of having shared in the proceedings of the previous parliamentary secretaries." Queen Elizabeth II, after twenty-one years on the Throne, enjoys this advantage and it will augment: at the time of writing she has known no less than six Prime Ministers.

Bagehot recognized that the monarchy has no veto. The Queen, he maintained, "must sign her own death warrant if the two houses unanimously send it up to her." Later constitutional writers have not all agreed with Bagehot. Sir William Anson at the time of the Home Rule controversy, immediately before the first world war, supported the Tory view that the King had residual powers as "guardian of the Constitution"[1]. Professor Jennings thought that the monarch had a right of veto in that he could refuse to assent to a policy "which subverted the democratic basis of the Constitution"[2]. The difficulty here is that what constitutes such a measure is largely a matter of opinion arising from pre-conceived political views. Whatever the theory of the matter, there has been no example of the use of the veto since the reign of Queen Anne, and the attempt to invoke it would be less likely to result in the preservation of "the democratic basis of the Constitution" than to bring the institution of monarchy itself to an end.

Choice of Prime Minister

At the same time Bagehot did not view the monarch as a mere ceremonial cypher and recognized that the sovereign had certain personal prerogatives, exercised on his own will, and not necessarily on the advice of ministers. Bagehot accepted that if a party commanded a clear majority in the House of Commons and possessed a recognized leader, then the leader must be chosen by the Crown as Prime Minister. At the same time he recognized two situations where the Crown had a personal choice of Prime Minister, first where no one party commanded a clear majority, and secondly where the majority party possessed no recognized leader. Both exceptions still exist today.

The first exception was of particular importance during Queen Victoria's reign, for

1 King George V, on the throne at the time, did not deny Anson's contention but was not keen to act upon it. His view, contained in a letter written to the Prime Minister, Asquith in July 1914, but never despatched, is characteristically sane and commonsensical: "Much has been said and written in favour of the proposition that the Assent of the Crown should be withheld from the measure. (The Home Rule Bill). On the other hand, the King feels strongly that that extreme course should not be adopted in this case unless there is convincing evidence that it would avert a national disaster, or at least have a tranquillising effect on the distracting conditions of the time. There is no such evidence." *Royal Archives*, K.2553 VI. 56.

2 *Cabinet Government* (2nd edn) Cambridge, 1951, *p* 381. Bagehot also denied that the sovereign has the right to dismiss a ministry on his own initiative but the existence of the right was subsequently asserted by Dicey. "I entirely agree", he wrote, "that the King can do nothing except on the advice of his ministers. I totally disagree with the doctrine drawn from this principle that he can never dismiss ministers in order that he may ascertain the will of the nation." *See* Colvin, *The Life of Lord Carson*, II: 240.

owing to the split in the Conservative party from 1846 until the victory of Gladstone in 1868, over the repeal of the Corn Laws, no general election yielded a result which the Crown was bound to accept. The multiplicity of parties, not only Whigs, Tories and Peelites, but also Radicals and Irish, cast a further burden on the Crown of cabinet making. During Queen Victoria's reign there were no less than eight minority and two coalition governments. A similar situation arose under George V, when the Labour Party was displacing the Liberal as one of the major political parties and England had for a time three party government. Bagehot had foreseen the weakness of such a system declaring that it was one in which cabinet government "is more sure to exhibit its defects, and least likely to exhibit its merits. The defining characteristic of that government is the choice of the executive ruler by the legislative assembly; but when there are three parties a satisfactory choice is impossible"[1].

The second exception, when a majority party has no recognized leader, was of great practical importance when Bagehot was writing, and for a considerable time thereafter but is no longer so today, when both the Labour and Conservative parties have machinery for electing their leaders[2]. Both the party leaders are elected by members of the parliamentary parties. This was always the position in the Labour Party and the Tory Party adopted a similar procedure after the electoral defeat of 1964. Mr Edward Heath was the first leader of the Tory party to be elected under the new procedure. Previous Tory leaders had "emerged" by a process of elimination and consultation. The Crown is thus left with no scope for selection. But what if a Prime Minister resigns or dies in office?[3]. A spokesman for the Labour party has declared that in such an eventuality only the elected leader of the Parliamentary Labour Party could accept the Premiership from The Queen. The Tory Party has not even gone as far as that. Presumably the monarch would ask a member of the cabinet to act as "caretaker" Prime Minister until the party had gone through its electoral process[4]. Clearly if the "caretaker" was one of

1 *The English Constitution.*

2 As an example Bagehot pointed to the situation which would arise at the death of Lord Palmerston, then Prime Minister, but in fact there was little freedom of choice for the Crown, as Lord John Russell was the obvious successor. A better example of the importance of the royal power was the resignation of Lord Derby in 1868, when the Queen might have sent for the Duke of Richmond or Lord Stanley, but summoned Disraeli instead. In the same year she sent for Gladstone when she might have chosen Lord John Russell.

3 The most dramatic exercise of the royal prerogative came in 1923, when Bonar Law who had contracted cancer of the throat laid down his office. He was too ill to discuss the succession with the King. The Conservative party was divided between Baldwin and Curzon. The final decision was the King's and according to Sir Harold Nicolson, his decision in favour of Baldwin was determined by his view that a Prime Minister in the House of Lords was not possible when the largest opposition party was confined to the Commons. On the resignation of Sir Anthony Eden the royal prerogative came into play again when The Queen, after consulting Conservative leaders, sent for Mr Macmillan instead of Mr Butler and in 1963 when Mr Butler was again passed over in favour of Sir Alec Douglas-Home.

4 The practice followed in Australia is of some interest. When Mr A. J. Lyons, Australian Prime Minister died in office in 1939, the United Australian Party, which he headed, possessed no deputy leader. The Governor General called on the leader of the Country party and deputy Prime Minister to form a caretaker cabinet until the UAP elected a successor to Mr Lyons. Sir Earle Page, who had been selected resigned nineteen days later when Mr Menzies was elected UAP Leader. Similar action was taken some years later when Mr Curtin died in office. Mr Forde, deputy Prime Minister and deputy Leader of the Labour Party held office for six days until the Labour Party met to elect Mr J. B. Chifley Leader. Mr Forde was an unsuccessful candidate in the ballot. For a discussion of this point and a recommendation that it should be followed, if necessary, in Canada, see Edward McWhinney, "Constitutional Convention", *The Canadian Bar Review,* XXXV, No. 1, January 1957.

the candidates for the leadership of the party the royal choice could still be of considerable significance since possession remains nine points of the law.

Appointment and Dismissal of Ministers

Ministers other than the Prime Minister are also appointed by the Crown but on the nomination of the Prime Minister. Since the death of Queen Victoria no potential ministers have been excluded from office by the Crown, but she was much more active in this respect than Bagehot suspected. From 1841 the practice recommended by Lord Melbourne had been followed, and before appointment the list of ministers was submitted to The Queen for her approval. She was entitled to raise objections, and on numerous occasions did so. She succeeded in keeping Charles Dilke from office, refusing to accept him in 1886, because he had been cited as co-respondent in a divorce suit, and again in 1892. The Queen undoubtedly took the title of "Her Majesty's Ministers" not as fiction but as fact, but her successors have recognized that the Cabinet no longer rests on royal but on popular approval. As to dismissal of ministers, the Crown could in theory take this unusual step, but there is no modern example of this having been done without the advice of the Prime Minister. Bagehot denied that the Crown had any right to dismiss the entire Ministry and this has not happened since 1835.

Dissolution of Parliament

A personal prerogative of the Crown, which some have thought to exist, concerns the dissolution of Parliament. Can the monarch dissolve Parliament without the advice of the Prime Minister? Bagehot thought not, as long as a ministry remained undefeated in Parliament, and this would seem to be correct. He conceded the right of dissolution in theory but thought it could not be exercised in practice. "Nothing", he wrote, "perhaps, would more surprise the English people than if The Queen by a *coup d'etat* and on a sudden, destroyed a ministry firm in the allegiance and secure of a majority in Parliament. That power, indisputably, in theory, belongs to her; but it has passed so far away from the minds of men that it would terrify them, if she used it, like a volcanic eruption from Primrose Hill"[1]. If the Crown cannot dissolve Parliament, can it refuse to grant a dissolution? "There are vestiges of doubt", wrote Bagehot, "whether in *all* cases a sovereign is bound to dissolve Parliament when the Cabinet asks him to do so. But neglecting such small and dubious exceptions, the Cabinet which was chosen by one House of Commons has an appeal to the next House of Commons." Elsewhere he states: "The Queen can hardly now refuse a defeated minister the chance of a dissolution, any more than she can dissolve in the time of an undefeated one, and without his consent." Queen Victoria did not accept this view and maintained that the granting of a dissolution was within the personal prerogatives of the sovereign. "She considers", she wrote in 1846, "the power of dissolving Parliament a most valuable and powerful instrument in the hands of the Crown, but which ought not be used except in the extreme cases and with certainty of success. To use the instrument and be defeated is a thing most lowering to the Crown and hurtful to the country"[2]. She clearly believed that a government defeat at a general election was a personal affront to the Crown, as the ministers were *her* government. Yet zealous as the Queen was in maintaining the existence of her right in theory she never in practice refused a dissolution.

Subsequent monarchs have followed the same course. In November 1918 George V tried to dissuade Lloyd George from dissolving and took the same course with Baldwin

1 *The English Constitution.*

2 *Letters of Queen Victoria* 1st series II *p* 108.

in 1923 but in each case eventually granted the request: he was here exercising his undoubted prerogative of warning his chief minister. The position would seem to be that despite the absence of any refusal for over a hundred years, the Prime Minister has no absolute right to a dissolution and the sovereign can dispense with his advice if he can find an alternative Prime Minister. The danger of this course is that the second Minister may be defeated and the sovereign obliged to grant to the second what he has refused to the first, and thus be drawn into the party political conflict. Precisely this occurred in Canada in 1926, when the Governor General although not the King was involved[1].

Creation of Peers

The fourth prerogative in which the personal wishes of the sovereign may play a part is the creation of peers. Bagehot named this power the "safety valve" of the Constitution. "The head of the executive", he wrote, "can overcome the resistance of the second chamber by choosing new members of that chamber; if he does not find a majority, he can make a majority. This is a safety valve of the truest kind. It enables the popular will—the will of which the executive is the exponent, the will of which it is the appointee—to carry out within the Constitution desires and conceptions which one branch of the Constitution dislikes and resists. It lets forth a dangerous accumulation of inhibited power, which might sweep this Constitution before it, as like accumulations have often swept away like Constitutions"[2].

Fount of Honour

The last of the sovereign's personal prerogatives is concerned with patronage and the conferment of honours. The sovereign is the fount of honour, but honours, with a few exceptions, are conferred on the advice of the Prime Minister. The sovereign may refuse to grant an honour but nowadays this is rare. The Royal Victorian Order is awarded personally by the Crown, and—since December 1946—the Orders of the Garter and the Thistle. The conferring of the Order of Merit is entirely in the Sovereign's personal prerogative.

The Commonwealth

One aspect of the monarchy hardly mentioned by Bagehot is its role in the Empire and Commonwealth. He did not in the sixties devote much thought to imperialism, and this is not surprising, since it did not become pronounced in England until Disraeli's administration of 1874. He could not have foreseen the developments which culminated in the Statute of Westminster and left the Crown as the only visible link between the Commonwealth nations. The members of the British Commonwealth, declared the statute, are a free association of nations, "united by a common allegiance to the Crown."

1 In September 1925, Mr Mackenzie King requested a dissolution from the Governor General, Lord Byng, which was granted. His Conservative opponents, led by Mr Meighen gained a majority of fifteen, but the Liberals remained in office supported by the Labour Party. In June 1926 after a vote of censure, he requested a dissolution, but was refused by Lord Byng, first because Mr Meighen's party being the largest single party in the chamber should be given a chance of forming a government, and second because it would mean a second general election within nine months. Mr Meighen thereupon formed a government, was defeated three days later by one vote and requested a dissolution. This time the request was granted but a Liberal majority was returned. Lord Byng was severely criticised for his decision. In 1926 the Imperial Conference passed a resolution maintaining that the Governor General's functions were "similar in all essentials" to those of the Sovereign. This obscure resolution does not shed much light on the question.

2 *The English Constitution.*

Full legislative autonomy was conferred on the Dominion Parliaments, and after the passing of the statute, no law passed by the United Kingdom Parliament was to extend to any Dominion without its express request and consent, declared in the relevant act. A further development came in 1949 when the Crown became the symbol of India's membership of the Commonwealth, but surrendered all prerogative powers. India became a Republic but remained within the commonwealth. Other Commonwealth nations have since taken this course.

Finances

The role of the monarchy was subjected to sharp, although indirect scrutiny in 1971 when after a message from The Queen to the Commons asking for additional financial provision for the Royal Family, a Select Committee was appointed to consider the question[1]. At the beginning of each reign the monarch surrenders the hereditary revenues from the Crown estates for the duration of the reign and, in return, is granted a fixed sum of money, a procedure which has been followed since the accession of George III in 1860. By the Civil List Act of 1952, on the accession of Queen Elizabeth II, Parliament provided a sum of £475,000 a year for the support of The Queen together with annuities for certain members of the Royal Family, anticipating that this would suffice for the whole of the reign. Owing to inflation at an unprecedently high rate, the sums voted proved inadequate and by 1970 total civil list expenditure had reached £745,000, leaving a deficit of £240,000 which had to be met from the Privy Purse, hence the royal message and the subsequent appointment of the Select Committee.

The committee considered a wide range of evidence and published its report in November 1971. For the first time the evidence submitted was published so that the report constitutes a unique and valuable document on the working of the monarchy in the second half of the twentieth century[2]. The report was not, however, unanimous, and a split occurred along party lines. The Conservative members of the committee supported an increased sum for the monarchy to be granted in the traditional manner while the Labour and Liberal members although not dissenting from the need for a larger provision for the monarch and her family, voted for the setting up of a separate department of the Crown. This department, under a permanent secretary, would be supported by a separate vote and would be directly responsible to Parliament[3]. In the event, the committee approved by majority an increase in the civil list to £980,000 a year for The Queen and her household and increased annuities for other members of the Royal Family. The committee also recommended that the royal trustees should report from

1 The committee consisted of seventeen members: Mr Joel Barnett, Mr John Boyd-Carpenter (now Lord Boyd-Carpenter), the Chancellor of the Exchequer (Mr Anthony Barber), Mr Robin Chichester-Clark, Mrs Peggy Fenner, Mr William Hamilton, Mr Douglas Houghton, Mr Roy Jenkins, Miss Joan Lestor, Sir Fitzroy Maclean, Mr Charles Pannell, Mr Norman St John-Stevas, Mr John Thomas, Mr Jeremy Thorpe, Sir Robin Turton, Mr William Whitelaw and Mr Harold Wilson.

2 Notable amongst the documents considered was a memorandum from Sir Michael Adeane (now Lord Adeane) then Private Secretary to The Queen, on The Queen's activities.

3 One member of the committee, Mr William Hamilton, submitted a separate report which while granting the Queen an annual salary of £100,000 would have reduced or abolished the payments to other members of the Royal Family and confiscated the revenues of the Duchies of Lancaster and Cornwall. Mr John Boyd-Carpenter suggested that the amount voted to the Monarch should be expressed as a percentage of the revenue from the crown estates, Thus providing a built-in protection against inflation since the estates revenues increase year by year. Some members of the committee were sympathetic to this plan, but it did not command majority support.

time to time on royal expenditure and that following receipt of such reports the sums charged on the consolidated fund should be increasable by treasury order: "Such reports, which would be laid before Parliament, to be made when necessary, and in any event not less frequently than once every ten years". In this way the committee provided for a means of reviewing the royal finances but avoided the embarrassment of annual inquiries into royal expenditure.

These proposals were subsequently incorporated into a statute which was approved by Parliament[1]. Members were satisfied with the provision for decennial reviews, thus putting into practice Bagehot's principle of protecting the monarchy from continual inquisition. "Above all things", he wrote in *The English Constitution,* "our royalty is to be reverenced, and if you begin to poke about it you cannot reverence it. When there is a select committee on The Queen, the charm of royalty will be gone. Its mystery is its life. We must not let in daylight upon magic"[2].

Criticism of the Monarchy

The monarchy, like other institutions, is not immune from criticism, and in recent years some doubts about its continued utility have been voiced, although there has been nothing equivalent to the republican movement which grew up in England in the 1860s. Led by Charles Bradlaugh, it commanded support at various times from men such as Dilke, Joseph Chamberlain, Bright and John Morley. In 1871 the movement was stimulated by the proclamation of the French Republic, but the illness of the Prince of Wales, and the subsequent outburst of popular rejoicing on his recovery finished the movement as an effective force.

It is sometimes argued that the hereditary principle is not supportable in any institution playing a prominent role in a modern state. This theoretical objection is reinforced in practice by the argument that it involves a lottery in genetics and sooner or later a losing ticket is bound to be drawn. Bagehot's criticism was sharp:

> "A constitutional sovereign must in the common course of government be a man of but common ability. I am afraid, looking to the early acquired feebleness of hereditary dynasties, that we must expect him to be a man of inferior ability. Theory and experience both teach that the education of a prince can be but a poor education and that a royal family will generally have less ability than other families. What right then have we to expect the perpetual entail on any family of an exquisite discretion, which if it be not a sort of genius, is at least as rare as genius?"

1 The Civil List Act, 1972. The report was debated in the Commons on 14 December 1971 and an Opposition amendment to pave the way for the setting up of a separate department of the Crown defeated by 300 votes to 263. The report itself was then approved by 300 votes to 27. *Hansard,* 828: 278—399. The Bill to give effect to the report was given a second reading on 21 December 1971, for debate see *Hansard,* 828: 1323—1382, the Bill being passed by 166 votes to 45. The remaining stages of the Bill were taken on 19 January 1972, see *Hansard,* 829: 495—557. The principal points of controversy were the annuities payable to other members of the Royal Family and the tax exemption of The Queen.

2 *Cf* the following comment by Bagehot: "An English Sovereign, to exist at all, must not be liable to be cross-examined in a Tichborne case, must not be allowed by etiquette to hold controversy with a subject, must not be directly or rudely criticised in public, and must not, above all, have his or her privacy invaded by Parliament at discretion. He must be a figure, and not a mere person liable to criticism even for vices, unless indeed he forces those vices as George IV did upon the public notice". "Sir Charles Dilke on the Civil List": *The Economist,* 10 January 1874.

The hereditary principle is, however, quite defensible both in theory and in practice. The basic unit of our society remains the family and so long as this is so the Royal Family is not so much an anomaly as an apotheosis. In any case what more acceptable alternative is there? An elective monarchy has grave drawbacks not least that it would open the highest position in the country to competition. This would increase the scramble for social distinction which is moderated by the hereditary character of the monarchy. The English are a theatrical people and care about the show and would be eager to take part in it. If the highest post in conspicuous life were thrown open to public competition, wrote Bagehot, "this low sort of ambition and envy would be fearfully increased. Politics would offer a prize too dazzling for mankind; clever base people would strive for it and stupid base people would envy it". In a society which is becoming increasingly a mobile and competitive meritocracy there is value in preserving an institution whose hereditary basis points to another scale of values.

Another charge which opponents of the monarchy level against it is that it is an expensive and extravagant institution.

Surveying the available figures it would be absurd to pretend that the British monarchy is cheap but equally it is in no way extravagant. It has a certain splendour and style but that is in accordance with the wishes of a people who like pageantry and pomp. There is something to be said for a splendid monarchy and something to be said for no monarchy but a mean monarchy has nothing to be said for it at all[1]. "It is better", Bagehot wrote, "to spend a million in dazzling when you wish to dazzle, than three-quarters of a million in trying to dazzle and yet not dazzling". "Cheap princes", he observed, "are sure to cost the nation dear"[2]. And he was specific if a little exaggerated in his criticism of Queen Victoria's retirement: "From causes which it is not difficult to define the Queen has done almost as much injury to the popularity of the monarchy by her long retirement from public life as the most unworthy of her predecessors did by his profligacy and frivolity"[3].

Apart from alleged extravagance the criticism most often levelled against the Crown is that it has failed to change sufficiently rapidly with the times. A picture is built up of a monarch surrounded by a crowd of stuffy courtiers and hemmed in by a small circle of the socially privileged, unrepresentative of modern Britain. Criticism of The Queen's choice of personal friends does not deserve to be treated seriously as in this respect at any rate she must be accorded the same freedom of choice as her subjects. The criticisms of the "court" are of a different order, but are equally devoid of content. The Queen has a remarkably small staff to assist her discharge her constitutional and ceremonial duties and they are noted for their unobtrusiveness and efficiency. Recently the whole royal system of administration was subjected to a radical overhaul by modern efficiency experts, a trial which the House of Commons has yet to experience.

Under the guidance of Prince Philip the monarchy far from remaining static is

1 It is worth noting that the republican movement grew up in England in the 1860s not because of any ostentation in the court, but because Queen Victoria had virtually withdrawn from public life. The people, in fact, wanted to see more of her not less.

2 "The income of the Prince of Wales", *The Economist,* 10 October 1874.

3 "The Monarchy and the People", *The Economist* 22 July, 1871, The Works. Bagehot gave a good reason to guard against envy of royal splendour: "But instead of feeling any jealousy of all that somewhat hollow splendour, we ought really to look upon their lives as, in a very real sense, sacrificed to external effect for the good of the nation, and feel much more a sympathy with them in their grandeur than of envy of its pleasure". "The Prince of Wales's Indian Visit:" *The Economist* 10 July 1875, *The Works.*

constantly altering and developing[1]. His keen interest in science and British industry has connected the monarch with areas of the national life which otherwise might have been remote from her. The Queen's Awards for Industry have been instituted and proved highly successful. The presentation parties for debutantes have been abolished and cocktail parties and informal luncheon parties for people of widely different backgrounds have been introduced. The dangers of becoming identified with a declining class have been avoided. Special garden parties are held from time to time for such organizations as the Women's Institutes, the Commonwealth universities, etc. Garden parties have become national rather than social events. The whole protocol that formerly surrounded royalty has been greatly simplified and informality emphasized wherever possible. The Queen attends press receptions both at home and abroad and Prince Philip gives interviews. Ceremonial is confined to official and diplomatic occasions when it is meticulously carried out. This process of gradual and judicious modernization is continuing.

Conclusion

Today the British monarchy is as firmly established as at any time in its long history. Maintaining its role as one of the "dignified" parts of the constitution it has nevertheless changed with the times and brought itself up to date. The Queen's dedicated discharge of her duties constitutes both a challenge and an example to the country. The nation reveres The Queen, but the excessive adulation which threatened the monarchy in the 1950s has declined. The British monarchy seems destined to serve the nation for many years to come.

1 "To survive," he has stated, "the monarchy has to change". His outspokenness has at times being criticised, but a consort should have greater freedom of speech than the sovereign and by his utterances Prince Philip has facilitated the adaption of the monarchy to changed conditions by projecting a new "image" of its character.

The Role of the Prince Consort

BY ELIZABETH LONGFORD

"The role of a Prince Consort has never been easy to assess", wrote the Republican MP, William Hamilton, a member of the Select Committee on the Civil List, 1971. At least one can agree with him in that. Prince Philip himself had an illuminating thought a few years earlier. "It's almost like being self-employed", he said, "in the sense that you decide what to do." That clue will be followed up in due course.

Our Queens Regnant in their own right are five in number. Their Consorts, however, far from being as like in function as the five fingers of a hand, are remarkable for their differences. So much so, that one is quickly driven to focus on the person rather than the role. It seems to be the personality which has formed the role, not vice versa.

Our five Consorts have none the less some things in common. Constitutionally each exists, and exists solely, as husband of the Queen. That is their place in the Constitution. They have no other. Not only do they share this bare constitutional upland, but they also can be seen as typical of their own age, and forming together some sort of five-point pattern in history. Philip II of Spain, husband of Mary I, was not so much King Consort as King in his own right, and because his kingdom was Spain he appeared as a villain of sixteenth century melodrama. William III was King jointly with Mary II and if he had not existed he would have had to be invented to make the Settlement work. Queen Anne's Consort, George of Denmark, waxed happily fat, like so many seventeenth century characters, on the love of his Queen, of news, and of his bottle. Queen Victoria's Consort, Prince Albert of Saxe-Coburg-Gotha, was earnestly creative like much of his age. Prince Philip is astringently dynamic, as so much of his age would also like to see itself. That Prince Albert and Prince Philip gradually appeared to epitomise their own period does not necessarily mean they influenced it or it them. But it may be so. If we add a sixth Prince by way of prelude to the list, the pattern is still there. For the "Nine day Queen", Lady Jane Grey, was married at sixteen to nineteen-year-old Lord Guildford Dudley. When her aspiring Consort asked Lady Jane to make him King Consort, we are told that she was "quite tart" with him. No wonder. The very sound of "King Guildford" was unsuitable. In a violent age the Consort, like his Queen, was put to death.

Lastly, the five Princes seem to form a changing pattern of power. Philip of Spain was potentially so powerful that the country's whole concern was to see that he had no power in England at all. With poor old George of Denmark, even the post of Lord High Admiral got him into a scrape and he turned to making model ships. When we reach Albert the decibels of power, *de facto* rather than *de jure,* have risen to their peak; some say his was the Albertian age rather than the Victorian. For every one of Prince Albert's honorary posts Prince Philip probably holds fifty, his appointments and responsibilities filling many pages of print; yet no one seriously accuses him, as they did Prince Albert, of being the real ruler of England.

* * *

Prince Albert arrived in England to marry Queen Victoria in 1840. They were both twenty. He brought with him a store-house of shining qualities and an albatross which hung round his neck until the end of the Crimean War. (Prince Philip tells us in his *Birds from Britannia* that he had seen six kinds of albatross, the Sooty, Wandering, Black-browed, Buller and Shy. Albert's must have been the shy species.) He was a foreigner. Not that Britain was particular xenophobic, but Albert was exceptionally aloof. His shy manner was wrongly ascribed to arrogance. In addition, he never went about without an equerry or indeed went about at all in general society, for fear of getting involved in some scandal. (He regarded society as basically immoral up to the 1850s, when he began to reform it.) So the albatross round his neck thumped him on the chest until his efficiency and competency during the Crimean War made the "foreigner" deeply respected if not popular. That was 1855. In the same year Prince Albert's German adviser, Baron Stockmar, left Britain for good. He also had been a bit of an albatross.

A foreign adviser is not advisable for a foreign prince. Stockmar's radiantly unselfish love for Prince Albert did not compensate for his misreading of the British Constitution. Any mistakes which the Prince made can reasonably be put down to Stockmar's promptings. On the psychological plane the Baron's operations were hardly more felicitous. He had been dismayed to find his pupil uninterested in politics at the advanced age of eighteen. He therefore tried to tighten and screw up a temperament which was already too taut for comfort. His motto for Prince Albert was "Never relax, never relax, never relax"; a motto which helped to bring the unfortunate man to death from fever at the age of only forty-two.

In order to understand the development of his role as Prince Consort it is necessary to trace briefly the story of his first decade in Britain. After preliminary skirmishes with the Tory opposition, the Prince Consort's early battles to establish himself were waged, strangely enough, against the Queen and her entourage. The anti-Tory skirmishes concerned matters which have often proved thorns in the flesh of Consorts, both before and since. First, his "annuity" (income). A Queen Consort regularly received £50,000 a year, and this the adoring Victoria felt was the least her "perfect Angel" Albert should be offered. Unhappily, the royal wedding was taking place at the beginning of the Hungry Forties. Chiefly, one must admit, as a party ploy, the Tory opposition managed to get the Prince's annuity reduced to £30,000. When Queen Victoria reflected that "stupid old George of Denmark", as she called Prince Albert's predecessor, had received £100,000, she exploded in royal wrath against the Tory "monsters" and "scoundrels". (The original annuity of her great-great-grandson, £40,000, voted at a time when money was worth very much less than in the nineteenth or seventeenth centuries, would no doubt have inspired in her even stronger language.) As Prince Consort, Albert well understood the inflammable nature of money where the Monarchy was concerned. In writing to Stockmar about a large legacy the Queen had received from an old miser named Nield, he noted with a burst of bi-lingual anxiety that its terms "*vielleicht ein* subject of popular animadversion *werden könnte*"—"perhaps could become a subject of popular animadversion".

Second, the question of precedence. This hit Prince Albert mainly as a "foreigner". In their professed desire to protect the rights of the old Royal Dukes (Cumberland, Cambridge, Sussex) the Tories did not wish to concede the "Coburg lad" his precedence next to the Queen. When Queen Victoria was expecting her first baby many of the nobility objected to bowing to the Prince when he presided at a Levée in her place. Yet, if the Prince Consort had any obvious, undeniable and outstanding role, that was it. To assist the Queen. When the Prince of Wales reached the age of seventeen, the question of precedence again raised its ugly head. "Wicked men", wrote Prince Albert to his brother, were plotting to claim precedence for Bertie above his own father, the Queen's husband, the danger being particularly acute during Continental visits. So in 1857 Queen Victoria formally created her husband Prince Consort. It is improbable that any future Prince Consort will be hampered in his role by this matter of precedence. In the case of Prince Philip, there have been no "wicked men" to make trouble; nor does it seem the least likely that he will ever receive the formal title of Prince Consort.

It may be added that Prince Albert, as a Royal Duke, had a constitutional right to take his seat in the House of Lords. Less than a dozen years before his advent, two other Royal Dukes had made fiery speeches about Catholic Emancipation, speaking on opposite sides. But when the unlucky Albert entered the House of Commons in 1846 simply to hear the Tory Prime Minister, Sir Robert Peel, speak on Corn Law reform, he was violently attacked by Peel's extreme "right-wing" opponents. Prince Albert was never present at a debate in Parliament again. Since then, the Prince Consort's role seems to have stopped short at any form of parliamentary contribution. As Duke of Edinburgh, Prince Philip has indeed taken his seat in the Lords but he has not spoken. With his gifts, this is a loss to the man and to the nation. Perhaps it is time that Prince Albert's débâcle should be forgotten. Perhaps Royal Dukes might be seen on the cross-benches, at least on non-party political occasions. It would be a return to the robust tradition of the past. It could also enhance the emergent picture of a modern Monarchy supported on all counts by actively contributing, normally functioning human beings.

Third, Prince Albert's religion. At a time of religious controversy, the Prince's role as husband of the Queen had its difficulties. Like Prince George of Denmark before him, he was suspected at first of Roman Catholicism. Even after this unfounded fear was laid to rest, Prince Albert's religion was questioned both by the High and Low Church. Nevertheless, it was his enquiring, scientific mind and Broad Church views which finally came nearest to the spirit of his age. His descendant, born into the Greek Orthodox Church and received into the Church of England before his marriage, has never been troubled by echoes of this ancient strife.

We come now to Prince Albert's chief role, and the supreme preoccupation of every Prince Consort—to support his wife. For a couple of years the Prince was greatly handicapped by two unexpected factors. Queen Victoria, though heart and soul in love, felt curious twinges of jealousy at sharing any of her responsibilities. She had been on the Throne for well over two years before she married. She was hot-tempered and accustomed, as she was the first to declare, to having her own way. After a few months of marriage the Prince was forced to lament to a young German friend, that he was only the husband but not the master in the house. A considerable and perennial human problem is concealed in those few words. In what sense can a Prince Consort be master in the Queen's house? Prince Philip has told an interviewer that (unlike Prince Albert) he began in 1947, when he married, with a normally authoritative position in his own home and then, in 1952, when The Princess Elizabeth became Queen he had to work out new ways of serving her and leading a meaningful existence. With Prince Albert the two adjustments had to come simultaneously. His position in the home had to be established at the same time as he developed his role as Prince Consort in his adopted country.

After no more than two strenuous years, this forbearing but determined Prince had accomplished his twin tasks. The woman whom he saw as the Queen's evil genius—Baroness Lehzen—was quietly but firmly sent back to Germany and the Court purged of certain uppish noble families. His position *vis à vis* the government of the day was even more satisfactory. He was encouraged by two Prime Ministers in turn (Melbourne and Peel) to see all the Queen's State papers, to help her in drafting documents and to attend Ministerial interviews. By 1846 he was hand in glove with Peel, enjoying a splendid working partnership based on mutual understanding and appreciation. As for his position with the Queen, he had become her majordomo, her time-and-motion expert in the Palace economy, her Capability Brown in the royal gardens, her principal and indeed only private secretary, her teacher, "walking dictionary", interpreter, father, husband and lover all rolled into one.

If one seeks a cause for this unprecedented result it must be found in the fecundity of the royal marriage and the barrenness of the royal household. Queen Victoria gave birth to nine children in seventeen years—all of them high spirited and some of them quite a handful. Prince Philip's creative impact on the upbringing of his children is well known. How much more did his great-great-grandmother need the unremitting help of a husband, having as she did a far less serene temperament than the present Queen, as well as over double the number of children in rather less time? At the same time, Queen Victoria's Household provided nothing which today would be recognised as a secretariat. In this it was not unique. Public figures like the great Duke of Wellington himself were forced to inveigle nieces and other kind women into copying their letters. In the 1840s and 1850s, Ministers were only too glad that their Sovereign had in Prince Albert such a magnificent secretary-substitute. If Prince Philip were magically transported back a century he would undoubtedly fill Prince Albert's secretarial role with equal aplomb. Fortunately or not, the boot today is on the other foot, or rather, the pen is in other hands. It was the descent of an immensely comprehensive secretariat upon the young couple at the time of Elizabeth II's Accession which drove Prince Philip to serve Queen and country in new directions.

It should now be possible to understand the constitutional traumas which came to afflict Queen Victoria's Consort, roughly during the eight years following Peel's fall. Up till then, the Prince had been riding high. That the Queen had once been prevented from creating her treasure "King-Consort" now seemed ludicrously irrelevant. He was King in all but name. And it had all happened so smoothly, so inevitably, with such noble intentions, that no one called it unconstitutional. Then came 1846, Peel's fall, and a new Foreign Secretary, that launcher of Liberal gun-boats, Lord Palmerston.

Now the Prince's idea of his role had special relevance to foreign affairs. He had been encouraged by his foreign advisers to groom himself as a kind of unofficial Foreign Minister. It was true that his foreign birth, correspondence with foreign relatives, and assiduous reading of the newspapers, had given him far more knowledge than ninety-nine out of a hundred British Ministers. Unfortunately for him Lord Palmerston was the hundredth man. Not only did he know his business, but his policies differed widely from the Prince's and Palmerston did not brook interference. Incidentally, how did it come about that the Prince Consort had a policy at all? According to the Constitution, only Ministers had policies; Prince Consorts had wives and children. But Prince Albert did not see it like this. He had a "vocation" which was in his own words to increase the "power, stability and symmetry" of the Monarchy, by transforming the Sovereign from the nodding "Mandarin figure" envisaged by Palmerston, into a kind of super-Premier. It was at this point that the Prince's thinking entered dangerous waters. What did he mean by a "symmetrical" Monarchy? Perhaps "systematic", a word of Germanic flavour not suited to an unwritten Constitution. "The Crown supports the Ministry of the time", he wrote, "whatever it may be, *so long as it commands a majority, and governs with integrity for the welfare of the country*". That qualification introduced by the Prince (and put here in italics) led him even further among the shoals. He saw it as his vocation not merely to raise the Monarchy into a "neutral between parties" but also gradually to mould it into an "arbiter" or "mediator" between them, taking advice from both sides in order to form an opinion. This mistaken concept of the Crown was roundly denounced by H. H. Asquith many years later. It was this idea which caused Benjamin Disraeli sarcastically to write that, if Prince Albert had lived into old age, he would have "given us the benefit of absolute government".

The benefits of old age were tragically withheld from Prince Albert. A longer life would perhaps have enabled him to see his true role more clearly. In association with Mr Gladstone, so like himself in public ponderosity and flashes of private gaiety, Prince Albert's astute intelligence might swiftly have divested itself of old, anachronistic ideas. But despite his misunderstanding of the Crown's role, and so of his own, Prince Albert mapped out other areas of the land with conspicuous success. It is here that we can discover some resemblances between his interpretation of the role and Prince Philip's.

The industrial welfare of the country seemed to Prince Albert his peculiar province. Industry, especially engineering, was forging ahead but the mechanics and engineers themselves, the navvies and ballast-heavers in the docks led a hard, harsh existence. Again and again Prince Albert spoke up for "that class of our community which has most of the toil and least of the enjoyment of this world". Though self-help was ultimately the only solution he could see for them, he did succeed in getting the ballast-heavers paid in money rather than in drink. In twice visiting Birmingham during periods of economic unrest he showed courage and social concern. Ministers had warned him against going. Engineering and commerce also appealed to him as likely to stimulate contemporary art, in which he was passionately interested. The Great Exhibition of 1851 marked his highest point in this direction. Not only did it "immortalise" Albert, as the Queen fondly wrote, but it established his right to deploy a creative imagination; to change a corner of England physically, leaving a Crystal Palace of glass and steel and a yearning for international brotherhood, where before had been some empty acres of Hyde Park and an obsessive fear of revolutionaries. No doubt it was the cold steel rather than the crystal which proved more durable and swiftly reappeared in the Crimean War. The Prince Consort's dream survived notwithstanding, linking itself with the advances of science as well as art and industry. The ever-growing nucleus of buildings at South Kensington is a testimony to the vigour of his role, and a reminder that there was a Science Museum, an Albert Hall, and a Victoria and Albert Museum long before twentieth century European revolutions had written their amiable postscripts with Peoples' Palaces of Art and Culture.

It is tempting to delve for comparisons between our most recent Royal Consorts.

(The two Philips have nothing in common but their name.) Stories have appeared that Prince Philip, during his engagement, spent long hours studying the precedents set up by Prince Albert. There is no reason to believe them. Indeed, so utterly remote are the circumstances of Queen Victoria's Consort, that references to them could justifiably provoke in Prince Philip the same impatience with which Victoria as a young Queen swept aside "that eternal Prince George of Denmark".

* * *

The most striking difference between their roles has in a sense been deliberately created by Prince Philip. Prince Albert's purpose, as we have seen, was to arrest the Monarchy's slide into the semblance of a "nodding Mandarin" and to re-establish its power as the umpire between the political parties and final arbiter of politics. In other words, to move in a constitutional direction which can only be called historically backwards. Prince Philip's vocation, on the contrary, has been to carry the Monarchy forward into the second half of the twentieth century. How has he set about it?

Two outstanding alterations have taken place in the life of the Sovereign compared with Her Majesty's predecessors. First, more mobility. Second, greater informality. There can be little doubt that her Consort has been one of the aiders and abettors in these welcome changes. Not only do they accord with his known views on the new "style" of Monarchy, but they are also in line with his own personality. One very hard fact and some other more intangible signs must here suffice as evidence. On the mobility issue it is accepted that he was the prime mover in breaking the ban on royal air travel. How else could a modern Queen get around a modern Commonwealth, now composed of thirty-one members? It is noteworthy that when Her Majesty's former private secretary, Sir Michael Adeane (now Lord Adeane) informed the Select Committee on the Civil List in a most enlightening memorandum about these changes, including the increase in travel, he spoke of "travelling in aeroplane, yacht, train and motor car"—putting the aeroplane first. Prince Philip's own zest and expertise in piloting an aeroplane contribute to the same picture. As for the informality, this is not the place to enumerate the many ways in which the modern Monarchy has become more accessible to the people. One only need compare the starchy pathos of Queen Victoria and Prince Albert in rigid checks and stripes, a topper gleaming above the absent smile, with the gaiety, the open-neck shirt, the summer dress and cardigan of a hundred years later, to appreciate the visual difference. Dignity was the theme of the 1850s, naturalness that of the 1960s. While the later Consort studiously avoids what he calls "fundungus" (false trappings), the earlier Consort would have been well satisfied to know that his widow maintained to the end of her life his legacy of "Balmorality".

Prince Philip's role in the changing scene is stamped on every word he writes, every joke he makes, every photograph he takes. He discusses a fixture with his secretary in the least pompous idiom. "I can chopper from Goodwood, should be quite easy. An hour? Start the thing, lunch, chop back". He photographs a marine iguana on the Galápagos Islands with its little leathery arm round its mate, calling it his favourite and luckiest photograph. His captions are all informal: one gull "pinches" another gull's egg instead of stealing it. And his text is full of "can'ts", "isn'ts", "doesn'ts"; partly to emphasise his amateur status as a naturalist, partly to avoid any trace of pomposity. He can raise a laugh on any occasion, however serious, because he is not inhibited about cracking jokes against himself—something unthinkable in Prince Albert's day. At a banquet to commemorate the tercentenary of the Resettlement of Jews in Britain he said: "You at least have had more lasting good fortune at making a living in these islands, and you have done the country more good than my ancestors at any rate; danegeld was never popular I gather". His speeches rarely lack bold touches: for instance, in opening a hostel for deaf youths, he declared that much as he admired the work of the Institute, "I admire still more the fortitude and the courage of those it sets out to help". Two linked ideas sum up his attitude to speech-making: "I have no axe to grind and nothing to sell. I have to make speeches as a matter of duty but the line I take is my own". Prince Albert, an equally original mind in his own way, was all too seldom allowed to take his own line in public.

There were, nevertheless, not a few resemblances between the two Princes, enough at least to make their roles comparable. Each was free, though within very different limits, to make the role what he wished. They have both had an efficiency-drive in the Palace, Prince Albert in 1840, Prince Philip in 1962. There have been the same bouts of duelling with the Press; but few public figures who try to do anything can altogether avoid sporadic clashes. There was a similar stringency over money, relieved in Prince Philip's case on 1 January 1972, when his annuity was raised from £40,000 to £65,000 (though Lord Cobbold, the Lord Chamberlain, emphasised that the annuity "was pretty well pared to the bone in the case of The Duke of Edinburgh", implying that The Queen might have once more to subsidise his annuity from her own, before the next review.) When Prince Albert had to pay income tax on its re-introduction in 1842, Queen Victoria realised it was going to be hard for "poor dear Albert".

By far the most important resemblance in their roles, however, lies in the accepted vocation of each to help those who needed it most; to fill important gaps, especially those which the State might have overlooked. In Prince Albert's time, as has been seen, it was the industrial workers who seemed to him in direst need. In the Fifties of our own century, The Duke of Edinburgh advanced the over-riding claims of deprived youth. The Playing Fields Association, the Outward Bound Trust and The Duke of Edinburgh's Award Scheme speak for themselves. It is surely significant that one of the Duke's most eloquent and moving passages occurred in a speech celebrating the achievements of the Trust: "Outward Bound . . . seeks, first, to show the boy the stuff he is made of, to find himself, to become even dimly aware of his own possibilities. It may seem ridiculous that this can be done in a month at a school near the sea or in the mountains, but that is the fact of the matter; it is being done. It may take a given time to acquire skill or to become physically fit; but that doesn't mean to say that you need a three-year syllabus to touch a man's soul".

Curiously enough, neither Prince Albert nor Prince Philip have been called upon to visit the Empire or the Commonwealth in its political heyday; the former, because the royal couple were not to be entrusted to seas wider than the English or Irish Channels; the latter, because the political links with the Commonwealth had already changed. But the most recent and absorbing of Prince Philip's responses to a crying need—Conservation—has in fact drawn him into ever closer contact with the independent Commonwealth.

It would need a whole page just to enumerate the multitudinous interests which Conservation has opened up: what Prince Philip's collaborator on *Wildlife Crisis* James Fisher, calls "the great debate on pollution, conservation, amenity, landscape, recreation, natural ecological change, and planning of new towns, roads, reservoirs, airports, mines and industry". It seems a far cry from Prince Philip's national parks, green belts and indeed the whole environment, to Prince Albert's small plot in Hyde Park and short row of model cottages on Kennington Common. But the inspiration is the same, namely, to give a unique voice to the foremost need of the time. Behind it all lies the same fundamental duty. To serve the country and The Queen.

1 *HRH The Princess Margaret, Countess of Snowdon*
by Bryan Organ, 1970. (Reproduced by kind permission of the Treasurer and Masters of the Bench of Lincoln's Inn)

The Royal Image

BY ROY STRONG

The public is seldom moved to vehemence over a modern work of art. The advent of a royal portrait is, however, an exception. Everyone feels that he or she is entitled to express a view about the image of their sovereign. Pietro Annigoni's two portraits of Her Majesty The Queen, and Bryan Organ's portrait of HRH The Princess Margaret (*Fig* 1), are instances of how likenesses of members of our Royal Family suddenly become world-wide news. From Harwich to Hong Kong every human being feels qualified to pronounce. High security surrounds the manufacture of these images, they are revealed amidst frenzies of public excitement, and the institution where they hang is promptly surrounded by huge queues of enthusiastic and indignant members of the general public. It is ironical that a form of art which has produced so little that is of any aesthetic merit or that is memorable should arouse such passions. It reveals the depths of feeling that such representations are still capable of evoking. And yet paintings of the Royal Family in 1972 are only one aspect of their iconography. Portraiture today embraces not only the aesthetic, but the mechanical media. In a hundred years time the recent television film of Her Majesty The Queen may be more highly rated as a portrait than a painting by, for example, Sir William Hutchinson. All forms of images of our Royal Family are interesting for they are historical evidence of how we think about a person or a group of persons, and how we visualize people affects how we think about them and how we see their role within our society.

The fundamental image of royalty is embodied in the state portrait, those icons of majesty, compilations of velvet, ermine, jewels, embroidery, regalia and swagged curtains. These images, in which it is almost incidental that the sovereign is a human being at all, purvey the living embodiment of an abstract principle. Their display and their use on ordinary artefacts represent adherence to an order of government. In this way the present Queen's features, crowned or wearing a tiara, appear on the banknotes and coinage, on postage stamps and seals of state, besides adorning the walls of official residences of ambassadors and other representatives of the head of state. In recent years some of these areas have been eroded: The Queen's profile, shrunk to minute size, is tucked into a corner of the endless vulgar commemorative stamps and historical heroes such as the Duke of Wellington have crept onto the banknotes. The changing royal image is proliferated through the mass production of coloured prints of "official" portraits and by periodic releases of "official" photographs to mark royal events: births, marriages, coronations or royal tours. Framed and adorning the walls of a million government buildings, offices, factories, shops, public houses and private homes, a visual gesture is made of loyalty to monarchical government.

Historically the state portrait was born of an alliance of the new art form of the portrait, evolved during the renaissance, with the rise of absolutism. In these images in paint, bronze and marble a ruler was deliberately exulted by adorning and surrounding him with the emblems of his office. Gradually a royal repertory evolved of crowns and sceptres, vast curtains and vaster columns, distant views of royal palaces and attendant deities or servants. In England Van Dyck created for Charles I (*Fig* 2) the formulae for depicting our Royal Family, one which has lived on, little changed, ever since, suffering only modifications at the hands of Lely and Kneller, Gainsborough and Reynolds, Winterhalter and Lavery. It is a fixed formula, a secular equivalent of some of the conventions governing religious art, although the latter has been more successful in this century in using the visual repertory of the age. There are, in sharp contrast, no equivalents of Henry Moore's Madonna and Child or John Piper's stained glass within the royal canon. Bryan Organ's portraits of Princess Margaret represent a lonely flirtation with the present.

The Royal Family also occupies within the eye of vision a role as the First Family, the model upon which every household within the realm should pattern itself in the exercise of the domestic virtues. However far from reality this arcadia might be, no dynasty since the advent of the exaltation of family life as a virtue, has been able quite to ignore this essential ingredient of their official visual image.

For the Tudors and Stuarts such family groups represented in microcosm a principle of monarchical rule, the patriarchal one. Just as a father rules over his family so a king reigns over his subjects, so the argument ran for kingship based on the Law of Nature. Family groups too were genealogical trees made flesh and blood, statements of the hereditary principle and images of succession. The hierarchical royal family group begins with Holbein's lost monumental wall painting in the Privy Chamber of Whitehall Palace and stems down through the centuries by way of Van Dyck's lyrical arrangements of Charles I and Henrietta Maria and their children to Lavery's silvery grey solemnity of the family of George V. From these Byzantine confrontations fan out other patterns of relationship of the family set apart by dint of being of the blood royal.

All royal relationships must be super-perfect and ideal. As husband and wife, king and consort are generally depicted over the centuries in terms of an amorous idyll dressed in the love etiquette of successive periods. Charles I and Henrietta Maria are glorified as knight and lady, leaving for the chase, for example, while a putto showers them with roses, the flowers of love; George III and Queen Charlotte are the perfection of the distant reserved marital relationships of the Age of Reason; while Queen Victoria and Prince Albert live out in their public images a passionate romantic story, she pale and wilting, he tender yet masculine and assertive. Since the advent of mass media every royal marriage has been built up as a romance within the quintessential visual terms of its period.

If royal marriages must always be portrayed as perfect, family life as propagated through the visual media, is too one of eternal harmony. In spite of all that we know concerning royal relationships, over the centuries the media disseminate the official image of parents and children, brother and sister, as being always harmonious. From the

2

3

THE STATE PORTRAIT

2 *Charles I* by Sir Anthony Van Dyck (Reproduced by gracious permission of HM The Queen)

3 *George II* Studio of Charles Jervois (National Portrait Gallery)

4 *Queen Elizabeth II* by James Gunn (Reproduced by gracious permission of HM The Queen)

4

5 *Queen Charlotte and the Princess Royal* by Francis Cotes (Reproduced by gracious permission of HM The Queen)

6 *The First of May 1851*: The Duke of Wellington, Prince Albert, Queen Victoria and the infant Duke of Connaught (Reproduced by gracious permission of HM The Queen)

7 *Princess Elizabeth and Prince Charles* by Baron (Camera Press)

8 *Conversation Piece at the Royal Lodge, Windsor* by James Gunn, 1950 (National Portrait Gallery)

9 *The Bible* by R. Turner after T. J. Barker (National Portrait Gallery)

10 *The Crown* by Grace Wheatley
(The Palace Theatre: reproduced by kind permission of Mr Emile Littler)

11 *George V*: Postage Stamp, Barbados
(From the collection of Mr Peter Hill)

moment the Queen clasps her first born in her arms, a romantic gesture of fairy tale fulfilment recorded as vividly by Cotes for Queen Charlotte (*Fig* 5), as by Winterhalter for Queen Victoria (*Fig 6*) and by Baron for the present Queen (*Fig 7*), the family is always "united" and "perfect". Whether in paint or print, film or photograph, the Royal Family must officially be a pool without a ripple. This is reflected in the vast groups of Victoria and her family as much as in James Gunn's Royal Lodge group of George VI and his Family in the National Portrait Gallery (*Fig* 8). Such a painting alone, if it were examined in a century's time as iconographical evidence on the idea of the Royal Family, would make a fascinating and revealing statement. The choice of a tea party as against any other meal, the absence of domestics (The Queen Mother pours tea), the modesty of the fare (one fruit cake), the dogs, the simplicity of dress, the presence of the portrait of George IV over the fireplace, all reveal a myriad of thought attitudes concerning the presentation of our Royal Family within the context of the immediate post-war era. Its equivalent in our period would be the recent Royal film to which we are still too close to objectively disentangle the subtle threads governing their iconographical presentation.

The allegorical royal portrait, in contrast, has vanished forever along with the philosophical basis which made it a valid vehicle for the communication of monarchical ideas. Springing from a thought attitude basically platonic in which seeing was believing, the representation of a monarch as a god or hero of classical or any other mythology momentarily assimilated him to the prototype of which on earth he was the living embodiment. In this way profound truths of the mystery of the crown could be revealed and monarchs could live out in art, whether in paint, poetry or the more ephemeral form of court theatre, their heroic exemplars, thus providing their subjects with patterns for imitation in the path of the virtues. Allegory enabled abstract ideas, of which the monarch was the embodiment, to be made manifest. James I identified himself with Solomon to epitomise his belief in the divinity of his rule as the Old Testament king reincarnate. William III was apotheosised at Hampton Court by Verrio, at Greenwich by Thornhill, and in the medals of his reign, as the mighty British Hercules, hero of the Labours, but whose own labours were laying low the forces of *le Roi Soleil,* whose sunbeams sometimes lay beneath the feet of his horse's hooves. Charles II rides along in a vast sea shell as Neptune, the ruler of the seas, an assertion of British sea power as old as the glorification of Queen Elizabeth I as Diana, the moon goddess ruling over the ocean, and as modern as this century's stamps depicting George V riding along in a marine chariot on the stamps of the island of Barbados (*Fig* 11). There are still occasional lapses into this lost world of apprehension as in Grace Wheatley's *The Crown* (*Fig* 10), in which The Queen, in full coronation robes, finds herself in the middle of a jungle happily acknowledging the salute of natives, by now no longer subject to the Crown. Such a painting is a fascinating glimpse of the final use of one of the allegorical formulae evolved for the now vanished British Empire. As a *motif* for the monarchy it first gained currency in late Victorian England.

Although this language of mythological allusion ceased to be a mode of thinking applied to the monarchy much beyond the early nineteenth century, it has been replaced by another visual repertory designed to celebrate the bounty and goodness of the Crown, this time by making them the living personifications of the achievements of their subjects. This is reflected in groups of Queen Victoria presenting the bible to colonial chieftains (*Fig* 9) or presiding over the opening of the Great Exhibition as much as in newspaper photographs or in television coverage of our Royal Family at services of thanksgiving for a national triumph, launching a new ship, or visiting a factory floor. There may be many instances more of this kind of image of our Royal Family today but the sets of circumstances governing their appearance remains remarkably small and unchanging.

The dilemma of the moment might be said to be that no new visual vocabulary has replaced that evolved four hundred years ago, and as circumstances change these become progressively less meaningful. The art of this country, unfortunately for the monarchy, is not related for its pattern of communication to crowns. Hence the Crown may be said to be isolated in its visual language and imagery and forced back into redeploying the archaic repertory of the age of absolutism, attributes now often having little more significance than leitmotifs of revivalist romance. One of the present problems facing the monarchy therefore is this one of its visual language and how it can create a new meaningful iconography for itself.

The Royal Residences

BY MARK BENCE-JONES

During the thousand years since the coming of William the Conqueror, the Kings and Queens of England and Great Britain have lived in a succession of palaces. Some of these, like Hampton Court, are intact and perfectly maintained, though they have long been abandoned by the reigning Sovereign. Of others, such as Whitehall or Eltham, only fragments survive; while others again, like Nonesuch or Carlton House, have vanished without trace.

In contrast to the relatively modern Buckingham Palace—which did not become a Royal residence until 1762 and was mostly built by George IV— or to those former Royal residences which came into favour at various times and were later abandoned, there are three palaces which have been continually associated with the Crown throughout the past thousand years. Only one of these, Windsor Castle, is now a Royal residence in the strict sense; but the other two, the Palace of Westminster and the Tower of London, are still the background to some of the pageantry surrounding the Sovereign. Westminster was a Royal palace from the reign of Canute, and was enlarged by Edward the Confessor. The Great Hall (*Fig* 1), originally built by William Rufus in 1097, was given its hammer-beam roof by Richard II. With its length of 240 feet, it is the largest and finest mediaeval hall of its kind in Europe; and is the only major part of the ancient palace to have survived the fires of 1512 and 1835. A few years after the first of these fires, Westminster ceased to be a Royal residence; but as the meeting place of Parliament it has remained a Royal palace in theory, and is still under the control of the Lord Great Chamberlain. Similarly, the Tower, which was lived in by various mediaeval Kings, notably Henry III, has never lost its Royal status; we are reminded of this by the presence of the Yeomen Warders, and the Crown Jewels.

Tradition has it that the Tower was founded by Julius Caesar; but the present structure was begun in 1078 by William the Conqueror. He built another fortification at the opposite end of the City, the now vanished Baynard's Castle; and as the outer defences of his capital, he surrounded London with a ring of castles including Hertford to the north, Rochester to the south-east and Windsor to the west. He and his immediate successors moved between these castles as politics, and the victualling of the Court, required—a mediaeval monarch could only stay in a particular place so long as the food supplies of the neighbourhood held out. In time, however, Windsor became the most favoured of these Royal castles; not only for strategic reasons, but also because it was situated in what had been a Royal domain since Saxon times. While at Windsor, the monarch could command the river which was the main thoroughfare of this part of the kingdom, at the same time as he enjoyed the pleasures of the chase.

And so William the Conqueror's stronghold on a hill overhanging the Thames—represented today by the Mound, on which the Round Tower stands—grew into the present fortified palace. Henry II built most of the curtain wall; Edward III—with William of Wykeham as his overseer—built the Royal lodgings in the Upper Ward; Edward IV built St George's Chapel, intending it to outshine the chapel of his rival, Henry VI, across the river at Eton. Elizabeth I built a long gallery which survives as the present Library; Charles II reconstructed the Sovereign Apartments (*Fig* 2) and decorated them in magnificent style, with carvings by Grinling Gibbons and ceilings painted by Verrio. George III, after the Castle had been neglected by his two predecessors, carried out modest alterations; while George IV employed Sir Jeffry Wyatville to give the Upper Ward and the rest of the Castle a more romantic appearance, and to provide a larger and more splendid series of State and private apartments—at the cost of sacrificing all but three of Charles II's interiors.

At the same time as Edward III and William of Wykeham built the Royal lodgings at Windsor, they undertook various works at Eltham Palace in Kent (*Fig* 3), about eight miles south-east of London, which had been a Royal residence in the reign of Henry III, but had then been granted to one of the great mediaeval clerical statesmen, Anthony Bek, Bishop of Durham, who had left it back to the Crown when he died in 1311. During the next two centuries, Eltham was a favourite Royal residence; it was here that Froissart came to present his book to Richard II; it was here that Erasmus conversed with the children of Henry VII[1]. The fact that Eltham was not so much a castle as a rambling country house of brick, stone and half-timber, built round several courtyards—rather like those two other great Kentish houses, Knole and Penshurst—shows how, despite such upheavals as the Wars of the Roses, the monarchs of the later Middle Ages were able to concentrate less on security and more on comfort. The main quadrangle, containing the hall, chapel and Royal apartments, was surrounded by a moat.

Henry VI may have begun the hall which was completed by Edward IV, and which became the principal feature of the palace, rising above the other buildings. A vast concourse of people would feast beneath its hammer-beam roof when the Court was here for Christmas. Henry VII rebuilt the Royal apartments, adorning them with projecting oriels and tapering cupolas; Henry VII made a garden linked to the palace by a bridge across the moat. From the time of Henry VIII, however, Eltham fell out of favour; though it was maintained as a Royal palace until the seventeenth century, and occasionally occupied by James I. After that it was allowed to decay; the buildings were still largely intact at the beginning of the eighteenth century, but a hundred years later they had mostly disappeared, except for the hall, which was used as a barn. In the nineteen-thirties it was restored by Sir Stephen Courtauld, who built a modern house adjoining it; the buildings are now occupied by the Institute of Army Education.

The palace for which Henry VIII forsook Eltham was only a couple of miles away, at Greenwich on the southern bank of the Thames. Here, early in the previous century, Humphrey, Duke of Gloucester had built what he called his "Manor of Pleasance", which gave Greenwich its alternative name of Placentia or Plesshy. The manor reverted to the Crown at Duke Humphrey's death in 1447, and Edward IV and Henry VII both

1 *The Story of Eltham Palace* by Roy Brook (Harrap, 1960). See also *Erasmus of Rotterdam* by George Faludy (Eyre & Spottiswoode, 1970).

1 Palace of Westminster: Westminster Hall (National Monuments Record—Crown Copyright)

2 Windsor Castle: the Queen's Presence Chamber (Reproduced by gracious permission of HM The Queen)

carried out improvements to it; while Henry VIII spent large sums in making it a "pleasant, perfect and princely palace". From a view of it drawn in 1558 it appears to have consisted of several irregular ranges dominated by two groups of battlemented towers.

Greenwich remained a Royal residence until the end of the seventeenth century. James I gave it to his Queen, Anne of Denmark, as a peace-offering after he had scolded her too severely for accidentally shooting his favourite hound; and she commissioned Inigo Jones to build her a miniature palace bridging the public road from London to Woolwich, which separated the main palace from its park. Before the Queen's House (*Fig* 5), as it came to be known, was finished, Anne of Denmark was dead, but it was completed and furnished for her daughter-in-law, Queen Henrietta Maria. With its perfect Classical proportions, its Ionic loggia, its painted ceilings by Jakob Jordaens and Orazio Gentileschi, its gilded decoration and its bust of Charles I by Bernini, it must have been the most elegant and sophisticated house in the England of its time; a testimony to Charles I's exquisite taste and love of the arts. Henrietta Maria returned to the Queen's House after the Restoration, and Jones's nephew, John Webb, was employed to enlarge it. Charles II also commissioned Webb to rebuild the main palace, but this was unfinished at the time of his death, and in 1695 it was given over to be the Royal Hospital for Seamen. Mary II, however, insisted that the view to the river from the Queen's House should not be closed, and so the Royal Hospital was finally built in the form of twin palaces, flanking the much smaller Queen's House in the centre. Henry, Earl of Romney, who became Ranger of Greenwich Park in 1667, moved the road to its present line between the Queen's House and the Royal Hospital; but the arches through which it formerly passed under the house can still be seen. After being used for various purposes, the Queen's House was beautifully restored and redecorated 1934-36[1].

No sooner had Henry VIII improved Greenwich than he turned his attention to Wolsey's palace of Hampton Court, which the Cardinal had prudently surrendered to him. For the remainder of Henry's reign, and during the five reigns that followed, Hampton Court was a favourite Royal residence. Mary I and Charles II both spent their honeymoons here; Shakespeare and his company acted in the Great Hall before James I, and also perhaps before Elizabeth I.

Hampton Court was less frequently occupied from the time of Charles II onwards; but William III so liked its situation that he commissioned Wren to rebuild it. The project however was incomplete at the time of King William's death; so that today, there is the pleasing contrast between the gateway (*Fig* 6), courtyard, Great Hall and gallery dating from Tudor times and the partially-built Wren palace that lies beyond them; with its grand front (*Fig* 7) facing along the canal and its enfilades of State rooms. Wren's Hampton Court is architecturally the finest palace which the British Crown possesses, the nearest equivalent to Versailles on this side of the Channel. It was unfortunate that it should have been abandoned by George III, who associated it with the unhappy quarrels between his father, Frederick, Prince of Wales, and his grandfather, George II; though its continuance as a Royal residence would probably have meant the giving up of Windsor Castle.

In return for Hampton Court, Henry VIII allowed Wolsey for a time the use of another Thames-side palace, a few miles closer to London. This had been a Royal manor as far back as the reign of Edward I, when it was known as Sheen. Richard II cursed the place and "caused it to be thrown down and defaced" on account of his Queen, Anne of Bohemia, having died here; Henry V rebuilt it, and it was rebuilt again, after a fire, by Henry VII, who renamed it Richmond in memory of his former title.

1 Further renovations made 1969.

3 Eltham Palace (Reproduced from Buck's *Cornwall, Devonshire and Kent* by permission of Royal Institute of British Architects)

4 Nonesuch Palace (Reproduced from Sir Thomas Jackson's *The Renaissance of Roman Architecture, Part II*: *England* by permission of the publishers, Cambridge University Press)

5 Greenwich: the Great Saloon of the Queen's House (Country Life)

With the fall of Wolsey, Richmond reverted to the Crown and became once again an occasional Royal residence; here Elizabeth I died, propped up among cushions on the floor almost to the last. Henry, Prince of Wales, the elder son of James I, embellished the palace at great expense; and his brother, Charles I, added to its grounds the deer park now known as Richmond Park. The Commonwealth put an end to the glories of Richmond. The palace was partly dismantled, and though it was occupied by Henrietta Maria after the Restoration, and used by James II as a nursery for his son, it fell into decay, and was eventually parcelled into tenements. All that now remains of it is a gateway and a few other relics.

As a builder of palaces, Henry VIII was equalled, among British monarchs, only by George IV. Not content with Hampton Court, Greenwich, Richmond, Windsor and Eltham, Henry built Nonesuch, near Cheam in Surrey (*Fig* 4), a fantasy of gilded half-timber decorated by Italians, which survived until the reign of Charles II. And in London, after the partial destruction of Westminster Palace by fire, he acquired two new palaces, St James's and Whitehall.

St. James's was on the site of a twelfth century hospital for leprous women under the patronage of St James the Less which Henry obtained from its custodians, the Fellows of Eton College, in exchange for lands in Suffolk. Of the palace he built here, little now remains save the familiar gateway facing up St James's Street, which bears the cyphers of Henry and Anne Boleyn, and dates the structure to about 1535 when that lady was still in favour. Wren enlarged the State Apartments towards the Park which were embellished by later architects, notably William Kent. After the burning of Whitehall in 1698 St James's became what it still officially is: the metropolitan palace of the Sovereign—and it is to the Court of St James that ambassadors are accredited. In the eighteenth century, it was generally regarded as quite unworthy of this function; but we now can admire the quiet dignity of its rooms, which are of comfortable proportions and rely for effect on portraits and tapestries rather than on any elaborate ornamentation.

York Place, the residence of the Archbishop of York from 1248, came into the possession of the Crown with the fall of Wolsey, and was renamed Whitehall. A hundred years later it had grown into a warren of lodgings, galleries, courtyards and gardens stretching for nearly half a mile along the bank of the river (*Fig* 8); and was not just the principal London residence of the King, but the seat of government of state that was growing increasingly complex, with dependencies overseas. Londoners regarded Whitehall as "mean and inelegant", and in 1619 James I initiated a scheme for rebuilding it, with Inigo Jones as architect. Jones and his nephew John Webb produced designs for a palace (*Fig* 9) which, in its final form, was one of the grandest architectural concepts of the Renaissance, enclosing seven courtyards including a circular "Persian Court" and covering an area twice the size of the Escurial; but which, unfortunately for posterity, was far beyond the exchequer of both James and Charles I. With the outbreak of the Civil War, the scheme was finally dropped; however Jones had already built the Banquetting House, which had a ceiling painted by Rubens. Through one of its upper windows, Charles I, the monarch who had the taste but not the resources to bring this great palace into being, stepped out onto the scaffold.

Whitehall is, of course, chiefly remembered as it was during the reign of Charles II, when the Stone Gallery was the centre of the gaiety, the brilliance and the intrigue of Restoration London. Off this gallery opened Charles's private apartments: a withdrawing room, a bedchamber and a closet, guarded by the faithful Chiffinch, where the King kept his special treasures. It was very different from the splendid settings created by architects like Mansard or Bernini for his brother-monarchs of Europe; but this did not

6 Hampton Court: the Tudor Front
(Crown Copyright: reproduced by permission of Controller of Her Majesty's Stationery Office)

7 Hampton Court: the Wren Fronts
(Crown Copyright: reproduced by permission of Controller of Her Majesty's Stationery Office)

mean that his tastes were particularly simple; rather, that his interests, in the matter of building, lay elsewhere. We have seen how he began to rebuild Greenwich, and constructed the magnificent State apartments at Windsor. His most ambitious project was still further afield: at Winchester, which, after his experience of the London mob during the Exclusion crisis, he contemplated making his capital. Here, Wren began to build him a palace that would have outdone Hampton Court as the English Versailles. It was to have had colonnades and cupolas, high enough for the King to see his warships riding at Spithead; it would have been approached by a street two hundred feet broad leading from Winchester Cathedral, lined on each side with noblemens' houses. The palace was just about to be roofed when Charles's death put a stop to the whole scheme; in the nineteenth century, the surviving buildings were made into barracks. Charles II's death virtually marked the end of Whitehall although, during the brief reign of his brother James II, there were some improvements carried out by Wren. William III declared that he could not live there because he could not stand the fogs and impure air of London; and then, in 1698, the whole conglomeration of buildings, except for the Banquetting House, went up in flames owing, it was said, to the carelessness of a Dutch laundrymaid. Wren set to work to design a new palace, but this was merely a matter of form. Apart from the Banquetting House, Whitehall has, since the time of the fire, been no more than a memory.

To provide himself with a residence where he could breathe the country air, but which was closer to London than Hampton Court, William III bought the house of the former Lord Chancellor, Heneage Finch, Earl of Nottingham, near the village of Kensington; which henceforth came into prominence as the "Court Suburb". The Kensington Palace of today, elegant and comfortable in its warm red brick, is largely the work of Wren, who, with Nicholas Hawksmoor as his clerk of works rebuilt Nottingham House after it had been purchased by the King. William III's three successors on the Throne all preferred Kensington to their other palaces. Queen Anne built the Orangery, according to Vanbrugh's or Hawksmoor's design; while during the reign of George I, William Kent added a new set of State apartments, as well as the King's Staircase (*Fig* 10): its walls painted with courtiers and ladies, pages and Yeomen of the Guard, looking down from *trompe-l'oeil* balconies. After the accession of George III, Kensington was deserted, only to come into prominence again as the childhood home of Queen Victoria. In later years it was the childhood home of Queen Mary; who after her husband had ascended the Throne as George V, considered the possibility of making Kensington the London residence of the King and Queen, in preference to Buckingham Palace.

Even with Kent's additions, Kensington was remarkably modest compared with Schönbrunn, Caserta, the Palacio Real at Madrid and the other royal palaces which, during the first half of the eighteenth century, were springing up in or near most European capitals; indeed, there was many a Margrave or Prince-Bishop in Germany who could boast of a new rococo *Residenz* that far exceeded it in grandeur. The first three Georges were less splendidly housed than some of their own subjects, though, paradoxically, there was a greater degree of formality at the Court of James's than at most other eighteenth century Courts. At various times during the century there were plans for giving London the sort of Royal palace which the growing wealth and power of Britain seemed to demand: thus Kent provided George II with designs for a rather dull palace in Hyde Park. But during the reign of "Farmer George" and his homely Consort, Queen Charlotte, the tendency was in the opposite direction: Kensington and Hampton Court were deserted in favour of Richmond Lodge, a rather unpretentious nobleman's villa consisting of a centre with two lower wings. It had been built about

8 Whitehall: An early Seventeenth Century view
(Reproduced from Visscher's *View of London*
by permission of the Trustees of the British Museum)

9 Whitehall Palace: the designs of Inigo Jones and John Webb
(Reproduced from W. Kent's *Designs of Inigo Jones* by permission of Royal Institute of British Architects)

fifty years before by the second Duke of Ormonde close to the old Royal palace of Richmond, and became Crown property as a result of the Duke's attainder.

By 1770 the house was too small for the King and Queen and their growing family, and Sir William Chambers produced designs for a new palace nearby. Work had begun on the foundations when the King abandoned the project owing to the death of his mother, the Princess of Wales, which enabled him to move into the White House, her villa at Kew. This had originally belonged to Lord Capel, and had then been remodelled by Kent for Frederick, Prince of Wales, the King's father. Like Richmond Lodge, it consisted of a centre and wings, but was on a larger scale and contained an enfilade of painted and gilded rooms. In 1802 the White House was demolished—as Richmond Lodge had been thirty years earlier—prior to the building of a castellated palace by the riverside, according to the design of James Wyatt. Only the shell of this Wyatt castle was completed; a few years later George IV ordered materials from it to be used in the building of Buckingham Palace, and the walls were eventually blown up with gunpowder.

George IV, a Royal builder in the grand manner, made up for his father's love of simplicity. He had taste, like Charles I and Charles II; but unlike them, he was able to bring his schemes into being. In 1783, at the age of twenty-one, long before he was King or even Prince Regent, he started to transform Carlton House, his official residence, into the most spectacular palace London had yet known; the masterpiece of Henry Holland, after whose death it was completed by Wyatt, John Nash and Thomas Hopper. The exterior—the Corinthian entrance front, guarded by its Ionic screen, facing up what is now Lower Regent Street, the garden front overlooking St James's Park—had something of Holland's characteristic restraint; but within, all was of the utmost splendour: columns of porphyry or yellow Siena, with bronze or silver capitals; walls hung with crimson damask; a circular drawing room (*Fig* 11) with the ceiling painted like the sky, from which crystal chandeliers cascaded down and were endlessly reflected in pier glasses; a Gothick dining room. By the time he became King, George IV had grown bored with this palace of enchantment; and a few years later, he ordered it to be pulled down. Fortunately, however, his other extravagance, the Brighton Pavilion (*Fig* 12), a Royal fantasy that compares only with Nonesuch, is still there for us to enjoy; its colourful and exotic furnishings fully restored; though when Queen Victoria, who associated it with the more raffish side of her uncle's career, gave it up, its future must have been very much in doubt. The Prince Regent commissioned Nash to build him this vision of the Gorgeous East in the year of Waterloo; the style is at once Chinese and Hindu, with a dash of Tartar; inside it is a riot of red and gold, of dragons and bamboos, pagodas and banana foliage.

If George IV were to be remembered only by the Brighton Pavilion, it would be fair to regard him as frivolous; but we have already seen how he undertook a formidable programme of reconstruction at Windsor Castle, where St George's Hall, the Waterloo Chamber and his other apartments are essentially suited to great State occasions rather than to parties of pleasure. And while with characteristic fickleness he robbed London of Carlton House almost as soon as it was built, he gave the capital the imposing Royal palace which it had hitherto lacked. In 1762 George III bought Buckingham House which was built at the beginning of the eighteenth century for John Sheffield, Duke of Buckingham, according to the design of the Dutch architect, Captain Wynne or Wynde. With its spacious grounds, more like a country house park than a town garden, Buckingham House was the finest private house in London, but not on the scale of a Royal palace. As such, it would have appealed to George III, who occupied it as his London residence while using St James's for ceremonial. When George IV ascended the Throne he commissioned Nash to turn Buckingham House into a palace large enough for Royal

10 Kensington Palace: the King's Staircase
(Reproduced by gracious permission of HM The Queen)

11 Carlton House: the Circular Drawing Room
(Reproduced from W. H. Pyne's *Royal Residences* by permission of Royal Institute of British Architects)

entertaining. Nash built the new palace round a three-sided courtyard, the open side facing the Mall and approached through a triumphal arch. The main front overlooked the garden (*Fig* 13), and incorporated the shell of the original house. Unfortunately, Wynne's painted staircase and his other interiors were not preserved; but Nash's State apartments are certainly well suited to their purpose, and manage to recreate something of the sumptuousness of Carlton House; particularly the Blue Drawing Room, with its Siena columns, and the Music Room, with its bold reliefs of *putti* in the spandrels of the domed ceiling.

Both George IV and Nash were dead before Buckingham Palace—as it finally came to be known, having at times been called St George's, and also sarcastically Pimlico, Palace—was completed. Queen Victoria and Prince Albert found it inconvenient and lacking in accommodation; at one time there was even the idea of adapting it for some cultural use and building a new palace elsewhere. Instead, Edward Blore provided rooms for the Queen's growing family by enclosing the courtyard with a rather dull range facing the Mall—Nash's triumphal arch being banished to Tyburn, where it became familiar to later generations of Londoners as the Marble Arch. Then, Sir James Pennethorne added the south wing containing the vast Ballroom and Supper Room, which was not completed until 1855. Six years later occurred the death of the Prince Consort; the palace was deserted for much of Queen Victoria's long widowhood, so that it can be said to have not really come into its own until within living memory, when it was the setting for the brilliant Drawing Rooms and Court Balls held by Edward VII and Queen Alexandra. After George V and Queen Mary had dropped the idea of returning to Kensington, the Mall front was given a more imposing façade of Portland stone designed by Sir Aston Webb; it is this façade of 1913, rather than Nash's work, which for most people signifies Buckingham Palace.

As well as completing Buckingham Palace, Queen Victoria contributed to the saga of the Royal residences by purchasing an estate in the Isle of Wight and another in Aberdeenshire, and building a large country house on each—the Italianate Osborne, and the Scottish Baronial Balmoral. The idea of the monarch leading a simple country life as a change from pomp and circumstance was, of course, nothing new; but whereas George III's rural retreats had been near London, and adjacent to an old Royal park, Osborne and Balmoral were in parts of the country which had no traditional connections with the Sovereign. Moreover, they belonged to the Queen as a private individual, whereas previous Royal residences had all been Crown property. As another new departure, Prince Albert was himself largely responsible for the design of both houses, assisted respectively by the great London builder, Thomas Cubitt, and by William Smith of Aberdeen. Osborne later became unique among the Royal residences in having a room specially dedicated to Queen Victoria's new function as Empress of India: the Durbar Hall (*Fig* 14). The State and private apartments at Osborne remain furnished as they were in Queen Victoria's time, though the rest of the house was given up by Edward VII to be a convalescent home for officers. He already had a country house of his own in England: Sandringham, rebuilt for him in the Elizabethan style when he was Prince of Wales, on the Norfolk estate which he had acquired largely for the shooting. To the long line of Royal residences, his grandson added Fort Belvedere, a small Georgian castle, adjoining Windsor Great Park, which was an enlargement of a folly originally built for William, Duke of Cumberland. Having been the Prince of Wales's weekend retreat, it remained his favourite residence after he had ascended the Throne as Edward VIII.

Queen Victoria's decision to spend part of every year at Balmoral was greatly welcomed by the Scottish people, who had seen little of their Sovereigns since James VI ascended the English throne as James I. Before the Union of the Crowns, there were a

12 Brighton Pavilion
(National Monuments Record—Crown Copyright)

13 Buckingham Palace: the Garden Front
(Reproduced by gracious permission of HM The Queen)

number of Royal residences in Scotland, which have survived remarkably well considering the vicissitudes of the country's history. There is Edinburgh Castle, dominating the city from its rock, which includes among its buildings the eleventh or early twelfth century St Margaret's Chapel, as well as an ancient hall and the newer apartments occupied by the Regent, Mary of Guise, and her daughter, Mary Queen of Scots. There is the even more impregnable Stirling Castle, enclosing a Renaissance palace built by James V, whose sophisticated taste can also be seen at Falkland and Linlithgow. Falkland, a palace dedicated to sport and pleasure, seems to have come straight from the France of François Premier; in its time, it was the most advanced building in Britain. After a fire during the Cromwellian occupation it fell into decay, but was restored at the end of the last century by the third Marquess of Bute. Linlithgow, the birthplace of Mary Queen of Scots, was also the victim of a fire started by English troops—who were quartered there following the collapse of the '45—and is now a spectacular and well-preserved ruin.

One alone among the ancient Royal palaces of Scotland has continued to be the abode of her Kings and Queens down to the present time, though it was deserted for long periods in the past. This, of course, is Holyrood, crouching below the cliffs of Arthur's Seat (*Fig* 15) at the opposite end of Edinburgh to the Castle. It was originally built between 1501 and 1503, for the reception of Margaret Tudor, the bride of James IV, adjoining an abbey of Canons Regular founded by David I in 1128. The abbey church became the Chapel Royal, which has been a ruin since the roof collapsed in the eighteenth century. Much of the palace was burnt while it was occupied by Cromwell's troops; the parts that survived included Mary Queen of Scots' apartments, the scene of the murder of David Riccio. A new quadrangle was built by Charles II, under the supervision of Robert Mylne and to the design of Sir William Bruce of Kinross. Owing to shortage of money, its style was austere, the plain walls being relieved in places by typically Scottish turrets. Inside, however, were rich furnishings and tapestries; the gallery was adorned with 100 fanciful portraits of Scottish Kings, painted at £2 a head by an artist named de Witte.

During the eighteenth century, the most notable Royal visitor to Holyrood was Prince Charles Edward. The old palace saw nothing of the Georges until George IV held court here in 1822; then Queen Victoria started the custom, continued by her successors, of occupying Holyrood for a brief period every year. For all its somewhat forbidding appearance, Holyrood is one of the most fascinating of Royal palaces; little changed from the time of Charles II and with a combination of intimacy and grandeur that is particularly Scottish. Its special character is enhanced on State occasions by the presence of the Archers in their picturesque uniform, many of them descended from forebears who frequented the palace in the days before the Stuart Kings deserted it for Whitehall, Windsor and Hampton Court.

14 Osborne House: the Durbar Hall
(Mr G. Nuttall)

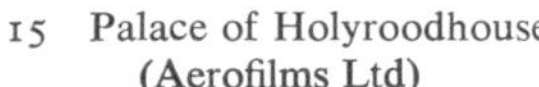

15 Palace of Holyroodhouse
(Aerofilms Ltd)

Royal Heraldry

BY J. P. BROOKE-LITTLE

Richmond Herald of Arms

Arms of England

1 *The Royal Arms until 1603*

The royal heraldry of England starts officially in about 1198 when three lions passant guardant, in those days termed leopards, appeared on the second Great Seal of King Richard I cut some time after 1195. These golden lions, with their blue tongues and claws, on a red shield have remained the arms of England as personified by the Sovereign until the present day.

Although the three lions were first used by Richard, there is evidence that earlier monarchs used shields on which lions featured. We know that as early as 1127 King Henry I gave his son-in-law Geoffrey, Count of Anjou, the ancestor of our Plantagenet kings, a blue shield decorated with little gold lions. This shield, *azure, six lions rampant or,* can be seen on the beautiful enamel which marked Geoffrey's grave at Le Mans and is now in the museum there. This same shield appears again a century later as the arms of William Longespée, Earl of Salisbury, bastard son of Henry II. They still adorn his splendid tomb in Salisbury Cathedral.

Arms of France (Ancient) and England

The chronicler Ernoul records that a company of troops raised at Henry's expense for the defence of Jerusalem in 1187 was ordered to show on its banners "les armes le roi d'Engletiere". Unfortunately we do not know what these arms were but it seems more than probable that they were lions. King John, when Lord of Ireland and Count of Mortain, had two lions on his shield as depicted on his seal in 1177. Richard I himself had a lion rampant on his shield in his first great seal, cut at his accession in 1189. Here only one half of the shield is visible so that it is anyone's guess as to whether a second lion lurked round the corner.

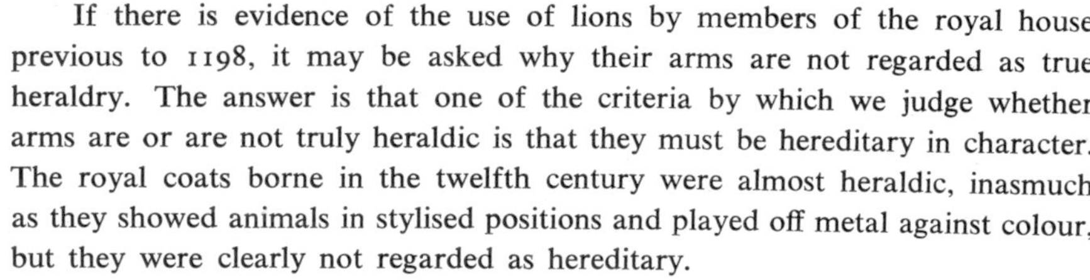

If there is evidence of the use of lions by members of the royal house previous to 1198, it may be asked why their arms are not regarded as true heraldry. The answer is that one of the criteria by which we judge whether arms are or are not truly heraldic is that they must be hereditary in character. The royal coats borne in the twelfth century were almost heraldic, inasmuch as they showed animals in stylised positions and played off metal against colour, but they were clearly not regarded as hereditary.

Arms of France (modern)

The simple, noble coat of the three lions was borne alone by King John, King Henry III and the three Edwards. During this period armory developed apace and one noted innovation was the idea of quartering: that is of marshalling more than one coat on a single shield by the simple device of dividing it into four quarters and placing a coat in each, or, if only two coats were to be displayed, repeating the first in the last quarter and the second in the third. One of the earliest quartered shields seen in England was that of Queen Eleanor, first wife of Edward I, whom she married in 1254, and daughter of Ferdinand III King of Castile and Leon. The union of these two kingdoms, which finally happened in 1230, was admirably symbolized by quartering the golden castle on red of Castile with the purple lion on silver of Leon.

Arms of St Edward the Confessor

In 1337 King Edward III formally claimed the throne of France. Edward's mother Isabella was the only daughter, and eventually sole heir of Philip IV of France. However, when her brother Charles IV died in 1328, the throne passed to Isabella's first cousin Philip, as in France a woman could not succeed to the throne. Edward's contention was that although his mother could not succeed because of her sex, she could transmit the sovereignty to him. Thus began the Hundred Years' War. Edward illustrated his claim by quartering the royal arms of France, *azure semy-de-lys or* with the arms of England. In doing this he gave the French coat pride of place, putting it in the first and fourth quarters. He may have done this in order to underline his claim but more probably he put France first as it was the senior Kingdom according to the scale of precedence laid down by the Pope. Also, the King of England had customarily done homage to the King of France for his French possessions.

The quartered coat of France and England was borne by all the sovereigns of England until the death of Queen Elizabeth I in 1603. The only minor alteration was in the way in which the arms of France were depicted. Most of the French kings down to the time of King Charles V had used the blue shield powdered with gold fleurs-de-lys but in 1376 Charles reduced the number of fleurs-de-lys to three and it remained that way ever since. Various theories have been put forward as to why he did this. One is that the three lilies illustrated the Holy Trinity; another states that they represent the three lines of kings from which Charles claimed descent, whilst a third story is that a legend, popular in the fourteenth century, had it that in 496 a hermit gave Queen Clothilde a holy cloth embroidered with three lilies, symbolising the Blessed Virgin, which she in turn gave to her husband King Clovis. Whatever the reason Charles certainly used the three fleurs-de-lys and King Henry IV followed his lead when a new Great Seal was struck in 1405. There is evidence of earlier use of the three lilies in the English royal arms but the seal of 1405 made this use official.

Arms of Egbert

It was the custom of mediaeval and later heralds to attribute arms to pre-heraldic notables. Old and new testament characters were assigned arms and so were the kings who reigned before Richard I. Some of these attributed arms have become quite famous, principally those of St Edward the Confessor, azure, a cross patonce between five (or sometimes four) martlets or. This coat was attributed to the Confessor by Geoffrey of Monmouth (died 1154) and was based on a design which appeared on the reverse of a penny of Edward's reign. This showed a voided cross between four birds. This coat was so closely associated with St Edward that it came to be equally closely associated with his Abbey at Westminster and later with the City of Westminster. The coat forms part of the arms of the former and present Cities of Westminster; is included

Arms of Alfred

Arms of Ethelred

in the arms of Ampleforth Abbey, which claims direct descent from the old Benedictine Abbey of Westminster, and it occurs in several other coats. King Richard II had a particular devotion to St Edward and frequently, though not invariably, impaled his royal arms with the attributed arms of his patron. That is, he divided his shield down the centre and placed the arms of the Confessor in the dexter and more honourable portion, whilst the quartered royal arms were shown on the sinister side. The painting on the reverse of the Wilton Diptych affords an excellent example of Richard's rather charming heraldic conceit.

Some of the early kings have had more than one coat attributed to them by heralds and historians but those which are shown here are perhaps the most popular, being taken from a seventeenth century manuscript (*L* 14) in the College of Arms.

It is frequently forgotten that Mary I's husband Philip of Spain, son of the Emperor Charles V, was crowned King and was indeed King regnant jointly with Mary. After their marriage in July 1554 the regnal year was no longer styled 2 Mary but 1 and 2 Philip and Mary and the royal style began, "Philip and Mary, by the Grace of God, King and Queen of England, France, Ireland, Naples and Jerusalem, Defenders of the Faith, Princes of Spain and the two Sicilies . . .". On the Great Seal struck after the marriage the dexter half of the complex coat of King Philip, together with the pomegranate in point, impales Mary's quartered coat. Philip's full coat may be blazoned:—Quarterly 1 and 4, sub-quarterly i and iv, Castile quartering Leon (*vide supra*); ii and iii, or, four palets gules (Aragon) impaling per saltire or, four palets gules, and argent, in each flaunch an eagle displayed sable (Sicily); 2 and 3, sub-quarterly i, gules, a fess argent (for Austria); ii, France ancient within a bordure company argent and gules (Burgundy modern); iii, bendy or and azure, a bordure gules (Burgundy ancient); iv, sable, a lion rampant or (Brabant), over all an escutcheon or, a lion rampant sable (Flanders) impaling, argent, an eagle displayed gules (Tyrol). A point in base argent, charged with a pomegranate slipped and leaved vert, seeded gules.

Arms of Edmund Ironside

2 *The Crest*

A great many people, unversed in armorial semantics, refer to the coat of arms as a crest. In fact the expression "coat of arms" should really refer simply to what is emblazoned on the shield. The crest is a separate hereditary emblem which did not evolve until about a century after arms came into common use. It consisted of a device modelled onto the top of the helmet. This evolved from a simple fan crest, possibly decorated with some armorial device. It is interesting to note that in Richard I's great seal a fan crest adorns the King's helm and is decorated with a royal lion. However, this vestigial crest disappears until the reign of King Edward III when, on the Great Seal, is found a representation of the crest of a lion statant guardant crowned with an open crown and standing on a chapeau. In essence this device has remained the crest of England. At first minor variations can be noted but from the reign of King Henry VIII the royal crest has invariably been; upon the royal crown proper, a lion statant guardant or, crowned with a like crown.

Arms of William I

As the crest was actually fixed to the helm it has been customary when depicting the crest, to show also the helm of which it was part. This in turn argues representing the mantling, which was a short cape fixed to the back of the helm. Its purpose appears to have been defensive; it would help to deaden a sword blow on the back of the neck and might also help to keep the helmet cool in hot climes. Whatever its original purpose it has proved a great boon to the heraldic artist who, by exaggerating its length, parting and scalloping it, has been able to unite arms and crest in a single, harmonious design.

Arms of Philip and Mary

Since the early seventeenth century rules have existed regulating the type and position of helmet which may be used by gentlemen, esquires, knights, baronets and peers. However, in earlier days the royal crest was shown on any appropriate style of helm. King Henry VIII favoured a golden, barred helmet facing the front and this design thereafter became peculiar to royalty, lesser men having to put up with less glorious head-gear.

Until the reign of Queen Elizabeth I the royal mantling was red lined with ermine but she altered this to gold and ermine and so it has remained to this day.

Just as there have been minor variations in the royal crests so have there been in the royal crown. The evidence of seals and coins suggests that until the middle of the fifteenth century the royal diadem was an open circlet, the rim decorated with stylised leaves or fleurs-de-lys. On a seal of Henry VI an open crown is shown with crosses formy on the rim and the crown in the third Great Seal of Edward IV has arches which thenceforth become a permanent feature of the royal crown. The number of arches as also the arrangement of leaves, fleurs-de-lys and crosses varies but from the reign of Elizabeth there have normally been four crosses formy alternating with four fleurs-de-lys. Until early Stuart times the four-arched crown was popular but from the time of King Charles I the two-arched crown, similar to that later made by Sir Robert Vyner for the coronation of Charles II in 1662, has been used in official representations of the royal arms. Today the heraldic crown is of gold, the rim ornamented with pearls and with a sapphire in the centre between two emeralds and two rubies at either end. Three crosses formy interspersed with two fleurs-de-lys are visible. The arches spring from the crosses, the outer arches sporting nine pearls and the centre arch showing five. The arches support a green orb decorated with gold and surmounted by a golden cross formy. The cap of crimson velvet turned up below the rim with ermine can be shown.

Crest of Edward III

3 *The Supporters*

The crest was not the last hereditary device to be introduced into heraldry, The fifteenth century saw the development of supporters. These were creatures, placed on either side of the shield and which literally supported it. Originally it seems that artists and seal engravers added to the arms of great magnates, some of the family beasts and badges to support the shield. At first the choice of beasts was capricious and it was not until Tudor times that the heralds took cognizance of supporters, made rules for their use and granted them to certain persons and institutions.

Representations, though not on seals nor coins, of supporters to the arms of fifteenth century kings include a variety of beasts. Henry IV's and Henry V's arms are traditionally supported by an heraldic antelope (a very distant relative of the actual beast) and a swan; creatures associated with the Bohun family, Mary Bohun being Henry V's mother.

Crest of Edward IV

Crest of Edward VI

Two silver antelopes and also a golden lion and an antelope are associated with the arms of Henry VI. Edward IV's arms are found supported by the two silver lions of Mortimer, a lion and a hart and a lion and a black bull. The bull was a beast of the house of Clare and was used *jure uxoris* by Lionel Duke of Clarence, by virtue of descent from whom Edward claimed the throne. Richard III used two white boars and a lion and a boar.

The red dragon garnished with gold was traditionally associated with Cadwalader, the last native ruler of Britain. Owen Tudor used it as a badge, claiming descent from Cadwalader and his son, Henry VII, used it as a royal supporter. Although it was never used after the Tudor line ended it has always remained the royal badge for Wales. All the Tudor monarchs used various combinations of the dragon, the crowned English lion and a silver greyhound, a beast associated with the Earldom of Richmond which the Tudors held. Philip and Mary used a black imperial eagle armed and crowned gold, as a dexter supporter, the sinister being the lion. Queen Elizabeth I used the lion and dragon.

When James VI of Scotland succeeded as James I of England the royal arms of England were altered and the supporters, as used today, were adopted. The dexter supporter is the golden lion royally crowned and the sinister is the silver unicorn of Scotland, about its neck an open crown like the circlet of the royal crown, to which is attached a golden chain reflexed over the beast's back. Its hooves, mane, horn and tufts of hair are also gold. The unicorn was established as a royal Scottish beast by at least the early fifteenth century. Indeed a pursuivant named Unicorn was appointed in 1426 and a coin called a Unicorn was struck during the reign of James III (1466-1488), because the royal arms on the reverse were supported by this beast. But why it was adopted and so much favoured is still one of the many mysteries of heraldry.

Arms of Stuart

4 *The Royal Arms from 1603*

In 1542 the royal titles were altered and Henry VIII was styled King of Ireland rather than Lord of Ireland, which title he and his predecessors had used since the time of King John. However no arms were assumed to represent this new kingdom so, when James I came to the throne the opportunity was taken to add to the royal arms a coat for Ireland. This coat, based on the badge previously used for Ireland, consisted of a golden harp with silver strings (now normally shown as seven) on a blue field.

As the new royal arms had to feature the arms of Scotland (or, a lion rampant within a double tressure flory counterflory gules), they were marshalled as follows: Quarterly 1 and 4, France modern and England quarterly; 2, Scotland; 3, Ireland. This coat was used by James I, Charles I, Charles II, James II, William and Mary and Anne until after the Act of Union 1707.

When William III and Mary II were proclaimed joint sovereigns in 1689 an escutcheon of the arms of Nassau (azure, billety and a lion rampant or) was placed in the centre of the royal coat. This was used on the Great Seal of the joint rulers and after Mary's death in 1694 by William alone. There are examples of the royal arms with the Nassau inescutcheon impaling the royal arms without it but this marshalling does not appear to have been used officially. On a half-crown struck in 1689 the royal arms are shown as the coats of England, France, Scotland and Ireland quartered with Nassau in pretence but this marshalling is found nowhere else.

Arms of Nassau

Arms of Anne

On 1 May 1707, the two kingdoms of England and Scotland were united, in the words of Article I of The Act for the Union with Scotland, "into one Kingdom by the Name of Great Britain and that the Ensigns Armorial of the said United Kingdom be such as Her Majesty shall appoint". On the 17 April following, it was decreed by Order in Council that the royal arms should be:—Quarterly 1 and 4, England impaling Scotland; 2, France; 3, Ireland. It should be noticed that, according to armorial practice, the double tressure of Scotland is not continued down the palar line.

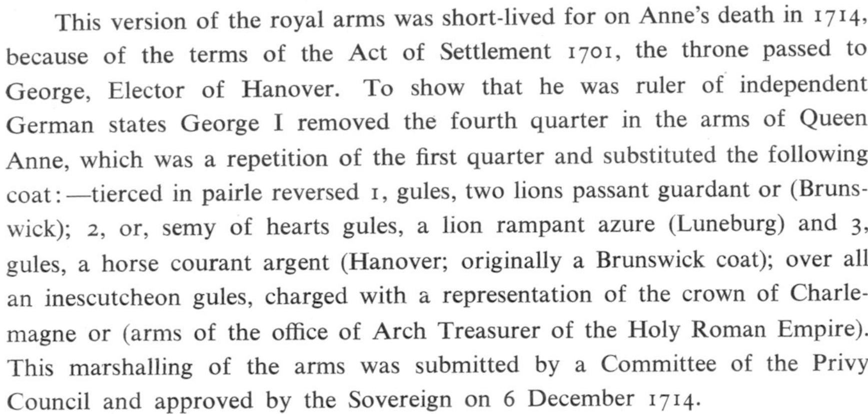

This version of the royal arms was short-lived for on Anne's death in 1714, because of the terms of the Act of Settlement 1701, the throne passed to George, Elector of Hanover. To show that he was ruler of independent German states George I removed the fourth quarter in the arms of Queen Anne, which was a repetition of the first quarter and substituted the following coat:—tierced in pairle reversed 1, gules, two lions passant guardant or (Brunswick); 2, or, semy of hearts gules, a lion rampant azure (Luneburg) and 3, gules, a horse courant argent (Hanover; originally a Brunswick coat); over all an inescutcheon gules, charged with a representation of the crown of Charlemagne or (arms of the office of Arch Treasurer of the Holy Roman Empire). This marshalling of the arms was submitted by a Committee of the Privy Council and approved by the Sovereign on 6 December 1714.

Arms of Hanover

The arms were next altered by Royal Proclamation on 1 January 1801, in persuance of Article 1 of an Act for Union with Ireland 1800. This stated that the "ensigns armorial, flags and banners" of the new Kingdom of Great Britain and Ireland "shall be such as his Majesty, by his royal proclamation under the Great Seal" shall appoint. On this occasion the opportunity was taken to omit the arms of France and adopt the simple quartered coat still used today:—Quarterly 1 and 4, England; 2, Scotland; 3, Ireland. The arms of the German dominions were placed on an inescutcheon surmounted by the electoral bonnet of crimson velvet, surmounted by a gold tassel and turned up with ermine. In 1816 the bonnet was replaced by a gold crown consisting of a circlet adorned with eight strawberry leaves from which spring four arches supporting an orb. This was done to symbolize the fact that under the terms of the Congress of Vienna the Electorate of Hanover, abolished by Napoleon, was raised into a Kingdom.

On the death of William IV in 1837 the German dominions passed to his brother owing to the operation of the Salic Law and so Queen Victoria naturally dropped the crowned inescutcheon from the royal arms. Since 1837 no further alterations have been made in the royal arms.

5 *Mottoes, Insignia and Badges*

Mottoes were not in common use before the seventeenth century but the famous royal motto "Dieu et mon droit" has been used, though not necessarily beneath the arms, from the time of Henry V. Not every monarch has favoured this motto. Henry IV was much attached to the word "Souverayne" whilst Queen Elizabeth I and Queen Anne liked "Semper eadem". Mary I sometimes used "Veritas tempora filia", James I "Beati pacifici" and William III "Pax quaeritur bello".

Electoral Bonnet

Crown of Hanover

A familiar part of the royal arms is the blue garter, garnished and bearing the motto "Honi soit qui mal y pense" in gold, which environs the shield. Although this order was founded by Edward III in about 1348 the garter itself did not normally surround the royal arms until more than a hundred years later.

A variety of badges which are devices used by those who bear arms to mark their servants and property, has been widely used by monarchs. Badges tend to be associated with a particular place or function so it is not surprising that the Crown, having so many and various activities, has need of many badges. For example The Queen has a badge for the House of Windsor, for Wales, for England, for Ireland, for Scotland, for the Union, for the Palace of Westminster, for her Officers of Arms, and so on. The subject is too vast to be explored further here but it is one of great interest. The best advice I can give to anyone interested in royal beasts and badges is to study *Royal Beasts* by H. Stanford London, FSA, Norfolk Herald Extraordinary (The Heraldry Society 1956).

The marginal illustrations in the above article were drawn by Alison Urwick

Of the coloured illustrations of arms of the Royal Family which now follow, the armorial bearings of HM The Queen, HRH The Princess Margaret, Countess of Snowdon, HRH the late Prince William of Gloucester, HRH Prince Richard of Gloucester, HRH The Duke of Kent, HRH Prince Michael of Kent and HRH Princess Alice, Countess of Athlone were drawn by Persephone Jackson; and those of HRH The Prince Andrew, HRH The Princess Anne and HRH The late Duke of Windsor by C. W. West.

THE ARMORIAL BEARINGS OF
HER MAJESTY THE QUEEN

Quarterly: first and fourth, gules, three lions passant guardant in pale, or (England); second, or a lion rampant within a double tressure flory counter-flory, gules (Scotland); and third, azure, a harp or stringed argent (Ireland); the whole encircled with the Garter.

Crown A circle of gold, issuing therefrom four crosses patée and four fleurs-de-lis, arranged alternatively: from the crosses patée arise two golden arches ornamented with pearls, crossing at the top under a mound, surmounted by a cross patée, also gold, the whole enriched with precious stones. The cap is of crimson velvet, turned up ermine.

Crest Upon the Royal helmet the Crown proper, thereon a lion statant guardant, or, royally crowned, also proper.

Supporters On the dexter a lion guardant or, crowned as the crest; and on the sinister a unicorn argent armed, crined and unguled or, and gorged with a coronet composed of crosses patée and fleurs-de-lis, a chain affixed thereto passing between the forelegs and reflexed over the back, of the last.

Motto Dieu et mon Droit.

THE ARMORIAL BEARINGS OF
HIS ROYAL HIGHNESS THE PRINCE PHILIP
DUKE OF EDINBURGH

Quarterly: first, or, semée of hearts gules three lions passant in pale azure, ducally crowned of the first; second, azure, a cross argent; third, argent, two pallets sable; fourth argent, upon a rock proper a castle triple-towered sable, masoned argent, windows, port turret, caps and vanes gules.

Crest A plume of five ostrich feathers alternatively sable, and argent issuant from a ducal coronet or.

Supporters On the dexter side a representation of Heracles girt about the loins with a lion skin, crowned with a chaplet of oak leaves and holding in the dexter hand a club proper, and on the sinister side a lion queue fourchée ducally crowned or and gorged with a naval coronet azure.

Motto God is my help.

THE ARMORIAL BEARINGS OF HER MAJESTY QUEEN ELIZABETH THE QUEEN MOTHER

Within the Garter ensigned with the Royal Crown, the arms of the United Kingdom of Great Britain and Ireland, impaling quarterly: first and fourth (for LYON) Argent, a lion rampant azure, armed and langued gules, within a double tressure flory counter-flory of the second; second and third (for BOWES) Ermine, three bows, strings palewise proper.

Supporters On the dexter side a lion guardant or, imperially crowned proper, and on the sinister side a lion per fesse or and gules.

THE ARMORIAL BEARINGS OF
HIS ROYAL HIGHNESS THE PRINCE OF WALES

THE ROYAL ARMS, differenced by a label of three points argent and in the centre an escutcheon of the arms of the Principality of Wales, *viz,* quarterly or and gules, four lions passant guardant counterchanged, ensigned by the coronet of His degree.

Crest The Royal Crest, differenced with a label of three points argent, but the coronets those of the Heir Apparent.

Supporters Same as the Royal Arms differenced by a label of three points argent, the dexter crowned with the Heir-Apparent coronet, and the sinister gorged with a coronet of fleur-de-lis and crosses patée, a chain affixed thereto passing between the fore-legs and reflexed over the back, or.

Badges Dexter, a plume of three ostrich feathers argent, enfiled by a coronet, composed of fleur-de-lis or alternatively with motto "Ich Dien"; sinister, a representation of the Badge of Wales, namely on a mount vert, a dragon passant gules, differenced as in the Crest with a label of three points argent.

Motto Ich dien.

THE ARMORIAL BEARINGS OF HIS ROYAL HIGHNESS THE PRINCE ANDREW

THE ROYAL ARMS differenced by a label of three points argent, the centre point charged with an anchor azure.

Crest On a coronet composed of crosses patée and fleurs-de-lis, a lion statant and guardant, or, crowned with a like coronet and differenced with a label as in the arms.

Supporters The Royal Supporters differenced with the like coronet and label.

THE ARMORIAL BEARINGS OF
HER ROYAL HIGHNESS THE PRINCESS ANNE

THE ROYAL ARMS differenced by a label of three points argent, the first and third points charged with a St George's Cross, and the centre point with a heart gules.

Supporters The Royal Supporters differenced with similar labels. Surmounting the lozenge the Royal Coronet of her rank.

THE ARMORIAL BEARINGS OF
HER ROYAL HIGHNESS THE PRINCESS MARGARET
COUNTESS OF SNOWDON

THE ROYAL ARMS differenced by a label of three points argent, the centre point charged with a thistle slipped and leaved proper, and each of the outer points with a Tudor Rose, the whole encircled with the Royal Victorian Order.

Supporters The Royal Supporters with similar labels.

Summounting the lozenge the Royal Coronet of her rank, *viz* a coronet composed of crosses patée and fleurs-de-lis.

NOTE: For an illustration of the Earl of Snowdon's arms—*see* BURKE'S *Peerage*.

THE ARMORIAL BEARINGS OF THEIR ROYAL HIGHNESSES THE DUKE AND DUCHESS OF GLOUCESTER

Arms (of HRH The Duke of Gloucester) THE ROYAL ARMS, differenced by a label of three points argent, the first and third points charged with a St George's Cross, and the centre point charged with a lion passant guardant gules, the whole encircled with the Garter.

Supporters The Royal Supporters each differenced with a like coronet and label.

Crest On a coronet composed of crosses patée and fleurs-de-lis, a lion statant guardant or, crowned with a like coronet and differenced with a label as in the arms.

Arms (of HRH The Duchess of Gloucester) Quarterly, 1st, The Royal Arms of King Charles II (quarterly, 1st and 4th, counter-quartered, *France* and *England;* 2nd *Scotland;* 3rd, *Ireland*), debruised by a baton sinister argent; 2nd, or, on a bend azure a mullet of six points between two crescents of the field (for SCOTT): 3rd, quarterly, 1st and 4th, argent, a human heart gules, crowned with an imperial crown or, and on a chief azure three mullets of the field (for DOUGLAS), 2nd and 3rd, azure, a bend between six cross crosslets fitchée or (for MAR), the whole quarter within a bordure or, charged with the double tressure of Scotland gules; 4th, quarterly, 1st, argent three lozenges conjoined in fesse gules, a bordure sable (for MONTAGU); 2nd, or an eagle displayed vert, beaked and membered gules (for MONTHERMER): 3rd, sable a lion rampant argent, on a canton of the last a cross gules (for CHURCHILL): 4th, argent, a chevron gules, between three chapeaux to the sinister azure (for BRUDENELL).

THE ARMORIAL BEARINGS OF
HIS LATE ROYAL HIGHNESS PRINCE WILLIAM OF
GLOUCESTER

THE ROYAL ARMS differenced by a label of five points argent, the centre point and two outer points charged with a lion passant guardant, gules, and the inner points with a St George's Cross.

Crest On a coronet composed of crosses patée and strawberry leaves, a lion statant guardant, or, crowned with the like coronet and differenced with a label as in the arms.

Supporters The Royal Supporters each differenced with the like coronet and label.

THE ARMORIAL BEARINGS OF
HIS ROYAL HIGHNESS PRINCE RICHARD OF
GLOUCESTER

THE ROYAL ARMS differenced by a label of five points argent, the centre point and two outer points charged with a St George's Cross, and the inner points with a lion passant guardant, gules.

Crest On a coronet composed of crosses patée and strawberry leaves, a lion statant guardant, or, crowned with the like coronet and differenced with a label as in the arms.

Supporters The Royal Supporters each differenced with the like coronet and label.

THE ARMORIAL BEARINGS OF
HIS ROYAL HIGHNESS THE DUKE OF KENT

THE ROYAL ARMS differenced by a label of five points argent, the centre point and two outer points charged with an anchor azure, and the inner points with a St George's Cross.

Crest On a coronet composed of crosses patée and strawberry leaves, a lion statant guardant, or, crowned with the like coronet and differenced with a label as in the arms.

Supporters The Royal Supporters each differenced with the like coronet and label.

THE ARMORIAL BEARINGS OF
HIS ROYAL HIGHNESS PRINCE MICHAEL OF KENT

THE ROYAL ARMS differenced by a label of five points argent, the centre point and two outer points charged with a St George's Cross, and the inner points with an anchor azure.

Crest On a coronet composed of crosses patée and strawberry leaves, a lion statant guardant, or, crowned with the like coronet and differenced with a label as in the arms.

Supporters The Royal Supporters each differenced with the like coronet and label.

THE ARMORIAL BEARINGS OF
HER ROYAL HIGHNESS PRINCESS ALEXANDRA,
THE HONOURABLE MRS ANGUS OGILVY

THE ROYAL ARMS differenced by a label of five points argent, the centre point charged with a St. George's Cross, the two inner points with an anchor azure, and the two outer points with a heart gules.

Crest The Royal Coronet of her Rank.

Supporters The Royal Supporters each differenced with the like coronet and label.
NOTE: For an illustration of the OGILVY arms—*see* BURKE'S *Peerage*, AIRLIE, E.

THE ARMORIAL BEARINGS OF
HER ROYAL HIGHNESS PRINCESS ALICE
COUNTESS OF ATHLONE

THE ROYAL ARMS differenced with a label of five points argent, the centre point charged with a St George's Cross, and the outer points with hearts gules.

Supporters The Royal Supporters with similar labels.

Surmounting the lozenge the Royal Coronet of her rank, *viz* a coronet composed of crosses patée and strawberry leaves.

THE ARMORIAL BEARINGS OF
HIS LATE ROYAL HIGHNESS THE DUKE OF WINDSOR

THE ROYAL ARMS differenced by a label of three points argent, the centre point charged with an Imperial Crown proper, the whole encircled with the Garter.

Crest On a coronet composed of crosses patée and fleurs-de-lis, a lion statant guardant, or, crowned with the like coronet and differenced with a label as in the arms.

Supporters The Royal Supporters each differenced with the like coronet and label.

The Royal Family

Biographies compiled by Hugo Vickers

Introduction

This section contains the biographies of the Royal Family. They are set out in the following order:—(1) birth, parentage and education; (2) titles, orders and decorations (British and foreign); (3) connections with the Armed Forces and active service; (4) civilian appointments; (5) Presidencies and Patronages; (6) official travel overseas; (7) constitutional details and personal interests; (8) details of marriage and issue; (9) references to coats of arms and Lineage; (10) residences and clubs. *The Report from the Select Committee on The Civil List (Session 1971-72)* has been used throughout. Whereas all the Presidencies and Patronages of the Royal Family have been included, it was not possible to list the Patronages of HM The Queen, HRH The Prince Philip, Duke of Edinburgh and HM Queen Elizabeth The Queen Mother, as these are too numerous. Photographs of every member of the Royal Family accompany their entries.

All the biographies have been compiled with the co-operation of the Royal Household. The kind help of the Press Office and Household Offices at Buckingham Palace, the Household Offices at Clarence House, Kensington Palace and St James's Palace, and the Household of HRH The late Duke of Windsor in Paris is gratefully acknowledged. Among the numerous organisations and official sources that have assisted with information and advice are the Central Office of Information, the Ministry of Defence, the City Livery Companies, and certain Embassies. Miss Clarissa Harris helped in the preparation of the text, and Sergeant-Major C. W. West of the Royal Hospital drew the crowns and coronets.

The deaths of HRH The Duke of Windsor and HRH Prince William of Gloucester occurred after work on this book had begun. Their entries appear in this section with the agreement of their Private Secretaries.

Cecil Beaton

HER MAJESTY THE QUEEN

H M The Queen

ELIZABETH THE SECOND, By The Grace of God, of The United Kingdom of Great Britain and Northern Ireland and of Her Other Realms and Territories Queen, Head of the Commonwealth, Defender of the Faith** is the elder daughter of HM KING GEORGE VI (*see* reference to **Lineage** *below*) and HM QUEEN ELIZABETH THE QUEEN MOTHER (*see p* 133). She was born at 17 Bruton Street, W1 21 April 1926, baptized Elizabeth Alexandra Mary, and educated privately. On the death of her Father, 6 February 1952, she succeeded to the Throne, and was crowned at Westminster Abbey 2 June 1953.

The Queen is Sovereign of all the British Orders of Knighthood, the Order of Merit, the Order of Victoria and Albert, the Crown of India, the Companions of Honour, the Distinguished Service Order, the Imperial Service Order, and Sovereign of the Order of St John of Jerusalem in the British Realm, and of the Order of Canada (founded 1967). Her Majesty has the following foreign decorations: the Order of the Elephant (1947) Denmark, Grand Cordon of the Order of El Kamal (1948) Egypt, Grand Cross of the Legion of Honour (1948) France, the Order of Ojaswi Rajanya (1949) Nepal, Grand Cross of the Order of St Olga and St Sophia (1950) Greece, Grand Cross of the Order of the Lion (1950) Netherlands, the Order of the Seraphim (1953) Sweden, Gold Collar of the Order of Manuel Amador Guerrero (1953) Panama, the Order of Qeladet El-Hussein Ibn Ali (1953) Jordan, Grand Collar of the Order of Idris I (1954) Libya, Chain and Collar of the Order of the Seal of Solomon (1954) Ethiopia, Grand Cross with Chain of the Order of St Olav (1955) Norway, Grand Sash and Cross of the United Orders of Christ, Aviz and Santiago (1955) Portugal, the Order of the Hashimi with Chain (1956) Iraq, Grand Cross and Grand Cordon of the Order of Merit of the Republic (1958) Italy, Special Grand Cross with Star of the Order of Merit (1958) Federal Republic of Germany, Grand Cross with diamonds of the Order of the Sun (1960) Peru, First Class of Nishan-i-Pakistan (1960) Pakistan, Grand Collar of the Order of Liberator General San Martin (1960) Argentine, Grand Cross and Collar of the Order of the Royal House of Chakri (1960) Thailand, Collar of the Order of the White Rose (1961) Finland, Grand Cross of the National Order (1961) Senegal, Grand Cordon of the Order of Knighthood of the Pioneers of the Republic (1961) Liberia, Grand Collar of the Order of Independence (1961) Tunisia, the Mahendra Chain (1961) Nepal, Grand Cross of the National Order (1962) Ivory Coast, Collar and Grand Cordon of the Order of the Chrysanthemum (1962) Japan, Grand Band of the Star of Africa (1962) Liberia, Grand Cross of the Order of Valour (1963) Cameroon Republic, Grand Cordon of the Order of Leopold (1963) Belgium, Grand Cross of the Order of the Redeemer (1963) Greece, Grand Cross, with Chain, of the Order of the Falcon (1963) Iceland, the Chain of Honour (1964) Sudan, Grand Collar of the Order of Merit (1965) Chile, Grand Cross of the Decoration of Honour (1966) Austria, Grand Cordon of the Order of Merit (1966) Austria, Grand Collar of the Order of the Southern Cross (1968) Brazil, Grand Cross of the National Order of Niger (1969) Nigeria, First Class of the Order of Al Nehayyan (1969) Abu Dhabi, Grand Cross of the Order of the Equatorial Star (1970) Gabon, the Order of Temasek (1972) Singapore, Darjah Utama Seri Mahkota Negara (1972) Malaysia, the Most Esteemed Family Order, 1st class (1972) Brunei, the

Distinguished Order of Ghaazi (1972) Maldives, the Order of the Golden Heart (1972) Kenya, and the Order of the Golden Lion of the House of Nassau (1972) Luxembourg. Her Majesty, when Princess Elizabeth, was appointed a Lady of the Garter (1947), member of the Order of the Crown of India (1947), and Dame Grand Cross of the Order of St John of Jerusalem (1947).

Her Majesty is Lord High Admiral of the United Kingdom (1964), Captain-General of Royal Regiment of Artillery, The Honourable Artillery Company, Combined Cadet Force, Royal Regiment of Canadian Artillery, Royal Regiment of Australian Artillery, Royal New Zealand Artillery, and Royal New Zealand Armoured Corps, Colonel-in-Chief of The Life Guards, The Blues and Royals (Royal Horse Guards and 1st Dragoons), The Royal Scots Dragoon Guards (Carabiniers and Greys), 16th/5th The Queen's Royal Lancers, Royal Tank Regiment, Corps of Royal Engineers, Grenadier Guards, Coldstream Guards, Scots Guards, Irish Guards, Welsh Guards, The Royal Welch Fusiliers, The Queen's Lancashire Regiment, The Royal Green Jackets, The Argyll and Sutherland Highlanders (Princess Louise's), Royal Army Ordnance Corps, Royal Corps of Canadian Engineers, Royal *22e* Regiment, Royal Canadian Ordnance Corps, King's Own Calgary Regiment, Governor General's Foot Guards, Canadian Grenadier Guards, Le Régiment de la Chaudière, The Royal New Brunswick Regiment (Carleton and York), 48th Highlanders of Canada, The Argyll and Sutherland Highlanders of Canada (Princess Louise's), Royal Australian Engineers, Royal Australian Infantry Corps, Royal Australian Army Ordnance Corps, Royal Australian Army Nursing Corps, Royal New Zealand Engineers, Royal New Zealand Infantry Regiment, and Malawi Rifles, hon Colonel-in-Chief of The Duke of Lancaster's Own Yeomanry, hon Commissioner of Royal Canadian Mounted Police, Air Commodore-in-Chief of Royal Auxiliary Air Force, Royal Air Force Regiment, Royal Observer Corps, Royal Canadian Air Force Auxiliary, The Australian Citizen Air Force, and The Territorial Air Force of New Zealand, Commandant-in-Chief of Royal Air Force College, Cranwell, Head of The Civil Defence Corps, and Master of the Merchant Navy and Fishing Fleets. The Queen was formerly Colonel-in-Chief of Royal Malta Artillery 1953-71, Auckland Regiment (Countess of Ranfurly's Own) 1953-64, Wellington Regiment (City of Wellington's Own) 1953-64, Royal West African Frontier Force, The Ghana Regiment of Infantry, The Nigerian Army, Royal Sierra Leone Military Forces, Regiment of Canadian Guards 1954-70, Royal Durban Light Infantry 1947-61, Railways and Harbours Brigade 1947-61, The Royal Northern Rhodesia Regiment 1953-65, Imperial Light Horse 1956-61, Royal Natal Carbineers 1956-61, Kaffrarian Rifles 1958-61, and hon Air Commodore of City of Edinburgh Squadron RAAF, City of Edinburgh LAA Squadron and City of Edinburgh Fighter Control Unit 1951-57.

The Queen is Sovereign of the Faculty of Advocates of Scotland, Visitor of University College, Oriel College, and Christ Church, Oxford, Pembroke College, Gonville and Caius College, Trinity Hall, Queens' College, St Catharine's College, Trinity College, and Downing College, Cambridge, the Universities of London, Manchester, Birmingham, Liverpool, Leeds, Sheffield, Bristol, Reading, Southampton, Exeter, Leicester, Sussex, and East Anglia, the National University of Ireland, the University of Wales, Queen's University (Belfast), the University College of Fourah Bay, the University College of the West Indies, the City and Guilds of London Institute, St George's Chapel, Windsor, Westminster Abbey, Wellington College, Westminster School, the Royal College of Physicians, the Royal College of Surgeons of England, and the Imperial College of Science and Technology, Canon of St David's Cathedral, Pembroke, and a Royal Governor of Charterhouse. She received the Gold Albert Medal of the Royal Society of Arts 1958. Her Majesty, when Princess Elizabeth, received the following honorary degrees: DCL Oxford (1948), LLD Edinburgh (1949), and London (1951), Mus Bach London (1946), and Mus D Wales (1949). She was made a Freeman of the Royal Borough of Windsor 1947, the City of London 1948, the City of Cardiff 1948, the City of Edinburgh 1949, and the City of Belfast 1949, Burgess of Stirling 1948, and received the hon Freedom of the Worshipful Company of Drapers 1947. She was also appointed a Fellow of the Royal Society 1947, hon Fellow of the Royal College of Surgeons of England 1951, and of the Royal College of Obstetricians and Gynaecologists 1951. She acted as Counsellor of State in 1944 and 1951. Her Majesty is Patron, Protector and Supporter of the Royal Academy of Arts, and Patron of numerous other organizations.

Her Majesty has made many overseas visits, always accompanied by The Duke of Edinburgh. As Princess Elizabeth, she visited South Africa (accompanied The King and Queen, and Princess Margaret) 1947, France (opened exhibition) 1948, Malta 1949 and 1950, Gibraltar, Greece (as guests of King Paul), Malta and Libya 1950, Italy (had audience of the Pope) 1951, Canada (two month tour) and the USA (as guests of President Truman) 1951, and Kenya (succeeded to the Throne, and cancelled proposed visit to Australia and New Zealand) 1952. Since her accession, Her Majesty has visited Bermuda, Jamaica, Fiji, Tonga, New Zealand, Australia, Ceylon, Uganda, Malta, Gibraltar (Commonwealth tour), and Libya (received by King Idris) 1953-54, Norway (State Visit) 1955, Nigeria (three week tour) 1956, Sweden (State Visit, and attended equestrian events of Olympic Games) 1956, Portugal (State Visit) 1957, France (State Visit) 1957, Denmark (State Visit) 1957, Canada (opened 23rd Canadian Parliament) and the USA (attended Jamestown Festival, stayed as guests of President Eisenhower, and addressed a special meeting of UN General Assembly in New York) 1957, the Netherlands (State Visit) 1958, Canada (opened new St Lawrence Seaway, made six week tour of the Provinces), and the USA (visited Chicago) 1959, Cyprus, India, Pakistan, Nepal (State Visit), Iran (State Visit), and Turkey (in total six week tour) 1961, Italy and the Vatican (State Visits) 1961, Ghana, Liberia, Sierra Leone and The Gambia 1961, the Netherlands (for the Silver Wedding celebrations of Queen Juliana and Prince Bernhardt) 1962, Canada, Fiji, New Zealand, Australia (in total two month tour) 1963, Canada (attended the centennial celebrations commemorating the visits of the Fathers of the Confederation to Charlottetown and Quebec City, and visited Ottawa) 1964, Ethiopia and the Sudan (State Visits) 1965, the Federal Republic of Germany (State Visit, and visit to Berlin) 1965, British Guiana, Trinidad and Tobago, Grenada, St Vincent, Barbados, St Lucia, Dominica, Montserrat, Antigua, St Kitts-Nevis-Anguilla, British Virgin Islands, Turks and Caicos Islands, Bahamas and Jamaica (month's Caribbean tour) 1966, Belgium (State Visit) 1966, Canada (attended 100th anniversary celebrations of the Confederation, and visited EXPO '67) 1967, the Federal Republic of Germany (reviewed Royal Tank Regiment) 1967, Malta 1967, Brazil and Chile (State Visits), and Senegal (laid foundation stone of British Institute) 1968, Austria (State Visit) 1969, Fiji, Tonga, New Zealand and Australia (for bicentenary of Captain Cook's 1st landing there) 1970, Canada (for centenary celebrations of the North West Territories and Manitoba) 1970, Canada (for the British Columbia Centennial Celebrations) 1971, Turkey (State Visit) 1971, Thailand (State Visit), Singapore, Malaysia, Brunei, the Maldive Islands, the Seychelles, Mauritius and Kenya (in total 25,000 mile tour) 1972, France (State Visit) 1972, and Yugoslavia (State Visit) 1972.

Her Majesty has also received State Visits from King Gustav VI Adolf of Sweden 1954, Emperor Haile Selassie of Ethiopia 1954, President Cravero Lopes of Portugal 1955, King Feisal of Iraq 1956, President Gronchi of Italy 1958, President Heuss of Germany 1958, The Shahanshah of Iran 1959, President de Gaulle of France 1960, King Bhumibol of Thailand 1960, King Mahendra of Nepal 1960, President Tubman of

Liberia 1962, King Olav V of Norway 1962, King Baudouin of Belgium 1963, President Radhakrishan of India (Commonwealth Visit) 1963, King Paul I of Greece 1963, President Ferik Ibrahim Abbood of Sudan 1964, President de Frei of Chile 1965, President Jonas of Austria 1966, King Hussein of Jordan 1966, President Ayub Khan of Pakistan (Commonwealth Visit) 1966, King Faisal of Saudi Arabia 1967, President Cevdet Sunay of Turkey 1967, President Saragat of Italy 1969, President Kekkonen of Finland 1969, Emperor Hirohito of Japan 1971, King Zahir Shah of Afghanistan 1971, Queen Juliana of the Netherlands 1972, Grand Duke Jean of Luxembourg 1972, and President Heinemann of the Federal Republic of Germany 1972.

The Queen's own duties in her capacity as Sovereign of the United Kingdom, and of the ten other self-governing Commonwealth Monarchies and the remaining colonial Territories, and as Supreme Governor of the Church of England and with her special responsibility to the Established Church of Scotland, fall under four main heads. First there is the work arising from the normal operations of Government in the form of information she receives both from Ministers at home and representatives abroad, and submissions which she has to approve and sign. The Queen receives copies of all important Government papers—reports from Ambassadors and Ministers abroad and instructions or replies from the Foreign Office, copies of Parliamentary papers, copies of memoranda and minutes of Cabinet meetings and minutes of all important conferences such as meetings of Commonwealth Ministers. There is therefore a continuing burden of unseen work involving some hours' reading of papers each day in addition to Her Majesty's more public duties. Secondly, The Queen receives a large number of important people in audience. These include those about to be appointed to, or retire from, senior public posts and discussions with the Prime Minister and other Ministers. She also holds meetings of the Privy Council and some fourteen investitures each year at which she personally bestows over two thousand orders, decorations and medals. Thirdly, The Queen attends numerous State occasions such as the State Opening of Parliament, The Queen's Birthday Parade, Remembrance Day and various services at St Paul's Cathedral and Westminster Abbey. There are many engagements both public and private involving visits to all parts of the United Kingdom, many of them including visits to local universities, hospitals, factories and units of the Armed Forces. Fourthly Her Majesty is directly involved both in State Visits to this country of the Heads of Foreign and Commonwealth States of which there have been more than twenty since the beginning of her reign, and in tours and visits overseas to Commonwealth countries and in State Visits to foreign countries, of which there have so far been over thirty. In particular Her Majesty's programme has increasingly included visits for specific occasions to monarchical countries of the Commonwealth. The Queen also has a variety of public commitments in her capacity as Head of the Armed Services.

The Queen's greatest interest is racing. In 1972, Her Majesty had fifteen horses in training, twenty-two mares at stud, eleven yearlings, fifteen foals and two stallions at Sandringham, *Aureole,* wholly owned, and part of the syndicated *Ribero.* She has two trainers, W. R. Hern and I. A. Balding. Since 1952, Her Majesty has won over 200 races under Flat-Race Rules, virtually all with home-bred horses, and has had some notable successes. *Aureole* won the Derby Trial at Lingfield and finished second to *Pinza* in the Derby in 1953, and the following year won the Coronation Cup at Epsom, and the Hardwicke Stakes and the King George VI and Queen Elizabeth Stakes at Ascot. *Alexander* won the Hunt Cup at Ascot 1956, and *Doutelle* won seven races between 1956 and 1958, but died prematurely after a successful start to his stud career. *Pall Mall,* racing 1957-58, won seven races including the Two Thousand Guineas at Newmarket (Her Majesty's first Classics Winner), and *Agreement* won seven races between 1957 and 1961, including the Doncaster Cup twice. *Almeria,* racing 1957-58, won the Ribblesdale Stakes at Ascot, the Yorkshire Oaks, the Park Hill Stakes at Doncaster, and was second in the King George VI and Queen Elizabeth Stakes at Ascot. *Above Suspicion* won the St James's Palace Stakes at Ascot and the Gordon Stakes at Goodwood in 1959, and *Canisbay* won the Eclipse Stakes at Sandown in 1965. *Magna Carta,* racing 1969-70, won eight races including the Ascot Stakes and the Doncaster Cup; *Albany,* racing 1970-71, won two races including the Prix Psyche at Deauville, and *Charlton,* also racing 1970-71, won five races including the William Hill Gold Trophy at Doncaster and the Henry II Stakes at Sandown. *Example,* racing since 1971, has won four races to date, including the Park Hill Stakes at Doncaster, the Prix de Royallieu at Longchamp, and the Prix Jean de Chaudenay at St Cloud. The Queen attends race meetings and horse trials and enjoys riding at Windsor, Sandringham and Balmoral.

Her Majesty married at Westminster Abbey 20 November 1947, HIS ROYAL HIGHNESS THE PRINCE PHILIP, DUKE OF EDINBURGH, KG (*see separate biography, p* 125), and has issue,

1 •HRH THE PRINCE CHARLES PHILIP ARTHUR GEORGE, PRINCE OF WALES (*see separate biography, p* 137).

2 •HRH THE PRINCE ANDREW ALBERT CHRISTIAN EDWARD, born at Buckingham Palace 19 February 1960, educated at Heatherdown School, Ascot, enrolled as Boy Scout 1971.

3 •HRH THE PRINCE EDWARD ANTONY RICHARD LOUIS, born at Buckingham Palace 10 March 1964, educated at Heatherdown School, Ascot.

1 •HRH THE PRINCESS ANNE ELIZABETH ALICE LOUISE (*see separate biography, p* 139).

Arms *see p* 101.

Badges ENGLAND—The red and white rose united, slipped and leaved proper. SCOTLAND—A thistle slipped and leaved proper. IRELAND—1 A shamrock leaf slipped vert. 2 A harp or, stringed argent. UNITED KINGDOM—1 The Rose of England, the Thistle of Scotland, and the Shamrock of Ireland engrafted on the same stem proper. 2 An escutcheon charged as the Union Flag. All these badges are ensigned with the Royal Crown. WALES—1 Upon a mount vert a dragon passant, wings elevated, gules. 2 THE AUGMENTED BADGE—Within a circular riband argent, fimbriated or bearing the motto Y Ddraig Goch Ddyry Cychwyn in letters vert and ensigned with a representation of the Crown proper and escutcheon per fesse argent and vert and thereon the Red Dragon passant. THE ROYAL HOUSE OF WINDSOR—On a mount vert the Round Tower of Windsor Castle argent masoned sable, flying thereon the Royal standard the whole within two branches of oak, fruited and ensigned with the Royal Crown.

Crest of Scotland On the Crown proper, a lion sejant affrontee, gules, crowned or, holding in the dexter paw a sword and in the sinister a sceptre erect, also proper.

Crest of Ireland On a wreath or and azure, a Tower triple-towered of the first, from the portal a hart springing argent, attired and hoofed gold.

Arms of the three Royal Dynasties of Wales 1 NORTH WALES—Quarterly: or and gules, four lions passant guardant counterchanged. 2 SOUTH WALES—Gules, a lion rampant, within a bordure indented, or. 3 POWYS—Argent, a lion rampant, sable.

Lineage *see* ROYAL LINEAGE, *p* 185.

Royal Residences Buckingham Palace, SW1; Windsor Castle, Berkshire; Balmoral Castle, Aberdeenshire; Sandringham House, Norfolk.

Anthony Buckley

HIS ROYAL HIGHNESS THE PRINCE PHILIP, DUKE OF EDINBURGH
The Duke wears the uniform of Admiral of the Fleet, the riband and star of the Order of the Garter, the star of the Order of the Thistle, and the badge of the Order of Merit.

H R H The Prince Philip Duke of Edinburgh

HIS ROYAL HIGHNESS THE PRINCE PHILIP, DUKE OF EDINBURGH, EARL OF MERIONETH and BARON GREENWICH, KG, KT, PC, OM, GBE, is the only son of HRH the late Prince Andrew of Greece and Denmark, GCVO, by his wife HRH the late Princess (Victoria) Alice Elizabeth Julia Marie, RRC, elder daughter of 1st Marquess of Milford Haven, PC, GCB, GCVO, KCMG (*see* reference to **Lineage** *below*). He was born at Mon Repos, Corfu 10 June 1921, and educated at Cheam School, Salem (Baden), Gordonstoun, and the Royal Naval College, Dartmouth.

He was naturalized a British subject 28 February 1947 adopting the surname of MOUNTBATTEN (the surname adopted by his maternal grandfather HSH Prince Louis of Battenberg, for himself and his issue by Royal Licence dated 14 July 1917, when he renounced his foreign princely titles), granted the title, style and attribute of Royal Highness 19 November 1947, and created BARON GREENWICH, *of Greenwich, co London,* EARL OF MERIONETH, and DUKE OF EDINBURGH (in the Peerage of the United Kingdom) 20 November 1947. He was introduced and took his seat in the House of Lords 21 July 1948, and was granted the style and titular dignity of Prince of the United Kingdom and Northern Ireland 22 February 1957. He is a Knight of the Garter (1947), a Knight of the Thistle (1952), a member of the Order of Merit (1968), Grand Master and First or Principal Knight of the Order of the British Empire (1953), and was sworn of the Privy Council of Great Britain (1951), and the Privy Council of Canada (1957). Prince Philip also has the following foreign orders: Grand Cross of the Order of George I, with swords, Grand Cross of the Order of the Phoenix, Grand Cross of the Order of the Redeemer, the Order of St George and St Constantine, 4th class with swords (Greek Orders received before his marriage), the Order of the Elephant (1947) Denmark, Grand Cross of the Order of St Charles (1951) Monaco, Grand Cross of the Order of St Olav (1952) Norway, Grand Cross of the Order of Manuel Amador Guerrero (1953) Panama, member of the Order of the Seraphim (1954) Sweden, Chain of the Order of The Queen of Sheba (1954) Ethiopia, Grand Cross or the Order of The Tower of the Sword (Civil) (1955) Portugal, Grand Cross of the Order of King Feisal I (1956) Iraq, Grand Cross of the Legion of Honour (1957) France, Grand Cross of the Order of Merit (1958) Italy, Grand Cross of the Order of the Lion (1958) Netherlands, Grand Cross of the Order of Merit, 1st class (1958) Federal Republic of Germany, the Order of Ojaswi Rajanya (1960) Nepal, Grand Band of the Order of the Star of Africa (1961) Liberia, the Order of Gran Cruz and Grand Cross Extraordinary of the Order of Boyaca (1962) Colombia, Grand Cross of the National Order of Merit (1962) Ecuador, Great Cross of the Order of the Sun with Brilliantes (1962) Peru, Grand Cross of the Order of the Condor of the Andes (1962) Bolivia, Chain of the Order of Merit (1962) Chile, the National Order of Merit (1962) Paraguay, Grand Cross of the National Order of the Southern Cross (1962)

Brazil, Grand Cross of the Order of San Martin (1962) Argentina, Grand Cordon of the Order of Leopold (1963) Belgium, Decoration of the Republic, 1st class (1964) Sudan, Grand Cross of the Order of the Falcon (1964) Iceland, the Collar of the Order of the Aztec Eagle (1964) Mexico, Grand Cross of the Decoration of Honour for Services to the Republic (1966) Austria, the Star and Riband of the Order of Al Nahda (1966) Jordan, Grand Commander of the Order of Maritime Merit (1968) USA, the Order of the Brilliant Star, 1st class (1968) Zanzibar, Grand Cross of the Order of Rio Branco (1968) Brazil, Grand Cross of the Order of the White Rose (1969) Finland, Medal of the Order of Dogwood (1971) Canada, Grand Cordon of the Supreme Order of the Chrysanthemum (1971) Japan, the Order of the Superior Sun (1971) Afghanistan, the Most Esteemed Family Order (1972) Brunei, hon member of the Order of Temasek (1972) Singapore, and the Order of the Golden Lion of the House of Nassau (1972) Luxembourg.

His Royal Highness was appointed Admiral of the Fleet 1953 (joined Royal Navy 1939, served in World War II with the Mediterranean Fleet in Home Waters, and with the British Pacific Fleet in SE Asia and the Pacific (despatches, Cape Matapan 1942), Croix de Guerre with Palm (1948) France, War Cross (1950) Greece, Sub-Lieutenant 1942, Lieutenant 1942, Lieutenant-Commander 1950, commanded HMS *Magpie* 1950-51, and Commander 1952), Field Marshal 1953, Marshal of the Royal Air Force 1953, Admiral of Sea Cadet Corps 1952, Captain-General of Royal Marines 1953 and Extra Master of Merchant Navy from 1954. He is Colonel-in-Chief of Army Cadet Force (1952), The Queen's Royal Irish Hussars (1958), The Duke of Edinburgh's Royal Regiment (Berkshire and Wiltshire) (1959), Queen's Own Highlanders (Seaforth and Camerons) (1961), and Royal Electrical and Mechanical Engineers (1969), Colonel of Welsh Guards (1953), hon Colonel of University of Edinburgh and Heriot Watt Officer Training Corps (1953), a member of The Honourable Artillery Company (1957) (hon member 1954-57), and Air Commodore-in-Chief of Air Training Corps (1952).

He is Admiral of the Fleet in the Royal Australian Navy (1954), Field Marshal in the Australian Military Forces (1954), Marshal of the Royal Australian Air Force (1954), Colonel-in-Chief of Royal Australian Electrical and Mechanical Engineers (1959), and Australian Cadet Corps (1963), Admiral of the Fleet in the Royal New Zealand Navy (1958), and Colonel-in-Chief of Royal New Zealand Electrical and Mechanical Engineers (1970), Admiral of Royal Canadian Sea Cadets (1953), Colonel-in-Chief of Royal Canadian Army Cadets (1953), Royal Canadian Regiment (1953), Cameron Highlanders of Ottawa (Militia) (1967), Queen's Own Cameron Highlanders (Militia) (1967), and Seaforth Highlanders (Militia) (1967) and Air Commodore-in-Chief of Royal Canadian Air Cadets (1953), hon Colonel of Honourable Order of Kentucky Colonels (1967), and hon member of Ancient and Honourable Artillery Company of Massachusetts (1952) USA, hon Colonel of Trinidad and Tobago Regiment (1964) West Indies, and hon Pilot in the Chilean, and the Colombian Air Forces (1962). He was a Personal ADC to HM King George VI 1948-52.

The Duke of Edinburgh is Master of the Corporation of Trinity House (1969) (Elder Brother from 1952), and Chancellor of the Universities of Wales (1948), Edinburgh (1952), and Salford 1967-76. He has the following honorary degrees: LLD Wales (1949), London (1951), Cambridge (1952), Edinburgh (1952), Karachi (1959), Malta (1964), DCL Durham (1951), DSc Delhi (1959), Reading (1960), Salford, Lancs (1967), Southampton (1967), Victoria, BC (1969), Dr of Engineering, Lima, Peru (1962), DCL by diploma Oxford (1964), Dr of Law, California, Los Angeles (1966), is Visitor of Upper Canada College (1955), Manchester College of Science and Technology (1957), Churchill College, Cambridge (1959), and St Catherine's College, Oxford (1962), and hon Fellow of University College, Oxford (1953). He is hon Freeman of London (1948), Edinburgh (1948), Greenwich (1948), Belfast (1949), Cardiff (1952), Glasgow (1955), Melbourne (1956), Dar-es-Salaam (1961), Nairobi (1963), Guadalajara (1964), Acapulco (1964), Bridgetown, Barbados (1964), and Los Angeles (1966).

He is Lord High Steward of Plymouth (1960) and a member of the Court of Assistants of the Fishmongers' Company 1950 (Freeman and Liveryman 1947, Prime Warden for 1961, 4th Warden 1962-63), hon member of the Company of Merchants, Edinburgh 1948 (Master 1965-66), Grand Master of the Guild of Air Pilots and Navigators (1952), Freeman of the Mercers' Company (1953) (Liveryman 1959), hon member of the Incorporation of Hammermen of Glasgow (1955), Permanent Master of the Shipwrights' Company (1955), Guild Brother of Glasgow of Craft Rank Qua Hammermen, Trade Houses of Glasgow (1955), and Admiral of the Master Mariners' Company (1957) (Master 1954-57). He is a Fellow of the Royal Society (1951), hon Fellow of the Royal Society of Edinburgh (1951), and the Royal Society of Canada (1957), Patron and 1st hon Fellow of the Ghana Academy of Sciences (1961) (hon President 1959-61), and hon Fellow of the Botanical Society of Edinburgh (1950), The Royal Institute of British Architects (1951), the Royal Institute of British Chemistry (1951), the Royal Aeronautical Society (1953) (hon President for 1966), the Royal College of Surgeons of England (1953), the North Coast Institution of Engineers and Shipbuilders (1953), the Permanent Way Institution (1953), the Institute of Welding (1953), the Royal College of Surgeons of Edinburgh (1954, also Patron), the Royal Society of Medicine (1954), the Royal College of Art (1955), the Pharmaceutical Society of Great Britain (1955), the Royal Incorporation of Architects in Scotland (1956), Heriot Watt College, Edinburgh (1958), the Institute of Building (1958), the Institute of Structural Engineers (1958), the Illuminating Engineering Society (1959), the Australian Academy of Science (1961), the Royal Zoological Society of Scotland (1963), the Institute of Petroleum (Permanent Fellow 1963), the Royal Microscopical Society (1966) (President for 1966), the Institute of Public Health Engineers (1966), the Royal Numismatic Society (1967), the British Institute of Management (1969) (President 1968-69), the Institute of Mathematics and Its Applications (1969), the Institute of Public Cleansing (1969), the Institute of Water Pollution Control (1970), the Institute of Sales Engineers (1972), the Medical Society of London (1972), and the Chemical Society (1972), a Master of the Bench of the Inner Temple (1954) (Treasurer for 1961), a Freemason (1952), Ranger of Windsor Great Park (1952), a member of the Council of the Duchy of Cornwall (1952), hon Brother of the Corporation of Hull Trinity House (1953), Life-Governor of King's College, London (1954), and Royal Governor of Charterhouse (1953).

Prince Philip is directly associated as Chairman, President or Patron with several hundred organizations. He accepts many of these commitments for a limited period of time. He is Chairman of the Committee charged with organising Conference on Pollution (1973), the Schools Science and Technology Committee (1968), the Tiger Club (1968), the Combined General Council of the United Service and Royal Aero Club (1971), the Council of the British Red Cross Society (1970-73), Trustee of the National Maritime Museum, Greenwich (1948-76), and the Tower Hill Trust (1969), Patron and Chairman of Trustees of The Duke of Edinburgh's Award Scheme from 1961, and Patron of the Council of St George's House, Windsor (1965). His Royal Highness is President of the Australian Conservation Foundation (1971-76), the British Amateur Athletic Board (1952), the British Commonwealth Games Federation (1955), the British Sportsman's Club (1958), the Central Council of Physical Recreation (1951), the Cheam School Association (1952), the City and Guilds of London Institute (1951), the Council of Engineering Institutions (1965-75), the Council of Trustees of the Air Centre (1968-

73), the Council for National Academic Awards (1964-75), "Countryside in 1970" (1953), the Crafts Centre of Great Britain (1952-64 and from 1967), the English-Speaking Union of the Commonwealth (1952), Game Conservancy (1964), the Guards Polo Club (1955), the Guinea Pig Club (1960), the Historic Churches Preservation Trust (1952), the Institute of Work Study Practitioners (1972-77), the Maritime Trust (1969-79), the National Association for the Blind and Disabled Incorporated (1972-75), the National Council of Social Service (1970-73), the National Playing Fields Association (1949-75), the Royal Agricultural Society of the Commonwealth (1958), the Royal College of General Practitioners (1972-73), the Royal Commission for the Exhibition of 1851 (1965), the Royal Household Cricket Club (1953), the Royal Merchant Navy School (1952), the Royal Mint Advisory Committee (1952), the Royal Society of Arts (1952), the Royal Yachting Association (1956-1970 and 1975-77), the Scottish-Icelandic Association (1965), the Standing Conference on Schools Science and Technology (1971-76), UK National Committee of European Architectural Year 1975 (from 1972), and President-in-Chief of the British Racing Drivers' Club (1952). He was President of the Air League 1969, the Association of Technical Institutions 1964-66, the Automobile Association 1951-61, the British Association for the Advancement of Science 1951-53, the British Dairy Farmers' Association 1957, the British Medical Association 1959-60, the British Sub-Aqua Club 1960-63, the Canadian Medical Association 1959-60, the Company of Veteran Motorists 1959-62, the Cornish Cricket Society 1961-62, the Council for Volunteers Overseas 1964-68, the Crafts Council of Great Britain 1964-69, the English Association 1967-68, the Federation Equestre Internationale 1964-72, the Football Association 1955-58, the Friends of Malta, GC 1965-67, the Helicopter Club of Great Britain 1968-71, the Highland Society of London 1962-63, the Council of the Institute of Marine Engineers 1960-61, the Institute of Sports Medicine 1967-70, the Institution of Highway Engineers 1960-61, the International Lawn Tennis Club of Great Britain 1962-65, the King William IV Naval Foundation 1969-72, the Licensed Victuallers' National Homes (both in 1966 and 1974), the Marylebone Cricket Club 1949-50, the Medical Commission on Accident Prevention 1968-72, Missions to Seamen 1956-57, the National Association of Workshops for the Blind Incorporated 1960-68, the National Book League 1963-66, the National Federation of Parent Teachers' Associations 1960-65, the National Federation of Young Farmers' Clubs 1961-64, the National Safety Campaign 1971-72, the Printers' Pension, Almshouse and Orphan Asylum Corporation 1963 (Life Vice-President from 1963), the Royal Aero Club 1964-71, the Royal Agricultural Society of England 1957 and 1963 (Trustee from 1957), the Royal Air Forces Association 1967-69, the Royal Association of British Dairy Farmers 1965 (and again 1973-74), the Royal Caledonian Curling Club 1964-65, the Royal Smithfield Club 1972, the Royal Society for the Prevention of Accidents 1966-68, the Society of Film and Television Arts 1958-65, the Smeatonian Society of Civil Engineers 1971, and the Spastics Society 1957-65, and was Chairman of The Duke of Edinburgh Committee of The Queen's Award to Industry 1965. He is Vice-President of the Society of Friends of St George's and Descendants of the Knights of the Garter (1947), and was Vice-President of the British Horse Society 1957-67, and the Board of Patrons for European Conservation Year 1970. He is Admiral of the House of Lords Yacht Club (1951), the Royal Motor Yacht Club (1952), the Royal Naval Sailing Association (1952), the Royal Southern Yacht Club (1952), the Royal Yacht Squadron (1952) (Commodore 1961-68), the Bar Yacht Club (1954), the Royal Gibraltar Yacht Club (1954), the Royal Yacht Club of Victoria, Australia (1956), the Great Navy of the State of Nebraska, USA (1958), and the Royal Dart Yacht Club (1966). Prince Philip also has numerous other Patronages, and is a member of a large number of clubs.

Besides always accompanying Her Majesty The Queen on her visits overseas, Prince Philip also travels extensively on his own account. He has visited the Middle East (while serving in the Royal Navy, visited King Ibn Saud of Iran, and King Abdullah of Jordan) 1950, Turkey (visited the President) 1950, Gibraltar (opened new Legislative Council) 1950, Finland (attended the Olympic Games with The Duke of Kent), Norway and Sweden 1952, France (visited the President) 1952, Malta (presented The Queen's Colour to the Royal Marine Commando Brigade) 1952, Federal Republic of Germany (visited British forces) 1953, France (visited SHAPE) and Germany 1954, Canada (10,000 mile tour, visited the British Empire Games at Vancouver, the Yukon and an Eskimo settlement in the Arctic Circle) 1954, Malta and the Mediterranean (watched naval manoeuvres) 1955, Germany (visited British Army and RAF units) 1955, Denmark (visited British Trade Fair) 1955, Germany (presented Colours to 2nd Battalion, the Royal Canadian Regiment) 1955, the Mediterranean and Gibraltar (for Combined Fleet Operations) 1956, Australia (opened Olympic Games in Melbourne), the Seychelles, Ceylon, Papua, New Guinea, Malaya, Australia, New Zealand, the Antarctic, island territories of the Commonwealth, the Gambia and Gibraltar 1956-57, Germany (attended his niece's wedding and inspected British Army Units) 1957, Germany 1958, Belgium (for International Exhibition) 1958, Germany 1958, Canada (presided at two meetings during World Conference of English-Speaking Union of the Commonwealth) 1958, India and Pakistan (attended two scientific congresses as representative of the British Association), Rangoon, Singapore, Sarawak, Brunei, North Borneo, Hong Kong, the Solomon Islands, the Gilbert and Ellice Islands, Christmas Island, the Bahamas and Bermuda 1959, Ghana (visited development schemes) 1959, Malta (watched Royal Marines' exercises) and Switzerland 1960, Germany 1960, Canada and the USA (opened British Exhibition) 1960, Germany (visited 1st Battalion, Welsh Guards) 1961, Tanganyika (represented The Queen at the Independence celebrations) 1961, British Guiana, Venezuela, Colombia, Ecuador, Peru, Bolivia, Chile, Paraguay, Uruguay, Brazil and Argentina (36,000 mile tour) 1962, Canada (opened 2nd Commonwealth Study Conference), and the USA 1962, the USA (for the World Branches' Conference of the English-Speaking Union of the Commonwealth and the United States at San Francisco), Australia (opened Commonwealth Games) and Italy 1962, Germany (visited Royal Canadian Regiment) 1962, the USA (represented The Queen at the funeral of President Kennedy in Washington) 1963, Zanzibar (represented The Queen at the Independence celebrations), Kenya (represented The Queen at the Independence celebrations), Northern Kenya and Sudan 1963, Greece (represented The Queen at the funeral of King Paul) 1964, Iceland 1964, Malawi (represented The Queen at the Independence celebrations) 1964, Greece (represented The Queen at the wedding of King Constantine and Princess Anne-Marie of Denmark), and Malta (represented The Queen at the Independence celebrations) 1964, the Bahamas, Mexico, the Galapagos Islands, Panama, Trinidad and Tobago, Grenada, St Vincent, Barbados, St Lucia, Dominica, St Kitts, Montserrat and Antigua 1964, Germany, France (addressed NATO Defence College) and Belgium (attended FEI Conference) 1964, Morocco (as guest of King Hassan) 1964, Saudi Arabia (as guest of King Feisal), Pakistan, India, Singapore, Australia, Sarawak, Brunei, Sabah, Malaya, Thailand, India, Nepal, Pakistan, Bahrain, and Greece (21,000 mile tour) 1965, Italy (attended Bilderberg Conference) 1965, France (attended International Air Rally) 1965, Germany 1965, Italy (visited British Week, Milan) 1965, France (saw construction work on *Concorde*) 1965, Switzerland (visited Headquarters of the World Wildlife Fund, and the International Union for the Conservation of Nature) 1965, Belgium (attended meetings of FEI) 1965, the USA (visited Miami, Houston, Texas, Dallas, Palm Springs, Chicago, Los Angeles, and New York) and

Canada (Toronto and Ottawa) 1966, the Netherlands (attended the wedding of his nephew, Prince Karl of Hesse) 1966, Norway (visited the British Trade Fair) 1966, Germany (official visit to Schleswig-Holstein) 1966, Jamaica (opened the 8th British Empire and Commonwealth Games) 1966, Argentina (represented The Queen at the 150th anniversary celebrations of the founding of the republic) 1966, Germany 1966, Monaco (visited British Week) 1966, Italy (attended the General Council of the FEI in Rome) 1966, France (attended the celebrations for the 50th anniversary of the France-Great Britain Association) 1966, Iran (as guest of The Shah) 1967, Greece, Jordan, Iran, Pakistan, Singapore, Australia, Thailand, Pakistan, Qatar, and the Lebanon 1967, France (attended commemoration ceremonies at Vimy Ridge) 1967, France (attended FEI Horse Trials at Nice with The Prince of Wales and Princess Anne) 1967, the Netherlands (attended a board meeting of the World Wildlife Fund) 1967, Italy (attended the International Horse Show, Rome for the FEI) 1967, Canada (opened the Pan American Games at Winnipeg) 1967, Canada (opened the Royal Agricultural Winter Fair and attended a conference) 1967, Oman, Jaipur, Malaysia, Indonesia, Thailand, Bali, Australia (for 3rd Commonwealth Study Conference), New Zealand, Singapore and Malta 1968, Mexico (attended the Olympic Games) 1968, Ethiopia and Kenya (visited game reserves for the World Wildlife Fund) 1969, France (for the Paris Air Show) 1969, Germany (visited international show-jumping championship, Aachen) 1969, Canada (made tour in connection with his Award scheme), and the USA 1969, Switzerland (visited International Horse Show, Geneva) 1969, France (attended the Council of Europe's European Conservation Conference at Strasbourg) 1970, the USA (visited Cape Kennedy to see developments in US Space programme) 1970, Finland (visited the Helsinki International Trade Fair) 1970, Italy and Germany (two visits) 1970, Belgium 1970, the Canal Zone (visited Howard Air Force Base), the Galapagos Islands (visited Tower Island, Albemarle Island, Charles Island, Indefatigable Island, Baltra Island and Chatham Island), Easter Island, Pitcairn Island, Raratonga (Cook Island), Samoa, Fiji, the New Hebrides, the Solomon Islands, Bougainville, New Guinea, Australia (for the 50th anniversary celebrations of the RAAF) 1971, Germany 1971, France (for the FEI) 1971, Hungary (visited the European Driving Championship for the FEI) 1971, Iran (attended the 2,500th anniversary celebrations of the Iranian Monarchy at Persepolis) 1971, Sweden (as guest of the Swedish Academy of Naval Science) 1971, Denmark (represented The Queen at the state funeral of King Frederik IX) 1972, Kenya (visited Lake Nakuru National Park for the World Wildlife Fund) 1972, Germany (for the World Driving Championships) 1972, and Germany (attended the Olympic Games at Munich) 1972.

The Duke of Edinburgh is a member of the Counsel of State, though he has never been acting Counsellor. Besides the many engagements he undertakes for all his organizations, he takes a special interest in The Duke of Edinburgh's Award Scheme, which he founded in 1956, the Federation Equestre Internationale, St George's House, where he frequently takes part in discussions, the World Wildlife Fund, Conservation and ecology. His other interests include photography and painting, and, since giving up polo, he has taken up driving. He has published *Birds from Britannia* (1962) and *Wildlife Crisis* (jointly with James Fisher) (1970).

Creation (for Historical Note on the Dukedom of Edinburgh *see* TITLES TRADITIONALLY ASSOCIATED WITH THE ROYAL FAMILY, *p* 336) 20 November 1947.

Arms *see p* 102.

Lineage *see* LINEAGE OF HRH THE PRINCE PHILIP, DUKE OF EDINBURGH, *p* 327; THE ROYAL LINEAGE, *p* 185; and BURKE'S Peerage, MILFORD HAVEN, M.

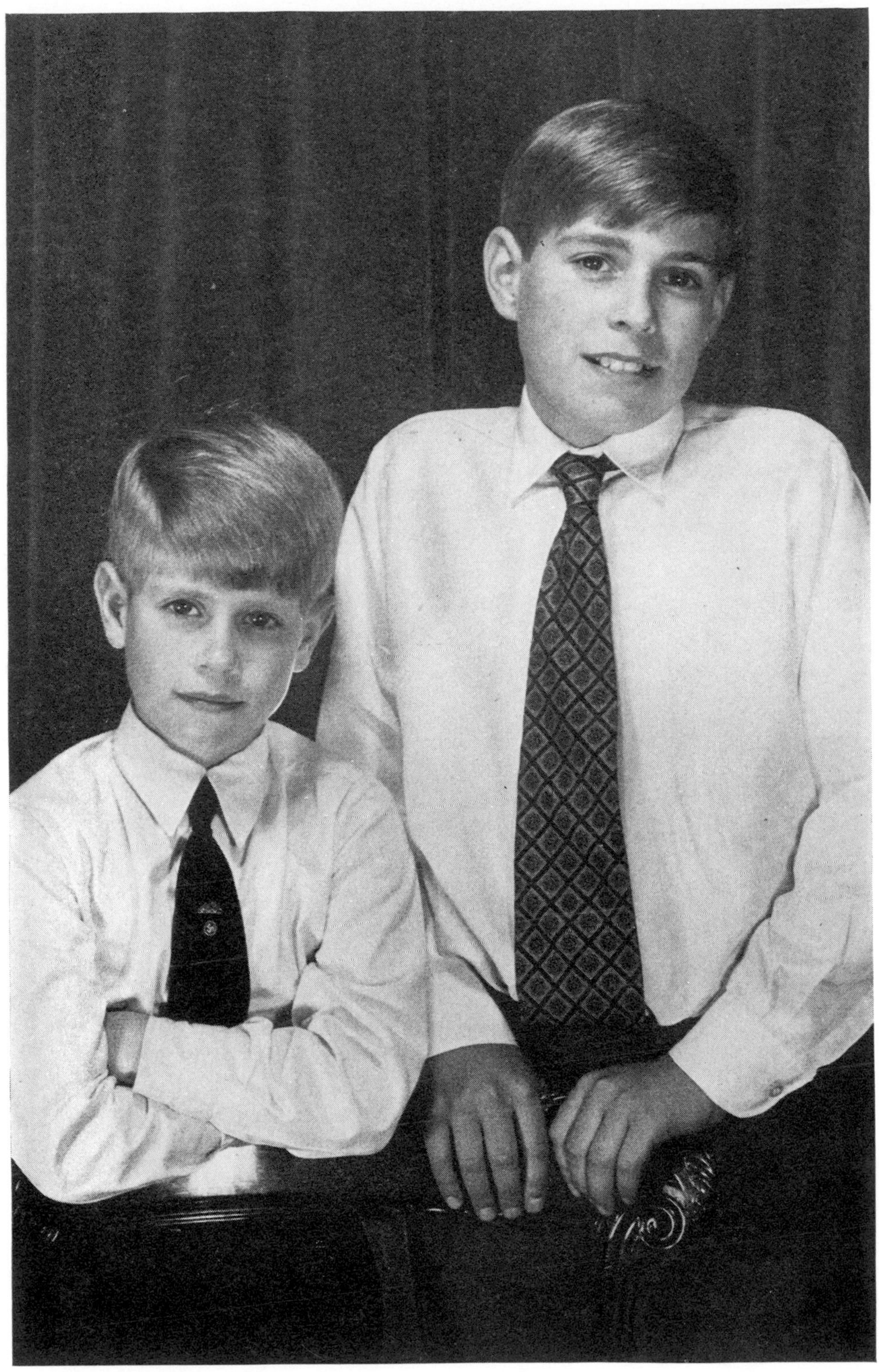

Tom Blau/Camera Press

THEIR ROYAL HIGHNESSES THE PRINCE EDWARD and THE PRINCE ANDREW

Anthony Buckley

HER MAJESTY QUEEN ELIZABETH THE QUEEN MOTHER

H M Queen Elizabeth The Queen Mother

HER MAJESTY QUEEN ELIZABETH THE QUEEN MOTHER, widow of HIS MAJESTY KING GEORGE VI, is the youngest daughter of the 14th Earl of Strathmore and Kinghorne, KG, KT, GCVO, TD, by his wife Nina Cecilia, GCVO, eldest daughter of The Reverend Charles William Frederick Cavendish-Bentinck (*see* reference to **Lineage** *below*). She was born 4 August 1900 at St Paul's Waldenbury, Herts, and was christened Elizabeth Angela Marguerite. She was educated privately, and in 1922 was bridesmaid at the wedding of HRH The late Princess Royal. Her Majesty, then Lady Elizabeth Bowes-Lyon, married at Westminster Abbey 26 April 1923, HRH PRINCE ALBERT FREDERICK ARTHUR GEORGE, DUKE OF YORK, who ascended the Throne as KING GEORGE VI on the abdication of his brother King Edward VIII 10 December 1936 (*see* ROYAL LINEAGE, *p* 308). Their Majesties were crowned at Westminster Abbey 12 May 1937, and His Majesty died at Sandringham 6 February 1952.

Queen Elizabeth is a Lady of the Garter (1936), Lady of the Thistle (1937), Lady of the Crown of India (1931), Grand Master and Dame Grand Cross of the Royal Victorian Order (1937), has the Royal Victorian Chain (1937), Dame Grand Cross of the Order of the British Empire (1927), and Dame Grand Cross of the Order of St John of Jerusalem (1926). She also has the Grand Cross of the Order of St Sava (1923) Serbia, Grand Cross of the Order of Lernor Ala (1928) Afghanistan, Grand Cross of the Order of the Crown (1938) Roumania, Grand Cross of the Order of St Olga and St Sophia (1938) Greece, Grand Cross of the Legion of Honour (1938) France, Red Cross Medal (1945) France, Norwegian War Cross, the Order of Ojaswi Rajanya (1949) Nepal, Grand Cross of the Order of the Lion (1950) Netherlands, Grand Cross of the Order of the Sun (1960) Peru, and Grand Cross of the Order of Independence (1961) Tunisia.

Her Majesty is Colonel-in-Chief of 1st The Queen's Dragoon Guards, The Queen's Own Hussars, the 9th/12th Royal Lancers (Prince of Wales's), The King's Regiment, The Royal Anglian Regiment, The Light Infantry, The Black Watch (Royal Highland Regiment), Royal Army Medical Corps, The Black Watch (Royal Highland Regiment) of Canada, the Toronto Scottish Regiment, Royal Australian Army Medical Corps and the Royal Canadian Army Medical Corps. She is hon Colonel of the Inns of Court and City Yeomanry Cadre, The Royal Yeomanry, The London Scottish (The Gordon Highlanders) Cadre, and University of London Officers Training Corps. She is also Commandant-in-Chief of the Royal Air Force Central Flying School, Women's Royal Naval Service, Women's Royal Army Corps, and Women's Royal Air Force, is Air Chief Commandant of Women's Royal Australian Air Force, and Commandant-in-Chief of Nursing Corps and Divisions, The St John Ambulance Brigade.

Her Majesty is Chancellor of London University (1955), and Dundee University (1967), was 1st President of the University College of Rhodesia and Nyasaland 1957-70 and is Visitor of Girton College, Cambridge. She has received the following honorary degrees: LLD Belfast (1924), St Andrews (1929), Glasgow (1932), Edinburgh (1937), Cape Town (1947), Cambridge (1948), Manchester (1951), Leeds (1954), Columbia (New York) (1954), Melbourne (1958), Liverpool (1958), Auckland (1966), Dalhousie (Halifax, NS) (1967), and Dundee (1967), DCL Oxford (1931), DMus Sheffield (1966), DLitt London (1937), and West Indies (1965), and Litt D Keele (1965). The Queen Mother has the Freedom of Glasgow (1927), Stirling (1928), Dunfermline (1928), Perth (also on behalf of The Black Watch) (1935), Edinburgh (1936), Inverness (jointly with Queen's Own Cameron Highlanders) (1953), London (1953), King's Lynn (1954), Dundee (1954) and Forfar (1956) (both also on behalf of The Black Watch), Musselburgh (1956), Wick (1956), Aberdeen (1959), and St Albans (1961). She is Fellow of the Royal Society (1956), hon Fellow of the Royal College of Obstetricians and Gynaecologists (1949), the Royal College of Surgeons of England (1950), the Royal College of Physicians of Edinburgh (1953), the Royal College of Physicians of London (1962), Royal Fellow of the Society of Antiquaries (1958), a Master of the Bench, Middle Temple (1944) (Treasurer 1949). She is hon Freeman of the Worshipful Companies of Shipwrights (1933), Grocers (1953), Merchant Taylors (1960), Musicians (1966), and Barbers (1969). She is an hon member of the Company of Merchants of Edinburgh (1967) and the Faculty of Advocates of Edinburgh (1965), and received the Gold Albert Medal of the Royal Society of Arts 1952.

Queen Elizabeth The Queen Mother is associated either as President or Patron with about 300 organisations including the Royal Agricultural Society, The British Red Cross Society, the Women's Section of the Royal British Legion, the Victorian Order of Nurses for Canada, the Royal Academy of Music, the Botanical Society of the British Isles, the British Drama League, the British Orthopaedic Association, the Church Army, the Royal Commonwealth Society, Dr Barnardo's Homes, the Franco-British Society, the Friends of St Paul's, the Girl Guides Association, the Royal Horticultural Society, the Hostel of God (Clapham), the Museums Association, the National Association of Youth Clubs, the National Hunt Committee, the National Trust, the Nuffield Foundation, the Royal School of Needlework, the Royal Society for the Prevention of Cruelty to Animals, Toc H, the United Association of Great Britain and France, the Women's Voluntary Service for Civil Defence, and the Young Women's Christian Association.

The Queen Mother has paid many visits to foreign countries: as Duchess of York, with the Duke, to Serbia (for christening of Crown Prince (later King) Peter of Yugoslavia) 1923, East Africa 1924-25, and Australia (the Duke opened Federal Parliament in Canberra and visited every State), New Zealand, West Indies, Panama, Polynesia, Mauritius, Malta and Gibraltar, January–June 1927; as Queen, with The King, to Paris (State Visit) 1938, Canada (six week coast-to-coast tour) and the USA (guests of President Roosevelt and visited World Fair, New York) 1939, and South Africa (four month tour with Princess Elizabeth and Princess Margaret) 1947; as Queen Mother, Southern Rhodesia (opened Central Africa Rhodes Centenary Exhibition, and made a short tour) and Uganda 1953, the USA (bicentennial ceremonies of Columbia University and as guest of President Eisenhower) and Ottawa, Canada 1954, Paris (opened Franco-

Scottish Exhibition) 1956, Dunkirk (unveiled war memorial) 1957, Federation of Rhodesia and Nyasaland (installed at the University) 1957, New Zealand and Australia (called at Montreal, Vancouver, Honolulu and Fiji on outward journey, and Cocos, Mauritius, Uganda and Malta on return) 1958, Kenya and Uganda (three week tour) 1959, Rhodesia (opened Kariba Dam) and Nyasaland 1960, Tunisia (visited Ruins of Carthage) 1961, Canada (for centenary celebrations of Black Watch of Canada) 1962, West Indies 1964, Jamaica and Barbados 1965, Federal Republic of Germany (visited the British Army of the Rhine) 1965, Australia (visited Adelaide Festival of Arts, opened new Flinders University in Adelaide, visited Perth, Canberra, Snowy Mountains and Melbourne), Fiji, New Zealand (visited Wanaka, Queenstown, Arrowtown, Timaru, Wanganni and Auckland) 1966, Northern France 1967, Canada (toured Atlantic provinces, visited New Brunswick, Nova Scotia, Prince Edward Island and Newfoundland) 1967, and Denmark (for wedding of Princess Benedicte, her god-daughter) 1968.

Her Majesty is the first Queen Dowager to be appointed a Counsellor of State. As Queen Consort, she acted on The King's behalf on occasions in the war and during His Majesty's illness of 1951. Since 1953 she has acted as Counsellor of State on every occasion that The Queen has been absent from the United Kingdom, and has undertaken numerous Investitures on The Queen's behalf. Her Majesty also undertakes a large number of engagements for London University, and for her regiments and the other organizations with which she is associated as President or Patron. Her Majesty normally spends part of the summer in Scotland at the Castle of Mey, and Birkhall. She is a keen racing enthusiast and has won over 200 races under National Hunt rules, and also enjoys fishing on the Dee, and gardening.

Her Majesty is the mother of HM THE QUEEN and HRH THE PRINCESS MARGARET, COUNTESS OF SNOWDON (*see separate biographies, pps* 119 *and* 143 *respectively*).

Arms *see p* 103.

Lineage *see* BURKE'S *Peerage,* STRATHMORE AND KINGHORNE, E, and PORTLAND, D.

Residences Clarence House, St James's SW1; The Royal Lodge, Windsor, Berkshire; The Castle of Mey, Thurso, Caithness.

Patrick Lichfield

HIS ROYAL HIGHNESS THE PRINCE OF WALES

Prince Charles wears the uniform of a Sub-Lieutenant in the Royal Navy and the Star of the Order of the Garter

HRH The Prince of Wales

HIS ROYAL HIGHNESS THE PRINCE CHARLES PHILIP ARTHUR GEORGE, PRINCE OF WALES and EARL OF CHESTER, DUKE OF CORNWALL AND ROTHESAY, Earl of Carrick and Baron of Renfrew, Lord of the Isles and Great Steward of Scotland, KG, is the eldest son and heir of HER MAJESTY QUEEN ELIZABETH II (*see p* 119), and of HRH THE PRINCE PHILIP, DUKE OF EDINBURGH (*see p* 125). He was born at Buckingham Palace 14 November 1948, and educated at Hill House School, Cheam School (Captain of Soccer XI and a School Monitor), Gordonstoun (won Silver Award Duke of Edinburgh's Award 1965, member of the Cadet Force, undertook sea training with Royal Navy, Portsmouth, took title role in school's production *Macbeth* 1965, Guardian (head boy) 1967), Geelong Grammar School, Melbourne (January to August 1966), Trinity College, Cambridge (BA 1970, appeared in the college revues 1968, 1969 and 1970, and was awarded half-blue Polo 1969) and the University College of Wales, Aberystwyth.

On the accession of his mother, HM QUEEN ELIZABETH II, to the throne, 6 February 1952, His Royal Highness became DUKE OF CORNWALL *in the Peerage of England,* in accordance with the charter of 17 March 1337, and upon the same occasion, DUKE OF ROTHESAY, EARL OF CARRICK, and BARON OF RENFREW, *in the Peerage of Scotland,* Lord of the Isles, and Great Steward of Scotland. He was created PRINCE OF WALES and EARL OF CHESTER 26 July 1958, and a Knight of the Garter 1958 (invested and installed 1968). He was invested by HM The Queen with the insignia of Prince of Wales and Earl of Chester at Caernarvon Castle 1 July 1969. He took his seat in the House of Lords 11 February 1970. His Royal Highness was appointed Grand Cross of the Order of the White Rose (1969) Finland, Grand Cordon of the Supreme Order of the Chrysanthemum (1971) Japan, Grand Cross of the Order of the House of Orange (1972) Netherlands, and Grand Cross of the Order of the Oak Crown (1972) Luxembourg. He has the Queen Elizabeth II Coronation Medal.

The Prince of Wales made his first solo flight with the RAF 1969. From March to July 1971 he served at RAF College, Cranwell (obtained his wings, made first solo jet flight in a Jet Provost, co-piloted a supersonic Phantom jet, and parachuted into the sea from an Andover aircraft at 1,200 feet), and he entered the Royal Navy in September 1971 (served in HMS *Norfolk* 1971-72, and HMS *Minerva* from 1972). His Royal Highness is Colonel-in-Chief of the Royal Regiment of Wales (1969) and a member of The Honourable Artillery Company (1970).

His Royal Highness has the Freedom of Cardiff (1969), New Windsor (1970), London (1971), is a Royal Fellow of the Society of Antiquaries (1971), hon Freeman of the Drapers' Company (1971), and hon Freeman and Liveryman of the Fishmongers' Company (1971).

He is Chairman of The Prince of Wales' Committee (1971-75), was Chairman of the Steering Committee for Wales "Countryside in 1970" Conference 1968-70, and is President of the Welsh Environment Foundation from 1971. He is a Vice-President of the Society of the Friends of St George's (1968), Patron of the "Wales in Bloom" Campaign, the Royal Regiment of Wales Officers' Dining Club and Regimental Association (1969), and was Patron of the National Co-ordinating Committee of the United Nations Organization 25th Anniversary (1970) 1969-70, and of the Joint Services Expedition to the Elephant Island Group 1970-71.

His Royal Highness has undertaken a number of official visits abroad: to Libya, Malta and Gibraltar (joined his parents at the end of their Commonwealth tour) 1954, Greece (attended the wedding of King Constantine to Princess Anne-Marie of Denmark) 1964, Mexico and Jamaica (for Commonwealth Games) 1966, France (attended FEI Horse Trials with The Duke of Edinburgh and Princess Anne) 1967, Australia (represented The Queen at the funeral service for Harold Holt, the Prime Minister) 1967, Germany (attended the funeral of his aunt, Princess Theodora of Baden) 1969, Malta (for bicentenary celebrations of the Royal University of Malta and inaugurated a new campus at Msida) 1969, France (for the Council of Europe's Conservation Conference at Strasbourg) 1970, New Zealand and Australia (with The Queen, Prince Philip and Princess Anne) and Japan (for EXPO '70, Osaka) 1970, Canada (with The Queen, Prince Philip and Princess Anne) and the USA (with Princess Anne as guests of President Nixon's family) 1970, Fiji (represented The Queen at the Independence celebrations), Gilbert and Ellice Islands, Bermuda (attended the 350th Anniversary of the Parliament on behalf of The Queen) and Barbados 1970, France (represented The Queen at the memorial service for General de Gaulle) 1970, Kenya (with Princess Anne) 1971, the Federal Republic of Germany (visited 1st Battalion, Royal Regiment of Wales at Osnabruck) 1971, and France (joined The Queen and The Duke of Edinburgh during their State Visit) 1972.

The Prince of Wales has acted as Counsellor of State during Her Majesty's absence abroad and carried out a large number of public engagements between leaving University and entering the RAF College, Cranwell. He is especially interested in Wales and made a week's tour of Wales after his Investiture. He is a member of the Game Research Association, Punch Table, RAF Association, Royal Naval Saddle Club, Zoological Society of London, British Deer Society, Lord's Taverners, and Tiger Club. His Royal Highness has a wide variety of interests, including angling, archaeology, music, surfing, polo (captain of Young England Team 1972), shooting, and water-skiing. At present he is a full-time officer in the Royal Navy.

Arms *see p* 104.

Personal Flag in Wales Quarterly or and gules, four lions passant guardant counterchanged, over all an inescutcheon vert charged with the coronet of The Prince of Wales.

Lineage *see* ROYAL LINEAGE, *p* 185. For Historical Note on the Titles of the Heir-Apparent *see* TITLES TRADITIONALLY ASSOCIATED WITH THE ROYAL FAMILY, *p* 336.

Residence Buckingham Palace, SW1.

Clubs White's; Turf; United Oxford and Cambridge University; RAF; New (Edinburgh); Cornish; Norfolk (Norwich); Naval; Royal Yacht Squadron; Island Sailing; Royal London Yacht; Royal Dart Yacht; Cowes Corinthian Yacht.

H R H The Princess Anne

HER ROYAL HIGHNESS THE PRINCESS ANNE ELIZABETH ALICE LOUISE is the only daughter of HM QUEEN ELIZABETH II (*see p* 119), and of HRH THE PRINCE PHILIP, DUKE OF EDINBURGH (*see p* 125). She was born at Clarence House 15 August 1950, and educated at Benenden School. She is a Dame of Justice of the Order of St John of Jerusalem (1971), and has the Order of Merit (1969) Austria, the Order of the White Rose (1969) Finland, the Order of the Precious Crown, 1st class (1971) Japan, Darjah Utama Bakti Chemerlang (1972) Singapore, the Most Esteemed Family Order (1972) Brunei, Grand Cross of the Order of the Crown of the House of Orange (1972) Netherlands, and Grand Cross of the Order of the Oak Crown (1972) Luxembourg. She has the hon Freedom of the Companies of Farriers (1971), Loriners (1972), and Fishmongers (1972), and is Yeoman of the Saddlers' Company (1971).

Her Royal Highness is Colonel-in-Chief of the 14th/20th King's Hussars (1969), The Worcester and Sherwood Foresters Regiment (29th/45th Foot) (1969), and the 8th Canadian Hussars (1972), and Commandant-in-Chief of Ambulance and Nursing Cadets, St John Ambulance Brigade (1970). She is President of the Save The Children Fund (1970), and the Society of Film and Television Arts Ltd (1972), and Patron of the Riding for the Disabled Association (1971), and the Jersey Wildlife Preservation Trust (1972), and has acted as Counsellor of State on several occasions.

Her Royal Highness's overseas visits include: Libya, Malta and Gibraltar (joined her Parents at the end of their Commonwealth tour) 1954, France (educational visit) 1962, Greece (train-bearer to Princess Anne-Marie of Denmark at her wedding to King Constantine) 1964, Jamaica (visit to the Commonwealth Games with The Duke of Edinburgh and The Prince of Wales) 1966, France (attended the FEI Horse Trials with The Duke of Edinburgh and The Prince of Wales) 1967, Austria (accompanied The Queen and The Duke of Edinburgh on their State Visit) 1969, Germany (three day visit to visit 14th/20th Hussars at Paderborn) 1969, Fiji, Tonga, New Zealand and Australia (accompanied The Queen and The Duke of Edinburgh) 1970, Germany (laid the foundation stone of the Florence Nightingale Hospital at Dusseldorf-Kaiserwerth, and visited army units at Paderborn) 1970, Canada (with The Queen and The Duke of Edinburgh) and the USA (with The Prince of Wales as guests of President Nixon's family) 1970, Germany (visited RAF at Bruggen, and presented The Queen's colours to RAF Germany, on behalf of The Queen) 1970, Kenya (for the Save the Children Fund; HRH was later seen in a BBC television film for *Blue Peter*) 1971, Canada (with The Queen

Fox Photos

HER ROYAL HIGHNESS THE PRINCESS ANNE

and The Duke of Edinburgh) 1971, Norway (for 25th anniversary of Redd Barna, the Norwegian Branch of the Save The Children Fund) 1971, Iran (with The Duke of Edinburgh, attended the 2,500th anniversary celebrations of the Iranian Monarchy at Persepolis), and Turkey (joined The Queen on her State Visit) 1971, Hong Kong (visited 14th/20th King's Hussars, toured hospitals, schools and nurseries for the Save The Children Fund) 1971, Thailand, Singapore, Brunei, Sarawak and Malaysia (accompanied The Queen and The Duke of Edinburgh) 1972, Monaco (as guest of Prince Rainier), and Spain (witness at the wedding of Crown Prince Alexander of Yugoslavia) 1972, Germany (attended the equestrian events of the Olympic Games at Munich) 1972, and Yugoslavia (accompanied The Queen and The Duke of Edinburgh on their State Visit) 1972.

Princess Anne is a keen and talented horse-woman. She has taken part in the Horse of the Year Show, Wembley, came in fifth at the Badminton Horse Trials 1971, and won the Raleigh trophy in the Individual Three-day Event at Burghley, Lincs (European Championships). She was named Sportswoman of the Year, by the Sports Writers' Association, the *Daily Express,* and *World Sport* (now *Sportsworld*) (journal of the British Olympic Association), and was elected the BBC's Sports Personality of the Year 1971. Her Royal Highness has undertaken several skiing holidays and enjoys sailing. She is a member of the Island Sailing Club (Cowes), Lady Associate member of the Royal Yacht Squadron, and Royal hon member of the Royal Thames Yacht Club.

Arms *see p* 106.

Lineage *see* ROYAL LINEAGE, *p* 185.

Residence Buckingham Palace, SW1.

David Bailey

HER ROYAL HIGHNESS THE PRINCESS MARGARET, COUNTESS OF SNOWDON and THE EARL OF SNOWDON

H R H The Princess Margaret Countess of Snowdon

HER ROYAL HIGHNESS THE PRINCESS MARGARET ROSE, COUNTESS OF SNOWDON, CI, GCVO, is the younger daughter of HM KING GEORGE VI (*see* reference to **Lineage** *below*) and of HM QUEEN ELIZABETH THE QUEEN MOTHER (*see p* 133). She was born at Glamis Castle, Angus 21 August 1930, and educated privately. Her Royal Highness is a Lady of the Crown of India (1947), Dame Grand Cross of the Royal Victorian Order (1953), Dame Grand Cross of the Order of St John of Jerusalem (1956) (Dame of Justice 1948), and has the Grand Cross of the Order of the Lion (1948) Netherlands, the Order of the Brilliant Star (1956) Zanzibar, Grand Cross of the Order of the Crown (1960) Belgium, Grand Cross of the Order of the Crown, Lion and Spear of Toro Kingdom (1965) Uganda, and the Order of the Precious Crown, 1st class (1971) Japan.

Princess Margaret is Colonel-in-Chief of 15th/19th The King's Royal Hussars, The Royal Highland Fusiliers (Princess Margaret's Own Glasgow and Ayrshire Regiment), Queen Alexandra's Royal Army Nursing Corps, Women's Royal Australian Army Corps, The Highland Light Infantry of Canada, and The Princess Louise's Fusiliers, and Deputy Colonel-in-Chief of The Royal Anglian Regiment. She is Chancellor and hon Dr of Letters of Keele University (1962), hon DMus London (1957), and hon LLD Cambridge (1958), hon Fellow of the Royal Institute of British Architects (1953), the Royal Society of Medicine (1957), the Royal College of Surgeons of England (1963), the Royal College of Obstetricians and Gynaecologists (1966), and hon Life Fellow of the Zoological Society of London (1959). Her Royal Highness has the Freedom of London (1966), and Queensferry (1972), and of the Haberdashers' Company (1966), and is a Master of the Bench of Lincoln's Inn (1956) (Treasurer 1967).

Her Royal Highness is Grand President of the St John Ambulance Association and Brigade from 1972, President and Chairman of the Council of Invalid Children's Aid Association, and President of the following organizations for which she carries out a number of engagements each year: the Royal Ballet, the Chorley Wood College for Training Girls with little or no sight, the Dockland Settlements, Dr Barnardo's, the English Folk Dance and Song Society, the Friends of the Poor and Gentlefolk's Help, the Girl Guides Association, the Horder Centre for Arthritics, the Royal National Institute for the Blind (Sunshine Homes and Schools for Blind Children), the National

Society for the Prevention of Cruelty to Children, the Royal Scottish Society for the Prevention of Cruelty to Children, the Sadlers Wells Foundation, the Scottish League of Pity, and the Victoria League for Commonwealth Friendship, joint President of the Lowland Brigade Club, and was President of the Royal Agricultural Society for 1966.

Princess Margaret is Patron-in-Chief of the English Harbour Repair Fund, Patron of the Architects' Benevolent Society, the Barristers' Benevolent Association, the Bristol Royal Workshops for the Blind, the British Sailors' Society Guild, the Canadian Cancer Society Auxiliary of the Princess Margaret Hospital and Lodge (Toronto), the Royal College of Nursing and National Council of Nurses of the United Kingdom, the Coventry Cathedral Ten Year Development Plan, the Friends of Southwark Cathedral, the Grand Antiquity Society of Glasgow (and hon member), the Guild of St Margaret's Chapel (Edinburgh Castle), the Joint Services Expedition to Chilean Patagonia 1972/73, the Light Infantry Club, the Mary Hare Grammar School for the Deaf, the Mathilda and Terence Kennedy Institute of Rheumatology, the Migraine Trust, the National Pony Society, the Princess Margaret Rose Hospital (Edinburgh), the QARANC Association, the Services Kinema Corporation, the Suffolk Regimental Association, Tenovus, the Union of Girls' Schools for Social Service, the University of London Choir, and the Zebra Trust, Vice-Patron of the Royal Anglian Regimental Association, and a Life Member of the Women's Section, the Royal British Legion.

Her Royal Highness has been acting Counsellor of State on many occasions during The Queen's absence abroad, and has also paid many visits overseas herself. She visited South Africa (with The King and Queen, and Princess Elizabeth) 1947, the Netherlands (represented The King at the enthronement of Queen Juliana) 1948, Italy (received by the Pope, and entertained by the Italian President), Switzerland and France 1949, Malta and Tripoli (joined Princess Elizabeth) 1950, France (attended a gala ball in aid of Hertford British Hospital) 1951, Norway (represented The Queen at the wedding of Princess Ragnhild) 1953, Southern Rhodesia (with Queen Elizabeth The Queen Mother) 1953, the Federal Republic of Germany (inspected British Army and RAF Units, met President Heuss and Chancellor Adenauer) 1954, Trinidad, the Windward Islands, Barbados, the Leeward Islands, St Vincent, Bermuda, Jamaica and the Bahamas 1955, Sweden (with The Duke and Duchess of Gloucester, joined The Queen and The Duke of Edinburgh to attend the equestrian events of the Olympic Games) 1956, Mauritius, Zanzibar, Tanganyika, and Kenya 1956, Germany (inspected Highland Light Infantry) 1958, Trinidad (inaugurated the legislature of the new West Indies Federation on behalf of The Queen), British Guiana and British Honduras 1958, Canada (represented The Queen at the British Columbia centenary celebrations, and toured Canada) 1958, Belgium (visited the Brussels Exhibition) 1958, Portugal (visited the Federation of British Industries Fair) 1959, Belgium (represented The Queen at the wedding of King Baudouin) 1960, Norway (represented The Queen at the wedding of Princess Astrid) 1961, Jamaica (represented The Queen at the Independence celebrations) 1962, Germany (visited King's Royal Hussars) 1963, Germany (visited 1st Battalion, The Royal Highland Fusiliers at Iserlohn) 1963, Germany (visited the NATO air base) 1964, Uganda (ten-day tour) 1965, the Netherlands (opened British Week) 1965, the USA (visited San Francisco, Los Angeles, Arizona, Washington and New York, dined with President Johnson), and Bermuda (presented colours to the Bermuda Regiment) 1965, Hong Kong (opened British Week) 1966, France (attended 60th anniversary ball of the foundation of the British American Hospital in Nice, and visited Cannes) 1966, Belgium (visited British Week) 1967, the USA (attended a theatrical performance in aid of the Invalid Children's Aid Association in New York) 1968, France (inaugurated British Railways' Hovercraft cross-Channel service and travelled to Boulogne) 1968, Japan (opened British Trade Week), Hong Kong,

Cambodia, Thailand and Iran (opened a British Day at 2nd Asian Trade Fair) 1969. Yugoslavia (made a week's tour as guest of President Tito) 1970, France (opened exhibition of British commercial and industrial design) 1971, Canada (opened a new art gallery in Winnipeg) 1971, the British Virgin Islands (for the Tercentenary celebrations) 1972, Italy (visited Henry Moore exhibition in Florence) 1972, Germany (visited 15th/19th King's Royal Hussars, a Military Hospital at Hanover, and Berlin) 1972 and the Seychelles (for Tercentenary Festival), Western Australia, and Singapore (visited The Royal Highland Fusiliers) 1972.

Princess Margaret is interested in all forms of art, often attends the theatre and ballet, and has a fine collection of china and modern art. She is an accomplished pianist and singer, and enjoys riding. As a young girl she was Patrol Leader of the Buckingham Palace Girl Guide Company and Commodore of the Sea Rangers, and with her sister, The Queen, took part in amateur theatricals at Windsor during the war.

Her Royal Highness married in Westminster Abbey 6 May 1960, Antony Charles Robert Armstrong-Jones (THE EARL OF SNOWDON—*see p* 146), and has issue,

•DAVID ALBERT CHARLES, *Viscount Linley,* born at Clarence House 3 November 1961, educated at Ashdown House.

•*Lady* Sarah Frances Elizabeth (*Armstrong-Jones*), born 1 May 1964, enrolled as Girl Guide 1971.

Arms *see p* 107.

Lineage *see* ROYAL LINEAGE, *p* 185.

Residence Kensington Palace, W8.

The Earl of Snowdon

THE RIGHT HONOURABLE THE EARL OF SNOWDON, GCVO, husband of HRH THE PRINCESS MARGARET, is the only son of the late Ronald Owen Lloyd Armstrong-Jones, MBE, DL, JP, QC, of Plâs Dinas, Caernarvonshire (High Sheriff 1936), by his wife Anne (who married secondly, 6th Earl of Rosse, MBE), only daughter of the late Lieutenant-Colonel Leonard Charles Rudolph Messel, OBE, TD, MA, of Nymans, Handcross, Sussex (*see* reference to **Lineage** below). He was born 7 March 1930, christened Antony Charles Robert, and educated at Eton, and Jesus College, Cambridge (University Boat Cox in winning crew 1950).

He was created EARL OF SNOWDON, VISCOUNT LINLEY, *of Nymans, co Sussex* in the Peerage of the United Kingdom 6 October 1961, and Knight Grand Cross of the Royal Victorian Order 1969. He is Grand Officer of the Order of Leopold II (1961) Belgium, and has the Grand Cross of the Order of the Crown (1963) Belgium. He was appointed Constable of Caernarvon Castle 1963, and is hon Fellow of the Institute of Incorporated Photographers (1961), the Manchester College of Art and Design (1967), and the Royal Photographic Society of Great Britain (1968), and a Liveryman of the Worshipful Company of Clothworkers (1959).

Lord Snowdon is President of the British Theatre Museum Association, the Civic Trust for Wales, the Contemporary Art Society for Wales, the Welsh Association of Youth Clubs, and the Welsh Theatre Club, and Patron of the British Water Ski Federation, the National Youth Theatre, the Welsh National Rowing Club, the Windsor and Eton Regatta, and the Metropolitan Union of YMCAs. He is a member of the Council of Action for the Crippled Child, the Committee of Mental Health Trust, the Arts Council, the National Union of Journalists, the Association of Cinematograph, Television, and Allied Technicians, and hon member of the North Wales Society of Architects, the South Wales Institute of Architects, and the Royal Welsh Yacht Club, Caernarvon, and was formerly a member of the Council of RADA. He is Artistic Adviser to the *Sunday Times* and *Sunday Times* Publications Ltd, Adviser to the Design Council, and is Editorial Advisor to *Design* Magazine.

Lord Snowdon accompanies Princess Margaret to many of her engagements. He has accompanied her on seventeen out of twenty-two overseas visits undertaken, and opened British Week in Belgium on her behalf in 1967. He has also travelled extensively in connection with his work as a full-time professional photographer, photographing many social problems varying from mental health and cruelty to children, to aspects of loneliness and old age. He has worked in most European countries as well as India, Japan, Yugoslavia, Czechoslovakia (twice) and Peru for the *Sunday Times*, and has undertaken many industrial tours for the Design Council. He had his first one man exhibition, *Photocall* in London 1957, exhibited photographs in Cologne 1972, and has published *Malta* (with Sacheverell Sitwell) (1957), *London* (1958), *Private View* (with John Russell and Bryan Robertson) (1965), *Assignments* (1972), and *View of Venice* (1972). Lord Snowdon has directed three documentary films, *Don't Count the Candles* (won two Hollywood "Emmys", St George Prize at Venice, and prizes at film festivals in Prague and Barcelona) (1968), *Love of a Kind* (1969), and *Born to be Small* (1971). He designed the Snowdon Aviary at the London Zoo (1964), and recently a Chairmobile (a new type of invalid transport). He was responsible for the design of the Investiture Ceremony at Caernarvon Castle 1969.

Arms *see* BURKE'S *Peerage,* SNOWDON, E.

Lineage *see* BURKE'S *Peerage,* SNOWDON, E; and BURKE'S *Landed Gentry,* MESSEL *of Nymans.*

Clubs Buck's; Leander (hon Life member); Hawks (Cambridge); United Oxford and Cambridge University (hon member).

Snowdon/Camera Press

VISCOUNT LINLEY and LADY SARAH ARMSTRONG-JONES

East African Newspapers Ltd

HIS ROYAL HIGHNESS THE DUKE OF GLOUCESTER

The Duke wears the tropical uniform of the Royal Inniskilling Fusiliers, the riband of the Order of St Patrick (of which he is the only surviving Knight), the Great Master's badge of the Order of the Bath, and the Royal Victorian Chain. *Kenya* 1962.

H R H The Duke of Gloucester

HIS ROYAL HIGHNESS THE PRINCE HENRY WILLIAM FREDERICK ALBERT, DUKE OF GLOUCESTER, EARL OF ULSTER and BARON CULLODEN, KG, KT, PC, KP, GCB, GCMG, GCVO, is the third and only surviving son of HM KING GEORGE V and HM QUEEN MARY (*see* reference to **Lineage** below). He was born at York Cottage, Sandringham 31 March 1900, and educated at Eton, Royal Military College, Sandhurst, and Trinity College, Cambridge.

His Royal Highness was created DUKE OF GLOUCESTER, EARL OF ULSTER and BARON CULLODEN *in the Peerage of the United Kingdom,* by Letters Patent 31 March 1928. He was appointed a Knight of the Garter 1921, Knight of the Thistle 1933, Knight of St Patrick 1934, Great Master and Knight Grand Cross of the Order of the Bath 1942, Knight Grand Cross of the Order of St Michael and St George 1935, and Knight Grand Cross of the Royal Victorian Order 1922. He has the Royal Victorian Chain (1932), was sworn of the Privy Council 1925, and appointed Grand Prior and Bailiff Grand Cross of the Order of St John of Jerusalem 1930. He has the Grand Cross of the Order of the Elephant (1924) Denmark, Grand Cross with Chain of the Order of St Olav (1924) Norway, the Grand Cordon of the Order of Leopold (1926) Belgium, the Gold Collar of the Order of the Chrysanthemum (1929) Japan, the Order of the Seal of Solomon (1930) Ethiopia, the Order of El Rafidian (1933) Iraq, the Grand Cross of the Order of Carol I (1937) Roumania, Grand Cross of the Legion of Honour (1939) France, the Order of the Royal House of Chakri (1940) Siam, the Order of the Redeemer (1942) Greece, and the Order of Mohamed Ali (1948) Egypt.

The Duke is a Field Marshal in the Army (1955) (Captain 1927, Brevet Major 1934, Major 1935, Major-General 1937, Lieutenant-General 1941, General 1944), Colonel-in-Chief of The Royal Irish Rangers (27th (Inniskilling) 83rd and 87th), The Gloucestershire Regiment (1935), The Gordon Highlanders, Royal Corps of Transport, Royal Canadian Army Service Corps (1947), Royal Winnipeg Rifles (1950), Royal Australian Armoured Corps, Royal Army Service Corps, Royal New Zealand Army Service Corps, Ceylon Light Infantry, and the Natal Mounted Rifles (1937). He was formerly Colonel-in-Chief of 10th Royal Hussars. He is Deputy Colonel-in-Chief of The Royal Green Jackets, and is Colonel of Scots Guards (Senior Colonel in the Household Brigade), and hon Colonel of Royal Regiment of Artillery (Territorial and Army Volunteer Reserve), and Cambridge University Officers Training Corps (1934), hon Captain Royal Naval

Volunteer Reserve (1937) and hon Commodore Royal Naval Reserve (1958). He is Marshal of the RAF (1958) (Air Vice-Marshal 1937, Air Marshal 1941, Air Chief Marshal 1944), was Personal ADC to HM King George V 1929-36, to HM King Edward VIII 1936, to HM King George VI 1936-52 and to HM The Queen from 1952. He served in World War II as Chief Liaison Officer to the British Expeditionary Force 1939 (wounded slightly, and despatches for service in France 1940), and Chief Liaison Officer, GHQ, Home Forces 1940 (toured military posts in Britain and military missions and British troops abroad).

His Royal Highness was Governor General of Australia 1945-47, Lord High Commissioner to the General Assembly of the Church of Scotland 1949 and 1963, is an Elder Brother of Trinity House (1942) (Master 1942-69), High Steward of King's Lynn (1924) and of Windsor (1936), and Ranger of Epping Forest (1943). He has the hon degrees of LLD Cambridge (1930), Adelaide (1934), Melbourne (1934), and Sydney (1934), is hon Freeman of the Worshipful Companies of Mercers (Liveryman 1921), Grocers (1927), Vintners (Liveryman 1936, member of the Court of Assistants 1952 and Master 1953), Fishmongers (1937), Goldsmiths (Liveryman 1938), Merchant Taylors (1939), the Society of Apothecaries (1959), and Gardeners (Liveryman 1963), is a Fellow of the Royal Society (1938), hon Fellow of the Royal College of Surgeons of England (1945), and the Royal Institute of British Architects (1937), and a Barrister-at-law and Master of the Bench of Gray's Inn (1926) (Treasurer 1954).

The Duke of Gloucester is Chairman of King George's Jubilee Trust (1936), and the Grand Military Race Meeting and Committee. He was formerly Grand President of the League of Mercy and Chairman (now Vice-President) of The British Red Cross Society. He is President of the Royal Alexandra and Albert School, the Army and Navy Club, the Army Football Association, the Army Polo Association, the Australian Club, the Australian Rheumatism Council, the British Empire Cancer Campaign for Research, the Royal Caledonian Hunt, Royal Cambridge Home for Soldiers' Widows, the Cavalry Club, Cheltenham Races, Christ's Hospital (Horsham), the Civil Service Sports Council, the Royal Commonwealth Society, The Duke of York's Royal Military School (Dover), the Fairbridge Society, the Friends of St George's Chapel and Descendants of the Knights of the Garter, the Gardeners' Royal Benevolent Society, the Royal Household Bowling Society, the Royal Humane Society, The Imperial War Museum, the Kennel Club, the King Edward VII Hospital for Officers, the National Association of Boys' Clubs, the National Rifle Association, the Newmarket and Worlington Golf Club, The Royal Patriotic Fund Corporation, the Peterborough Royal Foxhound Show Society, the Printers' Pension, Almshouse and Orphan Asylum Corporation, the Roehampton Club, Royal School for Daughters of Officers of the Army (Bath), the Scout Association, the Windsor Branch of the RSPCA, and the Royal United Services Institute. He was formerly President of the Imperial War Museum, the King Edward's Hospital Fund, the Boy Scouts' Association, the Royal Humane Society, the Imperial War Graves Commission and Wellington College 1936-69. He is hon President of the King Edward VII Hospital for Officers (Windsor), and St Bartholomew's Hospital, Vice-President of the Royal Norfolk Agricultural Association and a life-Governor of the Connaught Hospital, E17.

The Duke is Patron-in-Chief of Scottish Naval, Military and Air Force Veterans' Residences and the Union Jack Services Club, Patron of the Royal Air Force Reserves Club, Aldershot Horse Show, Aldershot Races, the Royal Armoured Corps Club, the Army Athletic and Cross Country Association, the Army Hockey Association, the Army Point-to-Point, the Asthma Research Council, the Belfast Royal Victoria Hospital, the British Boys' Movement for Australia, the British Commonwealth Ex-Services League, the British Hospitals Association, the King's Lynn and Leicester Branches of the Royal British Legion, the Cambridge Amateur Dramatic Club, the Cheshire Ploughing and Hedgecutting Society, the Cheyne and Hip Hospital for Children (Sevenoaks), the City of London Club, the Combined Cavalry Old Comrades' Association, the Royal Epping Forest Golf Club, the Essex Field Club, the Northants Local Area Council of the Fire Services National Benevolent Fund, the Friends of Gloucester and Peterborough Cathedrals and Tewkesbury Abbey, the Gloucester Society in London, the Grand Antiquity Society of Glasgow, the Hakluyt Society, the Lawrence Memorial Military School (Shaawar, India), the Institute of the Royal Army Service Corps, the Invalid and Crippled Children's Society's Hospital (Plaistow), the Royal London Homeopathic Hospital, the Lord Kitchener Memorial Hospital, the Melton War Memorial Hospital, the Metropolitan Drinking Fountain and Cattle Trough Association, the Royal Military Museum (Sandhurst), the National Burns Memorial Cottage Homes, the Royal National Orthopaedic Hospital, the Gloucester branch of the NSPCC, the Mansfield Orthopaedic Hospital (Northampton), the Northants and Huntingdonshire Association of Small Bore Rifle Clubs, the Royal Northern Hospital (Holloway Road, N7), the Old Contemptibles' Association, the Old Etonians' Rifles Association, the Peel Institute, Prince Henry's Grammar School (Evesham), Queen Mary's Hospital for East End (Stratford), the Returned Service League of Australia, St John's School Leatherhead, the Scottish Kennel Club, the Gloucester and Norfolk Scout Associations, the Society of Engineers, the Staff College Club, the Suffolk Sheep Society, Surbiton New Hospital, the Thames Rowing Club, the Royal Tournament, the Royal Veterinary College and Hospital, the Victoria Hospital for Children (Tite Street, SW), the Royal Wanstead School, the Welsh Back Cattle Society, and Wembley Hospital, Vice-Patron of the British Olympic Association, the Royal Overseas League, and the Yorkshire Agricultural Society. He is Commodore of the Royal Ulster Yacht Club and hon member of the Jockey Club.

His Royal Highness visited Kenya (on safari with The Prince of Wales), Tanganyika and Northern Rhodesia 1928, Japan (invested Emperor Hirohito with the Order of the Garter on behalf of King George V) 1929, Ethiopia (represented The King at the coronation of Emperor Haile Selassie) 1930, Australia (represented The King at the centenary celebrations of Victoria), Ceylon (returned the crown to the Kings of Kandy) 1934-35, Gibraltar (on military missions) 1941 and 1942, the Middle East (visited the battlefields of Alamein and Tobruk), India and Ceylon (visited troops), Egypt, Iran, Palestine, Lebanon, Cyprus, Syria, Jordan, Bahrain, India, Ceylon, Eritrea, Aden, the Somaliland Protectorate and Kenya (tour of three months in total) 1942, Australia (Governor General) 1945-47, Malta (opened legislature of new constitution on behalf of King George VI) 1947, Ceylon (opened 1st session of Parliament as self-governing Commonwealth country) 1948, Denmark (opened the British Exhibition, presented the late King Frederik with commission as hon Admiral) 1948, the Netherlands (as guest of Prince Bernhard) 1948, Kenya (attended ceremony raising Nairobi to status and dignity of a city) 1950, Germany (inspected British Army Units) 1950, Sweden (represented The King at the funeral of King Gustav V) 1950, France (unveiled Green Jackets War Memorial at Calais) 1951, Germany (inspected British Army Units), and France (visited war cemeteries) 1952, Sweden (as guest of The King) 1952, Iraq (represented The Queen at the enthronement of King Feisal) and Jordan (met King Hussein) 1953, Norway (represented The Queen at the funeral of Crown Princess Martha) 1954, Germany (visited British troops) 1955, Italy (toured British Commonwealth war cemeteries and had audience of the Pope) 1955, France (unveiled war memorial at Rouen) 1955, Germany (visited British troops) 1956, Sweden (joined The Queen and The Duke of Edinburgh, and watched the equestrian events of the Olympic

Games) 1956, the Netherlands and Germany (visited war cemeteries) 1957, France (was present when Queen Elizabeth The Queen Mother unveiled the Dunkirk War Memorial) 1957, Malaya (represented The Queen at the Independence celebrations) 1957, Norway (represented The Queen at the funeral of King Haakon) 1957, Ethiopia (as guest of the Emperor), the Somaliland Protectorate and Aden 1958, Germany (visited units of the British Army of the Rhine) 1959, Nigeria (represented The Queen at the self-government celebrations in Northern Nigeria, visited Kaduna, Enugu, Lagos and Ibadan) and Southern Cameroons 1959, Germany (visited British troops) 1960, Cyprus (visited units of the RAF) 1960, Italy (joined The Queen and The Duke of Edinburgh after their State Visit), and Greece (travelled in HM Yacht *Britannia,* unveiled Commonwealth war memorial, visited war cemeteries in Macedonia, Salonika and Crete) and Turkey (visited Istanbul, Ankara and toured the cemeteries and battlefields of the Gallipoli Peninsula) 1961, Germany (two visits to see army units) 1961, Malta and Kenya (visited army units) 1962, Jordan (as guest of King Hussein), and Cyprus 1963, Australia (five-week tour of the States of Victoria, New South Wales, Queensland and Tasmania, represented The Queen at the 50th anniversary ANZAC ceremonies in Canberra) 1965, and Singapore and Malaysia (made fortnight's tour and visited British Forces) 1966.

His Royal Highness has acted as Counsellor of State on numerous occasions since the final illness of King George V in 1936. He witnessed the abdication document, and under the Regency Act 1937, he was named as Regent in the event of the death of King George VI, his brother, before Princess Elizabeth attained her majority in 1947 (for this reason he had to return to England from Australia before The King's South African tour 1947).

Besides his interest in the Army and Australia, the Duke is a keen practical farmer. After his return from Australia, he personally supervised the redesigning of the Home Farm at Barnwell. As a young man he was a keen sportsman and represented his University and Regiment at Polo. His Royal Highness has now retired from public life, and lives at Barnwell.

His Royal Highness married at Buckingham Palace 6 November 1935, Lady Alice Christabel Montagu-Douglas-Scott (HRH THE DUCHESS OF GLOUCESTER—*see separate biography, p* 153), and has had issue,

1 HRH the late PRINCE WILLIAM HENRY ANDREW FREDERICK (*see separate biography, p* 157).

2 •HRH PRINCE RICHARD ALEXANDER WALTER GEORGE (*see separate biography, p* 159).

Arms *see p* 108.

Lineage *see* ROYAL LINEAGE, *p* 185. For Historical Note on the Dukedom of Gloucester *see* TITLES TRADITIONALLY ASSOCIATED WITH THE ROYAL FAMILY, *p* 336.

Residences Kensington Palace, W8; Barnwell Manor, Peterborough.

Clubs Army and Navy; Cavalry; Bath.

H R H The Duchess of Gloucester

HER ROYAL HIGHNESS THE DUCHESS OF GLOUCESTER, CI, GCVO, GBE, is the third daughter of the 7th Duke of Buccleuch and (9th Duke of) Queensberry, KT, GCVO, HML, JP, by his wife Lady Margaret Alice, 2nd daughter of 4th Earl of Bradford, DL, JP (*see* reference to **Lineage** *below*). She was born in London 25 December 1901, baptized Alice Christabel, and educated at West Malvern, and in Paris. She is a Lady of the Crown of India (1937), Dame Grand Cross of the Royal Victorian Order (1948), Dame Grand Cross of the Order of the British Empire (1937), Dame Grand Cross of the Order of St John of Jerusalem (1936) and has the Star and Badge of Grand Cross of the Order of the Crown (1938) Roumania, the Grand Cordon of Al Kamal (1950) Egypt, and the Badge and Star of the Order of the Queen of Sheba (1958) Ethiopia.

Her Royal Highness is Colonel-in-Chief of The King's Own Scottish Borderers, and The Royal Hussars (Prince of Wales's Own) (1969), Deputy Colonel-in-Chief of The Royal Anglian Regiment, Air Marshal of the Women's Royal Air Force (1968) (Air Chief Commandant 1943) and Deputy Commandant-in-Chief of Nursing Corps and Divisions, The St John Ambulance Brigade (1937).

She has the honorary Freedoms of Edinburgh (1937), Gloucester (1939), and Belfast (1952), and of the Worshipful Companies of Fanmakers (1949), Gardeners (1963), Mercers (1967), and Vintners (1969).

The Duchess is President of the Charterhouse Rheumatism Clinic, the Royal Academy of Music, the East of England Show (Peterborough), the Gilbert and Sullivan Society, the Guild of Aid for Gentlepeople, the King's College Hospital Group, the Ladies' Guild of the Hospital of St John of Jerusalem, the Northamptonshire Yeomanry Association, the North London Collegiate and Camden School for Girls (Frances Mary Buss Foundation), the Princess Christian Nursing Home (Windsor), the Princess Helena College (Hitchin), the Scottish and English Branch of the Queen's Institute of District Nursing, the Scottish Society of Women Artists, the Women's Guild of St Bartholomew's Hospital, the Women's Royal Air Force Officers' Association, and the North Midland Region of the Women's Royal Voluntary Services, Joint President of the Royal Caledonian Hunt, and the Lowland Brigade Club, and a member of the Council of the British Red Cross Society.

She is Patron of the Australian Musical Association, the Australian Terrier Club of

Lenare

HER ROYAL HIGHNESS THE DUCHESS OF GLOUCESTER

England, the Badminton Association of England, Bible Days and Bible Ways, the Bookham School of Stitchery, the British Limbless Ex-Servicemen's Association, the Central Company for District Nursing in London, the Church of England's Children's Society (Children's Union), the Northants Branch of the Council for the Preservation of Rural England, the Crosby Hall Association Ltd, the Dominion Students Hall Trust (London House and William Goodenough House), the East African Conservatoire of Music, the England Branch of the East African Women's League, the Edinburgh Children's Holiday Fund, the Embroiderers' Guild, the Fraternity of the Abbey of St Alban, the Royal Free Hospital, the Association of the Friends of Lichfield Cathedral, the Girls' Brigade, Girls of the Realm, the Girls' Public Day-Schools Trust, Queen Margaret College, the Royal Green Jackets Ladies' Guild, the Kenya Arts and Crafts Society, the London Orpheus Choir, the London Union of Youth Clubs, the Methodist International House, the Nakuru War Memorial Hospital, the National Adoption Society, the National Baby Welfare Council, the National Burns Memorial Cottage Homes, the Northamptonshire Nursing Association, the Oundle Choral Society, the Peterborough Arts Council, the Postal Sunday School Movement (Australia), the Princess Tsahai Memorial Hospital Association, the Redlands Hospital for Women (Glasgow), the St Andrews Society of Denmark, the Scottish Association for Mental Health, the Royal Scottish Society for the Self-Aid of Gentlewomen, the Jessop Hospital for Women (Sheffield), the Sir Oswald Stoll Foundation, the Royal Society for the Relief of Indigent Gentlewomen of Scotland, the Royal Society of British Artists, the Society of Scottish Artists, the Surrey Convalescent Homes, the Ulster Hospital for Children and Women (Belfast), and the West London Hospital (Hammersmith), and Vice-Patron of the Royal Air Forces Association and the Soldiers', Sailors' and Airmen's Association.

Before her marriage, the Duchess frequently visited her uncle Colonel Lord (Henry) Francis Montagu-Douglas-Scott in Kenya. She accompanied the Duke on most of his foreign visits, and, on her own account, visited Germany and Austria (inspected units of the WRAF and military units of her regiments) 1949, Germany (inspected WRAF units) 1956, Germany (inspected military units, April and November) 1969, Cyprus (visited WRAF units) 1970, and Norway (represented The Queen at the centenary celebrations of the birth of late King Haakon) 1972.

She is interested in cine-photography, and painting in water-colours (she is a Friend and hon member of the Royal Scottish Society of Painters in Water Colours, and held several exhibitions before her marriage), and was a fully-trained Red Cross nurse (formerly assistant Commandant of her local Scottish Division of the Voluntary Aid Detachment). Besides the engagements she undertakes for her own commitments, Her Royal Highness has also assumed responsibility for many of the Duke's, and she continues to take part in State occasions on his behalf.

Arms *see p* 108.

Lineage *see* BURKE'S *Peerage*, BUCCLEUCH, D, and BRADFORD, E.

Tom Hustler

HIS late ROYAL HIGHNESS PRINCE WILLIAM OF GLOUCESTER

H R H the late Prince William of Gloucester

HIS late ROYAL HIGHNESS PRINCE WILLIAM HENRY ANDREW FREDERICK OF GLOUCESTER, was the elder son of TRH THE DUKE AND DUCHESS OF GLOUCESTER (*see pps* 149 *and* 153 *respectively*). He was born at Barnet, Hertfordshire 18 December 1941, and educated at Eton, Magdalene College Cambridge (BA 1963), and Stanford University, California.

He was a Knight of Justice of the Order of St John of Jerusalem (1968), was Commandant-in-Chief of the St John Ambulance Brigade (1968), hon Freeman of the Worshipful Companies of Mercers (1963), Merchant Taylors (1971), and Grocers (Liveryman 1972), a member of the Guild of Air Pilots and Air Navigators (1968), and a Fellow of the Royal Geographical Society (1970).

After six months with Lazards, the merchant bankers, Prince William joined the Commonwealth Relations Office 1965, was 3rd Secretary, HM Diplomatic Service, Lagos 1965-68, and 2nd (Commercial) Secretary, British Embassy, Tokyo 1968-70. He was President of the British Light Aviation Centre (1969) (Chairman from 1971), the National Ski Federation Supporters' Association (1965), the Magdalene Society (Cambridge), Cambridge House, the East Midlands Tourist Board, the Royal African Society (1972), and the Guild of Centurions (Peterborough), President of Trustees of the Kettering and District Medical Foundation, Vice-Chairman of the United Service and Royal Aero Club, and Patron of the Royal Anthropological Institute of Great Britain, the British Schools Exploring Society, the Northants and Peterborough Association of Youth Clubs, and Talyllyn Railway Preservation Society, and hon member of the International Association of Aviation Historians, the Farmers' Club, Tiger Club (Redhill), and *Air Britain*.

Prince William acted as Counsellor of State on several occasions from 1963, and visited many foreign countries—Australia (when the Duke was Governor General) 1945-47, Malaya (accompanied the Duke and Duchess) 1957, Europe, North and East Africa (made an overland safari trip with friends via the Middle East and the Sudan, made a film in Ethiopia, which was shown on BBC Television) 1963, the USA (at Stanford University) 1963-64, Australia (month's visit) 1964, Nigeria (at British High Commission) 1965-68, Japan (with the Embassy) 1968-70, Tonga (represented The Queen at the celebrations to mark the termination of Tonga's status as a protected state) 1970, Malta (for an air rally, and some official engagements) 1971, Congo (for British Trade Fair) 1971, and Ethiopia and Kenya (on safari) 1971 and 1972.

His Royal Highness undertook a number of engagements on his father's behalf and had recently taken on engagements for St John's and his other organisations. Prince William was a qualified pilot and owned an aircraft from 1967. His interest in flying brought him into close contact with the RAF. He farmed the 2,500 acre family estate at Barnwell, and his other interests included ski-ing, photography, Skin-diving and polo.

Prince William was killed in a flying accident while taking part in the Goodyear Air Race, near Wolverhampton 28 August 1972, and was buried at Frogmore 2 September 1972. He was unmarried.

Arms *see p* 109.

Lineage *see* ROYAL LINEAGE, *p* 185.

Tom Hustler

HIS ROYAL HIGHNESS PRINCE RICHARD OF GLOUCESTER

H R H Prince Richard of Gloucester

HIS ROYAL HIGHNESS PRINCE RICHARD ALEXANDER WALTER GEORGE OF GLOUCESTER is the younger son and heir of TRH THE DUKE AND DUCHESS OF GLOUCESTER (*see pps* 149 *and* 153 *respectively*). He was born at Northampton 26 August 1944. He was educated at Eton, and Magdalene College, Cambridge (BA 1966, MA 1968, Diploma of Architecture 1969).

Prince Richard is a Freeman of the City of London (1971), Liveryman of the Vintners' Company (1965), President of the Institute of Advanced Motorists from 1971, Vice-President of LEPRA (British Leprosy Relief Association), Patron-in-Chief of New Islington and Hackney Housing Association, and a member of the Anglo-Nepalese Society. He first acted as a Counsellor of State in 1966.

His Royal Highness has travelled extensively: to Australia (when the Duke was Governor General) 1945-47, Norway (with Eton College Cadet Corps) 1962, Singapore and Australia (two month tour, joined The Queen and The Duke of Edinburgh at the end of their tour) 1963, Italy (visited Florence, Rome and Venice, studying buildings of architectural interest) 1963, Germany and Italy 1964, Greece (for the wedding of King Constantine) 1964, Germany, Austria, Turkey, Syria and Jordan (camping) 1965, Tonga, Fiji, New Guinea, the Philippines, Hong Kong, Japan, Cambodia, Thailand, India, Nepal (as guest of Crown Prince (now King) Birendra), Pakistan, Afghanistan, and Iran 1969, and Nepal (represented The Queen at the wedding of Crown Prince Birendra) 1970.

Prince Richard worked with the Offices Development Group of the Ministry of Public Building and Works 1967-68. He was elected a corporate member of the Royal Institute of British Architects 1972, and at present is practising as a partner in a firm of London architects. He carries out a number of royal engagements, and is especially interested in art and photography. He illustrated *On Public View* (1971).

His Royal Highness married at Barnwell Parish Church, Northants 8 July 1972, Miss Birgitte van Deurs (HRH PRINCESS RICHARD OF GLOUCESTER—*see p* 161).

Arms *see p* 110.

Lineage *see* ROYAL LINEAGE, *p* 185.

Residence Kensington Palace, W8.

Office Kensington Palace, W8.

Tom Hustler

HER ROYAL HIGHNESS PRINCESS RICHARD OF GLOUCESTER

H R H Princess Richard of Gloucester

HER ROYAL HIGHNESS PRINCESS RICHARD OF GLOUCESTER is the younger daughter of Asger Preben Wissing Henriksen, lawyer, of Odense, Denmark, by his former wife Mrs Vivian Marx-Nielsen, of Fruens Bøge, Denmark, daughter of the late Waldemar Oswald van Deurs, of Copenhagen, Denmark. She was born in Odense, Island of Funen, Denmark 20 June 1946 and named Birgitte Eva. She used the surname van Deurs. She was educated in Odense, at Brillantmont, Lausanne, at a language school, Cambridge, the Niels Brock Commercial College, Copenhagen (passed Higher Commercial Examinations 1970), and at a language College, London 1970-71. From 1971 until her marriage she was a secretary at the Royal Danish Embassy, London.

Barry Lategan/Camera Press

HIS ROYAL HIGHNESS THE DUKE OF KENT

The Duke wears the uniform of the Royal Regiment of Fusiliers, the badge, riband and star of the Grand Master of the Order of St Michael and George

HRH The Duke of Kent

HIS ROYAL HIGHNESS PRINCE EDWARD GEORGE NICHOLAS PAUL PATRICK, 2nd DUKE OF KENT, EARL OF ST ANDREWS, and BARON DOWNPATRICK, GCMG, GCVO is the elder son of HRH The late DUKE OF KENT, KG, and HRH The late PRINCESS MARINA, DUCHESS OF KENT (*see* reference to **Lineage** *below*). He was born at 3 Belgrave Square, W1 9 October 1935. and educated at Eton, Le Rosey (Switzerland) and the Royal Military Academy, Sandhurst (awarded the Sir James Moncrieff Grierson foreign languages prize, and passed French interpretership examination). He succeeded his father as 2nd Duke 25 August 1942, and took his seat in the House of Lords 9 December 1959.

He is Grand Master and Knight Grand Cross of the Order of St Michael and St George (1967), Knight Grand Cross of the Royal Victorian Order (1960), has the Order of St George and St Constantine, 1st class, Greece, the Order of Tri Shakta Patta, 1st class with Chain (1960) Nepal, the Grand Band of the Order of the Star of Africa (1962) Liberia, and the Order of Al Nahda, 1st class (1966) Jordan.

His Royal Highness is Colonel-in-Chief of The Royal Regiment of Fusiliers (1969). He is a Major in The Royal Scots Dragoon Guards (Carabiniers and Greys) 1967 (Lieutenant 1955, Captain 1960, attended the Army Staff Course 1966, served on staff in Eastern Command, commanded a squadron of his regiment in Cyprus (United Nations Force) 1970, served in Northern Ireland 1971), Personal ADC to HM The Queen from 1966, and a member of The Honourable Artillery Company (1967). He is hon DCL Durham University (1961), and has the honorary Freedom of Kampala, Uganda (1962), and Georgetown, Guyana (1966), is Freeman and hon Liveryman of the Clothworkers' Company (1958), Freeman and Liveryman of the Salters' Company (1965), and hon Freeman of the Mercers' Company (1972).

The Duke of Kent is Grand Master of the United Grand Lodge of England from 1967 (Freemason 1964). He is President of the Royal Air Force Benevolent Fund, the All England Lawn Tennis and Croquet Club (Wimbledon), the Civil Service Motoring Association, the Royal Choral Society, Commonwealth War Graves Commission, the Football Association, the Royal Geographical Society, the Leukaemia Research Fund, the Royal Masonic Benevolent Institute, the Royal Masonic Hospital, the Royal Masonic Institution for Boys, the Royal Masonic Institution for Girls, the Royal National Lifeboat Institution, and Wellington College. He is Patron of the Army Ski Association, the

Association of Men and Kentish Men, the Buckinghamshire County Show, the Distinguished Conduct Medal League, Iver Fair, the Kandahar Ski Club, Kent County Cricket Club, the Ski Club of Great Britain, and the Society for Army Historical Research.

His Royal Highness has travelled with his regiment and also to undertake royal duties abroad: Switzerland (at school) 1951-53, Finland (joined The Duke of Edinburgh to attend the Olympic Games), Norway and Sweden 1952, Malaya, Singapore, Sarawak, North Borneo, Brunei and Hong Kong (accompanied his mother, The Duchess of Kent) 1952, Greece (attended the funeral of his grand-mother, Princess Nicholas) 1957, Germany (with the Royal Scots Greys) 1958, Sierra Leone (represented The Queen at the Independence celebrations) 1961, Uganda (represented The Queen at the Independence celebrations), Kenya and Tanganyika 1962, Hong Kong (with his regiment) 1962-63, Germany (with his regiment) 1964-65, The Gambia (represented The Queen at the Independence celebrations) 1965, Belgium (attended a ball celebrating the 150th anniversary of the Battle of Waterloo) 1965, Guyana (represented The Queen at the Independence celebrations) 1966, France (opened British Week at Lyons) 1966, Barbados (represented The Queen at the Independence celebrations) 1966, Tonga (represented The Queen at the Coronation of King Taufa'ahau Topou IV), the Cook Islands, Western Samoa and Fiji 1967, Canada (opened the Calgary Stampede and Exhibition) 1968, Switzerland (attended the Kandahar Ski Club races) 1969, Switzerland (represented The Queen at the funeral of Queen Victoria Eugenie of Spain) 1969, India (represented The Queen at the funeral of President Husain) 1969, Australia (visited Canberra, Darwin for its centenary, and toured the North, South and West), Papua, New Guinea (opened the 3rd South Pacific Games), the British Solomon Islands, and the New Hebrides 1969, Cyprus (with his regiment) 1970, Switzerland (attended the Army ski-ing championships) 1971, Denmark (for British Trade Drive) 1972, and the USA (attended premiere of *Young Winston* in New York in aid of Winston Churchill Foundation of the United States) 1972.

The Duke first acted as Counsellor of State in 1957. When he is stationed in England he undertakes certain royal engagements and has deputised for The Queen at an investiture. He is at present employed in the Department of the Master-General of the Ordnance, and is also a Member of the National Electronics Council. He is interested in sport, learned to fly in 1962, and has often captained his regimental ski team. He is interested in electronics and mechanical developments, music and opera, and is also a keen photographer.

His Royal Highness married in York Minster 8 June, 1961, Katharine Lucy Worsley (HRH THE DUCHESS OF KENT—*see p* 167), and has issue,

1 •GEORGE PHILIP NICHOLAS, *Earl of St Andrews,* born at Coppins 26 June 1962, educated at Eton End, PNEU, Datchet, and Heatherdown School, Ascot.

2 •*Lord* Nicholas Charles Edward Jonathan (*Windsor*), born at Coppins 25 July 1970.

1 •*Lady* Helen Marina Lucy (*Windsor*), born at Coppins 28 April 1964, educated at Eton End, PNEU, Datchet, and St Paul's Preparatory School, London.

Arms *see p* 111.

Lineage *see* ROYAL LINEAGE, *p* 185. For Historical Note on the Dukedom of Kent *see* TITLES TRADITIONALLY ASSOCIATED WITH THE ROYAL FAMILY, *p* 336.

Residence York House, St James's Palace, SW1.

Clubs White's; St James's; Boodle's; Travellers' (hon member); Buck's; Naval and Military; Cavalry; RAF; Royal Automobile; Union; New (Edinburgh); Royal Thames Yacht; British Racing Drivers'.

THE EARL OF
ST ANDREWS and
LADY HELEN WINDSOR
(above)

Barry Lategan/Camera Press

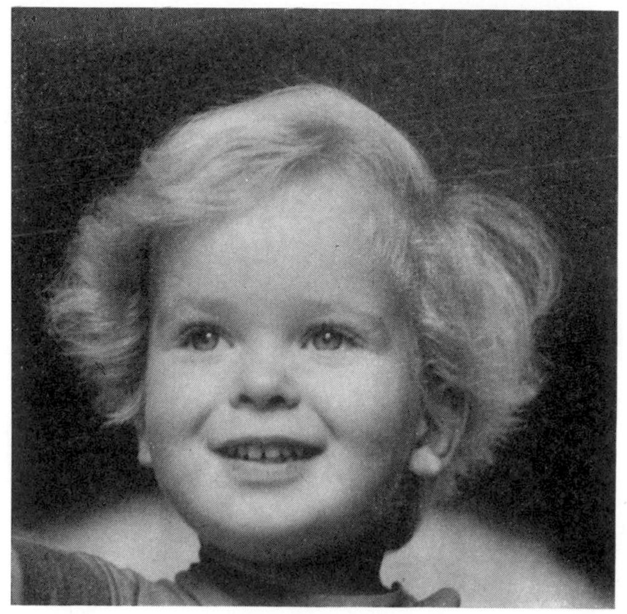

LORD NICHOLAS
WINDSOR (right)

Barry Lategan/Camera Press

HER ROYAL HIGHNESS THE DUCHESS OF KENT

H R H The Duchess of Kent

HER ROYAL HIGHNESS THE DUCHESS OF KENT is the youngest child and only daughter of Colonel Sir William Arthington Worsley, 4th Bt, DL, JP, late The Green Howards, formerly Lord Lieutenant of the North Riding of Yorkshire by his wife Joyce Morgan, only daughter of Sir John Fowler Brunner, 2nd Bt, JP (*see* reference to **Lineage** *below*). She was born 22 February 1933, christened Katharine Lucy Mary, and educated in Yorkshire and at an Oxford finishing school.

Her Royal Highness is Controller Commandant of the Women's Royal Army Corps (with hon rank of Major-General) 1967, Colonel-in-Chief of the Army Catering Corps, hon Colonel of the Yorkshire Volunteers (Territorial and Army Volunteer Reserve), and Air Chief Commandant of the Royal Australian Air Force Nursing Service. She is Chancellor of Leeds University (1965), and has the honorary Freedom of the Companies of Clothworkers (1967), Dyers (1968), and Glaziers (1971).

Her Royal Highness is President of the ATS/WRAC Joint Benevolent Fund, the Distressed Gentlefolk's Aid Association, and the WRAC Association. She is Patron of "Age Concern", the Arthritis and Rheumatism Council for Research in Great Britain and the Commonwealth, the British Epilepsy Association, the Buckinghamshire Branch of the British Red Cross Society, the Buckinghamshire Association of Youth Clubs, the Derwen Training College for the Disabled (Oswestry), the Georgian Theatre (Richmond, Yorkshire), International Social Service of Great Britain, Iver Fair, the Kent Country Playing Fields Association, the Leeds International Pianoforte Competition, the National Society for Cancer Relief, the "Not Forgotten" Association, the Nuffield Orthopaedic Centre (Headington, Oxford), the Robert Jones and Agnes Hunt Orthopaedic Hospital (Oswestry, Shropshire), the Samaritans, St George's Hospital, the Spastics Society, the UK Committee for UNICEF, the York Civic Trust, the York Mystery Plays, the Yorkshire County Cricket Club, and the National Women's Auxiliary of the Young Men's Christian Association, and is a Life member of the Women's Section of the Royal British Legion.

Besides accompanying the Duke on his important overseas engagements and to some of his regimental stationings, Her Royal Highness has also travelled on her own account to: Germany (visited detachments of the Women's Royal Army Corps stationed on the Rhine) 1969, Hong Kong and Singapore (visited units of the Women's Royal Army Corps) 1970, and Canada (opened the United Appeal for Metropolitan Toronto) 1970.

The Duchess of Kent undertakes a large number of royal engagements on her own. She is an accomplished pianist and enjoys riding and country pursuits.

Lineage *see* BURKE'S *Peerage,* WORSLEY, Bt, and BRUNNER, Bt.

Press Association

HIS ROYAL HIGHNESS PRINCE MICHAEL OF KENT

H R H Prince Michael of Kent

HIS ROYAL HIGHNESS PRINCE MICHAEL GEORGE CHARLES FRANKLIN OF KENT is the younger son of HRH THE late DUKE OF KENT, KG and HRH THE late PRINCESS MARINA, DUCHESS OF KENT (*see* reference to **Lineage** *below*). He was born at Coppins 4 July 1942 (the late Franklin D. Roosevelt, 31st President of the USA was sponsor), and educated at Eton, and the Royal Military Academy, Sandhurst.

His Royal Highness trained with the Royal Armoured Corps, Bovington Camp, Dorset and was commissioned into the 11th Hussars (Prince Albert's Own) (now The Royal Hussars (Prince of Wales's Own)) 1963 (Lieutenant 1964, Captain 1968). He commanded a Centurion tank troop 1963-64, underwent a training course at Bovington 1964-66, was posted to the Army School of Education, Wilton Park, Beaconsfield (2nd-class interpretership in Russian) 1966-68, was appointed to the Foreign Liaison Section (Army) at the Ministry of Defence 1968, took the Junior Command and Staff Course, Warminster 1970, spent six months with the United Nations Forces in Cyprus (UNFICYP) 1971, and is currently serving with his regiment at Tidworth, Wiltshire. He is a member of The Honourable Artillery Company (1967) and hon Liveryman of the Worshipful Company of Clothworkers (1968).

Prince Michael's overseas visits include Italy, Greece and Germany, Greece (attended the funeral of his grandmother, Princess Nicholas) 1957, Norway (with Eton College Cadet Corps) 1960, Libya, Cyprus and France (with Sandhurst cadets) 1961/62, Germany (served with his regiment) 1963/66, France (completed his Army Russian Language Course) 1967, Japan (as a competitor in The International Winter Sports at Sapporo) 1971, and Switzerland (as reserve for his regimental ski team, competed in the bobsleigh championships at St Moritz 1966, 1967, 1969, and 1971, and won the British bobsleigh championship 1972).

Prince Michael is interested in mechanics, and learnt to fly in 1962 (he took part in the *Daily Mail* transatlantic air race 1969, and the London to Mexico World Cup Rally 1970). He has also sailed regularly at Cowes since 1959 and is an hon member of the Royal Yacht Squadron (1972). Prince Michael participates in certain State occasions, but undertakes no royal engagements of his own.

Arms *see p* 112.

Lineage *see* ROYAL LINEAGE, *p* 185.

Residence Kensington Palace, W8.

Cecil Beaton

HER ROYAL HIGHNESS PRINCESS ALEXANDRA, THE HONOURABLE MRS ANGUS OGILVY

H R H Princess Alexandra
The Hon Mrs Angus Ogilvy

HER ROYAL HIGHNESS PRINCESS ALEXANDRA HELEN ELIZABETH OLGA CHRISTABEL, THE HONOURABLE MRS ANGUS OGILVY, GCVO, is the only daughter of HRH THE late DUKE OF KENT, KG and HRH THE late PRINCESS MARINA, DUCHESS OF KENT (*see* reference to **Lineage** *below*). She was born at 3 Belgrave Square, W1 25 December 1936, educated at Heathfield, in Paris, and took a short nursing course at the Great Ormond Hospital for Sick Children, WC 1.

Her Royal Highness is Dame Grand Cross of the Royal Victorian Order (1960), and has the Order of the Aztec Eagle, 1st class (1959) Mexico, Grand Cross of the Order of the Sun (1959) Peru, Grand Cross of the Order of Merit (1959) Chile, Grand Cross of the Order of the Southern Cross (1959) Brazil, the Order of the Sacred Crown, 1st class (1962) Japan, Grand Cross of the Order of the White Rose (1969) Finland, and Grand Cross of the Order of the Oak Crown (1972) Luxembourg.

The Princess is Colonel-in-Chief of 17th/21st Lancers (1969), and 3rd Militia Battalion, The Queen's Own Rifles of Canada (1970), Deputy Colonel-in-Chief of The Light Infantry (1968), hon Colonel of the North Irish Horse (T) (1957), hon Commandant-General of the Royal Hong Kong Police Force (1969) and the Royal Hong Kong Auxiliary Police Force (1969), and hon Commandant of the Women's Royal Australian Naval Service (1969).

Princess Alexandra is Chancellor of Lancaster University (1964), is hon LLD of Queensland University (1961) and Hong Kong University (1961), has hon Freedom of the Clothworkers' Company (1961), and is hon Fellow of the Royal College of Physicians and Surgeons of Glasgow (1960), the Faculty of Anaesthetists in the Royal College of Surgeons of England (1967), and the Royal College of Obstetricians and Gynaecologists (1969).

Her Royal Highness is President of Alexandra Day (1969), the Queen Alexandra's House Association (1956), the Children's Country Holidays Fund (1957), the Royal Commonwealth Society for the Blind (1960), the Star and Garter Home for Disabled Sailors, Soldiers and Airmen (1964), and the British School at Rome (1969), and Vice-President of the British Red Cross Society (1965).

The Princess also Patron and Air Chief Commandant of Princess Mary's Royal Air Force Nursing Service, Patron of Alexandra House (Newquay), the Bethlam Royal and Maudsley Hospitals, the British Junior Red Cross, the Canadian Junior Red Cross, the Australian Junior Red Cross, Central School of Speech and Drama, Cystic Fibrosis Research Trust, the Durham Light Infantry Association, Ernest Read Music Association, Friends of the Osborne and Lillian H. Smith Collections (Toronto), Girls Venture Corps and Scottish Girls Training Corps, the Guide Dogs for the Blind Association, the Light

Infantry Club, the London Academy of Music and Dramatic Art, London Association for the Blind, the Motor and Cycle Trades Benevolent Fund, National Association for Mental Health, the National Birthday Trust, National Florence Nightingale Memorial Committee of Great Britain and Northern Ireland, National Heart Hospital, the National Kidney Research Fund, the New Bridge, the Poor Clergy Relief Corporation, Royal Alexandra Hospital for Sick Children (Brighton), the Companions of the Royal Commonwealth Society, the Twentieth Century Group of the Royal Over-Seas League, the Royal Soldiers' Daughters' School (Hampstead), Scottish Artists' Benevolent Association, the Tavistock Clinic, Queen Alexandra's Royal Naval Nursing Service, Vice-Patron of the YWCA, and a temporary Governor of King Edward's Hospital Fund for London.

Her Royal Highness was a Counsellor of State in 1959, and has visited France 1953-54, Canada and the USA (accompanied her mother, The Duchess of Kent on her tour) 1954, Greece (attended the funeral of her grandmother, Princess Nicholas 1957), South America (accompanied her mother, The Duchess of Kent on her tour of Latin America, visited Mexico, Peru, Chile and Brazil) 1959, Australia (visited Queensland for centenary celebrations, and made a tour), Thailand, Cambodia, India, Iran and Turkey 1959, Germany (visited 2nd Battalion, The Queen's Own Rifles of Canada) 1960, Nigeria (represented The Queen at the Independence celebrations) 1960, Canada, Honolulu, Wake Island, Hong Kong (for 50th Anniversary of the University), Japan, Burma, Thailand, Aden and Tripoli 1961, the Netherlands (for the silver wedding celebrations of Queen Juliana and Prince Bernhard) 1962, Sweden (opened the British Trade Fair) 1962, Greece (bridesmaid at Princess Sophie's marriage to Don Juan Carlos of Spain) 1962, France 1965, Japan (for the British Exhibition), Hong Kong, Iran (as guest of the Shah), Jordan (as guest of King Hussein), Jerusalem, and Malta 1965, the Netherlands (witness at the wedding of Princess Beatrix) 1966, Burma, Hong Kong, Australia, Canada (opened British Columbia international trade fair, and made extensive tour) 1967, Sweden (opened British Petroleum's new refinery at Gothenburg) 1967, the USA (opened British Fortnight in Dallas), and Canada (for British Week in Toronto) 1967, Sweden (opened British Week) 1968, Singapore (represented The Queen during 150th Anniversary celebrations of the founding of modern Singapore) 1969, Kenya, Swaziland (for the first anniversary of independence), Malagasy Republic and Mauritius 1969, Austria (opened British Week in Vienna) 1969, Sweden (named a tanker built for the World Wide Shipping Group) 1970, the USA (opened the new British Overseas Airways Corporation passenger terminal at Kennedy Airport) 1970, Argentina (opened the British Industrial Exhibition as Patron) 1970, New Zealand (for the centenary celebrations of Auckland, visited Napier and Wellington) 1971, the USA (visited San Francisco for the opening of British Week, and Los Angeles) 1971, Germany (visited regiments, and presented new colours to 1st Battalion, The Light Infantry on behalf of The Queen) 1972, Afghanistan (as guest of Princess Bilqis) and Hong Kong (visited the Royal Hong Kong Police Force, and the Royal Hong Kong Auxiliary Police Force) 1972.

Princess Alexandra enjoys a wide variety of music and plays the piano. Her interests include travel, ski-ing, swimming and other outdoor recreations.

Her Royal Highness married at Westminster Abbey 24 April 1963, HON ANGUS JAMES BRUCE OGILVY (*see p* 175), and has issue,

- James Robert Bruce (*Ogilvy*), born at Thatched House Lodge, Richmond 29 February 1964.
- Marina Victoria Alexandra (*Ogilvy*), born at Thatched House Lodge, Richmond 31 July 1966.

Arms *see p* 113.
Lineage *see* ROYAL LINEAGE, *p* 185.
Residence Thatched House Lodge, Richmond Park, Surrey.
Office Kensington Palace, W8.

JAMES OGILVY

Central Press

MARINA OGILVY

Norman Parkinson

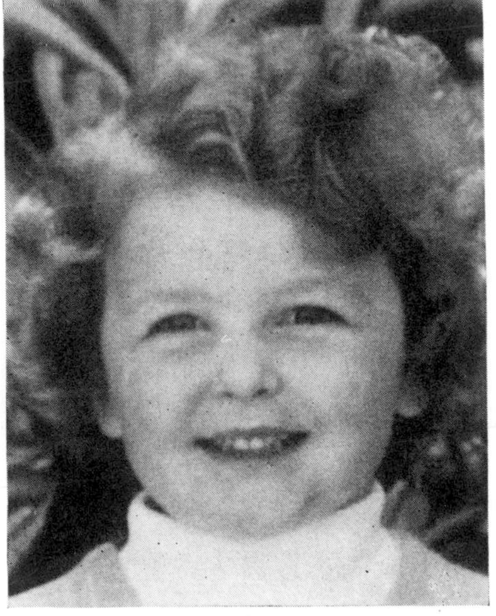

Cecil Beaton

THE HONOURABLE ANGUS OGILVY

The Honourable Angus Ogilvy

THE HONOURABLE ANGUS JAMES BRUCE OGILVY, husband of HRH PRINCESS ALEXANDRA, is the 2nd son of the 12th Earl of Airlie, KT, GCVO, MC, formerly Lord Lieutenant of Angus, by his wife Lady Alexandra Marie Bridget, younger daughter of 3rd Earl of Leicester, GCVO, CMG (*see* reference to **Lineage** *below*). He was born 14 September 1928 and educated at Eton, and Trinity College, Oxford (BA 1950).

Mr Ogilvy is Grand Officer of the Order of the Lion (1969) Finland, and the Order of the Oak Crown (1972) Luxembourg. He is Freeman and Liveryman of the Worshipful Companies of Goldsmiths (1964), and Tallow Chandlers (1964). Mr Ogilvy was commissioned in the Scots Guards 1946 (Captain Reserve of Officers from 1948), and is a member of the Royal Company of Archers (The Queen's Body Guard for Scotland) (1958). He is President of the British Rheumatism and Arthritis Association, the Imperial Cancer Research Fund, the National Association of Youth Clubs, and the Scottish Wildlife Trust, Vice-President of the Friends of the Poor and Gentlefolk's Help and Vice-Patron of Toc H.

He is Chairman of the Investment Trusts of the Drayton Group, and a Director of the Canadian Imperial Bank of Commerce, Clive Holdings Ltd, Guardian Royal Exchange Assurance Ltd, Metropolitan Estate and Property Corporation Ltd, Midland Bank Ltd, Rank Organization Ltd, and Robeco, and a member of the Council of the Institute of Directors.

Mr Ogilvy assists Princess Alexandra in her engagements whenever possible, and has accompanied her on most of her foreign visits.

Arms *see* BURKE'S *Peerage,* AIRLIE, E.

Lineage *see* BURKE'S *Peerage,* AIRLIE, E, and LEICESTER, E.

Club White's.

Yevonde

HER ROYAL HIGHNESS PRINCESS ALICE, COUNTESS OF ATHLONE

H R H Princess Alice Countess of Athlone

HER ROYAL HIGHNESS PRINCESS ALICE, COUNTESS OF ATHLONE, VA, GCVO, GBE is the only daughter of HRH PRINCE LEOPOLD GEORGE DUNCAN ALBERT, 1ST DUKE OF ALBANY, KG (4th son of HM QUEEN VICTORIA), by his wife Princess Helen Frederica Augusta, daughter of HSH Reigning Prince George Victor of Waldeck and Pyrmont (*see* reference to **Lineage** *below*). She was born at Windsor Castle 25 February 1883, and educated privately. She married in St George's Chapel, Windsor 10 February 1904, HSH PRINCE ALEXANDER OF TECK, later Major-General The Right Honourable the EARL OF ATHLONE, KG, PC, GCB, GCMG, GCVO, DSO, FRS (*see* ROYAL LINEAGE, *p* 293). He died at Kensington Palace 16 January 1957.

Her Royal Highness is a Lady of the Order of Victoria and Albert (1898), Dame Grand Cross of the Royal Victorian Order (1948), Dame Grand Cross of the Order of the British Empire (1937), Dame Grand Cross of the Order of St John of Jerusalem (1926) (Dame of Justice 1904), Dame Grand Cross of the Order of Christ (1918) Portugal, and Dame Grand Cross of the Legion of Honour (1945) France.

Princess Alice is Commandant-in-Chief of the Women's Transport Service (FANY) from 1940, and was formerly hon Air Commandant RCAF, and hon Commandant WRCNS. She was Chancellor of the University of the West Indies 1950-71, and has the following honorary degrees: DLitt London (1933), Queen's University of Kingston (Ontario) (1943), McGill (1944), Birmingham (1946), and St Andrews (1951). She has the honorary Freedom of the Royal Borough of Kensington (1961), the Weavers' Company (1947) and the Vintners' Company (1956).

Her Royal Highness is President of the National Children's Adoption Association (1917), the Deptford Fund (succeeded her mother 1922), the King Edward VII District Nursing Association (also in South Africa 1924-30), and the Royal School of Needlework. She was Chairman of the Soldiers', Sailors' and Airmen's Families Association, and the War Pensions Fund during World War I, and also served in the Forestry Corps Canteen (Windsor Great Park) and the Hayes Munition Canteen. She was Chairman of the Governors of the Royal Holloway College 1936-58 (now a member of the Governing Body), and was 1st President of the Women's Section of the British Legion 1918-23. Her Royal Highness was President of the Royal Victoria League for Commonwealth Friendship 1931-71, and The Queen's Institute of District Nursing 1957-68.

Besides numerous private visits to relatives in Europe (most often to her brother, the Duke of Coburg 1899-1903, and 1948), Her Royal Highness has travelled extensively, to Colombo, Malaya, Singapore and Siam (Lord Athlone represented HM King George V at the coronation of The King of Siam) 1911-12, South Africa (Lord Athlone was Governor General, Commander-in-Chief and High Commissioner, received HRH The Prince of Wales (later Duke of Windsor), and toured parts of the Union each year) 1924-30, Rhodesia, Uganda (made safari), Egypt, Palestine and Turkey (five months journey back to England) 1931, South Africa (founded The Princess Alice Orthopaedic Hospital at Musenburg, near Cape Town) 1930, the USA, the Bahamas and Antigua 1933, India 1934, Egypt and Arabia 1938, Canada (Lord Athlone was Governor General of the Dominion, visited the USA as guests of President Roosevelt 1940, toured parts of Canada regularly and acted as hosts to President Roosevelt and Mr Winston Churchill at the Quebec Conferences 1943 and 1944) 1940-45, the USA, Nassau and Trinidad (journey back to England) 1946, South Africa (on invitation of Field Marshal Smuts) 1948, the Netherlands (for the enthronement of Queen Juliana) 1948, and the West Indies (for installation as Chancellor of the University College) 1950. Since 1950 Princess Alice visited the West Indies each year until 1971 (except 1957) (she received The Queen and The Duke of Edinburgh at the University 1966), she visited Germany (for the funeral of her sister-in-law, the Duchess of Coburg) 1970, and revisited South Africa for two months 1972.

Her Royal Highness, who is The Queen's great-aunt, was present at the Diamond Jubilee celebrations of HM Queen Victoria 1897, and has attended four Coronations. She takes an active interest in all the organisations with which she is connected. Her other interests include gardening and needlework. Princess Alice published her memoirs *For My Grandchildren* 1966.

Her Royal Highness has had issue (*see* ROYAL LINEAGE, *p.* 294).

Arms *see p* 114.

Lineage *see* ROYAL LINEAGE, *p* 185.

Residence Clock Tower, Kensington Palace, W8.

H R H The late Duke of Windsor

HIS late ROYAL HIGHNESS THE PRINCE EDWARD ALBERT CHRISTIAN GEORGE ANDREW PATRICK DAVID, DUKE OF WINDSOR, KG, KT, KP, GCB, GCSI, GCMG, GCIE, GCVO, GBE, ISO, MC, formerly HIS MAJESTY KING EDWARD VIII, was the eldest son of HM KING GEORGE V and HM QUEEN MARY (*see* reference to **Lineage** *below*). He was born at White Lodge, Richmond Park 23 June 1894 (baptised 16 July), educated privately, and subsequently at the Royal Naval Colleges Osborne and Dartmouth, and Magdalen College, Oxford (matriculated 1912).

On the accession of his father, HM King George V, to the Throne, 6 May 1910, His Royal Highness became DUKE OF CORNWALL, *in the Peerage of England* in accordance with the charter of 17 March 1337, and became DUKE OF ROTHESAY, EARL OF CARRICK, and BARON OF RENFREW, *in the Peerage of Scotland,* LORD OF THE ISLES and GREAT STEWARD OF SCOTLAND. His Royal Highness was created PRINCE OF WALES and EARL OF CHESTER 2 June 1910, and a Knight of the Garter 1910 (invested and installed 1911). He was invested by HM King George V, with the insignia of Prince of Wales and Earl of Chester at Caernarvon Castle 13 July 1911. He took his seat in the House of Lords 19 February 1918. His Royal Highness was appointed a Knight of the Thistle 1922, a Knight of St Patrick 1927, an extra Knight Grand Cross of the Order of the Bath 1936, an extra Knight Grand Commander of the Order of the Star of India 1921, a Knight Grand Cross of the Order of St Michael and St George 1917 (Grand Master 1917-36), an extra Knight Grand Commander of the Order of the Indian Empire 1921, a Knight Grand Cross of the Royal Victorian Order 1920, Knight Grand Cross of the Order of the British Empire 1917 (Grand Master and first or principal Knight 1917-36), a member of the Imperial Service Order 1937, Bailiff Grand Cross of the Order of St John of Jerusalem 1926 (Knight of Justice 1917, and Prior for Wales until 1936), received the Royal Victorian Chain 1921, and was introduced into the Privy Council 1920, and the Privy Council of Canada 1927. He also received the Order of the Golden Fleece (1912) Spain, Grand Cross of the Legion of Honour (1912) France, the Order of the Elephant (1914) Denmark, Grand Cross of the Order of St Olav with chain (1914) Norway, the Order of the Annunziata (1915) Italy, the Order of St George (1916) Russia, the Order of Michael the Brave (1918) Roumania, the Grand Cordon of the Order of Mohamed Ali (1922) Egypt, Knight of the Order of the Seraphim (1923) Sweden, the Collar of the Order of Carol (1924) Roumania, the Order of Merit, 1st class (1925) Chile, the Order of the Sun (1931) Peru, Grand Cross of the Condor of the Andes (1931) Bolivia, the United Orders of Christ and Aviz (1931) Portugal, Grand Cross of the Order of the Southern Cross (1933) Brazil, and Grand Cross of the Order of Knighthood of St Agatha (1935) San Marino. He was an Admiral in the Royal Danish Navy and a General in the Japanese Army.

He was Admiral of the Fleet 1936 (Midshipman 1911, Lieutenant 1913, Captain 1929, Vice-Admiral 1930), and Master of the Merchant Navy and Fishing Fleets 1928-36. He was a Field Marshal in the Army 1936, and as Prince of Wales, Colonel of Welsh Guards (1919), Colonel-in-Chief of 12th Royal Lancers (Prince of Wales's) (1919), The Royal Scots Fusiliers (1919), The South Wales Borderers (1922), The Duke of Cornwall's Light Infantry (1919), The Prince of Wales's Volunteers (South Lancashire) (1923), The Middlesex Regiment (Duke of Cambridge's Own) (1921), The Seaforth Highlanders (Ross-shire Buffs, The Duke of Albany's) (1920), The Royal Wiltshire Yeomanry (Prince of Wales's Own) (1919), The Toronto Regiment, Canadian Militia, 14th Prince of Wales's Own Scinde Horse, 17th Dogra Regiment, 6th Rajputana Rifles, 12th Frontier Force Regiment, 8th Punjab Regiment, and 4th Prince of Wales's Own Gurkha Rifles, hon Colonel of the 5th (Prince of Wales's) Battalion, The Devonshire Regiment (Territorial) (1919), 4th/5th (Earl of Chester's) Battalion, The Cheshire Regiment (1917), 16th Battalion London Regiment (Queen's Westminster and Civil Service Rifles) (1919), Oxford University Contingent of the Senior Division, Officers Training Corps (1934), 3rd Prince of Wales's Canadian Dragoons, and The Ceylon Light Infantry, and Colonel of The Ceylon Planters' Rifle Corps. He was Marshal of the Royal Air Force 1936 (Group Captain 1922, Air Marshal 1930, Air Chief Marshal 1935), and hon Air Commodore-in-Chief of Auxiliary Air Force 1932-36. On his accession to the Throne, he became Colonel-in-Chief of The Life Guards, Royal Horse Guards (The Blues), Royal Regiment of Artillery, Corps of Royal Engineers, Grenadier Guards, Coldstream Guards, Scots Guards, Irish Guards, Welsh Guards, Canadian Grenadier Guards, The Seaforth Highlanders of Canada, Lord Strathcona's Horse (Royal Canadians), Royal Canadian Artillery, Royal Canadian Engineers, Australian Infantry, Queen Alexandra's (Wellington West Coast) Mounted Rifles, Regiment of New Zealand Artillery, Auckland Regiment (Countess of Ranfurly's Own), 1st and 2nd Mounted Rifles (Natal Carabiniers), Transvaal Scottish 8th Infantry Regiment, Imperial Light Horse, Ceylon Defence Force, Royal West African Frontier Force, and The King's African Rifles, and Captain-General of Honourable Artillery Company. He served in World War I in France and Italy with 1st Battalion, Grenadier Guards (Lieutenant 1914, Captain 1916, temporary Major 1918, Colonel 1919, Lieutenant-General 1930, General 1935, ADC to the Commander-in-Chief British Expeditionary Force 1914, on active service, Staff Captain Deputy Assistant Quartermaster-General and General Staff Officer (2nd Grade) 1916, Military Cross (1916), War Cross (1915) France, and War Merit Cross (1919) Italy). His Royal Highness was Personal ADC to HM King George V 1919-36.

His Royal Highness was an Elder Brother of Trinity House from 1919, Freemason in the Household Brigade Lodge, Senior Grand Warden of the United Grand Lodge of Ancient and Accepted Masons of England, Provincial Grand Master of Surrey 1924-36 and Grand Supernumerary of Royal Arch Masonry for Surrey (1930), High Steward of Windsor 1918-36, Plymouth 1919-36, Chancellor of the University of Wales 1920-36, and had the following honorary degrees: LLD Edinburgh (1919), Toronto (1919), Alberta (1919), Queen's University (Kingston, Canada) (1919), Cambridge (1921), Calcutta (1921), St Andrews (1922), Hong Kong (1922), and Witwatersrand (South Africa) (1925), DCL Oxford (1921), DSc and hon Master of Commerce London 1921, and DLitt Benares 1921. He received the hon Freedom of London 1919, Plymouth

1919, Windsor 1919, and Rothesay 1933, was 1st Master of the Honourable Company of Master Mariners 1928-36 (Admiral 1936), hon Freeman of the Worshipful Company of Fishmongers (1919), Mercers (1919), Goldsmiths (1920), Musicians (1921), Merchant Taylors (1921), Stationers and Newspaper Makers (Liveryman 1933, Master 1934-36), and Gardeners (1935), hon Licentiate in Medicine and Surgery, Society of Apothecaries (1926), and Fellow of the Royal Society (1919), hon Fellow of the Royal College of Surgeons of England (1919), the Royal College of Physicians of Edinburgh (1919), and the Royal Institute of British Architects (1921), hon member of the Institute of Civil Engineers (1919), a Master of the Bench of Middle Temple 1919, and Captain of the Royal and Ancient Golf Club, St Andrews 1922-23.

He was Grand President of the League of Mercy 1919-39, Chairman of the Royal Patriotic Fund 1916-36, and King George's Jubilee Trust 1935-36, Governor of Wellington College 1918-36, Governor and President of St Bartholomew's Hospital 1919-37, Trustee of the British Museum 1919-36, and the National Gallery 1930-36, and President of Westminster Hospital 1915-36, the Royal College of Music 1918-36, King Edward's Hospital Fund for London 1918-36, the King Edward VII Hospital Fund for Officers 1919-36, the Royal National Lifeboat Institution 1919-36, the British Empire Exhibition 1924, the British Association 1926, the British Legion 1919-36, the Royal Society for Prevention of Cruelty to Animals, Housing Association for Officers' Families, and the National Council of Social Service 1928-36, hon President of the Royal Statistical Society 1921-36, Patron of Toc H, the Lord Mayor of London's Fund for Distressed Miners, and the Feathers Association, and Chief Scout for Wales 1911-36.

As Prince of Wales, His Royal Highness travelled extensively, his first visit being to Denmark 1898, then to France (four-month educational visit) 1912, Germany (as guest of King Wilhelm of Wurttemburg, visited Count Zeppelin) 1913, Germany (as guest of Grand Duke Adolphus of Mecklenburg-Strelitz, visited Prince Henry of Prussia, the Duke of Saxe-Coburg-Gotha, and Emperor William II) 1913, Denmark and Norway 1914, France (on active service) 1914-18, Egypt (inspected defences of the Suez Canal) 1916, Italy 1917, Germany, France and Belgium (visited British Army Units) 1919, Canada (three month tour) and the USA (visited President Wilson) 1919, Barbados, San Diego (California), Honolulu, Fiji, New Zealand (month's tour), Australia (two month tour), Fiji, Samoa, Honolulu, Acapulco, the West Indies, and Bermuda (in total 46,000 mile journey) 1920, Gibraltar, Malta, Aden, India (four month tour), Ceylon, Malaya, Singapore, Hong Kong, Japan, (month's return visit to Prince Regent Hirohito) Manila, North Borneo, Penang, and Egypt (visited King Fuad) 1921-22, Belgium 1923, Canada 1923, the USA (visited President Calvin Coolidge) and Canada 1924, Gambia, Sierra Leone, the Gold Coast, Nigeria, South Africa (three month tour), South America 1925, France, Spain (as guest of King Alfonso) and Canada (attended celebrations of the Diamond Jubilee of the Confederation and made five week tour) 1927, Kenya (with The Duke of Gloucester), Uganda, Tanganyika (on safari) 1928, South Africa, Kenya, Uganda the Sudan, Egypt (on safari) 1930, Jamaica, South America (visited Peru, Bolivia, the Argentine and Brazil (trade mission) and opened British Empire Exhibition in Buenos Aires) 1931, Greece and Malta (visited the Mediterranean Fleet) 1932, Denmark (opened the Anglo-Danish Exposition), Sweden (visited King Gustav V), Germany and the Netherlands 1932, Portugal, Majorca, Italy and Switzerland 1934, Austria, Hungary and France (two visits) 1935; as King, France (inaugurated Canadian war memorial at Vimy Ridge) 1936, and Turkey, Bulgaria, Yugoslavia and Austria (semi-official visits during his summer holidays) 1936.

His Royal Highness acted as Counsellor of State during King George V's illness 1928-29, and during his final illness 1936. He ascended the Throne as **KING EDWARD**

Karsh of Ottawa/Camera Press

THE DUKE AND DUCHESS OF WINDSOR

VIII of Great Britain, Ireland, and the British Dominions beyond the seas, and Emperor of India 20 January 1936, when his honours created by Patent merged with the crown. On 10 December 1936, confirmed by the Declaration of Abdication Act on the following day, he renounced the throne for himself and his descendants, and was succeeded by his brother, HRH The Duke of York. He was created DUKE OF WINDSOR in the Peerage of the United Kingdom, by Letters Patent 8 March 1937, and the title of Royal Highness was reconferred for himself only and not for his wife or descendants if any, by Letters Patent 27 May 1937. His Royal Highness temporarily relinquished the rank of Field Marshal, and assumed that of Major-General 1939, and served on Staff as liaison officer at the French Army General Headquarters. He was Governor and Commander-in-Chief of the Bahama Islands 1940-45. He married at the Chateau de Candé, Monts, France 3 June 1937, Mrs Wallis Warfield (THE DUCHESS OF WINDSOR—*see p* 184).

The Duke of Windsor gave many years of devoted service to the Crown and his extensive travelling brought the monarchy close to many parts of the British Empire, besides boosting trade. In England he undertook the normal royal engagements, and also undertook a number of visits to the unemployed in industrial areas. After his abdication he lived mainly in France and always spent part of the spring in the USA. He published his memoirs *A King's Story* (1951) (made into a film by Jack Le Vien with the co-operation of the Duke and Duchess 1965), *The Crown and The People 1902-1953* (1953), and *A Family Album* (1960). An interview with the Duke and Duchess by Kenneth Harris was shown on BBC Television 1970. The Duke and Duchess visited England privately on a number of occasions. Their first public engagement in England since the abdication was the Memorial Service for HRH The Princess Royal in Westminster Abbey 1 April 1965. They subsequently attended the unveiling of a plaque to HM Queen Mary at Marlborough House with The Queen and other members of the Royal Family 7 June 1967. His Royal Highness last visited England to attend the funeral of HRH Princess Marina, Duchess of Kent at Windsor 30 August 1968. In his youth, the Duke enjoyed point-to-pointing, hunting and flying (he first flew 1916, made his first solo flight December 1929, and owned a De Havilland Gypsy Moth), and his other interests included golf and gardening.

On 5 October 1971, The Duke and Duchess of Windsor received Emperor Hirohito and Empress Nagako of Japan at their home on the Emperor's request, and The Queen, The Duke of Edinburgh and The Prince of Wales visited the Duke and Duchess during their State Visit to France, 18 May 1972.

His Royal Highness died at his Paris home 28 May 1972, and after Lying-in-State in St George's Chapel, Windsor, he was buried in the Royal Family's private burial ground at Frogmore 5 June 1972.

Arms *see p* 115.

Lineage *see* ROYAL LINEAGE, *p* 185.

The Duchess of Windsor

THE DUCHESS OF WINDSOR, widow of HRH THE DUKE OF WINDSOR, KG (*see p* 179), is the only child of Teackle Wallis Warfield (died 1896), of Baltimore, Maryland, by his wife Alice (who married secondly 1908, John Freeman Rasin, of Baltimore, Maryland (died 4 April 1913); and thirdly 1923, Charles Gordon Allen, of Washington, and died 2 November 1929), daughter of William Montague, of Virginia. She was born at Blue Ridge Summit, Monterey, Pennsylvania 19 June 1896 and christened (Bessie) Wallis.

She married first 8 November 1916 (marriage dissolved by divorce 1927), Lieutenant (later Captain) Earl Winfield Spencer, Jr, USN, of Chicago. He died at San Diego 29 May 1950. She married secondly, as his second wife, 21 July 1928 (marriage dissolved by divorce 1936), Ernest Aldrich Simpson, son of Ernest Louis Simpson, of New York, USA. He died in London 30 November 1958. She resumed by Deed Poll her maiden name of WARFIELD 7 May 1937, and married thirdly 3 June 1937, HRH THE DUKE OF WINDSOR, KG. He died 28 May 1972.

During World War II, the Duchess joined the Colis de Trianon relief organization and the Section Sanitaire of the French Red Cross. When the Duke was Governor of the Bahamas, she worked with the Red Cross and organized a canteen for the Royal Air Force. Fashion was an interest she shared with the Duke, and she is also interested in interior decorating. The Duchess was named first woman Governor of the American Hospital in Paris 1972, and published her memoirs *The Heart Has Its Reasons* 1956. **Residence** 4 Route du Champ D'Entrainement, Paris XVIe, France.

The Royal Lineage

Compiled by David Williamson and Jeffrey Finestone

Introduction

This section comprises as accurate and complete an account as possible of the Royal Lineage. An attempt has been made for the first time to give the places of birth, marriage, death and burial of every individual member with the exception of the descendants in the female line from King George II. Among entirely new features in the Royal Lineage are accounts of the Saxon Kings of Wessex before Egbert, of the Kings and Princes of Wales, and of the direct male line ancestry of HRH The Duke of Edinburgh. It is hoped, too, that the inclusion of all the descendants of King George II will greatly add to the interest and general utility of the work as a whole.

Burke's usual narrative style of pedigree has been followed and will be familiar to most readers. A new departure is the indication by the use of italics of the usual christian name by which an individual is known—a very necessary procedure when one considers that some continental families have been in the habit of bestowing as many as twenty names upon each of their children. Also, from the time of George II royal styles and titles and dynastic or family names are given at each entry. In this connection it should be mentioned that for all reigning or formerly reigning families the word "of" has been used (*e.g.* Prince of Schleswig-Holstein), but for other families the words "von", "zu", "de", etc, have not been translated (*e.g.* Prince zu Hohenlohe-Langenburg). The only exceptions to this rule are the Princes of Battenberg and the Princes and Dukes of Teck, families which have become so closely allied to the British Royal Family that it would be wrong to give them a German style. In the cases where male members of certain German families have contracted marriages which do not conform to the requirements of the house laws of the families concerned, and therefore convey no rank or status to the wives or children of such a marriage, the title of *Prinz* (or *Prinzessin*) has been shown in parentheses before the names of the children without any qualification.

It is interesting to note that every Sovereign now reigning in Europe, with two exceptions (the Princes of Liechtenstein and Monaco), is a descendant of King George II, as well as the heads of many families which were reigning until 1918 and the heads of the Balkan kingdoms of Bulgaria, Roumania and Yugoslavia who were reigning until the last World War or shortly after. A common descent of all the reigning Sovereigns of Europe, including the Princes of Liechtenstein and Monaco, is shown in the table in the Appendices (*p* 338).

It has never been *Burke*'s practice to cite the authority for every statement made in its pages, but some mention should be made of those works which have been principally consulted and found most useful in the compilation of the Royal Lineage. H. M. Lane's *The Royal Daughters of England* (1910) and Professor F. M. Powicke's *Handbook of British Chronology* (1939) have been invaluable throughout. G.E.C.'s *Complete Peerage, The Dictionary of National Biography,* Sir John Edward Lloyd's *History of Wales,* and *The Dictionary of Welsh Biography* have also been extremely useful, while for the descendants of George II Mr A. C. Addington's monumental work *The Royal House of Stuart* and the series of genealogical handbooks published by the firm of C. A. Starke have also proved to be of great value.

It remains to express gratitude for the contributions of those persons without whom the Royal Lineage would not be the full and up-to-date record it is ventured to claim that it is. First and foremost to the people shown in the pedigrees who so readily supplied facts and dates when requested to do so; then to Miss Monica Andrew, Miss Carole Brown, Mr T. Y. Cocks, Major Francis Jones, Wales Herald Extraordinary, Mr Charles Kidd, Sir Iain Moncreiffe of that Ilk, Bt, Albany Herald, Mr Felix Pryor, Mr T. W. E. Roche and Mr Hugo Vickers, all of whom made valuable additions or gave advice and encouragement.

The Anglo-Saxon Kingdoms

The English settlement dates traditionally from 449 when Hengest and Horsa were invited by the British King Vortigern to assist in repelling the Picts and Scots, whose raids had become more frequent after the withdrawal of the Romans early in the fifth century. A wave of Angle, Jute and Saxon invaders followed and kingdoms were established throughout the land. The pedigrees of the Kings of Kent, Wessex, Bernicia, East Anglia, Essex, Deira, Mercia and Lindsey, as recorded in the Anglo-Saxon Chronicle and by Bede and other historians, all derive from Woden, a mythical God-King, and have been critically examined by Mr Kenneth Sisam (see his "Anglo-Saxon Royal Genealogies" in *The Proceedings of the British Academy,* Volume XXXIX, 1953). The Kingdom of the West Saxons (or Wessex) finally became pre-dominant and absorbed the other kingdoms, and as its Kings are the direct ancestors of our present Royal Family they alone are dealt with here. Descents from some of the other royal families (notably those of Kent and Mercia), although highly probable, cannot be established with any degree of certainty.

The Kings of Wessex

519-534 CERDIC, King of Wessex; son of Elesa, son of Esla, son of Gewis, son of Wig, son of Freawine, son of Frithugar, son of Brand, son of Baeldaeg, son of Woden (according to the *Anglo-Saxon Chronicle*); said to have come to Britain with his son Cynric and five ships 495, obtained the kingdom of the West Saxons 519, obtained possession of IoW 530, and *d* 534, leaving issue,

534-560 CYNRIC, King of Wessex (according to some authorities son of Creoda, son of Cerdic), appears to have reigned jtly with his father (or grandfather ?) and to have *s* him 534. He gave the Isle of Wight to his (or Cerdic's) two *nefan* (grandsons or nephews) Stuf and Wihtgar. Cynric *d* 560, leaving issue,

1 CEAWLIN, *s* his father.
2 Cutha, fought against the Britons with his brother King Ceawlin and was *k* in battle at *Fethanleag,* nr Stoke-Lyne, Oxon 584, leaving issue,
1 CEOL, or CEOLRIC, reigned jtly with his uncle King Ceawlin and *s* him.
2 CEOLWULF, *s* his brother King Ceol.
3 Cuthwulf (possibly identical with Cutha), fought against the Britons, *d* 571.
4 (?) Cwichelm, *d* 593.

King Cynric was *s* by his eldest son,

560-593 CEAWLIN, King of Wessex, according to Bede the second acknowledged overlord (*Bretwalda*) of the Southern English. He either associated his nephew Ceol in the kingdom or was deposed by him 591, and *d* 593, leaving issue,

Cuthwine, fought against the Britons with his father in 577 and perhaps *dvp* leaving issue,
1 Cynebald, who had issue,
Æthelbald, who had issue,
Oswald, who fought with King Æthelheard (probably contesting the succession) in 728, and *d* 730.
2 Cedda, who had issue,
Coenberht, probably a *regulus* or sub-King, who *d* 661, leaving issue,
1*a* CAEDWALLA, *s* King Centwine.
2*a* Mul, laid waste Kent and IoW with his brother King Caedwalla 686, and was burned to death in Kent 687.
3 Cutha, who had issue,
Ceolwald, who had issue,
Cenred, a sub-King according to Florence of Worcester, who had issue,
1*b* INE, *s* his kinsman King Caedwalla.
2*b* Ingild, *d* 718, leaving issue,
Eoppa, who had issue,
Eafa, who may have *m* a Princess and heiress of the Royal House of Kent (the Oiscings), and had issue,
Ealhmund, King or sub-King in Kent 784, who had issue,
EGBERT, *s* King Beorhtric.
1*b* Cwenburh.
2*b* Cuthburh, founder of the monastic community at Wimborne, *m* Aldfrith, King of Northumbria, and had issue, but separated from him "during their lifetime". He *d* at Driffield, ER Yorks 14 Dec 705.

King Ceawlin was *s* by his nephew,

591-597 CEOL, *or* **CEOLRIC, King of Wessex,** assoc in the kingdom from 591 and *s* as sole King 593, presumably *d* 597, leaving issue,

CYNEGILS, *s* his uncle King Ceolwulf.

King Ceol was *s* by his brother,

597-611 CEOLWULF, King of Wessex, who spent his whole reign fighting the Angles, the Welsh, the Picts, or the Scots, and *d* 611, leaving issue,

Cuthgils, who had issue,
Cenferth, who had issue,
CENFUS, who *s* Queen Seaxburh.

King Ceolwulf was *s* by his nephew, the son of King Ceol,

611-643 CYNEGILS, King of Wessex, who was converted to Christianity and *bapt* by Birinus, Bishop of Dorchester 635, and *d* 643, having had issue,

1 Cwichelm, assoc in the kingdom with his father from 626 or earlier, *bapt* at Dorchester and *dvp* the same year 636, leaving issue,
Cuthred, *bapt* at Dorchester by Bishop Birinus 639, apparently assoc in the kingdom with his grandfather and uncle, *d* 661.
2 CENWALH, *s* his father.
3 CENTWINE, *s* his kinsman King Æscwine.

1 A dau (? Cyneburg), *m ca* 635, St Oswald, King of Northumbria, and had issue. He was *k* in battle with Penda, King of Mercia at Oswestry, Salop 5 Aug 641.
2 (?) St Egelwine, or Ethelwine, venerated at Athelney according to William of Malmesbury.

King Cynegils was *s* by his 2nd son,

643-672 CENWALH, King of Wessex, expelled from Wessex by Penda, King of Mercia 645 and lived in exile in East Anglia until 648, *bapt* 646, founded the Old Minster at Winchester 648, *m* 1st —, sister of Penda, King of Mercia, whom he repudiated 645. He *m* 2ndly 645, SEAXBURH, who *s* him, and d 672, when he was *s* by his widow,

672-674 SEAXBURH, Queen of Wessex, who *d* or was deposed 674 and was *s* by her husband's kinsman,

674 CENFUS, King of Wessex, who *d* the same year and was *s* by his son,

674-676 AESCWINE, King of Wessex, who *d* 676 and was *s* by the brother of King Cenwalh,

676-685 CENTWINE, King of Wessex, *m* —, a sister of Eormenburh, the 2nd wife of Ecgfrith, King of Northumbria, and was overthrown and probably *k* by his kinsman Caedwalla 685, leaving issue,

Bugge (dau).

King Centwine was *s* as stated by

685-688 CAEDWALLA, King of Wessex, abdicated and went to Rome 688, being *bapt* there by the name of Peter by Pope Sergius I 10 April 689, *b ca* 659, *m* Centhryth, and *dsp* in Rome 20 April 689, (*bur* St Peter's). He was *s* on his abdication by his kinsman,

688-726 INE, King of Wessex, founded the monastery of Glastonbury, abdicated and went to Rome 726, *m* Æthelburh, who accompanied him to Rome, sister of Æthelheard his successor, and *d* in Rome in or *post* 726. King Ine was *s* on his abdication by his brother-in-law and kinsman,

726-740 AETHELHEARD, King of Wessex, of the lineage of Cerdic, *m* Frithugyth, who went to Rome 737, and *dsp* 740, when he was *s* by his kinsman,

740-756 CUTHRED, King of Wessex, of the lineage of Cerdic, *d* 756, having had issue,

Cynric, *kvp* 748.

King Cuthred was *s* by his kinsman,

756-757 SIGEBERHT, King of Wessex, of the lineage of Cerdic, deposed by his kinsman Cynewulf "for unlawful actions" and was stabbed by a herdsman at Privett, nr Petersfield, Hants in or *post* 757. His kinsman and successor,

757-786 CYNEWULF, King of Wessex, of the lineage of Cerdic, was surprised and *k* at *Merantun* (? Merton, Surrey) by Cyneheard, the brother of his predecessor 786 (*bur* Winchester). Cyneheard was also *k* in the fray (*bur* Axminster, Devon). King Cynewulf was *s* by his kinsman,

786-802 BEORHTRIC, King of Wessex, of the lineage of Cerdic, *m* 789, Eadburh (*d* a beggar at Pavia), dau of Offa, King of Mercia, by his wife Cynethryth, and *dsp* being accidentally poisoned by his wife 802 (*bur* Wareham, Dorset), when he was *s* by his kinsman,

802-839 EGBERT, King of Wessex and All England (*see* KINGS OF ALL ENGLAND, *p* 189).

Kings of all England

802-839 EGBERT, King of England, son of Ealhmund, sub-King of Kent (*see p* 188), expelled from England "to the land of the Franks" by Offa, King of Mercia and Beorhtric, King of Wessex 789 (?), *s* Beorhtric as King of Wessex 802, acknowledged in Kent, Surrey, Sussex, Essex and East Anglia after his victory over the Mercians at *Ellendun* (nr Wroughton, Wilts) 825, conquered Mercia 829, reckoned as the eighth *Bretwalda* ("Ruler of Britain"), *b ca* 770-75, *m* Raedburh (Redburga), of unknown (possibly Frankish) origin, and *d* 839 (*bur* Winchester Cathedral), leaving issue,

839-855 ÆTHELWULF, King of England, sub-King in Kent, Essex, Sussex and Surrey 825-39, *s* his father 839, resigned Wessex to his son Ethelbald 855, retaining Kent, Sussex and Essex, *b ca* 795-800, *m* 1st, Osburh (Osburga) (*d ca* 853 ?), dau of Ealdorman Oslac (of Hampshire ?), the royal cup-bearer (*pincerna*), a descendant of Wihtgar, the nephew of Cerdic (*see p* 187), and had issue,

1 Athelstan*, sub-King in Kent, Essex, Sussex and Surrey 839, *dvp ca* 851.
2 ÆTHELBALD, *s* his father.
3 ÆTHELBERT, *s* his brother King Æthelbald.
4 ÆTHELRED I, *s* his brother King Æthelbert.
5 ALFRED, *s* his brother King Ethelred I.
1 Æthelswith, *m* at Chippenham, Wilts *post* Easter (2 April) 853, Burhred, King of Mercia, and *dsp* on the way to Rome (*bur* Pavia). He *d* in Rome *post* 874 (*bur* St Mary's Church in the "School of the English" there).

King Æthelwulf *m* 2ndly at Verberie-sur-Oise 1 Oct 856, Judith (*b ca* 844; *m* 2ndly 858 or 859 (*m* annulled), her stepson, King Æthelbald; and 3rdly 863, Baldwin I, Count of Flanders (*d* 879), and had issue), dau of Charles II *the Bald,* King of France and Holy Roman Emperor, by his 1st wife Ermentrude, dau of Odo, Count of Orleans, and *d* 13 Jan 858 (*bur* Winchester Cathedral).

King Æthelwulf was *s* by his 2nd (but eldest surv) son,

855-860 ÆTHELBALD, King of England, *s* to Wessex on his father's resignation 855 and to all England 858, *m* 858 or 859 (*m* annulled) his stepmother, Judith (*see above*), and *dsp* 860 (*bur* Sherborne Abbey), when he was *s* by his next brother,

860-866 ÆTHELBERT, King of England, sub-King in Kent, Essex, Sussex and Surrey 858-60, *d unm* (?) 866 (*bur* Sherborne Abbey), and was *s* by his brother,

866-871 ÆTHELRED I, King of England, *m* —, and *d* of wounds received at Merton in fighting the Danish invaders *post* Easter (15 April) 871 (*bur* Wimborne Minster), leaving issue,

1 Æthelhelm.
2 Æthelwold, rebelled against his cousin King Edward the Elder and was *k* in battle 904.

King Æthelred I was *s* by his brother,

871-899 ALFRED *THE GREAT,* **King of England,** went to Rome as a child with his father and was anointed there by Pope Leo IV 855, a great national leader in the struggle against the Danish invaders and a renowned patron of learning, *b* at Wantage, Berks 849, *m* 869, Ealhswith (*d* 904), dau of Æthelred Mucil, Ealdorman of the Gaini, by his wife Eadburh, a descendant of the Kings of Mercia, and *d* 26 Oct 899 (*bur* New Minster (afterwards Hyde Abbey), Winchester), having had issue, with several children who *d* as infs,

1 EDWARD, *s* his father.
2 Æthelweard, *b ca* 880, *m* —, and *d* 16 Oct 922, leaving issue,
1 Thurcytel, Chancellor under Kings Athelstan, Edmund I and Edred, later Abbot of Croyland, Lincs, *b ca* 907; *d* at Croyland 975.
2 Ælfwine, *k* at the Battle of Brunanburh 937.
3 Æthelwine, *k* at the Battle of Brunanburh 937.
1 Æthelfled, "Lady of the Mercians", *m ante* end of 889, Æthelred, Ealdorman of the Mercians, and *d* at Tamworth 12 June 918 (*bur* St Peter's Church, Gloucester), leaving issue, one dau. He *d* 912.
2 Æthelgiva, Abbess of Shaftesbury.
3 Ælfthryth (Elftrudis), *m* between 893 and 899, Baldwin II *the Bald,* Count of Flanders, son of Baldwin I, Count of Flanders, by his wife Judith, widow of Kings Æthelwulf and Æthelbald, and dau of Charles II, King of France (*see above*), and *d* 929 (?) (*bur* St Peter's Abbey, Ghent), leaving issue, two sons and two daus. He *d* 10 Sept 918 (*bur* St Peter's Abbey, Ghent).

King Alfred was *s* by his elder son,

899-925 EDWARD (I) *THE ELDER,* **King of England,** crowned at Kingston-upon-Thames 8 June 900, annexed the Danelaw south of the Humber and was acknowledged as overlord by Rægnald I, King of York, Constantine II, King of Scots, the King of the Strathclyde Britons, and others 923, *b ca* 871-72, *m* 1st, Ecgwynn (Egwina), of unknown origin, and had issue,

1 ATHELSTAN, *s* his father.
1 A dau, *m* at Tamworth 30 Jan 926, as his 2nd wife, Sihtric Caoch, King of York. He *d* 927.

King Edward the Elder *m* 2ndly, Ælflaed (Elfleda), dau of Ealdorman Æthelhelm, and by her had issue,

2 Ælfweard, *d* at Oxford 2 Aug 925 (*bur* Winchester Cathedral).
3 Edwin, drowned in the English Channel 933 (*bur* St Bertin's Abbey, St Omer).
2 Eadflaed, a nun (*bur* Wilton).
3 Eadgifu (Ogive), *m* 1st between 916 and 919, as his 2nd wife, Charles III *the Simple,* King of France, and had issue. He *d* 7 Oct 929. She *m* 2ndly, Herbert of Vermandois, Count of Meaux, and *d* 948, having had further issue.
4 Æthelhild, a nun (*bur* Wilton).
5 Eadhild, *m* 926, as his 1st wife, Hugh the Great, Duke of France and Count of Paris, and *dsp ante* 938. He *d* 956.
6 Eadgyth, *m* 930, as his 1st wife, Otto I *the Great,* Holy Roman Emperor and Duke of Saxony, and *d* 26 Jan 946 (or 947), leaving issue. He *d* 973.
7 Ælfgifu (Adiva), *m* "some King not far from the Jupiter Mountains" (*ie* the Alps), who has recently

* Some authorities make him a yr son of King Egbert.

been identified* as Boleslaw II, Duke of Bohemia. He *d* 999.

King Edward the Elder *m* 3rdly Eadgifu (*d* 25 Aug 968), dau of Sigehelm, and *d* at Farndon-on-Dee 17 July 925 (*bur* Winchester Cathedral), having by her had issue,

4 EDMUND I, *s* his half-brother King Athelstan.
5 EDRED, *s* his brother King Edmund I.
8 Eadburh (St), a nun at Winchester.
9 Eadgifu, *m* "Louis of Aquitaine, King of Arles", who has not been satisfactorily identified.

King Edward the Elder was *s* by his eldest son,

925-939 ATHELSTAN, King of England, crowned at Kingston-upon-Thames by Wulfhelm, Archbishop of Canterbury 5 Sept 925, annexed the Danish kingdom of York 927, *b ca* 895; *d unm* at Gloucester 27 Oct 939 (*bur* Malmesbury Abbey), and was *s* by his half-brother,

939-946 EDMUND I *THE MAGNIFICENT,* **King of England,** *b ca* 921, *m* 1st, (St) Ælfgifu (*d* 944), and had issue,

1 EDWY, *s* his uncle King Edred.
2 EDGAR, *s* his brother King Edwy.

King Edmund I *m* 2ndly, Æthelflaed of Damerham (who *m* 2ndly, Ealdorman Athelstan, and *d post* 975), dau of Ealdorman Ælfgar, and was murdered by Liofa, an outlaw, at Pucklechurch, Glos 26 May 946 (*bur* Glastonbury Abbey), when he was *s* by his brother,

946-955 EDRED, King of England, crowned at Kingston-upon-Thames by Oda, Archbishop of Canterbury, *b ca* 923; *d unm* (?) at Frome, Somerset 23 Nov 955 (*bur* Winchester Cathedral), and was *s* by his nephew, the elder son of King Edmund I (*see above*),

955-959 EDWY *THE FAIR,* **King of England,** crowned at Kingston-upon-Thames by Oda, Archbishop of Canterbury Jan 956 (?), *b ca* 941, *m* 955 or early 956 (*m* annulled on grounds of consanguinity 958), his near relation Ælfgifu (*d* at Gloucester *ca* Sept 959), dau of ——, by his wife Æthelgifu, and *dsp* at Gloucester 1 Oct 959, when he was *s* by his brother,

959-975 EDGAR *THE PEACEFUL,* **King of England,** reigned in Mercia and the Danelaw 957-59, crowned at Bath by Dunstan, Archbishop of Canterbury and Oswald, Archbishop of York 11 May 973, *b* 943 or 944, *m* 1st, Æthelflaed, dau of Ealdorman Ordmaer, and had issue,

1 EDWARD (II), *s* his father.

King Edgar *m* 2ndly 965, Ælfthryth (Elfrida) (*b ca* 945; *d* a nun at Wherwell 1000), widow of Ealdorman Æthelwold of East Anglia, and dau of Ealdorman Ordgar of Devon, and *d* 8 July 975 (*bur* Glastonbury Abbey), having by her had issue,

2 Edmund, *d* 971 (*bur* Romsey Abbey).
3 ÆTHELRED II, *s* his half-brother King Edward II.

* The identification is based on convincing numismatic evidence brought to light by the researches of Dr Pavel Radomersky, of the National Museum, Prague (see *Tracing a Lost Princess,* by Bernard Orna, in *Coins and Medals,* Vol II, No 3, Oct 1965).

King Edgar also had an illegitimate dau by one Wulfthryth (Wulfrida), a nun,

St Eadgyth, a nun at Wilton, *b* at Kemsing *ca* 961; *d* at Wilton 16 Sept 984.

King Edgar was *s* by his eldest son,

975-979 EDWARD (II) *THE MARTYR,* **King of England,** crowned at Kingston-upon-Thames 975, *b ca* 962; *d unm* being murdered at the instigation of his stepmother Queen Elfrida at Corfe Castle, Dorset 18 March 979 (*bur* first at Wareham, later transferred to Shaftesbury Abbey), and was *s* by his half-brother,

979-1013 and 1014-1016 ÆTHELRED II *THE UNREADY* (or *THE REDELESS*), **King of England,** crowned at Kingston-upon-Thames 14 April 979, fled to Normandy, following the Danish invasion autumn 1013, restored to the throne on the death of Sweyn Feb 1014, *b ca* 968, *m* 1st Ælfgifu (Elfgiva), dau of Ealdorman Thored of Northumbria, and had issue,

1 Athelstan, *d ca* 1012.
2 Egbert, *d ca* 1005.
3 EDMUND II, *s* his father.
4 Edred, *d ca* 1012.
5 Edwy, *d* murdered by King Canute 1017 (*bur* Tavistock).
6 Edgar, *d ca* 1008.
1 Eadgyth, *m* 1st 1009, Eadric Streona, Ealdorman of Mercia. He was *k* in London by King Canute 1017. She *m* 2ndly, Earl Thorkell Hávi.
2 Ælfgifu, *m* as his 3rd wife, Uchtred, Earl of Northumbria (*d* 1016), and had issue,
Ealdgyth, *m* Maldred, Lord of Allerdale, son of Crinan, Hereditary Abbot of Dunkeld, and had issue (*see* KINGS AND QUEENS OF SCOTLAND, *p* 313).
3 Wulfhild, *m* Ulfcytel *Snilling,* Ealdorman of East Anglia. He was *k* in battle with the Danes 1016.
4 A dau, *m* Athelstan, who was *k* at the Battle of Ringmere May 1010.
5 A dau, Abbess of Wherwell, Hants, living 1051.

King Æthelred II *m* 2ndly spring 1002, Emma (called Ælfgifu in England) (*b* in Normandy *ca* 985; *m* 2ndly 2 July 1017, Canute I, King of England, Denmark and Norway (*see p* 192); *d* at Winchester 6 March 1052, *bur* Winchester Cathedral), eldest dau of Richard I, Duke of Normandy (*see p* 310), and *d* in London 23 April 1016 (*bur* St Paul's Cathedral), having by her had issue,

7 EDWARD (III), *s* his half-brother King Hardicanute.
8 Alfred, *d* at Ely after being blinded 5 Feb 1037.
6 Godgifu (Goda), *m* 1st Drogo (Dreux), Count of Mantes and the Vexin, and had issue, three sons. He *d* at Nicæa 1035. She *m* 2ndly *ca* 1036, as his 1st wife, Eustace II, Count of Boulogne, and *d ante* 1049. He *d* 1093.

King Æthelred II was *s* by his eldest surv son,

April-Nov 1016 EDMUND II *IRONSIDE,* **King of England,** chosen as King by "all the councillors who were in London, and the citizens" after his father's death April 1016, *b ca* 993, *m* summer 1015, Ealdgyth, widow of Sigeferth, an Anglo-Scandinavian thegn, and *d* 30 Nov 1016 (*bur* Glastonbury Abbey), leaving issue,

1 Edmund, sent to Hungary by King Canute, *b* 1016, *m* in Hungary, Hedwig (who *m* 2ndly, Eppo, Count of Nellenburg), 2nd dau of (St) Stephen I, King of Hungary, by his wife Gisela, dau of Heinrich II *the Quarrelsome,* Duke of Bavaria, and *dsp.*

2 Edward *Atheling,* sent to Hungary with his brother, *b* (? twin) 1016, *m* in Hungary, Agatha, probably dau of Bruno, later Bishop of Augsburg, brother of the Holy Roman Emperor Heinrich II, and *d* in London shortly after his return from exile 1057 (*bur* St Paul's Cathedral), leaving issue,

1 Edgar *Atheling,* chosen King by the citizens of London after the death of Harold II at Hastings 1066, but submitted to William the Conqueror and swore an oath of fealty to him, went to Scotland with his mother and sisters 1067, *d unm post* 1126.

1 (St) Margaret, *b* in Hungary ca 1045, *m* at Dunfermline *ca* 1069, as his 2nd wife, Malcolm III *Canmore,* King of Scots, and *d* at Edinburgh Castle 16 Nov 1093 (*bur* Church of the Holy Trinity, Dunfermline), leaving issue (*see* KINGS AND QUEENS OF SCOTLAND, *p* 313). He *d* at Alnwick, Northumberland 13 Nov 1093 (*bur* Church of the Holy Trinity, Dunfermline). Queen Margaret was canonized by Pope Innocent IV 1250.

2 Christina, a nun at Romsey, Hants.

On the death of King Edmund II the crown passed to the Anglo-Danish dynasty (*see p* 192) until 1042, when the Saxon line was restored in the person of his half-brother,

1042-1066 EDWARD (III) *THE CONFESSOR,* **King of England,** crowned at Winchester Cathedral by Eadsige, Archbishop of Canterbury and Æthelric, Archbishop of York 3 April 1043, *b* at Islip, Oxon *ca* 1004, *m* 23 Jan 1045, Eadgyth (Edith) (*d* at Winchester 18 Dec 1075, *bur* Westminster Abbey), dau of Godwin, Earl of Wessex, by his wife Gytha, sister of Earl Ulf (*see p* 192), and *dsp* 5 Jan 1066 (*bur* Westminster Abbey). King Edward the Confessor was canonized by Pope Alexander III 1161. He was *s* by his wife's brother Harold (*see p* 192).

The Anglo-Danish Kings of England

1013-1014 SWEYN *FORKBEARD,* **King of England;** son of Harald *Bluetooth,* King of Denmark; *s* his father as King of Denmark *ca* 986, conquered England and was acknowledged as King autumn 1013, *m* 1st, Gunhild, dau of Mieszko I, Duke of Poland, by 1st wife Dubrawka, dau of Boleslaw I, Duke of Bohemia, and had issue,

1 Harald, King of Denmark 1014-19.
2 CANUTE, *s* his father in England.
1 Gytha, *m* Earl Eric Hakonson, and had issue.
2 Estrith (Astrid), or Margaret, *m* 1st 1017 (repudiated) as his 2nd wife, Richard II *the Good,* Duke of Normandy (*see p* 310). She *m* 2ndly, Earl Ulf, son of Thorgils Sprakalegg, and was ancestress by him of the later Kings of Denmark.

King Sweyn *m* 2ndly, Sigrid *the Haughty,* formerly wife of Eric *the Victorious,* King of Sweden, and dau of Skogul Toste, and *d* at Gainsborough 3 Feb 1014 (*bur* Roskilde Cathedral).

King Sweyn's yr son,

1016-1035 CANUTE *THE GREAT,* **King of England,** was chosen King by the Danish fleet on his father's death but at first failed to establish his position, secured the Danelaw and Mercia by agreement with King Edmund II *Ironside* 1016 and became sole King on the latter's death Nov 1016, *s* his brother as King of Denmark 1019, conquered Norway 1030, *b ca* 995, *m* 1st, Ælfgifu (whom he repudiated), dau of Ælfhelm, Ealdorman of Northampton, and had issue,

1 Sweyn, King of Norway, *d* 1036.
2 HAROLD I, *s* his father.

King Canute *m* 2ndly 2 July 1017, Emma, also called Ælfgifu (*b* in Normandy *ca* 985; *d* 6 March 1052, *bur* Winchester Cathedral), widow of King Æthelred II (*see p* 190), and eldest dau of Richard I, Duke of Normandy (*see p* 310), and *d* at Shaftesbury, Dorset 12 Nov 1035 (*bur* Winchester Cathedral), having by her had issue,

3 HARDICANUTE, *s* his half-brother King Harold I.
1 Gunhild (renamed Kunigunde after her marriage), *m* at Nimeguen June 1036, as his 1st wife, Heinrich (later Emperor Heinrich III), German King and Duke of Bavaria, only son of Emperor Conrad II, and *d* in Italy 18 July 1038, leaving issue, one dau. He *d* at Bodfeld 5 Oct 1056 (*bur* Speyer).
2 A dau, *d* young (*bur* Bosham, Sussex).

King Canute was *s* by his 2nd son,

1035-1040 HAROLD I *HAREFOOT,* **King of England,** chosen jt King with his half-brother Hardicanute, but acknowledged as sole King 1037, *b ca* 1016; *d unm* at Oxford 17 March 1040 (*bur* Winchester Cathedral), and was *s* by his half-brother,

1040-1042 HARDICANUTE, King of England, *s* his father in Denmark and was nominally jt-King of England with his half-brother King Harold I 1035-37, *b ca* 1018; *d unm* at Lambeth 8 June 1042 (*bur* Winchester Cathedral). He was *s* by his half-brother (on his mother's side) King Edward the Confessor (*see p* 191), who on his death was *s* by his brother-in-law,

1066 HAROLD II, King of England, son of Godwin, Earl of Wessex, by his wife Gytha, dau of Thorgils Sprakalegg, son of Styrbjorn, by his wife Thyra, dau of Harald *Bluetooth,* King of Denmark, and sister of King Sweyn (*see above*), crowned at Westminster Abbey by Ealdred, Archbishop of York 5 Jan 1066, *b ca* 1020, *m* 1065, Ealdgyth, widow of Gruffydd ap Llywelyn, King of Gwynedd and Powys (*see* KINGS AND PRINCES OF WALES, *p* 324), and dau of Aelfgar, Earl of Mercia, and was *k* in battle with William, Duke of Normandy nr Hastings 14 Oct 1066 (*bur* Waltham Abbey), leaving issue,

Harold.

King Harold II also had issue by Eadgyth Swanneshals, an earlier wife or mistress,

1 Godwin.
2 Edmund.
3 Magnus.
4 Ulf.
1 Gytha (Gyda), *m ca* 1070, as his 1st wife, Vladimir II *Monomakh,* Great Prince of Kieff, and had issue. He *d* on the banks of the Alta 19 May 1125 (*bur* Kieff).
2 Gunhild, a nun at Wilton.

The Kings and Queens of England (and Great Britain) since the Conquest

1066-1087 WILLIAM I *THE CONQUEROR,* **King of England** (styled *Willielmus Rex Anglorum*), *s* his father as (William II) Duke of Normandy 1035, conquered Maine 1063, obtained the crown of England by conquest 14 Oct 1066, crowned at Westminster Abbey by Ealdred, Archbishop of York 25 Dec 1066, *b* at Falaise, Normandy *ca* autumn 1028, *m* at Eu *ca* 1051, Matilda, crowned at Westminster Abbey 11 May 1068 (*b ca* 1031; *d* at Caen 2 Nov 1083, *bur* there in the Church of the Holy Trinity, which she had founded), dau of Baldwin (Baudouin) V, Count of Flanders (a direct descendant of Alfred the Great), by his wife Adèle, widow of Richard III, Duke of Normandy, and dau of Robert II *the Pious,* King of France, and *d* at the Priory of St Gervais, nr Rouen 9 Sept 1087 (*bur* Abbey of St Stephen Caen, which he had founded), having had issue,

1 Robert (II) *Curthose,* DUKE OF NORMANDY, *s* his father in Normandy and Maine 1087, joined the First Crusade and pledged his duchy to his brother King William II 1096-1100, ceded the county of Evreux to his brother King Henry I 1104, defeated and taken prisoner at the Battle of Tinchebrai 28 Sept 1106, *b* in Normandy ca 1051-54, *m* at Apulia 1100, Sibylla (*d* at Rouen Feb or March 1103, *bur* Caen Cathedral), dau of Geoffrey, Count of Conversano, and *d* (a prisoner of his brother King Henry I) at Cardiff Castle 10 Feb 1134 (*bur* Gloucester Cathedral), having had issue,

1 William *Clito,* COUNT OF FLANDERS, received the county of Flanders from Louis VI, King of France spring 1127, *b* 1101, *m* 1st 1123 (*m* annulled on the grounds of consanguinity 1124), Sibylla (*b* 1112; *m* 2ndly 1134, Thierry of Alsace, Count of Flanders (*d* 1168); *d* a nun in the Abbey of St Lazarus, Bethlehem 1165), yr dau of Fulk (Foulques) V, Count of Anjou and Maine (later King of Jerusalem), by his 1st wife Heremburge, dau and heiress of Hélie I, Count of Maine. He *m* 2ndly Jan 1128, Joan (Giovanna), half-sister of Adelaide of Savoy, 2nd wife of Louis VI, King of France, and dau of Ranieri, Marquis of Montferrat, by his wife Gisla (Gisèle), widow of Umberto II, Count of Savoy and Maurienne, and dau of Guillaume I, Count of Burgundy, and *d* of a wound received five days previously in a sortie at Alost, at the Abbey of St Bertin, St Omer 27 July 1128, *spvp* (*bur* there).

2 Henry, *b* 1102; *k* while hunting in the New Forest, *unm vp.*

2 Richard, *b* in Normandy *ante* 1056; *k* while hunting in the New Forest, *unm vp* 1081 (?) (*bur* Winchester Cathedral).

3 WILLIAM II, *s* his father.

4 HENRY I, *s* his brother King William II.

1* Cecilia (Cecily), professed a nun in the Benedictine convent of the Holy Trinity, Caen 5 April 1075, elected Abbess 1112, *b* in Normandy *ca* 1055; *d* at Caen 30 July 1126 (*bur* there in the Church of the Holy Trinity).

---

* The number, names and order of birth of the daughters of William the Conqueror have been the subject of much dispute. We here follow the listing of Prof David C. Douglas in his recent (1964) biography *William the Conqueror,* but have transferred Cecily to the head of the list as she is almost always spoken of as the eldest daughter.

2 Agatha, said to have been betrothed successively to Harold Godwinsson, Earl of Wessex (later KING HAROLD II—*see p* 192), and to Alfonso VI, King of Leon, *d unm* (*bur* Bayeux).

3 Adeliza, said to have become a nun.

4 Adela, *b* in Normandy *ca* 1062, *m* at Chartres *ca* 1081, Stephen (Etienne), Count of Blois and Chartres, eldest son of Thibaut III, Count of Blois and Champagne, by his wife Alix, dau of Raoul III, Count of Crépy and Valois. He joined the First Crusade and was *k* at Ramleh 19 May 1102. The Countess Adela, who acted as regent of the counties of Blois and Chartres during her husband's absences and the minority of her son Count Thibaut IV, became a nun in the Cluniac Priory of Marcigny-sur-Loire *ca* 1122, and *d* there 8 March 1138 (*bur* Church of the Holy Trinity, Caen), having had issue, with one or more other daus,

1 William (Guillaume), Lord of Sully *jure uxoris,* excluded from the succession to Blois and Chartres for lack of capacity, *m* Agnès, yr dau and coheiress of Gilon, Lord of Sully, by his wife Eldeburge, sister and heiress of Etienne, Viscount of Bourges, and had issue, three sons and two daus.

2 Theobald (Thibaut) IV, Count of Blois and Chartres 1102-52, and of Champagne 1125-52, *b ca* 1085, *m* 1123, Matilda (*b ca* 1105; *d* 1160), dau of Engelbert II, Duke of Carinthia, by his wife Uta, dau of Udalrich, Count of Passau, and *d* 8 Jan 1152, leaving issue.

3 STEPHEN, *s* his uncle King Henry I.

4 Henry, Abbot of Glastonbury 1126-71, consecrated Bishop of Winchester 17 Nov 1129, *b ca* 1099, *educ* Cluny, *d* 6 Aug 1171 (*bur* Winchester Cathedral).

5 Philippe, Bishop of Châlons.

1 Matilda (or Maud), *m* 1115, Richard d'Avranches, 2nd Earl of Chester (*see* BURKE'S *Dormant and Extinct Peerages*), and was drowned with him in the wreck of the White Ship off Barfleur 25 Nov 1120, *sp.*

2 Agnes, *m* Hugues III, Seigneur du Puiset, and had issue (Hugh du Puiset, Treas of York 1143-53, and Bishop of Durham 1153-95).

5 Constance, *m* at Caen 1086, as his 1st wife, Alain IV, Count of Brittany, and *dsp* 13 Aug 1090 (*bur* St Melans, nr Rhedon). He *d* 13 Oct 1119.

6 Matilda, mentioned in *Domesday Book, d unm ante* 1112.

King William I was *s* in England by his 3rd son,

1087-1100 WILLIAM II *RUFUS,* **King of England** (styled *Dei Gratia Rex Anglorum*), crowned at Westminster Abbey by Lanfranc, Archbishop of Canterbury 26 Sept 1087, held the duchy of Normandy in pledge 1096-1100 but was never Duke, *b* in Normandy *ca* 1056-60; *k* while hunting in the New Forest 2 Aug 1100 (*bur* Winchester Cathedral), *unm,* and was *s* by his brother,

1100-1135 HENRY I *BEAUCLERC,* **King of England** (styled the same as William II), crowned at Westminster Abbey by Maurice, Bishop of London 6 Aug 1100, annexed the duchy of Normandy after the Battle of Tinchebrai 28 Sept 1106, *b* at Selby, Yorks latter half of 1068, *m* 1st at Westminster Abbey 11 Nov 1100 (she being crowned the same day), Matilda (formerly called Edith) (*b* at Dunfermline 1079; *d* at Westminster Palace 1 May 1118, *bur* Westminster Abbey), elder dau of Malcolm III *Canmore,* King of Scots, by his 2nd wife St Margaret, dau of Edward *Atheling,* and grand-dau of Edmund II *Ironside,* King of England (*see p* 191), and had issue, with a child (sex unknown) *b ca* July 1101 and *d* an inf,

1 William (called William the Atheling), DUKE OF NORMANDY, invested with the duchy of Normandy by Louis VI, King of France 1120, *b* at Winchester *ante* 5 Aug 1103 (possibly twin with his sister Matilda), *m* at Lisieux June 1119, Matilda (formerly called Alice) (*b* 1107; *d* as Abbess of Fontévrault 1154), elder dau of Fulk (Foulques) V, Count of Anjou and Maine (later King of Jerusalem), by his 1st wife Heremburge, dau and heiress of Hélie I, Count of Maine, and was drowned in the wreck of the White Ship off Barfleur during the passage from Normandy to England 25 Nov 1120, *sp vp*.

2 Richard, drowned with his brother William 25 Nov 1120, *unm vp*. He is often described as an illegitimate son of King Henry I, but the *Anglo-Saxon Chronicle* implies his legitimacy and Piers of Langtoft and Robert of Gloucester both refer to him specifically as a son of Queen Matilda.

1 MATILDA (formerly called Alice or Aethelic), received the oath of fealty as heiress-presumptive to the crown following the deaths of her two brothers Christmas 1126, proclaimed LADY OF THE ENGLISH by a legatine council of the English Church at Winchester 7 April 1141 but was never crowned, renounced her claim in favour of Stephen for his life with remainder to her son Henry 1152, *b* at Winchester *ca* 1102 (possibly twin with her brother William), *m* 1st at Mainz 7 Jan 1114 (being crowned Empress the same day), Heinrich V, Holy Roman Emperor and King of Germany. He *dsp* at Utrecht 23 May 1125 (*bur* Speyer). She *m* 2ndly at Le Mans 22 May 1127, Geoffrey V *Plantagenet,* Count of Anjou and Maine (*b* 24 Aug 1113; *d* at Château-du-Loir 7 Sept 1151, *bur* Le Mans Cathedral), brother of her sister-in-law Matilda, Duchess of Normandy (*see above*), and *d* at Rouen 10 Sept 1169 (*bur* Bec Abbey), having had issue by her 2nd husband*,

1 HENRY II, *s* his mother's cousin King Stephen.

2 Geoffrey (VI) *Martel,* COUNT OF NANTES, *b* at Argentan 1 June 1134; *d unm* at Nantes 26 July 1158 (*bur* there).

3 William, *b* at Angers (?) Aug 1136; *d unm* at Rouen 30 Jan 1164 (*bur* Nôtre Dame, Rouen).

King Henry I *m* 2ndly at Windsor Castle 29 Jan 1121, Adeliza, crowned at Westminster Abbey by Ralph d'Escures, Archbishop of Canterbury 3 Feb 1121 (*b ca* 1104; *m* 2ndly 1138, William d'Aubigny, 1st Earl of Arundel (*d* 12 Oct 1176), and *d* at Afflighem, Flanders 23 March or April 1151 (*bur* there), leaving issue (*see* BURKE'S *Dormant and Extinct Peerages*)), dau of Godfrey I the Bearded, Duke of Lower Lorraine, Marquis of Antwerp and Count of Louvain (*see* BURKE'S *Peerage,* MILFORD HAVEN, M), and *d* at St Denis-le-Fermont, nr Rouen 1 Dec 1135 (*bur* Reading Abbey, which he had founded).

King Henry I was *s* in spite of the oath of fealty to his dau Matilda, by his nephew,

1135-1154 STEPHEN, King of England (styled *Rex Anglorum, Dux Normannorum*), crowned at Westminster Abbey by William de Corbeil, Archbishop of Canterbury 26 Dec 1135, captured by adherents of Matilda 2 Feb 1141, released 1 Nov 1141, re-crowned 25 Dec 1141, lost the duchy of Normandy to Geoffrey V, Count of Anjou, the husband of his rival Matilda 1144, *b* at Blois *ca* 1096, *m* 1125, Matilda, Countess of Boulogne, crowned at Westminster Abbey 22 March 1136 (*b ca* 1105; *d* at Hedingham Castle, Essex 3 May 1152, *bur* Faversham Abbey), only dau and heiress of Eustace III, Count of Boulogne, by his wife Mary, yr dau of Malcolm III *Canmore,* King of Scots, and *d* at Dover 25 Oct 1154 (*bur* Faversham Abbey, which he had founded), having had issue,

1 Baldwin, *b ca* 1126; *d ante* 2 Dec 1135 (*bur* Holy Trinity Church, Aldgate).

2 Eustace IV, COUNT OF BOULOGNE, *s* 1147, *b ca* 1130/1, *m* at Paris *post* Feb 1140, Constance (*b ca* 1128; *m* 2ndly 1154, Raymond V, Count of Toulouse; *d* at Rheims 16 Aug 1176), only dau of Louis VI, King of France, by his 2nd wife Adelaide, dau of Umberto II, Count of Savoy and Maurienne, and *dspvp* at Bury St Edmunds 10 Aug 1153 (*bur* Faversham Abbey).

3 William II, COUNT OF BOULOGNE, *s* 1153 and *jure uxoris* EARL OF WARENNE AND SURREY, *b ca* 1134, *m ca* 1149, Isabel (*b ca* 1137; *m* 2ndly 1164, Hameline, *jure uxoris* Earl of Warenne and Surrey (*d* April 1202), natural son of Geoffrey V, Count of Anjou, and consequently half-brother of King Henry II; *d* 13 July 1199, *bur* Chapter House, Lewes Priory), dau and heiress of William de Warenne, 3rd Earl of Warenne and Surrey (*see* BURKE'S *Dormant and Extinct Peerages*), and was *k* at the siege of Toulouse 11 Oct 1159, *sp*.

1 Matilda, *b ca* 1133; *d ca* 1135 (*bur* Holy Trinity Church, Aldgate).

2 Mary, COUNTESS OF BOULOGNE, Abbess of Romsey, Hants before she *s* her brother Count William II 1159, later resumed the monastic life at St Austrebert, nr Montreuil, *b ca* 1136, *m ca* 1160 (*m* annulled on the grounds of her previous vow of chastity 1169), as his 1st wife, Matthew I, Count of Boulogne *jure uxoris,* son of Thierry of Alsace, Count of Flanders, by his 2nd wife Sibylla, yr dau of Fulk V, Count of Anjou and Maine (*see above*), and *d* at St Austrebert 1182 (*bur* there), leaving issue, two daus. He *d* of a wound received at the siege of Driencourt 25 July 1173.

King Stephen was *s* by the son of the Empress Matilda and grandson of King Henry I (*see above*),

1154-1189 HENRY II *CURTMANTLE,* **King of England** (styled *Rex Angliae, Dux Normanniae et Aquitaniae et Comes Andegaviae*), *s* his father as Count of Anjou and Maine and Duke of Normandy 1151, Duke of Aquitaine *jure uxoris* 1152, recognized as Stephen's heir by the Treaty of Winchester 1153, crowned at Westminster Abbey by Theobald, Archbishop of Canterbury 19 Dec 1154, *b* at Le Mans 5 March 1133, *m* at Bordeaux 18 May 1152, Eleanor, Duchess of Aquitaine, crowned with her husband (*b* at Bordeaux or at Belin 1122; *d* at Fontévrault 31 March/1 April 1204, *bur* there), formerly wife of Louis VII, King of France (*m* annulled on the grounds of consanguinity 11 March 1152), and elder dau and co-heiress of Guillaume X, Duke of Aquitaine and Count of Poitou, by his wife Aënor, dau of Aimery I, Viscount of Châtellerault, and *d*

* It is sometimes stated that Emma, the sister of King Henry II who *m ante* Michaelmas 1174, Dafydd I, Prince of Gwynedd (*see* KINGS AND PRINCES OF WALES, *p* 322), was dau of the Empress Matilda, but it seems more likely that she was an illegitimate dau of Geoffrey V, Count of Anjou, and had been *m* 1st to Guy, Sire de Laval.

at Chinon 6 July 1189 (*bur* Fontévrault), having had issue,

1 William, *b* in Normandy 17 Aug 1153; *d* at Wallingford Castle Berks *ca* April 1156 (*bur* Reading Abbey).

2 Henry, DUKE OF NORMANDY and COUNT OF ANJOU, associated in the kingdom with his father and styled *Henry the Young King,* crowned at Westminster Abbey by Roger of Pont l'Eveque, Archbishop of York 14 June 1170, and again with his consort at Winchester by Rotrou, Archbishop of Rouen 27 Aug 1172, *b* at Bermondsey 28 Feb 1155, *m* at Newburgh, Normandy 2 Nov 1160, Margaret (*b* early 1158; *m* 2ndly 1185, as his 2nd wife, Bela III, King of Hungary; *d* at Acre 1197 or 1198), dau of (his mother's 1st husband) Louis VII, King of France, by his 2nd wife Constance, dau of Alfonso VII, King of Castile, and *dvp* at Martel 11 June 1183 (*bur* first Le Mans, later transferred to Rouen), having had issue,

A son, *b* at Paris 19 June, *d* 22 June 1177.

3 RICHARD I, *s* his father.

4 Geoffrey, DUKE OF BRITTANY *jure uxoris, b* 23 Sept 1158, *m* July 1181, Constance, Duchess of Brittany (*b* 1161; *m* 2ndly 1186/88 (*m* diss 1199), Ranulf de Blundeville, 4th Earl of Chester (*see* BURKE'S *Dormant and Extinct Peerages*); and 3rdly at Angers 1199, Guy, brother of Aimery, Viscount of Thouars, by whom she had further issue; *d* at Nantes 4 Sept 1201, *bur* Villeneuve), only dau and heiress of Conan IV *the Little,* Duke of Brittany, by his wife Margaret, yr dau of Henry, Earl of Huntingdon (*see* BURKE'S *Dormant and Extinct Peerages,* and KING'S AND QUEENS OF SCOTLAND, *p* 314), and was *k* in a tournament at Paris 19 Aug 1186 (*bur* Nôtre Dame Cathedral), having had issue,

1 Arthur, DUKE OF BRITTANY, declared *heir presumptive* to the crown by his uncle King Richard I 11 Nov 1190 but excluded from the succession by his uncle John, *b* (posthumously) at Nantes 29 March 1187; murdered at Rouen 3 April 1203 (*bur* Bec Abbey).

1 Eleanor, heiress of Brittany, known as "The Damsel of Brittany", kept in captivity by her uncle King John and cousin King Henry III, *b* 1184; *d unm* at Bristol Castle 10 Aug 1241 (*bur* first St James's Church, Bristol, later transferred to Amesbury, Wilts).

2 Matilda, *b* 1185 or 1186; *d* an inf.

5 JOHN, *s* his brother King Richard I.

1 Matilda, *b* in London 1156, *m* at Minden 1 Feb 1168, as his 2nd wife, Heinrich V *the Lion,* Duke of Saxony and Bavaria, and *d* 28 June 1189 (*bur* Cathedral of St Blasius, Brunswick), leaving issue, four sons and one dau. He *d* at Brunswick 6 Aug 1195 (*bur* Cathedral of St Blasius).

2 Eleanor, *b* at Domfront, Normandy 13 Oct 1162, *m* at Burgos Sept 1177, Alfonso VIII, King of Castile, and *d* at Burgos 31 Oct 1214 (*bur* Las Huelgas), having had issue, four sons and eight daus. He *d* 6 Oct 1214 (*bur* Las Huelgas).

3 Joan, *b* at Angers Oct 1165, *m* 1st at Palermo 13 Feb 1177, Guglielmo II, King of Sicily, and had issue, one son (who *d* an inf). He *d* at Palermo 18 Nov 1189 (*bur* Monreale). She *m* 2ndly at Rouen Oct 1196, as his 4th wife, Raymond VI, Count of Toulouse, son of Raymond V, Count of Toulouse, by his wife Constance, widow of Eustace IV, Count of Boulogne (son of King Stephen—*see p* 194), and dau of Louis VI, King of France, and *d* 4 Sept 1199 (*bur* Fontévrault), having had further issue, two sons. He *d* Aug 1222.

King Henry II was *s* by his 3rd (but eldest surv) son,

1189-1199 RICHARD I *CŒUR DE LION,* **King of England** (styled the same as Henry II), crowned at Westminster Abbey by Baldwin, Archbishop of Canterbury 3 Sept 1189, spent the greater part of his reign overseas fighting in the Crusades, *b* at Beaumont Palace, Oxford 8 Sept 1157, *m* at the Chapel of St George, Lemesos, Cyprus 12 May 1191 (she being crowned the same day by John Fitz Luke, Bishop of Evreux), Berengaria (*b ca* 1163; *d* at Espans Abbey, nr Le Mans *ca* 1230, *bur* there), dau of Sancho VI *the Wise,* King of Navarre, by his wife Beatrice (or Sanchia), dau of Alfonso VII, King of Castile, and *d* of a wound received while besieging the Castle of Châlus, Aquitaine 6 April 1199 (*bur* Fontévrault), *spl* when he was *s* by his yst and only surv brother,

1199-1216 JOHN *LACKLAND,* **King of England** (styled *Rex Angliae, Dominus Hiberniae, Dux Normanniae, et Dux Aquitaniae*), formerly Count of Mortain and *jure uxoris* Earl of Gloucester, crowned at Westminster Abbey by Hubert Walter, Archbishop of Canterbury 27 May 1199, *b* at Beaumont Palace, Oxford 24 Dec 1167, *m* 1st at Marlebridge 29 Aug 1189 (*m* annulled on the grounds of consanguinity 1200), Isabella, Countess of Gloucester (who *m* 2ndly 1213, Geoffrey de Mandeville, 5th Earl of Essex, one of the twenty-five peers who enforced observance of Magna Carta (*dsp* 1216) (*see* BURKE'S *Dormant and Extinct Peerages*); and 3rdly *ca* Oct 1217, as his 2nd wife, Hubert de Burgh, 1st Earl of Kent (*d* 4 March 1243) (*see* BURKE'S *Dormant and Extinct Peerages*), and *dsp ca* 18 Nov 1217, *bur* Canterbury Cathedral), 3rd and yst dau and co-heiress of William, Earl of Gloucester, by his wife Hawise, dau of Robert (*Bossu*) de Beaumont, 2nd Earl of Leicester, Justice of England (*see* BURKE'S *Dormant and Extinct Peerages*). He *m* 2ndly at Bordeaux 24 Aug 1200, Isabella, crowned at Westminster Abbey 8 Oct 1200 (who *m* 2ndly *ca* 1220, Hugh de Lusignan, Count of La Marche, and *d* at Fontévrault 31 May 1246 (*bur* there), leaving further issue), only dau and heiress of Aymer Taillefer, Count of Angoulême, by his wife Alice, dau of Pierre de Courtenay, yst son of Louis VI, King of France, and *d* at Newark Castle 19 Oct 1216 (*bur* Worcester Cathedral), having by her had issue,

1 HENRY III, *s* his father.

2 Richard, *cr* Count of Poitou *ante* 14 Aug 1225 (renounced *ca* Dec 1243), EARL OF CORNWALL 30 May 1227, co-Regent of England with Queen Eleanor during Henry III's absence in Gascony Aug 1253—May 1254, sole Regent May-Dec 1254, elected KING OF THE ROMANS at Frankfurt 13 Jan 1257, crowned at Aachen by Konrad von Hochstaden, Archbishop of Cologne 17 May 1257, *b* at Winchester Castle 5 Jan 1209, *m* 1st at Fawley, Bucks 13 March 1231, Isabella (*b* at Pembroke Castle 9 Oct 1200; *d* at Berkhamstead, Herts 15 Jan 1240, *bur* Beaulieu Abbey), widow of Gilbert de Clare, 5th Earl of Hertford and 1st Earl of Gloucester (*see* BURKE'S *Dormant and Extinct Peerages*), and 3rd dau of William Marshal, 1st Earl of Pembroke (*see* BURKE'S *Dormant and Extinct Peerages*), and had issue,

1 John, *b* at Marlow, Bucks 2 Feb 1232; *d* there 22 Sept 1233 (*bur* Reading Abbey).

2 Henry (called *Henry of Almayne*), ktd at Aachen by his father 18 May 1257, *b* at Haughley Castle, Suffolk 12 Nov 1235, *m* at Windsor 15 May 1269, Constance (*d ca* 1299), widow of Alfonso, Infante of Aragon (son and heir of Jaime I, King of Aragon), and eldest dau and co-heiress

of Gaston VII, Viscount of Béarn, by his 1st wife Mathe, dau of Boson de Mastas, Seigneur de Cognac, by his wife Petronelle, Countess of Bigorre, and was murdered by his cousins Simon and Guy de Montfort in the Church of San Silvestro, Viterbo 13 March 1271 (*bur* Hayles Abbey), *sp vp*.

3 Nicholas, *b* and *d* at Berkhamsted Jan 1240 (*bur* Beaulieu Abbey).

1 Isabella, *b* at Marlow 9 Sept 1233; *d* there 10 Oct 1234 (*bur* Reading Abbey).

The King of the Romans *m* 2ndly at Westminster Abbey 23 Nov 1243, Sanchia, crowned Queen of the Romans at Aachen with her husband (*b* at Aix-en-Provence *ca* 1225; *d* at Berkhamsted 9 Nov 1261, *bur* Hayles Abbey), sister of his sister-in-law Queen Eleanor, and 3rd dau and co-heiress of Raymond Bérenger V, Count of Provence, by his wife Beatrice, dau of Tommaso I, Count of Savoy, and by her had issue,

4 Richard (?), *b* at Wallingford, Berks July 1246; *d* there Aug 1246 (*bur* Grove Mill).

5 Edmund (called *Edmund of Almayne*), 2nd EARL OF CORNWALL, invested with his father's earldom and ktd by King Henry III 13 Oct 1272, *b* at Berkhamsted 26 Dec 1249, *m* at Ruislip, Middx 7 Oct 1272 (*m* diss 1293/4), Margaret (*b* 1249; *d* Feb 1313, *bur* Chertsey Abbey), dau of Richard de Clare, 6th Earl of Hertford and 2nd Earl of Gloucester (*see* BURKE'S *Dormant and Extinct Peerages*), and *dsp* at Ashbridge Abbey, Bucks (which he had founded 1283) 1 Oct 1300 (*bur* Hayles Abbey).

6 (?)* Richard, *b ca* 1252; *k* at the siege of Berwick 1296, *unm*.

The King of the Romans *m* 3rdly at Kaiserslautern 16 June 1269, Beatrix (*b ca* 1253; *d* 17 Oct 1277, *bur* Church of the Friars Minors, Oxford), 2nd dau of Dirk (or Dieter) II, Lord of Falkenburg (brother of Engelbert, Archbishop of Cologne), by his 2nd wife Johanna van Loon, aud *d* at Berkhamsted 2 April 1272 (*bur* Hayles Abbey, which he had founded).

1 Joan, *b* 22 July 1210, *m* at York 19 June 1221, as his 1st wife, Alexander II, King of Scots (*see* KINGS AND QUEENS OF SCOTLAND, *p* 315), and *dsp* nr London 4 March 1238 (*bur* Tarrant Crawford, Dorset). He *d* at the Island of Kerrera 8 July 1249 (*bur* Melrose Abbey).

2 Isabella, *b* 1214, *m* at Worms 20 July 1235, as his 3rd wife, Friedrich II, Holy Roman Emperor and King of Sicily, etc, and *d* at Foggia 1 Dec 1241 (*bur* Andria), having had issue, two sons and two daus. He *d* at Firenzuola 13 Dec 1250.

3 Eleanor, *b* 1215, *m* 1st 23 April 1224, as his 2nd wife, William Marshal, 2nd Earl of Pembroke (*see* BURKE'S *Dormant and Extinct Peerages*). He *dsp* 24 April 1231 (*bur* New Temple Church, London). She *m* 2ndly at the King's private chapel at Westminster 7 Jan 1239, Simon de Montfort, 2nd and last (of that creation) Earl of Leicester, the statesman and soldier, and *d* at Montargis, France 13 April 1275 (*bur* there), having had issue, five sons and one dau (*see* BURKE'S *Dormant and Extinct Peerages*). He was *k* at the Battle of Evesham 4 Aug 1265 (*bur* Evesham Abbey).

King John was *s* by his elder son,

1216-1272 HENRY III, King of England (styled the same as John until 1259, then *Rex Angliae, Dominus Hiberniae et Dux Aquitaniae*), crowned at Gloucester Cathedral by Peter des Roches, Bishop of Winchester 28 Oct 1216, and again at Westminster Abbey by Stephen Langton, Archbishop of Canterbury 17 May 1220, *b* at Winchester Castle 1 Oct 1207, *m* at Canterbury 14 Jan 1236, Eleanor, crowned at Westminster Abbey 20 Jan 1236 (*b* at Aix-en-Provence *ca* 1217; *d* at Amesbury, Wilts (having taken the veil there 7 July 1284) 24 June 1291, *bur* there), 2nd dau and co-heiress of Raymond Bérenger V, Count of Provence, by his wife Beatrice, dau of Tommaso I, Count of Savoy, and *d* at Westminster Palace 16 Nov 1272 (*bur* Westminster Abbey), having had issue,

1 EDWARD I, *s* his father.

2 Edmund (*Crouchback*), *cr* EARL OF LEICESTER 26 Oct 1265, EARL OF LANCASTER 30 June 1267, nominated King of Sicily by Pope Innocent IV 1252 but never obtained possession of the kingdom, *b* in London 16 Jan 1245, *m* 1st at Westminster Abbey 8 or 9 April 1269, Aveline (*b* 20 Jan 1259; *d* at Stockwell 10 Nov 1274, *bur* Westminster Abbey), only surv dau and heiress of William de Forz, Earl of Aumale, by his 2nd wife Isabella, dau and heiress of Baldwin de Redvers, 7th Earl of Devon (*see* BURKE'S *Dormant and Extinct Peerages*). He *m* 2ndly at Paris *ante* 3 Feb 1276, Blanche (*b ca* 1245-50; *d* abroad 2 May 1302, probably *bur* Minoresses' Convent, Aldgate), widow of Henri I, King of Navarre, and only dau of Robert I, Count of Artois (3rd son of Louis VIII, King of France), by his wife Mahaut, dau of Henri II, Duke of Brabant, and *d* at Bayonne 5 June 1296 (*bur* Westminster Abbey), having by her had issue,

1 Thomas, 2nd EARL OF LANCASTER and *jure uxoris* EARL OF LINCOLN, Steward of England, joined the confederation of nobles against Piers Gaveston, the favourite of his cousin King Edward II, *b ca* 1279-80, *m ca* 1310 (*m* diss *ca* 1318), Alice, styled Countess of Lincoln and Salisbury (*b* 1281; *m* 2ndly 1331, Eubule l'Estrange, Lord Strange (*dsp* 1335); and 3rdly 1336, Hugh de Fresnes, and *dsp* 2 Oct 1348, *bur* Birling, Kent), dau and heiress of Henry de Lacy, 3rd Earl of Lincoln, (*see* BURKE'S *Dormant and Extinct Peerages*) and was beheaded outside Pontefract 22 March 1322 (*bur* Pontefract Abbey), *sp*.

2 Henry, 3rd EARL OF LANCASTER and LEICESTER, Steward of England, Capt-Gen of all the King's forces in the marches of Scotland, *b* at Grosmont Castle, Mon *ca* 1281, *m ante* 2 March 1297, Maud (*b* 1282; *d ante* 3 Dec 1322), only dau and heiress of Sir Patrick de Chaworth, Kt, Lord of Kidwelly, by his wife Isabel, dau of William de Beauchamp, 1st Earl of Warwick (*see* BURKE'S *Dormant and Extinct Peerages*), and *d* at Leicester 22 Sept 1345 (*bur* Leicester Abbey), having had issue,

(1) Henry (*the Wryneck*), KG (founder kt) (1349), *cr* EARL OF DERBY 16 March 1337, *s* his father as 4th EARL OF LANCASTER and LEICESTER 1345, Steward of England, Lord Lieut of Aquitaine, Kt of the Round Table, *cr* EARL OF LINCOLN 20 Aug 1349, and DUKE OF LANCASTER 6 March 1352 (the 2nd Duke ever *cr* in England), known as the "Good Duke", *b* at Grosmont Castle *ca* 1314, *m ca* 1334, Isabel (living 24 March 1356; *bur* Leicester Abbey), 4th dau of Henry, Earl of Buchan and 1st Baron Beaumont, PC, Lord of the IoM, Constable of England (*see* BURKE'S *Peerage*, BEAUMONT, Bt), and *d* of the plague at Leicester 24 March 1361 (*bur* Leicester Abbey), leaving issue,

1*a* Maud (Matilda), *b* 4 April 1335, *m* 1st, Ralph Stafford, son and heir of Ralph, 1st Earl of Stafford (*see* BURKE'S *Dormant and Extinct Peerages*). He *dvp sp ca* 1349. She *m* 2ndly 1352, Wilhelm I, Duke of Bavaria, Count of Zeeland, Holland and Hainault, son of the Emperor Ludwig IV, by his wife Margarete, dau of Guillaume I Count of Hainault (and sister of Queen Philippa—*see below*), and *dsp* in

* There is some doubt as to the existence of this yst son of Richard, Earl of Cornwall and King of the Romans. It seems likely that he has been confused with Richard's illegitimate son by Jeanne de Valletort, Richard de Cornwall, who received the manor of Thunnock, Lincs from his half-brother Edmund 1280. This Richard was ancestor of John Cornwall, Baron Fanhope and Milbroke, KG, who *m* Elizabeth, dau of John of Gaunt, Duke of Lancaster (*see below*), and of the Cornwalls of Burford (*see* BURKE'S *Dormant and Extinct Peerages*).

England 10 April 1362. He *d* April 1389 (*bur* Valenciennes).
2*a* Blanche, *b* 25 March 1345, *m* at the Queen's Chapel, Reading 13 May 1359, as his 1st wife, John (of Gaunt), Earl of Richmond, later Duke of Lancaster, 4th son of King Edward III, and *d* at Bolingbroke Castle 12 Sept 1369 (*bur* St Paul's Cathedral), having had issue (*see below, p* 199). He *d* Leicester Castle 3 Feb 1399.
(1) Blanche, *b ca* 1305, *m ante* 24 Nov 1320, Thomas Wake, 2nd Lord Wake (*see* BURKE'S *Peerage,* WAKE, Bt), and *dsp* 10 July 1380 (her tombstone in Norman French was found in Stamford 1967 and is now in the museum there). He *d* 30 May 1349.
(2) Maud, *b ca* 1310, *m* 1st *ca* 1330, William de Burgh, 3rd Earl of Ulster, and had issue, one dau. (Elizabeth, who *m* Lionel (of Antwerp), Duke of Clarence, 3rd son of King Edward III, and had issue—*see below, p* 199). He *d* 7 June 1333. She *m* 2ndly *ante* 6 July 1345, as his 2nd wife, Ralph de Ufford, Justiciary of Ireland, brother of Robert de Ufford, 1st Earl of Suffolk (*see* BURKE'S *Dormant and Extinct Peerages*), and *d* at Campsey Abbey, Suffolk (having taken the veil there 1347 or 1348) *ante* 5 May 1377 (*bur* Bruisyard, Suffolk), having had further issue, one dau. He *d ante* 14 June 1346.
(3) Joan, *b ca* 1312, *m* (Royal Assent given 28 Feb 1327) John, 3rd Lord Mowbray (*see* BURKE'S *Peerage,* MOWBRAY, SEGRAVE AND STOURTON, B), and *d post* 6 Feb 1345 (*bur* Bella Landa), leaving issue, one son and two daus. He *d* at York 4 Oct 1361 (*bur* Grey Friars Church, York).
(4) Isabel, Prioress of Amesbury, professed a nun *ante* 6 April 1337, *b ca* 1317; *d post* 1 Feb 1347.
(5) Eleanor, *b ca* 1318, *m* 1st *ante* 23 Aug 1337, John, 2nd Baron Beaumont (brother of Isabel, Duchess of Lancaster—*see above*) (*see* BURKE'S *Peerage,* BEAUMONT, Bt), and had issue, one son and one dau. He *d* between 24 Feb 1342 and 25 May 1342. She *m* 2ndly at Ditton 5 Feb 1345, as his 2nd wife, Richard Fitzalan, 9th Earl of Arundel, KG, and *d* at Arundel Castle 11 Jan 1372 (*bur* Lewes Priory), having had further issue, four sons and three daus (*see* BURKE'S *Dormant and Extinct Peerages*). He *d* at Arundel Castle 24 Jan 1376 (*bur* Lewes Priory)
(6) Mary, *b ca* 1321, *m* (Royal Assent given 14 Aug 1334) 1341, as his 1st wife, Henry Percy, 3rd Baron Percy of Alnwick, and had issue, two sons (*see* BURKE'S *Dormant and Extinct Peerages*). He *d* 17 June 1368.
3 John, Lord of Beaufort and Nogent Lartauld, *b ante* May 1286; *d unm* in France *ante* 1327.
1 Mary, *d* young.
3 Richard, *b ca* 1247; *d ante* 1256 (*bur* Westminster Abbey).
4 John, *b ca* 1250; *d ante* 1256 (*bur* Westminster Abbey).
5 Henry, *d* young (*bur* Westminster Abbey).
1 Margaret, *b* at Windsor Castle 29 Sept 1240, *m* at York 26 Dec 1251, as his 1st wife, Alexander III, King of Scots, and *d* at Cupar Castle, Fife 26 Feb 1275 (*bur* Dunfermline), leaving issue (*see* KINGS AND QUEENS OF SCOTLAND, *p* 316). He *d* nr Kinghorn 19 March 1286 (*bur* Dunfermline).
2 Beatrice, *b* at Bordeaux 25 June 1242, *m* at St Denis, 22 Jan 1260, Jean de Dreux, Earl of Richmond, later Duke of Brittany, and *d* in London 24 March 1275 (*bur* Grey Friars Church, Newgate, London), leaving issue, four sons and three daus. He *d* at Lyons 18 Nov 1305 (*bur* Carmelite Church, Ploermel).
3 Katherine, *b* at Westminster Palace 25 Nov 1253; *d* at Windsor Castle 3 May 1257 (*bur* Westminster Abbey).

King Henry III was *s* by his eldest son,

1272-1307 EDWARD I *LONGSHANKS,* **King of England** (styled the same as Henry III), *cr* Earl of Chester 14 Feb 1254, crowned at Westminster Abbey by Robert Kilwardby, Archbishop of Canterbury 19 Aug 1274, *b* at Westminster Palace 17 or 18 June 1239, *m* 1st at Burgos between 13 and 31 Oct 1254, Eleanor (Leonor), crowned with her husband (*b ca* 1244; *d* at Herdeby Lincs 28 or 29 Nov 1290, *bur* Westminster Abbey), dau of (St) Fernando III, King of Castile and Leon, by his 2nd wife Jeanne, Countess of Ponthieu, dau and heiress of Simon de Dammartin, Count of Ponthieu and Aumâle, and had issue,
1 John, *b* at Winchester or at Windsor 10 June or July 1266; *d* at Westminster Palace 1 or 3 Aug 1271 (*bur* Westminster Abbey).
2 Henry, *b* at Windsor 13 July 1267; *d* at Merton, Surrey 14 Oct 1274 (*bur* Westminster Abbey).
3 Alfonso, *cr* EARL OF CHESTER *ca* 1284, *b* at Bayonne or at Maine 24 Nov 1273; *d* at Windsor Castle 19 Aug 1284 (*bur* Westminster Abbey).
4 EDWARD II, *s* his father.
1 Eleanor, *b* at Windsor Castle *ca* 17 June 1264, *m* at Bristol 20 Sept 1293, Henri III, Count of Bar, and *d* at Ghent 12 Oct 1297 (*bur* Westminster Abbey), leaving issue, one son and one (or possibly two) daus. He *d* 1302 (*bur* Naples Cathedral).
2 Joan, *d* an inf *ante* 7 Sept 1265 (*bur* Westminster Abbey).
3 Julian (or Katherine), *b* in the Holy Land 1271; *d* there 5 Sept (?) 1271.
4 Joan (*of Acre*), *b* at Acre spring 1272, *m* 1st at Westminster Abbey 30 April 1290, as his 2nd wife, Gilbert de Clare, 3rd Earl of Gloucester and 7th Earl of Hertford, and had issue, one son and three daus (*see* BURKE'S *Dormant and Extinct Peerages*). He *d* at Monmouth Castle 7 Dec 1295 (*bur* Tewkesbury Abbey). She *m* 2ndly Jan 1297, as his 1st wife, Ralph de Monthermer, 1st Baron Monthermer, who enjoyed the Earldoms of Gloucester and Hertford during her lifetime (*see* BURKE'S *Dormant and Extinct Peerages*), and *d* at Clare, Suffolk 23 April 1307 (*bur* Clare Priory), leaving further issue, two sons and two daus. He *d* between 6 Feb 1325 and 18 Feb 1326.
5 Margaret, *b* at Windsor Castle 11 Sept 1275, *m* at Westminster Abbey 8 July 1290, Jean II, Duke of Brabant, and *d* 1318 (*bur* Collegiate Church of St Gudule, Brussels), leaving issue, one son. He *d* at Terveuren 27 Oct 1312 (*bur* St Gudule).
6 Berengaria, *b* at Kennington 1276; *d* 1279 (?) (*bur* Westminster Abbey).
7 Mary, professed a nun at Amesbury 15 Aug 1285, *b* at Windsor Castle 11 March 1278; *d* at Amesbury *ante* 8 July 1332 (*bur* there).
8 Alice, *b* at Woodstock, Oxon 12 March 1279; *d* 1291.
9 Elizabeth, *b* at Rhuddlan Castle Aug 1282, *m* 1st at Ipswich, Suffolk 18 Jan 1297, Jan I, Count of Holland. He *dsp* at Haarlem 10 Nov 1299. She *m* 2ndly at Westminster 14 Nov 1302, Humphrey de Bohun, 4th Earl of Hereford and Essex, Lord of Brecknock and Constable of England (*see* BURKE'S *Dormant and Extinct Peerages*), and *d ca* 5 May 1316 (*bur* Walden Priory, Essex), having had issue, six sons and four daus. He was *k* at Boroughbridge, Yorks 16 March 1321.
10 Beatrice, *b* in Aquitaine *ca* 1286; *d* young.
11 Blanche, *b* 1290; *d* young.

King Edward I *m* 2ndly at Canterbury Cathedral 8 or 10 Sept 1299, Marguerite* (*b* 1279; *d* at Marlborough Castle 14 Feb 1317, *bur* Grey Friars Church, London), dau of Philippe III, King of France, by his wife Marie, only dau of Henri III, Duke of Brabant, and *d* at Burgh-on-the-Sands, nr Carlisle 8 July 1307 (*bur* Westminster Abbey), having by her had issue,
5 Thomas (*of Brotherton*), *cr* EARL OF NORFOLK by Special Charter 16 Nov 1312, Earl

* She appears to have been the first Queen Consort since the conquest not to have been crowned.

Marshal of England, *b* at Brotherton, Yorks 1 June 1300, *m* 1st *ca* 1316, Alice (*d post* 8 May 1326), dau of Sir Roger Hayles, Kt, of Harwich, and had issue,

1 Edward, *b ca* 1319, *m ca* 1327, Beatrice (who *m* 2ndly *ca* 1334, Thomas de Braose, 1st Baron Braose (*d* 1361), and *d* 16 Oct 1383, leaving issue (*see* BURKE'S *Dormant and Extinct Peerages*)), 7th dau of Roger Mortimer, 1st Earl of March (*see* BURKE'S *Dormant and Extinct Peerages*), and *dspvp ca* 1332.

1 Margaret, as Countess of Norfolk claimed to execute the office of Earl Marshal of England by deputy at the coronation of King Richard II but was disallowed, *cr* DUCHESS OF NORFOLK for life 29 Sept 1397, *b ca* 1320, *m* 1st (Royal Assent given 3 March 1327), John de Segrave, 4th Baron Segrave (*see* BURKE'S *Dormant and Extinct Peerages*, and BURKE'S *Peerage*, MOWBRAY, SEGRAVE AND STOURTON, B.), and had issue, two daus. He *d* 20 March 1353 (*bur* Chacombe Priory, Northants). She *m* 2ndly *ante* 30 May 1354, Walter Manny, 1st Baron Manny, KG, and *d* 24 March 1400 (*bur* Carthusian Church, London) (*see* BURKE'S *Dormant and Extinct Peerages*), having had further issue, one son and one dau. He *d* at Great Chesterford, Essex 15 Jan 1372 (*bur* Carthusian Church, London, which he had founded).
2 Alice, *m ante* 16 Jan 1339, as his 1st wife, Edward de Montagu, 1st Baron Montagu (*see* BURKE'S *Dormant and Extinct Peerages*), and *d ante* 16 Nov 1351, leaving issue, three daus. He *d* July 1361.

He *m* 2ndly *ca* 1328, Mary (*d* 9 June 1362), widow of Sir Ralph de Cobham, and dau of William, 2nd Baron de Ros (*see* BURKE'S *Peerage*) and *d* Aug 1338 (will dated 4 Aug 1338) (*bur* Bury St Edmunds).
6 Edmund (*of Woodstock*), *cr* EARL OF KENT by Charter 28 July 1321, summoned to Parl by Writ 5 Aug 1320, *b* at Woodstock 5 Aug 1301, *m ca* Christmas 1325, Margaret, Baroness Wake (*b ca* 1299; *d* 29 Sept 1349), widow of John Comyn, Lord of Badenoch, and only dau of John, 1st Baron Wake, and heiress of her brother Thomas, 2nd Baron Wake (*see* BURKE'S *Peerage*, WAKE, Bt), and was beheaded at Winchester for his part in the conspiracy to rescue King Edward II from prison 19 March 1330 (*bur* Church of the Friars Minors, Winchester), leaving issue,

1 Edmund, 2nd EARL OF KENT, etc, restored in blood to his father's honours 1331, *b ca* 1326; *d* 5 Jan 1333.
2 John, 3rd EARL OF KENT, etc, *s* his brother, *b* at Arundel Castle, Sussex 7 April 1330, *m ca* 1352, Elizabeth (who *m* 2ndly Sept 1360, Sir Eustace Dabridgecourt, and *d* 6 June 1411, *bur* Winchester), dau of Wilhelm V, Duke of Jülich, by his wife Jeanne, dau of Guillaume I, Count of Hainault (sister of Queen Philippa), and *dsp* 26 or 27 Dec 1352.
1 Joan ("The Fair Maid of Kent"), *s* her brother as COUNTESS OF KENT, BARONESS WOODSTOCK and BARONESS WAKE 1352, *b* 29 Sept 1328, *m* 1st *ante* 15 Oct 1348 (*m* annulled by Papal Bull on the grounds of her pre-contract with Sir Thomas de Holand 13 Nov 1349), as his 1st wife, William de Montacute, 2nd Earl of Salisbury, KG (*see* BURKE'S *Dormant and Extinct Peerages*). He *d* 3 June 1397. She *m* 2ndly (having been affianced since 1346), Sir Thomas de Holand, KG, *cr* Earl of Kent and Baron Wake *jure uxoris* (*see* BURKE'S *Dormant and Extinct Peerages*), and had issue, three sons and two daus. He *d* in Normandy 26 or 28 Dec 1360. She *m* 3rdly at Windsor 10 Oct 1361, her 1st cousin once removed, Edward, Prince of Wales, eldest son and heir of King Edward III, and *d* at Wallingford Castle, Berks 8 Aug 1385 (*bur* Stamford, Lincs), having had further issue (*see below, p* 199). He *d* at Westminster Palace 8 June 1376 (*bur* Canterbury Cathedral).

12 Eleanor, *b* at Winchester 4 May 1306; *d* at Amesbury, Wilts 1311 (*bur* either Beaulieu Abbey, Hants, or Westminster Abbey).

King Edward I was *s* by his 4th (but eldest surv) son,

1307-1327 EDWARD II, King of England (styled the same as Henry III), had a grant of the Principality of Wales and Earldom of Chester 7 Feb 1301, crowned at Westminster Abbey by Henry Merewell (*alias* Woodlock), Bishop of Winchester 24 Feb 1308, deposed by Parl 20 Jan 1327, *b* at Caernarvon Castle 25 April 1284, *m* at Boulogne *ca* 25 Jan 1308, Isabelle, crowned with her husband (*b* 1295; *d* at Hertford Castle 22 Aug 1358, *bur* Grey Friars Church, London), eldest dau of Philippe IV, King of France, by his wife Jeanne I, Queen of Navarre, and was murdered at Berkeley Castle 21 Sept 1327 (*bur* Gloucester Cathedral), leaving issue,

1 EDWARD III, *s* his father.
2 John (*of Eltham*), *cr* EARL OF CORNWALL 16-31 Oct 1328, Guardian of the Realm May-June 1329 and April 1331, *b* at Eltham Palace, Kent *ca* 15 Aug 1316; *d unm* at Perth 13 or 14 Sept 1336 (*bur* Westminster Abbey).
1 Eleanor, *b* at Woodstock 18 June 1318, *m* at Nimeguen May 1332, as his 2nd wife, Rainald II, Count (later Duke) of Gueldres, Vicar-Gen of the Empire under the Emperor Ludwig of Bavaria, and *d* at Deventer 22 April 1355 (*bur* there), leaving issue, two sons. He *d* at Arnhem 12 Oct 1343.
2 Joan ("Joan Makepeace"), *b* in the Tower of London 5 July 1321, *m* at Berwick-on-Tweed 17 July 1328, as his 1st wife, David II, King of Scots (*see* KINGS AND QUEENS OF SCOTLAND, *p* 317) and *dsp* at Hertford 7 Sept 1362 (*bur* Grey Friars Church, London). He *d* at Edinburgh Castle 22 Feb 1371 (*bur* Holyrood Abbey).

King Edward II was *s* on his deposition by his elder son,

1327-1377 EDWARD III, King of England (styled the same as Henry III until 1340, then *Rex Angliae et Franciae et Dominus Hiberniae*), *cr* Earl of Chester 24 Nov 1312, Count of Ponthieu and Montreuil 2 Sept 1325, Duke of Aquitaine 10 Sept 1325, proclaimed Keeper of the Realm 26 Oct 1326, proclaimed King 25 Jan 1327, crowned at Westminster Abbey by Walter Reynolds, Archbishop of Canterbury 2 Feb 1327, claimed the crown of France 1340, renounced the claim 1360, resumed it June 1369, founded the Most Noble Order of the Garter 1348, *b* at Windsor Castle 13 Nov 1312, *m* at York Minster 24 Jan 1328, Philippa, crowned at Westminster Abbey 20 Feb 1328 (*b ca* 1312; *d* at Windsor Castle 15 Aug 1369, *bur* Westminster Abbey), 3rd dau of Guillaume I, Count of Hainault, by his wife Jeanne, 2nd dau of Charles, Count of Valois (and sister of Philippe VI, King of France), and *d* at Sheen Palace, Surrey 21 June 1377 (*bur* Westminster Abbey), having had issue,

1 Edward (*of Woodstock*), KG (1348), *cr* EARL OF CHESTER by Charter 18 May 1335, DUKE OF CORNWALL in Parl 3 March 1337, and PRINCE OF WALES in Parl 12 May 1343, Lieut of the Duchy of Aquitaine 1355-72, *cr* PRINCE OF AQUITAINE by Charter 19 July 1362, *cr* Lord of Biscay and Castro Urdiales in Spain by Pedro I, King of Castile 23 Sept 1366, known to posterity as "The Black Prince", *b* at Woodstock 15 June 1330, *m* at Windsor 10 Oct 1361, his 1st cousin once removed, Joan, *suo jure* Countess of Kent, etc (*b* 29 Sept 1328; *d* at Wallingford Castle, Berks 8 Aug 1385, *bur* Stamford, Lincs), widow of Thomas de

Holand, 1st Earl of Kent, KG (*see* BURKE'S *Dormant and Extinct Peerages*), and only dau of Edmund *of Woodstock*, Earl of Kent (*see above, p* 198), and *dvp* at Westminster Palace 8 June 1376 (*bur* Canterbury Cathedral), having had issue,

1 Edward (*of Angoulême*), *b* at Angoulême 27 Jan 1365; *dvp* at Bordeaux 1372, (*bur* Austin Friars, London).

2 RICHARD II, *s* his grandfather.

2 William (*of Hatfield*), *b* at Hatfield, Herts *ante* 16 Feb 1337; *d ante* 8 July 1337 (*bur* Kings Langley, Herts).

3 Lionel (*of Antwerp*), KG (1361), *cr* in full Parl DUKE OF CLARENCE 13 Nov 1362, EARL OF ULSTER *jure uxoris*, Chief Gov of Ireland 1361-64, 1364-65 and 1367, *b* at Antwerp 29 Nov 1338, *m* 1st at the Tower of London 9 Sept 1342, Elizabeth (*b* probably at Carrickfergus Castle 6 July 1332; *d* at Dublin 10 (?) Dec 1363, *bur* Clare Priory, Suffolk), only dau and heiress of William de Burgh, 3rd Earl of Ulster (*see* BURKE'S *Dormant and Extinct Peerages*) and had issue,

Philippa, *b* at Eltham Palace, Kent 16 Aug 1355, *m* at the Queen's Chapel, Reading *post* 15 Feb 1359, Edmund Mortimer, 3rd Earl of March, Marshal of England and Lieut of Ireland (*b* 1 Feb 1352; *d* at Cork 26 or 27 Dec 1381, *bur* Wigmore, Herefordshire), eldest son and heir of Roger Mortimer, 2nd Earl of March, KG (*see* BURKE'S *Dormant and Extinct Peerages*), and *d* on or *ante* 7 Jan 1378 (*bur* Wigmore), leaving issue,

(1) Roger Mortimer, 4th EARL OF MARCH and 7th EARL OF ULSTER, Lieut of Ireland 1381, declared heir to the throne by King Richard II 1387, *b* at Usk 1 Sept 1373, *m ca* 7 Oct 1388, Eleanor (*b ca* 1373; *m* 2ndly *post* 19 June 1399, Edward de Cherleton, 4th Baron Cherleton of Powys, KG (*d* 14 March 1421), and *d* 23 Oct 1405, leaving further issue (*see* BURKE'S *Dormant and Extinct Peerages*)), eldest dau of Thomas de Holand, 2nd Earl of Kent, KG (half-brother of King Richard II) (*see* BURKE'S *Dormant and Extinct Peerages*), and was *k* in a skirmish with the Irish at Kenlis 20 July 1398 (*bur* Wigmore), leaving issue,

1*a* Edmund Mortimer, 5th EARL OF MARCH and 8th EARL OF ULSTER, *de jure* King of England on the death of King Richard II but did not succeed in asserting his claim against the House of Lancaster, *b* in the New Forest 4 Nov 1391, *m ca* 1415, Anne (who *m* 2ndly John, Earl of Huntingdon (later Duke of Exeter), and *d* 20 Sept 1432, leaving issue (*see* BURKE'S *Dormant and Extinct Peerages*)), eldest dau of Edmund Stafford, 5th Earl of Stafford, KG (*see* BURKE'S *Dormant and Extinct Peerages*), by his wife Anne, eldest dau of Thomas, Duke of Gloucester (*see p* 202), and *dsp* at Trim Castle, co Meath 19 Jan 1425 (*bur* Stoke Clare, Suffolk).

2*a* Roger Mortimer, *b* 24 March 1393; *d unm ca* 1409/10.

1*a* Anne Mortimer, *b* 27 Dec 1390, *m ca* May 1406, as his 1st wife, Richard, Earl of Cambridge, son of Edmund, Duke of York, and *d* Sept 1411 (*bur* Kings Langley), leaving issue (*see p* 201). He was beheaded at Southampton 6 Aug 1415.

2*a* Eleanor Mortimer, *b ca* 1395, *m* 1408/9, Edward, Lord Courtenay, KB, Adm of the Fleet, son and heir of Edward Courtenay, 3rd Earl of Devon (*see* BURKE'S *Peerage*) and *dsp*. He *dvp* 1 May 1418.

(2) Edmund Mortimer (Sir), *b* Nov 1377, *m ca* Nov 1402, Katherine (*d ante* 1 Dec 1413, *bur* St Swithin's Church, London), dau of Owain, Lord of Glyndyfrdwy (Owen Glendower), sometime Prince of Wales, by his wife Margaret, dau of Sir David Hanmer, of Hanmer, Flint (*see* BURKE'S *Peerage*, HANMER, Bt), and *d ante* 13 May 1411, having had issue, one son and two or more daus, who *d* young and were *bur* with their mother.

(1) Elizabeth Mortimer, *b* at Usk 12 Feb 1371, *m* 1st *ante* 1 May 1380, Henry Percy, Lord Percy, KG (*Hotspur*), eldest son and heir of Henry Percy, 1st Earl of Northumberland, and had issue, one son and one dau (*see* BURKE'S *Peerage*, NORTHUMBERLAND, D). He was *k* at the Battle of Shrewsbury 21 July 1403. She *m* 2ndly, as his 2nd wife, Thomas, 1st Baron Camoys, KG (*see* BURKE'S *Peerage*), and *d ca* 1417/18 (*bur* Trotton, Sussex). He *d* 28 March 1419 (*bur* Trotton).

(2) Philippa Mortimer, *b* at Ludlow 21 Nov 1375, *m* 1st *ca* 1385, as his 2nd wife, John Hastings, 3rd Earl of Pembroke (formerly husband of Elizabeth, 2nd dau of John *of Gaunt*, Duke of Lancaster—*see below*) (*see* BURKE'S *Dormant and Extinct Peerages*). He *d* 30 Dec 1389. She *m* 2ndly *ante* 15 Aug 1390, as his 2nd wife, Richard Fitzalan, 10th Earl of Arundel, KG (*see* BURKE'S *Dormant and Extinct Peerages*) and had issue, one son (who *d* young). He was beheaded at Cheapside 21 Sept 1397 (*bur* Austin Friars, London). She *m* 3rdly, as his 2nd wife, Thomas Poynings, 5th Baron St John of Basing (*see* BURKE'S *Dormant and Extinct Peerages*) and *dsps* 26 Sept 1400 (*bur* Boxgrove, Sussex). He *d* 7 March 1429.

Lionel, Duke of Clarence *m* 2ndly at Milan 28 May 1368, Violante (*b ca* 1353; *m* 2ndly at Pavia 2 Aug 1377, Ottone Paleologo, Marquis of Montferrat (murdered at Langhirano nr Parma Dec 1378); and 3rdly 18 April 1381, her 1st cousin, Lodovico Visconti, Lord of Lodi (*d* 1404), and *d* Nov 1386), yr dau of Galeazzo II (Visconti), Lord of Milan, by his wife Bianca Maria, dau of Aimone, Count of Savoy, and *dspm* at Alba (Longuevil), Piedmont 17 Oct 1368 (*bur* first Pavia, later transferred to Clare Priory, Suffolk).

4 John (*of Gaunt*), KG (1361), *cr* EARL OF RICHMOND 20 Nov 1342 (confirmed 6 March 1351), DUKE OF LANCASTER 13 Nov 1362, and DUKE OF AQUITAINE *for life* 2 March 1389, EARL OF LANCASTER, DERBY, LINCOLN and LEICESTER *jure uxoris*, Steward of England, titular King of Castile and Leon, *b* at the Abbey of St Bavon, Ghent March 1340, *m* 1st at the Queen's Chapel, Reading 13 May 1359, Blanche (*b* 25 March 1345; *d* at Bolingbroke Castle 12 Sept 1369, *bur* St Paul's Cathedral), yr dau and co-heiress of Henry, 4th Earl and 1st Duke of Lancaster, KG (*see p* 197), and had issue,

1 John, *b ca* 1362; *d* young (*bur* St Mary's Church, Leicester).

2 Edward, *b ca* 1365; *d* young (*bur* St Mary's Church, Leicester).

3 John, *b ante* 4 May 1366; *d* young (*bur* St Mary's Church, Leicester).

4 HENRY IV, *s* his cousin King Richard II.

1 Philippa, *b* at Leicester 31 March 1360, *m* at Oporto 11 Feb 1387, João I, King of Portugal, and *d* at Odivelas, nr Lisbon 19 July 1415 (*bur* Batalha), having had issue, six sons and two daus. He *d* at Lisbon 14 Aug 1433 (*bur* Batalha).

2 Elizabeth, *b ante* 21 Feb 1363, *m* 1st at Kenilworth 24 June 1380 (*m* diss *ca* 1383), as his 1st wife, John Hastings, 3rd Earl of Pembroke (who *m* 2ndly, Lady Philippa Mortimer—*see above*) (*see* BURKE'S *Dormant and Extinct Peerages*). He *dsp* 30 Dec 1389. She *m* 2ndly *ca* 1384, John de Holand, 1st Duke of Exeter, KG (half-brother of King Richard II) (*see* BURKE'S *Dormant and Extinct Peerages*), and had issue, three sons and two daus. He was beheaded at Pleshey, Essex 9 Jan 1400 (*bur* Collegiate Church there). She *m* 3rdly ante 3 July 1401, John Cornwall, 1st Baron Fanhope of Fanhope and Milbroke of Milbroke, KG (descended from a natural son of Richard, Earl of Cornwall and King of the Romans—*see above, p* 196, and BURKE'S *Dormant and Extinct Peerages*), and *d* 24 Nov 1425 (*bur* Burford, Salop). He *dsp* 11 Dec 1443.

3 Isabel, *b ca* 1368; *d* young.

John, Duke of Lancaster *m* 2ndly at Roquefort, Guienne Sept 1371, Constance, titular Queen of Castile and Leon (*b* at Castro Kerez 1354; *d* at Leicester 24 March 1394, *bur* St Mary's Church there), 2nd dau of Pedro I *the Cruel*, King of Castile and Leon, by his mistress Maria de Padilla (whom he claimed to have *m* secretly), and by her had issue,

5 John (*of Gaunt*), *b* at Ghent 1374; *d* an inf.

4 Catherine, *b* at Hertford between 6 June 1372 and 31 March 1373, *m* at Burgos 1393, Enrique III, King of Castile and Leon, and *d* 2 June 1418 (*bur* Toledo), having had issue, one son and two daus. He *d* at Toledo 25 or 26 Dec 1406 (*bur* there).

John, Duke of Lancaster *m* 3rdly at Lincoln 13 Jan 1396, Catherine (*b* 1350; *d* at Lincoln 10 May 1403, *bur* Lincoln Cathedral), widow of Sir Hugh Swynford, Kt, and dau of Sir Payn Roet, Kt, of Hainault, Guienne King of Arms, and *d* at Leicester Castle 3 Feb 1399 (*bur* St Paul's Cathedral), having by her had issue (surnamed *Beaufort*) all born prior to their marriage and legitimated by Statute 9 Feb 1397 for all purposes save succession to the crown,

6 John Beaufort, KG (1397), *cr* EARL OF SOMERSET 10 Feb 1397, and MARQUESS OF DORSET AND SOMERSET 29 Sept 1397, Lord High Adm, Great Chamberlain of England, Capt of Calais, *b* at Beaufort Castle, Anjou *ca* 1373, *m ante* 23 April 1399, Margaret (*b* 1385; *m* 2ndly 1412, Thomas, Duke of Clarence, KG, 2nd son of King Henry IV (*see below, p* 202), and *d* 31 Dec 1439, *bur* Canterbury Cathedral), 3rd dau of Thomas de Holand, 2nd Earl of Kent, KG (*see* BURKE'S *Dormant and Extinct Peerages*), and *d* 21 April 1410 (*bur* Canterbury Cathedral), leaving issue,

(1) Henry Beaufort, 2nd EARL OF SOMERSET, *b* Oct 1401; *d* 25 Nov 1418.

(2) John Beaufort, 3rd EARL OF SOMERSET, KG (1440), *cr* DUKE OF SOMERSET and EARL OF KENDAL 28 Aug 1443, *b ante* 25 March 1404, *m* 1439, Margaret (who *m* 3rdly, as his 2nd or 3rd wife, Leo, 6th Baron Welles, KG, KB (*k* at Towton 29 March 1461) (*see* BURKE'S *Dormant and Extinct Peerages*), and *d* 8 Aug 1482, leaving further issue), widow of Sir Oliver St John, of Bletso, Beds (*see* BURKE'S *Peerage*, ST JOHN OF BLETSO, B), only dau of John Beauchamp, 3rd Baron Beauchamp of Bletso, and sister and heiress of John Beauchamp, 4th Baron Beauchamp of Bletso (*see* BURKE'S *Dormant and Extinct Peerages*), and *d* 27 May 1444 (*bur* Wimborne Minster, Dorset), leaving issue,

Margaret Beaufort, *b* at Bletso, Beds, April 1441, *m* 1st 1455, Edmund Tudor, 1st Earl of Richmond (*b* at Hadham, Beds *ca* 1430; *d* at Carmarthen 3 Nov 1456, *bur* St David's Cathedral), son of Owen Tudor, by his wife Catherine, widow of King Henry V (*see below, p* 203), and dau of Charles VI, King of France, and had issue,

HENRY VII, *s* King Richard III.

She *m* 2ndly *ca* 1459, Lord Henry Stafford, 2nd son of Humphrey, 1st Duke of Buckingham (*see* BURKE'S *Dormant and Extinct Peerages*). He *d* 1481. She *m* 3rdly, as his 2nd wife, Thomas Stanley, 1st Earl of Derby, KG, Constable of England (*see* BURKE'S *Peerage*), and *d* at Westminster Palace 5 July 1509 (*bur* Westminster Abbey). He *d* 29 July 1504.

(3) Thomas Beaufort, styled EARL OF PERCHE, *b* 1405; *d unm* 1432.

(4) Edmund Beaufort, KG (1436), 4th EARL OF SOMERSET, *cr* MARQUESS OF DORSET 24 June 1443, and DUKE OF SOMERSET 31 March 1448, Lord High Constable of England, sometime Regent of France (for King Henry VI) and Count of Mortain in Normandy, *b* 1406, *m* 1431/35, Eleanor (*b* 1408; *d* at Baynard's Castle, London 6 March 1468), widow of Thomas, 9th Baron de Ros (*see* BURKE'S *Peerage*), and 2nd dau of Richard Beauchamp, 5th Earl of Warwick, KG (*see* BURKE'S *Dormant and Extinct Peerages*), and was *k* at the first Battle of St Albans 22 May 1455, leaving issue,

1*a* Henry Beaufort, 2nd Duke of Somerset, etc, *b* 26 Jan 1436; beheaded after a fight at Hexham with the Yorkists 15 May 1464, *unm* (*bur* Tewkesbury Abbey)*.

2*a* Edmund Beaufort, sometimes styled (3r Duke of Somerset, but never restored to h brother's honours, *b ante* 1440; *d unm* bein beheaded two days after the Battle of Tewkesbu 6 May 1471.

3a John Beaufort, *k* at the Battle of Tewkesbu 4 May 1471.

4*a* Thomas Beaufort, *d* young *ante* 1463.

1*a* Margaret Beaufort, *m* 1st Humphrey Staffor 7th Earl of Stafford (*see* BURKE'S *Dormant an Extinct Peerages*), and had issue, two sons. H was *k* at the Battle of St Albans 22 May 145 She *m* 2ndly Sir Richard Dayrell, Kt, of Lillin stone Dayrell, Bucks, and *d* 1474 (Inquisitio *post mortem* 8 May 1474), leaving further issu one dau.

2*a* Eleanor Beaufort, *m* 1st, as his 2nd wif James Butler, 5th Earl of Ormonde and 1st Ea of Wiltshire, KG, sometime Lord Dep of Irelan and Lord High Treas of England (*see* BURKE' *Peerage*, ORMONDE, M). He was beheade at Newcastle 1 May 1461. She *m* 2ndly S Robert Spencer, Kt, of Spencercombe, Devo He was living 13 March 1492.

3*a* Elizabeth Beaufort, *m* Sir Henry Lewes, K and *d ante* 1492, leaving issue, one dau.

4*a* Margaret (or Mary) Beaufort, *m* —— Burgh and had issue, two sons.

5*a* Anne Beaufort, *m* Sir William Paxton, K and had issue, one son and two daus.

6*a* Joan Beaufort, *m* 1st, Robert Howth, Lor of Howth in Ireland; and 2ndly, Sir Richard Fr Kt, and was living *sp* 1492.

(1) Joan Beaufort, *m* 1st at the Church of S Mary Overy, Southwark 2 Feb 1424, James I, Kin of Scots, and had issue (*see* KINGS AN QUEENS OF SCOTLAND, *p* 319). He was mu dered at Perth 21 Feb 1437 (*bur* in the Carthusia Church there). She *m* 2ndly 1439, Sir Jame Stewart, the "Black Knight of Lorne", and *d* a Dunbar Castle 15 July 1445 (*bur* Carthusia Church, Perth), leaving further issue.

(2) Margaret Beaufort.

7 Henry Beaufort, Dean of Wells 1397, conse crated Bishop of Lincoln 14 July 1398, Chancello of Oxford Univ 1399, Chancellor of Englan 1403-04, Bishop of Winchester 1404, agai Chancellor of England 1413 and 1424-26, nominate Cardinal-Priest of St Eusebius by Pope Martin V 23 June 1426, legate in Germany, Hungary an Bohemia, *b* at Beaufort Castle *ca* 1375, *educ* Pete house, Camb, Oxford Univ, and Aachen, *d* 11 Apri 1447 (*bur* Winchester Cathedral).

8 Thomas Beaufort, KG (1400), Capt of Calai 1407, Chancellor of England 1410-12, *cr* EARL O DORSET 5 July 1411 or 1412, and DUKE O EXETER *for life* 18 Nov 1416, Count of Harcour in Normandy 1 July 1418, Capt of Rouen 1419, *b* at Beaufort Castle *ca* Jan 1377, *m* Margaret, da and co-heiress of Sir Thomas Neville, Kt, of Hornby Lincs, and *d* 27 Dec 1426 (*bur* Bury St Edmunds) having had issue,

Henry Beaufort, *d* young *vp*.

5 Joan Beaufort, *b* at Beaufort Castle *ca* 1379, *m* 1st Robert Ferrers, 2nd Baron Ferrers of Wemme and had issue, two daus (*see* BURKE'S *Dorman and Extinct Peerages*). He *d ante* 29 Nov 1396 She *m* 2ndly *ante* 20 Feb 1397, as his 2nd wife Ralph Nevill, 1st Earl of Westmoreland, KG (*se* BURKE'S *Dormant and Extinct Peerages*), and *d* a Howden, Yorks 13 Nov 1440 (*bur* Lincol Cathedral), having had further issue, eight sons and five daus. He *d* at Raby Castle 21 Oct 1425.

5 Edmund (*of Langley*), KG (1361), *cr* EARL OF CAMBRIDGE 13 Nov 1362, Constable of Dove Castle and Lord Warden of the Cinque Ports 1376-81, *cr* DUKE OF YORK 6 Aug 1385, Chief Justic of Chester and Flint 1385-87, Guardian and Lieu of England 1394-95, and again 1396 and 1399, *b* a Kings Langley, Herts 5 June 1341, *m* 1st at Hertford (?) *ca* 1 March 1372, Isabel (*b* at Morales, or a Tordesillas 1355; *d* 23 Nov 1393, *bur* Kings Langley), 3rd and yst dau of Pedro I *the Cruel*, King of Castile and Leon, by his mistress Maria de Padilla (whom he claimed to have *m* secretly), and had issue,

* He left a natural son, Charles Somerset, *b ca* 1460, *cr* Lord Herbert of Raglan 1506 and Earl of Worcester 1514, ancestor of the present Duke of Beaufort (*see* BURKE'S *Peerage*).

1 Edward, KG (1387), PC (1399), *cr* EARL OF RUTLAND 25 Feb 1390, Adm of the North and West 1391-98, Constable of the Tower of Lond 1392, and again 1406, Jt Amb to France 1395, Constable of Dover Castle and Lord Warden of the Cinque Ports 1396-98, Gov of Jersey, Guernsey, Sark and Alderney 1396, Lord of IoW and Carisbrooke Castle 1397, *cr* DUKE OF ALBEMARLE 29 Sept 1397, again Constable of the Tower of Lond 1397-99, Constable of England 1398-99, Jt Amb to Scotland 1399, deprived of the Dukedom of Albemarle 6 Oct 1399, Lieut of the Duchy of Aquitaine 1400-13, Warden and Gov of N Wales 1401, *s* his father as 2nd DUKE OF YORK 1402, Jt Founder of Fotheringay Coll 1411, Warden and Commissary-Gen of the East Marches towards Scotland and Capt of the Castle and town of Berwick 1414-15, Constable and Marshal of the King's Army in France Sept-Oct 1415, *b* 1373, *m ca* 1398, Philippa (who is said to have *m* 4thly, John Vesey, and *d* 17 July 1431, *bur* Westminster Abbey), widow of (1) Sir John Golofre, Kt, of Langley, Oxon, and (2) Walter Fitzwalter, 4th Baron FitzWalter (*see* BURKE'S *Peerage*), and dau and co-heiress of John de Mohun, 2nd Baron Mohun of Dunster (*see* BURKE'S *Dormant and Extinct Peerages*), and was *k* at the Battle of Agincourt 25 Oct 1415, *sp* (*bur* Fotheringay).

2 Richard, *s* his father as EARL OF CAMBRIDGE 1402, attainted for high treason 1415, *b* at Conisborough Castle, Yorks *ca* Sept 1376, *m* 1st *ca* May 1406, Anne (*b* 27 Dec 1390; *d* Sept 1411, *bur* Kings Langley), elder dau of Roger Mortimer, 4th Earl of March (*see above, p* 199), and had issue,

Richard, KG (1433), *s* his uncle as 3rd DUKE OF YORK 1415, *s* as EARL OF MARCH and ULSTER 1425, Lieut and Gov-Gen of France and Normandy 1436-37 and 1440-47, Jt Amb to treat with France 1436, Lieut and Capt-Gen of the Duchy of Aquitaine, Chief Commissary, Amb and Dep to treat with France 1442, Lieut of Ireland 1447-53 and 1457-59, Protector and Defender of the Realm and Church of England and Chief of the Council 3 April 1454 and 1455-56, attainted Nov 1459, restored Oct 1460, declared heir to the crown 25 Oct 1460, assumed the surname of *Plantagenet* 1448, *b* 20 Sept 1411, *m ca* 1437, Cicely (*b* at Raby Castle 3 May 1415; *d* at Berkhamsted Castle 31 May 1495, *bur* Fotheringay), 12th and yst dau of Ralph Nevill, 1st Earl of Westmorland, KG, by his 2nd wife Joan (Beaufort), dau of John *of Gaunt*, Duke of Lancaster (*see above, p* 200) (*see* BURKE'S *Dormant and Extinct Peerages*) and was *k* at Wakefield 31 Dec 1460 (*bur* first Pontefract, later transferred to Fotheringay), having had issue,

1*a* Henry, *b* at Hatfield, Herts 10 Feb 1441; *d* young.

2*a* EDWARD IV, *s* King Henry VI.

3*a* Edmund, *cr* EARL OF RUTLAND *post* 21 Dec 1445, attainted Nov 1459, restored Oct 1460, *b* at Rouen 17 May 1443; *k* at the Battle of Wakefield 31 Dec 1460 (*bur* Fotheringay).

4*a* William, *b* at Fotheringay 7 July 1447; *d* young.

5*a* John, *b* at Neyte, nr Worcester 7 Nov 1448; *d* young.

6*a* George, KG (1461), *cr* DUKE OF CLARENCE 28 June 1461, and EARL OF WARWICK AND SALISBURY 25 March 1472, Lord Great Chamberlain, Lord of Richmond and Lord Lieut of Ireland, attainted 1477, *b* in Dublin 2 Oct 1449, *m* at Calais 11 July 1469, Isabel (*b* at Warwick Castle 5 Sept 1451; *d* there 12 Dec 1476, *bur* Tewkesbury Abbey), eldest dau and co-heiress of Richard Nevill, 1st Earl of Warwick and 2nd Earl of Salisbury, KG (*see* BURKE'S *Dormant and Extinct Peerages*), and was put to death in the Tower of London (said to have been drowned in a butt of Malmsey) 18 Feb 1478 (*bur* Tewkesbury Abbey), having had issue,

1*b* Edward, styled Earl of Warwick, *s* his mother as EARL OF SALISBURY 1476, and his maternal grandmother as EARL OF WARWICK 1490, kept prisoner in the Tower of London by King Henry VII, *b* at Warwick Castle 21 Feb 1474; beheaded on Tower Hill on a charge of high treason 24 Nov 1499, *unm* (*bur* Bisham Abbey, Berks), when the legitimate male line of King Henry II became *extinct*.

2*b* Richard, *b* at Tewkesbury Abbey 6 Oct 1476; *d* at Warwick Castle 1 Jan 1477 (*bur* Warwick).

1*b* Anne (?), *b* at sea off Calais April 1470; *d* an inf (*bur* Calais).

2*b* Margaret, declared COUNTESS OF SALISBURY by King Henry VIII 14 Oct 1513, *b* at Farley Castle, Somerset 14 Aug 1473, *m ante* 22 Sept 1494, Sir Richard Pole, KG, son of Sir Geoffrey Pole, Kt, by his wife Edith, dau of Sir Oliver St John (and half-sister of Margaret, Countess of Richmond and Derby—*see above, p* 200), and was beheaded on Tower Hill (having been attainted 1539) 27 May 1541 (*bur* Chapel of St Peter ad Vincula in the Tower), leaving issue, four sons and one dau. He *d ante* 15 Nov 1504.

7*a* Thomas, *b ca* 1450/51; *d* an inf.

8*a* RICHARD III, *s* King Edward V.

1*a* Anne, *b* at Fotheringay 10 Aug 1439, *m* 1st (*m* diss 12 Nov 1472), Henry Holland, 2nd Duke of Exeter (*see* BURKE'S *Dormant and Extinct Peerages*), and had issue, one dau. He was found dead in the English Channel 1473. She *m* 2ndly 1472 or 1473, Sir Thomas St Leger, Kt, and *d* 14 Jan 1476 (*bur* St George's Chapel, Windsor), having had further issue, one dau. He was executed at Exeter for his part in Buckingham's rebellion Nov 1483 (*bur* St George's Chapel Windsor.)

2*a* Elizabeth, *b* at Rouen 22 April 1444, *m ante* Oct 1460, John de la Pole, 2nd Duke of Suffolk, KG (*see* BURKE'S *Dormant and Extinct Peerages*), and *d post* Jan 1503, having had issue, six sons* and two daus. He *d* 1491 (*bur* Collegiate Church, Wingfield).

3*a* Margaret, *b* at Fotheringay 3 May 1446, *m* at Dame 3 July 1468, as his 3rd wife, Charles, Duke of Burgundy, KG, and *dsp* at Malines 28 Nov 1503 (*bur* Church of the Cordeliers there). He *d* 5 Jan 1477 (*bur* St George's Church, Nancy).

4*a* Ursula, *b ca* 1453/54; *d* young.

Isabel, *b* 1409, *m* 1st (Royal Assent given 18 Feb 1413) (*m* diss *ante* 1430), Thomas Grey, of Werke. He *d ante* 26 July 1443. She *m* 2ndly *ca* 1430, Henry Bourchier, 1st Earl of Essex, KG (*see* BURKE'S *Dormant and Extinct Peerages*), and *d* 2 Oct 1484, having had issue, eight sons and two daus. He *d* 4 April 1483.

Richard, Earl of Cambridge *m* 2ndly 1411-15, Maud (who *m* 2ndly, John Nevill, 5th Baron Latimer of Danby (*dsp* 1430) (*see* BURKE'S *Dormant and Extinct Peerages*), and *d* 26 Aug 1446), dau of Thomas de Clifford, 4th Baron Clifford (*see* BURKE'S *Dormant and Extinct Peerages*), and was beheaded on Southampton Green 6 Aug 1415 (*bur* Chapel of God's House, Southampton).

1 Constance, *b ca* 1374, *m ante* 7 Nov 1379, Thomas Le Despencer, 6th Baron Le Despencer, and 1st and last Earl of Gloucester, KG, and *d* 28 Nov 1416 (*bur* Reading Abbey), having had issue, one son and two daus (*see* BURKE'S *Peerage*, FALMOUTH, V, *Barony of* LE DESPENCER). He was beheaded at Bristol 16 Jan 1400 (*bur* Tewkesbury Abbey).

Edmund, Duke of York *m* 2ndly *ante* 4 Nov 1393, Joan (*b ca* 1380; *m* 2ndly *ante* 26 March 1406, as his 2nd wife, William Willoughby, 5th Baron Willoughby de Eresby, KG (*d* 30 Nov 1410) (*see* BURKE'S *Peerage*, ANCASTER, E); 3rdly *ante* 9 Dec 1410, as his 2nd wife, Henry Scrope, 3rd Baron Scrope of Masham, KG (*d* 5 Aug 1415) (*see* BURKE'S *LG*, SCROPE *of Danby*); and 4thly *ante* 14 Aug 1416, Henry Bromflete, 1st Baron Vesey (*d* 6 Jan 1468) (*see* BURKE'S *Dormant and Extinct*

---

* The eldest son, John, styled Earl of Lincoln, was declared heir-presumptive to the crown by King Richard III 1484. He was *k* at the Battle of Stoke 16 June 1487.

Peerages), and *dsp* 12 April 1434), 2nd dau of Thomas de Holand, 2nd Earl of Kent, KG (half-brother of King Richard II) (*see* BURKE'S *Dormant and Extinct Peerages*), and *d* at Kings Langley 1 Aug 1402 (*bur* Church of the Mendicant Friars there).

6 William (*of Windsor*), *b* at Windsor Castle *ante* 24 June 1348; *bur* St Edmund's Chapel, Westminster Abbey 5 Sept 1348.

7 Thomas (*of Woodstock*), KG (1380), *cr* EARL OF BUCKINGHAM 16 July 1377, and DUKE OF GLOUCESTER 6 Aug 1385, Justice of Chester 1387, *b* at Woodstock 7 Jan 1355, *m* 1374, Eleanor (*b* 1366; *d* a nun at Barking Abbey, Essex 3 Oct 1399, *bur* Westminster Abbey), eldest dau and co-heiress of Humphrey de Bohun, 7th Earl of Hereford KG (*see* BURKE'S *Dormant and Extinct Peerages*), and was murdered at Calais 8 or 15 Sept 1397 (*bur* Westminster Abbey), leaving issue,

1 Humphrey, 2nd DUKE OF GLOUCESTER, *b ca* April 1382; *d* at Chester 2 Sept 1399 (*bur* Walden Priory, Essex).

1 Anne, *b* April 1383, *m* 1st *ca* 1390, Thomas Stafford, 3rd Earl of Stafford (*see* BURKE'S *Dormant and Extinct Peerages*). He *d* 4 July 1392. She *m* 2ndly *ca* 28 June 1398, Edmund Stafford, 5th Earl of Stafford, KG, brother of her 1st husband (*see* BURKE'S *Dormant and Extinct Peerages*), and had issue, one son and two daus. He was *k* at the Battle of Shrewsbury 21 July 1403 (*bur* Stafford). She *m* 3rdly *ca* 1408, Sir William Bourchier, Kt, Count of Eu in Normandy, and *d* 16 Oct 1438 (*bur* Llanthony Priory, Mon), having had further issue, four sons (of whom the eldest, Henry, *m* Isabel, only dau of Richard, Earl of Cambridge—*see p* 201) and one dau. He *d* at Troyes 1420 (*bur* Llanthony Priory).

2 Joan, *b* 1384; *d* 16 Aug 1400 (*bur* Walden Priory).

3 Isabel, professed a nun of the Order of St Clare at the Minoresses, Aldgate 23 April 1399, *b* 12 March 1386; *d ca* April 1402.

4 Philippa, *b ca* 1389; *d ante* 3 Oct 1399.

1 Isabel, *b* at Woodstock 16 June 1332, *m* at Windsor 27 July 1365, as his 1st wife, Enguerrand VII, Lord of Coucy, *cr* Earl of Bedford and Count of Soissons by his father-in-law, KG, only son of Enguerrand VI, Lord of Coucy, by his wife Catherine, dau of Leopold II, Duke of Austria, and *d ante* 7 Oct 1382 (*bur* Grey Friars, London), leaving issue, two daus. He *d* at Bursa, Anatolia 18 Feb 1397.

2 Joan, *b* at Woodstock *ca* Feb 1335; *d* at Loremo *en route* for Spain 2 Sept 1348 (*bur* Bayonne Cathedral).

3 Blanche, *b* and *d* at the Tower of London March 1342 (*bur* Westminster Abbey).

4 Mary, *b* at Waltham, nr Winchester 9 or 10 Oct 1344, *m* at Woodstock summer 1361, as his 1st wife, Jean V, Duke of Brittany, KG, and *dsp* autumn 1361 or early 1362 (*bur* Abingdon Abbey, Berks). He *d* at Nantes 1 Nov 1399 (*bur* Nantes Cathedral).

5 Margaret, *b* at Windsor 20 July 1346, *m* at the Queen's Chapel, Reading 19 May 1359, as his 1st wife, John Hastings, 2nd Earl of Pembroke, KG (*see* BURKE'S *Dormant and Extinct Peerages*), and *dsp post* 1 Oct 1361 (*bur* Abingdon Abbey, Berks). He *d* between Paris and Calais 16 April 1375.

King Edward III was *s* by his grandson,

1377-1399 RICHARD II, King of England (styled the same as Edward III), *cr* Earl of Chester, Duke of Cornwall and Prince of Wales 20 Nov 1376, KG 23 April 1377, crowned at Westminster Abbey by Simon Sudbury, Archbishop of Canterbury 16 July 1377, deposed 29 Sept 1399, *b* at Bordeaux 6 Jan 1367, *m* 1st at Westminster Palace 14 or 20 Jan 1382, Anne, crowned at Westminster Abbey by William Courtenay, Archbishop of Canterbury 22 Jan 1382 (*b* at Prague 11 May 1366; *d* at Sheen Palace *ante* 3 June 1394, *bur* Westminster Abbey), dau of Karl IV, Holy Roman Emperor and King of Bohemia, by his 4th wife Elisabeth, dau of Bogislaw V, Duke of Pomerania. He *m* 2ndly at the Church of St Nicholas Calais 4 Nov 1396, Isabelle, crowned at Westminster Abbey 8 Jan 1397 (*b* at the Louvre Paris 9 Nov 1389; *m* 2ndly at Compiègne 2 June 1406, Charles, Duke of Orleans (*d* 4 Ja 1465), and *d* at Blois 13 Sept 1409, *bur* firs Abbey of St Laumer, Blois, later (*ca* 1624 transferred to the Celestines, Paris), 2nd da of Charles VI, King of France, by his wif Isabelle (Isabeau), dau of Stephan II, Duk of Bavaria-Ingolstadt, and *dsp* (supposedl murdered) at Pontefract Castle, Yorks 6 Ja 1400 (*bur* Westminster Abbey).

King Richard II was *s* on his deposition by hi 1st cousin,

1399-1413 HENRY IV, King of Englan (styled the same as Edward III), styled Ear of Derby, KG 1377, *cr* Duke of Hereford 2 Sept 1397, banished from England followin his quarrel with the Duke of Norfolk 1398 returned secretly to recover his estates whic had been confiscated on the death of his fathe and eventually obtained the resignation of th crown in his favour 29 Sept 1399, crowned a Westminster Abbey by Thomas Arundel Archbishop of Canterbury 13 Oct 1399 founded the Order of the Bath 1399, *b* a Bolingbroke Castle, Lincs 3 April 1367, *m* 1s at Arundel Castle between July 1380 an March 1381, Mary (*b ca* 1370; *d* at Peter borough Castle 4 June (or July ?) 1394, *bu* St Mary's Church, Leicester), yr dau and co heiress of Humphrey de Bohun, 7th Earl o Hereford, 6th Earl of Essex, and 2nd Earl o Northampton, KG (*see* BURKE'S *Dorman and Extinct Peerages*), and had issue,

1 A son, *b* April 1382; *d* an inf.

2 HENRY V, *s* his father.

3 Thomas, KG (1399), Lieut of Ireland 1401, Cap of Guines 1407, *cr* DUKE OF CLARENCE an EARL OF ALBEMARLE 9 July 1412, Lieut o France 1421, *b* at Kenilworth, Warwicks *ante* 3 Sept (and ? May) 1388, *m* 1412, Margaret (*b* 1385 *d* 31 Dec 1439, *bur* Canterbury Cathedral), widow o his father's half-brother, John Beaufort, Earl o Somerset, KG (*see above, p* 200), and dau of Thoma de Holand, 2nd Earl of Kent, KG (half-brother o King Richard II) (*see* BURKE'S *Dormant an Extinct Peerages*), and was *k* at the Battle of Beaug 22 March 1421, *sp*, (*bur* Canterbury Cathedral).

4 John, KG (1400), *cr* DUKE OF BEDFORD an EARL OF KENDAL *for life* 16 May 1414 (titl confirmed with limitation extended to heirs mal 8 July 1433), and EARL OF RICHMOND 24 No 1414, Lieut of England 1415 and 1421, Regent o France and Protector of England 1422-35, *b* 20 Jun 1389, *m* 1st at Troyes 17 April 1423, Anne (*b* 1404 05; *d* at the Hôtel de Bourgogne, Paris, 14 Nov 1432 *bur* Célestines Church, Paris), 6th dau of Jean (*San Peur*), Duke of Burgundy, by his wife Marguerite dau of Albert, Count of Holland and Hainault, an had issue,

A child, *b* and *d* at Paris Nov 1432.

He *m* 2ndly at Therouenne 22 April 1433, Jacquett (*b ca* 1416; *m* 2ndly *ca* 1436, Richard Woodville 1st Earl Rivers, KG (beheaded at Northampton 1 Aug 1469) (*see* BURKE'S *Dormant and Extinc Peerages*), and *d* 30 May 1472, leaving issue), dau o Pierre de Luxembourg, Count of St Pol, by his wif Marguerite, eldest dau of Francisco del Balzo (d Baux), Duke of Andria, and *dsps* at Rouen 15 Sep 1435 (*bur* Rouen Cathedral).

5 Humphrey, KG (1400), Great Chamberlain of England 1413, *cr* DUKE OF GLOUCESTER and EARL OF PEMBROKE 16 May 1414, Gov of Rouen 1419, Regent of England 1420-21, Protector 1422 and 1427-29, Lieut of the Kingdom 1430-32, a great patron of literature, *b* Aug or Sept 1390, *m* 1st 1422 (*m* annulled by decree of Pope Martin V 1428), Jacqueline (who *m* 4thly, Floris van Borselen, Count of Ostrevant and Stadtholder of Holland (*d* 1470), and *d* at Teilingen 8 Oct 1436, *bur* the Hague), formerly wife of Jean IV, Duke of Brabant, previously widow of Jean of France, Dauphin of Viennois (4th son of Charles VI, King of France), and only dau of Willem VI, Count of Holland, by his wife Marguerite, eldest dau of Philippe, Duke of Burgundy. He *m* 2ndly *ante* 1431, Eleanor (*d* 1454 ?), dau of Reginald de Cobham, 2nd Baron Cobham of Sterborough (*see* BURKE'S *Dormant and Extinct Peerages*), and *dspl* (supposedly murdered) at Bury St Edmunds 23 Feb 1447 (*bur* St Albans Abbey).

1 Blanche, *b* at Peterborough Castle spring 1392, *m* at Cologne 6 July 1402, as his 1st wife, Ludwig III, Duke of Bavaria, Elector Palatine of the Rhine, and *d* 22 May 1400 (*bur* Neustadt, Alsace), having had issue, one son. He *d* at Heidelberg 29 Dec 1436.

2 Philippa, *b* probably at Peterborough Castle 4 July 1394, *m* at Lund 26 Oct 1406 (being crowned there 1 Nov 1406), Erik (IX) of Pomerania, King of Denmark, Sweden and Norway, and *dsps* in the Convent of Wadstena 5 Jan 1430 (*bur* there). He *d* at Rügenwalde Castle, Pomerania 1459.

King Henry IV *m* 2ndly at Winchester Cathedral 7 Feb 1403, Joan, crowned at Westminster Abbey 26 Feb 1403 (*b ca* 1370; *d* at Havering Bower, Essex 9 July 1437, *bur* Canterbury Cathedral), widow of Jean V, Duke of Brittany, and 2nd dau of Charles II, King of Navarre, by his wife Jeanne, eldest dau of Jean II, King of France, and *d* in the Jerusalem Chamber at Westminster Abbey 20 March 1413 (*bur* Canterbury Cathedral).

King Henry IV was *s* by his eldest surv son,

1413-1422 HENRY V, King of England (styled the same as Edward III until 1420, then *Rex Angliae, Haeres et Regens Franciae, et Dominus Hiberniae*), *cr* Prince of Wales, Duke of Cornwall and Earl of Chester 15 Oct 1399, and Duke of Aquitaine and Duke of Lancaster 10 Nov 1399, crowned at Westminster Abbey by Thomas Arundel, Archbishop of Canterbury 9 April 1413, declared heir and regent of France by the Treaty of Troyes 1420, *b* at Monmouth 16 Sept 1387, *m* at Troyes 2 June 1420, Catherine, crowned at Westminster Abbey 24 Feb 1421 (*b* at the Hôtel St Pol, Paris 27 Oct 1401; *m* 2ndly *ca* 1428, Owen Tudor (*d* 2 Feb 1461), and had issue (*see p* 325); *d* at Bermondsey Abbey 3 Jan 1437, *bur* Westminster Abbey), 6th and yst dau of Charles VI, King of France, by his wife Isabelle (Isabeau), dau of Stephan II, Duke of Bavaria-Ingolstadt, and *d* at Bois de Vincennes 31 Aug 1422 (*bur* Westminster Abbey), leaving issue,

1422-1461 and 1470-1471 HENRY VI, King of England (styled *Rex Angliae et Franciae et Dominus Hiberniae*), crowned at Westminster Abbey by Henry Chichele, Archbishop of Canterbury 6 Nov 1429, crowned King of France at Nôtre Dame Cathedral, Paris by Cardinal Beaufort 17 Dec 1431, declared of age 12 Nov 1437, deposed 4 March 1461, recovered the crown 3 Oct 1470, again deposed 11 April 1471, *b* at Windsor Castle 6 Dec 1421, *m* by proxy at Nancy Nov 1444 and in person at Titchfield, Hants 23 April 1445, Margaret, crowned at Westminster Abbey by John Stafford, Archbishop of Canterbury 30 May 1445 (*b* at Pont-à-Mousson, Lorraine 23 March 1429; *d* at Château Dampierre 25 Aug 1482, *bur* Angers), 2nd dau of René, Duke of Anjou, titular King of Naples and Sicily, by his 1st wife Isabelle, Duchess of Lorraine, eldest dau and co-heiress of Charles I, Duke of Lorraine, and *d* (supposedly murdered) in the Tower of London 21 May 1471 (*bur* first Chertsey Abbey, later transferred to St George's Chapel, Windsor), having had issue,

Edward, Duke of Cornwall at birth, *cr* PRINCE OF WALES and EARL OF CHESTER 15 March 1454, *b* at Westminster Palace 13 Oct 1453, *m* at Amboise Aug 1470, Anne (*b* at Warwick Castle 11 June 1456; *m* 2ndly at Westminster 12 July 1472, Richard Duke of Gloucester, later King Richard III (*see p* 204); *d* at Westminster Palace 16 March 1485, *bur* Westminster Abbey), yr dau and co-heiress of Richard Nevill, 1st Earl of Warwick and 2nd Earl of Salisbury, KG (*see* BURKE'S *Dormant and Extinct Peerages*), and was *k* after the Battle of Tewkesbury 4 May 1471, *spvp* (*bur* Tewkesbury Abbey).

King Henry VI was *s* on his deposition by the Yorkist claimant to the throne,

1461-1470 and 1471-1483 EDWARD IV, King of England (styled the same as Henry VI), *cr* Earl of March *post* 21 Dec 1445, *s* his father as (4th) Duke of York 1460, declared King in Parliament 4 March 1461, crowned at Westminster Abbey by Cardinal Bourchier, Archbishop of Canterbury 29 June 1461, deposed in favour of Henry VI 3 Oct 1470, regained the crown 11 April 1471, *b* at Rouen 28 April 1442, *m* at Grafton Regis, Northants 1 May 1464, Elizabeth, crowned at Westminster Abbey 26 May 1465 (*b* at Grafton Regis *ca* 1437; *d* at Bermondsey Abbey 8 June 1492, *bur* St George's Chapel, Windsor), widow of John Grey, 2nd Baron Grey of Groby (*see* BURKE'S *Dormant and Extinct Peerages*), and eldest dau of Richard Woodville, 1st Earl Rivers, KG (*see* BURKE'S *Dormant and Extinct Peerages*), by his wife Jacquette, widow of John, Duke of Bedford (*see p* 202), and dau of Pierre de Luxembourg, Count of St Pol, and *d* at Westminster Palace 9 April 1483 (*bur* St George's Chapel, Windsor), having had issue,

1 EDWARD V, *s* his father.

2 Richard, KG (1475), KB (1475), declared DUKE OF YORK 1473 and so *cr* 28 May 1474, *cr* EARL OF NOTTINGHAM 12 June 1476, and EARL OF WARENNE and DUKE OF NORFOLK 7 Feb 1478, Lieut of Ireland 5 May 1479, *b* at Shrewsbury 17 Aug 1473, *m* at St Stephen's Chapel, Westminster 15 Jan 1478, Anne (*b* at Framlingham 10 Dec 1472; *d* at Greenwich 19 Nov 1481, *bur* first at Westminster Abbey, then in the Minoresses, Stepney, where her body was discovered 1965 and reinterred in Westminster Abbey), only dau and heiress of John Mowbray, 4th Duke of Norfolk and 9th Baron Mowbray, KG, Earl Marshal of England (*see* BURKE'S *Peerage*, MOWBRAY, SEGRAVE AND STOURTON, B), and being confined in the Tower of London with his brother King Edward V was presumed to have been murdered there in or *post* 1483.

3 George, designated but never formally *cr* Duke of Bedford, *b* at Windsor Castle March 1477; *d*

there March 1479 (*bur* St George's Chapel, Windsor),
1 Elizabeth, *b* at Westminster Palace 11 Feb 1465, *m* at Westminster 18 Jan 1486, Henry VII, King of England, and had issue (*see below*).
2 Mary, *b* at Windsor Castle Aug 1466; *d* at Greenwich 23 May 1482 (*bur* St George's Chapel, Windsor).
3 Cicely, *b* 20 March 1469, *m* 1st *ante* Dec 1487, John Welles, 1st Viscount Welles, KG, (*see* BURKE'S *Dormant and Extinct Peerages*), half-brother of Margaret, Countess of Richmond and Derby (*see above, p* 200), and had issue, two daus. He *d* in London 9 Feb 1499. She *m* 2ndly *ante* Jan 1504, Thomas Kyme, and *d* at Quarr Abbey, IoW 24 Aug 1507 (*bur* there), having had, according to some authorities, further issue, one son and one dau.
4 Margaret, *b* 10 April, *d* 11 Dec 1472 (*bur* Westminster Abbey).
5 Anne, *b* at Westminster Palace 2 Nov 1475, *m* 4 Feb 1495, as his 1st wife, Thomas Howard, 3rd Duke of Norfolk, KG (*see* BURKE'S *Peerage*), and *d* 23 Nov 1511 (*bur* first Thetford, Norfolk, later transferred to Framlingham, Suffolk), having had issue, four sons (who all *d* young). He *d* 25 Aug 1554.
6 Catherine, *b* at Eltham Palace, Kent *ca* 14 Aug 1479, *m ante* Oct 1495, William Courtenay, Earl of Devon, KB (*see* BURKE'S *Peerage*), and *d* at Tiverton, Devon 15 Nov 1527 (*bur* Tiverton Parish Church), having had issue, two sons and one dau. He *d* at Greenwich 9 June 1511 (*bur* Black Friars Church, London).
7 Bridget, a nun at Dartford, Kent, *b* at Eltham Palace 10 Nov 1480; *d* at Dartford 1517 (*bur* Dartford Priory).

King Edward IV was *s* by his eldest son,

April-June 1483 EDWARD V, King of England (styled the same as Henry VI), *cr* Prince of Wales and Earl of Chester 26 June 1471, Duke of Cornwall 17 July 1471, KG 1475, Earl of March and Earl of Pembroke 8 July 1479, *s* his father 9 April 1483, deposed by an assembly of Lords and Commons on the grounds of the supposed invalidity of his parents' marriage* 25 June 1483 without having been crowned and confined in the Tower of London, *b* in Sanctuary at Westminster 4 Nov 1470; presumed to have been murdered in the Tower of London in or *post* July 1483†.

King Edward V was *s* on his deposition by his uncle,

1483-1485 RICHARD III, King of England (styled the same as Henry VI), *cr* Duke of Gloucester 1461, KG 1466, Lord High Constable and Lord Adm of England, Lord High Protector on the accession of his nephew King Edward V 9 April 1483, proclaimed King 26 June 1483, crowned at Westminster Abbey by Cardinal Bourchier, Archbishop of Canterbury 6 July 1483, *b* at Fotheringay Castle 2 Oct 1452, *m* at Westminster 12 July 1472, Anne, crowned with her husband (*b* at Warwick Castle 11 June 1456; *d* at Westminster Palace 16 March 1485, *bur* Westminster Abbey), widow of Edward, Prince of Wales (*see p* 203), and yr dau and co-heiress of Richard Nevill, 1st Earl of Warwick and 2nd Earl of Salisbury, KG (*see* BURKE'S *Dormant and Extinct Peerages*), and was defeated and *k* at Bosworth Field 22 Aug 1485 (*bur* Grey Friars Abbey, Leicester), having had issue,

Edward, *cr* EARL OF SALISBURY 15 Feb 1478, DUKE OF CORNWALL on his father's accession, *cr* PRINCE OF WALES and EARL OF CHESTER 24 Aug 1483, *b* at Middleham Castle, Yorks *ca* Dec 1473; *d* there 9 April 1484 (*bur* Sheriff Hutton, Yorks).

King Richard III was *s* by his successful rival,

1485-1509 HENRY VII, King of England (styled the same as Henry VI), *s* his father as Earl of Richmond at birth, attainted 26 Jan 1484, obtained the crown of England on the defeat and death of King Richard III at Bosworth 22 Aug 1485, crowned at Westminster Abbey by Cardinal Bourchier, Archbishop of Canterbury 30 Oct 1485, *b* at Pembroke Castle 28 Jan 1457, *m* at Westminster 18 Jan 1486, Elizabeth, crowned at Westminster Abbey 25 Nov 1487 (*b* at Westminster Palace 11 Feb 1465; *d* in the Tower of London 11 Feb 1503, *bur* Westminster Abbey), eldest dau of King Edward IV (*see above*), and *d* at Sheen Palace 21 April 1509 (*bur* Westminster Abbey), having had issue,

1 Arthur, Duke of Cornwall at birth, *cr* PRINCE OF WALES and EARL OF CHESTER 29 Nov 1489, installed KG 8 May 1491, *b* at Winchester Castle 19 Sept 1486, *m* at St Paul's Cathedral, London 14 Nov 1501, Catherine (Catalina) (*b* at Alcala de Henares 15 Dec 1483; *m* 2ndly at Greenwich 11 June 1509, as his 1st wife, her brother-in-law King Henry VIII (*see p* 205), and *d* at Kimbolton Castle, Hunts 7 Jan 1536, *bur* Peterborough Cathedral), 4th and yst dau of Fernando V, King of Aragon, by his 1st wife Isabel I, Queen of Castile and Leon, and *dspvp* at Ludlow Castle 2 April 1502 (*bur* Worcester Cathedral).
2 HENRY VIII, *s* his father.
3 Edmund, said to have been *cr* Duke of Somerset immediately after his birth, but no enrolment of any patent is to be found, *b* at Greenwich Palace 20 Feb 1499; *d* at Hatfield, Herts 19 June 1500 (*bur* Westminster Abbey).
1 Margaret, *b* at Westminster Palace 29 Nov 1489, *m* 1st at Holyrood House, Edinburgh 8 Aug 1503, James IV, King of Scots (*k* at the Battle of Flodden 9 Sept 1513), and had, with other issue (*see* KINGS AND QUEENS OF SCOTLAND, *p* 319), an only surv son,

James V, King of Scots (*see* KINGS AND QUEENS OF SCOTLAND, *p* 320 *for fuller details*) *b* 10 April 1512, *m* 2ndly 12 June 1538, Marie (*d* 10 June 1560), widow of Louis II, Duke of Longueville, and eldest dau of Claude I de Lorraine, Duke of Guise, and *d* 14 Dec 1542, having by her had, with other issue,

Mary, Queen of Scots, *b* 4 Dec 1542, *m* 2ndly 29 July 1565, Henry Stuart, Lord Darnley, *cr* Duke of Albany, Earl of Ross and Lord Ardmannoch (*d* 10 Feb 1567), and was beheaded at Fotheringay Castle 8 Feb 1587, having had issue,

JAMES I, *s* Queen Elizabeth I.

She *m* 2ndly at Kinnoull 4 Aug 1514 (*m* diss 11 March 1527), as his 2nd wife, Archibald Douglas, 6th Earl of Angus (*d* 1557), and had further issue,

Margaret Douglas, *b* at Harbottle Castle, Northumberland 7 or 8 Oct 1515, *m* at St James's Palace, London 6 July 1544, Matthew Stuart, 4th Earl of Lennox, sometime Regent of Scotland (*d* 4 Sept 1571), and *d* at Hackney, Middx 9 March

---

* King Edward IV was stated on the evidence of Robert Stillington, Bishop of Bath and Wells, to have been contracted to Lady Eleanor Butler, widow of Sir Thomas Butler, Kt, and dau of John Talbot, 1st Earl of Shrewsbury, which lady was still living at the time of his marriage to Elizabeth, Lady Grey.

† The deaths of King Edward V and his brother the Duke of York were long attributed to their uncle King Richard III; but recent research has done much to rehabilitate the character of that greatly maligned monarch and the responsibility for the deaths of the Princes still remains unproven.

1578 (*bur* Westminster Abbey), having had, with other issue, a 2nd son,

Henry Stuart, Lord Darnley, *cr* Duke of Albany, Earl of Ross and Lord Ardmannoch, *b* 7 Dec 1545, *m* 29 July 1565, Mary, Queen of Scots, and *d* 10 Feb 1567, leaving issue (*see above*).

She *m* 3rdly *ante* 2 April 1528, as his 2nd wife, Henry Stewart, 1st Lord Methven (*see* BURKE'S *Dormant and Extinct Peerages*), and *d* at Methven Castle 24 Nov 1541 (*bur* St John's Abbey, Perth), having had further issue, one dau (who *d* an inf).

2 Elizabeth, *b* 2 July 1492; *d* at Eltham 14 Sept 1495 (*bur* Westminster Abbey).

3 Mary, *b* at Richmond Palace 18 March 1496, *m* 1st at Abbeville 9 Oct 1514 (being crowned at St Denis 5 Nov 1514), as his 3rd wife, Louis XII, King of France. He *d* at the Palais du Tournelles, Paris 1 Jan 1515. She *m* 2ndly privately in Paris 3 March and publicly at the Grey Friars, Greenwich 13 May 1515, as his 3rd wife, Charles Brandon, 1st Duke of Suffolk KG (*b* 1484; *d* at Guildford Palace 24 Aug 1545, *bur* Windsor), and *d* at Westhorpe, Suffolk 24 June 1533 (*bur* first in Bury Abbey, later transferred to St Mary's Church, Bury), having by him had issue,

1 Henry Brandon, *cr* EARL OF LINCOLN 18 June 1525, *b* at Bath Place, London 11 March 1516; *d unm* at Suffolk House, Southwark, *ante* 8 March 1534.

1 Frances Brandon, *b* at Hatfield, Herts 16 July 1517, *m* 1st *ca* 1534, as his 2nd wife, Henry Grey, 1st Duke of Suffolk, and 3rd Marquess of Dorset, KG (beheaded on Tower Hill 23 Feb 1554), and had issue,

(1) A son, *d* an inf.

(1) A dau, *d* an inf.

(2) JANE, *s* King Edward VI as the "nine days Queen".

(3) Catherine Grey, *b ca* 1539, *m* 1st at Durham House 21 May 1553 (*m* diss 1554), as his 1st wife, Henry Herbert, Lord Herbert (afterwards 2nd Earl of Pembroke, KG (*see* BURKE'S *Peerage*). He *d* 19 Jan 1601. She *m* 2ndly at his house in Canon Row, Westminster *ca* Nov 1560, as his 1st wife, Edward Seymour, 1st Earl of Hertford (*see* BURKE'S *Dormant and Extinct Peerages*), and *d* at Cockfield Hall, Suffolk 26 or 27 Jan 1568 (*bur* Yoxford, Suffolk), leaving issue, two sons. He *d* 6 April 1621 (*bur* Salisbury Cathedral).

(4) Mary Grey, *b* 1545, *m* at Westminster 10 Aug 1565, Thomas Keyes, Serjeant Porter to Queen Elizabeth I, and *dsp* at the Barbican by Red Cross Street, London 20 April 1578 (*bur* St Botolph's Church, Aldersgate). He *d* at Lewisham, or at Sandgate Castle, Kent Sept 1571.

She *m* 2ndly 9 March 1554, as his 1st wife, Adrian Stokes (*d ca* 1581), and *d* at the Charterhouse, London 11 Nov 1559 (*bur* Westminster Abbey), having had further issue,

(5) Elizabeth Stokes, *b* and *d* 20 Nov 1554.

2 Eleanor Brandon, *b ca* 1520, *m* at Southwark June 1537, as his 1st wife, Henry Clifford, 2nd Earl of Cumberland, KB (*see* BURKE'S *Dormant and Extinct Peerages*), and *d* at Brougham Castle, Westmorland Nov 1547 (*bur* Skipton), having had issue, two sons (who *d* young) and one dau. He *d* at Brougham Castle 6 Jan 1570 (*bur* Skipton).

4 Catherine, *b* in the Tower of London 2 Feb 1503; *d* aged a few weeks (*bur* Westminster Abbey).

King Henry VII was *s* by his 2nd (but only surv) son,

1509-1547 HENRY VIII, King of England (styled the same as Henry VI until 1521, then *King of England and France, Defender of the Faith, Lord of Ireland, and of the Church of England on Earth Supreme Head* until 1542, then *King of England, France and Ireland, Defender of the Faith and of the Church of England and also of Ireland in Earth the Supreme Head*), Constable of Dover Castle and Lord Warden of the Cinque Ports 5 April 1493, Lieut of Ireland 12 Sept 1494, KB 31 Oct 1494, *cr* Duke of York 1 Nov 1494 (patent cancelled 1503), KG 17 May 1495, Earl Marshal of England 1495, *s* his brother Arthur as Duke of Cornwall 2 April 1502, *cr* Prince of Wales and Earl of Chester 18 Feb 1503, crowned at Westminster Abbey by William Warham, Archbishop of Canterbury 24 June 1509, received the title of Defender of the Faith (*Fidei Defensor*) from Pope Leo X 1521, the first English sovereign to be styled *Majesty, b* at Greenwich Palace 28 Jan 1491, *m* 1st at Greenwich (with Papal dispensation) 11 June 1509 (*m* declared null and void by Thomas Cranmer, Archbishop of Canterbury 23 May 1533, and "utterly dissolved" by Act of Parl March 1534), Catherine (Catalina), crowned with her husband (*b* at Alcala de Henares 16 Dec 1485; *d* at Kimbolton Castle, Hunts 7 Jan 1536, *bur* Peterborough Cathedral), widow of his brother Arthur, Prince of Wales (*see above, p* 204), and 4th and yst dau of Fernando V, King of Aragon, by his 1st wife Isabel I, Queen of Castile and Leon, and had issue,

1 Henry, DUKE OF CORNWALL, *b* at Richmond Palace 1 Jan, *d* there 22 Feb 1511 (*bur* Westminster Abbey).

2 A Prince, DUKE OF CORNWALL, *b* and *d* at Richmond Palace Nov 1513 (*bur* Westminster Abbey).

3 A Prince, *b* and *d* (? stillborn) Dec 1514.

1 A Princess, stillborn 31 Jan 1510.

2 MARY I, *s* her half-brother King Edward VI.

3 A Princess, stillborn 10 Nov 1518.

King Henry VIII *m* 2ndly at Whitehall, or at Westminster 25 Jan 1533 (*m* declared valid 28 May 1533 and invalid 17 May 1536), Anne, Marchioness of Pembroke (so *cr* 1 Sept 1532), crowned at Westminster Abbey 1 June 1533 (*b* at Blickling Hall, Norfolk, or at Hever Castle, Kent *ca* 1507; beheaded on Tower Green 19 May 1536, *bur* Chapel of St Peter ad Vincula in the Tower), dau of Thomas Boleyn, 1st Earl of Wiltshire and Ormonde, KG (*see* BURKE'S *Dormant and Extinct Peerages*), by his wife Elizabeth, dau of Thomas Howard, 2nd Duke of Norfolk, KG (*see* BURKE'S *Peerage*), and by her had issue,

4 A Prince, stillborn at Greenwich 29 Jan 1536.

4 ELIZABETH I, *s* her half-sister Queen Mary I.

King Henry VIII *m* 3rdly at Wolf Hall, Savernake, Wilts, 30 May 1536, Jane (*b ca* 1509; *d* at Hampton Court Palace 24 Oct 1537, *bur* St George's Chapel, Windsor), dau of Sir John Seymour, Kt, of Wolf Hall (*see* BURKE'S *Peerage*, SOMERSET, D), and by her had issue,

5 EDWARD VI, *s* his father.

King Henry VIII *m* 4thly at Greenwich 6 Jan 1540 (*m* annulled 9 July 1540), Anne (*b* at Düsseldorf 22 Sept 1516; *d* at Chelsea, Middx 17 July 1557, *bur* Westminster Abbey), 2nd dau of Johann III, Duke of Cleves, by his wife Marie, dau and heiress of Wilhelm III, Duke of Jülich. He *m* 5thly at Hampton Court Palace 28 July 1540, Catherine (*b* at Lambeth (?) *ca* 1521/22; beheaded on Tower Green 13 Feb 1542, *bur* Chapel of St Peter ad Vincula in the Tower), dau of Lord Edmund Howard, son of Thomas Howard, 2nd Duke of

Norfolk, KG (*see* BURKE'S *Peerage*). He *m* 6thly at Hampton Court Palace 12 July 1543, Catherine (*b* at Kendal Castle, Westmorland *ca* 1512; *m* 4thly April or May 1547, Thomas Seymour, 1st Baron Seymour of Sudeley, KG, Lord High Adm, brother of Queen Jane (*see* BURKE'S *Dormant and Extinct Peerages*); *d* at Sudeley Castle, Glos 5 Sept 1548, *bur* chapel there), widow of (1) John Nevill, 3rd Baron Latimer (*see* BURKE'S *Dormant and Extinct Peerages*), and (2) Edward Borough, 2nd Baron Borough, and dau of Sir Thomas Parr, Kt, of Kendal, by his wife Maud, dau and co-heiress of Sir Thomas Green, Kt, of Boughton and Green's Norton, Northants, and *d* at Whitehall 28 Jan 1547 (*bur* St George's Chapel, Windsor).

King Henry VIII was *s* by his only surv son,

1547-1553 EDWARD VI, King of England (styled the same as Henry VIII), Duke of Cornwall at birth, called but never formally *cr* Prince of Wales, crowned at Westminster Abbey by Thomas Cranmer, Archbishop of Canterbury 20 Feb 1547, *b* at Hampton Court Palace 12 Oct 1537; *d* at Greenwich 6 July 1553 (*bur* Westminster Abbey), when he should have been succeeded by his half-sister Mary, but his 1st cousin once removed, Lady Jane Dudley, having been declared heiress-presumptive 21 June 1553, was proclaimed Queen.

10-19 July 1553 JANE, Queen of England (styled the same as Henry VIII), proclaimed 10 July 1553, dethroned in favour of the rightful heir Mary 19 July 1553, tried and condemned to death for high treason 13 Nov 1553, *b* at Bradgate, Leics Oct 1537, *m* at Durham House, London 21 May 1553, Lord Guildford Dudley (beheaded on Tower Hill 12 Feb 1554, *bur* Chapel of St Peter ad Vincula in the Tower), 6th son of John Dudley, 1st Duke of Northumberland, KG (*see* BURKE'S *Dormant and Extinct Peerages*), and *dsp* being beheaded on Tower Green 12 Feb 1554 (*bur* Chapel of St Peter ad Vincula in the Tower).

King Edward VI was *s* after the brief intrusion of Jane by his half-sister,

1553-1558 MARY I, Queen of England (styled the same as Henry VIII until her marriage, when she and her husband were styled *Philip and Mary, by the Grace of God, King and Queen of England and France, Naples, Jerusalem and Ireland, Defenders of the Faith, Princes of Spain and Sicily, Archdukes of Austria, Dukes of Milan, Burgundy and Brabant*), crowned at Westminster Abbey by Stephen Gardiner, Bishop of Winchester 1 Oct 1553, *b* at Greenwich Palace 18 Feb 1516, *m* at Winchester Cathedral 25 July 1554, as his 2nd wife, her 1st cousin once removed, Philip (Felipe) II, King of Spain (from 1555) (*b* at Valladolid 21 May 1527; *d* at Madrid 13 Sept 1598, *bur* the Escorial), only son of the Emperor Karl V (Carlos I, King of Spain), by his 1st wife Isabel, dau of Manoel I, King of Portugal, and *dsp* at St James's Palace 17 Nov 1558 (*bur* Westminster Abbey), when she was *s* by her half-sister,

1558-1603 ELIZABETH I, Queen of England (styled *by the Grace of God, Queen of England, France and Ireland, Defender of the Faith*), crowned at Westminster Abbey by Owen Oglethorpe, Bishop of Carlisle 15 Jan 1559, *b* at Greenwich Palace 7 Sept 1533; *d unm* at Richmond Palace 24 March 1603 (*bur* Westminster Abbey), when she was *s* by her kinsman, James VI, King of Scots (*see* KINGS AND QUEENS OF SCOTLAND, *p* 320), who became

1603-1625 JAMES I (Charles James), **King of England** (styled *King of England, Scotland, France and Ireland, Defender of the Faith*), *s* his mother as King of Scots 24 July, and was crowned at Stirling 29 July 1567, crowned as King of England at Westminster Abbey by John Whitgift, Archbishop of Canterbury 25 July 1603, *b* at Edinburgh Castle 19 June 1566, *m* by proxy at Kronborg 20 Aug and in person at Oslo, Norway 23 Nov 1589 (the ceremony being again repeated at Kronborg 21 Jan 1590), Anna, crowned Queen of Scots at Holyrood 17 May 1590 and Queen of England with her husband (*b* at Skanderborg Castle, Jutland, 14 Oct 1574*; *d* at Hampton Court Palace 4 March 1619*, *bur* Westminster Abbey), 2nd dau of Frederik II, King of Denmark and Norway, by his wife Sophie, dau of Ulrich III, Duke of Mecklenburg-Güstrow, and *d* at Theobalds Park, Herts 27 March 1625 (*bur* Westminster Abbey), having had issue,

1 Henry Frederick, KG (1603), DUKE OF ROTHESAY and PRINCE AND STEWARD OF SCOTLAND at birth, DUKE OF CORNWALL on his father's accession to the English throne, *cr* PRINCE OF WALES and EARL OF CHESTER 4 June 1610, *b* at Stirling Castle 19 Feb 1594; *dvp* at St James's Palace 6 Nov 1612 (*bur* Westminster Abbey).

2 CHARLES I, *s* his father.

3 Robert, styled DUKE OF KINTYRE, MARQUIS OF WIGTOUN, EARL OF CARRICK and LORD OF ANNERDAIL 2 May 1602 (the day of his baptism), *b* at Dunfermline 18 Jan 1602; *d* there 27 May 1602 (*bur* there).

4 A Prince, stillborn at Stirling May 1603.

1 Elizabeth, *b* at Dunfermline† 19 Aug 1596, *m* at the Chapel Royal, Whitehall 14 Feb 1613, Friedrich V, Elector Palatine of the Rhine, Duke of Bavaria, Cupbearer and High Steward of the Empire, who was elected King of Bohemia and crowned at Prague 3 Nov 1619 (she being crowned there 6 Nov 1619), but lost the throne 1620 (*b* at Amberg 16 Aug 1596; *d* at Mentz 29 Nov 1632), son of Friedrich IV, Elector Palatine of the Rhine, etc, by his wife Louise Juliana, dau of Willem I *the Silent*, Prince of Orange, and *d* at Leicester House, London 13 Feb 1662 (*bur* Westminster Abbey), having had issue,

1 Heinrich Friedrich, *b* at Heidelberg 2 Jan 1614; drowned in Haarlem Meer 7 Jan 1629 (*bur* Cloister Church, The Hague).

2 Karl Ludwig, KG (1633), Elector Palatine of the Rhine, etc, *b* at Heidelberg 1 Jan 1618, *m* 1st at Cassel 12 Feb 1650 (*m* said to have been diss by div 1657), Charlotte (*b* at Cassel 20 Nov 1627; *d* there 16 March 1686, *bur* Heidelberg), 4th dau of Wilhelm V, Landgrave of Hesse-

* These are the dates on her coffin plate, but most authorities say she was *b* 12 Dec 1574 and *d* 2 March 1619.

† Not at Falkland Palace as often stated.

Cassel, by his wife Amalie Elisabeth, dau of Philipp Ludwig, Count of Hanau, and had issue, two sons and one dau, who being Roman Catholics were excluded from the line of succession to the British throne. He *m* 2ndly (probably bigamously) at Schwetzingen 6 Jan 1658, Marie Louise, who bore the title of *Raugräfin* (*b* at Strassburg 28 Nov 1634; *d* at Mannheim 18 March 1677, *bur* there), dau of Baron Christoph von Degenfeld, and *d* at Edinger, nr Heidelberg 28 Aug 1680 (*bur* Heidelberg), having by her had issue, fourteen children.

3 Rupert, KG (1642), *cr* BARON OF KENDAL, co Westmorland, EARL OF HOLDERNESS and DUKE OF CUMBERLAND by his uncle King Charles I 24 June 1644, served as a celebrated Royalist cmdr throughout the Civil War, credited by John Evelyn with the invention of mezzotint engraving, *b* at Prague 17 Dec 1619; *d unm* at his house in Spring Gardens London 29 Nov 1682 (*bur* Westminster Abbey).

4 Maurice, KG (1649), served as a Royalist cmdr in the Civil War; *b* at Cüstrin Prussia 6 Jan 1621; lost at sea 1653, *unm.*

5 Ludwig, *b* at The Hague 21 Aug 1623; *d* there 24 Dec 1624.

6 Edward, KG (1649), *b* at The Hague 6 Oct 1624, *m* at Paris 4 May 1645, Anne (*b* at Mantua 1616; *d* at Paris 6 July 1684), formerly wife of Henri de Lorraine, Duc de Guise, and 2nd dau of Charles de Gonzague, Duke of Nevers and Mantua, by his wife Catherine, eldest dau of Charles de Lorraine, Duc de Mayenne, and *d* at Paris 13 March 1663, having had issue, four daus, who as Roman Catholics were excluded from the line of succession to the British throne.

7 Philip, *b* at The Hague 16 Sept 1627; *k* in battle at Rethel 15 Dec 1650, *unm* (*bur* Heidelberg).

8 Gustavus, *b* at The Hague 4 Jan 1632; *d* there 9 Jan 1641.

1 Elisabeth, Princess-Abbess of Herford 1667-81, *b* at Heidelberg 26 Dec 1618; *d unm* at Herford 11 Feb 1681 (*bur* there).

2 *Louise* Hollandine, Abbess of Maubuisson 1664-1709, a talented artist, *b* at The Hague 17 April 1622; *d* at Maubuisson 11 Feb 1709.

3 Henrietta Maria, *b* at The Hague 17 July 1626, *m* at Patak 4 April 1651, Sigismund Rákóczy, Prince of Siebenbürgen, brother of George Rákóczy, Prince of Transylvania, and *dsp* at Fogaras, Hungary 18 Sept 1651 (*bur* St Michael's Cathedral, Karlsberg). He *d* at Fogaras 4 Feb 1652 (*bur* with her).

4 Charlotte, *b* at The Hague 19 Dec 1628; *d* there 23 Jan 1631 (*bur* Cloister Church, The Hague).

5 Sophia, upon whom and upon whose descendants (being Protestant) the crown of England was settled by Act of Parl 12 June 1701, Heiress-Presumptive 1702-14, *b* at The Hague 14 Oct 1630, *m* at Heidelberg 30 Sept 1658, Ernst August, Elector and Duke of Hanover, Duke of Brunswick-Lüneburg (*b* at Herzberg 20 Nov 1629; *d* at Herrenhausen 23 Jan 1698, *bur* Hanover), and *d* at Herrenhausen 8 June 1714 (*bur* Hanover), having had issue,

(1) GEORGE I, *s* his 2nd cousin Queen Anne (*see below, p* 209).

(2) Friedrich August, *b* at Hanover 3 Oct 1661; *k* in battle against the Turks at Siebenbürgen 10 Jan 1691, *unm.*

(3) Maximilian Wilhelm, fought under Marlborough at the Battle of Blenheim 1704, *b* at Schloss Iburg 14 Dec 1666; *d unm* at Vienna 27 July 1726.

(4) A prince (twin with Maximilian Wilhelm), stillborn at Schloss Iburg 14 Dec 1666.

(5) Karl Philipp, *b* at Schloss Iburg 13 Oct 1669; *k* in battle with the Turks at Pristine, Albania 31 Dec 1690, *unm.*

(6) Christian, *b* at Schloss Iburg 19 Sept 1671; *d unm* being drowned in the Danube nr Ulm 31 July 1703.

(7) Ernst August, KG (1717), Prince-Bishop of Osnabrück 1715-28, *cr* DUKE OF YORK AND ALBANY and EARL OF ULSTER by his brother King George I 5 July 1716, *b* at Osnabrück 18 Sept 1674; *d* there *unm* 14 Aug 1728.

(1) Sophie Charlotte, *b* at Schloss Iburg 12 Oct 1662, *m* at Herrenhausen 28 Sept 1684, as his 2nd wife, Friedrich I, King of Prussia, and *d* at Hanover 1 Feb 1705 (*bur* Berlin), having had issue, two sons. He *d* at Berlin 25 Feb 1713.

2 Margaret, *b* at Dalkeith Palace 24 Dec 1598; *d* at Linlithgow March 1600.

3 Mary, *b* at Greenwich Palace 8 April 1605; *d* at Stanwell Park, Middx 16 Sept 1607 (*bur* Westminster Abbey).

4 Sophia, *b* at Greenwich Palace 22 June, *d* there 23 June 1606 (*bur* Westminster Abbey).

King James I was *s* by his 2nd (but only surv) son,

1625-1649 CHARLES I, King of England (styled the same as James I), *cr* Duke of Albany Marquis of Ormond, Earl of Ross and Baron of Ardmannoch (in the Peerage of Scotland) 23 Dec 1603, KB 1605, *cr* Duke of York (in the Peerage of England) 6 Jan 1605, KG 1611, *s* his elder brother as Duke of Cornwall and Duke of Rothesay, etc 6 Nov 1612, *cr* Prince of Wales and Earl of Chester 4 Nov 1616, crowned at Westminster Abbey by George Abbot, Archbishop of Canterbury 2 Feb 1626, and in Edinburgh by John Spottiswood, Archbishop of St Andrews 18 June 1633, *b* at Dunfermline 19 Nov 1600, *m* by proxy at Nôtre Dame Cathedral, Paris 1 May 1625 and in person at Canterbury 13 June 1625, Henrietta Maria* (*b* at the Louvre, Paris 25 Nov 1609; *d* at Colombe, nr Paris 31 Aug 1669, *bur* St Denis), 3rd and yst dau of Henri IV, King of France and Navarre, by his 2nd wife Marie, dau of Francesco I (dei Medici), Grand Duke of Tuscany, and, having been defeated by the Parliamentarians and illegally tried and condemned to death, was beheaded outside Whitehall Palace 30 Jan 1649 (*bur* St George's Chapel, Windsor), having had issue,

1 Charles James, DUKE OF CORNWALL and DUKE OF ROTHESAY, etc at birth, *b* and *d* at Greenwich Palace 13 May 1629 (*bur* Westminster Abbey).

2 CHARLES II, *s* his father as King *de jure* 1649 and was restored as King *de facto* 1660.

3 JAMES II, *s* his brother King Charles II.

4 Henry, KG (1653), *cr* DUKE OF GLOUCESTER and EARL OF CAMBRIDGE 13 May 1644, *b* at Oatlands, Surrey 8 July 1640; *d unm* at Whitehall Palace 13 Sept 1660 (*bur* Westminster Abbey).

1 Mary, Princess Royal (the first to bear that title), *b* at St James's Palace 4 Nov 1631, *m* at the Chapel Royal, Whitehall 2 May 1641, Willem II, Prince of Orange, Stadholder of the United Provs of the Netherlands (*d* 27 Oct 1650, *bur* Delft), and *d* at Whitehall Palace 24 Dec 1660 (*bur* Westminster Abbey), leaving issue,

William Henry, later KING WILLIAM III.

2 Elizabeth, *b* at St James's Palace 29 Dec 1635; *d* at Carisbrooke Castle, Isle of Wight 8 Sept 1650 (*bur* St Thomas's Church, Newport, IoW).

3 Anne, *b* at St James's Palace 17 March 1637; *d* at Richmond Palace 5 Nov 1640 (*bur* Westminster Abbey).

4 Catherine, *b* and *d* at Whitehall Palace 29 June 1639.

5 Henrietta Anne†, *b* at Bedford House, Exeter 16 June 1644, *m* at the Chapel of the Palais Royal,

---

* She was never crowned owing to the religious difficulties involved.

† She was baptized *Henrietta* only; the name *Anne* being probably added at her confirmation in compliment to Anne of Austria, Queen Regent of France, her mother's sister-in-law.

Paris 31 March 1661, as his 1st wife, her 1st cousin, Philippe, Duke of Orleans, yr son of Louis XIII, King of France and Navarre, and *d* at St Cloud 30 June 1670 (*bur* St Denis), having had issue, one son and three daus. He *d* 9 June 1701. The representation of the Royal Houses of Stuart, Tudor, Plantagenet and Normandy is vested in the descendants of the Princess Henrietta, Duchess of Orleans, but being Roman Catholics they were excluded from the succession to the throne by the Act of Settlement 1701. The present rep is HRH Duke Albrecht of Bavaria, who is also descended from King George II (*see p* 255).

King Charles I was *s* by his 2nd (but eldest surv) son,

1649 (1660)-1685 CHARLES II, King of England (styled the same as James I), Duke of Cornwall and Duke of Rothesay, etc at birth, declared (but never *cr*) Prince of Wales 1638, crowned King of Scots at Scone 1 Jan 1651, lived in exile in France, Germany and Holland 1651-60, restored to the throne 29 May 1660, crowned at Westminster Abbey by William Juxon, Archbishop of Canterbury 23 April 1661, *b* at St James's Palace 29 May 1630, *m* at Portsmouth 21 May 1662, *Catherine* Henrietta* (*b* at Vila Vicosa, Lisbon 25 Nov 1638; *d* at the Palace of Bemposta, Lisbon 31 Dec 1705, *bur* Belém), dau of João IV, King of Portugal, by his wife Luisa Maria, dau of Juan Manuel Domingo Perez de Guzmán, 8th Duke of Medina Sidonia, and *dspl*† at Whitehall Palace 6 Feb 1685 (*bur* Westminster Abbey), when he was *s* by his brother,

1685-1688 JAMES II (VII of Scotland), **King of England** (styled the same as James I), KG 1642, *cr* Duke of York 27 Jan 1643 (having been so designated from his birth), PC 1649, Lord High Adm of England 1649, *cr* Earl of Ulster in Ireland 10 May 1659, Constable of Dover Castle and Lord Warden of the Cinque Ports 1660-73, *cr* Duke of Albany in Scotland 31 Dec 1660, Lord High Adm of England, Ireland and Wales, and of the town and marches of Calais, Normandy, Gascony and Aquitaine 1661-73, FRS 1665, Capt-Gen of the Forces 1670-73, Lord High Adm of Scotland 1673, Generalissimo and C-in-C of all the Forces (against Holland) April-June 1673, PC (Scotland) 1674 and 1682, Lord High Commr to the Parl of Scotland 1681, Lord High Adm of England and Ireland 1684, crowned at Westminster Abbey by William Sancroft, Archbishop of Canterbury 23 April 1685 (having been privately crowned with his consort with Roman Catholic rites at Whitehall the previous day), left the country 11 Dec 1688 and was declared by Parl to have abdicated the throne on that day 28 Jan 1689, remained *de facto* King of Ireland until his defeat at the Battle of the Boyne 1 July 1690, *b* at St James's Palace 14 Oct 1633, *m* 1st (secretly) at Breda 24 Nov 1659 and (publicly) at Worcester House, London 3 Sept 1660, Anne (*b* at Cranbourne Lodge nr Windsor 12 March 1638; *d* at St James's Palace 31 March 1671, *bur* Westminster Abbey), eldest dau of Edward Hyde, 1st Earl of Clarendon, PC, Lord High Chancellor of England (*see* BURKE'S *Dormant and Extinct Peerages*), and had issue,

1 Charles, styled (but never *cr*) DUKE OF CAMBRIDGE, *b* at Worcester House, London 22 Oct 1660; *d* at Whitehall Palace 5 May 1661 (*bur* Westminster Abbey).

2 James, KG (1666), *cr* DUKE and EARL OF CAMBRIDGE and BARON DAUNTSEY 23 Aug 1664, *b* at St James's Palace 12 July 1663; *d* at Richmond Palace 20 June 1667 (*bur* Westminster Abbey).

3 Charles, styled (but never *cr*) DUKE OF KENDAL, *b* at St James's Palace 4 July 1666; *d* there 22 May 1667 (*bur* Westminster Abbey).

4 Edgar, *cr* DUKE and EARL OF CAMBRIDGE and BARON DAUNTSEY 7 Oct 1667, *b* at St James's Palace 14 Sept 1667; *d* at Richmond Palace 8 June 1671 (*bur* Westminster Abbey).

1 MARY II, proclaimed Queen jtly with her husband William, Prince of Orange.

2 ANNE, *s* her brother-in-law King William III.

3 Henrietta, *b* at Whitehall Palace 13 Jan, *d* at St James's Palace 15 Nov 1669 (*bur* Westminster Abbey).

4 Catherine, *b* at Whitehall Palace 9 Feb, *d* at St James's Palace 5 Dec 1671 (*bur* Westminster Abbey).

King James II *m* 2ndly (while still Duke of York) by proxy at Modena 30 Sept 1673 and in person at Dover 21 Nov 1673, *Mary* Beatrice Eleanora*, crowned with her husband (*b* at Modena 25 Sept 1658; *d* at St Germain-en-Laye 7 May 1718, *bur* Chaillot), only dau of Alfonso IV (d'Este), Duke of Modena, by his wife Laura, dau of Count Girolamo Martinozzi, and *d* in exile at St Germain-en-Laye, France 6 Sept 1701 (*bur* first the Church of the English Benedictines, rue St Jacques, Paris, later removed to St Germain), having by her had issue,

5 Charles, styled (but never *cr*) DUKE OF CAMBRIDGE, *b* at St James's Palace 7 Nov, *d* there 12 Dec 1677 (*bur* Westminster Abbey).

6 *JAMES* FRANCIS EDWARD, DUKE OF CORNWALL and DUKE OF ROTHESAY, etc at birth, styled (but never *cr*) PRINCE OF WALES, proclaimed King JAMES III at St Germain on the death of his father, proclaimed in Scotland as King JAMES VIII 6 Sept 1715 and again at Perth 1745. *b* at St James's Palace 10 June 1688, *m* by proxy at Bologna 19 May and in person at Monte Fiascone 3 Sept 1719, Maria Casimire *Clementina* (*b* 18 July 1702; *d* at the Palazzo Apostoli, Rome 18 Jan 1735, *bur* St Peter's Rome), 5th dau of Prince Jakob Ludwik Sobieski (eldest son of Jan III, King of Poland), by his wife Hedwig Elisabeth, 7th dau of Philipp Wilhelm, Elector Palatine of the Rhine, and *d* at Rome 1 Jan 1766 (*bur* St Peter's), leaving issue,

1 *CHARLES EDWARD* LOUIS JOHN CASIMIR SILVESTER MARIA, styled PRINCE OF WALES, etc from his birth, proclaimed Prince Regent in Scotland 12 Aug 1745, defeated at Culloden 16 April 1746, assumed the title of Count of Albany, recognized by his adherents as King CHARLES III on the death of his father, *b* at Rome 31 Dec 1720, *m* at Macerata 17 April 1772, *Louise* Maximilienne Caroline Emanuele (*b* at Mons 20 Sept 1752; *d* at Florence 29 Jan 1824, *bur* Church of Santa Croce there), dau of Gustavus Adolphus, Prince of Stolberg-Gedern, by his wife Elisabeth Philippine Claudine, yr dau and co-heiress of Maximilian Emmanuel, Prince of Hornes, by his 1st wife Lady Mary Theresa Charlotte, dau of Thomas Bruce, 3rd Earl of Elgin and 2nd Earl of

* Like her mother-in-law she was never crowned.

† The present Dukes of Buccleuch and Queensberry; Grafton; Richmond and Gordon; and St Albans descend from four of the natural sons of King Charles II (*see* BURKE'S *Peerage*).

* Her names are also given as Mary Beatrice Anne Margaret Isabella by some authorities.

Ailesbury (*see* BURKE'S *Peerage*, AILESBURY, M), and *dspl** at Rome 31 Jan 1788 (*bur* in St Peter's).

2 *HENRY BENEDICT* THOMAS EDWARD MARIA CLEMENT FRANCIS XAVIER, styled DUKE OF YORK from birth, *cr* Cardinal Deacon with the title of *Santa Maria in Campitelli* by Pope Benedict XIV 3 July 1747, ordained priest 1 Sept 1748, Camerlengo April 1758, consecrated Archbishop of Corinth *in partibus infidelium* 19 Nov 1758, apptd Bishop of Frascati 7 July (enthroned 13 July) 1761, Dean of the Sacred Coll and Bishop of Ostia and Velletri, recognized by his adherents as King HENRY IX on the death of his brother, *b* at the Palazzo Muti-Papazurri, Rome 6 March 1725; *d* at Frascati 13 July 1807 (*bur* St Peter's, Rome).

5 Catherine Laura, *b* at St James's Palace 10 Jan, *d* there 3 Oct 1675 (*bur* Westminster Abbey).

6 Isabella, *b* at St James's Palace 18 Aug 1676; *d* there 2 March 1681 (*bur* Westminster Abbey).

7 Charlotte Maria, *b* at St James's Palace 16 Aug, *d* there 6 Oct 1682 (*bur* Westminster Abbey).

8 Louisa Maria Theresa†, *b* at St Germain-en-Lave 28 June 1692; *d* there *unm* 8 April 1712 (*bur* Church of the English Benedictines, Paris).

After King James II was declared to have abdicated by Act of Parl the crown was offered to his daughter and son-in-law who ascended the Throne jtly as

1689-1694 WILLIAM III and MARY II, King and Queen of England (styled *King and Queen of England, Scotland, France and Ireland, Defenders of the Faith*), proclaimed 13 Feb 1689, crowned at Westminster Abbey by Henry Compton, Bishop of London (Archbishop Sancroft, who had crowned King James II, having declined to officiate) 11 April 1689. Queen Mary II was *b* at St James's Palace 30 April 1662, *m* there 4 Nov 1677, her 1st cousin, William Henry, Prince of Orange, Count of Nassau-Dillenburg, only son of Willem II, Prince of Orange, etc, by his wife Mary, Princess Royal, eldest dau of King Charles I (*see above*), and *dsp* at Kensington Palace 28 Dec 1694 (*bur* Westminster Abbey), when her husband continued to reign alone as

1694-1702 WILLIAM III, King of England, *b* (posthumously) at The Hague 4 Nov 1650; *dsp* at Kensington Palace 8 March 1702 (*bur* Westminster Abbey), and was *s* by his sister-in-law and 1st cousin, the 2nd dau of King James II (*see above*),

1702-1714 ANNE, Queen of England (styled *Queen of England, Scotland, France and Ireland, Defender of the Faith* until the Act of Union with Scotland 6 March 1707 and thereafter *Queen of Great Britain, France and Ireland, Defender of the Faith*), crowned at Westminster Abbey by Thomas Tenison, Archbishop of Canterbury 23 April 1702, *b* at St James's Palace 6 Feb 1665, *m* at the Chapel Royal, St James's 28 July 1683, her 2nd cousin once removed, Prince George of Denmark, KG (1684), *cr* Duke of Cumberland 9 April 1689, Lord High Adm of England 20 May 1702 (of Great Britain from 1707) (*b* at Copenhagen 2 April 1653; *d* at Kensington Palace 28 Oct 1708, *bur* Westminster Abbey), yr son of Frederik III, King of Denmark, by his wife Sophie Amalie, dau of Georg, Duke of Brunswick-Lüneburg (and sister of Ernst August, Elector of Hanover—*see p* 207), and *dsps* at Kensington Palace 1 Aug 1714 (*bur* Westminster Abbey), having had issue, with six other stillbirths or miscarriages of unknown sex,

1 A son, stillborn 22 Oct 1687 (*bur* Westminster Abbey).

2 William KG (1696), declared (but never *cr*) DUKE OF GLOUCESTER 27 July 1689, *b* at Hampton Court Palace 24 July 1689; *d* at Windsor Castle 30 July 1700 (*bur* Westminster Abbey).

3 George, *b* and *d* at Sion House, Brentford, Middx 17 April 1692 (*bur* Westminster Abbey).

4 A son, stillborn at Windsor 20 Sept 1696 (*bur* St George's Chapel, Windsor).

5 A son, stillborn 15 Sept 1698.

1 A dau, stillborn 12 May 1684 (*bur* Westminster Abbey).

2 Mary, *b* at Whitehall Palace 2 June 1685; *d* at Windsor Castle 8 Feb 1687 (*bur* Westminster Abbey).

3 Anne Sophia, *b* at Windsor Castle 12 May 1686; *d* there 2 Feb 1687 (*bur* Westminster Abbey).

4 Mary, *b* and *d* at St James's Palace 14 Oct 1690 (*bur* Westminster Abbey).

5 A dau, stillborn at Berkeley House 23 March 1693 (*bur* Westminster Abbey).

6 A dau, stillborn 18 Feb 1696.

7 A dau, stillborn 25 Jan 1700 (*bur* Westminster Abbey).

Queen Anne was *s* in accordance with the terms of the Act of Settlement by her 2nd cousin,

1714-1727 GEORGE I (George Louis), **King of Great Britain** (styled *King of Great Britain, France and Ireland, Duke of Brunswick-Lüneburg, Elector of Hanover, Defender of the Faith*), *s* his father as Duke and Elector of Hanover 1698, KG 1701, naturalized an English subject 1705, crowned at Westminster Abbey by Thomas Tenison, Archbishop of Canterbury 20 Oct 1714, *b* at Osnabrück 28 May 1660, *m* at Zelle 21 Nov 1682, his 1st cousin, Sophia Dorothea* (*b* at Zelle 5 Sept 1666; *d* at Ahlden 2 Nov 1726, *bur* Zelle), only surv dau and heiress of Georg Wilhelm, Duke of Brunswick-Lüneburg and Zelle, KG, by his wife Eleonore, dau of Alexandre Desmier, Seigneur d'Olbreuse, and *d* in his carriage *en route* to Osnabrück 11 June 1727 (*bur* Hanover), leaving issue,

GEORGE II, *s* his father.

Sophia Dorothea, *b* at Hanover 16 March 1687, *m* at Berlin 17 Nov 1706, her 1st cousin, Friedrich Wilhelm I, King of Prussia, and *d* at Monbijou, nr Berlin 28 June 1757 (*bur* Potsdam), having had issue, seven sons and seven daus. He *d* at Berlin 31 May 1740 (*bur* Potsdam).

King George I was *s* by his only son,

1727-1760 GEORGE II (George Augustus), **King of Great Britain** (styled the same as George I), naturalized an English subject 1705, KG 1706, *cr* Duke and Marquess of Cambridge, Earl of Milford Haven, Viscount Northallerton and Baron Tewkesbury 9 Nov 1706, Duke of

---

* His natural dau (by Clementina Walkinshaw) Charlotte Stuart was legitimated by Louis XVI, King of France and *cr* Duchess of Albany by her father. She *d unm* 1789, having herself had three natural children.

† She was baptized *Louise Marie* and received the last name at her confirmation.

* She was separated from her husband 1694 and confined in the Castle of Ahlden and, although never formally div., was never acknowledged as Queen of Great Britain.

Cornwall and Duke of Rothesay, etc on his father's accession, *cr* Prince of Wales and Earl of Chester 22 Sept 1714, crowned at Westminster Abbey by William Wake, Archbishop of Canterbury 11 Oct 1727, *b* at Hanover 30 Oct 1683, *m* there 22 Aug 1705, Wilhelmina Charlotte *Caroline,* crowned with her husband (*b* at Anspach 1 March 1683; *d* at St James's Palace 20 Nov 1737, *bur* Westminster Abbey), 3rd and yst dau of Johann Friedrich, Margrave of Brandenburg-Anspach, by his wife Eleonore Erdmuthe Louise, eldest dau of Johann Georg, Duke of Saxe-Eisenach, and *d* at Kensington Palace 25 Oct 1760 (*bur* Westminster Abbey), having had issue*,

1 HRH Prince *Frederick* Louis, KG (1717), styled (but never *cr*) DUKE OF GLOUCESTER 1717-26, *cr* DUKE OF EDINBURGH, MARQUESS OF ELY, EARL OF ELTHAM, VISCOUNT LAUNCESTON and BARON SNOWDON 26 July 1726, DUKE OF CORNWALL and DUKE OF ROTHESAY, etc on his father's accession, *cr* PRINCE OF WALES and EARL OF CHESTER 8 Jan 1729, *b* at Hanover 20 Jan 1707, *m* at the Chapel Royal, St James's 8 May 1736, HSH Princess Augusta (*b* at Gotha 30 Nov 1719; *d* at Carlton House, London 8 Feb 1772, *bur* Westminster Abbey), 6th and yst dau of HSH Friedrich II, Duke of Saxe-Gotha-Altenburg, by his wife HSH Princess Magdalene Auguste, only dau of HSH Karl Wilhelm, Prince of Anhalt-Zerbst, and *dvp* at Leicester House, London 31 March 1751 (*bur* Westminster Abbey), having had issue,

1 GEORGE III, *s* his grandfather.

2 HRH Prince Edward Augustus, KG (1752), PC (1760), FRS (1760), *cr* DUKE OF YORK AND ALBANY and EARL OF ULSTER 1 April 1760, Midshipman RN 1758, Post Capt 1759, Rear Adm of the Blue 1761, Vice-Adm of the Blue 1762, High Steward of Plymouth 1762, Pres of Lond Hosp 1764, Keeper and Lieut of Windsor Forest, Parks and Warrens 1766, Keeper and Ranger of Cranbourne Chace, in Windsor Forest 1766, *b* at Norfolk House, St James's Square, London 14 March 1739; *d unm* at Monaco 17 Sept 1767 (*bur* Westminster Abbey).

3 HRH Prince William Henry, KG (1762), PC (1764), FRS (1780), *cr* DUKE OF GLOUCESTER AND EDINBURGH and EARL OF CONNAUGHT 17 Nov 1764, Gen in the Army 1772, Field Marshal 1793, *b* at Leicester House 14 Nov 1743, *m* at her house in Pall Mall, London 6 Sept 1766, Maria (*b* 3 July 1739; *d* at Brompton 23 Aug 1807, *bur* St George's Chapel, Windsor), widow of James Waldegrave, 2nd Earl Waldegrave, KG, PC (*see* BURKE'S *Peerage*), and 2nd natural dau of Hon Sir Edward Walpole, KB (2nd son of Robert Walpole, 1st Earl of Orford, KG—*see* BURKE'S *Dormant and Extinct Peerages*), by Dorothy Clement, and *d* at Gloucester House, London 25 Aug 1805 (*bur* St George's Chapel, Windsor), having had issue,

(1) HRH Prince William Frederick, KG (1794), PC (1806), FRS (1797), 2nd DUKE OF GLOUCESTER, etc, Col of 1st Foot Guards in Flanders 1794, Major-Gen 1795, Gen 1808, Field Marshal 1816, Chancellor of Camb Univ 1811, Gov of Portsmouth 1827, *b* at Rome 15 Jan 1776, *m* at the Queen's House, St James's 22 July 1816, his 1st cousin, HRH Princess Mary (*b* at the Queen's House 25 April 1776; *d* at Gloucester House 30 April 1857, *bur* St George's Chapel, Windsor), 4th dau of HM King George III, and *dsp* at Bagshot Park, Surrey 30 Nov 1834 (*bur* St George's Chapel, Windsor).

(1) HRH Princess Sophia Matilda, Ranger of Greenwich Park, *b* at Gloucester House 29 May 1773; *d unm* at the Ranger's House, Blackheath 29 Nov 1844 (*bur* St George's Chapel, Windsor).

(2) HH Princess *Caroline* Augusta Maria, *b* at Gloucester House 24 June 1774; *d* there 14 March 1775 (*bur* St George's Chapel, Windsor).

4 HRH Prince Henry Frederick KG (1767), PC (1767), *cr* DUKE OF CUMBERLAND AND STRATHEARN and EARL OF DUBLIN 18 Oct 1766, Adm of the White, *b* at Leicester House 27 Oct 1745, *m* at her house in Hertford Street, Mayfair 2 Oct 1771, Hon Anne (*b* in London 24 Jan 1743; *d* at Trieste 28 Dec 1808), widow of Christopher Horton, of Catton Hall, Derbys, and eldest dau of Simon Luttrell, 1st Baron Irnham, later (1781) Viscount Carhampton and (1785) Earl of Carhampton (*see* BURKE'S *Dormant and Extinct Peerages*) and *dsp** at Cumberland House, Pall Mall 18 Sept 1790 (*bur* Westminster Abbey).

5 HRH Prince Frederick William, *b* at Leicester House, 13 May 1750; *d* there 29 Dec 1765 (*bur* Westminster Abbey).

1 HRH Princess Augusta, *b* at St James's Palace 31 July 1737, *m* there 16 Jan 1764, her 2nd cousin, HH *Karl* II (Wilhelm Ferdinand), Duke of Brunswick-Wolfenbüttel (*b* 9 Oct 1735; *d* at Altona (of wounds received at the Battle of Jena) 10 Nov 1806), and *d* at her house in Hanover Square, London 23 March 1813 (*bur* St George's Chapel, Windsor), having had issue,

(1) HSH Hereditary Prince *Karl Georg* August of Brunswick-Wolfenbüttel, *b* 8 Feb 1766, *m* 14 Oct 1790, HH Princess *Friederike* Louise Wilhelmina (*b* 28 Nov 1770; *d* 15 Oct 1819), only dau of HH Willem V, Prince of Orange (*see p* 217), and *dspvp* 20 Sept 1806.

(2) HSH Prince Georg Wilhelm Christian of Brunswick, renounced his rights of succession to the Duchy of Brunswick-Wolfenbüttel in favour of his yst brother, *b* 17 June 1769; *d unm* 16 Sept 1811.

(3) HSH Prince August of Brunswick, Major in the Hanoverian Army, renounced his rights of succession to the Duchy of Brunswick-Wolfenbüttel in favour of his yst brother, *b* 18 Aug 1770; *d unm* 18 Dec 1820.

(4) HH Duke *Friedrich Wilhelm* of Brunswick (1806-1815), Major-Gen in the Prussian Army, *b* 9 Oct 1771, *m* 1 Nov 1802, HSH Princess *Marie* Elisabeth Wilhelmine (*b* 7 Sept 1782; *d* 20 April 1808), 5th dau of HSH Hereditary Prince Karl Ludwig of Baden, by his wife HSH Princess Amalie Friederike, 3rd dau of HSH Landgrave Ludwig IX of Hesse-Darmstadt (*see* BURKE'S *Peerage,* MILFORD HAVEN, M), and was *k* at the Battle of Quatre Bras 16 June 1815, having had issue,

1*a* HH Duke *Karl* III (Friedrich August Wilhelm) of Brunswick (1815-1830), abdicated 7 Sept 1830, *b* 30 Oct 1804; *d unm* 19 Aug 1873.

2*a* HH Duke August Ludwig *Wilhelm* Maximilian Friedrich of Brunswick (1830-1884), KG (1831), *b* 25 April 1806; *d unm* 18 Oct 1884, when this branch of the House of Guelph became *extinct* in the male line.

1*a* A Princess, *b* and *d* April 1808.

(1) HSH Princess *Auguste* Caroline Friederike Luise of Brunswick, *b* 3 Dec 1764, *m* 11 Oct 1780, as his 1st wife, *Friedrich* Wilhelm Karl, Hereditary Prince (later HM King Friedrich I) of Württemberg (*b* 6 Nov 1754; *d* 30 Oct 1816), and *d* 27 Sept 1788, having had issue,

* All the descendants of George II are now shown and their styles are also indicated.

* In 1820 Mrs Olivia Serres (1772-1834), wife of the marine painter John Thomas Serres (1759-1825) and herself an artist of some merit who had exhibited at the Royal Acad, assumed the style and title of *HRH Princess Olive of Cumberland,* claiming to be the legitimate dau of Prince Henry Frederick, Duke of Cumberland by a secret marriage to one Olive Wilmot contracted 4 March 1767. Her claim found favour with some members of the royal family for a time, but in 1821 she was arrested for debt and eventually died within the rules of the King's Bench. The elder of her two surv daus, Lavinia Janetta Horton Serres (1797-1871) later claimed to have been *cr* Duchess of Lancaster by King George III. She *m* Antony Thomas Ryves, a portrait painter, and had six children.

1*a* HM King *Wilhelm* I (Friedrich Karl) of Württemberg (1816-1864), KG (1830), *b* 27 Sept 1781, *m* 1st 8 June 1808 (*m* diss by div 1814), HRH Princess *Charlotte* Auguste (b 8 Feb 1792; *d* 9 Feb 1873), 3rd dau of HM King Maximilian I of Bavaria. He *m* 2ndly 24 Jan 1816, HIH Grand Duchess Catherine Pavlovna (*b* 21 May 1788; *d* 19 Jan 1819), widow of HH Duke Georg of Oldenburg, and 4th dau of HIM Emperor Paul I of all the Russias, and by her had issue,

1*b* HRH Princess *Marie* Friederike Charlotte of Württemberg, *b* 30 Oct 1816, *m* 19 March 1840, *Alfred* August Karl Franz Kamill, Count von Neipperg (*b* 26 Jan 1807; *d* 16 Nov 1865), and *dsp* 4 Jan 1887.

2*b* HRH Princess *Sophie* Friederike Mathilde of Württemberg, *b* 17 June 1818, *m* 18 June 1839, as his 1st wife, HM King Willem III of the Netherlands (*b* 19 Feb 1817; *d* 23 Nov 1890), and *d* 3 June 1877, having had issue (*see p* 215).

King Wilhelm I of Württemberg *m* 3rdly 15 April 1820, HRH Duchess *Pauline* Therese Luise (*b* 4 Sept 1800; *d* 10 March 1873), 3rd dau of HRH Duke Ludwig of Württemberg, by his 2nd wife HSH Princess Henriette, dau of HSH Prince Karl of Nassau-Weilburg (*see p* 258), and *d* 25 June 1864, having by her had issue,

1*b* HM King *Karl* I (Friedrich Alexander) of Württemberg (1864-1891), KG (1890), *b* 6 March 1823, *m* 13 July 1846, HIH Grand Duchess Olga Nikolaievna (*b* 30 Aug 1822; *d* 30 Oct 1892), 3rd dau of HIM Emperor Nicholas I of all the Russias, by his wife HRH Princess Charlotte (Alexandra Feodorovna), 2nd dau of HM King Friedrich Wilhelm III of Prussia, and *dsp* 6 Oct 1891.

3*b* HRH Princess *Katharina* Friederike Charlotte of Württemberg, *b* 24 Aug 1821, *m* 20 Nov 1845, her 1st cousin, HRH Prince *Friedrich* Karl August of Württemberg (*b* 21 Feb 1808; *d* 9 May 1870), and *d* 6 Dec 1898, leaving issue (*see below*).

4*b* HRH Princess *Auguste* Wilhelmine Henriette of Württemberg, *b* 4 Oct 1826, *m* 17 June 1851, HH Prince *Hermann* Bernhard Georg of Saxe-Weimar-Eisenach, Duke of Saxony (*b* 4 Aug 1825; *d* 31 Aug 1901), and *d* 3 Dec 1898, having had issue,

1*c* HH Prince *Wilhelm* Carl Bernhard Hermann of Saxe-Weimar-Eisenach, Duke of Saxony, *b* 31 Dec 1853, *m* 11 April 1885, HSH Princess *Gerta* Auguste zu Ysenburg und Büdingen in Wächtersbach (*b* 18 Jan 1863; *d* 27 Nov 1945), yr dau of HSH Ferdinand Maximilian, 1st Prince zu Ysenburg und Büdingen (*see p* 263) and *d* 15 Dec 1924, having had issue,

1*d* HH Prince *Hermann* Carl Bernhard Ferdinand Friedrich Wilhelm August Paul Philipp of Saxe-Weimar-Eisenach, Duke of Saxony, renounced his rights as a member of the Grand Ducal House of Saxe-Weimar-Eisenach and was *cr* Count von Ostheim 2 Aug 1909, *b* 14 Feb 1886, *m* 1st 5 Sept 1909 (*m* diss by div 1911), Wanda Paola Lottero (*b* 14 July 1884). He *m* 2ndly 4 Aug 1918, Suzanne Aagot Midling (*b* 3 March 1886; *d* 16 Oct 1931), and by her had issue,

Count *Alexander-Kyrill* Wilhelm Hermann Nikolaus von Ostheim, *b* 7 Aug 1922; *d unm* 23 March 1943.

He *m* 3rdly 28 Nov 1932, •Isabel, has Order of Bene Merençia of Portugal (*b* 3 Feb 1895) [*68 Eaton Square, SW1; Ribalonga, Cascais, Portugal*], dau of Francis Nielsen, and *d* 4 June 1964.

2*d* HH Prince *Albert* Wilhelm Carl Hermann Bernhard August Friedrich of Saxe-Weimar-Eisenach, Duke of Saxony, *b* 31 Dec 1886; *k* in action in World War I 9 Sept 1918, *unm.*

1*d* HH Princess *Sophie* Auguste Ida Caroline Pauline Agnes Elisabeth Ernestine of Saxe-Weimar-Eisenach, Duchess of Saxony, *b* 25 July 1888; *d unm* 18 Sept 1913.

2*c* HH Prince *Bernhard* Wilhelm Georg Hermann of Saxe-Weimar-Eisenach, Duke of Saxony, renounced his rights as a member of the Grand Ducal House of Saxe-Weimar-Eisenach and was *cr* Count von Crayenberg 24 May 1901, *b* 10 Oct 1855, *m* 1st 10 Oct 1900, Elisabeth Brockmüller (*b* 6 May 1866; *d* 11 March 1903). He *m* 2ndly 1 April 1905, Countess Elisabeth (*b* 1 April 1869; *d* 25 Dec 1940), dau of Count Hermann von der Schulenburg, and *dsp* 23 Dec 1907.

3*c* HH Prince Alexander Wilhelm Bernhard Carl Hermann of Saxe-Weimar-Eisenach, Duke of Saxony, *b* 22 June 1857; *d unm* 5 Sept 1891.

4*c* HH Prince *Ernst* Carl Wilhelm of Saxe-Weimar-Eisenach, Duke of Saxony, *b* 9 Aug 1859; *d unm* 19 Jan 1909.

1*c* HH Princess *Pauline* Ida Maria Olga Henriette Katharina of Saxe-Weimar-Eisenach, Duchess of Saxony, *b* 25 July 1852, *m* 26 Aug 1873, HRH Hereditary Grand Duke *Karl August* Wilhelm Nikolaus Alexander Michael Bernhard Heinrich Friedrich Stephan of Saxe-Weimar-Eisenach (*b* 31 July 1844; *d* 20 Nov 1894), and *d* 17 May 1904, leaving issue (*see below*).

2*c* HH Princess *Olga Marie* Ida Sophie Pauline Auguste of Saxe-Weimar-Eisenach, Duchess of Saxony, *b* 8 Sept 1869, *m* 22 April 1902, as his 1st wife, HSH Prince *Leopold* Wolfgang Ernst Maria Ferdinand Karl Michael Anton Viktor Ludwig Joseph Johann Baptist Franz zu Isenburg (*b* 10 March 1866; *d* 30 Jan 1933), and *d* 12 Jan 1924, leaving issue,

HSH Prince *Wilhelm Karl* Hermann zu Isenburg, author of many genealogical works, *b* 16 Jan 1903, *m* (civil) 12 April and (religious) 30 April 1930, •Countess Helene (*b* 6 April 1900) [*5628 Heiligenhaus, Bez Düsseldorf, Sauerbruchstrasse 8, Germany*], dau of Count Alfred von Korff gen Schmising-Kerssenbrock, and *dsp* 23 Nov 1956.

2*a* HRH Prince *Paul* Heinrich Karl Friedrich August of Württemberg, *b* 19 Jan 1785, *m* 28 Sept 1805, HSH Princess Catherine *Charlotte* Georgine (*b* 17 June 1787; *d* 12 Dec 1847), eldest dau of HH Duke Friedrich of Saxe-Hildburghausen, and *d* 16 April 1852, having had issue,

1*b* HRH Prince *Friedrich* Karl August of Württemberg, *b* 21 Feb 1808, *m* 20 Nov 1845, his 1st cousin, HRH Princess *Katharina* Friederike Charlotte (*b* 24 Aug 1821; *d* 6 Dec 1898), 3rd dau of HM King Wilhelm I of Württemberg (*see above*), and *d* 9 May 1870, leaving issue,

HM King *Wilhelm* II (Karl Paul Heinrich Friedrich) of Württemberg (1891-1918), abdicated 29 Nov 1918, *b* 25 Feb 1848, *m* 1st 15 Feb 1877, HSH Princess Georgine Henriette *Marie* (*b* 23 May 1857; *d* 30 April 1882), 3rd dau of HSH Georg Viktor, Prince of Waldeck and Pyrmont, and had issue,

1*d* HRH Prince Christoph *Ulrich* Ludwig of Württemberg, *b* 29 July, *d* 28 Dec 1880.

1*d* HRH Princess *Pauline* Olga Helene Emma of Württemberg, *b* 19 Dec 1877, *m* 29 Oct 1898, HSH Wilhelm *Friedrich* Hermann Otto Karl, 6th Prince zu Wied (*b* 27 June 1872; *d* 18 June 1945), and *d* 9 May 1965, having had issue,

1*e* HSH Hereditary Prince *Hermann* Wilhelm Friedrich zu Wied, *b* 18 Aug 1899, *m* 29 April 1930, •H Ill H Countess Marie Antonia (*b* 6 Feb 1909; *m* 2ndly 31 Aug 1943, Edward Franz von Gordon [*Dierdorf, Bez Koblenz, Kupferhaus, Germany*], elder dau of H Ill H Count Carl zu Stolberg-Wernigerode, and *d* 5 Nov 1941, leaving issue,

1*f* •HSH *Friedrich Wilhelm* Heinrich Konstantin, 7th Prince zu Wied [*Schloss Neuwied, Rhineland, Germany*], *b* 2 June 1931, *educ* Gordonstoun, *m* 1st 9 Sept 1958 (*m* diss by div 1967), HSH Princess Guda (*b* 22 Aug 1939), yst dau of HSH Josias,

Prince of Waldeck and Pyrmont (*see p 221*), and has issue,
1g •HSH Hereditary Prince Johann Friedrich *Alexander* Hermann Josias Wilhelm zu Wied, *b* 29 Sept 1960.
2g •HSH Prince Friedrich August Maximilian Wilhelm *Carl* zu Wied, b 27 Oct 1961.
He *m* 2ndly 15 July 1967, •HSH Princess *Sophie* Charlotte Agnes zu Stolberg-Stolberg (*b* 4 Oct 1943), yr dau of HSH Wolf Heinrich, 3rd Prince and Count zu Stolberg, and by her has issue,
1g •HSH Princess *Christina Elisabeth* Sophie Wilhelmine Friederike zu Wied, *b* 9 June 1970.
2f •HSH Prince *Metfried* Alexander Wilhelm Friedrich zu Wied [6251 *Burg Runkel über Limburg a d Lahn, Germany*], *b* 25 April 1935, *m* 17 Feb 1968, •Baroness *Felicitas* (*Fairy*) Gisela Sylvia (*b* 31 Dec 1948), yst dau of Baron Hans Georg von der Pahlen, and has issue,
•HSH Prince *Friedrich Christian* Hermann Wilhelm Alexis zu Wied, *b* 5 Aug 1968.
1f •HSH Princess Wilhelmine Friederike Elisabeth Henriette Anastasia *Osterlind* zu Wied, *b* 8 April 1939, *m* 7 Sept 1964, *Werner* Manfred Fritz von Klitzing (*b* 3 Aug 1934) [*Frankfurt a M, Wiesenau 25, Germany*], and has issue,
1g •*Sophie* Antonie Margarete von Klitzing, *b* 13 Sept 1965.
2g •*Franziska* Christiane Hilde Elisabeth von Klitzing, *b* 30 Nov 1966.
3g •*Valeska* Marie Natalie Henriette von Klitzing, *b* 3 July 1970.
2e •HSH Prince *Dietrich* Wilhelm Friedrich Karl Paul zu Wied [*Ludwigsburg, Marienwahl, Württemberg, Germany*], *b* 31 Oct 1901, *m* 18 July 1928, •Countess *Antoinette* Julia Marie Amilie Ethel Amerika Thyra Gustava (*b* 9 Oct 1902), 3rd dau of Count Otto von Grote, and has issue,
1f •HSH Prince Wilhelm Friedrich Otto Hermann *Maximilian* zu Wied [*Siegfriedstrasse 11, Munich, Bavaria, Germany*], *b* 30 May 1929.
2f •HSH Prince Wilhelm Friedrich *Ulrich* zu Wied [*Schrandolphstrasse 9, Munich, Bavaria, Germany*], *b* 12 June 1931, *m* 2 Dec 1968, •Ilke Fischer (*b* 9 Dec 1936), and has issue,
•HSH Prince *Wilhelm* Friedrich Ulrich zu Wied, *b* 26 June 1970.
3f •HSH Prince Wilhelm Friedrich Dietrich *Ludwig* Eugen zu Wied [*Hohenzollernstrasse 34, Munich, Bavaria, Germany*], *b* 27 Aug 1938, *m* 8 June 1966, •Helga Gemeinert (*b* 7 May 1941), and has issue,
•HSH Prince Karl *Edzard* zu Wied, *b* 16 Jan 1968.
2d A Princess, stillborn 27 April 1882.
King Wilhelm II of Württemberg *m* 2ndly 8 April 1886, HSH Princess *Charlotte* Marie Ida Luise Hermine Mathilde (*b* 10 Oct 1864; *d* 16 July 1946), eldest dau of HSH Prince Wilhelm of Schaumburg-Lippe, and *d* 2 Oct 1921.
2b HRH Prince Karl Paul Friedrich of Württemberg, *b* 7 March 1809; *d* 28 May 1810.
3b HRH Prince Friedrich *August* Eberhard of Württemberg, Col-Gen in the Prussian Army, *b* 24 Jan 1813, *m* (morganatically) Marie Bettige, *cr* Frau von Wardenburg (*b* 1 April 1830; *d* 16 Feb 1869), and *d* 12 Jan 1885, leaving issue,
Helene *Katharina* Wilhelmine von Wardenburg, *b* 18 April 1865, *m* 2 Oct 1884, Dedo von Schenck (*b* 11 Feb 1853; *d* 28 April 1918), and *d* 25 Sept 1938, having had issue,
1d Albrecht von Schenck, *b* 20 Sept 1885; *d* 10 June 1888.
2d •Eberhard Friedrich August von Schenck, *b* 15 Nov 1887, *m* 14 Sept 1918, •Irmgard Ecker (*b* 1 July 1895), and has had issue,
1e •Dedo Otto Eberhard Kersten von Schenck, *b* 29 March 1922, *m* 19 April 1944, •Maria Margarethe (*b* 3 Aug 1922), dau of Heinz Louis Sander, and has issue,
1f •Ulrike von Schenck, *b* 12 Jan 1949.
2f •Kersten von Schenck, *b* 10 Nov 1951.
2e Albrecht Kurt Hermann von Schenck, *b* 25 Nov 1923; *d unm* 25 Dec 1941.
3d Dedo von Schenck, *b* 23 July, *d* 15 Aug 1892.
1d *Freda* Katharina von Schenck, *b* 21 March 1890, *m* 1st 28 June 1910 (*m* diss by div 1916), Baron Kurt von Reibnitz (*b* 12 Nov 1877; *d* 26 June 1937). She *m* 2ndly 29 Feb 1916, Count Ernst August *Werner* Achaz Alexander von der Schulenburg (*b* 31 Oct 1886; *d* 5 Feb 1945), and *d* 2 March 1946, leaving issue,
•Count *Johannes Heinrich* (*Jonny*) Dedo Carlotto Bruno Ferdinand Antonius Mariano von der Schulenburg [*Halle, Kr Holzminden, Germany*], *b* 20 Dec 1916, *m* 1 Nov 1946, •Inge (*b* 27 July 1920), dau of Friedrich Guht, and has issue,
1f •Count *Friedrich Werner* von der Schulenburg, *b* 30 Aug 1947.
2f •Count *Christian Günther* von der Schulenburg, *b* 23 Nov 1954.
1f •Countess *Marie Christine* von der Schulenburg, *b* 2 Sept 1949.
2f •Countess Ingeborg von der Schulenburg, *b* 3 Nov 1951.
3f •Countess Gabriele von der Schulenburg, *b* 10 June 1961.
1b HRH Princess Friederike *Charlotte* Marie (Grand Duchess *Helena Pavlovna*) of Württemberg, *b* 9 Jan 1807, *m* 20 Feb 1824, HIH Grand Duke Michael Pavlovitch of Russia (*b* 8 Feb 1798; *d* 9 Sept 1849), yst son of HIM Emperor Paul I of all the Russias, and *d* 21 Jan 1873, having had issue,
1c HIH Grand Duchess Marie Mikhailovna of Russia, *b* 9 March 1825; *d unm* 19 Nov 1846.
2c HIH Grand Duchess Elisabeth Mikhailovna of Russia, *b* 26 May 1826, *m* 31 Jan 1844, as his 1st wife, HH Duke *Adolf* Wilhelm Karl August Friedrich of Nassau, later (HRH) Grand Duke of Luxembourg (*b* 24 July 1817; *d* 17 Nov 1905), and *d* 28 Jan 1845, having had issue,
A Princess, *b* and *d* Jan 1845.
3c HIH Grand Duchess Catherine Mikhailovna of Russia, *b* 28 Aug 1827, *m* 16 Feb 1851, HH Duke *Georg* August Ernst Adolf Karl Ludwig of Mecklenburg-Strelitz (*b* 11 Jan 1824; *d* 20 June 1876), and *d* 12 May 1894, having had issue,
1d HH Duke Nikolaus Georg Michael Karl of Mecklenburg-Strelitz, *b* and *d* 11 July 1854.
2d HH Duke *Georg Alexander* Michael Friedrich Wilhelm Franz Karl of Mecklenburg-Strelitz, *b* 6 June 1859, *m* (morganatically) 14 Feb 1890, Natalia, *cr* Countess von Carlow by Grand Duke Friedrich Wilhelm of Mecklenburg-Strelitz 18 Nov 1890 (*b* 16 May 1858; *d* 14 March 1921), dau of Feodor Ardalionovitch Wonlarsky, and *d* 5 Dec 1909, leaving issue,
1e HH Duke *Georg Alexander* Michael Friedrich Wilhelm Albert Theodor Franz of Mecklenburg-Strelitz (recognized as Duke of Mecklenburg-Strelitz 1928/29, assumed the style of Highness 18 Dec 1950), *b* 5 Oct 1899, *m* 1st 7 Oct 1920, Irina (*b* 18 Aug 1892; *d* 25 July 1955), dau of Mikhail Nikolaievitch Raievsky, and had issue,
1f •HH Duke *Georg Alexander* Andreas Carl Michael Peter Philipp Ignatius Maria of Mecklenburg-Strelitz [*78 Freiburg i Br, Bugerwehrstrasse 4, Germany; Culleen, Mullingar, co Westmeath*], *b* 27 Aug 1921, *m* 30 April 1946, •HI and RH Archduchess Helene (*Ilona*) (*b* 20 April 1927), 2nd dau of HI and RH Archduke Joseph Franz of Austria, and has issue,
1g •HH Duke Georg *Borwin* Friedrich Franz Carl Stephan Konrad Hubertus

Maria of Mecklenburg-Strelitz, *b* 10 June 1956.
1*g* ●HH Duchess Elisabeth *Christine* Auguste Louisa Irene Anna Cecilie Margarethe Maria Immaculata Scholastika Katharina Gabriele et omnes sancti of Mecklenburg-Strelitz, *b* 22 March 1947.
2*g* ●HH Duchess *Marie* Katharina Elisabeth Henriette Friederike Sophie Josephine et omnes sancti of Mecklenburg-Strelitz, *b* 14 Nov 1949.
3*g* ●HH Duchess Caroline Luise *Irene* Margarethe Helene Albertine Konrada of Mecklenburg-Strelitz, *b* 18 April 1952.
2*f* ●HH Duke *Carl Gregor* Georg Friedrich Franz Heinrich Norbert Wenzeslaus Johann Nepomuk Lazarus Clemens Maria de Mercede et omnes sancti of Mecklenburg-Strelitz [*Villa Silberburg, 745 Hechingen, Germany*], *b* 14 March 1933, *m* 24 April 1966, ●HSH Princess *Maria Margarete* Anna Viktoria Luise Josephine Mathilde Theresia Kinde Jesu (*b* 2 Jan 1928), only dau of HSH late Prince Franz Joseph of Hohenzollern-Emden (*see p* 235).
1*f* HH Duchess *Helene* Cecilie Therese Maria Immaculata Viktoria Sophie Franziska Monika of Mecklenburg-Strelitz, *b* 15 Nov 1924, *m* 18 Feb 1955, ●*Hassan* Sayed Kamil (*b* 14 Nov 1918), and was *k* in a flying accident 7 July 1962, leaving issue,
●Sheila Kamil [*61 Restelbergstrasse, Zürich, Switzerland*], *b* 26 July 1958.
He *m* 2ndly 25 July 1956, ●HI and RH Archduchess *Charlotte* Hedwig Franziska Josepha Maria Antonia Roberta Ottonia Pia Anna Ignatia Marcus d'Aviano (*b* 1 March 1921), 2nd dau of HIM Emperor Karl I of Austria, Apostolic King of Hungary (*see p* 240), and *d* 6 July 1963.
1*d* Countess *Catherine* Helene von Carlow, *b* 7 Aug 1891, *m* 23 Feb 1913, as his 1st wife, Prince Vladimir Emmanuelovitch Galitzine (*b* 18 June 1884; *d* 13 July 1954), and was *k* by enemy action in an air raid in London 8 Oct 1940, leaving issue,
1*f* ●Prince Nicholas Galitzine, served in World War II as Lieut RNVR [*225 Robertson Street, Victoria, BC, Canada*], *b* 2 Jan 1914, *m* 1st 11 Dec 1946 (*m* diss by div 1955), *Elizabeth* Beatrice (*b* 26 Oct 1924), yr dau of Col Cyril Denzil Branch, MC, and has issue,
1*g* ●Prince Andrew Galitzine, *b* 22 June 1949.
He *m* 2ndly 4 May 1956, ●Anita (*b* 22 Dec 1933), dau of Harold Frisch, and by her has issue,
2*g* ●Prince Alexander Galitzine, *b* 6 Feb 1957.
3*g* ●Prince Peter Galitzine, *b* 26 Nov 1958.
1*g* ●Princess Marina Galitzine, *b* 13 Jan 1962.
2*f* ●Prince George Galitzine, late Major Welsh Guards, served in World War II [*113 Eaton Square, SW1*], *b* 3 May 1916, *m* 1st 11 Sept 1943 (*m* diss by div 1954), Baroness Anne Marie (*b* 12 Nov 1916), dau of Major-Gen Baron Sir Rudolf von Slatin Pasha, GCVO, KCMG, CB, and has issue,
1*g* ●Prince *Alexander* Peter Galitzine, *b* 6 Sept 1945, *educ* Harrow.
2*g* ●Prince *George* Rudolf Galitzine, *b* 3 Dec 1946, *educ* Harrow.
1*g* ●Princess *Caroline* Marie Galitzine, *b* 14 June 1944, *m* 1 Jan 1966, ●*Jonathan* Walter Peter Hazell, MA, MB, BChir (*b* 28 March 1942) [*Hilton, Hunts*], son of late Major Peter Hazell, and has issue,
1*h* ●*Alexander* Jonathan Peter Hazell, *b* 4 Sept 1969.
1*h* ●*Lara* Emma Hazell, *b* 28 June 1967.
He *m* 2ndly 5 May 1963, ●Jean (*b* 22 March 1925), dau of Frederick Dawnay, and by her has issue,
2*g* ●Princess Catherine Galitzine, *b* 20 Sept 1964.
3*f* ●Prince Emmanuel Galitzine, served in World War II with RAFVR [*The Abbey, Abbotsbrook, Bourne End, Bucks*], *b* 28 May 1918, *m* 23 Feb 1943, ●Gwendoline (*b* 4 July 1920), yr dau of Capt Stanley Rhodes, and has issue,
1*g* ●Prince Nicholas Galitzine [*3466 East 48, Vancouver, BC, Canada*], *b* 19 Oct 1944, *m* 17 April 1971, ●Anne, dau of William Ramsey.
2*g* ●Prince Michael Galitzine, *b* 25 Jan 1949.
3*g* ●Prince Emmanuel Galitzine, *b* 11 March 1951.
2*e* ●Countess *Marie* Catherine Sophie von Carlow, *b* 1 Nov 1893, *m* 1st 14 Nov 1916, HSH Prince Boris Dimitrievitch Galitzine (*b* 24 Jan 1892; *d* 6 June 1919), and has had issue,
1*f* HSH Prince Dimitri Borisovitch Galitzine, Capt S Wales Bdrs, served in World War II (wounded twice), *b* 16 Nov 1917, *educ* Brighton Coll, *d* of wounds received in action in NW Europe 26 Oct 1944, *unm.*
1*f* ●HSH Princess Natalia Borisovna Galitzine [*1261 Bogis-Bossey, Geneva, Switzerland*], *b* 15 Jan 1920, *m* 14 Aug 1938 (*m* diss by div 1947), Nigel Heseltine (*b* 3 July 1916), and has issue,
●Elizabeth Heseltine [*c/o Countess Kleinmichel, 21 Upper Phillimore Gardens, W8*], *b* 27 May 1939, *m* 1st 30 July 1962 (*m* diss by div 1966), Graham Nesbitt (*b* 25 Sept 1936). She *m* 2ndly 1 April 1967 (*m* diss by div 1971), Michael Ronald Ward, and has issue,
1*h* ●Catherine Ward, *b* 30 May 1968.
2*h* ●Natalia Ward, *b* 27 June 1969.
She *m* 2ndly 14 June 1929, ●Count Vladimir Petrovitch Kleinmichel, CVO (*b* 19 Jan 1901) [*21 Upper Phillimore Gardens, W8*], and has further issue,
2*f* ●Countess Sophie (*Sonia*) Vladimirovna Kleinmichel, *b* 27 March 1930, *m* 17 May 1957, ●*Philip* Henry Russell Goodman (*b* 17 June 1931) [*56 Mortlake Road, Kew Gardens, Richmond, Surrey*], elder son of late Sir Victor Martin Reeves Goodman, KCB, OBE, MC, by his 1st wife Julian Ottoline (later Mrs Igor Vinogradoff), only dau of Philip Edward Morrell, JP, of Garsington Manor, Oxford (*see* BURKE'S *LG*, 1952 *Edn*, MORRELL *of Headington Hill Hall*), and has issue,
1*g* ●Mary Goodman, *b* 20 Oct 1959.
2*g* ●*Catherine* Anne Goodman, *b* 22 April 1961.
3*g* ●*Elizabeth* Ottoline Goodman, *b* 21 Jan 1964.
4*g* ●Sophie Goodman, *b* 11 Sept 1965.
5*g* ●*Xenia* Alexandra Goodman, *b* 5 Sept 1969.
3*e* Countess *Natalia* Catherine Helene von Carlow, *b* 20 Nov 1894; *d unm* 4 Dec 1913
3*d* HH Duke *Karl Michael* Wilhelm August Alexander, Head of the Grand Ducal House of Mecklenburg-Strelitz (1918-1934), *b* 17 June 1863; *d unm* 6 Dec 1934.
1*d* HH Duchess *Helene* Marie Alexandra Elisabeth Auguste Caroline of Mecklenburg-Strelitz, *b* 16 Jan 1857, *m* 13 Dec 1891, HH Prince *Albert* Heinrich Joseph Karl Viktor Georg Friedrich of Saxe-Altenburg, Duke of Saxony (*b* 14 April 1843; *d* 22 May 1902) (*see* (*p* 247), and *dsp* 28 Aug 1936.
4*c* HIH Grand Duchess Alexandra Mikhailovna of Russia, *b* 28 Jan 1831; *d* 27 March 1832.
5*c* HIH Grand Duchess Anna Mikhailovna of Russia, *b* 27 Oct 1834; *d* 22 March 1836.
2*b* HRH Princess *Pauline* Friederike Marie of Württemberg, *b* 25 Feb 1810, *m* 23 April 1829, HH Duke *Wilhelm* Georg August Heinrich Belgicus of Nassau (*b* 14 June 1792; *d*

20 Aug 1839), and *d* 7 July 1856, having had issue (*see p* 220).

1*a* HRH Princess Friederike *Katharine* Sophie Dorothea of Württemberg, *b* 21 Feb 1783, *m* 23 Aug 1807, as his 2nd wife, HM King Jérôme Napoléon of Westphalia (1807-1813), later (1816) *cr* Prince of Montfort by the King of Württemberg, Marshal of France (1850) (*b* 15 Nov 1784; *d* 24 June 1860), yst brother of HIM Napoléon I, Emperor of the French and King of Italy, and *d* 28 Nov 1835, leaving issue,

1*b* HIH Prince *Jérôme*-Napoléon-Charles (Bonaparte), *Prince français,* Prince of Montfort, Col in the army of Württemberg, *b* 24 Aug 1814; *d unm* 12 May 1847.

2*b* HIH Prince *Napoléon*-Joseph-Charles-Paul (Bonaparte), *Prince français,* called Prince Napoléon-Jérôme, called Comte de Meudon after 1870, *cr* Count of Moncalieri by letters patent of the King of Italy, Nov 1870, Head of the Imp House of Bonaparte 1891-1926, *b* 18 July 1862, *m* 30 Jan 1859, HRH Princess *Clothilde*-Marie-Thérèse-Louise of Savoy (*b* 2 March 1843; *d* 25 June 1911), eldest dau of HM King Vittorio Emanuele II of Italy, and *d* 18 March 1891, leaving issue,

1*c* HIH Prince Napoléon-*Victor*-Jérôme-Frédéric, Prince Napoléon, Head of the Imp House of Bonaparte 1891-1926, *b* 18 July 1862, *m* 14 Nov 1910, HRH Princess *Clémentine*-Albertine-Marie-Léopoldine (*b* 30 July 1872; *d* 8 March 1955), yst dau of HM King Léopold II of the Belgians (*see p* 258), and *d* 3 May 1926, leaving issue,

1*d* •HIH Prince Napoléon-*Louis*-Jérôme-Victor-Emmanuel-Léopold-Marie, Prince Napoléon, Head of the Imp House of Bonaparte from 1926 [*10 Boulevard Suchet, Paris XVIe, France; Villa de Prangins, Vaud, Switzerland*], *b* 23 Jan 1914, *m* 16 Aug 1949, •*Alix*-Thérèse-Henriette (*b* 4 April 1926), dau of Comte Albéric de Foresta, and has issue,

1*e* •HIH Prince *Charles*-Marie-Jérôme-Victor Napoléon, *b* 19 Oct 1950.

2*e* •HIH Prince *Jérôme*-Xavier-Marie-Joseph-Victor Napoléon, *b* 14 Jan 1957.

1*e* •HIH Princess *Catherine*-Elisabeth-Albérique-Marie Napoléon, *b* (twin with Prince Charles) 19 Oct 1950.

2*e* •HIH Princess *Laure*-Clémentine-Geneviève Napoléon, *b* 8 Oct 1952.

1*d* •HIH Princess *Marie-Clothilde*-Eugénie-Alberte-Laetitia-Geneviève Napoléon, *b* 20 March 1912, *m* 17 Oct 1938, •Count Serge de Witt (*b* 30 Dec 1891) [*Château de la Pommerie, par Cendrieux, Dordogne, France; 57bis rue Spontini, Paris XVIe, France*], and has had issue,

1*e* Napoléon-Serge de Witt, *b* 2 Nov, *d* 4 Nov 1942.

2*e* •*Baudouin*-Napoléon de Witt, *b* 24 Jan 1947.

3*e* •*Jean*-Jérôme de Witt, *b* 12 April 1950.

4*e* •Wladimir de Witt, *b* 26 Jan 1952.

1*e* •Marie-Eugénie de Witt, *b* 29 Aug 1939, *m* 9 Nov 1959, •Count Peter Petrovitch Cheremeteff (*b* 14 Sept 1931).

2*e* •Hélène de Witt, *b* 22 Nov 1941, *m* 17 Oct 1959, •Comte Henri de Lau d'Allemans (*b* 17 March 1925) [*Château de Montardy, par Grand Brassac, Dordogne, France; 22 rue Spontini, Paris XVIe, France*], and has issue,

1*f* •*Jean*-Wladimir de Lau d'Allemans, *b* 18 Dec 1960.

2*f* •*Alexandre*-Serge-Marie de Lau d'Allemans, *b* 19 May 1962.

1*f* •*Astrid*-Françoise-Marie-Laetitia de Lau d'Allemans, *b* 19 Sept 1964.

3*e* Yolande de Witt, *b* 9 Sept 1943; *d* 6 July 1945.

4*e* •*Véra*-Geneviève de Witt, *b* 7 Nov 1945, *m* 11 April 1966, •Raymond Godefroy, Marquis de Commargue (*b* 18 Dec 1938) [*Château de la Bourlie, Urval, par Le Buisso 24, Dordogne, France*], and has issue,

•Grégoire-Ludovic-Wladimir de Commargue *b* 22 April 1967.

5*e* •Isabelle de Witt, *b* 27 Jan 1949, *m* 1970, •Remmest Laasi.

6*e* •*Anne*-Clémentine de Witt, *b* 28 Sep 1953.

2*c* HIH Prince Napoléon-*Louis*-Joseph-Jérôme Napoléon, Gen in the Imp Russian Army, *b* 16 July 1864; *d unm* 14 Oct 1932.

1*c* HIH Princess Marie-*Laetitia*-Eugénie-Catherine-Adélaïde Napoléon, *b* 20 Dec 1866, *m* 11 Sept 1888, as his 2nd wife, her uncle, HRH Prince *Amedeo* Ferdinando Maria of Savoy, 1st Duke of Aosta, King of Spain (1870-73) (*b* 30 May 1845; *d* 18 Jan 1890), and *d* 25 Oct 1926, having had issue,

HRH Prince *Umberto* Maria Vittorio Amedeo Giuseppe of Savoy-Aosta, Count of Salemi, *b* 22 June 1889; *d unm* 18 Oct 1918.

1*b* HIH Princess *Mathilde*-Laetitia-Wilhelmine (Bonaparte), *b* 27 May 1820, *m* 1 Nov 1840, Anatole Nikolaievitch Demidoff, 1st Principe di San Donato (*b* 5 April 1813; *d* 29 April 1870), and *dsp* 2 Jan 1904.

2*a* HH Princess Sophie Dorothea of Württemberg, *b* 24 Dec 1783; *d* 3 Oct 1784.

(2) HSH Princess *Caroline* Amelia Elizabeth of Brunswick, *b* 17 May 1768, *m* 8 April 1795, her 1st cousin, HRH George Augustus Frederick, Prince of Wales, afterwards HM King George IV (*b* 12 Aug 1762; *d* 23 June 1830), and *d* 7 Aug 1821, having had issue (*see p* 294).

(3) HSH Princess Amalie Caroline Dorothea Luise of Brunswick-Wolfenbüttel, *b* 22 Nov 1772; *d* 2 April 1773.

2 HRH Princess *Elizabeth* Caroline, *b* at Norfolk House, St James's Square, London 30 Dec 1740; *d unm* at Kew Palace 4 Sept 1759 (*bur* Westminster Abbey).

3 HRH Princess Louisa Anne, *b* at Leicester House 8 March 1749; *d unm* at Carlton House 13 May 1768 (*bur* Westminster Abbey).

4 HRH Princess Caroline Matilda, *b* at Leicester House 11 July 1751, *m* by proxy at the Chapel Royal, St James's 1 Oct 1766, and in person at Christianborg 8 Nov 1766, her 1st cousin, HM King Christian VII of Denmark (*b* 29 Jan 1749; *d* 13 March 1808), and *d* at Zelle 10 May 1775, leaving issue (*see p* 286).

2 A Prince, stillborn 9 Nov 1716.

3 HRH Prince George William, *b* at St James's Palace 2 Nov 1717; *d* at Kensington Palace 6 Feb 1718 (*bur* Westminster Abbey).

4 HRH Prince *William* Augustus, KG (1730), PC (1742), *cr* DUKE OF CUMBERLAND, MARQUESS OF BERKHAMPSTED, EARL OF KENSINGTON, VISCOUNT TREMATON and BARON OF THE ISLE OF ALDERNEY 27 July 1726, Col Coldstream Guards 1740, trans to 1st Guards 1742, Major-Gen 1742, Lieut-Gen 1743, Capt-Gen of British Land Forces 1745, cmd'd 2nd army against Prince Charles Edward 1745, and defeated him at Culloden 1746, earned the nickname of "Butcher Cumberland" from the severity with which he pursued the rebels, Chancellor of St Andrews Univ 1746, and of Dublin Univ 1751, *b* at Leicester House 15 April 1721; *d unm* at his house in Upper Grosvenor Square, London 31 Oct 1765 (*bur* Westminster Abbey).

1 HRH Princess Anne, Princess Royal (from her father's accession in 1727), *b* at Hanover 2 Nov 1709, *m* at the French Chapel, St James's 25 March 1734, HH *Willem IV* (Karel Hendrik), Prince of Orange, KG (*b* 1 Sept 1711; *d* 22 Oct 1751), and *d* at The Hague 12 Jan 1759, having had issue,

1 A Prince, *b* and *d* 1735.

2 HH *Willem V* (Batavus), Prince of Orange, KG (1752), *b* 8 March 1748, *m* 4 Oct 1767, HRH Princess Friederike Sophie *Wilhelmine* (*b* 7 Aug 1751; *d* 9 June 1820), only dau of HRH Prince August Wilhelm of Prussia, and *d* 9 April 1806, having had issue,

(1) A Prince, stillborn 23 March 1769.

(2) HM King *Willem I* (Frederik) of the Netherlands, Grand Duke of Luxembourg, KG (1814),

was Prince of Fulda and Corvey 1802, deprived of all his territory by the Treaty of Tilsit 1807, restored 1813, proclaimed King of the Netherlands and Grand Duke of Luxembourg 21 March 1815, abdicated 7 Oct 1840 and assumed the style of King Willem Frederik, Count of Nassau, *b* 24 Aug 1772, *m* 1st 1 Oct 1791, HRH Princess Friederike Luise *Wilhelmine* (*b* 18 Nov 1774; *d* 12 Oct 1837), 3rd dau of HM King Friedrich Wilhelm II of Prussia, and had issue,

1a HM King *Willem II* (Frederik Georg Lodewijk) of the Netherlands, Grand Duke of Luxembourg (1840-1849), *b* 6 Dec 1792, *m* 21 Feb 1816, HIH Grand Duchess Anna Pavlovna (*b* 18 Jan 1795; *d* 1 March 1865), 6th and yst dau of HIM Emperor Paul I of all the Russias, and *d* 17 March 1849, having had issue,

1b HM King *Willem III* (Alexander Paul Frederik Lodewijk) of the Netherlands, Grand Duke of Luxembourg (1849-1890), KG (1882), *b* 19 Feb 1817, *m* 1st 18 June 1839, HRH Princess *Sophie* Friederike Mathilde (*b* 17 June 1818; *d* 3 June 1877), 2nd dau of HM King Wilhelm I of Württemberg (*see p* 211), and had issue,

1c HRH Prince *Willem* Nicolaas Alexander Frederik Karel Hendrik of the Netherlands, Prince of Orange, *b* 4 Sept 1840; *d unm* 11 June 1879.

2c HRH Prince Willem Frederik *Maurits* Alexander Hendrik Karel of the Netherlands, *b* 15 Sept 1843; *d* 4 June 1850.

3c HRH Prince Willem *Alexander* Karel Hendrik Frederik of the Netherlands, Prince of Orange, *b* 25 Aug 1851; *d unm* 21 June 1884.

He *m* 2ndly 7 Jan 1879, HSH Princess Adelaide *Emma* Wilhelmine Therese, Queen Regent of the Netherlands 1890-1898 (*b* 2 Aug 1858; *d* 20 March 1934), 4th dau of HSH Georg Viktor, Prince of Waldeck and Pyrmont (*see p* 223), and *d* 23 Nov 1890, having by her had issue,

1c HM Queen *Wilhelmina* Helena Pauline Maria of the Netherlands (1890-1948), KG (1944), VA, abdicated 4 Sept 1948 and assumed the style of Princess of the Netherlands, *b* 31 Aug 1880, *m* 7 Feb 1901, HH Duke *Heinrich* Wladimir Albrecht Ernst of Mecklenburg-Schwerin, *cr* HRH Prince Hendrik of the Netherlands 26 Jan 1901 (*b* 19 April 1876; *d* 3 July 1934), 8th and yst son of HRH Grand Duke Friedrich Franz III of Mecklenburg-Schwerin, and *d* 28 Nov 1962, leaving issue,

•HM Queen *Juliana* Louise Emma Marie Wilhelmina of the Netherlands, KG (1958), Princess-Regent of the Netherlands 14 Oct-1 Dec 1947 and 14 May-30 Aug 1948, *s* to the throne on her mother's abdication 4 Sept 1948 and was inaugurated at Amsterdam 6 Sept 1948, Col-in-Chief The Royal Sussex Regt from June 1953, received Royal Victorian Chain 1950 [*Palace Soestdijk, Baarn, Prov Utrecht, Netherlands*], *b* 30 April 1909, *m* 7 Jan 1937, •HSH Prince *Bernhard* Leopold Friedrich Eberhard Julius Karl Gottfried Peter of Lippe-Biesterfeld (*cr* HRH and Prince of the Netherlands 7 Jan 1937; HRH The Prince of the Netherlands 6 Sept 1948), GCB, GCVO, GBE (*b* 29 June 1911), and has issue,

1e •HRH Crown Princess *Beatrix* Wilhelmina Armgard of the Netherlands, Princess of Orange-Nassau and Lippe-Biesterfeld, GCVO, *b* 31 Jan 1938, *m* 10 March 1966, •HRH Prince Claus of the Netherlands, Jonkheer van Amsberg (so *cr* 16 Feb 1966), formerly *Claus* Georg Wilhelm Otto Friedrich Gerd von Amsberg (*b* 6 Sept 1926) [*Kasteel Drakesteyn, Lage Vuursche, Prov Utrecht, Netherlands*], and has issue,

1f •HRH Prince *Willem Alexander* Claus Georg Ferdinand of the Netherlands, Prince of Orange-Nassau, Jonkheer van Amsberg, *b* 27 April 1967.

2f •HRH Prince *Johan Friso* Bernhard Christiaan David of the Netherlands, Prince of Orange-Nassau, Jonkheer van Amsberg, *b* 25 Sept 1968.

3f •HRH Prince *Constantijn* Christopher Frederik Aschwin of the Netherlands, Prince of Orange-Nassau, Jonkheer van Amsberg, *b* 11 Oct 1969.

2e •HRH Princess *Irene* Emma Elisabeth of the Netherlands, Princess of Orange-Nassau and Lippe-Biesterfeld, *b* 5 Aug 1939, *m* 29 April 1964, HRH Prince Carlos Hugo of Bourbon-Parma (*b* 8 April 1930) [*Villa Valcarlos, 64 Arbonne, France*], and has issue,

1f •HRH Prince *Carlos* Xavier Bernardo Sixtus Marie of Bourbon-Parma, *b* 27 Jan 1970.

2f •HRH Prince Jaime Bernardo of Bourbon-Parma, *b* 13 Oct 1972.

1f •HRH Princess Marguarita Maria Beatrice of Bourbon-Parma, *b* (twin with Prince Jaime) 13 Oct 1972.

3e •HRH Princess *Margriet* Francisca of the Netherlands, Princess of Orange-Nassau and Lippe-Biesterfeld, *b* 19 Jan 1943, *m* 10 Jan 1967, •Pieter van Vollenhoven (*b* 30 April 1939) [*Palace Het Loo, Apeldoorn, Gelderland, Netherlands*], and has issue,

1f •HH Prince *Maurits* Willem Pieter Hendrik of Orange-Nassau, Van Vollenhoven, *b* 17 April 1968.

2f •HH Prince *Bernhard* Lucas Emmanuel of Orange-Nassau, Van Vollenhoven, *b* 25 Dec 1969.

3f •HH Prince *Pieter Christiaan* Michael of Orange-Nassau, Van Vollenhoven, *b* 22 March 1972.

4e •HRH Princess Maria *Christina* of the Netherlands, Princess of Orange-Nassau and Lippe-Biesterfeld, *b* 18 Feb 1947.

2b HRH Prince Willem *Alexander* Frederik Constantijn Nikolaas Michiel of the Netherlands, *b* 2 Aug 1818; *d unm* 20 Feb 1848.

3b HRH Prince Willem Frederik *Hendrik* of the Netherlands, Lieut of the Grand Duchy of Luxembourg 1850-79, *b* 13 June 1820, *m* 1st 19 May 1853, HH Princess *Amalie* Maria da Gloria Auguste (*b* 20 May 1830; *d* 1 May 1872), 4th and yst dau of HH Prince Bernhard of Saxe-Weimar-Eisenach. He *m* 2ndly 24 Aug 1878, HRH Princess *Marie* Elisabeth Luise Friederike (*b* 14 Sept 1855; *d* 20 June 1888), eldest dau of HRH Prince Friedrich Karl of Prussia, and *dsp* 13 Jan 1879.

4b HRH Prince Willem Alexander *Ernst* Frederik Casimir of the Netherlands, *b* 21 May, *d* 22 Oct 1822.

1b HRH Princess Wilhelmine Marie *Sophie* Louise of the Netherlands, *b* 8 April 1824, *m* 8 Oct 1842, HRH Grand Duke Karl Alexander of Saxe-Weimar-Eisenach (*b* 24 June 1818; *d* 5 Jan 1901), and *d* 23 March 1897, leaving issue (*see below*).

2a HRH Prince Willem *Frederik* Karel of the Netherlands, *b* 28 Feb 1797, *m* 21 May 1825, HRH Princess *Luise* Auguste Wilhelmine Amalie (*b* 1 Feb 1808; *d* 6 Dec 1870), 5th and yst dau of HM King Friedrich Wilhelm III of Prussia, KG, and *d* 8 Sept 1881, having had issue,

1b HRH Prince Willem *Frederik* Nicolaas Albert of the Netherlands, *b* 6 July 1833; *d* 1 Nov 1834.

2b HRH Prince *Willem* Frederik Nicolaas Albert of the Netherlands, *b* 22 Aug 1836; *d* 23 Jan 1846.

1b HRH Princess Wilhelmina Frederica Alexandrine Anna *Louise* of the Netherlands, *b* 5 Aug 1828, *m* 19 June 1850, HM King Karl XV of Sweden and Norway (*b* 3 May 1826; *d* 18 Sept 1872), and *d* 30 March 1871, having had issue,

HRH Hereditary Prince *Karl* Oskar Wilhelm Frederik of Sweden and Norway, Duke of Södermanland, *b* 14 Dec 1852; *d* 13 March 1854.

HRH Princess *Louise* Josephine Eugenie of Sweden and Norway, *b* 31 Oct 1851, *m* 28 July 1869, HM King Frederik VIII of Denmark (*b* 3 June 1843; *d* 14 May 1912), and *d* 20 March 1926, leaving issue (*see p* 278).

2*b* HRH Princess Wilhelmina Frederica Alexandrine Anna Louise *Marie* of the Netherlands, *b* 5 July 1841, *m* 18 July 1871, HSH *Wilhelm* Adolf Maximilian Karl, 5th Prince zu Wied (*b* 22 Aug 1845; *d* 22 Oct 1907), and *d* 22 June 1910, having had issue,

1*c* HSH Wilhelm *Friedrich* Hermann Otto Karl, 6th Prince zu Wied, *b* 27 June 1872, *m* 29 Oct 1898, HRH Princess *Pauline* Olga Helene Emma (*b* 19 Dec 1877; *d* 9 May 1965), only dau of HM King Wilhelm II of Württemberg, and *d* 18 June 1945, having had issue (*see p* 211).

2*c* HSH Prince Wilhelm Alexander Friedrich Karl *Hermann* zu Wied, *b* 28 May 1874; *d* 15 Jan 1877.

3*c* HH Prince *Wilhelm* Friedrich Heinrich zu Wied, accepted the crown of Albania 6 Feb 1914 and was proclaimed as Wilhelm I, Prince (*Mbret*) of Albania 7 March 1914, left the country reserving his rights 5 Sept 1914, *b* 23 March 1876, *m* 30 Nov 1906, HSH Princess *Sophie* Helene Cäcilie (*b* 21 May 1885; *d* 3 Feb 1936), only dau of HSH Hereditary Prince Victor von Schönburg-Waldenburg, and *d* 17 April 1945, leaving issue,

●HH Hereditary Prince *Carol Victor* Wilhelm Friedrich Ernst Günther of Albania, Prince zu Wied [*8 München 71 (Solln), Heinrich-Vogl-Strasse 18, Germany*], *b* 19 May 1913, *m* 8 Sept 1966, ●Eileen (*b* 3 Sept 1922), widow of André de Coppet, and dau of George Johnston.

HSH Princess *Marie Eleonore* Elisabeth Cecilie Mathilde Lucie of Albania, Princess zu Wied, *b* 19 Feb 1909, *m* 1st 16 Nov 1937, her 1st cousin, HSH Prince Alfred von Schönburg-Waldenburg (*b* 30 Oct 1905; *d* 10 March 1941). She *m* 2ndly 5 Feb 1949, ●*Ion* Octavian Bunea (*b* 1 Nov 1899) [*8 München (Solln), Knotestrasse 24, Germany*], son of Aureliu Bunea, and *dsp* in a prison camp in Roumania 29 Sept 1956.

4*c* HSH Prince Wilhelm Friedrich Adolf Hermann *Viktor* zu Wied, *b* 7 Dec 1877, *m* 6 June 1912, ●H Ill H Countess *Gisela* Klementine Christophora Karola (*b* 30 Dec 1891) [*Oberammergau, Schwedenhaus, Germany*], yst dau of H Ill H Friedrich Magnus, 4th Count zu Solms-Wildenfels, and *d* 1 March 1946, leaving issue,

1*d* ●HSH Princess *Marie Elisabeth* Charlotte Sophie Anna Pauline Luise Solveig zu Wied [*Valhallavägen 129, Stockholm, Sweden*], *b* 14 March 1913.

2*d* ●HSH Princess *Benigna Viktoria* Ingeborg Anna Wilhelmine zu Wied [*Gorsel/Gelderland, Netherlands*], *b* 23 July 1918, *m* 19 Dec 1939, Baron *Ernst Hartmann* Günther von Schlotheim (*b* 27 Dec 1914; *d* 31 Oct 1952), and has issue,

1*e* ●Baroness *Victoria* Elisabeth Sibylla Agnete von Schlotheim, *b* 11 April 1948.

2*e* ●Baroness *Christiana Maria* Gisela von Schlotheim, *b* 22 July 1950.

1*c* HSH Princess Wilhelmine Friederike Auguste Alexandrine Marie Elisabeth *Luise* zu Wied, *b* 24 Oct 1880; *d unm* 29 Aug 1965.

2*c* HSH Princess Wilhelmine Auguste Friederike Marie Luise *Elisabeth* zu Wied, *b* 28 Jan 1883; *d unm* 14 Nov 1968.

1*a* HH Princess Wilhelmina Frederica Louise Pauline *Charlotte* of Orange, *b* 1 March 1800; *d* 22 Dec 1806.

2*a* HRH Princess Wilhelmina Frederica Louise Charlotte *Marianne* of the Netherlands, *b* 9 May 1810, *m* 1st 14 Sept 1830 (*m* diss by div 1849), as his 1st wife, HRH Prince Friedrich Heinrich *Albrecht* of Prussia (*b* 4 Oct 1809; *d* 14 Oct 1872), yst son of HM King Friedrich Wilhelm III of Prussia, and had issue,

1*b* HRH Prince Friedrich Wilhelm Nikolaus *Albrecht* of Prussia, Regent of the Duchy of Brunswick 1885, *b* 8 May 1837, *m* 19 April 1873, HH Princess *Marie* Friederike Leopoldine Georgine Auguste Alexandrine Elisabeth Therese Josephine Helene Sophie (*b* 2 Aug 1854; *d* 8 Oct 1898), only dau of HH Duke Ernst I of Saxe-Altenburg, and *d* 13 Sept 1906, leaving issue,

1*c* HRH Prince Wilhelm Ernst Alexander *Friedrich Heinrich* Albrecht of Prussia, *b* 15 July 1874; *d unm* 13 Nov 1940.

2*c* HRH Prince Wilhelm Friedrich Karl Ernst *Joachim Albrecht* of Prussia, *b* 27 Sept 1876, *m* 1st 3 Sept 1919, Marie Sulzer (*b* 16 Oct 1872; *d* 9 Nov 1919). He *m* 2ndly 9 Oct 1920 (*m* diss by div 1936), Karoline (*Lilly*) Cornelia Stockhammer (*b* 5 Sept 1891), and *dsp* 24 Oct 1939.

3*c* HRH Prince *Friedrich Wilhelm* Viktor Karl Ernst Alexander Heinrich of Prussia, *b* 12 July 1880, *m* 8 June 1910, HSH Princess *Agathe* Charlotte Pauline Marie von Ratibor und Corvey, Princess zu Hohenlohe-Schillingsfürst (*b* 24 July 1888; *d* 12 Dec 1960), elder dau of HSH Viktor II, 2nd Duke von Ratibor and 2nd Prince von Corvey, Prince zu Hohenlohe-Schillingsfürst, and *d* 9 March 1925, leaving issue,

1*d* ●HRH Princess *Marie Therese* Auguste Viktoria Friederike Henriette Charlotte Agathe of Prussia, *b* 2 May 1911, *m* 13 May 1932, ●*Aloys* Rudolf Hug (*b* 21 Oct 1885) [*6946 Lützelsachsen über Weinheim an der Bergstrasse, Weinheimer Strasse 72, Germany*], and has had issue,

1*e* ●*Friedrich Wilhelm* Hug, *b* 13 Oct 1932.

2*e* *Alois Rudolf* Hug, *b* (twin with Friedrich Wilhelm) and *d* 14 Oct 1932.

3 ●Joachim *Albrecht* Silvester Hug, *b* 31 Dec 1933.

4*e* ●Rudolf-*Siegismut* Dietrich Hug, *b* 7 Oct 1939.

5*e* ●Rudmarth *Wolfdietrich* Franz Joseph Hug, *b* 7 Oct 1945.

6*e* ●Rudolf-*Philipp* Friedrich Wilhelm Ernst Günther Hug, *b* 22 June 1957.

1*e* ●*Charlotte* Henriette Marie Therese Hug, *b* 28 June 1935, *m* 30 June 1961, ●Erich Brehm (*b* 10 July 1930) [*7141 Beihingen (Neckar), Panoramastrasse, Germany*], and has issue,

1*f* ●*Bernhard* Rudolf Friedrich Brehm, *b* 1 Aug 1962.

2*f* ●Michael-*Ulrich* Erwin Albrecht Brehm, *b* 3 April 1967.

2*e* ●*Oda* Marie Therese Hug, *b* 8 July 1937, *m* 12 July 1963, ●*Hans-Hermann* Piltz (*b* 16 Sept 1930) [*605 Offenbach (Main), Dreieichring 6, Germany*], and has issue,

●Luise-*Dorothea* Marie Therese Caroline Sieglinde Piltz, *b* 25 May 1965.

3*e* ●*Siegilde* Marie Therese Hug, *b* 26 Sept 1941.

4*e* ●*Liutgard*-Luise Marie Therese Hug, *b* 25 Nov 1943, *m* 12 May 1967, ●Klaus Beckenbauer.

5*e* ●*Angela* Griseldis Theodora Charlotte Maria-Anna Marie Therese Hug, *b* 4 July 1951.

2*d* ●HRH Princess *Luise Henriette* Wilhelmine Sophie Albertine Marie Elisabeth Ernestine Viktoria Margarete of Prussia, *b* 21 July 1912, *m* 30 Nov 1936, ●Lt-Gen Wilhelm Schmalz (*b* 1 March 1901) [*6291 Leimbach über Weilburg, Germany*], and has issue,

1*e* ●*Hubertus* Ernst Wilhelm Victor Friedrich Schmalz, Lieut Fed German Navy [*23 Kiel 14, Drewsstrasse 27, Germany*], *b* 13 Nov 1938, *m* ●*Ulrike* Gertrud Feuerborn, and has issue,

1*f* ●Alexandra Schmalz.

2*f* ●Franziska Schmalz.

2*e* ●*Bernhard* Hans Heinrich Walter Karl Egon Schmalz, *b* 17 May 1941.

3*e* ●*Friedrich-Wilhelm* Martin Julius Eck Conrad Ludwig Schmalz, Lieut Fed German Army, *b* 19 Sept 1943, *m* ●Sybille Spring, and has issue,

●Alexander Schmalz.

•Silke Schmalz.
1e •*Agathe* Friederike Henriette Margarethe Auguste Brunhilde Eleonore Marianne Elisabeth Schmalz, *b* 23 Oct 1937.
3*d* •HRH Princess *Marianne* Cecilie Auguste Friederike Wilhelmine Elisabeth Johanna of Prussia [*3443 Herleshausen a d Werra, Schloss Augustenau, Germany*], *b* 23 Aug 1913, *m* 30 Jan 1933, HH Prince and Landgrave *Wilhelm* Ernst Alexis Hermann of Hesse (*b* 1 March 1905; *k* in action 30 April 1942), and has issue,
1*e* •HH Prince and Landgrave *Wilhelm* Chlodwig Friedrich Ernst Hermann Paul Philipp Heinrich of Hesse [*3443 Herleshausen a d Werra, Schloss Augustenau, Germany*], *b* 14 Aug 1933, *m* 5 Aug 1961, •*Oda-Mathilde* (*b* 12 Feb 1935), dau of Hilmar von Garmissen, and has issue,
1*f* •(Prinz) Wilhelm von Hessen, *b* 1 Jan 1963.
2*f* •(Prinz) Otto von Hessen, *b* 19 Jan 1965.
2*e* •HH Prince and Landgrave *Hermann* Ernst Ludwig Joachim Hans Georg Hugo Alexander Wilhelm of Hesse [*3443 Herleshausen a d Werra, Schloss Augustenau, Germany*], *b* 21 Aug 1935, *m* 9 May 1962, •Countess *Monika* Toska Renata (*b* 11 July 1939), anly dau of Count Manfred Strachwitz von Gross-Zauche und Camminetz.
1*e* •HH Princess and Landgravine Johanna of Hesse, *b* 22 Nov 1937, *m* 1st 30 Sept 1957 (*m* diss by div 1961), Alfons Kuhn (*b* 10 Dec 1924), and has issue,
1*f* •*Vera-Maria* Kuhn, *b* 21 Jan 1959.
She *m* 2ndly 8 June 1963, •Bruno Riek (*b* 19 May 1927) [*2 Hamburg-Rahlstedt, Timmendorfer Strasse 31, Germany*], and has further issue,
1*f* •*Bruno* Arnim Riek, *b* 9 Jan 1964.
2*f* •*Monika* Marianne Riek, *b* 18 April 1965.
3*f* •*Renata* Johanna Riek, *b* 13 Feb 1968.
4*d* HRH Princess *Elisabeth* Auguste Wilhelmine Viktoria Margarete Franziska Karoline of Prussia, *b* 9 Feb 1919, *m* 5 Aug 1948, •Heinz Mees (*b* 6 April 1918) [*6229 Erbach, Rheingau, Schloss Reinhartshausen, Germany*], and *dsp* 24 Aug 1961.
1*b* HRH Princess Friederike Luise Wilhelmine Marianne *Charlotte* of Prussia, *b* 21 June 1831, *m* 18 May 1850, as his 1st wife, HH Duke Georg II of Saxe-Meiningen (*b* 2 April 1826; *d* 25 June 1914), and *d* 30 March 1855, leaving issue (*see p* 265).
2*b* HRH Princess Friederike Luise Wilhelmine Elisabeth of Prussia, *b* 27 Aug, *d* 9 Oct 1840.
3*b* HRH Princess Friederike Wilhelmine Luise Elisabeth *Alexandrine* of Prussia, *b* 1 Feb 1842, *m* 9 Dec 1865, HH Duke Friedrich *Wilhelm* Nikolaus of Mecklenburg-Schwerin (*b* 5 March 1827; *d* 28 July 1879), and *d* 25 March 1906, leaving issue,
HH Duchess Friederike Wilhelmine Elisabeth Alexandrine Auguste Marianne *Charlotte* of Mecklenburg-Schwerin, *b* 7 Nov 1868, *m* 1st 17 Nov 1886, HSH Prince Heinrich XVIII Reuss (Younger Line) (*b* 14 May 1847; *d* 15 Aug 1911), and had issue,
1*d* HSH Prince Heinrich XXXVII Reuss (Younger Line), *b* 1 Nov 1888, *m* 1st 14 Nov 1922 (*m* diss by div 1930), Friedel (*b* 25 Sept 1892, formerly wife of — von Hoff, and dau of — Mijotki. He *m* 2ndly 7 Aug 1933, •Stefanie (*b* 25 Dec 1900) [*81 Garmisch-Partenkirchen, Georgenhof, Germany*], formerly wife of Karl Ludwig Diehl, and dau of Gustav Clemm von Hohenberg, and *d* 9 Feb 1964, having by her had issue,
•HSH Prince *Heinrich XI Licco* Reuss (Younger Line) [*62 Wiesbaden, Beethovenstrasse 5, Germany*], *b* 28 Aug 1934, *m* 21 July 1961, •Baroness Ulfa (*b* 17 April 1935), dau of Baron Siegfried von Dörnberg, and has issue,
•HSH Prince Heinrich XVI Reuss (Younger Line) *b* 8 Dec 1965.
•HSH Princess *Henriette* Charlotte Sophie Stefanie Marie-Elisabeth Reuss (Younger Line), *b* 24 April 1964.
•HSH Princess *Marianne* Charlotte Katharina Stefanie Reuss (Younger Line) [*81 Garmisch-Partenkirchen, Georgenhof, Germany*], *b* 29 July 1936.
2*d* HSH Prince Heinrich XXXVIII Reuss (Younger Line), *b* 6 Nov 1889; *k* in action 22 March 1918, *unm*.
3*d* HSH Prince Heinrich XLII Reuss (Younger Line), *b* 22 Sept 1892, *m* 1st 28 Dec 1923, Charlotte (*b* 30 Nov 1893; *d* 16 Sept 1944), formerly wife of — Lent, and dau of — Nawrath. He *m* 2ndly 3 Nov 1947, •Anneliese (*b* 11 July 1915) [*81 Garmisch-Partenkirchen, Georgenhof, Germany*], formerly wife of Harald Weberstedt, and dau of Karl Ludwig Ernst Taube, and *d* 10 March 1949, having by her had issue,
•(Prinzessin) *Alexandrine* Charlotte Marianne Luise Reuss, *b* 27 April 1948.
She *m* 2ndly 4 Feb 1921, Col Robert Schmidt, and *d* 20 Dec 1944.
She *m* 2ndly, Johan van Rossum (*d* 1873), and *d* 29 May 1883, having had further issue (? legitimated *per subsequens matrimonium*),
2*b* Johan Willem von Reinhartshausen, *b* 1848; *d* 1860.
King Willem I of the Netherlands *m* 2ndly (morganatically) 16 May 1841, Countess *Henrietta* Adrienne Ludovica Flora (*b* 28 Feb 1792; *d* 26 Oct 1864), dau of Ferdinand Louis, Comte d'Oultremont de Wégimont, and *d* 12 Dec 1843.
(3) HH Prince *Frederik* Willem Georg of Orange, *b* 15 Feb 1774; *d unm* 6 Jan 1799.
(1) HH Princess *Frederica* Louise Wilhelmine of Orange, *b* 28 Nov 1770, *m* 14 Oct 1790, HSH Hereditary Prince *Karl Georg* August of Brunswick-Wolfenbüttel (*b* 8 Feb 1766; *d* 20 Sept 1806) (*see p* 210), and *dsp* 15 Oct 1819.
1 A Princess, *b* and *d* 19 Dec 1736.
2 A Princess, *b* and *d* 10 Dec 1739.
3 HH Princess Caroline of Orange, *b* 28 Feb 1743, *m* 5 March 1760, HSH *Karl* Christian, Prince of Nassau-Weilburg (1763-1788) (*b* 16 Jan 1735; *d* 28 Nov 1788), and *d* 6 May 1787, having had issue,
(1) HSH Prince Georg Wilhelm Belgicus of Nassau-Weilburg, *b* 18 Dec 1760; *d* 27 May 1762.
(2) HSH Hereditary Prince *Ludwig* Flamand of Nassau-Weilburg, *b* 12 Dec 1761; *d* 26 April 1770.
(3) HSH *Friedrich Wilhelm*, Prince of Nassau-Weilburg (1788-1816), *b* 25 Oct 1768, *m* 31 July 1788, Luise *Isabelle* Alexandrine Auguste, Countess of Sayn-Hachenburg (*b* 19 April 1772; *d* 6 Jan 1827), dau of Wilhelm Georg, Burggrave of Kirchberg, Count of Sayn-Hachenburg, and *d* 9 Jan 1816, leaving issue,
1*a* HH Duke *Wilhelm* Georg August Heinrich Belgicus of Nassau, *s* his father as Prince of Nassau-Weilburg 9 Jan 1816 and Duke Friedrich August of Nassau-Usingen 24 March 1816 thus becoming Duke of Nassau, *b* 14 June 1792, *m* 1st 24 June 1813, HH Princess Charlotte *Luise* Friederike Amalie Alexandrine (*b* 28 Jan 1794; *d* 6 April 1825), 3rd dau of HH Duke Friedrich of Saxe-Altenburg, and had issue,
1*b* HRH Grand Duke *Adolf* Wilhelm Karl August Friedrich of Luxembourg, Duke of Nassau (1839-1866), *s* King Willem III of the Netherlands (*see p* 215) as Grand Duke of Luxembourg 1890, *b* 24 July 1817, *m* 1st 31 Jan 1844, HIH Grand Duchess Elisabeth Mikhailovna (*b* 26 May 1826; *d* 28 Jan 1845), 2nd dau of HIH Grand Duke Michael Pavlovitch of Russia (*see p* 212), and had issue,
1*c* A Princess, *b* and *d* Jan 1845.
He *m* 2ndly 23 April 1851, HH Princess *Adelheid* Marie (*b* 25 Dec 1833; *d* 24 Nov 1916), eldest dau of HH Prince Friedrich of Anhalt (*see p* 285), and *d* 17 Nov 1905, having by her had issue,
1*c* HRH Grand Duke *Guillaume IV* (Alex-

andre) of Luxembourg (1905-1912), Duke of Nassau, Lieut-Rep of the Grand Duchy of Luxembourg 1902-05, *b* 22 April 1852, *m* 21 June 1893, HRH Infanta *Maria Ana* (*Marie-Anne*) do Carmo Henrique Adelaide Joana Carolina Inés Sofia Eulália Leopoldina Isabel Francisca de Assis e de Paula Inácia Gonzaga, Lieut of the Grand Duchy 19 March-18 Nov 1908, Regent 1908-12 (*b* 13 July 1861; *d* 31 July 1942), 5th dau of HRH Infante Miguel of Portugal, Duke of Braganza, sometime (1828-1834) King of Portugal, and *d* 25 Feb 1912, leaving issue,

1*d* HRH Grand Duchess *Marie-Adélaïde*-Thérèse-Hilda-Wilhelmine of Luxembourg (1912-1919), Duchess of Nassau, abdicated 5 Jan 1919, and became a nun, *b* 14 June 1894; *d unm* 24 Jan 1924.

2*d* ●HRH Grand Duchess *Charlotte*-Adelgunde-Elisabeth-Marie-Wilhelmine of Luxembourg (1919-1964), Duchess of Nassau, GCVO, abdicated in favour of her elder son 12 Nov 1964 [*Fischbach, Luxembourg*], *b* 23 Jan 1896, *m* 6 Nov 1919, HRH Prince *Félix*-Marie-Vincent of Bourbon-Parma, *cr* Prince of Luxembourg 5 Nov 1919 (*b* 28 Sept 1893; *d* 8 April 1970), son of HRH Duke Roberto I of Parma, and has issue,

1*e* ●HRH Grand Duke *Jean*-Bénoît-Guillaume-Robert-Antoine-Louis-Marie-Adolphe-Marc d'-Aviano of Luxembourg, Duke of Nassau, Prince of Bourbon-Parma, KG (1972), Lieut of the Grand Duchy 4 May 1961, *s* as Grand Duke on his mother's abdication 12 Nov 1964, [*Colmar-Berg, Luxembourg*], *b* 5 Jan 1921, *m* 9 April 1953, ●HRH Princess *Joséphine-Charlotte* - Ingeborg - Elisabeth-Marie-Josèphe-Marguerite-Astrid (*b* 11 Oct 1927), eldest dau of HM King Léopold III of the Belgians (*see p* 226), and has issue,

1*f* ●HRH Hereditary Grand Duke *Henri*-Albert-Gabriel-Félix-Marie-Guillaume of Luxembourg, Prince of Bourbon-Parma and Nassau, *b* 16 April 1955.

2*f* ●HRH Prince *Jean*-Félix-Marie-Guillaume of Luxembourg, Bourbon-Parma and Nassau, *b* 15 May 1957.

3*f* ●HRH Prince Guillaume of Luxembourg, Bourbon-Parma and Nassau, *b* 1 May 1963.

1*f* ●HRH Princess *Marie-Astrid*-Charlotte-Léopoldine - Wilhelmine - Ingeborg - Antonia-Elisabeth-Anne-Alberte of Luxembourg, Borbon-Parma and Nassau, *b* 17 Feb 1954.

2*f* ●HRH Princess *Marguerite*-Antonia Marie-Felicité of Luxembourg, Bourbon-Parma and Nassau, *b* (twin with Prince Jean) 15 May 1957.

2*e* ●HRH Prince *Charles*-Frédéric-Louis Guillaume-Marie of Luxembourg, Bourbon-Parma and Nassau [*Luxembourg*], *b* 7 Aug 1927, *m* 1 March 1967, ●*Joan* Douglas (*b* 31 Jan 1935), formerly wife of James B. Monseler, and dau of Clarence Douglas Dillon, sometime Min of Finance, USA, and has issue,

●HRH Prince *Robert*-Louis-François-Marie of Luxembourg, Bourbon-Parma and Nassau, *b* 14 Aug 1968.

●HRH Princess Charlotte of Luxembourg, Bourbon-Parma and Nassau, *b* 15 Sept 1967.

1*e* ●HRH Princess *Elisabeth*-Hilda-Zita-Marie - Anne - Antonia-Frédérique-Wilhelmine-Louise of Luxembourg, Bourbon-Parma and Nassau, *b* 22 Dec 1922, *m* 9 May 1956, ●HH *Franz Ferdinand* Friedrich Ernst Josef Karl Leopold Mauritius Hubertus Maria, 3rd Prince and Duke von Hohenberg (*b* 13 Sept 1927) [*7951 Eberhardzell, Württemberg, Germany*] (*see p* 239), and has issue,

1*f* ●HSH Princess *Anna* Charlotte Euphemie Marie Helene von Hohenberg, *b* 18 Aug 1958.

2*f* ●HSH Princess Sophie von Hohenberg, *b* 5 May 1960.

2*e* ●HRH Princess *Marie-Adélaïde*-Louise-Thérèse-Wilhelmine of Luxembourg, Bourbon-Parma and Nassau, *b* 21 May 1924, *m* 10 April 1958, ●Count Maria *Carl Josef* Erdmann Jakob Edwin Lazarus Andreas Alois Henckel von Donnersmarck (*b* 7 Nov 1928) [*Schloss Wolfsberg, Kärnten, Austria; Austrasse 2, CH-5400 Baden, Kt Aargau, Switzerland*], and has issue,

1*f* ●Count Maria *Andreas* Lazarus Alexius Felix Mauritius Erdmann Sigismund Johannes von Capistran Henckel von Donnersmarck, *b* 30 March 1959.

2*f* ●Count Maria *Felix* Lazarus Franziskus Erdmann Edwin Jakob Wilhelm Robert Karl Henckel von Donnersmarck, *b* 2 March 1960.

3*f* ●Count Maria *Heinrich* Carl Erdmann Winfried Felix Lazarus Didacus Henckel von Donnersmarck, *b* 13 Nov 1961.

1*f* ●Countess Maria *Charlotte* Therese Franziska Dominique Henckel von Donnersmarck, *b* 4 Aug 1965.

3*e* ●HRH Princess *Marie-Gabrielle*-Adelgunde-Wilhelmine-Louise of Luxembourg, Bourbon-Parma and Nassau, *b* 2 Aug 1925, *m* 6 Nov 1951, ●*Knud* Johan Ludvig, Count von Holstein-Ledreborg (*b* 2 Oct 1919) [*Ledreborg, Denmark*], and has issue,

1*f* ●Countess *Monica* Charlotte Louise Maria von Holstein-Ledreborg, *b* 29 July 1952.

2*f* ●Countess *Lydia* Adelaide Maria von Holstein-Ledreborg, *b* 22 Feb 1955.

3*f* ●Countess *Véronica* Birgitte Maria von Holstein-Ledreborg, *b* 19 Jan 1956.

4*f* ●Countess *Silvia* Charlotte Maria von Holstein-Ledreborg, *b* 1 Jan 1958.

5*f* ●Countess *Camilla* Josephine Marie von Holstein-Ledreborg, *b* 26 March 1959.

6*f* ●Countess *Tatiana* Alix Marie von Holstein-Ledreborg, *b* 25 April 1961.

7*f* ●Countess *Antonia* Charlotte Jeannette Marie von Holstein-Ledreborg, *b* 19 June 1962.

4*e* ●HRH Princess *Alix*-Marie-Anne-Antonia-Charlotte-Gabrielle of Luxembourg, Bourbon-Parma and Nassau, *b* 24 Aug 1929, *m* 17 Aug 1950, ●HH Prince *Antoine*-Marie-Joachim-Lamoral de Ligne (*b* 8 March 1925) [*Château de Beloeil, Hainaut, Belgium*], and has issue,

1*f* ●HH Prince *Michel*-Charles-Eugène-Marie-Lamoral de Ligne, *b* 26 May 1951.

2*f* ●HH Prince *Wauthier*-Philippe-Félix-Marie-Lamoral de Ligne, *b* 10 July 1952.

3*f* ●HH Prince *Antoine*-Lamoral-Charles-Joseph-Marie de Ligne, *b* 28 Dec 1959.

1*f* ●HH Princess *Anne-Marie*-Jeanne-Isabelle de Ligne, *b* 3 April 1954.

2*f* ●HH Princess *Christine*-Marie-Elisabeth de Ligne, *b* 11 Aug 1955.

3*f* ●HH Princess *Sophie*-Léontine-Charlotte-Marie-Gabrielle de Ligne, *b* 23 April 1957.

4*f* ●HH Princess *Yolande*-Marie-Gabrielle de Ligne, *b* 16 June 1964.

3*d* ●HGDH Princess *Hilda*-Sophie-Marie-Adélaïde-Wilhelmine of Luxembourg and Nassau [*Villa Ella, Bordighera, Italy, Villa Annagallis, Colmar-Berg, Luxembourg*], *b* 15 Feb 1897, *m* 29 Oct 1930, HSH *Adolf* Johann Maria Franz Josef Hubertus Agapit, 10th Prince zu Schwarzenberg (*b* 18 Aug 1890; *dsp* 27 Feb 1950).

4*d* HGDH Princess *Antoinette*-Roberta-Sophie-Wilhelmine of Luxembourg and Nassau, *b* 7 Oct 1899, *m* 7 April 1921, as his 2nd wife, HRH Crown Prince *Rupprecht* Maria Luitpold Ferdinand of Bavaria (*b* 18 May 1869; *d* 2 Aug 1955), and *d* 31 July 1954, leaving issue (*see p* 225).

5*d* HGDH Princess *Elisabeth*-Marie-Wilhelmine of Luxembourg and Nassau, *b* 7 March 1901, *m* 14 Nov 1922, HSH Prince *Ludwig Philipp* Maria Friedrich Joseph Maximilian Antonius Ignatius Lamoral von Thurn und

Taxis (*b* 2 Feb 1901; *d* 22 April 1933), and *d* 2 Aug 1950, having had issue,
HSH Prince *Anselm* Albert Ludwig Maria Lamoral von Thurn und Taxis, *b* 14 April 1924; *k* in action 25 Feb 1944.
●HSH Princess *Iniga* Anna Margarete Wilhelmine Louisa von Thurn und Taxis [*8131 Aufhausen b Starnberg, Wolfratshauserstrasse 2, Germany; Schloss Lichtenstein, Württemberg, Germany*], *b* 25 Aug 1925, *m* 18 May 1948, HSH Rupprecht *Eberhard* Wilhelm Gero Maria, 4th Duke von Urach, Count von Württemberg (*b* 24 Jan 1907; *d* 29 Aug 1969), and has issue,
1*f* ●HSH *Karl-Anselm* Franz-Joseph Wilhelm Louis-Philippe, 5th Duke von Urach, Count von Württemberg, *b* 5 Feb 1955.
2*f* ●HSH Prince *Wilhelm-Albert* Raphael Maria von Urach, Count von Württemberg, *b* 9 Aug 1957.
3*f* ●HSH Prince Eberhard Friedrich *Inigo* Maria von Urach, Count von Württemberg, *b* 12 April 1962.
1*f* ●HSH Princess Marie *Amélie* Margit Elisabeth Anna von Urach, Countess von Württemberg, *b* 6 April 1949.
2*f* ●HSH Princess *Elisabeth* Maria Immaculata Alberta Wilhelmine von Urach, Countess von Württemberg, *b* 10 Dec 1952.
6*d* HGDH Princess *Sophie*-Caroline-Marie-Wilhelmine of Luxembourg and Nassau, *b* 14 Feb 1902, *m* 14 April 1921, as his 1st wife, HRH Prince *Ernst Heinrich* Ferdinand Franz Joseph Otto Maria Melchiades of Saxony (*b* 9 Dec 1896; *d* 14 June 1971), 2nd son of HM King Friedrich August III of Saxony, and *d* 31 May 1941, leaving issue,
1*e* ●HRH Prince Albrecht Friedrich August Johannes Gregor *Dedo* of Saxony [*Ballyhook Demesne, PO Grange Con, co Wicklow*], *b* 9 May 1922.
2*e* ●HRH Prince Georg *Timo* Michael Nikolaus Maria of Saxony [*355 Marburg an der Lahn, Im Stiftfeld 1, Germany*], *b* 2 Dec 1923, *m* 1st 7 Aug 1952, Margrit (*b* 9 May 1932; *d* 6 June 1957), dau of Carl Lucas, and has issue,
1f ●(Prinz) *Rüdiger* Karl-Ernst Timo Aldi von Sachsen [*433 Mülheim an der Ruhr-Saarn, Saarbrücker Weg 5, Germany*], *b* 23 Dec 1953.
1*f* ●(Prinzessin) *Iris* Hildegard Sophie Margrit Gisela von Sachsen [*433 Mülheim an der Ruhr-Saarn, Saarbrücker Weg 5, Germany*], *b* 21 Sept 1955.
He *m* 2ndly 5 Feb 1966, ●Charlotte (*b* 11 March 1919), dau of Peter Gottfried Schwindack.
3*e* ●HRH Prince Rupprecht Hubertus *Gero* Maria of Saxony [*Ballyhook Demesne, PO Grange Con, co Wicklow*], *b* 12 Sept 1925.
2*c* HH Prince *Friedrich* Paul Wilhelm of Nassau, *b* 23 Sept 1854; *d* 23 Oct 1855.
3*c* HH Prince *Franz* Joseph Wilhelm of Nassau, *b* 30 Jan 1859; *d* 2 April 1875.
2*c* HH Princess Marie Bathildis of Nassau, *b* 14 Nov, *d* 28 Dec 1857.
3*c* HH Princess *Hilda* Charlotte Wilhelmine of Nassau, *b* 5 Nov 1864, *m* 20 Sept 1885, HRH Grand Duke Friedrich II of Baden (*b* 9 July 1857; *d* 9 Aug 1928) (*see p* 288), and *dsp* 8 Feb 1952.
2*b* HSH Prince *Wilhelm* Karl Heinrich Friedrich of Nassau, *b* 8 Sept 1819; *d* 22 April 1823.
3*b* HSH Prince *Moritz* Wilhelm August Karl Heinrich of Nassau, *b* 21 Nov 1820; *d unm* 23 March 1850.
4*b* HSH Prince *Wilhelm* Karl August Friedrich of Nassau, *b* 12 Aug 1823; *d* 28 Aug 1828.
1*b* HSH Princess *Auguste* Luise Friederike Maximiliane Wilhelmine of Nassau-Weilburg, *b* 13 April, *d* 3 Oct 1814.
2*b* HSH Princess *Therese* Wilhelmine Friederike Isabelle Charlotte of Nassau, *b* 17 April 1815, *m* 23 April 1837, HH Duke Constantin Friedrich *Peter* of Oldenburg (*b* 26 Aug 1812; *d* 14 May 1881), and *d* 8 Dec 1871, having had issue,
1*c* HH Duke *Nikolaus* Friedrich August of Oldenburg, *b* 9 May 1840, *m* (morganatically) 29 May 1863, Marie Bulazel, *cr* Countess von Osternburg by HRH Grand Duke Peter I of Oldenburg 13 July 1863 (*b* 8 July 1845; *d* 29 Jan 1909), and *d* 20 Jan 1886, having had issue,
1*d* Countess Alexandra von Osternburg, *b* 4 June 1864, *m* 8 June 1885, Paul Verola (*b* 13 July 1863), and *d* 23 July 1952, having had issue,
1*e* Raymond Verola, *b* 3 May 1888; *d* 23 March 1895.
1*e* Marie Claire Verola, *b* 9 May 1886, *m* 25 Sept 1911, Count Alexander Alexandrovitch Mordvinoff (*b* 20 Dec 1887; *d* 13 Feb 1950), and *d* 26 April 1943, leaving issue,
●Countess Marie Madeleine Mordvinoff, *b* 17 Jan 1913.
2*d* Countess Olga von Osternburg, *b* May 1868; *d* 1874.
3*d* Countess Vera von Osternburg, *b* 4 June 1871; *d* 1887.
2*c* HIH (*cr* by Imperial Ukase) Duke *Alexander* Friedrich Constantin of Oldenburg, *b* 2 June 1844, *m* 19 Jan 1868, HIH Princess Eugenie Maximilianovna Romanowsky, Duchess of Leuchtenberg (*b* 1 April 1845; *d* 4 April 1925), 3rd dau of HIH Maximilian Joseph, 3rd Duke of Leuchtenberg, by his wife HIH Grand Duchess Maria Nikolaievna, dau of HIM Nicholas I, Emperor of all the Russias, and *d* 6 Sept 1932, having had issue,
HH Duke *Peter* Friedrich Georg of Oldenburg, *b* 21 Nov 1868, *m* 1st 9 Aug 1901 (*m* diss by div 1916), HIH Grand Duchess Olga Alexandrovna (*b* 13 June 1882; *d* 24 Nov 1960), yr dau of HIM Emperor Alexander III of all the Russias. He *m* 2ndly 3 May 1922, Olga (*b* 1 Nov 1878; *d* 1955), dau of Vladimir Ratkow Rojnow, and *dsp* 11 March 1924.
3*c* HH Duke *Georg* Friedrich Alexander of Oldenburg, *b* 17 April 1848; *d unm* 17 March 1871.
4*c* HH Duke *Constantin* Friedrich Peter of Oldenburg, *b* 9 May 1850, *m* (morganatically) 20 Oct 1882, Agrafena Djaparidize, *cr* Countess von Zarnekau (*b* 6 Nov 1855; *d* 1929), and *d* 18 March, 1906, leaving issue,
1*d* Count Nikolaus von Zarnekau, *b* 22 Feb 1886, *m* 11 June 1935, ●Adrienne (*b* 18 Aug 1898), dau of Jean-Baptiste Haristoy.
2*d* Count Alexis von Zarnekau, *b* 16 July 1887; *d unm* 16 Sept 1918.
3*d* Count Peter von Zarnekau, *b* 26 May 1889, *m* 1st 24 Oct 1914, Princess Tamara (*b* 20 Nov 1896; *d* 27 Feb 1931), dau of Prince Prokopi Levanovitch Schervaschidze, and had issue,
●Count Constantin von Zarnekau, *b* 25 May 1916, *m* 1947, ●Marcelle Tricaud (*b* 17 Jan 1922), and has issue,
●Count Peter von Zarnekau, *b* 12 Nov 1947.
●Countess Nina von Zarnekau, *b* 16 July 1919.
He *m* 2ndly 8 July 1934, ●Alexandra (*b* 25 June 1906), dau of Feodor Annenkoff, and *d* 4 Nov 1961.
1*d* Countess Alexandra von Zarnekau, *b* 10 May 1883, *m* 1st 16 Feb 1900 (*m* diss by div 1908), HSH Prince George Alexandrovitch Yourievsky (*b* 30 April 1872; *d* 14 Sept 1913), son of HIM Emperor Alexander II of all the Russias, and had issue (*see below*). She *m* 2ndly 17 Oct 1908, Lev Vassilievitch Narishkine (*b* Dec 1876; *d* 4 April 1931), and *d* 28 May 1957.
2*d* Countess Catherine von Zarnekau, *b* 16 Sept 1884, *m* 1907, Jean de Ploën (*b* 1878; *d* 1955), and *d* 24 Dec 1963, having had issue,
Tatiana de Ploën, *b* 13 Dec 1908, *m* 15 Feb 1933, Nikolai Vladimirovitch Eltchaninoff (*b* 18 Feb 1906; *d* March 1952), and *d* 9 June 1960, leaving issue,

●Nikolai Nikolaievitch Eltchaninoff, *b* 29 May 1934, *m* 7 July 1957, ●Kyra (*b* 10 Oct 1935), dau of Boris Gandourine, and has issue,

1*g* ●Ariane Eltchaninoff, *b* 12 May 1958.

2*g* ●Isabelle-Anne Eltchaninoff, *b* 30 April 1959.

3*d* Countess Nina von Zarnekau, *b* 13 Aug 1892; *d unm* 1922.

1*c* HH Duchess *Alexandra* Friederike Wilhelmine of Oldenburg, *b* 2 June 1838, *m* 6 Feb 1856, HIH Grand Duke Nicholas Nikolaievitch of Russia (*b* 8 Aug 1831; *d* 25 April 1891), 3rd son of HIM Emperor Nicholas I of all the Russias, and *d* 25 April 1900, leaving issue,

1*d* HIH Grand Duke Nicholas Nikolaievitch of Russia, *b* 18 Nov 1856, *m* 12 May 1907, HRH Princess Anastasia (Stana) (*b* 4 Jan 1868; *d* 15 Nov 1935), formerly wife of HIH George Maximilianovitch (de Beauharnais), 3rd Prince Romanowsky, 6th Duke of Leuchtenberg, and 3rd dau of HM King Nicholas I of Montenegro, and *dsp* 5 Jan 1929.

2*d* HIH Grand Duke Peter Nikolaievitch of Russia, *b* 22 Jan 1864, *m* 7 Aug 1889, HRH Princess Militza (*b* 26 July 1866; *d* 5 Sept 1951), 2nd dau of HM King Nicholas I of Montenegro, and *d* 17 June 1931, leaving issue,

1*e* ●HH Prince Roman Petrovitch of Russia [*79 Via Panama, Rome, Italy*], *b* 17 Oct 1896, *m* 16 Nov 1921, ●Countess Prascovia (*b* 15 Oct 1901), dau of Count Dimitri Sergeievitch Cheremeteff, and has issue,

1*f* ●HSH Prince Nikolai Romanovitch Romanoff, *b* 26 Sept 1922, *m* 21 Jan 1952, ●Countess Sveva (*b* 15 July 1930), dau of Count Walfredo della Gherardesca, and has issue,

1*g* ●HSH Princess Natalia Nikolaievna Romanoff, *b* 4 Dec 1952.

2*g* ●HSH Princess Elisabeth Nikolaievna Romanoff, *b* 7 Aug 1956.

3*g* ●HSH Princess Tatiana Nikolaievna Romanoff, *b* 12 April 1961.

2*f* ●HSH Prince Dimitri Romanovitch Romanoff, *b* 17 May 1926, *m* 21 Jan 1959, ●Inge Magna *Jeanne* Mimi (*b* 1 June 1936), dau of late Axel von Kauffman.

1*e* ●HH Princess Marina Petrovna of Russia, *b* 11 March 1892, *m* 4 Feb 1927, ●Prince Alexander Nikolaievitch Galitzine (*b* 25 Oct 1885) [*La Bastide Galitzine, Le Brusc, Var, France*].

2*e* ●HH Princess Nadejda Petrovna of Russia [*53 3C Avenue Lamorlay-Oise, France*], *b* 15 March 1898, *m* 10 April 1917 (*m* diss by div 1940), Prince Nikolai Vladimirovitch Orloff (*b* 12 March 1896; *d* 30 May 1961), and has issue,

1*f* ●Princess Irina Nikolaievna Orloff, *b* 27 March 1918, *m* 1st 27 April 1940 (*m* diss by div 1946), Baron Herbert von Waldstätten (*b* 1 Jan 1913), and has issue,

●Baroness Elisabeth (*Maya*) von Waldstätten, *b* 7 Feb 1941, *m* 27 July 1970, ●Christopher M. Wynkoop [*44 Hillcrest Road, Fair Haven, NJ, USA*], and has issue,

●Mark B. Wynkoop, *b* 21 July 1972.

She *m* 2ndly 8 Jan 1960, ●Anthony Adama-Zylstra (*b* 9 Jan 1902) [*21 rue Grande, 25077 Villecerf, Moret sur Loinc, France*].

2*f* Princess Xenia Nikolaievna Orloff, *b* 27 March 1921, *m* 1st 1 April 1943 (*m* diss by div 1951), Paul de Montaignac de Pessotte, and had issue,

●*Calixte*-Nicolas-Auguste de Montaignac de Pessotte, *b* 24 Sept 1944.

She *m* 2ndly 14 March 1951, ●Vicomte *Jean-Albert*-Louis-Marie d'Almont (*b* 27 Nov 1909 [*Château de l'Echeneau, par Ennordres Cher, France*], and *d* 17 Aug 1963, leaving further issue,

●*Marie*-Isabelle-Nadejda d'Almont, *b* 20 March 1952.

2*c* HH Duchess *Marie* Friederike Cecilie of Oldenburg, *b* 27 Feb 1842; *d* 11 Jan 1843.

3*c* HH Duchess *Catherine* Friederike Pauline of Oldenburg, *b* 21 Sept 1846; *d unm* 23 June 1866.

4*c* HH Duchess *Therese* Friederike Olga of Oldenburg, *b* 30 March 1852, *m* 11 May 1879, as his 1st wife, HIH George Maximilianovitch (de Beauharnais), 3rd Prince Romanowsky, 6th Duke of Leuchtenberg (*b* 29 Feb 1852; *d* 3 May 1912), and *d* 19 April 1883, leaving issue,

HIH Alexander Gueorguievitch (de Beauharnais), 4th Prince Romanowsky, 7th Duke of Leuchtenberg, *b* 13 Nov 1881, *m* 22 April 1917, Nadejda (*b* 15 July 1883), formerly wife of — Ignatieff, and dau of Nikolai Caralli, and *dsp* 26 Sept 1942.

3*b* HSH Princess *Marie* Wilhelmine Luise Friederike Henriette of Nassau, *b* 5 April 1822; *d* 3 April 1824.

4*b* HSH Princess *Marie* Wilhelmine Friederike Elisabeth of Nassau, *b* 29 Jan 1825, *m* 20 June 1842, HSH Wilhelm *Hermann* Karl, 4th Prince zu Wied (*b* 22 May 1814; *d* 5 March 1864), and *d* 24 March 1902, having had issue,

1*c* HSH *Wilhelm* Adolf Maximilian Karl, 5th Prince zu Wied, *b* 22 Aug 1845, *m* 18 July 1871, HRH Princess Wilhelmina Frederica Alexandrine Anna Louise *Marie* (*b* 5 July 1841; *d* 22 June 1910), yr dau of HRH Prince Frederik of the Netherlands, and *d* 22 Oct 1907, leaving issue (*see p* 216).

2*c* HSH Prince *Otto* Nikolaus zu Wied, *b* 22 Nov 1850; *d* 18 Feb 1862.

1*c* HSH Princess Pauline *Elisabeth* Ottilie Louise zu Wied, authoress and poetess writing under the name of *Carmen Sylva*, *b* 29 Dec 1843, *m* 15 Nov 1869, HM King Carol I of Roumania (*b* 27 April 1839; *d* 10 Oct 1914), and *d* 3 March 1916, having had issue,

HSH Princess Marie of Roumania, *b* 8 Sept 1870; *d* 1874.

Duke Wilhelm of Nassau *m* 2ndly 23 April 1829, HRH Princess *Pauline* Friederike Marie (*b* 25 Feb 1810; *d* 7 July 1856), yr dau of HRH Prince Paul of Württemberg (*see p* 213), and *d* 20 Aug 1839, having by her had issue,

5*b* HSH Prince *Nikolaus* Wilhelm of Nassau, *b* 20 Sept 1832, *m* (morganatically) 1 July 1868, Natalia, *cr* Countess von Merenberg by HSH Prince Georg Viktor of Waldeck and Pyrmont 29 July 1868 (*b* 4 June 1836; *d* 23 March 1913), formerly wife of Gen Michael Leontievitch von Dubelt, and yr dau of Alexander Sergeievitch Pushkin, the famous poet, and *d* 18 Sept 1905, leaving issue,

1*c* Count *Georg* Nikolaus von Merenberg, *b* 13 Feb 1871, *m* 1st 12 May 1895, HSH Princess Olga Alexandrovna Yourievsky (*b* 9 Nov 1873; *d* 10 Aug 1925), dau of HIM Emperor Alexander II of all the Russias, and had issue,

1*d* Count — von Merenberg, *b* Sept 1896; *d* 27 April 1897.

2*d* Count *Georg* Michael Alexander von Merenberg, *b* 16 Oct 1897, *m* 1st 7 Jan 1926 (*m* diss by div), Paulette de Kövér de Gyergyós-Zent-Miklós. He *m* 2ndly 27 July 1940, Elisabeth Müller-Uri (*b* 1 July 1903; *d* 18 Nov 1963), and *d* 11 Jan 1965, having by her had issue,

●Countess Elisabeth Clothilde von Merenberg, *b* 14 May 1941, *m* 27 May 1965, ●Enno von Rintelen (*b* 9 Nov 1921), and has issue,

●Alexander von Rintelen, *b* 23 March 1966.

1*d* ●Countess *Olga* Katharina Adda von Merenberg, *b* 3 Oct 1898, *m* 14 Nov 1923, ●Count Michael Loris-Melikoff (*b* 21 June 1900), and has issue,

●Count Alexander Mikhailovitch Loris-Melikoff, *b* 26 May 1926, *m* 27 Sept 1958 ●Micheline Prunier (*b* 21 June 1932), and has issue,

1*f* ●Count Michael Alexandrovitch Loris-Melikoff, *b* 18 Dec 1964.

1*f* ●Countess Ann-Elisabeth Alexandrovna Loris-Melikoff, *b* 23 July 1959.

2*f* •Countess Dominique Alexandrovna Loris-Melikoff, *b* 23 March 1961.
3*f* •Countess Nathalie Alexandrovna Loris-Melikoff, *b* 28 Dec 1962.
He *m* 2ndly 2 Jan 1930, Ada (*d* 12 May 1942), dau of Frank Moran-Brambeer, and *d* 31 May 1948.
1*c* Countess Sophie von Merenberg, *cr* Countess de Torby by the Grand Duke of Luxembourg 1891, *b* 1 June 1868, *m* 26 Feb 1891, HIH Grand Duke Michael Mikhailovitch of Russia (*b* 16 Oct 1861; *d* 26 April 1929), and *d* 14 Sept 1927, leaving issue,
1*d* Count Mikhail Mikhailovitch de Torby, naturalized in GB Nov 1938, *b* 8 Oct 1898; *d unm* 25 April 1959.
1*d* •Countess Anastasia (*Zia*) de Torby, CBE (1956) (OBE 1946), DStJ, granted the style and precedence of the dau of an Earl by Royal Warrant of HM King George V 1 Sept 1917, *b* 9 Sept 1892, *m* 20 July 1917, •Major-Gen Sir *Harold* Augustus Wernher, 3rd Bt, GCVO, TD, DL (*b* 16 Jan 1893) [*Luton Hoo, Luton, Beds; 15 Grosvenor Square, W1*] (*see* BURKE'S *Peerage*), and has had issue,
1*e* *George* Michael Alexander Wernher, Capt 17th/21st Lancers, served in World War II, *b* 22 Aug 1918; *k* in action in N Africa 4 Dec 1942.
1*e* •Georgina Wernher, SSStJ, *b* 17 Oct 1919, *m* 10 Oct 1944, •Lt-Col *Harold* Pedro Joseph Phillips, FRGS, Coldstream Guards (*b* 6 Nov 1909) [*Checkendon Court, Checkendon, Reading, Berks; 15 Grosvenor Square, W1; Ardhuncart Lodge, Alford, Aberdeenshire*] (*see* BURKE'S *LG*, PHILLIPS *formerly of Sunningdale and Royston*), and has issue,
1*f* •*Nicholas* Harold Phillips, *b* 23 Aug 1947, *educ* Eton.
1*f* •*Alexandra* Anastasia Phillips, *b* 27 Feb 1946, *m* 20 Oct 1966, •James Hamilton, Marquess of Hamilton (*b* 4 July 1934) [*7 Upper Belgrave Street, SW1; Barons Court, Omagh, co Tyrone*], elder son of 4th Duke of Abercorn (*see* BURKE'S *Peerage*), and has issue,
•*James* Harold Charles Hamilton, Viscount Strabane, *b* 19 Aug 1969.
2*f* •*Fiona* Mercedes Phillips, *b* 30 March 1951, *m* 7 July 1971, •*James* Comyn Burnett of Leys (*b* 24 July 1941) [*Crathes Castle, Banchory, Kincardineshire*] (*see* BURKE'S *Peerage*, AMHERST OF HACKNEY, B).
3*f* •*Marita* Georgina Phillips, *b* 28 May 1954.
4*f* •*Natalia* Ayesha Phillips, *b* 8 May 1959.
2*e* •*Myra* Alice Wernher, *b* 8 March 1925, *m* 5 Nov 1946, •Major David Henry Butter of Pitlochry, MC, late Scots Guards (*b* 18 May 1920) [*Eastwood, Dunkeld, Perthshire; 15 Grosvenor Square, W1*] (*see* BURKE'S *LG*), and has issue,
1*f* •*Charles* Harold Alexander Butter, *b* 10 April 1960.
1*f* •*Sandra* Elizabeth Zia Butter, *b* 26 July 1948.
2*f* •*Marilyn* Davina Butter, *b* 22 March 1950.
3*f* •*Rohays* Georgina Butter, *b* 9 April 1952.
4*f* •*Georgina* Marguerite Butter, *b* 9 July 1956.
2*d* Countess Nadejda (*Nada*) de Torby, *b* 28 March 1896, *m* 15 Nov 1916, *George* Louis Victor Henry Sergius Mountbatten, 2nd Marquess of Milford Haven, GCVO (*b* 6 Nov 1892; *d* 8 April 1938), and *d* 22 Jan 1963, leaving issue (*see* p 303, and BURKE'S *Peerage*).
2*c* Countess Alexandra von Merenberg, *b* 14 Dec 1869, *m* 1914, Don Massimo de Elia (*d* 1929), and *dsp* 29 Sept 1950.

5*b* HSH Princess *Helene* Wilhelmine Henriette Pauline Marianne of Nassau, *b* 12 Aug 1831, *m* 26 Sept 1853, as his 1st wife, HSH Georg Viktor, Prince of Waldeck and Pyrmont (*b* 14 Jan 1831; *d* 12 May 1893), and *d* 27 Oct 1888, leaving issue,
1*c* HSH *Friedrich* Adolf Hermann, Prince of Waldeck and Pyrmont (1893-1918), ceased to reign 13 Nov 1918, *b* 20 Jan 1865, *m* 9 Aug 1895, HSH Princess *Bathildis* Marie Leopoldine Anna Auguste (*b* 21 May 1873; *d* 6 April 1962), 2nd dau of HSH Prince Wilhelm of Schaumburg-Lippe, and *d* 26 May 1946, leaving issue,
1*d* HSH *Josias* Georg Wilhelm Adolf, Prince of Waldeck and Pyrmont, *b* 13 May 1896, *m* 25 Aug 1922, •HH Duchess *Altburg* Marie Mathilde Olga (*b* 19 May 1903) [*3548 Schloss Arolsen, Germany; 6251 Schloss Schaumburg über Diez an der Lahn, Germany*], yst dau of HRH Grand Duke Friedrich August of Oldenburg, and *d* 30 Nov 1967, leaving issue,
1*e* •HSH *Wittekind* Adolf Heinrich Georg Wilhelm, Prince of Waldeck and Pyrmont [*3548 Schloss Arolsen, Germany*], *b* 9 March 1936.
1*e* •HSH Princess *Margarethe* Sophie Charlotte of Waldeck and Pyrmont, *b* 22 May 1923, *m* 27 March 1952, •H Ill H *Franz August* Gustav Adam Hubertus Friedrich Wilhelm Hans Karl, Count zu Erbach-Erbach (*b* 5 Feb 1925) [*6121 Jagdschloss Eulbach, Post Würzberg, Odenwald, Germany; 6122 Schloss Erbach, Odenwald, Germany*], and has issue,
•H Ill H Hereditary Count Franz *Eberhard* Wittekind Botho Heinrich Nikolaus Georg Wilhelm zu Erbach-Erbach, *b* 2 June 1958.
•H Ill H Countess *Alexandra* Polyxene Elisabeth Bathildis Ingrid Amelie zu Erbach-Erbach, *b* 2 Aug 1955.
2*e* •HSH Princess *Alexandra* Bathildis Elisabeth Luise Helene Emma of Waldeck and Pyrmont, *b* 25 Sept 1924, *m* 28 June 1949, •HSH Prince *Botho* Alexander Adolf zu Bentheim und Steinfurt (*b* 29 June 1924) [*35 Kassel, Adolfstrasse 70, Germany*] (*see* p 223), and has issue,
1*f* •HSH Prince *Georg-Viktor* Karl Josias zu Bentheim und Steinfurt, *b* 30 May 1950.
2*f* •HSH Prince *Wolfgang* Manfred Friedrich Christian zu Bentheim und Steinfurt, *b* 17 Feb 1952.
3*e* •HSH Princess Ingrid of Waldeck and Pyrmont [*3548 Schloss Arolsen, Germany; 6251 Schloss Schaumburg über Diez an der Lahn, Germany*], *b* 2 Sept 1931.
4*e* •HSH Princess Guda of Waldeck and Pyrmont, *b* 22 Aug 1939, *m* 1st 9 Sept 1958 (*m* diss by div 1967), HSH Friedrich Wilhelm, 7th Prince zu Wied (*b* 2 June 1931), and has issue (*see* p 211). She *m* 2ndly 4 March 1968, •Horst Dierkes (*b* 21 Feb 1939) [*Feldkirch-Hüllenbach, Auf dem Schneeberg, Germany*].
2*d* •HSH Prince *Max* Wilhelm Gustav Hermann of Waldeck and Pyrmont [*3548 Schloss Arolsen, Germany*], *b* 13 Sept 1898, *m* 12 Sept 1929, •Countess *Gustava* Frieda Betty Wilhelmine Paula (*b* 7 Dec 1899), 2nd dau of Count Karl von Platen-Hallermund, and has issue,
1*e* •HSH Prince *Friedrich-Carl* Georg Viktor of Waldeck and Pyrmont [*3548 Arolsen, Heliosteig 31, Germany*], *b* 21 Aug 1933, *m* 26 Jan 1959, •Ingeborg (*b* 2 July 1932), dau of Wolf von Biela, and has issue,
1*f* •HSH Princess Caroline Gustava Adelheid of Waldeck and Pyrmont, *b* 8 Jan 1960.
2*f* •HSH Princess Donata Altburg Helene-Sophie of Waldeck and Pyrmont, *b* 2 Feb 1961.
3*f* •HSH Princess Juliane Bathildis of Waldeck and Pyrmont, *b* 25 June 1962.
2*e* •HSH Prince *Georg-Viktor* Ludwig Adolf of Waldeck and Pyrmont [*577 Arns-*

berg, Westf, Ringstrasse 152, Germany], *b* 11 July 1936, *m* 6 Feb 1963, •*Margarete* Charlotte Barbara (*b* 7 Feb 1938), only dau of late Kurt von Klitzing, and has issue,

1*f* •HSH Prince *Christian-Ludwig* Friedrich-Carl Albrecht Hubertus Claus of Waldeck and Pyrmont, *b* 16 May 1967.

1*f* •HSH Princess Friederike of Waldeck and Pyrmont, *b* 28 Dec 1963.

2*f* •HSH Princess Barbara Ingemarie Helene-Sophie of Waldeck and Pyrmont, *b* 15 March 1965.

1*e* •HSH Princess *Marie-Louise* Bathildis Elfrieda Olga of Waldeck and Pyrmont, *b* 3 Nov 1930, *m* 23 May 1951, •HSH *Albrecht* Friedrich Carl, 3rd Prince zu Castell-Castell (*b* 13 Aug 1925) [*8711 Castell uber Kitzingen, UFranken, Germany*], and has had issue,

1*f* •H Ill H Hereditary Count *Maximilian* Friedrich Carl zu Castell-Castell, *b* 23 May 1953.

2*f* •H Ill H Count *Alexander* Friedrich Carl zu Castell-Castell, *b* 8 Nov 1954.

3*f* •H Ill H Count *Georg* Friedrich zu Castell-Castell, *b* 26 Nov 1956.

4*f* •H Ill H Count *Ferdinand* Friedrich Carl zu Castell-Castell, *b* 20 May 1965.

1*f* •H Ill H Countess *Philippa* Emma zu Castell-Castell, *b* 23 Jan 1952.

2*f* •H Ill H Countess *Johanna* Bathildis zu Castell-Castell, *b* (twin with Countess Philippa) 23 Jan 1952.

3*f* H Ill H Countess Christina zu Castell-Castell, *b* 4 March 1962; *d* 11 Nov 1964.

4*f* •H Ill H Countess Stephanie zu Castell-Castell, *b* 26 Sept 1966.

2*e* •HSH Princess *Helene-Sophie* Ingeborg Margarethe Elisabeth Gustava of Waldeck and Pyrmont [*3548 Schloss Arolsen, Germany*], *b* 27 Oct 1943.

3*d* •HSH Prince *Georg Wilhelm* Karl Viktor of Waldeck and Pyrmont [*3548 Schloss Arolsen, Germany*], *b* 10 March 1902, *m* 20 Jan 1932, •Countess *Ingeborg* Elfriede Gabriele Sophie Ilke Wilhelmine (*b* 27 Feb 1902), 3rd dau of Count Karl von Platen-Hallermund, and has issue,

1*e* •HSH Prince *Josias* Friedrich Wilhelm of Waldeck and Pyrmont [*78 Freiburg-i-Br, Germany*], *b* 23 Nov 1935.

2*e* •HSH Prince *Georg-Friedrich* Nikolaus of Waldeck and Pyrmont [*230 Flensburg-Weiche, Försterstieg 2, Germany*], *b* 22 Nov 1936, *m* (civil) 29 Aug and (religious) 30 Aug 1961, •HSH Princess Irmgard *Sixtina* Juliana zu Stolberg-Stolberg (*b* 4 Nov 1933), elder dau of HSH Wolff-Heinrich, 3rd Prince and Count zu Stolberg, and has issue,

1*f* •HSH Prince *Philipp-Heinrich* Wittekind of Waldeck and Pyrmont, *b* 12 April 1967.

1*f* •HSH Princess Christine *Henriette* Bathildis of Waldeck and Pyrmont, *b* 6 April 1963.

2*f* •HSH Princess Marie *Isabelle* of Waldeck and Pyrmont, *b* 29 Aug 1965.

3*e* •HSH Prince *Volkwin* Georg Ludwig of Waldeck and Pyrmont [*3548 Arolsen, Hauptstrasse 27, Germany; 54 Koblenz, Alte Heerstrasse 149, Germany*], *b* 20 Sept 1940, *m* (civil) 1 Dec 1967 and (religious) 2 March 1968, •Baroness *Orlinda* Clara Hedwig (*b* 11 Aug 1938), only dau of Baron Eccard von Gablenz.

4*e* •HSH Prince *Christian-Peter* of Waldeck and Pyrmont, *b* 9 Jan 1945, *m* 1971, •Sibylle Pieper.

1*e* •HSH Princess *Rixa* Bathildis Elfriede of Waldeck and Pyrmont [*3548 Schloss Arolsen, Germany*], *b* 14 July 1939.

1*d* HSH Princess *Helene* Bathildis Charlotte Maria Friederike of Waldeck and Pyrmont, *b* 22 Dec 1899, *m* 26 Oct 1921, as his 1st wife, HRH Hereditary Grand Duke *Nikolaus* Friedrich Wilhelm of Oldenburg (*b* 10 Aug 1897; *d* 3 April 1970) (*see p* 252), and *d* 18 Feb 1948, having had issue,

1*e* •HRH Duke *Anton Günther* Friedrich August Josias, Head of the Grand Ducal House of Oldenburg [*2902 Schloss Rastede, Oldenburg, Germany*], *b* 16 Jan 1923, *m* 7 Aug 1951, •HSH Princess *Ameli* Gertrud Pauline Antonie Madeleine Wanda Elisabeth (*b* 4 March 1923), eldest dau of HSH Udo, 6th Prince zu Löwenstein-Wertheim-Freudenberg, and has issue,

•HRH Duke *Christian* Nikolaus Udo Peter of Oldenburg, *b* 1 Feb 1955.

•HH Duchess *Helene* Elisabeth Bathildis Margarete of Oldenburg, *b* 3 Aug 1953.

2*e* •HH Duke *Peter* Friedrich August Max of Oldenburg [*2432 Lensahner Hof, Post Lensahn, Ostholstein, Germany*], *b* 7 Aug 1926, *m* 7 Aug 1951, •HSH Princess *Gertrud* Olga Ilka Emma Agnes Magdalena Mechtild (*b* 24 Jan 1926), 2nd dau of HSH Udo, 6th Prince zu Löwenstein-Wertheim-Freudenberg, and has issue,

1*f* •HH Duke *Friedrich August* Nikolaus Udo Peter Philipp of Oldenburg, *b* 26 Sept 1952.

2*f* •HH Duke *Nikolaus* Anton-Günther Max Johann Alfred Ernst of Oldenburg, *b* 21 May 1955,

3*f* •HH Duke *Georg-Moritz* Friedrich Ferdinand Egilmar Huno of Oldenburg, *b* 25 June 1957.

1*f* •HH Duchess *Margarete* Elisabeth Bathildis Ameli Eilika Barbara Marie-Alix Altburg of Oldenburg, *b* 16 May 1954.

3*e* •HH Duke *Egilmar* Friedrich Franz Stephan Wilhelm of Oldenburg [*2432 Güldenstein, Post Lensahn, Ostholstein, Germany*], *b* 14 Oct 1934.

4*e* •HH Duke *Friedrich August* Wilhelm Christian Ernst of Oldenburg [*2432 Sievershagen, Ostholstein, Germany*], *b* 11 Jan 1936, *m* (civil) 3 Dec and (religious) 4 Dec 1965, •HRH Princess *Marie Cécile* Kira Victoria Louise (*b* 28 May 1942), eldest dau of HI and RH Prince Louis Ferdinand of Prussia, Head of the Royal House of Prussia (*see p* 301), and has issue,

•HH Duke *Paul-Wladimir* Nikolaus Louis-Ferdinand Peter Max Karl-Emich of Oldenburg, *b* 16 Aug 1969.

•HH Duchess *Rixa* Marie-Alix Kira Altburg of Oldenburg, *b* 17 Sept 1970.

5*e* •HH Duke *Huno* Friedrich Peter Max of Oldenburg [*D-2359 Henstedt-Ulzburg 1, Lohering 16, Germany*], *b* 3 Jan 1940, *m* 6 June 1970, •Countess Felicitas Anita (*Fenita*) Siegfriede (*b* 5 July 1941), yst dau of Count Johann Ludwig (Lutz) Schwerin von Krosigk, and has issue,

•HH Duchess Beatrix of Oldenburg, *b* 27 May 1971.

6*e* •HH Duke *Johann* Friedrich Adolf of Oldenburg [*2432 Güldenstein, Post Lensahn, Germany*], *b* (twin with Duke Huno) 3 Jan 1940, *m* 9 Oct 1971, •H Ill H Countess *Ilka* Irmgard Pauline Hanna Lili Harriet (*b* 29 June 1942), elder dau of H Ill H Count Alfred-Friedrich zu Ortenburg (*see p* 270).

1*e* HH Duchess *Rixa* Elisabeth Bathildis Emma Cecilie of Oldenburg, *b* 28 March 1924; *d* 1 April 1939.

2*e* •HH Duchess *Eilika* Stephanie Elisabeth Thekla Juliana of Oldenburg, *b* 2 Feb 1928, *m* 10 Aug 1950, •HSH *Emich* Cyril Ferdinand Hermann, 7th Prince zu Leiningen (*b* 18 Oct 1926) [*Fürstliche Palais, Amorbach, Odenwald, Germany*], and has issue (*see p* 297).

3*e* •HH Duchess *Altburg* Elisabeth Hilda Ingeborg Marie Luise Mathilde of Oldenburg, *b* 14 Oct 1938, *m* 8 July 1967, •Baron Alfred Dietrich *Rüdiger* Hartmann von Erffa (*b* 19 April 1936) [*433 Mülheim an der Ruhr, Fischenbeck 43, Germany*].

1*c* HSH Princess *Sophie* Nikoline of Waldeck and Pyrmont, *b* 27 July 1854; *d* 5 Aug 1869.

2c HSH Princess *Pauline* Emma Auguste Hermine of Waldeck and Pyrmont, *b* 19 Oct 1855, *m* 7 May 1881, HSH *Alexis* Carl Ernst Louis Ferdinand Eugen Bernhard, 4th Prince zu Bentheim und Steinfurt (*b* 17 Nov 1845; *d* 21 Jan 1919), and *d* 3 July 1925, having had issue,

1d HSH Prince *Eberwyn* Ludwig Georg Friedrich zu Bentheim und Steinfurt, *b* 10 April 1882, *m* 1st 26 Oct 1906 (*m* diss by div 1914), Pauline (Lilly) (*b* 11 Feb 1884), dau of Christian Langenfeld, and had issue,

(Prinzessin) *Ellen* Ingeborg Sophie Henriette Marie Ruperte Pauline Maximilliene Constance Caroline Johanna Huberta (zu Bentheim und Steinfurt), *b* 24 April 1911, *m* Alfred Weitmann, and *d* 12 Sept 1954.

He *m* 2ndly 24 Aug 1918 (*m* diss by div 1919), Ellen Bischoff-Korthaus (*b* 6 Nov 1894; *d* 27 March 1936). He *m* 3rdly 16 Aug 1920, Luise Husser (*b* 2 July 1891; *d* 19 Oct 1951).

2d HSH *Viktor Adolf* Wilhelm Otto, 5th Prince zu Bentheim und Steinfurt, *b* 18 July 1883, *m* 1st 9 Sept 1921, HSH Princess *Stephanie* Alexandrine Hermine Thyra Xenia Bathildis Ingeborg (*b* 19 Dec 1899; *d* 2 May 1925), yr dau of HSH Prince Friedrich of Schaumburg-Lippe, and had issue,

1e HSH Hereditary Prince *Alexis* Friedrich Karl Christian zu Bentheim und Steinfurt, *b* 30 July 1922; *k* in action in World War II 2 Dec 1943, *vp*.

2e ●HSH *Christian* Max Gustav Albrecht, 6th Prince zu Bentheim und Steinfurt [*443 Burgsteinfurt, Westfalen, Germany*], *b* 9 Dec 1923, *m* 7 Aug 1950, ●Countess *Sylvia* Marie-Agnes Olga Vera (*b* 16 May 1930), elder dau of Count Sylvius von Pückler, Baron von Groditz.

He *m* 2ndly 30 June 1931, HSH Princess *Rosa Helene* (*b* 14 Aug 1901; *d* 14 April 1963), eldest dau of HSH Reinhard, Prince zu Solms-Hohensolms-Lich, and *d* 4 June 1961, having by her had issue,

3e ●HSH Prince *Reinhard* Georg zu Bentheim und Steinfurt [*Bremen, Holler Alle 29a, Germany*], *b* 27 March 1934.

4e ●HSH Prince *Ferdinand* Ludwig Franz zu Bentheim und Steinfurt [*Bonn 1, Fährgasse 6, Germany*], *b* 13 Aug 1938.

5e ●HSH Prince *Otto Victor* zu Bentheim und Steinfurt [*443 Burgsteinfurt, Westfalen, Germany*], *b* 24 July 1940.

6e ●HSH Prince *Oskar* Arnold zu Bentheim und Steinfurt [*443 Burgsteinfurt, Westfalen, Germany*], *b* 8 March 1946.

1e ●HSH Princess *Juliane* Henriette Eleonore zu Bentheim und Steinfurt [*443 Burgsteinfurt, Westfalen, Germany*], *b* 22 Dec 1932.

2e ●HSH Princess *Marie Adelheid* zu Bentheim und Steinfurt, *b* 14 April 1935, *m* 30 Dec 1965, ●István von Beliczey de Baicza (*b* 10 Nov 1936), and has issue,

●Katharina Maritta Charlotte von Beliczey de Baicza, *b* 3 Nov 1966.

3e ●HSH Princess *Charlotte* Elisabeth zu Bentheim und Steinfurt, *b* 3 July 1936, *m* 23 May 1964, ●Wolfgang Paul Winkhaus (*b* 11 May 1929) [*Telgte, Kr Münster, Westfalen, Vechtrup 66, Germany*], and has issue,

1f ●*Sofie* Charlotte Winkhaus, *b* 13 March 1965.

2f ●Christine Irene Juliane Margarete Winkhaus, *b* 6 June 1966.

3d HSH Prince *Karl* Georg zu Bentheim und Steinfurt, *b* 10 Dec 1884, *m* 24 July 1914, ●HSH Princess Margarete von Schönaich-Carolath (*b* 5 June 1888) [*443 Burgsteinfurt, Westfalen, Germany*], dau of HSH Prince Emil von Schönaich-Carolath-Schilden, and *d* 14 Feb 1951, having had issue,

1e HSH Prince *Georg Viktor* Alexis Emil Wilhelm Friedrich Ottfried Max Karl zu Bentheim und Steinfurt, *b* 26 May 1915; *dvp unm* 3 May 1940.

2e ●HSH Prince *Manfred* Alexander Josias Ludwig Friedrich Sieghard zu Bentheim und Steinfurt [*Hamburg-Nieustedten, Elbchaussee 448, Germany*], *b* 31 July 1918, *m* 1st 1 Sept 1953 (*m* diss by div 1956), Karin-Annabel (*b* 6 July 1929), dau of Wilhelm von Grumme-Douglas. He *m* 2ndly 22 Oct 1957, ●Erna Martha Hertha *Irene* (*b* 2 June 1931), only dau of Kurt-Victor von Sydow.

3e ●HSH Prince *Hubertus* Friedrich Gustav Leopold Johann Georg Christian-Ernst zu Bentheim und Steinfurt [*Schloss Bentheim, Kr Gfschaft Bentheim, Niedersachsen, Germany*], *b* 26 Oct 1919, *m* 6 Aug 1957, ●Eva Luise (*b* 20 Oct 1925), dau of Artur Wagner, and has issue,

1f ●HSH Prince *Rudolf-Alexander* Botho Georg Manfred Christian zu Bentheim und Steinfurt, *b* 28 April 1959.

2f ●HSH Prince *Nikolaus* Friedrich-Christian Karl Reinhard Peter zu Bentheim und Steinfurt, *b* 3 Oct 1962.

1f ●HSH Princess *Huberta* Sylvia Juliane Maria Irene Dorothea Gerda Luise zu Bentheim und Steinfurt, *b* 19 June 1961.

4e ●HSH Prince *Botho* Alexander Adolf zu Bentheim und Steinfurt [*35 Kassel, Adolfstrasse 70, Germany*], *b* 29 June 1924, *m* 28 June 1949, ●HSH Princess *Alexandra* Bathildis Elisabeth Luise Helene Emma (*b* 25 Sept 1924), 2nd dau of HSH Josias, Prince of Waldeck and Pyrmont, and has issue (*see p* 221).

4d ●HSH Prince *Friedrich* Georg Ludolf zu Bentheim und Steinfurt [*Berlin-Wilmersdorf, Durlaucher Strasse 29, Germany*], *b* 27 May 1894, *m* 7 Aug 1934, Louise von Gülich (*b* 6 June 1893; *d* 3 March 1949).

1d HSH Princess *Elisabeth* Sophie Marie Helene zu Bentheim und Steinfurt, *b* 12 July 1886; *d unm* 8 May 1959.

2d HSH Princess *Victoria* Charlotte Hermine Auguste zu Bentheim und Steinfurt, *b* 18 Aug 1887; *d unm* 30 Jan 1961.

3d HSH Princess *Emma* Marie Bertha Wilhelmine zu Bentheim und Steinfurt, *b* 19 Feb 1889; *d* 25 April 1905.

3c HSH Princess Georgine Henriette *Marie* of Waldeck and Pyrmont, *b* 23 May 1857, *m* 15 Feb 1877, as his 1st wife, HM King Wilhelm II of Württemberg (*b* 25 Feb 1848; *d* 2 Oct 1921), and *d* 30 April 1882, having had issue (*see p* 211).

4c HSH Princess Adelaide *Emma* Wilhelmine Therese of Waldeck and Pyrmont, *b* 2 Aug 1858, *m* 17 Jan 1879, as his 2nd wife, HM King Willem III of the Netherlands (*b* 19 Feb 1817; *d* 23 Nov 1890), and *d* 20 March 1934, leaving issue (*see p* 215).

5c HSH Princess *Helene* Friederike Augustine of Waldeck and Pyrmont, *b* 7 Feb 1861, *m* 27 April 1882, HRH Prince *Leopold* George Duncan Albert of Great Britain and Ireland, 1st Duke of Albany, KG (*b* 7 April 1853; *d* 28 March 1884), and *d* 1 Sept 1922, leaving issue (*see p* 299).

6c HSH Princess Luise *Elisabeth* Hermine Erika Pauline of Waldeck and Pyrmont, *b* 6 Sept 1873, *m* 3 May 1900, HSH *Alexander* Ludwig Alfred Eberhard, 2nd Prince and Count zu Erbach-Schönberg (*b* 12 Sept 1872; *d* 18 Oct 1944), son of HSH Gustav, 1st Prince and Count zu Erbach-Schönberg, by his wife HSH Princess Marie Caroline of Battenberg (*see* BURKE'S *Peerage*, MILFORD HAVEN, M), and *d* 23 Nov 1961, having had issue,

1d ●HSH *Georg Ludwig* Friedrich Viktor Carl-Eduard Franz-Joseph, 3rd Prince and Count zu Erbach-Schönberg [*Bensheim-Schönberg, Kastanienalle, Germany*], *b* 1 Jan 1903, *m* 2 July 1925, ●Marie Margaretha (*b* 25 Dec 1903), dau of Alfons Deringer, and has issue,

1e ●HSH Hereditary Prince *Ludewig* Wilhelm-Ernst Andreas Georg-Wilhelm Joachim zu Erbach-Schönberg, *b* 17 Oct 1926, *m* 10 March 1950, ●Rosemarie (*b* 22 Sept 1927), dau of Karl Moshage, and has issue,

1f ●HSH Prince *Burckhard* Alexander Maynolf Wittekind zu Erbach-Schönberg, *b* 7 April 1951.
2f ●HSH Prince *Dietrich* Wilhelm zu Erbach-Schönberg, *b* 27 March 1954.
1f ●HSH Princess *Uta* Edda Marie Jutta Annemarie zu Erbach-Schönberg, *b* 1 Aug 1955.
2e ●HSH Prince *Maynolf* Wilhelm Viktor Richard Josias Ludwig-Christian Waldemar zu Erbach-Schönberg [*Frankfurt a M, Mousonstrasse 10, Germany*], *b* 13 May 1936, *m* 14 May 1959, ●Marie-Katherine Markert (*b* 16 Jan 1921).
1e ●HSH Princess *Edda-Marie* Luise Imma Helene Sophie Viktoria zu Erbach-Schönberg, *b* 28 April 1930, *m* 2 May 1951, ●Karl Josef Dierkes (*b* 16 Nov 1929) [*Darmstadt, Luisenstrasse 24, Germany*], and has issue,
1f ●Anja Dierkes, *b* 11 April 1952.
2f ●Petra Dierkes, *b* 5 July 1953.
3f ●Tatjana Dierkes, *b* 29 April 1960.
2d HSH Prince *Wilhelm-Ernst* Heinrich Alfred zu Erbach-Schönberg, *b* 4 Jan 1904, *m* 4 Oct 1938, ●H Ill H Countess *Alexandra* Anna Sophia Katharina Emilia Adrienne (*b* 24 Sept 1910) [*Schlitz, OHessen, Hallenburg, Germany*], eldest dau of H Ill H Wilhelm, Count Schlitz gen von Görtz, and *d* in a Russian p o w camp 27 Sept 1947, having had issue,
HSH Princess Marianne zu Erbach-Schönberg, *b* 15, *d* 16 Dec 1939.
1d HSH Princess *Imma* Gustave Marie Luise Pauline Edda Adolfine Hermine zu Erbach-Schönberg, *b* 11 May 1901, *m* 1st 31 May 1923, Baron *Hans-Carl* Friedrich Wilhelm Ernst von Dörnberg (*b* 23 Dec 1875; *d* 22 March 1924). She *m* 2ndly 1 July 1940, Neil McEachan (*b* 28 Dec 1885; *d* 18 April 1964), and *dsp* 14 March 1947.
2d ●HSH Princess *Helene* Sophie Luise Hedwig Emilie Martha zu Erbach-Schönberg [*Göppingen, Württemberg, Fauerndauer Strasse 8, Germany*], *b* 8 April 1907.
6b HSH Princess *Sophie* Wilhelmine Marianne Henriette of Nassau, *b* 9 July 1836, *m* 6 June 1857, HM King Oscar II of Sweden and Norway, KG (*b* 21 Jan 1829; *d* 8 Dec 1907), and *d* 30 Dec 1913, having had issue,
1c HM King (Oscar) *Gustaf V* (Adolf) of Sweden (1907-1950), KG (1905), GCB (1901), hon Adm in British Navy *b* 16 June 1858, *m* 20 Sept 1881, HGDH Princess Sophie Marie *Victoria* (*b* 7 Aug 1862; *d* 4 April 1930), only dau of HRH Grand Duke Friedrich I of Baden (*see p* 288), and *d* 29 Oct 1950, having had issue,
1d ●HM King (Oscar Fredrik Vilhelm Olaf) *Gustaf VI Adolf of Sweden*, KG (1954), GCB (1905), GCVO, Royal Victorian Chain (1923), Col-in-Chief The Cameronians (Scottish Rifles) [*Royal Palace, Stockholm, Sweden; Drottningholm, nr Stockholm; Sofiero, nr Hälsingborg, Sweden*], *b* 11 Nov 1882, *m* 1st 15 June 1905, HRH Princess *Margaret* Victoria Augusta Charlotte Norah, VA, CI, DJStJ (*b* 15 Jan 1882; *d* 1 May 1920), elder dau of HRH Prince *Arthur* William Patrick Albert of Great Britain and Ireland, 1st Duke of Connaught and Strathearn, KG, etc (*see p* 298), and has had issue,
1e HRH Hereditary Prince *Gustaf Adolf* Oscar Fredrik Arthur Edmund of Sweden, Duke of Västerbotten, GCVO, *b* 22 April 1906, *m* 20 Oct 1932, ●HH Princess *Sibylla* Calma Marie Alice Bathildis Feodora (*b* 18 Jan 1908) [*Royal Palace, Stockholm, Sweden; Hagaberg, nr Borgholm, Isle of Öland*], elder dau of HRH Karl Eduard (Charles Edward), Duke of Saxe-Coburg and Gotha, Prince of Great Britain and Ireland, 2nd Duke of Albany, etc (*see p* 299), and was *k* in a flying accident at Copenhagen 26 Jan 1947, leaving issue,
1f ●HRH Crown Prince *Carl Gustaf* Folke Hubertus of Sweden, Duke of Jämtland [*Royal Palace, Stockholm, Sweden*], *b* 30 April 1946.
1f ●HRH Princess *Margaretha* Désirée Victoria of Sweden, now styled HRH Princess Margaretha, Mrs Ambler, *b* 31 Oct 1934, *m* 30 June 1964, ●John Ambler (*b* 6 June 1924) [*Chippinghurst Manor, Oxon*], son of late Capt Charles Ambler, 60th Rifles, of Rapkyns, Horsham, Sussex (*see* BURKE'S *LG*, 1952 *Edn*, AMBLER *of Lawkland Hall*), and has issue,
1g ●Charles *Edward* Ambler, b 14 July 1966.
2g ●*James* Patrick Ambler, *b* 10 June 1969.
1g ●*Sybilla* Louise Ambler, *b* 14 April 1965.
2f ●HRH Princess *Birgitta* Ingeborg Alice of Sweden, *b* 19 Jan 1937, *m* 30 May 1961, ●HSH Prince *Johann Georg* Carl Leopold Eitel-Friedrich Meinrad Maria Hubertus Michael of Hohenzollern (*b* 31 Jan 1932) [*8022 Grünwald bei München, Dr-Max-Strasse 70, Germany*], and has issue,
1g ●HSH Prince *Carl Christian* Friedrich Johannes Maria Meinrad Hubertus Edmund of Hohenzollern, *b* 5 April 1962.
2g ●HSH Prince *Hubertus* Gustav Adolf Veit Georg Meinrad Maria Alexander of Hohenzollern, *b* 10 June 1966.
1g ●HSH Princess *Désirée* Margarethe Victoria Louise Sibylla Catarina Maria of Hohenzollern, *b* 27 Nov 1963.
3f ●HRH Princess *Désirée* Elisabeth Sibylla of Sweden, relinquished the style of Royal Highness and title of Princess of Sweden on her marriage and became Princess Désirée, Baroness Silfverschiöld, *b* 2 June 1938, *m* 5 June 1964, ●Baron Niclas Silfverschiöld (*b* 31 May 1934) [*Koberg, 460 30 Sollebrunn, Sweden*], and has issue,
1g ●Baron *Carl Otto* Edmund Silfverschiöld, *b* 22 March 1965.
1g ●Baroness *Christina-Louise* Ewa Madelaine Silfverschiöld, *b* 29 Sept 1966.
2g ●Baroness *Hélène* Ingeborg Sibylla Silfverschiöld, *b* 20 Sept 1968.
4f ●HRH Princess *Christina* Louise Helena of Sweden, *b* 3 Aug 1943.
2e ●HRH Prince *Sigvard* Oscar Fredrik of Sweden, Duke of Uppland, renounced his rights of succession and style and titles as a Prince of Sweden and assumed the surname of Bernadotte 7 March 1934, *cr* Count Bernadotte af Wisborg by HRH the Grand Duchess of Luxembourg 2 July 1951 [*Villagatan 10, S114 32 Stockholm, Sweden*], *b* 7 June 1907, *m* 1st 8 March 1934 (*m* diss by div 1943), *Erika* Maria Regina Rosalie (*b* 12 July 1911), dau of Anton Patzek. He *m* 2ndly 26 Oct 1943 (*m* diss by div), *Sonja* Helene (*b* 12 Oct 1909), dau of Reeders Robbert, and by her has issue,
●Count *Michael* Sigvard Bernadotte af Wisborg, *b* 21 Aug 1944.
He *m* 3rdly 30 July 1961, ●Gullan *Marianne* (*b* 15 July 1924), dau of Helge Lindberg.
3e ●HRH Prince *Bertil* Gustaf Oscar Carl Eugen of Sweden, Duke of Halland [*Villa Solbacken, Djurgardsbrunn, Stockholm, Sweden*], *b* 28 Feb 1912.
4e ●HRH Prince *Carl Johan* Arthur of Sweden, renounced his rights of succession and style and titles as a Prince of Sweden and assumed the surname of Bernadotte 22 Feb 1946, *cr* Count Bernadotte af Wisborg by HRH the Grand Duchess of Luxembourg 2 July 1951 [*Room 909, 527, Fifth Avenue, New York City 17, USA; Linnégatan 3, Stockholm, Sweden; 308, Algö Vagen, Saltsjöboden, Sweden*], *b* 31 Oct 1916, *m* 19 Feb 1946, ●Elin *Kerstin* Margareta (*b* 4 March 1910), formerly wife of Axel Johnson, and dau of Dr Henning Wijkmark.
1e ●HRH Princess *Ingrid* Victoria Sofia Louise Margareta of Sweden [*Amalienborg*

Palace, Copenhagen, Denmark], *b* 28 March 1910, *m* 24 May 1935, HM King Frederik IX of Denmark, KG (*b* 11 March 1899; *d* 14 Jan 1972), and has issue (*see p* 278).
HM the King of Sweden *m* 2ndly 3 Nov 1923, Lady *Louise* Alexandra Marie Irene Mountbatten, RRC, formerly HSH Princess Louise of Battenberg (*b* 13 July 1889; *d* 7 March 1965), yr dau of Louis Alexander Mountbatten, 1st Marquess of Milford Haven, formerly HSH Prince Louis of Battenberg (*see p* 303 and BURKE'S *Peerage*).
2*d* HRH Prince Carl *Vilhelm* Ludvig of Sweden, Duke of Södermanland, *b* 17 June 1884, *m* 3 May 1908 (*m* diss by div 1914), HIH Grand Duchess Maria Pavlovna (*b* 18 April 1890; *d* 13 Dec 1958), dau of HIH Grand Duke Paul Alexandrovitch of Russia (*see p* 281), and *d* 5 June 1965, leaving issue,
●HRH Prince Gustaf *Lennart* Nicolaus Paul of Sweden, Duke of Småland, renounced his rights of succession and style and titles as a Prince of Sweden and assumed the surname of Bernadotte 11 March 1932, *cr* Count Bernadotte af Wisborg by HRH the Grand Duchess of Luxembourg 2 July 1951 [*Schloss Mainau, Lake Constance, Germany*], *b* 8 May 1909, *m* 1st 11 March 1932 (*m* diss by div 1972), *Karin* Emma Louise (*b* 7 July 1911), dau of Sven Nissvandt, and has issue,
1*f* ●Count Carl Johan (*Jan*) Gustaf Vilhelm Bernadotte af Wisborg [*D7750 Konstanz, Schulthaissstrasse 10, Germany*], *b* 9 Jan 1941, *m* 1st 3 May 1965 (*m* diss by div 1967), Gunilla (*b* 3 Sept 1941), dau of Erik Stampe. He *m* 2ndly 26 June 1967 (*m* diss by div 1970), Anna Skarne (*b* 18 April 1944), and by her has issue,
●Countess Sophia Magdalena Birgitta Bernadotte af Wisborg, *b* 3 May 1968.
He *m* 3rdly 23 June 1972, ●Annegret (*b* 15 Nov 1938), formerly wife of — Drenckhahn, and dau of —Thomssen.
1*f* ●Countess Birgitta Bernadotte af Wisborg, *b* 3 May 1933, *m* 16 June 1955, ●Fritz Straehl (*b* 20 Nov 1922) [*CH 8280 Kreuzlingen, Gaisbergstrasse 26, Switzerland*], and has issue,
1*g* ●*Friedrich* Lennart Straehl, *b* 10 April 1956.
2*g* ●Andreas Straehl, *b* 16 July 1957.
3*g* ●Stephan Straehl, *b* 16 July 1964.
1*g* ●Maria Christina Straehl, *b* 23 April 1960.
2*g* ●Désirée Straehl, *b* 20 Oct 1961.
2*f* ●Countess Marie Louise Bernadotte af Wisborg, *b* 6 Nov 1935, *m* 11 Sept 1956, ●Rudolf Kautz (*b* 24 Aug 1930) [*D7750 Konstanz, Mozartsstrasse 14, Germany*], and has issue,
1*g* ●Henric Kautz, *b* 16 July 1957.
1*g* ●Karin Kautz, *b* 13 Oct 1958.
2*g* ●*Madeleine* Cecilia Kautz, *b* 23 Aug 1961.
3*f* ●Countess Karin Cecilia Bernadotte af Wisborg, *b* 9 April 1944, *m* 31 March 1967, ●Hansjörg Baenkler (*b* 24 Sept 1939) [*D7750 Konstanz, Am See 4, Germany*].
He *m* 2ndly 6 May 1972, ●Sonja Haunz (*b* 7 May 1944).
3*d* HRH Prince *Erik* Gustaf Ludvig Albert of Sweden, Duke of Vestmanland, *b* 20 April 1889; *d unm* 19 Sept 1918.
2*c* HRH Prince *Oscar* Carl August of Sweden, Duke of Gotland, Vice-Adm in the Royal Swedish Navy, renounced his rights of succession and style and titles as a Prince of Sweden and assumed the style and title of HH Prince Bernadotte 15 March 1888, *cr* Count af Wisborg by HRH the Grand Duke Adolf of Luxembourg 2 April 1892, *b* 15 Nov 1859, *m* 15 March 1888, *Ebba* Henrietta (*b* 24 Oct 1858; *d* 16 Oct 1946), dau of Carl Munck af Fulkila, and *d* 4 Oct 1953, having had issue,
1*d* ●Count *Carl Oscar* Bernadotte af Wisborg [*Malmsjö-Värsta, Sweden*], *b* 27 May 1890, *m* 1st (*m* diss by div 1935), Baroness Marianne (*b* 6 Oct 1893), dau of Baron Louis De Geer af Leufsta, and has had issue,
1*e* Count *Nils* Carl Oscar Bernadotte af Wisborg, *b* 9 Feb 1918; *d* 21 April 1920.
2*e* ●Count *Oscar* Carl Emanuel Bernadotte af Wisborg [*Frötuna, Rasbo, Sweden*], *b* 12 July 1921, *m* 1st 18 March 1944 (*m* diss by div 1950), Baroness *Ebba* Anna Ida Louise (*b* 26 July 1918), dau of Baron Nils Gyllenkrok, and has issue,
1*f* ●Countess *Ebba* Marianne Charlotte Bernadotte af Wisborg, *b* 2 March 1945.
He *m* 2ndly 18 Oct 1950, ●Gertrud (*b* 10 May 1916), dau of Johannes Ollén, and by her has issue,
1*f* ●Count *Carl Louis* Bernadotte af Wisborg, *b* 1 June 1955.
2*f* ●Countess Christina Bernadotte af Wisborg, *b* 21 Dec 1951.
3*f* ●Countess Birgitta Bernadotte af Wisborg, *b* 21 Dec 1953.
1*e* ●Countess *Dagmar* Ebba Märtha Marianne Bernadotte af Wisborg, *b* 10 April 1916, *m* 16 Oct 1936, ●Col Nils-Magnus von Arbin, Royal Swedish Navy (*b* 17 Aug 1910), and has issue,
1*f* ●Elsa Ebba *Marianne* von Arbin, *b* 2 Aug 1937, *m* 5 Sept 1958, ●*Miles* Carl Gustaf Flack (*b* 10 Aug 1934), and has issue,
●Camilla Jana Gabrielle Flack, *b* 22 Dec 1960.
2*f* ●Dagmar Märtha *Louise* von Arbin, *b* 27 May 1940, *m* 29 July 1961, Per-Erik Sven *Richard* Bergström (*b* 22 Oct 1936), and has issue,
●Dick Michael Bergström, *b* 10 Dec 1965.
●Therese Marianne Bergström, *b* 10 Sept 1963.
3*f* ●Eva Wibeke *Catherine* von Arbin, *b* 26 June 1946.
4*f* ●Lise-Lotte *Jeanette* von Arbin, *b* 19 May 1951.
5*f* ●Susanne Maud *Madeleine* von Arbin, *b* 27 Jan 1955.
2*e* ●Countess Märtha Elsa *Catherina* Bernadotte af Wisborg, *b* 14 April 1926, *m* 9 Oct 1948, ●*Tore Henrik* Nilert (*b* 9 Feb 1915) [*2 East 67th Street, New York City, USA*], and has issue,
1*f* ●Jan Nilert, *b* 11 March 1950.
1*f* ●Charlotte Nilert, *b* 20 May 1952.
2*f* ●Anna-Marie Nilert, *b* 1 March 1954.
Count Carl Oscar Bernadotte af Wisborg *m* 2ndly 20 April 1937, ●Gerty (*b* 30 Oct 1910), dau of Fritz Börjesson, and by her has issue,
3*e* ●Count *Claës Oscar* Carl Bernadotte af Wisborg, *b* 17 July 1942.
2*d* Count Folke Bernadotte af Wisborg, hon KBE (1947), hon MD Univs of Copenhagen, Oslo and Uppsala, Pres Swedish Red Cross, Pres Swedish Boy Scouts, apptd United Nations Mediator in Israel 1948, had Grand Cross of Orders of the North Star (Sweden), Dannebrog (Denmark), Crown of Belgium, Léopold II (Belgium), Orange-Nassau (Netherlands), White Rose (Finland), St Olav (Norway), and Polonia Restituta, Grand Offr Legion of Honour (France), author of *The Fall of the Curtain, Instead of Arms,* and *To Jerusalem*, *b* 2 Jan 1895, *m* 1 Dec 1928, ●*Estelle* Romaine (*b* 26 Sept 1904) [*Dragongarden, Stockholm, Sweden*], dau of Edward Manville, of USA, and was assassinated in Jerusalem 17 Sept 1948, having had issue,
1*e* Count Gustaf Edward Bernadotte af Wisborg, *b* 30 Jan 1930; *d* 2 Feb 1936.
2*e* ●Count *Folke* Bernadotte af Wisborg [*Luthagesplanaden 11, Uppsala, Sweden*], *b* 8 Feb 1931, *m* 2 July 1955, ●Christine (*b* 9 Jan 1932), dau of Gunnar Glahns, and has issue,
1*f* ●Count Carl Folke Bernadotte af Wisborg, *b* 2 Dec 1958.

2*f* ●Count Gunnar Fredrik Bernadotte af Wisborg, *b* 24 Nov 1963.
1*f* ●Countess Anne Christine Bernadotte af Wisborg, *b* 22 Nov 1956.
2*f* ●Countess Marie Estelle Bernadotte af Wisborg, *b* 27 April 1962.
3*e* Count Fredrik Oscar Bernadotte af Wisborg, *b* 10 Jan, *d* 20 Aug 1934.
4*e* ●Count Bertil Oscar Bernadotte af Wisborg, *b* 6 Oct 1935.
1*d* ●Countess *Maria* Sophia Henriette Bernadotte af Wisborg [*Linnégatan 21, Stockholm, Sweden*], *b* 28 Feb 1889.
2*d* Countess Ebba *Sophia* Bernadotte af Wisborg, *b* 17 May 1892, *m* 14 May 1917, ●Baron Carl-Marten Fleetwood (*b* 1885), and *dsp* 21 June 1936.
3*d* ●Countess Elsa Victoria Bernadotte af Wisborg, *b* 3 Aug 1893, *m* 18 Sept 1929, ●Hugo Cedergren, CBE (*b* 26 July 1891) [*Skeppargatan 56, Stockholm, Sweden*].
3*c* HRH Prince Oscar *Carl* Vilhelm of Sweden, Duke of Västergötland, *b* 27 Feb 1861, *m* 27 Aug 1897, HRH Princess *Ingeborg* Charlotta Carolina Friederika Louisa (*b* 2 Aug 1878; *d* 11 March 1958), 2nd dau of HM King Frederik VIII of Denmark (*see p* 278), and *d* 24 Oct 1951, having had issue,
1*d* ●HRH Prince *Carl* Gustaf Oscar Fredrik Christian of Sweden, Duke of Östergötland, renounced for himself and his descendants his rights of succession to the throne and style and titles as a Prince of Sweden and was *cr* Prince Bernadotte by HM King Léopold III of the Belgians 6 July 1937 [*Apelvägen 18, Stockholm, Sweden*], *b* 10 Jan 1911, *m* 1st 6 July 1937 (*m* diss by div 1951), Countess Elsa (*b* 7 Feb 1904), formerly wife of Count Victor Gösta Adolf von Rosen, and dau of Count Eugen von Rosen, and has issue,
●Countess *Madelaine* Ingeborg Ella Astrid Elsa Bernadotte, *b* 8 Oct 1938, *m* 6 Oct 1962, ●Count Charles-Albert Ullens de Schooten Whettnall (*b* 16 Nov 1927).
He *m* 2ndly 1954, ●Anne Larson.
1*d* ●HRH Princess *Margaretha* Sofia Lovisa Ingeborg of Sweden [*Bernstorffshøj bei Gentofte, Denmark*], *b* 25 June 1899, *m* 22 May 1919, HRH Prince *Axel* Christian Georg of Denmark (*b* 12 Aug 1888; *d* 14 July 1964), and has issue (*see p* 281).
2*d* HRH Princess *Märtha* Sofia Lovisa Dagmar Thyra of Sweden, *b* 28 March 1901, *m* 21 March 1929, ●HRH Crown Prince Olav of Norway (now HM King Olav V of Norway) (*b* 2 July 1903) [*Skaugum, Asker, nr Oslo, Norway*], and *d* 5 April 1954, leaving issue (*see p* 307).
3*d* HRH Princess *Astrid* Sofia Lovisa Thyra of Sweden, *b* 17 Nov 1905, *m* (civil) 4 Nov and (religious) 10 Nov 1926, as his 1st wife, ●HM King Léopold III of the Belgians, KG, GCVO, Royal Victorian Chain (*b* 3 Nov 1901) [*Domaine d'Argenteuil, nr Brussels, Belgium*], and was *k* in a motor accident 29 Aug 1935, leaving issue,
1*e* ●HM King *Baudouin I* (Albert-Charles-Léopold-Axel-Marie-Gustave) of the Belgians, KG (1963), hon Air Chief Marshal RAF (1963), *s* to the throne on the abdication of his father 17 July 1951 [*Palais de Bruxelles, Belgium; Laeken, nr Brussels, Belgium*], *b* 7 Sept 1930, *m* 15 Dec 1960, ●Doña *Fabiola* Fernanda Maria de las Victorias Antonia Adelaida Mora y Aragon (*b* 11 June 1928), yst dau of late Don Gonzalo Mora y Fernández, Conde de Mora, Marqués de Casa Riera.
2*e* ●HRH Prince *Albert*-Félix-Humbert-Théodore-Christian-Eugène-Marie of Belgium, Prince of Liège, GCVO [*Château de Belvédère, Laeken, Belgium*], *b* 6 June 1934, *m* 2 June 1959, ●Donna *Paola* Margherita Maria Antonia Consiglia Ruffo di Calabria (*b* 11 Sept 1937), yst dau of late Don Fulco, Principe Ruffo di Calabria, Duca di Guardia Lombarda, and has issue,
1*f* ●HRH Prince *Philippe*-Léopold-Louis-Marie of Belgium, *b* 15 April 1960.
2*f* ●HRH Prince *Laurent*-Bénoit-Baudouin-Marie of Belgium, *b* 19 Oct 1963.
1*f* ●HRH Princess *Astrid*-Joséphine-Fabrizia-Elisabeth-Paola-Marie of Belgium, *b* 5 June 1962.
1*e* ●HRH Princess *Joséphine-Charlotte*-Ingeborg-Elisabeth-Marie-Josèphe - Marguerite-Astrid of Belgium, *b* 11 Oct 1927, *m* 9 April 1953, ●HRH Grand Duke Jean of Luxembourg, KG (*b* 5 Jan 1921), and has issue (*see p* 218).
4*c* HRH Prince *Eugen* Napoléon Nicolaus of Sweden, Duke of Nerike, a distinguished artist, *b* 1 Aug 1865; *d unm* 17 Aug 1947.
2*a* HSH Prince *Friedrich* Wilhelm of Nassau, *b* 15 Dec 1799, *m* 7 June 1840, Anna (*b* 21 June 1803; *d* 17 June 1864), dau of Josef Ritter von Vallyemare, and *dsp* 6 Jan 1845.
1*a* HSH Princess Auguste Luise Wilhelmine of Nassau-Weilburg, *b* 5 Jan 1794; *d* 11 April 1796.
2*a* HSH Princess *Henriette* Alexandrine Friederike Wilhelmine of Nassau, *b* 30 Oct 1797, *m* 17 Sept 1815, HI and RH Archduke *Karl* Ludwig Johann Joseph Laurencius of Austria, Duke of Teschen (*b* 5 Sept 1771; *d* 30 April 1847), 2nd son of HIM Emperor Leopold II, and *d* 29 Dec 1829, leaving issue,
1*b* HI and RH Archduke *Albrecht* Friedrich Rudolf of Austria, Duke of Teschen, *b* 3 Aug 1817, *m* 1 May 1844, HRH Princess *Hildegarde* Luise Charlotte Therese Friederike (*b* 10 June 1825; *d* 2 April 1864), 3rd dau of HM King Ludwig I of Bavaria, and *d* 18 Feb 1895, having had issue,
1*c* HI and RH Archduke *Karl* Albrecht Ludwig of Austria, *b* 3 Jan 1847; *d* 19 July 1848.
1*c* HI and RH Archduchess *Maria Theresia* Anna of Austria, *b* 15 July 1845, *m* 18 Jan 1865, HRH Duke Philipp Alexander Maria Ernst of Württemberg (*b* 30 July 1838; *d* 11 Oct 1917), and *d* 8 Oct 1927, having had issue,
1*d* HRH Duke *Albrecht* Maria Alexander Philipp Joseph of Württemberg, *s* as Head of the Royal House of Württemberg on the death of King Wilhelm II (*see p* 211) 1921, *b* 23 Dec 1865, *m* 24 Jan 1893, HI and RH Archduchess *Margarete Sophie* Marie Annunciata Theresia Karoline Luise Josephine Johanna (*b* 13 May 1870; *d* 24 Aug 1902), eldest dau of HI and RH Archduke Karl Ludwig of Austria, and *d* 29 Oct 1939, leaving issue,
1*e* ●HRH Duke *Philipp Albrecht* Carl Maria Joseph Ludwig Hubertus Stanislaus Leopold of Württemberg, Head of the Royal House of Württemberg from 1939 [*7963 Schloss Altshausen, Kreis Saulgau, Württemberg, Germany; 799 Schloss Friedrichshafen, Württemberg, Germany*], *b* 14 Nov 1893, *m* 1st 24 Oct 1923, HI and RH Archduchess *Helene* Marie Alice Christine Josepha Anna Margareta Madeleine Walburga Blandina Caecilie Philomena Carmela Ignazia Rita de Cascia (*b* 30 Oct 1903; *d* 8 Sept 1924), elder dau of HI and RH Archduke Peter Ferdinand of Austria, Prince of Tuscany (*see p* 238, and has issue,
1*f* ●HRH Duchess *Marie Christine* Helene Philippine Albertine Margarethe Amélie Elisabeth Therese Rosa Josepha Antonia Hedwig Aloysia of Württemberg, *b* 2 Sept 1924, *m* 23 Sept 1948, ●HSH Prince *Georg* Hartmann Maria Josef Franz de Paula Aloys Ignatius Benediktus Martin of Liechtenstein (*b* 11 Nov 1911) [*Alserbachstrasse 16, A-1090 Vienna, Austria*], and has issue,
1*g* ●HSH Prince *Christoph* Alois Maria Ferdinand Josef Philipp Pius Konrad Thaddäus Ruppert Paulus Ignatius of Liechtenstein, *b* 15 Jan 1958.
1*g* ●HSH Princess *Margarita* Maria Helene Rosa Aloisia Philippine Elisabeth

Georgine Josefa Konrada Pia Ignatia of Liechtenstein, *b* 1 May 1950.

2*g* ●HSH Princess *Maria Assunta* Elisabeth Philippine Rosa Helena Aloisia Georgine Josefa Benedikta Pia Ignatia of Liechtenstein, *b* 28 April 1952.

3*g* ●HSH Princess *Isabelle* Marie Helene Caroline Alfreda Josefa Monika Pia Georgina Hemma Henriette Ignatia of Liechtenstein, *b* 17 May 1954.

4*g* ●HSH Princess *Marie Helene* Diane Rosa Elisabeth Aloysia Philippine Josefa Gabriella Pia Antonia Ignatia of Liechtenstein, *b* 8 Sept 1960.

5*g* ●HSH Princess *Georgine* Maria Agnes Philippine Elisabeth Ignatia of Liechtenstein, *b* 13 Nov 1962.

HRH the Duke of Württemberg *m* 2ndly 1 Aug 1928, ●HI and RH Archduchess *Rosa* Maria Antonie Roberta Josepha Anna Walburga Carmela Ignazia Rita de Cascia (*b* 22 Sept 1906), yr sister of his 1st wife, and by her has issue,

1*f* ●HRH Duke *Ludwig* Albrecht Maria Philipp Peter Ferdinand Karl Gottfried Georg Alfons of Württemberg, renounced his rights of succession and membership of the Royal House of Württemberg 29 June 1959 and 19 Jan 1960 [*7302 Nellingen, Württemberg, Friedrich-List-Strasse 20*], *b* 23 Oct 1930, *m* 16 Feb 1960, ●Baroness Adelheid (*Heidi*) (*b* 3 Aug 1938), dau of Baron Johann Franz von und zu Bodman, and has issue,

1*g* ●*Christoph* Albrecht Philipp Maria Bernhard Rudolf Andreas von Württemberg, *b* 30 Nov 1960.

1*g* ●*Isabelle* Helene Maria Rositta Christina Alix Andrea von Württemberg, *b* (twin with Christoph) 30 Nov 1960.

2*g* ●*Sybilla* Rositta Maria-Christina Maria-Magdalena von Württemberg, *b* 29 May 1963.

2*f* ●HRH Duke *Carl* Maria Peter Ferdinand Philipp Albrecht Joseph Michael Pius Konrad Robert Ulrich of Württemberg [*799 Schloss Friedrichshafen, Württemberg, Germany*], *b* 1 Aug 1936, *m* (civil) 18 July and (religious) 21 July 1960, ●HRH Princess *Diane*-Françoise-Maria da Gloria of France (*b* 24 March 1940), 4th dau of HRH Prince Henri, Count of Paris, Head of the Royal House of France, and has issue,

1*g* ●HRH Duke *Friedrich* Philipp Carl Franz Maria of Württemberg, *b* 1 June 1961.

2*g* ●HRH Duke *Eberhard* Alois Nikolaus Heinrich Johannes Maria of Württemberg, *b* 20 June 1963.

3*g* ●HRH Duke *Philipp* Albrecht Christoph Ulrich Maria of Württemberg, *b* 1 Nov 1964.

4*g* ●HRH Duke *Michael* Heinrich Albrecht Alexander Maria of Württemberg, *b* 1 Dec 1965.

1*g* ●HRH Duchess *Mathilde* Marie-Antoinette Rosa Isabelle of Württemberg, *b* 11 July 1962.

2*f* ●HRH Duchess *Helene* Maria Christine Margaretha Albertine Philippine Amélie Therese Josepha Antonia Alix Petrine Paula Pia of Württemberg, *b* 29 June 1929, *m* 23 Aug 1961, ●*Friedrich* Alexander Karl Maria Alfons, Markgraf von Pallavicini (*b* 23 Dec 1924) [*7967 Schloss Altshausen, Kreis Saulgau, Württemberg, Germany*], and has issue,

1*g* ●*Gian-Carlo* Maria Emanuel Friedrich Albert, Markgraf von Pallavicini, *b* 8 April 1967.

1*g* ●*Maria-Cristina* Rosa Carolina Elisabeth, Markgräfin von Pallavicini, *b* 4 Jan 1963.

2*g* ●*Antonietta* Maria Claudia Margerita, Markgräfin von Pallavicini, *b* 9 Jan 1964.

3*g* ●*Gabriella* Maria Helene Georgina Josefa, Markgräfin von Pallavicini, *b* 23 April 1965.

3*f* ●HRH Duchess *Elisabeth* Maria Margarethe Alix Helene Rosa Philippine Christine Josepha Therese vom Kinde Jesu of Württemberg, *b* 2 Feb 1933, *m* (civil) 18 July and (religious) 19 July 1958, HRH Prince *Antonio* Maria Giuseppe Alfonso Adamo et omnes sancti of the Two Sicilies (*b* 20 Jan 1929) [*77 par la Ferté Gaucher, Lecherolles, Seine-Oise, France*] (*see p* 237), and has issue,

1*g* ●HRH Prince *Francesco* Filippo Maria Giuseppe Gabriele of the Two Sicilies, *b* 20 June 1960.

2*g* ●HRH Prince *Gennaro* Maria Pio Casimiro of the Two Sicilies, *b* 27 Jan 1966.

1*g* ●HRH Princess Maria *Carolina* Giovanna Rosa Cecilia of the Two Sicilies, *b* 18 July 1962.

4*f* ●HRH Duchess *Marie-Therese* Nadejda Albertine Rosa Philippine Margarethe Christine Helene Josepha Martina Leopoldine of Württemberg, *b* 12 Nov 1934, *m* 5 July 1957, ●HRH Prince *Henri*-Philippe-Pierre-Marie of France, Count of Clermont (*b* 14 June 1933) [*131 rue Lecourbe, F-75 Paris 15ème, France*], eldest son of HRH Prince Henri, Count of Paris, Head of the Royal House of France, and has issue,

1*g* ●HRH Prince *François*-Henri-Louis-Marie of France, *b* 7 Feb 1961.

2*g* ●HRH Prince *Jean*-Charles-Pierre-Marie of France, *b* 19 May 1965.

3*g* ●HRH Prince *Eudes*-Thibaut-Joseph-Marie of France, *b* 18 March 1968.

1*g* ●HRH Princess *Marie*-Isabelle-Marguerite-Anne-Genevieve of France, *b* 3 Jan 1959.

2*g* ●HRH Princess Blanche of France, *b* 10 Sept 1962.

5*f* ●HRH Duchess *Marie Antoinette* Conrada Rosa Helene Michaela Josepha Christine Margarethe Pia of Württemberg [*7967 Schloss Altshausen, Kreis Saulgau, Württemberg, Germany*], *b* 31 Aug 1937.

2*e* HRH Duke *Albrecht Eugen* Maria Philipp Carl Joseph Fortunatus of Württemberg, *b* 8 Jan 1895, *m* 24 Jan 1924, HRH Princess *Nadejda* Klementine Maria Pia Majella (*b* 30 Jan 1899; *d* 15 Feb 1958), yr dau of HM King Ferdinand of the Bulgarians (*see p* 246), and *d* 24 June 1954, leaving issue,

1*f* ●HRH Duke *Ferdinand Eugen* Albrecht Maria Joseph Ivan Rilsky Philipp August Clemens Karl Robert Ludwig Boris Cyrill Franz de Paula of Württemberg [*7 Stuttgart, Hölderlinstrasse 32, Württemberg, Germany*], *b* 3 April 1925.

2*f* ●HRH Duke *Eugen Eberhard* Albrecht Maria Joseph Ivan Rilsky Robert Ulrich Philipp Odo Carl Hubert of Württemberg [*4 Düsseldorf, Tiergartenstrasse 43, Germany*], *b* 2 Nov 1930, *m* (civil) 31 Aug and (religious) 3 Sept 1962, ●HI and RH Archduchess Alexandra (*b* 21 May 1935), 2nd dau of HI and RH Archduke Anton of Austria, Prince of Tuscany (*see p* 296).

3*f* ●HRH Duke *Alexander Eugen* Philipp Albrecht Ferdinand Maria Joseph Ivan Rilsky Johannes-Joseph vom Kreuz of Württemberg [*8 München 80, Prinzregentenstrasse 87, Germany*], *b* 5 March 1933.

1*f* ●HRH Duchess *Margarethe Louise* Eudoxie Nadejda Maria Josepha Albertine Therese Amélie Elisabeth Benedicta Rosa Catharina Elisabetha-Bona of Württemberg, *b* 25 Nov 1928, *m* Aug 1970, ●*François*-Luce, Vicomte de Chevigny.

2*f* ●HRH Duchess *Sophie* Eudoxie Marie Louise Josepha Margarethe Theresia vom Kinde Jesu Konrada Donata of Württemberg, *b* 16 Feb 1937, *m* 18 Feb 1969, ●Dr Antonio de Ramos-Bandeira.

3*e* HRH Duke *Carl Alexander* Maria Philipp Joseph Albrecht Gregor of Württemberg, *b* 12 March 1896; *d unm* 27 Dec 1964.

1*e* HRH Duchess *Maria Amélie* Theresia Annunziata Assunta Margarethe Sophie Caroline Albertine Josepha of Württemberg, *b* 15 Aug 1897; *d unm* 13 Aug 1923.

2*e* HRH Duchess *Maria Theresia* Margarethe Annunziata Sophie Elisabeth Albertine Josepha of Württemberg, *b* 16 Aug 1898; *d unm* 26 March 1928.

3*e* HRH Duchess *Marie Elisabeth* of Württemberg, *b* 12 Sept 1899; *d* 15 April 1900.

4*e* HRH Duchess *Margarethe* Maria Annunziata Sophie Theresia Elisabeth Josepha Albertine of Württemberg, *b* 4 Jan 1902; *d unm* 22 April 1945.

2*d* HRH Duke *Robert* Maria Klemens Philipp Josef of Württemberg, *b* 14 Jan 1873, *m* 29 Oct 1900, HI and RH Archduchess *Maria Immakulata* Rainiera Josepha Ferdinande Theresia Leopoldine Antonia Henriette Franziska Karoline Aloysia Januaria Christina Philomena Rosalia (*b* 3 Sept 1878; *d* 25 Nov 1968), yst dau of HI and RH Archduke Karl Salvator of Austria, Prince of Tuscany (*see p* 245), and *dsp* 12 April 1947.

3*d* HRH Duke *Ulrich* Maria Ludwig Joseph Anton of Württemberg, *b* 13 June 1877; *d unm* 13 June 1944.

1*d* HRH Duchess *Marie* Amalie Hildegart Philippine Theresia Josephine of Württemberg, *b* 24 Dec 1865; *d* 16 Dec 1883.

2*d* HRH Duchess *Maria Isabella* Philippine Theresia Mathilde Josephine of Württemberg, *b* 30 Aug 1871, *m* 5 April 1894, HRH Prince *Johann Georg* Pius Karl Leopold Maria Januarius Anacletus of Saxony (*b* 10 July 1869; *d* 24 Nov 1938), 2nd son of HM King Georg of Saxony, and *dsp* 24 May 1904.

2*c* HI and RH Archduchess *Mathilde* Maria Adelgunde of Austria, *b* 25 Jan 1849; *d* 6 June 1867.

2*b* HI and RH Archduke *Karl Ferdinand* of Austria, *b* 29 July 1818, *m* 18 April 1854, HI and RH Archduchess *Elisabeth* Franziska Maria (*b* 17 Jan 1831; *d* 14 Feb 1903), widow of HI and RH Archduke Ferdinand of Austria-Este (*see p* 255), and elder dau of HI and RH Archduke Joseph of Austria, Palatine of Hungary (*see p* 255), and *d* 20 Nov 1874, having had issue,

1*c* HI and RH Archduke Franz Joseph of Austria, *b* 5, *d* 13 March 1855.

2*c* HI and RH Archduke *Friedrich* Maria Albrecht Wilhelm Karl of Austria, Duke of Teschen, *b* 4 June 1856, *m* 8 Oct 1878, HSH Princess *Isabelle* Hedwige Françoise Nathalie (*b* 27 Feb 1856; *d* 5 Sept 1931), elder dau of HSH Rudolf, 11th Duke von Croy, and *d* 30 Dec 1936, leaving issue,

1*d* HI and RH Archduke *Albrecht* Franz Joseph Karl Friedrich Georg Hubert Maria of Austria, *b* 24 July 1897, *m* 1st 16 July 1930 (*m* diss by div 1937), *Irene* Dora (*b* 22 Dec 1897), formerly wife of Dr Louis Rudnay de Rudno et Divékujfalu, and dau of Johann Lelbach. He *m* 2ndly 9 May 1938 (*m* diss by div), Juliana (*b* 1 Nov 1911), dau of Béla Bocskay de Felsó-Bánya, and by her had issue,

1*e* •*Charlotte* Isabella Maria Christine Esther Katharina Pia Habsburg-Lothringen, *b* 3 March 1940.

2*e* •*Ildiko* Katharina Isabella Henriette Alice Maria Habsburg-Lothringen, *b* 19 Feb 1942.

He *m* 3rdly, •Lydia Strauss, and *d* 23 July 1955.

1*d* HI and RH Archduchess *Maria Christina* Isabelle Natalie of Austria, *b* 17 Nov 1879, *m* 10 May 1902, HSH Hereditary Prince *Emanuel* Alfred Leopold Franz zu Salm und zu Salm-Salm, Wild- und Rheingraf (*b* 30 Nov 1871; *d* 19 Aug 1916), and *d* 6 Aug 1962, leaving issue,

1*e* •HSH *Nikolaus Leopold* Heinrich Alfred Emmanuel Friedrich Antonius, 13th Prince zu Salm and 8th Prince zu Salm-Salm [*Haus Rhéde, Rhéde bei Bocholt, Westfalen, Postfach 44, Germany*], *b* 14 Feb 1906, *m* 1st 19 July 1928 (*m* diss by div 1948), HSH Princess Maria *Ida* Leonhardine Hedwig Mechtildis Balthasara (*b* 26 Feb 1909), yst dau of HSH Carl Philipp, 4th Prince von Wrede, and has had issue,

1*f* HSH Hereditary Prince *Alfred* Franz Emmanuel Christophorus Bruno Melchior zu Salm und Salm-Salm, Wild- und Rheingraf, *b* 6 Oct 1930; *k* in an air raid 21 March 1945.

2*f* •HSH Hereditary Prince *Carl Philipp* Josef Petrus Cœlestinus Balthasar zu Salm und Salm-Salm [*Düsseldorf, Kaiserswerth, Niederheinstrasse 358, Germany*], *b* 19 May 1933, *m* 8 Feb 1961, •*Erika* Carla Eleonora Helga Sophie-Luise (*b* 19 March 1935), 3rd dau of Ernst von Morgen, and has issue,

1*g* •HSH Prince *Emanuel* Philipp Nikolaus Johann Felix zu Salm und Salm-Salm, Wild- und Rheingraf, *b* 6 Dec 1961.

2*g* •HSH Prince *Philipp* Petrus Andreas Antonius Joachim zu Salm und Salm-Salm, Wild- und Rheingraf, *b* 5 July 1963.

1*f* •HSH Princess *Konstance* Maria Theresia Jakobea Kaspara zu Salm und Salm-Salm, Wild- und Rheingräfin [*Anholt, Westfalen, Haus Hardenberg, Germany*], *b* 25 July 1929.

2*f* •HSH Princess *Anna* Huberta Maria Alfonsa Kaspara zu Salm und Salm-Salm, Wild- und Rheingräfin [*Anholt, Westfalen, Haus Hardenberg, Germany*], *b* 2 Aug 1935.

3*f* •HSH Princess *Margarethe* Cecile Johanna Alfonsa Melchiora zu Salm und Salm-Salm, Wild- und Rheingräfin [*Moulin du bac, Olivet, Loiret, France*], *b* (twin with Princess Anna) 2 Aug 1935, *m* 23 Sept 1957, György Szolnoki-Scheffsik (*b* 11 July 1926; *d* 30 April 1965), and has issue,

1*g* •*Stephan* Jean Georges Scheffsik de Szolnok, *b* 10 May 1958.

2*g* •Jean Stephan Georges Scheffsik de Szolnok, *b* 2 Aug 1963.

1*g* •Portia Isadora Constance Scheffsik de Szolnok, *b* 15 Jan 1960.

2*g* •Cecile Scheffsik de Szolnok, *b* 9 July 1961.

He *m* 2ndly 19 Oct 1950 (*m* diss by div 1961), *Eleonore* Sophie Eveline (*b* 24 Nov 1919), 2nd dau of late Wilhelm Siegfried von Zitzewitz, and by her had issue,

3*f* •HSH Prince *Ludwig-Wilhelm* Carl Emanuel Jörg Nikolaus zu Salm und Salm-Salm, Wild- und Rheingraf, *b* 15 April 1953.

He *m* 3rdly 23 March 1962, •Maria (*b* 23 June 1930), dau of Léon Moret, and by her has issue,

4*f* •HSH Prince *Christian-Nikolaus* Lucius Piero Angelus zu Salm und Salm-Salm, Wild- und Rheingraf, *b* 25 Aug 1964.

1*e* •HSH Princess *Isabella* Maria Rosa Katharina Antonia zu Salm und Salm-Salm, Wild- und Rheingräfin [*Kevelaer, Niederrhein, Friedenstrasse 53, Germany*], *b* 13 Feb 1903, *m* 8 Sept 1925, Count *Felix* Maximilian Ludwig Georg Aloysius Hubertus Joseph Maria von Loë (*b* 1 Sept 1896; *k* in action 25 July 1944), and has had issue,

1*f* •Count *Friedrich* (*Fritz*) Paul Emanuel Christoph Hubertus Maria von Loë [*4179 Wissen, Post Weeze, Niederrhein, Germany*], *b* 8 June 1926, *m* •*Inez* Helene Elisabeth Dorothea Konrad Hubertus Maria (*b* 6 Feb 1935), eldest dau of Baron Maximilian von Boeselager, and has issue,

1*g* •Baron *Raphael* Felix Maximilian Pius Maria von Loë, *b* 30 Aug 1958.

2*g* •Baron *Wessel* Martin Wolfgang Philipp Maria von Loë, *b* 10 Nov 1959.

3*g* •Baron *Winfried* Johannes Benedikt Maria von Loë, *b* 29 July 1961.

4*g* •Baron *Augustinus* von Loë, b 12 June 1966.
1*g* •Baroness Paula von Loë, *b* 17 May 1963.
2*f* •Baron Clemens *Wessel* Albrecht Cyriakus Joseph Hubertus Maria von Loë [*5307 Wachtberg-Adendorf, Germany*], *b* 8 Aug 1928, *m* 7 May 1957, •H Ill H Countess *Marie Sophie* Josepha Elisabeth Walburga (*b* 5 Dec 1932), 4th dau of H Ill H Count Georg von Waldburg-Zeil, by his wife HI and RH Archduchess Gertrud of Austria, Princess of Tuscany (*see p* 244), and has issue,
1*g* •Baron *Georg* Friedrich Benedikt Maria von Loë, *b* 18 April 1958.
2*g* •Baron *Felix* Franz Martin von Loë, *b* 30 Aug 1960.
3*g* •Baron *Philipp* Joseph Bonifatius Christophorus Maria von Loë, *b* 11 Oct 1961.
1*g* •Baroness *Maria Annunciata* von Loë, *b* 15 Feb 1963.
2*g* •Baroness Agnes von Loë, *b* 25 April 1966.
3*g* •Baroness *Marie Sophie* von Loë, *b* 31 May 1969.
3*f* •Baron *Franz* Raphael Viktor Hubertus Christoph von Loë [*Kevelaer, Niederrhein, Friedenstrasse 53, Germany*], *b* 24 Oct 1936.
1*f* •Baroness *Christine* Maria Georgia Ignatia von Loë, *b* 31 July 1927, *m* 30 Aug 1949, •HSH Prince Maria *Johannes* Paul Kilian Joseph Alois Anton Michael zu Löwenstein-Wertheim-Rosenberg (*b* 8 July 1919) [*Schluifeld, Post Wessling, OBayern, Germany*], and has issue,
1*g* •HSH Prince Maria *Michael* Aloysius Felix Thomas Cyriacus Bernhard Johannes zu Löwenstein-Wertheim-Rosenberg, *b* 20 Dec 1950.
2*g* •HSH Prince Maria *Karl* Emanuel Ludger Petrus zu Löwenstein--Wertheim-Rosenberg, *b* 18 Jan 1952.
3*g* •HSH Prince Maria *Felix* Friedrich Johannes Pius Faustinus zu Löwenstein-Wertheim-Rosenberg, *b* 15 Feb 1954.
4*g* •HSH Prince Maria *Martin* Carl Wolfgang Franz Rasso zu Löwenstein-Wertheim-Rosenberg, *b* 15 April 1961.
5*g* •HSH Prince *Stephan* Wenzeslaus Erwein Korbinian Maria Rosario zu Löwenstein-Wertheim-Rosenberg, *b* 7 Oct 1968.
1*g* •HSH Princess Maria *Isabella* Josephine Ulrike Ludmilla Christine zu Löwenstein-Wertheim-Rosenberg, *b* 2 Nov 1956.
2*g* •HSH Princess Maria *Josephine* Sophie Konrada Monika Afra zu Löwenstein-Wertheim-Rosenberg, *b* 23 April 1958.
2*f* •Baroness Maria *Elisabeth* Leopoldine Josepha Theresia von Loë, *b* 15 March 1930, *m* 22 Sept 1954, •Baron *Philipp* Neri Maria Assumpta Georg Hubert Anselm Kasimir José Rudolf Markus d'Aviano Wambolt von Umstadt (*b* 15 Aug 1918) [*Münster i W, Heerdestrasse 6, Germany*].
3*f* Baroness Paula Therese Franziska Maria von Loë, *b* 1 March 1931; *d unm* 29 Oct 1950.
4*f* •Baroness *Maria* Rosa Maximiliane Klothilde Huberta von Loë [*Kevelaer, Niederrhein, Friedenstrasse 53, Germany*], *b* 3 June 1939.
2*e* •HSH Princess *Rosemary* Friederike Isabelle Eleonore Henriette Antonia zu Salm und Salm-Salm, Wild- und Rheingräfin [*Schloss Persenbeug, N Austria*], *b* 13 April 1904, *m* 25 Nov 1926, HI and RH Archduke *Hubert Salvator* Rainer Maria Joseph Ignatius of Austria, Prince of Tuscany (*b* 30 April 1894; *d* 24 March 1971) (*see p* 242), and has issue,
1*f* •HI and RH Archduke *Friedrich Salvator* Franz Karl Rainer Gabriel Matthäus Vincentius Hubert Maria Joseph Ignatius of Austria, Prince of Tuscany [*Schloss Rorregg, Post Ysper, N Austria*], *b* 27 Nov 1927, *m* 18 June 1955, •Countess *Margarethe* Isabella Maria Gemma (*b* 13 May 1926), 3rd dau of Count Sándor Kálnoky von Köröspatak, and has issue,
1*g* •HI and RH Archduke *Leopold Salvator* Hubert Maria Rainer Judas Thaddäus Alexander Maximilian Stephan Franziskus Pius Alois of Austria, Prince of Tuscany, *b* 16 Oct 1956.
2*g* •HI and RH Archduke *Alexander Salvator* Maria Josef Raphael Pius of Austria, Prince of Tuscany, *b* 12 April 1959.
1*g* •HI and RH Archduchess Maria *Bernadette* Christa Agnes Josepha Raphaella of Austria, Princess of Tuscany, *b* 10 Feb 1958.
2*g* •HI and RH Archduchess *Katharina* Mathilde Aloisia Maria Elisabeth Raphaella of Austria, Princess of Tuscany, *b* 1 Nov 1960.
2*f* •HI and RH Archduke *Andreas Salvator* Gabriel Gottfried Petrus Paulus Augustinus Severinus Maria Josephus Hubertus Ignatius of Austria, Prince of Tuscany [*Granja 4, Calle 1a, Madrid, Spain*], *b* 28 April 1936.
3*f* •HI and RH Archduke *Markus* Emanuel *Salvator* Franziskus de Paula Stanislaus Gregorius Josaphat Florian Joseph Hubert Ignatius of Austria, Prince of Tuscany, *b* 2 April 1946.
4*f* •HI and RH Archduke *Johann* Maximilian Salvator Benedictus Ambrosius Pius Lukas Wolfgang Maria Joseph Hubert Ignatius of Austria, Prince of Tuscany, *b* 18 Sept 1947.
5*f* •HI and RH Archduke *Michael Salvator* Konrad Johannes Aloisius Franziskus Xaverius Barnabas Antonius Maria Josephus Hubertus Ignatius of Austria, Prince of Tuscany, *b* (twin with Archduke Johann) 18 Sept 1947.
1*f* •HI and RH Archduchess *Agnes* Christina Franziska Caroline Theresia Raphaella Johanna Magdalena Huberta Josepha Ignatia of Austria, Princess of Tuscany, *b* 14 Dec 1928, *m* 17 Feb 1949, •HSH Prince *Karl Alfred* Maria Johannes Baptista Heinrich Aloys Georg Hartmann Ignatius Benediktus Franz Joseph Rochus of Liechtenstein (*b* 16 Aug 1910) [*Alserbachstrasse 16, A-1090 Vienna, Austria*], and has issue,
1*g* •HSH Prince *Dominik* Volkmar Hubert Alois Maria Josef Thaddäus Thomas Paulus Karl Ignatius Severius of Liechtenstein, *b* 20 June 1950.
2*g* •HSH Prince *Andreas* Duarte Emanuel Ulrich Benedikt Josef Maria Karl Rafael Ignatius Matthias Paulus of Liechtenstein, *b* 25 Feb 1952.
3*g* •HSH Prince *Gregor* Heinrich Augustinus Judas Thaddäus Josef Maria Pius Paulus Antonius Stefan Salvator of Liechtenstein, *b* 18 April 1954.
1*g* •HSH Princess *Alexandra* Maria Christina Aloisia Ulrike Henriette Agnes Ignatia Pia Gabriela Anastasia of Liechtenstein, *b* 25 Dec 1955.
2*g* •HSH Princess *Maria* Pia of Liechtenstein, *b* 6 Aug 1960.
3*g* •HSH Princess *Katharina* Maria Christina Henriette Valerie Agnes of Liechtenstein, *b* 27 Jan 1964.
4*g* •HSH Princess *Brigitta* Ulrike Rosa Marie Elisabeth Aloisia Hermengilde of Liechtenstein, *b* 13 April 1967.
2*f* •HI and RH Archduchess *Maria Margaretha* Elisabeth Franziska Josepha Valeria Emanuela Michaela Philippa Rosa Huberta Ignatia of Austria, Princess of Tuscany [*Schloss Persenbeug, N Austria*], *b* 29 Jan 1930.

3*f* ●HI and RH Archduchess *Maria Ludowika* Isabelle Alfonsa Anna Thaddea Ferdinanda Katharina Huberta Marie Josepha Ignatia of Austria, Princess of Tuscany [*Schloss Persenbeug, N Austria*], *b* 31 Jan 1931.

4*f* ●HI and RH Archduchess *Maria Adelheid* (*Alix*) Theodora Antonia Bartholomea Leopolda Amalia Mathilde Markus d'Aviano Huberta Josepha Ignatia of Austria, Princess of Tuscany [*Schloss Persenbeug, N Austria*], *b* 28 July 1933.

5*f* ●HI and RH Archduchess *Elisabeth* Mathilde Karoline Alberta Jacobea Martina Helena Lucia Maria Josepha Huberta Ignatia of Austria, Princess of Tuscany, *b* 18 March 1935, *m* 6 July 1959, ●HSH Prince *Heinrich* Weikhard Rudolf Gobertus Felix Maria von Auersperg-Breunner (*b* 21 May 1931) [*Schloss Wald, bei St Pölten, N Austria*], and has issue,

1*g* ●HSH Prince Johann *Weikhard* Karl Thaddäus Severin Gobertus Maria von Auersperg-Breunner, *b* 23 Oct 1961.

2*g* ●HSH Prince *Maximilian* Andreas Karl Blasius Thaddäus Gobertus Maria von Auersperg-Breunner, *b* 3 Feb 1964.

1*g* ●HSH Princess *Isabel* Maria Ernestina Silvester Thaddäa Leopoldina Gobertina von Auersperg-Breunner, *b* 31 Dec 1962.

2*g* ●HSH Princess *Dominica* von Auersperg-Breunner, *b* 28 Feb 1970.

6*f* ●HI and RH Archduchess *Josepha* Hedwig Georgia Henriette Barbara Agathe Stefana Matthia Koloman Maria Huberta Ignatia of Austria, Princess of Tuscany, *b* 2 Sept 1939, *m* 3 Sept 1969, ●Count *Clemens* Eugen Josef Leopold Maria von Waldstein, Herr von Wartenberg (*b* 17 June 1935) [*A-2081 Niederfladnitz Karlslust, N Austria*].

7*f* ●HI and RH Archduchess *Valerie* Isabelle Maria Anna Alfonsa Desideria Brigitte Sophia Thomasia Huberta Josepha Ignatia of Austria, Princess of Tuscany, *b* 23 May 1941, *m* 30 Sept 1966, ●HRH *Maximilian* Andreas Friedrich Gustav Ernst August Bernhard, Margrave of Baden, Head of the Grand Ducal House of Baden (*b* 3 July 1933) [*7777 Schloss Salem, Baden, Germany*], and has issue (*see p* 290).

8*f* ●HI and RH Archduchess *Maria Alberta* Dominika Benedikta Dorothea Felicitas Beatrix Simon Josaphat Huberta Josepha Ignatia of Austria, Princess of Tuscany, *b* 1 June 1944, *m* 10 May 1969, ●Baron Konrad *Alexander* von Kottwitz-Erdödy (*b* 24 Sept 1943) [*A-7512 Kohfidisch, Burgenland, Austria*].

3*e* ●HSH Princess *Cäcilie* Marie Alphonsine Emmanuela Antonia zu Salm und Salm-Salm, Wild- und Rheingräfin [*Schloss Dyck, über Neuss 2, Rheinland, Germany*], *b* 8 March 1911, *m* 27 May 1930, HSH *Franz Joseph* Alfred Leopold Hermann Maria, 6th Prince and Altgraf zu Salm-Reifferscheidt-Krautheim und Dyck (*b* 7 April 1899; *d* 13 June 1958), and has issue,

1*f* ●H Ill H Altgräfin *Marie Christine* Erwine Isabella Innocentia Thaddäa zu Salm-Reifferscheidt-Krautheim und Dyck, *b* 4 Jan 1932, *m* 27 July 1955, ●Count Levinus *Peter* Georg Henning Antonius Maria Apollonia Wolff-Metternich zur Gracht (*b* 5 March 1929) [*D-3404 Schloss Adelebsen, Kr Northeim, Germany*], and has issue,

1*g* ●Count *Simeon* Peter Stanislas Heinrich Maria Apollonia Wolff-Metternich zur Gracht, *b* 30 April 1965.

1*g* ●Countess Georgina (*Gina*) Cäcilia Sophia Paula Maria Appolonia Wolff-Metternich zur Gracht, *b* 18 Oct 1956.

2*g* ●Countess *Helene* Christine Salome Maria Apollonia Wolff-Metternich zur Gracht, *b* 22 Oct 1957.

3*g* ●Countess *Maria del Pilar* Emanuel[a] Johanna Thomasine Apollonia Wolff[-] Metternich zur Gracht, *b* 21 Dec 1959.

2*f* ●H Ill H Altgräfin *Marie-Anne* Friede[-]rike Christine Leopoldine Emmanuel[a] Helena zu Salm-Reifferscheidt-Krautheim und Dyck [*Petersham Lodge, Richmond, Surrey*], *b* 18 Aug 1933, *m* 27 July 1964, as his 2n[d] wife, Hon Alexander Campbell Geddes, OBE, MC, TD (*b* 24 Sept 1910; *d* 22 Sep[t] 1972), 2nd son of 1st Baron Geddes, PC, GCMG, KCB, TD (*see* BURKE'S *Peerage*), and has issue,

●Stephen George Geddes, *b* 28 June 1969.

●Camilla Joanna Geddes, *b* 10 Dec 1966.

3*f* ●H Ill H Altgräfin *Rosemary* Ferdinand[e] Dorothea Matthea Michaela Joseph[a] Thaddäa zu Salm-Reifferscheidt-Krautheim und Dyck, *b* 24 Feb 1937, *m* 11 Sept 1959, ●Count *Johannes* Georg Carl Friedrich Huyn (*b* 3 July 1930) [*Neuburg, a d Donau-Burgwaldhof, Bayern, Germany*], and ha[s] issue,

1*g* ●Count *Johannes* Joseph Felix Maria Victor Franziskus Xavier Huyn, *b* 28 July 1960.

2*g* ●Count Franz Ferdinand Christian Paul Joseph Maria Emanuel Huyn, *b* 16 March 1964.

1*g* ●Countess *Marie Christine* Helena Irmgard Cäcilia Ignatia Immaculata Huyn, *b* 27 Nov 1961.

2*g* ●Countess *Maria Assunta* Ernestine Michaela Katherina Natalie Huyn, *b* 30 April 1965.

4*f* ●H Ill H Altgräfin *Isabella* Marie Franziska Gabrielle Pia zu Salm-Reifferscheidt-Krautheim und Dyck, *b* 19 Feb 1939, *m* 2 Oct 1962, ●HSH *Franz Albrecht* Maximilian Wolfgang Josef Thaddäus Maria Metternich-Sándor, 4th Duke von Ratibor, 4th Prince von Corvey, Prince zu Hohenlohe-Schillingsfürst (*b* 23 Oct 1920) [*347 Höxter Corvey, Germany*], and has issue,

1*g* ●HSH Hereditary Prince *Victor* von Ratibor und Corvey, Prince zu Hohenlohe-Schillingsfürst, *b* 31 March 1964.

2*g* ●HSH Prince *Tassilo Ferdinand* von Ratibor und Corvey, Prince zu Hohenlohe-Schillingsfürst, *b* 23 Oct 1965.

3*g* ●HSH Prince *Stephan Aloysius* von Ratibor und Corvey, Prince zu Hohenlohe-Schillingsfürst, *b* 2 July 1968.

4*g* ●HSH Prince *Benedikt Christian* von Ratibor und Corvey, Prince zu Hohenlohe-Schillingsfürst, *b* 25 Jan 1971.

5*f* ●H Ill H Altgräfin *Gabrielle* Louisanne Huberta Theodora Maria Immaculata Michaela Thaddäa zu Salm-Reifferscheidt-Krautheim und Dyck, *b* 9 Nov 1941, *m* 12 Dec 1961, ●Count *Ernst-Friedrich* Johann Maria Josef Benedictus Adam Zeno Gregor von Goëss (*b* 12 March 1932) [*Staupitzhof, 9061 Wölfnitz, Austria*], and has issue,

1*g* ●Count *Moritz-Heinrich* von Goëss, *b* 5 June 1966.

1*g* ●Countess *Sveva* Cäcilia von Goëss, *b* 16 July 1962.

2*g* ●Countess *Philippa* Cäcilia von Goëss, *b* 8 July 1964.

6*f* ●H Ill H Altgräfin *Cäcilie* Christine Caroline Maria Immaculata Michaela Thaddäa zu Salm-Reifferscheidt-Krautheim und Dyck, *b* 14 Dec 1943.

2*d* HI and RH Archduchess *Maria Anna* Isabelle Epiphanie Eugenie Gabriele of Austria, *b* 6 Jan 1882, *m* 25 May 1903, HRH Prince *Elie* Roberto Carlos Maria Pio José of Bourbon, Head of the Ducal House of Parma (*b* 23 July 1880; *d* 27 June 1959), and *d* 25 Feb 1940, having had issue,

1*e* HRH Prince *Carlo* Luigi Federigo Antonio Roberto Elias Maria of Bourbon-Parma, *b* 22 Sept 1905; *d* 26 Sept 1912.

2*e* ●HRH *Roberto* (II) Ranieri Alexis Luigi Enrico Deodato Elias Pio Maria of Bourbon,

Head of the Ducal House of Parma [*Schloss Schwarzau, nr Vienna, Austria; Metternichgasse 7, A-1030 Vienna, Austria*], *b* 7 Aug 1909.
3*e* HRH Prince *Francesco* Alfonso Gabriele Luigi Enrico Roberto Pio Carlo Elias Maria of Bourbon-Parma, *b* 14 June 1913; *d unm* 29 May 1939.
1*e* ●HRH Princess *Elisabetta* Maria Anna Pia Luisa of Bourbon-Parma [*Metternichgasse 7, A-1030 Vienna, Austria*], *b* 17 March 1904.
2*e* ●HRH Princess *Maria* Francesca Giuseppa Raniera Enrichetta Pia Luisa of Bourbon-Parma [*Metternichgasse 7, A-1030 Vienna, Austria*], *b* 5 Sept 1906.
3*e* HRH Princess *Giovanna* Isabella Alfonsina Pia Luisa Maria of Bourbon-Parma, *b* 8 July 1916; *d unm* 1 Nov 1949.
4*e* ●HRH Princess *Alice* Maria Francesca Luisa Pia Ana Valeria of Bourbon-Parma [*Hermanos Pinzon 4, Madrid 16, Spain*], *b* 13 Nov 1917, *m* 16 April 1936, HRH Prince *Alfonso* Maria Leone Cristino Alfonso di Liguori Antonio Carlos Andres Francisco Saverio of Bourbon-Two Sicilies, Infante of Spain (*b* 30 Nov 1901; *d* 3 Feb 1964) (*see p* 234), and has issue,
1*f* ●HRH Prince *Carlos* Maria Alfonso Marcelo of Bourbon-Two Sicilies [*José Ortej Gasset 26, Madrid, Spain*], *b* 16 Jan 1938, *m* 12 May 1965, ●HRH Princess *Anne*-Marguerite-Brigitte-Marie of France (*b* 4 Dec 1938), 3rd dau of HRH Prince Henri, Count of Paris, Head of the Royal House of France, and has issue,
1*g* ●HRH Prince *Pedro* Juan Maria Alejo Saturnino y todos los Santos of Bourbon-Two Sicilies, *b* 16 Oct 1968.
1*g* ●HRH Princess *Cristina* Isabella Maria Luisa of Bourbon-Two Sicilies, *b* 20 March 1966.
2*g* ●HRH Princess *Maria* Paloma Diana Irene of Bourbon-Two Sicilies, *b* 5 April 1967.
3*g* ●HRH Princess *Inés* Maria Alicia Ana Isabel of Bourbon-Two Sicilies, *b* 20 April 1971.
1*f* ●HRH Princess *Teresa* Maria Francisca Dorotea of Bourbon-Two Sicilies, *b* 6 Feb 1937, *m* 16 April 1961, ●Don Iñigo Moreno y Arteaga, 12th Marqués de Laula (*b* 2 Jan 1935) [*Zurbano 36, Madrid, Spain*], and has issue,
1*g* ●Don Rodrigo Moreno y Borbón, *b* 1 Feb 1962.
2*g* ●Don Alfonso Moreno y Borbón, *b* 19 Oct 1965.
3*g* ●Don Fernando Moreno y Borbón, *b* 8 July 1969.
1*g* ●Doña Alicia Moreno y Borbón, *b* 6 June 1964.
2*g* ●Doña Beatriz Moreno y Borbón, *b* 10 May 1967.
3*g* ●Doña Clara Moreno y Borbón, *b* 14 June 1971.
4*g* ●Doña Delia Moreno y Borbón, *b* 30 Aug 1972.
2*f* ●HRH Princess *Inés* Maria Alicia of Bourbon-Two Sicilies, *b* 18 Feb 1940, *m* 21 Jan 1965, ●Don Luis Morales y Aguado (*b* 8 Oct 1933), and has issue,
1*g* ●Don Manuel Morales y Borbón, *b* 16 Dec 1971.
1*g* ●Doña *Isabel* Ana Maria Morales y Borbón, *b* 10 April 1966.
2*g* ●Doña *Eugenia* Maria Morales y Borbón, *b* 14 Dec 1967.
3*g* ●Doña Sonia Morales y Borbón, *b* 9 Dec 1969.
5*e* ●HRH Princess *Maria Cristina* Albertina Enrichetta Luisa Pia Carlotta of Bourbon-Parma [*Metternichgasse 7, A-1030 Vienna, Austria*], *b* 7 June 1925.
3*d* HI and RH Archduchess *Maria Henriette* Caroline Gabriele of Austria, *b* 10 Jan 1883, *m* 3 June 1908, HSH Prince *Gottfried* Maximilian Maria zu Hohenlohe-Waldenburg-Schillingsfürst, Prince von Ratibor und Corvey (*b* 8 Nov 1867; *d* 7 Nov 1932), and *d* 2 Sept 1956, having had issue,
1*e* HSH Prince *Friedrich* Konrad Konstantin Gottfried Marie zu Hohenlohe-Waldenburg-Schillingsfürst, Prince von Ratibor und Corvey, *b* 18 Feb 1913; *d* in a Russian p o w camp Dec 1945, *unm.*
1*e* ●HSH Princess Marie *Elisabeth* Henriette zu Hohenlohe-Waldenburg-Schillingsfürst, Princess von Ratibor und Corvey, *b* 27 Sept 1909.
2*e* ●HSH Princess *Natalie* Isabelle Marie zu Hohenlohe-Waldenburg-Schillingsfürst, Princess von Ratibor und Corvey, *b* 28 July 1911.
4*d* HI and RH Archduchess *Natalie* Maria Theresia of Austria, *b* 12 Jan 1884; *d* 23 March 1898.
5*d* HI and RH Archduchess *Stephanie* Marie Isabelle of Austria, *b* 1 May 1886; *d* 29 Aug 1890.
6*d* HI and RH Archduchess *Gabrielle* Maria Theresia of Austria, *b* 14 Sept 1887; *d unm* 15 Nov 1954.
7*d* ●HI and RH Archduchess *Isabella* Maria Theresia Christine Eugenie of Austria [*22 avenue Bel Air, CH-1814 La Tour-de-Peilz, Kt Waadt, Switzerland*], *b* 17 Nov 1888, *m* 10 Feb 1912 (*m* annulled 1913), HRH Prince *Georg* Franz Joseph Luitpold Maria of Bavaria (*b* 2 April 1880; *d* 31 May 1943).
8*d* HI and RH Archduchess *Marie Alice* Emanuele Agnes Anna of Austria, *b* 15 Jan 1893, *m* 8 May 1920, Baron *Friedrich-Heinrich* Karl Maria Waldbott von Bassenheim (*b* 17 Sept 1889; *d* 16 Dec 1959), and *d* 1 July 1962, leaving issue,
1*e* ●Baron *Anton* Friedrich Martin Bartholomäus Waldbott von Bassenheim, *b* 24 Aug 1922, *m* ●Thea Schanderer (*b* 13 Jan 1938), and has issue,
1*f* ●Baron Christian Friedrich Anton Waldbott von Bassenheim, *b* 19 April 1961.
2*f* ●Baron Peter Josef Waldbott von Bassenheim, *b* 24 Jan 1966.
1*f* ●Baroness Christine Maria Alice Waldbott von Bassenheim, *b* 6 Aug 1963.
2*f* ●Baroness Alice Stefanie Waldbott von Bassenheim, *b* (twin with Baron Peter Josef) 24 Jan 1966.
2*e* ●Baron *Paul* Albrecht Friedrich Cyrille Maria Waldbott von Bassenheim [*Halbturn, Burgenland, Austria*], *b* 9 Feb 1924, *m* 16 June 1958, ●Countess Marie Theresia (*b* 17 Aug 1929), dau of Count Eduard Capello von Wickenburg.
3*e* ●Baron *Joseph* Clemens Alexius Friedrich Polycarp Maria Waldbott von Bassenheim [*München, Elisabethstrasse 28, Germany*], *b* 26 Jan 1931.
1*e* ●Baroness *Maria Immaculata* Hedwig Isabella Waldbott von Bassenheim, *b* 27 July 1921, *m* 10 Dec 1947, as his 2nd wife, Count *Hans Heribert* Wilhelm Veit Adolf zu Toerring-Jettenbach (*b* 25 Dec 1903) [*8031 Schloss Seefeld, Kr Starnberg, OBayern, Germany*], and has issue,
1*f* ●Count *Hans-Kaspar* Heribert Veit Friedrich zu Toerring-Jettenbach, *b* 22 July 1953.
2*f* ●Count *Maximilian-Gaudenz* Karl Ludwig Wilhelm zu Toerring-Jettenbach, *b* 29 Jan 1955.
1*f* ●Countess *Alice* Maria Immaculata Sophie Isabella zu Toerring-Jettenbach, *b* 5 June 1949.
2*f* ●Countess *Marie-José* Gabriele Stefanie zu Toerring-Jettenbach, *b* 27 Oct 1950.
3*f* ●Countess *Sophie* Maria Antonia Eleonore zu Toerring-Jettenbach, *b* 26 March 1957.
2*e* ●Baroness *Isabella* Klementine Hedwig Theodore Maria Waldbott von Bassenheim, *b* 20 April 1926, *m* 23 April 1952, ●Count

Pongrác Somssich von Sáard (*b* 12 Aug 1920) [*Usumbura, Burundi, Africa*], and has issue,
1*f* ●Count István László Friedrich Marie-Gobert Somssich von Sáard, *b* 23 May 1953.
2*f* ●Count Gabor Hans Heribert Pongrác Somssich von Sáard, *b* 14 March 1955.
3*f* ●Count Christoph László Paul Frederic Somssich von Sáard, *b* 26 July 1960.
3*e* ●Baroness *Stefanie* Elisabeth Alice Maria Waldbott von Bassenheim, *b* 19 Nov 1929, *m* 27 Sept 1955, ●H Ill H *Johannes* von Nepomuk Maria Eusebius Pius, Count zu Königsegg-Aulendorf (*b* 13 April 1925) [*Königseggwald über Aulendorf, Württemberg, Germany*], and has issue,
1*f* ●H Ill H Hereditary Count Maximilian Ulrich Philipp Eusebius Benno zu Königsegg-Aulendorf *b* 16 June 1958.
2*f* ●Count Markus Maximilian Eusebius Johannes zu Königsegg-Aulendorf, *b* 16 May 1963.
1*f* ●Countess Isabelle Gabrielle Maria Appolonia Eusebia zu Königsegg-Aulendorf, *b* 23 July 1956.
3*c* HI and RH Archduke *Karl Stephan* Eugen Viktor Felix Maria of Austria, *b* 5 Sept 1860, *m* 28 Feb 1886, HI and RH Archduchess *Maria Theresia* Antonia Immakulata Josephe Ferdinande Leopoldine Franziska Karoline Isabella Januaria Aloysia Christina Anna (*b* 18 Sept 1862; *d* 10 May 1933), eldest dau of HI and RH Archduke Karl Salvator of Austria, Prince of Tuscany, and *d* 7 April 1933, leaving issue,
1*d* HI and RH Archduke *Karl Albrecht* Nikolaus Leo Gratianus of Austria, *b* 18 Dec 1888, *m* 8 Nov 1920, ●*Alice* Elizabeth, who bears the title of Princess von Altenburg (*b* 18 Dec 1889) [*Engelbrektsgatan 23, Stockholm Ö, Sweden*], widow of Count Ludwig Badeni, and dau of Major Oscar Ankarcrona, and *d* 17 March 1951, having had issue,
1*e* ●Prince *Karl-Stefan* Maximilian Ferdinand Narcissus Maria von Altenburg [*Östervik 4, S-13011 Saltsjö-Duvnäs, Sweden*], *b* 29 Oct 1921, *m* 18 Sept 1952, ●Marie-Louise (*b* 4 Nov 1910), dau of August af Petersens, and has had issue,
Prince *Karl-Albrecht* Ferdinand Leopold Philipp Joseph Rafael Maria von Altenburg, *b* 24 Oct 1956; *d* 26 May 1957.
●Princess *Maria-Christina* Ninfa Renata Margarita Isabella Clara Eugenia Anselma von Altenburg, *b* 21 April 1953.
2e Prince *Karl-Albrecht* Maximilian Leon Maria Dominique von Altenburg, *b* 4 Aug 1926; *d* 19 Dec 1928.
1*e* ●Princess *Maria-Christina* Immaculata Elisabeth Renata Alice Gabriele von Altenburg [*Haus Roweida, CH-7270 Davos Platz, Switzerland*], *b* 8 Dec 1923.
2*e* ●Princess *Renata* Maria Theresia Alice Elisabeth von Altenburg, *b* 13 April 1931, *m* 26 June 1957, ●Don Eduardo de Zulueta y Dato (*b* 4 Dec 1923) [*O'Donnell 15, Madrid 9, Spain*], and has issue,
1*f* ●Don Carlos Eduardo Ernesto Maria George Rámon Anthony de Zulueta y Altenburg, *b* 19 Oct 1958.
2*f* ●Don Ernesto Maria Jaime Antonio Rámon Cristóbal de Zulueta y Altenburg, *b* 7 July 1961.
1*f* ●Doña Isabelle Maria Christina Immaculada Renata Tomasa de Zulueta y Altenburg, *b* 7 March 1965.
2*d* HI and RH Archduke *Leo Karl* Maria Kyrill Method of Austria, renounced his Imp and Royal style and titles on marriage and assumed the title of Count von Habsburg-Lothringen for himself and issue, *b* 5 July 1893, *m* 4 Oct 1922, ●Countess *Maria Klothilde* (*b* 6 Nov 1893), dau of Count Karl de Thuillieres von Montjoye-Vaufrey et de la Roche, and *d* 28 April 1939, leaving issue,
1*e* ●Count *Leo-Stephan* Maria Carl Wolfgang Rudolf Fidelis von Habsburg-Lothringen, *b* 12 June 1928, *m* 31 March 1962, ●Gabriele (*b* 15 June 1935), dau of Julius Kunert, and has issue,
●Count Albrecht Stanislaus Bernhard Matthias Manfred von Habsburg-Lothringen, *b* 6 Sept 1963.
●Countess Maria Isabella Klara von Habsburg-Lothringen, *b* 21 Dec 1962.
2*e* ●Count *Hugo Carl* Maria Leo Fidelis von Habsburg-Lothringen [*Vienna IV, Schikanedergasse 2, Austria*], *b* 27 Sept 1930.
1*e* ●Countess *Maria Desiderata* Theresa Fidelis Irene von Habsburg-Lothringen, *b* 3 Aug 1923, *m* 6 April 1947, ●Count *Wolfgang* Maria Benedikt Karl Edmund Ignatius Hartig (*b* 13 Aug 1922) [*Arsenal Objekt V, Vienna III, Austria*], and has issue,
1*f* ●Count *Karl Johann* Leo Maria Franz de Paula Wolfgang Edmund Hartig, *b* 8 June 1949.
2*f* ●Count *Andreas Maria* Franz de Paula Wolfgang Edmund Leopold Hartig, *b* 6 Feb 1952.
2*e* ●Countess *Mechtildis* Maria Irene Fidelis von Habsburg-Lothringen, *b* 14 Aug 1924, *m* 29 April 1948, ●*Manfred* Rambald Wenzeslaus Anton Maria, Count and Marquis von Piatti (*b* 22 July 1924) [*Schloss Loosdorf bei Mistelbach, N Austria*], and has issue,
1*f* ●Count *Alfons* Maria Ferdinand Leo Karl Judas Thaddäus Josef von Piatti, *b* 13 Sept 1950.
2*f* ●Count Michael von Piatti, *b* 23 Jan 1955.
3*f* ●Count Ferdinand von Piatti, *b* 23 March 1962.
4*f* ●Count Benedikt von Piatti, *b* 21 Jan 1966.
1*f* ●Countess *Andrea* Maria Anna Alexandra Theckla Gabriele von Piatti, *b* 3 Feb 1949.
3*e* ●Countess *Elisabeth* Irene Maria Fidelis von Habsburg-Lothringen [*Vienna IV, Schikanedergasse 2, Austria*], *b* 13 March 1927.
3*d* HI and RH Archduke *Wilhelm* Franz Joseph Karl of Austria, *b* 10 Feb 1895; *d* in a Russian concentration camp 1954.
1*d* ●HI and RH Archduchess *Eleonora* Maria Immakulata Christina Josepha Sosthenesia of Austria [*Karlsgasse 2b, Baden bei Wien, Austria*], *b* 28 Nov 1886, *m* 9 Jan 1913, Alfons von Kloss (*b* 9 June 1880; *d* 25 Aug 1953), and has had issue,
1*e* ●*Albrecht* Karl Stephan von Kloss, *b* 13 Oct 1913, *m* 4 Sept 1942, ●Erika (*b* 13 Oct 1920), dau of Guido Kaiser, and has issue,
1*f* ●Karl Stephan von Kloss, *b* 4 Oct 1943.
1*f* ●Maria Elisabeth Franziska von Kloss, *b* 3 Dec 1944.
2*f* ●Barbara Eleonore von Kloss, *b* 5 June 1946.
2*e* *Karl* Albrecht von Kloss, *b* 15 Feb 1915; *k* in action in World War II 5 Sept 1939.
3*e* ●*Rainer* Albrecht von Kloss, *b* 12 Oct 1916, *m* 17 Jan 1944, ●Cornelia (*b* 15 Jan 1920), dau of Cornelius Schoute, and has issue,
●Georg von Kloss, *b* 5 Sept 1954.
●Elisabeth von Kloss, *b* 26 Feb 1945.
4*e* ●*Ernst* Jerome von Kloss, *b* 19 Jan 1919, *m* 11 July 1953, ●*Rixta Maria* (*b* 27 April 1925), dau of Julius Eugen Hartig, and has issue,
1*f* ●Florian von Kloss, *b* 12 March 1954.
2*f* ●Thomas von Kloss, *b* 29 Dec 1956.
3*f* ●Nikolaus von Kloss, *b* 24 Sept 1957.
1*f* ●Andrea von Kloss, *b* 24 Dec 1958.
5*e* ●*Alfons* Salvator von Kloss [*5020 Salzburg, Judenbergweg 9, Austria*], *b* 3 May 1920, *m* 12 July 1947, ●Countess *Theresia* Bianca (*b* 12 March 1923), elder dau of late Count Max von Coreth zu Coredo, and has issue,
1*f* ●Andreas von Kloss, *b* 5 May 1948.
2*f* ●Johannes von Kloss, *b* 21 Nov 1949.

3f ●Alfons von Kloss, *b* 19 Sept 1953.
6e *Friedrich* Anton von Kloss, *b* 13 Feb 1922; *k* in action in World War II, Feb 1943.
7e ●*Stefan* Maximilian von Kloss, *b* 23 Nov 1933, *m* 3 Sept 1955, ●Ingrid (*b* 24 May 1936), dau of Wolfgang Morocutti, and has issue,
1f ●Christoph von Kloss, *b* 18 Feb 1959.
2f ●Marcus von Kloss, *b* 12 June 1960.
1f ●Michaela von Kloss, *b* 3 June 1956.
2f ●Marina von Kloss, *b* 28 Jan 1958.
1e ●*Maria* Theresia Franziska von Kloss, *b* 7 May 1925, *m* 30 April 1949, ●Walter Kaiser (*b* 5 Oct 1918), and has issue,
1f ●Martin Kaiser, *b* 20 April 1950.
2f ●Michael Guido Joseph Kaiser, *b* 23 March 1951.
3f ●Marius Kaiser, *b* 7 April 1952.
4f ●Christian Kaiser, *b* 2 Oct 1957.
1f ●Claudia Kaiser, *b* 7 Oct 1954.
2d HI and RH Archduchess *Renata Maria* Caroline Rainera Theresia Philomena Desideria Macaria of Austria, *b* 2 Jan 1888, *m* 16 Jan 1909, as his 1st wife, HSH Prince *Hieronim* Nikolaj Melchior Konstanty Dominik Maria Radziwill (*b* 6 Jan 1885; *d* in the Russian Deportation 6 April 1945), and *d* 16 May 1935, having had issue,
1e ●HSH Prince *Dominik* Rainer Karol Hieronim Maria Nikolaj Alfons Radziwill [*Palazzo Taverna, 36 via Monte Giordano, I-00186 Rome, Italy*], *b* 23 Jan 1911, *m* 1st 30 May 1938 (*m* diss by div 1946), HRH Princess Eugénie (*b* 10 Feb 1910), only dau of HRH Prince George of Greece and Denmark (*see p* 280), and has issue,
1f ●HSH Prince *Jerzy* Andrzej Dominik Hieronim Piotr Leon Radziwill, *b* 4 Nov 1942.
1f ●HSH Princess *Tatiana* Maria Renata Eugenia Elzbieta Malgorzata Radziwill, *b* 28 Aug 1939, *m* 26 March 1966, ●John Fruchaud (*b* 1 April 1937) [*35 rue de Grenelle, F-75 Paris 7, France*], and has issue,
●Alexis Fruchaud, *b* 25 Nov 1969.
●Fabiola Fruchaud, *b* 7 Feb 1967.
He *m* 2ndly 8 Jan 1947, ●*Lida* Lacey (*b* 1 Feb 1923), dau of John Van Schaick Bloodgood, and by her has issue,
2f ●HSH Princess Lida Maria *Renata* Radziwill, *b* 11 July 1954.
3f ●HSH Princess Maria *Ludwika* Jadwiga Radziwill, *b* 23 Jan 1956.
4f ●HSH Princess *Lida* Dominica Radziwill *b* 29 Aug 1959.
2e ●HSH Prince *Karol Hieronim* Celestyn Maria Konstanty Stanislaw Radziwill [*Calle Posadas 1683, Buenos Aires, Argentina*], *b* 3 May 1912, *m* 21 March 1949, ●Doña *Maria Luisa* (*b* 11 July 1913), dau of Don Eugenio de Alvear.
3e HSH Prince *Olbracht Hieronim* Maria Karol Zydor Stanislaw Radziwill, *b* 10 April 1914; *d* 23 June 1932.
4e ●HSH Prince *Leon Hieronim* Stanislaw Karol Maria Tadeusz Radziwill [*Avenida Pueyrredon 1867, Buenos Aires, Argentina*], *b* 28 Oct 1922.
1e ●HSH Princess *Maria Teresa* Kanuta Dominika Karolina Renata Radziwill [*A2572 Kaumberg, St Corona am Schöpfl, N Austria*], *b* 19 Jan 1910.
2e ●HSH Princess *Eleonora* Maria Aniela Alberta Renata Karolina Radziwill, *b* 2 Aug 1918, *m* 1st 21 April 1938, Count Benedykt Ladislaus Tyszkiewicz (*b* 2 Aug 1905; *d* 6 Feb 1956). She *m* 2ndly 16 Nov 1959, ●Roger de Froidcourt (*b* 13 Jan 1931) [*4 rue Charles Vildrac, F-94 Mont Mesly-Créteil, Val-de-Marne, France*].
3d HI and RH Archduchess *Mechtildis* Maria Christina Leona Theresia Rosario Nikosia of Austria, *b* 11 Oct 1891, *m* 11 Jan 1913, ●HSH Prince Aleksander *Olgierd* Johann Paul Anton Czartoryski (*b* 25 Oct 1888) [*Avenida Copacabana 74, Apt 402, Rio de Janeiro, Brazil*], and *d* 6 Feb 1966, leaving issue,
1e ●HSH Prince *Konstanty Stefan* Aleksander Adam Gracjan Czartoryski [*Calle Suipacha 1080, Buenos Aires, Argentina*], *b* 9 Dec 1913, *m* 21 Dec 1941, ●Countess Karolina (*b* 7 Dec 1917), dau of Count Henryk Plater-Zyberk, and has issue,
1f ●HSH Prince *Karol* Henryk Czartoryski, *b* 9 Dec 1942, *m* 29 Aug 1964, ●Aline (*b* 1940), dau of René Ternynck, and has issue,
●HSH Princess Maria Dolores Dorota Czartoryska, *b* 16 Sept 1965.
2f ●HSH Prince *Krzysztof* Hubert Czartoryski, *b* 25 Aug 1946.
2e ●HSH Prince *Aleksander* Chrystian Antoni Józef Czartoryski [*Rua São Bento 279, andor 11, São Paulo, Brazil*], *b* 21 Oct 1919.
1e ●HSH Princess *Cecylia* Teresa Immakulata Ilona Felicyta Elzbieta Helena Czartoryska, *b* 9 April 1915, *m* 25 June 1947, ●Jerzy Rostworowski (*b* 10 Sept 1910) [*Alameda Rocha Azevedo 644, São Paulo, Brazil*], and has issue,
1f ●Karol Stefan Rostworowski, *b* 27 May 1950.
2f ●Jerzy Olgierd Rostworowski, *b* 12 Feb 1953.
1f ●Isabella Maria Teresa Adelajda Rostworowska, *b* 30 March 1948.
2f ●Malgorzata Rostworowska, *b* 20 Dec 1956.
2e ●HSH Princess *Izabella* Maria Karolina Zuzanna Róza Marcelina Cypriana Dezyderia Felicja Mechtylda Czartoryska [*59 rue Maurice Wilmotte, Brussels, Belgium*], *b* 8 Aug 1917, *m* 8 Dec 1942, Count *Rafal* Ignaz Adalbert Adolf Lukas Maria Bninski (*b* 27 Feb 1918; *d* 13 Oct 1943), and has issue,
●Count *Karol* Andrzej Rafal Antoni Jósef Aleksander Konstanty Maria Bninski, *b* (posthumously) 15 Nov 1943.
4c HI and RH Archduke *Eugen* Ferdinand Pius Bernhard Felix Maria of Austria, *b* 21 May 1863; *d unm* 30 Dec 1954.
1c HI and RH Archduchess *Maria Christine* Desideria Henriette Felicitas Rainera of Austria, Queen-Regent of Spain 1885-1902, *b* 21 July 1858, *m* 29 Nov 1879, as his 2nd wife, HM King Alfonso XII of Spain, KG (*b* 28 Nov 1857; *d* 25 Nov 1885), and *d* 6 Feb 1929, having had issue,
1d HM King *Alfonso XIII* (Léon Fernando Maria Jaime Isidro Pascual Antonio) of Spain, KG (1902), GCVO (1897), Royal Victorian Chain, hon DCL Oxford (1926), Field Marshal in the British Army (1928) (Gen 1905), Col-in-Chief 16th/5th Lancers (1922) (Col-in-Chief 16th Lancers 1905-22), left the country 14 April 1931, *b* (posthumously) 17 May 1886, *m* 31 May 1906, HRH Princess *Victoria Eugénie* Julia Ena of Battenberg (*b* 24 Oct 1887; *d* 15 April 1969), only dau of HRH Prince Henry of Battenberg, by his wife HRH Princess Beatrice, yst dau of HM Queen Victoria, and *d* 28 Feb 1941, having had issue (*see p* 305).
1d HRH Infanta *Maria de las Mercedes* Isabel Teresa Cristina Alfonsa Jacinta of Spain, Princess of the Asturias, *b* 11 Sept 1880, *m* 14 Feb 1901, as his 1st wife, HRH Prince *Carlo* Maria Francesco d'Assisi Pasquale Ferdinando Antonio di Padova Francesco di Paula Alfonso Andrea Avelino Tancredi of the Two Sicilies, Infante of Spain, who renounced his rights of succession to the Two Sicilies 14 Dec 1900 and was naturalized in Spain 7 Feb 1901 (*b* 10 Nov 1870; *d* 11 Nov 1949), and *d* 17 Oct 1904, leaving issue,
1e HRH Prince *Alfonso* Maria Leone Cristino Alfonso di Liguori Antonio Carlos Andres Francisco Saverio of the Two Sicilies,

Infante of Spain, *b* 30 Nov 1901, *m* 16 April 1936, ●HRH Princess *Alice* Maria Francesca Luisa Pia Ana Valeria of Bourbon-Parma (*b* 13 Nov 1917) [*Hermanos Pinzon 4, Madrid 16, Spain*], 4th dau of HRH Prince Elie of Bourbon, Head of the Ducal House of Parma, and *d* 3 Feb 1964, leaving issue (*see p* 231).

2*e* HRH Prince *Fernando* Maria Antonio Alfonso Carlos Fadrique Ignacio Olegario of Bourbon-Two Sicilies, Infante of Spain, *b* 6 March 1903; *d* 4 Aug 1905.

1*e* ●HRH Princess *Isabel Alfonsa* Maria Teresa Antonietta Cristina Mercedes Carolina Adelaide Raffaela of Bourbon-Two Sicilies, Infanta of Spain, *b* 16 Oct 1904, *m* 9 March 1929, Count Jan Kanty Zamoyski (*b* 17 Aug 1900; *d* 28 Sept 1961), and has had issue,

1*f* ●Count *Karol* Alfons Maria Józef Zamoyski, *b* 2 Sept 1932, *m* 18 Dec 1956, ●Doña Maria de la Esperanza Rey y Luque, dau of Don Mariano Rey y Iglesia, and has issue,

●Countess *Maria del Rocio* Zamoyska, *b* 1 Jan 1958.

2*f* ●Count *Józef* Michal Maria Leon Zamoyski, *b* 27 June 1935.

1*f* Countess *Maria Krystyna* Zamoyska, *b* 2 Sept 1932; *d unm* 6 Dec 1959.

2*f* ●Countess *Maria Teresa* Zamoyska, *b* 18 April 1938.

2*d* HRH Infanta *Maria Teresa* Isabel Eugénia Patrocinio Diega of Spain, *b* 12 Nov 1882, *m* 12 Jan 1906, HRH Prince *Fernando* Maria Luis Francisco de Asis Isabellus Adalberto Ildefonso Martino Bonifacio José Isidro of Bavaria, Infante of Spain, naturalized in Spain 20 Oct 1905, renounced his rights of succession to Bavaria 29 June 1914 (*b* 10 May 1884; *d* 5 April 1958), and *d* 23 Sept 1912, leaving issue,

1*e* ●HRH Infante *Luis Alfonso* Fernando Cristino Adalberto Teresa Maria de Guadalupe Santiago Isidro Raimundo José Antonio Maria de la Espectación de Todos los Santos of Spain, Mil Gov of Madrid [*Joaquin Costa 20, Madrid, Spain*], *b* 12 Dec 1906.

2*e* HRH Infante *José Eugenio* Alfonso Fernando Mariano Teresa Antonio Jesus Santiago Isidro Raimundo Branlio de Todos los Santos of Spain, *b* 26 March 1909, *m* 25 July 1933, ●Doña Maria Solange (*Marisol*) Messia y de Lesseps, Condesa de Odiel (*b* 30 Sept 1911) [*Calle Henares, Madrid, Spain; Villa Pumpenia, F-64 Ciboure, Basses-Pyrénées, France*], dau of Don Fernando Messia y Stuart, Conde de Mora, Duque de Tamames (nephew of HIM the Empress Eugénie), by his wife Doña Maria Solange de Lesseps, of the Vicomtes de Lesseps, and *d* 16 Aug 1966, leaving issue,

1*f* ●Don Fernando de Baviera y Messia, [*Hontares 8, Puerta de Hierro, Madrid 16, Spain*], *b* 1937, *m* 1966 ●Doña Sofia Arquer Arig (*b* 13 Oct 1941).

2*f* Don Luis de Baviera y Messia, *b* 1942; *d unm* Dec 1966.

1*f* ●Doña Maria *Cristina* de Baviera y Messia, *b* 6 Feb 1935, *m* 12 July 1967,● Don Juan Manuel de Urquijo [*Darro 22, Madrid 2, Spain*].

2*f* ●Doña Maria *Teresa* de Baviera y Messia, *b* 11 Jan 1941, *m* 23 Nov 1963, ●Don Alfonso Marquez y Patiño Castillejo y Losada, Marqués de Castro (*b* 7 Aug 1936), and has issue,

1*g* ●Doña *Myrta* Sofia Marquez y de Baviera, *b* 27 Oct 1965.

2*g* ●Doña *Sonia* Victoria Eugénia Marquez y de Baviera, *b* 6 June 1969.

1*e* HRH Infanta *Maria de las Mercedes* Teresa Maria de la Paz Fernanda Adalberta Cristina Antonia Isidra Raimunda Josefa Jesusa Fausta y Todos los Santos Francisca de Borja of Spain, *b* 3 Oct 1911, *m* 29 Aug 1946, as his 2nd wife, ●Prince Irakly Bagration-Mukhransky (*b* 21 March 1909) [*Calle Serrano 154, Madrid, Spain; Palacio di Santillana del Mar, Santander, Spain*], and *d* 11 Sept 1953, leaving issue,

●Prince Bagrat Bagration-Mukhransky, *b* 12 Jan 1949.

●Princess Maria de la Paz Bagration-Mukhransky, *b* 27 June 1947, *m* 24 Oct 1968, ●Don José Luis Blanco de Briones (*b* 23 Dec 1937) [*Spanish Embassy, Paris*], and has issue,

●Tamara Blanco de Briones, *b* 14 Oct 1969.

2*e* HRH Infanta *Maria del Pilar* Adelgonda Luitpolda Maria de la Paz Teresa Luisa Fernanda Cristina Antonia Isidra Romana Atocha Maria de las Mercedes Simona de Rojas y Todos los Santos of Spain, *b* 15 Sept 1912; *d* 9 May 1918.

3*b* HI and RH Archduke *Friedrich* Ferdinand Leopold of Austria, *b* 14 May 1821; *d unm* 5 Oct 1847.

4*b* HI and RH Archduke Rudolf of Austria, *b* 25 Sept, *d* 24 Oct 1822.

5*b* HI and RH Archduke *Wilhelm* Franz Karl of Austria, *b* 21 April 1827; *d unm* 29 July 1894.

1*b* HI and RH Archduchess *Maria Theresia* Isabella of Austria, *b* 31 July 1816, *m* 27 Jan 1837, as his 2nd wife, HM King Ferdinando II of the Two Sicilies (*b* 12 Jan 1810; *d* 22 May 1859), and *d* 8 Aug 1867, having had issue,

1*c* HRH Prince *Lodovico* Maria of Bourbon-Two Sicilies, Count of Trani, *b* 1 Aug 1838, *m* 5 June 1861, HRH Duchess *Mathilde* Ludovika (*b* 30 Sept 1843; *d* 18 June 1925), yr dau of HRH Duke Maximilian Joseph in Bavaria, and *d* 8 June 1886, leaving issue,

HRH Princess *Maria Teresa* Maddalena of Bourbon-Two Sicilies, *b* 15 Jan 1867, *m* 27 June 1889, HRH *Wilhelm* August Karl Joseph Peter Ferdinand Benedikt, Prince of Hohenzollern (*b* 7 March 1864; *d* 22 Oct 1927), and *d* 1 March 1909, leaving issue,

1*e* HRH *Friedrich Viktor* Pius Alexander Leopold Karl Theodor Ferdinand, Prince of Hohenzollern, *b* 30 Aug 1891, *m* 2 June 1920, HRH Princess *Margarete* Karola Wilhelmine Viktoria Adelheid Albertine Petrussa Bertram Paula (*b* 24 Jan 1900; *d* 19 Oct 1962), eldest dau of HM King Friedrich August III of Saxony, and *d* 6 Feb 1965, leaving issue,

1*f* ●HH *Friedrich Wilhelm* Ferdinand Joseph Maria Manuel Georg Meinrad Fidelis Benedikt Michael Hubert, Prince of Hohenzollern [*Landhaus Josefslust, Sigmaringen, Hohenzollern, Germany*], *b* 3 Feb 1924, *m* 3 Feb 1951, ●HSH Princess *Margarita* Ileana Viktoria (*b* 9 May 1932), 2nd dau of HSH Karl, 6th Prince zu Leiningen, and has issue (*see p* 297).

2*f* ●HSH Prince *Franz Joseph* Hubertus Maria Meinrad Michael of Hohenzollern [*748 Schloss Sigmaringen, Sigmaringen, Hohenzollern, Germany*], *b* 15 March 1926, *m* 1st 15 July 1950 (*m* diss by div 1951), HSH Princess *Maria Ferdinanda* Eudoxia Michaela Gabriela Raphaela (*b* 19 Dec 1927), yst dau of HSH Franz Joseph, 9th Prince von Thurn und Taxis. He *m* 2ndly 16 April 1955 (*m* diss by div 1961), HRH Princess *Diana* Margherita (*b* 22 May 1932), only dau of HRH late Prince Gaetano of Bourbon-Parma, and by her has issue,

●HSH Prince *Alexander* Friedrich Ferdinand Meinrad Fidelis Maria of Hohenzollern, *b* 2 June 1957.

3*f* ●HSH Prince *Johann Georg* Carl Leopold Eitel-Friedrich Meinrad Maria Hubertus Michael of Hohenzollern [*8022 Grünwald bei München, Dr-Max-Strasse 70, Germany*], *b* 31 Jan 1932, *m* 30 May 1961, ●HRH Princess *Birgitta* Ingeborg Alice (*b* 19 Jan 1937), 2nd dau of HRH the late Hereditary Prince Gustaf Adolf of Sweden, Duke of Västerbotten, and has issue (*see p* 224).

4*f* ●HSH Prince *Ferfried* Maximilian Pius Meinrad Maria Hubert Michael Justinus of

Hohenzollern, *b* 14 April 1943, *m* 21 Sept 1968, ●*Angela* Elisabeth Ernestine Hermine Gerda Renata (*b* 11 Nov 1942), 4th dau of Ernst von Morgen, and has issue,

1*g* ●(Prinzessin) *Valerie Alexandra* Henriette Margarethe von Hohenzollern, *b* 14 April 1969.

2*g* ●(Prinzessin) Stefanie von Hohenzollern, *b* 8 May 1971.

1*f* ●HSH Princess Benedikta *Maria Antonia* Mathilde Anna of Hohenzollern [*7951 Schloss Heinrichburg, Post Eberhardzell über Biberach a d Riss, Germany*], *b* 19 Feb 1921, *m* 4 Jan 1942, H Ill H Count *Heinrich* Maria Willibald Benedikt Albrecht Philipp Ulrich von Waldburg zu Wolfegg und Waldsee (*b* 16 Sept 1911; *d* 25 May 1972), and has issue,

1*g* ●H Ill H Count Maria *Friedrich* Maximilian Wunibald Meinrad Michael Gebhard Konstantin von Waldburg zu Wolfegg und Waldsee, *b* 21 May 1948.

2*g* ●H Ill H Count Maria *Joseph* Anton Willibald Fidelis Petrus Canisius von Waldburg zu Wolfegg und Waldsee, *b* 15 Dec 1950.

3*g* ●H Ill H Count Maria *Hubert* Willibald Pius Johannes Nepomuk von Waldburg zu Wolfegg und Waldsee, *b* 25 June 1956.

1*g* ●H Ill H Countess Maria *Sidonie* Margarete Elisabeth Walburga Caspara Meinrada Barbara von Waldburg zu Wolfegg und Waldsee, *b* 4 Dec 1942, *m* ●Count *Alexander* Moritz Kasimir Paul Maria Eustachius Esterházy, Baron zu Galántha (*b* 15 July 1943).

2*g* ●H Ill H Countess Maria *Sophie* Therese Viktoria Walburga Elisabeth von Waldburg zu Wolfegg und Waldsee, *b* 9 July 1946, *m* ●Matthäus Lill von Rastern.

3*g* ●H Ill H Countess Maria *Margaretha* Theresa Walburga Dionysia von Waldburg zu Wolfegg und Waldsee, *b* 26 Feb 1953.

4*g* ●H Ill H Countess Maria *Anna* Adelheid Jacobe Walburga Petrusa Bernhardine von Waldburg zu Wolfegg und Waldsee, *b* 20 Aug 1954.

5*g* ●H Ill H Countess Maria *Theresia* Viktoria Walburga Franziska Epiphania von Waldburg zu Wolfegg und Waldsee, *b* 8 Jan 1958.

6*g* ●H Ill H Countess Maria *Jacobe* Walburga Meinrada Sebastiana von Waldburg zu Wolfegg und Waldsee, *b* 20 Jan 1960.

7*g* ●H Ill H Countess *Ludmila* Walburga Martha Ida Johanna Vianney von Waldburg zu Wolfegg und Waldsee, *b* 29 July 1964.

2*f* ●HSH Princess *Maria Adelgunde* Alice Luise Josephine of Hohenzollern [*7801 Schloss Umkirch uber Freiburg i Br, Germany*], *b* 19 Feb 1921, *m* 1st 31 Aug 1942 (*m* diss by div 1948), HRH Prince *Konstantin* Leopold Ludwig Adalbert Georg Thaddäus Josef Petrus Johannes Antonius Franz von Assisi Assumption et omnes sancti of Bavaria (*b* 15 Aug 1920; *d* 30 July 1969), and has issue,

1*g* ●HRH Prince *Leopold* Rupprecht Ludwig Ferdinand Adalbert Friedrich Maria et omnes sancti of Bavaria [*8 München 23, Tengstrasse 48, Germany*], *b* 21 June 1943.

2*g* ●HRH Prince *Adalbert* Friedrich Johannes Maria et omnes sancti of Bavaria [*8 München 23, Klopstockstrasse 1b, Germany*], *b* 27 Dec 1944.

She *m* 2ndly 25 March 1950 (*m* diss by div 1962), Dr Werner Hess (*b* 20 Sept 1907), and has further issue,

1*g* ●Monika Elisabeth Maria Hess, *b* 3 Nov 1953.

2*g* ●Angelica Diana Maria Hess, *b* 28 April 1955.

3*f* ●HSH Princess *Maria Theresia* Ludovika Cecilie Zita Elisabeth Hilda Agnes of Hohenzollern [*8022 Grünwald bei München, Hugo-Junkers-Strasse 19, Germany*], *b* 11 Oct 1922.

2*e* HSH Prince *Franz Joseph* Maria Ludwig Karl Anton Tassilo of Hohenzollern-Emden, *b* 30 Aug 1891, *m* 25 May 1921, ●HRH Princess *Maria Alix* Luitpolda Anna Henriette Germana Agnes Damiana Michaela (*b* 27 Sept 1901) [*D-7450 Hechingen, Villa Silberburg, Germany*], 2nd dau of HM King Friedrich August III of Saxony, and *d* 3 April 1964, leaving issue,

1*f* ●HSH Prince *Karl Anton* Friedrich Wilhelm Ludwig Maria Georg Manuel Rupprecht Heinrich Benedikt Tassilo of Hohenzollern [*D-7450 Hechingen, Villa Eugenia, Germany*], *b* 28 Jan 1922, *m* 15 Aug 1951, ●Alexandra (*b* 16 Nov 1919), dau of Alexander de Afif.

2*f* ●HSH Prince *Meinrad* Leopold Maria Friedrich Christian Ferdinand Albert of Hohenzollern [*D-7450 Hechingen, Villa Eugenia, Germany*], *b* 17 Jan 1925, *m* 11 Sept 1971, ●Baroness *Edina* Verena Valeria Gabrielle Mona (*b* 23 Aug 1938), only dau of Baron Alfred von Kap-Herr.

3*f* ●HSH Prince *Emanuel* Joseph Maria Wilhelm Ferdinand Burkhard of Hohenzollern [*D-7450 Hechingen, Villa Eugenia, Germany*], *b* 23 Feb 1929, *m* 25 May 1968, ●HH Princess *Katharina* Feodora Adelheid Sabine Sophie Felicitas Sieglinde (*b* 30 Nov 1943), only dau of HH Prince Bernhard Friedrich of Saxe-Weimar-Eisenach (*see p* 266), and has issue,

●HSH Prince *Carl Alexander* Franz Joseph Wilhelm Ernst Meinrad of Hohenzollern, *b* 26 Oct 1970.

●HSH Princess *Eugenia* Maria Margarethe Adelheid Felicitas Luise Henrietta of Hohenzollern, *b* 13 March 1969.

1*f* ●HSH Princess *Maria Margarete* Anna Viktoria Luise Josephine Maria Theresia vom Kinde Jesu of Hohenzollern, *b* 2 Jan 1928, *m* 23 April 1966, ●HH Duke *Carl Gregor* Georg Friedrich Franz Heinrich Norbert Wenzeslaus Johann Nepomuk Lazarus Clemens Maria de Mercede et omnes sancti of Mecklenburg-Strelitz (*b* 14 March 1933) [*D-7450 Hechingen, Villa Silberburg, Germany*] (*see p* 213).

1*e* HSH Princess *Auguste Viktoria* Wilhelmine Antonie Mathilde Ludovika Josephine Maria Elisabeth of Hohenzollern, *b* 19 Aug 1890, *m* 1st 4 Sept 1913, HM King Manoel II of Portugal, KG, GCVO, hon FRGS, (*b* 15 Nov 1889; *d* 2 July 1932). She *m* 2ndly 23 April 1939, Count Carl *Robert* Douglas (*b* 24 April 1880; *d* 26 Aug 1955), and *dsp* 29 Aug 1966.

2*c* HRH Prince *Alberto* Maria Francesco of Bourbon-Two Sicilies, Count of Castrogiovanni, *b* 17 Sept 1839; *d* 12 July 1844.

3*c* HRH Prince *Alfonso* Maria Giuseppe Alberto of Bourbon-Two Sicilies, Count of Caserta, *s* his half-brother King Francesco II as Head of the Royal House of the Two Sicilies 1894, *b* 28 March 1841, *m* 8 June 1868, HRH Princess *Maria Antonietta* Giuseppina Leopoldina (*b* 16 March 1851; *d* 12 Sept 1938), eldest dau of HRH Prince Francesco of the Two Sicilies, Count of Trapani, and *d* 26 May 1934, having had issue,

1*d* HRH Prince *Ferdinando* Pio Maria, Duke of Calabria, Head of the Royal House of the Two Sicilies (1934-1960), *b* 25 July 1869, *m* 31 May 1897, HRH Princess *Maria* Ludwiga Theresia (*b* 6 July 1872; *d* 10 June 1954), 2nd dau of HM King Ludwig III of Bavaria, and *d* 7 Jan 1960, having had issue,

1*e* HRH Prince *Ruggiero* Maria of Bourbon-Two Sicilies, Duke of Noto, *b* 7 Sept 1901; *dvp* 1 Dec 1914.

1*e* HRH Princess Maria *Antonietta* Leonia of Bourbon-Two Sicilies, *b* 16 April 1898; *d unm* 11 Jan 1957.

2e ●HRH Princess *Maria Cristina* of Bourbon-Two Sicilies [*1601 La Colina, Quito, Ecuador*], *b* 4 May 1899, *m* 3 March 1948, Don Manuel Sotomayor Luna, Vice-President of Ecuador (*b* 27 Nov 1884; *d* 16 Oct 1949).

3e HRH Princess *Barbara* Maria Antonietta Luitpolda of Bourbon-Two Sicilies, *b* 14 Dec 1902, *m* 31 May 1922, H Ill H Count *Franz Xaver* Marie Joseph Martin Anton Hubertus Ignatius Sebastian Georg Willibald Vincenz von Paul Leo zu Stolberg-Wernigerode (*b* 19 July 1894; *d* as a p o w 4 May 1947), and *d* 1 Jan 1927, leaving issue,

1f ●H Ill H Count Ferdinand *Anton* Maria Christian Friedrich Leopold Franz Josef Pius Gabriel zu Stolberg-Wernigerode [*Greifenberg am Ammersee, OBayern, Germany*], *b* 4 July 1925.

1f ●H Ill H Countess *Elisabeth* Bona Maria Alfonsa Ferdinanda Josefa Antonie Juliane zu Stolberg-Wernigerode, *b* 17 April 1923, *m* 26 Jan 1944, ●Count Rüdiger Josef Maria Martin von Stillfried-Rattonitz (*b* 14 July 1923) [*899 Lindau im Bodensee, Bäuerlinshalde 13, Germany*], and has had issue,

1g Countess Barbara von Stillfried-Rattonitz, *b* 22 Dec 1948; *d* 29 March 1951.

2g ●Countess Maria *Gabriele* Christine von Stillfried-Rattonitz, *b* 13 Aug 1950.

3g ●Countess *Pia* Maria von Stillfried-Rattonitz, *b* 20 April 1956.

2f ●H Ill H Countess *Maria* Josefa Gabriele Antonia Gebharda zu Stolberg-Wernigerode [*899 Lindau im Bodensee, Bäuerlinshalde 13, Germany*], *b* 11 May 1924.

3f ●H Ill H Countess *Sophie* Marie Antonie Henrike Thaddea Gabriele zu Stolberg-Wernigerode [*899 Lindau im Bodensee, Bäuerlinshalde 13, Germany*], *b* 21 Dec 1926.

4e ●HRH Princess *Lucia* Maria Raniera of Bourbon-Two Sicilies, *b* 9 July 1908, *m* 29 Oct 1938, ●HRH Prince *Eugenio* Alfonso Carlo Maria Giuseppe of Savoy-Genoa, Duke of Ancona (*b* 13 March 1906) [*Rua Peixoto Gomide 1618, Apt 82, São Paulo, Brazil*], and has issue,

●HRH Princess *Maria Isabella* Elena Immacolata Barbara Anna Paz of Savoy-Genoa, *b* 23 June 1943, *m* 29 April 1971, ●Alberto Frioli (*b* 7 April 1943), and has issue,

●*Vittorio Eugenio* Frioli, *b* 27 Feb 1972.

5e ●HRH Princess *Urraca* Maria Isabella Carolina Aldegonda Carmela of Bourbon-Two Sicilies [*Schloss Amsee 8991, Esserats-weiler über Lindau, Bavaria, Germany*], *b* 14 July 1913.

2d HRH Prince *Carlo* Maria Francesco d'Assisi Pasquale Ferdinando Antonio di Padova Francesco di Paola Alfonso Andrea Avelino Tancredi of Bourbon-Two Sicilies, Infante of Spain, *b* 10 Nov 1870, *m* 1st 14 Feb 1901, HRH Infanta *Maria de las Mercedes* Isabel Teresa Cristina Alfonsa Jacinta (*b* 11 Sept 1880; *d* 17 Oct 1904), elder dau of HM King Alfonso XII of Spain, KG, and had issue (*see p* 233). He *m* 2ndly 16 Nov 1907, HRH Princess *Louise*-Françoise-Marie-Laure of France (*b* 24 Feb 1882; *d* 18 April 1958), yst dau of HRH Prince Louis-Philippe, Count of Paris, Head of the Royal House of France, and *d* 11 Nov 1949, having by her had issue,

1e HRH Prince *Carlos* Maria Fernando Luis Felipe Lorenzo Giustiniano of Bourbon-Two Sicilies, *b* 5 Sept 1908; *k* in action 27 Sept 1936.

1e ●HRH Princess *Maria de los Dolores* Vittoria Filipina Maria de las Mercedes Luisa Carlota Eugénia of Bourbon-Two Sicilies, *b* 15 Nov 1909, *m* 1st 16 Aug 1937, HSH Prince *Józef August* Antoni Maria Pius Czartoryski (*b* 20 Oct 1907; *d* 1 July 1946), and has had issue,

1f ●HSH Prince *Adam* Karol Czartoryski, *b* 2 Jan 1940.

2f HSH Prince Ludwik Piotr Czartoryski, *b* 13 March 1945; *d* 3 May 1946.

She *m* 2ndly 29 Dec 1950, ●Don Carlos Chias y Osorio (*b* 26 Feb 1925) [*Dos Hermanos, Seville, Spain*].

2e ●HRH Princess *Maria de las Mercedes* Cristina Gennara Isabel Luisa Carolina Vittoria of Bourbon-Two Sicilies, *b* 23 Dec 1910, *m* 12 Oct 1935, ●HRH Infante Don *Juan* Carlos Teresa Silvestre Alfonso, Count of Barcelona, Head of the Royal House of Spain (*b* 20 June 1913) [*Villa Giralda, Estoril, Portugal*], and has had issue (*see p* 305).

3e ●HRH Princess *Maria de la Esperanza* Amalia Raniera of Bourbon-Two Sicilies, *b* 14 June 1914, *m* 18 Dec 1944, ●HRH Prince *Pedro* de Alcantara *Gastão João* Maria Filipe Lourenço Huberto Miguel Rafael Gabriel Gonzaga of Orleans and Braganza (*b* 19 Feb 1913) [*Palácio do Grão Pará, Petrópolis, Brazil; F-76 Château d'Eu, Seine Maritime, France; Villamanrique de la Condesa, Seville, Spain*], and has issue,

1f ●HRH Prince *Pedro* de Alcantara *Carlos* João Lourenço Miguel Rafael Gabriel Gonzaga of Orleans and Braganza, *b* 31 Oct 1945.

2f ●HRH Prince *Afonso* Duarte Francisco Marcos Miguel Rafael Gabriel Gonzaga of Orleans and Braganza, *b* 25 April 1948.

3f ●HRH Prince *Manoel* Alvaro Raniero Miguel Gabriel Rafael Gonzaga of Orleans and Braganza, *b* 17 June 1949.

4f ●HRH Prince *Francisco* Humberto Miguel Rafael Gabriel Gonzaga of Orleans and Braganza, *b* 9 Dec 1956.

1f ●HRH Princess *Maria da Gloria* Henriqueta Dolores Lucia Miguela Rafaela Gabriela Gonzaga of Orleans and Braganza, *b* 13 Dec 1946, *m* 1 July 1972, ●HRH Crown Prince Alexander of Yugoslavia (*b* 17 July 1945), only son of HM late King Peter II of Yugoslavia (*see p* 296).

2f ●HRH Princess *Cristina* Maria de Rosário Leopoldina Miguela Gabriela Rafaela Gonzaga of Orleans and Braganza, *b* 16 Oct 1950.

3d HRH Prince *Francesco di Paola* of Bourbon-Two Sicilies, *b* 14 July 1873; *d* 26 June 1876

4d HRH Prince *Gennaro* Maria Francesco di Paola of Bourbon-Two Sicilies, *b* 24 Jan 1882, *m* 27 June 1922, Beatrice Bordessa, Contessa di Villa-Colli (*b* 29 Dec 1881; *d* 20 Aug 1963), and *dsp* 11 April 1944.

5d ●HRH Prince *Ranieri* Maria Gaetano of Bourbon-Two Sicilies, Duke of Castro, *s* his brother the Duke of Calabria as Head of the Royal House of the Two Sicilies 1960 [*Villa Carmen, Ave des Mesanges, F-83 Boulouris, Var, France*], *b* 3 Dec 1883, *m* 12 Sept 1923, Countess Maria *Karolina* Franciszka Józefa Antonia Eustachia Konstancja (*b* 22 Sept 1896; *d* 9 May 1968), 4th dau of Count Andrzej Zamoyski, by his wife HRH Princess Carolina of the Two Sicilies, and has issue,

●HRH Prince *Ferdinando* Maria Andrea Alfonso Marco of Bourbon-Two Sicilies, Duke of Calabria [*Il Castellucio, Les Rives d'Or, F-83 St Aygulf, Var, France*], *b* 28 May 1926, *m* 23 July 1949, ●Chantal (*b* 10 Jan 1925), dau of Joseph-Pierre, Comte de Chevron-Villette, and has issue,

1f ●HRH Prince Carlo of Bourbon-Two Sicilies, Duke of Noto, *b* 24 Feb 1963.

1f ●HRH Princess *Beatrice* Maria Carolina Luisa Francesca of Bourbon-Two Sicilies, *b* 13 June 1950.

2f ●HRH Princess *Anna* Maria Carolina Carmen of Bourbon-Two Sicilies, *b* 24 April 1957.

●HRH Princess *Maria del Carmen* Carolina Antonietta of Bourbon-Two Sicilies [*La*

Combe, près Roquebrune sur Argens (83520), France], *b* 13 July 1924.
6*d* HRH Prince *Filippo* Maria Alfonso Antonio Ferdinando Francesco di Paola Luigi Enrico Alberto of Bourbon-Two Sicilies, *b* 10 Dec 1885, *m* 1st 12 Jan 1916 (*m* diss by div 1925), HRH Princess *Marie-Louise*-Ferdinande-Charlotte-Henriette (*b* 31 Dec 1896), eldest dau of HRH Prince Philippe-Emmanuel of Bourbon-Orleans, Duke of Vendôme, and had issue,
●HRH Prince *Gaetano* Maria Alfonso Enrico Paolo of Bourbon-Two Sicilies [9 *Derbyshire Road, Water Falls, Induna, Salisbury, Rhodesia*], *b* 16 April 1917, *m* 16 Feb 1946, ●Olivia (*b* 16 July 1917), dau of Lt-Cmdr Charles Arthur Yarrow, RM, and has issue,
1*f* ●Adrian Philip de Bourbon, *b* 7 April 1948.
2*f* ●Gregory Peter de Bourbon, *b* 2 Jan 1950.
He *m* 2ndly 10 Jan 1927, ●Odette (*b* 22 Nov 1902), formerly wife of Dino Ceretti, and dau of Fernand Labori, and *d* 9 March 1949.
7*d* HRH Prince *Francesco d'Assisi* Maria Ferdinando Eudo of Bourbon-Two Sicilies, *b* 13 Jan 1888; *d unm* 26 March 1914.
8*d* ●HRH Prince *Gabriele* Maria Giuseppe Carlo Ignazio Antonio Alfonso Pietro Giovanni Gerardo di Majella et omnes sancti of Bourbon-Two Sicilies [*Hú, 13.300 (SP), Rua da Convenção 144, Brazil*], *b* 11 Jan 1897, *m* 1st 25 Aug 1927, HSH Princess Izabella *Malgorzata (Margherita)* Maria Magdalena Antonina Jacento Jósefa Ludwika (*b* 17 Aug 1902; *d* 8 March 1929), eldest dau of HSH Adam, 12th Prince Czartoryski, and has issue,
1*e* ●HRH Prince *Antonio* Maria Giuseppe Alfonso Adamo et omnes sancti of Bourbon-Two Sicilies [*Schloss Altshausen, Kr Saulgau, Württemberg, Germany*], *b* 20 Jan 1929, *m* 19 July 1958, ●HRH Duchess *Elisabeth* Maria Margarethe Alix Helene Rosa Philippine Christine Josepha Therese vom Kinde Jesu (*b* 2 Feb 1933), 3rd dau of HRH Duke Philipp Albrecht of Württemberg, Head of the Royal House of Württemberg, and has issue (*see p* 227).
He *m* 2ndly 15 Sept 1932, ●HSH Princess *Cecylia (Cecilia)* (*b* 28 June 1907), only dau of HSH Prince Kazimierz Lubomirski, and by her has issue,
2*e* ●HRH Prince *Giovanni* Maria Casimiro of Bourbon-Two Sicilies [*73, rue de Lille, Paris VII, France*], *b* 30 June 1933.
3*e* ●HRH Prince *Casimiro* Maria Alfonso Gabriele of Bourbon-Two Sicilies [*Rua Raul Pompeja, Rio de Janeiro 3037, Brazil*], *b* 8 Nov 1938, *m* 29 Jan 1967, ●HRH Princess *Maria Cristina* Giusta Elena Giovanna of Savoy-Aosta (*b* 12 Sept 1933), yr dau of HRH Prince Amedeo of Savoy, 3rd Duke of Aosta, Viceroy of Ethiopia, and has issue,
1*f* ●HRH Prince *Luis-Afonso* of Bourbon-Two Sicilies, *b* 28 Nov 1970.
1*f* ●HRH Princess *Anna-Cecilia* of Bourbon-Two Sicilies, *b* 24 Dec 1971.
1*e* ●HRH Princess *Maria Margherita* Teresa Antonietta Alfonsina Casimira of Bourbon-Two Sicilies, *b* 16 Nov 1934, *m* 11 June 1962, ●Don *Luís Gonzaga* Maldonado y Gordon (*b* 17 Nov 1932) [*Paseo de Pintor Rogales 82, Madrid 14, Spain*], and has issue,
1*f* ●Doña *Maria Margarita* Maldonado y Borbón, *b* 24 Sept 1963.
2*f* ●Doña *Maria Claudia* Maldonado y Borbón, *b* 31 March 1965.
3*f* ●Doña *Maria Cecilia* Maldonado y Borbón, *b* 31 March 1967.
2*e* ●HRH Princess *Maria Immacolata* of Bourbon-Two Sicilies, *b* 25 June 1937, *m* 29 June 1970, ●Don Miguel García de Sáez, [*Finca St Miguel, La Moraleja, Madrid, Spain*], and has issue,
●Don *José Luis* Miguel Maria Garcia y Borbón, *b* 3 March 1972.
1*d* HRH Princess *Maria Immacolata* Cristina Pia Isabella of Bourbon-Two Sicilies, *b* 30 Oct 1874, *m* 30 Oct 1906, as his 2nd wife, HRH Prince *Johann Georg* Pius Karl Leopold Maria Januarius Anakletus of Saxony (*b* 10 July 1869; *d* 24 Nov 1938), 2nd son of HM King Georg of Saxony, and *dsp* 28 Nov 1947.
2*d* HRH Princess *Maria Cristina* Carolina Pia of Bourbon-Two Sicilies, *b* 10 April 1877, *m* 8 Nov 1900, HI and RH Archduke *Peter Ferdinand* Salvator Karl Ludwig Maria Joseph Leopold Anton Rupert Pius Pancraz of Austria, Head of the Grand Ducal House of Tuscany (*b* 12 May 1874; *d* 8 Nov 1948), and *d* 4 Oct 1947, having had issue,
1*e* ●HI and RH Archduke *Gottfried* Maria Joseph Peter Ferdinand Hubert Anton Rupert Leopold Heinrich Ignaz Alfons of Austria, Head of the Grand Ducal House of Tuscany [*St Gilden, Salzburg, Austria*], *b* 14 March 1902, *m* 3 Aug 1938, ●HRH Princess *Dorothea* Therese Marie Franziska (*b* 25 May 1920), yst dau of HRH late Prince Franz of Bavaria, and has issue,
1*f* ●HI and RH Archduke *Leopold Franz* Peter Ferdinand Maria Joseph Gottfried Georg Karl Otto Rudolf Michael of Austria, Prince of Tuscany [*Pueyrredon 2345 p 7, Buenos Aires, Argentina*], *b* 25 Oct 1942, *m* 26 July 1965, ●*Laetitia* Marie Magdeleine Suzanne Valentine de Belzunce d'Arenberg (*b* 2 Sept 1941), dau of late Henri, Marquis de Belzunce, and step and adopted dau of HSH Prince and Duke Erik von Arenberg, and has issue,
1*g* ●HI and RH Archduke *Sigismund* Otto Maria Josef Gottfried Heinrich Erik Leopold Ferdinand of Austria, *b* 21 April 1966.
2*g* ●HI and RH Archduke *Guntram* Maria Josef of Austria, *b* 21 July 1967.
1*f* ●HI and RH Archduchess *Elisabeth* Maria Dorothea Josefa Theresia Ludmilla of Austria, Princess of Tuscany, *b* 22 Oct 1939, *m* 24 April 1965, ●Friedrich von Braun (*b* 26 Dec 1934), and has issue,
●Bernadette von Braun, *b* 21 July 1966.
2*f* ●HI and RH Archduchess *Alice* Marie Christine Margarete Antoinette Josefa Rosa Helene Adelgunde Eleonore of Austria, Princess of Tuscany, *b* 29 April 1941, *m* 7 May 1970, ●Baron Don Vittorio Manno (*b* 31 July 1938) [*Blauwe Kamerlaan 12a, The Hague, Netherlands*].
3*f* ●HI and RH Archduchess *Marie Antoinette* Christine Josefa Rosa Margaretha Pia Angela Theresia Gabriele Isabella Ludmilla Zita Ruperta of Austria, Princess of Tuscany, *b* 16 Sept 1950.
2*e* HI and RH Archduke *Georg* Maria Rainer Joseph Peter Hubert Gottfried Eustach Rupert Ignaz of Austria, Prince of Tuscany, *b* 22 Aug 1905, *m* 29 April 1936, ● H Ill H Countess *Marie Valerie* Klementine Franziska Elisabeth Walburga (*b* 28 June 1913) [*Schwarzenbenberg-Prom 28, A-5026 Salzburg-Aigen, Austria*], eldest dau of H Ill H Count Georg von Waldburg-Zeil, by his wife HI and RH Archduchess Elisabeth Franziska of Austria (*see p* 243), and *d* 21 March 1952, having had issue,
1*f* HI and RH Archduke *Guntram* Maria Georg Otto Joseph Peter Franz Leopold Karl Gabriel Walpurgis Ludwig of Austria, Prince of Tuscany, *b* 19 Aug 1937; *d* 9 May 1943.
2*f* ●HI and RH Archduke *Radbot Ferdinand* Maria Johann Georg Gottfried Otto Joseph Anton Raphael Willibald Linus of Austria, Prince of Tuscany, *b* 23 Sept 1938.
3*f* HI and RH Archduke *Johann* of Austria, Prince of Tuscany, *b* and *d* 27 Dec 1946.
4*f* ●HI and RH Archduke *Georg* Maria Otto Joseph Leopold Philipp Michael Vitus

Augustinus of Austria, Prince of Tuscany, *b* 28 Aug 1952.

1*f* HI and RH Archduchess Marie Christine Elisabeth Franziska Klementine Helene Rosa Josepha Agnes Walburga Michaela Notgera of Austria, Princess of Tuscany, *b* 8 April 1941; *d* 4 Jan 1942.

2*f* •HI and RH Archduchess *Walburga* Rosa Maria Christine Elisabeth Clementine Helene Caroline Zita Stephanie Michaela Apollinaria of Austria, Princess of Tuscany, *b* 23 July 1942, *m* 17 Feb 1969, •Dom Carlos Tasso de Saxe-Coburgo e Bragança (*b* 16 July 1931) (*see p* 245).

3*f* HI and RH Archduchess Verena Gertrud Maria Josepha Christine Elisabeth Georgine Walburga Paula Johanna Gabriele Aloysia of Austria, Princess of Tuscany, *b* 21 June 1944; *d* 5 Jan 1945.

4*f* •HI and RH Archduchess *Katharina* Maria Christina Josefa Clementine Elisabeth Walburga Theresia Gertrud Georgine Agnes Gabriele of Austria, Princess of Tuscany, *b* 24 April 1948.

5*f* •HI and RH Archduchess *Agnes* Maria Gertrud Elisabeth Josepha Pia Theresia Walburga Raphaela of Austria, Princess of Tuscany, *b* 20 April 1950.

1*e* HI and RH Archduchess *Helene* Marie Alice Christine Josepha Anna Margareta Madeleine Walburga Blandina Caecilie Philomena Carmela Ignazia Rita de Cascia of Austria, Princess of Tuscany, *b* 30 Oct 1903, *m* 24 Oct 1923, as his 1st wife, •HRH Duke Philipp Albrecht of Württemberg, Head of the Royal House of Württemberg (*b* 14 Nov 1893), and *d* 8 Sept 1924, leaving issue (*see p* 226).

2*e* •HI and RH Archduchess *Rosa* Maria Antonie Roberta Josepha Anna Walburga Carmela Ignazia Rita de Cascia of Austria, Princess of Tuscany, *b* 22 Sept 1906, *m* 1 Aug 1928, as his 2nd wife, her brother-in-law, •HRH Duke Philipp Albrecht of Württemberg, Head of the Royal House of Württemberg (*b* 14 Nov 1893) [*7963 Schloss Altshausen, Kr Saulgau, Württemberg, Germany*], and has issue (*see p* 227).

1*d* •HRH Princess *Maria* de Grazia *Pia* Chiara Anna of Bourbon-Two Sicilies [*Château de Lude, Sarthe* (72), *France*], *b* 12 Aug 1878, *m* 4 Nov 1908, HI and RH Prince *Luiz* Maria Filipe Pedro de Alcântara Gastão Miguel Rafael Gonzaga of Orleans and Braganza (*b* 26 Jan 1878; *d* 26 March 1920), and has had issue,

1*e* •HI and RH Prince *Pedro Henrique* Alfonso Filipe Maria Gabriel Rafael Gonzaga of Orleans and Braganza, Head of the Imp House of Brazil [*Sitio Santa Maria, Caixa Postal 2, Vassouras, Estado do Rio, Brazil*], *b* 13 Sept 1909, *m* 19 Aug 1937, •HRH Princess *Marie* Elisabeth Franziska Josepha Therese (*b* 9 Sept 1914), eldest dau of HRH late Prince Franz of Bavaria, and has had issue,

1*f* •HRH Prince *Luiz* Gastão Maria José Pio of Orleans and Braganza [*Sitio Santa Maria, Caixa Postal 2, Vassouras, Estado do Rio, Brazil*], *b* 6 June 1938.

2*f* •HRH Prince *Eudo* Maria Raniero Pedro José of Orleans and Braganza [*205 Rua Joaquin Nabuco, Rio de Janeiro, Brazil*], *b* 8 June 1939, *m* 8 May 1967, •*Ana Maria* Moraes Barros, and has issue, one child.

3*f* •HRH Prince *Bertrão* Maria José Pio Januario of Orleans and Braganza [*69 Rua Martim Francisco, São Paulo, Brazil*], *b* 2 Feb 1941.

4*f* •HRH Prince *Pedro* de Alcântara Henrique Maria of Orleans and Braganza, *b* 1 Dec 1945.

5*f* •HRH Prince *Fernando* Diniz Maria José of Orleans and Braganza, *b* 2 Feb 1948.

6*f* •HRH Prince *Antonio* João Maria José of Orleans and Braganza, *b* 24 June 1950.

7*f* •HRH Prince *Francisco* Maria José Rasso Miguel Gabriel Rafael Gonzaga of Orleans and Braganza, *b* 6 April 1955.

8*f* •HRH Prince *Alberto* Maria José João Miguel Gabriel Rafael Gonzaga of Orleans and Braganza, *b* 23 June 1957.

1*f* •HRH Princess *Isabel* Maria Josefa Henriqueta Francisca of Orleans and Braganza, *b* 5 April 1944.

2*f* HRH Princess *Leonor* Maria Josefa Filipa Miguela Gabriela Rafaela Gonzaga of Orleans and Braganza, *b* 20 May 1953; *d* 25 Nov 1954.

3*f* •HRH Princess Maria *Teresa* Adelgunde Luiza Josa Miguela Gabriela Rafaela Gonzaga of Orleans and Braganza, *b* 14 July 1959.

4*f* •HRH Princess Maria *Gabriela* Dorothea Isabel José Miguela Gonzaga of Orleans and Braganza, *b* (twin with Princess Teresa) 14 July 1959.

2*e* HRH Prince *Luiz Gastão* Antonio Maria Filipe of Orleans and Braganza, *b* 19 Feb 1911; *d unm* 8 Sept 1931.

1*e* •HRH Princess *Pia* Maria Raniera Isabel Antoineta Vitória Teresa Amélia Gerarda Raimunda Ana Miguela Rafaela Gonzaga of Orleans and Braganza [*Château de Lude, Sarthe* (72), *France*], *b* 4 March 1913, *m* 12 Aug 1948, Count René de Nicolay (*b* 17 Jan 1910; *d* 25 Nov 1954), and has issue,

1*f* •*Louis-Jean* de Nicolay, *b* 18 Sept 1949.

2*f* •Robert de Nicolay, *b* 17 Feb 1952.

4*d* HRH Princess *Maria Giuseppina* Antonietta of Bourbon-Two Sicilies, *b* 25 March 1880; *d unm* 22 July 1971.

4*c* HRH Prince *Gaetano* Maria Federigo of the Two Sicilies, Count of Girgenti, *b* 12 Jan 1846, *m* 13 May 1868, HRH Infanta Maria *Isabel* Francisca de Asis Cristina Francisca de Paula Dominga of Spain, sometime Princess of the Asturias (*b* 20 Dec 1851; *d* 23 April 1931), eldest dau of HM Queen Isabel II of Spain, and *dsp* 26 Nov 1871.

5*c* HRH Prince *Giuseppe* Maria of the Two Sicilies, Count of Lucera, *b* 4 March 1848; *d* 28 Sept 1851.

6*c* HRH Prince *Vincenzo* Maria of the Two Sicilies, Count of Melazzo, *b* 26 April 1851; *d* 13 Oct 1854.

7*c* HRH Prince *Pasquale* Baylen Maria del Carmine Giovanni Battista Vincenzo-Ferreri Michele of the Two Sicilies, Count of Bari, *b* 15 Sept 1852, *m* 20 Nov 1878, Louise-*Blanche* de Marconnay (*b* 27 Aug 1848; *d* 12 April 1926), and *dsp* 21 Dec 1904.

8*c* HRH Prince *Gennaro* Maria Immacolata Luigi of the Two Sicilies, Count of Caltagirone, *b* 28 Feb 1857; *d* 13 Aug 1867.

1*c* HRH Princess *Maria Annunziata* Isabella Filomena Sabasia of the Two Sicilies, *b* 24 March 1843, *m* 21 Oct 1862, HI and RH Archduke *Karl Ludwig* Joseph Marie of Austria (*b* 30 July 1833; *d* 19 May 1896), and *d* 4 May 1871, leaving issue,

1*d* HI and RH Archduke *Franz Ferdinand* Karl Ludwig Joseph Maria of Austria, Heir-Presumptive to the Austro-Hungarian Empire, *b* 18 Dec 1863, *m* (morganatically) 1 July 1900, Countess *Sophie* Maria Josephine Albina, *cr* HSH Princess von Hohenberg 1900, and HH Duchess von Hohenberg 4 Oct (confirmed 17 Dec) 1909 by Emperor Franz Joseph of Austria (*b* 1 March 1868; assassinated with her husband 28 June 1914), dau of Count Bohuslaw Chotek von Chotkowa und Wognin, and was assassinated at Sarajevo 28 June 1914, having had issue,

1*e* HH *Maximilian* Karl Franz Michael Hubert Anton Ignatius Joseph Maria, 2nd Prince and Duke von Hohenberg, *b* 29 Sept 1902, *m* 16 Nov 1926, •H Ill H Countess Maria *Elisabetha* Bona Walburga Josefa Laurentia (*b* 10 Aug 1904) [*A-3661 Artstetten, N Austria; Ziegelstadlstrasse 7a, A-5026 Salz-*

burg-Aigen, Austria], yst dau of HSH Maximilian, Hereditary Grand Seneschal of the Holy Roman Empire, 4th Prince von Waldburg zu Wolfegg und Waldsee, and *d* 8 Jan 1962, leaving issue,

1f ●HH *Franz Ferdinand* Friedrich Ernst Josef Karl Leopold Mauritius Hubertus Maria, 3rd Prince and Duke von Hohenberg [*7951 Eberhardzell, Württemberg, Germany*]. *b* 13 Sept 1927, *m* 9 May 1956, ●HRH Princess *Elisabeth* Hilda Zita Maria Anna Antonia Friederike Wilhelmine Luise of Luxembourg, Bourbon-Parma and Nassau (*b* 22 Dec 1922), eldest dau of HRH Grand Duchess Charlotte of Luxembourg, GCVO, and has issue (*see p* 218).

2f ●HSH Prince *Georg Friedrich* Maximilian Jaroslav Petrus Canisius Josef Markus Hubertus Maria von Hohenberg [*Wien III, Salesianergasse 4, Austria*], *b* 25 April 1929, *m* 8 Sept 1960, ●HSH Princess *Eleonore* Marie Gobertine Henriette von Auersperg-Breunner (*b* 12 Sept 1928), eldest dau of HSH Karl, 10th Prince von Auersperg, and has issue,

1g ●HSH Prince *Nikolaus* von Hohenberg, *b* 3 July 1961.

2g ●HSH Prince *Maximilian* Andreas Gerhard Paul Severin Karl Martin Franz Leopold Josef Maria von Hohenberg, *b* 25 Jan 1970.

1g ●HSH Princess Henriette von Hohenberg, *b* 9 Nov 1962.

3f ●HSH Prince *Albrecht* Philipp Leopold Josef Andreas Hubertus Maria von Hohenberg, *b* 4 Feb 1931, *m* 12 May 1962, ●Countess Leontine (*b* 3 Aug 1933), dau of Count Leo de Cassis-Faraone, and has issue,

1g ●HSH Prince Leo von Hohenberg, *b* 28 Sept 1964.

1g ●HSH Princess Margarethe von Hohenberg, *b* 19 June 1963.

2g ●HSH Princess *Johanna* Sophia Carolina Maria von Hohenberg, *b* 29 April 1966.

3g ●HSH Princess *Katharina* Aglae Franziska Maria von Hohenberg, *b* 9 March 1969.

4f ●HSH Prince *Johannes* Andreas Josef Antonius Michael Severinus Alexander Hubertus Maria von Hohenberg, *b* 3 May 1933, *m* (civil) 28 Aug and (religious) 11 Oct 1969, ●Elisabeth Meilinger-Rehrl (*b* 30 May 1947), dau of Franz Meilinger and adopted dau of Prof Hermann Rehrl, and has issue,

●HSH Prince Stephan von Hohenberg, *b* 3 July 1972.

●HSH Princess *Sophie* Christina Philippa Elisabetha Bona Bernadette Maria von Hohenberg, *b* 26 May 1970.

5f ●HSH Prince *Peter* Friedrich Benedikt Josef Emanuel Gerhard Judas Thaddäus Hubertus Maria von Hohenberg, *b* 26 March 1936, *m* (civil) 14 April and (religious) 16 May 1970, ●Christine-Maria Meilinger-Rehrl (*b* 17 April 1945), dau of Franz Meilinger and adopted dau of Prof Hermann Rehrl, and has issue,

1g ●HSH Princess *Marie-Christine* Anna Katharina Elisabetha Bona von Hohenberg, *b* 25 Nov 1970.

2g HSH Princess *Maria Theresia* von Hohenberg, *b* 31 July 1972.

6f ●HSH Prince *Gerhard* Josef Anton Stephan Jakob Wenzel Pius Hartmann Hubertus Maria von Hohenberg, *b* 23 Dec 1941.

2e HSH Prince *Ernst* Alphons Karl Franz Ignaz Joseph Maria Anton von Hohenberg, *b* 27 May 1904, *m* 25 May 1936, ●Marie-Thérèse (*b* 9 May 1910) [*A-8795 Radmer, Steiermark, Austria*], only dau of Capt George Jervis Wood, OBE (*see* BURKE'S *LG,* 1952 *Edn,* WOOD *formerly of Hetton*), and *d* 5 March 1954, leaving issue,

1f ●HSH Prince *Franz Ferdinand* Maximilian Georg Ernst Maria Josef Zacharius Ignaz von Hohenberg, *b* 14 March 1937.

2f ●HSH Prince *Ernst-Georg* Elemer Albert Josef Antonius Peregrinus Rupert Maria von Hohenberg, *b* 1 March 1944.

1e ●HSH Princess *Sophie* Maria Franziska Antonia Ignatia Alberta von Hohenberg, *b* 24 July 1901, *m* 8 Sept 1920, ●*Friedrich* Leopold Joseph Hubertus Maria, Count von Nostitz-Rieneck (*b* 1 Nov 1893) [*A-5026 Salzburg-Aigen, Ziegelstadelstrasse 7, Austria*], and has had issue,

1f Count *Erwein* Maximilian Franz Peter Paul Hubertus Conrad Maria von Nostitz-Rieneck, *b* 29 June 1921; *d* as a Russian prisoner-of-war 11 Sept 1949.

2f Count *Franz* von Assisi Friedrich Ernst Leopold Joseph Maria von Nostitz-Rieneck, *b* 2 Feb 1923; *k* in action in World War II 23 Feb 1945.

3f ●Count *Alois* Karl Josef Maria von Nostitz-Rieneck [*A-8790 Eisenerz, Schloss Geyeregg, Steiermark, Austria*], *b* 12 Aug 1925, *m* 12 Sept 1962, ●H Ill H Countess *Marie Therese* Walburga Elisabeth Antonia (*b* 8 Aug 1931), 2nd dau of HSH Erich August, 6th Prince von Waldburg zu Zeil und Trauchburg, and has issue,

1g ●Count *Friedrich* Erich Thaddäus Vincenz Jakob Alois Josef Maria von Nostitz-Rieneck, *b* 19 July 1963.

1g ●Countess *Monika* Maria Theresia Walburga Henriette von Nostitz-Rieneck, *b* 15 April 1965.

2g ●Countess *Sophie-Bernadette* Maria Hyacintha Thaddäa Walburga von Nostitz-Rieneck, *b* 17 Aug 1967.

1f ●Countess *Sophie* Amalia Therese Quirina Henriette Lukretia Magdalena Maria Ignatia von Nostitz-Rieneck, *b* 4 June 1929, *m* 18 Aug 1953, ●Baron *Ernst Gordian* Paul Franz Xaver Josef Ignaz Jakob Isidor Pelagius Leonhard Maximilian Maria Emanuel von Gudenus (*b* 26 March 1916) [*A-8160 Werz, Schloss Thannhausen, Steiermark, Austria*], and has issue,

1g ●Baron Erwein Friedrich Maria Gordian Andreas Balthasar Leonhard Josef Felix von Gudenus, *b* 30 Aug 1958.

2g ●Baron Ferdinand von Gudenus, *b* 27 July 1960.

1g ●Baroness *Sophie* Maria Amelie Florence Norberta Leonarda Margaretha Henriette Kaspara Michaela von Gudenus, *b* 6 June 1954.

2g ●Baroness Maria Sidonia von Gudenus, *b* 20 Aug 1955.

2d HI and RH Archduke *Otto* Franz Joseph Karl Ludwig Maria of Austria, *b* 21 April 1865, *m* 2 Oct 1886, HRH Princess *Maria Josepha* Luise Philippine Elisabeth Pia Angelika Margarete (*b* 31 May 1867; *d* 28 May 1944), yr dau of HM King Georg I of Saxony, and *d* 1 Nov 1906, leaving issue,

1e HIM *Karl I* (Franz Josef Ludwig Hubert Georg Otto Maria), Emperor of Austria, Apostolic King of Hungary, King of Bohemia, etc (1916-1918), abdicated 11 Nov 1918, *b* 17 Aug 1887, *m* 21 Oct 1911, ●HRH Princess *Zita* Maria delle Grazie Adelgonda Michaela Raffaela Gabriela Giuseppina Antonia Luisa Agnese (*b* 9 May 1892) [*Johannesstift, Zizers, Kanton Graubünden, Switzerland*], 10th dau of HRH Duke Roberto I of Parma, and *d* 1 March 1922, leaving issue,

1f ●HI and RH Archduke Franz Joseph *Otto* Robert Maria Anton Karl Max Heinrich Sixtus Xaver Felix Renatus Ludwig Gaetan Pius Ignatius of Austria, Head of the Imp House of Austria [*8134 Pöcking bei Starnberg, Hindenburgstrasse 15, Germany*], *b* 20 Nov 1912, *m* 10 May 1951, ●HH Princess *Regina* Helene Elisabeth Margarete (*b* 6 Jan 1925), yr dau of HH late Duke

Georg III of Saxe-Meiningen (*see p* 266), and has issue,

1g ●HI and RH Archduke *Karl Thomas* Robert Maria Franziskus Bahnam of Austria, *b* 11 Jan 1961.

2g ●HI and RH Archduke *Paul Georg* of Austria, *b* 16 Dec 1964.

1g ●HI and RH Archduchess *Andrea* Maria of Austria, *b* 30 May 1953.

2g ●HI and RH Archduchess *Monika* Maria Roberta Antonia Raphaele of Austria, *b* 13 Sept 1954.

3g ●HI and RH Archduchess *Michaela* Maria Madeleine Kiliana Elisabeth of Austria, *b* (twin with Archduchess Monika) 13 Sept 1954.

4g ●HI and RH Archduchess *Gabriela* Maria Charlotte Felicitas Elisabeth Antonia of Austria, *b* 14 Oct 1956.

5g ●HI and RH Archduchess *Walburga* Maria Franziska Helene Elisabeth of Austria, *b* 5 Oct 1958.

2f ●HI and RH Archduke *Robert* Karl Ludwig Maximilian Michael Maria Anton Franz Ferdinand Joseph Otto Hubert Georg Pius Johannes Marcus d'Aviano of Austria-Este [*42 avenue Thierry, F-92 Ville d'Avray, France*], *b* 8 Feb 1915, *m* 28 Dec 1953, ●HRH Princess *Margherita* Isabella Maria Vittoria Emanuela Elena Gennara of Savoy-Aosta (*b* 7 April 1930), elder dau of HRH Prince Amedeo of Savoy, 3rd Duke of Aosta, Viceroy of Ethiopia, and has issue,

1g ●HI and RH Archduke *Lorenz* Otto Carl Amadeus Thadeus Maria Pius Andreas Marcus d'Aviano of Austria, *b* 16 Dec 1955.

2g ●HI and RH Archduke *Gerhard* Thaddäus Anton Marcus d'Aviano Maria Umberto Otto Carl Amadeus of Austria, *b* 30 Oct 1957.

3g ●HI and RH Archduke *Martin* Carl Amadeo Maria of Austria, *b* 21 Dec 1959.

1g ●HI and RH Archduchess *Maria Beatrix* Anna Felicitas Zita Charlotte Adelheid Cristina Elisabeth Gennara of Austria, *b* 11 Dec 1954.

2g ●HI and RH Archduchess *Isabella* Marie Laura Helena Antonia Zita Anna Gennara of Austria, *b* 2 March 1963.

3f ●HI and RH Archduke *Felix* Friedrich August Maria vom Siege Franz Joseph Peter Karl Anton Robert Otto Pius Michael Benedikt Sebastien Ignatius Marcus d'Aviano of Austria [*Reyna 85, San Angel, Mexico DF, Mexico*], *b* 31 May 1916, *m* 19 Nov 1952, ●HSH Princess and Duchess *Anna-Eugénie* Pauline Gabrielle Robertine Marie de Mercedes Melchiore (*b* 5 July 1925), yr dau of HSH Prince and Duke Robert von Arenberg, and has issue,

1g ●HI and RH Archduke *Carl Philipp* Maria Otto Lukas Markus d'Aviano Melchior of Austria, *b* 18 Oct 1954.

2g ●HI and RH Archduke *Raimund* Joseph Carl Ludwig Maria Gabriel Markus d'Aviano Caspar of Austria, *b* 28 Jan 1958.

3g ●HI and RH Archduke *István* Franz-Leopold Johannes Maria Rudolph Theresius Marcus d'Aviano Balthasar of Austria, *b* 22 Sept 1961.

1g ●HI and RH Archduchess *Maria del Pilar* Sophie Valerie Charlotte Zita Johanna Marcus d'Aviano Caspara of Austria, *b* 18 Oct 1953.

2g ●HI and RH Archduchess *Kinga* Barbara Maria Carlota Jakobea Markus d'Aviano Balthasara of Austria, *b* 13 Oct 1955.

3g ●HI and RH Archduchess *Myriam* Adelheid Hugoline Omnes Sancti Marcus d'Aviano Melchiora of Austria, *b* 21 Nov 1959.

4g ●HI and RH Archduchess *Viridis* Aloisia Marie-Eleonore Elisabeth Marcus d'Aviano Caspara of Austria, *b* (twin wi Archduke István) 22 Sept 1961.

4f ●HI and RH Archduke *Carl Ludw* Maria Franz Joseph Michael Gabriel Ant nius Robert Stephan Pius Gregor Ignati Marcus d'Aviano of Austria [*57 Rou Gouvernmentale, Brussels 15, Belgium*], 10 March 1918, *m* 17 Jan 1950, ●HH Pri cess *Yolande*-Marie-Jeanne-Charlotte (*b* May 1923), yr dau of HH Eugène, 12 Prince de Ligne, and has issue,

1g ●HI and RH Archduke *Rudolf* Mar Carl Eugen Anna Antonius Marc d'Aviano of Austria, *b* 17 Nov 1950.

2g ●HI and RH Archduke *Carl Christic* Maria Anna Rudolf Anton Marc d'Aviano of Austria, *b* 26 Aug 1954.

1g ●HI and RH Archduchess *Alexand* Maria Anna Philippa Athina of Austri *b* 10 July 1952.

2g ●HI and RH Archduchess Maria *Co stanza* Anna Rosario Roberta of Austri *b* 19 Oct 1957.

5f ●HI and RH Archduke *Rudolf Syring* Peter Karl Franz Joseph Robert Ot Antonius Maria Pius Benedikt Ignati Laurentius Justiniani Marcus d'Aviano c Austria [*6 Corniche Verte, 1150 Brussel Belgium*], *b* 5 Sept 1919, *m* 1st 22 Jur 1953, Xenia Sergeievna (*b* 11 June 1929 *k* in a motor accident 21 Sept 1968), dau c Sergei Alexandrovitch Besobrasow, of th house of the Counts Tchernyschew-Krugl kow-Besobrasow, and has issue,

1g ●HI and RH Archduke *Carl Pete* Otto Serge Joseph Paul Leopold Heinric of Austria, *b* 5 Nov 1955.

2g ●HI and RH Archduke *Simeon* Ca Eugen Joseph Leopold of Austria, *b* 2 June 1958.

3g ●HI and RH Archduke *Johannes* Ca Ludwig Clemens Maria Joseph Marcu d'Aviano Leopold of Austria, *b* 11 De 1962.

1g ●HI and RH Archduchess *Maria Anna* Charlotte Zita Elisabeth Regin Therese of Austria, *b* 19 May 1954.

He *m* 2ndly 15 Oct 1971, ●HSH Princes *Anna Gabriele* Maria Theresia Kaspara (11 Sept 1940), elder dau of HSH Carl, 5t Prince von Wrede.

1f HI and RH Archduchess *Adelhai* Maria Josepha Sixta Antonia Roberta Ottc nia Zita Charlotte Luise Immakulata Pi Theresia Beatrix Franziska Isabelle Henriett Maximiliana Genoveva Ignatia Marcu d'Aviano of Austria, *b* 3 Jan 1914; *d unm* 1971.

2f ●HI and RH Archduchess *Charlott* Hedwig Franziska Josepha Maria Antoni Roberta Ottonia Pia Anna Ignatia Marcu d'Aviano of Austria, social worker [*München 13, Rankestrasse 14, Germany*], *b* March 1921, *m* 25 July 1956, as his 2n wife, HH Duke *Georg Alexander* Michae Friedrich Wilhelm Albert Theodor Franz o Mecklenburg-Strelitz (*b* 5 Oct 1899; *d* July 1963 (*see p* 213).

3f ●HI and RH Archduchess *Elisabet* Charlotte Alphonsa Christina Theresi Antonia Josepha Roberta Ottonia Franzisk Isabella Pius Marcus d'Aviano et omne sancti of Austria, *b* 31 May 1922, *m* 12 Sep 1949, ●HSH Prince *Heinrich* Karl Vincen Maria Benediktus Justinus of Liechtenstei (*b* 5 Aug 1916) [*A-8122 Schloss Waldstei bei Peggau, Steiermark, Austria*], and ha issue,

1g ●HSH Prince *Vincenz* Karl Alfre Maria Michael et omnes sancti of Liechtenstein, *b* 30 July 1950.

2g ●HSH Prince *Michael* Karl Alfred o Liechtenstein, *b* 10 Oct 1951.

3g ●HSH Prince *Christof* Karl Alfre Maria Michael Hugo Ignatius et omne sancti of Liechtenstein, *b* 11 April 1956.

4*g* ●HSH Prince *Karl* Maria Alfred Georg et omnes sancti of Liechtenstein, *b* 31 Aug 1957.

1*g* ●HSH Princess *Charlotte* Maria Benedikta Eleonore Adelheid et omnes sancti of Liechtenstein, *b* 3 July 1953.

2*e* HI and RH Archduke *Maximilian* Eugen Ludwig Friedrich Philipp Ignatius Joseph Maria of Austria, *b* 13 April 1895, *m* 29 Nov 1917, ●HSH Princess *Franziska* Maria Anna (*b* 21 June 1897) [*A-5087 Anif 61, Salzburg, Austria*], yst dau of HSH Prince Konrad zu Hohenlohe-Waldenburg-Schillingsfürst, Prince von Ratibor und Corvey, and *d* 19 Jan 1952, leaving issue,

1*f* ●HI and RH Archduke *Ferdinand* Karl Max Franz Otto Konrad Maria Joseph Ignatius Nikolaus of Austria [*84 Grand Rue, Garches, Seine-et-Oise, France*], *b* 6 Dec 1918, *m* 10 April 1956, ●Countess *Helene* Marina Elisabeth (*b* 20 May 1937), only dau of H Ill H Carl Theodor, Count zu Toerring-Jettenbach, by his wife HRH Princess Elisabeth, 2nd dau of HRH Prince Nicholas of Greece and Denmark (*see p* 280), and has issue,

1*g* ●HI and RH Archduke *Maximilian* Heinrich Ferdinand of Austria, *b* 8 Feb 1961.

1*g* ●HI and RH Archduchess *Elisabeth* Caecilia Helen Antonia of Austria, *b* 15 May 1957.

2*g* ●HI and RH Archduchess *Sophie* Maria Germaine Franziska of Austria, *b* 19 Jan 1959.

2*f* HI and RH Archduke *Heinrich* Karl Maria of Austria [*Dolderstrasse 79, CH-8000 Zürich, Switzerland*], *b* 7 Jan 1925, *m* 17 Oct 1961, ●Countess *Ludmilla* Wladimira Antonia Huberta Maria Silveria Wilhelmine Cornelia (*b* 20 June 1939), yst dau of Count Christoph-Bernhard von Galen, and has issue,

1*g* ●HI and RH Archduke *Philipp* Joachim Franz Max Clemens Gallus of Austria, *b* 16 Oct 1962.

2*g* ●HI and RH Archduke *Ferdinand* Karl Augustinus Maria of Austria, *b* 28 May 1965.

1*g* ●HI and RH Archduchess *Marie-Christine* Franziska Sophie of Austria, *b* 14 March 1964.

3*f* HI and RH Archduke *Ferdinand Karl Ludwig* Joseph Johann Maria of Austria, *b* 27 Dec 1868, *m* (morganatically) 15 Aug 1909 Bertha (*b* 1879), dau of Emanuel Czuber, and *dsp* 10 March 1915.

1*f* HI and RH Archduchess *Margarete Sophie* Marie Annunciata Theresia Caroline Luise Josephe Johanna of Austria, *b* 13 May 1870, *m* 24 Jan 1893, HRH Duke *Albrecht* Maria Alexander Philip Josef of Württemberg, Head of the Royal House of Württemberg (*b* 23 Dec 1865; *d* 29 Oct 1939), and *d* 24 Aug 1902, leaving issue (*see p* 226).

2*c* HRH Princess *Maria Immacolata* Clementina of the Two Sicilies, *b* 14 April 1844, *m* 19 Sept 1861, HI and RH Archduke *Karl Salvator* Maria Joseph Johann Baptist Philipp Jakob Januarius Ludwig Gonzaga Rainer of Austria, Prince of Tuscany (*b* 30 April 1839; *d* 18 Jan 1892), and *d* 18 Feb 1899, leaving issue,

1*d* HI and RH Archduke *Leopold Salvator* Marie Joseph Ferdinand Franz von Assisi Karl Anton von Padua Johann Baptist Xaver Aloys Gonzaga Rainer Venceslaus Gallus of Austria, Prince of Tuscany, *b* 15 Oct 1863, *m* 24 Oct 1889, HRH Princess *Blanca* de Castille Maria de la Concepción Teresa Francisca d'Asis Margarita Juana Beatriz Carlotta Luisa Fernanda Aldegonda Elvira Ildefonsa Regina Josefa Michaela Gabriele Raffaela (*b* 7 Sept 1868; *d* 25 Oct 1949), eldest dau of HRH Prince Carlos of Bourbon, Duke of Madrid, and *d* 4 Sept 1931, having had issue,

1*e* HI and RH Archduke *Rainer Karl* Leopold Blanka Anton Margarete Beatrix Peter Joseph Raphael Michael Ignaz Stephan of Austria, Prince of Tuscany, *b* 21 Nov 1895; *d unm* 25 May 1930.

2*e* HI and RH Archduke *Leopold* Maria Alfons Blanka Karl Anton Beatrix Raphael Michael Joseph Peter Ignaz of Austria, Prince of Tuscany, *b* 30 Jan 1897, *m* 1st 12 April 1919 (*m* diss by div), Baroness Dagmar (*b* 15 July 1898), dau of Baron Wladimir von Nicolics-Podrinje, and had issue,

●Gabriele Habsburg-Lothringen, *b* 12 Feb 1922, *m* ●Jan von der Muhle.

He *m* 2ndly ●Alice Coburn, and *d* 14 March 1958.

3*e* ●HI and RH Archduke *Anton* Maria Franz Leopold Blanka Karl Joseph Ignaz Raphael Michael Margareta Nicetas of Austria, Prince of Tuscany [*Emerberg 2, Post Winzendorf, N Austria*], *b* 20 March 1901, *m* 26 July 1931 (*m* diss by div 1954), HRH Princess Ileana (*b* 5 Jan 1909), yst dau of HM King Ferdinand of Roumania, KG, and has issue (*see p* 296).

4*e* ●HI and RH Archduke *Franz Joseph* Karl Leopold Blanka Adelgonde Ignatius Raphael Michael Vero of Austria, Prince of Tuscany [*Franz-Josef-Hof, Berndorf IV, N Austria*], *b* 4 Feb 1905, *m* 22 July 1927, ●*Marta Aloisia* (*b* 30 Sept 1906), dau of Alois Baumer.

5*e* HI and RH Archduke *Karl* Pius Maria Adelgonde Blanka Leopold Ignaz Raphael Michael Salvator Kyrill Angelus Barbara of Austria, Prince of Tuscany, *b* 4 Dec 1909, *m* 10 May 1938 (*m* diss by div), Christa (*b* 4 Dec 1914), dau of Géza Satzger de Bálványos, and *d* 24 Dec 1952, leaving issue,

1*f* ●Alexandra Blanca von Habsburg-Lothringen, *b* 20 Jan 1941, *m* 1 Feb 1960, ●Don José Maria Riera de Leyva (*b* 13 Nov 1934), and has issue,

●Doña Alejandra Matilde Riera de Leyva y Habsburgo-Lothringen, *b* 4 Nov 1960.

2*f* ●Immaculata Pia von Habsburg-Lothringen, *b* 3 July 1945.

1*e* ●HI and RH Archduchess Maria de los *Dolores* Beatrix Carolina Blanka Leopoldina Margaretha Anna Josepha Pia Raphaela Michaela Sixta Stanislawa Ignatia Hieronyma Gregoria Georgia Cäcilia Carmino Barbara of Austria, Princess of Tuscany [*Viareggio, Italy*], *b* 5 May 1891.

2*e* ●HI and RH Archduchess Maria *Immakulata* Carolina Margarita Blanka Leopoldina Beatrix Anna Josepha Raphaela Michaela Stanislawa Ignatia Hieronyma Carmino Katherina Petra Cäcilia of Austria, Princess of Tuscany [*Viareggio, Italy*], *b* 9 Sept 1892, *m* 14 July 1932, Nob Igino Neri Serneri (*b* 22 July 1891; *d* 1 May 1950).

3*e* ●HI and RH Archduchess *Margarita* Raniera Maria Antonia Blanka Leopoldina Beatrix Anna Josepha Raphaela Michaela Stanislawa Ignatia Alice Cäcilia of Austria, Princess of Tuscany, *b* 8 May 1894, *m* 27 Nov 1937, ●Marchese Francesco Taliani (*b* 22 Oct 1887).

4*e* ●HI and RH Archduchess *Maria Antonia* Roberta Blanka Leopoldina Beatrix Margarita Karoline Josepha Raphaela Michaela Ignatia Aurelia of Austria, Princess of Tuscany, *b* 13 July 1899, *m* 1st 16 July 1924, Don Ramón Orlandis y de Villalonga (*b* 24 Dec 1896; *d* 10 Nov 1936), and has issue,

1*f* ●Don Juan Orlandis y Habsburgo, *b* 2 Jan 1928, *m* March 1951, ●Doña Hildegarde Bragagnolo y Daiqui Chevalier (*b* 25 July 1932), dau of Don Teobaldo Bragagnolo, and has issue,

1*g* ●Don Ramón Orlandis y Bragagnolo, *b* 28 April 1953.

2*g* ●Don Luís Felipe Orlandis y Bragagnolo, *b* 13 June 1954.

1g ●Doña Maria del Carmen Orlandis y Bragagnolo, *b* 13 Feb 1952, *m* 1971, ●Count *Wladimir* Anton Friedrich Peter Maria Halka von Ledóchow, Count Ledóchowski (*b* 17 June 1946).

2g ●Doña Maria del Pilar Orlandis y Bragagnolo, *b* 28 May 1955.

3g ●Doña Hildegarda Orlandis y Bragagnolo, *b* (twin with Doña Maria del Pilar) 28 May 1955.

4g ●Doña Marta Orlandis y Bragagnolo, *b* 6 Jan 1957.

1f ●Doña Blanca Maria de las Nieves Orlandis y Habsburgo, *b* 17 Sept 1926, *m* 15 April 1948, ●Don Juan Ereñú y Ferreira (*b* 27 Jan 1908), and has issue,

1g ●Don Joaquin Alfonso Ereñú y Orlandis, *b* 25 June 1949.

2g ●Don Carlos Alberto Ereñú y Orlandis, *b* 8 Sept 1951.

3g ●Don Eugenio Ereñú y Orlandis, *b* 20 May 1959.

1g ●Doña Maria Antonia Ereñú y Orlandis, *b* 13 June 1950.

2g ●Doña Cristina Eugenia Ereñú y Orlandis, *b* 7 Jan 1958.

2f ●Doña Isabel Orlandis y Habsburgo, *b* 12 March 1931, *m* 8 Jan 1954, ●Don Fausto Morell y Rovira (*b* 9 Dec 1916), and has issue,

1g ●Don Fausto Morell y Orlandis, *b* 18 Dec 1954.

2g ●Don Francisco Javier Morell y Orlandis, *b* 5 Dec 1955.

3g ●Don Carlos Morell y Orlandis, *b* 24 Jan 1957.

1g ●Doña Maria Immaculada Morell y Orlandis, *b* 14 May 1958.

She *m* 2ndly 1942, Don Luís Perez Sucre.

5e ●HI and RH Archduchess *Assunta* Alix Ferdinanda Blanka Leopoldina Margaretha Beatrix Josepha Raphaela Michaela Philomena of Austria, Princess of Tuscany [*San Antonio, Texas, USA*], *b* 10 Aug 1902, *m* 17 Sept 1939 (*m* diss by div 1950), Joseph Hopfinger (*b* 14 April 1905).

2d HI and RH Archduke *Franz Salvator* Maria Joseph Ferdinand Karl Leopold Anton von Padua Johann Baptist Januarius Aloys Gonzaga Rainer Benedikt Bernhard of Austria, Prince of Tuscany, *b* 21 Aug 1866, *m* 1st 31 July 1890, HI and RH Archduchess *Marie Valerie* Mathilde Amalie (*b* 22 April 1868; *d* 6 Sept 1924), yst dau of HIM Emperor Franz Joseph I of Austria, Apostolic King of Hungary, etc, and had issue,

1e HI and RH Archduke *Franz Carl Salvator* Marie Joseph Ignaz of Austria, Prince of Tuscany, *b* 17 Feb 1893; *d unm* 10 Dec 1918.

2e HI and RH Archduke *Hubert Salvator* Rainer Maria Joseph Ignatius of Austria, Prince of Tuscany, *b* 30 April 1894, *m* 25 Nov 1926, ●HSH Princess *Rosemary* Friederike Isabelle Eleonore Henriette Antonia (*b* 13 April 1904) [*Schloss Persenbeug, N Austria*], 2nd dau of HSH Hereditary Prince Emanuel zu Salm und Salm-Salm, and *d* 24 March 1971, leaving issue (*see p* 229).

3e ●HI and RH Archduke *Theodor Salvator* Petrus Realinus Maria Josef Ignatius of Austria, Prince of Tuscany [*Schloss Wallsee, N Austria*], *b* 9 Oct 1899, *m* 28 July 1926, ●H Ill H Countess *Maria Therese* Walpurga Antonia Josepha Felicitas (*b* 18 Oct 1901), eldest dau of HSH Georg, 5th Prince von Waldburg zu Zeil und Trauchburg, and has issue,

1f ●HI and RH Archduke *Franz Salvator* Georg Josef Maria Thaddäus of Austria, Prince of Tuscany [*Schloss Wallsee, N Austria*], *b* 10 Sept 1927, *m* 26 April 1962, HSH Princess *Anna-Amelie* Madeleine Charlotte Marie Therese Sibylle Ulrike (*b* 22 Jan 1936; *d* 7 Oct 1966), eldest dau of HSH Prince George von Schönburg-Walder burg (*see p* 268).

2f ●HI and RH Archduke *Carl Salvato* Otto Maximilian Johannes Maria of Austria Prince of Tuscany [*Schloss Wallsee, N Austria*], *b* 23 June 1936.

1f ●HI and RH Archduchess *Theresi* Monika Maria Valerie Elisabeth Ludovik Walburga Anna of Austria, Princess o Tuscany, *b* 9 Jan 1931, *m* 17 Oct 1955 ●HRH Prince *Rasso* Maximilian Rupprech of Bavaria (*b* 24 May 1926) [*Leutstette über Starnberg, Wangener Strasse, German*] (*see p* 256), and has issue,

1g ●HRH Prince *Franz-Josef* Michae Maria Ignatius of Bavaria, *b* 21 Sept 1957

2g ●HRH Prince *Wolfgang* Rupprech Maria Theodor of Bavaria, *b* 28 Jan 1960

3g ●HRH Prince *Christoph* Ludwig Mari of Bavaria, *b* 5 May 1962.

1g ●HRH Princess *Maria-Theresia* Ann Walburga Irmingard of Bavaria, *b* 10 Sep 1956.

2g ●HRH Princess *Elisabeth* Maria Immaculata Anastasia of Bavaria, *b* 22 Ja 1959.

3g ●HRH Princess *Benedikta* Mari Gabrielle of Bavaria, *b* 13 March 1961.

4g ●HRH Princess Gisela of Bavaria, *b* 10 Sept 1964.

2f ●HI and RH Archduchess *Maria* Immakulata Mathilde Elisabeth Gabriele Walburga Huberta of Austria, Princess of Tuscany, *b* 7 Dec 1933, *m* 9 June 1959, ●Count *Reinhart* Heinrich Hubertus Maria von und zu Hoensbroech (*b* 15 Oct 1926) [*517 Schloss Kellenberg, Jülich, Germany*], and has issue,

1g ●Count Franz Lothar *Branco* Ignatius Georg von und zu Hoensbroech, *b* 23 April 1961.

2g ●Count Faustus *Florian* Lothar Felix von und zu Hoensbroech, *b* 1 March 1969

1g ●Countess *Alexandra* Maria Margarete Josefa von und zu Hoensbroech, *b* 19 March 1960.

2g ●Countess Maria *Consuelo* Pia Felicitas von und zu Hoensbroech, *b* 30 May 1962.

3g ●Countess *Donata* Theodora Carlotta Maria von und zu Hoensbroech, *b* 23 Aug 1963.

4g ●Countess *Elena* Maria Victoria Ingeborg von und zu Hoensbroech, *b* 1 May 1965.

4e ●HI and RH Archduke *Clemens* Salvator Leopold Benedikt Antonius Maria Joseph Ignatius of Austria, Prince of Tuscany, renounced his Imp and Royal styles and titles on his marriage and assumed the title of Prince von Altenburg [*Unterburgau, Post Unterach am Attersee, Austria*], *b* 6 Oct 1904, *m* 20 Feb 1930, ●Countess *Elisabeth* Marie Thaddea (*b* 28 Oct 1906), eldest dau of Count Friedrich Rességuier de Miremont, and has issue,

1f ●Prince *Clemens* Maria Franz Salvator Friedrich Christian Joseph Johannes a Mata von Altenburg, *b* 8 Feb 1932, *m* 17 Oct 1964, ●Laurence (*b* 3 June 1942), dau of Henry, Marqués de Costa de Beauregard, and has issue,

●Prince Philipp von Altenburg, *b* 15 March 1966.

2f ●Prince *Georg* Adam Maria Friedrich Leopold Joseph Michael von Altenburg [*Salzburg, Arenbergstrasse 2, Atelier Ferch, Austria; Unterad am Attersee, Austria*], *b* 23 Sept 1933, *m* 7 Feb 1963, ●*Maria Roswitha* Wickl (*b* 2 March 1941), and has issue,

●Prince Aegidus von Altenburg, *b* 4 Jan 1964.

3f ●Prince *Peter* Friedrich Christian Clemens Maria Leopold Joseph Matthäus von Altenburg [*Wien III, Reisnerstrasse*

5/13, *Austria; Unterach am Attersee, Austria*], *b* 18 Sept 1935, *m* 2 Oct 1965, ●Countess *Juliane* Maria Christiane Hermine Elisabeth (*b* 22 May 1940), yr dau of Count Eugen von Waldstein-Wartenberg.

4*f* ●Prince *Christoph* Theodor Johannes Leopold Joseph Maria Vitalis von Altenburg [*c/o Mr M. Morrison, Durmosa, Victoria, Australia*], *b* 28 April 1937.

5*f* ●Prince *Franz Joseph* Georg Clemens Maria Leopold von Altenburg [*Graz, Brockmanngasse 70, Kunstgewerbeschule, Austria*], *b* 15 March 1941.

6*f* ●Prince *Nikolaus* Gottfried Salvator Maria Joseph Leopold Johannes Vianney von Altenburg [*Unterach am Attersee, Germany*], *b* 22 May 1942.

7*f* ●Prince *Johannes* Maria Karl Salvator Leopold Ignatius Florian von Altenburg, *b* 21 Jan 1949.

1*f* ●Princess *Marie Valerie* Christiane Elisabeth Clementine Franziska Josepha Marcella von Altenburg, *b* 16 Jan 1931, *m* 20 July 1959, ●Count *Mario* Heinrich von Ledebur-Wicheln (*b* 28 July 1931) [*CH-3000 Bern, Gerechtigkeitgasse 40, Switzerland*], and has issue,

1*g* ●Count Johann Maria *Heinrich* von Ledebur-Wicheln, *b* 27 July 1964.

1*g* ●Countess *Maria Josepha* Anna Pauline Martha Elisabeth Johanna Henriette Fatima von Ledebur-Wicheln, *b* 25 May 1962.

2*g* ●Countess *Maria Clementine* Sophie Anna Josepha Walburga Franziska Pauline Fatima von Ledebur-Wicheln, *b* 25 Jan 1963.

3*g* ●Countess *Anna* Maria de Mercede Vendeline Michaela Josepha von Ledebur-Wicheln, *b* 29 Sept 1965.

4*g* ●Countess *Maria Benedicta* Carolina Mathilde Henriette Beatrice Josepha Michaela von Ledebur-Wicheln, *b* 13 Nov 1969.

2*f* ●Princess *Elisabeth* Maria Christiane Magdalena Walburga von Altenburg [*Wien III, Reisnesstrasse 5/13, Austria; Unterach am Attersee, Austria*], *b* 11 Dec 1938.

1*e* HI and RH Archduchess *Elisabeth Franziska* Marie Karoline Ignatia of Austria, Princess of Tuscany, *b* 27 Jan 1892, *m* 19 Sept 1912, as his 1st wife, H Ill H Count *Georg* Julius Kaspar Konrad von Waldburg-Zeil (*b* 7 Jan 1878; d 26 Oct 1955), and *d* 29 Jan 1930, leaving issue,

1*f* ●H Ill H Count *Franz Joseph* Vitus Xaver Georg Wunibald von Waldburg-Zeil [*A-6845 Hohenems, Vorarlberg, Austria*], *b* 7 March 1927, *m* 21 June 1956, ●H Ill H Countess *Priscilla* Irene Franziska Elisabeth Maria Barbara (*b* 5 Feb 1934), elder dau of H Ill H late Count Clemens von Schönborn-Wiesentheid, and has had issue,

1*g* ●H Ill H Count *Franz-Clemens* Marie Josef Willibald von Waldburg-Zeil, *b* 5 March 1962.

2*g* ●H Ill H Count *Stephan-Georg* Manfred Rupert Wunibald von Waldburg-Zeil, *b* 3 Aug 1963.

1*g* ●H Ill H Countess *Maria Rosario* Clara Dorothea Walburga von Waldburg-Zeil, *b* 2 April 1957.

2*g* ●H Ill H Countess *Carolina* Josepha Graziella Maria Walburga von Waldburg-Zeil, *b* 15 Dec 1958.

3*g* H Ill H Countess *Elisabeth* Maria Sophie Aloisia Walburga von Waldburg-Zeil, *b* 28 Jan 1960; *d* 30 April 1966.

4*g* ●H Ill H Countess *Philippa* Charlotte Gertrud Walburga Maximiliana von Waldburg-Zeil, *b* 2 Dec 1968.

1*f* ●H Ill H Countess *Marie Valerie* Klementine Franziska Elisabeth Walburga von Waldburg-Zeil [*A-5026 Salzburg-Aigen, Schwarzenberg-promenade 28, Austria*], *b* 28 June 1913, *m* 29 April 1936, HI and RH Archduke *Georg* Maria Rainer Joseph Peter Hubert Gottfried Eustach Rupert Ignaz of Austria, Prince of Tuscany (*b* 22 Aug 1905; *d* 21 March 1952), and has issue (*see p* 237).

2*f* H Ill H Countess *Klementine* Marie Hedwig Elisabeth Agnes Walburga von Waldburg-Zeil, *b* 5 Oct 1914; *d unm* 21 Sept 1941.

3*f* ●H Ill H Countess *Elisabeth* Hedwig Maria Franziska Walburga Xaveria von Waldburg-Zeil [*7989 Schloss Syrgenstein, Post Eglofs über Wangen, Allgäu, Germany*], *b* 23 Feb 1917.

2*e* HI and RH Archduchess *Hedwig* Maria Immakulata Michaela Ignatia of Austria, Princess of Tuscany, *b* 24 Sept 1896, *m* 24 April 1918, H Ill H Count *Bernhard* Friedrich Hubertus Aloisius Maria zu Stolberg-Stolberg (*b* 20 Jan 1881; *d* 22 Sept 1952), and *d* 1 Nov 1970, having had issue,

1*f* ●H Ill H Count *Franz Josef* Hubert Bernhard Stephan Martin Maria zu Stolberg-Stolberg [*Wien IV, Prinz-Eugen-Strasse 68, Austria*], *b* 30 April 1920, *m* 5 Aug 1957, ●Countess *Elisabeth Christiane* Maria Johanna Antonia Bonaventura (*b* 16 May 1936), yr dau of Count Rudolf Kinsky von Wchinitz und Tettau, and has issue,

1*g* ●H Ill H Countess *Marie-Valerie* Aglaë Hedwig Elisabeth zu Stolberg-Stolberg, *b* 6 June 1958.

2*g* ●H Ill H Countess *Marie-Christine* Sybille Hedwig Elisabeth zu Stolberg-Stolberg, *b* 20 July 1959.

3*g* ●H Ill H Countess *Marie-Antoinette* Mathilde Hedwig zu Stolberg-Stolberg, *b* 8 Sept 1960.

4*g* ●H Ill H Countess *Marie-Sophie* Elisabeth Hedwig zu Stolberg-Stolberg, *b* 14 Dec 1961.

2*f* ●H Ill H Count *Friedrich Leopold* Martin Maria zu Stolberg-Stolberg [*Silz in Tirol, Austria*], *b* 23 May 1921, *m* 24 March 1948, ●Aloysia (*b* 24 July 1923), dau of Ernst von Pachmann, and has issue,

1*g* ●H Ill H Count *Christoph* Bernhard Maria zu Stolberg-Stolberg, *b* 28 July 1948.

2*g* ●H Ill H Count *Peter* Franziskus Theodor Raphael Blasius Maria zu Stolberg-Stolberg, *b* 3 Feb 1951.

3*g* ●H Ill H Count *Johannes* Ernst Bonifaz Maria zu Stolberg-Stolberg, *b* 14 May 1952.

4*g* ●H Ill H Count *Markus* Eugenius Bernhard Maria zu Stolberg-Stolberg, *b* 19 May 1953.

1*g* ●H Ill H Countess *Marie* Elisabeth Emanuela zu Stolberg-Stolberg, *b* 19 Dec 1949.

2*g* ●H Ill H Countess *Eleonora* Maria zu Stolberg-Stolberg, *b* 7 June 1959.

3*f* H Ill H Count *Bernhard* Hubert Josef Martin Maria zu Stolberg-Stolberg, *b* 30 Aug 1922; *d unm* 6 Oct 1958.

4*f* ●H Ill H Count *Carl* Franz Georg Petrus Canisius Hubert Martin Maria zu Stolberg-Stolberg [*Kühtai, Tirol, Austria*], b 7 June 1925, *m* 22 Aug 1951, ●Edith (*b* 25 May 1923), dau of Adolf Winkelbaur and has issue,

1*g* ●H Ill H Count *Christian Friedrich* Bernhard Adolf Franz Bonifatius zu Stolberg-Stolberg, *b* 9 June 1952.

2*g* ●H Ill H Count *Andreas* Rudolf Hubert Martin zu Stolberg-Stolberg, *b* 8 Oct 1954.

1*g* ●H Ill H Countess *Claudia* Maria Edina Hedwig zu Stolberg-Stolberg, *b* 25 May 1956.

5*f* ●H Ill H Count *Ferdinand* Maria Immaculata Joseph Martin Hubert zu Stolberg-Stolberg [*Pfeilgasse 32, Vienna, Austria*], *b* 8 Dec 1926, *m* 23 April 1966, ●Baroness Jutta (*b* 15 March 1938), elder dau of late Baron Adalbert von Cramm.

1f ●H Ill H Countess *Marie Elisabeth* Valerie Josefa Anna zu Stolberg-Stolberg [*Ban Me Thuot, Centre Vietnam, Vietnam*], *b* 21 May 1919.

2f ●H Ill H Countess *Therese* Marie Valerie Anne Hedwig zu Stolberg-Stolberg, *b* 11 Oct 1923, *m* 7 Aug 1945, ●Count *Paul Joseph* Hugo Ferdinand Alfred Alexander Wolff-Metternich zur Gracht (*b* 4 June 1916) [*Burg Heppingen bei Bad Neuenahr, Rheinland, Germany*], and has issue,

1g ●Count *Michael Donatus* Joseph Hugo Bernhard Karl Maria Wolff-Metternich zur Gracht, *b* 10 May 1946.

2g ●Count *Franz Joseph* Matern Paul Maria Wolff-Metternich zur Gracht, *b* 7 Oct 1947.

3g ●Count *Paul Christoph* Martin Laurentius Kuno Maria Wolff-Metternich zur Gracht, *b* 14 April 1952.

1g ●Countess *Theresa-Margarita* Flaminia Hedwig Walburga Maria Consuelo Wolff Metternich zur Gracht, *b* 29 March 1956.

2g ●Countess Maria Valeria Wolff-Metternich zur Gracht, *b* 26 June 1960.

3f ●H Ill H Countess *Anna Regina* Emmanuela Maria zu Stolberg-Stolberg, *b* 20 Dec 1927, *m* 9 Oct 1954, ●Chevalier Jack de Spirlet (*b* 3 April 1930) [*Dréve des Capucins, Nôtre Dame au Bois, nr Brussels, Belgium*], and has issue,

1g ●Guy - Bernard - Pierre - Edouard-Jack-Marie de Spirlet, *b* 13 May 1962.

2g ●Nicolas - Jean - François - Madeleine - Marie de Spirlet, *b* 10 Oct 1964.

1g ●Beatrice - Marie-Valerie-Hedwig-Ghislaine de Spirlet, *b* 21 June 1955.

2g ●Isabelle-Astrid-Paule-Marie de Spirlet, *b* 26 June 1957.

3g ●Marie-Elisabeth-Ferdinande-Catherine-Louise de Spirlet, *b* 30 April 1960.

4f ●H Ill H Countess *Magdalena* Maria Mathilde Emmanuela Walpurgis zu Stolberg-Stolberg, *b* 19 Dec 1930, *m* 8 Sept 1958, ●Baron *Martin* Sigismund Joseph Johannes Thomas Maria von Kripp zu Prunberg und Krippach (*b* 25 Dec 1924) [*Ansitz Knillenberg, Meran-Obermais, Dantestrasse 30, Germany*], and has issue,

1g ●Baron *Paul Bernhard* Bonifacius Joseph Georg von Kripp zu Prunberg und Krippach, *b* 24 April 1959.

2g ●Baron *Hans Jacob* Karl Martin Joseph von Kripp zu Prunberg und Krippach, *b* 10 Sept 1960.

3g ●Baron *Sigismund* Otto Bonifacius Antonius Joseph von Kripp zu Prunberg und Krippach, *b* 5 June 1962.

4g ●Baron *Franz-Xaver* Friedrich Blasius Maria Joseph von Kripp zu Prunberg und Krippach, *b* 2 Feb 1964.

1g ●Baroness *Marie-Agnes* Hedwig Elisabeth Mathilde von Kripp zu Prunberg und Krippach, *b* (twin with Baron Paul Bernhard) 24 April 1959.

3e HI and RH Archduchess *Gertrud* Maria Gisela Elisabeth Ignatia of Austria, Princess of Tuscany, *b* 19 Nov 1900, *m* 29 Dec 1931, as his 2nd wife, her brother-in-law, H Ill H Count *Georg* Julius Kaspar Konrad von Waldburg-Zeil (*b* 7 Jan 1878; *d* 26 Oct 1955), and *d* 22 Dec 1962, leaving issue,

●H Ill H Count *Josef* Klemens Georg Vitus Willibald Konrad von Parzham von Waldburg-Zeil [*7989 Schloss Syrgenstein, Post Eglofs, über Wangen, Allgäu, Germany*], *b* 12 April 1934, *m* 21 May 1960, ●Baroness *Maria Benedikta* Helene Elisabeth Franziska Sophie (*b* 12 April 1937), 3rd dau of Baron Alfons von Redwitz, and has issue,

1g ●H Ill H Count *Vitus Franziskus* Rupert Benedikt Josef Wunibald Maria von Waldburg-Zeil, *b* 17 March 1961.

2g ●H Ill H Count *Alois* Willibald Johann Baptist Paul Maria von Waldburg-Zeil, *b* 23 June 1963.

1g ●H Ill H Countess *Marie-Christine* Sophie Eugenie Walburga Benedikta Josefa von Waldburg-Zeil, *b* 2 July 1962.

2g ●H Ill H Countess *Maria* Josefa Gabriele Philippa von Waldburg-Zeil, *b* 29 Aug 1964.

●H Ill H Countess Marie *Sophie* Josepha Elisabeth Walburga von Waldburg-Zeil, *b* 5 Dec 1932, *m* 7 May 1957, ●Baron Clemens *Wessel* Albrecht Cyriakus Joseph Hubertus Maria von Loë (*b* 8 Aug 1928) [*3509 Schloss Adendorf über Rheinbach bei Bonn, Germany*], and has issue (*see p* 229).

4e HI and RH Archduchess *Maria* Elisabeth Therese Philomena Ignatia of Austria, Princess of Tuscany, *b* 19 Nov 1901; *d unm* 29 Dec 1936.

5e ●HI and RH Archduchess *Mathilde* Maria Antonia Ignatia of Austria, Princess of Tuscany, *b* 9 Aug 1906, *m* 10 April 1947, ●Ernst Hefel (*b* 25 Nov 1888).

6e HI and RH Archduchess Agnes of Austria, Princess of Tuscany, *b* and *d* 26 June 1911.

3d HI and RH Archduke *Albrecht Salvator* Marie Joseph Ferdinand Karl Anton Johannes Xaver Aloys Rainer Klemens Roman of Austria, Prince of Tuscany, *b* 22 Nov 1871; *d unm* 27 Feb 1896.

4d HI and RH Archduke *Rainer Salvator* Maria Joseph Ferdinand Leopold Karl Anton von Padua Franz von Assisi Johann Baptist Xaver Aloys Gonzaga Stephan Protomartyr Alexander of Austria, Prince of Tuscany, *b* 27 Feb 1880; *d* 4 May 1889.

5d HI and RH Archduke *Ferdinand Salvator* Franz von Assisi Anton von Padua Johann Baptist Xaver Aloys Gonzaga Rainer Erasmus of Austria, Prince of Tuscany, *b* 2 June 1888; *d* 28 July 1891.

1d HI and RH Archduchess *Maria Theresia* Antonia Immakulata Josephe Ferdinande Leopoldine Franziska Karoline Isabella Januaria Aloysia Christina Anna of Austria, Princess of Tuscany, *b* 18 Sept 1862, *m* 28 Feb 1886, HI and RH Archduke *Karl Stephan* Eugen Viktor Felix Maria of Austria (*b* 5 Sept 1860; *d* 7 April 1933), and *d* 10 May 1933, leaving issue (*see p* 232).

2d HI and RH Archduchess *Caroline* Maria Immakulata Josepha Ferdinanda Theresia Leopoldine Antoinette Franziska Isabelle Luise Januaria Christine Benedikta Laurencia Justiniana of Austria, Princess of Tuscany, *b* 5 Sept 1869, *m* 30 May 1894, HH Prince *August Leopold* Philipp Maria Michael Gabriel Raphael Gonzaga of Saxe-Coburg and Gotha, Duke of Saxony (*b* 6 Dec 1867; *d* 11 Oct 1922), and *d* 12 May 1945, having had issue,

1e HH Prince *August Klemens* Karl Joseph Maria Michael Gabriel Raphael Gonzaga of Saxe-Coburg and Gotha, Duke of Saxony, *b* 27 Oct 1895; *d* 22 Sept 1909.

2e HH Prince *Rainer* Maria Joseph Florian Ignatius Michael Gabriel Raphael Gonzaga of Saxe-Coburg and Gotha, Duke of Saxony, *b* 4 May 1900, *m* 1st 15 Dec 1930 (*m* diss by div 1935), Johanna (*b* 17 Sept 1906), dau of Caroly Károlyi von Károly-Patti, and had issue,

●HH Prince *Johannes Heinrich* Friedrich Werner Konrad Rainer Maria of Saxe-Coburg and Gotha, Duke of Saxony [*8 München 13, Lerchenauer Strasse 2, Germany*], *b* 28 March 1931, *m* 1st 24 Oct 1957 (*m* diss by div 1968), Baroness Maria *Gabriele* Huberta Louise Klara Karoline (*b* 22 June 1921), 2nd dau of late Baron Franziskus von Fürstenberg, and has issue,

●HH Princess *Felicitas* Franziska of Saxe-Coburg and Gotha, Duchess of Saxony, *b* 6 April 1958.

He *m* 2ndly 1969, ●HRH Princess *Mathilde* Maria Josepha Anna Xavera (*b* 17 Jan 1936), yst dau of HRH Prince Friedrich Christian of Saxony, Margrave of Meissen, Head of the Royal House of Saxony (*see p* 255), and by her has issue,

●HH Prince Johannes Albert of Saxe-Coburg and Gotha, Duke of Saxony, *b* 197-.

He *m* 2ndly 13 Feb 1940, ●Edith (*b* 31 May 1913) [*A-5020 Salzburg, Makartkai 15, Austria*], dau of Alexander Kozol, Dir of the National Bank of Hungary, and was *k* in action in Word War II 7 Jan 1945.

3*e* ●HH Prince *Philipp Josias* Maria Joseph Ignatius Michael Gabriel Raphael Gonzaga of Saxe-Coburg and Gotha, Duke of Saxony [*A-1010 Wien, Seilerstätte 3, Austria*], *b* 18 Aug 1901, *m* 1945, ●*Sarah* Aurelia Hálas, and has issue,

●(Prinz) Philipp von Sachsen-Coburg und Gotha.

4*e* ●HH Prince *Ernst* Franz Maria Joseph Ignatius Thaddeus Felix Michael Gabriel Rafael Gonzaga of Saxe-Coburg and Gotha, Duke of Saxony [*A-8970 Schladming, Steiermark, Austria*], *b* 25 Feb 1907, *m* 4 Sept 1939, ●Irmgard Roll (*b* 22 Jan 1912).

1*e* ●HH Princess *Klementine* Maria Theresa Josepha Leopoldine Viktoria Raphaele Michaele Gabriele Gonzaga of Saxe-Coburg and Gotha, Duchess of Saxony [*Bougy, St Martin, CH-1770 Aubonne, Kt Waadt, Switzerland*], *b* 23 March 1897, *m* 17 Nov 1925, Eduard von Heller (*b* 21 March 1877, and has issue,

●Athlone Alexander August Georg von Heller, *b* 22 July 1938.

●Marie Amelie von Heller, *b* 9 Aug 1926, *m* 19 Dec 1949, ●Carlo Felice Nicolis dei Conti di Robilant e Cereaglio (*b* 11 July 1927), and has issue, one child.

2*e* HH Princess *Maria* Karoline Philomena Ignatia Pauline Josepha Michaela Gabriela Raphaela Gonzaga of Saxe-Coburg and Gotha, Duchess of Saxony, *b* 10 Jan 1899; *d unm* 6 June 1941.

3*e* ●HH Princess *Theresia* Christiane Maria Josepha Ignatia Benizia Michaela Gabriele Raphaele Gonzaga of Saxe-Coburg and Gotha, Duchess of Saxony [*Villazzano di Trento, Italy; Rua Sà Ferreira 171, Copacabana, Rio de Janeiro, Brazil*], *b* 23 Aug 1902, *m* 6 Oct 1930, Baron Lamoral Alexander Anton Josef Maria Taxis von Bordogna und Valnigra (*b* 7 Dec 1900; *d* 28 Jan 1966), and has issue,

1*f* ●Dom Lamoral *Carlos* Tasso de Saxe-Coburgo e Bragança, *b* 16 July 1931, *m* 1st 15 Dec 1956, Doña Denyse (*b* 27 April 1936), dau of Dom Sebastião Páes de Almeida. He *m* 2ndly 17 Feb 1969, ●HI and RH Archduchess *Walburga* Rosa Maria Christine Elisabeth Clementine Helene Caroline Zita Stephanie Michaela Apollinaria (*b* 23 July 1942), 2nd dau of HI and RH Archduke Georg of Austria, Prince of Tuscany (*see p* 238).

2*f* ●Baron Tassilo *Philipp* Taxis von Bordogna und Valnigra, *b* 3 Jan 1939.

1*f* ●Doña *Alice* Carolina Teresa Francisca Clementina Antonia Josefina Maria Tasso de Saxe-Coburgo e Bragança, *b* 7 June 1936, *m* 7 Jan 1956, ●Count *Michele* Carlo di Formentini (*b* 3 Jan 1929) [*Via Margotti II, Gorizia, Italy; San Floriano, nr Gorizia, Italy*], and has issue,

1*g* ●Count Leonardo Alessandro di Formentini, *b* 28 Oct 1956.

2*g* ●Count Filippo di Formentini, *b* 1 May 1964.

1*g* ●Donna Isabella Teresa Cristina Leopoldina di Formentini, *b* 3 Jan 1958.

2*f* ●Baroness Maria-Cristina Taxis von Bordogna und Valnigra, *b* 31 Jan 1945.

4*e* ●HH Princess *Leopoldine* Blanka Maria Josepha Ignazia Pankrazia Michaela Gabriela Raphaela Gonzaga of Saxe-Coburg and Gotha, Duchess of Saxony, *b* 13 May 1905.

3*d* HI and RH Archduchess *Maria* Antoinette Immakulata Josepha Ferdinande Theresia Leopoldine Franziska Caroline Isabella Januaria Luise Christine Appolonie of Austria, Princess of Tuscany, *b* 18 April 1874; *d* 14 Jan 1891.

4*d* HI and RH Archduchess *Maria Immakulata* Raniera Josepha Ferdinande Theresia Leopoldine Antonia Henrietta Franziska Karolina Aloysia Januaria Christina Philomena Rosalia of Austria, Princess of Tuscany, *b* 3 Sept 1878, *m* 29 Oct 1900, HRH Duke *Robert* Maria Klemens Philipp Josef of Württemberg (*b* 14 Jan 1873; *d* 12 April 1947) (*see p* 228), and *dsp* 25 Nov 1968.

5*d* HI and RH Archduchess *Henriette* Marie Immakulata Adelgunde Josepha Ferdinande Theresia Leopoldine Franziska Karoline Isabella Januaria Luise Christine Eleonore of Austria, Princess of Tuscany, *b* 20 Feb 1884; *d* 13 Aug 1886.

3*c* HRH Princess Maria delle Grazie *Pia* of Bourbon-Two Sicilies, *b* 2 Aug 1849, *m* 5 April 1869, as his 1st wife, HRH Duke Roberto I of Parma (*b* 9 July 1848; *d* 16 Nov 1907), and *d* 29 Sept 1882, having had issue,

1*d* HRH Prince *Ferdinando* Maria Carlo Pio Luigi Francesco Giuseppe Pietro Paolo Roberto Antonio of Bourbon-Parma, *b* 5 March 1871; *d* 14 April 1872.

2*d* HRH *Enrico I* (Mario Alberto Ferdinando Carlo Pio Luigi Antonio) of Bourbon, Head of the Ducal House of Parma (1907-1939), *b* 13 June 1873; *d unm* 10 May 1939.

3*d* HRH *Giuseppe I* (Maria Pietro Paolo Francesco Roberto Tomaso d'Aquino Andreas-Avellino Biago Mauro Carlo Stanislao Luigi Filippo Neri Leone Bernardo Antonin Ferdinando) of Bourbon, Head of the Ducal House of Parma (1939-1950), *b* 30 June 1875; *d unm* 7 Jan 1950.

4*d* HRH *Elie I* (Roberto Carlo Maria Pio Giuseppe) of Bourbon, Head of the Ducal House of Parma (1950-1959), *b* 23 July 1880, *m* 25 May 1903, HI and RH Archduchess *Maria Anna* Isabelle Epiphanie Eugenie Gabriele (*b* 6 Jan 1882; *d* 25 Feb 1940), 2nd dau of HI and RH Archduke Friedrich of Austria, Duke of Teschen, and *d* 27 June 1959, leaving issue (*see p* 230).

5*d* HRH Prince Augusto of Bourbon-Parma, *b* and *d* 29 Sept 1882.

1*d* HRH Princess *Maria Luisa* Pia Teresa Anna Ferdinanda Francesca Antonietta Margherita Giuseppina Carolina Bianca Lucia Apolonia of Bourbon-Parma, *b* 17 Jan 1870, *m* 20 April 1893, as his 1st wife, HM King Ferdinand I of the Bulgarians (*b* 26 Feb 1861; *d* 10 Sept 1948), and *d* 31 Jan 1899, leaving issue,

1*e* HM King *Boris III* (Klemens Robert Maria Pius Ludwig Stanislaus Xaver) of the Bulgarians (1918-1943), *b* 30 Jan 1894, *m* 25 Oct 1930, ●HRH Princess *Giovanna* Elisabetta Antonia Romana Maria of Savoy (*b* 13 Nov 1907) [*Casa Iantra, Rua de Sousa Martins 3, Estoril, Portugal*], 3rd dau of HM King Vittorio Emanuele III of Italy, and *d* 28 Aug 1943, leaving issue,

●HM King Simeon II of the Bulgarians (1943-1946), left Bulgaria following a plebiscite 9 Sept 1946 [*Avenida del Valle 3, Madrid, Spain*], *b* 16 June 1937, *m* 21 Jan 1962, ●Doña Margarita Gómez-Acebo y Cejuela (*b* 6 Jan 1935), dau of late Don Manuel Gómez-Acebo y Modet (of the family of the Marqués de Cortina), and has issue,

1*g* ●HRH Crown Prince Kardam of Bulgaria, Prince of Tirnovo, *b* 2 Dec 1962.

2*g* ●HRH Prince Kyril of Bulgaria, Prince of Preslav, *b* 11 July 1964.

3*g* ●HRH Prince Kubrat of Bulgaria, Prince of Panagiuriste, *b* 5 Nov 1965.

4*g* ●HRH Prince Konstantin-Assen of Bulgaria, Prince of Vidin, *b* 5 Dec 1967.

1*g* •HRH Princess Kalina of Bulgaria, *b* 19 Jan 1972.

•HRH Princess Marie-Louise of Bulgaria, *b* 13 Jan 1933, *m* 1st 20 Feb 1957 (*m* diss by div 1969), HSH Prince *Karl* Vladimir Ernst Heinrich zu Leiningen (*b* 2 Jan 1928), and has issue (*see p* 297). She *m* 2ndly 16 Nov 1969, •Bronislaw Chrobok (*b* 27 Aug 1933) [*372 Russell Hill Road, Toronto, Ontario, Canada*], and has further issue,

•*Pawel* Alistair Antoni Chrobok, *b* 3 May 1972.

•*Alexandra* Nadejda Chrobok, *b* 14 Sept 1970.

2*e* HRH Prince *Kyril* Heinrich Franz Ludwig Anton Karl Philipp of Bulgaria, Prince of Preslav, *b* 17 Nov 1895; *d unm* 1 Feb 1945.

1*e* •HRH Princess *Eudoxie* Augusta Philippine Klementine Marie of Bulgaria [*7963 Schloss Altshausen, Kr Saulgau, Württemberg, Germany*], *b* 17 Jan 1898.

2*e* HRH Princess *Nadejda* Klementine Maria Pia Majella of Bulgaria, *b* 30 Jan 1899, *m* 24 Jan 1924, HRH Duke *Albrecht Eugen* Maria Philipp Carl Joseph Fortunatus of Württemberg (*b* 8 Jan 1895; *d* 24 June 1954), and *d* 15 Feb 1958, leaving issue (*see p* 227).

2*d* HRH Princess *Luisa* Maria Annunziata Enrichetta Teresa of Bourbon-Parma, *b* 24 March 1872; *d unm* 22 June 1943.

3*d* HRH Princess *Maria Immacolata* Luisa Francesca Praxedes Annunziata Teresa Pia Anna Ferdinanda Antonietta Giuseppina Lucia Apolonia Filomena Clotilda Emerentiana Maria Giulia of Bourbon-Parma, *b* 21 July 1874; *d unm* 16 May 1914.

4*d* HRH Princess *Maria Teresa* Pia Luisa Immacolata Ferdinanda Enrichetta Giuseppina Alfonsa of Bourbon-Parma, *b* 15 Oct 1876; *d unm* 25 Jan 1959.

5*d* HRH Princess Maria *Pia* Antonietta Carolina of Bourbon-Parma, *b* 9 Oct 1877; *d unm* 29 Jan 1915.

6*d* HRH Princess *Beatrice* Colomba Maria Immacolata Leonia of Bourbon-Parma, *b* 9 Jan 1879, *m* 12 Aug 1906, Count Pietro Lucchesi-Palli dei Principi di Campofranco (*b* 7 Feb 1870; *d* 5 Dec 1939), and *d* 11 March 1946, having had issue,

1*e* Count Antonio Lucchesi-Palli, *b* 1 June 1907; *d* 4 Jan 1911.

2*e* •Count Ludovico *Roberto* Lucchesi-Palli [*Brunnsee, Steiermark, Austria; Sticciano, Certaldo, Florence, Italy; Santa Flavia, Palermo, Italy*], *b* 7 May 1908, *m* 7 June 1941, •Donna *Stefania* Margherita Francesca Maria Luisa (*b* 25 Aug 1909), only dau of Don Umberto Ruffo di Calabria dei Principi di Scilla, and has issue,

1*f* •Count *Pietro* (*Pio*) Maria Umberto Lucchesi-Palli, *b* 4 Jan 1943.

2*f* •Count Umberto *Antonio* Lucchesi-Palli, *b* 5 Oct 1944.

3*f* •Count Adinolfo *Roberto* Lucchesi-Palli, *b* 20 July 1946.

4*f* •Count Ferrante *Emanuele* Lucchesi-Palli, *b* 11 Jan 1952.

3*e* •Count *Adinolfo* Antonio Sisto Lucchesi-Palli [*Weinburg 35, Post Brunnsee, Steiermark, Austria; Collefiorito Stabbia, Florence, Italy*], *b* 18 June 1911, *m* 2 June 1946, •Countess *Sarolta* Elisabeth (*b* 29 March 1923), eldest dau of Count Michael Teleki von Szék, and has issue,

1*f* •Count *Michele* Alfredo Lucchesi-Palli, *b* 5 Feb 1949.

2*f* •Count Pio Lucchesi-Palli, *b* 17 March 1955.

1*f* •Donna Maria Beatrice Lucchesi-Palli, *b* 25 April 1947.

2*f* •Donna Eva Maria Lucchesi-Palli, *b* 18 Sept 1951.

3*f* •Donna Maria Bernadetta Lucchesi-Palli, *b* 27 May 1957.

7*d* HRH Princess *Maria Anastasia* Antonietta Cristina Enrichetta of Bourbon-Parma, *b* 25 Aug, *d* 7 Sept 1881.

4*c* HRH Princess Maria Immacolata *Luisa* of Bourbon-Two Sicilies, *b* 21 Jan 1855, *m* 25 Nov 1873, HRH Prince *Enrico* Carlo Luigi Giorgio Abraham Paolo Maria of Bourbon-Parma Count of Bardi (*b* 12 Feb 1851; *d* 14 April 1905), and *dsp* 23 Aug 1874.

2*b* HI and RH Archduchess *Maria* Caroline Ludovika Christina of Austria, *b* 10 Sept 1825 *m* 21 Feb 1852, HI and RH Archduke *Rainer* Ferdinand Maria Johann Evangelist Franz Ignaz of Austria (*b* 11 Jan 1827; *d* 27 Jan 1913), and *dsp* 17 July 1915.

(4) HSH Prince Karl Ludwig of Nassau-Weilburg *b* 19 July, *d* 27 July 1772.

(5) HSH Prince Karl Wilhelm Friedrich of Nassau-Weilburg, *b* 1 May 1775; *d unm* 11 May 1807.

(1) HSH Princess Auguste Marie Karoline of Nassau-Weilburg, *b* 5 Feb 1764; *d unm* 20 Jan 1802.

(2) HSH Princess Wilhelmine *Luise* of Nassau-Weilburg, *b* 28 Sept 1765, *m* 9 Jan 1786, HSH Heinrich XIII, Prince Reuss-Greiz (Elder Line) (*b* 16 Feb 1747; *d* 29 Jan 1817), and *d* 10 Oct 1837, having had issue,

1*a* HSH Prince Heinrich XVIII Reuss-Greiz (Elder Line), *b* and *d* 31 March 1787.

2*a* HSH Heinrich XIX, Prince Reuss-Greiz (1817-1836) (Elder Line), *b* 1 March 1790, *m* 7 Jan 1822, HSH Princess Gasparine (*b* 27 Sept 1799; *d* 27 July 1871), 3rd dau of HSH Prince Charles-Louis de Rohan-Rochefort et Montauban, and *d* 31 Oct 1836, leaving issue,

1*b* HSH Princess *Luise* Karoline Reuss-Greiz (Elder Line), *b* 3 Dec 1822, *m* 1st 8 March 1842, HH Prince *Eduard* Karl Wilhelm Christian of Saxe-Altenburg, Duke of Saxony (*b* 3 July 1804; *d* 16 May 1852), and had issue,

1*c* HH Prince *Albert* Heinrich Joseph Carl Viktor Georg Friedrich of Saxe-Altenburg, Duke of Saxony, *b* 14 April 1843, *m* 1st 6 May 1885, HRH Princess *Marie* Elisabeth Luise Friederike (*b* 14 Sept 1855; *d* 20 June 1888), eldest dau of HRH Prince Friedrich Karl of Prussia, and had issue,

1*d* HH Princess *Olga Elisabeth* Karola Viktoria Marie Anna Agnes Antoinette of Saxe-Altenburg, Duchess of Saxony, *b* 17 April 1886, *m* 20 May 1913, *Carl-Friedrich* Wilhelm Lothar Erdmann, Count von Pückler-Burghauss, Baron von Groditz (*b* 7 Oct 1886; *d* 13 May 1945), and *d* 13 Jan 1955, having had issue,

1*e* Count *Carl Rüdiger* von Pückler, *b* 2 Oct, *d* 23 Dec 1923.

1*e* •Countess *Ella-Viola* Helene Alberta Maria Eleonore Isabella Josephe Henriette von Pückler, *b* 8 April 1914, *m* 8 Nov 1941, •*Andreas* Friedrich Clement Werner von Flotow (*b* 16 April 1913) [*Siggen über Leutkirch, Allgäu, Germany*], and has issue,

1*f* •*Adrian Hyacinth* Carl Friedrich Wolf Tiedecke von Flotow, *b* 5 June 1943, *m* 10 July 1968, •Silvia Colck (*b* 27 March 1945), and has issue,

•*Constantin-Andreas* von Flotow, *b* 11 July 1969.

2*f* •*Cyrill-Andreas* Pierre Jürgen Konstantin Friedrich von Flotow, *b* 1 Dec 1955.

1*f* •*Viola* Isabelle von Flotow, *b* 27 March 1945.

2*e* •Countess *Eleonora Renata* von Pückler *b* 25 Nov 1919, *m* 1st 19 Sept 1939 (*m* diss by div 1948), Baron Rudolf *Manfred* von Schröder (*b* 11 June 1914), and has issue,

1*f* •Baron Rudolf Manfred *Rüdiger* von Schröder, *b* 10 March 1943.

1*f* •Baroness *Caroline* Eleonore von Schröder, *b* 26 Sept 1940, *m* 12 June 1965, •Rudolf Menzer (*b* 10 Aug 1924), and has issue,

•Robin Rudolf Rüdiger Menzer, *b* 29 June 1966.

She *m* 2ndly 21 April 1949, ●Jürgen Petersen (*b* 17 Sept 1913) [*Heimhuder Strasse 59, Hamburg, Germany*], and has further issue,

2*f* ●Marcus Hieronymus Nikolaus Petersen, *b* 6 Dec 1950.

3*f* ●Sylvius Hieronymus Petersen, *b* 12 Jan 1959.

2*d* HH Princess *Maria* of Saxe-Altenburg, Duchess of Saxony, *b* 6 June 1888, *m* 20 April 1911 (*m* diss by div 1921), HSH Prince Heinrich XXXV Reuss (*b* 1 Aug 1887; *d* 17 Jan 1936), and *dsp* 12 Nov 1947.

He *m* 2ndly 13 Dec 1891, HH Duchess *Helene* Marie Alexandra Elisabeth Auguste Caroline (*b* 16 Jan 1857; *d* 28 Aug 1936), only dau of HH Duke Georg of Mecklenburg-Strelitz (*see p* 213), and *d* 22 May 1902.

1*c* HH Princess *Marie* Gasparine Amalie Antoinette Caroline Charlotte Elisabeth Luise of Saxe-Altenburg, Duchess of Saxony, *b* 28 June 1845, *m* 12 June 1869, HSH Karl Günther, Prince of Schwarzburg-Sondershausen (*b* 7 Aug 1830; *d* 28 March 1909), and *dsp* 5 July 1930.

She *m* 2ndly 27 Dec 1854, HSH Heinrich IV, Prince Reuss-Köstritz (Younger Line) (*b* 26 April 1821; *d* 25 July 1894), and *d* 28 May 1875, having had further issue,

2*c* HSH Heinrich XXIV, Prince Reuss-Köstritz (1894-1910) (Younger Line), *b* 8 Dec 1855, *m* 27 May 1884, HSH Princess Emma *Elisabeth* (*b* 10 July 1860; *d* 2 Dec 1931), yr dau of HSH Prince Heinrich LXXIV Reuss (Younger Line), and *d* 2 Oct 1910, leaving issue,

1*d* HSH Prince Heinrich XXXIX Reuss (1910-1918) (Younger Line), *b* 23 June 1891, *m* 7 Aug 1918, H Ill H Countess *Antonie* Emma Elisabeth (*b* 18 April 1896; *d* 4 May 1971), eldest dau of HSH Friedrich Karl, 1st Prince zu Castell-Castell, and *d* 24 Feb 1946, having had issue,

1*e* ●HSH Heinrich IV, Prince Reuss (Younger Line), Head of the Princely House of Reuss [*A-2155 Schloss Ernstbrunn, N Austria*], *b* 26 Oct 1919, *m* 10 June 1954, ●HSH Princess *Marie Luise* Eleonore Adelma Rosa (*b* 18 Aug 1918), yr dau of HSH Otto II, 3rd Prince and Rheingraf zu Salm-Horstmar, and has issue,

1*f* ●HSH Hereditary Prince Heinrich XIV Reuss (Younger Line), *b* 14 July 1955.

1*f* ●HSH Princess Anna Elisabeth *Johanetta* Reuss (Younger Line), *b* 29 June 1957.

2*f* ●HSH Princess *Caroline* Adelma Henriette Anna Elisabeth Reuss (Younger Line), *b* 23 June 1959.

3*f* ●HSH Princess *Espérance* Anna Elisabeth Eleonore Reuss (Younger Line), *b* 22 July 1962.

2*e* HSH Prince Heinrich VI Reuss (Younger Line), *b* 27 June 1922; *k* in action 5 Dec 1942.

3*e* ●HSH Prince Heinrich VII Reuss (Younger Line) [*8 München 13, Clemensstrasse 111, Germany*], *b* 14 May 1927, *m* ●Baroness—van Tuyll van Serooskerten.

1*e* ●HSH Princess *Amadea* Caroline Anna Elisabeth Gertrud Viola Eleonore Reuss (Younger Line), *b* 23 July 1923, *m* 2 Jan 1959, ●Reinhold Sachs (*b* 28 July 1922) [*1 Berlin 22 (Kladow), Krampnitzer Weg 105a, Germany*].

2*e* ●HSH Princess *Gertrud Renata* Anna Elisabeth Jutta Gasparine Reuss (Younger Line), *b* 15 Nov 1924, *m* 14 Oct 1950, ●Henri Grand d'Esnon (*b* 24 Jan 1918) [*34 rue de la Faisanderie, F-75 Paris XVI, France*], and has issue,

1*f* ●Henri-Ferdinand-Antoine-Gaston Grand d'Esnon *b* 10 Jan 1953.

2*f* ●Jérôme-Donatien-Etienne Grand d'Esnon, *b* 13 Feb 1956.

3*f* ●Vincent-Cornelis-Eugène Grand d'Esnon, *b* 7 May 1959.

4*f* ●Marc-Fredéric-Charles-Prosper Grand d'Esnon, *b* 8 Sept 1961.

1*f* ●Gasparine-Amadea-Charlotte-Christiane Grand d'Esnon, *b* 17 July 1951.

3*e* ●HSH Princess *Elisabeth Donata* Regina Emma Clementine Reuss (Younger Line), *b* 8 June 1932, *m* 14 May 1960, ●Rev Peter Everard Coleman (*b* 28 Aug 1928) [*7 Mortimer Road, Bristol 8*], and has issue,

1*f* ●*Basil* Henry Everard Coleman, *b* 1 May 1963.

2*f* ●*Benedict* Amadeus Michael Coleman, *b* 17 Sept 1965.

1*f* ●*Antonia* Emma Elisabeth Coleman, *b* 22 Aug 1961.

2*f* ●*Elena* Louise Regina Coleman, *b* 21 April 1969.

2*d* HSH Prince Heinrich XLI Reuss (Younger Line), *b* 2 Sept 1892; *k* in action 29 Nov 1916.

1*d* ●HSH Princess *Regina* Felicitas Helene Luise Amadea Reuss (Younger Line) [*A 8842 Forsthaus Katsch an der Mur, Steiermark, Austria*], *b* 4 April 1886, *m* 12 July 1916, H Ill H Count *Georg* Ernst Maria Karl Joseph Anton zu Stolberg-Stolberg (*b* 25 Feb 1883; *d* 25 Feb 1965), and has had issue,

1*e* H Ill H Count *Hermann Josef* Bonifacius Petrus Heinrich Maria zu Stolberg-Stolberg, *b* 4 March 1925; missing in Russia from Jan 1945.

2*e* ●H Ill H Count *Lukas* Ernst Heinrich Petrus Konrad Arnold Maria zu Stolberg-Stolberg [*A 8090 Graz-Ragnitz, Preventweberweg 3, Germany*], *b* 19 Oct 1926, *m* 28 Dec 1962, ●Lydia (*b* 24 May 1937), dau of Felix Perko Edler von Monshoff, and has issue,

1*f* ●H Ill H Count *Georg* Heinrich Felix Petrus zu Stolberg-Stolberg, *b* 18 Jan 1966.

1*f* ●H Ill H Countess *Sophie* Elisabeth Regina Margaretha zu Stolberg-Stolberg, *b* 17 Oct 1963.

2*f* ●H Ill H Countess *Regina* Dorothea Eleonore Maria zu Stolberg-Stolberg, *b* 21 Nov 1964.

1*e* ●H Ill H Countess *Elisabeth* Maria Theresia zu Stolberg-Stolberg, *b* 2 June 1918, *m* 1st 22 Jan 1941, Walter Eisenbach (*b* 12 Aug 1906; *k* in action in World War II 20 Aug 1944), and has issue,

1*f* ●Georg Michael Gottfried Eisenbach, *b* 17 Jan 1942.

2*f* ●Franziskus Maria Eisenbach, *b* 1 May 1943.

3*f* ●Martin Ferdinand Eisenbach, *b* 26 July 1944.

She *m* 2ndly 12 Aug 1951, ●Baron *Alexander* Oskar Gustav Maria Hubert von Warsberg (*b* 3 Nov 1910) [*Neckarsteinach bei Heidelberg, Germany*], and has further issue,

4*f* ●Baron Alexander Georg *Johannes* Maria Boëmund von Warsberg, *b* 28 Dec 1952.

5*f* ●Baron Hermann Heinrich *Markus* Maria Augustinus von Warsberg, *b* 19 Feb 1954.

6*f* ●Baron Karl Bernhard Stephan Maria Amadeus von Warsberg, *b* 15 Aug 1961.

1*f* ●Baroness *Katharina* Maria Regina Elisabeth Pia von Warsberg, *b* 25 April 1956.

2*e* ●H Ill H Countess *Eleonore* Maria Theresia Sibylla Sofie zu Stolberg-Stolberg [*Gusterheim Post Pöls bei Judenburg, Steiermark, Austria*], *b* 8 Aug 1920, *m* 30 Nov 1946, HSH Prince *Heinrich* Karl Borromäus Maria Franz von Sales zu Schwarzenberg (*b* 29 Jan 1903; *d* 18 June 1965), and has issue,

●HSH Princess *Elisabeth* Regina Maria Gabriele zu Schwarzenberg, *b* 1 Oct 1947.

3*e* ●H Ill H Countess *Maria Andrea* Ferdinande Antonia Ida zu Stolberg-Stolberg [*Salzburg, Abtei Nonnberg, Germany*], *b* 24 Nov 1921.

4*e* H Ill H Countess *Maria Christiane* Johanna Elisabeth zu Stolberg-Stolberg, *b* (twin with Countess Maria Andrea) 24 Nov 1921; *d unm* 23 June 1948.

2*d* ●HSH Princess *Sibylle* Gabriele Reuss (Younger Line) [*8711 Castell über Kitzingen, Germany*], *b* 26 Sept 1888, *m* 5 Oct 1920, H Ill H Count *Wolfgang* Friedrich Julius Magnus zu Castell-Castell (*b* 27 May 1877; *d* 8 Feb 1940), and has issue,

1*e* ●H Ill H Count *Prosper* Friedrich Karl Gustav Heinrich zu Castell-Castell [*München 27, Schumannstrasse 10, Germany*], *b* 4 Sept 1922, *m* 4 Aug 1961, ●HSH Princess *Elisabeth* Ilka Friederike Anna Luise (*b* 8 Dec 1940), only dau of HSH Prince Christian of Lippe-Weissenfeld, and has issue,

●H Ill H Count *Johannes* Friedrich zu Castell-Castell, *b* 17 Aug 1962.

2*e* ●H Ill H Count *Friedrich Ludwig* Hubertus Anton zu Castell-Castell [*Kreuzwertheim, Fürstin-Margarethe-Strasse 4, Germany*], *b* 5 Oct 1927, *m* 16 May 1958, ●Countess *Amélie* Helene Barbara Marta Elise (*b* 26 May 1930), eldest dau of Count Otto von Pfeil und Klein-Ellguth, and has issue,

1*f* ●H Ill H Count *Andreas* Wolfgang Otto Prosper Heinrich Friedrich zu Castell-Castell, *b* 15 May 1959.

2*f* ●H Ill H Count *Johann-Philipp* Carl Alexander Ulrich Friedrich zu Castell-Castell, *b* 14 Sept 1960.

3*f* ●H Ill H Count *Hubertus* Friedrich Aurel Georg-Michael zu Castell-Castell, *b* 16 Sept 1961.

1*f* ●H Ill H Countess *Désirée* Sibylle Elise Barbara Margarethe Isa zu Castell-Castell, *b* (twin with Count Johann-Philipp) 14 Sept 1960.

2*f* ●H Ill H Countess *Friederike-Christiane* Amélie Marie-Louise zu Castell-Castell, *b* 18 April 1964.

3*d* ●HSH Princess Gasparine Eleonore *Viola* Reuss (Younger Line) [*8 München 13, Clemensstrasse 111, Germany*], *b* 5 April 1898.

2*c* HSH Princess *Eleonore* Karoline Gasparine Luise Reuss-Köstritz (Younger Line), *b* 22 Aug 1860, *m* 1 March 1908, as his 2nd wife, HM King Ferdinand I of the Bulgarians (*b* 26 Feb 1861; *d* 10 Sept 1948), and *dsp* 12 Sept 1917.

3*c* HSH Princess *Elisabeth* Johanna Auguste Dorothea Reuss-Köstritz (Younger Line), *b* 2 Jan 1865; *d unm* 8 April 1937.

2*b* HSH Princess Elisabeth *Henriette* Reuss-Greiz (Elder Line), *b* 23 March 1824, *m* 4 Nov 1844, HSH Karl Egon III, Prince zu Fürstenberg (*b* 4 March 1820; *d* 15 March 1892), and *d* 7 May 1861, leaving issue,

HSH *Karl Egon IV* (Maria Friedrich Emil Caspar Heinrich Wilhelm Camill Max Ludwig Viktor), Prince zu Fürstenberg, *b* 25 Aug 1852, *m* 6 July 1881, Marie-*Dorothée*-Louise (*b* 17 Nov 1862; *d* 17 June 1948), only dau of Louis de Talleyrand-Perigord, Duc de Talleyrand et de Sagan, and *dsp* 27 Nov 1896.

HSH Princess *Amélie* Caroline Gasparine Leopoldine Henriette Luise Elisabeth Franziska Maximilienne zu Fürstenberg, *b* 25 May 1848; *d unm* 8 March 1918.

3*a* HSH Heinrich XX, Prince Reuss-Greiz (1836-1859) (Elder Line), *b* 29 June 1794, *m* 1st 25 Nov 1834, HSH Princess *Sofie* Marie Therese (*b* 18 Sept 1809; *d* 21 July 1838), 3rd dau of HSH Karl, Prince zu Löwenstein-Wertheim-Rosenberg. He *m* 2ndly 1 Oct 1839, HH Princess *Karoline* Amelie Elisabeth (*b* 19 March 1819; *d* 18 Jan 1872), elder dau of HH Gustav, Landgrave of Hesse-Homburg, and *d* 8 Nov 1859, having by her had issue,

1*b* HSH Prince Heinrich XXI Reuss-Greiz (Elder Line), *b* 11 Feb, *d* 14 June 1844.

2*b* HSH Heinrich XXII, Prince Reuss (1859-1902) (Elder Line), *b* 28 March 1846, *m* 8 Oct 1872, HSH Princess *Ida* Mathilde Adelaide (*b* 28 July 1852; *d* 28 Sept 1891), 3rd dau of HSH Adolf Georg, Prince of Schaumburg-Lippe, and *d* 19 April 1902, leaving issue,

1*c* HSH Heinrich XXIV, Prince Reuss (1902-1918) (Elder Line), *b* 20 March 1878; *d unm* 13 Oct 1927, when the Elder Line of the House of Reuss became *extinct*.

1*c* HSH Princess *Emma* Karoline Hermine Marie Reuss (Elder Line), *b* 17 Jan 1881, *m* 14 May 1903, Count Erich Künigl zu Ehrenburg, Baron von Warth (*b* 20 June 1880; *d* 3 Dec 1930), and *d* 6 Dec 1961, having had issue,

1*d* ●Count *Carl* Heinrich Künigl zu Ehrenburg, Baron von Warth [*Schloss Ehrenburg (Casteldarne), Post Chiènes, Pustertal, Italy*], *b* 17 April 1905, *m* 10 Dec 1931, Countess Helga *Ilsa Liane* Daniela (*b* 26 March 1908; *d* 4 Feb 1955), elder dau of Count Julius von Platen-Hallermund, and has issue,

1*e* ●Count *Erich* Julius Otto Künigl zu Ehrenburg, Baron von Warth, *b* 17 Dec 1942.

1*e* ●Countess *Maria-Elisabeth* Künigl zu Ehrenburg, Baroness von Warth, *b* 7 July 1932, *m* 20 May 1953, ●Gilbert Durst (*b* 6 June 1912) [*Ansitz, Vilsegg, Brixen-Milland, Italy*], and has issue

1*f* ●Alice Maria Christina Durst, *b* 17 Feb 1954.

2*f* ●Evelyn Andrea Durst, *b* 18 July 1955.

3*f* ●Irina Michaela Vivian Patrizia Durst, *b* 22 Jan 1961.

2*e* ●Countess *Erica* Gabriele Hermine Carola Künigl zu Ehrenburg, Baroness von Warth, *b* 24 Jan 1935, *m* 23 April 1955, ●Count Maria *Leopold* Adolf Emil Giselbert Alexander Künigl zu Ehrenburg, Baron von Warth (*b* 9 Feb 1917) [*A-5440 Golling an der Salzach, Obergau, Austria*], and has issue,

1*f* ●Count *Christian* Georg Gisbert Paul Leopold Karl Künigl zu Ehrenburg, Baron von Warth, *b* 15 Sept 1955.

2*f* ●Count *Marcus* Gilbert Kaspar Ignaz Leopold Künigl zu Ehrenburg, Baron von Warth, *b* 25 July 1958.

3*f* ●Count *Thomas* Stephan Alexander Leopold Künigl zu Ehrenburg, Baron von Warth, *b* 9 June 1965.

1*f* ●Countess Alexandra Künigl zu Ehrenburg, Baroness von Warth, *b* 3 July 1962.

3*e* ●Countess *Margarethe* Gabriele Eleonore Künigl zu Ehrenburg, Baroness von Warth, *b* 26 Aug 1939, *m* 26 Nov 1961, ●Jürgen Teckemeyer (*b* 26 July 1937) [*8 München 60, Wallnerstrasse 11, Germany*], and has issue,

●Hans Eric Teckemeyer, *b* 25 May 1962.

●Marion Teckemeyer, *b* 23 May 1964.

4*e* ●Countess *Christiane* Adelheid Künigl zu Ehrenburg, Baroness von Warth, *b* 26 Aug 1939, *m* 5 Oct 1963, ●Ulrich Nörtemann (*b* 25 Oct 1933), and has issue,

●Stephan Michael Lennart Nörtemann, *b* 13 April 1964.

2*d* Count Ferdinand Karl Erich Künigl zu Ehrenburg, Baron von Warth, *b* 12 June 1906; *d unm* 11 May 1931.

1*d* ●Countess *Marie-Hermine* Karoline Martha Künigl zu Ehrenburg, Baroness von Warth [*A-9201 Schloss Hornstein bei Krumpendorf, Kärnten, Austria*], *b* 7 March 1904, *m* 6 Sept 1924, Baron Otto Daublebsky von Sterneck zu Ehrenstein (*b* 13 Jan 1902; *k* in action in World War II 19 Oct 1942), and has issue,

1*e* ●Baron Walther Erich Ferdinand Heinrich Max Daublebsky von Sterneck zu Ehrenstein, *b* 20 July 1929, *m* 24 Aug 1954, ●Eva (*b* 5 Nov 1926), dau of Hans Ortner.

2*e* ●Baron Erich Richard Ferdinand Carl Daublebsky von Sterneck zu Ehrenstein, *b* 7 Dec 1931.

1*e* ●Baroness Rosmarie Martha Ida Emma Daublebsky von Sterneck zu Ehrenstein, *b* 19 Aug 1926, *m* 20 Aug 1955, ●Count Anton Bolza (*b* 13 June 1916), and has issue,

●Count Peter Béla Otto Stephan Bolza, *b* 3 Oct 1960.

●Countess Antoinette Felicitas Marie-Hermine Rudolfine Bolza, *b* 2 Jan 1958.

2*e* ●Baroness Felicitas Ferdinanda Elisabeth Gertrude Hermine Daublebsky von Sterneck zu Ehrenstein, *b* 27 March 1933, *m* 15 Aug 1959, ●Baron Johannes Evangelist (*Hans*) Georg von Steeb (*b* 25 June 1927) [*Graz, Johann Fuxgasse 12, Austria*], and has issue,

1*f* ●Baron Christian Heinrich Otto Raoul Johannes Maria von Steeb, *b* 2 Nov 1960.

2*f* ●Baron Richard Erich Ferdinand Felix Johannes Maria von Steeb, *b* 31 Oct 1961.

3*f* ●Baron Heinrich Octavian Felix Johannes Maria von Steeb, *b* 28 Jan 1963.

2*c* HSH Princess *Marie* Agnes Reuss (Elder Line) *b* 26 March 1882, *m* 4 Feb 1904, Baron Ferdinand von Gnagnoni (*b* 6 Sept 1878; *d* 8 July 1955), and *dsp* 1 Nov 1942.

3*c* HSH Princess *Karoline* Elisabeth Ida Reuss (Elder Line), *b* 13 July 1884, *m* 30 April 1903, as his 1st wife, HRH Grand Duke Wilhelm Ernst of Saxe-Weimar-Eisenach (*b* 10 June 1876; *d* 24 April 1923) (*see below*), and *dsp* 17 Jan 1905.

4*c* HSH Princess Hermine Reuss (Elder Line), *b* 17 Dec 1887, *m* 1st 7 Jan 1907, HSH Prince *Johann Georg* Ludwig Ferdinand August von Schönaich-Carolath (*b* 11 Sept 1873; *d* 7 April 1920), and had issue,

1*d* HSH Prince *Hans Georg* Heinrich Ludwig Friedrich Hermann Ferdinand von Schönaich-Carolath, *b* 3 Nov 1907, *m* 24 June 1939, ●Baroness *Sibylle* Anna Helene (*b* 4 July 1910) [*8311 Schlossgut Ast, Post Oberast über Landshut, NBayern, Germany*], yst dau of Baron Günther von Zedlitz und Leipe, and was *k* in action in World War II 9 Aug 1943, leaving issue,

●HSH Prince *Georg-Dietrich* Heinrich Günther Wilhelm Hubertus von Schönaich-Carolath [*8311 Schlossgut Ast, Post Oberast über Landshut, N Bayern, Germany*], *b* 4 Jan 1943.

●HSH Princess *Marina* Hermine Ilse Sibylle Huberta von Schönaich-Carolath, *b* 8 May 1940, *m* 28 Oct 1967, ●Baron *Peter* Karl Maria Josef Johann Eduard Faustinus Jovitta Wiedersperger von Wiedersperg (*b* 1943) [*8311 Sshlossgut Ast, Post Oberast über Landshut, N Bayern, Germany*], and has issue,

●Baroness Mariette Wiedersperger von Wiedersperg, *b* 1968.

2*d* HSH Prince *Georg Wilhelm* Johann Armand Viktor Heinrich Ferdinand von Schönaich-Carolath, *b* 16 March 1909; *d* 1 Nov 1927.

3*d* ●HSH Prince *Ferdinand* Johann Georg Hermann Heinrich Ludwig Wilhelm Friedrich August von Schönaich-Carolath [*8 München 2, Brienner Strasse 42 IV, Germany*], *b* 5 April 1913, *m* 1st 8 Nov 1938 (*m* diss by div), Rose Rauch (*b* 1917). He *m* 2ndly (civil) 18 Jan and (religious) 9 Nov 1963, ●Baroness *Margarethe* (*Margret*) Catharina Julia Marie (*b* 2 Jan 1908), formerly wife of Hermann Meyer, and 2nd dau of Baron Oscar von Seckendorff.

1*d* ●HSH Princess *Hermine Caroline* Wanda Ida Luise Feodora Viktoria Augusta von Schönaich-Carolath [*1 Berlin-Charlottenburg, Riehlstrasse 7, Germany*], *b* 9 May 1910, *m* 12 Dec 1936, Hugo Herbert Hartung (*b* 3 July 1908; *d* in a Russian p o w camp 31 Dec 1945).

2*d* ●HSH Princess *Henriette* Hermine Wanda Ida Luise von Schönaich-Carolath, *b* 25 Nov 1918, *m* (civil) 1 Oct and (religious) 5 Oct 1940 (*m* diss by div 1946), HRH Prince Karl *Franz Joseph* Wilhelm Friedrich Eduard Paul of Prussia (*b* 15 Dec 1916), and has issue (*see p* 302).

She *m* 2ndly 5 Nov 1922, as his 2nd wife, HIM Wilhelm II, German Emperor and King of Prussia (*b* 27 Jan 1859; *d* 4 June 1941) (*see p* 300), and *d* 7 Aug 1947.

5*c* ●HSH Princess *Ida* Emma Antoinette Charlotte Viktoria Reuss (Elder Line) [*6474 Ortenberg über Stockheim, OHessen, Germany*], *b* 4 Sept 1891, *m* 7 Nov 1911, HSH *Christoph Martin*, 3rd Prince zu Stolberg-Rossla (*b* 1 April 1888; *d* 27 March 1949), and has issue,

1*d* ●HSH *Heinrich Botho*, 4th Prince zu Stolberg-Rossla [*6474 Ortenberg über Stockheim, OHessen, Germany*], *b* 13 Dec 1914.

2*d* ●HSH Prince *Johann Martin* zu Stolberg-Rossla, *b* 6 Oct 1917.

1*d* ●HSH Princess *Caroline Christine* Hedwig Marie Hermine Luise Friederike zu Stolberg-Rossla [*Schleiden, Eifel, Jahnstrasse 3, Germany*], *b* 3 Dec 1912, *m* 1st 30 Nov 1935, Hans Albert von Boltenstein (*b* 14 Oct 1905; *k* in action 4 Sept 1940), and has issue,

1*e* ●Ruth Ingrid von Boltenstein, *b* 6 May 1937.

2*e* ●Gisela von Boltenstein, *b* 17 Nov 1938.

She *m* 2ndly 12 April 1944, Wilhard von Eberstein (*b* 11 Nov 1894; *d* 10 May 1964).

2*d* ●HSH Princess *Marie Elisabeth* Ida Emma Cecilie Mathilde zu Stolberg-Rossla [*Schleiden, Eifel, Jahnstrasse 3, Germany*], *b* 1 Oct 1921, *m* 27 Sept 1939, HSH Prince Wilhelm von Schönburg-Waldenburg (*b* 3 April 1913; *k* in action 11 June 1944), and has issue (*see p* 269).

3*b* HSH Prince Heinrich XXIII Reuss-Greiz (Elder Line), *b* 27 June 1848; *d* 22 Oct 1861.

1*b* HSH Princess Christiane *Hermine* Amalie Luise Henriette Reuss-Greiz (Elder Line), *b* 25 Dec 1840, *m* 29 April 1862, HSH Prince Hugo von Schönburg-Waldenburg (*b* 29 Aug 1822; *d* 9 June 1897), and *d* 4 Jan 1890, leaving issue,

1*c* HSH Prince Heinrich von Schönburg-Waldenburg, *b* 8 June 1863, *m* 1st 5 Oct 1898 (*m* diss by div 1920), HSH Princess *Olga* Amalie Wilhelmine Ernestine Marie Pauline (*b* 25 Oct 1880; *d* 1 July 1961), eldest dau of HSH Prince Alfred zu Löwenstein-Wertheim-Freudenberg, and had issue,

1*d* HSH Prince Alfred von Schönburg-Waldenburg, *b* 30 Oct 1905, *m* 16 Nov 1937, HSH Princess *Marie Eleonore* Elisabeth Cecilie Mathilde Lucie (*b* 19 Feb 1909; *m* 2ndly 5 Feb 1948, Ion Octavian Bunea; *d* 29 Sept 1956), only dau of HH Prince Wilhelm I of Albania, Prince zu Wied (*see p* 216), and *dsp* 10 March 1941.

2*d* HSH Prince Hugo von Schönburg-Waldenburg, *b* 15 Oct 1910, *m* 4 Nov 1937, ●Waltraut (*b* 2 July 1918), dau of Wilko von Klüchtzner, and was *k* in action 16 Jan 1942, leaving issue,

●HSH Princess Michaela von Schönburg-Waldenburg, *b* 9 March 1940, *m* 7 June 1963, ●HSH Hereditary Prince *Alexander* Maria Ladislaus Johannes Carl Ludwig zu Hohenlohe-Jagstberg (*b* 25 Aug 1937) [*Schloss Haltenbergstetten, Post Niederstetten, Württemberg, Germany*], and has issue,

●HSH Princess Antoinette zu Hohenlohe-Jagstberg, *b* 24 Feb 1964.

1*d* ●HSH Princess *Hermine* von Schönburg-Waldenburg [*484 Rheda-Wiedenbrück, Pixeler Strasse 4, Germany*], *b* 18 Sept 1899, *m* 5 Oct 1919 HSH Prince Heinrich XXXVI Reuss (Younger Line) (*b* 10 Aug 1888; *d* 10 April 1956), and has issue,

1*e* ●HSH Princess *Magdalene* Pauline Reuss (Younger Line) [*647 Büdingen, OHessen, Oberhof, Germany*], *b* 20 Aug 1920, *m* 5 June 1943, HRH Prince *Hubertus* Karl Wilhelm of Prussia (*b* 30 Sept 1909; *d* 8 April 1950), and has issue (*see p* 301).

2*e* ●HSH Princess Caroline Reuss (Younger Line), *b* 7 May 1923, *m* 4 Oct 1950, ●Count *Alfred* Robert Clemens von Wedel, Baron Wedel-Jarlsberg (*b* 22 Feb 1895) [*5 Köln-Sülz, Hermeskeiler Strasse 3, Germany*], and has issue,

●Count *Christian Alfred* Ernst August Georg von Wedel, Baron Wedel-Jarlsberg, *b* 24 May 1951.

2*d* ●HSH Princess Amelie von Schönburg-Waldenburg [*484 Rheda-Wiedenbrück, Pixeler Strasse 4, Germany*], *b* 27 April 1902, *m* 26 July 1922, HSH *Adolf* Moritz Kasimir Karl Adalbert Hugo Arthur, 5th Prince zu Bentheim-Tecklenburg (*b* 29 June 1889; *d* 4 Jan 1967), and has issue,

1e ●HSH *Moritz-Casimir* Widukind Gumprecht, 6th Prince zu Bentheim-Tecklenburg [*484 Rheda-Wiedenbrück, Haus Bosfeld, Germany*], *b* 12 Oct 1923, *m* 26 July 1958, ●Countess *Huberta* Elisabeth-Maria Henriette (*b* 28 Feb 1923), only dau of Count Dietrich-Werner von Hardenberg, and has issue,

1f ●HSH Hereditary Prince *Carl-Gustav* Moritz-Casimir zu Bentheim-Tecklenburg, *b* 2 June 1960.

2f ●HSH Prince *Philipp* Adolf Moritz-Casimir zu Bentheim-Tecklenburg, *b* 15 June 1964.

3f ●HSH Prince *Christoph* zu Bentheim-Tecklenburg, *b* 29 May 1966.

4f ●HSH Prince *Maximilian* Nicolaus Moritz-Casimir zu Bentheim-Tecklenburg, *b* 1969.

2e ●HSH Prince *Nikolaus* Moritz Casimir zu Bentheim-Tecklenburg [*Via di Grotta Pinta 19, Rome, Italy*], *b* 12 March 1925, *m* 15 Sept 1951, ●Countess *Franziska* Ladislaja Maria Josepha Bernhardine Philomena Wenzeslaja Agnes (*b* 28 Sept 1921), 2nd dau of late Count Friedrich Hoyos.

3e ●HSH Prince *Heinrich* Karl Moritz Casimir zu Bentheim-Tecklenburg, *b* 1 Feb 1940.

1e ●HSH Princess Gustava zu Bentheim-Tecklenburg, *b* 21 Oct 1929, *m* 14 Oct 1952, ●Count *Botho* Werner von Hohenthal (*b* 9 July 1926) [*8026 Ebenhausen, Isartal, Ulrich-von-Hassel-Strasse 21, Germany*], and has issue,

●Count *Karl* Gustaf Adolf von Hohenthal, *b* 13 Nov 1955.

●Countess *Tatiana* Amélie Yvonne von Hohenthal, *b* 19 Aug 1958.

He *m* 2ndly 14 July 1921, HSH Princess *Adelheid* Wilhelmine Olga Emilie Mathilde of Lippe-Biesterfeld (*b* 14 Oct 1884; *d* 9 March 1961), eldest dau of H Ill H Count Friedrich of Lippe-Biesterfeld, and *d* 28 Dec 1945, having by her had issue,

3d ●HSH Princess Marie von Schönburg-Waldenburg, *b* 29 March 1922, *m* 20 Sept 1944, ●Baron *Wolff-Dietrich* Hermann Paul von Wolzogen und Neuhaus (*b* 5 June 1910) [*Kalbach über Frankfurt-Bonames, Schöne Aussicht 1, Germany*], and has issue,

1e ●Baron *Wolf-Heinrich* Hans von Wolzogen und Neuhaus, *b* 25 Aug 1947.

2e ●Baron *Hans-Christoph* Walter von Wolzogen und Neuhaus, *b* 25 Aug 1948.

1c HSH Princess Margarete von Schönburg-Waldenburg, *b* 18 July 1864, *m* 4 Oct 1888, HSH Prince *Heinrich* Ludwig Erdmann Ferdinand von Schönaich-Carolath (*b* 24 April 1852; *d* 20 June 1920), and *dsp* 26 Jan 1937.

2c HSH Princess Elisabeth von Schönburg-Waldenburg, *b* 8 Nov 1867; *d unm* 1943.

2b HSH Princess *Marie* Henriette Auguste Reuss (Elder Line), *b* 19 March 1855, *m* 20 July 1875, Hereditary Count *Friedrich* Casimir Wolfgang Adolf Georg Ferdinand Julius Heinrich zu Ysenburg and Büdingen in Meerholz (*b* 10 Aug 1847; *d* 29 March 1889), and *dsp* 6 Dec 1909.

(3) HSH Princess *Karoline* Luise Friederike of Nassau-Weilburg, *b* 14 Feb 1770, *m* 4 Sept 1787, HSH *Karl Ludwig* Friedrich Alexander, Prince von Wied-Runkel (*b* 29 Sept 1763; *d* 9 March 1824), and *dsp* 8 July 1828.

(4) HSH Princess *Amalie* Wilhelmine Luise of Nassau-Weilburg, *b* 6 Aug 1776, *m* 1st 29 Oct 1793, HSH Prince *Viktor II* (Karl Friedrich) of Anhalt-Bernburg-Schaumburg (*b* 2 Nov 1767; *d* 22 April 1812), and had issue,

1a HSH Princess Hermine of Anhalt-Bernburg-Schaumburg, *b* 2 Dec 1797, *m* 30 Aug 1815, as his 2nd wife, HI and RH Archduke *Joseph* Anton Johann Baptist of Austria, Palatine of Hungary (*b* 9 March 1776; *d* 13 Jan 1847), 7th son of HIM Emperor Leopold II, and *d* 14 Sept 1817, leaving issue,

HI and RH Archduke *Stephan* Franz Viktor of Austria, *b* 14 Sept 1817; *d unm* 19 Feb 1867.

HI and RH Archduchess *Hermine* Amalie Maria of Austria, *b* (twin with her brother) 14 Sept 1817; *d unm* 13 Feb 1842.

2a HSH Princess Adelheid of Anhalt-Bernburg-Schaumburg, *b* 23 Feb 1800, *m* 24 July 1817, as his 1st wife, HRH Grand Duke (Paul Friedrich) *August* of Oldenburg (*b* 13 July 1783; *d* 27 Feb 1853), and *d* 13 Sept 1820, leaving issue,

1b HH Duchess Marie Friederike *Amalie* of Oldenburg, *b* 21 Dec 1818, *m* 22 Nov 1836, HM King *Otto I* of Greece (*b* 1 June 1815; *d* 26 July 1867), and *dsp* 20 May 1875.

2b HH Duchess Elisabeth Marie *Friederike* of Oldenburg, *b* 8 June 1820, *m* 15 Aug 1855, Baron Maximilian von Washington (*b* 2 Aug 1829; *d* 3 July 1903), and *d* 20 March 1891, leaving issue,

1c Baron Peter Elimar Otto Karl Georg von Washington, *b* 31 July 1856, *m* 27 March 1883, Countess Gisela (*b* 25 Aug 1857; *d* 1 July 1913), dau of Count Vincenz Welser von Welsersheimb, and *dsp* 22 Dec 1930.

2c Baron Stephan Ludwig von Washington, *b* 17 June 1858; *d unm* 10 Sept 1899.

3a HSH Princess Emma of Anhalt-Bernburg-Schaumburg, *b* 20 May 1802, *m* 26 June 1823, HSH Prince *Georg II* (Friedrich Heinrich) of Waldeck and Pyrmont (*b* 20 Sept 1789; *d* 15 May 1845), and *d* 1 Aug 1858, having had issue,

1b HSH Hereditary Prince Josef Friedrich Heinrich of Waldeck and Pyrmont, *b* 24 Nov 1825; *d* 27 Jan 1829.

2b HSH Prince *Georg Viktor* of Waldeck and Pyrmont (1845-1893), *b* 14 Jan 1831, *m* 1st 26 Sept 1853, HSH Princess *Helene* Wilhelmine Henriette Pauline Marianne (*b* 12 Aug 1831; *d* 27 Oct 1888), 5th dau of HH Prince Wilhelm of Nassau-Weilburg, and had issue (*see p* 221). He *m* 2ndly 29 April 1891, HH Princess *Luise* Karoline Juliane (*b* 6 Jan 1858; *d* 2 July 1936), 2nd dau of HH Duke Friedrich of Schleswig-Holstein-Sonderburg-Glücksburg, and *d* 12 May 1893, having by her had issue,

HSH Prince Viktor *Wolrad Friedrich* Adolf Wilhelm Albert of Waldeck and Pyrmont, *b* 26 June 1892; *k* in action in World War I 14 Oct 1914, *unm*

3b HSH Prince *Wolrad* Melander of Waldeck and Pyrmont, *b* 24 Jan 1833; *d unm* 20 Jan 1867.

1b HSH Princess *Auguste* Amelie Ida of Waldeck and Pyrmont, *b* 21 July 1824, *m* 15 June 1848, HSH Alfred, 1st Prince zu Stolberg-Stolberg (*b* 23 Nov 1820; *d* 24 Jan 1903), and *d* 4 Sept 1893, having had issue,

1c HSH *Wolfgang* Georg, 2nd Prince zu Stolberg-Stolberg, *b* 15 April 1849, *m* 19 May 1897, H Ill H Countess *Irmgard* Thekla Bertha Emma Helene (*b* 11 July 1868; *d* 4 July 1918), 3rd dau of H Ill H Count Carl zu Ysenburg und Büdingen in Meerholz, and *d* 27 Jan 1903, leaving issue,

HSH *Wolf-Heinrich,* 3rd Prince zu Stolberg-Stolberg, *b* 28 April 1903, *m* 22 Jan 1933, ●Irma (*b* 28 April 1910) [*Neuwied, Feldkirchstrasse 20a, Germany*], dau of Willy Erfert, and *d* 2 Jan 1972, having had issue,

1e HSH Hereditary Prince *Johann Wolfgang* zu Stolberg-Stolberg, *b* 27 March 1935; *d unm* 26 Sept 1964.

2e ●HSH *Jost Christian,* 4th Prince zu Stolberg-Stolberg [*Neuwied, Feldkircherstrasse 20a, Germany; 27A Avenue d'Orbaix, Brussels 18, Belgium*], *b* 19 July 1940.

1e ●HSH Princess Irmgard *Sixtina* Juliana zu Stolberg-Stolberg, *b* 4 Nov 1933, *m* 30 Aug 1961, ●HSH Prince *Georg-Friedrich* Nikolaus of Waldeck and Pyrmont (*b* 22 Nov 1936), and has issue (*see p* 222).

2e ●HSH Princess *Sophie-Charlotte* Agnes zu Stolberg-Stolberg, *b* 4 Oct 1943, *m* 15 July 1967, ●HSH *Friedrich Wilhelm* Heinrich Konstantin, 7th Prince zu Wied (*b* 2 June 1931), and has issue (*see p* 212).

2c HSH Prince *Eberhard* Berengar zu Stolberg-Stolberg, *b* 15 June, *d* 20 Aug 1851.

3*c* HSH Prince *Vollrath* Elinger zu Stolberg-Stolberg, *b* 9 Nov 1852; *d unm* 18 May 1906.
4*c* HSH Prince *Heinrich* Ottomar zu Stolberg-Stolberg, *b* 6 March 1854; *d unm* 15 Dec 1935.
5*c* HSH Prince *Albrecht* Ilger zu Stolberg-Stolberg, *b* 16 Jan 1861; *d unm* 29 July 1903.
6*c* HSH Prince *Volkwin* Udo zu Stolberg-Stolberg, *b* 15 Sept 1865; *d unm* 25 May 1935.
1*c* HSH Princess *Erika* Juliane zu Stolberg-Stolberg, *b* 15 July 1856, *m* 12 Sept 1878, H Ill H Count (Franz) *Georg Albrecht IV* zu Erbach-Erbach (*b* 22 Aug 1844; *d* 19 April 1915), and *d* 20 March 1928, having had issue,
H Ill H Count Franz *Erasmus* zu Erbach-Erbach, *b* 23 March 1883, *m* 1st 1 Sept 1905, Dora (*b* 1884), dau of Ludwig Fischer. He *m* 2ndly, — Hellwig, and *dsp* 10 Feb 1920.
2*b* HSH Princess Hermine of Waldeck and Pyrmont, *b* 29 Sept 1827, *m* 25 Oct 1844, HSH Prince Georg *Adolf* of Schaumburg-Lippe (*b* 1 Aug 1817; *d* 8 May 1893), and *d* 16 Feb 1910, having had issue,
1*c* HSH Prince Stephan Albrecht *Georg* of Schaumburg-Lippe (1893-1911), *b* 10 Oct 1846, *m* 16 April 1882, HH Princess Maria Anna (*b* 14 March 1864; *d* 3 May 1918), eldest dau of HH Prince Moritz of Saxe-Altenburg, and *d* 29 April 1911, having had issue,
1*d* HSH Prince *Adolf* Bernhard Moritz Ernst Waldemar of Schaumburg-Lippe (1911-1918), *b* 23 Feb 1883, *m* 10 Jan 1920, Elisabeth *Franziska* (*b* 6 Nov 1894; *k* in an air accident 26 March 1936), dau of Franz August von Bischoff-Korthaus, and was *k* in an air accident 26 March 1936, *sp*.
2*d* HSH Prince *Moritz* Georg of Schaumburg-Lippe, *b* 11 March 1884; *d unm* 10 March 1920.
3*d* HSH Prince Peter of Schaumburg-Lippe, *b* 6 Jan, *d* 17 May 1886.
4*d* HSH Prince Ernst *Wolrad* of Schaumburg-Lippe, Head of the Princely House of Schaumburg-Lippe (1936-1962), *b* 19 April 1887, *m* 16 April 1925, •HSH Princess *Bathildis* Wera Thyra Adelheid Hermine Mathilde Mary (*b* 11 Nov 1903), only dau of HSH Prince Albrecht of Schaumburg-Lippe, and *d* 14 May 1962, having had issue,
1*e* HSH Hereditary Prince Albrecht *Georg-Wilhelm* Eugen of Schaumburg-Lippe, *b* 26 Jan 1926; *k* in action in World War II 29 April 1945.
2*e* HSH Prince Friedrich August *Philipp-Ernst* Wolrad of Schaumburg-Lippe, Head of the Princely House of Schaumburg-Lippe from 1962, *b* 26 July 1928, *m* 3 Oct 1955, •Baroness *Eva-Benita* Viktoria Maria (*b* 18 Nov 1927), elder dau of late Hans-Werner, Count von Tiele-Winckler, and has issue,
1*f* •HSH Hereditary Prince Adolf Friedrich *Georg-Wilhelm* Wolrad Hans-Werner of Schaumburg-Lippe, *b* 14 July 1956.
2*f* •HSH Prince Ernst August *Alexander* Christian Victor Hubert of Schaumburg-Lippe, *b* 25 Dec 1958.
3*e* •HSH Prince *Konstantin* Carl-Eduard Ernst-August Stephan Alexander of Schaumburg-Lippe [*Bielefeld, Wertherstrasse 69, Germany*], *b* 22 Dec 1930, *m* 28 Dec 1956, •Sigrid (*b* 2 Sept 1929), dau of Gerhard Knape, and has issue,
•HSH Prince *York* Karl-Albrecht Konstantin of Schaumburg-Lippe, *b* 4 June 1960.
1*e* •HSH Princess Elsa *Viktoria-Luise* Marie Barbara Elisabeth Bathildis Wera of Schaumburg-Lippe, *b* 31 July 1940, *m* 1967, •Baron *Carl Georg* von Stackelberg, and has issue,
1*f* •Baron Arved Andre von Stackelberg, *b* 26 June 1967.
2*f* •Baron Stefan Matthias von Stackelberg, *b* 20 Sept 1968.
5*d* HSH Prince *Stephan* Alexander Viktor of Schaumburg-Lippe, *b* 21 June 1891, *m* 4 June 1921, •HH Duchess *Ingeborg Alix* (*b* 20 July 1901) [*8136 Kempfenhausen 54, Post Percha über Starnberg, Germany*], 2nd dau of HRH Grand Duke August of Oldenburg, and *d* 10 Feb 1965, leaving issue (*see p* 252).
6*d* HSH Prince *Heinrich* Konstantin Friedrich Ernst of Schaumburg-Lippe, *b* 25 Sept 1894, *m* 10 June 1933, Countess *Marie-Erika* Gisella Ada Elisabeth Alberta (*b* 10 Feb 1903; *d* 15 July 1964), only dau of Count Albert von Hardenberg, and *d* 11 Nov 1952, leaving issue,
•HSH Princess *Dagmar* Marie Elisabeth of Schaumburg-Lippe, *b* 18 Feb 1934, *m* 7 May 1956, •Christoph Kalau vom Hofe (*b* 16 Sept 1931) [*Travesia San Telmo 3, Colonia Las Magnolias, Madrid 16, Spain*], and has issue,
1*f* •Alexander Christoph Heinrich Fabian Kalau vom Hofe, *b* 13 March 1957.
2*f* •Fabian Georg Friedrich Kalau vom Hofe, *b* 16 Dec 1964.
1*f* •Caroline Marie-Anne Kalau vom Hofe, *b* 23 Aug 1962.
7*d* •HSH Prince *Friedrich Christian* Wilhelm Alexander of Schaumburg-Lippe [*757 Baden-Baden, Lichtenthaler Allee 6, Germany*], *b* 5 Jan 1906, *m* 1st 25 Sept 1927, H Ill H Countess *Alexandra* Hedwig Johanna Bertha Marie (*b* 29 June 1904; *d* 9 Sept 1961), only dau of H Ill H Count Wolfgang zu Castell-Rüdenhausen, and has had issue,
1*e* •HSH Prince Albrecht-Wolfgang Friedrich Wolrad Ruppert of Schaumburg-Lippe, *b* 5 Aug 1934, *m* 7 Jan 1961, •Catherine Whitenack-Hurt (*b* 13 Dec 1941), and has issue,
•HSH Prince *Stefan* Wilhelm Ernst of Schaumburg-Lippe, *b* 10 Sept 1965.
1*e* HSH Princess *Marie-Elisabeth* Hermina Hedwig Bathildis of Schaumburg-Lippe, *b* 19 Dec 1928; *d* 4 Dec 1945.
2*e* •HSH Princess *Christine* Marie-Luise Auguste Friederike of Schaumburg-Lippe, *b* 16 Oct 1936, *m* 21 Sept 1958, •Baron *Albrecht* Richard Max von Süsskind-Schwendi (*b* 20 Feb 1937) [*Johanneshus b Ronneby, Sweden*].
He *m* 2ndly 8 Oct 1962, HH Princess Viktoria *Marie Luise* Agnes Calma Elisabeth Irmgard (*b* 8 Dec 1908; *d* 1969), formerly wife of Baron Rudolf Carl von Stengel, eldest dau of HH Prince Albert of Schleswig-Holstein-Sonderburg-Glücksburg, and adopted dau of HH Duke Ernst Günther of Schleswig-Holstein. He *m* 3rdly 1971, •Helene Mayr (*b* 12 March 1913).
1*d* HSH Princess *Elisabeth* Hermine Auguste Viktoria of Schaumburg-Lippe, *b* 31 May 1908, *m* 1st 1 Aug 1928 (*m* diss by div Nov 1928), Benvenuto Hauptmann. She *m* 2ndly 10 Jan 1930, •Baron Johann Herring von Frankensdorf (*b* 1 Sept 1891), and *d* 25 Feb 1933, leaving issue,
•Baron Hans Georg Friedrich Christian Herring von Frankensdorf, *b* 5 Feb 1933, *m* 13 June 1964, •Anneliese (*b* 4 May 1941), dau of Richard Buchholz, and has issue, one dau.
•Baroness Sibylle Herring von Frankensdorf, *b* 13 March 1932, *m* 13 March 1955, •Emil Eugene Jemail (*b* 19 Nov 1929).
2*c* HSH Prince Peter *Hermann* of Schaumburg-Lippe, *b* 19 May 1848; *d unm* 29 Dec 1918.
3*c* HSH Prince *Otto* Heinrich of Schaumburg-Lippe, *b* 13 Sept 1854, *m* (morganatically) 28 Nov 1893, *Anna* Luise (*b* 3 Feb 1860; *d* 27 March 1932), dau of Heinrich von Köppen, and *d* 18 Aug 1935, leaving issue,
1*d* Count *Wilhelm* Hermann Heinrich Albrecht Otto von Hagenburg, *b* 15 Jan 1895, *m* 1st 29 June 1920 (*m* diss by div 1928), Maria Holzfuss (*b* 11 Nov 1893; *d* 16 March 1953). He *m* 2ndly 10 Nov 1928, •Wilhelmine (*b* 4 Sept 1898), dau of Johann Bisch, and was *k* in action in World War II, 19 April 1945, having by her had issue,
•Countess Gisela Anna Hermine Edeltraut von Hagenburg, *b* 15 April 1930, *m* 21 May

1955, ●Heinrich Silbernagel (*b* 31 Oct 1925), and has issue,
1*f* ●Ralph Wilhelm Ewald Heinrich Silbernagel, *b* 6 Nov 1955.
2*f* ●Ronald Peter Alexander Silbernagel, *b* 2 May 1964.
1*f* ●Claudia Ute Gisela Silbernagel, *b* 7 March 1961.
2*d* ●Count *Otto-Heinrich* Hermann Gottlieb Hubertus von Hagenburg [*Hinnang, Post Altstädten, Allgäu, Germany*], *b* 13 Oct 1901, *m* 27 May 1935, ●Gertrud (*b* 1 Nov 1909), dau of Josef Carnier.
1*d* Countess Hermine Franziska Maria von Hagenburg, *b* 27 Aug 1898, *m* 11 May 1920, ●Baron *Felix* Georg Otto Karl Alfred von Quernheim (*b* 29 April 1891) [*Holterhöfe, Post Anrath, Bez Düsseldorf, Zu den Tannen 25, Germany*], and *d* 11 March 1963, leaving issue,
●Baron *Elmar* Otto Heinrich Hans von Quernheim [*Bergen-Enkheim, Bischofsheimer Strasse 9, Germany*], *b* 12 May 1921.
●Baroness *Hermine* Elisabeth Maria von Quernheim, *b* 16 June 1923, *m* 23 Oct 1948, ●Ewald Kempkens (*b* 30 April 1924) [*Krefeld, Rheinstrasse 99, Germany*], and has issue,
1*f* ●Franz Detlef Kempkens, *b* 1 July 1949.
2*f* ●Felix Harald Kempkens, *b* 13 Nov 1953.
4*c* HSH Prince *Adolf* Wilhelm Viktor of Schaumburg-Lippe, *b* 20 July 1859, *m* 19 Nov 1890, HRH Princess Friederike Amelia Wilhelmine *Viktoria* (*b* 12 April 1866; *d* 13 Nov 1929), 2nd dau of HIM Friedrich III, German Emperor and King of Prussia, KG (*see p* 302), and *dsp* 9 July 1916.
1*c* HSH Princess Hermine of Schaumburg-Lippe, *b* 5 Oct 1845, *m* 16 Feb 1876, HRH Duke Wilhelm Ferdinand *Maximilian* Karl of Württemberg (*b* 3 Sept 1828; *d* 30 July 1888), and *dsp* 23 Dec 1930.
2*c* HSH Princess *Emma* Friederike Ida of Schaumburg-Lippe, *b* 16 July 1850; *d* 25 Nov 1855.
3*c* HSH Princess *Ida* Mathilde Adelaide of Schaumburg-Lippe, *b* 28 July 1852, *m* 8 Oct 1872, HSH Prince Heinrich XXII Reuss (Er Line) (*b* 28 March 1846; *d* 19 April 1902), and *d* 28 Sept 1891, leaving issue (*see p* 248).
4*c* HSH Princess *Emma* Elisabeth Bathildis Auguste Agnes of Schaumburg-Lippe, *b* 13 July 1865; *d* 27 Sept 1868.
4*a* HSH Princess Ida of Anhalt-Bernburg-Schaumburg, *b* 10 March 1804, *m* 24 June 1825, as his 2nd wife, her brother-in-law, HRH Grand Duke (Paul Friedrich) *August* of Oldenburg (*b* 13 July 1783; *d* 27 Feb 1853), and *d* 31 March 1828, leaving issue,
HRH Grand Duke (Nikolaus Friedrich) *Peter II* of Oldenburg (1853-1900), *b* 8 July 1827, *m* 10 Feb 1852, HH Princess *Elisabeth* Pauline Alexandrine (*b* 26 March 1826; *d* 2 Feb 1896), 3rd dau of HH Duke Joseph of Saxe-Altenburg, and *d* 13 June 1900, leaving issue,
1*c* HRH Grand Duke (Friedrich) *August* of Oldenburg (1900-1918), *b* 16 Nov 1852, *m* 1st 18 Feb 1878, HRH Princess *Elisabeth* Anna (*b* 8 Feb 1857; *d* 28 Aug 1895), 2nd dau of HRH Prince Friedrich Karl of Prussia, and had issue,
1*d* HH Duchess *Sophie Charlotte* of Oldenburg, *b* 2 Feb 1879, *m* 1st 27 Feb 1906 (*m* diss by div 1926), HRH Prince Wilhelm *Eitel Friedrich* Christian Karl of Prussia (*b* 7 July 1883; *d* 8 Dec 1942), 2nd son of HIM Wilhelm II, German Emperor and King of Prussia (*see p* 301). She *m* 2ndly 24 Nov 1927, Harald von Hedemann (*b* 22 Sept 1887; *d* 12 June 1951), and *dsp* 29 March 1964.
2*d* HH Duchess Margarete of Oldenburg, *b* 13 Oct 1881; *d* 20 Feb 1882.
He *m* 2ndly 24 Oct 1896, HH Duchess *Elisabeth* Alexandrine Mathilde Auguste (*b* 10 Aug 1869; *d* 3 Sept 1955), 3rd dau of HRH Grand Duke Friedrich Franz II of Mecklenburg-Schwerin, and *d* 24 Feb 1931, having by her had issue,
1*d* HRH Hereditary Grand Duke *Nikolaus* Friedrich Wilhelm of Oldenburg, Head of the Grand Ducal House of Oldenburg (1931-1970), *b* 10 Aug 1897, *m* 1st 26 Oct 1921, HSH Princess *Helene* Bathildis Charlotte Maria Friederike (*b* 22 Dec 1899; *d* 18 Feb 1948), only dau of HSH Prince Friedrich of Waldeck and Pyrmont, and had issue (*see p* 222). He *m* 2ndly 20 Sept 1950, ●Anne-Marie (*b* 3 July 1903) [*2902 Schloss Rastede, Oldenburg, Germany*], formerly wife of Count Berchthold von Bernstorff, and dau of Rudolf von Schutzbar gen Milchling, Royal Prussian Chamberlain, and *d* 3 April 1970.
2*d* HH Duke *Friedrich August* of Oldenburg, *b* and *d* 25 March 1900.
3*d* HH Duchess Alexandrine of Oldenburg, *b* and *d* (twin with Duke Friedrich August) 25 March 1900.
4*d* ●HH Duchess *Ingeborg Alix* of Oldenburg [*8136 Kempfenhausen 54, Post Percha über Starnberg, Germany*], *b* 20 July 1901, *m* 4 June 1921, HSH Prince *Stephan* Alexander Viktor of Schaumburg-Lippe (*b* 21 June 1891; *d* 10 Feb 1965), and has had issue,
HSH Prince *Georg-Moritz* Friedrich August Otto Christian of Schaumburg-Lippe, *b* 9 March 1924; *d unm* 17 Oct 1970.
●HSH Princess Marie-Alix of Schaumburg-Lippe, *b* 2 April 1923, *m* 9 Oct 1947, ●HH Duke Friedrich Ernst *Peter* of Schleswig-Holstein-Sonderburg-Glücksburg (*b* 30 April 1922), and has issue (*see p* 298).
5*d* ●HH Duchess *Altburg* Marie Mathilde Olga of Oldenburg [*3548 Schloss Arolsen, Waldeck, Germany; 6251 Schloss Schaumburg über Diez an der Lahn, Germany*], *b* 19 May 1903, *m* 25 Aug 1922, HSH Prince *Josias* Georg Wilhelm Adolf of Waldeck and Pyrmont, Head of the Princely House of Waldeck and Pyrmont (*b* 13 May 1896; *d* 30 Nov 1967), and has issue (*see p* 221).
2*c* HH Duke *Georg* Ludwig of Oldenburg, *b* 27 June 1855; *d unm* 30 Nov 1939.
Princess Amalie of Nassau-Weilburg *m* 2ndly 15 Feb 1813, Baron Friedrich von Stein-Liebenstein zu Barchfeld (*b* 14 Feb 1777; *d* 4 Dec 1849), and *d* 19 Feb 1841, leaving further issue,
1*a* Baron Friedrich Gustav von Stein-Liebenstein zu Barchfeld, *b* 10 Dec 1813, *m* 18 May 1841, Caroline Luise (*b* 16 June 1815; *d* 5 Nov 1867), dau of Johann Schulze, and *dsp* 18 June 1875.
(5) HSH Princess Henriette of Nassau-Weilburg, *b* 22 April 1780, *m* 28 Jan 1797, as his 2nd wife, HRH Duke *Ludwig* Friedrich Alexander of Württemberg (*b* 30 Aug 1756; *d* 20 Sept 1817), and *d* 2 Jan 1857, leaving issue,
1*a* HRH Duke *Alexander* Paul Ludwig Konstantin of Württemberg, *b* 9 Sept 1804, *m* (morganatically) 2 May 1835, Countess *Claudine* Susanne, *cr* Countess von Hohenstein 16 May 1835 (*b* 21 Sept 1812; *d* 1 Oct 1841), dau of Count László Rhédey de Kis-Rhéde, by his wife Baroness Agnes Inczédy, and *d* 4 July 1883, leaving issue,
1*b* HH *Franz* Paul Karl Ludwig Alexander, 1st Prince (*cr* 1864) and Duke (*cr* 16 Sept 1871), of Teck, Count von Hohenstein, GCB (1866), *b* 27 Aug 1837, *m* 12 June 1866, HRH Princess *Mary Adelaide* Wilhelmina Elizabeth (*b* 27 Nov 1833; *d* 27 Oct 1897), yr dau of HRH Prince *Adolphus* Frederick of Great Britain and Ireland, 1st Duke of Cambridge, etc, KG, and *d* 20 Jan 1900, leaving issue (*see p* 293).
1*b* Countess *Claudine* Henriette Marie Agnes von Hohenstein, *cr* Princess of Teck, *b* 11 Feb 1836; *d unm* 18 Nov 1894.
2*b* Countess *Amalie* Josephine Henriette Agnes Susanne von Hohenstein, *cr* Princess of Teck, *b* 12 Nov 1838, *m* 24 Oct 1863, Count Paul von Hügel (*b* 13 April 1835; *d* 13 April 1897), and *d* 20 July 1893, leaving issue,

Count *Paul-Julius* Alexander Franz Klaudius von Hügel, *b* 30 Sept 1872, *m* Anna Pauline Homolatsch, and *d* 20 March 1912, leaving issue,

•Count Ferdinand Paul von Hügel, *b* 11 March 1901.

Countess Huberta Amelia Maximilienne Pauline von Hügel, *b* 8 Oct 1897; *d* 22 Dec 1912.

1*a* HRH Duchess *Marie Dorothea* Luise Wilhelmine Caroline of Württemberg, *b* 1 Nov 1797, *m* 24 Aug 1819, as his 3rd wife, HI and RH Archduke *Joseph* Anton Johann Baptist of Austria, Palatine of Hungary (*b* 9 March 1776; *d* 13 Jan 1847), and *d* 30 March 1855, having had issue,

1*b* HI and RH Archduke *Alexander* Leopold Ferdinand of Austria, *b* 6 June 1825; *d* 12 Nov 1837.

2*b* HI and RH Archduke *Joseph* Karl Ludwig of Austria, *b* 2 March 1833, *m* 12 May 1864, HH Princess *Klothilde* Marie Adelheid Amalie (*b* 8 July 1846; *d* 3 June 1927), elder dau of HH Prince August of Saxe-Coburg and Gotha, Duke of Saxony, and *d* 13 June 1905, having had issue,

1*c* HI and RH Archduke *Joseph August* Viktor Clemens Maria of Austria, *b* 9 Aug 1872, *m* 15 Nov 1893, HRH Princess *Auguste* Maria Luise (*b* 28 April 1875; *d* 25 June 1964), yr dau of HRH Prince Leopold of Bavaria, and *d* 6 July 1962, having had issue,

1*d* HI and RH Archduke *Joseph* Franz Leopold Anton Ignatius Maria of Austria, *b* 28 March 1895, *m* 4 Oct 1924, •HRH Princess *Anna* Monika Pia (*b* 4 May 1903) [*19 rue Henri Dumant, CH-1700 Fribourg, Switzerland*], yst dau of HM King Friedrich August III of Saxony, and *d* 25 Sept 1957, leaving issue,

1*e* •HI and RH Archduke *Joseph Arpád* Benedikt Ferdinand Franz Maria Gabriel of Austria [*8133 Feldafing, OBayern, Germany*], *b* 8 Feb 1933, *m* 12 Sept 1956, •HSH Princess *Maria* Aloisia Josephine Consolata Immaculata Benedicta Theresia Antonia Johanna Carla Conrada Leonharda (*b* 6 Nov 1935), eldest dau of HSH Karl, 8th Prince zu Löwenstein-Wertheim-Rosenberg, and has had issue,

1*f* HI and RH Archduke Joseph Karl of Austria, *b* 7 Aug, *d* 8 Aug 1957.

2*f* •HI and RH Archduke *Joseph Karl* Maria Arpád Stephan Pius Ignatius Aloysius Cyrillus of Austria, *b* 18 March 1960.

3*f* •HI and RH Archduke *Andreas-Augustinus* Maria Arpád Aloys Konstantin Pius Ignatius Peter of Austria, *b* 29 April 1963.

1*f* •HI and RH Archduchess *Monika-Ilona* Maria Carolina Stephanie Elisabeth Immakolata Benedicta Dominica of Austria, *b* 14 Sept 1958.

2*f* •HI and RH Archduchess *Maria Christina* Regina Stephanie Immacolata Carolina Monika Agidia of Austria, *b* 1 Sept 1961.

3*f* •HI and RH Archduchess *Alexandra* Lydia Pia Immacolata Josepha Petra Paula Maria of Austria, *b* 29 June 1965.

2*e* •HI and RH Archduke *István* Dominik Anton Umberto of Austria [*813 Starnberg, Ludwig-Thoma-Weg 28, Austria*], *b* 1 July 1934.

3*e* •HI and RH Archduke *Géza* Ladislaus Euseb Gebhard Rafael Albert Maria of Austria [*Chemin des Corneilles 10, Thônex, CH-1226 Moillesulaz, Kt Genf, Switzerland*], *b* 14 Nov 1940, m 7 July 1965, •Monika (*b* 1 Dec 1939), dau of Walther Decker, and has issue,

1*f* •Franz Ferdinand von Habsburg-Lothringen, *b* 8 May 1967.

2*f* •Ferdinand Leopold von Habsburg-Lothringen, *b* 14 July 1969.

4*e* •HI and RH Archduke *Michael* Kalman Pius Matthias Ludwig Emmerich Martin of Austria [*8 München-Nymphenburg, Hundingstrasse 11, Germany*], *b* 5 May 1942, *m* 13 April 1966, •HSH Princess *Christiana* Maria Josephine Aloisia Consolata Immaculata Theresia Antonia Johanna Carla Conrada Rita (*b* 18 Sept 1940), 4th dau of HSH Karl 8th Prince zu Löwenstein-Wertheim-Rosenberg, and has issue,

1*f* •HI and RH Archduke *Eduard Karl* Joseph Michael Marcus Antonius Kálmán Volkhold Maria of Austria, *b* 12 Jan 1967.

2*f* •HI and RH Archduke *Paul* Rudolph Michael Joseph Antal Petrus Maria of Austria, *b* 19 Oct 1968.

1*f* •HI and RH Archduchess *Margherita* Anastasia Maximiliana Anna Karolina Michaela Christiana Maria of Austria, *b* 26 July 1972.

1*e* •HI and RH Archduchess Margit of Austria, *b* 17 Aug 1925, *m* 17 Aug 1943, •Alexander Erba-Odescalchi, Prince of Monteleone (*b* 23 March 1914), son of Joseph Cech, by his wife Princess Amalie Erba-Odescalchi, and has issue,

•Princess *Sibylla* Maria-Pace Anna Amalia Augusta Erba-Odescalchi, *b* 7 April 1945.

2*e* •HI and RH Archduchess Ilona of Austria, *b* 20 April 1927, *m* 30 April 1946, •HH Duke *Georg Alexander* Andreas Carl Michael Peter Philipp Ignatius Maria of Mecklenburg-Strelitz (*b* 27 Aug 1921) [*Culleen, Mullingar, co Westmeath; 78 Freiburg i Br, Bürgerwehrstrasse 4, Germany*], and has issue (*see p 212*).

3*e* •HI and RH Archduchess *Anna Theresia* Gabriella of Austria [*8081 Breitbrunn am Ammersee, Germany*], *b* 19 April 1928.

4*e* •HI and RH Archduchess Maria *Kinga* Beatrix of Austria, *b* 27 Aug 1938, *m* 1959, •Ernst Kiss, and has issue,

•Mátyás Kiss, *b* 1964.

2*d* HI and RH Archduke *László* Luitpold Joseph Anton Ignaz Maria of Austria, *b* 3 Jan 1901; *d unm* 29 Aug 1946.

3*d* HI and RH Archduke *Mátyás* Joseph Albrecht Anton Ignaz Maria of Austria, *b* 26 June 1904; *d* 7 Oct 1905.

1*d* HI and RH Archduchess *Gisela* Augustine Anna Maria of Austria, *b* 5 July 1897; *d* 30 March 1901.

2*d* •HI and RH Archduchess *Sophie* Klementine Elisabeth Klotilde Maria of Austria, *b* 11 March 1899.

3*d* •HI and RH Archduchess *Magdalena* Maria Raniera of Austria [*8 München 13, Adalbertsstrasse 82, Germany*], *b* 6 Sept 1909.

2*c* HI and RH Archduke *László Philipp* Marie Vincent of Austria, *b* 16 July 1875; *d unm* 6 Sept 1895.

1*c* HI and RH Archduchess *Elisabeth* Clementine Clothilde Maria Amalie of Austria, *b* 18 March 1865; *d* 7 Jan 1866.

2*c* HI and RH Archduchess *Maria Dorothea* Amalie of Austria, *b* 14 June 1867, *m* 5 Nov 1896, HRH Prince Louis-*Philippe*-Robert d'Orléans, Duc d'Orléans, Head of the Royal House of France (*b* 6 Feb 1869; *d* 28 March 1926), and *dsp* 6 April 1932.

3*c* HI and RH Archduchess *Margarethe* Clementine Maria of Austria, *b* 6 July 1870, *m* 15 July 1890, HSH *Albert* Maria Joseph Maximilian Lamoral, 8th Prince von Thurn und Taxis (*b* 8 May 1867; *d* 22 Jan 1951), and *d* 2 May 1955, leaving issue,

1*d* HSH *Franz Joseph* Maximilian Maria Antonius Ignatius Lamoral, 9th Prince von Thurn und Taxis, *b* 21 Dec 1893, *m* 23 Nov 1920, HRH Infanta Maria *Isabel* Alberta Josefa Miguela Gabriela Rafaela Francisca de Paula e de Assis Teresa Adelaide Eulália Sofia Carolina (*b* 19 Nov 1894; *d* 12 Jan 1970), 2nd dau of HRH Infante Dom Miguel of Portugal, Duke of Braganza, and *d* 1971, having had issue,

1*e* HSH Hereditary Prince *Gabriel* Albert

Maria Michael Franz Joseph Gallus Lamoral von Thurn und Taxis, *b* 16 Oct 1922; *k* in action 17 Dec 1942.

1*e* ●HSH Princess *Helene* Maria Maximiliana Emanuela Michaela Gabriela Raphaela von Thurn und Taxis, *b* 27 May 1924, *m* 29 April 1947, ●H Ill H Count *Rudolf Erwein* von Schönborn-Wiesentheid (*b* 1 Oct 1918) [*St Gilgen am Wolfgangsee, Ischler Strasse, Austria*], and has issue,

1*f* ●H Ill H Count *Albert Ernst* von Schönborn-Wiesentheid, *b* 20 Feb 1948.

2*f* ●H Ill H Count *Johann Philipp* von Schönborn-Wiesentheid, *b* 3 July 1949.

3*f* ●H Ill H Count *Peter* Andreas von Schönborn-Wiesentheid, *b* 10 Nov 1954.

1*f* ●H Ill H Countess *Gabriela* Helene von Schönborn-Wiesentheid, *b* 16 Oct 1950, *m* 1969, HSH Alexander, 7th Prince zu Sayn-Wittgenstein-Sayn (*b* 22 Nov 1943) [*Bendorf-Sayn b Koblenz, Germany*], and has issue,

●HSH Hereditary Prince Heinrich zu Sayn-Wittgenstein-Sayn, *b* 1971.

2*e* ●HSH Princess *Maria Theresia* Michaela Raphaela Gabriela Carolina Ludovica von Thurn und Taxis, *b* 10 Sept 1925, *m* 19 June 1955, ●Count *Franz Eduard* Johannes Alexander Hubert Michael Maria von Oppersdorff (*b* 19 June 1919) [*München-Solln, Bichlesstrasse 35, Germany*], and has issue,

1*f* ●Count *Franz Joseph* Maria Albert Johannes Bernhard Friedrich Anton Hubertus Michael von Oppersdorff, *b* 24 May 1958.

2*f* ●Count Michael Ferdinand Johannes Eduard Karl Anton Joachim Hubertus Joseph Maria von Oppersdorff, *b* 18 June 1962.

1*f* ●Countess *Ferdinanda Franziska* Maria Hedwig Elisabeth Luise Gabrielle Margarethe Adelheid von Oppersdorff, *b* 23 March 1956.

2*f* ●Countess *Maria Gabrielle* Aloysia Margarethe Mathilde Elisabeth Josepha von Oppersdorff, *b* 25 March 1957.

3*f* ●*Margarethe Maria Louise* Elisabeth Helene Regina Hedwig Melanie Theodora von Oppersdorff, *b* 9 Nov 1959.

3*e* ●HSH Princess *Maria Ferdinanda* Eudoxia Michaela Gabriela Raphaela von Thurn und Taxis [*München, Maria-Theresia-Strasse 10, Germany; Regensburg, Schloss, Germany*], *b* 19 Dec 1927, *m* 15 July 1950 (*m* diss by div 1951), as his 1st wife, HSH Prince *Franz Joseph* Hubertus Maria Meinrad Michael of Hohenzollern (*b* 15 March 1926) (*see p* 234).

2*d* ●HSH *Karl August* Joseph Maria Maximilian Lamoral Antonius Ignatius Benediktus Valentin, 10th Prince von Thurn und Taxis [*8401 Schloss Höfling, Post Oberisling über Regensburg, Germany*], *b* 23 July 1898, *m* 18 Aug 1921, HRH Infanta *Maria Ana* Rafaela Miguela Gabriela Lourença (*b* 3 Sept 1899; *d* 1971), 5th dau of HRH Infante Dom Miguel of Portugal, Duke of Braganza, and has had issue,

1*e* ●HSH Hereditary Prince *Johannes Baptista* de Jesus Maria Ludwig Miguel Friedrich Bonifazius Lamoral von Thurn und Taxis, [*Oberpfaffenhofen bei München, Hauptstrasse 16, Germany*], *b* 5 June 1926.

2*e* HSH Prince *Albert* Maria Raimund Ildefons Paul Polycarp Lamoral von Thurn und Taxis, *b* 23 Jan 1929; *d* 21 Feb 1935.

1*e* ●HSH Princess *Clothilde* Alberta Maria Franziska Xaviera Andrea von Thurn und Taxis, *b* 30 Nov 1922, *m* 7 Nov 1944, ●HSH Prince *Johann* (Baptist) *Moritz* Heinrich Alfred Ildefons Benedikt Maria Josef of Liechtenstein (*b* 6 Aug 1914) [*Dietersdorf, A-3441 Judenau, N Austria*], and has issue,

1*f* ●HSH Prince *Gundakar* Albert Alfred Petrus of Liechtenstein, *b* (twin with Princess Diemut) 1 April 1949.

2*f* ●HSH Prince *Alfred* Heinrich Michael Benedikt Maria of Liechtenstein, *b* 17 Sept 1951.

3*f* ●HSH Prince Karl *Emmeran* Duarte Johannes Theobald Benedikt of Liechtenstein, *b* 1 July 1955.

4*f* ●HSH Prince Hugo Karl August of Liechtenstein, *b* 20 Feb 1964.

1*f* ●HSH Princess *Diemut Margarete* Maria Benedicta Anna of Liechtenstein, *b* 1 April 1949.

2*f* ●HSH Princess *Adelgunde* Maria Anna Therese Mafalda Eleonore of Liechtenstein, *b* 10 Aug 1953.

3*f* ●HSH Princess *Maria Eleonore* Bernadette Hildegard of Liechtenstein, *b* 14 Nov 1958.

2*e* ●HSH Princess *Mafalda* Theresia Franziska Josepha Maria von Thurn und Taxis, *b* 6 March 1924, *m* 22 Dec 1961, ●HSH Prince *Franz von Assisi* Josef Ferdinand Wilhelm Paulus Rudolf Emil Lamoral Alexander Ignatius Theodor Pius Marie von Thurn und Taxis (*b* 15 April 1915), and has issue,

●HSH Princess Daria Maria Gabriele von Thurn und Taxis, *b* 6 March 1962.

3*d* HSH Prince *Ludwig Philipp* Maria Friedrich Joseph Maximilian Antonius Ignatius Lamoral von Thurn und Taxis, *b* 2 Feb 1901, *m* 14 Nov 1922, HGDH Princess *Elisabeth* Marie Wilhelmine (*b* 7 March 1901; *d* 2 Aug 1950), 5th dau of HRH Grand Duke Guillaume IV of Luxembourg, and *d* 22 April 1933, leaving issue (*see p* 218).

4*d* ●HSH Prince *Max Emanuel* Maria Siegfried Joseph Antonius Ignatius Lamoral von Thurn und Taxis, *b* 1 March 1902.

5*d* ●HSH Prince *Raphael Rainer* Karl Maria Joseph Antonius Ignatius Hubertus Lamoral von Thurn und Taxis [*Schloss Bullachberg b Füssen, Germany*], *b* 30 May 1906, *m* 24 May 1924, ●HSH Princess *Margarete* Charlotte Klementine Maria Alexandra Melanie (*b* 19 Oct 1913), only dau of HSH Prince Maximilian Theodor von Thurn und Taxis (*see p* 272), and has issue,

●HSH Prince *Max Emanuel* Maria Albert Paul Isabella Klemens Lamoral von Thurn und Taxis [*Schloss Bullachberg b Füssen, Germany*], b 7 Sept 1935, *m* 23 May 1969 (*m* diss by div 1970), Countess Annemarie (*Mirzl*) Elisabeth (*b* 1 April 1944), elder dau of Count Konrad Albert di Pocci.

6*d* HSH Prince *Philipp Ernst* Maria Adalbert Joseph Maximilian Antonius Ignatius Stanislaus Lamoral von Thurn und Taxis, *b* 7 May 1908, *m* 8 Sept 1929, ●HSH Princess *Eulalie* (*Illa*) Maria Antonie Eleonore (*b* 21 Dec 1908) [*Schloss Hohenberg b Seeshupt, OBayern, Germany*], only dau of HSH Prince Friedrich von Thurn und Taxis, and *d* 23 July 1964, leaving issue,

1*e* ●HSH Prince *Albert Friedrich* Maria Lamoral Kilian von Thurn und Taxis [*Schloss Hohenberg b Seeshupt, OBayern, Germany*], *b* 5 July 1930, *m* 30 July 1962, ●Baroness *Alexandra* Beatrice Ursula Irma Carmen (*b* 31 Oct 1932), 2nd dau of Baron Schweter von der Ropp.

1*e* ●HSH Princess *Margarete Eleonore* Maria Franziska Antonius von Padua von Thurn und Taxis, *b* 1 Dec 1933.

2*e* ●HSH Princess *Antonia* Maria Margareta Theresia vom Kinde Jesu von Thurn und Taxis, *b* 28 Jan 1936.

1*d* ●HSH Princess *Elisabeth-Helene* Maria Valerie Franziska Maximiliane Antonie von Thurn und Taxis [*8 München 90, Wolkensteinstrasse 10, Germany*], *b* 15 Dec 1903, *m* 16 June 1923, HRH Prince *Friedrich Christian* Albert Leopold Anno Sylvester Makarius of Saxony, Margrave of Meissen, Head of the Royal House of Saxony (*b* 31 Dec 1893; *d* 9 Aug 1968), 2nd son of HM King Friedrich August III of Saxony, and has issue,

1*e* ●HRH Prince *Maria Emanuel* of Saxony, Margrave of Meissen, Head of the Royal House of Saxony [*CH-5430 Wettingen,*

Kt Aargau, Switzerland], *b* 31 Jan 1926, *m* 23 June 1962, ●HH Princess *Anastasia-Luise* Alexandra Elisabeth Jutta Sibylle Marie-Auguste Henriette (*b* 22 Dec 1940), only dau of HH Prince Eugen of Anhalt (*see p* 268).
2*e* ●HRH Prince *Albert* Joseph Maria Franz-Xaver of Saxony [*8 München 90, Wolkensteinstrasse 10, Germany*], *b* 30 Nov 1934.
1*e* ●HRH Princess *Maria Josepha* of Saxony [*8 München 13, Agnesstrasse 16, Germany*], *b* 20 Sept 1928.
2*e* ●HRH Princess Maria *Anna* Josepha of Saxony, *b* 13 Dec 1929, *m* 1 May 1953, ●Roberto Afif (*b* 30 Nov 1916) [*80 München 90, Jollystrasse 13, Germany*], and has issue,
1*f* ●Alexander Afif, *b* 12 Feb 1954.
2*f* ●Friedrich Wilhelm Afif, *b* 5 Oct 1955.
3*f* ●Charles August Afif, *b* 1 Jan 1958.
3*e* ●HRH Princess *Mathilde* Maria Josepha Anna Xaveria of Saxony, *b* 17 Jan 1936, *m* 1969, as his 2nd wife, ●HH Prince *Johannes Heinrich* Friedrich Werner Konrad Rainer Maria of Saxe-Coburg and Gotha, Duke of Saxony (*b* 28 March 1931), and has issue (*see p* 245).
4*c* HI and RH Archduchess *Elisabeth* Henriette Clothilde Maria Viktoria of Austria, *b* 9 March 1883; *d unm* 8 Feb 1958.
5*c* HI and RH Archduchess *Klothilde Maria Raineria* Amalia Philomena of Austria, *b* 9 May 1884; *d* 14 Dec 1903.
1*b* HI and RH Archduchess Franziska Maria Elisabeth of Austria, *b* 31 July, *d* 23 Aug 1820.
2*b* HI and RH Archduchess *Elisabeth* Franziska Maria of Austria, *b* 17 Jan 1831, *m* 1st 4 Oct 1847, HI and RH Archduke *Ferdinand* Karl Viktor of Austria-Este, Prince of Modena (*b* 19 July 1821; *d* 15 Dec 1849), and had issue,
HI and RH Archduchess *Maria Theresia* Henriette Dorothee of Austria-Este, Princess of Modena*, *b* 2 July 1849, *m* 20 Feb 1868, HM King *Ludwig III* (Leopold Joseph Marie Aloysius Alfred) of Bavaria (*b* 7 Jan 1845; *d* 18 Oct 1921), and *d* 3 Feb 1919, having had issue,
1*d* HRH Crown Prince *Rupprecht* Maria Luitpold Ferdinand of Bavaria, Head of the Royal House of Bavaria (1921-1955), *s* his mother as rep and heir-gen of King Charles I 1919, *b* 18 May 1869, *m* 1st 10 July 1900, HRH Duchess *Marie Gabriele* Mathilde Isabelle Therese Antoinette Sabine (*b* 9 Oct 1878; *d* 24 Oct 1912), yst dau of HRH Duke Karl Theodor in Bavaria, and had issue,
1*e* HRH Prince *Luitpold* Maximilian Ludwig Karl of Bavaria, *b* 8 May 1901; *d* 27 Aug 1914.
2*e* ●HRH Prince *Albrecht* Luitpold Ferdinand Michael of Bavaria, Duke of Bavaria, Head of the Royal House of Bavaria and rep and heir-gen of King Charles I [*8 München, Schloss Nymphenburg, Germany; 8131 Schloss Berg bei Starnberg, Germany*], *b* 3 May 1905, *m* 1st 3 Sept 1930, Countess Maria (*Marita*) Franziska Juliana Johanna (*b* 8 March 1904; *d* 10 June 1969), only dau of Count Dionys Draskovich von Trakostjan, by his wife HSH Princess Julia von Montenuovo, and has issue,
1*f* ●HRH Hereditary Prince *Franz* Bonaventura Adalbert Maria of Bavaria [*8 München 15, Mozartstrasse 18, Germany*], *b* 14 July 1933.
2*f* ●HRH Prince *Max Emanuel* of Bavaria, Duke in Bavaria as adopted heir of HRH Duke Ludwig Wilhelm in Bavaria from 18 March 1965 [*8185 Wildbad Kreuth bei Tegernsee, Germany*], *b* 21 Jan 1937, *m* 24 Jan 1967, ●Countess *Elizabeth* Christina (*b* 31 Dec 1940), elder dau of Count Carl Ludwig Douglas, and has issue,
1*g* ●HRH Princess *Sophie* Elizabeth Marie Gabrielle of Bavaria, *b* 28 Oct 1967.
2*g* ●HRH Princess Marie Caroline of Bavaria, *b* 26 June 1969.
1*f* ●HRH Princess Marie *Gabriele* of Bavaria, *b* 30 May 1931, *m* 23 Oct 1957, ●HSH Maria *Georg* Konstantin Ignatius Antonius Felix Augustinus Wunibald Kilian Boniface, 7th Prince von Waldburg zu Zeil und Trauchburg (*b* 5 June 1928) [*7971 Schloss Zeil über Leutkirch, Württemberg, Germany*], and has issue,
1*g* ●H Ill H Hereditary Count Maria *Erich* Wunibald Aloysius Georg von Waldburg-Zeil, *b* 21 Nov 1962.
1*g* ●H Ill H Countess Maria *Walburga* Monica Charlotte Matthäa von Waldburg-Zeil, *b* 21 Sept 1958.
2*g* ●H Ill H Countess Maria *Gabriele* Walburga Cäcilia Theresia von Waldburg-Zeil, *b* 22 Nov 1959.
3*g* ●H Ill H Countess Maria *Monika* Sofie Walburga Nikoletta von Waldburg-Zeil, *b* 22 March 1961.
4*g* ●H Ill H Countess Maria *Adelheid* Walburga Rufina von Waldburg-Zeil, *b* 28 Nov 1964.
5*g* ●H Ill H Countess Maria *Elisabeth* Walburga Priscilla Wiltrud von Waldburg-Zeil, *b* 30 July 1966.
2*f* ●HRH Princess Marie *Charlotte* of Bavaria, *b* (twin with Princess Gabriele) 30 May 1931, *m* 3 Sept 1955, ●HSH *Paul* Franz von Assisi Georg Ghislain Christoph Edmond Marie Alexander, 4th Prince von Quadt zu Wykradt und Isny (*b* 28 Nov 1930) [*7972 Schloss Isny, Allgäu, Germany*], and has issue,
1*g* ●H Ill H Hereditary Count *Alexander* Albrecht Maria Ghislain Peter Paul Georg Mauritius von Quadt zu Wykradt und Isny, *b* 18 Jan 1958.
2*g* ●H Ill H Count Bertram von Quadt zu Wykradt und Isny, *b* 1966.
1*g* ●H Ill H Countess *Maria-Anna* Gabrielle Ghislaine von Quadt zu Wykradt und Isny, *b* 8 April 1960.
2*g* ●H Ill H Countess Maria Georgina von Quadt zu Wykradt und Isny, *b* 1962.
He *m* 2ndly 27 April 1971, ●Countess *Maria-Jenke* (*Eugenie*) Clara Clementine Antonia Stephanie Walburga Paula (*b* 23 April 1921), only dau of Count Stephan Keglevich von Buzin.
3*e* HRH Prince *Rudolf* Friedrich Rupprecht of Bavaria, *b* 30 May 1909; *d* 26 June 1912.
1*e* HRH Princess *Irmingard* Maria Therese José Cäcilia Adelheid Michaela Antonia Adelgunde of Bavaria, *b* 21 Sept 1902; *d* 21 April 1903.
He *m* 2ndly 7 April 1921, HGDH Princess *Antonia* Roberta Sophie Wilhelmine (*b* 7 Oct 1899; *d* 31 July 1954), 4th dau of HRH Grand Duke Guillaume IV of Luxembourg, and *d* 2 Aug 1955, having by her had issue,
4*e* HRH Prince *Heinrich* Franz Wilhelm of Bavaria, *b* 28 March 1922, *m* 31 July 1951, ●Anne (*b* 28 Sept 1927) [*82 rue Vaneau, F-75 Paris 7, France; Iragana, rue François Rabelais, F-64 St Jean de Luz, Basses Pyrénées, France*], dau of Jean, Baron de Lustrac, and *dsp* 14 Feb 1958.
2*e* ●HRH Princess *Irmingard* Marie Josefa of Bavaria, *b* 29 May 1923, *m* 20 July 1950, ●HRH Prince *Ludwig* Karl Maria Anton Joseph of Bavaria (*b* 22 June 1913), and has issue (*see p* 256).
3*e* ●HRH Princess *Editha* Maria Gabriela Anna Cunigunde of Bavaria, *b* 16 Sept 1924, *m* 1st 12 Nov 1946, *Tito Tommaso* Brunetti (*b* 18 Dec 1906; *d* 13 July 1954), and has issue,
1*f* ●*Serena* Giovanna Sofia Antonia Brunetti, *b* 22 Dec 1947, *m* 17 April 1971, ●Vanni Pozzolini.

* On the death of her paternal uncle, Duke Francisco V of Modena, in 1875 she became the rep and heir-gen of King Charles I by virtue of her descent from Princess Henrietta, Duchess of Orléans (*see p* 208).

2*f* ●*Carlotta* Hilda Maria Anna Brunetti, *b* 10 June 1949, *m* 29 April 1972, ●Michael von Longueval, Count von Buquoy, Baron von Vaux (*b* 12 Jan 1941).
3*f* ●*Antonia* Hilda Eugenia Assunta Brunetti, *b* 12 June 1952.
She *m* 2ndly 29 Dec 1959, ●Prof Dr *Gustav Christian* Schimert (*b* 28 Nov 1910) [*813 Starnberg, Oberer Seeweg 3, Germany*], and has further issue,
1*f* ●*Andreas* Heinrich Rupprecht Marius Schimert, *b* 26 May 1961.
2*f* ●*Christian* Philipp Gabriel Johannes Schimert, *b* 18 March 1963.
3*f* ●*Konstantin* Maximilian Ludwig Karl Schimert, *b* 30 May 1968.
4*e* ●HRH Princess *Hilda* Hildegard Marie Gabriele of Bavaria, *b* 24 March 1926, *m* 12 Feb 1949, ●Juan *Bradstock* Edgard Lockett de Loayza (*b* 30 March 1912) [*Casilla 1816, Lima, Peru; 8221 Bergen, OBayern, Ramberger Weg 48, Eicherhof, Germany*], only son of late Garstang Bradstock Lockett (*see* BURKE'S *LG*, LOCKETT *of Clonterbrook*), and has issue,
1*f* ●Juan Bradstock *Christopher* Henry Anthony Rupprecht Lockett von Wittelsbach, *b* 10 April 1950.
2*f* ●Juan Bradstock *Miguel* Maria Alexander Lockett von Wittelsbach, *b* 3 May 1953.
3*f* ●Heinrich Maria *Alexander* Luitpold Bradstock Lockett von Wittelsbach, *b* 11 April 1958.
1*f* ●Hilda *Marie Isabel* Irmingard Bradstock Charlotte Claire Lockett von Wittelsbach, *b* 5 July 1960.
5*e* ●HRH Princess *Gabriele* Adelgunde Marie Theresia Antonia of Bavaria, *b* 10 May 1927, *m* 18 June 1953, ●HSH Hereditary Prince *Carl* Emanuel Ludwig Petrus Eleonore Alexander Rudolf Engelbert Benno von Croy (*b* 11 Oct 1914) [*4409 Schloss Merfeld über Dülmen, Westfalen, Germany*], and has issue,
1*f* ●HSH Prince *Rudolf* Carl Rupprecht von Croy, *b* 8 July 1955.
2*f* ●HSH Prince *Stefan* Klemens Philipp von Croy, *b* 17 May 1959.
1*f* ●HSH Princess *Maria-Theresia* Antonia Nancy Charlotte von Croy, *b* 29 March 1954.
6*e* ●HRH Princess *Sophie* Marie Theresia of Bavaria, *b* 20 June 1935, *m* 20 Jan 1955, ●HSH Prince and Duke Jean-Engelbert von Arenberg (*b* 14 July 1921) [*44 avenue Père Dupierreux, Tervuren, Brabant, Belgium*], and has issue,
1*f* ●HSH Prince and Duke *Léopold-Engelbert* Evrard Rupprecht Gaspard von Arenberg, *b* 20 Feb 1956.
2*f* ●HSH Prince and Duke *Charles* Louis Felix Melchior von Arenberg, *b* 13 March 1957.
3*f* ●HSH Prince and Duke *Henri* Antoine Marie von Arenberg, *b* 20 May 1961.
4*f* ●HSH Prince and Duke *Etienne* Albert Marie Melchior von Arenberg, *b* 11 Dec 1967.
1*f* ●HSH Princess and Duchess *Marie-Gabrielle* Elisabeth von Arenberg, *b* 2 June 1958.
2*d* HRH Prince *Karl* Maria Luitpold of Bavaria, *b* 1 April 1874; *d unm* 9 May 1927.
3*d* HRH Prince *Franz* Maria Luitpold of Bavaria, *b* 10 Oct 1875, *m* 8 July 1912, ●HSH Princess *Isabella* Antonia Eleonore Natalie Klementine (*b* 7 Oct 1890) [*8131 Leutstetten über Starnberg, Samerhof, Germany*], only dau of HSH Karl, 12th Duke von Croy, and *d* 25 Jan 1957, leaving issue,
1*e* ●HRH Prince *Ludwig* Karl Maria Anton Joseph of Bavaria [*8911 Schloss Kaltenberg über Landsberg am Lech, Germany*], *b* 22 June 1913, *m* 20 July 1950, ●HRH Princess *Irmingard* Marie Josefa (*b* 29 May 1923), 2nd dau of HRH Crown Prince Rupprecht of Bavaria (*see p* 255), and has issue,
●HRH Prince *Luitpold* Rupprecht Heinrich of Bavaria, *b* 14 April 1951.
2*e* ●HRH Prince *Rasso* Maximilian Rupprecht of Bavaria [*8131 Gut Rieden, Post Leutstetten über Starnberg, OBayern, Germany*], *b* 24 May 1926, *m* 17 Oct 1955, ●HI and RH Archduchess *Theresia* Monika Maria Valerie Elisabeth Ludovika Walburga Anna (*b* 9 Jan 1931), elder dau of HI and RH Archduke Theodor of Austria, Prince of Tuscany, and has issue (*see p* 242).
1*e* ●HRH Princess *Maria* Elisabeth Franziska Josepha Therese of Bavaria, *b* 9 Sept 1914, *m* 19 Aug 1937, ●HI and RH Prince *Pedro Henrique* Afonso Filipe Maria Gabriel Rafael Gonzaga of Orleans and Braganza, Head of the Imp House of Brazil (*b* 13 Sept 1909), and has had issue (*see p* 238).
2*e* ●HRH Princess *Adelgunde* Maria Antonia Elisabeth Josefa of Bavaria, *b* 9 June 1917, *m* 2 June 1948, ●Baron *Zdenko* Maria Gabriel Johann Georg Albrecht von Hoenning-O'Carroll (*b* 6 Aug 1906), [*8406 Schloss Sünching über Regensberg, Germany*], and has issue,
1*f* ●Baron *Franz* Johann Nepomuk Pius Karl Cyprian von Hoenning-O'Carroll, *b* 26 Sept 1950.
2*f* ●Baron *Joseph* Bernhard Maria Gabriel Pius Johann Capistran von Hoenning-O'Carroll, *b* 28 March 1953.
1*f* ●Baroness *Marie Gabrielle* Radegundis Pia Theresia vom Kinde Jesu Desideria Venazius von Hoenning-O'Carroll, *b* 18 May 1949.
2*f* ●Baroness *Hildegard* Maria Margarete Theresia Oktavia Ludolfa von Hoenning-O'Carroll, *b* 29 March 1952.
3*f* ●Baroness Maria *Dorothee* Rupertine Helene Pia Theresia Pitra von Hoenning-O'Carroll, *b* 25 May 1956.
3*e* ●HRH Princess *Eleonore* Therese Marie Josepha Gabriele of Bavaria, *b* 11 Sept 1918, *m* 14 Aug 1951, ●H Ill H Count Maria *Konstantin* Friedrich Georg Wunibald Wilhelm Josef Anton von Waldburg-Zeil (*b* 15 March 1909) [*8961 Wengen über Kempten, Allgäu, Germany*], and has issue,
1*f* ●H Ill H Count Maria *Erich* Franz Georg Wunibald von Waldburg-Zeil, *b* 25 Sept 1952.
2*f* ●H Ill H Count Maria *Georg* Konstantin Franz Wunibald Ulrich von Waldburg-Zeil, *b* 1 May 1955.
3*f* ●H Ill H Count Maria *Konstantin* Karl Ludwig Willibald Georg von Waldburg-Zeil, *b* 30 July 1958.
1*f* ●H Ill H Countess Maria *Elisabeth* Therese Eleonora Walburga Monika von Waldburg-Zeil, *b* 6 Jan 1954.
2*f* ●H Ill H Countess Maria *Eleonore* Gabriele Theresia Walburga Elisabeth von Waldburg-Zeil, *b* 22 Feb 1957.
3*f* ●H Ill H Countess Maria *Theresia* Monika Walburga von Waldburg-Zeil, *b* 19 Jan 1960.
4*e* ●HRH Princess *Dorothea* Therese Marie Franziska of Bavaria, *b* 25 May 1920, *m* 3 Aug 1938, ●HI and RH Archduke *Gottfried* Maria Joseph Peter Ferdinand Hubert Anton Rupert Leopold Heinrich Ignaz Alfons of Austria, Prince of Tuscany, Head of the Grand Ducal House of Tuscany (*b* 14 March 1902), and has issue (*see p* 237).
4*d* HRH Prince *Wolfgang* Maria Leopold of Bavaria, *b* 2 July 1879; *d* 31 Jan 1895.
1*d* HRH Princess *Adelgunde* Marie Auguste Therese of Bavaria, *b* 17 Oct 1870, *m* 20 Jan 1915, as his 2nd wife, HRH Prince *Wilhelm* August Karl Joseph Peter Ferdinand Benedikt of Hohenzollern (*b* 7 March 1864; *d* 22 Oct 1927), and *dsp* 4 Jan 1958.

2*d* HRH Princess *Maria* Ludwiga Therese of Bavaria, *b* 6 July 1872, *m* 31 May 1897, HRH Prince Ferdinando Pio Maria of the Two Sicilies, Duke of Calabria, Head of the Royal House of the Two Sicilies (*b* 25 July 1869; *d* 7 Jan 1960), and *d* 10 June 1954, having had issue (*see p* 235).

3*d* HRH Princess *Mathilde* Maria Theresia Henriette Christine Luitpolda of Bavaria, *b* 17 Aug 1877, *m* 1 May 1900, as his 1st wife, HH Prince *Ludwig* Gaston Klemens Maria Michael Gabriel Raphael Gonzaga of Saxe-Coburg and Gotha, Duke of Saxony (*b* 15 Sept 1870; *d* 23 Jan 1942) and *d* 6 Aug 1906, leaving issue,

•HH Prince *Antonius* Maria Ludwig Klemens Eugen Karl Heinrich August Luitpold Franz Wolfgang Peter Joseph Gaston Alexander Alfons Ignatius Aloysius Stanislaus of Saxe-Coburg and Gotha, Duke of Saxony, *b* 17 June 1901, *m* 14 May 1938, •*Luise* Josepha (*b* 22 June 1903), dau of Alois Mayrhofer.

HH Princess *Maria Immaculata* Leopoldine Franziska Theresia Ildefonsa Adelgunde Klementine Hildegard Anna Josepha Elisabeth Sancta-Angelina Nicoletta of Saxe-Coburg and Gotha, Duchess of Saxony, *b* 10 Sept 1904; *d unm* 18 March 1940.

4*d* HRH Princess *Hildegarde* Marie Christine Therese of Bavaria, *b* 5 March 1881; *d unm* 2 Feb 1948.

5*d* HRH Princess *Notburga* Josepha Marie Karoline Therese of Bavaria, *b* 19, *d* 24 March 1883.

6*d* •HRH Princess *Wiltrud* Maria Alice of Bavaria [*Kgl Jagdhaus, Ludwigstrasse 13, Allgaü Oberstdorf, Germany*], *b* 10 Nov 1884, *m* 26 Nov 1924, HSH *Wilhelm* Karl Florestan Gero Cresentius, 2nd Duke von Urach, Count von Württemberg (*b* 3 March 1864; *d* 24 March 1928).

7*d* •HRH Princess *Helmtrud* Marie Amalie of Bavaria [*Wildenwart, b Prien a Chiemsee, Germany*], *b* 22 March 1886.

8*d* HRH Princess *Dietlinde* Marie Therese Josepha Adelgunde of Bavaria, *b* 2 Jan 1888; *d* 14/15 Feb 1889.

9*d* •HRH Princess *Gundelinde* Maria Josepha of Bavaria [*8351 Schloss Moos b Langenisarhofen, Niederbayern, Germany*], *b* 26 Aug 1891, *m* 23 Feb 1919, *Johann Georg* Heribert Maria Joseph Benedikt Ignatius Christian, Count von Preysing-Lichtenegg-Moos (*b* 17 Dec 1887; *d* 17 March 1924), and has had issue,

Count Johann Kaspar Warmund Konrad Simon Thaddäus Raimund Gebhard Nemegion Pantaleon Sigmund Maria von Preysing-Lichtenegg-Moos, *b* 19 Dec 1919; *k* in action in World War II 14 Feb 1940.

•Countess *Maria Theresia* Christiane Anna Leopoldine Auguste Elisabeth Notburga Thaddäa Creszentia Walburga Josepha Angela Annunciata von Preysing-Lichtenegg-Moos, *b* 23 March 1922, *m* 1st 25 Jan 1940, Count Maria *Ludwig* Gottfried Engelbert Ignatius Franziskus Konrad Aloysius Judas Thaddäus Katharina Melchior von Arco-Zinneberg (*b* 25 Nov 1913; *k* in action in World War II 18 Feb 1942), and has issue,

1*f* •Count *Rupprecht Maximilian* Maria Ludwig Joseph Georg Konrad Thaddäus Hubertus Felix Sebastian Kaspar von Arco-Zinneberg [*8 München 2, Wittelsbacherplatz 1, Germany*], *b* 14 Jan 1941, *m* 11 July 1968, •Countess Katharina Henckel, Baroness von Donnersmarck (*b* 17 June 1943), dau of Count Karl Erdmann Henckel, Baron von Donnersmarck, and has issue,

•Count *Aloys-Maximilian* Peter Michael Karl Ludwig Guido Bonifatius von Arco-Zinneberg, *b* 5 July 1970.

She *m* 2ndly 26 Sept 1943, her brother-in-law, Count Maria *Ulrich Philipp* Kaspar von Arco-Zinneberg (*b* 12 Dec 1917) [*8351 Schloss Moos über Plattling, NBayern, Germany; 8 München 2, Wittelsbacherplatz 1, Germany*], and has had further issue,

2*f* Count Maria *Ludwig* Karl Hieronymus Ulrich Georg Joseph Sylverius Peter Paul Melchior von Arco-Zinneberg, *b* 20 June, *d* 14 Aug 1944.

3*f* •Count *Riprand* Maria Franz Ulrich Gaspare del Buffalo Christophorus Jakob Kaspar von Arco-Zinneberg, *b* 25 July 1955.

Archduchess Elisabeth *m* 2ndly 18 April 1854, HI and RH Archduke Karl Ferdinand of Austria (*b* 29 July 1818; *d* 20 Nov 1874), and *d* 14 Feb 1903, having had further issue (*see p* 228).

3*b* HI and RH Archduchess *Marie Henriette* Anna of Austria, *b* 23 Aug 1836, *m* 22 Aug 1853, HM King Léopold II (Louis-Philippe-Marie-Victor) of the Belgians, KG (*b* 9 April 1835; *d* 17 Dec 1909), and *d* 19 Sept 1902, having had issue,

1*c* HRH Prince *Léopold-Ferdinand*-Elie-Victor-Albert-Marie of Belgium, Duke of Brabant, *b* 12 June 1859; *d* 22 Jan 1869.

1*c* HRH Princess *Louise*-Marie-Amélie of Belgium, *b* 18 Feb 1858, *m* 4 Feb 1875, HH Prince *Philipp* Ferdinand Marie August Raphael of Saxe-Coburg and Gotha, Duke of Saxony (*b* 28 March 1844; *d* 3 July 1921), and *d* 1 March 1924, having had issue,

HH Prince *Leopold* Clemens Philipp August Maria of Saxe-Coburg and Gotha, Duke of Saxony, *b* 19 July 1878; *d unm* 27 April 1916.

HH Princess *Dorothea* Marie Henriette Auguste Luise of Saxe-Coburg and Gotha, Duchess of Saxony, *b* 30 April 1881, *m* 2 Aug 1898, HH Ernst Günther, Duke of Schleswig-Holstein (*b* 11 Aug 1863; *d* 22 Feb 1921), and *dsp* 21 Jan 1967.

2*c* HRH Princess *Stéphanie*-Clothilde-Louise-Hermine-Marie-Charlotte of Belgium, *b* 21 May 1864, *m* 1st 10 May 1881, HI and RH Crown Prince and Archduke *Rudolf* Franz Karl Joseph of Austria (*b* 21 Aug 1858; *d* 30 Jan 1889), and had issue,

HI and RH Archduchess *Elisabeth Marie* Henriette Stephanie Gisela of Austria, *b* 2 Sept 1883, *m* 1st 23 Jan 1902 (*m* diss by div 1924), HSH Prince *Otto* Weriand Hugo Ernst zu Windisch-Graetz (*b* 7 Oct 1873; *d* 25 Dec 1952,) and had issue,

1*e* •HSH Prince *Franz Joseph* Marie Otto Antonius Ignatius Oktavius zu Windisch-Graetz, *b* 22 March 1904, *m* 3 Jan 1934, •Countess *Ghislaine* Emma Marie (*b* 10 March 1912), dau of Count Guillaume d'Arschot-Schoonhoven, and has issue,

•HSH Prince *Guilleaume* Franz Joseph Maria zu Windisch-Graetz, *b* 19 Nov 1950.

•HSH Princess *Stephanie* Marie Eva zu Windisch-Graetz, *b* 17 Jan 1939, *m* 15 Feb 1967, •Major Dermot Blundell.

2*e* HSH Prince *Ernst Weriand* Maria Otto Antonius Expeditus Anselmus zu Windisch-Graetz, *b* 21 April 1905, *m* 1st 17 Oct 1927 (*m* diss by div 1938), Ellen (*b* 6 April 1906), dau of Henry Skinner, and had issue,

1*f* •HSH Prince *Otto* Ernst Wilhelm zu Windisch-Graetz [*Wickenburggasse 2, A-1080 Vienna, Austria*], *b* 5 Dec 1928, *m* 1st 27 April 1957 (*m* diss by div 1969), Countess Johanna (*b* 26 May 1936), 2nd dau of Count Franz von Wimpffen, and has issue,

1*g* •HSH Prince Philipp Amadeus Otto Ernst zu Windisch-Graetz, *b* 22 June 1960.

1*g* •HSH Princess Henriette Raphaela zu Windisch-Graetz, *b* 31 Jan 1958.

2*g* •HSH Princess Désirée Eleonore Marie Felizitas zu Windisch-Graetz, *b* 1 July 1959.

He *m* 2ndly 22 Dec 1969, •Maria Magdalena (*b* 7 Nov 1932), dau of Dr Hans Gamper, and by her has issue,

2*g* •HSH Prince Johannes Hubertus Maria zu Windisch-Graetz, *b* 7 Feb 1971.

1*f* •HSH Princess *Stephanie* Maria Mag-

dalena zu Windisch-Graetz, *b* 21 Jan 1933, *m* 2 May 1956, ●Joseph Christoforetti (*b* 27 Jan 1919) [*Moosstrasse 51b, A-5020 Salzburg, Austria*], and has issue,
1*g* ●Alexander Wilhelm Christoforetti, *b* 18 Jan 1958.
2*g* ●Nikolaus Josef Christoforetti, *b* 26 Oct 1962.
1*g* ●Angelika Maria Christoforetti, *b* 16 Nov 1956.
2*g* ●Claudia Maria Christoforetti, *b* 22 June 1960.
Prince Ernst Weriand *m* 2ndly 11 May 1947, ●Baroness Eva (*b* 5 April 1921) [*Fillgradergasse 12, A-1060 Vienna, Austria*], dau of Baron Lothar von Isbary, and *d* 23 Dec 1952, having by her had issue,
2*f* ●HSH Princess Eleonore zu Windisch-Graetz, *b* 25 Aug 1947, *m* 21 March 1968, ●Count *Friedrich Johann* zu Hardegg auf Glatz und im Machlande (*b* 5 Jan 1944).
3*f* ●HSH Princess Elisabeth zu Windisch-Graetz, *b* 24 Oct 1951.
3*e* HSH Prince *Rudolf* Johannes Maria Otto Joseph Antonius Andreas zu Windisch-Graetz, *b* 4 Feb 1907; *d unm* 9 June 1939.
1*e* ●HSH Princess *Stephanie* Eleonore Maria Elisabeth Kamilla Philomena Veronika zu Windisch-Graetz, *b* 9 July 1909, *m* 1st 22 July 1933, Count *Pierre*-Arnold-Alvar-Marie-Joseph-François-de-Borgia-Hubert-Grégoire d'-Alcantara de Querrieu (*b* 2 Nov 1907; *d* in Orienburg Concentration Camp 14 Oct 1944), and has issue,
1*f* ●Count Alvar-Etienne-Jean-Othon-Pierre-Marie-Joseph-Pie-François-de-Borgia d'Alcantara de Querrieu, *b* 30 Jan 1935, *m* 18 July 1956, ●Anita (*b* 15 Dec 1936), dau of Peter Damsten, and has issue,
1*g* ●Count Frédéric-Pierre-Othon-Jacques-François-de-Borgia d'Alcantara de Querrieu, *b* 9 April 1958.
1*g* ●Countess Patricia - Stéphanie - Anne d'Alcantara de Querrieu, *b* 19 Jan 1957.
2*g* ●Countess Véronique d'Alcantara de Querrieu, *b* 27 May 1960.
She *m* 2ndly 14 Nov 1945, ●Karl Axel Björklund (*b* 21 Dec 1906) [*42 Avenue Gustave, B-1640 Rhode-St-Genèse, Belgium*], and has further issue,
2*f* ●Björn Axel Björklund, *b* 20 Oct 1944.
Archduchess Elisabeth Marie *m* 2ndly 4 May 1948, Leopold Petznek (*b* 30 June 1881; *d* 27 July 1956), and *d* 22 March 1963.
Princess Stéphanie *m* 2ndly 22 March 1900, HSH Prince Elemér Lónyay de Nagy-Lónya et Vásáros-Namény (*b* 24 Aug 1863; *d* 10 Aug 1946), and *d* 23 Aug 1945.
3*c* HRH Princess *Clémentine*-Albertine-Marie-Léopoldine of Belgium, *b* 30 July 1872, *m* 14 Nov 1910, HIH Prince *Victor*-Jérôme-Frédéric Napoléon, Head of the Imp House of Bonaparte (*b* 18 July 1862; *d* 3 May 1926), and *d* 8 March 1955, leaving issue (*see p* 214).
2*a* HRH Duchess *Amelie* Therese Luise Wilhelmine Philippine of Württemberg, *b* 28 June 1799, *m* 24 April 1817, HH *Joseph* Friedrich Ernst Georg Karl, Duke of Saxe-Altenburg (*b* 27 Aug 1789; *d* 25 Nov 1868), and *d* 28 Nov 1848, having had issue,
1*b* HH Princess Alexandrine *Marie* Wilhelmine Catherine Charlotte Therese Henriette Louise Pauline Elisabeth Friederike Georgina of Saxe-Altenburg, Duchess of Saxony, *b* 14 April 1818, *m* 18 Feb 1843, HM King Georg V of Hanover, KG (*b* 27 May 1819; *d* 12 June 1878), and *d* 9 Jan 1907, having had issue (*see p* 290).
2*b* HH Princess *Pauline* Friederike Henriette Auguste of Saxe-Altenburg, Duchess of Saxony, *b* 24 Nov 1819; *d* 11 Jan 1825.
3*b* HH Princess Henriette Friederike *Therese* Elisabeth of Saxe-Altenburg, Duchess of Saxony, *b* 9 Oct 1823; *d unm* 3 April 1915.
4*b* HH Princess *Elisabeth* Pauline Alexandrine of Saxe-Altenburg, Duchess of Saxony, *b* 26 March 1826, *m* 10 Feb 1852, HRH Grand Duke (Nikolaus Friedrich) *Peter II* of Oldenburg (*b* 8 July 1827; *d* 13 June 1900), and *d* 2 Feb 1896, having had issue (*see p* 252).
5*b* HH Princess *Alexandra* Friederike Henriette Pauline Marianne Elisabeth of Saxe-Altenburg, Duchess of Saxony (Grand Duchess Alexandra Iossifovna), *b* 8 July 1830, *m* 11 Sept 1848, HIH Grand Duke Constantine Nikolaievitch of Russia (*b* 21 Sept 1827; *d* 25 Jan 1892), son of HIM Emperor Nicholas I of all the Russias, KG, and *d* 6 July 1911, having had issue,
1*c* HIH Grand Duke Nicholas Constantinovitch of Russia, *b* 14 Feb 1850, *m* 1882, Nadejda, *cr* HSH Princess Romanovsky-Iskander (*b* 1861; *d* 1929), dau of Alexander Dreyer, and was *k* in the Russian Revolution Feb 1918, leaving issue,
1*d* HSH Prince Artemi Nikolaievitch Romanovsky-Iskander, *b* 1883; *d unm* 1919.
2*d* HSH Prince Alexander Nikolaievitch Romanovsky-Iskander, *b* 15 Nov 1889, *m* 1st (*m* diss by div), Olga (*b* 1893), dau of Joseph Rogovsky. He *m* 2ndly, ●Natalia (*b* 30 Dec 1893), dau of Constantine Nikolaievitch Hanykow, and *d* 8 Oct 1935, having by her had issue,
●HSH Prince Cyrill Alexandrovitch Romanovsky-Iskander, *b* 5 Dec 1915.
●HSH Princess Natalia Alexandrovna Romanovsky-Iskander, *b* 10 Feb 1917.
2*c* HIH Grand Duke Constantine Constantinovitch of Russia, *b* 22 Aug 1858, *m* 15 April 1884, HH Princess *Elisabeth* Auguste Marie Agnes (Grand Duchess Elisabeth Mavrikievna) (*b* 25 Jan 1865; *d* 24 March 1927), 2nd dau of HH Prince Moritz of Saxe-Altenburg, Duke of Saxony, and *d* 14 June 1915, leaving issue (*see p* 267).
3*c* HIH Grand Duke Dimitri Constantinovitch of Russia, *b* 1 June 1860; *d unm* 28 Jan 1919.
4*c* HIH Grand Duke Viacheslav Constantinovitch of Russia, *b* 1 July 1862; *d* 27 Feb 1879.
1*c* HIH Grand Duchess Olga Constantinovna of Russia, *b* 3 Sept 1851, *m* 15 Oct 1867, HM King George I of the Hellenes, KG (*b* 24 Dec 1845; *d* 18 March 1913), and *d* 18 June 1926, having had issue (*see p* 279).
2*c* HIH Grand Duchess Vera Constantinovna of Russia, *b* 4 Feb 1854, *m* 8 May 1874, HRH Duke Wilhelm *Eugen* August Georg of Württemberg (*b* 20 Aug 1846; *d* 27 Jan 1877), and *d* 11 April 1912, having had issue,
1*d* HRH Duke Karl Eugen of Württemberg, *b* 8 April, *d* 11 Nov 1875.
1*d* HRH Duchess *Elsa* Mathilde Marie of Württemberg, *b* 1 March 1876, *m* 6 May 1897, HSH Prince Christian *Albrecht* Cajetan Karl Wilhelm of Schaumburg-Lippe (*b* 24 Oct 1869; *d* 25 Dec 1942), and *d* 27 May 1936, leaving issue (*see p* 285).
2*d* HRH Duchess *Olga* Alexandrine Marie of Württemberg, *b* 1 March 1876, *m* 3 Nov 1898, HSH Prince *Maximilian* August Jaroslav Adalbert Hermann of Schaumburg-Lippe (*b* 13 March 1871; *d* 1 April 1904), and *d* 21 Oct 1932, having had issue (*see p* 286).
6*b* HH Princess Luise Pauline Caroline Therese Marie of Saxe-Altenburg, Duchess of Saxony, *b* 4 June 1832; *d* 29 Aug 1833.
3*a* HRH Duchess *Pauline* Therese Luise of Württemberg, *b* 4 Sept 1800, *m* 15 April 1820, HM King Wilhelm I of Württemberg, KG (*b* 27 Sept 1781; *d* 25 June 1864), and *d* 10 March 1873, having had issue (*see p* 211).
4*a* HRH Duchess *Elisabeth* Alexandrine Constance of Württemberg, *b* 27 Feb 1802, *m* 16 Oct 1830, HGDH Prince *Wilhelm* Ludwig August of Baden (*b* 8 April 1792; *d* 11 Oct 1859), and *d* 5 Dec 1864, having had issue,
1*b* HSH Princess *Wilhelmine* Pauline Henriette Leopoldine Sophie Amelie Maximilienne of Baden, *b* 7 May 1833; *d* 7 Aug 1834.
2*b* HGDH Princess *Sophie* Pauline Henriette Marie Amelie Luise of Baden, *b* 7 Aug 1834, *m* 9 Nov 1858, HSH (Günther Friedrich) *Woldemar*, Prince of Lippe (*b* 18 April 1824; *d* 20 March 1895), and *dsp* 6 April 1904.

3*b* HGDH Princess Pauline Sophie *Elisabeth* Marie of Baden, *b* 18 Dec 1835; *d unm* 15 May 1891.

4*b* HGDH Princess *Leopoldine* Wilhelmine Pauline Amelie Maximilienne of Baden, *b* 22 Feb 1837, *m* 24 Sept 1862, HSH Hermann, 6th Prince zu Hohenlohe-Langenburg (*b* 31 Aug 1832; *d* 9 March 1913), and *d* 23 Dec 1903, having had issue,

1*c* HSH *Ernst* Wilhelm Friedrich Karl Maximilian, 7th Prince zu Hohenlohe-Langenburg, GCB, Regent of the Duchy of Saxe-Coburg and Gotha 1900-05, *b* 13 Sept 1863, *m* 20 April 1896, HRH Princess *Alexandra* Louise Olga Victoria, VA, CI (*b* 1 Sept 1878; *d* 16 April 1942), 3rd dau of HRH Alfred, Duke of Saxe-Coburg and Gotha, Duke of Edinburgh, Prince of Great Britain and Ireland KG, and *d* 11 Dec 1950, having had issue (*see p* 297).

1*c* HSH Princess *Elise* Victoria Feodora Sophie Adelheid zu Hohenlohe-Langenburg, *b* 4 Sept 1864, *m* 11 Nov 1884, HSH Heinrich XXVII, Prince Reuss (Younger Line) (*b* 10 Nov 1858; *d* 21 Nov 1928), and *d* 18 March 1929, having had issue,

1*d* HSH Prince Heinrich XL Reuss (Younger Line) ,*b* 17 Sept, *d* 4 Nov 1891.

2*d* HSH Prince Heinrich XLIII Reuss (Younger Line), *b* 25 July 1893; *d* 13 May 1912.

3*d* HSH Hereditary Prince Heinrich XLV Reuss (Younger Line), *b* 13 May 1895; missing since autumn 1945.

1*d* HSH Princess *Victoria-Feodora* Agnes Leopoldine Elisabeth Reuss (Younger Line), *b* 21 April 1889, m 24 April 1917 as his 1st wife, HRH Duke *Adolf Friedrich* Albrecht Heinrich of Mecklenburg-Schwerin (*b* 10 Oct 1873; *d* 5 Aug 1969), and *d* 18 Dec 1918, leaving issue,

•HH Duchess *Woizlawa* Feodora of Mecklenburg-Schwerin, *b* 17 Dec 1918, *m* 15 Sept 1939, •HSH Prince Heinrich I Reuss (Younger Line) (*b* 8 Oct 1910) [*647 Büdingen, OHessen, Marktplatz 5, Germany*], and has issue,

1*f* •HSH Prince Heinrich VIII Reuss (Younger Line), *b* 30 Aug 1944, *m* •Baroness *Dorit* Maria-Elisabeth (*b* 8 Jan 1948), yr dau of Franz-Anton, Baron von Ruffin.

2*f* •HSH Prince Heinrich IX Reuss (Younger Line), *b* 30 June 1947.

3*f* •HSH Prince Heinrich X Reuss (Younger Line), *b* 28 July 1948.

4*f* •HSH Prince Heinrich XIII Reuss (Younger Line), *b* 4 Dec 1951.

5*f* •HSH Prince Heinrich XV Reuss (Younger Line), *b* 9 Oct 1956.

1*f* •HSH Princess *Feodora* Elisabeth Sophie Reuss (Younger Line), *b* 5 Feb 1942, *m* 10 Sept 1967, •Count Gisbert zu Stolberg-Wernigerode (*b* 2 May 1942) [*6078 Neu-Isenburg, Akazienweg 9, Germany*].

2*d* HSH Princess *Luise Adelheid* Ida Helene Wilhelmine Reuss (Younger Line), *b* 17 July 1890; *d unm* 12 Aug 1951.

2*c* HSH Princess *Feodora* Victoria Alberta zu Hohenlohe-Langenburg, *b* 23 July 1866, *m* 12 July 1894, HSH *Emich* Eduard Karl, 5th Prince zu Leiningen (*b* 18 Jan 1866; *d* 18 July 1939), and *d* 1 Nov 1932, having had issue,

1*d* HSH Hereditary Prince *Emich Ernst* Hermann Heinrich Maximilian zu Leiningen, *b* 29 Dec 1896; *k* in action in World War I 21 March 1918.

2*d* HSH Friedrich *Karl* Eduard Erwin, 6th Prince zu Leiningen, *b* 13 Feb 1898, *m* 24 Nov 1925, HIH Grand Duchess Marie Kirillovna (*b* 2 Feb 1907; *d* 27 Oct 1951), elder dau of HIH Grand Duke Kirill Vladimirovitch of Russia, and *d* as a p o w in Russia 2 Aug 1946, leaving issue (*see p* 297).

3*d* •HSH Prince *Hermann* Viktor Maximilian zu Leiningen [*Amorbach, Germany*], *b* 4 Jan 1901, *m* 21 Dec 1938, •H Ill H Countess Irene (*b* 17 July 1895), formerly wife of Count Philipp von Berckheim, and elder dau of H Ill H Count Klemens von Schönborn-Wiesentheid.

4*d* •HSH Prince *Hesso* Leopold Heinrich zu Leiningen [*Burg Vilszelt, Post Unkel a Rh u Gut Waldhof b Vilshofen/Ndb, Germany*], *b* 29 July 1903, *m* 12 July 1933, •Countess *Marie-Louise* Agathe (*b* 31 July 1905), only dau of Franz, Count von Nesselrode.

1*d* •HSH Princess *Viktoria* Marie Leopoldine Elise Sophie zu Leiningen, *b* 12 May 1895, *m* 23 Feb 1922 (*m* diss by div 1937), H Ill H Count *Maximilian* Ludwig zu Solms-Rödelheim und Assenheim (*b* 24 Sept 1893), and has issue,

•H Ill H Hereditary Count *Markwart* Emich Otto Ernst zu Solms-Rödelheim und Assenheim, *b* 30 June 1925.

4 HH Princess Anne Marie of Orange, *b* 15 Nov, *d* 29 Dec 1746.

2 HRH Princess *Amelia* Sophia Eleanor, *b* at Herrenhausen 10 June 1711; *d unm* at her house in Cavendish Square, London 31 Oct 1786 (*bur* Westminster Abbey).

3 HRH Princess *Caroline* Elizabeth, *b* at Hanover 10 June 1713; *d unm* at St James's Palace 28 Dec 1757 (*bur* Westminster Abbey).

4 HRH Princess Mary, *b* at Leicester House 22 Feb 1723, *m* by proxy at St James's Palace 8 May and in person at Cassel 28 June 1740, as his 1st wife, HSH Friedrich II, Landgrave of Hesse-Cassel, KG (1741) (*b* at Cassel 14 Aug 1720; *d* at Schloss Weissenstein 31 Oct 1785), and *d* at Hanau 14 Jan 1772, having had issue,

1 HSH Prince Wilhelm of Hesse-Cassel, *b* 25 Dec 1741; *d* 1 July 1742.

2 HH Wilhelm I, Elector of Hesse, KG (1786), *s* his father as Landgrave Wilhelm IX of Hesse-Cassel 1785, took the title of Elector 27 April 1803, *b* 3 June 1743, *m* 1 Sept 1764, his 1st cousin, HH Princess Caroline (*b* 10 July 1747; *d* 14 Jan 1820), 2nd dau of HM King Frederik V of Denmark, by his 1st wife HRH Princess Louisa, yst dau of HM King George II (*see p* 289), and *d* 27 Feb 1821, having had issue,

(1) HSH Prince Friedrich of Hesse-Cassel, *b* 8 Aug 1772; *d* 20 July 1784.

(2) HH Wilhelm II, Elector of Hesse (1821-1831), abdicated 30 Sept 1831, *b* 28 July 1777, *m* 1st 13 Feb 1797, HRH Princess Friederike Christine *Auguste* (*b* 1 May 1780; *d* 19 Feb 1841), 4th dau of HM King Friedrich Wilhelm II of Prussia, and had issue,

1*a* HSH Prince Wilhelm Friedrich Karl Ludwig of Hesse-Cassel, *b* 9 April 1798; *d* 25 Oct 1800.

2*a* HH Friedrich Wilhelm, Elector of Hesse (1831-1866), abdicated 20 Sept 1866, when the Electorate of Hesse was annexed to the Kingdom of Prussia, *b* 30 Aug 1802, *m* (morganatically) 26 June 1831, Gertrud, *cr* Countess von Schaumburg 10 Oct 1831, and Princess von Hanau 2 June 1853, with qualification of Serene Highness 10 June 1862 (*b* 18 May 1803; *d* 9 July 1882), widow of Capt Lehmann, and dau of Gottfried Falkenstein, and *d* 6 Jan 1875, having had issue,

1*b* HSH Prince *Friedrich Wilhelm* von Hanau, Count von Schaumburg, *b* 18 Nov 1832, *m* 1st 23 Sept 1856 (*m* diss by div), Auguste (*b* 9 Nov 1837; *d* 29 June 1862), dau of Carl Birnbaum. He *m* 2ndly 8 April 1875, Bertha Luise *Ludovika* (*b* 6 May 1840; *d* 20 April 1912), dau of Friedrich Glaede, and *d* 14 May 1889, having by her had issue,

1*c* HSH Prince *Friedrich August* von Hanau, Count von Schaumburg, *b* 14 April 1864, *m* 1st 6 July 1899 (*m* diss by div), Countess Hildegard (*b* 10 March 1879; *d* 1 Feb 1933), dau of Count Almásy von Zsadány und Török-Szent-Miklós, and had issue,

1*d* •HSH Friedrich Wilhelm Tassilo Ludwig Hubertus *Heinrich*, 5th Prince von Hanau, Count von Schaumburg [*Schloss Messelberg, Post Maria-Saal, Kärnten, Austria; Wien IV, Karolinengasse 6, Austria*], *b* 27 Dec 1900, *m* 1 Aug 1921, •H Ill H Countess *Maria Theresia* Karoline Gigina (*b* 1 March 1899), yst dau of HSH Karl, 5th Prince Fugger von Babenhausen, and has issue,

1e ●HSH Prince Friedrich Wilhelm *Carl Heinrich* von Hanau, Count von Schaumburg [*8135 Söcking, Kr Starnberg, Germany*], *b* 27 April 1923, *m* 15 May 1948, ●Countess Maria Antonia (*b* 3 Sept 1922), yr dau of late Count Kurt Strachwitz von Gross-Zauche und Camminetz, and has issue,

●HSH Prince Friedrich Wilhelm *Philipp* Georg Heinrich Jakob von Hanau, Count von Schaumburg, *b* 26 June 1959.

●HSH Princess Franziska Elisabeth Maria Antonia von Hanau, Countess von Schaumburg, *b* 27 Oct 1954.

2e ●HSH Prince Friedrich Wilhelm Ferdinand *Leopold* Tassilo von Hanau, Count von Schaumburg [*Wien IV, Karolinengasse 6, Austria*], *b* 7 May 1924, *m* 17 Dec 1949, ●Baroness *Marie-Alice* Leopoldine Wilhelmine Henriette Elisabeth (*b* 7 July 1919), only dau of late Baron Ernst-Gideon von Loudon, and has issue,

●HSH Prince *Friedrich Wilhelm* Heinrich Antonius von Hanau, Count von Schaumburg, *b* 28 Feb 1956.

●HSH Princess Friederike Wilhelmine Elisabeth Viktoria Maria von Hanau, Countess von Schaumburg, *b* 23 Dec 1953.

3e ●HSH Prince *Friedrich-Wilhelm* von Hanau, Count von Schaumburg [*135 East Mulberry, San Antonio, Texas, USA*], *b* 3 Dec 1927, *m* 5 June 1954, ●Maria (*b* 9 Dec 1924), dau of Arpád Kossacky, and has issue,

●HSH Prince *Friedrich-Wilhelm* Heinrich Christoph von Hanau, Count von Schaumburg, *b* 5 June 1956.

1e ●HSH Princess *Eleonore* Marie Elisabeth Hildegarde von Hanau, Countess von Schaumburg, *b* 16 May 1925, *m* 1st 15 Jan 1946 (*m* diss by div), Adalbert von Spanyi (*b* 23 Feb 1921), and has issue,

1f ●Elisabeth Franziska Maria von Spanyi, *b* 28 Oct 1946.

2f ●Ellen Maria Theresia Irene Regina von Spanyi, *b* 12 Feb 1952.

She *m* 2ndly 26 May 1959, ●Herbert Joost (*b* 30 April 1908) [*Hamburg 39, Leinpfad 21, Germany*].

2d HSH Prince Tassilo *Karl* Friedrich Wilhelm Antonius Hubertus von Hanau, Count von Schaumburg, *b* 21 Dec 1901; *d unm* 16 May 1932.

1d ●HSH Princess *Hildegard* Marie Ludovika Mathilde Anna von Hanau, Countess von Schaumburg [*München 19, Wilhelm-Düll-Strasse 3, Germany*], *b* 12 March 1903, *m* 1st 10 Jan 1922 (*m* diss by div 1928), *Carl-Max* Raimund Samuel Ortolf Vollrath, Count von und zu Sandizell (*b* 4 Oct 1895; *d* 21 May 1962), and has issue,

●Count *Carl Hochbrand* Maximilian Ortolph Theodor Raimund Tassilo von und zu Sandizell [*8 München 71, Sollner Strasse 52, Germany*], *b* 9 Feb 1924, *m* 11 July 1957 (*m* diss by div 1966), Irene (*b* 1 Sept 1937), dau of Herbert Rohrer, and has issue,

1f ●Count *Nikolaus* Carl Max Emanuel Heinrich Tassilo von und zu Sandizell, *b* 20 Jan 1959.

2f ●Count Tassilo von und zu Sandizell, *b* 12 April 1963.

1f ●Countess Alexandra von und zu Sandizell, *b* 29 April 1960.

She *m* 2ndly 26 June 1928 (*m* diss by div 1941), H Ill H Count *Wulf Diether* Wolfgang Christian Ernst Otto Paul Karl zu Castell-Rudenhausen (*b* 20 Nov 1905).

2d ●HSH Princess *Emmerentiana* Philippina Ernestine Anna Marie von Hanau, Countess von Schaumburg, *b* 22 April 1913, *m* 5 Oct 1933, ●Count *Ludwig* Adolf Maximilian von Montgelas (*b* 15 Dec 1907) [*München Obermenzing, Bauseweinallee 79, Germany*], and has issue,

1e ●Count *Maximilian* Theodor Ludwig Tassilo von Montgelas, *b* 24 July 1934, *m* 24 Aug 1963, ●Baroness Astrid (*b* 17 Sept 1940), dau of Baron Bertram Riedesel zu Eisenbach, and has issue,

●Countess Caroline von Montgelas, *b* 25 Feb 1966.

2e ●Count *Tassilo* Heinrich Maximilian Evarest von Montgelas, *b* 2 April 1937.

1e ●Countess *Elisabeth* Anna Maria Hildegard von Montgelas, *b* 24 March 1939.

He *m* 2ndly 12 Dec 1932, ●Ernestine (*b* 29 Jan 1894), dau of Johann Detzer, and *d* 26 April 1940.

2c HSH Prince *Ludwig* Cäcilius Felix von Hanau, Count von Schaumburg, *b* 19 May 1872; *d unm* 8 Jan 1940.

2b HSH Prince *Moritz* Philipp Heinrich von Hanau, Count von Schaumburg, *b* 4 May 1834, *m* 15 April 1875, Anna (*b* 14 Aug 1829; *d* 27 Oct 1876), dau of Gen Karl Wilhelm von Lossberg, and *d* 25 March 1889.

3b HSH Wilhelm, 2nd Prince von Hanau, Count von Schaumburg, *b* 19 Dec 1836, *m* 1st 30 Jan 1866 (*m* diss by div 1868), HSH Princess *Elisabeth* Wilhelmine Auguste Marie (*b* 5 March 1841; *d* 30 Nov 1926), 5th (and yst) dau of HSH Prince Georg of Schaumburg-Lippe. He *m* 2ndly 12 May 1890, H Ill H Countess Elisabeth (*b* 1 July 1868; *d* 24 Oct 1952), 3rd dau of H Ill H Count Franz of Lippe-Weissenfeld, and *dsp* 3 June 1902.

4b HSH Karl, 3rd Prince von Hanau, Count von Schaumburg, *b* 29 Nov 1840, *m* 11 Nov 1882, Countess *Hermine* Helene Doraline (*b* 8 Oct 1859; *d* 31 March 1939), dau of Count August von Grote, and *dsp* 27 Jan 1905.

5b HSH Friedrich Wilhelm *Heinrich* Ludwig Hermann, 4th Prince von Hanau, Count von Schaumburg, *b* 8 Dec 1842, *m* 4 June 1917, Martha (*b* 26 Oct 1876; *d* 10 March 1943), dau of August Riegel, and *dsp* 15 July 1917.

6b HSH Prince Friedrich Wilhelm *Philipp* von Hanau, Count von Schaumburg, *b* 29 Dec 1844, *m* 29 March 1875, Albertine Stauber (*b* 7 Dec 1845; *d* 11 April 1912), and *d* 28 Aug 1914, having had issue (bearing the title of Count or Countess von Schaumburg only),

1c Count Philipp von Schaumburg, *b* 17 April 1868; *d unm* 19 Sept 1890.

2c Count Friedrich Wilhelm August von Schaumburg, *b* 18 Dec 1875; *d unm* 26 Dec 1898.

3c Count *Karl* August Friedrich Felix von Schaumburg, *b* 10 Aug 1878, *m* 28 Sept 1901, Anna (*b* 22 Dec 1870; *d* 15 Oct 1942), dau of August von Trott zu Solz, and *d* 2 Dec 1905, leaving issue,

1d ●Countess *Albertine* Eleonore Bertha von Schaumburg, *b* 23 Aug 1902, *m* 16 Sept 1922, ●Count Ernst Georg *Edwin* von Rothkirch und Trach (*b* 1 Nov 1888) [*Rettershof über Königstein, Taunus, Germany*], and has issue,

●Count Thilo Karl August *Leopold* von Rothkirch und Trach [*Römersberg über Wabern, Bez Kassel, Germany*], *b* 27 Dec 1923, *m* 26 Jan 1950, ●Gabriele (*b* 10 May 1927), dau of Georg Heintze, and has issue,

●Count Edwin Georg *Leonhard* von Rothkirch und Trach, *b* 28 Feb 1951.

●Countess Albertine von Rothkirch und Trach, *b* 19 Feb 1954.

2d ●Countess *Marielier* Hermine Lilli von Schaumburg [*Oberurf, Bez Kassel, Herrenhaus, Germany*], *b* 17 Dec 1903, *m* 2 June 1927, Baron *Hans* Arwed Gustav Hermann von Buttlar und Treusch von Buttlar-Brandenfels (*b* 5 May 1885; *d* 29 July 1946), and has issue,

1e ●Baron *Hans* Adolf Karl Ludwig Kurt von Buttlar und Treusch von Buttlar-Brandenfels, *b* 23 Feb 1933, *m* 21 Jan 1959, ●Inge Parpart (*b* 6 Sept 1931), and has issue,

●Baron Hans Bernhard von Buttlar und Treusch von Buttlar-Brandenfels, *b* 12 Oct 1961.

1e ●Baroness *Marielier* (*Lily*) Stephanie Sophie von Buttlar und Treusch von Buttlar-Brandenfels, *b* 25 April 1928, *m* 10 July 1951, ●Leopold Beierl (*b* 12 Sept 1915) [*Oberurf, Forsthaus Hammer, Germany*], and has issue,
●Franz Beierl, *b* 31 March 1953.
●Elisabeth Beierl, *b* 15 Aug 1955.
2e ●Baroness *Marianne* Philippine Wilhelmine Gabriele von Buttlar und Treusch von Buttlar-Brandenfels, *b* 9 May 1930, *m* 31 Oct 1960, ●Herbert Weigand (*b* 8 Jan 1936), and has issue,
1f ●Michael Weigand, *b* 28 Feb 1956.
2f ●Thomas Weigand, *b* 8 Dec 1958.
3f ●Mathias Weigand, *b* 15 April 1963.
1f ●Christine Weigand, *b* (twin with Mathias) 15 April 1963.
1b HSH Princess *Auguste* Marie Gertrud von Hanau, Countess von Schaumburg, *b* 21 Sept 1829, *m* 17 July 1849, HSH *Ferdinand Maximilian* Adolf Ernst Ludwig Philipp, 1st Prince zu Ysenburg und Büdingen (*b* 24 Oct 1824; *d* 5 June 1903), and *d* 18 Sept 1887, leaving issue,
1c HSH *Friedrich Wilhelm* Adolf Georg Kasimir Karl, 2nd Prince zu Ysenburg und Büdingen, *b* 17 June 1850, *m* 16 Sept 1879, Countess (*cr* by the Emperor of Austria 13 July 1879) *Anna* Elisabeth Ludovika Antonia Huberta (*b* 25 Feb 1852; *d* 21 Sept 1913), dau of Baron Prokop Dobrzensky von Dobrzenicz, and *d* 20 April 1933, having had issue,
1d HSH Hereditary Prince *Ferdinand Maximilian* zu Ysenburg und Büdingen in Wächtersbach, *b* 25 June 1880, *m* 19 Dec 1903, Countess Margarethe (*Margita*) Maria Alexandrine Jelka Dagmar (*b* 19 April 1876; *d* 22 Sept 1954), dau of Count Otto von Dönhoff Baron von Krafft, and *dvp* 11 March 1927, leaving issue,
●HSH *Otto Friedrich* Viktor Ferdinand Maximilian Gustav Richard Bogislav, 3rd Prince zu Ysenburg und Büdingen [*647 Schloss Büdingen, OHessen, Germany*], *b* 16 Sept 1904, *m* 3 Sept 1935, ●HSH Princess *Felizitas* Anna Eleonore Cecilie (*b* 5 July 1914), dau of HSH Prince Heinrich XXXIV Reuss (Younger Line), and has issue,
1f ●HSH Hereditary Prince *Wolfgang Ernst* Ferdinand Heinrich Franz Karl Georg Wilhelm zu Ysenburg und Büdingen in Wächtersbach [*6470 Büdingen, Am Pfaffenwald 24, Germany*], *b* 20 June 1936, *m* (civil) 27 Jan and (religious) 28 Jan 1967, ●HSH Princess *Leonille* Elisabeth Victoria Barbara Margarete (*b* 6 July 1941), only dau of HSH Prince Casimir Johannes zu Sayn-Wittgenstein-Berleburg (*see p* 271), and has issue,
1g ●HSH Prince Casimir *Alexander* Lucian Friedrich Peter Franz Ferdinand Benedikt Wittekind zu Ysenburg und Büdingen in Wächtersbach, *b* 30 Dec 1967.
2g ●HSH Prince *Ferdinand-Maximilian* zu Ysenburg und Büdingen in Wächtersbach, *b* 28 July 1969.
2f ●HSH Prince *Ferdinand Heinrich* Karl August Hermann Gotthard zu Ysenburg und Büdingen in Wächtersbach, *b* 19 Oct 1940.
3f ●HSH Prince *Christian Albrecht* Franz Nikolaus Heinrich Wolfgang zu Ysenburg und Büdingen in Wächtersbach, *b* 3 Jan 1943, *m* 17 Feb 1966, ●Baroness Maria *Monika* Octavia Mannella (*b* 29 Jan 1940), dau of Baron Johann Ludwig von Plessen, and has issue,
1g ●HSH Prince Johann *Albrecht* Philipp Alexander Stefan Axel Wittekind Leonille zu Ysenburg und Büdingen in Wächtersbach, *b* 10 July 1967.
1g ●HSH Princess *Margita Octavia* Alexandra Silvia Felizitas Irmgard Madeleine zu Ysenburg und Büdingen in Wächtersbach, *b* 7 Nov 1966.
2g ●HSH Princess *Donata Elisabeth* zu Ysenburg und Büdingen in Wächtersbach, *b* 22 Feb 1970.
4f ●HSH Prince Johann Ernst Friedrich Karl Diether Franz Alexander Heinrich *Sylvester* zu Ysenburg und Büdingen in Wächtersbach, *b* 31 Dec 1949.
1f ●HSH Princess Sophie *Alexandra* Cecilie Anna Maria Friederike Benigna Dorothea zu Ysenburg und Büdingen in Wächtersbach, *b* 23 Oct 1937, *m* 21 Sept 1960, ●HRH Prince *Welf Heinrich* Ernst August Georg Christian Berthold Friedrich Wilhelm Louis Ferdinand of Hanover, Duke of Brunswick and Lüneburg (*b* 11 March 1923) (*see p* 290).
●HSH Princess *Gabriele Georgine* Gustava Resita Klausine Karoline Imagina Marion zu Ysenburg und Büdingen in Wächtersbach, *b* 23 Nov 1911, *m* 21 Feb 1942, ●HSH Prince *Franz Wilhelm* Otto Alfred Konstantin Emil zu Sayn-Wittgenstein-Berleburg (*b* 24 Aug 1910) [*8 München 27, Holbeinstrasse 14, Germany*] (*see p* 270).
1d HSH Princess *Maria* Elisabeth Auguste Anna zu Ysenburg und Büdingen in Wächtersbach, *b* 13 Nov 1881, *m* 23 June 1910, Domingo Aloisi (*b* 21 July 1867; *d* 15 March 1945), and *d* 13 Nov 1958, leaving issue,
1e ●Mario Aloisi, *b* 27 Sept 1912.
2e ●*Carlo* Federigo Aloisi [*Villa Pirignano, Casciano, Val di Pesa, Firenze, Italy*], *b* 8 June 1918, *m* 3 June 1954, ●Countess Donna *Adriana* Maria Rosario Paola Crispina Gasparre Melchiore Baldassare (*b* 25 Oct 1929), eldest dau of Don Giovanni, 5th Prince and Count Ginori-Conti, 5th Prince di Trevignano, and has issue,
1f ●Giandomenico Aloisi, *b* 27 Aug 1956.
1f ●Maria Federica Aloisi, *b* 25 Sept 1957.
2f ●Andrea Aloisi, *b* 19 Sept 1959.
3f ●Raimonda Aloisi, *b* 4 Jan 1961.
1e ●Mariangela Aloisi, *b* 7 April 1911, *m* 31 March 1937, ●Count *Ludwig* Joseph Albert Franz Heinrich Dieter, zu Ysenburg-Philippseich (*b* 23 July 1893) [*Rua Maranduba 59, São Paulo, Brazil*], and has issue,
1f ●Count *Christian Wilhelm* Adolf zu Ysenburg-Philippseich, *b* 29 July 1938.
1f ●Countess *Gabriele* Maria Emma Adelheid zu Ysenburg-Philippseich, *b* 30 Aug 1939.
2f ●Countess *Elisabeth* Victoria Raimonda zu Ysenburg-Philippseich, *b* 9 Dec 1941.
2e ●Anna Aloisi, *b* 16 Jan 1916, *m* 20 April 1936, ●Count Gabriele Ginanni Fantuzzi (*b* 15 May 1905), and has issue,
●Maria Ginevra dei Conti Ginanni Fantuzzi, *b* 12 Nov 1943.
2d ●HSH Princess *Elisabeth* Maria Auguste zu Ysenburg und Büdingen in Wächtersbach [*12 rue de Regard, F-75 Paris, France; F-45 Solaire-les-Bordes, Loiret, France*], *b* 12 Nov 1883, *m* 21 May 1901, Comte Edouard Desrousseaux de Vandières, 1st (Papal) Duke de Vandières (*b* 31 May 1866; *d* 29 May 1935), and has issue.
1e ●Comte Edouard Desrousseaux de Vandières, 2nd Duke de Vandières, *b* 13 Feb 1909, *m* 21 July 1937, Marie-France Patas d'Illiers (*b* 30 Aug 1917; *d* 11 Sept 1957), and has issue,
1f ●Comte Edouard Desrousseaux de Vandières, *b* 18 Jan 1942.
2f ●Comte Jean-François Desrousseaux de Vandières, *b* 7 March 1954.
1f ●Marcelle Desrousseaux de Vandières, *b* 13 July 1938, *m* 5 Sept 1964, ●Count Alain de Beaumont de Verneuil d'Auty (*b* 19 Oct 1938).
2f ●Françoise Desrousseaux de Vandières, *b* 3 Oct 1939.
3f ●Elisabeth Desrousseaux de Vandières, *b* 26 Nov 1940.
4f ●Michele Desrousseaux de Vandières, *b* 3 Aug 1943.

5*f* •Nicole Desrousseaux de Vandières, *b* 20 May 1946.
6*f* •Marie-Christine Desrousseaux de Vandières, *b* 18 May 1948.
1*e* •Elisabeth Desrousseaux de Vandières, *b* 2 Aug 1902, *m* Aug 1925, •Antoine de Pasquier de Franclieu, Marquis de Franclieu (*b* 24 March 1897), and has issue,
1*f* •Comte Jean-Marie de Pasquier de Franclieu, *b* 16 June 1926, *m* 6 Aug 1947, •Christiane (*b* 25 Sept 1925), dau of Comte Camille de Pasquier de Franclieu, and has issue,
1*g* •Georges de Pasquier de Franclieu, *b* 25 May 1948.
2*g* •Robert de Pasquier de Franclieu, *b* 27 Nov 1950.
3*g* •Jacques de Pasquier de Franclieu, *b* 16 June 1960.
1*g* •Edith de Pasquier de Franclieu, *b* 30 May 1949.
2*g* •Véronique de Pasquier de Franclieu, *b* 23 Dec 1957.
2*f* •Comte Robert de Pasquier de Franclieu, *b* 21 July 1932, *m* 2 July 1955, •Claude (*b* 31 May 1931), dau of Georges Le Boulanger de Capelle, and has issue,
1*g* •Philippe de Pasquier de Franclieu, *b* 23 Oct 1955.
2*g* •Bruno de Pasquier de Franclieu, *b* 15 Oct 1956.
3*g* •Thibaut de Pasquier de Franclieu, *b* 13 July 1959.
1*f* •Marguerite-Marie-Charlotte-Louise de Pasquier de Franclieu, *b* 3 Nov 1927, *m* 7 Oct 1955, Vincent de Bataille-Furé (*b* 1 Nov 1914; *d* 21 Feb 1960), and has issue,
1*g* •Anne de Bataille-Furé, *b* 1 Oct 1956.
2*g* •Marie-France de Bataille-Furé, *b* 5 May 1948.
3*g* •Emmanuelle de Bataille-Furé, *b* 11 July 1960.
2*f* •*Marie-Thérèse*-Camille de Pasquier de Franclieu, *b* 23 Sept 1941, *m* 7 Aug 1962, •Gérard Bergeron (*b* 5 April 1940), and has issue,
1*g* •Christian Bergeron, *b* 29 Nov 1963.
1*g* •Elisabeth Bergeron, *b* 8 April 1965.
2*g* •Marie-Alix Bergeron, *b* 21 April 1966.
2*e* •Marie-Anne-Eulalie-Frédérique-Guillemette-Ida-Philippine Desrousseaux de Vandières, *b* 16 June 1904, *m* 9 Aug 1927, •Comte Olivier de Bourdoncle de Saint-Salvy (*b* 14 Feb 1905), and has issue,
1*f* •Comte Jacques-René-Edouard-Marie-Joseph de Bourdoncle de Saint-Salvy, *b* 30 Nov 1930, *m* 8 Sept 1953, •Jeanne (*b* 9 Sept 1930), dau of Comte Guy de Cardevac d'Havrincourt, and has issue,
1*g* •Bruno de Bourdoncle de Saint-Salvy, *b* 8 Aug 1955.
2*g* •Ludovic de Bourdoncle de Saint-Salvy, *b* 18 March 1963.
1*g* •Anne-Françoise de Bourdoncle de Saint-Salvy, *b* 31 Aug 1954.
2*g* •Myriam de Bourdoncle de Saint-Salvy, *b* 17 June 1958.
2*f* •Comte Alain-Marie-Joseph-Marcel de Bourdoncle de Saint-Salvy, *b* 6 June 1934, *m* 9 Aug 1956, •Françoise (*b* 5 June 1934), dau of Comte Pierre de La Rocque de Sévérac, and has issue,
1*g* •Olivier de Bourdoncle de Saint-Salvy, *b* 4 April 1964.
1*g* •Christine de Bourdoncle de Saint-Salvy, *b* 1 June 1957.
2*g* •Béatrice de Bourdoncle de Saint-Salvy, *b* 27 March 1959.
3*g* •Anne de Bourdoncle de Saint-Salvy, *b* 16 July 1960.
4*g* •Catherine de Bourdoncle de Saint-Salvy, *b* 21 Sept 1961.
3*f* •Comte Jean-Christian-Marie-Joseph-Edmé de Bourdoncle de Saint-Salvy, *b* 27 Jan 1944.
1*f* •Monique-Elisabeth-Marie-Josèphe de Bourdoncle de Saint-Salvy, *b* 11 Oct 1929, *m* 5 May 1962, •Noël Segoune (*b* 5 Nov 1923).
2*f* •Nicole-Marie-Josèphe de Bourdoncle de Saint-Salvy, *b* 22 April 1938, *m* 19 May 1962, •Antoine Serre (*b* 8 Feb 1932), and has issue,
1*g* •Patrick-Anne-Marie-Joseph Serre, *b* 26 Feb 1963.
2*g* •François-Alain Serre, *b* 16 Dec 1964.
3*d* HSH Princess *Ida* Auguste zu Ysenburg und Büdingen in Wächtersbach, *b* 9 Aug 1885, *m* 14 April 1916, *Thilo* Ernst Adolf von Trotha (*b* 27 July 1882; *d* 29 June 1966), and *d* 18 Oct 1964, having had issue,
1*e* *Wolf-Ulrich* Thilo Waldemar von Trotha, *b* 28 Oct 1923; *k* in action in World War II 26 June 1944.
2*e* Hans Christoph *Thilo* Friedrich Hermann von Trotha, *b* 4 Oct 1926, *m* 18 July 1959, •HSH Princess *Alexandra* Anne Marie Viktoria Caroline Elisabeth Vincenzia (*b* 19 July 1935) [*D 798 Ravensburg, Tettnangerstrasse 78, Germany*], dau of HSH Prince Karl Erwin zu Hohenlohe-Langenburg, and *d* 29 June 1966, leaving issue,
1*f* •Thilo von Trotha, *b* 20 April 1960.
2*f* •*Hans* Ulrich von Trotha, *b* 19 July 1965.
1*f* •*Irene* Eleonore von Trotha, *b* 27 May 1962.
1*e* •*Huberta* Alexandra Anna Marie Therese von Trotha, *b* 22 Jan 1917, *m* 1st 25 July 1936 (*m* diss by div 1938), *Albert-Heino* Kasimir Joachim, Baron von Beust (*b* 21 July 1911), and has issue,
1*f* •Baroness *Maria-Therese* von Beust, *b* 31 Aug 1937.
She *m* 2ndly 23 June 1939 (*m* diss by div 1943), *Angus* William Udo Raven, Count von Douglas (*b* 30 July 1913), and has further issue,
1*f* •Count *Angus* Marten Archibald Ulrich von Douglas, *b* 24 June 1940.
2*f* •Count *Gol* Sholto von Douglas, b 30 Jan 1942.
She *m* 3rdly 15 April 1945, •Hans Becker (*b* 28 Jan 1916).
2*e* •*Alexandra* Anna Elisabeth Gerta Victoria von Trotha [*Stuttgart-Bad Cannstatt, Daimlerstrasse 24, Germany*], *b* 24 Feb 1919, *m* 3 Sept 1938 (*m* diss by div 1950), *Alexander* Georg Karl Maria von Brandenstein (*b* 15 Jan 1909), and has issue,
•Gerd Franz Alexander von Brandenstein *b* 6 April 1942.
3*e* •*Elisabeth* Luitgard Maria von Trotha [*München, Arnoldstrasse 22-24, Germany*], *b* 7 July 1920, *m* 30 Dec 1944, HSH Hereditary Prince *Alois* Franz Josef Hieronymus Maria von Schönburg-Hartenstein (*b* 18 Aug 1916; *k* in action in World War II 13 May, 1945), and has issue,
•HSH *Aloys* Franz Josef Alexander Hieronymus Thilo Michael Maria, 6th Prince von Schönburg-Hartenstein, *b* 4 Oct 1945.
4*e* •*Irene-Eleonore* Bernhardine Gabriele von Trotha [*Heidelberg, Lenaustrasse 4, Germany*], *b* 28 Feb 1922.
4*d* •HSH Princess Therese (*Resita*) zu Ysenburg und Büdingen in Wächtersbach [*Spré di Povo, Prov Trient, Italy*], *b* 19 June 1887, *m* 3 June 1913, Count Franz Ceschi a Santa Croce (*b* 10 June 1872; *d* 6 April 1952), and has issue,
•Countess *Anna Leopoldine* Friederike Theodora Maria Ceschi a Santa Croce [*Spré di Povo, Prov Trient, Italy*], *b* 8 April 1914, *m* 19 Sept 1933 (*m* diss by div 1950), Count *Felix* Theobald Paul Anton Maria Czernin von und zu Chudenitz (*b* 7 March 1902), and has issue,
•Count *Paul* Franz Felix Jaromir Maria Czernin von und zu Chudenitz [*Wien IV*,

Argentinierstrasse 33, Austria], *b* 16 July 1934.

5*d* HSH Princess Anna (*Anita*) zu Ysenburg und Büdingen in Wächtersbach, *b* (twin with Princess Resita) 19 June 1887, *m* 9 Jan 1919 (*m* diss by div 1941), Hans Rausch (*b* 8 Oct 1886; *d* 22 April 1961), and *d* 5 Sept 1954, leaving issue,

1*e* •Ferdinand Rausch, *b* 30 March 1927, *m* 29 Dec 1951, •Dagmar Leitner (*b* 5 May 1928), and has issue,

1*f* •Marion Rausch, *b* 17 March 1953.

2*f* •Regina Rausch, *b* 4 Sept 1955.

1*e* •Helga Rausch, *b* 31 July 1921, *m* 31 July 1946, •Heinrich Vogelbacher (*b* 11 Dec 1922), and has issue,

1*f* •Dieter Vogelbacher, *b* 11 Nov 1946.

2*f* •Peter Vogelbacher, *b* 12 April 1958.

2*e* •Annemarie Rausch, *b* 2 Sept 1922, *m* 10 Oct 1959, •Emil Grigo (*b* 10 Sept 1908).

3*e* •Huberta Rausch, *b* 29 May 1924, *m* 26 Dec 1950, •Wilhelm Heiss (*b* 11 Feb 1920).

2*c* HSH Prince Wilhelm Philipp Otto *Maximilian* zu Ysenburg und Büdingen in Wächtersbach, *b* 21 June 1867; *d unm* 18 March 1904.

1*c* HSH Princess Gertrude Philippine *Alexandra* Marie Auguste Luise zu Ysenburg und Büdingen in Wächtersbach, *b* 28 Dec 1855, *m* 1st 18 Nov 1875 (*m* diss by div 1877), HSH Prince Adalbert zu Ysenburg und Büdingen in Büdingen (*b* 17 Feb 1839; *d* 29 Aug 1885). She *m* 2ndly 15 May 1878 (*m* diss by div 1899), Baron Robert von Pagenhardt (*b* 28 April 1852; *d* 16 Sept 1922), and *d* 24 Oct 1932, having had issue,

1*d* Baron Ferdinand Maximilian Friedrich Wilhelm Heinrich Alexander Robert von Pagenhardt, *b* 11 March 1881, *m* 1st 31 March 1908 (*m* diss by div), Marthe de La Roche-Burchard (*b* 7 Sept 1886; *d* 3 Jan 1932). He *m* 2ndly 13 March 1934, •Maria Margaretha von Salis-Soglio-Maienfeld (*b* 1 Jan 1899), and *dsp* 13 June 1960.

2*d* Baron Friedrich Wilhelm Eduard Alexander Robert von Pagenhardt, *b* 29 Dec 1882; *d unm* 25 Aug 1907.

3*d* Baron Maximilian Hugo von Pagenhardt, *b* 20 June 1884, *m* 25 May 1918, •Marie Dupuy (*b* 27 Nov 1896), dau of Arthur Adams, and *d* 25 Sept 1943, leaving issue,

•Baron Maximilian Ferdinand Robert von Pagenhardt, *b* 21 Aug 1923, *m* 1st 11 April 1946 (*m* diss by div), Hope (*b* 11 Nov 1923), dau of Thomas Lamb Allen, and has issue,

1*f* •Baroness Alexandra Theodora Maria von Pagenhardt, *b* 30 Aug 1951.

2*f* •Baroness Tania Christina Adelaide von Pagenhardt, *b* 27 April 1953.

He *m* 2ndly 8 Jan 1958 (*m* diss by div), Sylvia, dau of Carl Hommel. He *m* 3rdly 25 July 1962, •Heidi, dau of Hans Schweizer.

4*d* Baron Kraft Hippolyt von Pagenhardt, *b* 13 Feb 1889, *m* 2 Aug 1921, •Marion Schmidtt-Stawitz (*b* 5 April 1901), and *dsp* 10 March 1957.

1*d* Baroness Auguste Alexandra von Pagenhardt, *b* 4 March 1879; *d unm* 20 Oct 1941.

2*d* •Baroness Anna Josephine von Pagenhardt, *b* 14 Sept 1890, *m* 25 Dec 1914, •Christian Gustaf Fielfe-Fairwil (*b* 23 June 1883), and has issue,

•*Karin* Anna-Lisa Fielfe-Fairwil (known as Karin von Pagenhardt), *b* 2 Oct 1918.

2*c* HSH Princess *Gerta* Auguste zu Ysenburg und Büdingen in Wächtersbach, *b* 8 Jan 1863, *m* 11 April 1885, HH Prince *Wilhelm* Karl Bernhard Hermann of Saxe-Weimar-Eisenach, Duke of Saxony (*b* 31 Dec 1853; *d* 15 Dec 1924), and *d* 27 Nov 1945, having had issue (*see p* 211).

2*b* HSH Princess *Alexandrine* Friederike Wilhelmine von Hanau, Countess von Schaumburg, *b* 22 Dec 1830, *m* 12 June 1851, HSH Prince *Felix* Eugen Wilhelm Ludwig Albrecht Karl zu Hohenlohe-Oehringen (*b* 1 March 1818; *d* 8 Sept 1900), and *d* 20 Dec 1871, leaving issue,

1*c* HSH Prince Victor Hugo *Kraft* Friedrich Wilhelm Moritz zu Hohenlohe-Oehringen, *b* 19 Jan 1861, *m* 10 Oct 1885 (*m* diss by div 1901), Marguerite *Marie* Madeleine Nativité de Vassinhac, Comtesse d'Imécourt (*b* 25 Dec 1863; *d* 5 Jan 1924), dau of Charles-Louis de Vassinhac, Marquis d'Imécourt, and *dsp* 11 Sept 1939.

2*c* HSH Prince Ferdinand *Alexander* zu Hohenlohe-Oehringen, renounced his princely titles 30 May 1895 and was *cr* Baron von Gabelstein, *b* 20 Dec 1871, *m* 16 July 1895, Elsa (*b* 19 July 1870; *d* 2 Feb 1960), dau of Ulpiano de Ondarza, and *d* 30 Jan 1929, leaving issue,

•Prince *Kraft* Alexander Ulpiano zu Hohenlohe-Oehringen, Baron von Gabelstein, bears the name of Prince zu Hohenlohe-Oehringen following his adoption by his uncle Prince Kraft zu Hohenlohe-Oehringen 30 Aug 1939, *b* 9 March 1896, *m* 15 Sept 1924, Baroness *Margarethe* Elisabeth Dorothea Anna Walburga (*b* 6 Feb 1905; *d* 17 July 1935), dau of Baron Anton von Ow, and has issue,

1*e* •Prince *Kraft* Leo Ulrich zu Hohenlohe-Oehringen, Baron von Gabelstein, *b* 4 July 1925, *m* 30 March 1957, •Margit (*b* 10 March 1930), dau of Wilhelm Profanter, and has issue,

1*f* •Prince Stephan zu Hohenlohe-Oehringen, Baron von Gabelstein, *b* 30 Oct 1961.

1*f* •Princess Monika zu Hohenlohe-Oehringen, Baroness von Gabelstein, *b* 28 Dec 1957.

2*f* •Princess Christa zu Hohenlohe-Oehringen, Baroness von Gabelstein, *b* 19 Feb 1960.

1*e* •Princess *Elisabeth* Maria Anna zu Hohenlohe-Oehringen, Baroness von Gabelstein, *b* 25 July 1926.

2*e* •Princess *Marie Therese* Antoinette Margarete Auguste zu Hohenlohe-Oehringen, Baroness von Gabelstein, *b* 5 Nov 1928.

1*c* HSH Princess Friederike Wilhelmine *Jadwiga* zu Hohenlohe-Oehringen, *b* 6 Oct 1857, *m* 28 May 1879, Count *Franz-Erich* von Bentzel zu Sternau und Hohenau (*b* 2 March 1850; *d* 8 Feb 1922), and *d* 29 Jan 1940, having had issue,

1*d* Count Hugo Alexander Felix Paul Maria Hyacinth Friedrich Wilhelm Ludwig Eric von Bentzel zu Sternau und Hohenau, *b* 11 March 1881; *d unm* 28 Jan 1916.

2*d* Count *Franz-Moritz* Erich Alexander Aloys Felix Christian von Bentzel zu Sternau und Hohenau, *b* 3 April 1882, *m* 1st 3 Nov 1910 (*m* diss by div), Elisabeth Rosenow (*b* 21 Feb 1890), and had issue,

1*e* •Count *Franz-Hubertus* August Richard Maria Friedrich Karl Ernst Walter Erich von Bentzel zu Sternau und Hohenau, *b* 18 July 1911, *m* 1 April 1943, •Ingeborg (*b* 1 Aug 1916), dau of Wilhelm Kornfeld, and has had issue,

1*f* Count Thomas Christian von Bentzel zu Sternau und Hohenau, *b* 11 Sept 1947; *d* 13 July 1966.

2*f* •Count Martin Franz von Bentzel zu Sternau und Hohenau, *b* 17 Feb 1949.

2*e* Count *Götz-Kraft* Erich Alexander Maria von Bentzel zu Sternau und Hohenau, *b* 5 Aug 1913, *m* 6 March 1937, •Baroness Irmgard (*b* 14 Feb 1907), dau of Baron Ludwig von Sturmfeder-Brandt, and was reported missing in Russia from 8 Aug 1943, leaving issue,

•Count Johannes Friedrich Karl Götz-Kraft Maria von Bentzel zu Sternau und Hohenau, *b* 3 July 1939.

•Countess Mechtild Kunigunde Friederike Karoline Elisabeth Maria Josefa von Bentzel zu Sternau und Hohenau, *b* 27 Jan 1938, *m* 22 Sept 1958, •Count *Berthold* Maria Schenk von Stauffenberg (*b* 3 July 1934)

[*Bamberg, Schutzenstrasse 20, Germany*], and has issue,

1*g* ●Count Claus Philipp Johannes Gottfried Sebastian Maria Schenk von Stauffenberg, *b* 1 June 1959.

2*g* ●Count Sebastian Heimeran Alexander Maria Schenk von Stauffenberg, *b* 2 Dec 1961.

3*g* ●Count Gottfried Franz Ludwig Markwart Sebastian Schenk von Stauffenberg, *b* 7 Oct 1964.

1*e* ●Countess Elisabeth Maria Jadwiga von Bentzel zu Sternau und Hohenau, *b* 14 April 1919, *m* 29 Jan 1940, ●Heinz Frank (*b* 17 Feb 1914), and has issue,

1*f* ●Hellmut Ernst Eberhard Frank, *b* 24 March 1946.

1*f* ●Doris-Elisabeth Frank, *b* 3 Sept 1940, *m* 15 Aug 1962, ●Herbert Jungwirth (*b* 13 July 1939), and has issue,

1*g* ●Andreas Jungwirth, *b* 9 Dec 1962.

2*g* ●Thomas Jungwirth, *b* 13 Oct 1965.

2*f* ●Ilka-Marina Frank, *b* 4 Jan 1942, *m* 28 May 1965, ●Walter Frisch (*b* 9 May 1936), and has issue,

●Claudia Frisch, *b* 18 May 1966.

2*e* ●Countess Erika Mauritia Jadwiga Elisabeth von Bentzel zu Sternau und Hohenau, *b* 20 Nov 1920, *m* 15 Oct 1942, ●Hans Ehling (*b* 13 June 1916), and has issue,

●Götz-Ottfried Ehling, *b* 28 Sept 1943.

●Elena Mauritia Ehling, *b* 22 July 1946.

He *m* 2ndly 30 July 1938, ●Irma (*b* 24 Nov 1901), dau of Wilhelm Aben, and *d* 1 Oct 1945.

3*d* Count Waldemar Erich Kraft Hyacinth von Bentzel zu Sternau und Hohenau, *b* 20 June 1886; *d* 16 Aug 1898.

2*c* HSH Princess Gertrude Auguste Mathilde *Olga* zu Hohenlohe-Oehringen, *b* 3 April 1862, *m* 29 April 1889, her 1st cousin, HSH *Johann* Heinrich Georg, 6th Prince zu Hohenlohe-Oehringen, 3rd Duke von Ujest (*b* 24 April 1858; *d* 24 April 1945), and *d* 21 April 1935, leaving issue,

1*d* HSH Hugo Felix *August*, 7th Prince zu Hohenlohe-Oehringen, 4th Duke von Ujest, *b* 28 April 1890, *m* 1st 16 Jan 1928 (*m* diss by div 1930), *Ursula* Maria Ilse (*b* 20 May 1905), dau of Konstantin von Zedlitz. He *m* 2ndly 11 Nov 1930 (*m* diss by div 1946), *Valerie* Frieda Alexandra Minka (*b* 3 April 1908), dau of Robert de Carstanjen, and by her had issue,

1*e* ●HSH *Kraft* Hans Konrad, 8th Prince zu Hohenlohe-Oehringen, 5th Duke von Ujest [*7113 Neuenstein, Kreis Oehringen, Schloss, Germany*], *b* 11 Jan 1933, *m* 24 June 1959, ●Katharine (*b* 24 Dec 1939), dau of Pieter von Siemens, and has issue,

1*f* ●HSH Hereditary Prince *Kraft* Franz Constantin zu Hohenlohe-Oehringen, *b* 31 Oct 1966.

1*f* ●HSH Princess *Margarita* Katharina Elisabeth zu Hohenlohe-Oehringen, *b* 28 April 1960.

2*f* ●HSH Princess Christina zu Hohenlohe-Oehringen, *b* 27 Nov 1961.

1*e* ●HSH Princess *Alexandra* Olga Elsa zu Hohenlohe-Oehringen, *b* 11 March 1931, *m* 24 May 1960, ●Egid Hilz (*b* 24 June 1932), and has issue,

●Christian Kraft Alexander Helmuth Georg Rafael Hilz, *b* 21 April 1966.

●Gabriela Hilz, *b* 20 Feb 1963.

2*e* ●HSH Princess Dorothea *Elisabeth* zu Hohenlohe-Oehringen [*München 23, Hohenstaufenstrasse 10, Germany*], *b* 27 July 1935.

He *m* 3rdly 6 April 1948, ●Erika (*b* 2 Dec 1916), dau of Friedrich Konrad Himmelein, and *d* 2 Aug 1962, having by her had issue,

3*e* ●HSH Princess *Dagmar* Maria Victoria zu Hohenlohe-Oehringen, *b* 14 Sept 1948.

2*d* HSH Prince *Kraft* Friedrich Karl zu Hohenlohe-Oehringen, *b* 16 March 1892, *m* 31 Jan 1948, Nina (*b* 20 Nov 1898; *d* 27 Aug 1965), dau of Ilya Schischin, and *dsp* 2 Sept 1965.

1*d* HSH Princess *Alexandrine* Marie Margarethe zu Hohenlohe-Oehringen, *b* 12 May 1891; *d unm* 15 May 1959.

2*d* HSH Princess *Dorothea* Marie Friederike Wilhelmine zu Hohenlohe-Oehringen, *b* 16 March 1892; *d unm* 7 Dec 1931.

3*c* HSH Princess *Pauline* Marie Malvine Auguste zu Hohenlohe-Oehringen, *b* 4 April 1863; *d* 20 Nov 1874.

4*c* HSH Princess Marie *Louise* Augustine zu Hohenlohe-Oehringen, *b* 26 Jan 1867, *m* 1st 8 May 1886, HSH Prince Albrecht of Waldeck and Pyrmont (*b* 11 Dec 1841; *d* 11 Jan 1897), and had issue,

1*d* HSH Prince *Georg Friedrich* Hugo Felix Albert of Waldeck and Pyrmont, *b* 15 March 1887; *d* 29 March 1888.

2*d* HSH Prince *Karl Alexander* Ferdinand Wilhelm of Waldeck and Pyrmont, *b* 15 Sept 1891; *d* 28 Oct 1910.

She *m* 2ndly 4 Dec 1913 (*m* diss by div 1915), George Granville Hope-Johnstone, of Transvaal, S Africa (*b* 28 Nov 1880; *d* 29 Dec 1938), eldest son of William James Hope-Johnstone (*see* BURKE'S *Peerage*, LINLITHGOW, M), and *d* 23 July 1945, having had further issue,

3*d* ●William August Ludwig Vernon Alexander Hope-Johnstone, Major late Gren Guards, *b* 3 June 1914, *m* 27 March 1943 (*m* diss by div 1951), *Pamela* Maud (*b* 1 March 1920), elder dau of John Murray Cobbold, of Glemham Hall, Suffolk (*see* BURKE'S LG), and has issue,

1*e* ●Philip William Hope-Johnstone, Capt 13th/18th Royal Hus (QMO), *b* 27 Dec 1943, *educ* Radley, and RMA Sandhurst, *m* 7 Dec 1968, ●Antonia Jay, yst dau of J. Y. Hutton-Potts, of The Old Vicarage, Mentmore, Beds.

2*e* ●Charles John Victor Hope-Johnstone, *b* 26 Jan 1948, *educ* Radley.

3*b* HSH Princess *Marie* Auguste von Hanau, Countess von Schaumburg, *cr* Princess von Ardeck by the King of Prussia 28 July 1876, *b* 22 Aug 1839, *m* 27 Dec 1857 (*m* diss by div 1872), HH Prince *Wilhelm* Friedrich Ernst of Hesse-Philippsthal-Barchfeld (*b* 3 Oct 1831; *d* 17 Jan 1890), and *d* 26 March 1917, having had issue,

1*c* HSH Prince *Friedrich Wilhelm* von Ardeck, *b* 2 Nov 1858, *m* 17 Dec 1890, Anne Hollingsworth Price (*b* 25 Aug 1868), and *dsp* 1 April 1902.

2*c* HSH *Carl* Wilhelm, 2nd Prince von Ardeck, *b* 18 May 1861, *m* 16 April 1891, Anne *Elise* Strehlow (*b* 5 June 1862; *d* 26 Nov 1938), and *dsp* 18 Oct 1938.

1*c* HSH Princess Sophie Auguste *Elisabeth* von Ardeck, *b* 8 June 1864, *m* 11 Oct 1886, H Ill H Karl *Ferdinand* Ludwig Adolf Wolfgang Ernst Kasimir Georg Friedrich, Count zu Ysenburg und Büdingen in Philippseich (*b* 15 Oct 1841; *d* 5 Jan 1920), and *d* 4 March 1919, having had issue with one son, who *d* an inf,

1*d* H Ill H Countess *Marie* Bertha Agnes Klementine Auguste Luise Albertine zu Ysenburg und Büdingen in Philippseich, *b* 28 April 1890; *d unm* 17 Feb 1964.

2*d* H Ill H Countess *Irmgard* Marie Hermine Anna Elisabeth zu Ysenburg und Büdingen in Philippseich, *b* 17 March 1894; *d unm* 11 July 1921.

3*d* H Ill H Countess *Elisabeth* Philippine Marie Ferdinande zu Ysenburg und Büdingen in Philippseich, *b* 4 Aug 1897; *d unm* 17 Oct 1917.

2*c* HSH Princess Karoline *Luise* von Ardeck, *b* 12 Dec 1868, *m* 2 Nov 1889, HSH Prince *Rudolf* Wolfgang Ludwig Ernst Leopold of Lippe (*b* 27 April 1856; *d* 21 June 1931), and *d* 21 Nov 1959, having had issue,

1*d* HSH Prince August *Friedrich Wilhelm* of Lippe, *b* 27 Nov 1890, *m* 1 July 1932,

●*Gudela* Ilse (*b* 17 Dec 1906) [*Detmold, Bandelstrasse 16, Germany*], yr dau of Eberhard von Oven, and *d* 24 Oct 1938, leaving issue,

●HSH Prince *Rudolf* Ferdinand Ludwig Eberhard Bernhard of Lippe, *b* 8 Jan 1937.

2d HSH Prince *Ernst* Julius Adalbert Emil Wilhelm Gustav Karl Philipp of Lippe, *b* 20 Jan 1892; *k* in action in World War I 28 Aug 1914.

1d ●HSH Princess *Marie Adelheid* Mathilde Karoline Elise Alexe Auguste Albertine of Lippe [*29 Oldenburg-Eversten, Osterkampweg 71, Germany*], *b* 30 Aug 1895, *m* 1st 19 May 1920 (*m* diss by div 1921), HSH Prince Heinrich XXXII Reuss (Younger Line) (*b* 4 March 1878; *d* 6 May 1935). She *m* 2ndly 12 April 1921 (*m* diss by div 1923), HSH Prince Heinrich XXXV Reuss (Younger Line) (*b* 1 Aug 1887; *d* 17 Jan 1936), and had issue,

●HSH Prince Heinrich V Reuss [*2 Hamburg-Hochkamp, Meyerhofstrasse 7, Germany*], *b* 26 May 1921, *m* 22 June 1961, ●*Ingrid* Dora Helene (*b* 9 March 1936), dau of Ernst Eugen Jobst, and has issue,

1f ●Prinz *Heinrich Ico* Reuss, *b* 18 Oct 1964.

1f ●Prinzessin *Maria* Alexandra Luise Hermine Dora Helene Reuss, *b* 1 Sept 1963.

2f ●Prinzessin Caroline Reuss, *b* 1968.

She *m* 3rdly 24 Feb 1927 (*m* diss by div 1936), Hanno Konopath (*b* 24 Feb 1882; *dec*).

3a HH Prince Friedrich Wilhelm Ferdinand of Hesse-Cassel, *b* 9 Oct, *d* 21 Nov 1806.

1a HH Princess *Caroline* Friederike Wilhelmina of Hesse, *b* 29 July 1799; *d unm* 28 Nov 1854.

2a HH Princess *Luise* Friederike of Hesse-Cassel, *b* 3 April 1801; *d* 28 Sept 1803.

3a HH Princess *Marie* Friederike Wilhelmine Christine of Hesse, *b* 6 Sept 1804, *m* 23 March 1825, HH *Bernhard II* (Erich Freund), Duke of Saxe-Meiningen, KG (*b* 17 Dec 1800; *d* 3 Dec 1882), brother of HM Queen Adelaide (*see p* 294). and *d* 1 Jan 1888, having had issue,

1b HH Georg II, Duke of Saxe-Meiningen, *b* 2 April 1826, *m* 1st 18 May 1850, HRH Princess Friederike Luise Wilhelmine Marianne *Charlotte* (*b* 21 June 1831; *d* 30 March 1855), eldest dau of HRH Prince Albrecht of Prussia, and had issue,

1c HH *Bernhard III* (Friedrich Wilhelm Albert Georg), Duke of Saxe-Meiningen, *b* 1 April 1851, *m* 18 Feb 1878, HRH Princess Victoria Elisabeth Augusta *Charlotte* (*b* 24 July 1860; *d* 1 Oct 1919), eldest dau of HIM Friedrich III, German Emperor and King of Prussia, KG (*see p* 300), and *d* 16 Jan 1928, leaving issue,

●HH Princess *Feodora* Victoria Auguste Marianne Marie of Saxe-Meiningen, Duchess of Saxony, *b* 12 May 1879, *m* 24 Sept 1898, HSH Prince Heinrich XXX Reuss (Younger Line) (*b* 25 Nov 1864; *d* 23 March 1939), and *dsp* 26 Aug 1945.

2c HH Prince Georg *Albrecht* of Saxe-Meiningen, Duke of Saxony, *b* 12 April 1852; *d* 27 Jan 1855.

3c A Prince, *b* 29, *d* 30 March 1855.

1c HH Princess *Marie* Elisabeth of Saxe-Meiningen, Duchess of Saxony, *b* 23 Sept 1853; *d unm* 22 Feb 1923.

He *m* 2ndly 23 Oct 1858, HSH Princess *Feodora* Viktoria Adelheid Pauline Amélie Marie (*b* 7 July 1839; *d* 10 Feb 1872), 2nd dau of HSH Ernst, 5th Prince zu Hohenlohe-Langenburg, and by her had issue,

4c HH Prince *Ernst* Bernhard Viktor Georg of Saxe-Meiningen, Duke of Saxony, *b* 27 Sept 1859, *m* (morganatically) 20 Sept 1892, Katharina, *cr* Baroness von Saalfeld 20 Sept 1892 (*b* 25 Jan 1874; *d* 19 April 1945), dau of Dr Wilhelm Heinrich Jensen, and *d* 19 Dec 1941, having had issue,

1d Baron *Georg* Wilhelm von Saalfeld, *b* 11 June 1893; *k* in action in World War I 29 April 1916.

2d Baron *Ernst* Friedrich Heinrich Paul von Saalfeld, *b* 4 July 1896; *k* in action in World War I 28 May 1915.

3d Baron *Ralf* Erich von Saalfeld, *b* 28 March 1900, *m* 1st 11 Oct 1925, Marie (*b* 12 May 1903; *d* 24 June 1931), dau of Dr Karl Seitz, and had issue,

1e ●Baron *Hermann* Ernst von Saalfeld, *b* 27 June 1928, *m* 4 Aug 1956, ●Monika (*b* 17 April 1933), dau of Hans Deinhardt, and has issue,

1f ●Baron *Franz Georg* von Saalfeld, *b* 4 Oct 1961.

2f ●Baron Peter Alexander von Saalfeld, *b* 14 July 1963.

1f ●Baroness Katharina von Saalfeld, *b* 23 April 1959.

1e Baroness Karin von Saalfeld, *b* 30 Jan 1927; *d* 16 Sept 1944.

He *m* 2ndly 16 Aug 1936, ●Elisabeth Luise Helene *Melanie* (*b* 15 May 1911) [*München-Neugrünwald, Hubertusstrasse 4, Germany*], eldest dau of Wilhelm von Bismarck, and *d* 22 July 1947, having by her had issue,

2e ●Baron *Christian* Wilhelm Ernst von Saalfeld, *b* 16 July 1937.

3e ●Baron Klaus von Saalfeld, *b* 5 May 1939.

2e ●Baroness Bettina von Saalfeld, *b* 27 Nov 1942.

3e ●Baroness *Ulrike Karin* von Saalfeld, *b* 24 Sept 1946.

4d ●Baron Sven *Hans* Heinrich Bernhard von Saalfeld, *b* 18 Sept 1903, *m* 20 March 1936 (*m* diss by div), Elisabeth (*b* 29 Feb 1916), dau of Julius Faust, and has issue,

1e ●Baron Sven von Saalfeld, *b* 24 Jan 1946.

1e ●Baroness Maleen von Saalfeld, *b* 21 May 1937, *m* 26 July 1961, ●István Babotai (*b* 17 Aug 1939).

2e ●Baroness Inka von Saalfeld, *b* 8 July 1939, *m* 14 Aug 1964, ●Dieter Goder (*b* 15 March 1938).

3e ●Baroness Heike von Saalfeld, *b* 8 June 1941, *m* 25 Aug 1962, ●Axel Varekamp (*b* 21 Jan 1937), and has issue,

1f ●Maj Varekamp, *b* 22 July 1963.

2f ●Nanon Varekamp, *b* 5 July 1965.

4e ●Baroness Lerke von Saalfeld, *b* 25 Sept 1944.

5d Baron Heinrich (*Enzio*) Woldemar Carl von Saalfeld, *b* 7 July 1908, *m* 28 Feb 1936, ●*Rut* Martha (*b* 23 May 1910; *m* 2ndly Karlheinz Schnell), dau of Ernst Viererbe, and was *k* in action in World War II April 1941, leaving issue,

1e ●Baron Jörg von Saalfeld, *b* 17 Jan 1937, *m* 13 Aug 1966, ●Heidi Schmidt-Steinworth (*b* 21 July 1944).

2e ●Baron Jens von Saalfeld, *b* (twin with Baron Jörg) 17 Jan 1937.

3e ●Baron Jan von Saalfeld, *b* 11 Nov 1941.

1e ●Baroness Jay von Saalfeld, *b* 9 June 1938, *m* 7 March 1966, ●Hans Hermann Schmidt-Steinworth (*b* 18 June 1942).

1d Baroness *Elisabeth* Helene Adelheid Marie von Saalfeld, *b* 2 Feb 1895, *m* 25 April 1917, Dr Johann Duken (*b* 12 Jan 1889; *d* 1954), and *dsp* 4 June 1934.

5c HH Prince *Friedrich* Johann Bernhard Hermann Heinrich Moritz of Saxe-Meiningen, Duke of Saxony, *b* 12 Oct 1861, *m* 25 April 1889, HSH Princess *Adelheid* Karoline Mathilde Emilie Agnes Ida Sophie of Lippe (*b* 22 June 1870; *d* 3 Sept 1948), elder dau of H Ill H Count Ernst of Lippe-Biesterfeld, and was *k* in action in World War I 23 Aug 1914, leaving issue,

1d HH Georg (III), Duke of Saxe-Meiningen, took the title of Duke on succeeding his uncle Prince Ernst as Head of the Ducal House 1941, *b* 11 Oct 1892, *m* 22 Feb 1919, ●Countess *Klara-Marie* Agnes Johanna Huberta Gabriele Josepha Elisabeth (*b* 31 May 1895) [*8793 Seeheim, Post Ammerland, OBayern, Germany*], eldest dau of Count Alfred von Korff gen Schmising-Kerssenbrock, and *d* in a Russian p o w camp 5 Jan 1946, having had issue,

1*e* HH Prince *Anton-Ulrich* Bernhard Friedrich Ernst of Saxe-Meiningen, Duke of Saxony, *b* 23 Dec 1919; *k* in action in World War II 20 May 1940.

2*e* •HH Hereditary Prince *Friedrich-Alfred* Carl Ludwig Vincenz Maria of Saxe-Meiningen, Duke of Saxony [*Grande Chartreuse, nr Grenoble, France*], *b* 5 April 1921.

1*e* HH Princess Marie Gabriele of Saxe-Meiningen, Duchess of Saxony, *b* 18 Dec 1922; *d* 31 March 1923.

2*e* •HH Princess *Regina* Helene Elisabeth Margarete of Saxe-Meiningen, Duchess of Saxony, *b* 6 Jan 1925, *m* 10 May 1951, •HI and RH Archduke Franz Joseph *Otto* Robert Felix Renatus Ludwig Gaetan Pius Ignatius Maria Anton Karl Max Heinrich Sixtus Xaver of Austria, Head of the Imp House of Austria (*b* 20 Nov 1912), and has issue (*see p* 239).

2*d* HH Prince *Ernst* Leopold Friedrich Wilhelm Otto of Saxe-Meiningen, Duke of Saxony, *b* 23 Sept 1895; *k* in action in World War I 27 Aug 1914.

3*d* •HH Prince *Bernhard* Friedrich Julius Heinrich of Saxe-Meiningen, Duke of Saxony, Head of the Ducal House of Saxe-Meiningen [*Ziegenberg über Bad Nauheim, OHessen Germany*], *b* 30 June 1901, *m* 1st 25 April 1931 (*m* diss by div 1947), Margot (*b* 22 Jan 1911), dau of Friedrich Grössler, and has issue,

1*e* •HH Prince *Friedrich-Ernst* (*Frieder*) Georg Bernhard of Saxe-Meiningen, Duke of Saxony, *b* 21 Jan 1935, *m* 3 March 1962, •*Ehrengard* Maria Elisabeth (*b* 25 Oct 1933), yr dau of Helmut von Massow.

1*e* •HH Princess *Feodora* Adelheid Mary Luise of Saxe-Meiningen, Duchess of Saxony, *b* 27 May 1932.

He *m* 2ndly 11 Aug 1948, •Baroness *Wera* Emma Anna Marie-Luise (*b* 10 Aug 1914), yr dau of Baron Fritz Schäffer von Bernstein, and by her has issue,

2*e* •HH Prince Johann *Friedrich-Konrad* Carl Eduard Horst Arnold Matthias of Saxe-Meiningen, Duke of Saxony, *b* 14 April 1952.

2*e* •HH Princess Marie *Eleonore Adelheid* Feodora Sophie Helene Gisela Edelgarde of Saxe-Meiningen, Duchess of Saxony, *b* 9 Nov 1950.

3*e* •HH Princess *Almut* Huberta Anna Victoria of Saxe-Meiningen, Duchess of Saxony, *b* 25 Sept 1959.

1*d* HH Princess *Feodora* Karola Charlotte Marie Adelheid Auguste Mathilde of Saxe-Meiningen, Duchess of Saxony, *b* 29 May 1890, *m* 4 Jan 1910, as his 2nd wife, HRH Grand Duke *Wilhelm Ernst* (Carl Alexander Friedrich Heinrich Bernhard Albert Georg Hermann) of Saxe-Weimar-Eisenach (*b* 10 June 1876; *d* 24 April 1923), and *d* 12 March 1972, leaving issue,

1*e* •HRH Hereditary Grand Duke *Carl-August* Wilhelm Ernst Friedrich Georg Johann Albrecht of Saxe-Weimar-Eisenach, Duke of Saxony [*7805 Bötzingen über Freiburg i Br, Rankstrasse 7, Germany*], *b* 28 July 1912, *m* 4 Oct 1944, •Baroness *Elisabeth* Mathilde Isidore Caroline Magdalene Maria (*b* 16 Jan 1912), elder dau of Baron Othmar von Wangenheim, and has issue,

1*f* •HH Hereditary Prince *Michael-Benedict* Georg Jobst Karl Alexander Bernhard Claus Friedrich of Saxe-Weimar-Eisenach, Duke of Saxony, *b* 15 Nov 1946, *m* July 1970, •Renate Henkel.

1*f* •HH Princess *Elisabeth* Sophie Feodora Mathilde Dorothea Louise Adelaide Vera Renate of Saxe-Weimar-Eisenach, Duchess of Saxony, *b* 22 July 1945.

2*f* •HH Princess *Beatrice-Maria* Margareta Dorothea Felicitas Virginie of Saxe-Weimar-Eisenach, Duchess of Saxony, *b* 11 March 1948.

2*e* •HH Prince *Bernhard Friedrich* Viktor Rupprecht Adalbert Ernst Ludwig Hermann Heinrich of Saxe-Weimer-Eisenach, Duke of Saxony [*62 Wiesbaden-Bierstadt, Kolpingstrasse 2, Germany*], *b* 3 March 1917, *m* 12 March 1943 (*m* diss by div 1956), HSH Princess *Felicitas* Sophie Katharine Margarethe Hermine Irene (*b* 31 March 1920), yst dau of HSH late Prince Emich zu Salm-Horstmar, and has issue,

•HH Prince *Wilhelm Ernst* Emich Georg Rudolf of Saxe-Weimar-Eisenach, Duke of Saxony [*8 München 40, Wormser Strasse 3, Germany*], *b* 10 Aug 1946.

•HH Princess *Katharina* Feodora Adelheid Sabine Sophie Felicitas Sieglinde of Saxe-Weimar-Eisenach, Duchess of Saxony, *b* 30 Nov 1943, *m* 25 May 1968, •HSH Prince *Emanuel Joseph* Maria Wilhelm Ferdinand Burkhard of Hohenzollern (*b* 23 Feb 1929), and has issue (*see p* 235).

3*e* •HH Prince *Georg* Wilhelm Albert Bernhard of Saxe-Weimar-Eisenach, Duke of Saxony, renounced his titles and membership of the Grand Ducal House and assumed the name of Jörg Brena 22 Jan 1953, *b* 24 Nov 1921, *m* (civil) 5 Feb and (religious) 8 March 1953, •Gisela (*b* 5 May 1930), dau of Wilhelm Erich Jänisch, and has issue,

1*f* •Luise *Ariane* Brena, *b* 17 Jan 1954.

2*f* •Adelheid *Cornelie* Brena, *b* 22 June 1955.

3*f* •Isabel Magdalene Brena, *b* 14 Oct 1959.

1*e* •HH Princess *Sophie* Luise Adelheid Marie Olga Karola of Saxe-Weimar-Eisenach, Duchess of Saxony [*2 Hamburg 39, Beblallee 57c, Germany*], *b* 20 March 1911, *m* 7 March 1938 (*m* diss by div 1 Nov 1938), HSH Friedrich Günther, Prince of Schwarzburg (*b* 5 March 1901).

2*d* HH Princess *Adelheid* Erna Karoline Maria Elisabeth of Saxe-Meiningen, Duchess of Saxony, *b* 16 Aug 1891, *m* 3 Aug 1914, HRH Prince *Adalbert* Ferdinand Berengar Viktor of Prussia (*b* 14 July 1884; *d* 22 Sept 1948), 3rd son of HIM Wilhelm II, German Emperor and King of Prussia, and *d* 25 April 1971, having had issue (*see p* 301).

3*d* •HH Princess *Luise* Marie Elisabeth Mathilde Helene Katharine of Saxe-Meiningen, Duchess of Saxony [*Kassel-Wilhelmshöhe, Kunoldstrasse 42, Germany*], *b* 13 March 1899, *m* 25 Oct 1936, Baron *Götz* Ernst Moritz Hans von Wangenheim (*b* 18 Jan 1895; *k* in action in World War II 5 Oct 1941), and has issue,

•Baron *Ernst Friedrich* Klaus Georg Melchior von Wangenheim [*Bad Homburg v d H, Wilhelm-Meister-Strasse 1, Germany*], *b* 14 April 1941, *m* 4 July 1963, •Christa Margaret (*b* 20 March 1941), dau of Alfred Binninger, and has issue,

•Baroness Verena Regina von Wangenheim, *b* 20 Nov 1966.

•Baroness *Karin* Renate Adelheid Dorothea Feodora Luise von Wangenheim, *b* 29 Oct 1937, *m* 5 Aug 1963, •Hans Dieter Schwarze (*b* 30 Aug 1926) [*8381 Griesbach, Alter Batzihof, Germany*], and has issue,

•Daniel Schwarze, *b* 22 Aug 1965.

6*c* HH Prince Viktor of Saxe-Meiningen, Duke of Saxony, *b* 14, *d* 17 May 1865.

Duke Georg II *m* 3rdly (morganatically) 18 March 1873, Helene, *cr* Baroness von Heldburg (*b* 30 May 1839; *d* 24 March 1923), dau of Hermann Franz, and *d* 25 June 1914.

1*b* HH Princess *Auguste* Luise Caroline Ida of Saxe-Meiningen, Duchess of Saxony, *b* 6 Aug 1843, *m* 15 Oct 1862, HH Prince *Moritz* Franz Friedrich Constantin Alexander Heinrich August Carl Albert of Saxe-Altenburg, Duke of Saxony (*b* 24 Oct 1829; *d* 13 May 1907), and *d* 11 Nov 1919, leaving issue,

1*c* HH *Ernst II* (Bernhard Georg Johann Karl

Friedrich Peter Albert), Duke of Saxe-Altenburg (1908-1918), *b* 31 Aug 1871, *m* 1st 17 Feb 1898 (*m* diss by div 1920), HSH Princess Friederike *Adelheid* Marie Luise Hilda Eugenie (*b* 22 Sept 1875; *d* 27 Jan 1971), 3rd dau of HSH Prince Wilhelm of Schaumburg-Lippe, and had issue,

1d •HH Hereditary Prince Wilhelm *Georg-Moritz* Ernst Albert Friedrich Karl Konstantin Eduard Max of Saxe-Altenburg, Duke of Saxony, Head of the Ducal House of Saxe-Altenburg from 1935 [*Schloss Hamborn über Paderborn-Land, Germany*], *b* 13 May 1900.

2d •HH Prince *Friedrich Ernst* Karl August Albert of Saxe-Altenburg, Duke of Saxony, *b* 15 May 1905.

1d •HH Princess *Charlotte Agnes* Ernestine Auguste Bathildis Marie Therese Adolfine of Saxe-Altenburg, Duchess of Saxony, *b* 4 March 1899, *m* 11 July 1919, •HRH Prince Wilhelm Viktor Karl Auguste Heinrich *Sigismund* of Prussia (*b* 27 Nov 1896), and has issue (*see p* 302).

2d •HH Princess *Elisabeth* Karola Viktoria Adelheid Hermine Hilda Luise Alexandra of Saxe-Altenburg, Duchess of Saxony [*Ballenstadt a H, Kügelgenstrasse 34, Germany*], *b* 6 April 1903.

He *m* 2ndly 15 July 1934, •Maria Triebel (*b* 16 Oct 1893), and *d* 22 March 1935.

1c HH Princess *Marie Anna* of Saxe-Altenburg Duchess of Saxony, *b* 14 March 1864, *m* 16 April 1882, HSH (Stephan Albrecht) *Georg*, Prince of Schaumburg-Lippe (*b* 10 Oct 1846; *d* 29 April 1911), and *d* 3 May 1918, having had issue (*see p* 251).

2c HH Princess *Elisabeth* Auguste Marie Agnes of Saxe-Altenburg, Duchess of Saxony (Grand Duchess Elisabeth Mavrikievna), *b* 25 Jan 1865, *m* 27 April 1884, HIH Grand Duke Constantine Constantinovitch of Russia (*b* 22 Aug 1858; *d* 14 June 1915), and *d* 24 March 1927, having had issue,

1d HH Prince Ioann Constantinovitch of Russia, *b* 23 June 1886, *m* 21 Aug 1911, HRH Princess Helen (*b* 23 Oct 1884; *d* 16 Oct 1962), elder dau of HM King Peter I of Serbia, and *d* in the Russian Revolution 17/18 July 1918, leaving issue,

•HH Prince Vsevolode Ioannovitch of Russia [*7a Marloes Road, W8*], *b* 7 Jan 1914, *m* 1st 1 June 1939 (*m* diss by div 1956), Lady Mary Lygon (*b* 12 Feb 1910), 3rd dau of 7th Earl Beauchamp, KG, PC, KCMG (*see* BURKE'S *Peerage*). He *m* 2ndly 28 March 1956 (*m* diss by div 1961), Emilia (*b* 19 April 1914), formerly wife of Count Sigismund (Zsiga) Alexander Leopold Corfitz Otto Tiburtius Korsinus Heinrich von Berchtold, previously of Michael Aubrey Bankier, and before that widow of Robin Alexander Lyle (*see* BURKE'S *Peerage*, LYLE *of Glendelvyne*, Bt), and dau of Col Eugen de Gosztonyi, of Budapest. He *m* 3rdly 8 June 1961, •Valli (*b* 4 April 1930), dau of Cyril Knust, MC.

•HSH Princess Catherine Joannovna of Russia, *b* 25 July 1915, *m* 15 Sept 1937 (judicially separated 1945), Marchese Ruggero Farace (*b* 4 Aug 1909; *d* 1971), and has issue,

1f •Marchese Giovanni Farace, *b* 20 Oct 1943, *m* •Marie-Claude Tellier-Debresse, and has issue,

•Don Alessandro dei Marchesi Farace, *b* 29 Aug 1971.

1f •Nicoletta dei Marchesi Farace, *b* 23 July 1938, *m* •— de Grunelland, and has issue,

•Eduardo de Grunelland.

•Alessandra de Grunelland.

2f •Fiammetta dei Marchesi Farace, *b* 19 Feb 1942, *m* •Victor Arcelus.

2d HH Prince Gabriel Constantinovitch of Russia (assumed the title of Grand Duke and style of Imp Highness 15 May 1939), *b* 15 July 1887, *m* 1st 22 April 1917, Antonia Raphailovna (*b* 14 March 1890; *d* 7 March 1950), dau of Raphail Nesterovsky. He *m* 2ndly 11 May 1951, •Princess Irina Ivanovna (*b* 22 Sept 1903) [*5 avenue Mozart, F-75 Paris 16e, France*], 2nd dau of Prince Ivan Anatolievitch Kourakine, sometime Steward of the Imp Court, Marshal of the Nobility of the Govt of Yaroslavl, and later a Bishop in the Orthodox Church, and *dsp* 28 Feb 1955.

3d HH Prince Constantine Constantinovitch of Russia, *b* 20 Dec 1890; *k* in the Russian Revolution 17/18 July 1918.

4d HH Prince Oleg Constantinovitch of Russia, *b* 15 Nov 1892; *k* in action in World War I 12 Oct 1914.

5d HH Prince Igor Constantinovitch of Russia, *b* 29 May 1894; *k* in the Russian Revolution 17/18 July 1918.

6d HH Prince Georg Constantinovitch of Russia, *b* 6 May 1903; *d unm* 30 Nov 1939.

1d •HH Princess Tatiana Constantinovna of Russia, now Mother Abbess Tamara in the Russian Orthodox Convent at Jerusalem [*The Mount of Olives Convent, PO Box 19 229 Jerusalem, Israel*], *b* 23 Jan 1890, *m* 1st 6 Sept 1911, Prince Constantine Alexandrovitch Bagration-Mukhransky (*b* 14 March 1889; *d* 1 June 1915), and has issue,

•Prince Taymuraz Constantinovitch Bagration-Mukhransky, *b* 21 Aug 1912, *m* 1st 27 Oct 1940, Catherine (*b* 4 July 1919; *d* 20 Dec 1946), dau of Stepan Ratchitch. He *m* 2ndly 27 Nov 1947, •Countess Irina (*b* 26 Sept 1926), dau of Count Sergei Alexandrovitch Tchernycheff-Bezobrasoff.

•Princess Natalia (*Natasha*) Constantinovna Bagration-Mukhransky, CStJ, *b* 19 April 1914, *m* 22 April 1944, •Sir Charles Hepburn Johnston, GCMG, late Brit High Commr in Australia (*b* 11 March 1912) [*32 Kingston House South, SW7*], eldest son of Ernest Johnston, of Cocks Hut, Reigate, Surrey.

She *m* 2ndly 9 Nov 1921, Col Alexander Vassilievitch Korotchenzoff, late Imp Gren Guards Regt of Russia (*b* 29 Aug 1877; *d* 6 Feb 1922).

2d HH Princess Natalia Constantinovna of Russia, *b* 23 March, *d* 23 May 1905.

3d •HH Princess Vera Constantinovna of Russia [*1309 Madison Avenue, Apt 4c, New York, NY 10028, USA*], *b* 24 April 1906.

3c HH Princess *Margaretha* Marie Agnes Adelheid Caroline Friederike of Saxe-Altenburg, Duchess of Saxony, *b* 22 May 1867; *d* 17 June 1882.

4c HH Princess *Luise* Charlotte Marie Agnes of Saxe-Altenburg, Duchess of Saxony, *b* 11 Aug 1873, *m* 6 Feb 1895 (*m* diss by div 1918), HH *Eduard* Georg Wilhelm Maximilian, Duke of Anhalt (*b* 18 April 1861; *d* 13 Sept 1918), and *d* 14 April 1953, having had issue,

1d HH Prince *Leopold* Friedrich Moritz Ernst Constantin Aribert Eduard of Anhalt, *b* 10 Feb 1897; *d* 26 Dec 1898.

2d HH *Joachim Ernst* Wilhelm Karl Albrecht Leopold Friedrich Moritz Erdmann, Duke of Anhalt (Sept-Nov 1918), *b* 11 Jan 1901, *m* 1st 3 March 1927 (*m* diss by div 1929), Odile *Elisabeth* Strickrodt, who bears the title of Countess von Askanien (*b* 3 Sept 1903). He *m* 2ndly 15 Oct 1929, •Editha (*Edda*) Charlotte Wilhelmine (*b* 20 Aug 1905), formerly wife of Maximilian Edler von Rogister, adopted dau of Bertha von Stephani, and natural dau of Irmgard Marwitz, and *d* as a Russian p o w 18 Feb 1948, having by her had issue,

1e HH Hereditary Prince Leopold *Friedrich* Franz Sieghard Hubertus Erdmann of Anhalt, Head of the Ducal House of Anhalt, *b* 11 April 1938; *d unm.*

2e •HH Prince *Eduard* Julius Ernst August Erdmann of Anhalt, Head of the Ducal House of Anhalt, *b* 3 Dec 1941, *m* •Countess *Astrid* Sophie Maria Hedwig Antonia (*b* 17

Aug 1952), elder dau of Count Hubert Deym von Stritez.

1e •HH Princess *Marie Antoinette* Elisabeth Alexandra Irmgard Edda Charlotte of Anhalt, *b* 14 July 1930, *m* 24 May 1957, •Karl-Heinz Guttmann (*b* 13 March 1911).

2e •HH Princess *Anna Luise* Marie Friederike Elisabeth Alice of Anhalt, *b* 26 March 1933.

3e •HH Princess *Edda* Adelheid Antoinette Emma Elisabeth of Anhalt, *b* 30 Jan 1940.

3d •HH Prince *Eugen* Friedrich Ernst August Heinrich Adolf Aribert of Anhalt, *b* 17 April 1903, *m* 2 Oct 1935, *Anastasia* Marie Therese Karoline (*b* 25 July 1901; *d* 19 Feb 1970), dau of Max Jungmeier, of Straubing, Bavaria, and has issue,

•HH Princess *Anastasia-Luise* Alexandra Elisabeth Jutta Sibylle Marie-Auguste Henriette of Anhalt, *b* 22 Dec 1940, *m* 23 June 1962, •HRH Prince *Maria Emanuel* of Saxony, Margrave of Meissen, Head of the Royal House of Saxony (*b* 31 Jan 1926) (*see p* 254).

4d HH Prince *Wolfgang* Albrecht Moritz Friedrich Wilhelm Ernst of Anhalt, *b* 12 July 1912; *d unm* 10 April 1936.

1d HH Princess *Friederike Margarete* Antoinette Marie Auguste Agnes Therese Elisabeth of Anhalt, *b* 11 Jan, *d* 18 Nov 1896.

2d •HH Princess *Marie Auguste* Antoinette Friederike Alexandra Hilda Luise of Anhalt [*43 Essen, Kunigundenstrasse 9, Germany*], *b* 10 June 1898, *m* 1st 11 March 1916, HRH Prince *Joachim* Franz Humbert of Prussia (*b* 17 Dec 1890; *d* 18 July 1920), yst son of HIM Wilhelm II, German Emperor and King of Prussia, and has issue (*see p* 302). She *m* 2ndly 27 Sept 1926 (*m* diss by div 1935), Baron Johannes Michael von Loën (*b* 6 Sept 1902).

Wilhelm II, Elector of Hesse *m* 2ndly (morganatically) 8 July 1841, Emily, *cr* Countess von Reichenbach-Lessonitz (*b* 13 May 1791; *d* 12 Feb 1843), dau of Johann Christoph Ortlöpp, and by her had issue (all *b* before the marriage),

4a Count Julius Wilhelm von Reichenbach-Lessonitz, *b* 4 Oct 1815; *d* 15 Jan 1822.

5a Count Gustav Carl von Reichenbach-Lessonitz, *b* 24 Aug 1818, *m* Sept 1861, Clementine Marie Richter (*b* 29 Aug 1842; *d* 14 July 1902), and *dsp* 20 Sept 1861.

6a Count Wilhelm von Reichenbach-Lessonitz, *b* 23 June 1824, *m* 19 March 1857, Baroness Amélie (*b* 27 April 1838; *d* 14 March 1912), dau of Baron Leopold Göler von Ravensburg, and *d* 19 Jan 1866, leaving issue,

1b Countess *Pauline* Victoria Caroline Wilhelmine Emilie von Reichenbach-Lessonitz, *b* 5 June 1858, *m* 9 Feb 1880, HSH Prince *Alfred* Ludwig Wilhelm Leopold zu Löwenstein-Wertheim-Freudenberg (*b* 18 Oct 1855; *d* 20 April 1925), and *d* 21 Oct 1927, leaving issue,

1c •HSH *Udo* Amelung Karl Friedrich Wilhelm Oleg Paul, 6th Prince zu Löwenstein-Wertheim-Freudenberg [*6983 Schloss Kreuzwertheim a M, UFranken, Germany*], *b* 8 Sept 1896, *m* 3 May 1922, •H Ill H Countess Margarete (*b* 27 Oct 1899), 2nd dau of HSH Friedrich Karl, 1st Prince zu Castell-Castell, and has issue,

1d •HSH Hereditary Prince *Alfred-Ernst* Friedrich Karl Richard Otto Konstantin Kasimir Bernhard zu Löwenstein-Wertheim-Freudenberg, *b* 19 Sept 1924, *m* 9 Sept 1950, •Ruth-Erika (*b* 25 June 1922), dau of Hans Detlof von Buggenhagen, and has issue,

1e •HSH Prince *Ludwig* Udo Hans Peter Alfred zu Löwenstein-Wertheim-Freudenberg, *b* 24 May 1951.

2e •HSH Prince *Udo* Alexander Richard Albrecht zu Löwenstein-Wertheim-Freudenberg, *b* 17 June 1957.

1e •HSH Princess *Ameli* Margarete Marielies Ingeborg zu Löwenstein-Wertheim- Freudenberg, *b* 20 Feb 1953.

2e •HSH Princess *Dorothee* Antonie Brigitte Ingeborg zu Löwenstein-Wertheim-Freudenberg, *b* 30 Oct 1955.

3e •HSH Princess *Ruth* Marie-Luise Orlinda Heidelind zu Löwenstein-Wertheim-Freudenberg, *b* 30 Dec 1959.

1d •HSH Princess *Ameli* Gertrud Pauline Antonie Madeleine Wanda Elisabeth zu Löwenstein-Wertheim-Freudenberg, *b* 4 March 1923, *m* 7 Aug 1951, •HRH Duke *Anton* Günther Friedrich August Josias of Oldenburg, Head of the Grand Ducal House of Oldenburg (*b* 16 Jan 1923), and has issue (*see p* 222).

2d •HSH Princess *Gertrud* Olga Ilka Emma Agnes Magdalena Mechthild zu Löwenstein-Wertheim-Freudenberg, *b* 24 Jan 1926, *m* 7 Aug 1951, •HH Duke *Peter* Friedrich August Max of Oldenburg (*b* 7 Aug 1926), and has issue (*see p* 222).

3d •HSH Princess *Pauline* Elisabeth Renata Luitgard zu Löwenstein-Wertheim-Freudenberg, *b* 9 June 1928, *m* 29 Dec 1956, •Dr Hans *Günther* Horst (*b* 23 Oct 1913) [*8184 Gmund-am Tegernsee, Burgstaller Strasse 11, Germany*], and has issue,

•Peter-Michael Horst, *b* 19 Aug 1957.

•Monika-Daniela Horst, *b* 6 March 1963.

1c HSH Princess *Olga* Amalie Wilhelmine Ernestine Marie Pauline zu Löwenstein-Wertheim-Freudenberg, *b* 25 Oct 1880, *m* 1st 5 Oct 1898 (*m* diss by div 1920), HSH Prince Heinrich von Schönburg-Waldenburg (*b* 8 June 1863; *d* 28 Dec 1945) and had issue (*see p* 249). She *m* 2ndly 22 Oct 1920, HSH Prince *Wolfgang* Wilhelm Gustav Karl Ludwig zu Löwenstein-Wertheim-Freudenberg (*b* 25 Nov 1890; *d* 8/9 July 1945), and *d* 1 July 1961.

2c HSH Princess *Pauline* Amalie Adele zu Löwenstein-Wertheim-Freudenberg, *b* 16 Oct 1881, *m* 24 Feb 1900, HSH Prince *Ulrich* Georg von Schönburg-Waldenburg (*b* 25 Aug 1869; *d* 1 Dec 1939), and *d* 22 April 1945, having had issue,

1d •HSH *Wolf* Georg Alfred, 6th Prince von Schönburg-Waldenburg [*Palazzo Venturi, Asciano, Prov Siena, Italy*], *b* 26 Nov 1902, *m* 16 Oct 1944, •Countess Luciana (*b* 17 Jan 1921), dau of Marchese Luigi Bargagli-Stoffi, and has issue,

1e •HSH Princess *Grazia* Dorothea von Schönburg-Waldenburg, *b* 4 March 1946.

2e •HSH Princess *Alessandra* Luisa Carlotta von Schönburg-Waldenburg, *b* 18 April 1949.

3e •HSH Princess *Anna-Luisa* Ermanna Pia Cecilie von Schönburg-Waldenburg, *b* 31 Nov 1952.

2d •HSH Prince *Georg* Ulrich von Schönburg-Waldenburg [*5280 Überackern, Post Braunau, Upper Austria*], *b* 18 Nov 1908, *m* 4 May 1935, •H Ill H Countess *Pauline* Emma Amalie Gertrud Elisabeth Madeleine (*b* 5 Sept 1906), elder dau of H Ill H Count Otto zu Castell-Castell, and has had issue,

1e HSH Princess *Anna-Amélie* Madeleine Charlotte Marie Therese Sibylle Ulrike von Schönburg-Waldenburg, *b* 22 Jan 1936, *m* 24 April 1962, •HI and RH Archduke *Franz Salvator* Georg Josef Maria Thaddäus of Austria, Prince of Tuscany (*b* 10 Sept 1927) (*see p* 242), and *dsp* 7 Oct 1966.

2e •HSH Princess *Clementine* Pauline Hermine Dorothea Antonie Ottilie von Schönburg-Waldenburg, *b* (twin with Princess Anna Amélie) 22 Jan 1936.

3e •HSH Princess *Stephanie* Pauline Amélie Walpurgis Alexandrine von Schönburg-Waldenburg, *b* 22 Sept 1938, *m* 7 Sept 1960, •H Ill H Count *Ludwig* Karl Maximilian Hubert Willibald Modestus von Waldburg zu Wolfegg und Waldsee (*b* 15 June 1934) [*7109 Assumstadt, Post Züttlingen an der Jagst, Germany*] and has issue,

•H Ill H Count *Hubertus* Georg Karl Maria Willibald Johannes von Waldburg zu Wolfegg und Waldsee, *b* 15 May 1964.

•H Ill H Countess *Elisabeth* Pauline Anna Amelie Maria Walburga von Waldburg zu Wolfegg und Waldsee, *b* 7 June 1962.

4*e* •HSH Princess *Luise* Pauline Amélie Vibeke Emma von Schönburg-Waldenburg, *b* 12 Oct 1943, *m* 9 Sept 1968, •HSH Prince Georg *Andreas* Heinrich zu Hohenlohe-Langenburg (*b* 24 Nov 1938) (*see p* 297).

3*d* HSH Prince Wilhelm von Schönburg-Waldenburg, *b* 3 April 1913, *m* 27 Sept 1939, •HSH Princess *Marie Elisabeth* Ida Emma Cecilie Mathilde (*b* 1 Oct 1921) [*Schleiden, Eifel, Jahnstrasse 3, Germany*], yr dau of HSH Christoph Martin, 3rd Prince zu Stolberg-Rossla (*see p* 269), and was *k* in action in World War II 11 June 1944, leaving issue,

1*e* •HSH Prince Ulrich von Schönburg-Waldenburg, *b* 9 Oct 1940.

2*e* •HSH Prince Wolf Christoph von Schönburg-Waldenburg, *b* 3 April 1943.

1*d* •HSH Princess *Charlotte* Pauline Luise Amalie zu Schönburg-Waldenburg [*Espelkamp-Mittwald über Lübecke, Westfalen, Potsdamer Strasse 7, Germany*], *b* 3 Feb 1901.

2*d* •HSH Princess *Dorothea* Luise Pauline von Schönburg-Waldenburg, *b* 3 Oct 1905, *m* 5 Sept 1928, HSH Prince Karl Franz *Ferdinand* of Lippe-Weissenfeld (*b* 16 July 1903; *k in* action in World War II 26 Sept 1939) and has issue,

•HSH Prince *Franz* Clemens Ulrich of Lippe-Weissenfeld, *b* 14 Oct 1929.

•HSH Princess *Margarete* Friederike Pauline of Lippe-Weissenfeld, *b* 28 April 1932.

3*c* •HSH Princess *Amélie* Karoline Ludovika Gabriele zu Löwenstein-Wertheim-Freudenberg [*Hochburg, A-5122 Ach, Austria*], *b* 24 June 1883, *m* 5 Oct 1903, H Ill H Count *Otto* Friedrich zu Castell-Castell (*b* 12 May 1868; *d* 8 July 1939), and has had issue,

1*d* H Ill H Count *Luitpold Alfred* Friedrich Karl zu Castell-Castell, *b* 14 Nov 1904, *m* 22 Jan 1937, HH Princess *Alexandrine-Louise* Caroline-Mathilde Dagmar (*b* 12 Dec 1914; *d* 26 April 1962), yst dau of HRH Prince Harald of Denmark, and was *k* in action in World War II 6 Nov 1941, leaving issue,

1*e* •H Ill H Countess *Amélie* Alexandrine Helene Caroline Mathilde Pauline zu Castell-Castell, *b* 25 May 1938, *m* 5 Sept 1965, •*Oscar-Heinrich* Ritter von Miller zu Aichholz (*b* 7 July 1934), and has issue,

•Alexander Oscar Heinrich Christian Luitpold Ritter von Miller zu Aichholz, *b* 13 Aug 1966.

2*e* •H Ill H Countess *Thyra* Antonie Marie-Therese Feodora Agnes zu Castell-Castell, *b* 14 Sept 1939, *m* 3 Nov 1961, •Karl Moes (*b* 17 Oct 1937) [*Liqustervoenget 19, Virum, nr Copenhagen, Denmark*], and has issue,

•Marie-Luise Moes, *b* 7 July 1966.

2*d* H Ill H Count *Gustav* Friedrich Wilhelm Ernst Franz Ulrich Richard Udo Hermann zu Castell-Castell, *b* 9 Dec 1911, *m* 14 July 1937, •Baroness Vibeke (*b* 9 April 1915) [*Hindemae Mølle, 5540 Ullerslev, Denmark*], dau of Baron Christian von Lotzbeck, and was *k* in action 19 Jan 1941, leaving issue,

•H Ill H Count Friedrich *Carl* Otto Luitpold zu Castell-Castell [*Hochburg, A-5122 Ach, Austria*], *b* 5 July 1940, *m* 24 May 1967, •Baroness *Adelheid* (*Heidi*) Margarethe Antonie Maria Hemma (*b* 22 April 1939), yr dau of Hans, Baron Jordis von Lohausen, and has issue,

1*f* •H Ill H Countess *Amelie* Margarete Clementine zu Castell-Castell, *b* 18 Feb 1968.

2*f* •H Ill H Countess Marie Therese zu Castell-Castell, *b* 3 Aug 1972.

•H Ill H Countess *Christa* Fanny Amélie Friederike zu Castell-Castell, *b* 19 May 1938, *m* 18 Aug 1962, •Count *Franz* von Assisi Eduard Maria Hubertus Wilderich Leopold Wilhelm Aloysius Johannes Antonius Apolinaris von Walderdorff (*b* 20 Nov 1930) [*8011 Vaterstetten, nr Munich, Germany*], and has issue,

•Count *Carl* Gustav Leopold Maria von Walderdorff, *b* 6 July 1963.

•Countess *Franziska* Anna Maria von Walderdorff, *b* 8 March 1965.

1*d* •H Ill H Countess *Pauline* Emma Amalie Gertrud Elisabeth Madeleine zu Castell-Castell, *b* 5 Sept 1906, *m* 4 May 1935, •HSH Prince *Georg* Ulrich von Schönburg-Waldenburg (*b* 18 Nov 1908), and has issue (*see p* 268).

2*d* •H Ill H Countess *Marie Therese* Pauline Mechthild Ludmilla Antonie zu Castell-Castell, *b* 30 Dec 1917, *m* 3 July 1937, •HSH *Philipp Franz* Friedrich Konrad Wilhelm Chlodwig, 4th Prince and Rheingraf zu Salm-Horstmar (*b* 31 March 1909) [*Schloss Varler Post Osterwick über Coesfeld, Westfalen, Germany*], and has issue,

1*e* •HSH Hereditary Prince *Philipp-Otto* Luitpold Karl Christoph Hans Rupert zu Salm-Horstmar, *b* 2 June 1938, *m* 30 Sept 1971, •Katy Sauter.

2*e* •HSH Prince *Gustav* Friedrich Georg Heinrich Ludwig Ferdinand Philipp Franz zu Salm-Horstmar, *b* 22 Oct 1942.

3*e* •HSH Prince Johann Christoph Udo Albrecht Karl Adolf zu Salm-Horstmar, *b* 27 July 1949.

4*c* •HSH Princess *Madeleine* Wilhelmine Felice Ludovika zu Löwenstein-Wertheim-Freudenberg [*81 Garmisch-Partenkirchen, Storistrasse 33, Germany*], *b* 8 March 1885, *m* 21 Nov 1905, HSH *Richard* Hermann Gustav, 4th Prince zu Sayn-Wittgenstein-Berleburg (*b* 27 May 1882; *d* 25 April 1925), and has had issue,

1*d* HSH *Gustav Albrecht* Alfred Franz Friedrich Otto Emil Ernst, 5th Prince zu Sayn-Wittgenstein-Berleburg, *b* 28 Feb 1907, *m* 26 Jan 1934, •Margaretha (*b* 28 March 1909) [*592 Berleburg, Westfalen, Germany*], yr dau of Charles Fouché, 6th Duc d'Otrante, and was missing in Russia 1944, leaving issue,

1*e* •HSH *Richard* Casimir Karl August Robert Konstantin, 6th Prince zu Sayn-Wittgenstein-Berleburg [*592 Berleburg, Westfalen, Germany*], *b* 29 Oct 1934, *m* 3 Feb 1968, •HRH Princess *Benedikte* Astrid Ingeborg Ingrid (*b* 29 April 1944), 2nd dau of HM late King Frederik IX of Denmark (*see p* 278), and has issue,

•HSH Hereditary Prince *Gustav* Friedrich Philipp Richard zu Sayn-Wittgenstein-Berleburg, *b* 12 Jan 1969.

•HSH Princess *Alexandra* Rosemarie Ingrid Benedikte zu Sayn-Wittgenstein-Berleburg, *b* 20 Nov 1970.

2*e* •HSH Prince *Robin* Alexander Wolfgang Udo Eugen Wilhelm Gottfried zu Sayn-Wittgenstein-Berleburg, *b* 29 Jan 1938, *m* 29 Jan 1970, •*Charlotte* Birgitta Elisabeth (*b* 1 April 1942), dau of late Frederik af Klercke, and has issue,

•HSH Prince Sebastian zu Sayn-Wittgenstein-Berleburg, *b* 30 Jan 1971.

1*e* •HSH Princess *Madeleine* Olga Dora Edle Benedicte zu Sayn-Wittgenstein-Berleburg, *b* 22 April 1936, *m* 29 July 1958, •H Ill H Hereditary Count Otto zu Solms-Laubach (*b* 26 Aug 1926), and has issue,

1*f* •H Ill H Countess Tatiana zu Solms-Laubach, *b* 16 Dec 1958.

2*f* •H Ill H Countess Ariane zu Solms-Laubach, *b* (twin with Countess Tatiana) 16 Dec 1958.

3*f* •H Ill H Countess Anna Margareta zu Solms-Laubach, *b* 29 June 1960.

2*e* •HSH Princess *Tatiana* Louise Ursula Therese Elsa zu Sayn-Wittgenstein-Berleburg, *b* 31 July 1940, *m* 3 June 1964, •HRH Prince *Moritz* Friedrich Karl Emanuel Humbert of Hesse (*b* 6 Aug 1926), and has issue (*see p* 284).

3*e* ●HSH Princess *Pia* Margareta zu Sayn-Wittgenstein-Berleburg, *b* 8 Dec 1942.
2*d* ●HSH *Christian Heinrich* Wolfgang Amelung Karl Friedrich Beno, 5th Prince zu Sayn-Wittgenstein-Hohenstein [*Possenhofen, Post Pöcking über Starnberg, Feichtetstrasse 25, Germany*], *b* 20 Sept 1908, *m* 1st 28 March 1945 (*m* diss by div 1951), Countess *Beatrix* Asta Johanna (*b* 20 June 1921), only dau of late Count Nikolaus von Bismarck-Schönhausen, and has issue,
1*e* ●HSH Princess Loretta Augusta Brigitte Madeleine zu Sayn-Wittgenstein-Hohenstein, *b* 16 June 1946.
2*e* ●HSH Princess *Johanna* Elisabeth Margareta zu Sayn-Wittgenstein-Hohenstein, *b* 22 Oct 1948, *m* ●Count *Axel* Alfred Otto Wilhelm Douglas (*b* 22 July 1943).
He *m* 2ndly 4 Nov 1960, ●HSH Princess *Dagmar* Elisabeth Rosemarie (*b* 16 Jan 1919), elder dau of HSH late Prince Georg zu Sayn-Wittgenstein-Hohenstein, and by her has issue,
1*e* ●HSH Hereditary Prince Bernhart Otto Peter zu Sayn-Wittgenstein-Hohenstein, *b* 15 Nov 1962
3*e* ●HSH Princess Madeleine Elisabeth Maria zu Sayn-Wittgenstein-Hohenstein, *b* 17 March 1961.
3*d* HSH Prince *Ludwig Ferdinand* Paul Franz Stanislaus Ulrich Otto Ludolf zu Sayn-Wittgenstein-Berleburg, *b* 4 April 1910, *m* 5 Aug 1935, ●HSH Princess *Friederike Juliane* Luise Emilie Feodora Anna (*b* 5 Oct 1912) [*Horstmar, Westfalen, Germany*], elder dau of HSH Otto II, 3rd Prince and Rheingraf zu Salm-Horstmar, and was *k* in action in World War II 22 Nov 1943, leaving issue,
1*e* ●HSH Prince *Otto-Ludwig* Richard Hermann Franz Christian Adolf Erwin zu Sayn-Wittgenstein-Berleburg, *b* 25 Feb 1938.
2*e* ●HSH Prince *Johann-Stanislaus* Karl Friedrich Ludwig Sebastian zu Sayn-Wittgenstein-Berleburg, *b* 9 Aug 1939.
3*e* ●HSH Prince *Ludwig-Ferdinand* Friedrich Hans Rudolf Winrich Klaus zu Sayn-Wittgenstein-Berleburg, *b* 25 Jan 1942.
1*e* ●HSH Princess *Marita* Rosy Luise Olympia zu Sayn-Wittgenstein-Berleburg, *b* 15 Aug 1936.
2*e* ●HSH Princess *Ulrike-Christine* Madeleine Rosy Editha Olga Ingetrud Sabine zu Sayn-Wittgenstein-Berleburg, *b* 21 Jan 1944.
5*c* ●HSH Princess *Ilka* Wilhelmine Auguste Adolfine zu Löwenstein-Wertheim-Freudenberg [*8721 Bayerhof, Post Gädheim, Ufranken, Germany*], *b* 9 Jan 1887, *m* 26 July 1905, H Ill H Count *Friedrich* Joseph Franz Emanuel zu Ortenburg (*b* 23 July 1871; *d* 4 March 1940), and has had issue,
1*d* ●H Ill H Count *Alfred-Friedrich* Franz Otto Amelung zu Ortenburg [*8721 Bayerhof, Post Gädheim, UFranken, Germany*], *b* 12 May 1906, *m* 28 May 1936, ●Jutta (*b* 21 June 1906), yr dau of Leopold von Lücken, and has issue,
1*e* ●H Ill H Count *Botho* Friedrich Leopold Harald Manfred Otto Wolf zu Ortenburg, *b* 21 April 1937.
2*e* ●H Ill H Count *Engelbert* Wilhelm Udo Heinrich zu Ortenburg, *b* 11 March 1939, *m* 6 March 1965, ●Margot (*b* 5 Aug 1942), dau of Georg August Pöllmann.
3*e* ●H Ill H Count *Joachim* Christian Manfred Gustav-Albrecht zu Ortenburg, *b* 26 May 1944.
1*e* ●H Ill H Countess *Ilka* Irmgard Pauline Hanna Lili Harriet zu Ortenburg, *b* 29 June 1942, *m* 9 Oct 1971, ●HH Duke *Johann* Friedrich Adolf of Oldenburg (*b* 3 Jan 1940) (*see p* 222).
2*e* ●H Ill H Countess *Yvonne* Elisabeth Amélie Marie-Luise zu Ortenburg, *b* 2 Jan 1948.
2*d* H Ill H Count *Aribo* Paul Carl Wilhelm Ulrich zu Ortenburg, *b* 31 March 1908; *d unm* 18 May 1934.
3*d* H Ill H Count *Udo-Wilhelm* Richard Ernst zu Ortenburg, *b* 20 May 1915; *k* in action in World War II 11 June 1942.
4*d* H Ill H Count *Joachim* Friedrich-Karl Wendt zu Ortenburg, *b* 10 Oct 1918; *k* in action in World War II 1 Sept 1941.
5*d* H Ill H Count *Georg* Friedrich Karl zu Ortenburg, *b* 14 Feb 1922; *k* in action in World War II 30 Jan 1944.
1*d* ●H Ill H Countess *Amélie* Anastasia Pauline Madeleine Elisabeth zu Ortenburg [*81 Garmisch-Partenkirchen, Ehrwalder Strasse 10, Germany*], *b* 19 Dec 1909, *m* 10 April 1934, Count *Heinrich* Eberhard Adolf Friedrich Manfred Alexander zu Dohna-Schlobitten (*b* 24 April 1907; *k* in action 22 May 1940), and has issue,
1*e* ●Countess *Ilka* Mathilde Dorothea Rosa Pauline zu Dohna-Schlobitten [*Zürich, Dufourstrasse 154, Switzerland*], *b* 10 June 1937.
2*e* ●Countess *Amélie* Jutta Vera Friederike Margaretta zu Dohna-Schlobitten [*Garmisch-Partenkirchen, Ehrwalder Strasse 10, Germany*], *b* 10 Dec 1939.
2*d* ●H Ill H Countess *Pauline* Amélie zu Ortenburg, *b* 3 Dec 1913, *m* 17 Oct 1935, ●HSH Prince Theodor Georg Ludwig *Christian* of Lippe-Weissenfeld (*b* 12 Aug 1907) [*8743 Bischofsheim/Rhon, Kissinge Strasse 33, Germany*], and has issue,
1*e* ●HSH Prince *Clemens* Friedrich-Ludwig Bernhard Simon Ferdinand of Lippe-Weissenfeld, *b* 16 Sept 1937, *m* 11 Jan 1964, ●Heidi Feriv (*b* 23 Feb 1940), and has issue,
●HSH Prince *Jan-Hendrik* Christian of Lippe-Weissenfeld, *b* 26 Aug 1970.
2*e* ●HSH Prince *Friedrich* Christian Hermann Georg Heinrich of Lippe-Weissenfeld, *b* 18 March 1939.
3*e* ●HSH Prince *Ferdinand* Jobst Hermann Carl Ernst Joachim of Lippe-Weissenfeld, *b* 14 Nov 1942, *m* 19 June 1970, ●Baroness Karoline von Felitzsch, and has issue,
●HSH Princess Felizitas of Lippe-Weissenfeld, *b* 1971.
4*e* ●HSH Prince *Christian* Franz Georg of Lippe-Weissenfeld, *b* 18 Oct 1945.
5*e* ●HSH Prince *Georg* Christian Heinrich Herbert Bernhard of Lippe-Weissenfeld, *b* 25 June 1957.
1*e* ●HSH Princess *Elisabeth* Ilka Friederike Anna-Luise of Lippe-Weissenfeld, *b* 8 Dec 1940, *m* 4 Aug 1961, ●H Ill H Count *Prosper* Friedrich Carl Gustav Heinrich zu Castell-Castell (*b* 4 Sept 1922), and has issue (*see p* 248).
6*c* HSH Princess *Elisabeth* Ferdinande zu Löwenstein-Wertheim-Freudenberg, *b* 5 May 1890, *m* 1st 25 Sept 1909 (*m* diss by div 1923), HSH Prince *Otto-Konstantin* Emil Franz zu Sayn-Wittgenstein-Berleburg (*b* 11 June 1878; *d* 16 Nov 1955), and had issue,
1*d* ●HSH Prince *Franz* Wilhelm Otto Alfred Konstantin Emil zu Sayn-Wittgenstein-Berleburg [*München, Holbeinstrasse 14, Germany*], *b* 24 Aug 1910, *m* 21 Feb 1942, ●HSH Princess *Gabriele Georgine* Gustava Resita Klausine Karoline Imagina Marion (*b* 23 Nov 1911), only dau of HSH late Hereditary Prince Ferdinand Maximilian zu Ysenburg und Büdingen in Wächtersbach (*see p* 261).
2*d* HSH Prince *August-Richard* Victor Paul Udo zu Sayn-Wittgenstein-Berleburg, *b* 13 Feb 1913; *k* in action in World War II 22 Dec 1939.
3*d* ●HSH Prince *Casimir-Johannes* Ludwig Otto zu Sayn-Wittgenstein-Berleburg [*36 Ennismore Gardens Mews, SW7*], *b* 22 Jan 1914, *m* 1st 21 April 1939 (*m* diss by div 1949), Ingrid (*b* 12 April 1915), dau of Lucian Alsen, and has issue,
1*e* ●HSH Prince Christian *Peter* August Richard Udo Maria Casimir zu Sayn-Wittgenstein-Berleburg, *b* 5 Feb 1940.
1*e* ●HSH Princess *Leonille* Elisabeth Victoria Barbara Margarete zu Sayn-Wittgen-

stein-Berleburg, *b* 6 July 1941, *m* (civil) 27 Jan and (religious) 28 Jan 1967, •HSH Hereditary Prince *Wolfgang Ernst* Ferdinand Heinrich Franz Karl Georg Wilhelm zu Ysenburg und Büdingen in Wächtersbach (*b* 20 June 1936), and has issue (*see p* 261).

He *m* 2ndly 1 May 1950, •*Iris* Mary Emilie (*b* 16 May 1917), yst dau of late Edward Hewish Ryle (*see* BURKE'S *LG*, RYLE *formerly of Barkhale*), and by her has issue,

2*e* •HSH Prince *Richard* Casimir Roger William zu Sayn-Wittgenstein-Berleburg, *b* 21 March 1952.

3*e* •HSH Prince *Johannes* Carl Franz August zu Sayn-Wittgenstein-Berleburg, *b* 30 Sept 1953.

4*d* HSH Prince *Gottfried* Stanislaus Friedrich Paul zu Sayn-Wittgenstein-Berleburg, *b* 16 Sept 1920; *k* in action in World War II 28 Nov 1941.

2*b* Countess Caroline von Reichenbach-Lessonitz, *b* 23 May 1860; *d* 28 April 1874.

1*a* Countess Luise Wilhelmine Emilie von Reichenbach-Lessonitz, *b* 26 Feb 1813, *m* 15 May 1845, Count Carl August von Bose (*b* 7 Nov 1814; *d* 25 Dec 1887), and *dsp* 3 Oct 1883.

2*a* Countess Amalie Wilhelmine Emilie von Reichenbach-Lessonitz, *b* 31 Dec 1816, *m* 1st 3 Oct 1836 (*m* diss by div), Count Johann Heinrich *Wilhelm* von Luckner (*b* 29 Jan 1805; *d* 19 Feb 1865), and had issue,

1*b* Count Nikolaus *Alfred* Arthur von Luckner, *b* 1 Jan 1838, *m* 11 June 1862, *Elisabeth Clara* Hock, and *dsp* Nov 1864.

She *m* 2ndly 2 Oct 1840, Baron Karl Hermann von Watzdorff (*b* 9 March 1807; *d* 5 Dec 1846), and had further issue,

2*b* Baron Wilhelm Emil von Watzdorff, *b* 13 April 1842, *m* 11 June 1866, Laura (*b* 15 Aug 1842; *d* 13 March 1915), dau of Jobst Rudolf von Witzleben, and *d* 11 Jan 1915, leaving issue,

Baroness Armgard von Watzdorff, *b* 3 May 1867, *m* 1 April 1891, Georg Ludwig von Dawans (*b* 30 Aug 1860; *d* 4 Feb 1912), and *d* 16 Jan 1945, having had issue,

1*d* •*Sigismund-Helmut* Konrad Alfred Felix Georg von Dawans [*Konstanz, Rheingutstrasse 13, Germany*], *b* 23 Sept 1899, *m* 1st 6 April 1923 (*m* diss by div 1928), Ingeborg (*b* 10 May 1902), dau of Walter Hane, and has issue,

1*e* •*Horst* Sigismund Ludwig Albert von Dawans [*Walsum, Niederrhein, Friedenstrasse 18, Germany*], *b* 4 May 1924, *m* 22 June 1948, •Annemarie (*b* 22 June 1922), dau of Franz Schaub, and has issue,

1*f* •*Dorothée* von Dawans, *b* 4 Nov 1955.

2*f* •Barbara von Dawans, *b* 23 Sept 1957.

He *m* 2ndly 1 Aug 1931, •Ilse (*b* 25 June 1911), dau of Karl Friedrich Schneider, and by her has issue,

2*e* •*Achim* Felix Sigmund von Dawans, *b* 24 Nov 1935, *m* 17 Nov 1958, •Sylvia (*b* 16 Jan 1939), dau of Harald Johannsen, and has issue,

•Rüdiger von Dawans, *b* 27 July 1960.

•Miriam von Dawans, *b* 7 Feb 1964.

3*e* •Hans-Dieter von Dawans, *b* 13 April 1939.

1*e* •*Ingrid* Emilie Else von Dawans, *b* 17 July 1932, *m* 3 April 1956, •Hans-Gerd Wasum (*b* 16 May 1931).

2*e* •Christel von Dawans, *b* 21 July 1934, *m* 9 April 1960, •*Götz* Joachim Erich Hugo von Winterfeld (*b* 1 Feb 1928) [*507 Bergisch Gladbach, Kolpingstrasse 41, Germany*], and has issue,

1*f* •Claus-Heinrich von Winterfeld, *b* 23 Feb 1961.

2*f* •Christoph von Winterfeld, *b* 29 Jan 1964.

1*d* Pauline Amélie Wilhelmine Julie von Dawans, *b* 29 Jan 1892, *m* 29 Jan 1919, Karl Marckwort (*b* 16 Aug 1888; *d* 24 Jan 1944), and *d* 29 July 1952, leaving issue,

•Kasimir Marckwort.

•Marie-Luise Marckwort, *b* 22 Feb 1922, *m* •Herbert Anders (*b* 4 July 1919), and has issue,

•Gabriele Anders, *b* 15 Dec 1945.

2*d* Amélie Helene Emilie Gabriele von Dawans, *b* 22 Oct, *d* 22 Dec 1893.

3*d* *Margot* Amélie Wilhelmine Olga Mathilde Ilke von Dawans, *b* 7 Oct 1897; *d unm* 7 Dec 1959.

3*b* Baron Konrad von Watzdorff, *b* 22 Aug 1844, *m* 12 Jan 1870, Countess Emilie (*b* 1 July 1847; *d* 6 July 1935), dau of Count Felix von Zichy-Ferraris zu Zich und Vásonykeö (*see p* 273), and *d* 28 May 1922, leaving issue,

1*c* Baron Ludwig Konrad Felix von Watzdorff, *b* 3 Feb 1871, *m* 30 Oct 1899, Countess Theresia (*b* 5 Oct 1877; *d* 16 Jan 1940), dau of Count Emmerich Festetics von Tolna, and *d* 5 Feb 1952, having had issue,

1*d* Baron Konrad Maria Ludwig von Watzdorff, *b* 1 Nov 1900; *d unm* 1944.

2*d* Baron Emanuel Emmerich Maria Ludwig von Watzdorff, *b* 12 March 1904; *d unm* July 1946.

2*c* Baron Alfred Albert Emanuel von Watzdorf, *b* 28 Oct 1872; *d unm* 28 May 1927.

3*c* Baron Karl Konrad Stephan von Watzdorff, *b* 16 Feb 1879; *d unm* 19 Nov 1934.

1*c* Baroness *Wilhelmine* Emilie Karoline von Watzdorff, *b* 20 June 1877, *m* 28 May 1901, Count Otto Welser von Welsersheimb (*b* 5 Dec 1871; *d* 23 April 1945), and *d* 2 June 1958, leaving issue,

1*d* •Count *Zeno* Maria Franz Joseph Leopold Anton Welser von Welsersheimb [*Graz, Elisabethstrasse 46, Austria*], *b* 21 Sept 1902, *m* 12 March 1934, •Countess *Sophia* Maria Rudolfine Franziska (•*b* 9 Jan 1911), eldest dau of Count Friedrich Széchényi von Sárvár-Felsövidék, and has issue,

1*e* •Count Otto Welser von Welsersheimb, *b* 1 June 1935.

2*e* •Count Leopold Welser von Welsersheimb, *b* 6 Jan 1939.

3*e* •Count Josef Welser von Welsersheimb, *b* 15 Aug 1942.

1*e* •Countess *Carla* Maria Welser von Welsersheimb, *b* 5 March 1936.

2*e* •Countess Marie Welser von Welsersheimb, *b* 22 Sept 1947.

2*d* •Count Leopold Welser von Welsersheimb, *b* 24 March 1911.

1*d* •Countess Marie Emilie Welser von Welsersheimb, *b* 12 Sept 1903, *m* 8 July 1924, Baron Johann Ritter von Záhony (*b* 11 Dec 1898; *d* 26 Feb 1937), and has had issue,

1*e* •Baron Carl Wilhelm Ritter von Záhony, *b* 29 May 1927.

2*e* Baron Hans Friedrich Ritter von Záhony, *b* 2 April 1933; *d unm* 14 Nov 1959.

1*e* •Baroness Wilhelmine Maria Ritter von Záhony, *b* 3 Sept 1925, *m* 23 Sept 1961 (*m* diss by div), Baron Wolf-Christian von Lilgenau (*b* 15 Dec 1925).

2*d* •Countess Maria Emma Karoline Welser von Welsersheimb, *b* 11 Jan 1906, *m* 26 Sept 1937, •Béla Szmrecsányi de Szmrecsán (*b* 8 Nov 1904), and has issue,

1*e* •Bertalan Maria Béla Szmrecsányi de Szmrecsán, *b* 3 Nov 1942.

1*e* •Benedicta Maria Vilma Szmrecsányi de Szmrecsán, *b* 26 Sept 1938, *m* 14 Sept 1962, •Carl Friedrich Edler von Monshoff (*b* 14 May 1938).

2*e* •Fruzsina Maria Theresia Szmrecsányi de Szmrecsán, *b* 8 April 1940.

3*d* •Countess Hildegard Welser von Welsersheimb, *b* 14 Dec 1909.

Countess Amalie Wilhelmine Emilie von Reichenbach-Lessonitz remarried her 1st husband, Count Wilhelm von Luckner 21 Dec 1847, and *d* 28 July 1858, having had further issue,

4*b* Count *Nikolaus* Rudolf Gustav Alfred Felix von Luckner, *b* 2 June 1849, *m* 25 Sept 1886, Mathilde Zinck (*b* 6 Aug 1853; *d* 18 Dec 1934), and *d* 12 April 1902, leaving issue,

•Count Nikolaus *Felix* von Luckner [*Genf, Avenue de la Grenade 8, Switzerland*], *b* 3 April 1884, *m* 29 Aug 1918, •Andrea Gallay (*b* 3 Feb 1884).

3*a* Countess Emilie von Reichenbach-Lessonitz, *b* 9 June 1820, *m* 10 March 1839, Count Felix Zichy-Ferraris zu Zich und Vásonykeö (*b* 20 Nov 1810; *d* 8 Sept 1885), and *d* 30 Jan 1891, leaving issue,

1*b* Count Victor Zichy-Ferraris zu Zich und Vásonykeö, *b* 1 July 1842; *d unm* 28 May 1880.

2*b* Count Ludwig Zichy-Ferraris zu Zich und Vásonykeö, *b* 11 Aug 1844; *d unm* 29 May 1899.

3*b* Count Emanuel Zichy-Ferraris zu Zich und Vásonykeö, *b* 19 Feb 1852; *d unm* 2 June 1914.

1*b* Countess Melanie Zichy-Ferraris zu Zich und Vásonykeö, *b* 16 Aug 1843, *m* 9 May 1868, HSH *Paul* Clemens Lothar, 4th Prince von Metternich-Winneburg (*b* 14 Oct 1834; *d* 6 Feb 1906), and *d* 3 Aug 1925, having had issue,

1*c* HSH *Klemens-Wenzel* Lothar Richard Felix, 5th Prince von Metternich-Winneburg, *b* 9 Feb 1869, *m* 4 Oct 1905, •Doña Isabel de Silva y Carvajal, 9th Condesa de Castillejo (*b* 3 May 1880; *m* 2ndly June 1931, Ladislaus Skrzynski (*d* 26 Dec 1937)) [*Princesa 18, Madrid, Spain*], dau of Don Alvaro de Silva y Fernández de Côrdoba, 12th Marqués de Santa Cruz de Mudela, and *d* 13 May 1930, leaving issue,

•HSH *Paul* Alfons Maria Clemens Lothar Philippus Neri Felix Nikomedes, 6th Prince von Metternich-Winneburg [*6225 Schloss Johannisberg über Rüdesheim am Rhein, Germany*], *b* 26 May 1917, *m* 6 Sept 1941, •Princess Tatiana (*b* 1 Jan 1915), dau of Prince Ilarion Sergeievitch Wassiltchikoff.

1*c* HSH Princess Emilie Marie Felicitas von Metternich-Winneburg, *b* 24 Feb 1873; *d* 20 Jan 1884.

2*c* HSH Princess Pauline Felix Maria von Metternich-Winneburg, *b* 6 Jan 1880, *m* 5 Feb 1906, HSH Prince Maximilian Theodor von Thurn und Taxis (*b* 8 March 1876; *d* 3 Oct 1939), and *d* 19 May 1960, leaving issue,

•HSH Princess *Margarete* Charlotte Klementine Maria Alexandra Melanie von Thurn und Taxis, *b* 19 Oct 1913, *m* 24 May 1932, •HSH Prince *Raphael* Rainer Karl Maria Joseph Antonius Ignatius Hubertus Lamoral von Thurn und Taxis (*b* 30 May 1906), and has issue (*see p* 254).

2*b* Countess Caroline Zichy-Ferraris zu Zich und Vásonykeö, *b* 13 Oct 1845, *m* 6 July 1863, as his 1st wife, Count Gyula Széchényi von Sárvár-Felsövidék (*b* 11 Nov 1829; *d* 13 Jan 1921), and *d* 25 Dec 1871, leaving issue,

1*c* Count Andor Pál Széchényi von Sárvár-Felsövidék, *b* 13 June 1864, *m* 1st 13 Oct 1894, Countess Andrea (*b* 27 Dec 1870; *d* 20 June 1913), dau of Count Andreas Csekonics von Zsombolya und Janova, and had issue,

1*d* •Count Joseph Maria Andreas Széchényi von Sárvár-Felsövidék, *b* 26 Feb 1897, *m* 2 June 1945, •Hedwig (*b* 17 Feb 1919), dau of Florian Mórgo-Mórgowski, and has issue,

1*e* •Count Joséph Andreas Maria Julius Florian Széchényi von Sárvár-Felsövidék, *b* 15 Feb 1958.

1*e* •Countess Maria Andrea Karolina Emilia Julia Széchényi von Sárvár-Felsövidék, *b* 20 July 1946.

2*e* •Countess Beata Andrea Constancia Leonida Julia Széchenyi von Sárvár-Felsövidék, *b* 14 March 1948.

2*d* •Count Endre Maria Paul Julius Széchényi von Sárvár-Felsövidék, *b* 29 April 1902, *m* 2 June 1932, •Countess Ella (*b* 12 Jan 1907), dau of Count Anton Somssich de Sáard, and has issue,

•Countess Gabrielle Széchényi von Sárvár-Felsövidék, *b* 18 July 1936, *m* 31 July 1957, Count Tomas Semsey de Semse (*b* 28 Nov 1926), and has issue,

•Count András Semsey de Semse, *b* 10 Dec 1966.

•Countess Julia Gabriela Andrea Semsey de Semse, *b* 19 April 1964.

1*d* •Countess Juliana Maria Margarethe Eugenie Széchényi von Sárvár-Felsövidék, *b* 6 Dec 1900, *m* 15 Jan 1931, •Count János Széchényi von Sárvár-Felsövidék (*b* 7 Aug 1897), and has issue,

1*e* •Count János-Peter Maria Joseph Alexander Dénes Ignaz Christof Széchényi von Sárvár-Felsövidék, *b* 31 July 1934, *m* 10 Oct 1959, •Adrienne (*b* 7 Oct 1941), dau of Karl Anders, and has issue,

1*f* •Count Ferdinand Széchényi von Sárvár-Felsövidék, *b* 20 Jan 1962.

2*f* •Count Dénes-Philipp Széchényi von Sárvár-Felsövidék, *b* 7 May 1963.

1*f* •Countess Judith Széchényi von Sárvár-Felsövidék, *b* 27 Nov 1961.

2*e* •Count István Maria Dénes Jânos Imre Hubertus Eustachius András-Gellért Széchényi von Sárvár-Felsövidék, *b* 25 Sept 1941, *m* 6 April 1966, •Ursula (*b* 23 July 1937), dau of Johann Jakob Kneght.

1*e* •Countess Andrea Marie Johanna Emilie Julia Huberta Széchényi von Sárvár-Felsövidék, *b* 3 Nov 1941, *m* 23 Dec 1955, •Michael Somerville-Withers (*b* 17 June 1926), and has issue,

1*f* •Andrew Somerville-Withers, *b* 6 April 1961.

2*f* •Brian Somerville-Withers, *b* 4 Sept 1963.

1*f* •Anne Somerville-Withers, *b* 20 Feb 1957.

2*f* •Elizabeth Somerville-Withers, *b* 17 April, 1958.

3*f* •Adrienne Somerville-Withers, *b* 6 Nov 1959.

2*e* •Countess Susanna Marie Bernadette Denise Gabrielle Ursula Széchényi von Sárvár-Felsövidék, *b* 10 Dec 1932, *m* 7 Oct 1954, •HSH Ottokar, Prince von Lobkowicz (*b* 28 Jan 1922), and has issue,

1*f* •HSH Prince Georg von Lobkowicz, *b* 23 April 1956.

2*f* •HSH Prince Anton von Lobkowicz, *b* (twin with Prince Georg) 23 April 1956.

1*f* •HSH Princess Elisabeth von Lobkowicz, *b* 3 April 1959.

3*e* •Countess Maria-Alice Julia Margit Huberta Maria Piroska Széchényi von Sárvár-Felsövidék, *b* 29 July 1938.

He *m* 2ndly 25 March 1925, •Baroness Maria (*b* 21 April 1897), dau of Baron Alexander Szegedy-Ensch von Mezö-Szeged, and *d* 13 April 1943.

1*c* Countess Margareta Széchényi von Sárvár-Felsövidék, *b* 27 May 1866, *m* 20 April 1892, Count Eugen von Kesselstatt (*b* 10 June 1870; *d* 10 Nov 1933), and *d* 17 Feb 1915, leaving issue,

1*d* Count *Franz* de Paula Georg Eugen von Kesselstatt, *b* 17 July 1894, *m* 23 June 1925, •HSH Princess Marie *Gabriele* Olga Anna (*b* 2 May 1905; *m* 2ndly 20 Oct 1951 (*m* annulled 1954), Harrison Day Blair) [*10 Parc Château Banquet, CH-1200 Genf, Switzerland*], 2nd dau of HSH Prince *Eduard* Viktor Maria of Liechtenstein, and *d* 2 Sept 1938, leaving issue,

1*e* •Count Franz Eugen Eduard Clemens Maria von Kesselstratt, *b* 1 May 1926, *m* 27 Oct 1953, •Louisette (*b* 12 Jan 1926), dau of Rudolf von Laveran-Stiebar von Hinzberg, and has issue,

1*f* •Count Rudolf Georg Maria von Kesselstatt, *b* 31 Jan 1956.

2*f* •Count Georg Johannes Maria von Kesselstatt, *b* 26 Sept 1957.

3*f* •Count Clemens Friedrich Maria von Kesselstatt, *b* 7 June 1959.

4*f* •Count Franz Degenhardt Maria von Kesselstatt, *b* 26 May 1961.

1*f* •Countess Gabrielle Antoinette Maria von Kesselstatt, *b* 1 Nov 1954.

2*f* ●Countess Theresa Maria Bernadette von Kesselstatt, *b* 28 Feb 1964.

2*e* ●Count Johannes Gabriel Franz Georg Maria von Kesselstatt, *b* 21 May 1927.

2*d* Count Johannes Georg Julius Eugen Maria von Kesselstatt, *b* 16 April 1902, *m* 1st 3 Jan 1929, Countess Ferdinande-Johanna (*b* 1 July 1902; *d* 22 April 1944), dau of Count Ferdinand von Hahn, and had issue,

1*e* ●Count Ferdinand Hans Stephan Mulich Eugen Josef Maria von Kesselstatt, *b* 16 Dec 1930, *m* 2 Aug 1958, ●Hella (*b* 22 Aug 1937), dau of Rudolf Witte, and has issue,

1*f* ●Count Maximilian Franz Edmund Mulich Maria von Kesselstatt, *b* 14 July 1961.

2*f* ●Count Johannes Baptist Ferdinand Rudolf Helmut Maria von Kesselstatt, *b* 9 Feb 1964.

1*f* ●Countess Aiga Alice Eugenie Johanna Hedwig Maria von Kesselstatt, *b* 7 March 1959.

2*f* ●Countess Isabella Alexandra Agnes Maria von Kesselstatt, *b* 2 Aug 1965.

2*e* Count Eugen Georg Nikolaus Peter Franziskus Theresia Maria von Kesselstatt, *b* 23 Feb 1935; *d* 22 April 1944.

3*e* Count Franz Edmund Ekhard Johannes Theresia von Kesselstatt, *b* 6 April 1936; *d* 22 April 1944.

1*e* ●Countess Alice-Eugenie Johanna Margarete Paula Franziska Maria von Kesselstatt, *b* 4 May 1932, *m* 25 April 1966, ●Rolf Alfred Wirtz (*b* 25 April 1939).

He *m* 2ndly 28 June 1945, ●Countess Alexandra Elisabeth (*b* 28 June 1914), dau of Count Lazarus von Schmettow, and *d* 9 Jan 1963.

3*d* ●Count Georg Alois Franz Joseph Baldwin Maria von Kesselstatt, *b* 9 June 1905, *m* 5 Nov 1955, ●Baroness Adelma (*b* 11 May 1932), dau of Baron Ladislaus Vay de Vaja.

1*d* ●Countess Caroline Ida Maria Marguerite von Kesselstatt, *b* 17 July 1893, *m* 14 Jan 1920, Count Joseph von Spee (*b* 18 April 1876; *d* 10 Nov 1941), and has had issue,

1*e* Count Joseph Eugen Wilderich Ferdinand Hubertus Maria Gerhard von Spee, *b* 19 Oct 1920, *m* 16 Sept 1943, ●Edith (*b* 28 Feb 1925), dau of Walter von Kleinmayr, and was *k* in action in World War II 17 Feb 1945, *sp*.

2*e* ●Count Franz Wilhelm Joseph Hubertus Gerhard Maria von Spee, *b* 14 March 1923, *m* 1st 6 Aug 1953, Countess Anna Maria (*b* 14 Dec 1928; *d* 12 Nov 1954), dau of Count Georg Henckel von Donnersmarck, and has issue,

1*f* ●Countess Pia Theresia Huberta Maria Anna Ursula von Spee, *b* 17 July 1954.

He *m* 2ndly 4 June 1956, ●Baroness Marie Charlotte (*b* 9 Feb 1929), dau of Baron Joseph von Mylius, and by her has issue,

1*f* ●Count Mariano Antonius Peter Hubertus Pius Apollinarius von Spee, *b* 23 July 1958.

2*f* ●Count Johannes Maria Georg Ruppert Hubertus von Spee, *b* 4 Jan 1960.

3*f* ●Count Wilderich Rochus Paul Hermann-Joseph Hubertus Maria von Spee, *b* 16 April 1964.

4*f* ●Count Peter Pius Franz Martin Hubertus Maria von Spee, *b* 13 Nov 1966.

2*f* ●Countess Brigida Monika Maximiliana Anna Maria Huberta von Spee, *b* 28 May 1957.

3*e* ●Count Maximilian Friedrich Augustinius Hubertus Maria von Spee, *b* 28 Aug 1924, *m* 28 Dec 1955, ●Countess Marie-Elisabeth (*b* 17 March 1933), dau of Count Franz Georg von Ballestrem, and has issue,

1*f* ●Count Jan Seger von Spee, *b* 15 Dec 1956.

2*f* ●Count Per-Degenhardt von Spee, *b* 24 Oct 1958.

3*f* ●Count Franz-Hilarius von Spee, *b* 15 Jan 1965.

1*f* ●Countess Juliane-Hedwig von Spee, *b* 11 March 1960.

2*f* ●Countess Monika Antonia von Spee, *b* 28 Aug 1963.

4*e* ●Count Degenhardt-Wilderich Carl Gerhardt Maria Hubertus Luitpold von Spee-Mirbach, *b* 1 Nov 1926, *m* 3 July 1956, ●Countess Brigitta (*b* 26 Sept 1925), dau of Count Friedrich von Westphalen zu Fürstenberg.

5*e* ●Count Georg Seger Jakob Gerhard Maria Hubertus von Spee, *b* 10 March 1929, *m* 11 Feb 1966, ●Baroness Maria Zita (*b* 12 Nov 1928), dau of Baron Ferdinand von Pereira-Arnstein.

1*e* ●Countess Antonia Margaretha Maria Wilhelmine Elisabeth Julia von Spee, *b* 14 Feb 1922, *m* 20 May 1943, ●Baron Erich von Wendt (*b* 16 Oct 1917), and has issue,

1*f* ●Baron Franz Egon Ferdinand Hermann Joseph Maria Felix von Wendt, *b* 6 March 1944.

2*f* ●Baron Max Hubertus Wilderich von Wendt, *b* 17 March 1945.

3*f* ●Baron Clemens August Sturmius Hubertus Maria von Wendt, *b* 14 Aug 1946.

4*f* ●Baron Karl Michael Klemens Ferdinand Bonifatius Maria, *b* 10 May 1951.

1*f* ●Baroness Marie-Agnes Georgina Antonia Elisabeth von Wendt, *b* 25 Sept 1948.

2*c* Countess Karoline Széchényi von Sárvár-Felsövidék, *b* 8 March 1869, *m* 30 May 1890, Count Simon von Wimpffen (*b* 21 Aug 1867; *d* 11 April 1925), and *dsp* 27 April 1932.

3*c* Countess Pauline Széchényi von Sárvár-Felsövidék, *b* 25 Nov 1871, *m* 22 July 1902, Count Aloys Lexa von Aehrenthal (*b* 27 Sept 1854; *d* 17 Feb 1912), and had issue,

1*d* ●Count Johann Maria Felix Anton Carl Lexa von Aehrenthal, *b* 9 Aug 1905, *m* 7 Nov 1932, ●H Ill H Countess Ernestine von Harrach zu Rohrau und Thannhausen (*b* 11 Aug 1903), dau of H Ill H Count Otto von Harrach, and has issue,

1*e* ●Count Johann Aloys Otto Paul Ernst Carl Maria Stephan Lexa von Aehrenthal, *b* 28 Nov 1933, *m* 4 Aug 1963, ●Baroness Alice (*b* 7 July 1936), dau of Baron Oskar von Wassberg.

1*e* ●Countess Marie Caroline Lexa von Aehrenthal, *b* 24 Dec 1935, *m* 26 April 1960, ●Guy Debièvre (*b* 21 July 1931), and has issue,

●Jean-Luc Debièvre, *b* 23 Jan 1962.

●Françoise-Ernestine Debièvre, *b* 16 Nov 1960.

2*e* ●Countess Marie Pauline Lexa von Aehrenthal, *b* 17 Feb 1941.

1*d* ●Countess Caroline Marie Antoinette Henriette Luise Lexa von Aehrenthal, *b* 13 Sept 1904.

2*d* ●Countess Elisabeth Maria Josefa Antoinette Aloysia Lexa von Aehrenthal, *b* 9 Aug 1909, *m* 3 Jan 1943, ●Count Josef von Thun und Hohenstein (*b* 31 Dec 1907).

3*b* Countess Emilie Zichy-Ferraris zu Zich und Vásonykeö, *b* 1 July 1847, *m* 12 Jan 1870, Baron Konrad von Watzdorff (*b* 22 Aug 1844; *d* 28 May 1922), and *d* 6 July 1935, leaving issue (*see p* 271).

4*a* Countess Friederike von Reichenbach-Lessonitz, *b* 16 Dec 1821, *m* 3 Nov 1841, Baron *Wilhelm Heinrich* von Dungern (*b* 20 June 1809; *d* 3 July 1874), and *d* 23 Feb 1898, leaving issue,

Baroness Wilhelmine von Dungern, *b* 22 Sept 1842, *m* 16 June 1861, Baron *Hermann* Friedrich Wilhelm Karl August Theodor von Dungern (*b* 9 May 1836; *d* 16 Dec 1880), and *d* 13 May 1924, leaving issue,

1*c* Baron *Otto* Wilhelm von Dungern, *b* 14 July 1869, *m* 22 Sept 1892, Elise van Schreven (*b* 20 Feb 1873), and had issue,

1*d* ●Baroness Irene von Dungern, *b* 6 Aug 1893, *m* ●Wilhelm Brandt.

2d ●Baroness Vera von Dungern, *b* 3 April 1901.
3d ●Baroness Sibylle von Dungern, *b* 21 June 1911.
2c Baron *Hermann* Wilhelm Karl von Dungern, *b* 3 March 1874, *m* 2 June 1897, Maria (*b* 3 March 1874; *d* 22 July 1954), dau of Heinrich von Hesse, and *d* 7 March 1947, leaving issue,
1d ●Baron *Hermann-Heinrich* Alfred Alexander Karl von Dungern [*Waldschwind über Gerolzhofen, MFranken, Germany*], *b* 23 July 1898, *m* 24 May 1923, ●Adelheid Katharina Elsa Marie Thekla (*b* 19 April 1898), only dau of Ludolf von Veltheim, and has issue,
Baron *Maximilian* Ludolph Hermann Wolfram Franz Bernard von Dungern, *b* 12 Sept 1926, *m* 26 Sept 1952, ●Wanja (*b* 24 Feb 1932), dau of Swen Wawrinsky, and has issue,
1f ●Baron *Peter-Maximilian* Wawrinsky von Dungern, *b* 18 July 1953.
2f ●Baron *James* Swen von Dungern, *b* 1 Feb 1955.
3f ●Baron Frederic Wawrinsky von Dungern, *b* 1 April 1958.
4f ●Baron Eric Swen Henric von Dungern, *b* 19 Feb 1960.
●Baroness *Asta* Adelheid-Victoria Veltheimia Alix Adele Irmgard von Dungern [*Schweinfurt, Friedenstrasse 23, Germany*], *b* 1 Jan 1929.
2d ●Baron *Helgo* Waldemar Lutz von Dungern [*Schloss Ober-Schwappach, Germany*], *b* 22 July 1903, *m* 28 Nov 1929, ●Baroness Julia (*b* 8 Dec 1898), dau of Baron Philipp von Seefried auf Buttenheim, and has issue,
●Baron *Helwig* Philipp von Dungern, *b* 17 Jan 1931, *m* 30 April 1959, ●Adele (*b* 28 Feb 1939), dau of Michael Regnat, and has issue,
●Baron Alexander von Dungern, *b* 8 April 1960.
●Baroness *Elisabeth* Maria-Ida von Dungern, *b* 18 Feb 1934.
3d ●Baron *Camill* Friedrich von Dungern [*Isernhagen bei Hannover, Föhrenwinkel, Germany*], *b* 19 Sept 1904, *m* 28 Sept 1937, ●Mechtild Semper (*b* 17 Sept 1910), and has issue,
1e ●Baron Friedrich Camill von Dungern, *b* 10 Dec 1944.
1e ●Baroness Dorette von Dungern, *b* 29 March 1939, *m* 14 Aug 1964, ●Egbrecht Kühne-Wanzleben (*b* 2 July 1935), and has issue,
●Serena Isabella Caroline Kühne-Wanzleben, *b* 14 Jan 1966.
2e ●Baroness Maria *Cordula* von Dungern, *b* 18 Aug 1941.
4d ●Baron *Martin* Albert Heinrich von Dungern [*Schloss Ober-Schwappach, Germany*], *b* 26 Aug 1906, *m* 24 May 1938, ●Ulla-Brita (*b* 7 March 1909), dau of Otto Rudolf Nordenstierna, and has issue,
1e ●Baroness *Signe* Maria von Dungern, *b* 22 Aug 1941.
2e ●Baroness Wilhelme von Dungern, *b* 1 Feb 1946.
1d ●Baroness *Dorothée* Alix Emily Elisabeth von Dungern [*Schloss Ober-Schwappach, Germany*], *b* 9 May 1901.
1c Baroness Friederike Emilie Wilhelmine Dorothée Maximiliane von Dungern, *b* 17 June 1862, *m* 17 Jan 1884, Baron Reinhard von Gise (*b* 30 Nov 1854; *d* 7 Nov 1913), and *d* 21 Nov 1925, leaving issue,
1d Baron Johann Nepomuk Ludwig Hermann Maria von Gise, *b* 3 Feb 1887, *m* 26 Feb 1916, ●Lilla Fuchs (*b* 25 Jan 1896), and *d* 24 Sept 1946, having had issue,
Baron Rüdiger Konrad Rainhard Theodor Melchior von Gise, *b* 25 March 1921; *k* in action 4 March 1944.
●Baroness Gunhild Wilhelmine Friederike Marie Margarita von Gise, *b* 31 March 1917.
2d Baron Ernst August Maximilian Josef Otto Wilhelm Maria von Gise, *b* 17 July 1888, *m* 25 Feb 1930, ●Ilse Maria (*b* 12 March 1907), dau of Reinhold Lechler, and was reported missing in Russia May 1945, leaving Issue,
1e ●Baroness Verena Margarita Gabriele Waltraut Maria von Gise, *b* 7 June 1931, *m* 20 July 1961, ●Helmut Müller (*b* 10 July 1925), and has issue,
●Florian Müller, *b* 18 Sept 1962.
2e ●Baroness Jutta Siglinde Gertrud Friederike Franziska Maria von Gise, *b* 21 July 1934, *m* 7 May 1957, ●Walter Köppe (*b* 14 May 1928).
3e ●Baroness Ingrid Christine Luise Erna Katharina Maria von Gise, *b* 14 June 1935, *m* 28 Aug 1959, ●Max Hagenauer (*b* 4 July 1929), and has issue,
1f ●Ulrike Hagenauer, *b* 15 June 1960.
2f ●Sabine Hagenauer, *b* 11 Oct 1964.
3d ●Baron Guntram Ferdinand Maria von Gise, *b* 5 Feb 1892, *m* 30 July 1919, ●Else Mörs (*b* 25 May 1890), and has issue,
●Baron Harro Hilmar Zeno Reinhard Johannes Maria von Gise, *b* 3 June 1920, *m* 1st 22 Aug 1946, Josefine Thiel (*b* 22 Aug 1927; *d* 16 Oct 1956), and has issue,
1f ●Baron Harro Erlhard Maria von Gise, *b* 8 Jan 1948.
1f ●Baroness Hilde Friederike Maria von Gise, *b* 26 Jan 1952.
He *m* 2ndly 15 Oct 1961, ●Elfriede Altenfelder (*b* 19 May 1922), and by her has issue,
2f ●Baroness Gertraud Gunhild Ulrike Maria von Gise, *b* 18 July 1962.
4d ●Baron Zeno Sigmund Hermann Maria von Gise, *b* 18 Jan 1896, *m* 1st 10 Jan 1928 (*m* diss by div), Käthe Sprecher (*b* 25 Aug 1898). He *m* 2ndly 23 Dec 1944, ●Liselotte (*b* 6 Dec 1916), dau of Carl Hansen, and by her has issue,
●Baroness Ute von Gise, *b* 9 Sept 1946.
1d ●Baroness Gertrud Maria Christine Elisabeth Wilhelmine Dorothea von Gise, *b* 21 March 1890, *m* 10 Jan 1924, Egon Arendt (*b* 18 Aug 1889; *d* 14 Nov 1964).
2d ●Baroness Margarita Marie Wilhelmine von Gise, *b* 24 Oct 1893, *m* 26 March 1935, Erich Neumann (*b* 13 Dec 1876; *d* 7 Dec 1952), and has issue,
●Hans-Jürgen Neumann, *b* 10 Jan 1936, *m* 14 Oct 1960, ●Marianne Höske (*b* 13 Jan 1939), and has issue,
●Christiane Neumann, *b* 27 Oct 1961.
●Sieglinde Neumann, *b* 17 Oct 1938.
2c Baroness Isabelle Wilhelmine Auguste Adolfine Amalie von Dungern, *b* 23 June 1863, *m* 1st 15 July 1886, Baron Alfred Wolffskeel von Reichenberg (*b* 5 Oct 1851; *d* 21 Nov 1896). She *m* 2ndly 7 April 1908, Baron Kurt Truchsess von Wetzhausen (*b* 14 Nov 1859; *d* 18 March 1919), and *dsp* 1936.
3c Baroness Dora Auguste Marie Friederike von Dungern, *b* 20 May 1871, *m* 14 Sept 1893, Kurt Kollmann (*b* 7 Nov 1868; *d* 19 Aug 1900), and *d* 24 Oct 1930, having had issue,
Siegfried Kollmann, *b* 28 May 1898; *k* in action in World War I 31 Oct 1914.
●Erika Wilhelmine Clara Pauline Kollman, *b* 15 June 1896, *m* 15 Oct 1921, ●Erich Holthaus (*b* 20 Aug 1891).
4c Baroness Ilka Helene Klara Marie Friederike von Dungern, *b* 8 Aug 1880, *m* 8 Jan 1928, Baron Richard von Niemans (*b* 6 July 1876; *d* 1 June 1943), and *dsp* 16 Oct 1952.
5a Countess Helene von Reichenbach-Lessonitz, *b* 8 Aug 1825, *m* 4 Jan 1844, Baron Oswald von Fabrice (*b* 8 Jan 1820; *d* 3 June 1898), and *d* 14 May 1898, leaving issue,
1b Baron Wilhelm Friedrich Maximilian von Fabrice, *b* 30 Aug 1845, *m* 13 Sept 1874, Amalie (*b* 20 Feb 1842; *d* 27 Jan 1914), dau of Pál Almásy von Zsadany und Török-Szent-

Miklos, and *d* 18 Nov 1914, leaving issue,
1*c* Baroness *Ellinka* Helene Rosa von Fabrice, *b* 30 May 1875, *m* 1st 18 May 1896 (*m* diss by div), Paul von Gans (*b* 11 July 1866; *d* 18 April 1915) and had issue,
1*d* Joszi von Gans, *b* 1 March 1897, *m* 1st 13 Nov 1920 (*m* diss by div), Philimena Martinet (*b* 14 May 1896). He *m* 2ndly 28 June 1927 (*m* diss by div), Baroness Melitta (*b* 24 Jan 1906), dau of Baron Hans von Riedel, and by her had issue,
1*e* •Bianca Emma Alice Elinka von Gans, *b* 28 April 1928, *m* 22 Nov 1950, •Denys McCullough (*b* 10 April 1927), and has issue,
1*f* •Keith Gadsden McCullough, *b* 19 May 1953.
2*f* •Anthony Mark McCullough, *b* 21 July 1956.
2*e* •Isabel Victoria Nora Ilona von Gans, *b* 10 Jan 1932, *m* 26 April 1952, •Hanno Weiss (*b* 1 Aug 1926), and has issue,
•Carina-Bianca Beatrice Melitta Christine Isabelle Norberta Weiss, *b* 10 Jan 1956.
He *m* 3rdly 28 Feb 1939, •Maria Krieglstein (*b* 13 July 1915), and *d* 9 Jan 1963, having by her had issue,
1*e* •Anthony Paul von Gans, *b* 31 Oct 1940, *m* 1 Oct 1966, •Brigitte Kompach (*b* 16 Oct 1941).
2*e* •Randolph Charles von Gans, *b* 16 Jan 1944.
3*e* •Angela von Gans, *b* 6 Aug 1947.
1*d* •*Margot* Luigina Ilma von Gans, *b* 11 July 1899, *m* 1st 3 Jan 1917 (*m* diss by div 1925), Baron *Werner* Siegfried Dagobert Kraft von Bischoffshausen (*b* 23 Sept 1894), and has had issue,
1*e* Baron *Claus-Henning* Günther Mordian Gotthard Paul von Bischoffshausen, *b* 5 June 1919; *k* in action in World War II 23 April 1942.
She *m* 2ndly 1 Oct 1921 (*m* diss by div 1925), Count *Adolkar* von Einsiedel (*b* 28 April 1889), and has further issue,
1*e* •Countess *Ellinka* Karin Harriet von Einsiedel, *b* 26 July 1922, *m* 1st 21 Feb 1945 (*m* diss by div), Ernst Bierlein (*b* 26 Feb 1920), and has issue,
1*f* •Peter Michael Bierlein, *b* 3 Dec 1945.
1*f* •Marie Blanche Bierlein, *b* 10 Dec 1954.
She *m* 2ndly 2 Sept 1957, •Walter Rupprecht (*b* 26 Feb 1924), and has further issue,
2*f* •Karl Alexander Rupprecht, *b* 29 Oct 1962.
2*d* •*Marie-Blanche* von Gans, *b* 31 Oct 1905, *m* 1st 23 Aug 1922 (*m* diss by div 1926), Count *Othmar* Maria Alfred Wladimir Wenzel von Aichelberg (*b* 27 Sept 1901), and has issue,
•Countess *Elisabeth* Wilhelmine Christine Marie-Blanka Helene von Aichelburg, *b* 10 Aug 1923, *m* 22 Feb 1947 (*m* diss by div), Georges Pollak (*b* 22 July 1909), and has issue,
•Robert Pollak, *b* 28 Feb 1948.
She *m* 2ndly; and 3rdly.
She *m* 2ndly 11 Jan 1916, Count Haupt von Pappenheim (*b* 16 Feb 1869; *d* 26 Jan 1954), and *d* 19 Aug 1938.
2*c* Baroness *Luigina* Zoë Friederika Antoinette Victorine von Fabrice, *b* 30 July 1876, *m* 1st 24 May 1894, Walter Sturtzfopf (*b* 10 May 1871; *d* 5 Oct 1898), and had issue,
•Charley Sturtzfopf, *b* 10 May 1896, *m* 6 Sept 1948, •Eugenie Bleifuss (*b* 29 Aug 1929), and has issue,
•Robert Sturtzfopf, *b* 17 Feb 1951.
•Hermine Sturtzfopf, *b* 10 March 1895, *m* 5 June 1920, •Georg von Szebeny (*b* 7 Nov 1887), and has had issue,
•Dénes von Szebeny, *b* 27 April 1921, *m* 1st 29 Aug 1942 (*m* diss by div), Emily Leidenfrost (*b* 7 Nov 1919), and has issue,
•Denise von Szebeny, *b* 4 Sept 1943.
He *m* 2ndly 13 July 1960, •Irmgard Gericke (*b* 14 Feb 1931), and by her has issue,
•Gábor von Szebeny, *b* 26 Sept 1963.
Gina von Szebeny, *b* 4 March 1926, *m* 7 Oct 1953, Gábor Markus (*b* 8 June 1921), and *dsp* 4 Feb 1962.
She *m* 2ndly 20 Nov 1901 (*m* diss by div 1911), Edgar Böcking (*b* 1861). She *m* 3rdly 26 Aug 1913 (*m* diss by div 1924), Hans Hippolyte von Simpson (*b* 27 March 1885). She *m* 4thly 14 Sept 1926, Edwin Tietjens (*b* 20 March 1894; *d* 22 May 1944), and *d* 29 April 1958.
3*c* •Baroness *Ilma* Frieda Rosa von Fabrice, *b* 28 March 1877, *m* 26 Aug 1896, Carlo Halm-Nicolai (*b* 6 Aug 1876; *d* 23 Feb 1951), and has had issue,
1*d* •Ilma Halm-Nicolai, *b* 29 June 1897.
2*d* Ellinka Halm-Nicolai, *b* 26 Oct 1900; *d* 1901.
3*d* Ilka Halm-Nicolai, *b* 8 Nov 1902, *m* 22 Nov 1943, Ludwig von Bürkel (*b* 5 July 1877; *d* 11 June 1946), and *dsp* 14 April 1965.
4*c* •Baroness *Blanche* Stella Franziska von Fabrice [*Sommerhalde b Ludwigshafen am Bodensee, Germany*], *b* 5 April 1880, *m* 1st 7 Aug 1902 (*m* diss by div), Baron Emanuel von Bodman (*b* 23 Jan 1874; *d* 21 May 1946). She *m* 2ndly 26 May 1917, Wilhelm Schäfer (*b* 20 Jan 1868; *d* 19 Jan 1952), and has issue,
•Klaus Wilhelm Schäfer, *b* 16 Nov 1910, *m* •Roza Honstetter (*b* 1 June 1920), and has issue,
1*e* •Klaus Wilhelm Schäfer, *b* 25 May 1940.
2*e* •Hans-Georg Wilhelm Schäfer, *b* 30 Dec 1945.
3*e* •Hermann Wilhelm Schäfer, *b* 9 April 1950.
5*c* Baroness *Agnes* Goldi Luise Sophie von Fabrice, *b* 28 Dec 1881, *m* 26 June 1902, Walter von Stockar-Scherer-Castell (*b* 13 Oct 1878; *d* 12 Nov 1938), and *d* 5 Nov 1964, leaving issue,
1*d* •Maximilian von Stockar-Scherer-Castell, *b* 11 July 1904, *m* 1st 4 Jan 1927 (*m* diss by div), Louise (*b* 1 June 1907), dau of Frédéric de Meuron, and has issue,
1*e* •Sibylle von Stockar-Scherer-Castell, *b* 15 June 1930, *m* 15 June 1948 (*m* diss by div), Max Froelicher (*b* 13 Sept 1923), and has issue,
1*f* •Sibylle Luise Elisabeth Froelicher, *b* 15 June 1951.
2*f* •Christine Anna Gabriele Froelicher, *b* 14 July 1953.
2*e* •Barbara von Stockar-Scherer-Castell, *b* 27 Aug 1933, *m* 21 Jan 1958, •Anton Hegner (*b* 22 Feb 1926), and has issue,
1*f* •Wolfgang Hegner, *b* 4 June 1964.
1*f* •Isabelle Hegner, *b* 16 Nov 1960.
2*f* •Livia Hegner, *b* 15 April 1963.
He *m* 2ndly, Veronika (*b* 24 May 1919), dau of Hans Eduard Bühler.
2*d* •Walter Hans Bernhard Caspar von Stockar-Scherer-Castell, *b* 2 Sept 1906, *m* 1st 5 Jan 1933 (*m* diss by div), Renée (*b* 9 Dec 1912), dau of Alfred Dürler, and has issue,
1*e* •Marc Antoine Walter von Stockar-Scherer-Castell, *b* 17 Jan 1935, *m* 11 Dec 1958, •Monica (*b* 3 Nov 1936), dau of Franz Bruman, and has issue,
1*f* •Daniel Marc von Stockar-Scherer-Castell, *b* 4 Sept 1961.
2*f* •Thomas Caspar von Stockar-Scherer-Castell, *b* 10 Jan 1964.
He *m* 2ndly 11 Feb 1941, •Georgine Koch de Vigier (*b* 8 July 1910), dau of Ernst Koch, and by her has issue,
2*e* •Urs Caspar von Stockar-Scherer-Castell, *b* 17 July 1942.
1*e* •Monica Goldi von Stocker-Scherer-Castell, *b* 8 Aug 1944.
1*d* •Elisabeth von Stockar-Scherer-Castell, *b* 28 Jan 1908, *m* 28 Oct 1933, •Paul Felber (*b* 11 July 1889), and has issue,
•Urban Felber, *b* 23 Feb 1950.
•Julia Felber, *b* 11 Oct 1935, *m* 7 Oct 1962, •Karl Siegrist (*b* 2 Oct 1933), and has issue,

1*f* •Karl Siegrist, *b* 7 Oct 1964.
1*f* •Elisabeth Siegrist, *b* 23 Sept 1963.
2*f* •Kathrin Siegrist, *b* 28 Nov 1966.
1*b* Baroness Helene Emilie Charlotte von Fabrice, *b* 28 July 1846; *d unm* 11 May 1907.
Elector Wilhelm II of Hesse *m* 3rdly (morganatically) 28 Aug 1843, *Caroline* Christine Albine Albertine, *cr* Countess von Bergen (*b* 9 Jan 1820; *dsp* 21 Feb 1877), dau of Baron Ludwig Hermann von Berlepsch, and *d* 20 Nov 1847.
(1) HSH Princess Marie *Friederike* of Hesse-Cassel, *b* 14 Sept 1768, *m* 29 Nov 1794 (*m* diss by div 1817), as his 1st wife, HH *Alexis* Friedrich Christian, Duke of Anhalt-Bernburg (*b* 12 June 1767; *d* 24 March 1834), and *d* 17 April 1839, having had issue,
1*a* HSH Prince Friedrich Amadeus of Anhalt-Bernburg, *b* 19 April, *d* 24 May 1801.
2*a* HH *Alexander* Karl, Duke of Anhalt-Bernburg, *b* 2 March 1805, *m* 30 Oct 1834, HSH Princess *Friederike* Caroline Juliane (*b* 9 Oct 1811; *d* 10 July 1902), 2nd dau of HSH Wilhelm, Duke of Schleswig-Holstein-Sonderburg-Glücksburg, and *dsp* 19 Aug 1863.
1*a* HSH Princess Katharina Wilhelmine Karoline Friederike of Anhalt-Bernburg, *b* 1 Jan, *d* 24 Feb 1796.
2*a* HSH Princess Wilhelmine *Luise* of Anhalt-Bernburg, *b* 30 Oct 1799, *m* 21 Nov 1817, HRH Prince *Friedrich* Wilhelm Ludwig of Prussia (*b* 30 Oct 1794; *d* 27 July 1863), and *d* 9 Dec 1882, leaving issue,
1*b* HRH Prince Friedrich Wilhelm Ludwig *Alexander* of Prussia, *b* 21 June 1820; *d unm* 4 Jan 1896.
2*b* HRH Prince Friedrich Wilhelm *Georg* Ernst of Prussia, *b* 12 Feb 1826; *d unm* 2 May 1902.
(2) HSH Princess *Caroline* Amalie of Hesse-Cassel, *b* 11 July 1771, *m* 24 April 1802, as his 2nd wife, HSH Emil Leopold *August*, Duke of Saxe-Gotha (*b* 23 Nov 1772; *d* 17 May 1822), and *dsp* 22 Feb 1848.
3 HH Karl, Landgrave of Hesse-Cassel, Regent of Schleswig-Holstein, Field Marshal in the Danish Army, *b* 19 Dec 1744, *m* 30 Aug 1766, HH Princess Louise (*b* 30 Jan 1750; *d* 12 Jan 1831), yst dau of HM King Frederik V of Denmark (*see p* 289), and *d* 17 Aug 1836, having had issue,
(1) HSH Prince Wilhelm of Hesse-Cassel, *b* 15 Jan 1769; *d* 14 March 1772.
(2) HH Friedrich, Landgrave of Hesse-Cassel, Gov of Rendsborg, Field Marshal in the Danish Army, *b* 24 May 1771, *m* (morganatically) 21 May 1813, Klara, *cr* Baroness von Liliencron (*b* 16 Jan 1778; *d* 24 May 1836), dau of Detlev von Brockdorff, and *dsp* 24 Feb 1845.
(3) HSH Prince Christian of Hesse-Cassel, Lt-Gen in the Danish Army, *b* 14 Aug 1776; *d unm* 21 Nov 1814.
(1) HSH Princess *Marie* Sophie Friederike of Hesse-Cassel, *b* 28 Oct 1767, *m* 31 July 1790, HM King Frederik VI of Denmark (*b* 28 Jan 1768; *d* 3 Dec 1839), and *d* 22 March 1852, having had issue (*see p* 286).
(2) HH Princess *Juliane* Luise Amalie of Hesse-Cassel, Abbess of Itzehoe, *b* 19 Jan 1773; *d unm* 11 March 1860.
(3) HSH Princess *Luise* Caroline of Hesse-Cassel, *b* 28 Sept 1789, *m* 26 Jan 1810, HSH Friedrich *Wilhelm* Paul Leopold, Duke of Schleswig-Holstein-Sonderburg-Glücksburg (*b* 4 Jan 1785; *d* 17 Feb 1831), and *d* 13 March 1867, having had issue,
1*a* HH Karl, Duke of Schleswig-Holstein-Sonderburg-Glücksburg, *b* 30 Sept 1813, *m* 19 May 1838, HRH Princess *Wilhelmine* Marie (*b* 18 Jan 1808; *d* 30 May 1891), formerly wife of HRH Prince Frederik of Denmark (later King Frederik VII), and yst dau of HM King Frederik VI of Denmark (*see p* 287), and *dsp* 24 Oct 1878.
2*a* HH Friedrich, Duke of Schleswig-Holstein-Sonderburg-Glücksburg, *b* 23 Oct 1814, *m* 27 Nov 1885, HSH Princess *Adelheid* Christine Juliane Charlotte (*b* 9 March 1821; *d* 30 July 1899), 2nd dau of HSH Georg Wilhelm, Prince of Schaumburg-Lippe, and *d* 27 Nov 1885, leaving issue,
1*b* HH *Friedrich Ferdinand* Georg Christian Karl Wilhelm, Duke of Schleswig-Holstein-Sonderburg-Glücksburg, *b* 12 Oct 1855, *m* 19 March 1885, HH Princess Victoria Friederike Auguste Marie *Caroline Mathilde* (*b* 25 Jan 1860; *d* 20 Feb 1932), 2nd dau of HH Friedrich, Duke of Schleswig-Holstein (*see p* 287), and *d* 21 Jan 1934, leaving issue,
1*c* HH Wilhelm *Friedrich* Christian Günther Albert Adolf Georg, Duke of Schleswig-Holstein-Sonderburg-Glücksburg, *b* 23 Aug 1891, *m* 15 Feb 1916, HSH Princess *Marie Melita* Leopoldine Victoria Feodora Alexandra Sophie (*b* 18 Jan 1899; *d* 8 Nov 1967), eldest dau of HSH Ernst, 7th Prince zu Hohenlohe-Langenburg, and *d* 10 Feb 1965, leaving issue (*see p* 297).
1*c* HH Princess *Victoria Adelheid* Helena Luise Marie Friederike of Schleswig-Holstein-Sonderburg-Glücksburg, *b* 31 Dec 1885, *m* 11 Oct 1905, HRH Prince Leopold *Charles Edward* George Albert of Great Britain and Ireland, Duke of Saxe-Coburg and Gotha, 2nd Duke of Albany, KG (*b* 19 July 1884; *d* 6 March 1954), and *d* 3 Oct 1970, having had issue (*see p* 299).
2*c* HH Princess *Alexandra Viktoria* Auguste Leopoldine Charlotte Amalie Wilhelmine of Schleswig-Holstein-Sonderburg-Glücksburg, *b* 21 April 1887, *m* 1st 22 Oct 1908 (*m* diss by div 1920), HRH Prince *August Wilhelm* Heinrich Günther Viktor of Prussia (*b* 29 Jan 1887; *d* 25 March 1949), 4th son of HIM Wilhelm II, German Emperor and King of Prussia, and had issue (*see p* 301). She *m* 2ndly 7 Jan 1922 Arnold Rümann, and *d* 15 April 1957.
3*c* HH Princess *Helena* Adelheid Viktoria Marie of Schleswig-Holstein-Sonderburg-Glücksburg, *b* 1 June 1888, *m* 28 April 1909, HRH Prince *Harald* Christian Frederik of Denmark (*b* 8 Oct 1876; *d* 30 March 1949), and *d* 30 June 1962, having had issue (*see p* 278).
4*c* HH Princess *Adelheid* Luise of Schleswig-Holstein-Sonderburg-Glücksburg, *b* 19 Oct 1889, *m* 1 Aug 1914, HSH *Friedrich* Hermann Heinrich Christian Hans, 3rd Prince zu Solms-Baruth (*b* 25 March 1886; *d* 12 Sept 1951), and *d* 11 June 1964, leaving issue,
1*d* •HSH *Friedrich* Wilhelm Ferdinand Hermann Hans, 4th Prince zu Solms-Baruth [*Farm Dabib, PO Marienthal, SW Africa*], *b* 22 Dec 1926, *m* 17 Aug 1963, •Baroness *Birgitta* Ingrid Zoë Maria Cecilia (*b* 9 Jan 1924), only dau of Eduard, Count von Berchem-Königsfeld, and has issue,
1*e* •Hereditary Count Friedrich Eduard Philipp zu Solms-Baruth, *b* 27 Nov 1963.
2*e* •Count Julian Immanuel Friedrich Christian Hubertus zu Solms-Baruth, *b* 6 Aug 1965.
1*d* •Countess Victoria *Friederike-Louise* Karoline Mathilde Hedwig Dorothea Rosa Helene Marka Marie zu Solms-Baruth [*Salzburg, Münzgasse 2, Austria*], *b* 10 Oct 1916.
2*d* •Countess *Feodora* Hedwig Luise Victoria Alexandra Marie zu Solms-Baruth, *b* 5 April 1920, *m* 1st 28 Nov 1942, Gert Schenk (*b* 2 July 1910; *d* 23 Aug 1957), and has issue,
1*e* •Sebastian Heinrich Schenk, *b* 27 Aug 1946.
2*e* •Christian Eric Gisbert Schenk, *b* 18 Aug 1953.
She *m* 2ndly 6 Oct 1961, •HSH *Karl Adolf* Franz Joseph Marie Aloys Ferdinand Gobert, 10th Prince von Auersperg (*b* 13 March 1915), and has further issue,
1*e* •HSH Princess Karoline Mathilde Adelheid Gobertina von Auersperg, *b* 24 May 1962.
3*d* •Countess *Rosa* Cecilie Karoline-Mathilde Irene Sibylla Anna zu Solms-Baruth, *b* 15 May 1925, *m* 3 Nov 1955, •Neville Lewis (*b* 8 Oct 1895) [*42 Rowan Street, Stellenbosch, Cape Province, S Africa*], and has issue,
•Frederick Henry Lewis, *b* 23 Nov 1961.
•Caroline Isabelle Anne Lewis, *b* 30 Aug 1956.

4d •Countess *Caroline-Mathilde* Luise Adelheid Elisabeth zu Solms-Baruth, *b* 15 April 1929, *m* 12 May 1963, •Johann van Steenderen (*b* 8 June 1905).
5c HH Princess Viktoria Irene Adelheid Auguste Alberta Feodora *Caroline-Mathilde* of Schleswig-Holstein-Sonderburg-Glücksburg, *b* 11 May 1894, *m* 27 May 1920, •Count *Hans* Georg Eduard zu Solms-Baruth (*b* 3 April 1893), and *d* 1972, leaving issue,
1d •Count *Friedrich-Hans* Ferdinand Wilhelm zu Solms-Baruth [*St Veit a d Glan, Klagenfurter Strasse 32, Kärnten, Austria*], *b* 3 March 1923, *m* 30 April 1950, •HSH Princess Oda zu Stolberg-Wernigerode (*b* 10 June 1925), 2nd dau of HSH Botho, 3rd Prince zu Stolberg, and has issue,
1e •Count *Christian-Friedrich* zu Solms-Baruth, *b* 13 July 1954.
1e •Countess *Irina* Renata zu Solms-Baruth, *b* 25 July 1953.
2e •Countess *Huberta* Désirée zu Solms-Baruth, *b* 22 Aug 1958.
2d •Count *Hubertus* Conrad Ferdinand zu Solms-Baruth, *b* 7 Dec 1934, *m* 12 Aug 1961, *Elisabeth-Charlotte* (*b* 3 Dec 1935; *d* 1967), 4th dau of Ernst Otto von Kerssenbrock, and has issue,
1e •Count Rupprecht Caspar Friedrich zu Solms-Baruth, *b* 5 Aug 1963.
1e •Countess Friederike Donata zu Solms-Baruth, *b* 23 March 1965.
2e •Countess Eilika Sophie zu Solms-Baruth, *b* 8 Aug 1966.
1d •Countess *Victoria Louise* Friederike Caroline Mathilde zu Solms-Baruth, *b* 13 March 1921, *m* 1st 25 Jan 1942 (*m* diss by div 1946), HH Prince *Friedrich Josias* Carl Eduard Ernst Kyrill Harald of Saxe-Coburg and Gotha, Head of the Ducal House (*b* 29 Nov 1918), and has issue (*see p* 300). She *m* 2ndly 6 Nov 1947, •Richard Whitten (*b* 9 May 1910) [*1528 Eighth Street, New Orleans, Louisiana 70115, USA*], and has further issue,
•Franklin Gagnard, *b* 23 Aug 1948.
2b HH Prince *Albert* Christian Adolf Karl Eugen of Schleswig-Holstein-Sonderburg-Glücksburg, *b* 15 March 1863, *m* 1st 14 Oct 1906, Countess *Ortrud* Agnes Maria Auguste Klara (*b* 15 Jan 1879; *d* 28 April 1918), yst dau of H Ill H Karl, Count zu Ysenburg und Büdingen in Meerholz, and had issue,
1c HH Prince *Friedrich Wilhelm* August Ferdinand Alexander Karl Eduard Ernst Gustav of Schleswig-Holstein-Sonderburg-Glücksburg, *b* 29 Dec 1909; *k* in action in Word War II 6 June 1940.
2c HH Prince *Johann Georg* Wilhelm Viktor Heinrich Konstantin Günther Friedrich Christian of Schleswig-Holstein-Sonderburg-Glücksburg, *b* 24 July 1911; *k* in action in World War II 23 June 1941.
3c •HH Prince *Friedrich Ferdinand* Karl Ernst August Wilhelm Harald Kasimir Nicola of Schleswig-Holstein-Sonderburg-Glücksburg [*2392 Schloss Glücksburg/Ostsee, Germany*], *b* 14 May 1913, *m* 1 Sept 1943, •HH Duchess *Anastasia* Alexandrine Cecilie Marie Louise Wilhelmine (*b* 11 Nov 1922), yr dau of HRH Grand Duke Friedrich Franz IV of Mecklenburg-Schwerin, and has issue (*see p* 291).
1c HH Princess Viktoria *Marie-Louise* Agnes Calma Elisabeth Irmgard of Schleswig-Holstein-Sonderburg-Glücksburg, *b* 8 Dec 1908, *m* 1st 19 April 1934 (*m* diss by div 1955), Baron Rudolf Carl von Stengel (*b* 7 Dec 1899), and had issue,
•Baroness Hertha-Margarethe Elisabeth Ortrud Dorothea Leopoldine Maria von Stengel, *b* 10 Jan 1935, *m* 27 Dec 1955, •Adolfo de Ceno Clemares, and has issue,
1e •Adolfo-Carlos de Ceno Clemares Stengel, *b* 14 Nov 1957.
2e •Enrique-Antonio de Ceno Clemares Stengel, *b* 30 Jan 1959.
1e •Maria-Teresa de Ceno Clemares Stengel, *b* 1 Oct 1956.
She *m* 2ndly 8 Oct 1962, •HSH Prince *Friedrich Christian* Wilhelm Alexander of Schaumburg-Lippe (*b* 5 Jan 1906) (*see p* 251), and *d* Dec 1969.
He *m* 2ndly 15 Sept 1920, HSH Princess Hertha (*b* 27 Dec 1883; *d* 30 May 1972), 7th dau of HSH Bruno, 3rd Prince zu Ysenburg und Büdingen, and *d* 23 April 1948, having by her had issue,
2c •HH Princess *Ortrud* Bertha Adelheid Hedwig of Schleswig-Holstein-Sonderburg-Glücksburg, *b* 19 Dec 1925, *m* 4 Sept 1951, •HRH Prince *Ernst August* Georg Wilhelm Christian Ludwig Franz Josef Nikolaus of Hanover, Duke of Brunswick and Lüneburg, Head of the Royal House of Hanover (*b* 18 March 1914), and has issue (*see p* 290).
1b HH Princess Marie Caroline *Auguste* Ida Luise of Schleswig-Holstein-Sonderburg-Glücksburg, *b* 27 Feb 1844, *m* 6 Dec 1884, HH Prince *Wilhelm* Friedrich Ernst of Hesse-Philippsthal-Barchfeld (*b* 3 Oct 1831; *d* 17 Jan 1890), and *d* 16 Sept 1932, leaving issue,
HH Prince *Christian* Ludwig Friedrich Adolf Alexis Wilhelm Ferdinand of Hesse (-Philippsthal-Barchfeld), *b* 16 June 1887, *m* 1st (morganatically) 14 Jan 1915, Elisabeth, *cr* Baroness von Barchfeld 14 Jan 1915, Princess of Hesse from 14 Nov 1921 (*b* 17 Aug 1893; *d* 2 Feb 1957), dau of Richard Reid Rogers, and had issue,
1d •(Prinz) Wilhelm *Richard Christian* Chlodwig Albert Carl Eduard Alexis von Hessen (-Philippsthal-Barchfeld) [*136 Calle de Jardin, Tucson, Arizona, USA*], *b* 14 Oct 1917, *m* 8 April 1953, •Maria Lourdes (*b* 15 Oct 1926), dau of Carlos Lafontaine.
2d •(Prinz) *Waldemar* Christian Victor Heinrich Philipp von Hessen (-Philippsthal-Barchfeld) [*3108 Ella Lee Lane, Houston 19, Texas, USA*], *b* 20 Sept 1919, *m* 9 Feb 1952, •Ellen Jane (*b* 25 Nov 1922), dau of Robert Hamilton, and has issue,
1e •(Prinz) Alexander von Hessen (-Philippsthal-Barchfeld), *b* 31 Aug 1956.
2e •(Prinz) Henry Christian von Hessen (-Philippsthal-Barchfeld), *b* 15 March 1963.
1d •(Prinzessin) *Elisabeth Auguste* Eunice Bertha Caroline Luise Christiane von Hessen (-Philippsthal-Barchfeld), *b* 2 Nov 1915, *m* 6 Aug 1949 (*m* diss by div), Jacques Olivetti.
2d •(Prinzessin) Marie Louise *Olga* Elvira Victoria von Hessen (-Philippsthal-Barchfeld), *b* 30 Dec 1921, *m* 13 June 1952, •Michael Savich (*b* 25 July 1924) [*Eminvafi Corusu Muallim Naci Cadessi 105, Ortaköy-Istanbul, Turkey*].
He *m* 2ndly 25 June 1958, •Anne Everett (*b* 23 Aug 1906) [*CH-1200 Genf, 11 Quai du Mont Blanc, Switzerland; Villa Chantemerle, Avenue Justinia, F-06 Cannes, France*], and *d* 1971.
2b HH Princess *Luise* Karoline Juliane of Schleswig-Holstein-Sonderburg-Glücksburg, *b* 6 Jan 1858, *m* 29 April 1891, as his 2nd wife, HSH *Georg Viktor*, Prince of Waldeck and Pyrmont (*b* 14 Jan 1831; *d* 12 May 1893), and *d* 2 July 1936, leaving issue (*see p* 250).
3b HH Princess *Marie* Wilhelmine Luise Ida Friederike Mathilde Hermine of Schleswig-Holstein-Sonderburg-Glücksburg, Abbess of Itzehoe, *b* 31 Aug 1859; *d unm* 26 June 1941.
3a HH Prince Wilhelm of Schleswig-Holstein-Sonderburg-Glücksburg, *b* 10 April 1816; *d unm* 5 Sept 1893.
4a HM King Christian IX of Denmark (1863-1906), *b* 8 April 1818, *m* 26 May 1842, HH Princess *Luise* Wilhelmine Friederike Caroline Auguste Julie (*b* 7 Sept 1817; *d* 29 Sept 1898), 3rd dau of HH Wilhelm, Landgrave of Hesse-Cassel (*see p* 286), and *d* 29 Jan 1906, leaving issue,
1b HM King (Christian) *Frederik VIII* (Wilhelm Carl) of Denmark (1906-1912), *b* 3 June 1843, *m* 28 July 1869, HRH Princess *Louise* Josephine Eugenie (*b* 31 Oct 1851; *d* 20 March

1926), only dau of HM King Karl XV of Sweden, and Norway (*see p* 215), and *d* 14 May 1912, leaving issue,

1*c* HM King *Christian X* (Carl Frederik Albert Alexander Wilhelm) of Denmark (1912-1947), KG (1914), GCB (1908), GCVO (1901), had Royal Victorian Chain, hon Adm in British Navy, Col-in-Chief The Buffs, hon mem Inst of Naval Architects (1949), Assoc KStJ, *b* 26 Sept 1870, *m* 26 April 1898, HH Duchess *Alexandrine* Auguste (*b* 24 Dec 1879; *d* 28 Dec 1952), elder dau of HRH Grand Duke Friedrich Franz III of Mecklenburg-Schwerin, (*see p* 289), and *d* 20 April 1947, leaving issue,

1*d* HM King (Christian) *Frederik IX* (Franz Michael Carl Valdemar Georg) of Denmark (1947-1972), KG (1951), GCB (1948), GCVO, Col-in-Chief The Buffs 1947 (The QO Buffs 1961), hon Adm in Brit Navy 1948, hon Air Chief Marshal RAF 1959, had Order of the Seraphim of Sweden, etc, *b* 11 March 1899, *m* 24 May 1935, •HRH Princess *Ingrid* Victoria Sofia Louise Margareta (*b* 28 March 1910) [*Amalienborg Palace, Copenhagen, Denmark*], only dau of HM King Gustaf VI Adolf of Sweden (*see p* 224), and *d* 14 Jan 1972, leaving issue,

1*e* •HM Queen *Margrethe II* (Alexandrine Thorhildur Ingrid) of Denmark, *s* her father 1972 [*Amalienborg Palace, Copenhagen, Denmark*], *b* 16 April 1940, *m* 10 June 1967, •HRH Prince Henrik of Denmark (so *cr* 10 June 1967), formerly Comte Henri-Marie-Jean-André de Laborde de Monpezat (*b* 11 June 1934), and has issue,

1*f* •HRH Crown Prince *Frederik* André Henrik Christian of Denmark, *b* 26 May 1968.

2*f* •HRH Prince *Joachim* Holger Valdemar Christian of Denmark, *b* 7 June 1969.

2*e* •HRH Princess *Benedikte* Astrid Ingeborg Ingrid of Denmark, has Order of the Elephant of Denmark, *b* 29 April 1944, *m* 3 Feb 1968, •HSH *Richard* Casimir Karl August Robert Constantin, 6th Prince zu Sayn-Wittgenstein-Berleburg (*b* 29 Oct 1934), and has issue (*see p* 269).

3*e* •HRH Princess *Anne-Marie* Dagmar Ingrid of Denmark, *b* 30 Aug 1946, *m* 18 Sept 1964, •HM King Constantine II of the Hellenes (*b* 2 June 1940) and has issue (*see p* 279).

2*d* •HRH Hereditary Prince (from 5 June 1953) *Knud* Christian Friedrich Michael of Denmark [*Slot, 2800 Kgs, Sorgenfri Lyngby, Denmark*], *b* 27 July 1900, *m* 8 Sept 1933, •HH Princess *Caroline-Mathilde* Louise Dagmar Christiane Maud Augusta Ingeborg Thyra Adelheid (*b* 27 April 1912), 2nd dau of HRH Prince Harald of Denmark (*see below*), and has issue,

1*e* •HH Prince *Ingolf* Christian Frederik Knud Harald Gorm Gustav Viggo Valdemar Aage of Denmark, renounced his titles and rights of succession and received the title of Count of Rosenborg 4 Jan 1968, *b* 17 Feb 1940, *m* 13 Jan 1968, •Inge, dau of Georg Terney.

2*e* •HH Prince *Christian* Frederik Knud Harald Carl Oluf Gustav Georg Erik of Denmark, renounced his titles and rights of succession and received the title of Count of Rosenborg 27 Feb 1970, *b* 22 Oct 1942, *m* 27 Feb 1970, •Anne-Dorthe, dau of Villy Maltofte-Nielsen.

1*e* •HH Princess *Elisabeth* Caroline-Mathilde Alexandrine Helena Olga Thyra Feodora Estrid Margarethe Désirée of Denmark, *b* 8 May 1935.

2*c* HM King Haakon VII of Norway (1905-1957), formerly HRH Prince Christian Frederik *Carl* Georg Valdemar Axel of Denmark, KG (1906), GCB (1896), GCVO (1901), received Royal Victorian Chain 1902, hon Adm in Brit Navy 1906, hon Col 55th (Suffolk and Norfolk Yeo), Anti-Tank Regt RA (TA), hon Col 28th (King's Own Royal Regt) (Norfolk Yeo), Light AA Regt (TA) 1956, Col-in-Chief The Green Howards, KStJ, had Orders of the Seraphim of Sweden and the Elephant of Denmark, elected King of Norway 18 Nov 1905, *b* 3 Aug 1872, *m* 22 July 1896, HRH Princess *Maud* Charlotte Mary Victoria, VA, CI, GCVO, DGCStJ (*b* 26 Nov 1869; *d* 20 Nov 1938), yst dau of HM King Edward VII, and *d* 21 Sept 1957, leaving issue (*see p* 307).

3*c* HRH Prince *Harald* Christian Frederik of Denmark, had Order of the Elephant of Denmark, *b* 8 Oct 1876, *m* 28 April 1909, HH Princess *Helena* Adelheid Viktoria Marie (*b* 1 June 1888; *d* 30 June 1962), 3rd dau of HH Friedrich Ferdinand, Duke of Schleswig-Holstein-Sonderburg-Glücksburg (*see p* 276), and *d* 30 March 1949, leaving issue,

1*d* •HH Prince *Gorm* Christian Frederik Hans Harald of Denmark, has Order of the Elephant [*Lykkesholm, Nejede, Hillerod, Denmark*], *b* 24 Feb 1919.

2*d* •HH Prince *Oluf* Christian Carl Axel of Denmark, has Order of the Elephant, renounced his titles and rights of succession and received the title of Count of Rosenborg 13 Jan 1948 [*Heilsmindevej 2, Charlottenlund, Copenhagen, Denmark*], *b* 10 March 1923, *m* 4 Feb 1948, •Annie Helene *Dorrit* (*b* 8 Sept 1926), dau of Gunnar Puggaard-Müller, and has issue,

•Count *Ulrik* Harald Gunnar Oluf af Rosenborg, *b* 17 Dec 1950.

•Countess *Charlotte* Helene Annie Dorrit af Rosenborg, *b* 11 April 1953.

1*d* •HH Princess *Feodora* Louise Caroline Mathilde Viktoria Alexandra Frederikke Johanne of Denmark, *b* 3 July 1910, *m* 9 Sept 1937, •HSH Prince *Christian* Nikolaus Wilhelm Friedrich Albert Ernst Stephan of Schaumburg-Lippe (*b* 20 Feb 1898), and has issue (*see p* 285).

2*d* •HH Princess *Caroline-Mathilde* Louise Dagmar Christiane Maud Augusta Ingeborg Thyra Adelheid of Denmark, *b* 27 April 1912, *m* 8 Sept 1933, •HRH Hereditary Prince Knud of Denmark (*b* 27 July 1900), and has issue (*see above*).

3*d* HH Princess *Alexandrine-Louise* Caroline-Mathilde Dagmar of Denmark, *b* 12 Dec 1914, *m* 22 Jan 1937, H Ill H Count *Luitpold Alfred* Friedrich Karl zu Castell-Castell (*b* 14 Nov 1904; *k* in action in World War II 6 Nov 1941), and *d* 26 April 1962, leaving issue (*see p* 269).

4*c* HRH Prince Christian Frederik Wilhelm Valdemar *Gustav* of Denmark, *b* 4 March 1887; *d unm* 5 Oct 1944.

1*c* HRH Princess *Luise* Caroline Josephine Sophie Thyra Olga of Denmark, *b* 17 Feb 1875, *m* 5 May 1896, HSH Prince *Friedrich* Georg Wilhelm Bruno of Schaumburg-Lippe (*b* 30 Jan 1868; *d* 12 Dec 1945), and *d* 4 April 1906, leaving issue (*see p* 285).

2*c* HRH Princess *Ingeborg* Charlotta Carolina Friederike Louisa of Denmark, *b* 2 Aug 1878, *m* 27 Aug 1897, HRH Prince Oscar *Carl* Vilhelm of Sweden, Duke of Västergötland (*b* 27 Feb 1861; *d* 24 Oct 1951), and *d* 11 March 1958, having had issue (*see p* 226).

3*c* HRH Princess *Thyra* Louise Caroline Amalie Augusta Elisabeth of Denmark, *b* 14 March 1880; *d unm* 2 Nov 1945.

4*c* HRH Princess *Dagmar* Louise Elisabeth of Denmark, *b* 23 May 1890, *m* 23 Nov 1922, •Jørgen Castenskiold, Royal Danish Court Chamberlain (*b* 30 Nov 1893) [*Rungsted Kyst, Denmark*], and *d* 11 Oct 1961, leaving issue,

1*d* •Carl Frederik Anton Jørgen Castenskiold, *b* 13 Nov 1923, *m* 23 Oct 1948, •Benta (*b* 5 April 1927), dau of Helmuth Grevenkop-Castenskiold, and has issue,

1*e* •Helmuth Jørgen Frederik Carl Castenskiold, *b* 9 Aug 1949.

2*e* •Jørgen Axel Holten Castenskiold, *b* 16 Dec 1951.

1e •Dagmar Birgitte Margaretha Castenskiold, *b* 26 Jan 1956.
2d •Christian Ludvig Gustav Fritz Castenskiold [*15224 Encanto Drive, Sherman Oaks, California 91403, USA*], *b* 10 July 1926, *m* 11 Nov 1952, •Cecily (*b* 10 Aug 1927), dau of Richard W. Abbotts, and has issue,
•Alexandra Castenskiold, *b* 11 June 1965.
3d Jørgen Frederik Aage Erik Helge Castenskiold, *b* 16 March 1928, *m* 1st 14 July 1956 (*m* diss by div 1958), Kirsten (*b* 24 April 1934), dau of Christian Otto Schlichtkrull, and had issue,
1e •Susanne Helene Dagmar Castenskiold, *b* 13 April 1957.
He *m* 2ndly 17 Oct 1959, •Bridget (*b* 3 Sept 1932) [*Rônnebackshuse, Naestved, Denmark*], dau of Ernst Tengstedt, and *d* 5 May 1964, having by her had issue,
2e •Marie-Louise Dagmar Johanne Birgit Castenskiold, *b* 10 Oct 1960.
1d •Dagmar Louise Thyra Sophie Augusta Petra Castenskiold, *b* 11 Sept 1931, *m* 4 April 1950, •Poul Bitsch (*b* 5 Oct 1930) [*Raageleje, Denmark*], and has issue,
1e •Erik Jørgen Marius Poul Carl Christian Bitsch, *b* 9 Aug 1950.
2e •Hans Jørgen Gorm Bitsch, *b* 14 Jan 1954.
3e •Christian Axel Carl Bitsch, *b* 18 Aug 1959.
2b HM King George I of the Hellenes (1863-1913), formerly HRH Prince Christian *Wilhelm* Ferdinand Adolf Georg of Denmark, elected King of the Hellenes 6 June 1863, renounced his rights of succession to the throne of Denmark for himself and his descendants 12 Sept 1863, *b* 24 Dec 1845, *m* 27 Oct 1867, HIH Grand Duchess Olga Constantinovna, Regent of Greece Oct-Dec 1920 (*b* 3 Sept 1851; *d* 18 June 1926), elder dau of HIH Grand Duke Constantine Nikolaievitch of Russia (*see p* 258), and was assassinated at Salonica 18 March 1913, having had issue,
1c HM King Constantine I of the Hellenes (1913-1917 and 1920-1922), abdicated for himself and his eldest son 11 June 1917, resumed the throne following a plebiscite 19 Dec 1920, again abdicated in favour of his eldest son 28 Sept 1922, *b* 21 July 1868, *m* 27 Oct 1889, HRH Pss *Sophie* Dorothea Ulrike Alice (*b* 14 June 1870; *d* 13 Jan 1932), 3rd dau of HIM Friedrich III, German Emperor and King of Prussia (*see p* 302), and *d* 11 Jan 1923, having had issue,
1d HM King George II of the Hellenes (1922-1924, 1935-1941 and 1946-1947), KG (1938), GCMG (1936), GCVO (1909), DSO (1941), received Royal Victorian Chain 1934, hon LLD Camb Univ 1941, GCStJ, had Orders of the Elephant of Denmark, Carol I of Roumania (with collar), the Annunciata of Italy, etc, *s* to the throne on his father's second abdication 28 Sept 1922, left the country 25 March 1924, restored 3 Nov 1935, again forced to leave the country on the German invasion 23 April 1941, again restored after a plebiscite 28 Sept 1946, *b* 20 July 1890, *m* 27 Feb 1921 (*m* diss by div 1935), HRH Princess *Elisabeth* Charlotte Josephine Victoria Alexandra, VA (*b* 12 Oct 1894; *d* 14 Nov 1956), eldest dau of HM King Ferdinand of Roumania (*see p* 296), and *dsp* 1 April 1947.
2d HM King Alexander I of the Hellenes (1917-1920), *s* to the throne on his father's first abdication 11 June 1917, *b* 1 Aug 1893, *m* 14 Nov 1919, Aspasia, recognised as Princess Alexander of Greece by Royal Decree 10 Sept 1922 (*b* 4 Sept 1896; *d* 7 Aug 1972), dau of Col Petros Mano, and *d* 25 Oct 1920, leaving issue,
•HRH Princess Alexandra of Greece and Denmark [*Giardino Eden, 138 La Giudecca, Venice, Italy*], *b* 25 March 1921, *m* 20 March 1944, HM King Peter II of Yugoslavia (*b* 6 Sept 1923; *d* 3 Nov 1970), and has issue (*see p* 296).
3d HM King Paul I of the Hellenes (1947-1964), KG (1963), GCVO (1937), had the Orders of the Elephant of Denmark and Carol I of Roumania, etc, hon Adm in Brit Navy 1953, *b* 14 Dec 1901, *m* 9 Jan 1938, •HRH Princess *Frederika* Luise Thyra Viktoria Margarete Sophie Olga Cecile Isabelle Christa (*b* 18 April 1917), only dau of HRH Ernst August, Duke of Brunswick-Lüneburg, Head of the Royal House of Hanover (*see p* 290), and *d* 6 March 1964, leaving issue,
1e •HM King Constantine II of the Hellenes, *s* his father 1964, has Order of the Elephant of Denmark [*13 Via Appia Antica, Rome, Italy*], *b* 2 June 1940, *m* 18 Sept 1964, •HRH Princess *Anne-Marie* Dagmar Ingrid (*b* 30 Aug 1946), yst dau of HM late King Frederik IX of Denmark (*see p* 278), and has issue,
1f •HRH Crown Prince Paul of Greece, Duke of Sparta, *b* 20 May 1967.
2f •HRH Prince Nicholas of Greece and Denmark, *b* 1 Oct 1969.
1f •HRH Princess Alexia of Greece and Denmark, was Crown Princess of Greece from her birth until 20 May 1967, *b* 10 July 1965.
1e •HRH Princess Sophie (Sofia) of Greece and Denmark, *b* 2 Nov 1938, *m* 14 May 1962, •HRH Infante Don *Juan Carlos* Alfonso Victor Maria of Spain, Prince of the Asturias, The Prince of Spain (*b* 5 Jan 1938), and has issue (*see p* 305).
2e •HRH Princess Irene of Greece and Denmark, was Crown Princess of Greece from 6 March 1964 until 10 July 1965, *b* 11 May 1942.
1d •HRH Princess Helen of Greece and Denmark, now known as HM Queen Helen The Queen Mother of Roumania, has Grand Cross of the Order of St Olga and St Sophia of Greece [*Villa Sparta, San Domenico, Florence, Italy*], *b* 3 May 1896, *m* 10 March 1921 (*m* diss by div 1928), HM King Carol II of Roumania (*b* 16 Oct 1893; *d* 3 April 1953), and has issue (*see p* 295).
2d •HRH Princess Irene of Greece and Denmark, has Grand Cross of the Order of St Olga and St Sophia of Greece [*Villa Sparta, San Domenico, Florence, Italy*], *b* 13 Feb 1904, *m* 1 July 1939, HRH Prince *Aimone* Roberto Margherita Maria Giuseppe Torino of Savoy, 4th Duke of Aosta, formerly Duke of Spoleto and sometime HM King Tomislav II of Croatia (*b* 9 March 1900; *d* 29 Jan 1948), and has issue,
•HRH Prince *Amedeo* Umberto Constantino Giorgio Paolo Elena Maria Fiorenzo of Savoy, 5th Duke of Aosta [*Villa Diamino, Florence, Italy*], *b* 27 Sept 1943, *m* 22 July 1964, •HRH Princess *Claude*-Marie-Agnès-Catherine of France (*b* 11 Dec 1943), 5th dau of HRH Prince Henri, Comte de Paris, Head of the Royal House of France, and has issue,
1f •HRH Prince *Aimone* Emanuele Filiberto Luigi Amedeo Elena Maria Fiorenzo of Savoy, Duke of Apulia, *b* 13 Oct 1967.
1f •HRH Princess *Bianca* Irene Olga Elena Isabella Fiorenza Maria of Savoy, *b* 2 April 1966.
2f •HRH Princess *Mafalda* Giovanna Shams Maria Fiorenza of Savoy, *b* 20 Sept 1969.
3d •HRH Princess Katherine of Greece and Denmark, was granted the rank of a Duke's dau by HM King George VI 9 Sept 1947 and is known in England as Lady Katherine Brandram, has Grand Cross of the Order of St Olga and St Sophia (Greece), *b* 4 May 1913, *m* 21 April 1947, •Major *Richard* Campbell Andrew Brandram, MC, TD, RA (ret) (*b* 5 Aug 1911) [*Croft Cottage, Marlow-on-Thames, Bucks*], only son of late Richard Andrew Brandram of The Well House, Bickley, Kent (*see that family,* BURKE'S *LG*), and has issue,

●Richard *Paul* George Andrew Brandram, *b* 1 April 1948, *educ* Eton.
2*c* HRH Prince George of Greece and Denmark, GCB (1900), GCVO, Adm Greek Navy, Vice-Adm Danish Navy, High Commr for the Powers in Crete 1898-1906, had the Orders of the Elephant of Denmark, Seraphim of Sweden, etc, *b* 24 June 1869, *m* 21 Dec 1907, Princess Marie, author of many works on psycho-analysis (*b* 5 July 1882; *d* 21 Sept 1962), only dau of Prince Roland Bonaparte, and *d* 25 Nov 1957, leaving issue,
●HRH Prince Peter of Greece and Denmark, Lt-Col Greek Army Res, Pres Confed of Inter-Allied Res Offrs, anthropologist [*Lille Bernstorff, Jaegersborg Allé 115, 2820 Gentofte, Denmark*], *b* 3 Dec 1908, *m* 9 Sept 1939, ●Irene (*b* 2 June 1904), formerly wife of —, and dau of — Ovtchinnikoff.
●HRH Princess Eugénie of Greece and Denmark, has Order of St Olga and St Sophia of Greece [*132 Boulevard de la République, 92-St Cloud, France*], *b* 10 Feb 1910, *m* 1st 30 May 1938 (*m* diss by div 1946), HSH Prince *Dominik* Rainer Karl Hieronim Maria Nikolaj Alfons Radziwill (*b* 23 Jan 1911), and has issue (*see p* 233). She *m* 2ndly 28 Nov 1949 (*m* diss by div), HSH Prince *Raymund* Alexander Maria Louis Lamoral della Torre e Tasso, 2nd Duca di Castel Duino (*b* 16 March 1907), and has further issue,
●HSH Prince *Charles* Alexander George Peter Lucien Marie Raymund Luis Lamoral della Torre e Tasso, *b* 10 Feb 1952.
3*c* HRH Prince Nicholas of Greece and Denmark, GCB (1934), GCVO, Lt-Gen Greek Army, Kt of the Orders of the Elephant (Denmark), St Andrew (Russia), the Black Eagle (Prussia), the Annunziata (Italy) and Carol I (Roumania), author of *My Fifty Years* (1926). *b* 22 Jan 1872, *m* 29 Aug 1902, HIH Grand Duchess Helen Vladimirovna (*b* 17 Jan 1882; *d* 13 March 1957), only dau of HIH Grand Duke Vladimir Alexandrovitch of Russia, and *d* 8 Feb 1938, leaving issue,
1*d* ●HRH Princess Olga of Greece and Denmark, has Grand Cross of Order of St Olga and St Sophia of Greece, *b* 11 June 1903, *m* 22 Oct 1923, ●HRH Prince Paul of Yugoslavia, KG, GCVO, has Royal Victorian Chain, Regent of Yugoslavia 1934-41 (*b* 15 April 1893) [*31 rue Scheffer, Paris, France; Villa Reale di Pratolino, Florence, Italy*], and has had issue,
1*e* ●HRH Prince Alexander of Yugoslavia, *b* 13 Aug 1924, *m* 12 Feb 1955, ●HRH Princess *Maria Pia* Elena Elisabetta Margherita Milena Mafalda Ludovica Tecla Genna of Savoy (*b* 24 Sept 1934), eldest dau of HM King Umberto II of Italy, and has issue,
1*f* ●HRH Prince *Dmitri* Hubert Anton Peter Maria of Yugoslavia, *b* 18 June 1958.
2*f* ●HRH Prince *Michael* Nicolas Paul George Maria of Yugoslavia, *b* (twin with Prince Dmitri) 18 June 1958.
3*f* ●HRH Prince *Sergius* Wladimir Emanuel Maria of Yugoslavia, *b* 12 March 1963.
1*f* ●HRH Princess *Helene* Olga Lydia Tamara Maria of Yugoslavia, *b* (twin with Prince Sergius) 12 March 1963
2*e* HRH Prince Nicholas of Yugoslavia, *b* 29 June 1928; *d* as the result of a motor accident 12 April 1954.
1*e* ●HRH Princess Elisabeth of Yugoslavia, *b* 7 April 1936, *m* 1st 21 May 1960 (*m* diss by div 1966), Howard Oxenberg (*b* 1919), and has issue,
1*f* ●Catherine Oxenberg, *b* 22 Sept 1961.
2*f* ●Christina Oxenberg, *b* 27 Dec 1962.
She *m* 2ndly 23 Sept 1969, ●*Neil* Roxburgh Balfour (*b* 12 Aug 1944) [*215 Kings Road, SW3*], yst son of late Archibald Roxburgh Balfour, MC (*see* BURKE'S *LG*, BALFOUR *of Dawyck*), and has further issue,
1*f* ●*Nicholas* Augustus Balfour, *b* 6 June 1970.

2*d* HRH Princess Elisabeth of Greece and Denmark, *b* 24 May 1904, *m* 10 Jan 1934, H Ill H *Carl* Theodor Klemens, Count zu Toerring-Jettenbach (*b* 22 Sept 1900; *d* 14 May 1967), and *d* 11 Jan 1955, leaving issue,
●H Ill H *Hans Veit* Kaspar Nikolaus, Count zu Toerring-Jettenbach [*8 München 27, Mauerkircher Strasse 77, Germany*], *b* 11 Jan 1935, *m* 20 April 1964, ●HSH Princess *Henriette* Marie Amélie Margarethe Madeleine Therese zu Hohenlohe-Bartenstein (*b* 23 Aug 1938), 2nd dau of HSH Karl, 8th Prince zu Hohenlohe-Bartenstein-Bartenstein, and has issue,
●Hereditary Count *Ignatius* Maximilian Karl Veit zu Toerring-Jettenbach, *b* 30 March 1966.
●Countess *Clarissa* Beatrix Eleonora Maria zu Toerring-Jettenbach, *b* 31 March 1965.
●Countess *Helen* Marina Elisabeth zu Toerring-Jettenbach, *b* 20 May 1937, *m* 10 April 1956, ●HI and RH Archduke *Ferdinand* Karl Max Franz Otto Konrad Maria Joseph Ignatius Nikolaus of Austria (*b* 6 Dec 1918) and has issue (*see p* 241).
3*d* HRH Princess Marina of Greece and Denmark, CI (1937), GCVO (1948), GBE (1937), GCStJ, *b* 13 Dec 1906, *m* 29 Nov 1934, HRH Prince *George* Edward Alexander Edmund of Great Britain and Ireland, 1st Duke of Kent, KG, etc (*b* 20 Dec 1902; *k* in a flying accident on active service in World War II 25 Aug 1942), and *d* 27 Aug 1968, leaving issue (*see p* 307).
4*c* HRH Prince Andrew of Greece and Denmark, GCVO, Gen Greek Army, Kt of the Orders of the Elephant (Denmark), St Andrew (Russia), the Annunziata (Italy), and the Black Eagle (Prussia), author of *Towards Disaster—The Greek Army in Asia Minor in 1921* (translated into English by Princess Andrew 1930), *b* 2 Feb 1882, *m* 7 Oct 1903, HSH Princess Victoria *Alice* Elisabeth Julie Marie of Battenberg (*b* 25 Feb 1885; *d* 5 Dec 1969), elder dau of HSH Prince Louis of Battenberg, later 1st Marquess of Milford Haven (*see* BURKE'S *Peerage*), by his wife HGDH Princess Victoria Alberta, dau of HRH Grand Duke Ludwig IV of Hesse and by Rhine, by his wife HRH Princess Alice, 2nd dau of HM Queen Victoria (*see p* 303), and *d* 3 Dec 1944, having had issue,
1*d* ●HRH PRINCE PHILIP OF GREECE AND DENMARK, now HRH THE PRINCE PHILIP, DUKE OF EDINBURGH (*see separate biography, sub* THE ROYAL FAMILY, *p* 125; *and for account of earlier* Lineage *see p* 327).
1*d* ●HRH Princess Margarita of Greece and Denmark [*Schloss Langenburg, Württemberg, Germany*], *b* 18 April 1905, *m* 20 April 1931, HSH *Gottfried* Hermann Alfred Paul Maximilian Viktor, 8th Prince zu Hohenlohe-Langenburg (*b* 24 March 1897; *d* 11 May 1960), and has issue (*see p* 297).
2*d* HRH Princess Theodora of Greece and Denmark, *b* 30 May 1906, *m* 17 Aug 1931, HRH Prince *Berthold* Friedrich Wilhelm Ernst August Heinrich Karl, Margrave of Baden, Head of the Grand Ducal House of Baden (*b* 24 Feb 1906; *d* 27 Oct 1963), and *d* 16 Oct 1969, leaving issue (*see p* 290).
3*d* HRH Princess Cecilie of Greece and Denmark, *b* 22 June 1911, *m* 2 Feb 1931, HRH Hereditary Grand Duke *Georg* Donatus Wilhelm Nikolaus Eduard Heinrich Karl of Hesse and by Rhine (*b* 8 Nov 1906; *k* in an air accident 16 Nov 1937), and was *k* together with her husband, two sons and mother-in-law in an air accident at Steene, nr Ostend 16 Nov 1937, having had issue (*see p* 303).
4*d* ●HRH Princess Sophie of Greece and Denmark, *b* 26 June 1914, *m* 1st 15 Dec 1930, HH Prince *Christoph* Ernst August of Hesse (*b* 14 May 1901; *k* in action 7 Oct 1943), and has issue (*see p* 284). She *m* 2ndly (civil) 23

April and (religious) 24 April 1946, •HRH Prince *Georg Wilhelm* Ernst August Friedrich Karl of Hanover, Duke of Brunswick and Lüneburg (*b* 25 March 1915) and has further issue (*see p* 290).

5*c* HRH Prince Christopher of Greece and Denmark, Major-Gen Greek Army, Kt of the Orders of St Andrew (Russia), the Elephant (Denmark), and the Black Eagle (Prussia), author of *Memoirs of HRH Prince Christopher of Greece* (1938), *b* 29 July 1888, *m* 1st 1 Feb 1920, *Nancy* May (Anastasia) (*b* 20 Jan 1873; *d* 29 Aug 1923), widow of William Bateman Leeds, previously wife of George H. Worthington, and dau of W. E. Stewart. He *m* 2ndly 11 Feb 1929, HRH Princess *Françoise*-Isabelle-Louise-Marie of France (*b* 25 Dec 1902; *d* 25 Feb 1953), 2nd dau of HRH Prince Jean, Duke of Guise, Head of the Royal House of France, and *d* 21 Jan 1940, having by her had issue,

•HRH Prince Michael of Greece and Denmark, *b* 7 Jan 1939, *m* 7 Feb 1965, •Marina (*b* 17 July 1940), dau of Theodore Karella, and has issue,

•HRH Princess Alexandra of Greece and Denmark, *b* Oct 1968.

1*c* HRH Princess Alexandra of Greece and Denmark, *b* 18 Aug 1870, *m* 5 June 1889, as his 1st wife, HIH Grand Duke Paul Alexandrovitch of Russia (*b* 21 Sept 1860; *k* in the Russian Revolution 30 Jan 1919), and *d* 12 Sept 1891, leaving issue,

HIH Grand Duke Dimitri Pavlovitch of Russia, *b* 6 Sept 1891, *m* 21 Nov 1926 (*m* diss by div 1937), Anna *Audrey* (*b* 4 Jan 1904), 3rd dau of John Josiah Emery, of Cincinnati, Ohio, USA, and *d* 5 March 1942, leaving issue,

•HSH Prince Paul Dimitrievitch Romanovsky-Ilyinsky [279 *Queen's Lane, Palm Beach, Florida, USA*], *b* 27 Jan 1928, *m* 1st Oct 1949 (*m* diss by div 1952) Mary Evelyn, dau of William Prince. He *m* 2ndly 1 Oct 1952, •*Angelika* Philippa (*b* 22 March 1932), dau of Philip Kauffmann, and by her has issue,

1*f* •HSH Prince Dimitri Pavlovitch Romanovsky-Ilyinsky, *b* 1 May 1953.

2*f* •HSH Prince Michael Pavlovitch Romanovsky-Ilyinsky, *b* 4 Jan 1960.

1*f* •HSH Princess Paula Marie Pavlovna Romanovsky-Ilyinsky, *b* 18 May 1955.

2*f* •HSH Princess Ann Pavlovna Romanovsky-Ilyinsky, *b* 4 Sept 1959.

HIH Grand Duchess Marie Pavlovna of Russia, *b* 6 April 1890, *m* 1st 20 April 1908 (*m* diss by div 1914), HRH Prince Carl *Vilhelm* Ludvig of Sweden, Duke of Södermanland (*b* 17 June 1884; *d* 5 June 1965), and had issue (*see p* 265). She *m* 2ndly 6 Sept 1917 (*m* diss by div 1923), as his 1st wife, Prince Sergei Mikhailovitch Poutiatine (*b* 7 Dec 1893; *d* 1966), and *d* 13 Dec 1958, having had further issue,

Prince Roman Sergeievitch Poutiatine, *b* 15 June 1918; *d* 29 July 1919.

2*c* HRH Princess Marie of Greece and Denmark, *b* 20 Feb 1876, *m* 1st 30 April 1900. HIH Grand Duke George Mikhailovitch of Russia (*b* 11 Aug 1863; *k* in the Russian Revolution 30 Jan 1919), and had issue,

1*d* •HH Princess Nina Georgievna of Russia [*Wellfleet, Mass 02667, USA*], *b* 7 Jan 1901, *m* 3 Sept 1922, Prince Paul Alexandrovitch Chavchavadze (*b* 15 June 1899; *d* 8 July 1971), and has issue,

•Prince David Chavchavadze, *b* 20 May 1924, *m* 1st 13 Sept 1952 (*m* diss by div), Helen (*b* 1 Feb 1933), dau of Ellery Husted, and has issue,

1*f* •Princess Maria Chavchavadze, *b* 28 Aug 1953.

2*f* •Princess Alexandra Chavchavadze, *b* 24 Dec 1954.

He *m* 2ndly 28 Dec 1959, •Judith J. (*b* 26 March 1932), dau of John Clippinger, and by her has issue,

1*f* •Prince Michael Chavchavadze, *b* 1966.

3*f* •Princess Catherine Chavchavadze, *b* 29 Dec 1960.

2*d* HH Princess Xenia Georgievna of Russia, *b* 9 Aug 1903, *m* 1st 9 Oct 1921 (*m* diss by div 1930), William Bateman Leeds (*b* 19 Sept 1902), son of William Bateman Leeds, by his wife Nancy May Stewart (later Princess Christopher of Greece (*see above*), and had issue,

•*Nancy* Helen Marie Leeds, *b* 25 Feb 1925, *m* 22 Dec 1945, •Edward Judson Wynkoop (*b* 23 May 1917) [*24 River Street, Woodstock, Vermont 05091, USA*], son of Edward Judson Wynkoop, of Syracuse, New York, USA and has issue,

•Alexandra Wynkoop, *b* 30 March 1959.

She *m* 2ndly 10 Aug 1946, •Herman Jud (*b* 14 Feb 1911), and *d* 17 Sept 1965.

She *m* 2ndly 3 Dec 1922, Vice-Adm Pericles Joannides (*b* 1 Nov 1881; *d* 7 Feb 1965), and *d* 14 Dec 1940.

3*c* HRH Princess Olga of Greece and Denmark, *b* 26 March, *d* 20 Oct 1880.

3*b* HRH Prince Valdemar of Denmark, had Order of the Elephant of Denmark, Adm in the Danish Navy, *b* 27 Oct 1858, *m* 22 Oct 1885, HRH Princess *Marie*-Amélie-Françoise-Hélène (*b* 13 Jan 1865; *d* 4 Dec 1909), elder dau of HRH Prince Robert d'Orléans, Duke of Chartres, and *d* 14 Jan 1939, leaving issue,

1*c* HH Prince *Aage* Christian Alexander Robert, Count af Rosenborg, granted the qualification of Royal Highness 5 Feb 1904, renounced his royal titles and rights of succession to the throne of Denmark and assumed the style of HH Prince Aage, Count af Rosenborg 5 Feb 1914, had Order of the Elephant of Denmark, served as Cmdr 1st Regt French Foreign Legion 1923-40, had Orders of the Elephant (Denmark), the Black Eagle (Prussia), and the Seraphim (Sweden), author of *My Life in the Foreign Legion* (1928), *b* 10 June 1887, *m* 17 Jan 1914, *Mathilde* Emilie Francesca Maria (*b* 17 Sept 1885; *d* 16 Oct 1949), dau of Conte Giorgio Calvi di Bergolo, and *d* 29 Feb 1940, leaving issue,

•Count *Valdemar* Alexander Georg Luigi af Rosenborg, Kt of Honour and Devotion of the Sov Order of Malta [*88 Avenue Foch, Paris XVI, France*], *b* 3 Jan 1915, *m* 20 April 1949, •*Floria*-Marie-Josèphe-Pierrette-Charlotte (*b* 10 Aug 1925), dau of Baron Gérald d'Huart St Mauris.

2*c* HRH (from 5 Feb 1904) Prince *Axel* Christian Georg of Denmark, Adm Royal Danish Navy 1958, mem Internat Olympic Cttee 1932-64, had Orders of the Elephant (Denmark), the Seraphim (Sweden), and the Black Eagle (Prussia), *b* 12 Aug 1888, *m* 22 May 1919, •HRH Princess *Margaretha* Sofia Lovisa Ingeborg (*b* 25 June 1899) [*Bernstorffshøj bei Gentofte, Denmark*], eldest dau of HRH Prince Carl of Sweden (*see p* 226), and *d* 14 July 1964, leaving issue,

1*d* •HH Prince *Georg* Valdemar Carl Axel of Denmark, CVO, Def Attaché Royal Danish Embassy, London, Mil, Naval and Air Attaché Royal Danish Embassy, Paris [*81 Carlisle Mansions, Carlisle Place, SW1*], *b* 16 April 1920, *m* 16 Sept 1950, •*Anne* Ferelith Fenella (*b* 4 Dec 1917), formerly wife of Major Viscount Anson, Gren Guards (*see* BURKE'S *Peerage*, LICHFIELD, E), and 2nd dau of late Hon John Herbert Bowes-Lyon, DL (*see* BURKE'S *Peerage*, STRATHMORE AND KINGHORNE, E).

2*d* •*Flemming* Valdemar Carl Axel, Count af Rosenborg, formerly HH Prince Flemming of Denmark, renounced his style and title as a Prince of Denmark and received the title of Count af Rosenborg 14 June 1949, Cmdr Royal Danish Navy, has the Order of the Elephant of Denmark [*Skowangen 34, Charlottenlund, Denmark*], *b* 9 March 1922, *m* 24 May 1949, •Alice *Ruth* (*b* 8 Oct 1924), dau of Kaj Nielsen, and has issue,

1e •Count Valdemar Georg Flemming Kai *Axel* af Rosenborg, *b* 24 Jan 1950.
2e •Count *Birger* Valdemar Georg Flemming Kai Axel af Rosenborg, *b* (twin with Count Axel) 24 Jan 1950.
3e •Count *Carl Johann* Valdemar Georg Flemming Kai Axel af Rosenborg, *b* 30 May 1952.
1e •Countess *Désirée* Märtha Ingeborg af Rosenborg, *b* 2 Feb 1955.
3c HH Prince *Erik* Frederik Christian Alexander, Count af Rosenborg, granted the qualification of Royal Highness 5 Feb 1904, renounced his royal titles and rights of succession to the throne of Denmark and assumed the style of HH Prince Erik, Count af Rosenborg 2 Dec 1923, *b* 8 Nov 1890, *m* 11 Feb 1924 (*m* diss by div 1937), *Lois* Frances (*b* 2 Aug 1897; *d* 26 Feb 1941), dau of John Booth, and *d* 10 Sept 1950, leaving issue,
•Count *Christian* Edward Valdemar Jean Frederik Peter af Rosenborg, *b* 16 July 1932, *m* 10 Aug 1962, •Karin (*b* 12 Aug 1938), dau of Folmer Lüttichau, and has issue,
•Count Valdemar Erik Flemming Christian af Rosenborg, *b* 9 July 1965.
•Countess *Alexandra* Dagmar Frances Marie Margrethe af Rosenborg, *b* 5 Feb 1927, *m* 2 May 1951, •*Ivar* Emil Vind, Master of the Royal Hunt (*b* 5 Jan 1921), and has issue,
1e •Erik Ove Carl John Emil Vind, *b* 5 May 1954.
2e •Georg Christian Valdemar Vind, *b* 5 Aug 1958.
1e •Marie-Louise Frances Elisabeth Vind, *b* 7 Feb 1952.
4c HH Prince *Viggo* Christian Adolf Georg, Count af Rosenborg, granted the qualification of Royal Highness 5 Feb 1904, renounced his royal titles and rights of succession to the throne of Denmark and assumed the style of HH Prince Viggo, Count af Rosenborg 21 Dec 1923, had the Order of the Elephant (Denmark), *b* 25 Dec 1893, *m* 10 June 1924, *Eleanor* Margaret (*b* 5 Nov 1895; *d* 3 July 1966), dau of James Green, and *dsp* 4 Jan 1970.
1c •HRH (from 5 Feb 1904) Princess *Margrethe* Françoise Louise Marie Helene of Denmark [*7 rue du Mon-Valerien, Saint Cloud, Seine-et-Oise, France*], *b* 17 Sept 1895, *m* 9 June 1921, HRH Prince *René*-Charles-Marie-Joseph of Bourbon-Parma (*b* 17 Oct 1894; *d* 30 July 1962), and has had issue,
1d HRH Prince *Jacques*-Marie-Antoine-Robert-Valdemar-Charles-Félix-Sixte-Ansgar of Bourbon-Parma, *b* 9 June 1922, *m* 9 June 1947, •Countess *Birgitte* Alexandra Maria (*b* 29 June 1922) [*Fredshøj, D-K 4320, Lejr, Denmark*], dau of late Count Joseph Holstein-Ledreborg, and *d* 5 Nov 1964, leaving issue,
1e •HRH Prince Philippe of Bourbon-Parma, *b* 22 Jan 1949.
2e •HRH Prince Alain of Bourbon-Parma.
1e •HRH Princess Lorraine of Bourbon-Parma, *b* 27 July 1951.
2d •HRH Prince *Michel*-Marie-Xavier-Valdemar-Georges-Robert-Charles-Aymard of Bourbon-Parma [*F-78 Château de Crespières, Seine-et-Oise, France*], *b* 4 March 1926, *m* 9 June 1951, •HSH Princess Yolande (*b* 26 April 1928), dau of HSH Prince Joseph de Broglie-Revel, and has issue,
1e •HRH Prince Eric of Bourbon-Parma, *b* 28 Aug 1953.
2e •HRH Prince *Charles*-Emanuel of Bourbon-Parma, *b* 3 June 1961.
1e •HRH Princess Inez of Bourbon-Parma, *b* 9 May 1952.
2e •HRH Princess Sybil of Bourbon-Parma, *b* 10 Nov 1954.
3e •HRH Princess Victoire of Bourbon-Parma, *b* 8 Nov 1957.
3d •HRH Prince André of Bourbon-Parma [*75 rue du Cherche Midi, F-75 Paris 7e, France*], *b* 6 March 1928, *m* (civil) 2 May and (religious) 9 May 1960, •Marina (*b* 5 Sept 1935), dau of Paul Gacry, and has issue,
1e •Axel de Bourbon-Parme.
1e •Sophie de Bourbon-Parme, *b* 13 Nov 1961.
2e •Astrid de Bourbon-Parme.
1d •HRH Princess *Anne*-Antoinette-Françoise-Charlotte of Bourbon-Parma, has French Croix de Guerre, *b* 18 Sept 1923, *m* 10 June 1948, •HM King Michael of Roumania, GCVO (*b* 25 Oct 1921), and has issue (*see p* 295).
1b HRH Princess *Alexandra* Caroline Marie Charlotte Louisa Julia of Denmark, *b* 1 Dec 1844, *m* 10 March 1863, HM King Edward VII of Great Britain and Ireland, Emperor of India (*b* 9 Nov 1841; *d* 6 May 1910), and *d* 20 Nov 1925, having had issue (*see p* 306).
2b HRH Princess Marie Sophie Friederike *Dagmar* of Denmark (Marie Feodorovna after her conversion to Orthodoxy), *b* 27 Nov 1847, *m* 9 Nov 1866, HIM Alexander III, Emperor of all the Russias, KG (*b* 26 Feb 1845; *d* 20 Oct 1894), and *d* 13 Oct 1928, having had issue,
1c HIH Grand Duke Alexander Alexandrovitch of Russia, *b* Aug 1867; *d* 1869.
2c HIM Nicholas II, Emperor of all the Russias, KG (1893), GCB, had Royal Victorian Chain, hon Adm in the British Navy and Field Marshal in the British Army, Col-in-Chief Scots Greys 1894-1918, *s* his father 1 Nov 1894, abdicated for himself and his only son 3 March 1917, *b* 6 May 1868, *m* 26 Nov 1894, HGDH Princess *Alix* Victoria Helena Louise Beatrice (Alexandra Feodorovna after her conversion to Orthodoxy), VA (*b* 6 June 1872; murdered 16/17 July 1918), 4th dau of HRH Grand Duke Ludwig IV of Hesse and by Rhine, by his wife HRH Princess Alice, 2nd dau of HM Queen Victoria (*see p* 303), and was murdered with his wife and children at Ekaterinburg 16/17 July 1918, having had issue,
1d HIH Grand Duke Cesarevitch Alexis Nikolaievitch of Russia, *b* 12 Aug 1904; murdered 16/17 July 1918.
1d HIH Grand Duchess Olga Nikolaievna of Russia, *b* 15 Nov 1895; murdered 16/17 July 1918.
2d HIH Grand Duchess Tatiana Nikolaievna of Russia, *b* 10 June 1897; murdered 16/17 July 1918.
3d HIH Grand Duchess Marie Nikolaievna of Russia, *b* 16 June 1899; murdered 16/17 July 1918.
4d HIH Grand Duchess Anastasia Nikolaievna of Russia, *b* 18 June 1901; murdered 16/17 July 1918.
3c HIH Grand Duke Alexander Alexandrovitch of Russia, *b* 7 June 1869; *d* 2 May 1870.
4c HIH Grand Duke George Alexandrovitch of Russia, *b* 9 May 1871; *d unm* 10 July 1899.
5c HIH Grand Duke Michael Alexandrovitch of Russia, KG (1902), GCB (1901), refused to accept the crown after his brother's abdication in his favour 3 March 1917, *b* 4 Dec 1878, *m* (morganatically) 15 Oct 1911, Natalia Sergeievna, who assumed the style and title of HSH Princess Romanovsky-Brassoff 1935 (*b* 26 June 1880; *d* 26 Jan 1952), formerly wife of Vladimir Vladimirovitch Wulffert, and before that of Sergei Ivanovitch Mamontoff, and dau of Col Sergei Alexandrovitch Cheremetevsky, and was *k* in the Russian Revolution between 18 and 28 July 1918, leaving issue,
Prince George Mikhailovitch Brassoff, legitimated as Count Brassoff 1915, assumed the title of Prince Brassoff 1928, *b* 1 March 1910; *k* in a motor accident 21 July 1931.
1c HIH Grand Duchess Xenia Alexandrovna of Russia, *b* 6 April 1875, *m* 6 Aug 1894, HIH Grand Duke Alexander Mikhailovitch of Russia (*b* 13 April 1866; *d* 26 Feb 1933), 4th son of HIH Grand Duke Michael Nikolaievitch of Russia, by his wife HGDH Princess Cäcilie, yst dau of HRH Grand Duke Leopold of Baden (*see p* 288), and *d* at Wilderness House,

Hampton Court Palace 20 April 1960, leaving issue,

1*d* •HH Prince Andrew Alexandrovitch of Russia [*Provender, Faversham, Kent*], *b* 24 Jan 1897, *m* 1st 12 June 1918, Elisabeth (*b* 26 Dec 1886; *d* 29 Oct 1940), formerly wife of Alexander Alexandrovitch de Friderici, and yst dau of Don Fabrizio Ruffo, Duca di Sasso-Ruffo, by his wife Princess Natalia Alexandrovna Mestchersky, and has issue,

1*e* •HSH Prince Michael Romanoff [*6 Wallaroy Crescent, Roslyn Avenue, Double Bay, Sydney, NSW, Australia*], *b* 15 July 1920 *m* 1st 24 Feb 1953 (*m* diss by div Sept 1953), Esther Blanche (*Jill*) Murphy (*b* 21 Oct 1921). He *m* 2ndly 23 July 1954 •*Shirley* Elizabeth (*b* 4 March 1916), dau of Gordon Rowe Cramond.

2*e* •HSH Prince Andrew Romanoff, *b* 21 Jan 1923, *m* 1st 9 Sept 1951 (*m* diss by div), Helen (*b* 7 March 1927), dau of Constantine Afanasievitch Dourneff, and has issue,

1*f* •HSH Prince Alexis Romanoff, *b* 27 April 1953.

He *m* 2ndly 21 March 1961, •Kathleen Norris (*b* 1 March 1935), and by her has issue,

2*f* •HSH Prince Peter Romanoff, *b* 21 Nov 1961.

3*f* •HSH Prince Andrew Romanoff, *b* 20 Feb 1963.

1*e* •HSH Princess Xenia Romanoff, *b* 10 March 1919, *m* 1st 17 June 1945 (*m* diss by div 1954), Calhoun Ancrum (*b* 28 April 1915), son of late Col Calhoun Ancrum, US Marine Corps. She *m* 2ndly 7 April 1958, •*Geoffrey* Cuthbert Tooth, MD (*b* 1 Sept 1908) [*Grand Provillac, Plazac, 24580 Rouffignac, France*].

He *m* 2ndly 21 Sept 1942, •*Nadine* Sylvia Ada (*b* 5 June 1908), eldest dau of Lt-Col Herbert McDougall, of 23, Wilton Crescent, Belgrave Square, SW1, formerly of Cawston Manor, Norfolk, and by her has issue,

2*e* •HSH Princess Olga Romanoff, *b* 8 April 1950.

2*d* HH Prince Feodor Alexandrovitch of Russia, *b* 23 Dec 1898, *m* 31 May 1923 (*m* diss by div 1936), HSH Princess Irene Pavlovna Paley (*b* 21 Dec 1903), 2nd dau of HIH Grand Duke Paul Alexandrovitch of Russia, by his 2nd wife Olga (Princess Paley), and *d* 30 Nov 1968, leaving issue,

•HSH Prince Michael Romanoff, *b* 4 May 1924, *m* 15 Oct 1958, •Helga Staufenberger (*b* 22 Aug 1926), and has issue,

•HSH Prince *Michael* Paul Romanoff, *b* 31 July 1959.

3*d* •HH Prince Nikita Alexandrovitch of Russia [*14 Boulevard Eugéne Tripet, Palais Nôtre-Dame de Pins, 16400 Cannes, France*], *b* 16 Jan 1900, *m* 19 Feb 1922, •Countess Maria Ilarionovna (*b* 13 Feb 1903), dau of Count Ilarion Ilarionovitch Woronzow-Daschkow, and has issue,

1*e* •HSH Prince Nikita Romanoff [*30 East 68th Street, Apt 11-b, New York, NY 10021, USA*], *b* 13 May 1923, *m* 14 July 1961, •Janet (*b* 1933), dau of Michael Schoenwald.

2*e* •HSH Prince Alexander Romanoff [*1040 Park Avenue, Apt 13, New York, NY 10028, USA*], *b* 4 Nov 1929, *m* 18 July 1971, •Donna *Maria* Immaculata Rosalia Emmanuela Stefanie Margherita Valguarnera di Niscemi (*b* 29 Nov 1931), dau of late Don Corrado Valguarnera, Principe di Niscemi.

4*d* •HH Prince Dimitri Alexandrovitch of Russia, served in World War II as Lt-Cmdr RNVR, Pres Russian Benevolent Soc 1917 [*1 Bryan Court, 68 Seymour Place, W1*], *b* 15 Aug 1901, *m* 1st 25 Nov 1931 (*m* diss by div 1946), Countess Marina Sergeievna (*b* 20 Nov 1912; *d* 1969), dau of Count Sergei Alexandrovitch Golenistcheff-Koutouzoff, and has issue,

•HSH Princess Nadejda Romanoff, *b* 4 July 1933, *m* 20 Dec 1952, •Brian Allen (*b* 6 May 1931) [*42 Linden Avenue, Victoria, BC, Canada*], and has issue,

1*f* •Penelope Allen, *b* 27 Feb 1953.

2*f* •Marina Allen, *b* 10 July 1955.

3*f* •Alexandra Allen, *b* 10 Dec 1958.

He *m* 2ndly 29 Oct 1954, Margaret *Sheila* MacKellar (*b* 9 Sept 1898; *d* 13 Oct 1969), widow of W/Cmdr Sir John Charles Peniston Milbanke, 12th Bt, RAF (*see* BURKE'S *Peerage*, 1949 *Edn*), previously wife of Hon Francis Edward Scudamore St Clair-Erskine, styled Lord Loughborough (*see* BURKE'S *Peerage*, ROSSLYN, E), and dau of Harry Chisholm, of Sydney, NSW, Australia.

5*d* •HH Prince Rostislav Alexandrovitch of Russia, *b* 24 Nov 1902, *m* 1st 1 Sept 1928 (*m* diss by div 1944), Princess Alexandra Pavlovna (*b* 20 May 1905), yst dau of Prince Paul Petrovitch Galitzine, and has issue,

1*e* •HSH Prince Rostislav Rostislavovitch Romanoff [*Flat 11, 3 Hans Crescent, SW1*], *b* 3 Dec 1938, *m* 9 Sept 1960, •Stephena Verdel (*b* 15 Dec 1938), dau of Edgar J. Cook, and has issue,

•HSH Princess *Stephena* Alexandra Romanoff, *b* 21 Jan 1963.

He *m* 2ndly 7 May 1945 (*m* diss by div 1952), Alice Baker (*b* 30 May 1923), and by her had issue,

2*e* •HSH Prince Nicholas Romanoff, *b* 8 Sept 1945.

He *m* 3rdly 19 Nov 1954, •*Hedwig* Maria Gertrud Eva (*b* 6 Dec 1905), formerly wife of Berkeley Everard Foley Gage, CMG (now Sir Berkeley Gage, KCMG) (*see* BURKE'S *Peerage*, GAGE, V), and dau of Carl von Chappuis, of Liegnitz, Silesia.

6*d* •HH Prince Vassili Alexandrovitch of Russia, *b* 7 July 1907, *m* 23 July 1931, Princess Natalia Alexandrovna (*b* 26 Oct 1907), yst dau of Prince Alexander Vladimirovitch Galitzine, and has issue,

•HSH Princess Marina Romanoff, *b* 22 May 1940, *m* Jan 1967, William Lawrence Beadleston, and has issue,

1*f* •Nicholas Beadleston, *b* 1971.

1*f* •Tatiana Beadleston.

2*f* •Alexandra Beadleston.

1*d* HH Princess Irina Alexandrovna of Russia, *b* 15 July 1895, *m* 22 Feb 1914, Prince Felix Felixovitch Youssoupoff, Count Soumarokoff-Elston (*b* 23 March 1887; *d* 27 Sept 1967), and *d* 26 Feb 1970, leaving issue,

•Princess Irina Felixovna Youssoupoff, *b* 21 March 1915, *m* 19 June 1938, •Count Nikolai Dimitrievitch Cheremeteff (*b* 10 Nov 1904), son of Count Dimitri Sergeievitch Cheremeteff, and has issue,

•Countess Xenia Nikolaievna Cheremeteff, *b* 1 March 1942, *m* 20 June 1965, •Ilias Sfyrias (*b* 20 Aug 1932), and has issue,

•Tatiana Sfyrias, *b* 1968.

2*c* HIH Grand Duchess Olga Alexandrovna of Russia, *b* 13 June 1882, *m* 1st 9 Aug 1901 (*m* diss by div 1916), as his 1st wife, HH Duke *Peter* Friedrich Georg of Oldenburg (*b* 21 Nov 1868; *d* 11 March 1924), only son of HH Duke *Alexander* Friedrich Konstantin of Oldenburg (*see p* 219). She *m* 2ndly 14 Nov 1916, Col Nikolai Alexandrovitch Koulikovsky (*b* 5 Nov 1881; *d* 11 Aug 1958), and *d* at Toronto, Canada 24 Nov 1960, leaving issue,

1*d* •Tikhon Nikolaievitch Koulikovsky, *b* 25 Aug 1917, *m* 1st 1942 (*m* diss by div), Agnete (*b* 17 May 1920), dau of Carl Petersen. He *m* 2ndly 13 Sept 1959, •Livia (*b* 12 July 1925), dau of Aladár Sebestyén, and by her has issue,

•Olga Tikhonovna Koulikovsky, *b* 9 July 1964.

2*d* •Guri Nikolaievitch Koulikovsky, *b* 23 April 1919, *m* 1st 10 May 1940 (*m* diss by div), Ruth Schwartz (*b* 6 Feb 1921), and has issue,

1*e* •Leonid Gurievitch Koulikovsky, *b* 2 May 1943.

2*e* •Alexander Gurievitch Koulikovsky, *b* 29 Nov 1949.

1e ●Xenia Gurievna Koulikovsky, *b* 19 June 1941.
He *m* 2ndly ●Princess Asanta Tamara Gagarine (*b* 1 Aug 1924).
3b HRH Princess *Thyra* Amelie Caroline Charlotte Anne of Denmark, *b* 29 Sept 1853, *m* 21 Dec 1878, HRH Crown Prince *Ernst August* Wilhelm Adolf Georg Friedrich of Hanover, Duke of Brunswick and Lüneburg, 3rd Duke of Cumberland, etc (*b* 21 Sept 1845; *d* 14 Nov 1923), and *d* 26 Feb 1933, having had issue (*see p* 290).
5a HH Prince Julius of Schleswig-Holstein-Sonderburg-Glüksburg, *b* 14 Oct 1824, *m* 2 July 1883, Elisabeth (*b* 18 June 1856; *d* 20 Nov 1887), dau of Wolff von Ziegesar, and *dsp* 1 June 1903.
6a HH Prince Johann (*Hans*) of Schleswig-Holstein-Sonderburg-Glücksburg, *b* 5 Dec 1825; *d unm* 27 May 1911.
7a HH Prince Nikolaus of Schleswig-Holstein-Sonderburg-Glücksburg, *b* 22 Dec 1828; *d unm* 18 Aug 1849.
1a HH Princess Luise *Marie* Friederike of Schleswig-Holstein-Sonderburg-Glücksburg, *b* 23 Oct 1810, *m* 1st 19 May 1837, Friedrich von Lasperg (*b* 1 Dec 1796; *d* 9 May 1843). She *m* 2ndly 3 Oct 1846, Count Alfred von Hohenthal (*b* 5 Dec 1805; *d* 16 Nov 1860), and *dsp* 11 May 1869.
2a HH Princess *Friederike* Caroline Juliane of Schleswig-Holstein-Sonderburg-Glücksburg, *b* 9 Oct 1811, *m* 30 Oct 1834, HH *Alexander* Karl, Duke of Anhalt-Bernburg (*b* 2 March 1805; *d* 19 Aug 1863) (*see p* 276), and *dsp* 10 July 1902.
3a HH Princess Luise of Schleswig-Holstein-Sonderburg-Glücksburg, *b* 18 Nov 1820; *d unm* 30 Nov 1894.
4 HH Friedrich, Landgrave of Hesse-Cassel, Gen in the Dutch Army, *b* 11 Sept 1747, *m* 2 Dec 1786, HSH Princess *Caroline Polyxene* (*b* 4 April 1762; *d* 17 Aug 1823), elder dau of HSH Carl Wilhelm, Prince of Nassau-Usingen, and *d* 20 May 1837, having had issue,
(1) HH Wilhelm, Landgrave of Hesse-Cassel, *b* 24 Dec 1787, *m* 10 Nov 1810 HRH Princess Louise *Charlotte* (*b* 30 Oct 1789; *d* 28 March 1864), yst dau of HRH Prince Frederik of Denmark, and *d* 5 Sept 1867, leaving issue,
1a HH *Friedrich Wilhelm* Georg Adolf, Landgrave of Hesse, *b* 26 Nov 1820, *m* 1st 28 Jan 1844, HIH Grand Duchess Alexandra Nikolaievna (*b* 24 June 1825; *d* 10 Aug 1844), 5th dau of HIM Nicholas I, Emperor of all the Russias, KG, and had issue,
1b HH Prince Wilhelm of Hesse, *b* and *d* 10 Aug 1844.
He *m* 2ndly 26 May 1853, HRH Princess Marie *Anna* Friederike (*b* 17 May 1836; *d* 12 June 1918), yr dau of HRH Prince Karl of Prussia, and *d* 14 Oct 1884, having by her had issue,
2b HH *Friedrich Wilhelm* Nikolaus Carl, Landgrave of Hesse, *b* 15 Oct 1854; *d* while travelling from Batavia to Singapore 14 Oct 1888, *unm*.
3b HRH *Alexander Friedrich* Albrecht Georg, Landgrave of Hesse, Head of the Electoral House of Hesse, renounced his rights in favour of his brother Friedrich Karl 25 March 1925, *b* 25 Jan 1863, *m* 25 March 1925, Baroness *Gisela* Anna Caroline Amelie Ida Pauline (*b* 17 Jan 1884; *d* 22 June 1965), dau of Baron Otto Stockhorner von Starein, and *dsp* 26 March 1945.
4b HRH *Friedrich Karl* Ludwig Konstantin, Landgrave of Hesse, Head of the Electoral House of Hesse, elected King of Finland Oct 1918, withdrew acceptance Nov 1918, *b* 1 May 1868, *m* 25 Jan 1893, HRH Princess *Margarete* Beatrice Feodora (*b* 22 April 1872; *d* 22 Jan 1954), yst dau of HIM Friedrich III, German Emperor and King of Prussia, KG, by his wife HRH Princess Victoria, Princess Royal, eldest dau of HM Queen Victoria (*see p* 302), and *d* 28 May 1940, having had issue,
1c HH Prince *Friedrich Wilhelm* Sigismund Viktor of Hesse, *b* 23 Nov 1893; *k* in action in World War I 12/13 Sept 1916.
2c HH Prince *Maximilian* Friedrich Wilhelm Georg Eduard of Hesse, *b* 20 Oct 1894; *k* in action in World War I 13 Oct 1914.
3c ●HRH Philipp, Landgrave of Hesse, Head of the Electoral House of Hesse [*6242 Kronberg, Taunus, Schloss Friedrichshof*], *b* 6 Nov 1896, *m* 23 Sept 1925, HRH Princess *Mafalda* Maria Elisabetta Anna Romana of Savoy (*b* 19 Nov 1902; *d* in Buchenwald Concentration Camp 27 Aug 1944), 2nd dau of HM King Vittorio Emanuele III of Italy and has issue,
1d ●HRH Prince *Moritz* Friedrich Karl Emanuel Humbert of Hesse [*2321 Schloss Panker über Lütjenburg, Ostholstein, Germany*], *b* 6 Aug 1926, *m* 3 June 1964, ●HSH Princess *Tatiana* Louise Ursula Therese Elsa (*b* 31 July 1940), 2nd dau of HSH Gustav Albrecht, 5th Prince zu Sayn-Wittgenstein-Berleburg (*see p* 269), and has issue,
1e ●HH Prince *Heinrich* Donatus Philipp Umberto of Hesse, *b* 17 Oct 1966.
2e ●HH Prince Philipp Robin of Hesse, *b* 17 Sept 1970.
1e ●HH Princess *Mafalda* Margarethe of Hesse, *b* 6 July 1965.
2e ●HH Princess *Elena* Elisabeth Madeleine of Hesse, *b* 8 Nov 1967.
2d ●HH Prince *Heinrich* Wilhelm Konstantin Victor Franz of Hesse [*Villa Polissena, Via San Filippo Martire 6, Rome, Italy; Villa la Falconara, Forio d'Ischia, Italy*], *b* 30 Oct 1927.
3d ●HH Prince *Otto* Adolf of Hesse [*Via della Martellina 9, Bagni a Ripoli, Florence, Italy*], *b* 3 June 1937, *m* 6 April 1965 (*m* diss by div 1969), *Angela* Mathilde Agathe (*b* 12 Aug 1940), formerly wife of Hans Peter Schmeidler, and dau of Major-Gen Wilhelm von Doering.
1d ●HH Princess *Elisabeth* Margarethe Elena Johanna Maria Jolanda Polyxene of Hesse, *b* 8 Oct 1940, *m* 28 Feb 1962, ●Count *Friedrich Karl* Eduard Wilhelm Hans Franz Eusebius Michael Hubert Maria von Oppersdorff (*b* 30 Jan 1925) and has issue,
1e ●Count Friedrich Karl Philipp Wilhelm Hans Moritz Maria von Oppersdorff, *b* 1 Dec 1962.
2e ●Count Alexander Wolfgang Johannes Georg Victor Emanuel Maria von Oppersdorff, *b* 3 Aug 1965.
4c ●HH Prince *Wolfgang* Moritz of Hesse [*6242 Kronberg, Taunus, Schloss Friedrichshof, Germany*], *b* (twin with Landgrave Philipp) 6 Nov 1896, *m* 1st 17 Sept 1924, HGDH Princess *Marie Alexandra* Thyra Viktoria Luise Carola Hilda (*b* 1 Aug 1902; *k* in an air raid at Frankfurt-on-Main 29 Jan 1944), only dau of HRH Prince Max of Baden, Head of the Grand Ducal House of Baden (*see p* 291). He *m* 2ndly 7 Sept 1948, ●Ottilie (*b* 24 June 1903), dau of Ludwig Moeller.
5c ●HH Prince *Richard* Wilhelm Leopold of Hesse [*6242 Kronberg, Taunus, Schloss Friedrichshof, Germany*], *b* 14 May 1901.
6c HH Prince *Christoph* Ernst August of Hesse, *b* (twin with Prince Richard) 14 May 1901, *m* 15 Dec 1930, ●HRH Princess Sophie (*b* 26 June 1914; *m* 2ndly 24 April 1946, ●HRH Prince Georg Wilhelm of Hanover), yst dau of HRH Prince Andrew of Greece and Denmark, GCVO (*see p* 280), and was *k* in action in World War II 7 Oct 1943, leaving issue,
1d ●HH Prince *Karl* Adolf Andreas of Hesse [*8 München 27, Denninger Strasse 102, Germany*], *b* 26 March 1937, *m* (civil) 26 March and (religious) 18 April 1966, ●Countess *Yvonne* Margit Valerie (*b* 4 April 1944), only dau of Count Béla Szápáry von Muraszombath, Széchysziget und Szápár, and has issue,
●HH Prince Christoph of Hesse, *b* 18 July 1969.

•HH Princess Irina Verena of Hesse, *b* 1 April 1971.

2*d* •HH Prince *Rainer* Christoph Friedrich of Hesse [*8166 Neuhaus bei Schliersee, OBayern, Breitensteinstrasse 1, Germany*], *b* 18 Nov 1939.

1*d* •HH Princess *Christina* Margarethe of Hesse, *b* 10 Jan 1933, *m* 1st 2 Aug 1956 (*m* diss by div 1961), HRH Prince Andrej of Yugoslavia (*b* 28 June 1929), and has issue (*see p* 296). She *m* 2ndly 3 Dec 1962, •Robert van Eyck (*b* 3 May 1916), and has further issue,

•Mark Nicholas van Eyck, *b* 16 Feb 1966.

•Helen Sophia van Eyck, *b* 25 Oct 1963.

2*d* •HH Princess *Dorothea* Charlotte Karin of Hesse, *b* 24 July 1934, *m* 1 April 1959, •HSH Prince *Friedrich* Karl Hugo Maximilian Maria Cyrillus Felix Hubertus zu Windisch-Graetz (*b* 7 July 1917) [*Cà Lupo, Alserio, Prov Como, Italy*], and has issue,

1*e* •HSH Princess *Marina* Margherita Sophia Leontina Christiana zu Windisch-Graetz, *b* 3 Dec 1960.

2*e* •HSH Princess Clarissa Elisabetta Fiore zu Windisch-Graetz, *b* 6 August 1966.

3*d* •HH Princess *Clarissa* Alice of Hesse, *b* (posthumously) 6 Feb 1944, *m* 20 July 1971, •Claude-Jean Derrien [*La Duvallerie, Le Plessis 37 par Cangey, Indre et Loire, France*].

1*b* HH Princess *Elisabeth* Charlotte Alexandra Marie Louise of Hesse, *b* 13 June 1861, *m* 26 May 1884, HH Hereditary Prince *Leopold* Friedrich Franz Ernst of Anhalt (*b* 18 July 1855; *d* 2 Feb 1886), and *d* 7 Jan 1955, leaving issue,

HH Princess *Antoinette Anna* Alexandra Marie Luise Agnes Elisabeth Auguste Friederike of Anhalt, *b* 3 March 1885, *m* 26 May 1909, as his 2nd wife, HSH Prince *Friedrich* Georg Wilhelm Bruno of Schaumburg-Lippe (*b* 30 Jan 1868; *d* 12 Dec 1945), and *d* 3 April 1963, having had issue (*see below*).

2*b* HH Princess *Marie Polyxene* Olga Viktoria Dagmar Anna of Hesse, *b* 29 April 1872; *d* 16 Aug 1882.

3*b* HH Princess *Sibylle* Margarethe Christa Thyra Hedwig Catherina of Hesse, *b* 3 June 1877, *m* 3 Sept 1898 (*m* diss by div 1923), Baron *Friedrich* Alexander Karl von Vincke (*b* 24 July 1867; *d* 31 Dec 1925), and *d* 11 Feb 1952, leaving issue,

1*c* •Baron *Itel-Jobst* Christian Friedrich Kaspar Dietrich von Vincke [*Wiesbaden, Nerobergstrasse 5, Germany*], *b* 20 June 1899, *m* 14 May 1929, •*Marthe* Marie Josette (*b* 17 Nov 1909), dau of Alfred Hoeppe-Menée.

2*c* •Baron *Alfram-Dietrich* Friedrich-Karl Alexander Alfred Ebbeke Gisbert von Vincke [*Wiesbaden, Nerobergstrasse 5, Germany*], *b* 18 May 1903, *m* 7 Dec 1935, •*Gurli* Marie Luise Nielsen (*b* 14 March 1912).

1*a* HH Princess *Karoline* Friederike Marie Wilhelmine of Hesse-Cassel, *b* 15 Aug 1811; *d* 10 May 1829.

2*a* HH Princess *Marie* Luise Charlotte of Hesse-Cassel, *b* 9 May 1814, *m* 11 Sept 1832, HH Prince *Friedrich* August of Anhalt (*b* 23 Sept 1799; *d* 4 Dec 1864), 4th son of HH Hereditary Prince Friedrich of Anhalt-Dessau, and *d* 28 July 1895, leaving issue,

1*b* HH Princess *Adelheid* Marie of Anhalt, *b* 25 Dec 1833, *m* 23 April 1851, as his 2nd wife, HRH Grand Duke *Adolf* Wilhelm Karl August Friedrich of Luxembourg, Duke of Nassau (*b* 24 July 1817; *d* 17 Nov 1905), and *d* 24 Nov 1916, leaving issue (*see p* 217).

2*b* HH Princess *Bathildis* Amalgunde of Anhalt, *b* 29 Dec 1837, *m* 30 May 1862, HSH Prince *Wilhelm* Karl August of Schaumburg-Lippe (*b* 12 Dec 1834; *d* 4 April 1906), yr son of HSH *Georg* Wilhelm, Prince of Schaumburg-Lippe, and *d* 10 Feb 1902, having had issue,

1*c* HSH Prince Franz Josef Leopold Adolf Alexander August Wilhelm of Schaumburg-Lippe, *b* 8 Oct 1865; *d* 4 Sept 1881.

2*c* HSH Prince *Friedrich* Georg Wilhelm Bruno of Schaumburg-Lippe, *b* 30 Jan 1868, *m* 1st 5 May 1896, HRH Princess *Louise* Caroline Josephine Sophie Thyra Olga (*b* 17 Feb 1875; *d* 4 April 1906), eldest dau of HM King Frederik VIII of Denmark (*see p* 278), and had issue,

1*d* •HSH Prince *Christian* Nikolaus Wilhelm Friedrich Albert Ernst Stephan of Schaumburg-Lippe [*4967 Bückeburg, Am Hofgarten 20, Germany*], *b* 20 Feb 1898, *m* 9 Sept 1937, •HH Princess *Feodora* Louise Caroline-Mathilde Viktoria Alexandra Frederikke Johanne (*b* 3 July 1910), eldest dau of HRH late Prince Harald of Denmark (*see p* 278), and has issue,

1*e* •HSH Prince *Wilhelm* Friedrich Harald Christian Ernst-August Carl Gustav of Schaumburg-Lippe [*8 München 81 (Oberföhring), Regina-Ullmann-Strasse 52, Germany*], *b* 19 Aug 1939, *m* 7 Jan 1970, •*Ilona* Maria Theresia (*b* 17 Oct 1940), 2nd dau of late Georg-Alfred Ritter Hentschel von Gilgenheimb, and has issue,

•HSH Prince *Christian* Hubertus Clemens-August Friedrich-Sigismund Louis-Ferdinand Harald of Schaumburg-Lippe, *b* 4 Sept 1971.

2*e* •HSH Prince *Waldemar* Stephan Ferdinand Wolrad Friedrich Karl of Schaumburg-Lippe, *b* 19 Dec 1940.

3*e* •HSH Prince *Harald* Christian Leopold Gustav of Schaumburg-Lippe, *b* 27 March 1948.

1*e* •HSH Princess *Marie-Louise* Friederike Cecilie Alexandrine Helene Bathildis Stephanie of Schaumburg-Lippe, *b* 27 Dec 1945.

1*d* HSH Princess *Marie Luise* Dagmar Bathildis Charlotte of Schaumburg-Lippe, *b* 10 Feb 1897, *m* 27 April 1916, HRH Prince Joachim Viktor Wilhelm Leopold *Friedrich Sigismund* of Prussia (*b* 17 Dec 1891; *d* 6 July 1927), and *d* 1 Oct 1938, leaving issue (*see p* 287).

2*d* HSH Princess *Stephanie* Alexandra Hermine Thyra Xenia Bathildis Ingeborg of Schaumburg-Lippe, *b* 19 Dec 1899, *m* 9 Sept 1921, HSH *Viktor Adolf* Wilhelm Otto, 5th Prince zu Bentheim und Steinfurt (*b* 18 July 1883; *d* 4 June 1961), and *d* 2 May 1925, leaving issue (*see p* 223).

He *m* 2ndly 26 May 1909, HH Princess *Antoinette Anna* Alexandra Marie Luise Agnes Elisabeth Auguste Friederike (*b* 3 March 1885; *d* 3 April 1963), only dau of HH Hereditary Prince Leopold of Anhalt (*see above*), and *d* 12 Dec 1945, having by her had issue,

2*d* •HSH Prince *Leopold* Friedrich Alexander Wilhelm Eduard of Schaumburg-Lippe, *b* 21 Feb 1910.

3*d* HSH Prince *Wilhelm* Friedrich Karl Adolf Leopold Hilderich of Schaumburg-Lippe, *b* 24 Aug 1912; *d unm* 4 March 1938.

3*c* HSH Prince Christian *Albrecht* Cajetan Karl Wilhelm of Schaumburg-Lippe, *b* 24 Oct 1869, *m* 1st 6 May 1897, HRH Duchess *Elsa* Mathilde Marie (*b* 1 March 1876; *d* 27 May 1936), elder dau of HRH Duke Eugen of Württemberg (*see p* 258), and had issue,

1*d* •HSH Prince Wilhelm Eugen Konstantin Georg *Max* of Schaumburg-Lippe, *b* 28 March 1898, *m* 9 May 1933, •*Helga* Claire *Lee* Roderbourg (*b* 24 Feb 1911).

2*d* •HSH Prince *Franz Josef* Adolf Ernst of Schaumburg-Lippe, *b* 1 Sept 1899, *m* 29 Jan 1959, •Maria Theresia (*b* 29 July 1912), dau of Anton Peschel.

3*d* HSH Prince *Alexander* Ernst Friedrich Albrecht of Schaumburg-Lippe, *b* 20 Jan 1901; *d unm* 26 Nov 1923.

1*d* •HSH Princess *Bathildis* Wera Thyra Adelheid Hermine Mathilde Mary of Schaumburg-Lippe, *b* 11 Nov 1903, *m* 16 April 1925, HSH Ernst *Wolrad*, Prince of Schaumburg-Lippe (*b* 19 April 1887; *d* 14 May 1962), and has issue (*see p* 251).

He *m* 2ndly 24 June 1939, Maria Herget (*b*

26 July 1897; *d* 25 Dec 1942), and *d* 25 Dec 1945.

4*c* HSH Prince *Maximilian* August Jaroslav Adalbert Hermann of Schaumburg-Lippe, *b* 13 March 1871, *m* 3 Nov 1898, HRH Duchess *Olga* Alexandrine Ida (*b* 1 March 1876; *d* 21 Oct 1932), yr (twin) dau of HRH Duke Eugen of Württemberg (*see p* 258), and *d* 1 April 1904, having had issue,

1*d* HSH Prince Wilhelm *Eugen* Georg Friedrich August Albrecht of Schaumburg-Lippe, *b* 8 Aug 1899; *d unm* 7 Nov 1929.

2*d* ●HSH Prince *Albrecht* Adolf Konstantin Ernst Nikolaus Friedrich of Schaumburg-Lippe, *b* 17 Oct 1900, *m* 2 Sept 1930, ●Baroness Walburgis (*b* 26 March 1906), dau of Baron Karl von Hirschberg.

3*d* HSH Prince Bernhard of Schaumburg-Lippe, *b* 18 Dec 1902; *d* 24 June 1903.

5c A Prince, *b* 26, *d* 27 June 1874.

1*c* HSH Princess *Charlotte* Marie Ida Luise Hermine Mathilde of Schaumburg-Lippe, *b* 10 Oct 1864, *m* 8 April 1886, as his 2nd wife, HM King Wilhelm II of Württemberg (*b* 25 Feb 1848; *d* 2 Oct 1921), and *d* 16 July 1946 (*see p* 212).

2*c* HSH Princess *Bathildis* Marie Leopoldine Anna Auguste of Schaumburg-Lippe, *b* 21 May 1873, *m* 9 Aug 1895, HSH *Friedrich* Adolf Hermann, Prince of Waldeck and Pyrmont (*b* 20 Jan 1865; *d* 26 May 1946), and *d* 6 April 1962, leaving issue (*see p* 221).

3*c* HSH Princess Friederike *Adelheid* Marie Luise Hilda Eugenie of Schaumburg-Lippe, *b* 22 Sept 1875, *m* 17 Feb 1898 (*m* diss by div 1920), HH Ernst II, Duke of Saxe-Altenburg (*b* 31 Aug 1871; *d* 22 March 1935), and *d* 27 Jan 1971, leaving issue (*see p* 267).

4*c* HSH Princess *Alexandra* Karoline Marie Ida Henriette Juliane of Schaumburg-Lippe, *b* 9 June 1879; *d unm* 5 Jan 1949.

3*b* HH Princess *Hilda* Charlotte of Anhalt, *b* 13 Dec 1839; *d unm* 22 Dec 1926.

2*a* HH Princess *Luise* Wilhelmine Friederike Caroline Auguste Julie of Hesse-Cassel, *b* 7 Sept 1817, *m* 26 May 1842, HM King Christian IX of Denmark, KG (*b* 8 April 1818; *d* 29 Jan 1906), and *d* 29 Sept 1898, leaving issue (*see p* 277).

3*a* HH Princess *Auguste* Sophie Friederike Marie Caroline Julie of Hesse-Cassel, *b* 30 Oct 1823, *m* 1 June 1854, Baron *Carl* Friedrich von Blixen-Finecke (*b* 15 Aug 1822; *d* 6 Jan 1873), and *d* 17 July 1889, leaving issue,

1*b* Baron Vilhelm Carl Ferdinand Christian Frederik Hilda Rudolph Gustav von Blixen-Finecke, *b* 29 May 1857; *d unm* 31 Jan 1909.

2*b* Baron Vilhelm Carl Anna Otto Gunnar Axel von Blixen-Finecke, *b* 21 June 1863, *m* 9 Nov 1888, Bertha (*b* 29 July 1868; *d* 11 Feb 1951), dau of Carl Vilhelm Castenskiold, and *d* 7 July 1942, leaving issue,

Baron Carl August von Blixen-Finecke, *b* 20 Sept 1889, *m* 10 May 1917, ●Brita (*b* 6 Oct 1893), dau of Hugo Ekström, and *d* 5 Dec 1954, leaving issue,

Baron Gustav Frederik von Blixen-Finecke, *b* 1 Sept 1920, *m* 1st 1 Sept 1951, Charlotte (*b* 18 June 1930; *d* 13 May 1954), dau of Carl Brønnum Scavenius, and had issue,

●Baron Axel Henrik von Blixen-Finecke, *b* 15 May 1952.

He *m* 2ndly 3 March 1960, ●Carin (*b* 31 March 1933), dau of Eric von Rosen, and *d* 30 April 1966, having by her had issue,

●Baroness Brita Madeleine von Blixen-Finecke, *b* 8 Feb 1961.

●Baroness Anna Elisabeth von Blixen-Finecke, *b* 18 July 1918, *m* 23 Nov 1946, ●Thorbjørn Møller (*b* 22 Oct 1897), and has issue,

●Carl Gustaf Thorbjørn Blixen-Finecke Møller, *b* 29 Jan 1949.

●Agnes Elisabeth Gertrud Blixen-Finecke Møller, *b* 8 May 1947.

4*a* HH Princess Sophie Wilhelmine Auguste Elisabeth of Hesse-Cassel, *b* 18 Jan, *d* 20 Dec 1827.

(2) HH Prince *Karl* Friedrich of Hesse-Cassel, *b* 8 March 1789; *d* 10 Sept 1802.

(3) HH Prince *Friedrich Wilhelm* of Hesse-Cassel, Gen in the Prussian Army, *b* 24 April 1790; *d unm* 25 Oct 1876.

(4) HH Prince *Ludwig* Karl of Hesse-Cassel, *b* 12 Nov 1791; *d* 12 May 1800.

(5) HH Prince *Georg* Karl of Hesse-Cassel, Gen in the Prussian army, *b* 14 Jan 1793; *d unm* 4 March 1881.

(1) HH Princess *Luise* Caroline Marie Friederike of Hesse-Cassel, *b* 9 April 1794, *m* 4 April 1833, Count Georg von der Decken (*b* 23 Nov 1787; *d* 19 Aug 1859), and *dsp* 16 March 1881.

(2) HH Princess *Marie* Wilhelmine Friederike of Hesse-Cassel, *b* 21 Jan 1796, *m* 12 Aug 1817, HRH Grand Duke *Georg* Friedrich Karl Joseph of Mecklenburg-Strelitz (*b* 12 Aug 1779; *d* 6 Sept 1860), and *d* 30 Dec 1880, having had issue,

1*a* HRH Grand Duke *Friedrich Wilhelm* Karl Georg Ernst Adolf Gustav of Mecklenburg-Strelitz, *b* 17 Oct 1819, *m* 28 June 1843, his 1st cousin, HRH Princess *Augusta* Caroline Charlotte Elizabeth Mary Sophia Louisa (*b* 19 July 1822; *d* 5 Dec 1916), elder dau of HRH Prince Adolphus of Great Britain and Ireland, 1st Duke of Cambridge, etc, and *d* 30 May 1904, having had issue (*see p* 292).

2*a* HH Duke *Georg* August Ernst Adolf Carl Ludwig of Mecklenburg-Strelitz, *b* 11 Jan 1824, *m* 16 Feb 1851, HIH Grand Duchess Catherine Mikhailovna (*b* 28 Aug 1827; *d* 12 May 1894), 3rd dau of HIH Grand Duke Michael Pavlovitch of Russia, and *d* 20 June 1876, leaving issue (*see p* 212).

1*a* HH Duchess Caroline *Luise* Marie Friederike Therese Charlotte Wilhelmine Augusta of Mecklenburg-Strelitz, *b* 31 May 1818; *d unm* 1 Feb 1842.

2*a* HH Duchess *Caroline* Charlotte Marianne of Mecklenburg-Strelitz, *b* 10 Jan 1821, *m* 10 June 1841 (*m* diss by div 1846), HRH Crown Prince Frederik (later HM King Frederik VII) of Denmark (*b* 6 Oct 1808; *d* 15 Nov 1863), and *dsp* 1 June 1876.

(3) HH Princess *Auguste* Wilhelmine Luise of Hesse-Cassel, *b* 25 July 1797, *m* 1 June 1818, HRH Prince Adolphus of Great Britain and Ireland, 1st Duke of Cambridge, KG, etc (*b* 24 Feb 1774; *d* 8 July 1850), 7th son of HM King George III, and *d* 6 April 1889, leaving issue (*see p* 291).

5 HRH Princess Louisa, *b* at Leicester House 7 Dec 1724, *m* by proxy at Hanover 30 Oct and in person at Altona 11 Dec 1743, as his 1st wife, HM King Frederik V of Denmark (*b* 31 March 1723; *d* at Copenhagen 14 Jan 1766), and *d* at Copenhagen 8 Dec 1751, having had issue,

1 HH Prince Christian, Prince Royal of Denmark, *b* 7 July 1745; *d* 3 June 1747.

2 HM King Christian VII of Denmark (1766-1808), *b* 29 Jan 1749, *m* by proxy 1 Oct and in person 8 Nov 1766, his 1st cousin, HRH Princess Caroline Matilda (*b* 11 July 1751; *d* 10 May 1775), yst dau of HRH Frederick, Prince of Wales, KG (*see p* 214), and *d* 13 March 1808, leaving issue,

HM King Frederik VI of Denmark (1808-1839), Regent from 1784, KG 1822, *b* 28 Jan 1768, *m* 31 July 1790, his 1st cousin, HSH Princess *Marie* Sophie Friederike (*b* 28 Oct 1767; *d* 21 March 1852), dau of HSH Landgrave Karl of Hesse-Cassel, by his wife HH Princess Louisa, yst dau of HM King Frederik V of Denmark, and *d* 3 Dec 1839, having had issue,

1*a* HRH Prince Christian of Denmark, *b* 22, *d* 23 Sept 1791.

2*a* HRH Prince Christian of Denmark, *b* 1, *d* 5 Sept 1797.

1*a* HRH Princess Marie Louise of Denmark, *b* 19 Nov 1792; *d* 12 Oct 1793.

2*a* HRH Princess Caroline of Denmark, *b* 28 Oct 1793, *m* 1 Aug 1829, HRH Prince Frederik *Ferdinand* of Denmark (*b* 22 Nov 1792; *d* 29 June 1863), and *dsp* 30 March 1881.

3*a* HRH Princess Louisa of Denmark, *b* 21 Aug, *d* 7 Dec 1795.

4*a* HRH Princess Louisa Juliana of Denmark, *b* 12, *d* 23 Feb 1802.
5*a* HRH Princess Frederika Maria of Denmark, *b* 3 June, *d* 14 July 1805.
6*a* HRH Princess *Wilhelmina* Maria of Denmark, *b* 18 Jan 1808, *m* 1st 1 Nov 1828 (*m* diss by div 1837), HRH Prince Frederik of Denmark, afterwards HM King Frederik VII (*b* 6 Oct 1808; *d* 15 Nov 1863). She *m* 2ndly 19 May 1838, HH Duke Karl of Schleswig-Holstein-Sonderburg-Glücksburg (*b* 30 Sept 1813; *d* 24 Oct 1878), and *dsp* 30 May 1891.
HRH Princess Louisa Augusta of Denmark, *b* 7 July 1771, *m* 27 May 1786, HH Friedrich Christian Duke of Schleswig-Holstein-Sonderburg-Augustenburg (*b* 28 Sept 1765; *d* 14 June 1814), and *d* 13 Jan 1843, leaving issue,
1*a* HH *Christian* Karl Friedrich *August*, Duke of Schleswig-Holstein-Sonderburg-Augustenburg, *b* 19 July 1798, *m* 18 Sept 1820, Countess Louise Sophie (*b* 22 Sept 1796; *d* 11 March 1867), dau of Count Christian Conrad Sophus Danneskjold-Samsoë, and *d* 11 March 1869, having had issue,
1*b* HH Hereditary Prince Alexander of Schleswig-Holstein-Sonderburg-Augustenburg, *b* 20 July 1821; *d* 3 May 1823.
2*b* HH *Friedrich* Christian August, Duke of Schleswig-Holstein-Sonderburg-Augustenburg, *b* 6 July 1829, *m* 11 Sept 1856, HSH Princess *Adelheid* Viktoria Amalie Luise Marie Konstanze (*b* 20 July 1835; *d* 25 Jan 1900), 2nd dau of HSH *Ernst* Christian Carl, 4th Prince zu Hohenlohe-Langenburg, and *d* 14 Jan 1880, leaving issue,
1*c* HH Ernst Günther, Duke of Schleswig-Holsten-Sonderburg-Augustenburg, *b* 11 Aug 1863, *m* 2 Aug 1898, HH Princess *Dorothea* Marie Henriette Auguste Luise (*b* 30 April 1881; *d* 21 Jan 1967), only dau of HH Prince Philipp of Saxe-Coburg and Gotha, Duke of Saxony (*see p* 257), and *dsp* 22 Feb 1921.
1*c* HH Princess *Auguste Viktoria* Friederike Luise Feodora Jenny of Schleswig-Holstein, *b* 22 Oct 1858, *m* 27 Feb 1881, as his 1st wife, HIM Wilhelm II, German Emperor and King of Prussia (*b* 27 Jan 1859; *d* 4 June 1941), and *d* 11 April 1921, leaving issue (*see p* 300).
2*c* HH Princess Viktoria Friederike Auguste Marie *Karoline Mathilde* of Schleswig-Holstein, *b* 25 Jan 1860, *m* 19 March 1885, HH Friedrich Ferdinand, Duke of Schleswig-Holstein-Sonderburg-Glücksburg (*b* 12 Oct 1855; *d* 21 Jan 1934), and *d* 20 Feb 1932, leaving issue (*see p* 276).
3*c* HH Princess Feodora *Louise Sophie* Adelheid Henriette Amalie of Schleswig-Holstein, *b* 8 April 1866, *m* 24 June 1889, HRH Prince Friedrich Leopold of Prussia (*b* 14 Nov 1865; *d* 13 Sept 1931), and *d* 28 April 1952, having had issue,
1*d* HRH Prince Joachim Viktor Wilhelm Leopold *Friedrich Sigismund* of Prussia, *b* 17 Dec 1891, *m* 27 April 1916, HSH Princess *Marie Luise* Dagmar Bathildis Charlotte (*b* 10 Feb 1897; *d* 1 Oct 1938), elder dau of HSH Prince Friedrich of Schaumburg-Lippe (*see p* 285), and *d* 6 July 1927, leaving issue,
•HRH Prince *Friedrich Karl* Viktor Stephan Christian of Prussia [*Gmund am Tegernsee, Am Seeblick 6, Germany*], *b* 13 March 1919, *m* 13 Dec 1961, Lady *Hermione* Mary Morton (*b* 2 March 1925; *d* 2 Sept 1969), formerly wife of Cmdr John Oliver Roberts, RN, and only dau of Archibald John Morton Stuart, 19th Earl of Moray (*see* BURKE'S *Peerage*).
•HRH Princess *Luise* Viktoria Margarete Antoinette Sieglinde Alexandrine Thyra Stephanie of Prussia [*4967 Bückeburg, Schloss Westflügel, Germany*], *b* 23 Aug 1917, *m* 12 Sept 1942 (*m* diss by div 1949), Hanns Reinhold (*b* 20 Nov 1917), and has issue,
•*Manfred* Friedrich Karl Hubertus Axel Reinhold, *b* 13 Feb 1943.
2*d* HRH Prince Tassilo Wilhelm Humbert Leopold *Friedrich Karl* of Prussia, *b* 6 April 1893; *k* in action in World War I 6 April 1917.
3*d* HRH Prince Franz Joseph Oskar Ernst Patrick *Friedrich Leopold* of Prussia, *b* 27 Aug 1895; *d unm* 27 Nov 1959.
1*d* HRH Princess *Viktoria Margarete* Elisabeth Marie Adelheid Ulrike of Prussia, *b* 17 April 1890, *m* 17 May 1913, HSH Prince Heinrich XXXIII Reuss (Younger Line) (*b* 26 July 1879; *d* 15 Nov 1942), and *d* 9 Sept 1923, leaving issue,
•HSH Prince Heinrich II Reuss (Younger Line) [*776 Park Avenue, 71 East 71st Street, New York, USA*], *b* 24 Nov 1916.
•HSH Princess *Marie Luise* Friederike Viktoria Wilhelmina Renata Charlotte Reuss (Younger Line) [*8 München, Grillparzerstrasse 43, Germany*], *b* 9 Jan 1915, *m* 1st (civil) 5 June and (religious) 7 June 1941 (*m* diss by div 1946), Erich Theisen (*b* 7 June 1905; *d* 1954). She *m* 2ndly (civil) 23 March and (religious) 27 March 1954 (*m* diss by div 1956), Alexander Bodey (*b* 28 Dec 1920).
4*c* HH Princess *Feodora* Viktoria Adelheid Pauline Amalie Marie of Schleswig-Holstein, *b* 3 July 1874; *d unm* 21 June 1910.
3*b* HH Prince Friedrich *Christian* Karl August of Schleswig-Holstein, granted the style of Royal Highness in anticipation of his marriage 30 June 1866, KG (1866), PC, GCVO, Gen in the Army, Personal ADC to HM Queen Victoria, HM King Edward VII and HM King George V, hon Col 4th Vol Bn Royal Berks Regt, Bencher of Inner Temple, KJStJ, High Steward of Windsor and Ranger of Windsor Park, *b* 22 Jan 1831, *m* 5 July 1866, HRH Princess *Helena* Augusta Victoria, VA, CI, RRC (*b* 25 May 1846; *d* 9 June 1923), 3rd dau of HM Queen Victoria, and *d* 28 Oct 1917, having had issue (*see p* 304).
1*b* HH Princess Louise Auguste of Schleswig-Holstein, *b* 28 Aug 1824; *d unm* 30 May 1872.
2*b* HH Princess Amalie of Schleswig-Holstein, *b* 15 Jan 1826; *d unm* 3 May 1907.
3*b* HH Princess Wilhelmine Friederike of Schleswig-Holstein, *b* 24 March 1828; *d* 4 July 1829.
4*b* HH Princess Henriette of Schleswig-Holstein, *b* 2 Aug 1833, *m* 28 Feb 1872, Prof Johannes-Friedrich August von Esmarch, MD (*b* 9 Jan 1823), and *d* Oct 1916, having had issue,
1*c* A son, *b* and *d* 25 Dec 1872.
2*c* Karl Friedrich Johann Christian August von Esmarch, *b* 1 July 1874, *m* 15 Sept 1898, Emma Awiszus (*b* 5 March 1873; *d* 15 Jan 1929), and *dsp* 15 Jan 1929.
3*c* Heinrich von Esmarch, *b* 20, *d* 24 Jan 1877.
2*a* HH Prince Friedrich Emil August of Schleswig-Holstein, took the title of Prince of Noër, *b* 23 Aug 1800, *m* 1st 17 Sept 1829, Countess Henriette (*b* 9 May 1806; *d* 10 Sept 1858), dau of Count Christian Conrad Sophus Danneskjold-Samsoë, and had issue,
1*b* HH Prince Friedrich of Schleswig-Holstein, took the title of Count of Noër, *b* 16 Nov 1830, *m* 17 May 1870, *Carmelite* Henrietta Sophia Matilda Eisenblat a la Guayra (*b* 21 Aug 1848), and *d* 25 Dec 1881, leaving issue,
1*c* Countess *Carmelita* Luise Henriette Laila von Noër, *b* 22 April 1871, *m* 1st 14 Oct 1894 (*m* diss by div), Count Ernst von Rantzau (*b* 29 May 1869; *d* 27 Nov 1930), and had issue,
Count Friedrich August Julius Bertram Ulrich Michael Ludwig Ernst von Rantzau, *b* 12 Oct 1895, *m* 20 Jan 1944, •Countess Ehrengard (*b* 23 Oct 1906), dau of Count Albrecht von der Schulenburg, and *dsp* as a p o w Dec 1945.
She *m* 2ndly 7 Sept 1921, Rudolf Humbert (*d* 29 Oct 1954), and *d* 9 May 1948.
2*c* Countess Louise von Noër, *b* 1 Nov 1873, *m* 26 Nov 1899, her 1st cousin, Prince Charles Vlangali-Handjeri (*b* 28 July 1866; *d* 1 Nov 1933), son of Prince Michael Vlangali-Handjeri,

by his 1st wife HH Princess Louise of Schleswig-Holstein, and *d* 2 June 1955, leaving issue (*see below*).
2*b* HH Prince Christian of Schleswig-Holstein, *b* 13 Dec 1832; *d* 3 Feb 1834.
1*b* HH Princess *Louise* Caroline Henriette Auguste of Schleswig-Holstein, *b* 29 July 1836, *m* 24 Oct 1865, as his 1st wife, Prince Michael Vlangali-Handjeri (*b* 1823; *d* 11 Aug 1911), grandson of Prince Alexander Handjeri, Hospodar of Wallachia, and *d* 25 Sept 1866, leaving issue,
1*c* Prince Charles Vlangali-Handjeri, *b* 28 July, 1866, *m* 26 Nov 1899, his 1st cousin, Countess Louise von Noër (*b* 1 Nov 1873; *d* 2 June 1955), yr dau of HH Prince Friedrich of Schleswig-Holstein, Count von Noër (*see above*), and *d* 1 Nov 1933, leaving issue,
●Princess Caroline Vlangali-Handjeri, *b* 6 Oct 1900, *m* 19 Sept 1923, Louis Laur (*b* 1 Jan 1904; *d* 10 May 1957), and has issue,
●Christian Laur, *b* 9 March 1927, *m* 6 Oct 1948, ●Camille (*b* 1925), dau of Jean de Bret, and has issue,
●Bernard Laur, *b* 18 Dec 1949.
2*c* Prince Alexander Vlangali-Handjeri, *b* (twin with Prince Charles) 28 July 1866; *d* 4 Jan 1867.
2*b* HH Princess Marie of Schleswig-Holstein, *b* 8 Aug 1838; *d* 3 Feb 1839.
He *m* 2ndly 30 Nov 1864, Marie Esther (*b* 3 Oct 1838; *m* 2ndly 14 April 1874, Count Alfred von Waldersee), dau of David Lee, of New York, USA, and *d* 2 July 1865.
1*a* HH Princess Caroline Amalie of Schleswig-Holstein, *b* 28 Jan 1796, *m* 22 May 1815, as his 2nd wife, HM King Christian VIII of Denmark (*b* 18 Sept 1786; *d* 20 Jan 1848), and *dsp* 9 March 1881.
1 HH Princess Sophia Magdalena of Denmark, *b* 3 July 1746, *m* 4 Nov 1766, HM King Gustaf III of Sweden (*b* 24 Jan 1746; *d* 29 March 1792), and *d* 21 Aug 1813, having had issue,
(1) HM King Gustaf IV Adolf of Sweden (1792-1809), deposed 29 March 1809, *b* 1 Nov 1778, *m* 31 Oct 1797 (*m* diss by div 1812), HSH Princess *Friederike* Dorothea Wilhelmine (*b* 12 March 1781; *d* 25 Sept 1826), 4th dau of HSH Hereditary Prince Karl Ludwig of Baden, and *d* 7 Feb 1837, having had issue,
1*a* HRH Prince Gustaf, sometime Crown Prince of Sweden, took the title of Prince of Wasa 5 May 1829, *b* 9 Nov 1799, *m* 9 Nov 1830, HGDH Princess *Luise* Amalie Stephanie (*b* 5 June 1811; *d* 19 July 1854), eldest dau of HRH Grand Duke Karl of Baden, and *d* 4 Oct 1877, leaving issue,
A son, *b* 3, *d* 7 Feb 1832.
HRH Princess Caroline (*Carola*) Friederike Franziska Stephanie Amalie Cecilie of Wasa, *b* 5 Aug 1833, *m* 18 June 1853, HM King Albert of Saxony, KG (*b* 23 April 1828; *d* 19 June 1902), and *dsp* 15 Dec 1907.
2*a* HRH Prince Carl Gustaf of Sweden, *b* 2 Dec 1802; *d* 10 Sept 1805.
1*a* HRH Princess *Sophie* Wilhelmine of Sweden, *b* 21 May 1801, *m* 25 July 1819, HRH Grand Duke Leopold of Baden (*b* 29 Aug 1790; *d* 24 April 1852), and *d* 6 July 1865, having had issue,
1*b* Ludwig, *b* 26 Oct, *d* 16 Nov 1822.
2*b* HRH Grand Duke Ludwig II of Baden, *b* 15 Aug 1824; *d unm* 22 Jan 1858.
3*b* HRH Grand Duke *Friedrich I* (Wilhelm Ludwig) of Baden, KG (1906), Regent for his brother Grand Duke Ludwig II 1852-56, took the title of Grand Duke 5 Sept 1856, *b* 9 Sept 1826, *m* 20 Sept 1856, HRH Princess *Luise* Marie Elisabeth (*b* 3 Dec 1838; *d* 23 April 1923), only dau of HIM Wilhelm I, German Emperor and King of Prussia, KG, and *d* 28 Sept 1907, leaving issue,
1*c* HRH Grand Duke *Friedrich II* (Wilhelm Ludwig Leopold August) of Baden, abdicated 22 Nov 1918, *b* 9 July 1857, *m* 20 Sept 1885, HH Princess *Hilda* Charlotte Wilhelmine (*b* 5 Nov 1864; *d* 8 Feb 1952), yst dau of HRH Grand Duke Adolf of Luxembourg, Duke of Nassau (*see p* 219), and *dsp* 9 Aug 1928.
2*c* HGDH Prince *Ludwig Wilhelm* Karl Friedrich Berthold of Baden, *b* 12 June 1865; *d unm* 23 Feb 1888.
1*c* HGDH Princess Sophie Marie *Victoria* of Baden, *b* 7 Aug 1862, *m* 20 Sept 1881, HM King Gustaf V of Sweden, KG (*b* 16 June 1858; *d* 29 Oct 1950), and *d* 4 April 1930, having had issue (*see p* 224).
3*b* HGDH Prince Ludwig *Wilhelm* August of Baden, *b* 18 Dec 1829, *m* 11 Feb 1863, HIH Princess Maria Maximilianovna Romanovsky (b 16 Oct 1841; *d* 16 Feb 1914), 2nd dau of HIH Maximilian (de Beauharnais) 3rd Duke of Leuchtenberg, by his wife HIH Grand Duchess Maria, eldest dau of HIM Emperor Nicholas I of all the Russias, KG, and *d* 27 April 1897, leaving issue,
1*c* HRH Prince Maximilian (*Max*) Alexander Friedrich Wilhelm of Baden, Chancellor of the German Empire, *s* his cousin Grand Duke Friedrich II as Head of the Grand Ducal House of Baden 1928, *b* 10 July 1867, *m* 10 July 1900, HRH Princess Marie Louise (*b* 11 Oct 1879; *d* 31 Jan 1948), dau of HRH Crown Prince Ernst August of Hanover, 3rd Duke of Cumberland, etc, and *d* 6 Nov 1929, leaving issue (*see p* 290).
1*c* HGDH Princess Sophie *Marie* Louise Amalie Josephine, *b* 26 July 1865, *m* 2 July 1889, HH Duke Friedrich II of Anhalt (*b* 19 Aug 1856; *d* 21 April 1918), and *dsp* 29 Nov 1939.
4*b* HGDH Prince *Karl* Friedrich Gustav Wilhelm Maximilian of Baden, *b* 9 March 1832, *m* (morganatically) 17 May 1871, Baroness Rosalie Louise, *cr* Countess von Rhena 8 May 1871 (*b* 19 June 1845; *d* 15 Oct 1908), dau of Baron Wilhelm von Beust, and *d* 3 Dec 1906, leaving issue,
Count *Friedrich* Maximilian Alexander von Rhena, *b* 29 Jan 1877; *d unm* 19 Nov 1908.
1*b* HGDH Princess *Alexandrine* Luise Amalie Friederike Elisabeth Sophie of Baden, *b* 6 Dec 1820, *m* 3 May 1842, HH Duke Ernst II of Saxe-Coburg and Gotha, KG (*b* 21 June 1818; *d* 22 Aug 1893), brother of HRH the Prince Consort, and *dsp* 20 Dec 1904.
2*b* HGDH Princess *Marie* Amalie of Baden, *b* 20 Nov 1834, *m* 11 Sept 1858, HSH Ernst, 4th Prince zu Leiningen (*b* 9 Nov 1830; *d* 3 April 1904), and *d* 21 Nov 1899, leaving issue,
HSH *Emich* Eduard Karl, 5th Prince zu Leiningen, *b* 18 Jan 1866, *m* 12 July 1894, HSH Princess *Feodora* Viktoria Alberta (*b* 23 July 1866; *d* 1 Nov 1932), yr dau of HSH Hermann, 6th Prince zu Hohenlohe-Langenburg, and *d* 18 July 1939, having had issue (*see p* 259).
HSH Princess Albertine zu Leiningen, *b* 24 July 1863; *d unm* 30 Aug 1901.
3*b* HGDH Princess *Cäcilie* Auguste of Baden (Grand Duchess Olga Feodorovna), *b* 20 Sept 1839, *m* 28 Aug 1857, HIH Grand Duke Michael Nikolaievitch of Russia (*b* 25 Oct 1832; *d* 18 Dec 1909), yst son of HIM Emperor Nicholas I of all the Russias, and *d* 12 April 1891, leaving issue,
1*c* HIH Grand Duke Nicholas Mikhailovitch of Russia, historian, *b* 26 April 1859; *d* in the Russian Revolution 28 Jan 1919, *unm*.
2*c* HIH Grand Duke Michael Mikhailovitch of Russia, *b* 16 Oct 1861, *m* (morganatically) 26 Feb 1891, Countess Sophia, *cr* Countess de Torby by the Grand Duke of Luxembourg 1891 (*b* 1 June 1868; *d* 14 Sept 1927), elder dau of HH Prince Nikolaus of Nassau, by his (morganatic) wife Countess de Merenberg, and *d* 26 April 1929, leaving issue (*see p* 221).
3*c* HIH Grand Duke George Mikhailovitch of Russia, *b* 23 Aug 1863, *m* 12 May 1900, HRH Princess Marie (*b* 3 March 1876; *m* 2ndly 16 Dec 1922, Vice-Adm Pericles Joannides; *d* 13 Dec 1940), 2nd dau of HM King George I of the Hellenes, KG, and *d* in the Russian Revolution 28 Jan 1919, leaving issue (*see p* 281).

4c HIH Grand Duke Alexander Mikhailovitch of Russia, *b* 13 April 1866, *m* 6 Aug 1894, HIH Grand Duchess Xenia Alexandrovna (*b* 6 April 1875; *d* 20 April 1960), elder dau of HIM Emperor Alexander III of all the Russias, KG, and *d* 26 Feb 1933, leaving issue (*see p* 282).
5c HIH Grand Duke Serge Mikhailovitch of Russia, *b* 7 Oct 1869; *d* in the Russian Revolution 17/18 July 1918.
6c HIH Grand Duke Alexei Mikhailovitch of Russia, *b* 28 Dec 1875; *d unm* 2 March 1895.
1c HIH Grand Duchess Anastasia Mikhailovna of Russia, *b* 28 July 1860, *m* 24 Jan 1879, HRH Grand Duke Friedrich Franz III of Mecklenburg-Schwerin (*b* 19 March 1851; *d* 10 April 1897), and *d* 11 March 1922, leaving issue,
1d HRH Grand Duke Friedrich Franz IV (Michael) of Mecklenburg-Schwerin, *b* 9 April 1882, *m* 7 June 1904, HRH Princess *Alexandra* Luise Marie Olga Elisabeth Therese Vera (*b* 29 Sept 1882; *d* 30 Aug 1963), 2nd dau of HRH Prince Ernst August of Hanover, 3rd Duke of Cumberland, KG, and *d* 17 Nov 1945, leaving issue (*see p* 291).
1d HH Duchess *Alexandrine* Auguste of Mecklenburg-Schwerin, *b* 24 Dec 1879, *m* 26 April 1898, HM King Christian X of Denmark, KG (*b* 26 Sept 1870; *d* 20 April 1947), and *d* 28 Dec 1952, leaving issue (*see p* 278).
2d HH Duchess *Cecilie* Auguste Marie of Mecklenburg-Schwerin, *b* 20 Sept 1886, *m* 6 June 1905, HI and RH Crown Prince Friedrich *Wilhelm* Viktor August Ernst of the German Empire and of Prussia (*b* 6 May 1882; *d* 20 July 1951), eldest son of HIM Wilhelm II, German Emperor and King of Prussia, and *d* 6 May 1954, having had issue (*see p* 300).
2a HRH Princess *Amalie* Marie Charlotte of Sweden, *b* 22 Feb 1805; *d unm* 31 Aug 1853.
3a HRH Princess Cäcilie of Sweden, *b* 22 June 1807, *m* 5 May 1831, as his 3rd wife, HRH Grand Duke (Paul Friedrich) August of Oldenburg (*b* 13 July 1783; *d* 27 Feb 1853), and *d* 27 Jan 1844, leaving issue,
HH Duke Anton Günther Friedrich *Elimar* of Oldenburg, *b* 23 Jan 1844; *d* 17 Oct 1895.
(2) HRH Prince Carl Gustaf of Sweden, Duke of Smaland, *b* 25 Aug 1782; *d* 23 March 1783.
2 HH Princess Wilhelmina Caroline of Denmark, *b* 10 July 1747, *m* 1 Sept 1764, her 1st cousin, HRH Elector Wilhelm I of Hesse (*b* 3 June 1743; *d* 27 Feb 1821), and *d* 14 Jan 1820, having had issue (*see p* 259).
3 HH Princess Louisa of Denmark, *b* 30 Jan 1750, *m* 30 Aug 1766, her 1st cousin, HH Landgrave Karl of Hesse-Cassel (*b* 19 Dec 1744; *d* 17 Aug 1836), and *d* 12 Jan 1831, having had issue (*see p* 276).

King George II was *s* by his grandson,
1760-1820 GEORGE III (George William Frederick), **King of Great Britain and Ireland** (styled the same as George I until 1 Jan 1801, then *By the Grace of God, of the United Kingdom of Great Britain and Ireland, King, Defender of the Faith*), *s* his father as Duke of Cornwall, Duke of Rothesay, etc and also as Duke of Edinburgh, etc 1751, *cr* Prince of Wales and Earl of Chester 20 April 1751, crowned at Westminster Abbey by Thomas Secker, Archbishop of Canterbury 22 Sept 1761, founded the Order of St Patrick 5 Feb 1783, declared King of Hanover 12 Oct 1814, *b* at Norfolk House, St James's Square, London 4 June 1738, *m* at St James's Palace 8 Sept 1761, HSH Princess Sophia *Charlotte,* crowned with her husband (*b* at Mirow, 19 May 1744; *d* at Kew Palace 17 Nov 1818, *bur* St George's Chapel, Windsor), 5th and yst dau of HSH Duke Karl Ludwig Friedrich of Mecklenburg-Strelitz, by his wife HSH Princess Albertine Elisabeth, 2nd dau of HSH Ernst Friedrich, Duke of Saxe-Hildburghausen, and *d* at Windsor Castle 29 Jan 1820 (*bur* St George's Chapel, Windsor), having had issue,

1 HRH Prince GEORGE AUGUSTUS FREDERICK, *s* his father as KING GEORGE IV.
2 HRH Prince Frederick, DUKE OF YORK AND ALBANY, KG (1771), PC (1787), GCB (1815), GCH (1815), FRS (1789), elected Prince-Bishop of Osnabrück 27 Feb 1764, First and Prin Kt Companion of the Order of the Bath 1767, Col in the Army 1780, Major-Gen 1782, Lt-Gen 1784, Col Coldstream Guards 1784, *cr* DUKE OF YORK AND ALBANY and EARL OF ULSTER 27 Nov 1784, C-in-C of the Forces in the United Prov 1793, Gen in the Army 1793, Field Marshal 1795, Col-in-Chief 60th (Royal Americans) Regt of Foot 1797, C-in-C of the Forces in GB 1798, Capt-Gen of the Forces in GB and the Continent 1799, C-in-C in GB and Ireland 1801-09, Col 1st Regt of Foot Guards 1805, Warden and Keeper of the New Forest 1805, Keeper and Lieut of Windsor Forest 1805, High Steward of New Windsor 1811, C-in-C of the Forces 1811, Kt of the Order of the Holy Ghost (France) (1814), Grand Cross of the Order of Carlos III (Spain) (1814), and Grand Cross of the Order of Maria Theresa (Austria) (1814), Field Marshal in the Austrian Army 1814, *b* at Buckingham House, St James's Park, London 16 Aug 1763, *m* at Berlin 29 Sept and in London 24 Nov 1791, HRH Princess *Frederica* Charlotte Ulrica Catherine (*b* at Potsdam 7 May 1767; *d* at Oatlands, Surrey 6 Aug 1820, *bur* Weybridge, Surrey), eldest dau of HM King Friedrich Wilhelm II of Prussia, by his 1st wife HSH Princess Elisabeth Christine Ulrike, dau of HSH Duke Karl of Brunswick, and *dsp* at Rutland House, Arlington Street, London 5 Jan 1827 (*bur* St George's Chapel, Windsor).
3 HRH Prince WILLIAM HENRY, *s* his brother as KING WILLIAM IV.
4 HRH Prince Edward, DUKE OF KENT AND STRATHEARN, KG (1786), Brevet-Col 1786, Major-Gen 1793, *cr* DUKE OF KENT AND STRATHEARN and EARL OF DUBLIN 24 April 1799, Gen 1799, C-in-C of the Forces in British N America 1799-1800, Gov of Gibraltar 1802-03, Field Marshal 1805, Keeper of Hampton Court Palace 1806, *b* at Buckingham House, St James's Park 2 Nov 1767, *m* at Coburg 29 May and at Kew Palace 11 July 1818, HSH Princess *Victoria* Mary Louisa (*b* at Coburg 17 Aug 1786; *d* at Frogmore, nr Windsor 16 March 1861, *bur* first St George's Chapel, Windsor, later transferred Kent Mausoleum, Frogmore), widow of HSH Emich Karl, 2nd Prince zu Leiningen, and 4th dau of HSH Franz Friedrich Anton, Duke of Saxe-Saalfeld-Coburg, by his 2nd wife Countess Auguste Caroline Sophie, eldest dau of Heinrich XXIV, Count Reuss-Ebersdorf, and *d* at Sidmouth, Devon 23 Jan 1820 (*bur* first St George's Chapel, Windsor, later transferred Kent Mausoleum, Frogmore), leaving issue,
HRH Princess ALEXANDRINA *VICTORIA*, *s* her uncle King William IV.
5 HRH Prince *Ernest* Augustus, KG (1786), GCB (1815), DUKE OF CUMBERLAND, Lt-Col 9th Hanoverian Hus 1793, Major-Gen in the British and Hanoverian Armies 1794, *cr* DUKE OF CUMBERLAND AND TEVIOTDALE and EARL OF ARMAGH 24 April 1799, Gen 1803, Chancellor of Trin Coll Dublin 1805, Dep-Elector of Hanover 1813, Field Marshal 1813, *s* his brother King William IV as King of Hanover 20 June 1837, *b* at Queen's House, St James's Park 5 June 1771, *m* at Strelitz 29 May and at Carlton House, London 29 Aug 1815, HSH Princess *Frederica* Caroline Sophia Alexandrina (*b* at Hanover 2 March 1778; *d* at Hanover 21 June 1841, *bur* Herrenhausen), widow of HSH Prince Friedrich Wilhelm zu Solms-Braunfels and previously of HRH Prince Ludwig of Prussia, and 5th dau of HSH Karl, Duke of Mecklenburg-Strelitz, by his 1st wife HSH Princess Friederike, eldest dau of HSH Prince Georg Wilhelm of Hesse-

Darmstadt, and *d* at Herrenhausen 18 Nov 1851 (*bur* there), having had issue (with a dau stillborn 27 Jan 1817),

HM King *Georg V* (Friedrich Alexander Karl Ernst August) of Hanover (1851-1866), 2nd DUKE OF CUMBERLAND, etc, KG (1835), lost his throne when Hanover was annexed to the Kingdom of Prussia 20 Sept 1866, *b* at Berlin 27 May 1819, *m* at Hanover 18 Feb 1843, HH Princess Alexandrine *Marie* Wilhelmine Katharina Charlotte Therese Henriette Louise Pauline Elisabeth Friederike Georgine, VA (*b* at Hildburghausen 14 April 1818; *d* at Gmunden 9 Jan 1907, *bur* there), eldest dau of HH Duke Joseph of Saxe-Altenburg, by his wife HRH Duchess Luise *Amalie* Wilhelmine Philippine, 2nd dau of HRH Duke Ludwig of Württemberg (*see p* 258), and *d* at 7 rue Presbourg, Paris 12 June 1878 (*bur* St George's Chapel, Windsor), leaving issue,

(1) HRH Crown Prince *Ernst August* Wilhelm Adolf Georg Friedrich of Hanover, 3rd Duke of Cumberland, etc, KG (1878), GCH, Col in the British Army 1876, Major-Gen 1886, Lt-Gen 1892, Gen 1898, Col of Cav in the Austrian Army, *s* his kinsman Duke Wilhelm (*see p* 210) as Duke of Brunswick and Head of the Ducal House 1884, but was impeded to *s* by Council of the German Empire and renounced in favour of his only surv son 24 Oct 1913, struck off the roll of the Order of the Garter 13 May 1915, deprived of his peerages and title of Prince of GB and Ireland by Order in Council 28 March 1919, *b* at Hanover 21 Sept 1845, *m* at Christiansborg Castle, Copenhagen 21 Dec 1878, HRH Princess *Thyra* Amelia Caroline Charlotte Anne, CI (*b* at Copenhagen 29 Sept 1853; *d* at Gmunden 26 Feb 1933), 3rd and yst dau of HM King Christian IX of Denmark (*see p* 284) and *d* at Gmunden 14 Nov 1923, having had issue,

1*a* HRH Prince *Georg Wilhelm* Christian Albert Edward Alexander Friedrich Waldemar Ernst Adolf of Hanover, GCVO, Capt 42nd Regt of Inf in the Austrian Army, *b* at Gmunden 28 Oct 1880; *d unm* at Brandenburg 20 May 1912.

2*a* HRH Prince *Christian* Friedrich Wilhelm Georg Peter Waldemar of Hanover, *b* at Gmunden 4 July 1885; *d* there 3 Sept 1901.

3*a* HRH *Ernst August* Christian Georg, *s* as Duke of Brunswick-Lüneburg 1 Nov 1913 following his father's renunciation, abdicated 8 Nov 1918, deprived of his title of Prince of GB and Ireland by Order in Council 28 March 1919, *b* at Penzing, nr Vienna 17 Nov 1887, *m* at Berlin 24 May 1913, •HRH Princess *Viktoria Luise* Adelheid Mathilde Charlotte, has Grand Cross of Order of St Olga and St Sophia of Greece (*b* at Marmorpalais, nr Potsdam 13 Sept 1892) [*Stresemannstrasse 5, Braunschweig 33, Germany*], only dau of HIM Wilhelm II, German Emperor and King of Prussia (*see p* 302), and *d* at Schloss Marienburg, nr Nordstemmen 30 Jan 1953, leaving issue,

1*b* •HRH Prince *Ernst August* Georg Wilhelm Christian Ludwig Franz Josef Nikolaus of Hanover, Duke of Brunswick-Lüneburg, Head of the Royal House of Hanover, Dr jur, late Capt in the German Army, has the Order of the Elephant of Denmark and the Grand Cross of the Order of the Redeemer of Greece [*Calenberg, 3211 Schulenburg an der Leine über Elze, Hanover, Germany; A-4810 Gmunden, Königsvilla, Upper Austria*], *b* 18 March 1914, *educ* Univ Coll Oxford, *m* 4 Sept 1951, •HH Princess *Ortrud* Bertha Adelheid Hedwig (*b* 19 Dec 1925), 2nd dau of HH late Prince Albert of Schleswig-Holstein-Sonderburg-Glücksburg (*see p* 277), and has issue,

1*c* •HRH Prince *Ernst August* Albert Paul Otto Rupprecht Oskar Berthold Friedrich Ferdinand Christian Ludwig of Hanover, *b* 26 Feb 1954.

2*c* •HRH Prince *Ludwig Rudolph* Georg Wilhelm Philipp Friedrich Wolrad Maximilian of Hanover, *b* 21 Nov 1955.

3*c* •HRH Prince *Heinrich Julius* Christian Otto Friedrich Franz Anton Günther of Hanover, *b* 29 April 1961.

1*c* •HRH Princess *Marie* Viktoria Luise Hertha Friederike of Hanover, *b* 26 Nov 1952.

2*c* •HRH Princess *Olga* Sophie Charlotte Anna of Hanover, *b* 17 Feb 1958.

3*c* •HRH Princess *Alexandra* Irene Margaretha Elizabeth Bathildis of Hanover, *b* 18 Feb 1959.

2*b* •HRH Prince *Georg Wilhelm* Ernst August Friedrich Axel of Hanover, late Major 10th Cav Regt, sometime Headmaster of Salem Sch, has Grand Cross of the Order of the Redeemer of Greece [*Georgs Haus, 8166 Neuhaus/Schliewer, Germany*], *b* 25 March 1915, *educ* Göttingen Univ (LLD 1948), *m* 23 April 1946, •HRH Princess Sophie (*b* 26 June 1914), widow of HH Prince Christoph of Hesse (*see p* 284), and yst dau of HRH Prince Andrew of Greece and Denmark, GCVO (*see p* 280), and has issue,

1*c* •HRH Prince *Welf* Ernst August Andreas Philipp Georg Wilhelm Ludwig Berthold of Hanover, *b* 25 Jan 1947, *m* 1969, •Wibeke, dau of Harry von Gunsteren, and has issue,

•(Prinzessin) Tanya (von Hannover), *b* 1970.

2*c* •HRH Prince *Georg* Paul Christian of Hanover, *b* 9 Dec 1949.

1*c* •HRH Princess *Friederike Elisabeth* Viktoria Luise Alice Olga Theodora Helena of Hanover, *b* 15 Oct 1954.

3*b* •HRH Prince *Christian* Oskar Ernst August Wilhelm Viktor Georg Heinrich of Hanover, late Capt 13th Cav Regt, has Grand Cross of the Order of the Redeemer of Greece, *b* 1 Sept 1919, *m* 25 Nov 1963, •Mireille (*b* 10 Jan 1946), dau of Armand Dutry, and has issue,

1*c* •(Prinzessin) *Caroline Luise* Mireille Irene Sophie (von Hannover), *b* 1965.

2*c* •(Prinzessin) *Mireille* Viktoria Luise (von Hannover), *b* 1971.

4*b* •HRH Prince *Welf Heinrich* Ernst August Georg Christian Berthold Friedrich Wilhelm Louis Ferdinand of Hanover, Dr jur, has Grand Cross of the Order of the Redeemer of Greece, [*6 Frankfort a M-Niederrad, Neuwiesenstrasse 22, Germany*], *b* 11 March 1923, *m* 21 Sept 1960, •HSH Princess Sophie *Alexandra* Cecilie Anna Maria Friederike Benigna Dorothea zu Ysenburg und Büdingen in Wächtersbach (*b* 23 Oct 1937), only dau of HSH Otto Friedrich, 3rd Prince zu Ysenburg und Büdingen (*see p* 261).

1*b* •HRH Princess Friederike (*Frederika*) Luise Thyra Viktoria Margarete Sophie Olga Cecile Isabelle Christa of Hanover, has Grand Cross of the Order of St Olga and St Sophia of Greece, *b* 18 April 1917, *m* 9 Jan 1938, HM King Paul I of the Hellenes, KG, GCVO (*b* 14 Dec 1901; *d* 6 March 1964), and has issue (*see p* 279).

1*a* HRH Princess *Marie Louise* Victoria Caroline Amelie Alexandra Auguste Friederike of Hanover, *b* at Gmunden 11 Oct 1879, *m* there 10 July 1900, HRH Prince *Maximilian* Alexander Friedrich Wilhelm of Baden, Head of the Grand Ducal House of Baden 1928-1929, Chancellor of the German Empire Oct-Nov 1918 (*b* at Baden-Baden 10 July 1867; *d* at Constance 6 Nov 1929), and *d* at Salem, Baden 31 Jan 1948, having had issue,

HRH *Berthold* Friedrich Wilhelm Ernst August Heinrich Karl, Margrave of Baden, Head of the Grand Ducal House of Baden 1929-1963, *b* 24 Feb 1906, *m* 17 Aug 1931, HRH Princess Theodora (*b* 30 May 1906; *d* 16 Oct 1969), 2nd dau of HRH Prince Andrew of Greece and Denmark, GCVO (*see p* 280), and *d* 27 Oct 1963, leaving issue,

1*c* •HRH *Maximilian* Andreas Friedrich Gustav Ernst August Bernhard, Margrave of Baden, Head of the Grand Ducal House of Baden from 1963 [*7777 Schloss Salem, Baden, Germany*], *b* 3 July 1933, *educ* Gordonstoun, *m* 30 Sept 1966, •HI and RH Archduchess *Valerie* Isabelle Maria Anna Alfonsa Desideria Brigitte Sophia Thomasia Huberta Josepha Ignatia (*b* 23 May 1941), 7th dau of HI and RH late Archduke Hubert Salvator of Austria, Prince of Tuscany (*see p* 230), and has issue,

1*d* •HRH Hereditary Prince *Bernhard* Max Friedrich August Gustav Louis Kraft of Baden, *b* 27 May 1970.
2*d* •HGDH Prince *Leopold* Max Christian Ludwig Clemens Hubert of Baden, *b* 1 Oct 1971.
1*d* •HGDH Princess *Marie-Louise* Elisabeth Mathilde Theodora Cecilie Sarah Charlotte of Baden, *b* 3 July 1969.
2*c* •HGDH Prince *Ludwig* Wilhelm Georg Ernst Christoph of Baden [*6931 Schloss Zwingenberg über Eberbach, Bad Neckartal, Germany*], *b* 16 March 1937, *m* 21 Oct 1967, •HSH Princess Maria Anna (*Marianne*) Henriette Eleonore Gobertina (*b* 15 Dec 1943), 5th dau of HSH Prince Karl von Auersperg-Breunner.
1*c* •HGDH Princess *Margarita* Alice Thyra Viktoria Marie Louise Scholastica of Baden, *b* 14 July 1932, *educ* Cranborne Chase Sch, *m* 6 June 1957, •HRH Prince Tomislav of Yugoslavia (*b* 9 Jan 1928), and has issue (*see p* 296).
HGDH Princess *Marie Alexandra* Thyra Viktoria Louise Carola Hilda of Baden, *b* 1 Aug 1902, *m* 17 Sept 1924, •HH Prince *Wolfgang* Moritz of Hesse (*b* 6 Nov 1896), and was *k* in an air raid at Frankfurt a M 29 Jan 1944, *sp*.
2*a* HRH Princess *Alexandra* Luise Marie Olga Elisabeth Therese Vera of Hanover, *b* at Gmunden 29 Sept 1882, *m* there 7 June 1904, HRH Grand Duke Friedrich Franz IV of Mecklenburg-Schwerin (*b* at Palermo 9 April 1882; *d* at Flensburg 17 Nov 1945) (*see p* 289), and *d* at Glücksburg 30 Aug 1963, leaving issue,
1*b* •HRH Hereditary Grand Duke *Friedrich Franz* Michael Wilhelm Nikolaus Franz Joseph Ernst August Hans of Mecklenburg(-Schwerin), Head of the Grand Ducal House of Mecklenburg(-Schwerin) from 1945, formerly Sec to German Legation, Copenhagen, has Order of the Elephant of Denmark [*D2 Hamburg 55, Besterleystrasse 49, Germany*], *b* 22 April 1910, *m* 11 June 1941, •*Karin Elisabeth* Henrietta Lori Gudela (*b* 31 Jan 1920), eldest dau of late Dr Walter von Schaper.
2*b* •HRH Duke *Christian Ludwig* Ernst August Maximilian Johann Albrecht Adolf Friedrich of Mecklenburg, has Order of the Black Eagle of Prussia [*2331 Hemmelmark über Eckernförde, Germany*], *b* 29 Sept 1912, *m* 11 July 1954, •HRH Princess *Barbara* Irene Adelaide Viktoria Elisabeth Bathildis (*b* 2 Aug 1920), only dau of HRH Prince Sigismund of Prussia (*see p* 302), and has issue,
1*c* •HH Duchess Donata of Mecklenburg, *b* 11 March 1956.
2*c* •HH Duchess Edwina of Mecklenburg, *b* 25 Sept 1960.
1*b* •HH Duchess *Thyra* Anastasia Alexandrine Marie Louise Olga Cecilie Charlotte Elisabeth Emma of Mecklenburg [*2392 Schloss Glücksburg/Ostsee, Germany*], *b* 18 June 1919.
2*b* •HH Duchess *Anastasia* Alexandrine Cecilie Marie Louise Wilhelmine of Mecklenburg, *b* 11 Nov 1922, *m* 1 Sept 1943, •HH Prince *Friedrich Ferdinand* Karl Ernst August Wilhelm Harald Kasimir Nicola of Schleswig-Holstein-Sonderburg-Glücksburg (*b* 14 May 1913) [*2392 Schloss Glücksburg/Ostsee, Germany*], and has issue,
1*c* •HH Princess *Elisabeth* Marie Alexandra of Schleswig-Holstein-Sonderburg-Glücksburg, *b* 10 Sept 1945.
2*c* •HH Princess *Irene* Olga Adelheid of Schleswig-Holstein-Sonderburg-Glücksburg, *b* 11 Oct 1946.
3*c* •HH Princess *Margaretha* Friederike Luise of Schleswig-Holstein-Sonderburg-Glücksburg, *b* 10 Feb 1948.
4*c* •HH Princess *Sibylla* Ursula Ortrud of Schleswig-Holstein-Sonderburg-Glücksburg, *b* 11 Sept 1955.
3*a* HRH Princess *Olga* Adelheid Luise Marie Alexandrine Agnes of Hanover, *b* at Gmunden 11 July 1884; *d unm* at Hubertihaus, nr Gmunden 21 Sept 1958.

(1) HRH Princess *Friederike* Sophie Marie Henriette Amalie Therese of Hanover, CI, RRC, DJStJ, *b* at Hanover 9 Jan 1848, *m* at the private chapel, Windsor Castle 24 April 1880, Baron Luitbert Alexander Georg Lionel Alfons von Pawel-Rammingen, KCB, KCVO, KCH, Offr of the Hanoverian Ernst August Order, Offr of the Legion of Honour, Kt of the Order of Henry the Lion of Brunswick, etc, hon Col 3rd Vol Bn Essex Regt 1884-90 (*b* at Coburg 27 July 1843; *d* at Biarritz 20 Nov 1932), and *d* at Biarritz 16 Oct 1926, having had issue,
Baroness *Victoria* Georgina Beatrice Maud Anne von Pawel-Rammingen, *b* at Hampton Court Palace 7 March, *d* 29 March 1881 (*bur* St George's Chapel, Windsor).
(2) HRH Princess *Marie* Ernestine Josephine Adolfine Henriette Therese Elisabeth Alexandrine of Hanover, CI, *b* at Hanover 3 Dec 1849; *d unm* at Gmunden 4 June 1904 (*bur* there).
6 HRH Prince *Augustus* Frederick, DUKE OF SUSSEX, KG (1786), *cr* DUKE OF SUSSEX, EARL OF INVERNESS, and BARON ARKLOW 27 Nov 1801, *b* at Buckingham House, St James's Park 27 Jan 1773, *educ* Göttingen Univ, *m* 1st (in contravention of the Royal Marriage Act) at Rome 4 April 1793 and at St George's, Hanover Square, London 5 Dec 1793 (*m* declared null and void by the Prerogative Court 3 Aug 1794), Lady Augusta Murray, who assumed the surname of De Ameland by Royal Licence 13 Oct 1806 (*b* in London 27 Jan 1768; *d* at Ramsgate, Kent 5 March 1830), 2nd dau of 4th Earl of Dunmore (*see* BURKE'S *Peerage*), and had issue,
Sir Augustus Frederick d'Este, KGH (1830), Lt-Col 1824, Col 1838, Dep Ranger of St James's and Hyde Parks, unsuccessfully claimed the Dukedom of Sussex 1843, *b* 13 Jan 1794; *d unm* 28 Dec 1848.
Augusta Emma d'Este, called Mademoiselle d'Este, *b* in London 11 Aug 1801, *m* 13 Aug 1845, as his 2nd wife, Thomas Wilde, 1st Baron Truro, Lord High Chancellor of GB 1850-52 (*b* in London 7 July 1782; *d* in London, 11 Nov 1855) (*see* BURKE'S *Peerage*, 1899 *Edn*), and *dsp* in London, 21 May 1866.
The Duke of Sussex *m* 2ndly (again in contravention of the Royal Marriage Act) *ca* 2 May 1831, Lady *Cecilia* Letitia Underwood (who assumed that surname by Royal Licence 2 March 1834), *cr* Duchess of Inverness 10 April 1840 (*b* 1785; *d* at Kensington Palace 1 Aug 1873, *bur* Kensal Green), widow of Sir George Buggin, and dau of 2nd Earl of Arran, KP (*see* BURKE'S *Peerage*), and *d* at Kensington Palace 21 April 1843 (*bur* Kensal Green).
7 HRH Prince *Adolphus* Frederick, 1st DUKE OF CAMBRIDGE, KG (1786), PC (1802), GCB, GCMG, GCH, FSA, Col in the Hanoverian Army 1793, Lt-Gen 1798, Lt-Gen in the British Army 1803, *cr* DUKE OF CAMBRIDGE, EARL OF TIPPERARY, and BARON CULLODEN 27 Nov 1801, Field Marshal 1813, Viceroy of Hanover 1816-37, Chancellor of St Andrews Univ 1811-14, *b* at Buckingham House 24 Feb 1774, *m* at Cassel 7 May and at the Queen's House, St James's Park 1 June 1818, HSH Princess *Augusta* Wilhelmina Louisa (*b* at Cassel 25 July 1797; *d* at St James's Palace, 6 April 1889, *bur* first Kew, later removed St George's Chapel, Windsor), 3rd dau of HH Landgrave Friedrich of Hesse-Cassel (*see p* 286), and *d* at Cambridge House, Piccadilly, London 8 July 1850 (*bur* first Kew, later removed St George's Chapel, Windsor), leaving issue,
1 HRH Prince *George* William Frederick Charles, 2nd DUKE OF CAMBRIDGE, etc, KG, KT, KP, PC, GCB, GCSI, GCMG, GCH, GCIE, GCVO, Field Marshal in the Army, Chief Personal ADC to HM King Edward VII, C-in-C of the British Forces 1856-95, Grand Master of the Order of St Michael and St George, Ranger of St James's, Green, Hyde and Richmond Parks, *b* at Hanover 26 March 1819, *m* (in contravention of the Royal Marriage Act) at St John's Church, Clerkenwell, London 8 Jan 1847, Sarah (called *Louisa*), known as Mrs FitzGeorge (*b* at Bow Street, Covent Garden, London 1816; *d* at 6 Queen Street, Mayfair, London 12 Jan 1890, *bur* Kensal Green), dau of Robert Fairbrother, a

theatrical printer, by his wife, a dau of Thomas Freeman, of Wylecot, Shrewsbury, and *d* at Gloucester House, Piccadilly, London 17 March 1904 (*bur* Kensal Green), leaving issue,

(1) *George* William Adolphus FitzGeorge, Col Royal Welch Fus, late 20th Hus, served in Egyptian Campaign and was present at Battle of Tel-el-Kebir (despatches, medal with clasp, 4th cl. Order of Osmanieh, Khedive's Star), *b* in London, 27 Aug 1843, *m* in Paris, 25 Nov 1885, *Rosa* Fredericka (*b* 9 March 1854; *d* 10 March 1927), formerly wife of Capt Frank Wigsell Arkwright, Coldstream Guards, and dau of William Henry Baring, JP, of Norman Court, Hants (*see* BURKE'S *Peerage*, NORTHBROOK, B.), and *d* at Lucerne, Switzerland 2 Sept 1907, leaving issue,

1*a* *George* William Frederick FitzGeorge, Cmdr RN, joined RN 1905, served in World Wars I and II, attached British Embassy, Paris 1944-46, had Legion of Honour, French Croix de Guerre, and Order of St Benito of Aviz of Portugal, *b* 12 Oct 1892, *educ* RN Colls Osborne and Dartmouth, *m* 1st 1918 (*m* diss by div 1927). Esther Vignon (*b* 1888; *d ca* 1935). He *m* 2ndly 1934 (*m* diss by div 1955), France (*b* 1911), dau of Robert Bellanger, French *Senateur,* and *dsp* at Tours 13 June 1960.

1*a* •Mabel *Iris* FitzGeorge [*45 Eaton Place, SW1*], *b* 23 Sept 1886, *m* 1st at the Chapel Royal, St James's Palace 12 Dec 1912, Robert Shekelton Balfour (*b* 7 March 1869; *d* 1 Nov 1942), son of Robert Balfour, of Stirling, and has issue,

•Sir Robert George *Victor* FitzGeorge-Balfour, KCB (1968) (CB 1965), CBE (1945) (MBE 1943), DSO (1950), MC (1939), Gen, commn'd Coldstream Guards 1934, UK Mil Rep to NATO from 1971, Kt Cmdr of the Order of Orange-Nassau of the Netherlands (with swords) (1946) [*The Old Rectory, West Chiltington, Sussex*], *b* 15 Sept 1913, *educ* Eton, and Kings Coll Camb (BA 1934), *m* at the Chapel Royal, St James's Palace 4 Dec 1943, •Mary Diana (*b* 12 Oct 1914), elder dau of late Adm Arthur Henry Christian, CB, MVO (*see* BURKE'S LG, CHRISTIAN *formerly of Milntown and Ewanrigg*), and has issue,

•*Robin* Victor FitzGeorge-Balfour, *b* 5 June 1951, *educ* Eton.

•*Diana* Christian Mary FitzGeorge-Balfour, *b* 8 March 1946,

She *m* 2ndly 12 Aug 1945, as his 2nd wife, Prince Vladimir Emmanuelovitch Galitzine (*b* 5 June 1884; *d* 13 July 1954).

2*a* George Daphné FitzGeorge, served in World War I as Red Cross nurse (Silver Palm Medal of France), empd in operating theatre, Westminster Hosp in World War II (resigned owing to ill-health 1945), *b* 23 Feb 1889, *m* 8 Dec 1915 (*m* diss by div 1926), as his 1st wife, George Foster Earle, later Sir George Foster Earle, CBE (*b* 8 Feb 1890; *d* 11 Dec 1965), son of John Hudson Earle, and *dsp* 1 June 1954.

(2) Sir *Adolphus* Augustus Frederick FitzGeorge, KCVO (1904), Rear-Adm, entered RN 1859, Lieut 1866, Cmdr 1872, Capt 1881, ret 1893, Rear-Adm 1896, Equerry to his father FM HRH The Duke of Cambridge 1897-1904, *b* in London 30 Jan 1846, *m* 1st at Hessle, Yorks 21 Sept 1875, *Sophia* Jane (*b* 1857, *d* 3 Feb 1920), dau of Thomas Holden, of Winestead Hall, Hull, and had issue,

Olga Mary Adelaide FitzGeorge, *b* 11 June 1877, *m* 1st 18 Dec 1897 (*m* diss by div 1902), Charles Edward *Archibald* Watkin Hamilton (later Sir Archibald Hamilton, 5th and 3rd Bt) (*b* 10 Dec 1876; *d* 18 March 1939) (*see* BURKE'S *Peerage,* HAMILTON, Bt, *of Trebinshun House*), and had issue,

1*b* George Edward Archibald Augustus FitzGeorge Hamilton, *b* 30 Dec 1898; *k* in action in World War I 18 May 1918.

1*b* A dau, *b* and *d* 5 May 1902.

She *m* 2ndly 5 Jan 1905, S/Ldr Robert Charlton Lane, RAF, of Glebe Manor, Havant, Hants (*b* 26 Jan 1873; *d* 23 May 1943), eldest son of Charles Thomas Lane, and *d* at Rouen 15 Oct 1928, leaving further issue,

2*b* •Mary Alice Olga Sofia Jane Lane, *b* 4 Jan 1919, *m* 1st 14 Nov 1939 (*m* diss by div 1961), Edward Christopher Hohler (*b* 22 Jan 1917), 2nd son of late Lt-Col Arthur Preston Hohler, DSO and bar, Middx Regt, of Long Crendon Manor, Aylesbury, Bucks (*see* BURKE'S *LG*), and has issue,

1*c* •Frederick Christopher Gerald Hohler, *b* 30 Aug 1943, *educ* Eton, *m* •Sarah Virginia, yr dau of Ian Gilbert, of 45 Belgrave Mews North, SW1, and has issue,

1*d* •Alice Hohler, *b* 28 Aug 1970.

2*d* •a dau, *b* 5 Dec 1971.

2*c* •Robert Henry Adolphus Hohler, *b* 2 Oct 1947.

1*c* •Olga Mary Hohler, *b* 11 Oct 1940, *m* 5 July 1969, •Godfrey Hamilton Bland (*b* 3 July 1943), yr son of James Franklin McMahon Bland, of Newcastle, co Down (*see* BURKE'S *LG of Ireland,* BLAND *formerly of Derryquin Castle*), and has issue,

•a son, *b* 23 Feb 1972.

2*c* •Philippa Caroline Jane Hohler, *b* 13 Jan 1942, *m* 5 Feb 1966, •William Terence Sanders (*b* 30 April 1940), 2nd surv son of Terence Robert Beaumont Sanders, CB, DL, of Slough House, Buckland, Surrey (*see* BURKE'S *LG of Ireland,* SANDERS *of Coolnamuck, formerly of Charleville Park*), and has issue,

1*d* •Algernon William Robert Sanders, *b* 18 March 1967.

1*d* •Laline Marion Jane Sanders, *b* 18 Feb 1969.

2*d* •a dau, *b* 23 Feb 1971.

She *m* 2ndly 14 May 1962, •Ronald Stratford Scrivener, CMG, Amb to Czechoslovakia (*b* 29 Dec 1919) [*72 Bedford Gardens, W8*], only son of late Sir Patrick Stratford Scrivener, KCMG, of Great Bedwyn, Wilts.

Sir Adolphus *m* 2ndly at Pimlico 28 Oct 1920, *Margarita* Beatrice (*b* 1863; *d* 26 Feb 1934), dau of John Watson, and *d* in London 17 Dec 1922.

(3) Sir *Augustus* Charles Frederick FitzGeorge, KCVO (1904), CB (1895), Col 11th Hus, joined The Rifle Bde 1864, Capt 1877, joined 11th Hus 1878, Major 1881, Lt-Col 1886, Col 1890, ret 1900, Priv Sec to his father FM HRH The Duke of Cambridge 1886-96 and later Equerry, extra ADC to HRH The Prince of Wales 1871-76, ADC to Lord Napier of Magdala, C-in-C India 1870-75, Sec to Horse Commn 1882, Extra ADC to GOC Aldershot 1883-85, EsqStJ *b* in London 12 June 1847; *d unm* in London 30 Oct 1933.

1 HRH Princess *Augusta* Caroline Charlotte Elizabeth Mary Sophia Louisa, CI, *b* at the Palace of Montbrillant, nr Hanover 19 July 1822, *m* at Buckingham Palace 28 June 1843, HRH Grand Duke *Friedrich Wilhelm* Karl Georg Ernst Adolf Gustav of Mecklenburg-Strelitz, KG, GCB (*b* at Neustrelitz 17 Oct 1819; *d* there 30 May 1904), and *d* at Neustrelitz 4 Dec 1916, having had issue,

(1) A son, *b* and *d* 13 Jan 1845.

(2) HRH Grand Duke (Georg) *Adolf Friedrich V* (August Viktor Ernst Adalbert Gustav Wilhelm Wellington) of Mecklenburg-Strelitz (1904-1914), KG, GCB, *b* 22 July 1848, *m* 17 April 1877, HH Princess *Elisabeth* Marie Friederike Amalie Agnes (*b* 7 Sept 1857; *d* 20 July 1933), eldest dau of HH Friedrich, Duke of Anhalt, and *d* 11 June 1914, having had issue,

1*a* HRH Grand Duke *Adolf Friedrich VI* (Georg Ernst Albert Eduard) of Mecklenburg-Strelitz (1914-1918), *b* 17 June 1882; *d unm* 24 Feb 1918.

2*a* HH Duke *Karl Borwin* Christian Alexander Arthur of Mecklenburg-Strelitz, *b* 10 Oct 1888; *d* 24 Aug 1908.

1*a* HH Duchess Victoria *Marie* Auguste Luise Antoinette Karoline Leopoldine of Mecklenburg-Strelitz, *b* 8 May 1878, *m* 1st 22 June 1899 (*m* diss by div 1908), Count Georges Jametel, and had issue,

1*b* •Count Georges Jametel, *b* 3 Feb 1904, *m* Nov 1948, •Lise Barbet.

1*b* •Countess Marie Auguste Friederike Elisabeth von Nemerow (*cr* 26 Jan 1910) [*Auberge les Genets, Coye la Forêt, Oise, France*], *b* 11

Sept 1905, *m* 8 May 1928, Major Karl Barton genannt von Stedman (*b* 30 Sept 1875; *d* 30 Sept 1933), and has issue,

●Ralph Joachim Barton genannt von Stedman, *b* 24 Feb 1933, *m* 25 Nov 1964, ●Asta Helen (*b* 13 Jan 1948), dau of Wilhelm Knorr, and has issue,

●Gloria Veronika Barton genannt von Stedman, *b* 15 Dec 1964.

She *m* 2ndly 11 Aug 1914, HSH Prince *Julius Ernst* Rudolf Friedrich Franz Viktor of Lippe (*b* 2 Sept 1873; *d* 15 Sept 1952), and *d* 14 Oct 1948, leaving further issue,

2*b* ●HSH Prince *Ernst August* Bernhard Alexander Eduard Friedrich Wilhelm of Lippe, Head of the Princely House of Lippe from 1953 [*Haus Obercassel, nr Bonn-on-Rhine, Germany*], *b* 1 April 1917, *m* 3 March 1948, ●*Christa* Irene (*b* 2 July 1923), dau of Curt David von Arnim-Kitzscher, and has issue,

1*c* ●HSH Hereditary Prince *Friedrich Wilhelm* Ernst Viktor Alexander of Lippe, *b* 7 Sept 1947.

2*c* ●HSH Prince *Ernst August* Friedrich Karl Georg Wilhelm of Lippe, *b* 24 Dec 1952.

1*c* ●HSH Princess Marie *Stephanie* Elisabeth Karoline Gloria of Lippe, *b* 26 Aug 1949, *m* 8 May 1971, ●*Nikolaus* Wilfried Friedrich Karl von Itzenplitz (*b* 7 Feb 1943) [*D5300, Bonn-Oberkassel, Haus Obercassel, Germany*], and has issue,

●*Georg Friedrich* Nikolaus Wilfried Christian Ernst August von Itzenplitz, *b* 1 March 1972.

2*c* ●HSH Princess Regine *Marie Christine* Emanuela Anna Charlotte Friederike Juliane of Lippe, *b* 13 Dec 1959.

2*b* ●HSH Princess *Elisabeth Caroline* Adelheid Friederike Leopoldine Armgard of Lippe, *b* 23 Jan 1916, *m* 15 Feb 1939, ●HSH Prince *Ernst August* Adolf Friedrich Hermann Albrecht Bernhard Maria zu Solms-Braunfels (*b* 10 March 1892) [*Schloss Braunfels, Lahn, Rheinland, Germany*], and has issue,

●HSH Princess *Maria Angela* Elisabeth Friederike Uta Beatrice zu Solms-Braunfels, *b* 6 Aug 1940.

2*a* HH Duchess Augusta Charlotte *Jutta* Alexandra Georgine Adolfine of Mecklenburg-Strelitz (assumed the name of Militza on marriage), *b* 24 Jan 1880, *m* 15 July 1899, HRH Crown Prince *Danilo* Alexander of Montenegro, GCVO (*b* 17 June 1871; *d* 24 Sept 1939), and *dsp* 17 Feb 1946.

2 HRH Princess *Mary Adelaide* Wilhelmina Elizabeth, CI, RRC, *b* at Hanover 22 Nov 1833, *m* at Kew Church, Surrey 12 June 1866, HH *Francis* Paul Charles Louis Alexander, 1st Prince and Duke of Teck, GCB, GCVO, Major-Gen in the Army (*b* at Vienna 27 Aug 1837; *d* at White Lodge, Richmond Park, Surrey 20 Jan 1900), only son of HRH Duke Alexander of Württemberg (*see p* 252), and *d* at White Lodge, Richmond Park, Surrey 27 Oct 1897, leaving issue,

(1) *Adolphus* Charles Alexander Albert Edward George Philip Louis Ladislaus, 1st MARQUESS OF CAMBRIDGE, GCB, GCVO (1901), CMG, *s* his father as 2nd Prince and Duke of Teck 1900 but relinquished those titles and the style of Highness and was *cr* MARQUESS OF CAMBRIDGE, EARL OF ELTHAM, and VISCOUNT NORTHALLERTON 16 July 1917 (*see* BURKE'S *Peerage*), Gov and Constable of Windsor Castle, Personal ADC to HM King George V, *b* 13 Aug 1868, *educ* Wellington, and RMC Sandhurst, *m* 12 Dec 1894, Lady *Margaret* Evelyn Grosvenor (*b* 9 April 1873; *d* 27 March 1929), 4th dau of 1st Duke of Westminster, KG (*see* BURKE'S *Peerage*), and *d* 24 Oct 1927, leaving issue,

1*a* ●George Francis Hugh Cambridge, 2nd MARQUESS OF CAMBRIDGE, etc (*see* BURKE'S *Peerage*), GCVO (1935) (KCVO 1927), Capt RASC (TA) and late 16th Lond Regt and Shropshire Yeo (TA), formerly Reserve Regt of 1st Life Guards, ADC Personal Staff 1918-19, Royal Trustee of British Museum from 1947 [*The Old House, Little Abington, Cambs*], *b* 11 Oct 1895, *educ* Eton, and Magdalen Coll Oxford, *m* 10 April 1923, ●*Dorothy* Isabel Westenra, Lady Pres of Royal Cambridge Home for Soldiers' Widows (*b* 18 May 1899), 2nd dau of late Hon Osmond William Toone Westenra Hastings (*see* BURKE'S *Peerage*, HUNTINGDON, E), and has issue,

●Lady *Mary* Ilona Margaret Cambridge, *b* 24 Sept 1924, *m* 9 Nov 1950, ●Peter Whitley (*b* 22 Oct 1923) [*Penharbour, Hurstpierpoint, Sussex*], only son of late Sir Norman Henry Pownall Whitley, MC, and has issue,

●Charles Francis Peter Whitley, *b* 10 Sept 1961.

●Sarah Elizabeth Whitley, *b* 30 Nov 1954.

2*a* Lord *Frederick* Charles Edward Cambridge, Capt Coldstream Guards, served in Palestine 1936, and in World War II, *b* 23 Sept 1907, *educ* Trin Coll Camb (BA), *k* in action in France in World War II May 1940.

1*a* ●Lady Victoria Constance *Mary* Cambridge, CStJ, *b* 12 June 1897, *m* 14 June 1923, ●*Henry* Hugh Arthur FitzRoy Somerset, 10th Duke of Beaufort, KG, PC, GCVO, Master of the Horse (*b* 4 April 1900) [*Badminton House, Glos*] (*see* BURKE'S *Peerage*).

2*a* Lady *Helena* Frances Augusta Cambridge, *b* 23 Oct 1899, *m* 2 Sept 1919, Col John Evelyn Gibbs, MC, Coldstream Guards (*b* 22 Dec 1879; *d* 11 Oct 1932), 4th son of Antony Gibbs, DL, JP, of Tyntesfield and Charlton, Somerset, and Pytte, Clyst St George, Devon (*see* BURKE'S *Peerage*, ALDENHAM AND HUNSDON, B), and *dsp* 22 Dec 1969.

(2) HSH Prince *Francis* Joseph Leopold Frederick of Teck, GCVO, DSO, Major 1st Dragoons, served in S African War 1899-1900, KJStJ, *b* 9 Jan 1870, *educ* Wellington, and RMC Sandhurst, *d unm* 22 Oct 1910.

(3) HSH Prince *Alexander* Augustus Frederick William Alfred George of Teck, later 1st and last EARL OF ATHLONE, KG (1928), PC (1931), GCB (1911), GCMG (1923) (Chancellor 1934-36, Grand Master 1936-57), GCVO (1904) (KCVO 1898), DSO (1900), FRS (1937), had Royal Victorian Chain (1935), relinquished his princely titles and assumed the surname of Cambridge by Royal Licence 14 July 1917, *cr* VISCOUNT TREMATON *in the co of Cambridge* and *EARL OF* ATHLONE 16 July 1917, had Grand Cordon of Leopold (Belgium), Grand Cross of Orange-Nassau (Netherlands), Legion of Honour (France), 1st cl with swords of Order of St Anne (Russia), hon Major-Gen 1923, 2nd Lieut 7th Hus 1894, Lieut 1899, Capt 1900, Capt RHG (Blues) 1904, Major 2nd Life Guards 1911, Brevet-Col 1915, Brig-Gen Gen Staff 1918-19, hon Brig-Gen 1919, served in Matabele War 1896-97 (medal, despatches), with the Inniskilling Dragoons in S African War (ADC to Brig-Gen 1900-01, despatches, medal with five clasps, DSO), and in World War I (GSO 2nd Grade 1914-15, GSO 1st Grade and Brig-Gen 1915-18, despatches twice, CMG, Legion of Honour, Belgian Mil medal), Col of the Life Guards from 1936, and of 7th QO Hus, hon Col Univ of Lond contingent snr Div OTC, hon Air Cdre 907 (Co of Middx) (Balloon) Sqdn AAF 1938-49, Personal ADC to HM King George V 1919-36, HM King Edward VIII 1936, HM King George VI 1937-52, and to HM The Queen 1953-57, Gold Stick-in-Waiting to HM King Edward VIII 1936, and to HM King George VI 1937-52, nominated Gov-Gen of Dominion of Canada 1914 but did not proceed, Gov-Gen, C-in-C and High Cmmr of Union of S Africa 1923-31, Gov-Gen and C-in-C of Dominion of Canada 1940-46, Gov and Constable of Windsor Castle 1931-57, Chancellor of Lond Univ 1932-57, hon DCL Oxford (1932), hon LLD Witwatersrand (1929), Edin (1931), Lond (1932), Camb (1933), St Andrews (1934), McGill (1943), Laval (1944), and Toronto, Pres of the Royal African Soc, Vice-Pres of Royal Empire Soc, Dir Standard Bank of S Africa, GCStJ (1930), *b* at Kensington Palace 14 April 1874, *educ* Eton, and RMC Sandhurst, *m* 10 Feb 1904, ●HRH Princess

Alice Mary Victoria Augusta Pauline (HRH PRINCESS ALICE, COUNTESS OF ATHLONE *see separate biography, sub* THE ROYAL FAMILY, *p* 177), and *d* at Kensington Palace 16 Jan 1957 (*bur* Frogmore), when his titles became *extinct,* having had issue,

1*a* *Rupert* Alexander George Augustus, *Viscount Trematon, b* at Claremont 24 Aug 1907, *educ* Eton, *d* as the result of a motor accident in France 15 April 1928 (*bur* Frogmore), *unm.*

2*a* HSH Prince *Maurice* Francis George of Teck, *b* at Claremont 29 March, *d* 14 Sept 1910.

1*a* •Lady *May* Helen Emma Cambridge, CStJ, *b* at Claremont 23 Jan 1906, *m* 24 Oct 1931, •Col Sir *Henry* Abel Smith, KCMG, KCVO, DSO, DL, hon LLD, KStJ, former Gov of Queensland, Australia, late RHG (Blues) (*b* 8 March 1900) [*Barton Lodge, Winkfield, Windsor, Berks*], elder surv son of late Francis Abel Smith, of Wilford House, Notts (*see* BURKE'S *LG,* SMITH *formerly of Wilford House*), and has issue,

1*b* •*Richard* Francis Abel Smith, DL (1970) Notts, Major, late Capt RHG (Blues) [*Blidworth Dale, Linby, Notts*], *b* 11 Oct 1933, *educ* Eton, and RMA Sandhurst, *m* 28 April 1960, •*Marcia* (*b* 27 March 1940), only dau of Major-Gen Sir Douglas Anthony Kendrew, KCMG, CB, CBE, DSO, Gov of W Australia, by his wife Nora Elisabeth, dau of John Harvey, of Malin Hall, co Donegal, and has issue,

•Katharine Emma Abel Smith, *b* 11 March 1961.

1*b* •*Anne* Mary Sibylla, *b* 28 July 1932, *m* 14 Dec 1957, •*David* Ian Liddell-Grainger, DL [*Ayton Castle, Berwicks*], only son of late Capt Henry Herbert Liddell-Grainger, of Ayton Castle, Berwicks (*see that family,* BURKE'S *LG*), and has issue,

1*c* •Ian Richard Peregrine Liddell-Grainger, *b* 23 Feb 1959.

2*c* •Charles Montague Liddell-Grainger, *b* 23 July 1960.

3*c* •Simon Rupert Liddell-Grainger, *b* 27 Dec 1962.

4*c* •Malcolm Henry Liddell-Grainger, *b* 14 Dec 1967.

1*c* •Alice Mary Liddell-Grainger, *b* 3 March 1965.

2*b* •*Elizabeth* Alice Abel Smith, *b* 5 Sept 1936, *m* 29 April 1965, •*Peter* Wise (*b* 29 Dec 1929), son of Capt Anthony Forster Wise, of 40 Winchester Court, Vicarage Gate, W8.

(1) HSH Princess Victoria *Mary* Augusta Louisa Olga Pauline Claudine Agnes of Teck, *b* 26 May 1867, *m* 6 July 1893, HM King George V, and *d* 24 March 1953, having had issue (*see p* 307).

8 HRH Prince Octavius, *b* at the Queen's House, St James's Park 23 Feb 1779; *d* at Kew Palace 3 May 1783 (*bur* first Westminster Abbey, later transferred St George's Chapel, Windsor).

9 HRH Prince Alfred, *b* at Windsor Castle 22 Sept 1780; *d* there 20 Aug 1782 (*bur* first Westminster Abbey, later transferred St George's Chapel, Windsor).

1 HRH Princess *Charlotte* Augusta Matilda, Princess Royal, *b* at Buckingham House 29 Sept 1766, *m* at the Chapel Royal, St James's Palace 18 May 1797, as his 2nd wife, HM King Friedrich I of Württemberg (*b* at Treptow 6 Nov 1754; *d* at Stuttgart 30 Oct 1816), and *dsps* at Ludwigsburg 6 Oct 1828 (*bur* Stuttgart), having had issue,

A Princess, stillborn 27 April 1798.

2 HRH Princess *Augusta* Sophia, *b* at Buckingham House 8 Nov 1768; *d unm* at Clarence House, St James's 22 Sept 1840 (*bur* St George's Chapel, Windsor).

3 HRH Princess Elizabeth, *b* at Buckingham House 22 May 1770, *m* there 7 April 1818, HH *Friedrich VI* (Joseph Ludwig Karl August), Landgrave of Hesse-Homburg (*b* at Homburg 30 July 1769; *d* there 2 April 1829), and *dsp* at Frankfort on Main 10 Jan 1840 (*bur* Homburg).

4 HRH Princess Mary, *b* at the Queen's House, St James's 25 April 1776, *m* there 22 July 1816, her 1st cousin, HRH Prince William Frederick, 2nd Duke of Gloucester, KG (*b* 15 Jan 1776; *d* 30 Nov 1834), only son of HRH Prince William Henry, Duke of Gloucester, KG (*see p* 210), and *dsp* at Gloucester House, Piccadilly 30 April 1857 (*bur* St George's Chapel, Windsor).

5 HRH Princess Sophia, *b* at Buckingham House 3 Nov 1777; *d unm* at her house in Vicarage Place, Kensington 27 May 1848 (*bur* Kensal Green).

6 HRH Princess Amelia, *b* at The Lodge, Windsor 7 Aug 1783; *d unm* at Augusta Lodge, Windsor 2 Nov 1810 (*bur* St George's Chapel, Windsor).

King George III was *s* by his eldest son,

1820-1830 GEORGE IV (George Augustus Frederick), **King of Great Britain and Ireland** (styled the same as George III), *s* as Duke of Cornwall, Duke of Rothesay, etc at birth, *cr* Prince of Wales and Earl of Chester 17 Aug 1762, KG 1765, Regent of the United Kingdom from 5 Feb 1811 until his accession to the throne, crowned at Westminster Abbey by Charles Manners Sutton, Archbishop of Canterbury 19 July 1821, *b* at St James's Palace 12 Aug 1762, *m** at the Chapel Royal, St James's 8 April 1795, his 1st cousin, HSH Princess *Caroline* Amelia Elizabeth (*b* at Brunswick 17 May 1768; *d* at Brandenburg House, Hammersmith 7 Aug 1821, *bur* Brunswick), 2nd dau of HH Karl Wilhelm Ferdinand, Duke of Brunswick-Wolfenbüttel, by his wife HRH Princess Augusta, eldest dau of HRH Frederick, Prince of Wales (*see p* 214), and *d at* Windsor Castle 26 June 1830 (*bur* St George's Chapel, Windsor), having had issue,

HRH Princess *Charlotte* Augusta, *b* at Carlton House 7 Jan 1796, *m* there 2 May 1816, as his 1st wife, HSH Prince *Leopold* George Frederick of Saxe-Saalfeld-Coburg, Duke of Saxony, KG, afterwards HM King Léopold I of the Belgians (*b* at Coburg 16 Dec 1790; *d* at Laeken 10 Dec 1865), 3rd son of HH Franz Friedrich Anton, Duke of Saxe-Saalfeld-Coburg, by his 2nd wife *Auguste* Caroline Sophie, dau of Heinrich XXIV, Count Reuss-Ebersdorf (Younger Line), and *d* at Claremont House, nr Esher, Surrey 6 Nov 1817 (*bur* St George's Chapel, Windsor), having had issue,

A Prince, stillborn at Claremont House 5 Nov 1817 (*bur* St George's Chapel, Windsor).

King George IV was *s* by his brother,

1830-1837 WILLIAM IV (William Henry), **King of Great Britain and Ireland** (styled the same as George III), KG 1782, *cr* Duke of Clarence and St Andrews, and Earl of Munster 20 May 1789, Rear-Adm of the Blue 1790, Adm of the Fleet 1811, Lord High Adm of England 1827, Ranger of Bushy Park 1797, crowned at Westminster Abbey by William Howley, Archbishop of Canterbury 8 Sept 1831, *b* at Buckingham House, St James's Park 21 Aug 1765, *m* at Kew Palace 11 July 1818, HSH Princess *Adelaide* Louisa Theresa Caroline Amelia, crowned with her husband (*b* at Meiningen 13 Aug 1792; *d* at Bentley Priory, Middx 2 Dec 1849, *bur* St George's Chapel, Windsor), elder dau of HH Duke Georg I

---

*He had gone through a form of marriage (in contravention of the Royal Marriage Act) at her house in London, 21 Dec 1785, with Mary Anne (*b* 26 July 1756; *d* 27 March 1837), widow of Thomas Fitzherbert, of Norbury, Derby, and Swynnerton, Staffs, and previously of Edward Weld, of Lulworth Castle, Dorset (*see* BURKE'S *LG*), and dau of Walter Smythe, of Brambridge, Hants (*see* BURKE'S *Peerage,* 1939 *Edn,* SMYTHE, Bt).

(Friedrich Karl) of Saxe-Meiningen, by his wife HSH Princess Louise Eleonore, eldest dau of HSH Prince Christian Albrecht zu Hohenlohe-Langenburg, and *d* at Windsor Castle 20 June 1837 (*bur* St George's Chapel, Windsor), having had issue*,

1 HRH Princess *Charlotte* Augusta Louisa, *b* and *d* at the Fürstenhof, Hanover 27 March 1819 (*bur* Hanover).

2 HRH Princess *Elizabeth* Georgiana Adelaide, *b* at St James's Palace 10 Dec 1820; *d there* 4 March 1821 (*bur* St George's Chapel, Windsor).

King William IV was *s* by his niece,

1837-1901 VICTORIA (Alexandrina Victoria), **Queen of Great Britain and Ireland** (styled the same as George III until 1 Jan 1877 and then *By the Grace of God, of the United Kingdom of Great Britain and Ireland, Queen, Defender of the Faith, Empress of India*), crowned at Westminster Abbey by William Howley, Archbishop of Canterbury 28 June 1838, proclaimed Empress of India at Delhi 1 Jan 1877, founded the Victoria Cross (the highest award for personal bravery) 29 Jan 1856, the Order of the Star of India 1861, the Order of the Crown of India (for ladies) 1878, the Order of the Indian Empire 1878, the Order of Victoria and Albert (for ladies) 1862, the Royal Victorian Order 1896, and the Distinguished Service Order 1886, *b* at Kensington Palace 24 May 1819, *m* at the Chapel Royal, St James's Palace 10 Feb 1840, HH Prince Francis *Albert* Augustus Charles Emmanuel of Saxe-Coburg and Gotha, Duke of Saxony, granted the style of Royal Highness by Patent 6 Feb 1840, *cr* Prince Consort by Patent 26 June 1857, KG, KT, KP, PC, GCSI, GCMG, Great Master of the Order of the Bath, Field Marshal in the Army, Col of Gren Guards, Col-in-Chief of The Rifle Bde, Chancellor of Camb Univ, Lord Warden of the Stannaries, Chief Steward of the Duchy of Cornwall, Gov and Constable of Windsor Castle, Ranger of Windsor Great Park, Master of Trin House, Capt-Gen and Col HAC, Lord High Steward of Plymouth and of Windsor (*b* at Schloss Rosenau, nr Coburg 26 Aug 1819; *d* at Windsor Castle 14 Dec 1861, *bur* Royal Mausoleum, Frogmore), yr son of HH Duke Ernst I of Saxe-Coburg and Gotha, KG, by his 1st wife HH Princess Louise, dau of HH Duke August of Saxe-Gotha-Altenburg. HM Queen Victoria, who celebrated her Golden Jubilee 1887 and her Diamond Jubilee 1897, *d* at Osborne House, I of W, 22 Jan 1901 (*bur* Royal Mausoleum, Frogmore), after reigning longer than any other English sovereign, having had issue,

1 HRH Prince *ALBERT EDWARD*, Prince of Wales, *s* his mother as KING EDWARD VII.

2 HRH Prince *Alfred* Ernest Albert, DUKE OF EDINBURGH, KG (1863), KT, KP, PC, GCB, GCSI, GCMG, GCIE, GCVO, elected King of Greece 1862 but refused the crown on pol grounds, *cr* DUKE OF EDINBURGH, EARL OF ULSTER, and EARL OF KENT 24 May 1866, Master of Trinity House 1866, Rear-Adm 1878, Adm Supt RNR 1879-82, Vice-Adm 1882, cmd'd Channel Sqdn 1883-84, C-in-C Mediterranean Fleet 1886-89, Adm 1887, C-in-C at Devonport 1890-93, Adm of the Fleet 1893, *s* his paternal uncle Duke Ernst II as reigning Duke of Saxe-Coburg and Gotha 1893 in virtue of the renunciation of his brother the Prince of Wales, Adm in the German Navy, Gen in the Prussian Army, *b* at Windsor Castle 6 Aug 1844, *m* at the Winter Palace, St Petersburg 23 Jan 1874, HIH Grand Duchess *Marie* Alexandrovna, VA, CI (*b* at St Petersburg, 17 Oct 1853; *d* at Zürich 25 Oct 1920), 2nd dau of HIM Emperor Alexander II of all the Russias, by his 1st wife HGDH Princess Marie, dau of HRH Grand Duke Ludwig II of Hesse, and *d* at Schloss Rosenau 30 July 1900 (*bur* Coburg), having had issue,

1 HRH Prince *Alfred* Alexander William Ernest Albert of Great Britain and Ireland, Hereditary Prince of Saxe-Coburg and Gotha, Duke of Saxony, KG (1894), Capt 2nd Vol Bn Devonshire Regt, Lieut 1st Regt Prussian Guards, *b* at Buckingham Palace 15 Oct 1874; *dvp unm* at Meran, Tyrol 6 Feb 1899 (*bur* Friedenstein, nr Gotha).

1 HRH Princess *Marie* Alexandra Victoria of Great Britain and Ireland, Princess of Saxe-Coburg and Gotha, Duchess of Saxony, VA, CI, RRC, hon Col 4th Rosiori (Hus) Regt, DJStJ, *b* at Eastwell Park, Kent 29 Oct 1875, *m* at Sigmaringen 10 Jan 1893, HM King *Ferdinand* (Viktor Albert Meinrad) of Roumania, KG, GCB (*b* at Sigmaringen 24 Aug 1865; *d* at Sinaia, Roumania 20 July 1927), and *d* at Sinaia 10 July 1938, having had issue,

(1) HM King Carol II of Roumania (1930-1940), Prince of Hohenzollern, KG (1938), GCVO (1925), renounced his rights of succession to the throne of Roumania 28 Dec 1925, subsequently proclaimed King by Act of Parl 8 June 1930, abdicated in favour of his son Michael 6 Sept 1940, Grand Master of the Order of Carol I of Roumania, had the Orders of the Black Eagle (Prussia), the Annunziata (Italy), the White Eagle (Poland) and St Andrew (Russia), and was Bailiff Grand Cross of Honour and Devotion of the Sov Order of Malta and Bailiff Grand Cross of Justice of the Constantinian Order of St George, *b* 16 Oct 1893, *m* 1st 31 Aug 1918 (*m* annulled 1919), Joana (*Zizi*) (*b* 3 Oct 1898; *d* 11 March 1953), dau of Col Constantin Lambrino, and had issue,

1*a* •(Prince) Mircea Gregor *Carol* (of Roumania), recognised as legitimate by the French Courts 1959, *b* 8 Jan 1920, *m* 1st 22 March 1944 (*m* diss by div 1960), *Hélène*-Henriette Nagavitzine (*b* 26 May 1925), and has issue,

1*b* •(Prince) *Paul* Philip (of Roumania), *b* 13 Aug 1948.

He *m* 2ndly 20 Dec 1960, •Thelma *Jeanne* (*b* 15 Nov 1930), dau of Richard Williams, of Nashville, Tennessee, USA, and by her has issue,

2*b* •(Prince) Ion George Nicolas *Alexander* (of Roumania), *b* 1 Sept 1961.

King Carol II *m* 2ndly 10 March 1921 (*m* diss by div 1928), HRH Princess Helen (*b* 20 April 1896), eldest dau of HM King Constantine I of the Hellenes (*see p* 279), and by her has issue,

2*a* •HM King Michael of Roumania (1927-1930 and 1940-1947), Prince of Hohenzollern, reigned under a Regency 20 July 1927-8 June 1930, took the title of Crown Prince of Roumania, Grand Voivode of Alba Julia during his father's reign, *s* his father 6 Sept 1940, abdicated 30 Dec 1947, has the Chain of the Order of Carol I of Roumania, the Order of Victory (USSR), and the Order of the White Eagle (Poland), Cmdr US Legion of Merit [*106 Route de Suisse, Versoix/Génève, Switzerland*], *b* 25 Oct 1921, *m* 10 June 1948, •HRH Princess *Anne*-Antoinette-Françoise-Charlotte (*b* 18 Sept 1923), only dau of HRH late Prince René of

*Prior to his marriage King William IV had had ten illegitimate children by "Mrs Jordan" (Dorothy Bland), a well-known actress. On his accession to the throne he *cr* the eldest son Earl of Munster (*see* BURKE'S *Peerage*) and raised the yr sons and daus (with the exception of those who had already acquired higher rank by marriage) to the rank and precedence of the yr issue of a Marquess.

Bourbon-Parma, by his wife HRH Princess Margrethe of Denmark (*see p* 282), and has issue,

1*b* ●HRH Princess Margarita of Roumania, Princess of Hohenzollern, *b* 26 March 1949.

2*b* ●HRH Princess Elena of Roumania, Princess of Hohenzollern, *b* 15 Nov 1950.

3*b* ●HRH Princess Irina of Roumania, Princess of Hohenzollern, *b* 28 Feb 1953.

4*b* ●HRH Princess Sophie of Roumania, Princess of Hohenzollern, *b* 28 Oct 1957.

5*b* ●HRH Princess Maria of Roumania, Princess of Hohenzollern, *b* 13 June 1964.

King Carol II *m* 3rdly 3 June 1947, ●Elena (Magda) (*b* 15 Sept 1902) [*Vila Mar y Sol, Estoril, Portugal*], formerly wife of Ion Tampeanu, and dau of Nicolas Wolf (called Lupescu), and *d* 3 April 1953.

(2) ●HRH Prince Nicolas of Hohenzollern (formerly HRH Prince Nicolas of Roumania), Air Marshal of the Roumanian Air Force, hon Lieut RN, Knight of the Order of Ferdinand I of Roumania, Bailiff Grand Cross of the Sovereign Order of Malta, Grand Cross of the Legion of Honour, Grand Cross of the Orders of Leopold I of Belgium, the White Lion (Czechoslovakia), Karageorgevitch (Yugoslavia), and the Holy Redeemer (Greece), has the Chain of the Order of Carol I of Roumania and the Order of the White Eagle (Poland), was Chief of the three Regents of Roumania 1927-30, deprived of his Royal rank and prerogative by decision of the Crown Council 9 April 1937, and took the name of Nicolas Brana, assumed by Royal Decree 10 June 1942, the name of Hohenzollern and with the approval of Prince Friedrich of Hohenzollern assumed the title of Prince and Style of Royal Highness 15 Jan 1947 [*34 Calle Alfonso XII, Madrid, Spain; 65 Avenue de Béthusy, Lausanne 1012, Switzerland*], *b* 18 Aug 1903, *educ* Eton, *m* 1st 28 Oct 1931, Joana, who assumed her grandmother's name of Doleté 1928 (*b* 24 Sept 1907; *d* 19 Feb 1963), formerly wife of Radu Saveanu, and dau of Ion Dumitrescu-Doleté, by his wife Nella Theodoru (later Princess Tchkotoua). He *m* 2ndly 13 July 1967, ●Thereza (*b* 10 June 1913), formerly wife of Andres Boulton, and dau of Jerónymo de Avellar Figueira de Mello, Brazilian Amb in Caracas and Warsaw, by his wife Candida Ribeira Lisboa.

(3) HRH Prince Mircea of Roumania, Prince of Hohenzollern, *b* 3 Jan 1913; *d* 2 Nov 1916.

(1) HRH Princess *Elisabeth* Charlotte Josephine Alexandra Victoria of Roumania, Princess of Hohenzollern, VA, *b* 12 Oct 1894, *m* 27 Feb 1921 (*m* diss by div 1935), HM King George II of the Hellenes, KG, GCMG, GCVO, DSO (*b* 7 July 1890; *d* 1 April 1947) (*see p* 279), and *dsp* 14 Nov 1956, having resumed the title of Princess of Roumania after her div.

(2) HRH Princess Marie of Roumania, Princess of Hohenzollern, hon Col 5th Regt of Yugoslavia Cav and 9th Regt of Roumanian Cav, *b* 9 Jan 1900, *m* 8 June 1922, HM King Alexander I of Yugoslavia, GCB, GCVO (*b* 4 Dec 1888; assassinated at Marseilles 9 Oct 1934), and *d* 22 June 1961, leaving issue,

1*a* HM King Peter II of Yugoslavia, *s* his father under a Regency 9 Oct 1934, deprived of his throne by the Yugoslav Constituent Assembly 29 Nov 1945, an Assoc GCStJ, *b* 6 Sept 1923, *educ* Clare Coll Camb, *m* 20 March 1944, ●HRH Princess Alexandra (*b* 25 March 1921), only child of HM King Alexander I of the Hellenes (*see p* 279), and *d* 3 Nov 1970, leaving issue,

●HRH Crown Prince Alexander of Yugoslavia [*c/o Redlands Farm, Kirdford, Billingshurst, Sussex*], *b* 17 July 1945, *m* 1 July 1972, ●HRH Princess *Maria da Gloria* Henriqueta Dolores Lucia Miguela Rafaela Gabriela Gonzaga (*b* 13 Dec 1946), elder dau of HRH Prince Pedro Gastão of Orleans and Braganza (*see p* 236).

2*a* ●HRH Prince Tomislav of Yugoslavia [*Redlands Farm, Kirdford, Billingshurst, Sussex*], *b* 19 Jan 1928, *educ* Oundle, and Clare Coll Camb, *m* 6 June 1957, ●HGDH Princess *Margarita* Alice Thyra Viktoria Marie Louise Scholastica (*b* 14 July 1932), only dau of HRH the late Margrave Berthold of Baden, Head of the Grand Ducal House of Baden (*see p* 291), and has issue,

●HRH Prince Nikola of Yugoslavia, *b* 15 March 1958.

●HRH Princess Katarina of Yugoslavia, *b* 28 Nov 1959.

3*a* ●HRH Prince Andrej of Yugoslavia [*Villa Milidvor, Birre, Cascais, Portugal*], *b* 28 June 1929, *educ* Oundle, and Clare Coll Camb, *m* 1st (civil) 1 Aug and (religious) 2 Aug 1956 (*m* diss by div 1962), HH Princess *Christina* Margarita (*b* 10 Jan 1933), eldest dau of HH late Prince Christoph of Hesse (*see p* 285), and has issue,

1*b* ●HRH Prince Marko *Christopher* of Yugoslavia, *b* 4 Feb 1960.

1*b* ●HRH Princess Maria Tatiana of Yugoslavia, *b* 18 July 1957.

He *m* 2ndly (civil) 18 Sept and (religious) 12 Oct 1963, ●HSH Princess *Kira* Melita Feodora Marie Viktoria Alexandra (*b* 18 July 1930), eldest dau of HSH Karl, 6th Prince zu Leiningen (*see p* 297), and by her has issue,

2*b* ●HRH Prince Karl Vladimir of Yugoslavia, *b* 11 March 1964.

3*b* ●HRH Prince Dimitri of Yugoslavia, *b* 12 April 1965.

(3) ●HRH Princess Ileana of Roumania Princess

2*b* ●HI and RH Archduke Gregor of Austria, Prince of Tuscany, *b* 20 Nov 1968.

1*a* HI and RH Archduchess Marie Ileana of Austria, Princess of Tuscany, *b* 18 Dec 1933, *m* 8 Dec 1957, Count *Jaroslav* Franz Josef Ignazius Maria Kottulinsky (*b* 3 Jan 1917), son of Count Karl Kunata Kottulinsky, and was *k* with him in an air crash at Rio de Janeiro 11 Jan 1959, leaving issue,

●Countess Ileana Kottulinsky, *b* 25 Aug 1958.

2*a* ●HI and RH Archduchess Alexandra of Austria, Princess of Tuscany, *b* 21 May 1935, *m* 3 Sept 1962, ●HRH Duke *Eugen Eberhard* Albrecht Maria Joseph Ivan Rilsky Robert Ulrich Philipp Odo Carl Hubert of Württemberg (*b* 2 Nov 1930) (*see p* 227).

3*a* ●HI and RH Archduchess *Maria Magdalena* of Austria, Princess of Tuscany, *b* 2 Oct 1939, *m* 29 Aug 1959, ●Baron *Hans* Ulrich von Holzhausen (*b* 1 Sept 1929) [*23 Rennbahnstrasse, Salzburg-Parsch, Austria*], and has issue,

1*b* ●Baron *Johann* Friedrich Anton von Holzhausen, *b* 29 July 1960.

2*b* ●Baron *Georg* Ferdinand von Holzhausen, *b* 16 Feb 1962.

1*b* ●Baroness *Alexandra* Maria von Holzhausen, *b* 22 Jan 1963.

4*a* •HI and RH Archduchess Elisabeth of Austria, Princess of Tuscany, *b* 15 May 1942, *m* 3 Aug 1964, •*Friedrich* Josef Sandhofer, MD [*Walserberg, nr Salzburg, Austria*], and has issue,
1*b* •Anton Dominic Friedrich Sandhofer, *b* 26 Oct 1966.
1*b* •Margareta Elisabeth Sandhofer, *b* 10 Sept 1968.
2*b* •Andrea Alexandra Sandhofer, *b* 13 Dec 1969.
She *m* 2ndly 19 June 1954 (*m* diss by div 1965), Dr Stefan Issarescu (*b* 5 Oct 1905).

2 HRH Princess *Victoria Melita* of Great Britain and Ireland, Princess of Saxe-Coburg and Gotha, Duchess of Saxony, VA, CI, *b* at the Palace of San Antonio, Malta 25 Nov 1876, *m* 1st at Coburg 19 April 1894 (*m* diss by div 1901), HRH Grand Duke *Ernst Ludwig* of Hesse and by Rhine, KG, GCB (*b* 25 Nov 1868; *d* 9 Oct 1937), and had issue (*see p* 303). She *m* 2ndly at Tegernsee 8 Oct 1905, HIH Grand Duke Kirill Vladimirovitch of Russia, Head of the Imp House of Russia (*b* at Tsarskoie Selo 30 Sept 1876; *d* at Neuilly 13 Oct 1938), and *d* at Amorbach 2 March 1936, leaving further issue,
(1) •HIH Grand Duke Vladimir Kirillovitch of Russia, Head of the Imp House of Russia from 1938 [*Guisando 13, Ciudad de Puerta de Hierro, Madrid 20, Spain; Ker Argonid, F-35 St Briac sur Mer, Dept Ille-et-Vilaine, France*], *b* 30 Aug 1917, *educ* London Univ, *m* 13 Aug 1948, •Princess Leonida (*b* 23 Sept 1914), formerly wife of Sumner Moore Kirby, and only dau of Prince George Alexandrovitch Bagration-Mukhransky, and has issue,
•HIH Grand Duchess Maria Vladimirovna of Russia, *b* 23 Dec 1953.
(1) HIH Grand Duchess *Marie* Kirillovna of Russia, *b* 2 Feb 1907, *m* 25 Nov 1925, HSH Friedrich *Karl* Eduard Erwin, 6th Prince zu Leiningen (*b* 13 Feb 1898; *d* as a Russian p o w 2 Aug 1946), and *d* 27 Oct 1951, having had issue,
1*a* •HSH *Emich* Cyril Ferdinand Hermann, 7th Prince zu Leiningen [*Fürstliche Palais, Amorbach, Odenwald, Germany*], *b* 18 Oct 1926, *m* 10 Aug 1950, •HH Duchess *Eilika* Stephanie Elisabeth Thekla Juliana (*b* 2 Feb 1928), elder surv dau of HRH late Hereditary Grand Duke Nikolaus of Oldenburg (*see p* 222), and has issue,
1*b* •HSH Hereditary Prince *Karl* Emich Nikolaus Friedrich Hermann zu Leiningen, *b* 12 June 1952.
2*b* •HSH Prince Andreas zu Leiningen, *b* 27 Nov 1955.
1*b* •HSH Princess *Melita* Elisabeth Bathildis Helene Margarita zu Leiningen, *b* 10 June 1951.
2*b* •HSH Princess *Stephanie* Margarita zu Leiningen, *b* 1 Oct 1958.
2*a* •HSH Prince *Karl* Vladimir Ernst Heinrich zu Leiningen [*1024 Westdale Road, Oakville, Ontario, Canada*], *b* 2 Jan 1928, *m* 20 Feb 1957 (*m* diss by div 1969), HRH Princess Marie Louise (*b* 13 Jan 1933), only dau of HM King Boris III of the Bulgarians (*see p* 246), and has issue,
1*b* •HSH Prince Karl *Boris* Frank Markwart zu Leiningen, *b* 17 April 1960.
2*b* •HSH Prince *Hermann* Friedrich Roland Fernando zu Leiningen, *b* 16 April 1963.
3*a* •HSH Prince *Friedrich* Wilhelm Berthold zu Leiningen [*Fürstliche Palais, Amorbach, Odenwald, Germany*], *b* 18 June 1938, *m* 9 July 1960 (*m* diss by div 1962), *Karin* Evelyne Göss (*b* 27 May 1942).
4*a* HSH Prince *Peter* Victor zu Leiningen, *b* 23 Dec 1942; *d* 12 Jan 1943.
1*a* •HSH Princess *Kira* Melita Feodora Marie Viktoria Alexandra zu Leiningen, *b* 18 July 1930, *m* 28 Sept 1963, as his 2nd wife, •HRH Prince Andrej of Yugoslavia (*b* 28 June 1929), and has issue (*see p* 296).
2*a* •HSH Princess *Margarita* Ileana Viktoria zu Leiningen, *b* 9 May 1932, *m* 3 Feb 1951, •HH *Friedrich Wilhelm* Ferdinand Joseph Marie Manuel Georg Meinrad Fidelis Benedikt Michael Hubert, Prince of Hohenzollern (*b* 3 Feb 1924) [*Landhaus Josefslust, Sigmaringen, Hohenzollern, Germany*] (*see p* 234), and has issue,
1*b* •HSH Prince *Karl* Friedrich Emich Meinrad Benedikt Fidelis Maria Michael Gerold of Hohenzollern, *b* 20 April 1952.
2*b* •HSH Prince *Albrecht* Johannes Hermann Meinrad Hubertus Michael Stephan of Hohenzollern, *b* 3 Aug 1954
3*b* •HSH Prince *Ferdinand* Maria Fidelis Leopold Meinrad Valentin of Hohenzollern, *b* 14 Feb 1960.
3*a* •HSH Princess *Mechtilde* Alexandra zu Leiningen, *b* 2 Jan 1936, *m* 25 Nov 1961, •*Karl Anton* Bauscher (*b* 26 Aug 1931) [*8600 Bamberg, Georgenstrasse 10/12a, Germany*], and has issue,
1*b* •*Ulf* Karl Heinz Stephan Kraft Bauscher, *b* 20 Feb 1963.
2*b* •*Berthold* Alexander Bauscher, *b* 31 Oct 1965.
(2) HIH Grand Duchess *Kira* Kirillovna, *b* 9 May 1909, *m* 2 May 1938, •HI and RH Prince *Louis Ferdinand* Viktor Eduard Adalbert Michael Hubertus of Prussia, Head of the Royal House of Prussia (*b* 9 Nov 1907), and *d* 8 Sept 1967, leaving issue (*see p* 301).

3 HRH Princess *Alexandra* Louise Olga Victoria of Great Britain and Ireland, Princess of Saxe-Coburg and Gotha, Duchess of Saxony, *b* at Coburg 1 Sept 1878, *m* at Coburg 20 April 1896, HSH *Ernst* Wilhelm Friedrich Karl Maximilian, 7th Prince zu Hohenlohe-Langenburg, Regent of the Duchy of Saxe-Coburg and Gotha 1900-05 (*b* at Langenburg 13 Sept 1863; *d* there 11 Dec 1950), and *d* at Schwäbisch-Hall 16 April 1942, having had issue,
(1) HSH *Gottfried* Hermann Alfred Paul Maximilian Viktor, 8th Prince zu Hohenlohe-Langenburg, *b* 24 March 1897, *m* 27 April 1931, •HRH Princess *Margarita* (*b* 5 April 1905) [*Schloss Langenburg, Württemberg, Germany*], dau of HRH late Prince Andrew of Greece and Denmark, GCVO (*see p* 280), and *d* 11 May 1960, leaving issue,
1*a* •HSH Prince *Kraft* Alexander Ernst Ludwig Georg Emich, 9th Prince zu Hohenlohe-Langenburg (*Schloss Langenburg, Württemberg, Germany*], *b* 25 June 1935, *m* 5 June 1965, •HSH Princess *Charlotte* Alexandra Maria Clotilde (*b* 31 Dec 1938), elder dau of HSH Prince Alexander von Croy, and has issue,
1*b* •HSH Hereditary Prince *Philipp* Gottfried Alexander zu Hohenlohe-Langenburg, *b* 20 Jan 1970.
1*b* •HSH Princess *Cecile* Marita Dorothea zu Hohenlohe-Langenburg, *b* 16 Dec 1967.
2*b* •HSH Princess *Xenia* Margarita Anne, *b* 8 July 1972.
2*a* •HSH Prince Georg *Andreas* Heinrich zu Hohenlohe-Langenburg, *b* 24 Nov 1938, *m* 9 Sept 1968, •HSH Princess *Luise* Pauline Amelie Vibeke Emma (*b* 12 Oct 1943), yst dau of HSH Prince Georg von Schönburg-Waldenburg (*see p* 269).
3*a* •HSH Prince *Ruprecht* Sigismund Philipp Ernst zu Hohenlohe-Langenburg, *b* 7 April 1944.
4*a* •HSH Prince *Albrecht* Wolfgang Christof zu Hohenlohe-Langenburg, *b* (twin with Prince Ruprecht) 7 April 1944.
1*a* •HSH Princess *Beatrix* Alice Marie Melita Margarete zu Hohenlohe-Langenburg, *b* 10 July 1936.
(2) HSH Prince *Alfred* zu Hohenlohe-Langenburg, *b* 16, *d* 18 April 1911.
(1) HSH Princess *Marie Melita* Leopoldine Viktoria Feodora Alexandra Sophie zu Hohenlohe-Langenburg, *b* 18 Jan 1899, *m* 15 Feb 1916, HH Wilhelm *Friedrich* Christian Günther Albert Adolf Georg, Duke of Schleswig-Holstein-Sonderburg-Glücksburg (*b* 23 Aug 1891; *d* 10 Feb 1965), and *d* 8 Nov 1967, having had issue,
1*a* HH Prince *Hans* Viktor Alexander Friedrich Ernst Gottfried August Heinrich Albert Waldemar of Schleswig-Holstein-Sonderburg-Glücksburg, *b* 12 May 1917; *k* in action in Poland in World War II 10 Aug 1944.
2*a* HH Prince *Wilhelm* Alfred Ferdinand of Schleswig-Holstein-Sonderburg-Glücksburg, *b* 24 Sept 1919; *d* 17 June 1926.

3*a* ●HH Friedrich Ernst *Peter*, Duke of Schleswig-Holstein-Sonderburg-Glücksburg [*2331 Gutbienebeck, Post Sieseby über Eckernforde, Holstein, Germany*], *b* 30 April 1922, *m* 9 Oct 1947, ●HSH Princess *Marie Alix* (*b* 2 April 1923), only dau of HSH late Prince Stephan of Schaumburg-Lippe (*see p* 252), and has issue,

1*b* ●HH Hereditary Prince *Christoph* of Schleswig-Holstein-Sonderburg-Glücksburg, *b* 22 Aug 1949.

2*b* ●HH Prince *Alexander* of Schleswig-Holstein-Sonderburg-Glücksburg, *b* 9 July 1953.

1*b* ●HH Princess *Marita* of Schleswig-Holstein-Sonderburg-Glücksburg, *b* 5 Sept 1948.

2*b* ●HH Princess *Ingeborg* of Schleswig-Holstein-Sonderburg-Glücksburg, *b* 9 July 1956.

1*a* ●HH Princess *Marie-Alexandra* Caroline Mathilde Viktoria Irene zu Hohenlohe-Langenburg, *b* 9 July 1927, *m* 22 July 1970, ●*Douglas* Barton Miller (*b* 8 Dec 1929).

(2) HSH Princess *Alexandra* Beatrice Leopoldine zu Hohenlohe-Langenburg, *b* 2 April 1901; *d unm* 26 Oct 1963.

(3) ●HSH Princess *Irma* Helene zu Hohenlohe-Langenburg [*Schloss Langenburg, Württemberg, Germany*], *b* 4 July 1902.

4 HRH Princess *Beatrice* Leopoldine Victoria of Great Britain and Ireland, Princess of Saxe-Coburg and Gotha, Duchess of Saxony, VA (2nd cl), had Grand Cross of Order of Maria Luisa of Spain, *b* at Eastwell Park, Kent 20 April 1884, *m* at Coburg 15 July 1909, ●HRH Prince *Alfonso* Maria Francisco Antonio Diego of Bourbon-Orleans, Infante of Spain, 3rd Duke of Galliera, Gen Spanish AF (*b* at Madrid 12 Nov 1886) [*The Palace, Sanlucar de Barrameda, Spain*], and *d* at Sanlucar de Barrameda 13 July 1966, having had issue,

(1) ●HRH Prince *Alvaro* Antonio Fernando Carlos Felipe of Bourbon-Orleans, 4th Duke of Galliera (by Royal Decree 1937 on his father's cession) [*Via Luigi Capucci 42, 00147 Rome, Italy*], *b* 20 April 1910, *educ* Winchester, *m* 10 July 1937, ●*Carla* (*b* 13 Dec 1909), eldest dau of late Senator Leopoldo Parodi Delfino, and has issue,

1*a* ●Don *Alonso* de Orleans y Parodi Delfino [*Ramonal Vuelta de los Pejaros, Santacruz de Tenerife, Canary Islands*], *b* 23 Aug 1941, *m* ●*Emilia* Ferrara Pignatelli, and has issue,

1*b* ●Don *Alfonso* de Orleans y Ferrara Pignatelli, *b* 2 Jan 1968.

2*b* ●Don *Alvaro* de Orleans y Ferrara Pignatelli, *b* 4 Oct 1969.

2*a* ●Don *Alvaro* Jaime de Orleans y Parodi Delfino, *b* 1 March 1947.

1*a* ●Doña *Gerarda* de Orleans y Parodi Delfino, *b* 25 Aug 1939, *m* 26 July 1963, ●*Harry* Freeman Saint (*b* 13 Feb 1941) [*211 Central Park, New York, NY 10024, USA*], and has issue,

1*b* ●Marc d'Orléans-Bourbon Saint, *b* 20 March 1969.

1*b* ●Carla d'Orléans-Bourbon Saint, *b* 22 May 1967.

2*a* ●Doña *Beatriz* de Orleans y Parodi Delfino, Marquesa de Torre Breva, *b* 27 April 1943, *m* 25 April 1964, ●*Tomaso* dei Conti Farini (*b* 16 Sept 1938), and has issue,

1*b* ●*Gerardo* Farini, *b* 23 Nov 1967.

1*b* ●*Elena* Farini, *b* 27 Oct 1969.

(2) HRH Prince *Alonso* Maria Cristino Justo of Bourbon-Orleans, *b* 28 May 1912; *k* in Spanish Civil War 18 Nov 1936, *unm.*

(3) ●HRH Prince *Ataulfo* Alejandro Isabelo Carlos, *b* 20 Oct 1913, *educ* Winchester.

3 HRH Prince *Arthur* William Patrick Albert, 1st DUKE OF CONNAUGHT AND STRATHEARN, KG (1867), KT (1869), KP (1869), PC (1871), GMB (1901), GCSI (1877), GCMG, GCIE (1887), GCVO, GBE (1917), VD, TD, had Royal Victorian Chain (1902), Privy Councillor of Ireland (1900), *cr* DUKE OF CONNAUGHT AND STRATHEARN and EARL OF SUSSEX 24 May 1874, was Grand Prior and Bailiff Grand Cross of the Order of St John of Jerusalem, and had Order of Golden Fleece, Mil Order of Merit, and Order of Charles III (Spain), Medjidie (Turkey), Legion of Honour (France), Order of Leopold (Belgium), Orders of the Seraphim, the Sword, and Charles XII (Sweden), Order of St Olav (Norway), the Annunziata and Mil Order of Savoy (Italy), the Elephant (Denmark), the Redeemer (Greece), the Chrysanthemum (Japan), the Star of Ethiopia, the Netherlands and the Lion (Netherlands), Nichan Iftikhar (Tunis), Danilo, 1st cl (Montenegro), the Crown (Roumania), and St Charles (Monaco), Personal ADC to TM Queen Victoria, King Edward VII, King George V, King Edward VIII and King George VI, Field Marshal in the Army, Col-in-Chief of The Rifle Bde (The Prince Consort's Own), The Highland LI, RAMC, and RASC, Col Gren Guards (1904), hon Col 3rd Bn QO (Royal W Kent Regt), 3rd and 4th Bns Highlands LI, 97th (Kent Yeo), Royal Field Artillery (TA), 18th Bn Lond Regt (Lond Irish Rifles), and of Ceylon ASC, Col-in-Chief 6th Duke of Connaught's Own Lancers, 13th Duke of Connaught's Own Bombay Lancers, 7th Rajputs Regt, and IASC (all IA), hon Col of Royal Canadian Regt, 3rd Regt Victoria Rifles of Canada, and 6th Regt (Duke of Connaught's Own Rifles), Canada, Col-in-Chief of 6th Inf (Durban LI), and 11th Inf (Rand LI), S Africa, Col-in-Chief of NZ Rifle Bde, hon Capt RNR, Gen in Swedish Army, and hon Lt-Col 9th Erapiles Bn of Cazadores (Spanish Army). HRH was apptd Lieut RE June 1868, trans to RA Oct 1868, and to Rifle Bde 1869, trans as Capt to 7th Hus 1874, Major 1875, Lt-Col cmdg 1st Bn Rifle Bde 1876, Brev-Col and Major-Gen 1880, Lt-Gen 1888, Gen 1893, and FM 1902, was Bde Major 2nd Inf Bde, Aldershot 1873-74, Bde Major Cav Bde, Aldershot 1875, Assist Adjt-Gen Gibraltar 1875-76, Major-Gen Aldershot 1880-82, Major-Gen Expdny Force Egypt 1882, Aldershot 1883, Bengal 1883-85, and Punjab 1886, C-in-C of the Army in Bombay 1886-90, Lt-Gen cmdg Southern Dist 1890-93, and Troops Aldershot 1893-98, Gen cmdg Forces in Ireland 1900-04, Gen cmdg 3rd Army Corps 1901-04, Inspr-Gen of the Forces and Pres of Selection Bd 1904-07, FM cmdg-in-Chief and High Commr in Mediterranean 1907-09, and Gov-Gen and C-in-C of Dominion of Canada 1911-16. He opened 1st Parl of Union of S Africa on behalf of The King 1910, and visited India to inaugurate new Legislative Councils and perform the ceremony of the Opening of the Chamber of Princes winter 1920-21. He served there during the Fenian Raid into Canada 1870 (medal and clasp), and as Major-Gen cmdg Bde of Guards in Egyptian War 1882, was present at Mahuta and Tel-el-Kebir (despatches thrice, thanks of Parl, medal with clasp, Khedive's Bronze Star, 2nd cl Medjidie, CB). He was hon DCL Oxford, hon LLD Camb and Cape Univ, and hon Litt D Punjab, an Elder Brother of Trin House (Master 1910-42), Grand Master of the United Lodge of Freemasons, Ranger of Epping Forest, High Steward of Wokingham, a Bencher of Gray's Inn, Pres Wellington Coll, St Thomas's Hosp, Royal Westminster Ophthalmic Hosp, City of Lond Hosp for Diseases of the Chest, Royal Soc of Arts (Gold Albert Medal 1931), The Duke of York's Royal Mil Sch, Royal Empire Soc, Gen Council of Royal Patriotic Fund Corpn, and of Boy Scouts' Assoc, hon FRCS, hon Freeman of Lond, Master of Saddlers' co, and had Freedom of Merchant Taylors', Grocers', Haberdashers' and Fishmongers' Cos. HRH was *b* at Buckingham Palace 1 May 1850, *m* at St George's Chapel, Windsor 13 March 1879, HRH Princess *Louise Margaret* Alexandra Victoria Agnes, VA, CI, RRC, Col-in-Chief 199th Canadian Inf Bn (Duchess of Connaught's Own Irish Canadian Rangers), DJStJ (*b* at the Marmorpalais, Potsdam 25 June 1860; *d* at Clarence House, London 14 March 1917, *bur* Frogmore), 3rd dau of HRH Prince Friedrich Karl of Prussia, GCB, and *d* at Bagshot Park, Surrey 16 Jan 1942 (*bur* Frogmore), having had issue,

1 HRH Prince *Arthur* Frederick Patrick Albert, KG (1902), KT (1913), PC (1910), GCMG, GCVO, CB (1917/18), had Royal Victorian Chain (1906), Personal ADC to TM King Edward VII, King George V, King Edward VIII and King George VI, Col Res of Offrs, Col-in-Chief of The Royal Scots Greys and RAPC, an Elder Brother of Trin House, GCStJ, comm'd 7th Hus 1901, Lieut 1903, Capt Royal Scots Greys 1907, Brevet

Major 1913, Major 1915, Brevet Lt-Col 1919, hon Major-Gen 1920, Col 1922, hon Capt RNVR 1920, ADC to C-in-C BEF 1914-16, GSO (2) Canadian Corps 1917-18 (despatches twice, CB, French and Belgian Croix de Guerre avec palmes), one of the four Counsellors of State during the King's absence in India 1911-12, deputed by HM on mission to Japan to invest the Emperor with the Order of the Garter 1906, to attend the funeral of the Emperor and invest his successor with the Order of the Garter 1912, and to present the Emperor with his FM's baton 1918, Gov-Gen and C-in-C of Union of S Africa and High Commr 1920-24, had the Orders of Grand Collar of Charles III (Spain), Legion of Honour (France), Order of the Chrysanthemum (Japan), the Seraphim (Sweden), the Annunziata and Mil Order of Merit (Italy), St Saviour (Greece), St Olav (Norway), Manoel (Portugal), St Andrew and St Vladimir (3rd cl with swords), Leopold (Belgium), Mohammed Ali (Egypt), the Elephant (Denmark), and Carol I (Roumania). He was hon DCL Oxford, hon LLD Camb, and Univ of S Africa, 1st Chancellor of Witwatersrand Univ (1922), Bencher of Gray's Inn, FRS, FRGS, FRES, and FZS, Prov Grand Master of Freemasons of Berks 1925-38, Gov Wellington Coll, Chm Middx Hosp, Pres of W Lond Hosp and Royal Lond Ophthalmic Hosp, and High Steward of Reading 1935-38, *b* at Windsor Castle 13 Jan 1883, *m* at the Chapel Royal, St James's Palace 15 Oct 1913, HH Princess *Alexandra* Victoria Alberta Edwina Louise, Duchess of Fife, RRC, GCStJ (*b* at East Sheen Lodge 17 May 1891; *d* in Avenue Road, London 26 Feb 1959, cremated at Golders Green), elder dau and co-heiress of Alexander William George Duff, 1st Duke of Fife, KG, KT, PC, GCVO (*see* BURKE'S *Peerage*), by his wife HRH Princess Louise, Princess Royal, eldest dau of HM King Edward VII (*see p* 306), and *dvp* at Belgrave Square, London 12 Sept 1938, leaving issue,

HH Prince *Alastair* Arthur (until 1917), styled Earl of Macduff 1917-42, 2nd and last DUKE OF CONNAUGHT AND STRATHEARN, Lieut Royal Scots Greys, served in World War II, *b* at Mount Street, London 9 Aug 1914, *s* his grandfather as 2nd Duke 1942, *d* on active service, at Government House, Ottawa 26 April 1943, *unm*, when the titles became *extinct*.

1 HRH Princess *Margaret* Victoria Augusta Charlotte Norah, VA, CI, DGStJ, *b* at Bagshot Park 15 Jan 1882, *m* at St George's Chapel, Windsor, 15 June 1905, •HRH Crown Prince Oscar Frederik Vilhelm Olaf *Gustaf Adolf* of Sweden, Duke of Skåne, GCB, GCVO (now HM King Gustaf VI Adolf of Sweden) (*b* at Stockholm 11 Nov 1882), and *dvp* at Stockholm 1 May 1920, leaving issue (*see p* 224).

2 •HRH Princess Victoria *Patricia* Helena Elizabeth (Lady Patricia Ramsay), VA (1902), CI (1911), Col-in-Chief Princess Patricia's Canadian LI, mem Royal Soc of Painters in Water Colours, Royal West of England Acad, and New English Art Club, GCStJ (1934) (DJStJ 1910), was authorised by Royal Warrant 25 Feb 1919 to relinquish on her marriage the style of Royal Highness and the title of Princess of Great Britain and Ireland, and adopt that of Lady, with precedence before the Marchionesses of England [*Ribsden Holt, Windlesham, Surrey*], *b* at Buckingham Palace 17 March 1886, *m* at Westminster Abbey 27 Feb 1919, Adm Hon Sir *Alexander* Robert Maule Ramsay, GCVO, KCB, DSO (*b* 29 May 1881; *d* 8 Oct 1972), 3rd son of 13th Earl of Dalhousie, KT (*see* BURKE'S *Peerage*), and has issue,

•*Alexander* Arthur Alfonso David Maule Ramsay of Mar, FRICS, DL, Capt late Gren Guards, served 1938-47 (wounded in N Africa 1943), ADC to HRH The Duke of Gloucester 1944-47, a Page of Honour at the Coronation of HM King George VI 1937, Laird of Mar, Chm Exec Cttee Scottish Life-Boat Council, RNLI from 1965, Vice-Patron RNMDSF [*Cairnbulg Castle, Fraserburgh, Aberdeenshire; Mar Estate Office, Braemar, Aberdeenshire*], *b* 21 Dec 1919, *educ* Eton, and Trin Coll Oxford (MA), *m* 6 Oct 1956, •Hon *Flora* Marjory Fraser (*b* 18 Oct 1930), only dau and heiress of 19th Lord Saltoun (*see* BURKE'S *Peerage*), and has issue,

1*a* •*Katharine* Ingrid Mary Isabel Ramsay of Mar, *b* 11 Oct 1957.

2*a* •*Alice* Elizabeth Margaret Ramsay of Mar, *b* 8 July 1961.

3*a* •*Elizabeth* Alexandra Mary Ramsay of Mar, *b* 15 April 1963.

4 HRH Prince *Leopold* George Duncan Albert, 1st DUKE OF ALBANY, KG, KT, PC, GCSI, GCMG, hon DCL Oxford (1876), Col in the Army, *cr* DUKE OF ALBANY, EARL OF CLARENCE and BARON ARKLOW 24 May 1881, *b* at Buckingham Palace 7 April 1853, *m* at St. George's Chapel, Windsor 27 April 1882, HSH Princess *Helena* Frederica Augusta VA, CI, RRC (*b* at Arolsen 17 Feb 1861, *d* at Hinterriss, Tirol 1 Sept 1922), 3rd dau of HSH Georg Viktor, Prince of Waldeck and Pyrmont, GCB (*see p* 223), and *d* at Cannes 28 March 1884, (*bur* Albert Memorial Chapel, Windsor), leaving issue,

HRH Prince *Charles Edward* George Albert, late Reigning Duke of Saxe-Coburg and Gotha, Gen à la suite 1st Regt Prussian Guards, and 1st Saxon Hus, No 18, Col-in-Chief 95th Prussian Inf, 9th Prussian Hus, and 22nd Bulgarian Inf, had Orders of Black Eagle (Prussia), Elephant (Denmark), Seraphim (Sweden), St Hubert (Bavaria), St Cyril and St Methodius (Bulgaria), etc, *s* his father as 2nd Duke of Albany at birth, and *s* as Duke of Saxe-Coburg and Gotha on the death of his uncle, HRH Prince Alfred, Duke of Edinburgh 30 July 1900 (*see p* 295), *cr* KG 1902, but struck off the Roll of that Order 13 May 1915. His titles were removed from the Roll of Peers in pursuance of the Order of The King in Council 28 March 1919, *b* posthumously at Claremont House, Esher, Surrey 19 July 1884, *educ* Eton, and Bonn Univ, *m* at Glücksburg 11 Oct 1905, HH Princess *Victoria Adelheid* Helena Luise Marie Friederike (*b* at Grunholz 31 Dec 1885; *d* at Coburg 3 Oct 1970), eldest dau of HH Friedrich Ferdinand, Duke of Schleswig-Holstein-Sonderburg-Glücksburg, and *d* at Coburg 6 March 1954, having had issue,

(1) HH Hereditary Prince *Johann Leopold* Wilhelm Albert Ferdinand Viktor of Saxe-Coburg and Gotha, Duke of Saxony, was Prince of Great Britain and Ireland until 1917, *b* 2 Aug 1906, *m* 1st 4 March 1932 (*m* diss by div 1962), Baroness *Feodora* Maria Alma Margarete (*b* 7 July 1905), formerly wife of Baron Wolf Sigismund Pergler von Perglas, and elder dau of late Baron Bernhard von der Horst, and has issue,

1*a* •(Prinz) *Ernst Leopold* Eduard Wilhelm Josias von Sachsen-Coburg und Gotha [*81 Garmisch-Partenkirchen, Hauptstrasse 75/1, Germany*], *b* 14 Jan 1935, *m* 1st 4 Feb 1961 (*m* diss by div 1963), Ingeborg (*b* 16 Aug 1937), dau of Richard Henig, and has issue,

1*b* •(Prinz) *Hubertus* Richard Ernst Eduard von Sachsen-Coburg und Gotha [*74 Tübingen, Scheefstrasse 34, Germany*], *b* 8 Dec 1961.

He *m* 2ndly 29 May 1963, •Gertraude (*b* 1 July 1938), dau of Hermann Horst Pfeiffer, and by her has issue,

2*b* •(Prinz) *Ernst* Josias von Sachsen-Coburg und Gotha, *b* 13 May 1965.

3*b* •(Prinz) *Carl Eduard* von Sachsen-Coburg und Gotha, *b* 25 July 1966.

1*b* •(Prinzessin) *Victoria* von Sachsen-Coburg und Gotha, *b* 7 Oct 1963.

2*a* •(Prinz) *Peter* Albert Friedrich Josias von Sachsen-Coburg und Gotha [*Coburg bei Rothenheim, Germany*], *b* 12 June 1939, *m* 11 May 1964, •Roswitha Breuer (*b* 1 Sept 1945), and has issue,

•(Prinz) *Peter* von Sachsen-Coburg und Gotha, *b* 4 Oct 1964.

•(Prinzessin) *Malte* von Sachsen-Coburg und Gotha, *b* 6 Oct 1966.

1*a* •(Prinzessin) Caroline Mathilde Adelheid Sibylla *Marianne* Erika von Sachsen-Coburg und Gotha, *b* 5 April 1933, *m* 5 Dec 1953, •*Michael* Adalbert Wilfried Nielsen (*b* 12 Aug 1923) [*Kleinblittersdorf/Saar, Germany*], and has issue,

1*b* •*Margarete Brigitte* Nielsen, *b* 30 Sept 1954.

2*b* •*Renate Christine* Nielsen, *b* 4 Feb 1957.

He *m* 2ndly 3 May 1963, •Maria *Theresia* Elisabeth (*b* 13 March 1908) [*A-4360 Grein 322 an der Donau, Austria*], dau of Max Reindl, and *d* May 1972.

(2) HH Prince Dietmar *Hubertus* Friedrich Wilhelm Philipp of Saxe-Coburg and Gotha, Duke of Saxony, was Prince of Great Britain and Ireland until 1917, Courier Pilot, German AF, *b* 24 Aug 1909; *k* on active service in World War II 26 Nov 1943, *unm*.

(3) •HH *Friedrich Josias* Carl Eduard Ernst Kyrill Harald of Saxe-Coburg and Gotha, Head of the Ducal House of Saxe-Coburg and Gotha [*Schloss Greinburg 3, A-4360 Grein an der Donau, Upper Austria*], *b* 29 Nov 1918, *m* 1st 25 Jan 1942 (*m* diss by div 1946), Countess *Victoria Louise* Friederike Caroline Mathilde (*b* 13 March 1921), only dau of Count Hans zu Solms-Baruth (*see p* 277), and has issue,

1*a* •HH Prince *Andreas* Michael Armin Siegfried Friedrich Hans Hubertus of Saxe-Coburg and Gotha, Duke of Saxony, *b* 21 March 1943, *m* •—, and has issue,

He *m* 2ndly 14 Feb 1948 (*m* diss by div 1964), *Denyse* Henriette (*b* 14 Dec 1923), dau of late Robert Gaston de Muralt, and by her has issue,

2*a* •HH Prince *Adrian* Vincenz Edward of Saxe-Coburg and Gotha, Duke of Saxony [*Henri-Dunant Strasse 86, CH-3074, Muri bei Bern, Switzerland*], *b* 18 Oct 1955.

1*a* •HH Princess Maria *Claudia* Sibylla of Saxe-Coburg and Gotha, Duchess of Saxony, *b* 22 May 1949, *m* 27 March 1971, •Gion Schäffer [*Berne, Junkerngasse 27, Switzerland*], and has issue,

• a child, *b* 1972.

2*a* •HH Princess *Beatrice* Charlotte of Saxe-Coburg and Gotha, Duchess of Saxony [*Henri-Dunant Strasse 86, CH-3074, Muri bei Bern, Switzerland*], *b* 15 July 1951.

He *m* 3rdly 30 Oct 1964, •*Katherine* (*b* 22 April 1940), dau of Dietrich Karl Bremme.

(1) •HH Princess *Sibylla* Calma Marie Alice Bathildis Feodora of Saxe-Coburg and Gotha, Duchess of Saxony, was Princess of GB and Ireland until 1917 [*Royal Palace, Stockholm, Sweden*], *b* 18 Jan 1908, *m* 20 Oct 1932, HRH Hereditary Prince *Gustaf Adolf* Oscar Frederik Arthur Edmund of Sweden, Duke of Västerbotten, GCVO (*b* 22 April 1906; *k* in a flying accident at Copenhagen 26 Jan 1947), eldest son of HM King Gustaf VI Adolf of Sweden, and has issue (*see p* 224).

(2) •HH Princess *Caroline Mathilde* Helene Ludwiga Auguste Beatrice of Saxe-Coburg and Gotha, Duchess of Saxony, was Princess of GB and Ireland until 1917, *b* 22 June 1912, *m* 1st 14 Dec 1931 (*m* diss by div 1938), H Ill H Count *Friedrich Wolfgang* Otto zu Castell-Rüdenhausen (*b* 27 June 1906; *k* in action in World War II 11 June 1940), and has issue,

1*a* •H Ill H Count *Bertram* Friedrich zu Castell-Rüdenhausen [*Nibellungen Gasse 3/16, Vienna 1, Austria*], *b* 12 July 1932, *m* 10 Oct 1964, •Countess *Felizitas* (*Fee*) (*b* 20 Sept 1944), only dau of Count Hanno von Auersperg, and has issue,

1*b* •H Ill H Count Dominik zu Castell-Rüdenhausen, *b* 20 July 1965.

2*b* •H Ill H Count Michael zu Castell-Rüdenhausen, *b* 1967.

2*a* •H Ill H Count *Konradin* Friedrich zu Castell-Rüdenhausen [*Vesta, Finland*], *b* 10 Oct 1933, *m* 6 July 1961, •*Marta Catherina* (*b* 17 April 1939), dau of Bjarne Lonegren, and has issue,

1*b* •H Ill H Count *Carl Eduard* Friedrich Hubertus zu Castell-Rüdenhausen, *b* 15 March 1964.

1*b* •H Ill H Countess *Anne Charlotte* Catharine Victoria zu Castell-Rüdenhausen, *b* 7 April 1962.

1*a* •H Ill H Countess *Victoria Adelheid* Clementine Luise zu Castell-Rüdenhausen, *b* 26 Feb 1935, *m* 20 June 1960, •John *Miles* Huntington-Whiteley, VRD, Lt-Cmdr RNVR (*b* 18 July 1929) [*29 Drayton Gardens, SW10*], yst son of Capt Sir (Herbert) Maurice Huntington-Whiteley, 2nd Bt, RN (*see* BURKE'S *Peerage*), and has issue,

1*b* •*Leopold* Maurice Huntington-Whiteley, *b* 15 July 1965.

1*b* •Alice *Louise* Esther Margot Huntington-Whiteley, *b* 22 July 1961.

2*b* •*Beatrice* Irene Helen Victoria Huntington-Whiteley, *b* 6 Sept 1962.

She *m* 2ndly 22 June 1938, Capt Max Schnirring, German AF (*b* 20 May 1896; *k* in a flying accident 7 July 1944), and has had further issue,

3*a* Peter *Michael* Schnirring, *b* 4 Jan 1943; *d unm* 6 Feb 1966.

2*a* •*Calma* Barbara Schnirring, *b* 18 Nov 1938, *m* 5 July 1961, •Richard Berger [*228 Carswell Drive, Moses Lake, Washington 98837, USA*], and has issue,

1*b* •Sascha Berger, *b* 22 Sept 1961.

2*b* •Richard Berger, *b* 7 July 1962.

3*b* •Victor Berger, *b* 1963.

4*b* •a son.

5*b* •a son.

6*b* •a son.

3*a* •*Dagmar* Sibylla Schnirring, *b* 22 Nov 1940, *m* 26 Feb 1964, •Heinrich Walz [*Hohensteinstrasse 11, Memmelsdorf, Bamberg, Germany*], and has issue,

1*b* •Valesca Walz, *b* 14 Aug 1965.

2*b* •Larissa Walz, *b* 16 Sept 1967.

She *m* 3rdly 21 Dec 1948 (*m* annulled 1949), Jim Andree (*b* 10 Feb 1912).

•HRH Princess *Alice* Mary Victoria Augusta Pauline of Great Britain and Ireland (PRINCESS ALICE, COUNTESS OF ATHLONE) (*see separate biography sub* THE ROYAL FAMILY, *p* 177).

1 HRH Princess *Victoria* Adelaide Mary Louisa, Princess Royal, VA, CI, RRC, *b* at Buckingham Palace 21 Nov 1840, *m* at St James's Palace 25 Jan 1858, HIM *Friedrich III* (Wilhelm Nikolaus Karl), German Emperor and King of Prussia, KG, GCB (*b* at Neues Palais, nr Potsdam 18 Oct 1831; *d* there 15 June 1888), and *d* at Friedrichshof 5 Aug 1901, having had issue,

1 HIM (Friedrich) Wilhelm II (Viktor Albert), German Emperor and King of Prussia (1888-1918), KG, abdicated 28 Nov 1918, *b* 27 Jan 1859, *m* 1st 27 Feb 1881, HH Princess *Auguste Viktoria* Friederike Luise Feodora Jenny (*b* 22 Oct 1858; *d* 11 April 1921), eldest dau of HH Friedrich, Duke of Schleswig-Holstein-Sonderburg-Augustenburg (*see p* 287), and had issue,

(1) HI and RH Crown Prince Friedrich *Wilhelm* Viktor Ernst of the German Empire and of Prussia, renounced his rights to the throne 1 Dec 1918, *b* 6 May 1882, *m* 6 June 1905, HH Duchess *Cecilie* Auguste Marie (*b* 20 Sept 1886; *d* 6 May 1954), yr dau of HRH Grand Duke Fredrich Franz III of Mecklenburg-Schwerin (*see p* 289), and *d* 20 July 1951, having had issue,

1*a* HRH Prince *Wilhelm* Friedrich Franz Joseph Christian Olaf of Prussia, *b* 4 July 1906, *m* 3 June 1933, Dorothea (*b* 10 Sept 1907; *d* 1972), only dau of Alexander von Salviati, and *d* of wounds received in action in World War II 26 May 1940, leaving issue,

1*b* •HRH Princess *Felicitas* Cecilie Alexandrine Helene Dorothea of Prussia, *b* 7 June 1934, *m* 12 Sept 1958, •*Dinnies* Friedrich Karl von der Osten (*b* 21 May 1929) [*2055 Wohltorf, Lauenburg, Am Sachsenwald 3, Germany*], and has issue,

1*c* •*Dinnies* Wilhelm Karl Alexander von der Osten, *b* 15 Feb 1962.

2*c* •*Hubertus* Christoph Joachim Friedrich von der Osten, *b* 5 May 1964.

1*c* •*Friederike* Thyra Marion Wilhelmine Dorothea von der Osten, *b* 14 July 1959.

2*c* •*Cecilie* Felicitas Katharina Sophie von der Osten, *b* 12 March 1967.

2*b* •HRH Princess *Christa* Friederike Alexandrine Viktoria of Prussia [*53 Bonn-Ippendorf, Finkenweg 2 Germany*], *b* 31 Oct 1936, *m* 24 March 1960, *Peter* Paul Eduard Maria Clemens Maximilian Franz von Assisi Liebes (*b* 18 Jan 1926; *d* 5 May 1967).

2*a* •HI and RH Prince *Louis Ferdinand* Viktor

Eduard Albert Michael Hubertus of Prussia, Head of the Royal House of Prussia, Dr Phil, late 1st Lieut German Air Force, Grand Master of the Order of the Black Eagle [*28 Bremen-Borgfeld, Wümmehof; 1 Berlin 33 (Grunewald), Königsallee 9, Germany*], *b* 9 Nov 1907, *m* (civil) 2 May and (religious) 4 May 1938, HIH Grand Duchess Kira Kirillovna (*b* 9 May 1909; *d* 8 Sept 1967), yr dau of HIH Grand Duke Kirill Vladimirovitch of Russia (*see p* 297), and has issue,

1*b* ●HRH Prince Louis Ferdinand *Friedrich Wilhelm* Hubertus Michael Kirill of Prussia, renounced his rights of succession to the throne for himself and his descendants 18 Sept 1967 [*852 Erlangen, Rudelsweiherstrasse 22 Germany*], *b* 9 Feb 1939, *m* 22 Aug 1967 (*m* diss by div), Waltraud (*b* 14 April 1940), dau of Dr Alois Freydag, and has issue,

●(Prinz) *Philip* Kirill Friedrich Wilhelm Moritz Boris Tanko von Preussen, *b* 23 April 1968.

2*b* ●HRH Prince Wilhelm Heinrich *Michael* Louis Ferdinand Friedrich Franz Wladimir of Prussia, renounced his rights of succession to the throne for himself and his descendants 29 Aug 1966 [*1 Berlin 33 (Grunewald), Gneiststrasse 9, Germany*], *b* 22 March 1940, *m* (civil) 23 Sept and (religious) 25 Sept 1966, ●Jutta (*b* 27 Jan 1943), dau of Capt Otto Jörn, and has issue,

1*c* ●(Prinzessin) *Micaela* Maria von Preussen, *b* 5 March 1967.

2*c* ●(Prinzessin) *Nataly* Alexandra Caroline von Preussen, *b* 13 Jan 1970.

3*b* ●HRH Prince *Louis Ferdinand* Oskar Christian of Prussia [*28 Bremen-Borgfeld, Wümmehof, Germany*], *b* 25 Aug 1944.

4*b* ●HRH Prince *Christian Sigismund* Louis Ferdinand Kilian of Prussia [*1 Berlin 33 (Grunewald), Königsallee 9, Germany*], *b* 14 March 1946.

1*b* ●HRH Princess *Marie Cécile* Kira Viktoria Louise of Prussia, *b* 28 May 1942, *m* (civil) 3 Dec and (religious) 4 Dec 1965, ●HH Duke *Friedrich August* Wilhelm Christian Ernst of Oldenburg (*b* 11 Jan 1936), and has issue (*see p* 222).

2*b* ●HRH Princess *Kira* Auguste Viktoria Friederike of Prussia, *b* 27 June 1943.

3*b* ●HRH Princess *Xenia* Sophie Charlotte Cecilie of Prussia, *b* 9 Dec 1949.

3*a* HRH Prince *Hubertus* Karl Wilhelm of Prussia, *b* 30 Sept 1909, *m* 1st 29 Dec 1941 (*m* diss by div 1943), Baroness *Maria-Anna* Sybilla Margaretha (*b* 9 July 1916), only dau of Baron Alexander von Humboldt-Dachroeden. He *m* 2ndly 5 June 1943, ●HSH Princess *Magdalene* Pauline (*b* 20 Aug 1920), elder dau of HSH late Prince Heinrich XXXVI Reuss (*see p* 249), and *d* 8 April 1950, having by her had issue,

1*b* ●HRH Princess *Anastasia* Victoria Cecilie Hermine of Prussia, *b* 14 Feb 1944, *m* (civil) 8 Oct and (religious) 8 Nov 1965, ●HSH Hereditary Prince *Aloys-Konstantin* Karl Eduard Joseph Johann Konrad Antonius Gerhard Georg Benediktus Pius Eusebius Maria zu Löwenstein-Wertheim-Rosenberg (*b* 16 Dec 1941) [*8764 Schloss Kleinheubach bei Miltenberg, Germany*], and has issue,

1*c* ●HSH Prince *Carl Friedrich* Georg Eduardo Paolo Nickolo Franz Alois Ignatius Hieronimus Maria zu Löwenstein-Wertheim-Rosenberg, *b* 30 Sept 1966.

2*c* ●HSH Prince *Hubertus* Maximilian Gabriel Franz Louis Konstantin Dominik Wunibald Maria zu Löwenstein-Wertheim-Rosenberg, *b* 18 Dec 1968.

2*b* HRH Princess *Marie Christine* of Prussia, *b* 18 July 1947; *k* in a motor accident 29 May 1966.

4*a* HRH Prince *Friedrich* Georg Wilhelm Christoph of Prussia, *b* 19 Dec 1911, *m* 30 July 1945, ●Lady *Brigid* Katharine Rachel Guinness (*b* 30 July 1920; *m* 2ndly 3 June 1967, Major Anthony Patrick Ness) [*Patmore Hall, Little Hadham, Herts*], yst dau of 2nd Earl of Iveagh, KG, CB, CMG, FRS, DL (*see* BURKE'S *Peerage*), and *d* 20 April 1966, leaving issue,

1*b* ●HRH Prince Frederick *Nicholas* of Prussia, *b* 3 May 1946.

2*b* ●HRH Prince *William* Andrew of Prussia, *b* 14 Nov 1948.

3*b* ●HRH Prince *Rupert* Alexander Frederick of Prussia, *b* 28 April 1955.

1*b* ●HRH Princess *Victoria* Marina Cecilia of Prussia, *b* 22 Feb 1952.

2*b* ●HRH Princess *Antonia* Brigid Elizabeth Louise of Prussia, *b* (twin with Prince Rupert) 28 April 1955.

1*a* ●HRH Princess *Alexandrine* Irene of Prussia [*813 Starnberg, OBayern, Ottostrasse 5, Germany*], *b* 7 April 1915.

2*a* ●HRH Princess *Cecilie* Viktoria Anastasia Zita Thyra Adelheid of Prussia [*2410 Van Buren Street, Amarillo, Texas, USA*], *b* 5 Sept 1917, *m* 21 June 1949, *Clyde* Kenneth Harris (*b* 18 April 1918; *d* 2 March 1958), and has issue,

●*Kira* Alexandrine Brigid Cecilie Ingrid Harris, *b* 20 Oct 1954.

(2) HRH Prince Wilhelm *Eitel Friedrich* Christian Karl of Prussia, *b* 7 July 1883, *m* 27 Feb 1906 (*m* diss by div 1926), HH Duchess *Sophie Charlotte* (*b* 2 Feb 1879; *d* 29 March 1964), eldest dau of HRH Grand Duke Friedrich August of Oldenburg (*see p* 252), and *dsp* 8 Dec 1942.

(3) HRH Prince *Adalbert* Ferdinand Berengar Viktor of Prussia, *b* 14 July 1884, *m* 3 Aug 1914, HH Princess *Adelheid* Erna Karoline Marie Elisabeth (*b* 16 Aug 1891; *d* 25 April 1971), 2nd dau of HH Prince Friedrich of Saxe-Meiningen, Duke of Saxony, and *d* 22 Sept 1948, leaving issue,

●HRH Prince *Wilhelm Victor* Freund Ernst Friedrich Georg Adalbert of Prussia [*7 Stuttgart-N, Feuerbacher Heide 59, Germany*], *b* 15 Feb 1919, *m* 20 July 1944, ●Countess *Marie Antoinette* Franziska Ladislaja Josepha Paula Bernhardine Agnes (*b* 27 June 1920), eldest dau of Count Friedrich Hoyos-Sprinzenstein, Baron zu Stichsenstein, and has issue,

●HRH Prince *Adalbert-Adelhart* Alexander Friedrich Joachim Christian of Prussia, *b* 4 March 1948.

●HRH Princess *Marie Louise* Marina Franziska of Prussia, *b* 18 Sept 1945, *m* 22 May 1971, ●H Ill H Count *Rudolf* Maria Emil Franz Friedrich Carl Antonius Christophorus Hubertus Joseph Wenzel Michael von Schönburg-Glauchau (*b* 25 Sept 1932) [*Quinta Maria Luisa, Marbella, Spain*].

●HRH Princess *Victoria Marina* of Prussia, *b* 11 Sept 1917, *m* 26 Sept 1947, ●Kirby William Patterson (*b* 24 July 1907) [*12216 North 61st Street, Paradise Valley, Arizona 85254, USA*], and has issue,

1*b* ●*Berengar* Orin Bernhard Kirby Patterson, BS [*4637 Rockwood Parkway, Washington, DC, USA*], *b* 21 Aug 1948.

1*b* ●*Marina* Adelaide Emily Patterson [*12800 Lakewood Boulevard, Apt 5, Downey, California, USA*], *b* (twin with Berengar) 21 Aug 1948.

2*b* ●*Dohna*-Maria Patterson, *b* 7 Aug 1954.

(4) HRH Prince *August Wilhelm* Heinrich Günther Viktor of Prussia, *b* 29 Jan 1887, *m* 22 Oct 1908 (*m diss* by div 1920), HH Princess *Alexandra Viktoria* Auguste Leopoldine Charlotte Amalie Wilhelmine (*b* 21 April 1887; *d* 15 April 1957), 2nd dau of HH Friedrich Ferdinand, Duke of Schleswig-Holstein-Sonderburg-Glücksburg, and *d* 25 March 1949, leaving issue,

●HRH Prince *Alexander Ferdinand* Albrecht Achilles Wilhelm Joseph Viktor Karl Feodor of Prussia [*62 Wiesbaden-Sonnenberg, Bingert, Am Birnbaum 35, Germany*], *b* 26 Dec 1912, *m* 19 Dec 1938, ●Irmgard (*b* 22 Aug 1912), formerly wife of Werner Rosendorff, and dau of Major Friedrich Weygand, and has issue,

●(Prinz) *Stephan Alexander* Dieter Friedrich von Preussen [*3551 Bauerbach 122 über Marburg an der Lahn, Germany*], *b* 30 Sept 1939, *m* 28 Feb 1964, ●Heide (*b* 6 Feb 1939), dau of Ernst Arthur Julius Schmidt, and has issue,

●(Prinzessin) *Stephanie* Viktoria-Luise Irmgard Gertrud von Preussen, *b* 21 Sept 1966.

(5) HRH Prince *Oskar* Karl Gustav Adolf of Prussia, *b* 27 July 1888, *m* 31 July 1914, ●Countess *Ina Marie* Helene Adele Elise von Bassewitz (*b* 27 Jan 1888) [*53 Bonn, Johanniterstrasse 1, Germany*], yr dau of Count Karl von Bassewitz-Levetzow, and *d* 27 Jan 1958, having had issue,

1*a* HRH Prince *Oskar* Wilhelm Karl Hans Kuno of Prussia, *b* 12 July 1915; *k* in action in World War II 5 Sept 1939.

2*a* ●HRH Prince *Burchard* Friedrich Max Werner Georg of Prussia [*8 München 23, Kaulbachstrasse 93, Germany*], *b* 8 Jan 1917, *m* (civil) 20 Jan and (religious) 31 Jan 1961, ●H Ill H Countess *Eleonora* Vera Alexia Anna Maria (*b* 31 Jan 1925), formerly wife of Robert Bee, and eldest dau of H Ill H Count Leopold Fugger von Babenhausen.

3*a* ●HRH Prince *Wilhelm-Karl* Adalbert Erich Detloff of Prussia [*345 Holzminden, Einbecker Strasse 21, Germany*], *b* 30 Jan 1922, *m* 1 March 1952, ●*Armgard* Else Helene (*b* 17 Feb 1926), only dau of Friedrich von Veltheim, and has issue,

1*b* ●HRH Prince *Wilhelm-Karl* Oskar Friedrich of Prussia, *b* 26 Aug 1955.

2*b* ●HRH Prince *Oskar* Hans Karl Michael of Prussia, *b* 6 May 1959.

1*b* ●HRH Princess *Donata-Viktoria* Ina-Marie Ottonie of Prussia, *b* 24 Dec 1952.

1*a* ●HRH Princess *Herzeleide-Ina-Marie* Sophie Charlotte Else of Prussia, *b* 25 Dec 1918, *m* 16 Aug 1938, ●HSH *Karl* Peter François Andreas Alexander Prince Biron von Curland (*b* 15 June 1907) [*8 München 27, Flemingstrasse 6, Germany*], and has issue,

1*b* ●HSH Prince *Ernst Johann* Karl Oskar Franz Eitel-Friedrich Peter Burchard Biron von Curland [*8 München 83, Unterbibergerstrasse 10, Germany*], *b* 6 Aug 1940, *m* 15 Aug 1967, ●Countess *Elisabeth* Victoria Raimonda (*b* 9 Dec 1941), yr dau of Ludwig, Count von Ysenburg-Philippseich.

2*b* ●HSH Prince *Michael* Karl August Wilhelm Biron von Curland [*8 München 81, Freischützstrasse 110/X, Germany*], *b* 20 Jan 1944, *m* 2 July 1969, ●Kristin (*b* 6 Nov 1944), 2nd dau of Joachim von Oertzen, and has issue,

●HSH Prince *Alexander* Biron von Curland, *b* 18 Sept 1972.

●HSH Princess *Veronika* Biron von Curland, *b* 23 Jan 1970.

1*b* ●HSH Princess *Viktoria-Benigna* Ina-Maria Cecilie Friederike-Luise Helene Biron von Curland, *b* 2 July 1939, *m* 6 May 1968, ●Baron *John* Robert von Twickel (*b* 25 July 1940) [*8 München 80, Mauerkircher Strasse 10, Germany*], and has issue,

●Baron Nikaolaus von Twickel, *b* 1 April 1969.

(6) HRH Prince *Joachim* Franz Humbert of Prussia, *b* 17 Dec 1890, *m* 11 March 1916, ●HH Princess *Marie Auguste* Antoinette Friederike Alexandra Hilda Luise (*b* 10 June 1898; *m* 2ndly 27 Sept 1926 (*m* diss by div 1935), Baron Johannes-Michael von Loën; resumed her maiden name) [*43 Essen, Kunigundenstrasse 9, Germany*], dau of HH Duke Eduard of Anhalt, and *d* 18 July 1920, leaving issue,

●HRH Prince Karl *Franz Joseph* Wilhelm Friedrich Eduard Paul of Prussia [*Carbaya 478, Lima, Peru*], *b* 15 Dec 1916, *m* 1st (civil) 1 Oct and (religious), 5 Oct 1940 (*m* diss by div 1946), HSH Princess *Henriette* Hermine Wanda Ida Luise (*b* 25 Nov 1918), yr dau of HSH Prince Johann Georg von Schönaich-Carolath, and has had issue,

1*b* ●HRH Prince *Franz Wilhelm* Victor Christoph Stephan of Prussia [*6 Frankfurt a M-Niederrad, Rennbahnstrasse 44, Germany*], *b* 3 Sept 1943.

2*b* HRH Prince Franz Joseph *Friedrich Christian* Carl Erdmann Louis Ferdinand Oskar of Prussia, *b* (twin with Prince Franz Wilhelm) 3 Sept, *d* 26 Sept 1943.

3*b* ●HRH Prince *Franz Friedrich* Christian of Prussia [*6 Frankfurt a M, Unterlindau 74, Germany*], *b* 17 Oct 1944.

He *m* 2ndly 9 Nov 1946 (*m* diss by div), *Luise* Dora (*b* 5 Sept 1909; *d* 23 April 1961), formerly wife of Fritz Simon, and dau of Max Emil Theodor Hartung. He *m* 3rdly 1959, ●Eva Maria Herrera Valdeavellano, dau of Norberto Herrera, and by her has issue,

1*b* ●(Prinzessin) *Alexandra* Marie Auguste Juana Consuelo Eva von Preussen, *b* 29 April 1960.

2*b* ●(Prinzessin) *Désirée* Anastasia Maria Benedicta von Preussen, *b* 13 July 1961.

(1) ●HRH Princess *Viktoria Luise* Adelheid Mathilde Charlotte of Prussia [*33 Braunschweig, Stresemannstrasse 5, Germany*], *b* 13 Sept 1892, *m* 24 May 1913, HRH Prince *Ernst August* Christian Georg of Hanover, Duke of Brunswick and Lüneburg, Head of the Royal House of Hanover (*b* 17 Nov 1887; *d* 30 Jan 1953), and has issue (*see p* 290).

Emperor Wilhelm II *m* 2ndly 5 Nov 1922, HSH Princess Hermine (*b* 17 Dec 1887; *d* 7 Aug 1947), widow of HSH Prince Johann Georg von Schönaich-Carolath, and dau of HSH Prince Heinrich XXII Reuss (Elder Line) (*see p* 249), and *d* 4 June 1941.

2 HRH Prince Albert Wilhelm *Heinrich* of Prussia, Grand Adm Imp German Navy, KG, *b* 14 Aug 1862, *m* 24 May 1888, HGDH Princess *Irene* Luise Marie Anna (*b* 11 July 1866; *d* 11 Nov 1953), 3rd dau of HRH Grand Duke Ludwig IV of Hesse and by Rhine (*see p* 304), and *d* 20 April 1929, leaving issue,

(1) HRH Prince *Waldemar* Wilhelm Ludwig Friedrich Viktor Heinrich of Prussia, *b* 20 March 1889, *m* 14 Aug 1919, ●HSH Princess *Calixta Agnes* Adelheid Irmgard Helene Karoline Elise Emma (*b* 14 Oct 1895) [*6229 Schloss Reinhartshausen, Post Erbach, Rheingau, Germany*], elder dau of HSH Prince Friedrich Wilhelm of Lippe, and *dsp* 2 May 1945.

(2) ●HRH Prince Wilhelm Viktor Karl August Heinrich *Sigismund* of Prussia [*Estacion La Barranca, Finca San Miguel, Costa Rica*], *b* 27 Nov 1896, *m* 11 July 1919, ●HH Princess *Charlotte Agnes* Ernestine Auguste Bathildis Marie Therese Adolfine (*b* 4 March 1899), elder dau of HH Duke Ernst II of Saxe-Altenburg (*see p* 267), and has issue,

●HRH Prince *Alfred* Friedrich Ernst Heinrich Conrad of Prussia [*Estacion La Barranca, Finca San Miguel, Costa Rica*], *b* 17 Aug 1924.

●HRH Princess *Barbara* Irene Adelaide Viktoria Elisabeth Bathildis of Prussia, *b* 2 Aug 1920, *m* 11 July 1954, ●HRH Duke *Christian Ludwig* Ernst August Maximilian Johann Albrecht Adolf Friedrich of Mecklenburg (*b* 29 Sept 1912), and has issue (*see p* 291).

(3) HRH Prince *Heinrich* Victor Ludwig Friedrich of Prussia, *b* 9 Jan 1900; *d* 26 Feb 1904.

3 HRH Prince Franz Friedrich *Sigismund* of Prussia, *b* 15 Sept 1864; *d* 18 June 1866.

4 HRH Prince Joachim Friedrich Ernst *Waldemar* of Prussia, *b* 10 Feb 1868; *d* 27 March 1879.

1 HRH Princess Victoria Elisabeth Augusta *Charlotte* of Prussia, *b* 24 July 1860, *m* 18 Feb 1878, HH Duke Bernhard III of Saxe-Meiningen (*b* 1 April 1851; *d* 16 Jan 1928), and *d* 1 Oct 1919, leaving issue (*see p* 265).

2 HRH Princess Friederike Wilhelmine Amalie *Viktoria* of Prussia, *b* 12 April 1866, *m* 1st 19 Nov 1890, HSH Prince *Adolf* Wilhelm Viktor of Schaumburg-Lippe (*b* 20 July 1859; *d* 9 July 1916) (*see p* 252). She *m* 2ndly 19 Nov 1927, Alexander Zubkov (*b* 25 Sept 1900; *d* 28 Jan 1936), and *dsp* 13 Nov 1929.

3 HRH Princess *Sophie* Dorothea Ulrike Alice of Prussia, *b* 14 June 1870, *m* 27 Oct 1889, HM King Constantine I of the Hellenes (*b* 2 Aug 1868; *d* 11 Jan 1923), and *d* 13 Jan 1932, having had issue (*see p* 279).

4 HRH Princess *Margarete* Beatrice Feodora of Prussia, *b* 22 April 1872, *m* 25 Jan 1893, HRH *Friedrich Karl* Ludwig Konstantin, Landgrave of

Hesse (*b* 1 May 1868; *d* 28 May 1940), and *d* 22 Jan 1954, having had issue (*see p* 284).

2 HRH Princess *Alice* Maud Mary, VA, *b* at Buckingham Palace 25 April 1843, *m* at Osborne 1 July 1862, HRH Grand Duke *Ludwig IV* (Friedrich Wilhelm Karl) of Hesse and by Rhine (*b* at Bessungen 12 Sept 1837; *d* at Darmstadt 13 March 1892), and *d* at Darmstadt 14 Dec 1878, having had issue,

1 HRH Grand Duke *Ernst Ludwig* Albert Karl Wilhelm of Hesse and by Rhine, KG, GCB, *b* 25 Nov 1868, *m* 1st 19 April 1894 (*m* diss by div 1901), HRH Princess *Victoria Melita* (*b* 25 Nov 1876; *d* 1 March 1936), 2nd dau of HRH Prince Alfred of Great Britain and Ireland, Reigning Duke of Saxe-Coburg and Gotha, Duke of Edinburgh (*see p* 297), and had issue,

(1) HGDH Prince (un-named), *b* and *d* 1900.

(1) HGDH Princess *Elisabeth* Mary Alice Victoria, *b* 11 March 1895; *d* 16 Nov 1903.

He *m* 2ndly 2 Feb 1905 HSH Princess *Eleonore* Ernestine Marie (*b* 17 Sept 1871; *d* 16 Nov 1937), 2nd dau of HSH Hermann, 5th Prince zu Solms-Hohensolms-Lich, and *d* 9 Oct 1937, having by her had issue,

(1) HRH Hereditary Grand Duke *Georg* Donatus Wilhelm Nikolaus Eduard Heinrich Karl of Hesse and by Rhine, *b* 8 Nov 1906, *m* 2 Feb 1931, HRH Princess Cecilie (*b* 23 June 1911; *d* 16 Nov 1937), 3rd dau of HRH Prince Andrew of Greece and Denmark, GCVO, and was *k* in a flying accident together with his wife, two sons and mother, 16 Nov 1937, having had issue,

1*a* HRH Prince *Ludwig* Ernst Andreas of Hesse and by Rhine, *b* 25 Oct 1931; *d* 16 Nov 1937.

2*a* HGDH Prince *Alexander* Georg Karl Heinrich of Hesse and by Rhine, *b* 14 April 1933; *d* 16 Nov 1937.

1*a* HGDH Princess *Johanna* Marina Eleonore of Hesse and by Rhine, *b* 20 Sept 1936; *d* 14 June 1939.

(2) HRH Prince *Ludwig* Hermann Alexander Chlodwig of Hesse and by Rhine, Head of the Grand Ducal House of Hesse and by Rhine, *b* 20 Nov 1908, *m* 17 Nov 1937, •Hon *Margaret* Campbell Geddes (*b* 18 March 1913) [*Schloss Wolfsgarten (607), Langen, Hessen, Germany*], only dau of 1st Baron Geddes, GCMG, KCB (*see* BURKE'S *Peerage*), and *dsp* in Frankfurt a/Main 30 May 1968, when he was *s* as Head of the Grand Ducal House by his adopted son, HRH Prince Moritz of Hesse (*see p* 284).

2 HGDH Prince *Friedrich Wilhelm* August Viktor Leopold Ludwig, *b* 7 Oct 1870; *d* as the result of an accident 29 May 1873.

1 HGDH Princess *Victoria Alberta* Elisabeth Mathilde Marie, VA, discontinued title of Princess 1917, *b* 5 April 1863, *m* 30 April 1884, Adm of the Fleet HSH Prince *Louis* Alexander of Battenberg, later 1st Marquess of Milford Haven, PC, GCB (civ and mil), KCMG (*b* 24 May 1854; *d* 11 Sept 1921), eldest son of HGDH Prince Alexander of Hesse and by Rhine (*see* BURKE'S *Peerage*, MILFORD HAVEN, M), and *d* in London 24 Sept 1950, having had issue,

(1) (HSH Prince) *George* Louis Victor Henry Serge, 2nd MARQUESS OF MILFORD HAVEN, GCVO (1932), relinquished his princely titles 1917, a naval cadet 1905, Midshipman 1910, act Sub-Lieut 1912, Sub-Lieut 1914, Lt-Cmdr 1922, Cmdr 1927, and Capt RN 1937, served in Battle Cruiser Fleet in World War I present at Battle of Heligoland, Dogger Bank and Jutland, rec Order of St Vladimir (4th cl) (Russia), and Mil Order of Savoy (4th cl) (Italy) for war service, had Grand Cross of Order of Isabella the Catholic (Spain), and of Order of the Pole Star (Sweden), Freeman of Lond, *b* 6 Nov 1892, *m* 15 Nov 1916, Countess Nadejda (*Nada*) de Torby (*b* 28 March 1896; *d* 22 Jan 1963), yr dau of HIH Grand Duke Michael Michailovitch of Russia (*see p* 221), and *d* 8 April 1938, leaving issue,

David Michael Mountbatten, 3rd MARQUESS OF MILFORD HAVEN, OBE (1942), DSC (1943), mem Inst of Electronic and Radio Engrs (1967), Lieut RN (ret 1948), served in World War II (despatches twice), Freeman of Shipwrights' Co, was best man to HRH The Duke of Edinburgh 20 Nov 1947, Chm Atlas Copco (GB) Ltd, and Katrinafors Ltd, Dir George Brodie Co, *b* 12 May 1919, *educ* RNC Dartmouth, *m* 1st 4 Feb 1950 (*m* diss by div in Mexico 1954, and in England 1960), *Romaine* Dahlgren (*b* Jan 1924), formerly wife of William Simpson, and only dau of late Vinton Ulric Dahlgren Pierce, of USA. He *m* 2ndly 17 Nov 1960, •*Janet* Mercedes (*b* 29 Sept 1937) [*2 Wilton Terrace, SW1*], only dau of late Major Francis Bryce, OBE, KRRC, of Hamilton, Bermuda, and *d* at St Bart's Hosp, London 14 April 1970, leaving issue.

1*b* •*George* Ivar Louis Mountbatten, 4th MARQUESS OF MILFORD HAVEN (*see* BURKE'S *Peerage*), *b* 6 June 1961.

2*b* •Lord *Ivar* Alexander Michael Mountbatten, *b* 9 March 1963.

•Lady *Tatiana* Elizabeth Mountbatten [*2 Wilton Terrace, SW1*], *b* 16 Dec 1917.

(2) •(HSH Prince) *Louis* Francis Albert Victor Nicholas, 1st EARL MOUNTBATTEN OF BURMA (*see* BURKE'S *Peerage*), KG (1946), PC (1947), GCB (1955), OM (1965), GCSI (1947), GCIE (1947), GCVO (1937), DSO (1941), FRS (1966), *cr* VISCOUNT MOUNTBATTEN OF BURMA, *of Romsey, co Southampton* 23 Aug 1946, and subsequently EARL MOUNTBATTEN OF BURMA and BARON ROMSEY, *of Romsey, co Southampton* 28 Oct 1947, in the Peerage of the United Kingdom (with remainder to the heirs male to his body, and in default of such issue to his elder dau and the heirs male of her body, and to every other dau successively in order of seniority of age and priority of birth, and to the heirs male of their bodies), relinquished his princely titles 1917, KStJ, has the following foreign orders: Grand Cross of Order of Isabella the Catholic (Spain), and of Orders of Crown and Star (Roumania), Greek Mil Cross, Grand Cross of Order of George I, Legion of Merit and DSM (USA), Grand Cross of Legion of Honour and Croix de Guerre (France), Spec Grand Cordon of Cloud and Banner (China), Grand Cross of Order of Star (Nepal), Grand Cross of Order of White Elephant (Siam), Grand Cross of Order of the Lion (Netherlands), Order of Seraphim (Sweden), Grand Cross of Mil Order of Aviz (Portugal), Agga Maha Thiri Thuddhamma (Burma), Grand Cross of Dannebrog (Denmark), and Grand Cross of Order of Solomon (Ethiopia). He is Adm of the Fleet (1956) (entd RN as a cadet 1913, Midshipman 1916, Sub-Lieut 1918, Lieut 1920, Lt-Cmdr 1928, Cmdr 1932, Capt 1937, Rear-Adm 1946, Vice-Adm 1949, Adm 1953), served in Grand Fleet in World War I, Naval ADC to HRH The Prince of Wales on his Australian and Indian Tours 1920-22, served in World War II, cmd'd 5th Destroyer Flotilla, in HMS *Kelly* 1939-41 (despatches twice), cmd'd HMS *Illustrious* 1941, Cdre of Combined Operations 1941-42, Chief of Combined Operations, and mem British Chiefs of Staff Cttee 1942-43, Supreme Allied Cmdr SE Asia 1943-46, Flag Offr cmdg 1st Cruiser Sqdn 1948-49, a Lord Commr of Admiralty, Fourth Sea Lord and Chief of Supplies and Transport 1950-52, C-in-C Mediterranean 1952-54, and concurrently C-in-C Allied Forces Mediterranean 1953-54, First Sea Lord and Chief of Naval Staff 1955-59, Chief of the Def Staff and Chm Chiefs of Staff Cttee 1959-65, Gold Stick and Col of The Life Guards and Col Cmdt RM from 1965, Personal Naval ADC to HM King Edward VIII 1936, and to HM King George VI 1937-52, Pers ADC to HM The Queen from March 1953, hon Lt-Gen and hon Air Marshal 1942, hon Col 289 Parachute Light Regt RHA 1956, hon Col Calcutta Lt Horse 1947, hon Col 4/5 Bn Royal Hampshire Regt (TA) 1964. He was apptd Viceroy of India (the last) Feb 1947, and was Gov-Gen of New Dominion of India Aug 1947-June 1948, Gov of IoW from 1965, hon Fell Christ's Coll Camb (1946), hon LLD Camb 1946, Leeds 1950, Edin 1954, Southampton 1955, Sussex 1963, hon DCL Oxford 1946 and Pennsylvania 1972, hon DSc Delhi and Patna 1948, AMIEE 1927, hon MIEE and hon

MIERE 1965, Grand Pres British Commonwealth Ex-Services League, Royal Life Saving Soc and Royal Overseas League, Pres King George's Fund for Sailors, Soldiers and Airmen's Families Assoc, past Pres Inst of Electronic and Radio Engrs, Chm and founder of Nat Electronics Research Council, Pres Royal Naval Film Corpn, Royal Naval Saddle Club, Sailors' Home and Red Ensign Club (Lond), Gordon Smith Inst, Liverpool, and Soc of Genealogists, an Elder Brother of Trin House, Pres of RAC, and Hampshire Aeroplane Club, Pres British Computer Soc 1965, of Soc of Film and TV Artists 1965-71, Pres Internat Council of United World Coll 1968, Adm of the Cumberland Fleet of Royal Thames Yacht Club, Cdre of Sea Scouts, Past Prime Warden Shipwrights' Co, Freeman of Mercers', Vintners' and Grocers' Cos, hon mem Co of Master Mariners, mem Royal Swedish Naval Soc, Freeman of Lond (with Sword of Honour) (1946), High Steward (1940) and 1st Freeman (1946) of Romsey, Freeman of the City of Edin (1954), has on many occasions represented The Queen [*Broadlands, Romsey, Hants; Classiebawn Castle, Mullaghmore, co Sligo; 2 Kinnerton Street, SW1*], *b* 25 June 1900, *educ* RN Colls Osborne and Dartmouth, and Christ's Coll Camb, *m* 18 July 1922, Hon Edwina Cynthia Annette Ashley, CI (1947), GBE (1947), DCVO (1946), GCStJ, hon LLD Edin and Freeman of the City of Edin (simultaneously with her husband), had Order of Brilliant Star (China), Belgian and Netherlands Red Cross, 1st cl (despatches), American Red Cross Silver Medal, Pres of Honour of Internat Union for Child Welfare, Save the Children Fund, Returned Brit Prisoners-of-War Assoc, Nat Soc for Cancer Relief, and Our Dumb Friends League, Vice-Pres Royal Coll of Nursing, and Professional Nurses and Midwives Conf, and Patron of Nat Assoc of State Enrolled Assist Nurses (*b* 28 Nov 1901; *d* in N Borneo on a tour on behalf of St John Ambulance Bde of which she was Supt-in-Chief 1942-60, and was *bur* at sea from HMS *Wakeful* off Portsmouth), elder dau of 1st and last Baron Mount Temple, PC (*see* BURKE'S *Peerage*, SHAFTESBURY, E), and has issue,

1*a* •Lady *Patricia* Edwina Victoria Mountbatten, served in World War II in WRNS, *b* 14 Feb 1924, *m* 26 Oct 1946, •*John* Ulick Knatchbull, 7th Baron Brabourne (*b* 9 Nov 1924) [*Newhouse, Mersham, Ashford, Kent; 39 Montpelier Walk, SW7*] (*see* BURKE'S *Peerage*), and has issue,

1*b* •Hon *Norton* Louis Philip Knatchbull, *b* 8 Oct 1947, *educ* Gordonstoun, and Kent Univ.

2*b* •Hon *Michael John* Ulick Knachbull, *b* 24 May 1950, *educ* Gordonstoun.

3*b* •Hon *Philip* Wyndham Ashley Knatchbull, *b* 2 Dec 1961.

4*b* •Hon *Nicholas* Timothy Charles Knatchbull, *b* 18 Nov 1964.

5*b* •Hon *Timothy* Nicholas Sean Knatchbull (twin), *b* 18 Nov 1964.

1*b* •Hon *Joanna* Edwina Doreen Knatchbull, *b* 5 March 1955.

2*b* •Hon *Amanda* Patricia Victoria Knatchbull, *b* 26 June 1957.

2*a* •Lady *Pamela* Carmen Louise Mountbatten, a bridesmaid to HRH The Princess Elizabeth 20 Nov 1947, Lady in Waiting to HRH The Princess Elizabeth during her visit to Kenya 1952, and to HM The Queen for her Commonwealth Tour 1953-54, *b* 19 April 1929, *m* 13 Jan 1960, •*David* Nightingale Hicks, the designer (*b* 25 March 1929) [*23 St Leonard's Terrace, SW3; Britwell Salome, Watlington, Oxon; Place de l'Horloge, Roquebrune sur Argens 83, France*], son of late Herbert Hicks, of The Hamlet, Coggeshall, Essex, and has issue,

1*b* •*Ashley* Louis David Hicks, *b* 18 July 1963.

1*b* •*Edwina* Victoria Louise Hicks, *b* 24 Dec 1961.

2*b* •*India* Amanda Caroline Hicks, *b* 5 Sept 1967.

(1) HSH Princess Victoria *Alice* Elizabeth Julie Marie of Battenberg, RRC, worked with Red Cross during Balkan War 1912, and with Swedish and Swiss Red Cross in Greece during World War II, Life Pres of Christian Sisterhood of Martha and Mary, which she founded 1949, had Grand Cross of St Olga and St Sophia (Greece), *b* at Windsor Castle 25 Feb 1885, *m* at Darmstadt 7 Oct 1903, HRH Prince Andrew of Greece and Denmark, GCVO (*b* 2 Feb 1882; *d* 3 Dec 1944), and *d* at Buckingham Palace 5 Dec 1969 (*bur* St George's Chapel, Windsor), having had issue (*see p* 280).

(2) HSH Princess *Louise* Alexandra Marie Irene of Battenberg, RRC, relinquished princely titles 1917 and became Lady Louise Mountbatten, *b* at Heiligenberg Castle, Hesse 13 July 1889, *m* at the Chapel Royal, St James's Palace 3 Nov 1923, as his 2nd wife, •HM King *Gustaf VI Adolf* of Sweden (*b* 11 Nov 1882) (*see p* 224), and *dsp* in St Goran's Hosp, Stockholm 7 March 1965 (*bur* in Great Church, Stockholm).

2 HGDH Princess *Elisabeth* Alexandra Luise Alice of Hesse and by Rhine (Grand Duchess Elisabeth Feodorovna), VA, founder of the Order of Martha and Mary, *b* 1 Nov 1864, *m* 15 June 1884 HIH Grand Duke Serge Alexandrovitch of Russia, GCB (*b* 24 April 1857; assassinated 4 Feb 1905), and was murdered in the Russian Revolution 17/18 July 1918 (*bur* Gethsemane, Jerusalem), *sp*.

3 HGDH Princess *Irene* Luise Marie Anna of Hesse and by Rhine, *b* 11 July 1866, *m* 24 May 1888, Grand Adm HRH Prince Albert Wilhelm *Heinrich* of Prussia, KG (*b* 14 Aug 1862; *d* 21 April 1929), and *d* 11 Nov 1953, having had issue (*see p* 302).

4 HGDH Princess Victoria *Alix* Helena Luise Beatrix of Hesse and by Rhine (Alexandra Feodorovna after her conversion to Orthodoxy), VA, *b* 6 June 1872, *m* 26 Nov 1894, HIM Nicholas II, KG, GCB, Emperor of all the Russias (*b* 6 May 1868; murdered 16/17 July 1918), and was assassinated 16/17 July 1918, having had issue (*see p* 282).

5 HGDH Princess *Marie* Victoria Feodore Leopoldine of Hesse and by Rhine, *b* 24 May 1874; *d* 16 Nov 1878.

3 HRH Princess *Helena* Augusta Victoria, VA, CI, GBE (1918), RRC, *b* at Buckingham Palace 25 May 1846, *m* at the Private Chapel, Windsor Castle 5 July 1866, HH Prince Friedrich *Christian* Karl August of Schleswig-Holstein (*cr* HRH 1866), KG, PC, GCVO (*b* at Augustenburg 22 Jan 1831; *d* at Schomberg House, Pall Mall, London 28 Oct 1917), and *d* at Schomberg House, Pall Mall, London 9 June 1923 (*bur* Frogmore), having had issue,

1 HH Prince *Christian Victor* Albert Ludwig Ernest Anton of Schleswig-Holstein, GCB, GCVO, Capt KRRC, served in S African War, *b* 14 April 1867; *d unm* in Pretoria 29 Oct 1900.

2 HH *Albert* John Charles Frederick Alfred George, Duke of Schleswig-Holstein, GCVO, *b* 26 Feb 1869; *d unm* 27 April 1931.

3 HH Prince Frederick Christian Augustus Leopold Edward *Harold* of Schleswig-Holstein, *b* 12 May, *d* 20 May 1876.

1 HH Princess Victoria Louise Sophia Augusta Amelia Helena (*Helena Victoria*) of Schleswig-Holstein, relinquished her German titles 1917 and became known as HH Princess Helena Victoria, VA, CI (1889), GBE (1918), RRC, Lady Pres of Order of Mercy, Pres YMCA Women's Aux, GCStJ, *b* 3 May 1870; *d unm* 13 March 1948.

2 HH Princess Franzisca Josepha Louise Augusta Marie Christina Helena (*Marie Louise*) of Schleswig-Holstein, relinquished her German titles 1917 and became known as HH Princess Marie Louise, VA, CI (1893), GCVO (1953), GBE (1919), RRC, Lady Pres of Order of Mercy, GCStJ, author of *My Memories of Six Reigns* (1956), *b* 12 Aug 1872, *m* 6 July 1891 (*m* diss by div 1900), HH Prince *Aribert* Joseph Alexander of Anhalt, GCB (*b* 18 June 1864; *d* 24 Dec 1933), and *dsp* at 10 Fitzmaurice Place, Berkeley Square, W1 8 Dec 1956 (*bur* Frogmore).

4 HRH Princess *Louise* Caroline Alberta, VA, CI (1878), GCVO (1937), GBE (1918), RRC, hon LLD Glasgow, Col-in-Chief of Princess Louise's Argyll and Sutherland Highrs, Pres Scottish Branch of League of Mercy, and of Nat Trust, hon Freeman of Kensington, GCStJ, *b* at Buckingham Palace

18 March 1848, *m* at St George's Chapel, Windsor 21 March 1871, John Campbell, 9th Duke of Argyll, KG, KT, PC, GCMG, GCVO (*b* in London 6 Aug 1845; *d* at Kent House, Cowes, IoW 2 May 1914) (*see* BURKE'S *Peerage*), and *dsp* at Kensington Palace 3 Dec 1939 (cremated at Golders Green and *bur* Frogmore).

5 HRH Princess *Beatrice* Mary Victoria Feodore, VA, CI (1878), GCVO (1937), GBE (1919), RRC, Gov of IoW and of Carisbrooke Castle, hon Col 8th Bn The Hampshire Regt (TA), and of The Princess Beatrice's (Isle of Wight Rifles) Heavy Bde, RA, Pres of League of Remembrance, GCStJ, *b* at Buckingham Palace 14 April 1857, *m* at Whippingham Church, IoW 23 July 1885, HSH Prince *Henry* Maurice of Battenberg (*cr* HRH 23 July 1885), KG, PC, Col in the Army, Capt Gen and Gov of IoW and of Carisbrooke Castle (*b* at Milan 5 Oct 1858; *d* at sea from fever contracted in the Ashanti Expdn 20 Jan 1896, *bur* Whippingham), and *d* at Brantridge Park, Balcombe, Sussex 26 Oct 1944 (*bur* Whippingham), having had issue,

1 (HH Prince) *Alexander* Albert of Battenberg, 1st and last MARQUESS OF CARISBROOKE, GCB (1927), GCVO (1911), relinquished his princely titles 1917 and was *cr* MARQUESS OF CARISBROOKE, EARL OF BERKHAMSTED and VISCOUNT LAUNCESTON, *co Cornwall* 18 July 1917, served as a naval cadet and Midshipman, but trans to Gren Guards and served in World War I, served in RAF in World War II, *b* 23 Nov 1886, *m* 19 July 1917, Lady *Irene* Frances Adza Denison, GBE (1938), DJStJ, had Order of Maria Luisa (Spain) (*b* 4 July 1890; *d* 16 July 1956), only dau of 2nd Earl of Londesborough, KCVO (*see* BURKE'S *Peerage*), and *d* 23 Feb 1960, leaving issue,

●Lady *Iris* Victoria Beatrice Grace Mountbatten, *b* 13 Jan 1920, *m* 1st 15 Feb 1941, as his 1st wife (*m* diss by div 1946), Capt *Hamilton* Joseph Keyes O'Malley, Irish Guards (*b* 1910), eldest son of late Lt-Col Middleton O'Malley Keyes, RHA, of Ross House, Westport, co Mayo (*see* BURKE'S *LG of Ireland*). She resumed her maiden name of Mountbatten by Deed Poll 1949. She *m* 2ndly 5 May 1957 (*m* diss by div 1957), Michael Kelly Bryan, of Memphis, Tennessee, USA, and has issue,

●Robin Alexander Bryan, *b* 20 Dec 1957.

She *m* 3rdly 11 Dec 1965, ●William Kemp [*405 East 56th Street, New York City 22, USA*].

2 (HH Prince) *Leopold* Arthur Louis of Battenberg (later Lord Leopold Mountbatten), GCVO, relinquished his princely titles and assumed the surname of Mountbatten by Royal Licence 14 July 1917, and was granted the title and precedence of the yr son of a Marquess by Royal Warrant 11 Sept 1917, Capt KRRC, formerly 8th Bn The Hampshire Regt, ADC Personal Staff 1915, served in World War I (despatches), hon Major 1920, *b* 21 May 1889; *d unm* 23 April 1922.

3 HH Prince *Maurice* Victor Donald of Battenberg, KCVO, Lieut KRRC, served in World War I in 60th Rifles, *b* 3 Oct 1891; *k* in action during the retreat from Mons 27 Oct 1914, *unm*.

1 HRH Princess *Victoria Eugénie* Julia Ena of Battenberg, VA, Dame Grand Cross of the Sov Order of Malta, had Grand Cross of Order of Maria Luisa and of Order of Public Beneficence of Spain, received into RC Church 7 March 1906, granted style of Royal Highness 3 April 1906, *b* at Balmoral 24 Oct 1887, *m* 31 May 1906, HM King *Alfonso* XIII of Spain, KG, GCVO (*b* 17 May 1886; *d* 28 Feb 1941) (*see p* 233), and *d* in Lausanne, Switzerland 15 April 1969, having had issue,

(1) HRH Infante *Alfonso* Pio Cristino Eduardo Francisco Guillermo Enrique Eugenio Fernando Antonio Venancio of Spain, Prince of the Asturias, renounced his right of succession 11 June 1933 and took the title of Count of Covadonga, *b* 10 May 1907, *m* 1st 21 June 1933 (*m* diss by div 8 May 1937), Doña *Edelmira* Ignacia Adriana Sampedro-Ocejo y Robato (*b* 5 March 1906), dau of Don Luciano Sampedro-Ocejo. He *m* 2ndly 3 July 1937 (*m* diss by div 1938) Doña *Marta* Rocafort y Altuzarra, and *d* as the result of a motor accident at Miami, Florida, USA 6 Sept 1938, *sp*.

(2) ●HRH Infante *Jaime* Luitpold Isabelino Enrique Alejandro Alberto Alfonso Victor Acacio Pedro Pablo Maria of Spain, Duke of Segovia, has Order of Golden Fleece (Spain), renounced his right of succession 11 June 1933 [*18 Chemin de Primerose, Lausanne, Switzerland*], *b* 23 June 1908, *m* 1st 4 March 1935 (*m* diss by div 1947), Vittoria Jeanne Joséphine Pierre Marie *Emanuela* de Dampierre (*b* 8 Nov 1913), dau of Vicomte Roger de Dampierre, 2nd Duca di San Lorenzo, and has issue,

1*a* ●Don *Alfonso* Jaime de Borbón y Dampierre, Spanish Amb to Sweden from 1970, *b* 20 April 1936, *m* 8 March 1972, ●Doña *Maria del Carmen* Esperanza Alejandra de la Santisima Trinidad y de Todos los Santos Martinez-Bordíu y Franco (*b* 26 Feb 1951), eldest dau of Don Cristóbal Martinez-Bordíu, Marques de Villaverde.

2*a* ●Don *Gonzalo* Victor de Borbón y Dampierre, *b* 5 June 1937.

He *m* 2ndly 3 Aug 1949, ●*Charlotte* Auguste Luise (*b* 2 Jan 1919), formerly wife of — Hippler, and dau of Otto Tiedemann, of Konigsberg, E Prussia.

(3) ●HRH Infante *Juan* Carlos Teresa Silvestre Alfonso of Spain, Count of Barcelona, Head of the Royal House of Spain, a Midshipman RN 1933-35 (hon Lieut from 1936), has Order of the Golden Fleece (Spain) [*Villa Giralda, Estoril, Portugal*], *b* 20 June 1913, *m* 12 Oct 1935, ●HRH Princess *Maria de las Mercedes* (*b* 23 Dec 1910), 3rd dau of HRH Prince Carlos of Bourbon-Two Sicilies, Infante of Spain (*see p* 236), and has had issue,

1*a* ●HRH Infante *Juan Carlos* Alfonso Victor Maria of Spain, Prince of the Asturias, proclaimed The Prince of Spain in the Cortes 23 July 1969 [*Palácio de la Zarzuela, Madrid, Spain*], *b* 5 Jan 1938, *m* 14 May 1962, ●HRH Princess *Sophie* (Sofia) (*b* 2 Nov 1938), elder dau of HM late King Paul I of The Hellenes, KG (*see p* 279), and has issue,

1*b* ●HRH Infante *Felipe* Juan Pablo Alfonso y Todos los Santos of Spain, *b* 30 Jan 1968.

1*b* ●HRH Infanta *Elena* Maria Isabel Domenica y Todos los Santos of Spain, *b* 20 Dec 1963.

2*b* ●HRH Infanta *Cristina* Frederica Victoria Antonia y Todos los Santos of Spain, *b* 13 June 1965.

2*a* HRH Infante *Alfonso* Cristino Teresa Angel Francisco y Todos los Santos of Spain, *b* 3 Oct 1941; *d* as the result of a shooting accident 29 March 1956.

1*a* ●HRH Infanta *Maria del Pilar* Alfonsa Juana Victoria Luisa Ignacia y Todos los Santos of Spain, Duchess of Badajoz, *b* 30 July 1936, *m* 5 May 1967, ●Don *Luis* Gómez-Acebo y Duque de Estrada, Visconde de la Torre (*b* 23 Dec 1934) [*Los Jeronimos, Mirlo 12, Somosaguas, Madrid 11, Spain*], and has issue,

1*b* ●Don *Juan Filiberto* Nicolás Gómez-Acebo y de Borbón, *b* 6 Dec 1969.

2*b* ●Don *Bruno* Alejandre Gómez-Acebo y de Borbón, *b* 15 June 1971.

1*b* ●Doña Mariá de Fátima *Simoneta* Lutsar Gómez-Acebo y de Borbón, *b* 29 Oct 1968.

2*a* ●HRH Infanta *Margarita* Maria de la Victoria Esperanza Jacoba Felicidad y Todos los Santos of Spain, *b* 6 March 1939, *m* 12 Oct 1972, ●Don *Carlos* Zurita y Delgado (*b* 9 Oct 1943).

(4) HRH Infante *Gonzalo* Manuel Maria Bernardo Narciso Alfonso Mauricio of Spain, *b* 24 Oct 1914, *educ* Louvain Univ, *d* as the result of a motor accident at Pörtschach, Carinthia 13 Aug 1934, *unm*.

(1) ●HRH Infanta *Beatriz* Isabel Federica Alfonsa Eugénia Cristina Maria Teresia Bienvenida Ladislàa of Spain, *b* 22 June 1909, *m* 14 June 1935, ●Don Alessandro Torlonia, 5th Principe di Civitella-Cesi (*b* 7 Dec 1911) [*Palazzo Torlonia, 78 Via Bocca di Leone, Rome, Italy*], and has issue,

1*a* ●Don *Marco* Alfonso Torlonia de Principi di Civitella-Cesi, *b* 2 July 1937, *m* 1st 16 Sept 1960, Donna Orsetta Caracciolo die Principi di

Castagneto dei Duchi di Melito (*b* 17 May 1940), dau of Don Alfonso Caracciolo dei Principi di Castagneto, and has issue,

•Don *Giovanni* Torlonia dei Principi di Civitella-Cesi, *b* 17 April 1962.

He *m* 2ndly •*Philippa* McDonald.

2*a* •Don *Marino* Riccardo Francesco Maria Giuseppe Torlonia dei Principi di Civitella-Cesi- *b* 13 Dec 1939.

1*a* •Donna *Sandra* Vittoria Torlonia dei Principi di Civitella-Cesi, *b* 14 Feb 1936, *m* 20 June 1958, Conte *Clemente* Lequio di Assaba (*b* 9 Dec 1925; *d* 1971), and has issue,

1*b* •Nobile *Alessandro* Vittorio Eugenio Enrico Lequio di Assaba, *b* 20 June 1960.

1*b* •Nobile *Desideria* Beatrice Elyse Francesca Lequio di Assaba *b* 19 Sept 1962.

2*a* •Donna Olimpia Torlonia di Civitella-Cesi, *b* 27 Dec 1943, *m* 26 June 1965, •Paul-Annik Weiller (*b* 28 July 1933) [*Le Noviciat, 1 Rue de l'Ermitage, Versailles, Seine-et-Oise, France*], son of Paul-Louis Weiller, and has issue,

1*b* •*Paul-Alexandre* Weiller, *b* 12 Feb 1970.

1*b* •Aliki *Beatrice* Victoria Weiller, *b* 23 March 1967.

2*b* •*Sibilla* Sandra Weiller, *b* 12 June 1968.

(2) •HRH Infanta *Maria Cristina* Teresa Alejandro Guadalupe Maria de la Concepción Ildefonsa Victoria Eugénia of Spain [*Via Giannone 10, Torino, Italy*], *b* 12 Dec 1911, *m* 10 June 1940, Count Enrico di Marone Cinzano (*b* 15 March 1895; *d* 23 Oct 1968), and has issue,

1*a* •*Vittoria* Alfonsa Alberta Pilar Enrica Paola dei Conti Marone, *b* 5 May 1941, *m* 12 Jan 1961, •Don *Jose Carlos* Alvarez de Toledo y Gross (*b* 30 Nov 1929), and has issue,

1*b* •Don *Francisco* de Borja Alvarez de Toledo y Marone, *b* 27 May 1964.

2*b* •Don *Marco* Alfonso de Toledo y Marone, *b* 23 Jan 1965.

1*b* •Doña Vittoria Eugénia Alvarez de Toledo y Marone, *b* 8 Oct 1961.

2*a* •*Giovanna* Paola Gabriella dei Conti Marone, *b* 31 Jan 1943, *m* 24 July 1967, •Don Jaime Galobart y Satrustegui (*b* 1935), and has issue,

•*Alfonso* Alberto Galobart y Marone, *b* 12 April 1969.

3*a* •*Maria Teresa* Beatrice dei Conti Marone, *b* 4 Jan 1945, *m* 22 April 1967, •*José Ruis* de Arana Marques de Brenes (*b* 27 April 1933), and has issue,

1*b* •*Cristina* Carmen Margarita de Arana, *b* 24 March 1968.

2*b* •*Isabel* Alfonsa de Arana, *b* 17 May 1970.

4*a* •*Anna* Sandra dei Conti Marone, *b* 21 Dec 1948, *m* 21 June 1969, •*Gian Carlo* Stavro Santarossa (*b* 25 May 1944), and has issue,

•*Astrid* Cristina Antonia Santarossa, *b* 24 April 1972.

Queen Victoria was *s* by her eldest son,

1901-1910 EDWARD VII (Albert Edward), **King of Great Britain and Ireland** (styled *By the Grace of God, of the United Kingdom of Great Britain and Ireland and of the British Dominions beyond the Seas, King, Defender of the Faith, Emperor of India*), *s* as Duke of Cornwall, and Duke of Rothesay, etc at birth, *cr* Prince of Wales and Earl of Chester 8 Dec 1841, *cr* Earl of Dublin 17 Jan 1850, crowned at Westminster Abbey by Frederick Temple, Archbishop of Canterbury 9 Aug 1902, founder of the Imp Service Order (1902), and the Order of Merit (1902), *b* at Buckingham Palace 9 Nov 1841, *educ* Edin Univ (matric 8 Sept 1859), and Ch Ch Oxford, *m* at St George's Chapel, Windsor, 10 March 1863, HRH Princess *Alexandra* Caroline Mary Charlotte Louisa Julia, KG (1901), VA, CI, DJStJ, Col-in-Chief 15th/19th (Queen Alexandra's Own) Royal Hus, and Alexandra, Princess of Wales's Own Yorks Regt, Pres BRCS, hon DMus of Royal Univ of Ireland (1885), founder and Pres Alexandra Rose Day, crowned with her husband by William Dalrymple Maclagan, Archbishop of York (*b* at the Yellow Palace, Copenhagen 1 Dec 1844; *d* at Sandringham, Norfolk 20 Nov 1925, *bur* St George's Chapel, Windsor), eldest dau of HM King Christian IX of Denmark (*see p* 282), and *d* at Buckingham Palace 6 May 1910 (*bur* St George's Chapel, Windsor, having had issue,

1 HRH The Prince *Albert Victor* Christian Edward, KG (1883), *cr* DUKE OF CLARENCE AND AVONDALE, and EARL OF ATHLONE 24 May 1890, had the Order of the Osmanieh (Turkey), the Order of the Black Eagle (Prussia), the Collar of the Order of Carlos III (Spain), the Grand Cross of the Order of Orange-Nassau (Netherlands), the Order of the Annunziata (Italy), and the Order of the Star (Roumania), *b* at Frogmore 8 Jan 1864; *d unm* at Sandringham, Norfolk 14 Jan 1892 (*bur* Albert Memorial Chapel, Windsor).

2 HRH The Prince GEORGE FREDERICK ERNEST ALBERT, *s* his father as KING GEORGE V.

3 HRH The Prince Alexander *John* Charles Albert, *b* at Sandringham 6 April, *d* there 7 April 1871 (*bur* there).

1 HRH The Princess *Louise* Victoria Alexandra Dagmar, Princess Royal of Great Britain and Ireland (so declared 9 Nov 1905), VA, CI, DJStJ, Col-in-Chief 4th/7th Dragoon Guards, *b* at Marlborough House, London 20 Feb 1867, *m* at Buckingham Palace 27 July 1889, *Alexander* William George Duff, 1st Duke of Fife, KG, PC, KT, GCVO (*b* at Edinburgh 10 Nov 1849; *d* at Assuan, Egypt 29 Dec 1912), only son of 5th Earl of Fife, KT (*see* BURKE'S *Peerage*), by his wife Lady Agnes Georgiana Elizabeth Hay, 2nd dau of William George Hay, 18th Earl of Erroll, KT, GCH (*see* BURKE'S *Peerage*), by his wife Lady Elizabeth FitzClarence, 3rd natural dau of HM King William IV, and *d* at Portman Square, London 4 Jan 1931, having had issue,

1 A son, stillborn 16 June 1890.

1 HH Princess *Alexandra* Victoria Alberta Edwina Louise, DUCHESS OF FIFE, RRC, GCStJ, Col-in-Chief RAPC, acted as Counsellor of State during the King's absences abroad 1939, 1943 and 1944, styled Lady Alexandra Duff from her birth until 9 Nov 1905 when HM King Edward VII declared that she and her sister should bear the title of Princess and style of Highness with precedence immediately after all members of the Royal Family bearing the style of Royal Highness, *s* her father as Duchess of Fife 1912, *b* 17 May 1891, *m* 15 Oct 1913, HRH Prince *Arthur* Frederick Patrick Albert of Connaught, KG, KT, GCMG, GCVO, CB (*b* 18 Jan 1883; *d* 12 Sept 1938), only son of Field Marshal HRH Prince Arthur, 1st Duke of Connaught, KG, etc, and *d* in London 26 Feb 1959, having had issue (*see p* 299).

2 HH Princess *Maud* Alexandra Victoria Georgina Bertha, styled Lady Maud Duff from her birth until 1905, *b* 3 April 1893, *m* 12 Nov 1923, as his 1st wife, •Charles Alexander Carnegie, 11th Earl of Southesk, KCVO (*b* 23 Sept 1893) [*Kinnaird Castle, Brechin, Angus*] (*see* BURKE'S *Peerage*), and *d* 14 Dec 1945, leaving issue,

•*James* George Alexander Bannerman Carnegie, 3rd DUKE OF FIFE (*see* BURKE'S *Peerage*), *s* his aunt 1959, served in Malaya with Scots Guards 1948-50, Liveryman of Clothworkers' Co (1954), Pres ABA from 1959 [*Elswick House, Stonehaven, Kincardineshire*], *b* 23 Sept 1929, *m* 11 Sept 1956 (*m* diss by div 1966), Hon *Caroline* Cicely Dewar (*b* 12 Feb 1934), elder dau of 3rd Baron Forteviot, MBE, TD, JP (*see* BURKE'S *Peerage*), and has issue,

•*David* Charles Carnegie, Earl of Macduff, *b* 3 March 1961.

•Lady *Alexandra* Clare Carnegie, *b* 20 June 1959.

2 HRH The Princess *Victoria* Alexandra Olga Mary, VA, CI, GCStJ, *b* at Marlborough House 6 July 1868; *d unm* at Coppins, Iver, Bucks 3 Dec 1935 (*bur* Frogmore).

3 HRH The Princess *Maud* Charlotte Mary Victoria, VA, CI, GCVO (1937), GCStJ, *b* at Marlborough House 26 Nov 1869, *m* at Buckingham Palace 22 July 1896, HRH Prince Christian Frederik *Carl* Georg Valdemar Axel of Denmark, afterwards HM King Haakon VII of Norway, KG, GCB, GCVO (*b* at Charlottenlund 3 Aug 1872; *d* at Oslo 21 Sept 1957), 2nd son of HM King Frederik VIII of Denmark (*see p* 278), and *d* in London 20 Nov 1938, leaving issue,

•HM King Olav V (Alexander Edward Christian Frederik) of Norway, KG (1959), KT (1963), GCB (1946), GCVO (1923), Royal Victorian Chain (1955), hon Fell Balliol Coll Oxford, hon Adm in Brit Navy, hon Air Chief Marshal RAF (1959), Col-in-Chief The Green Howards, hon Col RA (TA), hon Col 308 (Suffolk and Norfolk Yeo), Field Regt RA (TA) from 1961, Freeman of Drapers' Co (1925), has Grand Cross of the Order of St Olav of Norway, the Orders of the Elephant of Denmark and the Seraphim of Sweden, and the French Croix de Guerre [*The Royal Palace, Oslo, Norway*], *b* 2 July 1903, *m* 21 March 1929, HRH Princess *Märtha* Sofia Lovisa Dagmar Thyra (*b* 28 March 1901; *d* 5 April 1954), 2nd dau of HRH Prince Carl of Sweden, Duke of Västergotland (*see p* 226), and has issue,

(1) •HRH Crown Prince Harald of Norway, GCVO (1955), Freeman of Drapers' Co (1960), has Grand Cross of Order of St Olav of Norway, and Orders of the Elephant of Denmark and Seraphim of Sweden [*Skaugum, Oslo, Norway*], *b* 21 Feb 1937, *educ* Balliol Coll Oxford, *m* 29 Aug 1968, •Sonja (*b* 4 July 1937), dau of late Karl August Haraldsen, and has issue,

•HRH Princess *Märtha Louise* of Norway, *b* 22 Sept 1971.

(1) •HRH Princess *Ragnhild* Alexandra of Norway, assumed the style of HH Princess Ragnhild, Mrs Lorentzen on marriage, *b* 9 June 1930, *m* 15 May 1953, •Erling Sven Lorentzen (*b* 28 Jan 1923), and has issue,

1a •Haakon Lorentzen, *b* 23 Aug 1954.
1a •Ingeborg Lorentzen, *b* 27 Feb 1957.
2a •*Ragnhild* Alexandra Lorentzen, *b* 8 May 1968.

(2) •HRH Princess *Astrid* Maud Ingeborg of Norway, assumed the style of HH Princess Astrid, Mrs Ferner on marriage, *b* 12 Feb 1932, *m* 12 Jan 1961, •Johan Martin Ferner (*b* 22 July 1927) [*Vinderen, nr Oslo, Norway*], and has issue,

1a •Alexander Ferner, *b* 15 March 1965.
2a •— Ferner, *b* 22 Oct 1972.
1a •Cathrine Ferner, *b* 22 July 1962.
2a •Benedikte Ferner, *b* 27 Sept 1963.
3a •Elisabeth Ferner, *b* 30 March 1969.

King Edward VII was *s* by his 2nd (but only surv) son,

1910-1936 GEORGE V (George Frederick Ernest Albert), **King of Great Britain and Ireland** (styled the same as Edward VII), KG 1884, *cr* Duke of York, Earl of Inverness, and Baron Killarney 24 May 1892, *s* as Duke of Cornwall, and Duke of Rothesay, etc, on his father's accession to the Throne 22 Jan 1901, *cr* Prince of Wales and Earl of Chester 9 Nov 1901, crowned at Westminster Abbey by Randall Thomas Davidson, Archbishop of Canterbury 22 June 1911, founded the Order of the British Empire (1917) and the Order of the Companions of Honour (1917), celebrated the Silver Jubilee of his reign 1935, *b* at Marlborough House 3 June 1865, *m* at the Chapel Royal, St James's Palace 6 July 1893, HSH Princess Victoria *Mary* Augusta Louisa Olga Pauline Claudine Agnes, KG (1910), GCSI (1911), VA, CI (1889), GCVO (1936), GBE (1917) (Grand Master 1936), had Royal Victorian Chain (1937), RRC (1910), GCStJ, had Grand Cross of the Legion of Honour (France), the Orders of El-Kemal (Egypt), Almar-i-Ala (Afghanistan), and Gold Chain of the Order of Saba (Ethiopia), Col-in-Chief 13th/18th Queen Mary's Own Hus, The Queen's Royal Regt (W Surrey), 53rd (Worcs Yeo), Air Landing Light Regt, RA and 38th Field Regt, RA, TA, Queen's Own (Oxfordshire Yeo) Hus and The QO Rifles of Canada, Cmdt-in-Chief Queen Mary's Women's Army Aux Corps, and Queen Alexandra's Royal Army Nursing Corps, Free Sister of Mercers' Co, hon Freeman of Basketmakers' Co, crowned with her husband (*b* at Kensington Palace 26 May 1867; *d* at Marlborough House 24 March 1953, *bur* St George's Chapel, Windsor), only dau of HH Francis, Prince and Duke of Teck (*see p* 294), and *d* at Sandringham 20 Jan 1936 (*bur* St George's Chapel, Windsor), having had issue,

1 HRH The Prince *EDWARD* ALBERT CHRISTIAN GEORGE ANDREW PATRICK DAVID, *Prince of Wales, s* his father as King EDWARD VIII.

2 HRH The Prince *ALBERT* FREDERICK ARTHUR GEORGE, DUKE OF YORK, *s* his brother as KING GEORGE VI.

3 •HRH The Prince *HENRY* WILLIAM FREDERICK ALBERT, DUKE OF GLOUCESTER (*see separate biography, sub* THE ROYAL FAMILY, *p* 149).

4 HRH The Prince *George* Edward Alexander Edmund, DUKE OF KENT, EARL OF ST ANDREWS and BARON DOWNPATRICK (*cr* 12 Oct 1934), KG (1923), KT (1935), PC (1937), GCMG (1934), GCVO (1924), had the Royal Victorian Chain, Lieut RN 1926, Cmdr 1934, Capt 1937, Rear-Adm 1939, Major-Gen in the Army, a Personal ADC to HM King George VI 1937-42, hon LLD Edin (1929), Sheffield (1930) and St Andrews (1936), hon DCL Durham (1935), Fell and mem Council King's Coll, Lon, Barrister-at-law and Bencher of Lincoln's Inn 1932, Pres Univ Coll Hosp 1928, Pres St George's Hosp 1935, hon Freeman of Cardiff 1932, and of Edin 1935, Lord High Commr to the Gen Assembly of the Church of Scotland 1935, Pres NSPCC 1935, Pres RCM and British Sch at Rome 1936, Pres Overseas League 1937, Chancellor Univ of Wales 1937, Pres Royal Commn for the Exhbn of 1851. HRH was apptd Col-in-Chief of QO Royal W Kent Regt 1935, and Col-in-Chief The Royal Fus City of Lond Regt 1937, Col-in-Chief 1st City Regt Grahamstown 1935, G/C RAF 1937, hon A/Cdre No 500 (Co of Kent) (Bomber) Sqdn AAF 1938, nominated Gov-Gen and C-in-C of the Commonwealth of Australia 1938 (but did not proceed), served in World War II in Intell Div, Admiralty 1939-40, and with Trg Cmd RAF 1940-42. HRH was hon Liveryman of Salters' Co (1932), Goldsmiths (1932) and Glaziers (mem Court of Assists 1935), Kt of the Order of the Chrysanthemum (Japan) and of the Order of the Seraphim (Sweden), and had the Grand Cross of the Order of Merit (Chile), of the Condor of the Andes (Bolivia), the Order of the Sun (Peru), the United Orders of Christ and St Aviz (Portugal), of the Order of the Southern Cross (Brazil), of the Order of the Redeemer (Greece), and GCStJ. HRH was *b* at Sandringham 20 Dec 1902, *m* at Westminster Abbey 29 Nov 1934, HRH Princess Marina, CI, GCVO, GBE, hon LLD Camb Univ (1953) and McGill Univ, Montreal (1954), hon Mus D Wales, hon DCL Univ of Kent at Canterbury (1966), Chancellor Univ of Kent at Canterbury 1966, GCStJ (Cmdt-in-Chief of Nursing Corps and Div for Wales), Chief Cmdt WRNS, hon Cmdt WRANS, Col-in-Chief The Queen's Regt, Col-in-Chief the

Devonshire and Dorset Regt, the Essex and Kent Scottish (Canadian Army), and Corps of REME, hon Col The Buckinghamshire Regt RA (T), hon Freeman of the Worshipful Cos of Clothworkers, Glaziers and Musicians, Pres All-England Lawn Tennis and Croquet Club, Pres Alexandra Rose Day, British Sch at Rome, Chest and Heart Assoc, RAF Benevolent Fund, RNLI, Royal Geographical Soc, WRNS Benevolent Trust, YWCA Central Club, Royal Choral Soc, Old Vic, and Working Ladies' Guild, had Grand Cross of Order of St Olga and St Sophia (Greece), Order of the Aztec Eagle, 1st cl (Mexico), Grand Cross of the Order of the Sun (Peru), of the Order of Merit (Chile), and of the Order of the Southern Cross (Brazil), represented HM The Queen at the Independence Celebrations of Ghana 1957, Botswana 1966, and Lesotho 1966 (*b* at Athens 30 Nov 1906; *d* at Kensington Palace 27 Aug 1968, *bur* Frogmore), yst dau of HRH Prince Nicholas of Greece and Denmark, GCB, GCVO (*see p* 280), and was *k* in a flying accident on active service in World War II 25 Aug 1942 (*bur* Frogmore), leaving issue,

1 •HRH Prince *EDWARD* GEORGE NICHOLAS PAUL PATRICK, 2nd DUKE OF KENT (*see separate biography, sub* THE ROYAL FAMILY, *p* 163).

2 •HRH Prince *MICHAEL* GEORGE CHARLES FRANKLIN (*see separate biography, sub* THE ROYAL FAMILY, *p* 169).

1 •HRH Princess *ALEXANDRA* HELEN ELIZABETH OLGA CHRISTABEL (*see separate biography, sub* THE ROYAL FAMILY, *p* 171).

5 HRH The Prince *John* Charles Francis, *b* at York Cottage, Sandringham 12 July 1905; *d* there 18 Jan 1919 (*bur* there).

1 HRH The Princess Victoria Alexandra Alice *Mary, The Princess Royal* (so declared 1 Jan 1932), CI (1919), GCVO (1937), GBE (1927), RRC (1953), TD (1951), CD, Col-in-Chief of The Royal Corps of Signals (1935), The Royal Scots (The Royal Regt) (1918), The Prince of Wales's Own Regt of Yorks (1958) (formerly The W Yorks Regt (Prince of Wales's Own) 1947-58, Controller-Comdt of WRAC (1949), Col-in-Chief The Royal Canadian Corps of Signals (1940), The Royal Australian Corps of Signals (1937), The Canadian Scottish Regt (1930), The Royal NZ Corps of Signals (1940), The Indian Corps of Signals (1936), The Pakistan Corps of Signals, The Royal Regt of Canada (1961), and The Royal Newfoundland Regt (1963), hon Col of The Barbados Regt, and hon Col of Leeds Univ OTC (1960), Controller-Cmdt ATS (1941), Major-Gen (1950), hon Gen (1956), Cmdt-in-Chief British Red Cross Detachments and GCStJ (1926), Air Chief Cmdt Princess Mary's RAF Nursing Service, Chancellor of Leeds Univ (1951), had hon degrees of LLD Leeds (1925), Sheffield (1926), Cambridge (1951), St Andrews (1954), Manchester (1954), Hull (1955), McGill (1955), Laval (1956), Lille (1956), Lond (1958), and Newfoundland (1963), hon FRCS (1927), hon FRCOG (1952), had hon Freedom of Glasgow (1923), Edin (1930), Leeds (1932), Harrogate (1951), Inverness (1951), York (1952), Ripon (1953), and Lusaka (1964), of the Cos of Fanmakers (1926), Gardeners (1933), Basketmakers (1954), hon mem Guild of Merchant Adventurers (1949), acted as Counsellor of State in 1939, 1943, 1944, 1947, 1951, 1953, 1954, 1956, 1957, represented HM The Queen at Independence celebrations in Trinidad (1962), and Zambia (1964), was Pres of Brit Sch at Rome, and Girl Guides Assoc, *b* at York Cottage, Sandringham 25 April 1897, *m* at Westminster Abbey 28 Feb 1922, Henry George Charles Lascelles, 6th Earl of Harewood, KG, GCVO, DSO, TD, DL, Lord Lieut WR Yorks (*b* 9 Sept 1882; *d* 23 May 1947) (*see* BURKE'S *Peerage*), and *d* at Harewood House, Leeds, Yorks 28 March 1965 (*bur* Harewood), leaving issue,

1 •*George* Henry Hubert Lascelles, 7th EARL OF HAREWOOD (*see* BURKE'S *Peerage*), hon LLD Leeds and Aberdeen, hon D Mus Hull, Chancellor York Univ 1962-67, Capt late Gren Guards, served in World War II (wounded, prisoner), a Train Bearer to HM King George VI at the Coronation 1937, ADC to Gov-Gen of Canada (the Earl of Athlone) 1945-46, a Counsellor of State during HM King George VI's absence in S Africa Jan-May 1947, and during HM The Queen's absence on Australian tour Nov 1953-May 1954, Dir Royal Opera House, Covent Garden 1951-53, Admin Exec 1953-60, Dir-Gen Leeds Musical Festival from 1958, Artistic Dir Edin Internat Festival 1961-65, Man Dir Sadler's Wells Opera Co from 1972, editor of magazine *Opera* 1950-53, Pres English Opera Group, Chm Musical Panel and mem Arts Council 1966-72, Artistic Advr to New Philharmonia Orchestra from 1966, Pres English Football Assoc 1964-71, Leeds Utd FC, and Royal Manchester Coll of Music, has Australian Order of Merit (1959) [*Harewood House, Leeds, Yorks; 3 Clifton Hill, NW8*], *b* 7 Feb 1923, *educ* Eton, and King's Coll Camb (BA 1948), *m* 1st 29 Sept 1949 (*m* diss by div 1967), Maria Donata (*Marion*) Nanetta Pauline Gustava Erwina Wilhelmina (*b* 18 Oct 1926), only dau of late Erwin Stein, of 22 Melbury Road, W14, and has issue,

(1) •*David* Henry George Lascelles, Viscount Lascelles, *b* 21 Oct 1950, *educ* Westminster.

(2) •Hon *James* Edward Lascelles, *b* 5 Oct 1953, *educ* Westminster.

(3) •Hon *Robert* Jeremy Hugh Lascelles, *b* 14 Feb 1955, *educ* Westminster.

He *m* 2ndly 31 July 1967, •*Patricia* Elizabeth (*b* 24 Nov 1926, formerly wife of Athol Shmith, and only dau of Charles Tuckwell, of Sydney, NSW, Australia, and by her has issue,

(4) •Hon *Mark* Hubert Lascelles, *b* 5 July 1964.

2 •Hon *Gerald* David Lascelles, Capt late The Rifle Bde, served in World War II 1944-45, Pres Brit Racing Drivers' Club, Fell Inst Motor Industry (1966), Pres 1969-70, Dir Silverstone Circuits Ltd, Chm Green Crop Conservation Ltd [*Fort Belvedere, Sunningdale, Berks; 95 Sloane Street, SW1*], *b* 21 Aug 1924, *educ* Eton, *m* 15 July 1952, •Angela (*b* 20 April 1919), dau of Charles Stanley Dowding, late of Dulwich, and of late Lady Fox, of 115A Hamilton Terrace, NW8, and has issue,

•*Henry* Ulick Lascelles, *b* 19 May 1953, *educ* Eton.

King George V was *s* by his eldest son,

Jan-Dec 1936 EDWARD VIII (Edward Albert Christian George Andrew Patrick David), **King of Great Britain and Ireland** (styled the same as Edward VII), who renounced the throne for himself and his descendants by instrument dated 10 Dec 1936, which was confirmed by the Declaration of Abdication Act passed on the following day. He was *cr* by Letters Patent 8 March 1937, DUKE OF WINDSOR (*see separate biography, sub* THE ROYAL FAMILY, *p* 179). King Edward VIII was *s* on his abdication by his brother,

1936-1952 GEORGE VI (Albert Frederick Arthur George), **King of Great Britain and Ireland** (styled the same as Edward VII until 22 June 1948, when he relinquished the title of Emperor of India), *cr* Duke of York, Earl of Inverness, and Baron Killarney in the Peerage of the United Kingdom 3 June 1920, KG 1916, KT 1923, KP 1936, PC 1925, GCMG 1926, GCVO 1921, had the Royal Victorian Chain (1927), joined RN as Midshipman 1913, Lieut 1918, Cmdr 1920, Capt 1925, Vice-Adm, Adm and Adm of the Fleet 1936, served in World War I with the Grand Fleet, and was present at the Battle of Jutland 1916 (despatches), Gen in the Army and Field Marshal 1936, was Personal ADC to HM King George V 1919-36, and to HM King Edward VIII 1936, Air Marshal, Air Vice Marshal and Marshal of the RAF 1936, Elder Brother of Trin House

1937, etc, crowned at Westminster Abbey by Cosmo Gordon Lang, Archbishop of Canterbury 12 May 1937, *b* at York Cottage, Sandringham 14 Dec 1895, *m* at Westminster Abbey 26 April 1923, •Lady *Elizabeth* Angela Marguerite Bowes-Lyon (HM QUEEN ELIZABETH THE QUEEN MOTHER *see separate biography, sub* THE ROYAL FAMILY, *p* 133), and *d* at Sandringham House 6 Feb 1952 (*bur* King George VI Memorial Chapel, St George's Chapel, Windsor), leaving issue,

1 •HRH The Princess *ELIZABETH* ALEXANDRA MARY, now HM QUEEN ELIZABETH II (*see biography, sub* THE ROYAL FAMILY, *p* 119).
2 •HRH The Princess *MARGARET* ROSE (*see separate biography, sub* THE ROYAL FAMILY, *p* 143).

The Dukes of Normandy

HALFDAN *THE OLD,* a Norwegian nobleman living in the latter half of the 8th century, was the father of

IVAR, EARL OF THE UPLANDS, the father of

EYSTEIN GLUMRA, the father of

1 ROGNVALD, of whom presently.

2 Sigurd, Earl of Orkney, where he settled in the time of Harald *the Fairhaired,* King of Norway (860-933), the father of

Guttorm, Earl of Orkney for one year after his father

The elder son,

ROGNVALD *THE MIGHTY,* EARL OF MORE, *m* Hild, dau of Rolf Nefja, and was burnt to death in his house by Halfdan Haaleg and Gudrod Ljome *ca* 890, leaving issue,

1 ROLF, or ROLLO, of whom presently.

2 Tore *the Silent,* Earl of Möre, m ca 890, Aalof Aarbot, dau of Harald *the Fairhaired,* King of Norway, and had issue,

Bergljot, *m* Sigurd, Earl of Lade.

By an earlier wife or concubine Rognvald had further issue,

1 Ivar.

2 Hallad.

3 Torf Einar, *s* his cousin Guttorm as Earl of Orkney and was ancestor of the later Earls of Orkney (*see* BURKE'S *Dormant and Extinct Peerages*).

4 Rollaug.

Rognvald's elder legitimate son,

ROLF, *or* **ROLLO** *THE GANGER,* after ravaging northern France from 876, had investiture of the Duchy of Normandy as a fief of the Crown from Charles III *the Simple,* King of France 911, *bapt* by the name of Robert 912, *b ca* 846, *m* 1st, Popa, or Papie (whom he repudiated and later remarried after the death of Giselle), dau of Berengar, Count of Bayeux, and had issue,

WILLIAM I, *s* his father.

Gerloc, or Adèle, *m* 933, as his 1st wife, William I, Count of Poitiers, III Duke of Aquitaine, and *d* 963, leaving issue.

He *m* 2ndly 912, Giselle (*dsp* 919), dau of Charles III *the Simple,* King of France, by his 1st wife Frederona, sister of Bovo, Bishop of Châlons, and *d ca* 932 (*bur* Rouen). He was *s* by his only son,

WILLIAM I *LONGSWORD,* **Duke of Normandy,** assoc in govt with his father from 927, *b ca* 900, *m* 1st Sprota, of Norse descent, and had issue,

RICHARD, *s* his father.

He *m* 2ndly, Liutgarde (who *m* 2ndly, Theobald II, Count of Blois and Chartres, and *d post* 9 Feb 978), 2nd dau of Herbert II, Count of Vermandois, by his wife Hildebrande of France, and was murdered by the Flemings 17 Dec 942, when he was *s* by his only son,

RICHARD I *THE FEARLESS,* **Duke of Normandy**, *b* at Fécamp 933, *m* 1st 960, Emma (*dsp* 19 March 968), dau of Hugh *the Great,* Duke of France and Count of Paris, by his 3rd wife Hedwig of Saxony. He *m* 2ndly, Gunnor (*d* 1031), formerly his mistress, and *d* 20 Nov 996, having by her had issue,

1 RICHARD II, *s* his father.

2 Robert, Count of Evreux, Archbishop of Rouen 989, *d* 1037.

3 Mauger, Count of Corbeil *jure uxoris, m* Germaine, Countess of Corbeil, dau of Albert, Count of Corbeil, and had issue (*see* BURKE'S *Peerage*, KINLOSS, B).

1 Emma, *b ca* 985, *m* 1st 1002, Æthelred II, King of England, and had issue (*see p* 190). He *d* in London 23 April 1016. She *m* 2ndly July 1017, Canute I *the Great,* King of England, Denmark and Norway, and *d* 6 March 1052 (*bur* Winchester Cathedral), having had further issue. He *d* at Shaftesbury 12 Nov 1035 (*bur* Winchester Cathedral).

2 Hawise, *m* Geoffrey I, Count of Brittany, and *d* 21 Feb 1034, leaving issue. He *d* 20 Nov 1008.

3 Matilda, *m* as his 1st wife, Eudes II, Count of Blois, Chartres and Troyes, and *dsp* 1017.

4 Beatrix, *m* Ebles, Viscount of Turenne.

Duke Richard I was *s* by his eldest son,

RICHARD II *THE GOOD,* **Duke of Normandy,** *m* 1st, Judith (*d* 1017), dau of Conan I, Count of Brittany, by his wife Ermengarde of Anjou, and had issue,

1 RICHARD III, *s* his father.

2 ROBERT II, *s* his brother.

3 William, a monk at Fécamp, *d* 1025.

1 Adeliza, or Adelais, *m ante* 1023, Renaud I, Count Palatine of Burgundy, and had issue. He *d* 4 Sept 1057.

2 Eleanor, *m* as his 2nd wife, Baldwin IV, Count of Flanders, and had issue. He *d* 30 May 1036.

He *m* 2ndly 1017, Margaret, or Estrith (who was repudiated and *m* 2ndly, Earl Ulf (*d ca* 1035), brother of Gytha, wife of Earl Godwin, and son of Thorgils Sprakalegg), dau of Sweyn, King of England, Denmark and Norway (*see p* 192). He *m* 3rdly, Papie, of unknown origin, and *d* 23 Aug 1027, having by her had issue,

4 William, Count of Arques, claimed Normandy on the death of Duke Robert II, *m* dau of Hugh II, Count of Ponthieu.

5 Mauger, Archbishop of Rouen 1037, drowned off Guernsey 1055.

Duke Richard II was *s* by his eldest son,

RICHARD III, Duke of Normandy, *m* Jan 1026, Adèle (who *m* 2ndly 1028, Baldwin V, Count of Flanders, and *d* a nun 8 Jan 1097), dau of Robert I, King of France, by his 2nd wife Constance of Provence, and dspl 6 Aug 1028, when he was *s* by his brother,

ROBERT II *THE DEVIL,* or *THE MAGNIFICENT,* **Duke of Normandy,** *d unm* at Nicaea while returning from pilgrimage to Jerusalem 2 July 1035, leaving issue by his mistress Harlette*, dau of Fulbert, a tanner or furrier of Falaise,

WILLIAM II, Duke of Normandy, the conqueror of England (*see p* 193).

---

* Harlette subsequently *m* Herluin de Conteville, by whom she had issue, Odo, Bishop of Bayeux and Earl of Kent; Robert, Count of Mortagne; and Adelaide, who *m* Lambert, Count of Lens, and had issue, Judith, who *m* Waltheof, Earl of Northampton and Huntingdon (*see* BURKE'S *Dormant and Extinct Peerages*).

The House of Anjou

GEOFFREY II DE CHATEAU-LANDON, COUNT OF GATINAIS, *m* Ermengarde, dau and eventual heiress of Fulk III *the Black,* (5th) Count of Anjou, and *d post* 1034, leaving issue,

1 GEOFFREY III, *s* his maternal uncle as Count of Anjou.
2 FULK IV, *s* his brother.
1 Hildegarde, *m ca* 1060, as his 2nd wife, Joscelin I, Lord of Courtenay, and had issue.

The elder son,

GEOFFREY III *THE BEARDED,* **Count of Anjou,** *s* his uncle Count Geoffrey II 1060 and was deposed in favour of his brother Fulk IV *ca* 1067, *m* Julienne, and *dsp ca* 1096.

His brother,

FULK IV *RECHIN,* **Count of Anjou,** *b* 1043, *m* 1st, Hildegarde, dau of Lancelin II Sire de Beaugency, and had issue,

1 Ermengarde, *m* 1st (*m* annulled *ante* 1093), as his 1st wife, William IX, Duke of Aquitaine. He *d* 10 Feb 1127. She *m* 2ndly 1093, Alain III *Fergent,* Count of Brittany, and *d* a nun *ca* 1146, leaving issue. He *d* a monk 13 Oct 1119.

He *m* 2ndly 1070 (*m* annulled 1081), Ermengarde (who *m* 2ndly, William, Sire de Jaligny), dau of Archambaud IV, Sire de Bourbon, and by her had issue,

1 Geoffrey IV *Martel,* Count of Anjou jtly with his father from 1098, *d* at the siege of Candé, in Normandy 19 May 1106, *unm vp.*

He *m* 3rdly 21 Jan 1087 (*m* annulled), Arengarde (*d* a nun), dau of Isambart, Sire de Châtel Aillon. He *m* 4thly 1089 (*m* annulled), Bertrade (who *m* 2ndly 1093, Philippe I, King of France, and *d* a nun *post* 1017), dau of Simon I, Sire de Montfort l'Amauri, by his 2nd wife Agnès of Evreux, and *d* 14 April 1109, having by her had issue,

2 FULK V, *s* his father.

The yr son,

FULK V *THE YOUNG,* **Count of Anjou,** reigned jtly with his father from 1106, Count of Maine *jure uxoris* 11 July 1110, resigned Anjou and Maine to his eldest son 1129, Count of Tyre and Ptolemais 1129, King of Jerusalem 21 Aug 1131, crowned 14 Sept 1131, *b* 1092, *m* 1st 1110, Eremburge, Countess of Maine (*d* 1126), only dau of Hélie I, Count of Maine, by his wife Matilda of Château-du-Loir, and had issue,

1 GEOFFREY V, *s* his father.
2 Hélie II, Count of Maine, *m* Philippa, dau of Rotrou II, Count of Perche, by his wife Matilda, natural dau of King Henry I, and *d* 15 Jan 1151, leaving issue,
Beatrix, *m* John I, Count of Alençon, and had issue. He *d* 24 Feb 1191.
1 Matilda, *b* 1111, *m* June 1119, William, Duke of Normandy, son and heir of King Henry I (*see p* 194), and *d* as Abbess of Fontévrault 1154. He was drowned 25 Nov 1120.
2 Sibylla, *b* 1116, *m* 1st 1123 (*m* annulled 1124), William *Clito,* Count of Flanders, son of Robert III, Duke of Normandy (*see p* 193). She *m* 2ndly 1134, Thierry of Alsace, Count of Flanders, and *d* a nun in the Abbey of St Lazarus, Bethlehem 1165, leaving issue. He *d* 1168.

He *m* 2ndly 1129, Melesende, Queen of Jerusalem (*d* 11 Sept 1160), dau and heiress of Baldwin II, King of Jerusalem, Count of Edessa, Lord of Bourg, by his wife Morphia of Armenia, and was accidentally *k* in the plain of Acre 13 Nov 1144, having by her had issue,

3 Baldwin III, King of Jerusalem, crowned 25 Dec 1144, *b* 1131, *m ca* 1157, Theodora (who *m* 2ndly 1167, Andronicus I Comnenus, Emperor of the East), eldest dau of Isaac Comnenus, son of John I, Emperor of the East, and *d* of poison at Beirut 11 Feb 1163, *sp.*
4 Amalric I, King of Jerusalem, crowned 18 March 1163, *b* 1136, *m* 1st (*m* annulled 1162), Agnes (who *m* 3rdly, Hugh I, Lord of Ibelin; and 4thly, Reginald de Sidon, and *d ca* 1180), widow of Reginald Sire de Mares, and dau of Joscelin III, Sire de Courtenay, Count of Edessa, and had issue,
1 Baldwin IV *the Leper,* King of Jerusalem, crowned 15 July 1175, *b* 1161; *d unm* 16 March 1183.
1 Sibylla, *s* her son Baldwin V as Queen of Jerusalem and was crowned 20 July 1186, *m* 1st Nov 1176, William, Count of Jaffa and Ascalon, Regent of Jerusalem, eldest son of William III, Marquis of Montferrat, and had issue. He *d* June 1177. She *m* 2ndly 1180, Guy de Lusignan, King of Jerusalem and later King of Cyprus, and *d* autumn 1190. He *d* April 1194.
He *m* 2ndly 29 Aug 1167, Maria (who *m* 2ndly *ca* 1176, Balian II, Lord of Ibelin, and *d post* 1206), dau of the Sebastocrator Isaac Comnenus, son of Alexius I, Emperor of the East, and *d* 11 July 1174, having by her had issue,
2 Isabella, Queen of Jerusalem on the resignation of her brother-in-law King Guy 1192, *b* 1172, *m* 1st 22 Nov 1183 (*m* annulled 1190), Humphrey IV, Lord of Toron. She *m* 2ndly 24 Nov 1190, as his 2nd wife, Conrad, Marquis of Montferrat, 2nd son of William III, Marquis of Montferrat, and had issue. He was assassinated 28 April 1192. She *m* 3rdly 5 May 1192, Henry I, King of Jerusalem, II as Count of Champagne and Brie, son of Henry I, Count of Champagne and Brie, and had further issue. He *d* at Acre 10 Sept 1197. She *m* 4thly Oct 1198, Aimery, King of Cyprus and *jure uxoris* King of Jerusalem, brother of King Guy (*see above*), and *d ante* May 1206, having had further issue. He *d* at Acre 1 April 1205.
3 A dau, *d* an inf.

The eldest son,

GEOFFREY V *PLANTAGENET,* **Count of Anjou and Maine,** *b* 24 Aug 1113, *m* 3 April 1127, Matilda, widow of the Emperor Heinrich V, and only dau and heiress of King Henry I, and had issue (*see p* 194).

Kings and Queens of Scotland

The Royal House of Scotland descended from Fergus Mor MacEre (*d ca* 501), a descendant of the Irish Kings of Dalriada (roughly corresponding to modern co Antrim), who, with his brothers Loarn and Angus, came from Ulster towards the end of the fifth century and established the Scottish Kingdom of Dalriada in Argyll. His descendants frequently fought with the Kings of the Picts (the northern and eastern parts of the country), who had already been long established. It was a peculiarity of the Pictish Kingdom that succession passed from brother to brother or from uncle to nephew and sometimes from cousin to cousin in the female line; whereas, in Dalriada the succession, although reckoned in the male line, passed to the *Tanistair* or appointed successor of the reigning King, chosen from among his brothers or cousins. Matrimonial alliances between the Picts and Scots led to the two Kingdoms occasionally being united under one ruler and union was finally effected under Kenneth MacAlpin in 844. The genealogy and succession of the Kings between Fergus Mor MacErc and Kenneth MacAlpin is somewhat confused and uncertain. The latter's grandfather, EOCHAID (IV) *the Poisonous,* King of Dalriada in 781, *m* his cousin, Fergusa, dau of his uncle and predecessor Fergus, King of Dalriada, by his wife, the sister and heiress of Ciniath II and Alpin II, Kings of the Picts, and had issue,

ALPIN, King of Kintyre March-Aug 834, *m* —, and was *k* in battle with the Picts in Galloway Aug 834, leaving issue,

1 KENNETH I, of whom presently.
2 DONALD I, *s* his brother.

The elder son,

844-859 KENNETH I MACALPIN, King of Scots, became King of Dalriada 841 and King of the Picts (as Ciniath III) 844, uniting the two Kingdoms and becoming the first King of Scots, or King of Alba, as he and his successors were sometimes styled, *m* —, and *d* 859, leaving issue,

1 CONSTANTINE I, *s* his uncle King Donald I.
2 AEDH, *s* his brother.
1 A dau, *m* Run, King of Strathclyde (reigned 872-77), and had issue,
EOCHAID, *s* his uncle King Aedh.

King Kenneth I was *s* by his brother,

859-863 DONALD I, King of Scots, who was *s* by his nephew, the son of King Kenneth I,

863-877 CONSTANTINE I, King of Scots, *m* —, and was *k* in battle with the Danes at the Black Cove, Angus 877 (*bur* Iona), leaving issue,

DONALD II, *s* his cousin King Eochaid.

King Constantine I was *s* by his brother,

877-878 AEDH *WHITEFOOT*, King of Scots, *m* —, and was *k* at Strathallan by Giric, Regent of Strathclyde, leaving issue,

1 CONSTANTINE II, *s* his cousin King Donald II.
2 Donald, elected King of Strathclyde (as Dyfnal V) 908. His descendants reigned in Strathclyde until 1018.

King Aedh was *s* by his nephew, the son of his sister and of Run, King of Strathclyde,

878-889 EOCHAID, King of Scots, *s* his father as King of Strathclyde under the regency of his paternal great-uncle Giric 877 and became King of Scots, or King of Alba, after Giric's defeat of King Aedh 878. He was deposed as King of Scots by his cousin,

889-900 DONALD II *DASACHTACH*, King of Scots, *m* —, and *d* 900 (*bur* Iona), leaving issue,

MALCOLM I, *s* King Constantine II.

King Donald II was *s* by his cousin, the son of King Aedh,

900-942 CONSTANTINE II, King of Scots, defeated at Brunanburh by Athelstan, King of England 937, abdicated 942 and became Abbot of St Andrews, *m* —, and *d* 952, having had issue,

1 Cellach, *k* at the Battle of Brunanburh 937.
2 INDULF, *s* King Malcolm I.
1 A dau, *m* Olav II Sihtricsson (Anlaf Cuaran), King of York (reigned 941-43) and later of Dublin (reigned 945-49 and 953-81).

King Constantine II was *s* by the son of King Donald II,

942-954 MALCOLM I, King of Scots, concluded a treaty with Edmund I, King of England, *m* —, and was *k* by the men of Moray 954 (*bur* Iona), leaving issue,

1 DUBH, *s* King Indulf.
2 KENNETH II, *s* King Culen.

King Malcolm I was *s* by the son of King Constantine II,

954-962 INDULF, King of Scots, *m* —, and was *k* by Norse invaders 962, leaving issue,

1 CULEN, *s* King Dubh.
2 Eochaid, *k* with his brother King Culen by Riderch of Strathclyde 971.
3 Olav, *k* by King Kenneth II *ca* 977.

King Indulf was *s* by the son of King Malcolm I.

962-967 DUBH, King of Scots, *m* —, and was *k* by the men of Moray at Forres 967, leaving issue,

Malcolm (I), King of Strathclyde 973-90.
2 KENNETH III, *s* King Constantine III.

King Dubh was *s* by the son of King Indulf,

967-971 CULEN (*or* **CUILEAN**), **King of Scots,** *m* —, and was *k* by his kinsman Riderch of Strathclyde 971, leaving issue,

1 CONSTANTINE III, *s* King Kenneth II.
2 Malcolm, co-benefactor with Donald MacRuadri of Moray of the Abbey of Deer *ca* 1000.

King Culen was *s* by the yr son of King Malcolm I,

971-995 KENNETH II, King of Scots, *m* —, and was murdered at Fetteresso 995 (*bur* Iona), leaving issue,

1 Dungal, *k* by his kinsman Gillacomgain MacKenneth 999.
2 MALCOLM II, *s* King Kenneth III.

King Kenneth II was *s* by the son of King Culen,

995-997 CONSTANTINE III, King of Scots, *k* at Rathinveramon by his kinsman and successor, the son of King Dubh,

997-1005 KENNETH III, King of Scots, *m* —, and was *k* at Monzievaird, nr the banks of the Earn *ca* 25 March 1005, leaving issue,

1 Giric, Mormaer or *Regulus* under his father, *k* at Monzievaird *ca* 25 March 1005.

2 Gillacomgain, *k* his father's 1st cousin and Tanist Dungal MacKenneth 999.

3 Boite (or Bodhe), who had issue,

A son, who had issue,

A son, last male of the senior line of the House of Alpin, murdered by King Malcolm II 1033.

Gruoch, *m* 1st, Gillacomgain, Mormaer of Moray, who was burned alive in his hall 1032, leaving issue,

LULACH, *s* his stepfather King Macbeth.

She *m* 2ndly, *post* 1032, Macbeth, King of Scots (*see below*).

King Kenneth III was *s* by his Tanist, who had *k* him, the son of King Kenneth II,

1005-1034 MALCOLM II, King of Scots, King of Strathclyde 990-995 and 997-1005, annexed Lothian after the Battle of Carham 1018, and obtained the Kingdom of Strathclyde for his grandson Duncan, *b ca* 954, *m* —, and *d* at Glamis 25 Nov 1034 (*bur* Iona), leaving issue,

1 Bethoc, *m ca* 1000, Crinan, Mormaer of Athole, Abthane of Dule and Lay Abbot of Dunkeld, and Steward of the Western Isles, son of Duncan, Mormaer of Athole, etc (*see* BURKE'S *Peerage,* O'NEILL, B, *and* BURKE'S *LG,* IRVING *of Dumfries*). Crinan was *k* in battle with Macbeth attempting to avenge the murder of his son King Duncan I 1045. Crinan and Bethoc had issue, with one dau,

1 DUNCAN I, *s* his grandfather King Malcolm II.

2 Maldred, Lord of Allerdale, Regent of the Kingdom of Strathclyde 1034-45, *m* Ealdgyth, dau of Uhtred, Earl of Northumbria, by his 3rd wife Ælfgifu, dau of Æthelred II, King of England (*see p* 190), and had issue,

(1) Gospatrick, Earl of Northumberland 1067-72, dispossessed by King William I, *cr* Earl of Dunbar by King Malcolm III, *m* —, and *d ca* 1075, leaving issue, with several other daus,

1*a* Dolfin, driven out of Carlisle by William Rufus 1092.

2*a* Gospatrick, 2nd Earl of Dunbar, *m* —, and was *k* at the Battle of the Standard 22 Aug 1138, leaving issue (*see* BURKE'S *Peerage,* DUNBAR *of Mochrum,* Bt).

3*a* Waltheof (Waldeve), Lord of Allerdale, Abbot of Crowland 1125-38.

1*a* Æthelreda, *m ca* 1090, Duncan II, King of Scots, and had issue (*see below*).

(2) Maldred, ancestor of the Nevills (*see* BURKE'S *Peerage,* ABERGAVENNY, M).

2 Donada, *m* as his 2nd wife, Sigurd II Digri, Jarl of Orkney and Caithness, and had issue. He was *k* at the Battle of Clontarf 23 April 1014.

King Malcolm II was *s* by his grandson,

1034-1040 DUNCAN I *THE GRACIOUS,* **King of Scots.** King of Strathclyde 1018-34, *b ca* 1001, *m ca* 1030, Sibylla, probably sister of Siward, Earl of Northumbria, and dau of Bjorn Bearsson, and was murdered by Macbeth at Bothnagowan (now Pitgaveny), nr Elgin 14 Aug 1040 (*bur* Iona), leaving issue,

1 MALCOLM III, *s* as King in 1058

2 DONALD III BANE, *s* his brother.

3 Melmare, *m* —, and had issue,

Madach, or Maddad, Earl of Atholl *ca* 1116, *m* 1st, —, and had issue,

(1) Malcolm, 2nd Earl of Atholl, *m,* and *d ca* Aug 1198, leaving issue (*see* BURKE'S *LG,* ROBERTSON *of Struan*).

He *m* 2ndly, Margaret, dau of Haakon Paulsson, Jarl of Orkney, by his 2nd wife Helga, dau of Moddan of Dair, and *d ca* 1152, having by her had issue,

(2) Harald (II) Maddadsson, co-Jarl of Orkney 1138-58, sole Jarl 1158-1206, Earl of half Caithness 1158, of all Caithness 1200-06, *b* 1130, *m* 1st, Aufrica, sister of Duncan, Earl of Fife, and had issue,

1*a* David Haraldsson, Jarl of Orkney, *d* 1214.

He *m* 2ndly, Gormflaeth (or Hvafleda), dau of Malcolm II, Mormaer of Moray, by his wife, a sister of Somerled, Lord of the Isles, and *d* 1206, having by her had issue,

2*a* John Haraldsson, Jarl of Orkney, *dspm* 1231.

King Duncan I was *s* by his murderer,

1040-1057 MACBETH, King of Scots, son of Findlaech, Mormaer of Moray*, *s* his cousin Gillacomgain as Mormaer of Moray 1032, murdered King Duncan I and usurped the crown 14 Aug 1040, *b ca* 1005, *m ca* 1032, Gruoch, widow of Gillacomgain, Mormaer of Moray, and dau of Boite (or Bodhe), yst son of Kenneth III, King of Scots (*see above*), and *dsp* being *k* at Lumphanan, Aberdeenshire by Malcolm, son of King Duncan I 15 Aug 1057 (*bur* Iona). He was *s* by his stepson,

1057-1058 LULACH *THE SIMPLE,* **King of Scots,** son of Gillacomgain, Mormaer of Moray, by his wife Gruoch, grand-dau of Kenneth III, King of Scots (*see above*), set on the Royal Seat at Scone by his stepfather's followers 1057, *b* ca 1032, *m* —, and was *k* at Essie in Strathbogie by Malcolm, son of King Duncan I 17 March 1058 (*bur* Iona), leaving issue,

Maelsnectai, Mormaer of Moray, expelled by King Malcolm III 1078 and became a monk, *d* 1085.

A dau, *m* Aedh (or Heth), Mormaer of Moray in 1078, possibly great-grandson of Donald, yst son of Ruadri, Mormaer of Moray, and had issue,

1 Oengus (Angus), Mormaer of Moray, *k* at Stracathro, Forfarshire 1130.

2 Malcolm (II), Mormaer of Moray 1130-34, deprived of his Mormaership by David I, King of Scots, imprisoned at Roxburgh 1134-57, *cr* Earl of Ross by King Malcolm IV 1157, *m* —, sister of Somerled, *Regulus* of Argyll, later Lord of the Isles (*see* BURKE'S *Peerage,* MACDONALD, B), and *d* 23 Oct 1168, leaving issue, with two sons and one other dau,

Gormflaeth (or Hvafleda), *m* as his 2nd wife, Harald II Maddadsson, Jarl of Orkney, and had issue (*see above*). He *d* 1206.

1 Gruaidh, *m* as his 1st wife, William, Earl of Moray, only son of Duncan II, King of Scots, and had issue (*see below*).

1058-1093 MALCOLM III *CANMORE* (Great Head, or Chief), **King of Scots,** made King of Strathclyde on his father's accession to the Scottish throne 1034, conquered Lothian 1054, obtained the Scottish throne after the defeat and death of Macbeth and of Lulach, crowned at Scone 25 April 1058, *b ca* 1031, *m* 1st *ca* 1059, Ingibiorg widow of Thorfinn II, Earl of Caithness and Jarl of Orkney, and dau of Finn Arnesson of Vrjar, Jarl of Halland, by his wife Bergljot, dau of Halfdan Sigurdsson,

---

*Macbeth's mother is variously stated to have been a sister or dau of King Malcolm II; but modern scholarship tends to refute this view.

half-brother of Olav II *the Saint,* King of Norway, and had issue,

1 DUNCAN II, of whom presently.

2 Malcolm, witnessed a charter of his brother King Duncan II 1094.

3 Donald, *dvp* 1085.

King Malcolm III *m* 2ndly at Dunfermline *ca* 1069, St Margaret (*b* in Hungary *ca* 1045; *d* at Edinburgh Castle 16 Nov 1093, *bur* Abbey Church of the Holy Trinity, Dunfermline, canonized by Pope Innocent IV 1250), elder dau of Edward *Atheling* (son of Edmund II *Ironside,* King of England), by his wife Agatha, probably dau of Bruno, later Bishop of Augsburg, brother of the Holy Roman Emperor Heinrich II, and was *k* in battle at Alnwick 13 Nov 1093 (*bur* first Tynemouth, later removed to Dunfermline by King Alexander I), having by her had issue,

4 Edward, wounded at Alnwick 13 Nov and *d* at Edwardsisle, nr Jedburgh 16 Nov 1093.

5 Edmund, supported his uncle Donald Bane against his half-brother King Duncan II, later became a monk and *d* at Montacute, Somerset.

6 Ethelred, Lay Abbot of Dunkeld, *d ante* 1097 (*bur* Kilremont Church).

7 EDGAR, *s* his uncle King Donald Bane.

8 ALEXANDER I, *s* his brother King Edgar.

9 DAVID I, *s* his brother King Alexander I.

1 Edith, later called Matilda, *b* at Dunfermline 1079, *m* at Westminster Abbey 11 Nov 1100 (being crowned the same day), as his 1st wife, Henry I, King of England, and *d* at Westminster Palace 1 May 1118 (*bur* Westminster Abbey), having had issue (*see p* 194). He *d* at St Denis-le-Fermont, nr Rouen 1 Dec 1135 (*bur* Reading Abbey).

2 Mary, *m* 1102, Eustace III, Count of Boulogne, and *d* 31 May 1116 (*bur* Bermondsey Abbey), having had issue, one son (who *d* young) and one dau (Matilda, who *m* Stephen, King of England—*see p* 194).

King Malcolm III was *s* by his brother,

1093-1094 and 1094-1097 DONALD III BANE, King of Scots, chosen King by the people, deposed by his nephew King Duncan II May 1094, regained the throne on the latter's death 12 Nov 1094, said to have shared the govt with his nephew Edmund, deposed and blinded by his nephew King Edgar Oct 1097, *b ca* 1033, *m* —, and *d* at Rescobie, Forfarshire 1099 (*bur* first Dunkeld, later transferred to Iona), leaving issue,

Bethoc, *m* Uhtred of Tynedale, and had issue, one dau.

King Donald Bane was deposed in May 1094 by his nephew, the eldest son of King Malcolm III,

May-Nov 1094 DUNCAN II, King of Scots, *b ca* 1060, *m ca* 1090, Æthelreda (*bur* Dunfermline Abbey), dau of Gospatrick, 1st Earl of Dunbar (*see above*), and was *k* at the instigation of his half-brother Edmund and his uncle Donald Bane by Malpeder MacLoen, Mormaer of the Mearns at Mondynes, Kincardineshire 12 Nov 1094 (*bur* Dunfermline Abbey), leaving issue,

William, Earl of Moray, Lord of Skipton and Craven, Yorks, *m* 1st, Gruaidh, dau of Aedh (or Heth), Mormaer of Moray, by his wife —, dau of Lulach, King of Scots (*see above*), and had issue,

1 Donald Macwilliam, headed a rising to regain the throne for his family and was *k* on Mamgarvia Moor on Speyside, 31 July 1187, leaving issue,

(1) Godfrey Macwilliam, headed a second unsuccessful rising and was beheaded at Kincardine 1213.

(2) Donald Macwilliam, headed a third unsuccessful rising and was *k* in Moray 15 June 1215.

(1) A dau. — Macewen, and had issue,

Gillespie Macewen, Lord of Badenoch, headed a fourth and last unsuccessful rising and was put to death with his two sons and dau at Forfar 1228.

2 Gospatrick Macwilliam, Lord of Airton, Yorks, *d* at a great age *ante* 1208, leaving issue which is still extant in the male line*.

He *m* 2ndly *ca* 1138, Alice, dau of Robert de Romilly, and *d ca* 1154, having by her had issue,

3 William, Lord of Egremont, Cumberland, *d* young, being accidentally drowned in the Wharfe at Bolton.

1 Cecily, heiress of Skipton, *m* William le Gros, 3rd Earl of Aumale, and had issue, two daus. He *d* 20 Aug 1179.

2 Amabel, heiress of Egremont, *m* Reginald de Lucy, and had issue.

3 Alice, *m* 1st, Gilbert Pipard, Sheriff of Glos and of Herefordshire; and 2ndly *ante* 1195, Robert de Courtenay, and *dsp* 1215.

After the murder of King Duncan II his uncle King Donald Bane was restored to the throne and was again deposed by his nephew, the 7th son of King Malcolm III,

1097-1107 EDGAR, King of Scots, *b ca* 1074; *d unm* at Edinburgh Castle 8 Jan 1107 (*bur* Dunfermline Abbey), and was *s* by his brother, the 8th son of King Malcolm III,

1107-1124 ALEXANDER I *THE FIERCE,* **King of Scots,** *b ca* 1077, *m* Sibylla (*d* at Loch Tay 12 July 1122, *bur* Dunfermline Abbey), natural dau of Henry I, King of England, by Sibylla Corbet, and *dsp*† at Stirling 23 April 1124 (*bur* Dunfermline Abbey), when he was *s* by his brother, the 9th (and yst) son of King Malcolm III,

1124-1153 DAVID I *THE SAINT,* **King of Scots,** ruler in Strathclyde and South Lothian from 1107, held the Earldom of Northampton and the Honour of Huntingdon *jure uxoris, b ca* 1080, *m ca* 1113/14, Matilda (*d* between 23 April 1130 and 22 April 1131, *bur* Scone), widow of Simon de St Liz, and dau and heiress of Waltheof, Earl of Northampton and Huntingdon (*see* BURKE'S *Dormant and Extinct Peerages*), by his wife Judith, dau of Lambert, Count of Lens, by his wife Adelaide, sister or half-sister of William I *the Conqueror,* King of England (*see p* 310), and *d* at Carlisle 24 May 1153 (*bur* Dunfermline Abbey), having had issue,

1 Malcolm, *d* young *vp*.

2 Henry, EARL OF HUNTINGDON (on his father's resignation Feb 1136), *b ca* 1115, *m* 1139, Ada (*d* 1178), dau of William de Warenne II, 2nd Earl of Surrey and Warenne, by his wife Isabelle, dau of Hugues *the Great,* Count of Vermandois, and *dvp* 12 June 1151 (*bur* Kelso), leaving issue,

1 MALCOLM IV, *s* his grandfather.

2 WILLIAM I, *s* his brother King Malcolm IV.

3 David, EARL OF HUNTINGDON on the resignation of his brother King William 1185, deprived 1215 or 1216, restored 13 March 1218, had a grant of the *comitatus* of Lennox but does not appear to have been styled Earl of Lennox, *b ca* 1144, *m* 26 Aug 1190, Maud (*d ante* 1231), dau and in her issue heiress of Hugh (called *of*

---

*See *William of Scotland* by A. G. Williamson (Dumfries, N.D.).

†He left a natural son Malcolm, who made two ineffectual attempts to gain the throne from King David I.

Cyfeiliog), Earl of Chester, by his wife Bertrade, dau of Simon, Count of Evreux, and *d* at Jerdelay 17 June 1219 (*bur* Sawtrey Abbey, Hunts), having had issue,
(1) Robert, *d* young *vp* (*bur* Lindores Abbey).
(2) Henry, *d* young *vp*.
(3) John *le Scot*, *s* his father as EARL OF HUNTINGDON 1219, *cr* EARL OF CHESTER 21 Nov 1232, *b ca* 1207, *m* 1222, Helen (who *m* 2ndly, Robert de Quincy (*d* 1257), son of Seher de Quincy, Earl of Winchester (*see* BURKE'S *Dormant and Extinct Peerages*), and *d* 1253), dau of Llewelyn *the Great*, Prince of Aberffraw and Lord of Snowdon (*see p* 323, and *dsp* shortly before 6 June 1237.
(1) Margaret, *m* 1209, Alan, Lord of Galloway (*d* 1234), and had issue,
1*a* Helen, *m ante* 1234, as his 1st wife, Roger de Quincy, 2nd Earl of Winchester (*see* BURKE'S *Dormant and Extinct Peerages*), and had issue, three daus. He *d* 25 April 1264.
2*a* Christian, *m* 1236, as his 1st wife, William de Forz, Earl of Aumale, and *dsp* 1246. He *d* at Amiens 23 May 1260.
3*a* Devorguilla, *m* 1233, John Balliol, founder of Balliol College, Oxford (*d* 1269), and *d* 28 Jan 1290, having had issue,
1*b* Hugh (Sir), of Barnard Castle, *dsp ante* 10 April 1271.
2*b* Alan, of Barnard Castle, *dsp*.
3*b* Alexander (Sir), of Barnard Castle, *dsp ante* 13 Nov 1278.
4*b* JOHN, the successful competitor for the crown 1292.
1*b* Cecilia, *d unm*.
2*b* Ada, *m* 1266, William Lindsay of Lambarton.
3*b* Alianora, *m* John Comyn of Badenoch, a competitor for the crown, and had issue.
(2) Isabella, *m* Robert de Brus (Bruce), Lord of Annandale (*d* 1245), and *d* 1251, leaving issue,
Robert de Brus (Bruce), Lord of Annandale, one of the fifteen Regents of Scotland 1255, a competitor for the crown 1291, *b ca* 1210, *m* 1240, Isabella, dau of Gilbert de Clare, 3rd Earl of Gloucester (*see* BURKE'S *Dormant and Extinct Peerages*), and *d* at Lochmaben Castle *ante* 3 May 1294, having had issue,
1*b* Robert Bruce, Lord of Annandale, Earl of Carrick *jure uxoris* 1271, resigned the Earldom to his eldest son 27 Oct 1292, *b* 1253, *m* 1271, Margaret, or Marjorie (*d ante* 27 Oct 1292), widow of Adam de Kilconquhar (*dsp* 1270), and dau and heiress of Neil, 2nd Earl of Carrick (*see* BURKE'S *Dormant and Extinct Peerages*), and *d ante* 14 June 1304, leaving issue,
1*c* ROBERT I, *s* as King of Scots 1306.
2*c* Edward, *cr* Earl of Carrick by his brother King Robert I shortly *ante* 24 Oct 1313, crowned King of Ireland 2 May 1316, *k* in battle at Dundalk 14 Oct 1318, *spl*. His natural son, Alexander Bruce, was *cr* Earl of Carrick *ca* 1330 and *dspm* 19 July 1333.
3*c* Thomas (Sir), captured in Galloway and executed at Carlisle 9 Feb 1307.
4*c* Alexander, Dean of Glasgow, captured and executed with his brother Sir Thomas 9 Feb 1307.
5*c* Nigel, taken prisoner at Kildrummie and executed at Berwick Sept 1306.
1*c* Isabella, *m ante* 25 Sept 1293, as his 2nd wife, Eric II, King of Norway, and had issue, one dau. He *d* 13 July 1299.
2*c* Mary, *m* 1st, *ca* 1312, as his 3rd wife, Sir Neil Campbell of Lochow, and had issue (*see* BURKE'S *Peerage*, ARGYLL, D). He *d ante* 1316. She *m* 2ndly 1316, Sir Alexander Fraser, Lord Great Chamberlain of Scotland.
3*c* Christian, *m* 1st, Gratney, 7th Earl of Mar, and had issue (*see* BURKE'S *Peerage*). He *d ante* Sept 1305. She *m* 2ndly, Sir Christopher Seton; and 3rdly, Sir Andrew Moray of Bothwell, and *d ca* 1356.
4*c* Matilda, *m* Hugh, Earl of Ross (*see* BURKE'S *Dormant and Extinct Peerages*), and had issue. He *d* 19 July 1333.
5*c* Margaret, *m* Sir William de Carlyle.
2*b* William, *m* Elizabeth, dau and heiress of Raymond de Sully.
3*b* Bernard (Sir), of Conington and Exton, Rutland, *m* 1st, Alicia de Clare; and 2ndly, Constance de Morleyn, and had issue,
John (Sir), of Exton, who left an only dau and heiress.
Jane, *m* Sir Nicholas Green, and had issue.
4*b* Richard, *dvp ante* 26 Jan 1287.
Beatrice, *m* Hugo de Neville.
(3) Matilda, *d unm*.
(4) Ada, *m* Henry de Hastings, and had issue, one son and two daus. He *d* end of 1250.
1 Ada, *m* 1161, Floris III, Count of Holland, and had issue, two sons. He *d* at Antioch while taking part in the Third Crusade 1190.
2 Margaret, *m* 1st 1160, Conan IV *the Little*, Duke of Brittany, and had issue, one dau. He *d* 20 Feb 1171. She *m* 2ndly, Humphrey de Bohun, and *d* 1201, having had further issue (*see* BURKE'S *Dormant and Extinct Peerages*, HEREFORD, E).
3 Matilda, *d* young 1152.
1 Claricia, *d unm*.
2 Hodierna, *d unm*.

King David I was *s* by his grandson,

1153-1165 MALCOLM IV *THE MAIDEN*, **King of Scots,** crowned and/or enthroned at Scone "according to the custom of the nation", *b* 20 March 1142; *d unm* at Jedburgh 9 Dec 1165 (*bur* Dunfermline Abbey), and was *s* by his brother,

1165-1214 WILLIAM I *THE LION*, **King of Scots,** assigned the Earldom of Northumberland by his grandfather King David I 1152, consecrated King at Scone by Richard, Bishop of St Andrews 24 Dec 1165, invaded England and was taken prisoner at Alnwick 13 July 1174, acknowledged Henry II, King of England as overlord of Scotland by the Treaty of Falaise 8 Dec 1174, released and returned to Scotland 2 Feb 1175, received the Earldom of Huntingdon from Henry II 1185, had his independence restored by quitclaim of Richard I, King of England at Canterbury 5 Dec 1189, *b* 1143, *m* at Woodstock, Oxon 5 Sept 1186, Ermengarde (*d* 11 Feb 1234, *bur* Balmerino Abbey, Fife), dau of Richard, Viscount de Beaumont (son of Roscelin, Viscount de Beaumont, by his wife Constance, natural dau of Henry I, King of England), and *d* at Stirling 4 Dec 1214 (*bur* Arbroath Abbey), leaving issue,
1 ALEXANDER II, *s* his father.
1 Margaret, *m* at York 1221, as his 3rd wife, Hubert de Burgh, 1st Earl of Kent, Justiciary of England and later of Ireland (*see* BURKE'S *Dormant and Extinct Peerages*), and had issue, one dau (who *d* young). He *d* 12 May 1243 (*bur* Blackfriars Church, London).
2 Isabella, *m* 1225, Roger le Bigod, 4th Earl of Norfolk (*see* BURKE'S *Dormant and Extinct Peerages*), and *dsp*. He *d* 3 (or 4) July 1270.
3 Marjorie, *m* at Berwick 1 Aug 1235, as his 2nd wife, Gilbert Marshal, 4th Earl of Pembroke, Marshal of England (*see* BURKE'S *Dormant and Extinct Peerages*), and *dsp* 17 Nov 1244 (*bur* London). He was *k* in a tournament 27 June 1241.

King William the Lion was *s* by his only (legitimate) son,

1214-1249 ALEXANDER II, King of Scots, consecrated King by William Malvoisine, Bishop of St Andrews and enthroned at Scone 6 Dec 1214, *b* at Haddington 24 Aug 1198, *m* 1st at York 19 June 1221, Joan (*b* 22

July 1210; *dsp* nr London 4 March 1238, *bur* Tarrant Crawford, Dorset), eldest dau of John, King of England, by his 2nd wife Isabella, only dau and heiress of Aymer Taillefer, Count of Angoulême. King Alexander II *m* 2ndly at Roxburgh 15 May 1239, Marie (who *m* 2ndly *ante* 6 June 1257, Jean de Brienne (called *of Acre*), son of Jean (de Brienne), King of Jerusalem), 2nd dau of Enguerrand III, Lord of Coucy, by his 3rd wife Marie, dau of Jean, Seigneur de Montmirel en Brie, and *d* at the Island of Kerrera 8 July 1249 (*bur* Melrose Abbey), having by her had issue,

1249-1286 ALEXANDER III, King of Scots, consecrated King by David de Bernham, Bishop of St Andrews and enthroned at Scone 13 July 1249, *b* at Roxburgh 4 Sept 1241, *m* 1st at York 26 Dec 1251, Margaret (*b* at Windsor Castle 29 Sept 1240; *d* at Cupar Castle, Fife 26 Feb 1275, *bur* Dunfermline Abbey), eldest dau of Henry III, King of England (*see p* 197), and had issue,

1 Alexander, Prince of Scotland, *b* at Jedburgh 21 Jan 1264, *m* at Roxburgh 15 Nov 1282, Marguerite (who *m* 2ndly *ca* 1290, Rainald I, Count of Gueldres, and *d* 1330), dau of Guy de Dampierre, Count of Flanders, and *dspvp* at Lindores Abbey, Fife 28 Jan 1284 (*bur* Dunfermline Abbey).

2 David, *b* 20 March 1273, *d* at Stirling Castle end of June 1281 (*bur* Dunfermline Abbey).

1 Margaret, *b* at Windsor Castle 28 Feb 1261, *m* at Bergen *ca* 31 Aug 1281, as his 1st wife, Eric II (Magnusson), King of Norway (who *m* 2ndly Isabella, sister of King Robert I—*see above*), and *d* at Tönsberg 9 April 1283 (*bur* Bergen), leaving issue, MARGARET, *s* her grandfather King Alexander III.

King Alexander III *m* 2ndly at Jedburgh 14 Oct 1285, Yolande, or Joletta (who *m* 2ndly May 1294, as his 2nd wife, Arthur II, Duke of Brittany, and *d* 1323), dau of Robert IV, Count of Dreux, and was *k* by a fall from his horse between Burntisland and Kinghorn 19 March 1286, when he was *s* by his grand-dau,

1286-1290 MARGARET, Queen of Scots (called *The Maid of Norway*), *b* in Norway *ante* 9 April 1283; *d* in Orkney on her way to Scotland *ca* 26 Sept 1290 (*bur* Bergen).

After the death of Queen Margaret the succession to the throne was disputed by thirteen competitors, who agreed to submit their claims to the arbitration of Edward I, King of England. The thirteen competitors, in the order in which their names were recorded in the Great Roll of Scotland 3 Aug 1291, were:—

1 Floris V, Count of Holland (*d* 27 June 1296), who claimed as son of Willem II, Count of Holland, son of Floris IV, Count of Holland, son of Willem I, Count of Holland, son of Floris III, Count of Holland, by his wife Ada, dau of Henry, Earl of Huntingdon (*see p* 315).

2 Patrick de Dunbar, 7th Earl of Dunbar (*d* 10 Oct 1308), who claimed as son of Patrick, 6th Earl, son of Patrick, 5th Earl, son of Patrick, 4th Earl, by his wife Ada, *natural* dau of King William the Lion. The 4th Earl of Dunbar was son of Waltheof, 3rd Earl, son of Gospatrick, 2nd Earl, son of Gospatrick, 1st Earl of Dunbar (*see p* 313).

3 William de Vesci, Baron de Vesci (*dspsl* 1297), who claimed as son of William de Vesci, son of Eustace de Vesci, by his wife, Margaret, *natural* dau of King William the Lion.

4 William de Ros, 2nd Baron de Ros (*d* 15 Aug 1316), who claimed as son of Robert de Ros, 1st Baron de Ros (*see* BURKE'S *Peerage*), son of William de Ros, of Hamlake, son of Robert de Ros, by his wife Isabella, *natural* dau of King William the Lion.

5 Robert de Pinkeny, who claimed as son of Henry de Pinkeny, son of Henry de Pinkeny, by his wife Alicia, dau of John Lindesay, by his wife Marjorie, an alleged *natural* dau of Henry, Earl of Huntingdon.

6 Nicholas de Soules, who claimed as son of — de Soules, by his wife Ermengarde, dau of Alan Durward, by his wife Marjorie, *natural* dau of King Alexander II.

7 Patrick Galithly, who claimed as son of Henry Galithly, a *natural* son of King William the Lion.

8 Roger de Mandeville, who claimed as son of — de Mandeville, by his wife Agatha, dau of Robert Wardone, by his wife Aufrica, dau of William de Say, by his wife Aufrica, *natural* dau of King William the Lion.

9 John Comyn, Lord of Badenoch, who claimed as son of John Comyn, son of Richard Comyn, son of William Comyn, son of Richard Comyn, by his wife Hextilda, dau of Uhtred of Tyndale, by his wife Bethoc, dau of King Donald Bane (*see p* 314).

10 John de Hastings, 2nd Baron Hastings (*d* 1313), who claimed as son of Henry de Hastings, 1st Baron Hastings (*see* BURKE'S *Dormant and Extinct Peerages*), son of Henry de Hastings by his wife Ada, 4th dau of David Earl of Huntingdon.

11 JOHN BALLIOL, the successful competitor.

12 Robert de Brus (*see p* 315), whose grandson eventually *s* as King Robert I.

13 Eric II, King of Norway, who claimed as father and heir of the deceased Queen Margaret.

The death of Queen Margaret was followed by

1290-1292 THE FIRST INTERREGNUM, which ended 17 Nov 1292 when the arbitrator, Edward I, King of England, pronounced at Berwick in favour of

1292-1296 JOHN (BALLIOL), King of Scotland (so styled), crowned at Scone 30 Nov 1292, acknowledged the overlordship of Edward I but later attempted to assert his independence and was forced to abdicate at Brechin 10 July 1296, a prisoner in England 1296-99, released and allowed to go to France, *b ca* 1250, *m ante* 7 Feb 1281, Isabella, dau of John de Warenne, 3rd Earl of Surrey and Warenne (*see* BURKE'S *Dormant and Extinct Peerages*), by his wife Alice (half-sister of Henry III, King of England—*see p* 196), dau of Hugh de Lusignan, Count de la Marche, and *d* at Bailleul-en-Gouffern, Normandy April 1313 (probably *bur* Church of St Waast there), leaving issue,

1 EDWARD, of whom presently.

2 Henry, *k* at Annan 16 Dec 1332, *sp*.

The abdication of King John was followed by

1296-1306 THE SECOND INTERREGNUM, in which Edward I, King of England took over the government and attempted to treat Scotland as a conquered country. A long struggle for independence followed, led first by Sir William Wallace and then by Robert Bruce, who eventually succeeded in establishing himself as

1306-1329 ROBERT I *THE BRUCE,* King of Scots, *s* as Earl of Carrick on his father's resignation 27 Oct 1292, chosen one of the Guardians of the Kingdom at Peebles 19 Aug

1299, *s* his father as Lord of Annandale 1304, assumed the crown 27 March 1306 and was crowned at Scone by Isabella, Countess of Buchan "in the presence, and with the consent of four bishops, five earls, and the people of the land" 27 March 1306, totally defeated the English at Bannockburn, nr Stirling 24 June 1314, thus re-establishing Scottish independence, *b* probably at Writtle, nr Chelmsford, Essex 11 July 1274, *m* 1st *ca* 1295, Isabella, dau of Donald, 6th Earl of Mar (*see* BURKE'S *Peerage*), by his wife Helen (widow of Malcolm, 7th Earl of Fife), said* to have been a dau of Llewelyn *the Great,* Prince of Aberffraw and Lord of Snowdon (*see p* 322), and had issue,

1 Marjorie, *m* 1315, Walter, 6th High Steward of Scotland (*d* 1326), and *d* at Paisley, Renfrewshire 2 March 1316, leaving issue,
ROBERT II, *s* his half-uncle King David II.

King Robert I *m* 2ndly 1302, Elizabeth (*d* at Cullen 26 Oct 1327, *bur* Dunfermline Abbey), dau of Richard de Burgh, 2nd Earl of Ulster, by his wife Margaret, dau of John de Burgh, and *d* at Cardross, Dumbartonshire 7 June 1329 (*bur* Dunfermline Abbey), having by her had issue,

1 DAVID II, *s* his father.
2 John, *d* young (*bur* Restennet Priory, Forfarshire).
2 Matilda, *m* Thomas Isaac, and *d* at Aberdeen 20 July 1353 (*bur* Dunfermline Abbey), leaving issue, two daus.
3 Margaret, *m ante* 28 Sept 1345, as his 1st wife, William Sutherland, 5th Earl of Sutherland, and *d ca* 1346, leaving issue (*see* BURKE'S *Peerage,* SUTHERLAND, D). He *d* between 27 Feb 1370 and June 1371.

King Robert I was *s* by his only surv son,

1329-1371 DAVID II, King of Scots, styled Earl of Carrick before his accession, anointed and crowned at Scone 24 Nov 1331†, absent in France 1334-41, captured by the English following his defeat at Neville's Cross, nr Durham 17 Oct 1346, prisoner in England 1346-57, *b* at Dunfermline 5 March 1324, *m* 1st at Berwick 17 July 1328, Joan, crowned with her husband (*b* in the Tower of London 5 July 1321; *d* at Hertford 7 Sept 1362, *bur* Grey Friars Church, London), yr dau of Edward II, King of England (*see p* 198). King David II *m* 2ndly at Inchmurdach, Fife *ca* 20 Feb 1364 (div *ca* 20 March 1370), Margaret (*d* soon *post* 31 Jan 1375), widow of Sir John Logie of that Ilk, and dau of Sir Malcolm Drummond (*see* BURKE'S *Peerage,* PERTH, E), and *dsp* at Edinburgh Castle 22 Feb 1371 (*bur* Holyrood Abbey), when he was *s* by his half-nephew, Robert II, of whom presently.

(1332 and 1333-1338 EDWARD (BALLIOL), King of Scotland, elder son and heir of King John (*see p* 316), landed with the support of an English army at Kinghorn, Fife 6 Aug 1332, crowned at Scone 24 Sept 1332, fled to England 16 Dec 1332, restored with English aid 1333, formally acknowledged Edward III, King of England as his overlord Nov 1333, again fled to England 1334, again restored 1335, finally ret to England 1338, surrendered all claim to the crown of Scotland to Edward III 20 Jan 1356, *dsp* in England 1363).

1371-1390 ROBERT II, King of Scots, declared Heir to the Crown in default of male issue of his maternal grandfather King Robert I by Parl at Scone 3 Dec 1318, *s* his father as (7th) High Steward of Scotland 9 April 1326, Guardian of the Kingdom 1338-41 and 1346-57, crowned at Scone by William de Landallis, Bishop of St Andrews 26 March 1371, *b* at Paisley 2 March 1316, *m* 1st (dispensation dated Avignon 22 Nov 1347), Elizabeth (*d ante* 1355), dau of Sir Adam Mure of Rowallan, and had issue (legitimated *per subsequens matrimonium*),

1 JOHN, who *s* his father as ROBERT III.
2 Walter, Earl of Fife *jure uxoris, m* Isabel, Countess of Fife (who *m* 3rdly *ante* April 1363, Sir Thomas Byset (*d ante* 17 April 1365); and 4thly, John de Dunbar (*d ante* 1371), and *dsp* soon *post* 12 Aug 1389), widow of William Ramsey, and only dau and heiress of Duncan, 8th Earl of Fife, and *dsp post* 14 Aug 1362.
3 Robert, 1st DUKE OF ALBANY, became Earl of Menteith *jure uxoris* 1361, Earl of Fife on the resignation of his sister-in-law Isabel 30 March 1371, *cr* Duke of Albany 28 April 1398, Earl of Atholl 2 Sept 1403 (resigned 4 April 1406), *s* his yr brother Alexander as Earl of Buchan 1405-06 (resigned 20 Sept 1406), Great Chamberlain of Scotland 1383-1408, Gov of the Kingdom 1388-1420, *b ca* 1340, *m* 1st (by dispensation dated 9 Sept 1361), Margaret, Countess of Menteith (*d* 1380), widow of Sir John Drummond, previously wife of Thomas, 9th Earl of Mar (*see* BURKE'S *Peerage*), before that widow of Sir John Moray, and only surv child and heiress of Sir John Graham, by his wife Mary, Countess of Menteith, dau and heiress of Alan de Menteith, 7th Earl of Menteith (*see* BURKE'S *Dormant and Extinct Peerages*), and had issue,
1 Murdoch, 2nd DUKE OF ALBANY, *s* his father as Gov of the Kingdom 1420, *b ca* 1362, *m* 17 Feb 1392, Isabella, Countess of Lennox (*d ca* 1456-58), eldest dau and co-heiress of Duncan, 8th Earl of Lennox (*see* BURKE'S *Dormant and Extinct Peerages*), and was attainted and beheaded at Stirling 25 May 1425, having had issue,
(1) Robert, Master of Fife, *dspvp ante* 1421.
(2) Walter (Sir), beheaded at Stirling 24 May 1425.
(3) Alexander (Sir), beheaded with his father at Stirling 25 May 1425.
(4) James, fled to Ireland and *d* there *spl* 1451.*
(1) Isabella, *m* Sir Walter Buchanan of that Ilk.
1 Janet, probably *d unm.*
2 Mary, *m* Sir William Abernethy of Saltoun, and had issue (*see* BURKE'S *Peerage,* SALTOUN, B). He *d* 1420.
3 Margaret, *m* 1st *ca* 1392, as his 3rd wife, Sir John de Swinton, 14th Lord of that Ilk, and had issue (*see* BURKE'S *LG*). He was *k* at the Battle of Homildon Hill 14 Sept 1402. She *m* 2ndly, Robert Stewart, Lord Lorn, and had further issue (*see* BURKE'S *Dormant and Extinct Peerages*).
4 Isabella, *m* 1st Alexander Leslie, 7th Earl of Ross, and had issue. He *d* 8 May 1402. She *m* 2ndly, Walter Haliburton of Dirleton, and had further issue.

Robert, Duke of Albany *m* 2ndly, Muriella (*d* 1449),

---

*But not recorded in any Welsh genealogies.

†The right to receive anointing and coronation was granted to King Robert I and his successors by Pope John XXII 13 June 1329 (six days after that King's death).

*He left seven natural sons, from one of whom descend the Earls of Castle Stewart (*see* BURKE'S *Peerage*).

eldest dau of Sir William Keith, Great Marischal of Scotland, and *d* at Stirling 3 Sept 1420 (*bur* Dunfermline Abbey), having by her had issue,

2 John, 3rd EARL OF BUCHAN (on his father's resignation 20 Sept 1406), Chamberlain of Scotland, head of the Scottish auxiliaries in France 1420, Constable of France 1421, *b ca* 1380, *m* 1413, Elizabeth (who *m* 2ndly, Sir Thomas Stewart; and 3rdly, as his 1st wife, William Sinclair, 3rd Earl of Orkney (*see* BURKE'S *Dormant and Extinct Peerages*)), dau of Archibald Douglas, 4th Earl of Douglas and Duke of Touraine in France (*see* BURKE'S *Dormant and Extinct Peerages*), by his wife Margaret, eldest dau of King Robert III (*see below*), and was *k* at the Battle of Verneuil 17 Aug 1424, leaving issue,

Margaret, *m* 1436, as his 1st wife, George Seton, 1st Lord Seton, and had issue (*see* BURKE'S *Peerage*, EGLINTON AND WINTON, E). He *d* at the Blackfriar's Edinburgh *post* 15 July 1478.

3 Andrew, *dspvp ante* 1413.

4 Robert, *k* at the Battle of Verneuil 17 Aug 1424, *sp*.

5 Marjory (or Marcellina), *m* as his 1st wife, Sir Duncan Campbell of Lochow, 1st Lord Campbell, and *d ante* Aug 1432, leaving issue (*see* BURKE'S *Peerage*, ARGYLL, D). He *d* 1453.

6 Elizabeth, *m* Malcolm Fleming of Biggar and Cumbernauld, and had issue. He *d* 1440.

4 Alexander, 1st EARL OF BUCHAN (*cr* 25 July 1382) and *jure uxoris* Earl of Ross, known as "The Wolf of Badenoch", *m ca* 24 July 1382, Euphemia, Countess of Ross (*d post* 5 Sept 1394), widow of Sir Walter Leslie, and eldest dau and heiress of William, 5th Earl of Ross, and *dsp ca* 1405-06.

1 Margaret, *m* (by dispensation dated 14 June 1350), as his 2nd wife, John Macdonald, Lord of the Isles, and had issue (*see* BURKE'S *Peerage*, MACDONALD, B). He *d* at Ardtornish Castle 1387.

2 Marjorie, *m* 1st (by dispensation dated 11 July 1370), John de Dunbar, 1st Earl of Moray, and had issue (*see* BURKE'S *Dormant and Extinct Peerages*). He *d* at York of wounds received in a tournament in London *ante* Feb 1392. She *m* 2ndly *ca* 1403, Sir Alexander Keith of Grantown.

3 Elizabeth, *m ante* 7 Nov 1372, Sir Thomas de la Haye, 7th Feudal Baron of Erroll and Constable of Scotland, and had issue (*see* BURKE'S *Peerage*, ERROLL, E). He *d* July 1406 (*bur* Cupar Angus Abbey).

4 Isabella, *m* 1stly (by dispensation dated 24 Sept 1371), James Douglas, 2nd Earl of Douglas (*see* BURKE'S *Dormant and Extinct Peerages*). He was *k* at the Battle of Otterburn 19 Aug 1388, *spl*. She *m* 2ndly *ante* 1390, Sir John Edmonstone, and had issue, one son.

5 Jean, *m* 1stly, Sir John Keith. She *m* 2ndly *ante* 4 Oct 1376, Sir John Lyon, Chamberlain of Scotland, and had issue (*see* BURKE'S *Peerage*, STATHMORE AND KINGHORNE, E). He was *k* 4 Nov 1382. She *m* 3rdly 1384, Sir James Sandilands of Calder, and had further issue (*see* BURKE'S *Peerage*, TORPHICHEN, B).

King Robert II *m* 2ndly (by dispensation dated 2 May 1355), Euphemia, crowned at Scone by Alexander de Kyninmund II, Bishop of Aberdeen 1372 (*d* 1387), widow of John Randolph, 3rd Earl of Moray, and dau of Hugh, 4th Earl of Ross, and *d* at Dundonald Castle, Ayrshire, 19 April 1390 (*bur* Scone Abbey), having by her had issue,

5 David, Earl Palatine of Stratherne *ante* 27 March 1371, *cr* Earl of Caithness between 21 Nov 1375 and 28 Dec 1377, *b ca* 1356-60, *m* —, and *d ante* 1389, leaving issue,

Euphemia, Countess Palatine of Stratherne and Countess of Caithness, resigned the latter Earldom *ante* July 1402, *b ante* 1375, *m* 1st *ante* Dec 1406, Patrick Graham of Kilpont, son of Sir Patrick Graham of Kincardine, and had issue, one son and two daus. He was *k* 10 Aug 1413. She *m* 2ndly, Sir Patrick Dunbar, and *d* in or *post* 1434.

6 Walter, Lord of Brechin, received a charter of the Earldom of Caithness on the resignation of his niece Euphemia *ante* July 1402, *cr* EARL OF ATHOLL shortly before 8 June 1404, resigned the Earldom of Caithness in favour of his yst son Alan *ca* 1428, resumed it on the latter's death 1431, was the chief organiser of the conspiracy in which King James I fell a victim, *m ante* 19 Oct 1378, Margaret, dau and heiress of Sir David de Barclay, Lord of Brechin, and was beheaded at Stirling for his part in the above mentioned conspiracy (his earldoms being forfeited) 26 March 1437, having had issue,

1 James, *m* —, and *dvp* in England when a hostage for King James I, leaving issue,

Robert (Sir), Master of Atholl, one of the assassins of King James I, beheaded at Edinburgh March 1437.

2 Alan, Earl of Caithness on his father's resignation *ca* 1428, *k* at Inverlochy, Inverness-shire 1431, *vp unm*.

6 Egidia, *m* 1387, Sir William Douglas of Nithsdale, natural son of Archibald Douglas, 3rd Earl of Douglas (*see* BURKE'S *Dormant and Extinct Peerages*), and had issue.

7 Katherine (also called Jean and Elizabeth), *m* 1380, David Lindsay, 1st Earl of Crawford, and had issue (*see* BURKE'S *Dormant and Extinct Peerages*). He *d* Feb 1407.

King Robert II was *s* by his eldest son,

1390-1406 ROBERT III, King of Scots, originally called John, *cr* Earl of Carrick by King David II 22 June 1368, declared heir to the crown by decree of Parl at Scone 27 March 1371, crowned at Scone 14 Aug 1390, styled Robert III instead of John with consent of the Estates of the Kingdom on and after 14 Aug 1390, *b ca* 1337, *m ca* 1366-67, Annabella (*d* at Scone "in harvest" 1401, *bur* Dunfermline Abbey), dau of Sir John Drummond of Stobhall (*see* BURKE'S *Peerage*, PERTH, E), and *d* at Dundonald Castle 4 April 1406 (*bur* Paisley Abbey), having had issue,

1 David, DUKE OF ROTHESAY (*cr* 28 April 1398), *b* 24 Oct 1378, *m* at Bothwell Feb 1400, Marjorie (who *m* 2ndly, Walter Haliburton), dau of Archibald Douglas, 3rd Earl of Douglas (*see* BURKE'S *Dormant and Extinct Peerages*), and *dspvp* at Falkland 26 March 1402 (*bur* Lindores Abbey).

2 Robert, *d* an inf.

3 JAMES I, *s* his father.

1 Margaret, *m* Archibald Douglas, 4th Earl of Douglas and Duke of Touraine in France, and had issue (*see* BURKE'S *Dormant and Extinct Peerages*). He was *k* at the Battle of Verneuil 17 Aug 1424.

2 Mary, *m* 1st 1397, George Douglas, 1st Earl of Angus, and had issue (*see* BURKE'S *Dormant and Extinct Peerages*). He *d* 1402. She *m* 2ndly 1404, James Kennedy yr of Dunure, and had further issue (*see* BURKE'S *Peerage*, AILSA, M). He *d ante* 8 Nov 1408. She *m* 3rdly 13 Nov 1413, as his 2nd wife, Sir William Graham of Kincardine, and had further issue (*see* BURKE'S *Peerage*, MONTROSE, D). She *m* 4thly 1425, Sir William Edmonstone of Duntreath, and had further issue (*see* BURKE'S *Peerage*, EDMONSTONE, Bt).

3 Elizabeth, *m* 1387, as his 1st wife, Sir James Douglas, 1st Lord Dalkeith, and had issue (*see* BURKE'S *Peerage*, MORTON, E). He *d ante* 22 May 1441.

4 Egidia, *d unm*.

King Robert III was *s* by his yst (but only surv) son,

1406-1437 JAMES I, King of Scots, possibly *cr* Duke of Rothesay and Earl of Carrick 10 Dec 1404, captured at sea by English sailors when on the way to France 4 April 1406, held a prisoner in London until 28 March 1424, declared King by the Estates of the Kingdom at Perth June 1406, crowned at Scone by Henry Wardlaw, Bishop of St Andrews 21 May 1424, *b* at Dunfermline Dec 1394, *m* at St Mary Overy, Southwark 2 Feb 1424, Joan, crowned with her husband (who *m* 2ndly 1439, Sir James Stewart, the "Black Knight of Lorne", and *d* at Dunbar Castle 15 July 1445, *bur* Carthusian Church, Perth), elder dau of John Beaufort, 1st Duke of Somerset, KG (*see p* 200), and was assassinated at Perth by his uncle Walter, Earl of Atholl and others 21 Feb 1437 (*bur* the Carthusian Church there), having had issue,

1 Alexander, Duke of Rothesay (at birth), *b* at Holyrood 16 Oct 1430; *d* an inf.
2 JAMES II, *s* his father.
1 Margaret, *b* 1424, *m* at Tours 24 June 1436, as is 1st wife, Louis, Dauphin of Viennois (afterwards Louis XI, King of France), and *dsp* at Châlons 16 Aug 1445 (*bur* first Châlons Cathedral, later transferred to St Leon of Thouars). He *d* 24 Aug 1483.
2 Isabella, *m* 30 Oct 1442, François I, Duke of Brittany, and *d* 1494, leaving issue. He *d* 1450.
3 Joan, *m ante* 15 May 1459, James Douglas, 1st Earl of Morton, and had issue (*see* BURKE'S *Peerage*). He *d ante* 22 Oct 1493.
4 Eleanor, *m* 12 Feb 1449, as his 1st wife, Sigismund, Duke of Austria, and *dsp* 1480. He *d* 26 Oct 1496.
5 Mary, *m* 1444, as his 1st wife, Wolfart van Borssele, Count of Grandpré and Lord of Campvere in Zealand, and *d* 20 March 1465, having had issue, two sons (who *d* young). He *d* at Ghent 29 April 1487.
6 Annabella, *m* 1st 14 Dec 1447 (*m* diss by div), as his 1st wife, Louis, Count of Geneva (later King of Cyprus *jure uxoris*), son of Louis, Duke of Savoy. He *d* April 1482. She *m* 2ndly *ante* 10 March 1459 (*m* diss by div 24 July 1471), as his 2nd wife, George Gordon, 2nd Earl of Huntly, and had issue (*see* BURKE'S *Peerage*, HUNTLY, M). He *d ca* 8 June 1501.

King James I was *s* by his only son,

1437-1460 JAMES II, King of Scots, *s* his elder (twin) brother as Duke of Rothesay 1430, crowned at Holyrood by Michael Ochiltree, Bishop of Dunblane 25 March 1437, *b* at Holyrood 16 Oct 1430, *m* there 3 July 1449 (she being crowned the same day), Marie (*d* 1 Dec 1463; *bur* Holy Trinity Church, Edinburgh), only dau of Arnold, Duke of Gueldres, and was *k* by the bursting of a cannon at the siege of Roxburgh 3 Aug 1460 (*bur* Holyrood), having had issue, with one son and one dau, who *d* as infs,

1 JAMES III, *s* his father.
2 Alexander, *cr* EARL OF MARCH *ante* 4 Aug 1455 and DUKE OF ALBANY *ante* 3 July 1458, forfeited his honours 1483, *b ca* 1454, *m* 1st (*m* diss on the ground of propinquity 1478), Catherine, dau of William Sinclair, 3rd Earl of Orkney (*see* BURKE'S *Dormant and Extinct Peerages*), by his 1st wife Elizabeth, dau of Archibald Douglas, 4th Earl of Douglas (*see* BURKE'S *Dormant and Extinct Peerages*), by his wife Margaret, dau of King Robert III (*see p* 318), and had issue,
1 Alexander, declared illegitimate by Act of Parl 13 Nov 1516, Prior of Whithorn, Abbot of Inchaffray, consecrated Bishop of Moray *ante* 16 April 1532, *d* 19 Dec 1537 (*bur* Scone).
Alexander, Duke of Albany *m* 2ndly 10 Feb 1480, Anne (who *m* 2ndly 15 Feb 1487, Louis, Comte de la Chambre, and *d* 13 Oct 1512, *bur* Carmelite Monastery of La Rochette, Savoy), 3rd dau of Bertrand de la Tour, Comte d'Auvergne, and was accidentally *k* in a tournament at Paris 1485 (*bur* Church of the Célestines there), having by her had issue,
2 John, 2nd DUKE OF ALBANY (restored *ca* 1505), Gov of Scotland during the minority of King James V 1515-24, *b ca* 1484, *m* 8 July 1505, his 1st cousin, Anne (*d* at St Saturnin), elder dau and co-heiress of Jean de la Tour, Comte d'Auvergne et de Lauraguais, by his wife Jeanne, eldest dau of Jean de Bourbon, Comte de Vendôme, and *dspl* 2 June 1536.
3 David, Earl of Moray (*cr* 12 Feb 1456), *b ca* 1455; *d ante* 18 July 1457.
4 John, Earl of Mar (*cr* between 21 June 1458 and 25 June 1459), *b ca* July 1457; *d unm* 1479.
1 Mary, *m* 1st *ante* 26 April 1467, Thomas Boyd, 1st Earl of Arran, and had issue (*see* BURKE'S *Dormant and Extinct Peerages*). He was attainted 1469 and *d ca* 1473. She *m* 2ndly *ante* April 1474 (Papal dispensation 25 April 1476), as his 2nd wife, James Hamilton, 1st Lord Hamilton, and had further issue (*see* BURKE'S *Peerage*, ABERCORN, D). He *d* 16 Nov 1479.
2 Margaret, had issue by William Crichton, 3rd Lord Crichton (*see* BURKE'S *Dormant and Extinct Peerages*).

King James II was *s* by his eldest son,

1460-1488 JAMES III, King of Scots, crowned at Kelso Abbey 10 Aug 1460, *b* at St Andrews Castle May 1452*, *m* at Holyrood 13 July 1469, Margaret (*d* at Stirling 14 July 1486, *bur* Cambuskenneth Abbey), dau of Christian I, King of Denmark, by his wife Dorothea, dau of Johann III, Elector of Brandenburg, and was murdered in a cottage at Milltown, nr Bannockburn following the Battle of Sauchieburn 11 June 1488 (*bur* Cambuskenneth Abbey), leaving issue,

1 JAMES IV, *s* his father.
2 James, *cr* DUKE OF ROSS 23 Jan 1481 and MARQUIS OF ORMOND and EARL OF EDIRDALE 29 Jan 1488, titular Archbishop of St Andrews 20 Sept 1497 (never consecrated), Chancellor of the Kingdom 1502, *b* March 1476; *d unm* 12 Jan 1504 (*bur* St Andrews Cathedral).
3 John, *cr* EARL OF MAR 2 March 1486, *b* Dec 1479; *d unm* 11 March 1503.

King James III was *s* by his eldest son,

1488-1513 JAMES IV, King of Scots, crowned at Scone 26 June 1488, *b* 17 March 1473, *m* at Holyrood 8 Aug 1503, Margaret (who *m* 2ndly at Kinnoul 4 Aug 1514 (*m* diss by div 11 March 1527), as his 2nd wife, Archibald Douglas, 6th Earl of Angus; and 3rdly *ante* 2 April 1528, as his 2nd wife, Henry Stewart, 1st Lord Methven (*see* BURKE'S *Dormant and Extinct Peerages*), and *d* at Methven Castle 24 Nov 1541, *bur* St John's Abbey, Perth), eldest dau of Henry VII, King of England (*see p* 204), and was *k* fighting the English at the Battle of Flodden in Northumberland 9 Sept 1513 (*bur* Sheen Abbey, Surrey), having had issue,

1 James, DUKE OF ROTHESAY (at birth), *b* at Holyrood 21 Feb 1507; *d* at Stirling Castle 27 Feb 1508.
2 Arthur, DUKE OF ROTHESAY (at birth), *b* at Holyrood 20 Oct 1509; *d* at Edinburgh Castle 14 July 1510.
3 JAMES V, *s* his father.
4 Alexander, DUKE OF ROSS (*cr* at birth), *b* (posthumously) at Stirling Castle 30 April 1514; *d* there 18 Dec 1515 (*bur* Cambuskenneth Abbey).
1 A dau, *b* and *d* at Holyrood 15 July 1508.
2 A dau, *b* and *d ca* 1513.

---

*Not at Stirling 10 July 1451 as formerly accepted.

King James IV was *s* by his 3rd (but eldest surv) son,

1513-1542 JAMES V, King of Scots, crowned at Stirling 21 Sept 1513, *b* at Linlithgow 10 April 1512, *m* 1st at Nôtre Dame Cathedral, Paris 1 Jan 1537, Madeleine (*b* at St Germain-en-Laye 10 Aug 1520; *dsp* at Holyrood 7 July 1537, *bur* there), 3rd dau of François I, King of France, by his 1st wife Claude, eldest dau of Louis XII, King of France. He *m* 2ndly at St Andrews 12 June 1538, Marie, crowned at Holyrood 22 Feb 1540, Regent of Scotland 1554-60 (*b* at Bar-le-Duc 22 Nov 1515; *d* at Edinburgh Castle 10 June 1560, *bur* Rheims), widow of Louis II, Duc de Longueville, and dau of Claude I de Lorraine, Duc de Guise, by his wife Antoinette, eldest dau of François de Bourbon, Duc de Vendôme, and *d* at Falkland Castle 14 Dec 1542 (*bur* Holyrood), having by her had issue,

1 James, DUKE OF ROTHESAY (at birth), *b* at St Andrews 22 May 1540; *d* there April 1541 (*bur* at Holyrood).

2 Arthur, DUKE OF ALBANY (*cr* at birth), *b* at Falkland Castle April 1541; *d* aged 8 days (*bur* Holyrood).

1 MARY, *s* her father.

King James V was *s* by his only surv legitimate child,

1542-1567 MARY, Queen of Scots, crowned at Stirling Castle 9 Sept 1543, forced to abdicate 24 July 1567, held prisoner in England 1568-87, *b* at Linlithgow 7 (or 8) Dec 1542, *m* 1st at Nôtre Dame Cathedral, Paris 24 April 1558, François II, King of France. He *d* at Orleans 5 Dec 1560. She *m* 2ndly at Holyrood 29 July 1565, Henry Stuart, Lord Darnley, *cr* Duke of Albany, Earl of Ross and Lord Ardmannoch and associated with her as King Consort (*b* 7 Dec 1545; *d* (murdered) at the Kirk of Field 10 Feb 1567), 2nd son of Matthew Stuart, 4th Earl of Lennox (*see* BURKE'S *Dormant and Extinct Peerages*), by his wife Margaret, dau of Archibald Douglas, 6th Earl of Angus, by his wife Margaret, widow of King James IV (*see above*), and dau of Henry VII, King of England (*see p* 204), and had issue,

JAMES VI, *s* his mother.

Queen Mary *m* 3rdly at Holyrood 15 May 1567, James Hepburn, 4th Earl of Bothwell, *cr* Duke of Orkney 12 May 1567, Great Adm of Scotland (*d* at Malmö, Sweden 14 April 1578) (*see* BURKE'S *Dormant and Extinct Peerages*), and after a long imprisonment in England was tried by a commn assembled at Fotheringay Castle, Northants and there beheaded 8 Feb 1587 (*bur* first Peterborough Cathedral, later transferred to Westminster Abbey).

Queen Mary was *s* by her only son,

1567-1625 JAMES VI, King of Scots, who *s* as JAMES I, KING OF ENGLAND on the death of Queen Elizabeth I 1603 (*see p* 206).

The Kings and Princes of Wales

The majority of the Welsh dynasties derived their descent from CUNEDDA WLEDIG, who with his eight sons came from Manaw Gododin (on the Firth of Forth) to drive the Irish out of Gwynedd *ca* 400. Cunedda's father EDEYRN (Eternus), grandfather PADARN BEISRUDD (Paternus of the Red Robe), and great-grandfather TEGID (Tacitus) are accepted as historical by Sir J. E. Lloyd and other authorities. One of his eight sons, EINION *YRTH,* was the father of CADWALLON *LAWHIR* (*the Long-handed*), the father of—

-547 MAELGWN GWYNEDD, or **MAELGWN** *HIR* (*the Tall*), **King of Gwynedd,** called "Maglocunus, the island dragon" by Gildas and Malgo by Geoffrey of Monmouth, who lists him as the 4th King to reign in Britain after Arthur. He *d* of the "yellow plague" at Rhos 547, and was *s* by his natural son,

547- RHUN AP MAELGWN GWYNEDD, or **RHUN** *HIR,* **King of Gwynedd,** who was *s* by his son*,

BELI AP RHUN, King of Gwynedd, who was *s* by his son,

-616 IAGO AP BELI, King of Gwynedd, a reputed benefactor of Bangor Cathedral, *d* 616, and was *s* by his son,

616-ca 625 CADFAN AB IAGO, King of Gwynedd, whose tombstone at Llangadwaladr Church, Anglesey is inscribed "Catamanus rex sapientisimus opinatisimus" (King Cadfan, most wise, most renowned), *d ca* 625 and was *s* by his son,

ca 625-633 CADWALLON AP CADFAN, King of Gwynedd, *m* a dau of Pebba, and sister of Penda, King of Mercia, and was *k* in battle with Oswald, King of Northumbria nr Hexham end of 633, leaving issue,

CADWALADR, of whom presently.

After the death of Cadwallon the throne of Gwynedd was usurped by

633-654 CADAFAEL AP CYNFEDW, or **CADAFAEL** *CADOMEDD,* who was not of the lineage of Maelgwn. He fled after his defeat at Winwaed Field by Penda, King of Mercia and lost the throne to the rightful heir,

654-664 CADWALADR FENDIGAID (*the Blessed*) **AP CADWALLON, King of Gwynedd,** who *d* of plague 664, and was *s* by his son,

664- IDWAL IWRCH AP CADWALADR, King of Gwynedd, who was *s* by his son,

-754 RHODRI MOLWYNOG, King of Gwynedd, who *d* 754, leaving issue,

1 HYWEL } *s* their father.
2 CYNAN }

*According to most pedigrees, although Sir J. E. Lloyd has pointed out that the number of generations between Maelgwn and Cadwaladr is suspect. A fragment of pedigree in Geoffrey of Monmouth makes Beli the brother of Rhun, which would fit better chronologically.

754-816 HYWEL AP RHODRI MOLWYNOG and **CYNAN TINDAETHWY, Kings of Gwynedd,** contested for the possession of Anglesey until Cynan's death 816, leaving issue,

Ethyllt, *m* Gwriad, a Manx chieftain descended from Llywarch Hen, a 6th century British Prince, and had issue,

MERFYN FRYCH, *s* his great-uncle King Hywel.

816-825 HYWEL AP RHODRI reigned alone and *d* 825, when he was *s* by his great-nephew,

825-844 MERFYN FRYCH (*the Freckled*) **King of Gwynedd,** added the three cantrefs of Arfon, Lleyn and Arllechwedd to Anglesey on the death of Hywel ap Caradog, the last King (a descendant of Cunedda), *m* Nest, dau of Cadell ap Brochwel, King of Powys (*see p* 325), and *d* 844, leaving issue,

1 RHODRI MAWR, *s* his father.
2 Gwriad, *k* with his brother 878.

844-878 RHODRI *MAWR* (*the Great*), **King of Gwynedd, Powys and part of Deheubarth,** *s* his father as King of Gwynedd 844, his maternal uncle Cyngen as King of Powys 855, and his brother-in-law Gwgon as King of Scisyllwg (Ceredigion and Ystrad Tywi) 872, *m* Angharad, dau of Meurig ap Dyfnwallon, King of Seisyllwg, and was *k* in battle with the English 878, leaving issue,

1 ANARAWD, *s* to Gwynedd.
2 CADELL, *s* to Seisyllwg.
3 Merfyn, *d* 904, leaving issue,
Afandreg (dau).
4 Aidan.
5 Meuric.
6 Morgan.
7 Tutwawl.
8 Elisse.

After the death of Rhodri his realm was partitioned between his two eldest sons.

I *The Line of Gwynedd*

878-916 ANARAWD, King of Gwynedd, acknowledged Alfred the Great as overlord, and *d* 916, leaving issue,

1 IDWAL FOEL, *s* his father.
2 Elisse, who had issue, a dau,
Prawst, *m* Seisyll, and had issue,
LLYWELYN AP SEISYLL, later King of Deheubarth and Gwynedd.

The elder son,

916-942 IDWAL FOEL (*the Bald*), **King of Gwynedd,** accepted English overlordship 918, *d* during an unsuccessful revolt against the English 942, leaving issue,

1 Meuric, *d* 986, leaving issue,
Idwal, *d* in exile 996, leaving issue,
IAGO, *s* as King of Gwynedd 1033.
2 IAGO, *s* with his brother Ieuaf 950.
3 IDWAL, or IEUAF, *s* with Iago.
4 Rhodri, *d* 968.
5 Agnan.

After the death of Idwal Foel his sons were expelled and Gwynedd passed to his cousin,

942-950 HYWEL *DDA,* **King of Deheubarth and Gwynedd** (*see below*), on whose death two sons of Idwal were restored.

950-969 IAGO and **IDWAL,** or **IEUAF,**

Kings of Gwynedd, reigned jtly but fought for supremacy, Ieuaf being defeated and driven out 969. He *d* 985, leaving issue,

1 HYWEL, *s* as King Gwynedd 979.
2 CADWALLON, *s* his brother.

969-979 IAGO continued to reign as sole King of Gwynedd and submitted to Edgar, King of England 973. He was deposed and imprisoned by his nephew,

978-985 HYWEL AP IEUAF, King of Gwynedd, who *d* 985 and was *s* by his brother,

985-986 CADWALLON AP IEUAF, King of Gwynedd, who *d* 986, when the throne of Gwynedd was usurped by

986-999 MAREDUDD AB OWAIN AP HYWELDDA, King of Deheubarth and Gwynedd (*see below*), who was *s* by his son-in-law,

999-1023 LLYWELYN AP SEISYLL, King of Deheubarth and Gwynedd (*see below*), on whose death the throne was usurped by

1023-1033 RHYDDERCH AB IESTYN, King of South Wales, on whose death the legitimate line was restored in the person of

1033-1039 IAGO AB IDWAL AP MEURIG, King of Gwynedd, who was murdered 1039, leaving issue,

Cynan, who took refuge in Ireland, *m* there Ragnhildr, dau of Olaf, son of Sitric of the Silken Beard, Norse King of Dublin, and *d ca* 1060, leaving issue,
GRUFFUDD AP CYNAN, who regained Gwynedd 1075.

On Iago's murder the throne was usurped by the son of Llywelyn ap Seisyll,

1039-1063 GRUFFYDD AP LLYWELYN, King of Gwynedd and Powys and (from 1055) of all Wales (*see below*) who was *s* by his half-brother,

1063-1075 BLEDDYN AP CYNFYN, King of Gwynedd and Powys (*see below*) on whose death in 1075 the throne was usurped by his cousin,

1075-1081 TRAHAEARN AP CARADOG, King of Gwynedd, who was finally defeated and *k* by the rightful heir,

1081-1137 GRUFFYDD AP CYNAN, King of Gwynedd, imprisoned by the Normans in England 1081-93, *b* in Dublin *ca* 1055, *m ca* 1095, Angharad (*d* 1162), dau of Owain ab Edwin (*see p* 323), and *d* 1137 (*bur* Bangor Cathedral), having had issue,

1 Cadwallon, *dvp* being *k* in battle with the men of Powys nr Llangollen 1132.
2 Owain Gwynedd, *s* his father.
3 Cadwaladr, *m* Alice, dau of Richard Fitz Gilbert de Clare, 1st Earl of Hereford (*see* BURKE'S *Dormant and Extinct Peerages*) and *d* 29 Feb 1172 (*bur* Bangor Cathedral), leaving issue,
Cadfan.
1 Gwenllian, *m* shortly *post* 1116, Gruffydd ap Rhys, Prince of Deheubarth, and was *k* while leading an attack on the Norman Castle at Kidwelly 1136, the spot being named Maes Gwenllian in her honour.
2 Marared.
3 Rannill.
4 Susanna, *m* Madog ap Maredudd, King of Powys. (*see p* 325).
5 Annest.

Gruffydd ap Cynan also had a natural dau,

Gwenllian, *b ca* 1080, *m* 1098, Cadwgan ap Bleddyn, Prince of Powys (*see p* 325), and had issue (*see* BURKE'S *LG*, LLOYD *of Blaenglyn*). He *d* 1111.

Gruffudd ap Cynan was *s* by his 2nd son,

1137-1170 OWAIN GWYNEDD, King of Gwynedd, acknowledged the overlordship of King Henry II of England and from *ca* 1152 changed his style from King to Prince, *b ca* 1100, *m* 1st Gwladus, dau of Llywarch ap Trahaearn ap Caradog, and had issue,

1 IORWERTH *DRWYNDWN*, *s* his father.
2 Maelgwn, *d post* 1173.

He *m* 2ndly, his 1st cousin, Christina, dau of Gronw ab Owain ab Edwin, and *d* 28 Nov 1170 (*bur* Bangor Cathedral), having by her had issue

3 DAFYDD I, *s* as Prince of Gwynedd 1175.
4 Rhodri, Lord of Anglesey and Arfon, *m* 1st, Nest, dau of Rhys ap Gruffydd ("The Lord Rhys"); and 2ndly, a dau of Reginald I, King of Man, and *d* 1195, leaving issue (*see* BURKE'S *LG*, JONES-LLOYD *formerly of Moelygarnedd and Plasyndre*).

Owain Gwynedd also had other issue,

5 Rhun, *d* 1146.
6 Hywel (whose mother was Pyfog, an Irishwoman), a soldier and poet, *k* in battle with his half-brothers nr Pentraeth, Anglesey 1170 (*bur* Bangor Cathedral).
7 Cynan, Lord of Eifionydd, Ardudwy and Meirionnydd, *d* 1173, leaving issue,
1 Gruffydd, Lord of Meirionnydd and (?) Ardudwy in 1188, *d* 1200, leaving issue,
Hywel, *d* 1216.
2 Maredudd, Lord of Eifionydd 1188, co-founder of Cymmer Abbey, *d* 1212, leaving issue,
(1) Llywelyn Fawr, who had issue,
Maredudd, *m* Gwenllian, dau of Maelgwn Fychan, and *d* 1255, leaving issue,
Llywelyn, *d* 1263.
(2) Llywelyn Fychan.
1 Angharad, *m* Gruffydd Maelor I, Lord of Northern Powys, and had issue (*see p* 326). He *d* 1191.
2 Gwenllian, *m* as his 1st wife, Owain Cyfeiliog, Prince of Southern Powys, and had issue (*see p* 326). He *d* 1197.

Owain Gwynedd was *s* by his eldest legitimate son,

1170- ca 1174 IORWERTH DRWYNDWN, Prince of Gwynedd, *m* Marared, dau of Madog ap Maredudd, King of Powys, and *d ca* 1174, leaving issue,

LLYWELYN II, of whom presently.

On the death of Iorwerth the throne of Gwynedd was usurped by his half-brother.

1174-1194 DAFYDD I, Prince of Gwynedd, dispossessed by his nephew Llywelyn ap Iorwerth 1194, ret to England 1198, *m* summer 1174, Emma, widow of Guy, Sire de Laval, and natural dau of Geoffrey, Count of Anjou (*see* footnote, *p* 194), and *d ca* May 1203, leaving issue,

Owain.
A dau.

His nephew,

1194-1240 LLYWELYN *FAWR* (*the Great*), **Prince of Gwynedd** (styled from 1230 *Prince of Aberffraw and Lord of Snowdon*), defeated his uncle Dafydd I 1194, and by 1203 regained the whole of Gwynedd, acknowledged as overlord by all the other Welsh Princes, *b* probably at Dolwyddelan 1173, *m* 1205, Joan (*d* at Aber 2 Feb 1237, *bur* Llanfaes), natural dau of John, King of England, and *d* at Aberconwy 11 April 1240 (*bur* Abbey there), leaving issue,

DAFYDD II, *s* his father.

Llywelyn the Great also had other issue,

1 Gruffydd (whose mother was Tangwystl, dau of Llywarch Goch, of Rhos), Lord of Lleyn, *b ante* 1205, *m* Senena, and was *k* attempting to escape from prison in the Tower of London 1 March 1244 (*bur* Aberconwy), leaving issue,

1 Owain *Goch* (*the Red*), Lord of part of Lleyn, *d ante* 1282.

2 LLYWELYN III, *s* his uncle Dafydd II.

3 Rhodri, *m* 1st 1281, Beatrice (*d* 1290), dau and heiress of David de Malpas. He *m* 2ndly, Catherine (who surv him), and *d ca* 1315, having by her had issue,

Thomas ap Rhodri, sold most of his Cheshire estates and lived at Tatsfield, Surrey, later acquired the Manors of Bidfield, Glos and Dinas in Mechain Iscoed, unsuccessfully claimed the Lordship of Lleyn, *b ca* 1295, *m* Cecilia, and *d* 1363, leaving issue,

Owain ap Thomas ap Rhodri (or Owain Lawgoch), a soldier in the service of King Philippe VI of France, deprived of his estates in England and Wales 1369, *b* probably at Tatsfield *ca* 1330; *k* at the siege of Mortagne-sur-Mer July 1378 (*bur* St Leger).

4 DAFYDD, *s* his brother LLYWELYN.

1 Gwladus, *m* Rhys ap Rhys Mechyll, of Dinefwr, and *d* 1261, leaving issue (*see p* 325). He *d* at Dinefwr 17 Aug 1271 (*bur* Talley).

1 Gwenllian, *m* William de Lacy, and *d* 1281. He *d* 1233.

2 Helen, *m* 1st *ca* 1220, John le Scot, Earl of Chester (*see* BURKE'S *Dormant and Extinct Peerages*). He *dsp* shortly *ante* 6 June 1237. She *m* 2ndly, Robert de Quincy, and *d* 1253, leaving issue (*see BURKE'S Dormant and Extinct Peerages,* WINCHESTER, E.). He *d* in the tournament at Blie 1257.

3 Gwladus *Ddu* (*the Black*), *m* 1st *ca* 1215, Reginald de Breos. He *d* June 1228. She *m* 2ndly 1230, Roger Mortimer, of Wigmore, and *d* at Windsor 1251, leaving issue. He *d* 1246.

4 Margaret, *m* 1st *ca* 1217, John de Breos, and had issue. He was *k* at Bramber 1232. She *m* 2ndly, Walter Clifford, and had further issue. He *d* 1263.

5 Angharad, *m* Maelgwn Fychan, son of Maelgwn ap Rhys, Lord of Ceredigion, and had issue. He *d* 1257.

Llywelyn the Great was *s* by his only legitimate son,

1240-1246 DAFYDD, Prince of Gwynedd, paid homage for Gwynedd to his maternal uncle King Henry III and was ktd and received the princely diadem at Gloucester 15 May 1240, *b ca* 1208, *m* 1230, Isabella (*d ante* Feb 1248), eldest dau of William de Breos, by his wife Eva, yst dau of William Marshal, Earl of Pembroke (*see* BURKE'S *Dormant and Extinct Peerages*), and *dsp* at Aber 25 Feb 1246 (*bur* Aberconwy). He was *s* by his nephew,

1246-1282 LLYWELYN (*Llywelyn the Last*), **Prince of Gwynedd,** re-united North Wales from the Dovey to the Dee and was acknowledged as overlord by the other native Princes 1258, when he assumed the style of PRINCE OF WALES, which was officially recognized by King Henry III by the Peace of Montgomery 1267, *m* at Worcester 13 Oct 1278, Eleanor (*b* at Kenilworth *ca* Michaelmas 1252; *d* June 1282, *bur* Llanfaes), dau of Simon de Montfort, 6th Earl of Leicester (*see* BURKE'S *Dormant and Extinct Peerages*), by his wife Eleanor, dau of King John (*see p* 196), and was *k* nr Builth fighting the English 11 Dec 1282, leaving issue,

Gwenllian, a nun at Sempringham, *b* 19 June 1282; *d* at Sempringham 7 June 1337.

Llywelyn III's brother,

1282-1283 DAFYDD III, Prince of Gwynedd, maintained resistance against King Edward I until June 1283, when he was captured, *b ca* 1235, *m* Elizabeth Ferrers, of the family of the Earls of Derby (*see* BURKE'S *Dormant and Extinct Peerages*), and was beheaded at Shrewsbury 3 Oct 1283, leaving issue, with several daus who all became nuns,

1 Llywelyn, *d* a prisoner in Bristol Castle 1288.

2 Owain, a prisoner in Bristol Castle 1305.

2 *The Line of Deheubarth*

878-909 CADELL AP RHODRI, King of Seisyllwg, *d* 909, leaving issue,

1 HYWEL *DDA*, *s* his father

2 CLYDOG, jt King of Seisyllwg with his brother, *dsp* 920.

The elder son,

909-950 HYWEL *DDA* (*the Good*), **King of All Wales,** *s* as King of Dyfed *jure uxoris ca* 904, King of Seisyllwg 909, King of Gwynedd 942, did homage to King Edward the Elder 918 and to King Athelstan 926, went on a pilgrimage to Rome 928, was the only Welsh ruler to mint his own coinage of silver pennies, *m ca* 904, Elen, dau and heiress of Llywarch ap Hyfaidd, King of Dyfed*, and *d* 950, leaving issue

1 RHODRI
2 EDWIN
3 OWAIN } *s* their Father.

The sons of Hywel *Dda*,

950-988 RHODRI, EDWIN and OWAIN, Kings of Deheubarth (Seisyllwg and Dyfed), reigned jtly until the deaths of Rhodri (953) and Edwin (954) left Owain as sole King. He *d* 988, having had issue,

1 Cadwallon, *dvp* 966.

2 Einon, *k* in a skirmish with the chiefs of Gwent 984, *vp*, leaving issue,

1 Edwin, who had issue,

(1) HYWEL, who *s* as King 1033.

(2) MAREDUDD, reigned jtly with HYWEL.

(3) Owain, who had issue,

1*a* MAREDUDD, *s* as King of Deheubarth 1063.

2*a* RHYS, *s* his brother.

3*a* Hywel, *d* 1078.

2 Gronw, who had issue,

Edwin, who had issue,

1*a* Uchtryd.

2*a* Owain, *d* 1105, leaving issue,

1*b* Llywarch, *d* 1118.

2*b* Gronw, *d* 1124, leaving issue,

Christina, *m* as his 2nd wife, her 1st cousin, Owain Gwynedd, King of Gwynedd, and had issue (*see p* 322). He *d* 28 Nov 1170.

3*b* Rhirid, *d* 1124.

4*b* Meilir, *d* 1124.

1*b* Angharad, *m ca* 1095, Gruffydd ap Cynan, King of Gwynedd, and *d* 1162, leaving issue (*see p* 322). He *d* 1137.

3 Tewdwr, *d* 994.

4 Cadell, who had issue,

Tewdwr, who had issue,

---

*The Kingdom of Dyfed (modern Pembrokeshire and western half of Carmarthenshire) was founded by a family of Irish origin. One of its most famous early Kings was Aircol *Lawhir* (Agricola of the Long Hand), *ca* 450-500, whose grandson Vortepor (the Vortiporius of Gildas) is commemorated by a memorial stone inscribed in Roman and Ogam, the earliest remaining royal monument in Britain.

1a Rhydderch, *m* Hunydd, dau of Bleddyn ap Cynfyn, King of Gwynedd and Powys (*see p* 325), and had issue,
1b Maredudd.
2b Owain.
2a RHYS, who *s* as King of Deheubarth 1081.
3 Idwallon, *dvp* 975.
4 MAREDUDD, *s* his father.

Owain ap Hywel *Dda* was *s* by his yst son,
988-999 MAREDUDD AB OWAIN, King of Deheubarth, also King of Gwynedd from 986, *d* 999, having had issue,

Cadwallon, *dvp* 992.
Angharad, *m 1st*, LLYWELYN AP SEISYLL, who *s* his father-in-law, and had issue (*see below*). He *d* 1023. She *m* 2ndly, Cynfyn ap Gwerstan, a noble of Powys, and had further issue,
1 BLEDDYN, *s* as King of Gwynedd 1063.
2 Rhiwallon, *k* at the Battle of Mechain 1070, leaving issue,
(1) Meilyr, *dsp* 1081.
(1) Gwladus, *m* Rhys ap Tewdwr, King of Deheubarth, and had issue (*see below*). He was *k* April 1093.
(2) Sioned, *m* Tudor "Walensis", Lord of Whittington, Chirk, Maelor Cymraeg and Nantheudwy, and had issue.

Maredudd was *s* by his son-in-law,
999-1023 LLYWELYN AP SEISYLL, King of Deheubarth and Gwynedd, son of Seisyll and Prawst, dau of Elise ab Anarawd (*see p* 321), made himself ruler or overlord of all Wales and *d* 1023, leaving issue by Angharad his wife,

GRUFFYDD, who later *s* as King of all Wales.

On the death of Llywelyn ap Seisyll the throne was usurped by
1023-1033 RHYDDERCH AB IESTYN, who *d* 1033, and was *s* by
1033-1044 HYWEL AB EDWIN, King of Deheubarth, reigned jtly with his brother **MAREDUDD** until the latter's death 1035, expelled by Gruffydd ap Llywelyn 1042 or 1043, returned with Danish aid 1044 and was *k* in battle at the mouth of the Towy, when Gruffydd was successful in establishing himself as
1044-1063 GRUFFYDD AP LLYWELYN, King of Deheubarth, had become King of Gwynedd and Powys 1039 contested Deheubarth with Gruffydd, son of Rhydderch ab Iestyn for many years, but by 1055 was King of all Wales, *m ca* 1056, Ealdgyth (who *m* 2ndly, Harold II, King of England—*see p* 192), dau of Aelfgar, Earl of Mercia, and was *k* "through the treachery of his own men" 1063, leaving issue,

1 Maredudd, *d* 1070.
2 Idwal, *d* 1070.
1 Nest, *m* Osbern Fitz Richard, Lord of Richard's Castle and Byton, and had issue,
Agnes, or Nest, *m* Bernard de Neufmarche.

On the death of Gruffydd the old line was restored in the person of
1063-1072 MAREDUDD AB OWAIN AB EDWIN, KING OF DEHEUBARTH, spent his reign in opposing the Norman invaders but finally allowed the occupation of Gwent and was rewarded by grants of land in England, *k* on the banks of the Rhymney 1072, leaving issue,

Gruffydd, lived in exile in England, *k* when attempting to regain his inheritance from Rhys ap Tewdwr 1091.

Maredudd was *s* by his brother,
1072-1078 RHYS AB OWAIN AB EDWIN, KING OF DEHEUBARTH, who was *k* by Caradog ap Gruffydd 1078 and was *s* by his 2nd cousin,
1078-1093 RHYS AP TEWDWR, KING OF DEHEUBARTH, *m* Gwladus, dau of Rhiwallon ap Cynfyn (*see above*), and was *k* nr Aberhonddu, Brecon April 1093, leaving issue,

1 GRUFFYDD, *s* as Prince of Deheubarth 1135.
2 Hywel.
1 Nest, *m ca* 1100, Gerald of Windsor, and had issue. Her amorous exploits rendered her notorious and she bore a son to King Henry I among others.

After the death of Rhys ap Tewdwr his son, **GRUFFYDD AP RHYS,** was taken to Ireland, but returned in 1113 and eventually established himself as **Prince of Deheubarth** 1135, *b ca* 1090, *m* shortly after 1016, Gwenllian (who was *k* leading her men in an attack on the Norman Castle of Kidwelly 1136), dau of Gruffydd ap Cynan, King of Gwynedd (*see p* 322), and *d* 1137, leaving issue,

1 MAREDUDD, *s* his half-brother Cadell.
2 RHYS, *s* his half-brother Cadell.

Gruffydd ap Rhys also had other issue,

1 ANARAWD, *s* his father.
2 CADELL, *s* his brother Anarawd.
1 Gwladus, *m* 1st, Caradog ab Iestyn of Morgannwg, and had issue. She *m* 2ndly, Seisyll ab Dyfnwal.
2 Nest, *m* Ifor Bach.

Gruffydd ap Rhys was *s* by his eldest son,
1137-1143 ANARAWD AP GRUFFYDD, Prince of Deheubarth, who *d* 1143, leaving issue,

Einion, who appears to have been *penteulu* (captain of the war band) to his cousin the "Lord Rhys", and was *k* 1163.

Anarawd was *s* by his brother,
1143-1153 CADELL AP GRUFFYDD, Prince of Deheubarth, set upon by a band of marauders while hunting and severely wounded 1151, resigned his lands to his half-brothers and went on pilgrimage to Rome 1153, *d* at Strata Florida Abbey 1175 (*bur* there).

His half-brothers,
1153-1197 MAREDUDD and **RHYS,** *s* jointly as **Princes,** *or* **Lords of Deheubarth.** Maredudd, who was *b* in Ireland *ca* 1130/1, *d* 1155, leaving Rhys as sole ruler. He was *b* in Ireland 1132 and acquired a dominant position in South Wales. He acknowledged the overlordship of King Henry II in 1158 and was known as *Yr Arglwydd Rhys* ("The Lord Rhys"). He *m* Gwenllian, dau of Madog ap Maredudd, King or Prince of Powys (*see p* 326), and *d* 28 April 1197 (*bur* St David's Cathedral), leaving issue,

1 GRUFFYDD, *s* his father.
2 Maredudd Ddall, *d* 1239.
3 Cynwrig, *d* 1237.
4 Rhys *Gryg* (the Hoarse), confirmed in the possession of the greater part of Cantref Mawr and Cantref Bychan and the commotes of Cydweli and Carnwyllion by Llywelyn II 1216, *m* Joan, dau of Richard de Clare, 3rd Earl of Hertford (*see* BURKE'S *Dormant and Extinct Peerages*), and was mortally wounded while attacking Carmarthen Castle and *d* at Llandeilo-fawr 1234 (*bur* St David's Cathedral), leaving issue,

1 Rhys Mechyll, Lord of Dinefwr, *m* Matilda de Breos, and *d* early 1244, leaving, with other issue,
Rhys Fychan (or Ieuanc), *m* Gwladus, dau of Gruffydd ap Llywelyn, Prince of Gwynedd (*see p* 323), and *d* 1271, leaving issue,
1*a* Rhys Wyndod.
2*a* Gruffydd.
3*a* Llywelyn.
Gwenllian, *m* Gilbert Talbot, and had issue (*see* BURKE'S *Peerage,* SHREWSBURY, E). He *d* 1274.
2 Maredudd, *d* 27 July 1271, leaving issue,
Rhys, *m* 1285, Auda, dau of Henry Hastings, and *d* 1292.
3 Hywel.
5 Maredudd, Lord of Cantref Bychan, *k* 2 July 1201.
6 Maelgwn, Lord of Ceredigion, *b ca* 1170; *d* at Llanerch-aeron late 1230 (*bur* Strata Florida Abbey), leaving issue,
Maelgwn Fychan (or Ieuanc), Lord of Ceredigion, *d* 1257, having had issue,
(1) Rhys, *dvp* June 1255 (*bur* Strata Florida Abbey), leaving issue,
1*a* Llywelyn, *d* 1265.
2*a* Rhys Ieuanc.
(1) Gwenllian, *m* Maredudd ap Llywelyn of Meirionydd and *d* at Llanfihangel y Creuddyn 25 Nov 1254 (*bur* Strata Florida Abbey).
(2) Marared, *m* Owain ap Maredudd of Cydewain, and *d* 25 Sept 1255 (*bur* Strata Florida Abbey).
7 Hywel Sais, *d* 1204 (*bur* Strata Florida Abbey), leaving issue,
Cynan.
8 Maredudd, Archdeacon of Cardigan, *d* 1227.
1 Gwenllian, *m* Ednyfed Fychan ap Cynwrig, Seneschal of Gwynedd (*d* 1246), and had, with other issue,
Goronwy ab Ednyfed, Seneschal of Gwynedd, *d* 1268, leaving issue,
Tudur Hen, who *d* 1311, leaving issue,
Tudur Fychan, *m* Margaret, dau of Thomas ap Llywelyn of Iscoed (*see below*), and *d* 1367, leaving issue,
Maredudd ap Tudur, *m* Margaret, dau of Dafydd Fychan ap Dafydd Llwyd, and had issue,
Owen Tudor, *b ca* 1400, *m ca* 1429, Catherine, widow of King Henry V, and dau of Charles VI, King of France, and was beheaded at Hereford, 1461, leaving issue (*see p* 200).

The Lord Rhys was *s* by his eldest son,

1197-1201 GRUFFYDD AP RHYS, *m* 1189, Matilda, dau of William de Breos, and *d* 25 July 1201 (*bur* Strata Florida Abbey), leaving issue,

1 Rhys Ieuanc, *d* Aug 1222 (*bur* Strata Florida Abbey).
2 Owain, *d* at Strata Florida 18 Jan 1236 (*bur* there), leaving issue,
Maredudd, *m* Eleanor, dau of Maelgwn Fychan, and *d* 1265, leaving issue,
(1) Owain, *m* Angharad, dau of Owain of Cydewain, and *d* 1275, leaving issue,
Llywelyn, of Iscoed, who *d* 1309, leaving issue,
Thomas, of Iscoed, who had issue,
1*c* Elen, *m* Gruffydd Fychan II, Lord of Glyndyfrdwy, and had issue (*see p* 326).
2*c* Margaret, *m* Tudur Fychan, and had issue (*see above*).
(2) Gruffydd.
(3) Cynan.

3 *The Line of Powys*

The first dynasty of Powys was established in the fifth century by Cadell *Deyrnllwg,* a contemporary of St Germanus (Garmon). Tenth in descent from him was Elisse, to whom the monument known as "Eliseg's Pillar" near Llangollen was erected by his great-grandson Cyngen, the last King of his line, who died while on pilgrimage at Rome *ca* 854. His sister Nest married Merfyn Frych (*see p* 321) and her son Rhodri Mawr *s* to Powys, which remained united to Gwynedd and/or Deheubarth until it regained its independence after the death of

1063-1075 BLEDDYN AP CYNFYN, King of Gwynedd and Powys, *s* his half-brother Gruffud ap Llywelyn (*see p* 324), reigning jtly with his brother Rhiwallon until 1070, acknowledged the overlordship of Edward the Confessor, *b ca* 1025, *m* 1st (the order of his wives is uncertain), —, dau of Brochwell ap Moelyn, of Nwrcelyn in Môn (Anglesey) and had issue,

1 Cadwgan, Prince of Powys jtly with his brothers, and Lord of Nannau (*see* BURKE'S *LG,* LLOYD *of Blaenglyn).*
2 Llywarch.
1 Hunydd (or Gwladus), *m* Rhydderch ap Tewdwr, 2nd son of Tewdwr ap Cadell (*see p* 324), and had issue.
2 Gwenllian, *m* Caradog ap Gruffydd ap Rhydderch ab Iestyn, King of Gwynllwg, and had issue. He was *k* at the battle of Mynydd Carn 1081.

He *m* 2ndly, —, and by her had issue,

3 Madog, *k* at Llech-y-crau by Rhys ap Tewdwr 1088.
4 Rhiryd, *k* with his brother 1088, leaving issue,
1 Madog.
2 Iorwerth.
3 Ithel, *d* 1124.
4 Cadwgan.
5 Cynwrig.

He *m* 3rdly, Haer, widow of Cynfyn Hirdref, and dau of Cillin ap y Blaidd Rhudd, of Gest, and by her had issue,

5 MAREDUDD, of whom presently.

He *m* 4thly, Morien, dau of Idnerth ap Cadwgan ab Elstan Glodrydd, and was *k* by Rhys ab Owain, King of Deheubarth at Ystrad Tywi, or at Powys Castle 1075, having by her had issue,

6 Iorwerth, invested with Powys and Ceredigion and half of Dyfed by King Henry I 1102, but was deprived the following year and imprisoned at Shrewsbury until 1110, when he was released against hostages, *k* at Caereinion 1111.
7 Llywelyn (or Rhiwallon), ancestor of the LLOYDS *of Rhiwlas,* the GETHINS *of Glasgoed, Llansilin* and the DAVIESES *of Trewylan, Montgomeryshire.*

Bleddyn's 5th son,

1075-1132 MAREDUDD AP BLEDDYN, Prince of Powys, reigned jtly with his brothers but surv them all and finally united all Powys under his rule, *m* 1st Hunydd, dau of Eunydd (or Efnydd) ap Gwernwy, and had issue,

1 MADOG, *s* his father.
2 Gruffydd, Lord of Mawddy, *m* Gwerfyl, dau and heiress of Gwrgeno ap Hywel, Lord of Caer or Clydewen, and *dvp* 1128, leaving issue,
1 OWAIN CYFEILIOG, of whom presently.
2 Meurig.
3 Hywel, *k* by his own men 1142.

He *m* 2ndly, Eva, dau of Bletrws ab Ednowain Bendew, and *d* 1132, having by her had issue,

4 Iorwerth *Goch* (the Red), made his submission to King Henry II and received Sutton, nr Wenlock and other Shropshire manors, granted possession of Chirk Castle 1166, later driven out of Mochnant by his nephews Owain ap Madog and Owain Cyfeiliog, *m* Maud, dau of Roger de Manley, and had issue,
Madog.

Maredudd ap Bleddyn's eldest son,

1132-1160 MADOG AP MAREDUDD,

Prince (sometimes styled **King) of Powys,** and Lord of Bromfield, gave Cyfeiliog to his nephews Owain and Meurig 1149, *m* Susanna, 4th dau of Gruffydd ap Cynan, King of Gwynedd (*see p* 322), and *d* at Winchester *ca* 9 Feb 1160 (*bur* Tysilio Church, Meifod), leaving issue,

1 Llywelyn, *d* 1160.
2 Gruffydd Maelor I, Prince of Northern Powys (Powys Fadog).
1 Marared, *m* Iorwerth Drwyndwn, a Prince of Gwynedd (*see p* 322).
2 Gwenllian, *m* Rhys ap Gruffydd, Prince of Deheubarth (*see p* 324).

Madog also left three natural sons, of whom
Owain Brogyntyn, held lands in Edeirnion and Dinmael 1188, *m* Margaret, dau of Einion ap Seisyll, of Mathafarn, and had issue,
1 Bleddyn, who had issue,
Owain.
2 Iorwerth, who had issue,
(1) Gruffydd.
(2) Elisse.
3 Gruffydd, who had issue,
David.

3*a* *Powys Wenwynwyn*

1160-1195 OWAIN CYFEILIOG, Prince of Southern Powys, received Cyfeiliog from his uncle Madog ap Maredudd 1149, abdicated in favour of his son Gwenwynwyn 1195 and ret to the monastery of Strata Marcella, *b ca* 1125, *m* 1st Gwenllian, dau of Owain Gwynedd, King of Gwynedd, and had issue,

1 Gwenwynwyn, *s* his father.
2 Caswallon.

He *m* 2ndly, a dau of Rhys ap Gruffydd, and *d* at Strata Marcella 1197 (*bur* there).

His elder son,

1195-1216 GWENWYNWYN, Prince or Lord of Southern Powys (which became known as Powys Wenwynwyn after him), acquired the Lordship of Arwystli 1197, deprived of his lands by King John 1208, but was restored 1210, swore an oath of homage to Llywelyn 1215, *m* Margaret, dau of Robert Corbet, of Caus, and *d* in exile 1216, leaving issue,

1 Gruffydd ap Gwenwynwyn, invested with the Lordship of Arwystli, Cyfeiliog, Mawddwy, Caereinion, Y Tair Swydd and Upper Mochnant by King Henry III 1241, trans his allegiance to Llywelyn 1263, *m ante* 1241, Hawise (*d* 1310), dau of John Lestrange, of Knockin, Salop, and *d* between 21 Feb 1286 and end of 1287, having had issue, with five other sons and one dau,
Owen de La Pole *m* Joanna Corbet, and had issue,
Gruffydd, *d* 1309.
Hawise *Gadarn* (*the Hardy*), *b* 1291, *m* John Cherleton, or Charlton, Lord of Powys *jure uxoris* and *d ante* 1353 (probably *bur* Grey Friars, Shrewsbury), leaving issue (*see* BURKE'S *Dormant and Extinct Peerages*).
2 Madog.

3*b* *Powys Fadog*

1160-1191 GRUFFYDD MAELOR I, Lord of Northern Powys, received Maelor and Iâl as his portion and later added Nanheudwy, and on the death of his half-brother Owain Fychan 1187, Cynllaith and Lower Mochnant *m* Angharad, dau of Owain Gwynedd, King of Gwynedd (*see p* 322), and *d* 1191, leaving issue,

1 Madog, *s* his father.
2 Owain, jt ruler with his brother, *d* 1197.

The elder son,

1191-1236 MADOG AP GRUFFYDD, Lord of Northern Powys (which came to be called Powys Fadog after him), *m* Isota, and *d* 1236 (*bur* Valle Crucis Abbey), leaving issue,

1 GRUFFYDD MAELOR II, of whom presently.
2 Gruffydd Iâl, *d* 1238.
3 Maredudd, *d* 1256.
4 Hywel, *d* 1268(?).
5 Madog Fychan, *d* 1269.
1 Angharad.

1236-1269 GRUFFYDD MAELOR II, Lord of Powys Fadog, *m* Emma, widow of Henry Touchet, and dau of Henry Audley, and *d* 1269, leaving issue,

1 Madog, *d* 1277.
2 Llywelyn.
3 Owain.
4 Gruffydd Fychan I *d* 1289, leaving issue,
Madog Crippil, *d ca* 1304, leaving issue,
Gruffydd, *d ca* 1365, leaving issue,
Gruffydd Fychan II, Lord of Glyndyfrdwy, *m* Elen, dau of Thomas ap Llywelyn, of Iscoed (*see p* 325), and had issue,
1*b* OWAIN GLYNDWR, who attempted unsuccessfully to restore Welsh independence at the end of the 14th century, *m* Margaret, dau of Sir David Hanmer (*see* BURKE'S *Peerage*), HANMER, Bt), and had issue,
1*b* Lowry, *m* Robert Puleston, and had issue,
2*b* Isabel, *m* Adda ap Iorwerth Ddu, and had issue.

Lineage of H R H The Prince Philip, Duke of Edinburgh

EGILMAR I, COUNT OF ALDENBURG, living 1108, *m* Richza, Countess in Dithmarschen, and had issue,

EGILMAR II, COUNT OF ALDENBURG, *m* Eilika, Countess of Rietberg, and had issue,

CHRISTIAN I, COUNT OF OLDENBURG, *m* Kunigunde, and *d* 1167, leaving issue,

MORITZ, COUNT OF OLDENBURG, *m* a Countess of Wickerode, and *d ca* 1209, leaving issue,

CHRISTIAN II, COUNT OF OLDENBURG, *m* Agnes, Countess of Altena, and *d* 1233, leaving issue,

JOHANN I, COUNT OF OLDENBURG AND DELMENHORST, *m ca* 1255, Richza, Countess of Hoya, and had issue,

CHRISTIAN V, COUNT OF OLDENBURG, *m* Hedwig, Countess of Oldenburg, and *d* 1316, leaving issue,

JOHANN II, COUNT OF OLDENBURG, *m* Hedwig, Countess of Diepholz, and had issue,

KONRAD, COUNT OF OLDENBURG, living 1347, *m* Ingeborg, Countess of Holstein, and had issue,

CHRISTIAN VI, COUNT OF OLDENBURG, *b ca* 1360, *m* Agnes, only dau of Heinrich VII, Count of Hohnstein, by his wife Anna, dau of Ernst, Duke of Brunswick-Grübenhagen, and *d ca* 1420, leaving, with other issue, an elder son,

DIETRICH II *THE FORTUNATE,* COUNT OF OLDENBURG AND DELMENHORST, obtained the whole county of Oldenburg (jointly with his brother Count Christian VII) on the death of his cousin Moritz 1420, and *s* his brother-in-law as Count of Delmenhorst 1432, *b ca* 1390, *m* 2ndly 23 Nov 1423, Heilwig (*b ca* 1400; *d* 1436), widow of Balthasar, Prince of Wenden, Lord of Güstrow (*d* 1421), sister and heiress of Adolf VIII, Count of Holstein and Duke of Schleswig, and dau of Gerhard VI, Count of Holstein*, by his wife Katharina, 7th dau of Magnus II *Torquatus,* Duke of Brunswick-Lüneburg, and *d* at Delmenhorst 22 Jan 1440, having by her had issue,

CHRISTIAN I, KING OF DENMARK, NORWAY AND SWEDEN, *s* his father as Count (Christian VIII) of Oldenburg and Delmenhorst 1440, elected King of Denmark 1448, of Norway 1450, and of Sweden 1457, *s* his maternal uncle Adolf VIII as Count of Holstein (erected into a Duchy 1474) and Duke of Schleswig, Stormarn, etc 1459, ceded Oldenburg and Delmenhorst to his brother Gerhard 1460 (male line *extinct* 1681), *b* 1426, *m* at Copenhagen 28 Oct 1449, Dorothea (*b* 1430; *d* at Kalundborg 25 Nov 1495), widow of Christopher III, King of Denmark, Norway and Sweden, and dau of Johann *the Alchemist,* Margrave of Brandenburg-Kulmbach, by his wife Barbara, dau of Rudolf III, Duke of Saxe-Wittenberg, and *d* at Copenhagen 21 May 1481, leaving, with other issue,

1 Hans, King of Denmark 1481-1513, father of Christian II, King of Denmark 1513-23.

2 FREDERIK I, of whom presently.

1 Margaret, *m* at Holyrood 13 July 1469, James III, King of Scots, and *d* at Stirling 14 July 1486, leaving issue (*see* KINGS AND QUEENS OF SCOTLAND, *p* 319). He *d* 11 June 1488.

The yr son,

FREDERIK I, KING OF DENMARK AND NORWAY, Duke of Schleswig and Holstein 1482, *s* as King on the deposition of his nephew King Christian II 1523, *b* 7 Oct 1471, *m* 1st at Stendal 10 April 1502, Anna (*b* at Berlin 27 Aug 1487; *d* at Kiel 3 May 1514), 2nd dau of Johann IV *Cicero,* Elector of Brandenburg, by his wife Margareta, dau of Wilhelm III, Duke of Saxony, Landgrave of Thuringia, and nominated King of Bohemia, and had issue,

1 CHRISTIAN III, of whom presently.

He *m* 2ndly 9 Oct 1518 Sophie (*b* 1498; *d* 13 May 1568), dau of Bogislaw X, Duke of Pomerania, by his wife Anna, dau of Casimir III, King of Poland, and *d* at Gottorp 10 April 1533, having by her had issue,

2 Hans, Duke of Schleswig-Holstein in Hadersleben, *d* 1580.

3 Adolf, Duke of Schleswig-Holstein in Gottorp, *d* 1586. He was ancestor of the Dukes of Holstein-Gottorp, Kings of Sweden (1751-1818), Emperors of Russia (1762-1918), and Grand Dukes of Oldenburg (1815-1918).

The eldest son,

CHRISTIAN III, KING OF DENMARK AND NORWAY, ceded the Duchies of Schleswig and Holstein by his father 1523, *b* at Gottorp 12 Aug 1503, *m* at Lauenburg 1525, Dorothea (*b* 9 July 1511; *d* at Sonderburg 27 Oct 1571), 2nd dau of Magnus II, Duke of Saxe-Lauenburg, by his wife Katharina, dau of Heinrich *Senior,* Duke of Brunswick-Wolfenbüttel, and *d* at Coldingen 1 Jan 1559, leaving, with other issue,

1 Frederik II, King of Denmark, ancestor of all succeeding Kings of Denmark until 1863. His dau Anna, *m* James VI, King of Scots, later James I, King of England (*see p* 206).

2 Magnus, King of Livonia, *d* 1583.

3 HANS, of whom presently.

*Gerhard VI, Count of Holstein, was son of Heinrich II, Count of Holstein, son of Gerhard III *the Great,* Count of Holstein-Rendsburg (*d* 1340), by his wife Sophie, dau of Nikolaus of Mecklenburg, by his wife Rikissa, dau of Erik Klipping, King of Denmark (*d* 1286), thus giving the House of Oldenburg a link with the earlier Kings of Denmark.

The yst son,

HANS, DUKE OF SCHLESWIG-HOLSTEIN-SONDERBURG, received Sonderburg and the Isles of Ahlsen and Arroe in Schleswig, and Plön, Arnsbeck, etc, in Holstein by a compact signed at Flensburg with his brother King Frederik II 1582, *b* at Coldingen 25 March 1545, *m* 1st at Coldingen 19 Sept 1568, Elisabeth (*b* 20 March 1550; *d* at Osterholm 11 Feb 1586), dau of Ernst V, Duke of Brunswick-Grübenhagen, by his wife Margarete, dau of Georg, Duke of Pomerania-Stettin, and *d* at Glücksburg 9 Oct 1622, leaving, with other issue, a 3rd son,

ALEXANDER, DUKE OF SCHLESWIG-HOLSTEIN-SONDERBURG, *b* at Sonderburg 20 Jan 1573, *m* at Oldenburg 26 Nov 1605, Dorothea (*b* at Sondershausen 25 Aug 1579; *d* at Sonderburg 5 July 1639), dau of Johann Günther I, Count of Schwarzburg-Sondershausen, by his wife Anna Sophie, 2nd dau of Anton I, Count of Oldenburg and Delmenhorst, and *d* at Sonderburg 13 May 1627, leaving, with other issue,

1 Ernst Günther, Duke of Schleswig-Holstein-Sonderburg-Augustenburg, whose male line became extinct 1931.

2 AUGUST PHILIPP, of whom presently.

The yr (actually 5th) son,

AUGUST PHILIPP, DUKE OF SCHLESWIG-HOLSTEIN-SONDERBURG-BECK, *b* at Sonderburg 11 Nov 1612, *m* 3rdly at Beck 12 April 1651, Marie Sibylla (*b* at Saarbrücken 6 Oct 1623; *d* at Alverdissen 9 April 1699), 5th dau of Wilhelm Ludwig, Count of Nassau-Saarbrücken, by his wife Anna Amalia, dau of Georg Friedrich, Margrave of Baden-Durlach, and *d* at Beck 31 Oct 1675, having by her had, with other issue, a 2nd son,

LUDWIG FRIEDRICH, DUKE OF SCHLESWIG-HOLSTEIN - SONDERBURG-BECK, Royal Prussian General Field Marshal and Statthalter in East Prussia, *b* at Beck 6 April 1654, *m* at Copenhagen 10 Jan 1685, his 1st cousin, Luise Charlotte (*b* at Augustenburg 13 April 1658; *d* at Königsberg 2 May 1740), 3rd dau of Ernst Günther, Duke of Schleswig-Holstein-Sonderburg - Augustenburg (*see above*), by his wife Auguste, 3rd dau of Philipp, Duke of Schleswig-Holstein-Glücksburg, and *d* at Königsberg 7 March 1728, leaving, with other issue, a 5th and yst son,

PETER AUGUST FRIEDRICH, DUKE OF SCHLESWIG-HOLSTEIN - SONDERBURG-BECK, Imp Russian General Field Marshal and Governor Gen of the Duchy of Esthonia, *b* at Königsberg 7 Dec 1697, *m* 1st at Rinteln 5 Sept 1723, Sophie (*b* at Philippsthal 6 April 1695; *d* at Marburg 8 May 1728), 6th dau of Philipp, Landgrave of Hesse-Philippsthal, by his wife Katharina Amalie, dau of Karl Otto, Count of Solms-Laubach, and *d* at Reval 22 March 1775, having had issue,

KARL *ANTON* AUGUST, *b* at Marburg 10 Aug 1727, *m* at Königsberg 30 May 1754, his 1st cousin, Friederike *Charlotte* Antoinette (*b* at Königsberg 3 July 1738; *m* 2ndly 22 May 1777, Friedrich Detlev Graf von Moltke, and *d* at Wolde 21 April 1785), dau of Albrecht Christoph, Burggraf zu Dohna-Schlodien in Leistenau, by his 3rd wife Sophie Henriette, 4th dau of Ludwig Friedrich, Duke of Schleswig-Holstein-Sonderburg-Beck (*see above*), and *dvp* at Stettin of wounds received at the battle of Kunnersdorf 12 Sept 1759, leaving issue, an only son,

FRIEDRICH KARL LUDWIG, DUKE OF SCHLESWIG-HOLSTEIN - SONDERBURG-BECK, *b* at Königsberg 20 Aug 1757, *m* there 9 March 1780, *Friederike* Amalie (*b* at Königsberg 28 Feb 1757; *d* at Schleswig 17 Dec 1827), dau of Karl Leopold, Count von Schlieben, Royal Prussian Minister of War, by his wife Marie Eleonore, dau of Ahasuerus Ernst, Count von Lehndorff, and *d* at Wellingsbüttel 25 March 1816, leaving, with other issue, an eldest son,

FRIEDRICH *WILHELM* PAUL LEOPOLD, DUKE OF SCHLESWIG-HOLSTEIN-SONDERBURG-BECK, granted the Duchy of Glücksburg by King Frederik VI of Denmark 1825 and took the title of Duke of Schleswig-Holstein-Sonderburg-Glücksburg, *b* at Lindenau 4 Jan 1785, *m* at Gottorp 26 Jan 1810, *Louise* Charlotte (*b* at Gottorp 28 Sept 1789; *d* at Ballenstadt, Anhalt 13 March 1867), 3rd and yst dau of Karl, Landgrave of Hesse-Cassel, by his wife Louise, 3rd dau of Frederik V, King of Denmark, by his wife Louisa, dau of King George II (*see p* 286), and *d* at Gottorp 17 Feb 1831, leaving, with other issue, a 4th son,

CHRISTIAN IX, KING OF DENMARK, whose 2nd son,

GEORGE I, KING OF THE HELLENES, had, with other issue, a 4th son,

HRH PRINCE ANDREW (ANDREAS) OF GREECE AND DENMARK, father of

HRH THE PRINCE PHILIP, DUKE OF EDINBURGH.

(*see pps* 277-280 *for fuller details of the last three generations*).

Index of Names in the Royal Lineage

Contrary to our usual practice compound surnames are indexed under the first name rather than the last as this is felt to be more convenient for the reader. Countries and sovereign states are shown in capitals.

Appendices

Appendix A lists "The Royal Line of Succession"; *Appendix B* explains the constitutional position of "The Counsellors of State"; *Appendix C* comprises historical notes on "Titles Traditionally Associated with the Royal Family"; *Appendix D* is a genealogical table showing "The Relationships between the Reigning Sovereigns of Europe"; *Appendix E* is an anthology from the works of William Shakespeare entitled "The Kings in Shakespeare"; and *Appendix F* sets out "The List of Royal Warrant Holders".

APPENDIX A

The Royal Line of Succession

This list shows the Order of Succession to the Throne. Dates of birth are given in parentheses.

1 HRH THE PRINCE OF WALES (1948)
2 HRH The Prince Andrew (1960)
3 HRH The Prince Edward (1964)
4 HRH The Princess Anne (1950)
5 HRH The Princess Margaret, Countess of Snowdon (1930)
6 Viscount Linley (1961)
7 Lady Sarah Armstrong-Jones (1964)
8 HRH The Duke of Gloucester (1900)
9 HRH Prince Richard of Gloucester (1944)
10 HRH The Duke of Kent (1935)
11 The Earl of St Andrews (1962)
12 Lord Nicholas Windsor (1970)
13 Lady Helen Windsor (1964)
14 HRH Prince Michael of Kent (1942)
15 HRH Princess Alexandra, the Hon Mrs Angus Ogilvy (1936)
16 James Ogilvy (1964)
17 Marina Ogilvy (1966)
18 The Earl of Harewood (1923)
19 Viscount Lascelles (1950)
20 Hon James Lascelles (1953)
21 Hon Robert Lascelles (1955)
22 Hon Gerald Lascelles (1924)
23 Henry Lascelles (1953)
24 The Duke of Fife (1929)
25 The Earl of Macduff (1961)
26 Lady Alexandra Carnegie (1959)
27 HM King Olav V of Norway (1903)
28 HRH Crown Prince Harald of Norway (1937)
29 HRH Princess Märtha Louise of Norway (1971)
30 HH Princess Ragnhild, Mrs Lorentzen (1930)
31 Haakon Lorentzen (1954)
32 Ingeborg Lorentzen (1957)
33 Ragnhild Lorentzen (1968)
34 HH Princess Astrid, Mrs Ferner (1932)
35 Alexander Ferner (1965)
36 Cathrine Ferner (1962)
37 Benedicte Ferner (1963)
38 Elisabeth Ferner (1969)
39 A 2nd son (1972) of HH Princess Astrid, Mrs Ferner
40 HRH Princess Margarita of Roumania (1949)
41 HRH Princess Helen of Roumania (1950)
42 HRH Princess Irina of Roumania (1953)
43 HRH Princess Sophie of Roumania (1957)
44 HRH Princess Maria of Roumania (1964)
45 HRH Prince Tomislav of Yugoslavia (1928)
46 HRH Prince Nikola of Yugoslavia (1958)
47 HRH Princess Katarina of Yugoslavia (1959)
48 HRH Prince Andrej of Yugoslavia (1929)
49 HRH Prince Christopher of Yugoslavia (1960)
50 HRH Prince Karl Vladimir of Yugoslavia (1964)

APPENDIX B

The Counsellors of State

Introduction

In the event of the Sovereign's absence abroad, it has always been recognized that he must delegate his powers to someone to carry on the government of the country on his behalf. Henry V, William III, and other kings who commanded their armies in person, and also the Hanoverian Kings, who spent long periods in Hanover, appointed a single person as Guardian of the Realm (Custos Regni), or a Commission of Lord Justices to act during their absences. In 1912, King George V appointed Counsellors of State during his three month visit to India for the Durbar, and the whole question was examined following his illness 1928-29. The Regency Acts of 1937, 1943 and 1953 provide powers under which, in the event of the Sovereign's illness or absence or intended absence from the United Kingdom, the Sovereign may appoint Counsellors of State "to prevent delay or difficulty in the despatch of public business". Counsellors of State are appointed by Letters Patent, which specify the reason for their appointment (for example, The Queen's "intention to be absent from Our United Kingdom for the purpose of visiting the Republic of France") and the functions which are delegated to them.

The Counsellors

The Regency Acts specify that the Counsellors of State shall be the wife or husband of the Sovereign and the next four people in succession to the Throne. During her lifetime Queen Elizabeth The Queen Mother is added to this number. The heir apparent or heir presumptive if under eighteen, any other persons under twenty-one, and any who do not qualify to the Throne (for example, a Roman Catholic) are excluded. At present the Six Counsellors of State are The Duke of Edinburgh, The Queen Mother, The Prince of Wales, The Princess Anne, The Princess Margaret and The Duke of Gloucester. The Prince Andrew and The Prince Edward will automatically become eligible to act as Counsellors when they reach the age of twenty-one. The Letters Patent normally specify that a quorum of two or more Counsellors may act jointly to exercise the Royal functions, and except from the Counsellors any of their number who are absent or intend to be absent from the United Kingdom during the Sovereign's absence. Thus during the State Visit to France in May 1972, The Duke of Edinburgh, who accompanied The Queen, The Prince of Wales, who was serving in the Royal Navy, and The Princess Margaret, who went abroad for part of this time, were excepted.

Their Duties

The Regency Acts preclude the delegation to the Counsellors of State of the power to dissolve Parliament otherwise than on the express instructions of the Sovereign, or to grant any rank, title or dignity of the peerage. With this proviso, the Letters Patent may delegate any or all powers and authorities belonging to the Crown, whether prerogative or statutory, and may also specifically command the Counsellors not to do certain things. For example, in recent years they have been expressly precluded from receiving homage required to be done to The Queen. The delegated functions are set out in a Schedule to the Letters Patent, and normally include the power to:

1 Hold Privy Councils, and signify The Queen's approval in Council.

2 Issue commissions for giving the Royal assent to Acts of Parliament (except Acts touching the Royal Style and titles or modifying the Act of Settlement).

3 Approve or sign proclamations, warrants, and other documents requiring The Queen's approval or signature which relate to the affairs of the United Kingdom or to colonies or territories for whose foreign affairs the United Kingdom Government is responsible.

4 To exercise the Royal prerogative and any statutory or other powers enabling The Queen to act for the safety or good government of the United Kingdom and Colonies.

The Counsellors have the discretion to refuse to act in any case in which it appears to them that they should not do so without The Queen's previous special approval.

Apart from the functions already mentioned above, the Counsellors of State are usually precluded from approving or signing documents for which The Queen's approval is required for or in connection with matters of honours and awards, precedence among nobility, disbandment of regiments and Church of Scotland affairs.

APPENDIX C

Titles Traditionally Associated with the Royal Family

1 *The Titles of the Heir-Apparent*

The position of Heir-Apparent to the throne can only be held by the heir male of the body of the reigning sovereign, who is *ipso facto* Duke of Cornwall in the Peerage of England and Duke of Rothesay, Earl of Carrick, Baron of Renfrew, Lord of the Isles and Great Steward of Scotland.

Cornwall was first conferred on a member of the Royal Family as an Earldom to Richard, second son of King John. This creation became extinct on the death of the second holder in 1300. After being held for a short time by Edward II's favourite Piers Gaveston, the title was conferred on that King's second son John of *Eltham* in 1328. He died unmarried in 1336 and on 3 March 1337 Edward III created his son Edward, Duke of Cornwall, the title to descend to his heirs the eldest sons of the Kings of England for ever. He died before his father and was succeeded in the dignity by his son Richard, afterwards King Richard II. On the latter's deposition and the accession of Henry IV it was deemed necessary to recreate the Dukedom (15 October 1399) and this was again done by Edward IV in 1471. Thereafter the title has descended in accordance with the terms of the original creation of 1337.

The Scottish titles were first conferred by King Robert III on his eldest son David 28 April 1398, and thereafter on the first born sons of the succeeding Kings at birth until 1469 when by Act of Parliament the Castle of Rothesay was conferred on the King's eldest son and the succession became automatic.

The title principally associated with the Heir-Apparent, however, is that of Prince of Wales, with which the Earldom of Chester has always been associated. The latter title was conferred on Edward, the eldest son of King Henry III, in 1254. He in turn conferred it on his eldest surviving son Alfonso who died in 1284. On 7 February 1301 he created his then eldest surviving son, Edward, Prince of Wales and Earl of Chester. He succeeded his father as King Edward II in 1307 and in 1312 conferred the Earldom of Chester (but not the Principality of Wales) on his infant son, Edward, later King Edward III, who again conferred the Principality and Earldom together on his son Edward 12 May 1343, since when the titles have always been conferred together and were declared inseparately linked by a Statute of 1398. On the death of a Prince of Wales and Earl of Chester in the lifetime of a sovereign parent the titles do not descend to his son, but become extinct and have to be re-created as was the case on the death of Frederick, Prince of Wales in 1751.

2 *Duke of York*

The title of Duke of York has always been a Royal title and has traditionally come to be associated with the second surviving son of the reigning sovereign, but was first conferred on Edmund, the fifth son of King Edward III, by his nephew King Richard II in 1385. The 4th Duke of this creation succeeded to the throne as Edward IV in 1461, and in 1474 he created his second son Richard, Duke of York. The title was next conferred on Prince Henry (afterwards Henry VIII), the second son of King Henry VII in 1494, but he resigned his patent on being created Prince of Wales and Earl of Chester in 1504 following the death of his elder brother Arthur. Subsequent holders of the title have been Prince Charles (afterwards King Charles I), second son of King James I, Prince James (afterwards King James II), Ernst August, Prince-Bishop of Osnabrück (brother of King George I), Prince Edward (brother of King George III), Prince Frederick (second son of King George III), Prince George (second son of Albert Edward, Prince of Wales and afterwards King George V), and Prince Albert (afterwards King George VI), second son of the last. If a well-established precedent is followed it is to be anticipated that HRH The Prince Andrew will in due course be the next holder of this title.

3 *Duke of Gloucester*

The Dukedom of Gloucester, like that of York, has always been a Royal title, although an Earldom of Gloucester had existed earlier. The first Duke was Thomas *of Woodstock,* sixth son of King Edward III, who received the honour from his nephew King Richard II 6 August 1385 (the same day as the creation of the Dukedom of York). After his death in 1397 Gloucester was again granted as an Earldom to Thomas, 6th Baron Le Despenser, who was beheaded in 1400. In 1414 the title was revived as a Dukedom for Humphrey, the fourth son of King Henry IV, who died without legitimate issue in 1447. In 1461 the title was again revived in favour of Richard, brother of King Edward IV, and merged in the Crown on his accession as King Richard III in 1483.

In 1659, King Charles II, while still in exile, created his brother Prince Henry, Duke of Gloucester. He died unmarried in 1660 and although the title was borne by Queen Anne's son at the end of the seventeenth century, he was never formally so created. In 1764, King George III conferred the Dukedom on his brother Prince William Henry and this creation became extinct on the death of the second holder in 1834. It was again revived in favour of HRH The Prince Henry, the present holder, in 1928.

4 *Duke of Kent*

The title of Kent has long been associated with the Royal Family. William the Conqueror conferred it as an Earldom on his half-brother Odo, Bishop of Bayeux soon after the Conquest, and in 1321, King Edward II created his half-brother Edmund *of Woodstock,* the youngest son of King Edward I, Earl of Kent. The title descended to his heirs until 1408 when it became extinct. It was re-created in favour of William Neville in 1461 and of Edmund Grey in 1465, remaining with the Greys until 1740, its last holder being created Marquess of Kent in 1706 and Duke of Kent in 1710. It reappeared as a Royal title in 1799 when King George III created his fourth son Prince Edward, Duke of Kent and Strathearn. The Duke, who was the father of Queen Victoria, died in 1820, and in 1866 the Queen conferred the title of Kent as an Earldom on her second son, the Duke of Edinburgh, in conjunction with the Earldom of Ulster. The revived title became extinct on his death in 1900, and was re-created as a Dukedom in favour of HRH The Prince George, fourth son of HM King George V, 12 October 1934.

5 *Duke of Edinburgh*

In 1726, Frederick Louis, eldest son of George, Prince of Wales (afterwards King George II) was created Duke of Edinburgh (spelt Edenburgh in the patent). He was subsequently created Prince of Wales in 1729 and died during his father's lifetime in 1751, leaving a son and successor, George, Prince of Wales, 2nd Duke of Edinburgh, etc, who ascended the throne as King George III in 1760, when the Dukedom of Edinburgh merged in the Crown. Four years later the King created his brother Prince William Henry, Duke of Gloucester and Edinburgh and Earl of Connaught. This creation became extinct in 1834. In 1866, Queen Victoria created her second son Prince Alfred, Duke of Edinburgh, but the title again became extinct on his death in 1900 and remained unappropriated until conferred on Lieutenant Sir Philip Mountbatten, KG, RN, on the day of his marriage to HM Queen Elizabeth II (then HRH The Princess Elizabeth) 20 November 1947.

6 *Other Royal Dukedoms*

Another Dukedom which has been used exclusively as a Royal title is that of Clarence (derived from the honour of Clare in Suffolk) which was first conferred on Lionel *of Antwerp,* the third son of King Edward III, by his father on 13 November 1362. He died without male issue in 1368 and the title was next conferred in 1412 on Thomas, the second son of King Henry IV, who died in 1421. The next holder (created 1461) was the unfortunate George, Duke of Clarence, brother of King Edward IV, who was attainted and killed in 1478. It was not conferred again until 1789, when Prince William Henry, third son of King George III, was created Duke of Clarence and St Andrews. He succeeded to the Throne as King William IV in 1830 when his peerage honours merged in the Crown. In 1890, Queen Victoria created her grandson Prince Albert Victor, the eldest son of the Prince of Wales, Duke of Clarence and Avondale. He died unmarried in 1892 and the title has not been revived since. It may be regarded as an unlucky one as all the holders, with the exception of King William IV, have died young or by violence.

Other Royal Dukedoms have been those of Albany (originally Scottish, often created in conjunction with the Dukedom of York, and now a suspended peerage —*see* BURKE'S *Peerage,* 1953 *Edn*); Cambridge (now in use as a Marquessate); Connaught (*see p* 298); Cumberland (a suspended peerage); Kendal (used for two of the infant sons of King James II); and Sussex (*see p* 291). Of these, the last is the one most likely to be revived, perhaps in favour of HRH The Prince Edward in due course.

A special mention should be made of Lancaster. Lancaster was first conferred as an Earldom on Edmund *Crouchback,* the youngest son of King Henry III in 1267. The 4th Earl was created a Duke in 1351 and died without male issue in 1361. The castle and honour of Lancaster passed to his son-in-law John *of Gaunt,* who was created Duke of Lancaster the following year. When the latter's son succeeded as King Henry IV in 1399 the Dukedom merged in the crown, to be re-created two months later in favour of the King's son and heir Henry. He succeeded his father as King Henry V in 1413 and from that date the Dukedom has never been separated from the crown. In Lancashire the loyal toast is "The Queen, Duke (*sic*) of Lancaster". It is of passing interest to note that Mrs Ryves claimed to have been created Duchess of Lancaster by George III (*see footnote on p* 210).

7 *The Princess Royal*

The title of Princess Royal is only borne by the eldest daughter of a sovereign and is borne for life so that the eldest daughter of a reigning sovereign may not bear it during the lifetime of the eldest daughter of a preceding sovereign. The title is not created but granted by Royal Declaration and the two last holders were declared Princess Royal following the deaths of the previous holders of the title. Only six Princesses have borne the title:

(a) The Princess Mary (afterwards Princess of Orange), eldest daughter of King Charles I, who died in 1660 and is styled Princess Royal in the burial registers of Westminster Abbey, probably in imitation of the usage of the French Court where the eldest daughter of the King was styled *Madame Royale.*

(b) The Princess Anne (afterwards Princess of Orange), eldest daughter of King George II, appears to have been styled Princess Royal on her father's accession 1727, armorial bearings being conferred upon her in that style by Royal Warrant dated 30 August 1727. She died in 1759.

(c) The Princess Charlotte (afterwards Queen of Württemberg), eldest daughter of King George III, granted the style of Princess Royal 22 June 1789. She died in 1828.

(d) The Princess Victoria (afterwards German Empress and Queen of Prussia), eldest daughter of Queen Victoria, granted the style of Princess Royal 19 January 1841 (at the age of two months). She died in 1901.

(e) The Princess Louise (Duchess of Fife), eldest daughter of King Edward VII, declared Princess Royal 9 November 1905. She died 4 January 1931.

(f) The Princess Mary (Countess of Harewood), only daughter of King George V, declared Princess Royal 1 January 1932.

Whether the title will be revived in the near future for HRH The Princess Anne is a matter for speculation.

APPENDIX D

The Relationships between the Reigning Sovereigns of Europe

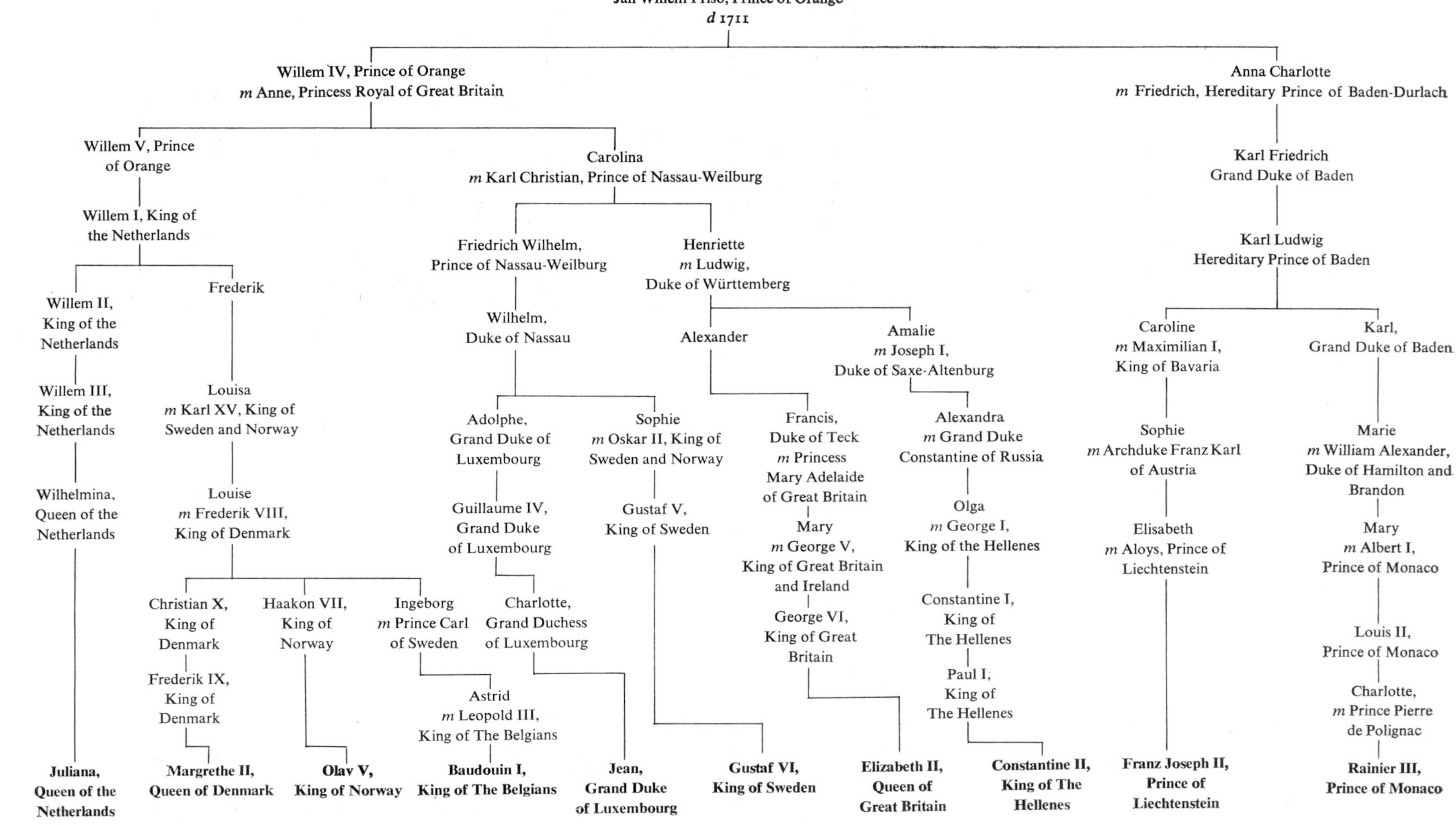

APPENDIX E

The Kings in Shakespeare

'There's such divinity doth hedge a king,
That treason can but peep to what it would.'
Hamlet IV, v.

THE DEPUTY ELECTED

Not all the water in the rough rude sea
Can wash the balm from an anointed King;
The breath of worldly men cannot depose
The deputy elected by the Lord.
For every man that Bolingbroke hath press'd
To lift shrewd steel against our golden crown,
God for his Richard hath in heavenly pay
A glorious angel: then, if angels fight,
Weak men must fall, for heaven still guards the right.
King Richard II, III, ii.

UPON THE KING!

Upon the king! let us our lives, our souls,
Our debts, our careful wives,
Our children, and our sins lay on the king!
We must bear all. O hard condition!
Twin-born with greatness, subject to the breath
Of every fool, whose sense no more can feel
But his own wringing. What infinite heart's ease
Must kings neglect that private men enjoy!

And what have kings that privates have not too,
Save ceremony, save general ceremony,
And what art thou, thou idle ceremony?
What kind of god are thou, that suffer'st more
Of mortal griefs than do thy worshippers?
What are thy rents? what are thy comings-in?
O ceremony! show me but thy worth:
What is thy soul of adoration?
Art thou aught else but place, degree, and form,
Creating awe and fear in other men?

'Tis not the balm, the sceptre and the ball,
The sword, the mace, the crown imperial,
The intertissued robe of gold and pearl,
The farced title running 'fore the king,
The throne he sits on, nor the tide of pomp
That beats upon the high shore of this world,
No, not all these, thrice-gorgeous ceremony,
Not all these, laid in bed majestical,
Can sleep so soundly as the wretched slave,
Who with a body fill'd and vacant mind
Gets him to rest, cramm'd with distressful bread;
Never sees horrid night, the child of hell,
But, like a lackey, from the rise to set
Sweats in the eye of Phoebus, and all night
Sleeps in Elysium; next day after dawn,
Doth rise and help Hyperion to his horse,
And follows so the ever-running year
With profitable labour to his grave:
And, but for ceremony, such a wretch,
Winding up days with toil and nights with sleep,
Had the fore-hand and vantage of a king.
King Henry V, IV, i.

YOUNG HARRY

I saw young Harry, with his beaver on,
His cushes on his thighs, gallantly arm'd,
Rise from the ground like feather'd Mercury,
And vaulted with such ease into his seat,
As if an angel dropp'd down from the clouds,
To turn and wind a fiery Pegasus
And witch the world with noble horsemanship.
King Henry IV, Part I, IV, i.

WHAT MUST THE KING DO NOW?

What must the king do now? Must he submit?
The king shall do it: must he be depos'd?
The king shall be contented: must he lose
The name of king? o' God's name, let it go:
I'll give my jewels for a set of beads,
My georgeous palace for a hermitage,
My gay apparel for an almsman's gown,
My figur'd goblets for a dish of wood,
My sceptre for a palmer's walking-staff,
My subjects for a pair of carved saints,
And my large kingdom for a little grave,
A little grave, an obscure grave;
Or I'll be buried in the king's highway,
Some way of common trade, where subjects' feet
May hourly trample on their sovereign's head;
For on my heart they tread now whilst I live;
And buried once, why not upon my head?
King Richard II, III, iii.

NOW SITS EXPECTATION

Now all the youth of England are on fire,
And silken dalliance in the wardrobe lies;
Now thrive the armourers, and honour's thought
Reigns solely in the breast of every man:
They sell the pasture now to buy the horse,
Following the mirror of all Christian kings,
With winged heels, as English Mercuries.
For now sits Expectation in the air
And hides a sword from hilts unto the point
With crowns imperial, crowns and coronets,
Promis'd to Harry and his followers.
King Henry V, II, Chorus.

BIRDS I' THE CAGE

Come, let's away to prison;
We two alone will sing like bird's i' the cage:
When thou dost ask me blessing, I'll kneel down,
And ask of thee forgiveness: so we'll live,
And pray, and sing, and tell old tales, and laugh

At gilded butterflies, and hear poor rogues
Talk of court news; and we'll talk with them too,
Who loses and who wins; who's in, who's out;
And take upon's the mystery of things,
As if we were God's spies: and we'll wear out,
In a wall'd prison, packs and sects of great ones
That ebb and flow by the moon.

King Lear, V, iii.

ACTION OF THE TIGER

Once more unto the breach, dear friends, once more;
Or close the wall up with our English dead!
In peace there's nothing so becomes a man
As modest stillness and humility:
But when the blast of war blows in our ears,
Then imitate the action of the tiger;
Stiffen the sinews, summon up the blood,
Disguise fair nature with hard-favour'd rage;
Then lend the eye a terrible aspect . . .
On, on, you noblest English!
Whose blood is fet from fathers of war-proof;
Fathers that like so many Alexanders,
Have in these parts from morn till even fought,
And sheath'd their sword for lack of argument.

And you, good yeomen,
Whose limbs were made in England, show us here
The mettle of your pasture.

King Henry V, III, i.

THE HOLLOW CROWN

For God's sake, let us sit upon the ground
And tell sad stories of the death of kings:
How some have been depos'd, some slain in war,
Some haunted by the ghosts they have depos'd,
Some poison'd by their wives, some sleeping kill'd;
All murder'd: for within the hollow crown
That rounds the mortal temples of a king
Keeps Death his court, and there the antick sits,
Scoffing his state and grinning at his pomp;
Allowing him a breath, a little scene,
To monarchize, be fear'd, and kill with looks,
Infusing him with self and vain conceit
As if this flesh which walls about our life
Were brass impregnable; and humour'd thus
Comes at the last, and with a little pin
Bores through his castle wall, and farewell king!
Cover your heads, and mock not flesh and blood
With solemn reverence: throw away respect,
Tradition, form, and ceremonious duty,
For you have but mistook me all this while:
I live with bread like you, feel want
Taste grief, need friends: subjected thus,
How can you say to me I am a king?

King Richard II, III, ii.

TO PAINT THE LILY

Therefore, to be possess'd with double pomp,
To guard a title that was rich before,
To gild refined gold, to paint the lily,
To throw a perfume on the violet,
To smooth the ice, or add another hue
Unto the rainbow, or with taper-light
To seek the beauteous eye of heaven to garnish
Is wasteful and ridiculous excess.

King John, IV, ii.

MYSELF A TRAITOR

Give me the crown. Here, cousin, seize the crown;
Here cousin,
On this side my hand and on that side thine.
Now is this golden crown like a deep well
That owes two buckets filling one another;
The emptier ever dancing in the air,
The other down, unseen and full of water:
That bucket down and full of tears am I,
Drinking my griefs, whilst you mount up on high.

With mine own tears I wash away my balm,
With mine own hands I give away my crown.

Mine eyes are full of tears, I cannot see:
And yet salt water blinds them not so much

But they can see a sort of traitors here.
Nay, if I turn mine eyes upon myself,
I find myself a traitor with the rest;
For I have given here my soul's consent
To undeck the pompous body of a king;
Made glory base and sovereignty a slave,
Proud majesty a subject, state a peasant.

King Richard II, IV, i.

UNEASY LIES THE HEAD

O sleep! O gentle sleep!
Nature's soft nurse, how have I frighted thee,
That thou no more wilt weigh my eyelids down
And steep my senses in forgetfulness?
Why rather, sleep, liest thou in smoky cribs,
Upon uneasy pallets stretching thee,
And hush'd with buzzing night-flies to thy slumber,
Than in the perfum'd chambers of the great,
Under the canopies of costly state,
And lull'd with sound of sweetest melody?

Wilt thou upon the high and giddy mast
Seal up the ship-boy's eyes, and rock his brains
In cradle of the rude imperious surge,
And in the visitation of the winds,
Who take the ruffian billows by the top,
Curling their monstrous heads, and hanging them
With deaf'ning clamour in the slippery clouds,
That with the hurly death itself awakes?

Then, happy low, lie down!
Uneasy lies the head that wears a crown.

King Henry IV, Part II, III, i.

THE BLOOD OF ENGLISH

My Lord of Hereford here, whom you call king,
Is a foul traitor to proud Hereford's king;
And if you crown him, let me prophesy,
The blood of English shall manure the ground
And future ages groan for this foul act . . .
And in this seat of peace tumultuous wars
Shall kin with kin and kind with kind confound;
Disorder, horror, fear and mutiny
Shall here inhabit, and this land be call'd
The field of Golgotha and dead men's skulls.
O! if you rear this house against this house,
It will the woefullest division prove
That ever fell upon this cursed earth.

King Richard II, IV, i.

CROOK'D WAYS

God knows, my son,
By what by-paths and indirect crook'd ways
I met this crown; and I myself know well
How troublesome it sat upon my head:
To thee it shall descend with better quiet,
Better opinion, better confirmation;
For all the soil of the achievement goes
With me into the earth.

King Henry IV, Part II, IV, v.

METHINKS IT WERE A HAPPY LIFE

O God! methinks it were a happy life,
To be no better than a homely swain;
To sit upon a hill, as I do now,
To carve out dials quaintly, point to point,
Thereby to see the minutes how they run,
How many make the hour full complete;
How many hours bring about the day;

How many days will finish up the year;
How many years a mortal man may live.
When this is known, then to divide the times:
So many hours must I tend my flock;
So many hours must I take my rest;
So many hours must I contemplate;
So many hours must I sport myself;
So many days my ewes have been with young;
So many weeks ere the poor fools will ean;
So many years ere I shall shear the fleece:
So minutes, hours, days, months, and years,
Pass'd over to the end they were created,
Would bring white hairs unto a quiet grave.

Ah! what a life were this! how sweet! how lovely!
Gives not the hawthorn bush a sweeter shade
To shepherds, looking on their silly sheep,
Than doth a rich embroider'd canopy
To kings, that fear their subjects' treachery?

King Henry VI, Part III, II, v.

I KNOW THEE NOT, OLD MAN

I know thee not, old man: fall to thy prayers;
How ill white hairs become a fool and jester!
I have long dream'd of such a kind of man,
So surfeit-swell'd, so old, and so profane . . .
Make less thy body hence, and more thy grace;
Leave gormandising; know the grave doth gape
For thee thrice wider than for other men.
Reply not to me with a fool-born jest:
Presume not that I am the thing I was;
so shall the world perceive
That I have turn'd away my former self;
So will I those that kept me company.

King Henry IV, Part II, V, v.

HAVE MERCY, JESU!

Give me another horse! bind up my wounds!
Have mercy, Jesu! Soft! I did but dream.
O coward conscience, how dost thou afflict me!

My conscience hath a thousand several tongues,
And every tongue brings in a several tale,
And every tale condemns me for a villain.
Perjury, perjury, in the high'st degree:
Murder, stern murder, in the dir'st degree;
All several sins, all us'd in each degree,
Throng to the bar, crying all, 'Guilty! guilty!'
I shall despair. There is no creature loves me;
And if I die, no soul will pity me:
Nay, wherefore should they, since that I myself
Find in myself no pity to myself?

King Richard III, V, iii.

TOMORROW AND TOMORROW AND TOMORROW

SEYTON:
The queen, my lord, is dead.
MACBETH:
She should have died hereafter;
There would have been a time for such a word.
Tomorrow, and tomorrow, and tomorrow,
Creeps in this petty pace from day to day,
To the last syllable of recorded time;
And all our yesterdays have lighted fools
The way to dusty death. Out, out, brief candle!
Life's but a walking shadow, a poor player
That struts and frets his hour upon the stage,
And then is heard no more; it is a tale
Told by an idiot, full of sound and fury,
Signifying nothing.

Macbeth, V, v.

APPENDIX F

The List of Royal Warrant Holders

Compiled from the *London Gazette* of 31 December 1971. List of Tradesmen who hold Warrants of Appointment to The Queen, The Duke of Edinburgh, The late King George VI, Queen Elizabeth The Queen Mother, The late King George V, The late Queen Mary, and The late Duke of Windsor (when Prince of Wales), with authority to display their Arms but not to fly the Royal Standard, nor to use the word "Royal". Warrant of Appointment is denoted by the marks shown below:

Key to the Royal Warrants of Appointment

a To HM THE QUEEN (Privy Purse Department)
b To HM The late KING GEORGE VI (Privy Purse Department)
c To HM The late KING GEORGE V (Privy Purse Department)
d To HM THE QUEEN (Master of the Household's Department)
e To HM The late KING GEORGE VI (Master of the Household's Department)
f To HM The late KING GEORGE V (Master of the Household's Department)
g To HM THE QUEEN (Lord Chamberlain's Office)
h To HM The late KING GEORGE VI (Lord Chamberlain's Office)
i To HM The late KING GEORGE V (Lord Chamberlain's Office)
j To HM The late QUEEN MARY (Lord Chamberlain's Office)
k To HM THE QUEEN (Royal Mews Department)
l To HM The late KING GEORGE V (Royal Mews Department)
m To HM QUEEN ELIZABETH THE QUEEN MOTHER
n To HRH THE DUKE OF EDINBURGH
o To HRH The late DUKE OF WINDSOR (when PRINCE OF WALES)

m Ackerman's Chocolates Ltd., London. Confectioners.
g Addo Ltd., Hatfield. Suppliers of Business Machines.
h Agnew, Thomas and Sons Ltd., London. Fine Art Publishers.
d Airwick Ltd., Hitchin. Manufacturers of Airwick.

a m Allan, James & Son, Ltd., Edinburgh. Boot and Shoemakers.
a Allen and Neale (Chemists) Ltd., King's Lynn. Chemists.
a Allflatt, Chas. D., Ltd., King's Lynn. Building Contractors.
d Allied Breweries (UK) Ltd., Burton on Trent. Brewers of Ale and Lager.
a Allis-Chalmers Great Britain Ltd., Essendine, Stamford. Manufacturers of Agricultural Machinery.
a Alvan Branch Development Co. Ltd., Malmesbury. Suppliers of Grain Driers

n Alvis Ltd., Coventry. Automobile Engineers.
a Amies, Hardy, Ltd., London. Dress-makers.
j Amor, Albert, Ltd., London. Fine Art Dealers.
a n Anderson, William & Sons, Ltd., Edinburgh. Tailors and Kiltmakers.
d Angostura Bitters (Dr J. G. B. Siegert & Sons) Ltd., Trinidad. Manufacturers of Angostura Automatic Bitters.
n Ansafone Ltd., London. Manufacturers and Distributors of Telephone Answering Machines.
k n Anstee & Co. Ltd., London. Forage Merchants.

m Aquascutum, Ltd., London. Makers of Weatherproof Garments.

a Archibald, James L. & Sons Ltd., Aberdeen. Cabinetmakers and Upholsterers.

d Ardath Tobacco Co. Ltd., London. Suppliers of Cigarettes.

BY APPOINTMENT TO HER MAJESTY THE QUEEN
SUPPLIERS OF CIGARETTES ARDATH TOBACCO CO. LTD.
PICCADILLY LONDON

d m Arden, Elizabeth, Ltd., London. Suppliers of Cosmetics.

a m Army & Navy Stores, Ltd., London. Suppliers of Household and Fancy Goods.

Army & Navy Stores Ltd
Victoria Street. London. SW1E 6QX
Tel: 01-834 1234

Army & Navy Stores (Bromley) Ltd
High Street. Bromley. Kent.
Tel: 01-460 9991

BY APPOINTMENT
TO H.M. THE QUEEN
SUPPLIERS OF HOUSEHOLD
AND FANCY GOODS

BY APPOINTMENT
TO H.M. QUEEN ELIZABETH
THE QUEEN MOTHER
SUPPLIERS OF HOUSEHOLD
AND FANCY GOODS

a Ashton and Mitchell Ltd., London. Theatre and Concert Ticket Agents.

a Ashwell and Nesbit, Ltd., Leicester. Heating, Ventilating and Stoker Engineers.

a m Asprey and Co. Ltd., London. Goldsmiths, Silversmiths and Jewellers.

By Appointment to Her Majesty the Queen Goldsmiths, Silversmiths & Jewellers Asprey & Company Ltd London

Asprey

By appointment to Her Majesty the Queen Goldsmiths, Silversmiths & Jewellers Asprey & Company Ltd London

GOLDSMITHS
SILVERSMITHS & JEWELLERS
165/169 New Bond Street, London W1Y 0AR
T.N. 01-493 6767

d Associated Fisheries and Foods Ltd., London. Fishmongers.

a Associated Portland Cement Manufacturers Ltd., The. London. Cement Manufacturers.

d Aylesbury Mushrooms Ltd., Black Bourton, nr Oxford. Purveyors of Mushrooms.

d j Baily, John & Son (Poulterers) Ltd., London. Purveyors of Poultry and Game.

e Baker, J. W. (China and Glass), Aberdeen. China and Glass Merchants.

a Bamfords, Ltd., Uttoxeter. Manufacturers of Farm Machinery and Engines.

n Barbour, J. & Sons, Ltd., South Shields. Manufacturers of Waterproof and Protective Clothing.

a Barclay, Ross & Hutchison Ltd., Aberdeen. Agricultural Engineers.

a Barkers & Lee Smith Ltd., Lincoln. Manufacturers and Suppliers of Animal Feeding Stuffs.

a Barrow Hepburn (Luggage & Equipment) Ltd., London. Manufacturers of Royal Maundy Purses.

BY APPOINTMENT TO HER MAJESTY THE QUEEN
MANUFACTURERS OF ROYAL MAUNDY PURSES
BARROW HEPBURN (LUGGAGE & EQUIPMENT) LTD.
LONDON SW8 4UZ

Barrow Hepburn Equipment Limited
Stewarts Road, S.W.8.
Tel: 01-622 9900 Telex 918741

Manufacturers:–
Industrial Safety Equipment,
Leather & Canvas Goods
to Industry.

d Bass Production Ltd., Burton on Trent. Brewers.

j Batsford, B. T., Ltd., London. Booksellers and Publishers.

d Baxter, G. G., Ltd., London. Suppliers of Pork Sausages.

By Appointment
to H.M. The Queen
Suppliers of
Pork Sausages

G. G. BAXTER LTD.
Suppliers of
Pork Sausages
52, 53, 54 & 56 Minories
E.C.3
T.N. 01-488 4351
Also at Sarre, Thanet
T.N. St. Nicholas at Wade 601/7

d m Baxter, James, & Son. Morecambe Purveyors of Potted Shrimps.

d m Baxter, W. A. & Sons, Ltd., Fochabers, Scotland. Purveyors of Scottish Specialities.

j Bayntun, George, Bath, Bookseller.

a Beaufort (Air-Sea) Equipment Ltd., Birkenhead. Suppliers of Life-Saving Equipment.

d Beecham Products, Brentford. Suppliers of Lucozade.

a Beeston Boiler Co. Ltd., Nottingham. Manufacturers of Cast Iron Sectional Boilers.

f Begg, John, Limited, Glasgow. Whisky Distillers.

n Beken of Cowes Ltd., Cowes, IoW. Marine Photographers.

g Bell, Lionel R., Streatham. Art Photographer.

a Belling & Co., Ltd., Enfield. Manufacturers of Electrical Appliances.

d Bendicks (Mayfair), Ltd., Winchester. Manufacturers of Chocolates.

d Bennett Opie & Moore, Ltd., Stanstead Abbots. Suppliers of Eggs.

a Bennett, R. S. & Co., Ltd., Downham Market. Suppliers of Argricultural Machinery and Farm Equipment.

d Benoist, V., Ltd., London. Purveyors of Table Delicacies.

b Benson and Clegg, Ltd., London. Tailors.

d Benson & Hedges Ltd., London. Tobacconists.

a Bentall, E. H. & Co. Ltd., Maldon. Manufacturers of Agricultural Provender Equipment.

a Bentley, Joseph, Ltd., Barrow on Humber. Suppliers of Horticultural Chemicals.

d Beresford & Hicks, Ltd., London. Upholsterers & Suppliers of Furnishing Materials.

d Berkel & Parnall, Ltd., Ponder's End. Manufacturers of Slicing Machines.

d Berry Bros. & Rudd, Ltd., London. Wine and Spirit Merchants.

a Bibby, J. Agriculture Ltd., Liverpool. Manufacturers of Animal Feeding Stuffs.

a Billings & Edmonds, Ltd., London. Tailors and Outfitters.

a Binns, Ltd., Edinburgh. House Furnishers.

d m Black & Edgington Ltd., Sidcup, Tent and Flag Makers.

e Block, Grey & Block Ltd., London. Wine Merchants.

a BOCM Silcock, Ltd., Basingstoke. Suppliers of Cattle Foods.

a Boddy, W. J. & Son, Ltd., Norwich. Suppliers of Dairy Equipment.

a Bond & Lacey, Ltd., Norwich. Bitumen Roofing Contractors.

d Booth's Distilleries Ltd., London. Gin Distillers.

a Boots Co. Ltd., The, Nottingham. Manufacturing Chemists.

a Boots Farm Sales Ltd., Nottingham. Suppliers of Horticultural and Agricultural Preparations.

a Boots The Chemists, Ltd., Nottingham. Chemists.

d Borelli, Charles & Sons Ltd., Farnham, Clock Makers.

g Bourlet, James & Sons, Ltd., London. Packers of Works of Art.

e Bovril, Ltd., Enfield. Suppliers of Bovril.

a Bowater Packaging, Ltd., London. Manufacturers of Packaging Materials.

a Bowker, A. & J., Ipswich. Suppliers of Animal Feeding Stuffs.

o Bowyers (Wiltshire) Ltd., Trowbridge Bacon Curers.

m Brannam, C. H., Ltd., Barnstaple. Pottery Makers.

d Brickwoods Ltd., Portsmouth. Brewers.

a Brintons, Ltd., Kidderminster. Carpet Manufacturers.

n British Equipment Co., Ltd., London. Suppliers of Office Machinery.

m British Legion Disabled Men's Industries, Ltd., Maidstone. Makers of Leather and Fancy Goods.

a British Legion Poppy Factory Ltd., Richmond, Surrey. British Legion Poppy Manufacturers & Suppliers of Rosettes.

k British Leyland (Austin-Morris) Ltd., Birmingham. Motor Car Manufacturers.

k British Nova Works Ltd., Southall, Middx. Manufacturers of Floor Maintenance Products and Waxes.

n British Olivetti Ltd., London. Office Equipment Manufacturers.

a British Overhead Irrigation Ltd., Shepperton. Manufacturers of Irrigation Equipment.

d j m Broadwood, John & Sons, Ltd., London. Pianoforte Manufacturers & Tuners.

d m Bronnley, H. & Co. Ltd., London. Toilet Soap Makers.

d Brook Bros. and Dean Ltd., London. Suppliers of Furnishing Trimming.

k Brooks Vitovia Ltd., Minningtree. Manufacturers of Horse Nuts.

m Brooks, W., & Son (Brook-Jones Ltd.), London. Purveyors of Fruit and Quick Frosted Foods.

a Brown, David Tractors, Ltd., Meltham. Manufacturers of Agricultural Machinery.

a Brown, William & Co. (Ipswich) Ltd., Ipswich. Timber Product Manufacturers.

d Bryant & May Ltd., London. Match Manufacturers.

d Buchanan, James & Co., Ltd., London. Scotch Whisky Distillers.

a n Buckley, Anthony Ltd., London. Photographers.

m Budgen & Company, Uxbridge. Grocers.

k m Bullens London Ltd., Borehamwood. Road Transport Contractors.

d Bulmer, H. P., Ltd., Hereford. Cider Makers.

a Bunning, Harry H., Ltd., King's Lynn. Suppliers of Seed Potatoes.

a m Burberrys Ltd., London. Weatherproofers.

d Burgess, John & Son, Ltd., London. Manufacturers of Potatoes and Creamed Horseradish.

b Burlingham, S. S., Ltd., King's Lynn. Clockmakers.

d m Burton, Montague, Ltd., Leeds/London. Tailors.

d Burton Son & Sanders, Ltd., Ipswich. Manufacturers of Fondant.

d Bury & Masco Industries Ltd., Bury. Felt and Carpet Manufacturers.

d m Cadbury Ltd., Bournville, Birmingham. Cocoa and Chocolate Manufacturers.

m Caithness Glass Ltd., Wick, Caithness. Glassmaker.

d Caldwell Brothers, Edinburgh. Printers.

a m Caleys (Cole Bros. Ltd.), Windsor, Berks. Suppliers of Household and Fancy Goods and Millinery.

a m Calman Links (Trading) Ltd., London. Furriers.

a Calor Gas, Ltd., Slough. Suppliers of Liquefied Petroleum Gas.

o Campbell and Co., Beauly. Suppliers of Highland Tweeds.

d Campbell Brothers (Edinburgh), Ltd., Purveyors of Meat and Poultry.

d Campbell, George & Sons., Edinburgh. Suppliers of Fish and Poultry.

a Camper & Nicholsons, Ltd., Southampton. Yacht Builders.

k Carawagon International, Ltd., Sunbury-on-Thames. Manufacturers of Specialized Trailers.

a Cargill, D. W. H. (Potatoes), Ltd., Benholm, Montrose. Suppliers of Seed Potatoes.

d Carlin, T. B., Ltd., London. Cigar Merchants.

d Carlsberg Distributors Ltd., London. Suppliers of Lager Beer.

k Carpenter, J. W., Ltd., Thame. Suppliers of Cleaning Stores.

d Carpet Manufacturing Company Ltd., The, Kidderminster. Carpet Manufacturers.

a m Carrington & Co. Ltd., London. Silversmiths and Jewellers.

d m Carr's of Carlisle Ltd., Carlisle. Biscuit Manufacturers.

d Cartem Engineering Ltd., Maidstone. Manufacturers of Sack Holders.

m Carters (J. & A.), Ltd., Westbury, Wilts. Invalid Furniture Manufacturers.

a m Carters Tested Seeds Ltd., London. Seedsmen.

a m Cartier Ltd., London. Jewellers and Goldsmiths.
a Cash, J. & J., Ltd., Coventry. Manufacturers of Woven Name Tapes.
a Cassie, William C., Aberdeen. Pianoforte Tuner.
k m Castrol, Ltd., London. Purveyors of Motor Lubricants.
n Central Audio Ltd., London. Suppliers of Sound Recording Equipment.
d Cerebos Limited, London. Suppliers of Table Salt and Pepper.
m Chad Valley Company, Ltd., Birmingham. Toymakers.
a Chafer, J. W., Ltd., Doncaster. Suppliers of Agricultural Chemicals.
b Chalmers, Robert, Oban. Suppliers of Highland Dress Accessories.
e Champagne Ayala, Ay-Champagne, Marne. Purveyors of Champagne.
d Champagne J. Bollinger, S.A., Ay-Champagne. Purveyors of Champagne.
d Champagne Heidsieck & Co., Monopole, S.A., Reims. Purveyors of Champagne.
d Champagne Lanson Pere et Fils., Reims. Purveyors of Champagne.
d Champagne Louis Roederer, Reims. Purveyors of Champagne.
e Champagne Perrier-Jouet, Epernay. Purveyors of Champagne.
k m Champion Sparking Plug Co., Ltd., Feltham. Suppliers of Sparking Plugs.
a Chandler, Fredk. J. (Saddler) Ltd., Marlborough. Saddlers.
d Charbonnel et Walker Ltd., London. Chocolate Manufacturers.
m Charles (1820), Ltd., London. Fishmongers.
a Charrington, Gardner, Locket (London) Ltd., London. Coal Merchants and Suppliers of Fuel Oil.
d m Chivas Bros. Ltd., Aberdeen. Purveyors of Provisions.
d m Chivers & Sons, Ltd., Cambridge. Purveyors of Jams, Jellies, English Canned Fruits, Vegetables, and Christmas Puddings.
d Christopher & Co., Ltd., London. Wine Merchants.
a Chubb & Sons, Lock and Safe Co. Ltd,. London. Patent Lock and Safe Makers.

a Clark, A. A. Ltd., Windsor. Automobile Engineers.
k Clarke, W., Eton. Saddler.
g Classic Restoration & Design, Ltd., London. Architectural Restorers.
d Coca-Cola Southern Bottlers, Ltd., Isleworth. Suppliers of Soft Drinks.
a Coe, C. & C. (Bircham) Ltd., Bircham, King's Lynn. Haulage Contractors.

a m Collingwood of Conduit Street Ltd., London. Jewellers and Silversmiths.
d Cognac Hine, S. A. Jarnac. Suppliers of Cognac.
a Cole & Son (Wallpapers) Ltd., London. Suppliers of Wallpapers.
a Comb Pluckers, Ltd., Wimbourne. Manufacturers of Poultry Plucking Machinery.
g Compton, J., Sons & Webb, Ltd., London. Uniform Makers.
g j Cooper, A. C. Ltd., London. Fine Art Photographers.
a Cooper Crowther, Ltd., Reading. Manufacturers of Dairy Cleansers.
d Cooper, Frank, Ltd., Oxford. Marmalade Manufacturers.
a Cooper, McDougall & Robertson, Ltd., Berkhamsted. Suppliers of Sheep and Cattle Dips and Veterinary Preparations.
d Cope & Timmins Ltd., London. Brass Finishers and Spring Makers.
d Corney & Barrow, Ltd., London. Wine Merchants.
a Cory Bros. (Hospital Contracts Co.) Ltd., London. Suppliers of Surgical Equipment.
d County Window Cleaning & Steam Carpet Beating Co., The, Reading, Window Cleaners.
e Courvoisier, Ltd., Jarnac. Purveyors of Cognac Brandy.
a Cox, Harold, Windsor. Jeweller.
d C.P.C. (United Kingdom), Ltd., Esher. Manufacturers of Corn Oil and Cornflower.
b Crabtree, J. A. & Co. Ltd., Walsall. Suppliers of Lighting Switches.
a Craig, James W., Drumoak. Manufacturers of Agricultural Machinery.
a Crane, Ltd., London. Suppliers of Heating Materials.
d Crawford, William & Sons, Ltd., Edinburgh. Biscuit Manufacturers.
a Crendon Concrete Co., Ltd. Aylesbury. Suppliers of Reinforced Concrete Buildings.
a Crompton Parkinson Ltd., London. Manufacturers of Electric Lamps.
k n Cross, G. R. & Son Ltd., Henley-on-Thames. Forage Merchants.
d m Crosse & Blackwell Ltd., Croydon. Purveyors of Preserved Provisions.
d Cullen, W. H., Dorking. Purveyors of Groceries and Provisions.
a Cyclax Ltd., London. Suppliers of Beauty Preparations.
m Daimler, Co. Ltd., The, Coventry. Motor Car Manufacturers.
k Daimler Hire, Ltd., London. Motor Car Hirers.
a Dairy Supply Co. Ltd., London. Suppliers of Dairy Appliances.
a Dale, Frank H., Ltd., Leominster. Suppliers of Farm Buildings and Tubular Equipment.
a Danarm Ltd., Stroud. Manufacturers and Suppliers of Chain Saws.
a Darby (Nursery Stock) Ltd., Thetford. Suppliers of Soft Fruit Stocks.

d Darville & Sons, Ltd., Windsor. Grocers.

d m Davidson, W. S. & Sons, Ballater. Purveyors of Meat and Poultry.

a Dawber Williamson Ltd., Hull. Suppliers of Building Materials.

a n Day, Son and Hewitt, Ltd., London/Bradford. Manufacturers of Animal Medicines and Veterinary Products.

l Day and Martin, Great Dunmow. Boot Polish Manufacturers.

d m Debenham & Freebody, London. Linen Drapers.

a DeCleene, Eric T., Bishops Stortford. Seedsmen.

a Deere, John, Ltd., Nottingham. Suppliers of Agricultural Equipment.

j de Faye, F. G., Ltd., Jersey, CI, Perfumers.

a Deimel Fabric Co., London. Manufacturers of Dr Deimel Garments.

a Dennis Bros. Ltd., Guildford. Motor Mower Manufacturers.

a Dennison Manufacturing Co. Ltd., Watford. Suppliers of Gift Wrapping Material.

d j Dewar, John & Sons Ltd., Perth/London. Scotch Whisky Distillers.

b Dickson, Alex. and Sons Ltd., Belfast. Nurserymen and Seedsmen.

d Dictograph Telephones Ltd., London. Suppliers of Dictograph Telephones.

a Dilloway, P. W., Ltd., Southall, Agricultural Engineers.

m Dipré, D., & Son, London. Cutlery Servicers, Knifegrinders and Suppliers of Kitchen Equipment.

j Dixey, C. W. and Son, Ltd., London. Opticians.

a Dobbie & Co. Ltd., Edinburgh. Seedsmen and Nurserymen.

d Dobbins, J. T., Ltd., Manchester. Suppliers of Household Cleaning Materials.

a Dodman, Alfred & Co., Ltd., King's Lynn. Engineers.

a Domestic Electric Rentals Ltd., Feltham. Suppliers of Television Receivers.

d Donaldson, Andrew, Ltd., King's Lynn. Suppliers of Fish and Ice.

g Dorling & Co. (Epsom) Ltd., Epsom. Manufacturers of Lapel Badges.

a Dorman Smith Britmac Ltd., Preston. Manufacturers of Electrical Accessories.

n Douglas (Sales & Service) Ltd., Bristol. Suppliers of Vespa Scooters & Mopeds.

d Doulton Fine China Ltd., Stoke-on-Trent. Suppliers of China.

a Drake & Fletcher, Ltd., Maidstone. Manufacturers of Agricultural Spraying Machinery.

d Drew, Clark & Co. Ltd., London. Manufacturers of Ladders.

a Driscoll, Eastbourne. Tailors.

a Duncton Quarrying Co. Ltd., Storrington. Suppliers of Crushed Chalk.

a Dunhill, Alfred, Ltd., London. Suppliers of Smokers' Requisites.

k m Dunlop, Ltd., London. Manufacturers of Motor Car Tyres.

a Dynatron Radio Ltd., Maidenhead. Suppliers of Television & Radiogramophones.

d Dyson & Sons Ltd., Windsor. Clock Makers and Silversmiths.

d Early and Marriott, Charles (Witney) Ltd., Witney. Manufacturers of Blankets.

a Eastern Counties Farmers Ltd., Ipswich. Suppliers of Agricultural Products.

g m n Ede & Ravenscroft, Ltd., London. Robe Makers.

d Edinburgh & Dumfriesshire Dairy Co. Ltd., Edinburgh. Purveyors of Ice Cream, Milk and Eggs.

a Edmondson, R. C. Ltd., Fakenham. Suppliers of Agricultural Machinery.

k Edmunds, Captain L., Cholderton. Breeder of Cleveland Bay Horses.

k Electro-Chemical Research Laboratories, Ltd., Iver. Makers of "Mordax" Studs.

d j m Electrolux Ltd., London/Luton. Suppliers of Suction Cleaners, Floor Polishers and Refrigerators.

a Elliott, Thomas, Ltd., Hayes, Kent. Suppliers of Fertilisers and Peat

a Ellis & McHardy Ltd., Aberdeen. Coal and Oil Distributors.

i Ellis, Richard, Valletta, Malta, GC. Photographer.

g Ellison, Clifford, London. Picture Restorer.

a Elsoms (Spalding) Ltd., Spalding. Seedsmen.

a Emile et Cie (London) Ltd., London. Hairdressers.

m Emmetts Store, Peasenhall, Suffolk. Curers & Suppliers of Sweet Pickled Hams

a En-tout-Cas, Ltd., Leicester. Manufacturers of Tennis Courts.

d Essex Flour & Grain Company Ltd., London. Suppliers of Tinned Meats, Vegetables, Fruits and Cereals.

k Esso Petroleum Co. Ltd., London. Purveyors of Motor Spirit.

d Express Dairy Co. (London) Ltd., London. Dairy Suppliers.

a Express Lift Co. Ltd., Northampton. Manufacturers and Suppliers of Passenger Lifts.

n Fairey Marine Ltd., Hamble. Boat Builders.

a Farman & Son., Salhouse, Norwich. Reed Thatchers.

a Farmers & Growers Industries Ltd., Worthing. Horticultural Sundriesmen.

d Farris, Charles Ltd., Hounslow, Chandlers.

d m Fenn, W., London. Poulterer.

d Ferrari, S. & Sons (Soho), Ltd., London. Suppliers of Kitchen Equipment.

d Findlater Mackie Todd & Co. Ltd., London. Wine and Spirit Merchants.

d m Findus Ltd., Croydon. Suppliers of Frozen Foods.

a Fine Art Engravers Ltd., Godalming. Fine Art Printers.

g m Firmin & Sons, Ltd., London. Button Makers.

a Fisher & Sons Fakenham) Ltd., Fakenham. Building Contractors.

a Fisons Ltd., (Fertiliser Division) Felixstowe. Makers of Chemical Fertilizers.

d Fitch & Son, Ltd., London. Provision Merchants.

d Floris, J. Ltd., London. Perfumers.

m Floris, The House of, London. Patissier and Confectioner.

b Fodens, Ltd., Sandbach. Steam Tractor Manufacturers.

n Fonadek International Ltd., Birmingham Suppliers of Telephone Amplifiers.

a m Forces Help Society and Lord Roberts Workshops, The, London. Manufacturers of Fancy Goods and Furniture Makers.

k m Ford Motor Co. Ltd., Brentwood, Essex. Motor Vehicle Manufacturers.

d m Fortnum & Mason, Ltd., London. Grocers and Provision Merchants and Suppliers of Leather and Fancy Goods.

a Foss Electric (UK) Ltd., York. Suppliers of Milk Meters.

d m Foster & Co., John, Ltd., London. Suppliers of Furnishing Fabrics.

a Fountain & Ansell Ltd., Reading. Suppliers of Game Food.

k Francis, G. C., Barnet. Heraldic Artist.

d Fraser, H. S. Ltd., London. Furniture Manufacturers.

m Frederick, John, Ltd., London. Carpet Cleaners.

g Freeman, W. & Son, Ltd., London. Picture Restorers.

d Frigicold, Ltd., London. Manufacturers of Deep Freeze Packaging.

d m Frodsham Charles & Co. Ltd., London. Clock and Watch Makers.

d Furnishing Contracts Ltd., London. Suppliers of Furnishing Requisites.

a Gallyon & Sons, Ltd., King's Lynn. Cartridge Makers.

a Galt, James & Co. Ltd., Cheadle. Manufacturers and Suppliers of Educational Aids.

j Ganeshi, Lall, and Son, Agra, UP India. Jewellers and Embroiderers.

k Gardiner & Co., London. Suppliers of Protective Clothing.

a Garford, P., Ltd., Walpole St. Andrew. Suppliers of Fertilisers and Baled Peat.

g m Garrard & Co. Ltd., London. Jewellers and Silversmiths.

d m Garrow, Robert, Ltd., Aberdeen. Fishmongers.

a Gascoigne, Cush & Dent Ltd., Alresford. Milking Machine Manufacturers.

d Gaunt, J. R. & Son, Ltd., London. Ribbon Makers.

a Gaybird Ltd., Great Missenden. Suppliers of Stock Game.

d Gaymer, William & Son Ltd., Attleborough. Cyder Manufacturers.

a General Trading Co., London. Suppliers of Fancy Goods.

a Gibbs, J., Ltd., Feltham. Suppliers of Agricultural Machinery and Implements.

k Gidden, W. & H., Ltd., London. Saddlers.

k n Gieves Ltd., London. Livery/Naval Tailors and Outfitters.

a m Gilbert, D. & Son. Newmarket. Suppliers of Racing Colours/Saddlers and Harness Makers.

a Gilbertson and Page, Ltd., Hertford. Manufacturers of Dog and Game Foods.

a Gilliam & Co. Ltd., Purley. Swimming Pool Contractors.

a Gillman & Spencer Ltd., Bletchley. Manufacturers and Suppliers of Liquid Supplements.

b Girlings Ferro-Concrete Co., Ltd., Hounslow East. Suppliers of Ferro-Concrete Work.

k Glover, Webb & Liversidge, Ltd., London. Coachbuilders.

k Glyn Protective Clothing, Ltd., Manchester. Manufacturers of State and Livery Waterproofs.

d m Goddard J. & Sons, Ltd., Camberley. Manufacturers of Silver Polishes and Suppliers of Dry Clean.

d j m Goode, Thomas & Co. (London) Ltd., London. Suppliers of China and Glass.

d m Goodyear, Edward, London. Florist.

d Gordon, Luis, & Sons Ltd., London. Suppliers of Domecq Sherry.

a	Gourock Ropework Co. Ltd., Port Glasgow. Manufacturers of Agricultural Twine.
d m	Gramophone Co. Ltd., Hayes, Middlesex. Manufacturers of Records, Radio, Television & Electrical Household Apparatus.
n	Grant, Pat, Aberdeen. Hairdresser.
k	Gray, Chas. & Co. (Stamford) Ltd., Stamford, Lincs. Suppliers of Shoeing Iron and Farriers' Equipment.
d	Gray, James & Son, Ironmongers & Electricians Ltd., Edinburgh. Suppliers of Cleaning Materials etc.
a	Gray, J. W. & Son, Ltd., London. Lightning Conductor Specialists.
a	Grima, Andrew Ltd., London. Jewellers.
m	Grosvenor Electrical (Belgravia, London) Ltd., London. Electrical Contractors.
m	Haggart, P. & J., Ltd., Aberfeldy, Scotland. Tartan and Woollen Manufacturers.
d	Haig, John & Co., Ltd., Markinch. Purveyors of Scotch Whisky.
a	Hall, Alexander & Son (Builders) Ltd., Aberdeen. Building Contractors.
o	Hall Brothers, Ltd., Oxford. Tailors and Hosiers.
a	Hall, Leslie, Ltd., Cottingham. Suppliers of Animal Feeding Stuffs.
j m n	Hamblin, Theodore, Ltd., London. Opticians.
i	Hamblin, W. T. and Co., Windsor. Upholsterers.
f	Hamer, Edward and Co., Llanidloes, North Wales. Suppliers of Welsh Mutton.
d	Hamilton & Inches Ltd., Edinburgh. Clock Specialists.
a j	Hamley Brothers Ltd., London. Toy and Sports Merchants.
m	Hancocks and Co. (Jewellers) Ltd., London. Goldsmiths and Silversmiths.
e	Hankey, Bannister & Co., London. Wine Merchants.
a	Hardie, R. G. & Co., Glasgow. Bagpipe Makers.
a	Hardy Brothers, Ltd., Sydney. Silversmiths.
a m n	Hardy, John G. Ltd., London. Mercers of Woollen Cloth.
d	Harris, C. & T. (Calne) Ltd., Calne. Manufacturers of Bacon, Sausages and Pies.

m	Harris, D. R. & Co. Ltd., London. Chemists.
a	Harris, L. G. & Co. Ltd., Stoke Prior. Manufacturers of Painting and Decorating Brushes.
j	Harris, M. & Sons, London. Dealers in Antique Furniture and Works of Art.
d	Harris Plating Works Ltd., The, London. Metal Finishing Specialists.
g m n	Harrison & Sons Ltd., High Wycombe. Printers.
a	Harrison & Wilson, King's Lynn. Saddlers and Cover Makers.
d m n	Harrods, Ltd., London. Suppliers of Provisions and Household Goods, China, Glass and Fancy Goods and Outfitters.

a	Harrold, A. J. & Co. Ltd., London. Builders and Decorators.
a m	Hartnell, Norman, Ltd., London. Dressmakers.
d	Harvey, John & Sons Ltd., Bristol. Wine Merchants.

j m	Harvey, Nichols, and Co. Ltd., London. General Drapers.
a m n	Hatchards, London. Booksellers.
b	Hawes and Curtis Ltd., London. Shirt Makers and Hosiers.
n	Hawes & Curtis (Tailors) Ltd., London. Tailors.
d	Hawker, James & Co. Ltd., Plymouth. Purveyors of "Pedlar" Sloe Gin.
a	Hayters, Ltd., Bishop's Stortford. Manufacturers of Agricultural Machinery.

a	Haythornthwaite & Sons, Ltd., Burnley. Manufacturers of Grenfell Cloth.
d	Heal & Son Ltd., London. Upholsterers and Suppliers of Bedding.
a m n	Heaton, Wallace, London. Suppliers of Photographic Equipment.
a	Heatstore Ltd., Wigan. Manufacturers of Storage Radiators.
d	Heering, Peter F., Copenhagen. Purveyors of Cherry Heering.
e	Heidsieck, Charles S. A., Reims. Purveyors of Champagne.
d	Heinz, H. J., Co. Ltd., London. Purveyors of Heinz Products.
a	Henderson's, Ballater. Outfitters.
d m	Hicks (Covent Garden) Ltd., Richard., London. Purveyors of Fruit and Vegetables.
a	Hill Construction Co. (Engineers) Ltd., Southampton. Manufacturers and Suppliers of Steel Buildings.
d	Hill Thomson & Co. Ltd., Edinburgh. Scotch Whisky Distillers.

g Hill, William, & Son, and Norman & Beard, Ltd., London. Organ Builders.
m Hillier & Sons, Winchester, Hants. Nurserymen and Seedsmen.
m Hillman-Douglas Ltd., Dudley, Worcs. Manufacturers of Handbags.
n Hodgkinson, T., Ltd., London. Tiemakers.
g Holder, W. & Son, London. Picture Restorers.
n Holland & Holland Ltd., London. Rifle Makers.
a Hollins, William, & Co. Ltd., Somercotes. Manufacturers of Viyella and Clydella.

d Hooper Struve & Co. Ltd., Brentford. Mineral Water Manufacturers.
d m Hoover Ltd., Greenford. Suppliers of Vacuum Cleaners.
e Horlicks, Ltd., Brentford. Purveyors of Malted Milk.
d Horne Brothers Ltd., London. Livery Tailors.
a Horrockses Fashions, Ltd., London. Dressmakers.
a Houseman and Thompson, Ltd., Burnham, Bucks. Specialists in Water Treatments and Descalents.

a Howard Rotavator Co. Ltd., West Horndon. Manufacturers of Agricultural & Horticultural Equipment.
d H.P. Sauce Ltd., Birmingham. Manufacturers of H.P. Sauce.
a Humber Manures, Ltd., Hull. Fertiliser Manufacturers.
d m Huntley & Palmers Ltd., Reading. Biscuit and Cake Manufacturers.
a Hurst Gunson Cooper Taber Ltd. Witham, Essex. Seedsmen.
a Ian Proctor Metal Masts Ltd., Southampton. Suppliers of Metal Masts.
a I.C.C. Machines Ltd., Enfield. Manufacturers of Paper Shredding Machines.
d m Idris Ltd., Brentford/London. Manufacturers of Mineral Water and Fruit Beverages.
g Imperial Typewriter Co. Ltd., Leicester. Typewriter Manufacturers.
k Incorporated Association for Promoting the General Welfare of the Blind, The, London. Suppliers of Stable Mats, etc., and Renovators of Mattresses.
g Inglis, Francis C. & Son, Ltd., Edinburgh. Photographers.
d Inglis Green Laundry Co. Ltd., Edinburgh. Launderers.
a Ironside, M. L., Ballater. Chemist.
d Jackson, Robert & Co. Ltd., London. Grocers.
d m Jacob & Co. W. & R. (Liverpool) Ltd., Liverpool. Biscuit Manufacturers.
d Jaeggi, Leon & Sons Ltd., London. Suppliers of Catering Utensils & Equipment.
m Jaguar Cars, Ltd., Coventry. Motor Car Manufacturers.
a James and Son (Grain Merchants) Ltd., London. Suppliers of Animal Feeding Stuffs.
d Jamieson & Sons, William, Edinburgh. Suppliers of Fruit and Vegetables.
g Janitorial Services Ltd., London. Office Cleaning Contractors.
a m Jarrolds (Sloane Street), Ltd., London. Suppliers of Leather Goods.
n Jekmoth Home Stores Ltd., London. Manufacturers of Garment Bags and Wardrobe Accessories.
d Jenners, Princes Street, Edinburgh, Ltd., Edinburgh. Suppliers of Furnishing Materials.
k Jeyes Group Ltd., Thetford. Manufacturers of Disinfectants.
m Joel, Walter C., Ltd., Crawley, Sussex. Clock and Watch Makers.
a John, C., London. Supplier of Carpets.

n Johns & Pegg Ltd., London. Military Tailors.
a m Johnson Brothers, Stoke-on-Trent. Manufacturers of Ceramic Tableware.
a Johnson, Herbert (Bond Street) Ltd., London. Hatters.
d m Johnson Wax Ltd., Camberley, Surrey. Manufacturers of Wax Polishes, Cleaner and Hygiene Products.

a Jollye, Leonard F. (Brookmans Park), Ltd., Hatfield. Forage Merchant.
d m n Jones, Yarrell & Co. Ltd., London. Newsagents.
e Jones, Peter, London. Suppliers of Furnishings.
d Justerini & Brooks Ltd., London. Wine Merchants.
a n Kagan Textiles, Ltd., Elland, Yorkshire. Manufacturers and Suppliers of Gannex Products.
d m Keen, G. H. & S. Ltd., High Wycombe. Furnishers and Upholsterers.
d Kellogg Co. of Great Britain Ltd., Manchester. Purveyors of Cereals.
k n Kenning Car Mart Ltd., London. Motor Car Distributors.
d Kent, G. B. and Sons Ltd., London. Brush Makers.
a Kidd, Archie Ltd., Devizes. Manufacturers of Farm Machinery.

a Kildew Mothproofing Ltd., London. Permanent Mothproofers.

m King Brothers (Fuel Merchants) Ltd., Eton. Coal and Coke Merchants.

a King, John K. & Sons, Ltd., Coggeshall. Seedsmen.

n Kiwi Polish Co. Pty. Ltd., London. Shoe Polish Manufacturers.

d m Kleen-Way (Berkshire) Co. Binfield/Bracknell. Chimney Sweepers.

a Knapp, Drewett & Sons Ltd., Kingston on Thames. Printers.

a Knight, Peter (Beaconsfield) Ltd., Beaconsfield. Suppliers of Fancy Goods.

a Knight, Peter (Esher) Ltd., Esher. Suppliers of Fancy Goods.

d Knowles & Sons (Fruiterers) Ltd., Aberdeen. Purveyors of Fruit and Vegetables.

d Knowles, Roger (Chemists) Ltd., (Wood's Pharmacy) Windsor. Pharmaceutical Chemists.

a Kodak, Ltd., London. Manufacturers of Photographic Supplies.

d Krug, Vins, Fins de Champagne S.A. Reims. Purveyors of Champagne.

a Lambert, James & Sons Ltd., Snettisham. Suppliers of Building Materials.

a Langton, W. E., Coventry. Suppliers of Milking Machine Components.

d Lansing Bagnall Ltd., Basingstoke. Manufacturers of Industrial Trucks.

a Latham, James, Ltd., London. Wood Merchants.

a Launer, S. & Co. (London) Ltd., London. Manufacturers of Handbags.

c Lavender and Bateman Ltd., Cambridge. Roadstone Merchants.

a Lawrie, R. G. Ltd., Glasgow. Bagpipe Makers.

d Lea & Perrins Ltd., Worcester. Purveyors of Worcestershire Sauce.

d Leith, G. & Son. Ballater. Bakers and Confectioners.

m Lenygon & Morant, Ltd., London. Decorators.

d m Lever Brothers Ltd., London. Soap Makers.

a Lewis East Ltd. Leicester. Manufacturers of Stationery.

j Lewis, F. (Publishers) Ltd., Leigh-on-Sea. Booksellers and Publishers.

a Lewmar Marine, Ltd., Havant. Suppliers of Yacht Fittings and Blocks.

a Leyland Motors Ltd., Leyland. Motor Vehicle Manufacturers.

j m Liberty and Co. Ltd., London. Silk Mercers.

d m Lidstone, John. London. Butchers.

a m Lilliman and Cox, Ltd., London. Dry Cleaners.

a Lillywhites, Ltd., London. Outfitters.

k Lincoln Bennett & Co. Ltd., Stockport. Hat Makers.

a Lincolnshire Drainage Co. Ltd., Boston. Drainage Contractors.

a Liner Concrete Machinery Co. Ltd., The, Gateshead. Manufacturers of Concrete Block and Mixing Machinery.

a Linfield, A. G. Ltd., Pulborough. Suppliers of Horticultural Products.

n Linguaphone Institute Ltd., London. Publishers of Recorded Language Courses.

d Linoleum Manufacturing Co. Ltd., Staines. Manufacturers of Linoleum.

d Lister & Co. Ltd., Bradford. Manufacturers of Furnishing Fabrics.

a Lister, R. A. & Co. Ltd., Dursley, Glos. Manufacturers of Agricultural Machinery & Dairy Appliances.

k n Lobb, John, London. Bootmaker.

n Lock, James & Co., Ltd., London. Hatters.

a Lock, S., Ltd., London. Embroiderers.

a London Brick Co. Ltd., London. Brick Makers.

d London Essence Co. Ltd., The. London. Manufacturers of Cleaning Compound.

a Longmate, E. C. Ltd., Wisbech. Agricultural Spraying Contractors.

a Lowe, F. C. & Son, Ltd., Sittingbourne. Dog and Game Food Manufacturers.

k Lucas, Joseph, Ltd., London. Manufacturers of Electrical Equipment.

d Lyons Bakery Ltd., London. Manufacturers of Cakes.

d m Lyons, J. & Co. Ltd., London. Caterers.

b Macdonald, Archibald, Forres. Decorator.

d Mackay, Hugh & Co. Ltd., Durham. Manufacturers of Wilton Carpeting.

d Macfarlane, Lang & Co. Ltd., Glasgow. Biscuit Manufacturers.

d Mac Fisheries Ltd., Windsor. Fishmongers.

b Mackenzie & Moncur, Ltd., Edinburgh. Hothouse Builders.

d Macvitties Guest & Co. Ltd. Edinburgh. Bakers and Confectioners and Purveyors.

d Malga Vita Ltd., Southall. Vitacream Manufacturers.

j Mallett and Son Ltd., London. Antique Dealers.

d Manbré & Garton Ltd., London. Suppliers of Coffee Sugar Crystals

g j Manley, J., Windsor. Guilder and Picture Frame Maker.

a Mann Egerton & Co. Ltd., Norwich. Automobile Engineers.

a Mappin & Webb, Ltd., London. Silversmiths.

m Marcyle, Madame, London. Corsetiére.

a Marley Buildings Ltd., Guildford. Building Manufacturers and Constructors.

a	Marley Tile Co. Ltd., Sevenoaks. Suppliers of Roof and Floor Tiles.
d	Marsh & Baxter Ltd., Brierley Hill, Staffs. Suppliers of Ham.
m	Marshall & Snelgrove, London. Drapers.
d m	Martini & Rossi Ltd., Brentford. Suppliers of Martini Vermouth.
a	Massey-Ferguson (United Kingdom) Ltd., London. Manufacturers of Agricultural Machinery.
a	Matthews, Frank P., Ltd., Tenbury Wells, Worcs. Suppliers of Fruit Trees.
m	Mayfair Window Cleaning Co. Ltd., London. Window Cleaners.
d m	McCallum & Craigie Ltd., High Blantyre. Manufacturers of Lan-Air-Cel Blankets.
d	McCarthy, D. & F. Ltd., Norwich. Fruit and Vegetable Merchants.
d	McVitie & Price Ltd., London. Biscuit Manufacturers.
d	Melroses Ltd., Edinburgh. Purveyors of Tea and Coffee.
m	Menzies, John, & Co. Ltd., Edinburgh. Booksellers.
a	Merryweather & Sons Ltd., London. Fire Engineers.
k	Metropolitan Window Cleaning Co. Ltd., London. Window Cleaners.
a	Meyer and Mortimer, Ltd., London. Military Outfitters.
a	Midland-Yorkshire Tar Distillers Ltd., The Warley. Suppliers of Creosote.
d	Miles Redfern Ltd., (General Marketing Division). Hyde, Cheshire. Manufacturers of Rubber Mats and Flooring.
m	J. Miller Calder, Thurso Caithness. Suppliers of Household Furnishings.
d	Milton, K. W. Dersingham. Purveyors of Meat and Poultry.
d j	Minear & Munday. London. Fruiterers and Greengrocers.
m	Minnesota Mining & Manufacturing Co. Ltd., London. Manufacturers of "Scotchbrite" Scouring Pads.
d	Minton Ltd., Stoke-on-Trent. China Manufacturers.
a m	Mirman, Simone, London. Milliner.
d	Mitchell & Muil, Aberdeen. Bakers and Confectioners.
a	Mobil Oil Co. Ltd., London. Suppliers of Petroleum Fuels and Lubricants.
d	Modern Fibre Glass Products Ltd., Tonbridge. Manufacturers of Fibre Glass Carrying Cases.
d	Moët & Chandon, Epernay. Purveyors of Champagne.
a	Moir, W., Aberdeen. Clock Repairer.
j	Moorcroft, W., Ltd., Burslem, Staffs. Potters.
a	Moreton Nurseries, Churt, Farnham, Surrey. Suppliers of Nosegays.
m n	Morny, Ltd., London. Manufacturers of Soap.
a	Morton Knight Ltd., London. Manufacturers of Sportswear.
a	Mowlem, John & Co., Ltd., Brentford. Building Contractors.
d m	Moyses Stevens, Ltd., London. Florists.
d	Mumm, G. H. & Co., Paris. Purveyors of Champagne.
f	Murchie's Creameries, Ltd. Edinburgh. Purveyors of Milk and Cream.
a	Murdins Typewriter Co. Ltd., King's Lynn. Suppliers of Office Stationery and Equipment.
a	Murkett Brothers, Ltd., Huntingdon. Suppliers of Motor Vehicles.
a	Murphy Chemical Ltd., Wheathampstead, St. Albans. Suppliers of Agricultural Insecticides.
f m o	Musk and Co., Newmarket. Purveyors of Meat and Sausage Manufacturers.
k	Nairn Floors. Kirkcaldy. Manufacturers of Floor-covering.
d m	Nairobi Coffee & Tea Co. Ltd., The, London. Coffee Merchants.
k m	National Benzole Co. Ltd., London. Suppliers of Motor Spirit.
g	National Cash Register Co. Ltd., London. Manufacturers of Accounting Machines.
f	National Flooring Co. Ltd., London. Parquet Flooring Manufacturers.
d	National Linen Co. Ltd., London. Suppliers of Linen.
a	Neaverson, A. & Sons Ltd., Peterborough. Dog Kennel Manufacturers.
a m	Nelson A. & Co. Ltd., London. Chemists.
e m	Nestle Co. Ltd., The, Croydon. Purveyors of Condensed Milk and Nestle Products.
d	Newbeam Ltd., London. Suppliers of Canned Foods.
d	Newbery, Henry & Co. Ltd., London. Suppliers of Furnishing Trimmings.
m	Newey Goodman Ltd., Birmingham. Pin Makers and Manufacturers of Hooks and Eyes.
g	Newman, Peter, London. Picture Restorers and Liners.
a	Nissen, Chas., & Co., London. Stamp Dealers.
d	Noilly Prat & Cie, Marseilles. Wine Producers.
a	Norfolk Paints (King's Lynn) Ltd., King's Lynn. Suppliers of Wallpaper and Paint.
a	Norfolk Reed Thatchers Ltd. Chorley Wood. Reed Thatchers.
k	North, W. A. & Son, Bourne. Forage Merchants.
a	Notcutts Nurseries Ltd., Woodbridge. Nurserymen.
a	Nuralite Co. Ltd., The, Rochester. Suppliers of Roofing Materials.
a	Nu-Way Heating Plant Ltd., Droitwich. Manufacturers of Combustion Equipment.
k	Offord, Gordon J., London. Coachbuilders.
a	O'Hanlon, W. M., & Co. Ltd., Manchester. Suppliers of Window Shade Fabrics.
d	Oliver, Janet, Edinburgh. Florist.
k	Orange Luxury Coaches Ltd., London. Coach Hirers.
m	Osmond & Sons Ltd., Grimsby. Suppliers of Animal Feeding Stuffs, Sheep Dips and Veterinary Medicines.
d	Overton Ltd., London. Fishmongers.
d	Oxley & Son (Windsor) Ltd., Windsor. Printers and Stationers.
a m	Papworth Industries. Cambridge. Travel Goods Makers.
a m	Paragon China Ltd., Stoke on Trent. China Potters.
a	Paris House, Ltd., London. Beltmakers.
m	Parker, George & Sons (Saddlers) Ltd., London. Saddlers.
a	Parker Pen Co. Ltd., London. Manufacturers of Pens, Pencils and Ink.
d	Patent Steam Carpet Cleaning Co. Ltd., London. Carpet Cleaners.
a	Patman, C., Cambridge. Clock Repairer.
a	Pattrick and Thompsons, Ltd., King's Lynn. Timber Merchants.
a	Pauls & Whites Foods Ltd., Ipswich. Manufacturers of Animal Feeding Stuffs.
d	Pears, A. & F. Ltd., London. Soap Manufacturers.

d m Peck, John & Co., Ltd., Liverpool. Suppliers of Overalls and Chefs Clothing.

d m Peek, Frean & Co. Ltd., London. Biscuit Manufacturers.

n Penhaligon's Ltd., London. Manufacturers of Toilet Requisites.

b Pennell & Sons Ltd., Lincoln. Seedsmen and Nurserymen.

a Perkins Engines Ltd., Peterborough. Manufacturers of Diesel Engines.

b Permutit Co. Ltd., London. Suppliers of Water Treating Equipment.

a Perry Heating Appliances Ltd., Eastbourne. Manufacturers of Heating Appliances.

a Pettifer, Thomas Ltd., Godalming. Manufacturers of Animal Medicines.

a Philip & Tracey, Ltd., Andover. Manufacturers and Designers of Educational Material.

n Philips Electrical Ltd., London. Suppliers of Dictation Machines.

j m Phillips, S. J. Ltd., London. Antique Dealer.

m Phonotas Co. Ltd., London. Telephone Cleaners and Sterilisers.

a n Pickfords Shipping & Forwarding Co. Ltd., London. Shipping and Forwarding Agents.

d Pilgrim Payne & Co. Ltd., London. Dyers and Cleaners of Soft Furnishings and Carpets.

a Pilkington Brothers Ltd., St. Helens. Manufacturers and Suppliers of Glass.

d Pink, W. & Sons Ltd., Portsmouth. Grocers and Provision Merchants.

m Pither, Edward, Ltd., Englefield Green, Surrey. Suppliers of Fish and Poultry.

l Pitt, Charles and Co. Ltd., London. Button Makers.

a j m n Plante & Johnson, Ltd., London. Silversmith and Jeweller.

k m Plessey Co. Ltd., The, Ilford, Essex. Suppliers of Car Radios.

a Plowright, Pratt and Harbage, Ltd., King's Lynn. Suppliers of Building Materials.

n Poole, E. C., Henley-on-Thames. Farrier.

k Poole, Henry, & Co. (Savile Row) Ltd., London. Livery Outfitters.

d Poulton & Nicholson Ltd., London. Upholsterers' Warehousemen.

a Powell, J. B. & Son, Ltd., Windsor. Suppliers of Animal Feeding Stuffs and Fertilizers.

k Power Petroleum Co. Ltd., The, London. Suppliers of Lubricating Oil.

a m Pratt & Leslie Jones Ltd., Windsor. Suppliers of China, Glass and Fancy Goods.

g Pratt, Thomas & Sons Ltd., London. Ecclesiastical Robe Makers.

a m Prestcold Ltd., Theale. Manufacturers of Refrigerating Machinery.

d Price's Patent Candle Co. Ltd., London. Candlemakers.

a Pringle, H. E., Ltd., Newmarket. Forage Merchants.

a m Pringle, John. Ballater. Motor Engineer.

a m Pringle of Scotland, Ltd., Hawick. Manufacturers of Knitted Garments.

d m Procter & Gamble, Ltd., Newcastle-upon-Tyne. Manufacturers of Soaps, Detergents and Shortening.

a Protim, Ltd., Marlow. Manufacturers of Wood Preservatives.

j k Pugh & Co. (London) Ltd., London. Coal Merchants.

a Pugh, Charles H., Ltd., Birmingham. Manufacturers of Motor Mowers.

a n Purdey, James & Sons, Ltd., London. Gun and Cartridge Makers.

n Pye Telecommunications Ltd., Cambridge. Manufacturers of Radio Telephone Equipment.

k Pyrene (Chubb Fire Security Ltd.), Sunbury-on-Thames. Manufacturers of Pyrene Fire Extinguishers.

a Pyrotenax, Ltd., Hebburn. Manufacturers and Suppliers of Electric Cable.

d Quaker Oats Ltd., Southall. Suppliers of Quaker Products.

k Radiomobile Ltd. London. Manufacturers of Car Radio Equipment.

k m Randall, H. E., Ltd., Kendal. Bootmakers.

a Rank, Joseph, Ltd., London. Manufacturers of Animal Feeding Stuffs.

a Rank Audio Visual Ltd. (Rank Film Equipment) Brentford. Manufacturers of Cinematograph Equipment.

g Rank Xerox, Ltd., London. Manufacturers and Suppliers of Xerographic Copying Equipment and Materials.

a Ransomes Sims and Jefferies, Ltd., Ipswich. Manufacturers of Agricultural and Horticultural Machinery.

a Ratsey & Lapthorn, Ltd., Cowes, IoW. Sail Makers.

d Rawlings, H. D., Ltd., London. Mineral Water Manufacturers.

a j m Rayne, H. & M., Ltd., London. Shoemakers.

k Reckitt & Colman Household Division, Hull. Manufacturers of Metal Polish, Shoe Polish & Leather Dressings.

d Reckitt & Colman, Food Division. Norwich. Manufacturers of Mustard & Sauces.

d Reckitt & Colman, Pharmaceutical Division. Hull. Manufacturers of Antiseptics.

k Reckitt & Colman, Industrial Division. High Wycombe. Manufacturers of Hygenol Polishing Preparations.

m Rediffusion London Ltd., London. Suppliers of Rediffusion.

a Redmayne, S. & Sons, Ltd., Wigton. Tailors.

d Reed Medway Sacks Ltd., Larkfield, nr Maidstone. Suppliers of Domestic Refuse Sacks.

d m Reeves, C. & Sons (Staines) Ltd., Windsor. Purveyors of Meat.

a Reid, C. J. (Eton), Eton. Chemists.

d n Remington Rand Division Sperry Rand Ltd., London. Suppliers of Office Machines and Equipment.

d m Renshaw, John F. & Co. Ltd., Mitcham. Purveyors of Almond Products.

a Rentokil, Ltd., East Grinstead. Contractors for Woodworm, Dry Rot and Pest Control.
a R.F.D.-G.Q. Ltd., Godalming. Manufacturers of Inflatable Boats.
g Rich, Arthur & Partners, Ltd., Belper. Suppliers of Leather Preservers and Dressings.
m Riche of Hay Hill, Ltd., London. Manicurists.
k Rickards, Charles (Tours) Ltd., London. Road Transport Contractors.
d m Ridgways Ltd., London. Tea and Coffee Merchants.
a Rigby, John & Co. (Gunmakers) Ltd., London. Rifle and Cartridge Makers.
a Rigby and Peller, London. Corsetiéres.
a Riverside Garage, Ballater. Automobile and Electrical Engineers.
a Rivington Carpets, Ltd., Bolton. Carpet Manufacturers.
a Rix, Oliver, Ltd., Fakenham. Suppliers of Agricultural Machinery.
a Roberts' Radio Co. Ltd., West Molesey. Radio Manufacturers.
d Robertson, James & Sons (PM) Ltd., Bristol. Marmalade Manufacturers.
d Roger & Gallet, Paris. Manufacturers of Soap.
k Rolls-Royce, Ltd., London. Motor Car Manufacturers.
d Romary, A. & Co. Ltd., York. Biscuit Manufacturers.
n Ronson Products Ltd., London. Suppliers of Electric Shavers.
d Rose, L. & Co. Ltd., St. Albans. Suppliers of Lime Juice Cordial.
a Ross Optical Ltd., Horsham. Manufacturers of Binoculars.
k Rossleigh, Ltd., Edinburgh. Motor Engineers.

k m Rover Co. Ltd., The, Birmingham/Solihull. Manufacturers and Suppliers of Motor Cars and Land Rovers.
a Rowe, Frank, Wellington, Somerset. Suppliers of Chrysanthemum Stock.
a Rowe's of Bond St. Ltd., London. Outfitters.
m Rowntree & Co. Ltd., York. Makers of Table Jellies.
a m Russell, Gordon, Ltd., Broadway, Worcs. Manufacturers and Suppliers of Furniture and Furnishings.
n Russell Taxis. Cowes, IoW. Motor Car Hirers.
e Ryvita Co. Ltd., The, Poole. Ryvita Manufacturers.
d S.A.B.D. Ltd., London. South African Brandy Suppliers.
k St. Cuthbert's Co-operative Association Ltd., Edinburgh. Coach Painters.
i Salt and Son, Ltd., Birmingham. Cutlers.
n Salter, J. & Son. Aldershot. Suppliers of Polo Sticks.
a Sampson, William G. & Son, Newbury. Farriers.
d Sandeman, George G. Sons & Co. Ltd., London. Wine Merchants.
a Sanderson, Arthur & Sons, Ltd., London. Suppliers of Wallpapers, Paints and Fabrics.
d m Sanderson, William & Son Ltd., West Lothian. Scotch Whisky Distillers.
d Sanitas Co. Ltd., The, London. Manufacturers of Hygiene Products.
b Sankey, Richard and Son Ltd., Nottingham. Makers of Horticultural Pottery.
n Saunders, Easton Grey, Ltd., Peter, Easton Grey. Makers of Peter Saunders Tweeds.
a m n Savory & Moore, Ltd., London. Chemists.
d m Schweppes Ltd., London. Mineral Water Manufacturers.
j Scott Adie, Ltd. London. Manufacturers of Scotch Tartan.
a Scott and Turner Co. The. Surbiton. Manufacturers of Delrosa Rose Hip Syrup.
a Scottish Agricultural Industries, Ltd., Edinburgh. Suppliers of Fertilisers and Seeds.
d Scottish & Newcastle Breweries Ltd., Edinburgh. Brewers.
a m Scottish Seed House, Perth. Seedsman.
m Scott's Fish Shop, Kirkwall, Orkney. Cheesemonger.
a Seemeel Ltd., London. Manufacturers of Animal Feeding Stuffs.
d Sekers Fabrics, Ltd., London. Manufacturers of Furnishing Fabrics.
m Sergent, Maurice Louis. London. Hairdresser.
a Sharpe, Charles & Co. Ltd., Sleaford. Seedsmen.
d m Sharp, Edward & Sons Ltd., Maidstone. Confectioners.
d Sharwood, J. A. & Co. Ltd., London. Manufacturers of Chutney and Indian Curry Powder.
d Shaw, Elizabeth, Ltd., London. Manufacturers of Confectionery.
a Shell & BP Scotland, Ltd., Glasgow. Suppliers of Motor Spirit and Gas Oil.
k Shell-Mex and BP Ltd., London. Purveyors of Motor Spirit.
a Shepherd's Aerosols, Ltd., Frant, Tunbridge Wells. Manufacturers of Aerovap.
a Sheringham & Overman Ltd., Fakenham. Seedsmen.
d Shippam, C., Ltd., Chichester. Manufacturers of Meat and Fish Pastes.
a Shirlaw, C. H. (Sailmakers) Ltd., Cowes, IoW. Sail Makers.
d Shirras, Laing & Co. Ltd., Aberdeen. Ironmongers.
a n Simpson (Piccadilly) Ltd., London. Outfitters.
d Singer Co. (UK) Ltd., The, Guildford. Manufacturers of Sewing Machines.
c j o Skinner, A. E. & Co., London. Jewellers and Silversmiths.
d Sleepeezee Ltd., Croydon. Bedding Manufacturers.

d m Slumberland, Ltd., Birmingham. Bedding Manufacturers.
m Smith, George & Co., Ballater, Aberdeenshire. Sporting Outfitters.
d m Smith, H. Allen, Ltd., London. Wine Cooper and Merchant.

d Smith, Tom & Co. Ltd., Norwich. Suppliers of Christmas Crackers.

a Smith and Wellstood, Ltd., Bonnybridge. Manufacturers of Esse Cooking Equipment.

a Smith, George & Co., Ballater. Sporting Outfitters.

a Smith, James (Scotland Nurseries) Ltd., Matlock. Nurserymen.

a Smiths Industries Ltd. (Clock & Watch Division), Wembley. Manufacturers of Clocks and Watches.

a Smythson, Frank. London. Stationers.

e Sodastream, Ltd., Harlow, Essex. Soda-water Machine Manufacturers.

a Soil Fertility, Dunns, Ltd., Corsham, Wilts. Seedsmen and Suppliers of Agricultural Fertilisers.

a Solignum Ltd., Crayford. Manufacturers of Wood Preservatives.

d Southwell, Charles & Co. Ltd., Ipswich. Manufacturers of Confectionery.

j m Sparks, John, Ltd., London. Antiquaries of Chinese Art.

g Spearman, George, Sunninghill. Fine Art Photographer.

a Spillers, Ltd., London. Manufacturers of Dog Foods and Animal Feeding Stuffs.

a n Spink & Son, Ltd., London. Medallists.

d Spode, Ltd., Stoke-on-Trent. Manufacturers of China.

a Spratt's Patent Ltd., Barking, Essex. Suppliers of Dog Foods.

d Sproston, W. F. Ltd., London. Suppliers of Fish.

a Spruce and Wright, Ltd., King's Lynn. Forage Merchants.

d Squire, F. & Sons Ltd., West Drayton. Contractors for the removal of Kitchen Waste.

a Sta-Dri (Cabs) Ltd., Bristol. Manufacturers of Tractor Cabs.

a Stanley Gibbons Ltd., London. Philatelists.

a Stanton Hope Ltd., Leigh-on-Sea. Suppliers of Forestry Equipment.

d Staples & Co. Ltd., Cricklewood, Manufacturers of Bedspreads and Bedding.

a Start-Rite Shoes Ltd., Norwich. Shoemakers.

a Steele, H. D. & Son (Agricultural) Ltd., Worthing. Manufacturers and Suppliers of Agricultural Eqiupment.

j Steiner, London. Hairdressers and Perfumers.

m Steiner, London. Chiropodists.

g Steinway & Sons, London. Pianoforte Manufacturers.

a Stenner of Tiverton Ltd., Tiverton. Manufacturers and Suppliers of Sawmilling Machinery.

b n Stephens Brothers Ltd., London. Hosiers.

a Stevens, A. B. Ltd., Goff's Oak, Waltham Cross. Florists.

d Stevens & Williams Ltd., Brierley Hill, Staffs. Suppliers of Table Glassware.

d m Stevenson Bros. (Dundee) Ltd., Aberdeen/Dundee. Launderers.

d Stewart, J. & G. Ltd., Edinburgh. Suppliers of Scotch Whisky.

d Still, W. M. & Sons, Ltd., Hastings. Manufacturers of Kitchen Equipment.

d Stoddard, A. F. & Co. Ltd., Johnstone, Scotland. Carpet Manufacturers.

d Strachan, George, Ltd., Crathie. General Merchants.

a Straker, S. & Sons, Ltd., London. Printers and Stationers.

k Stratstone Ltd., London. Motor Car Distributors.

a m Studio Lisa, Ltd., London/Welwyn. Photographers.

k Sturgess, Walter E. & Sons Ltd., Leicester. Suppliers of Horse & Carriage Conveyances.

d Sturtevant Welbeck, Ltd., Brighton. Manufacturers of Vacuum Cleaners.

a m Suttons Seeds Ltd., Reading. Seedsmen.

j k m Swaine Adeney Brigg and Sons, Ltd., London. Glove, Whip and Umbrella Manufacturers.

a Sykes International Ltd., Warminster. Live Poultry Suppliers.

m Symbol Biscuits Ltd., Blackpool. Biscuit Manufacturers.

d Tanqueray, Gordon, & Co. Ltd., London. Gin Distillers.

d Tate & Lyle Ltd., London. Sugar Refiners.

a Taylor, D. & R., King's Lynn. Upholsterers.

b Taylor and Henderson Ltd., Aberdeen. Printers and Stationers.

a Technoproof Ltd., Newbury. Roofing Contractors.

d Telfer, Henry, Ltd., London. Purveyors of Pork Pies.

d Temple & Crook Ltd., London. Suppliers of Brushes and Hardware.

a Thaarup, Aage, Ltd., London. Milliners.

d Thawpit, Ltd., Sheffield. Manufacturers of Thawpit.

d Thermos Ltd., London. Manufacturers of Vacuum Vessels.

j m Thomas, J. Rochelle, London. Dealers in Works of Art.

m Thomas Window Cleaning, Englefield Green. Window Cleaners.

m Thomson, Donald, Castletown, Caithness. Grocer.

a m Thorn Lighting Ltd., London. Manufacturers of Electric Lamps.

k m Thresher & Glenny, Ltd., London. Shirt Makers.

a	Timber, H. G. Ltd., Uxbridge. Suppliers of Timber Products.
j	Tomkins, H. J. & Son Ltd., London. Upholsterers.
d	Tong, E. G., Ltd., Earley, Berkshire. Muffin Makers.
g	Toye, Kenning & Spencer Ltd., London. Suppliers of Gold and Silver Laces, Insignia and Embroidery.
m	Trianco, Ltd., East Molesey, Surrey. Manufacturers of Domestic Boilers.
b	Trumper, Miss Georgina M., London. Hairdresser.
n	Truefitt & Hill (Products) Ltd., London. Hairdressers.
a	Tuck, Raphael, & Sons Ltd., London. Fine Art Publishers.
f	Turner, Thomas and Co. (Sheffield), Ltd., Sheffield, Cutlers.
d m	Twining, R. & Co. Ltd., London. Tea and Coffee Merchants.

Suppliers of Canadian Club Whisky.

d	Walker, John & Sons Ltd., London. Scotch Whisky Distillers.
g	Walker, J. W. & Sons, Ltd., Ruislip. Organ Builders.
d m	Wall, T. & Sons (Meat & Handy Foods) Ltd., London. Suppliers of Pork Sausages and Meat Pies.
a m	Wallace, Cameron & Co. Ltd., Glasgow. Manufacturers and Suppliers of Ultraplast First Aid Dressings.
a	Walpamur Co. Ltd., Darwen. Manufacturers of Paint.
d m	Walpole Brothers (London) Ltd., London. Linen Drapers.
a m	Ward, Thomas & Sons Ltd., Sheffield/Warrington. Cutlery Manufacturers.
d j m	Warner & Sons Ltd., London. Suppliers of Silks and Furnishing Fabrics.
a j m	Wartski Jewellers Ltd., London Jewellers.

Sons & Crisp, Ltd.,
den Contractors and

Vatson Ltd., London.
Manufacturers.
(London & Home
London. Brewers.
rnard, Ltd., London.
Outfitters and Livery

A., Ltd., Newmarket.
of Farm Machinery.
S., Castletown, Caith-
Contractors.
& J. Ltd., London.
Silversmiths.
Co. Ltd., Windsor.

fferies Ltd., London.

ar Refineries Ltd., The,
gar Refiners and Pur-

Super Lime Co. Ltd.,
ing's Lynn. Suppliers
rs of Agricultural Lime.
ge M., Ltd., London.
Gold Leaf.
Co. Ltd., London.

emlins Ltd., Maidstone,
s.
Distillers Ltd., Glasgow.
y Distillers.
uilders Merchants) Ltd.,
Suppliers of Building

Holdings, Ltd., Welling-
cessors and Packers of
Food Products.

m	Wholesale Fittings Co. Ltd., London. Suppliers of Electrical Equipment.
d	Whytock & Reid. Edinburgh. Decorators and Furnishers.
g m	Wiggins, Arnold & Sons (Carvers) Ltd., London. Picture Frame Makers.
a	Wilder, John (Agricultural) Ltd., Reading. Suppliers of Agricultural Machinery.
d	Wilkin & Sons, Ltd., Tiptree, Essex. Jam and Marmalade Manufacturers.

g n Wilkinson Sword Ltd., London. Sword Cutlers.

d Williamson, John & Son, Aberdeen. Purveyors of Meat and Poultry.

e j Wills and Segar, London. Florists.

g Wilson & Son, Edinburgh. Piano and Harpsichord Tuners.

d Wilson, Andrew & Sons Ltd., Edinburgh. Catering Equipment Hirers.

a Wilson, William & Co. (Aberdeen) Ltd., Aberdeen, Suppliers of Electrical and Plumbing Materials.

d Wilton Royal Carpet Factory Ltd., The, Wilton. Carpet Manufacturers.

k Windovers, Ltd., Hendon. Coachbuilders.

a Witney Blanket Co. Ltd., Witney. Bedding Manufacturers.

a Wolf Electric Tools, Ltd., London. Suppliers of Electrical Equipment.

d Wolfschmidt Ltd., London. Suppliers of Kummel.

a Wolseley Engineering, Ltd., Birmingham. Manufacturers of Agricultural Equipment.

d m Wolsey Ltd., Leicester. Manufacturers of Hosiery and Knitwear.

a m Wood, William & Son, Ltd., Taplow. Garden Contractors and Horticultural Builders.

f Woodford, Bourne and Co. Ltd., Cork. Wine Merchants.

d Woodhouse Hume Ltd. London. Suppliers of Meat and Poultry.

d Woodrow, J. & Sons Ltd., Stockport. Hatters and Trunk Merchants.

d Worcester Royal Porcelain Co. Ltd., The, Worcester. Manufacturers of China and Porcelain.

m Worham, Antony, Ltd., London. Suppliers of Tudor Queen Hams and Tongues.

a Wysall Tractor Co. Ltd., Wysall. Manufacturers of Agricultural Elevators.

d m Yardley & Co. Ltd., London. Perfumers & Manufacturers of Soap.

Addendum

The following information has been ascertained since the book went to press:—

The Royal Family

HM The Queen (*p* 119) has received Order of the Great Yugoslav Star (1972) Yugoslavia. **HRH The Prince Philip, Duke of Edinburgh** (*p* 125) has received Star of Yugoslavia with sash (1972) Yugoslavia; been installed as hon Fellow and President of the Royal College of General Practitioners (1972); and visited Germany (attended dinner in Munich in connection with "The British Trade Drive") 1972. **HM Queen Elizabeth The Queen Mother** (*p* 133) has had her 250th winner under National Hunt Rules. **HRH The Prince of Wales** (*p* 137) visited Germany (visited Prince of Wales's Division) 1972. **HRH The Princess Anne** (*p* 139) has received Grand Cross of the Yugoslav Flag (1972) Yugoslavia, and Grand Cross, 1st class, of the Order of Merit (1972) Federal Republic of Germany. **HRH The Princess Margaret, Countess of Snowdon** (*p* 143) has received Grand Cross, 1st class, of the Order of Merit (1972) Federal Republic of Germany. **HRH The Duchess of Kent** (*p* 167) is Chief Patron of The National Star Centre for Disabled Youth. **HRH Princess Alexandra, the Hon Mrs. Angus Ogilvy** (*p* 171) is Grand President of the Royal Life Saving Society from 1972 (for five years). **Hon Angus Ogilvy** (*p* 175) became MA Oxford 1972. **HRH Princess Alice, Countess of Athlone** also has hon Freedom of the Worshipful Company of Gold and Silver Wyre Drawers (1965); and visited Sweden (for 90th Birthday celebrations of King Gustaf VI Adolf) 1972.

The Royal Lineage

p 215, *col* 2. Issue of HRH Princess Sophie of the Netherlands and HRH Grand Duke *Karl Alexander* (August Johann) of Saxe-Weimar-Eisenach:

1*c* HRH Hereditary Grand Duke *Karl August* Wilhelm Nikolaus Alexander Michael Bernhard Heinrich Friedrich Stephan of Saxe-Weimar-Eisenach, Duke of Saxony, *b* 31 July 1844, *m* 26 Aug 1873, HH Princess *Pauline* Ida Marie Olga Henriette Catherine (*b* 25 July 1852; *d* 17 May 1904), elder dau of HH Prince Hermann of Saxe-Weimar-Eisenach, Duke of Saxony (*see p* 211), and *d* 20 Nov 1894, leaving issue,

1*d* HRH Grand Duke *Wilhelm Ernst* Karl Alexander Friedrich Heinrich Bernhard Albert Georg Hermann of Saxe-Weimar-Eisenach, *b* 10 June 1876, *m* 1st 30 April 1903, HSH Princess *Caroline* Elisabeth Ida (*b* 13 July 1884; *dsp* 17 Jan 1905), 3rd dau of HSH Heinrich XXII, Prince Reuss (Elder Line) (*see p* 249). He *m* 2ndly 4 Jan 1910, HH Princess *Feodora* Karola Charlotte Marie Adelheid Auguste Mathilde (*b* 29 May 1890; *d* 12 March 1972), eldest dau of HH Prince Friedrich of Saxe-Meiningen, Duke of Saxony, and *d* 24 April 1923, leaving issue (*see p* 266).

2*d* HH Prince *Bernhard Heinrich* Karl Alexander Hermann Wilhelm Oskar Friedrich Franz Peter of Saxe-Weimar-Eisenach, Duke of Saxony, *b* 18 April 1878; *d unm* 1 Oct 1900.

1*c* HH Princess *Marie Alexandrine* Anna Sophie Augusta Helene of Saxe-Weimar Eisenach, Duchess of Saxony, *b* 20 Jan 1849, *m* 6 Feb 1876, HSH Prince Heinrich VII Reuss (Younger Line) (*b* 14 July 1825; *d* 2 May 1906), and *d* 6 May 1922, having had issue,

1*d* HSH Prince Heinrich XXXII Reuss (Younger Line), *b* 4 March 1878, *m* 19 May 1920 (*m* diss by div 1921), HSH Princess *Marie Adelheid* Mathilde Karoline Elise Alexe Auguste Albertine (*b* 30 Aug 1895), only dau of HSH Prince Rudolf of Lippe (*see p* 265), and *dsp* 6 May 1935.

2*d* HSH Prince Heinrich XXXIII Reuss (Younger Line), *b* 26 July 1879, *m* 1st 17 May 1913, HRH Princess *Viktoria Margarete* Elisabeth Marie Adelheid Ulrike (*b* 17 April 1890; *d* 9 Sept 1923), only dau of HRH Prince Friedrich Leopold of Prussia, and had issue (*see p* 287). He *m* 2ndly 10 April 1929 (*m* diss by div 1935), Allene (*b* 7 July 1876; *d* 1 May 1955), widow of Anson Wood Burchard, and dau of Charles Henry Tew, and *d* 15 Nov 1942.

3*d* HSH Prince Heinrich XXXV Reuss (Younger Line), *b* 1 Aug 1887, *m* 1st 20 April 1911 (*m* diss by div 1921), HH Princess Maria (*b* 6 June 1888; *d* 12 Nov 1947), only dau of HH Prince Albert of Saxe-Altenburg, Duke of Saxony, and had issue: HSH Princess *Maria Helena* Cecilie Alexandra Olga Sophie Adelheid Reuss (Younger Line), *b* 23 Feb 1912; *d unm* 1 Aug 1933. He *m* 2ndly 12 April 1921 (*m* diss by div 1923), HSH Princess *Marie Adelheid* Mathilde Karoline Elise Alexe Auguste Albertine (*b* 30 Aug 1895), formerly wife of his brother Prince Heinrich XXXII (*see above*), and only dau of HSH Prince Rudolf of Lippe, and *d* 17 Jan 1936, having by her had issue (*see p* 265).

1*d* HSH Princess Johanna Reuss (Younger Line), *b* 8 June 1882; *d* 15 June 1883.

2*d* HSH Princess *Sophie Renata* Reuss (Younger Line), *b* 27 June 1884, *m* 12 Dec 1909, HSH Prince Heinrich XXXIV Reuss (Younger Line), (*b* 4 June 1887; *d* 30 April 1956), and *d* 19 Jan 1968, leaving issue,

1*e* ●HSH Prince Heinrich I Reuss (Younger Line) [*647 Büdingen, OHessen, Marktplatz 5, Germany*], *b* 8 Oct 1910, *m* 15 Sept 1939, ●HH Duchess *Woizlawa* Feodora (*b* 17 Dec 1918), only dau of HH Duke Adolf Friedrich of Mecklenburg-Schwerin, and has issue (*see p* 259).

2*e* ●HSH Prince Heinrich III Reuss (Younger Line) [*Danklerhube, A-8774 Mautern, Steiermark, Austria*], *b* 27 July 1919, *m* 1st 13 March 1944 (*m* diss by div 1955), Baroness *Franziska* Maria (*b* 12 Dec 1919; *d* 11 April 1964), elder dau of late Baron Franz Mayr von Melnhof, and has issue,

1*f* ●HSH Prince Heinrich XII Reuss (Younger Line), *b* 13 Oct 1950.

1*f* ●HSH Princess *Antoinette* Maria Anna Magdalena Cecilie Georgine Reuss (Younger Line), *b* 11 Jan 1945.

2*f* ●HSH Princess *Felizitas* Maria Gertrude Katharina Reuss (Younger Line), *b* 26 Oct 1946, *m* (civil) 1 July and (religious) 9 July 1967, ●HSH Prince Christian *Peter* August Richard Udo Maria Casimir zu Sayn-Wittgenstein-Berleburg (*b* 5 Feb 1940) [*5605 Hichdahl-Millrath Erlenweg 20, Germany*], eldest son of HSH

Prince Casimir Johannes zu Sayn-Wittgenstein-Berleburg (*see p* 270), and has issue: 1*g* ●HSH Prince *Carl-Constantin* Heinrich Egbert Franz Welf Casimir zu Sayn-Wittgenstein-Berleburg, *b* 2 June 1968; 2*g* ●HSH Prince *Johann-Philipp* Friedrich Benedict Heinrich Franz Richard zu Sayn-Wittgenstein-Berleburg, *b* 10 Nov 1970. He *m* 2ndly 5 Sept 1964, ●H Ill H Countess Odylia (*b* 26 Oct 1939), yr dau of H Ill H Count Constantin zu Castell-Castell, and by her has issue: 2*f* ●HSH Prince Heinrich XVII Reuss (Younger Line), *b* 1968.

1*e* ●HSH Princess *Felizitas* Anna Eleonore Cecilie Reuss (Younger Line), *b* 5 July 1914, *m* 3 Sept 1935, ●HSH *Otto Friedrich* Viktor Ferdinand Maximilian Gustav Richard Bogislav, 3rd Prince zu Ysenburg und Büdingen (*b* 16 Sept 1904), and has issue (*see p* 261).

2*c* HH Princess Marie Anna *Sophie* Elisabeth Ida Bernhardine Auguste Helene Amalie Charlotte of Saxe-Weimar-Eisenach, Duchess of Saxony, *b* 29 March 1851; *d* 26 May 1859.

3*c* HH Princess *Elisabeth* Sibylle Maria Dorothea Luise Anna Amalia of Saxe-Weimar-Eisenach, Duchess of Saxony, *b* 28 Feb 1854, *m* 6 Nov 1886, HH Duke *Johann Albrecht* Ernst Konstantin Friedrich Heinrich of Mecklenburg-Schwerin (*b* 8 Dec 1857; *d* 16 Feb 1920), 4th son of HRH Grand Duke Friedrich Franz II of Mecklenburg-Schwerin, and *dsp* 10 July 1908.

p 216, *col* 2. Siegismut Hug's address is 503 Hermülheim, Rheingoldstrasse 10, Germany. He *m* 18 July 1969, ●Annette Schervier (*b* 28 April 1942), and has issue, ●*Alexander* Wolf-Dietrich Hug, *b* 1 May 1971. His sister Oda has further issue: 1*f* ●Hellmut-*Albrecht* Gustav Freidrich Pilz, *b* 24 June 1969; 2*f* ●Hans-*Alexander* Rudolf August Bernhard Pilz, *b* (twin with Albrecht) 24 June 1969; 2*f* ●Angela-*Beatrice* Oda Margarethe Johanna Pilz, *b* 19 Feb 1968.

Siegilde Hug *m* 5 March 1971, ●Alessandro Goffredo Francesco Gatta (*b* 23 Nov 1946), and has issue, ●*Caterina* Angela Marie Therese Rossana Christiana Gatta, *b* 14 May 1972.

Liutgard Hug's husband Klaus Beckenbauer was *b* 11 Aug 1939. They have issue: ●*Wolf-Thilo* Friedrich Wilhelm Klaus Rudolf Beckenbauer, *b* 28 Nov 1969; ●*Bela* Charlotte Beckenbauer, *b* 3 March 1968.

p 219, *col* 2. Countess Alexandra von Zarnekau and Prince George Alexandrovitch Yourievsky had issue, ●HSH Prince Alexander Georgevitch Yourievsky, *b* 20 Dec 1900, *m* 23 Nov 1957, ●Ursula (*b* 30 May 1925), dau of Thomas Beer de Grüneck, and has issue, ●HSH Prince George Alexandrovitch Yourievsky, *b* 8 Dec 1961.

p 222, *col* 1. Prince Christian-Peter of Waldeck and Pyrmont's address is 3041 Alvern, Hermannshorst, Germany. He has issue, ●HSH Prince Georg-Wilhelm Karl of Waldeck and Pyrmont, *b* 18 Oct 1972.

p 222, *col* 2. Duke Johann of Oldenburg has issue, ●a dau, *b* 23 Aug 1972.

p 231, *col* 1. The address of Princess Teresa of Bourbon-Two Sicilies and her husband the Marqués de Laula is Juan Ramón Jiménez 55, Madrid, Spain. The address of her sister Princess Inés is Juan Bravo 26, Madrid, Spain.

p 242, *col* 1. Archduke Franz Salvator of Austria *m* 2ndly 28 April 1934, ●Baroness Melanie (*b* 20 Sept 1898), dau of Baron Philipp von Riesenfels, and *d* 20 April 1939.

p 243, *col* 2. Count Ferdinand zu Stolberg-Stolberg has issue: 1*g* ●H Ill H Count Bernhard Ferdinand Franz-Josef Heinrich Stanislaus Maria zu Stolberg-Stolberg, *b* 11 Oct 1970; 1*g* ●H Ill H Countess Katharina Maria Bonifatia Veronika Ruth Jadwiga zu Stolberg-Stolberg, *b* 2 Jan 1968; 2*g* ●H Ill H Countess Johanna Paula Irene Adelheid Maria zu Stolberg-Stolberg, *b* 13 Aug 1969.

p 251, *col* 2. Baron Hans Georg Herring von Frankensdorf has a dau, ●Baroness Elisabeth Herring von Frankensdorf, *b* 2 Oct 1964.

p 255, *col* 2. Full names of Count Bertram von Quadt zu Wykradt und Isny are Bertram Ernst Maria Ghislain Paul Ingbert. He was *b* 22 Oct 1966. His yr sister's full names are Maria Georgina Ghislaine Caroline. She was *b* 28 Dec 1962.

p 256, *col* 2. Count Konstantin von Waldburg-Zeil, husband of Princess Eleonore of Bavaria, *d* 1972.

p 262, *col* 2. Aloys, 6th Prince von Schönburg-Hartenstein, *d unm* April 1972.

p 270, *col* 1. Count Botho zu Ortenburg *m* 9 Jan 1971, ●Baroness Osterhold Anna Luise *Ilse* (*b* 16 April 1943), elder dau of Baron Hilmar von dem Bussche-Haddenhausen, and has issue. ●H Ill H Countess Anna-Madeleine zu Ortenburg, *b* 28 Oct 1971.

Count Engelbert zu Ortenburg has issue, ●H Ill H Count Peter-Jens zu Ortenburg, *b* 1 March 1970.

Count Joachim zu Ortenburg *m* 10 Oct 1970, ●Ilsabe von Brünneck (*b* 28 Sept 1945).

Countess Yvonne zu Ortenburg *m* 18 July 1970, ●*Ludwig* Borries Wolf von Breitenbuch (*b* 23 Sept 1935), and has issue, ●Georg-Ludwig von Breitenbuch, *b* 19 June 1971.

p 270, *col* 2. Prince Peter zu Sayn-Wittgenstein-Berleburg *m* 9 July 1967, ●HSH Princess Felizitas Reuss, and has issue (*see above*).

p 274, *col* 1. Baron Martin von Dungern's address is 8729 Eichelsdorf über Hassfurt/M, Germany. His elder dau, Baroness Signe von Dungern *m* 20 July 1968, ●Dr Wilhelm-Friedrich von Fischer-Francenfeld, and has issue, ●Wilhelmina von Fischer-Francenfeld, *b* 7 Oct 1972.

p 275, *col* 1. Marie-Blanche von Gans *m* 2ndly 6 Oct 1927 (*m* diss by div), Wilhelm Borgnis (*b* 17 Sept 1890). She *m* 3rdly 5 July 1940, ●Baron Otto von Leithner (*b* 1 Jan 1902).

p 277, *col* 1. Princess Marie-Louise of Schleswig-Holstein (Princess Friedrich Christian of Schaumburg-Lippe—*see p* 251, *col* 2) *d* 29 Dec 1969.

p 281, *col* 1. Prince Michael of Greece has a 2nd dau, ●HRH Princess Olga of Greece and Denmark, *b* 197-.

p 297, *col* 1. Archduchess Elisabeth of Austria and Dr Friedrich Sandhofer have further issue, 3*b* ●Elisabeth Victoria Magdalena Sandhofer, *b* 16 Nov 1971.

p 300, *col* 1. Prince Andreas of Saxe-Coburg and Gotha's address is Hamburg 52, Beckmannstrasse 3, Germany. He *m* 18 June 1971, ●Carin Dabelstein.

CONTENTS

First Published 2005 by Brown Watson
The Old Mill, 76 Fleckney Road,
Kibworth Beauchamp, Leics LE8 0HG

ISBN: 0-7097-1654-0

Printed in China

Illustrations by Stephen Holmes, Jane Swift, Lawrie Taylor

Text by Maureen Spurgeon

Brown Watson
ENGLAND

THE BARBECUE DRAGON

When Dilly the Dragon roared, flames came out of his mouth.

Then, it started to rain and Dilly got cold. There was no roar. No flames.

'My fire is out!' he said. 'I must breathe air to make flames. There is plenty of fresh air in the forest!'

In the forest there was a notice – BEWARE OF FIRE. 'Very wise,' said Dilly. 'But I need MY fire!' Another notice said – FIRE CAUSES DAMAGE. 'True,' said Dilly. 'But I NEED my fire!'

BEWARE
OF
FIRE

Another notice said – PUT FIRES OUT! Poor Dilly felt so cold!

'No fires, today!' a voice was saying. 'It is too cold and damp!'

'So, can we have our barbecue party, Linda?' a girl called out.

'I do not think so, Penny,' said Linda. 'It is raining again! Quick! We must shelter in the forest!'

Dilly went over to the barbecue. It was still warm. He breathed in, feeling warmer inside. Just as the rain stopped – R-OA-OA-RR! – flames came out of his mouth!

'What was that?' a boy called out. 'It sounded like thunder!' Everyone went to see.

'There is a fire for our barbecue!' cried Penny. 'We can have our party!'

'That dragon helped us!' said Holly. 'He roared like thunder and breathed flames! I saw him!'

'Dragons?' said Linda. 'Dragons are only for story books, Holly!'

'But I DID see him!' said Holly with a smile. 'Really, I did!' And just then, Dilly let out another roar.

R-OA-OA-RR!

READ THESE WORDS AGAIN!

roar
fire
breathe
beware
causes
damp
feeling
sounded

flames
mouth
plenty
another
damage
shelter
warmer
thunder

WHAT CAN YOU SEE HERE?

forest

barbecue

notice

story books

HIDE AND SEEK!

'Let's play Hide and Seek!' said Giraffe.

'Yes-s-s...' hissed Snake. 'Seeking is easy for you, Giraffe, with your long neck and tall legs!'

'I agree!' said Zebra.

'Then I will hide!' said Giraffe. One of you can do the seeking!'

'Sounds fun!' roared Tiger Cub. And off he ran. He hid behind a bush. But the sun cast his shadow on the ground. So, he laid down in the shade of a tree and waited.

Then, Tiger Cub got up and looked around. As he crept forward, he saw black and white shadows. Yet there was no sun!

'Zebra!' he roared. 'Come out from behind that bush!'

'You found me, Tiger Cub!' said Zebra. 'Well done!'

Next, Tiger Cub saw blossom hanging from the branches of a tree. He looked down at the trunk.

'Blossom does not grow on the trunk!' he roared. 'It is YOU, Snake, curled round and round!'

'Yes-s-s...' hissed Snake. 'You found me, Tiger Cub! Well done!'

'And only a tall tree can hide a tall Giraffe!' Tiger Cub went on. 'Come out, Giraffe!'

'You found me, Tiger Cub!' said Giraffe. 'Well done!'

'Yes!' roared Tiger Cub. 'But nobody came to find ME!'

'But YOU were the seeker!' said Zebra. 'Well done, Tiger Cub!'

'Let us have another game!' said Tiger Cub. 'And I really WILL be hiding this time!'

READ THESE WORDS AGAIN!

hissed	seeking
tall	agree
sounds	behind
bush	shadow
ground	forward
black	white
found	hanging
trunk	curled
nobody	another

WHAT CAN YOU SEE HERE?

BUZZ, BUZZ, BUSY BEES!

'Silly bees!' said Farmer. 'There is no pollen inside the flowers on these tiles on my kitchen wall!' He opened a window. 'Buzz off! Find real flowers!'

'Buzz! Buzz-z-z!' went the bees.

'These bees!' said Hector Horse. 'As they buzz around collecting pollen to make honey, they help plants to make new plants. They want pollen from the flowers on your hat, Donny Donkey!'

'But my flowers are plastic!' said Donny. 'Buzz off, bees!'

Clara Cow was eating grass in the meadow. 'These bees!' she mooed. 'They are all buzzing around these lovely buttercups!'

'They want pollen so that they can make honey!' said Hector.

'And as bees collect pollen, they help plants to make new plants,' said Donny. 'Look! They are going to the vegetable patch! Which flowers will they find there?'

'Let us go and see!' said Hector.

Peas, tomatoes and cabbages all grew in the vegetable patch.

The bees did not bother with those! They buzzed busily around the orange flowers of the runner beans and the yellow flowers of the marrows! 'Buzz-buzzzz!'

'See these bees!' said Donny. 'They are collecting pollen to make honey for the farmer!'

'And they are helping plants to make new plants,' said Hector again. 'That means new crops of winter feed for us!'

'What busy bees!' mooed Clara.

'Buzz-buzz-z-z!' went the bees.

READ THESE WORDS AGAIN!

silly	flowers
tiles	buzz
collecting	cabbages
plastic	grass
meadow	new
honey	peas
tomatoes	buttercups
orange	yellow
marrows	busy

WHAT CAN YOU SEE HERE?

bees

pollen

vegetable patch

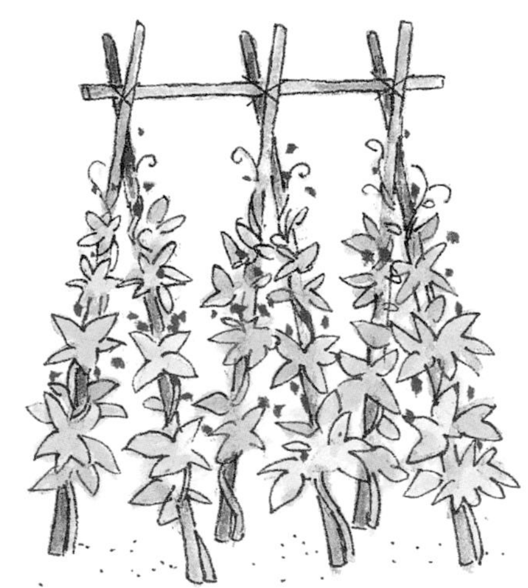

runner beans

marrows

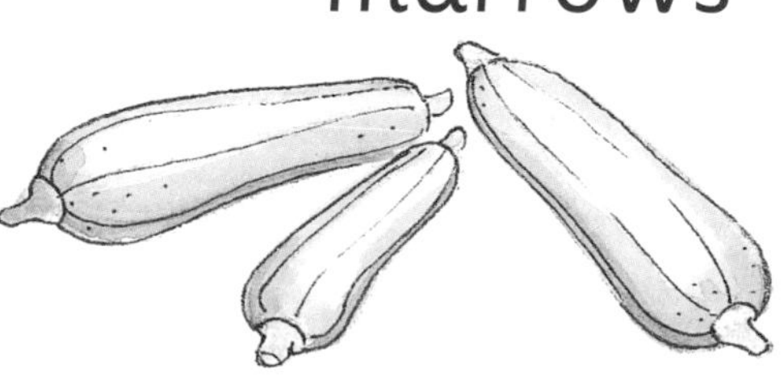

WHERE IS TINY?

Princess Fay loved her cat, Tiny. Tiny had been a present on her last birthday. 'So, what do you want this year?' asked the queen.

'I want to have Tiny with me all the time,' said Princess Fay.

'That is not easy,' said the queen. 'We must see what we can do!'

Next day, the princess called her cat. 'Tiny! Tiny, where are you?'

But Tiny did not appear until tea-time. She looked very pleased with herself.

'Tiny!' cried Princess Fay. 'Oh, Tiny, do not run off again!'

But Tiny was away for most of the next day and the day after. Princess Fay was nearly in tears. 'Oh, Tiny!' she cried. 'Where have you been?' But Tiny just looked pleased with herself.

Next day, Princess Fay got up early. 'My birthday!' she cried. 'Now, where is Tiny? Tiny!'

Then, as Princess Fay started searching, she saw the queen in the rose garden.

She was sitting at an easel with her painting things. And there beside her was Tiny! 'I have finished my painting!' smiled the queen. 'Come and see!'

Princess Fay looked. It was a painting of Tiny!

'I shall put the painting in a frame,' said the queen. 'So you CAN have Tiny with you all the time, just as you wanted. Happy birthday, Fay!'

Princess Fay was so happy, she had nothing to say. And, Tiny? She looked pleased with herself!

READ THESE WORDS AGAIN!

loved	present
birthday	what
called	appear
looked	pleased
herself	next
where	nearly
tears	searching
sitting	there
wanted	happy

WHAT CAN YOU SEE HERE?

princess

rose garden

queen

easel

painting in a frame

THEY LAUGHED AND LAUGHED!

The jungle animals were putting on a show! 'We can tap dance!' said the hippos. They stood on their hind legs, hooves tapping. Tap, tap, tap! Such fine dancing!

Monkey tried tap dancing. He got up on his hind legs. Tap, tap, tap! He tripped over his tail! The animals laughed and laughed.

Crocodile rolled balls of mud along his tail. He tossed the balls into the air, ready to catch on his snout. Such fine juggling!

Monkey tried juggling. He tossed a ball into the air. It fell – SPLAT! – all over his face. The animals laughed and laughed!

The elephants made trumpet sounds with their trunks. Ta-ra! Ta-ra! Such fine trumpeting!

Monkey tried making trumpet sounds. He puffed out his cheeks and blew. But no sound came out! The animals laughed and laughed.

Snakes bent themselves into strange shapes. Then they curled up in coils. Such fine contortions!

Monkey tried to do contortions. He put one arm around his head. Next, he curled one leg around his back. Then he tried putting his other leg behind his neck. BUMP! Monkey fell over.

'I cannot do contortions!' said poor Monkey. 'I cannot make trumpet sounds. I cannot juggle. I cannot tap dance. What CAN I do?' How the animals laughed!

'You make us laugh and laugh!' they said. 'Monkey, you are the funny clown, star of our show!'

READ THESE WORDS AGAIN!

show	tap
animals	dance
hind	hooves
tried	tripped
laughed	tossed
snout	juggling
trumpet	sounds
puffed	snakes
strange	shapes

WHAT CAN YOU SEE HERE?

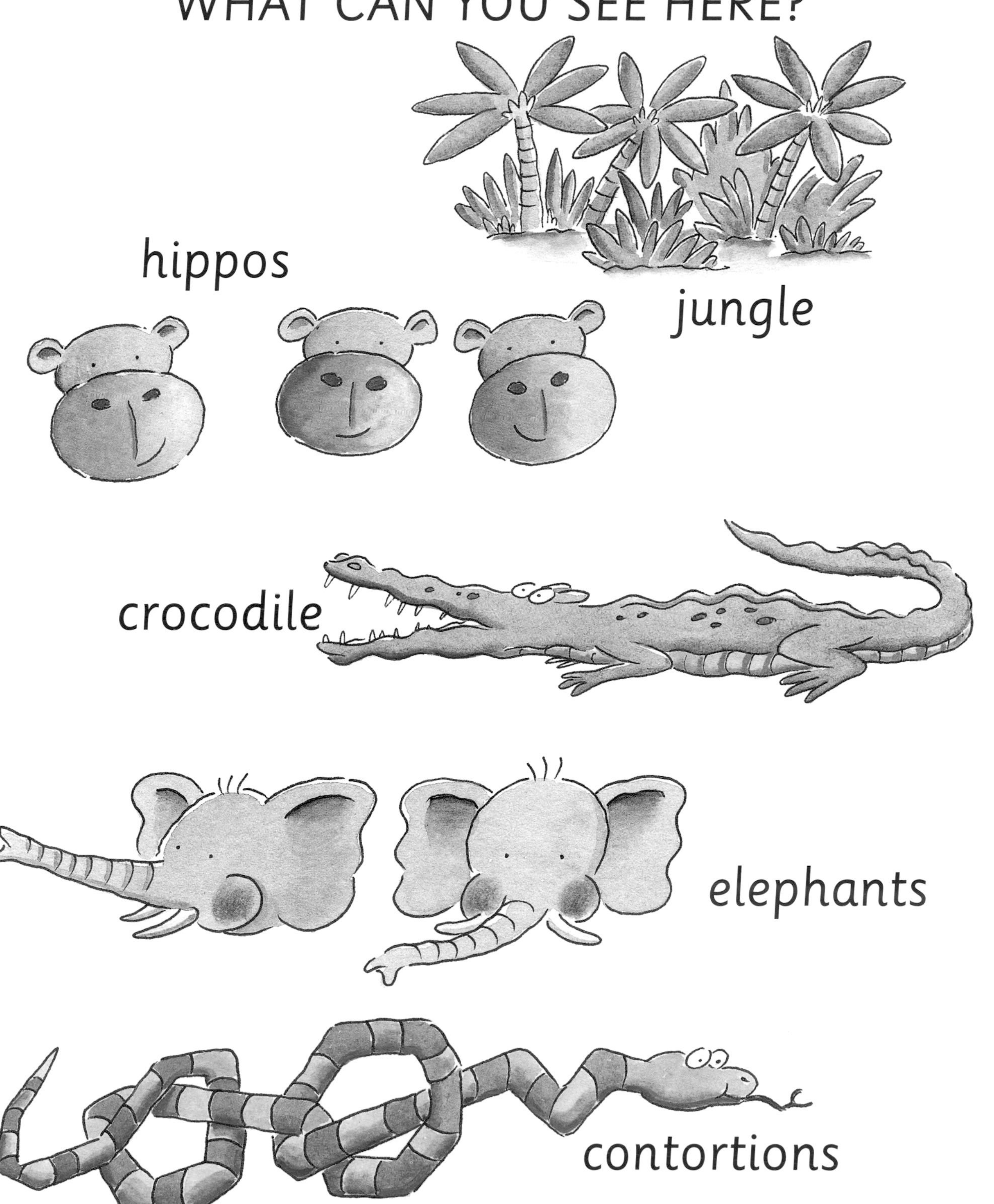

MOLE FINDS A HOME

Mole lived in a long, dark, damp tunnel. He did not like his home!

'This is where we are safe,' said Father Mole. 'It is fine for us!'

'It is not fine for ME!' said Mole to himself. 'I am leaving!'

He went along the tunnel. Just ahead was a hole. Sunshine beamed down. Mole climbed and poked his head outside. Just as he did, a spade appeared above him and almost hit him on the head! The man digging the hole hadn't even noticed Mole!

Mole ran under a hedge, as quickly as he could. Then, something round and hard landed on the ground next to him.

'What a hit!' came a voice. 'Where did that cricket ball go?'

Mole ran off and escaped down a rabbit hole. He bumped right into a big rabbit!

'Out of our home,' cried the rabbit, 'You are frightening my babies!'

Poor Mole! Suddenly, he felt very lonely and tired. Then he heard a voice he knew.

'So there you are, Mole! Where did you go?' It was Father Mole!

'I found a lawn,' panted Mole. 'But a man didn't notice me and almost hit me on the head with a spade! Then a cricket ball just missed me, so I ran down a hole and a rabbit shouted at me!'

'And now you are just in time for dinner!' said Mother Mole.

Mole opened his mouth to speak again. Then he looked around the tunnel, sniffing its smells and feeling the soft ground. It was so good to be home!

READ THESE WORDS AGAIN!

dark	damp
tunnel	where
leaving	sunshine
beamed	climbed
appeared	digging
another	cricket
escaped	suddenly
man	there
missed	sniffing

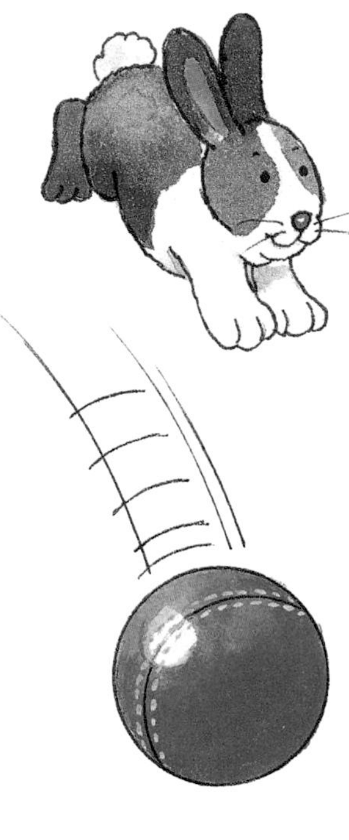

WHAT CAN YOU SEE HERE?

mole

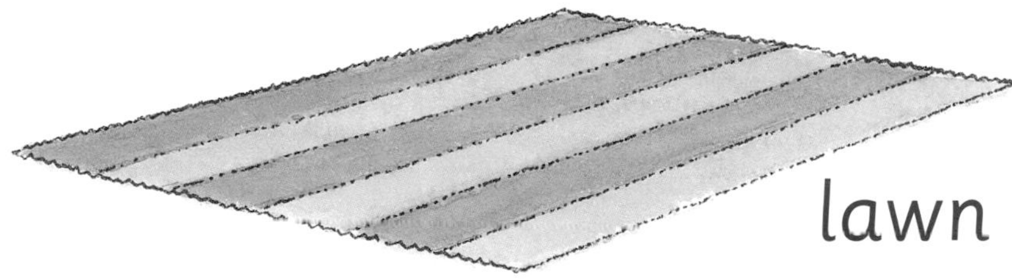

lawn

spade

hedge

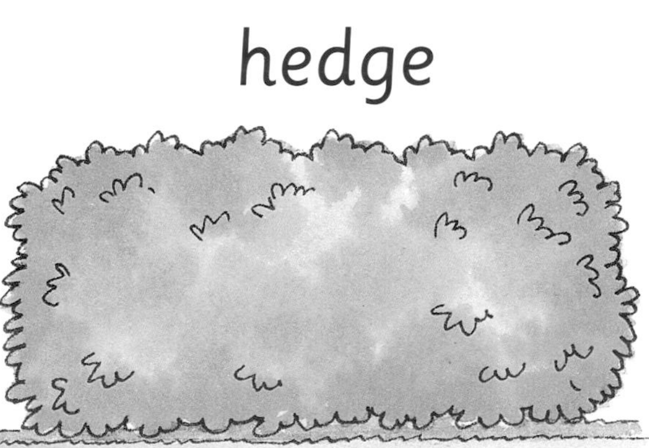

baby rabbits

HELLO, HOBBY-HORSE!

Hobby-Horse stood in the broom cupboard. He was a fine hobby-horse with knots all along his mane, reins and a harness with yellow bells. But, he was lonely.

'Nobody even knows I am here anymore,' he told himself.

But, one day, the door was pulled open. 'Hey! Nita!' said a voice he had never heard before. 'A Hobby-Horse! He must have been here before we came! You can ride him in the town parade on Sunday!'

'He is not a real horse, Max,' came a second voice. 'You know that...'

'But you can go where you like on Hobby-Horse!' said Max. 'He will be better than a real horse!'

Hobby-Horse did not know about that. 'A real horse can trot and gallop,' he said to himself. 'I can only move with someone pushing me along on my wheels.'

But on Sunday, Nita took him into the street. Then she sat across his back, pushing him along with her feet, so that his wheels went round.

'Money for the animal shelter, please!' she cried, holding out a bucket. In and out among the crowds they went, with everyone wanting to give money and to get to know Hobby-Horse!

'And I can get around on MY hobby-horse!' cried Max. 'Look!' Nita looked. And Hobby-Horse looked. Max was on a hobby-horse with black knots along his mane!

'Another hobby-horse!' said Hobby-Horse. 'I will never be lonely again!' And he never was.

READ THESE WORDS AGAIN!

knots	yellow
lonely	nobody
himself	pulled
voice	heard
parade	Sunday
second	know
gallop	pushing
wheels	another

WHAT CAN YOU SEE HERE?

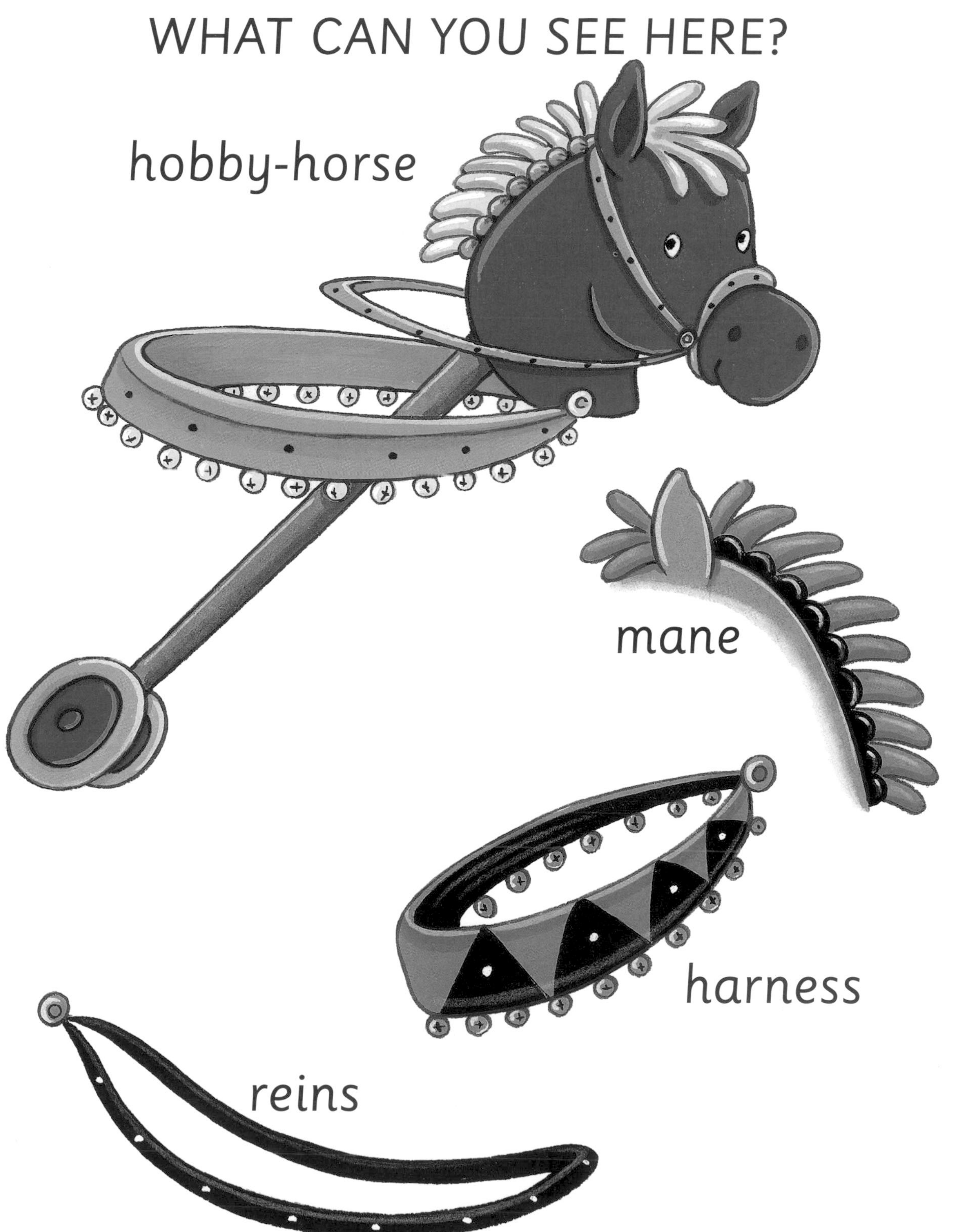

TEDDY'S SPRING CLEAN

'The toy room needs a spring clean!' said Teddy. 'So much dust! Lots of tidying up to do!'

'Well, I'm not going to help!' said Stripey Tiger.

'And I'm not going to help!' said Mermaid Doll. 'What can we do?'

'I will put spots on your face and put my paw in a sling!' said Tiger. 'Teddy will think we are poorly!'

So Tiger painted red spots on Mermaid Doll. She put his paw in a sling. They did look poorly!

All this time, Mr. Potato had been helping Teddy Bear.

'You have worked hard, Mr. Potato!' said Teddy. 'You deserve a reward!' He went to the toy cupboard. 'Here you are!' he said. 'A bag of marbles and a puzzle!'

'Oh, thank you!' said Mr. Potato.

'Marbles and a puzzle!' said Mermaid Doll. 'Just for helping with the spring cleaning!'

Mermaid Doll rubbed the spots off her face. Stripey Tiger took his paw from out of the sling.

Mermaid Doll and Stripey Tiger both wanted to have something nice from Teddy's toy cupboard!

'Mermaid Doll and Tiger!' cried Teddy. 'What can I do for you?'

'Er, we came to help with the spring cleaning!' said Tiger.

'We want to tidy the toy cupboard!' said Mermaid Doll.

'That has been done already!' said Teddy. 'But, never mind! I am sure I can find LOTS more spring cleaning for you to do!' And, he did!

READ THESE WORDS AGAIN!

spring	clean
tidying	poorly
painted	helping
deserve	reward
marbles	puzzle
rubbed	both
wanted	something
already	sure

WHAT CAN YOU SEE HERE?

Stripey Tiger

Mr. Potato

Mermaid Doll

toy cupboard

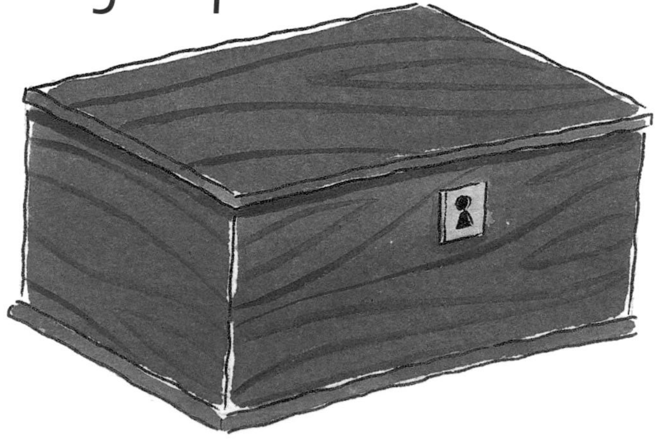

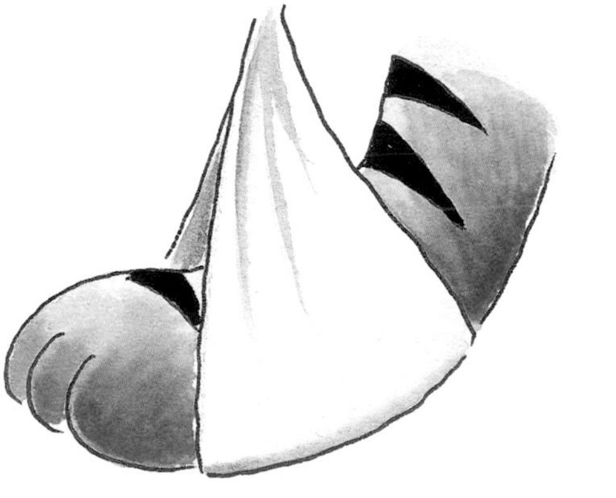

paw in a sling

THE MUSHROOM IN THE RAIN

Ladybird was in the wood. It began to rain. He looked around for a place to shelter. There was only a tiny mushroom, so Ladybird scuttled underneath. And, it kept him dry!

A big snail came crawling by.

'I hope that snail will not come under my mushroom,' said Ladybird. 'There is no room!'

But, the snail crawled in beside Ladybird out of the rain. And, they both kept dry.

Then a butterfly came fluttering by. ‘I hope that butterfly does not come under our mushroom!’ said Ladybird. ‘There is no room!’

But the butterfly fluttered down beside him. And, they all kept dry.

There was another flutter of wings. It was a baby owl.

‘I hope that owl will not come under our mushroom,’ said Ladybird. ‘There is no room!’

But the owl flew in under the mushroom. And Ladybird, the snail, the butterfly and the owl all kept dry.

The rain stopped. Out came the baby owl, the butterfly, the snail and Ladybird. ‘We all kept dry!’ he cried. ‘Yet we only had a tiny mushroom!’

‘Whoooo!’ hooted Mother Owl. ‘It WAS a tiny mushroom before the rain. Now, look!’

So, they looked. The top of the mushroom had spread out, getting bigger as the rain fell!

‘So, there WAS room for us all!’ said Ladybird. ‘And the mushroom helped us to keep dry!’

READ THESE WORDS AGAIN!

rain	around
shelter	tiny
scuttled	underneath
kept	dry
crawling	there
beside	fluttering
another	wings
flew	stopped
spread	bigger

WHAT CAN YOU SEE HERE?

mushroom

ladybird

snail

butterfly

WHATEVER THE WEATHER

Jan had a little weather house. If the weather was wet, Rainy-Day Man came out. If it was fine, he went inside and out came Sunshine Doll.

It began to rain. Out came Rainy-Day Man. Then, the sun came out. Rainy-Day Man went inside the weather house, and Sunshine Doll came out.

Just for a moment, Rainy-Day Man and Sunshine Doll saw each other. They wished they were able to spend some time together.

It started to rain. So, Sunshine Doll went in.

'See my weather house!' said Jan. 'Rainy-Day Man comes out as Sunshine Doll goes in! Then, she comes out and Rainy-Day Man goes in!'

'Rain one minute, sun the next!' said Mum. 'That is springtime!'

Just then, the weather house gave a wobble. 'It must be all this coming and going by Rainy-Day Man and Sunshine Doll!' said Mum. 'The little house is only fixed to the wall by a little peg!'

As Mum spoke, the peg snapped. CRASH! The weather house fell to the floor.

'Well,' said Mum. 'Rainy-Day Man and Sunshine Doll will not work, now.'

Jan and Mum managed to fit all the bits back together. Then Mum fixed Rainy-Day Man and Sunshine Doll by the front door.

Jan was pleased to see Rainy-Day Man and Sunshine Doll together!

'Look!' she cried. 'They are smiling at each other!' And, so they were.

READ THESE WORDS AGAIN!

little	inside
began	moment
each	other
wished	able
together	minute
spring	wobble
fixed	snapped
managed	smiling

WHAT CAN YOU SEE HERE?

Rainy-Day Man

weather house

Sunshine Doll

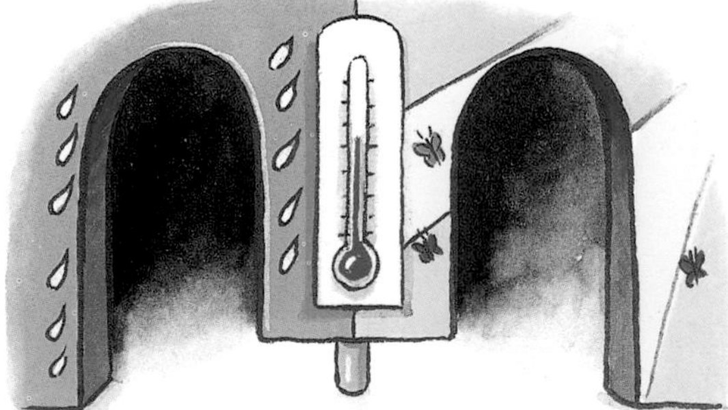

front door

peg

DOZY DORMOUSE!

Dozy Dormouse was fast asleep.

'Dozy Dormouse,' said Squirrel, 'is asleep AGAIN!'

'Quack!' went Duck. 'Sleep is no use at all!'

'So much to do, instead of sleeping!' said Rabbit.

Dozy slept until the next day. Then, as soon as he woke up, he began running about, picking up ears of corn and nuts and berries! Next, he dug a hole, deep in the ground!

'Dozy IS busy!' said Rabbit.

'Now, he is eating without stopping!' said Squirrel. 'He is hungry after all that work!'

Then, after Dozy had eaten all the food, he crawled into his hole and curled up into a ball.

'Well!' sniffed Rabbit. 'Dozy is going to sleep again!'

'Sleep is no use!' said Squirrel.

'You do not think so?' came the deep voice of Stag. 'See the falling leaves! Feel the cold wind! Winter is coming!'

'Winter!' quacked Duck. 'My pond will be frozen!'

'We will need to search for food!' said Squirrel.

'And try to keep warm!' said Rabbit with a shiver.

'But Dozy will sleep the winter away, until the warm weather comes,' said Stag.

They looked into the hole, where Dozy was already fast asleep.

'So, sleep is useful after all,' said Rabbit. 'See you in the spring, Dozy Dormouse!'

READ THESE WORDS AGAIN!

fast	asleep
duck	quack
instead	picking
about	ground
hungry	work
crawled	curled
sniffed	leaves
frozen	already

WHAT CAN YOU SEE HERE?

squirrel

berries

Dozy Dormouse

stag

rabbit

FAIRY PANSY

'How can I see a human child?' Fairy Pansy asked Fairy Moth.

'There is one at the end of our garden!' said Fairy Moth. 'Such lovely hair, tiny feet, a sweet face and a soft voice! Wait and see!'

So Fairy Pansy hid among the flowers, waiting. After a while, there came the sound of footsteps. Fairy Pansy peeped out – only to see big, flat feet with heavy boots. And the face did not look sweet at all!

'Fairies at the bottom of our garden, Meg?' came a voice. 'Huh!'

Fairy Pansy peeped out again. She still hoped to see a sweet face with long hair. But the face was round, with a snub nose and short hair.

'Mark!' came another voice. 'What are you staring at?'

'Er...' came the reply. 'For a moment, I was sure I saw...er...'

'Fairies at the bottom of our garden?' finished Meg. 'That is what I am always saying, Mark!'

Mark walked off, kicking at the grass. But Meg parted some of the flowers and looked more closely. Fairy Pansy sat among the flowers, her face in her tiny hands.

'Well!' breathed Meg. 'I SAID there were fairies at the bottom of our garden!'

Fairy Pansy took her hands away. She saw the lovely face, the long hair and the smooth skin.

'At last!' she said in her soft, tiny voice. 'I have seen a REAL human child!'

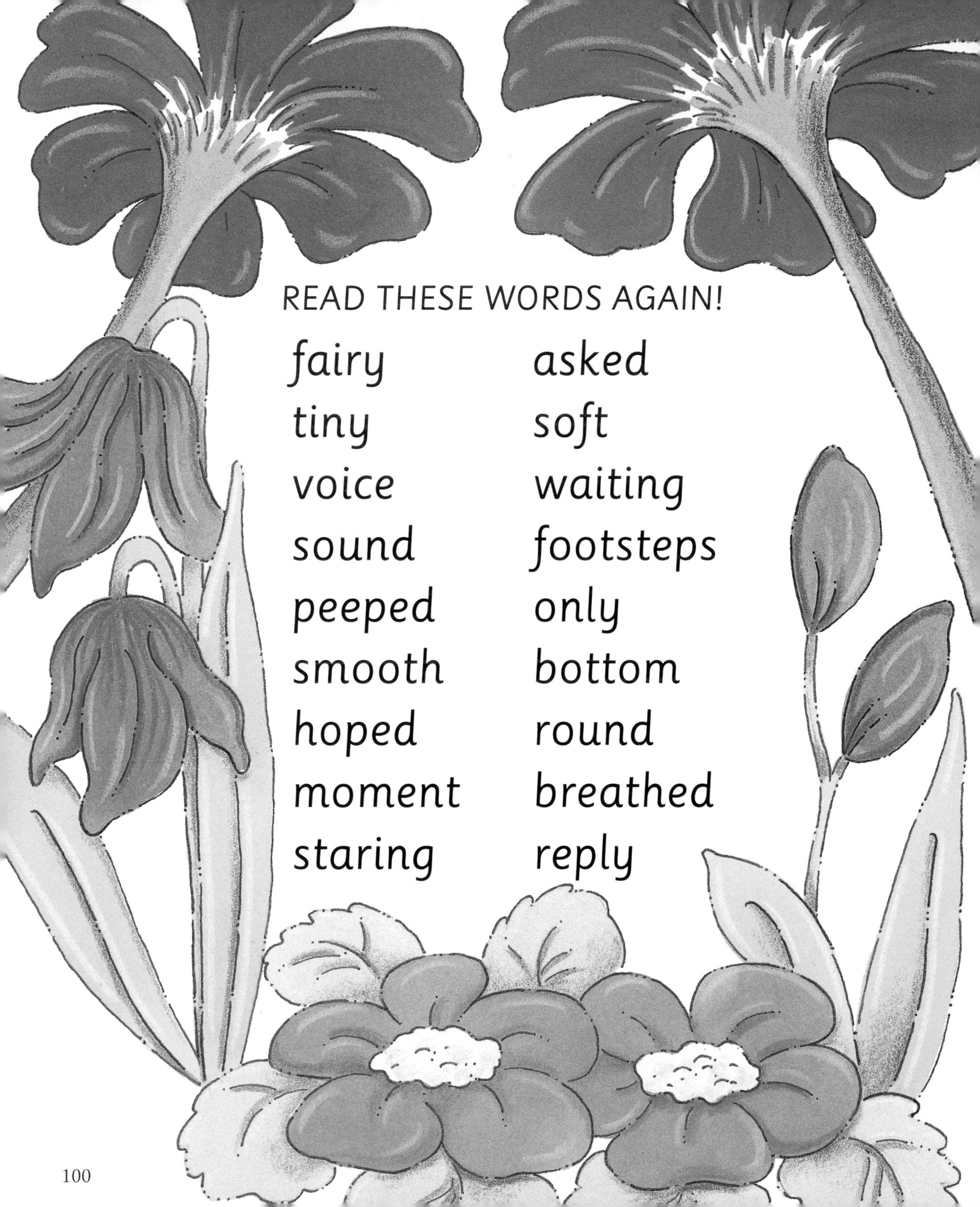

READ THESE WORDS AGAIN!

fairy	asked
tiny	soft
voice	waiting
sound	footsteps
peeped	only
smooth	bottom
hoped	round
moment	breathed
staring	reply

WHAT CAN YOU SEE HERE?

heavy boots

I KNOW!

Tim was always saying, 'I know!'

'Tim,' said Luke, 'we are all going to the park...'

'I know!' said Tim. 'I know!'

'We are going to see a puppet show!' said Amita. 'And...'

'I know!' said Tim. 'I KNOW!'

'It is my birthday...' said Dan.

'I know!' said Tim. 'I KNOW!'

Then, Tim went off to the park! But there was nobody there.

Tim gave a shout. 'Hey!'

'Hey!' a voice came from the Wendy house. It was the echo of his own voice, but Tim did not know that! 'Where is the puppet show?' he shouted.

'Puppet show!' came the echo.

'I know!' shouted Tim. 'It is over here!'

'Over here!' came the echo.

Tim searched the Wendy house. It was empty. 'Hey!' he cried. 'I want the puppet show!'

'Puppet show!' came the echo yet again. 'Puppet show!'

Tim marched off in a temper.

'Where is Tim?' he heard someone saying. 'He said he knew about the puppet show for my birthday!'

Tim looked over a fence. Everyone was in Dan's garden, enjoying the puppet show!

'Hello, Tim!' said Dan. 'You are a bit late for my party!'

'But you can come to the park for some games!' said Luke.

'Pity you missed the puppet show, Tim!' said Amita.

'Yes,' said Tim. 'I know.'

READ THESE WORDS AGAIN!

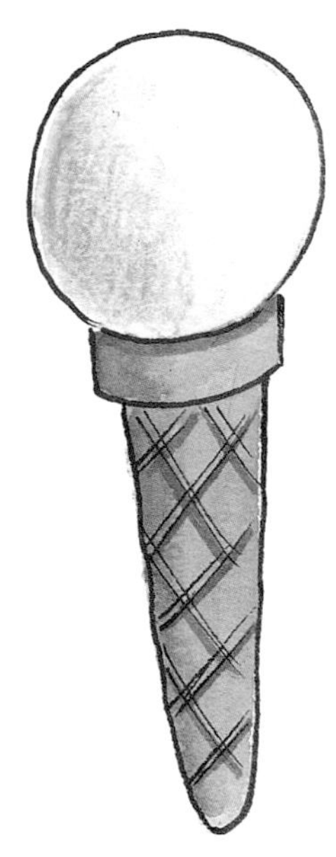

always
know
there
voice
shouted
searched
marched
knew
enjoying

saying
birthday
nobody
echo
here
empty
temper
everyone
missed

WHAT CAN YOU SEE HERE?

swing

puppet show

Wendy house

fence

garden

THE KING AND THE WIZARD

'Oh, dear!' King Cole said to his servant, Sam. 'Wizard Woo teases the children. He makes cats bark and dogs quack! Now, he has just sent this message!'

Sam began to read aloud.

'I will come to the palace today to see King Cole. If he can tell me the first thing I am thinking, I shall go away for ever! If not, I shall be king!'

'If only Wizard Woo DID go away for good!' said the king.

Sam was looking at the king's crown and his red velvet robe.

'Oh, dear!' said King Cole. 'Do something, Sam!'

Sam called a footman. 'Bring Wizard Woo to me when he arrives!' he said.

'Sam!' said the king. 'How can you smile at a time like this?'

Wizard Woo also smiled when he arrived, seeing the crown and the red velvet gown.

'King Cole!' said Wizard Woo. 'Can you tell me the first thing I am thinking?'

'You think I am King Cole!' came the reply. 'That is the first thing you were thinking! True?'

'Yes,' said the wizard, 'but...'

Off came the crown and the robe. It was Sam! 'And you were thinking I was the king!' he said.

Wizard Woo flew into a rage!

'You have made me look a fool!' he cried. 'I am going!' And off he went.

'Peace at last!' said King Cole. 'My crown, please, Sam!'

'Of course!' smiled Sam.

READ THESE WORDS AGAIN!

king	teases
children	quack
message	aloud
come	palace
first	something
called	arrives
smile	smiled
reply	rage
peace	last

WHAT CAN YOU SEE HERE?

BELLA'S UMBRELLA

Bella Bear had a new umbrella.

'Just see my new umbrella!' Bella kept saying. 'I can hardly wait for a rainy day, so that I can use it!'

She looked up at the sky, watching out for any sign of rain, just one, little black cloud! But the sky was a clear blue, without a cloud to be seen. She waited for the first shower of raindrops. But the sun shone high in the sky.

But Bella wanted to show off her new umbrella!

‘I will go to the park!’ she said at last. ‘The ducks will be splashing about in the pond. I can pretend to get wet and put up my umbrella!’

It seemed hotter than ever in the park! Even the ducks were hiding among the water weeds.

‘No sign of rain!’ said Bella with a sigh. ‘And I DID want to put up my pretty new umbrella!’

She walked on, getting hotter and hotter. Then – splash! Water splashed on her head. Then, again. Splash! Was it raining?

Bella put up her pretty new umbrella. Then she looked round. It was a splash from the water fountain! She felt very silly.

'Bella!' cried Pretty Bear. 'What a pretty parasol! A parasol to shade you from the sun!'

'A – a parasol?' said Bella. She looked up at her umbrella.

'Yes!' said Pretty. 'I must get one!'

'So, when it is fine, my umbrella is a parasol,' said Bella. 'And when it rains, my parasol is an umbrella!'

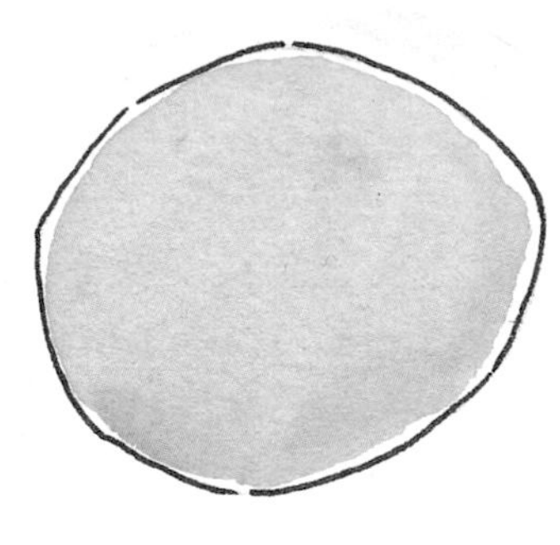

READ THESE WORDS AGAIN!

pretty	wait
looked	sky
sign	clear
shone	high
park	ducks
pretend	hiding
sigh	hotter
splash	fountain

WHAT CAN YOU SEE HERE?

black cloud

umbrella

shower of raindrops

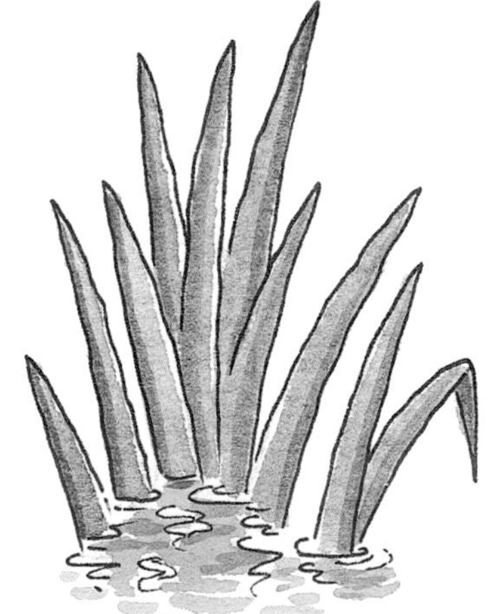

water weeds

parasol